BASIC DOCUMENTS IN
INTERNATIONAL LAW AND WORLD ORDER

Second Edition

Selected and Edited

By

Burns H. Weston
Bessie Dutton Murray Professor of Law
The University of Iowa

Richard A. Falk
Albert G. Milbank Professor of International Law and Practice
Princeton University

Anthony D'Amato
Judd and Mary Morris Leighton Professor of Law
Northwestern University

WEST PUBLISHING CO.
ST. PAUL, MINN., 1990

Printed in the United States of America

Library of Congress Cataloging-in-Publication Data

ISBN 0-314-67633-3

(W.F. & D.) Basic Doc. 2d Ed. ACB
1st Reprint—1991

Preface

This collection, like its predecessor, has been assembled for two reasons: first, to serve as a documentary supplement to our coursebook entitled *International Law and World Order—A Problem-Oriented Coursebook* (West Publishing Company, Second Edition, 1990); second, to provide a convenient general reference for students, instructors, governmental officials, and private practitioners in the international law field. Trying to serve these two purposes simultaneously has of course required that we be selective. However, in contrast to our first edition, this collection is more inclusive.

Our criteria for selection have been essentially four:

first, we have selected instruments largely according to the four world order problem areas we use in our coursebook (although in reverse order);

second, within the world order problem areas indicated, we have given preference to instruments which, both substantively and territorially, are more generic than specific in character;

third, we have omitted documents which, although of great importance, generally relate to more or less specialized areas of international law (*e.g.,* the Treaty of Rome, GATT, the Andean Pact, etc.); and

fourth, choosing to emphasize substance over form, we have excluded most preambles and most administrative or procedural articles not essential to a proper understanding of the substantive content of the instrument.

Irrespective of the selection criteria employed, however, we have presented all the instruments within each topical division in chronological order. Such an arrangement usefully shows the timing and evolution of international law in each area.

Three additional features merit attention also:

Appendix I, detailing the status, as of December 31, 1989, of the instruments contained in this volume and thereby contributing to the knowledge needed to assess the extent to which, if at all, any given instrument "counts as law";

Appendix II, listing the judgments and advisory opinions of the Permanent Court of International Justice and the International Court of Justice; and

Appendix III, constituting an expanded bibliography of other documentary texts of both general and specialized focus.

Each of these new features adds significantly, we believe, to the utility of this volume both within and beyond the classroom.

Finally, we hope that this collection will prove to be a practical tool for all who, like ourselves, find the study and practice of international law both fascinating and of immense importance for the progressive development of humankind. We have tried to be as thorough as space would permit, but nevertheless will welcome any suggestions for improvement should our effort warrant future editions.

January 1990

BURNS H. WESTON
Iowa City, Iowa

RICHARD A. FALK
Princeton, New Jersey

ANTHONY D'AMATO
Chicago, Illinois

Acknowledgments

Inasmuch as this second edition of *Basic Documents in International Law and World Order* builds upon the first edition, we continue to remain indebted to our law school, political science, and other colleagues who so graciously took the time to respond to our inquiries regarding the structure and content of the first edition. Their names are recorded therein and we salute them again.

We are indebted as well to James Anaya and to Cynthia Price Cohen for their heroic efforts in helping us to secure, respectively, the 1989 ILO Convention (No. 169) Concerning Indigenous and Tribal Peoples in Independent Countries (**Basic Document 3.47**) and the 1989 Convention on the Rights of the Child (**Basic Document 3.48**). For steady expert help in locating many different instruments, we also are indebted to Marilou M. Righini, Editor of *International Legal Materials,* and the staff of the Government Documents Section of the Main Library of The University of Iowa. To all our abundant thanks.

Especially deserving of appreciation for their help in assembling this collection are Sarah M. Bakheit, Shelly G. Dedmon, Donna M. Humpal, John E. Swartz, James C. Wherry, and Markus C. Zoeckler—all present or former students at The University of Iowa College of Law. However, we especially want to single out Sarah M. Bakheit, Shelly G. Dedmon, and Donna M. Humpal for their painstaking assistance in the preparation of Appendix I. Additionally, Mary E. Sleichter, Secretary to Professor Weston, merits more than a large round of applause.

Thus, we are not unmindful that this collection would not have come to fruition without the help of all these people. We alone, of course, take full responsibility for any and all errors.

*

Table of Abbreviations

The following abbreviations are used in the headnotes and footnotes to the documents included in this collection.

Abbreviations for United States Documentation

Bevans	C. Bevans, Treaties and Other International Agreements of the United States of America 1776–1949 (1968–1974, 12 vols.)
Dep't State Bull.	Department of State Bulletin
Dep't State Pub.	Department of State Publication
Gen'l For.Pol.Ser.	General Foreign Policy Series (of the Department of State)
Stat.	Statutes at Large
T.I.A.S.	Treaties and Other International Acts Series
T.S.	Treaty Series
U.S.C.	United State Code
U.S.T.	United States Treaties and Other International Agreements

Abbreviations for Regional Organization Documents

Europ.T.S.	European Treaty Series
O.A.S.Res.	Organization of American States Resolution
O.A.S.Off.Rec.	Organization of American States Official Records
OEA/Ser.	Organizacion Estados Americanos Series (Organization of American States Series)

Abbreviations for United Nations Documentation

A	General Assembly
Add.	Addendum
CONF	Conference
E	Economic and Social Council
E.S.C.	Economic and Social Council (abbreviation used with the Council's resolutions)
ESCOR	Economic and Social Council Official Records
INF	Information Series
Mtg.	Meeting
Res.	Resolution
Rev.	Revision

S	Security Council
SCOR	Security Council Official Records
Supp.	Supplement
U.N.Doc.	United Nations Document
U.N.G.A.	United Nations General Assembly (abbreviation used, in this collection, with the Assembly's resolutions)
U.N.GAOR	United Nations General Assembly Official Records
U.N.T.S.	United Nations Treaty Series
WP	Working Paper
Y.B.U.N.	Yearbook of the United Nations

Miscellaneous Abbreviations

I.L.M.	International Legal Materials
Int'l Legis.	M. Hudson, International Legislation—A Collection of the Text of Multipartite International Instruments of General Interest (1931–1950, 9 vols.)
J.Int'l Comm'n Jurists	Journal of the International Commission of Jurists
L.N.T.S.	League of Nations Treaty Series
No.	Number

Table of Contents

3. HUMAN RIGHTS

4. ECONOMIC DEVELOPMENT

6. MISCELLANEOUS

APPENDICES

BASIC DOCUMENTS IN
INTERNATIONAL LAW
AND WORLD ORDER

Second Edition

*

1. CONSTITUTIVE/ORGANIC

1.1 CONSTITUTION OF THE UNITED STATES OF AMERICA

* * *

ARTICLE I

* * *

SECTION 8. The Congress shall have Power To lay and collect Taxes, Duties, Imposts and Excises, to pay the Debts and provide for the common Defence and general Welfare of the United States; but all Duties, Imposts and Excises shall be uniform throughout the United States;

To borrow Money on the credit of the United States;

To regulate Commerce with foreign Nations, and among the several States, and with the Indian Tribes;

To establish an uniform Rule of Naturalization, and uniform Laws on the subject of Bankruptcies throughout the United States;

To coin Money, regulate the Value thereof, and of foreign Coin, and fix the Standard of Weights and Measures;

To provide for the Punishment of counterfeiting the Securities and current Coin of the United States;

To establish Post Offices and post Roads;

To promote the Progress of Science and useful Arts, by securing for limited Times to Authors and Inventors the exclusive Right to their respective Writings and Discoveries;

To constitute Tribunals inferior to the supreme Court;

To define and punish Piracies and Felonies committed on the high Seas, and Offences against the Law of Nations;

To declare War, grant Letters of Marque and Reprisal, and make Rules concerning Captures on Land and Water;

To raise and support Armies, but no Appropriation of Money to that Use shall be for a longer Term than two Years;

To provide and maintain a Navy;

To make Rules for the Government and Regulation of the land and naval Forces;

To provide for calling forth the Militia to execute the Laws of the Union, suppress Insurrections and repel Invasions;

To provide for organizing, arming, and disciplining, the Militia, and for governing such Part of them as may be employed in the Service of the United States, reserving to the States respectively, the Appointment of the Officers, and the Authority of training the Militia according to the discipline prescribed by Congress;

To exercise exclusive Legislation in all Cases whatsoever, over such District (not exceeding ten Miles square) as may, by Cession of particular States, and the Acceptance of Congress, become the Seat of the Government of the United States, and to exercise like Authority over all Places purchased by the Consent of the Legislature of the State in which the Same shall be, for the Erection of Forts, Magazines, Arsenals, dock-Yards, and other needful Buildings;—And

To make all Laws which shall be necessary and proper for carrying into Execution the foregoing Powers, and all other Powers vested by this Constitution in the Government of the United States, or in any Department or Officer thereof.

SECTION 9. The Migration or Importation of such Persons as any of the States now existing shall think proper to admit, shall not be prohibited by the Congress prior to the Year one thousand eight hundred and eight, but a Tax or duty may be imposed on such Importation, not exceeding ten dollars for each Person.

The Privilege of the Writ of Habeas Corpus shall not be suspended, unless when in Cases of Rebellion or Invasion the public Safety may require it.

No Bill of Attainder or ex post facto Law shall be passed.

No Capitation, or other direct, Tax shall be laid, unless in Proportion to the Census or Enumeration herein before directed to be taken.

No Tax or Duty shall be laid on Articles exported from any State.

No Preference shall be given by any Regulation of Commerce or Revenue to the Ports of one State over those of another; nor shall Vessels bound to, or from, one State, be obliged to enter, clear or pay Duties in another.

No Money shall be drawn from the Treasury, but in Consequence of Appropriations made by Law; and a regular Statement and Account of the Receipts and Expenditures of all public Money shall be published from time to time.

No Title of Nobility shall be granted by the United States: And no Person holding any Office of Profit or Trust under them, shall, without the Consent of the Congress, accept of any present, Emolument, Office, or Title, of any kind whatever, from any King, Prince or foreign State.

SECTION 10. No State shall enter into any Treaty, Alliance, or Confederation; grant Letters of Marque and Reprisal; coin Money; emit Bills of Credit; make any Thing but gold and silver Coin a Tender in Payment of Debts; pass any Bill of Attainder, ex post facto Law, or Law impairing the Obligation of Contracts, or grant any Title of Nobility.

No State shall, without the Consent of the Congress, lay any Imposts or Duties on Imports or Exports, except what may be absolutely necessary for executing its inspection Laws: and the net Produce of all Duties and Imposts, laid by any State on Imports or Exports, shall be for the Use of the Treasury of the United States; and all such Laws shall be subject to the Revision and Controul of the Congress.

No State shall, without the Consent of Congress, lay any Duty of Tonnage, keep Troops, or Ships of War in time of Peace, enter into any Agreement or Compact with another State, or with a foreign Power, or engage in War, unless actually invaded, or in such imminent Danger as will not admit of delay.

ARTICLE II

SECTION 1. The executive Power shall be vested in a President of the United States of America. He shall hold his Office during the Term of four Years. * * *

* * *

SECTION 2. The President shall be Commander in Chief of the Army and Navy of the United States, and of the Militia of the several States, when called into the actual Service of the United States; he may require the Opinion, in writing, of the principal Officer in each of the executive Departments, upon any Subject relating to the Duties of their respective Offices, and he shall have Power to grant Reprieves and Pardons for Offences against the United States, except in Cases of Impeachment.

He shall have Power, by and with the Advice and Consent of the Senate, to make Treaties, provided two thirds of the Senators present concur; and he shall nominate, and by and with the Advice and Consent of the Senate, shall appoint Ambassadors, other public Ministers and Consuls, Judges of the supreme Court, and all other Officers of the United States, whose Appointments are not herein otherwise provided for, and which shall be established by Law: but the Congress may by Law vest the Appointment of such inferior Officers, as they think proper, in the President alone, in the Courts of Law, or in the Heads of Departments.

The President shall have Power to fill up all Vacancies that may happen during the Recess of the Senate, by granting Commissions which shall expire at the End of their next Session.

SECTION 3. He shall * * * receive Ambassadors and other public Ministers.

* * *

ARTICLE III

SECTION 1. The judicial Power of the United States, shall be vested in one supreme Court, and in such inferior Courts as the Congress may from time to time ordain and establish. * * *

SECTION 2. The judicial Power shall extend to all Cases, in Law and Equity, arising under this Constitution, the Laws of the United States, and Treaties made, or which shall be made, under their Authority;—to all Cases affecting Ambassadors, other public ministers and Consuls;—to all Cases of admiralty and maritime Jurisdiction;—to Controversies to which the United States shall be a Party;—to Controversies between two or more States;—between a State and Citizens of another State;—between Citizens of different States;—between Citizens of the same State claiming Lands under Grants of different States, and between a State, or the Citizens thereof, and foreign States, Citizens or Subjects.

In all Cases affecting Ambassadors, other public Ministers and Consuls, and those in which a State shall be Party, the supreme Court shall have original Jurisdiction. In all the other Cases before mentioned, the supreme Court shall have appellate Jurisdiction, both as to Law and Fact, with such Exceptions, and under such Regulations as the Congress shall make.

* * *

SECTION 3. Treason against the United States, shall consist only in levying War against them, or in adhering to their Enemies, giving them Aid and Comfort. No Person shall be convicted of Treason unless on the Testimony of two Witnesses to the same overt Act, or on Confession in open Court.

The Congress shall have Power to declare the Punishment of Treason, but no Attainder of Treason shall work Corruption of Blood, or Forfeiture except during the Life of the Person attainted.

* * *

ARTICLE VI

This Constitution, and the Laws of the United States which shall be made in Pursuance thereof; and all Treaties made, or which shall be made, under the Authority of the United States, shall be the supreme Law of the Land; and the Judges in every State shall be bound thereby, any Thing in the Constitution or Laws of any State to the Contrary notwithstanding. * * *

* * *

AMENDMENT X

The powers not delegated to the United States by the Constitution, nor prohibited by it to the States, are reserved to the States respectively, or to the people.

* * *

1.2 GENERAL ACT FOR THE PACIFIC SETTLEMENT OF INTERNATIONAL DISPUTES. Done at Geneva, Sept. 26, 1928. Entered into force, Aug. 16, 1929. 93 L.N.T.S. 343, 25 A.J.I.L. Supp. 204 (1931)

CHAPTER I.

CONCILIATION.

Article 1.

Disputes of every kind between two or more Parties to the present General Act which it has not been possible to settle by diplomacy shall, subject to such reservations as may be made under Article 39, be submitted, under the conditions laid down in the present Chapter, to the procedure of conciliation.

Article 2.

The disputes referred to in the preceding article shall be submitted to a permanent or special Conciliation Commission constituted by the parties to the dispute.

Article 3.

On a request to that effect being made by one of the Contracting Parties to another Party, a permanent Conciliation Commission shall be constituted within a period of six months.

Article 4.

Unless the parties concerned agree otherwise, the Conciliation Commission shall be constituted as follows:

(1) The Commission shall be composed of five members. The parties shall each nominate one commissioner, who may be chosen from among their respective nationals. The three other commissioners shall be appointed by agreement from among the nationals of third Powers. These three commissioners must be of different nationalities and must not be habitually resident in the territory nor be in the service of the parties. The parties shall appoint the President of the Commission from among them.

(2) The commissioners shall be appointed for three years. They shall be re-eligible. The commissioners appointed jointly may be replaced during the course of their mandate by agreement between the parties. Either party may, however, at any time replace a commissioner whom it has appointed. Even if replaced, the commissioners shall continue to exercise their functions until the termination of the work in hand.

(3) Vacancies which may occur as a result of death, resignation or any other cause shall be filled within the shortest possible time in the manner fixed for the nominations.

Article 5.

If, when a dispute arises, no permanent Conciliation Commission appointed by the parties is in existence, a special commission shall be constituted for the examination of the dispute within a period of three months from the date at which a request to that effect is made by one of the parties to the other party. The necessary appointments shall be made in the manner laid down in the preceding article, unless the parties decide otherwise.

Article 6.

1. If the appointment of the commissioners to be designated jointly is not made within the periods provided for in Articles 3 and 5, the making of the necessary appointments shall be entrusted to a third Power, chosen by agreement between the parties, or on request of the parties, to the Acting President of the Council of the League of Nations.

2. If no agreement is reached on either of these procedures, each party shall designate a different Power, and the appointment shall be made in concert by the Powers thus chosen.

3. If, within a period of three months, the two Powers have been unable to reach an agreement, each of them shall submit a number of candidates equal to the number of members to be appointed. It shall then be decided by lot which of the candidates thus designated shall be appointed.

Article 7.

1. Disputes shall be brought before the Conciliation Commission by means of an application addressed to the President by the two parties acting in agreement, or in default thereof by one or other of the parties.

2. The application, after giving a summary account of the subject of the dispute, shall contain the invitation to the Commission to take all necessary measures with a view to arriving at an amicable solution.

3. If the application emanates from only one of the parties, the other party shall, without delay, be notified by it.

Article 8.

1. Within fifteen days from the date on which a dispute has been brought by one of the parties before a permanent Conciliation Commission, either party may replace its own commissioner, for the examination of the particular dispute, by a person possessing special competence in the matter.

2. The party making use of this right shall immediately notify the other party; the latter shall, in such case, be entitled to take similar action within fifteen days from the date on which it received the notification.

* * *

Article 10.

The work of the Conciliation Commission shall not be conducted in public unless a decision to that effect is taken by the Commission with the consent of the parties.

Article 11.

1. In the absence of agreement to the contrary between the parties, the Conciliation Commission shall lay down its own procedure, which in any case must provide for both parties being heard. In regard to enquiries, the Commission, unless it decides unanimously to the contrary, shall act in accordance with the provisions of Part III of the Hague Convention of October 18, 1907, for the Pacific Settlement of International Disputes.

2. The parties shall be represented before the Conciliation Commission by agents, whose duty shall be to act as intermediaries between them and the Commission; they may, moreover, be assisted by counsel and experts appointed by them for that purpose and may request that all persons whose evidence appears to them desirable shall be heard.

3. The Commission, for its part, shall be entitled to request oral explanations from the agents, counsel and experts of both parties, as well as from all persons it may think desirable to summon with the consent of their Governments.

Article 12.

In the absence of agreement to the contrary between the parties, the decisions of the Conciliation Commission shall be taken by a majority vote, and the Commission may only take decisions on the substance of the dispute if all its members are present.

Article 13.

The parties undertake to facilitate the work of the Conciliation Commission, and particularly to supply it to the greatest possible extent with all relevant documents and information, as well as to use the means at their disposal to allow it to proceed in their territory, and in accordance with their law, to the summoning and hearing of witnesses or experts and to visit the localities in question.

Article 14.

1. During the proceedings of the Commission, each of the commissioners shall receive emoluments the amount of which shall be fixed by agreement between the parties, each of which shall contribute an equal share.

2. The general expenses arising out of the working of the Commission shall be divided in the same manner.

Article 15.

1. The task of the Conciliation Commission shall be to elucidate the questions in dispute, to collect with that object all necessary information by means of enquiry or otherwise, and to endeavour to bring the parties to an agreement. It may, after the case has been examined, inform the parties of the terms of settlement which seem suitable to it, and lay down the period within which they are to make their decision.

2. At the close of the proceedings the Commission shall draw up a procès-verbal stating, as the case may be, either that the parties have come to an agreement and, if need arises, the terms of the agreement, or that it has been impossible to effect a settlement. No mention shall be made in the procès-verbal of whether the Commission's decisions were taken unanimously or by a majority vote.

3. The proceedings of the Commission must, unless the parties otherwise agree, be terminated within six months from the date on which the Commission shall have been given cognisance of the dispute.

Article 16.

The Commission's procès-verbal shall be communicated without delay to the parties. The parties shall decide whether it shall be published.

CHAPTER II.

JUDICIAL SETTLEMENT.

Article 17.

All disputes with regard to which the parties are in conflict as to their respective rights shall, subject to any reservations which may be made under Article 39, be submitted for decision to the Permanent Court of International Justice, unless the parties agree, in the manner hereinafter provided, to have resort to an arbitral tribunal.

It is understood that the disputes referred to above include in particular those mentioned in Article 36 of the Statute of the Permanent Court of International Justice.

Article 18.

If the parties agree to submit the disputes mentioned in the preceding article to an arbitral tribunal, they shall draw up a special agreement in which they shall specify the subject of the dispute, the arbitrators selected, and the procedure to be followed. In the absence of sufficient particulars in the special agreement, the provisions of the Hague Convention of October 18th, 1907, for the Pacific Settlement of International Disputes shall apply so far as is necessary. If nothing is laid down in the special agreement as to the rules regarding the substance of the dispute to be followed by the arbitrators, the tribunal shall apply the substantive rules enumerated in Article 38 of the Statute of the Permanent Court of International Justice.

Article 19.

If the parties fail to agree concerning the special agreement referred to in the preceding article, or fail to appoint arbitrators, either party shall be at liberty, after giving three months' notice, to bring the dispute by an application direct before the Permanent Court of International Justice.

Article 20.

1. Notwithstanding the provisions of Article 1, disputes of the kind referred to in Article 17 arising between parties who have acceded to the obligations contained in the present chapter shall only be subject to the procedure of conciliation if the parties so agree.

2. The obligation to resort to the procedure of conciliation remains applicable to disputes which are excluded from judicial settlement only by the operation of reservations under the provisions of Article 39.

3. In the event of recourse to and failure of conciliation, neither party may bring the dispute before the Permanent Court of International Justice or call for the constitution of the arbitral tribunal referred to in Article 18 before the expiration of one month from the termination of the proceedings of the Conciliation Commission.

CHAPTER III.

ARBITRATION.

Article 21.

Any dispute not of the kind referred to in Article 17 which does not, within the month following the termination of the work of the Conciliation Commission provided for in Chapter I, form the object of an agreement between the parties, shall, subject to such reservations as may be made under Article 39, be brought before an arbitral tribunal which, unless the parties otherwise agree, shall be constituted in the manner set out below.

Article 22.

The Arbitral Tribunal shall consist of five members. The parties shall each nominate one member, who may be chosen from among their respective nationals. The two other arbitrators and the Chairman shall be chosen by common agreement from among the nationals of third Powers. They must be of different nationalities and must not be habitually resident in the territory nor be in the service of the parties.

Article 23.

1. If the appointment of the members of the Arbitral Tribunal is not made within a period of three months from the date on which one of the parties requested the other party to constitute an arbitral tribunal, a third Power, chosen by agreement between the parties, shall be requested to make the necessary appointments.

2. If no agreement is reached on this point, each party shall designate a different Power, and the appointments shall be made in concert by the Powers thus chosen.

3. If, within a period of three months, the two Powers so chosen have been unable to reach an agreement, the necessary appointments shall be made by the President of the Permanent Court of International Justice. If the latter is prevented from acting or is a subject of one of the parties, the nominations shall be made by the Vice–President. If the latter is prevented from acting or is a subject of one of the parties, the appointments shall be made by the oldest member of the Court who is not a subject of either party.

Article 24.

Vacancies which may occur as a result of death, resignation or any other cause shall be filled within the shortest possible time in the manner fixed for the nominations.

Article 25.

The parties shall draw up a special agreement determining the subject of the disputes and the details of procedure.

Article 26.

In the absence of sufficient particulars in the special agreement regarding the matters referred to in the preceding article, the provisions of the Hague Convention of October 18th, 1907, for the Pacific Settlement of International Disputes shall apply so far as is necessary.

Article 27.

Failing the conclusion of a special agreement within a period of three months from the date on which the Tribunal was constituted, the dispute may be brought before the Tribunal by an application by one or other party.

Article 28.

If nothing is laid down in the special agreement or no special agreement has been made, the Tribunal shall apply the rules in regard to the substance of the dispute enumerated in Article 38 of the Statute of the Permanent Court of International Justice. In so far as there exists no such rule applicable to the dispute, the Tribunal shall decide *ex aequo et bono.*

CHAPTER IV.

General Provisions.

Article 29.

1. Disputes for the settlement of which a special procedure is laid down in other conventions in force between the parties to the dispute shall be settled in conformity with the provisions of those conventions.

2. The present General Act shall not affect any agreements in force by which conciliation procedure is established between the Parties or they are bound by obligations to resort to arbitration or judicial settlement which ensure the settlement of the dispute. If, however, these agreements provide only for a procedure of conciliation, after such procedure has been followed without result, the provisions of the present General Act concerning judicial settlement or arbitration shall be applied in so far as the parties have acceded thereto.

Article 30.

If a party brings before a Conciliation Commission a dispute which the other party, relying on conventions in force between the parties, has submitted to the Permanent Court of International Justice or an Arbitral Tribunal, the Commission shall defer consideration of the dispute until the Court or the Arbitral Tribunal has pronounced upon the conflict of competence. The same rule shall apply if the Court or the Tribunal is seized of the case by one of the parties during the conciliation proceedings.

Article 31.

1. In the case of a dispute the occasion of which, according to the municipal law of one of the parties, falls within the competence of its judicial or administrative authorities, the party in question may object to the matter in dispute being submitted for settlement by the different methods laid down in the present General Act until a decision with final effect has been pronounced, within a reasonable time, by the competent authority.

2. In such a case, the party which desires to resort to the procedures laid down in the present General Act must notify the other party of its intention within a period of one year from the date of the aforementioned decision.

Article 32.

If, in a judicial sentence or arbitral award, it is declared that a judgment, or a measure enjoined by a court of law or other authority of one of the parties to the dispute, is wholly or in part contrary to international law, and if the constitutional law of that party does not permit or only partially permits the consequences of the judgment or measure in question to be annulled, the parties agree that the judicial sentence or arbitral award shall grant the injured party equitable satisfaction.

Article 33.

1. In all cases where a dispute forms the object of arbitration or judicial proceedings, and particularly if the question on which the parties differ arises out of acts already committed or on the point of being committed, the Permanent Court of International Justice, acting in accordance with Article 41 of its Statute, or the Arbitral Tribunal, shall lay down within the shortest possible time the provisional measures to be adopted. The parties to the dispute shall be bound to accept such measures.

2. If the dispute is brought before a Conciliation Commission, the latter may recommend to the parties the adoption of such provisional measures as it considers suitable.

3. The parties undertake to abstain from all measures likely to react prejudicially upon the execution of the judicial or arbitral decision or upon the arrangements proposed by the Conciliation Commission and, in general, to abstain from any sort of action whatsoever which may aggravate or extend the dispute.

Article 34.

Should a dispute arise between more than two Parties to the present General Act, the following rules shall be observed for the application of the forms of procedure described in the foregoing provisions:

(a) In the case of conciliation procedure, a special commission shall invariably be constituted. The composition of such commission shall differ according as the parties all have separate interests or as two or more of their number act together.

In the former case, the parties shall each appoint one commissioner and shall jointly appoint commissioners nationals of third Powers not parties to the dispute, whose number shall always exceed by one the number of commissioners appointed separately by the parties.

In the second case, the parties who act together shall appoint their commissioner jointly by agreement between themselves and shall combine with the other party or parties in appointing third commissioners.

In either event, the parties, unless they agree otherwise, shall apply Article 5 and the following articles of the present Act, so far as they are compatible with the provisions of the present article.

(b) In the case of judicial procedure, the Statute of the Permanent Court of International Justice shall apply.

(c) In the case of arbitral procedure, if agreement is not secured as to the composition of the tribunal, in the case of the disputes mentioned in Article 17, each party shall have the right, by means of an application, to submit the dispute to the Permanent Court of International Justice; in the case of the disputes mentioned in Article 21, the above Article 22 and following articles shall apply, but each party having separate interests shall appoint one arbitrator and the number of arbitrators separately appointed by the parties to the dispute shall always be one less than that of the other arbitrators.

Article 35.

1. The present General Act shall be applicable as between the Parties thereto, even though a third Power, whether a party to the Act or not, has an interest in the dispute.

2. In conciliation procedure, the parties may agree to invite such third Power to intervene.

Article 36.

1. In judicial or arbitral procedure, if a third Power should consider that it has an interest of a legal nature which may be affected by the decision in the case, it may submit to the Permanent Court of International Justice or to the arbitral tribunal a request to intervene as a third Party.

2. It will be for the Court or the tribunal to decide upon this request.

Article 37.

1. Whenever the construction of a convention to which States other than those concerned in the case are parties is in question, the Registrar of the Permanent Court of International Justice or the arbitral tribunal shall notify all such States forthwith.

2. Every State so notified has the right to intervene in the proceedings; but, if it uses this right, the construction given by the decision will be binding upon it.

Article 38.

Accessions to the present General Act may extend:

A. Either to all the provisions of the Act (Chapters I, II, III and IV);

B. Or to those provisions only which relate to conciliation and judicial settlement (Chapters I and II), together with the general provisions dealing with these procedures (Chapter IV);

C. Or to those provisions only which relate to conciliation (Chapter I), together with the general provisions concerning that procedure (Chapter IV).

The Contracting Parties may benefit by the accessions of other Parties only in so far as they have themselves assumed the same obligations.

Article 39.

1. In addition to the power given in the preceding article, a Party, in acceding to the present General Act, may make his acceptance conditional upon the reservations exhaustively enumerated in the following paragraph. These reservations must be indicated at the time of accession.

2. These reservations may be such as to exclude from the procedure described in the present Act:

(a) Disputes arising out of facts prior to the accession either of the Party making the reservation or of any other Party with whom the said Party may have a dispute;

(b) Disputes concerning questions which by international law are solely within the domestic jurisdiction of States;

(c) Disputes concerning particular cases or clearly specified subject-matters, such as territorial status, or disputes falling within clearly defined categories.

3. If one of the parties to a dispute has made a reservation, the other parties may enforce the same reservation in regard to that party.

4. In the case of Parties, who have acceded to the provisions of the present General Act relating to judicial settlement or to arbitration, such reservations as they may have made shall, unless otherwise expressly stated, be deemed not to apply to the procedure of conciliation.

Article 40.

A Party whose accession has been only partial, or was made subject to reservations, may at any moment, by means of a simple declaration, either extend the scope of his accession or abandon all or part of his reservations.

Article 41.

Disputes relating to the interpretation or application of the present General Act, including those concerning the classification of disputes and the scope of reservations, shall be submitted to the Permanent Court of International Justice.

* * *

Article 45.

1. The present General Act shall be concluded for a period of five years, dating from its entry into force.

2. It shall remain in force for further successive periods of five years in the case of Contracting Parties which do not denounce it at least six months before the expiration of the current period.

3. Denunciation shall be effected by a written notification addressed to the Secretary–General of the League of Nations, who shall inform all the Members of the League and the non-Member States referred to in Article 43.

4. A denunciation may be partial only, or may consist in notification of reservations not previously made.

5. Notwithstanding denunciation by one of the Contracting Parties concerned in a dispute, all proceedings pending at the expiration of the current period of the General Act shall be duly completed.

* * *

1.3 CONVENTION ON THE RIGHTS AND DUTIES OF STATES. Done at Montevideo, Dec. 26, 1933. Entered into force, Dec. 26, 1934; for the United States, Dec. 26, 1934. 49 Stat. 3097, T.S. No. 881, Bevans 145, 165 L.N.T.S. 19

Article 1. The state as a person of international law should possess the following qualifications: (a) a permanent population; (b) a defined territory; (c) government; and (d) capacity to enter into relations with the other states.

Article 2. The federal state shall constitute a sole person in the eyes of international law.

Article 3. The political existence of the state is independent of recognition by the other states. Even before recognition the state has the right to defend its integrity and independence, to provide for its conservation and prosperity, and consequently to organize itself as it sees fit, to legislate upon its interests, administer its services, and to define the jurisdiction and competence of its courts.

The exercise of these rights has no other limitation than the exercise of the rights of other states according to international law.

Article 4. States are juridically equal, enjoy the same rights, and have equal capacity in their exercise. The rights of each one do not depend upon the power which it possesses to assure its exercise, but upon the simple fact of its existence as a person under international law.

Article 5. The fundamental rights of states are not susceptible of being affected in any manner whatsoever.

Article 6. The recognition of a state merely signifies that the state which recognizes it accepts the personality of the other with all the rights and duties determined by international law. Recognition is unconditional and irrevocable.

Article 7. The recognition of a state may be express or tacit. The latter results from any act which implies the intention of recognizing the new state.

Article 8. No state has the right to intervene in the internal or external affairs of another.

Article 9. The jurisdiction of states within the limits of national territory applies to all the inhabitants.

Nationals and foreigners are under the same protection of the law and the national authorities and the foreigners may not claim rights other or more extensive than those of the nationals.

Article 10. The primary interest of states is the conservation of peace. Differences of any nature which arise between them should be settled by recognized pacific methods.

Article 11. The contracting states definitely establish as the rule of their conduct the precise obligation not to recognize territorial acquisitions or special advantages which have been obtained by force whether this consists in the employment of arms, in threatening diplomatic representations, or in any other effective coercive measure. The territory of a state is inviolable and may not be the object of military occupation nor of other measures of force imposed by another state directly or indirectly or for any motive whatever even temporarily.

Article 12. The present Convention shall not affect obligations previously entered into by the High Contracting Parties by virtue of international agreements.

* * *

1.4 PACT OF THE LEAGUE OF ARAB STATES. Done at Cairo, March 22, 1945. Entered into force, May 10, 1945. 70 U.N.T.S. 237, 39 A.J.I.L. Supp. 266

Article 1. The League of Arab States is composed of the independent Arab States which have signed this Pact.

Any independent Arab State has the right to become a member of the League. If it desires to do so, it shall submit a request which will be deposited with the Permanent Secretariat General and submitted to the Council at the first meeting held after submission of the request.

Article 2. The League has as its purpose the strengthening of the relations between the member states; the coordination of their policies in order to achieve cooperation between them and to safeguard their independence and sovereignty; and a general concern with the affairs and interests of the Arab countries. It has also as its purpose the close cooperation of the member states, with due regard to the organization and circumstances of each state, on the following matters:

(A) Economic and financial affairs, including commercial relations, customs, currency, and questions of agriculture and industry.

(B) Communications; this includes railroads, roads, aviation, navigation, telegraphs, and posts.

(C) Cultural affairs.

(D) Nationality, passports, visas, execution of judgments, and extradition of criminals.

(E) Social affairs.

(F) Health problems.

Article 3. The League shall possess a Council composed of the representatives of the member states of the League; each state shall have a single vote, irrespective of the number of its representatives.

It shall be the task of the Council to achieve the realization of the objectives of the League and to supervise the execution of agreements which the member states have concluded on the questions enumerated in the preceding article, or on any other questions.

It likewise shall be the Council's task to decide upon the means by which the League is to cooperate with the international bodies to be created in the future in order to guarantee security and peace and regulate economic and social relations.

Article 4. For each of the questions listed in Article 2 there shall be set up a special committee in which the member states of the League shall be represented. These committees shall be charged with the task of laying down the principles and extent of cooperation. Such principles shall be formulated as draft agreements, to be presented to the Council for examination preparatory to their submission to the aforesaid states.

Representatives of the other Arab countries may take part in the work of the aforesaid committees. The Council shall determine the conditions under which these representatives may be permitted to participate and the rules governing such representation.

Article 5. Any resort to force in order to resolve disputes arising between two or more member states of the League is prohibited. If there should arise among them a difference which does not concern a state's independence, sovereignty, or territorial integrity, and if the parties to the dispute have recourse to the Council for the settlement of this difference, the decision of the Council shall then be enforceable and obligatory.

In such a case, the states between whom the difference has arisen shall not participate in the deliberations and decisions of the Council.

The Council shall mediate in all differences which threaten to lead to war between two member states, or a member state and a third state, with a view to bringing about their reconciliation.

Decisions of arbitration and mediation shall be taken by majority vote.

Article 6. In case of aggression or threat of aggression by one state against a member state, the state which has been attacked or threatened with aggression may demand the immediate convocation of the Council.

The Council shall by unanimous decision determine the measures necessary to repulse the aggression. If the aggressor is a member state, his vote shall not be counted in determining unanimity.

If, as a result of the attack, the government of the state attacked finds itself unable to communicate with the Council, that state's representative in the Council shall have the right to request the convocation of the Council for the purpose indicated in the foregoing paragraph. In the event that this representative is unable to communicate with the Council, any member state of the League shall have the right to request the convocation of the Council.

Article 7. Unanimous decisions of the Council shall be binding upon all member states of the League; majority decisions shall be binding only upon those states which have accepted them.

In either case the decisions of the Council shall be enforced in each member state according to its respective basic laws.

Article 8. Each member state shall respect the systems of government established in the other member states and regard them as exclusive concerns of those states. Each shall pledge to abstain from any action calculated to change established systems of government.

Article 9. States of the League which desire to establish closer cooperation and stronger bonds than are provided by this Pact may conclude agreements to that end.

Treaties and agreements already concluded or to be concluded in the future between a member state and another state shall not be binding or restrictive upon other members.

Article 10. The permanent seat of the League of Arab States is established in Cairo. The Council may, however, assemble at any other place it may designate.

Article 11. The Council of the League shall convene in ordinary session twice a year, in March and in October. It shall convene in extraordinary session upon the request of two member states of the League whenever the need arises.

Article 12. The League shall have a permanent Secretariat–General which shall consist of a Secretary–General, Assistant Secretaries, and an appropriate number of officials.

The Council of the League shall appoint the Secretary–General by a majority of two-thirds of the states of the League. The Secretary–General, with the approval of the Council shall appoint the Assistant Secretaries and the principal officials of the League.

The Council of the League shall establish an administrative regulation for the functions of the Secretariat–General and matters relating to the Staff.

The Secretary–General shall have the rank of Ambassador and the Assistant Secretaries that of Ministers Plenipotentiary.

Article 13. The Secretary–General shall prepare the draft of the budget of the League and shall submit it to the Council for approval before the beginning of each fiscal year.

Article 14. The members of the Council of the League as well as the members of the committees and the officials who are to be designated in the administrative regulation shall enjoy diplomatic privileges and immunity when engaged in the exercise of their functions.

The building occupied by the organs of the League shall be inviolable.

Article 15. The first meeting of the Council shall be convened at the invitation of the head of the Egyptian Government. Thereafter it shall be convened at the invitation of the Secretary–General.

The representatives of the member states of the League shall alternately assume the presidency of the Council at each of its ordinary sessions.

Article 16. Except in cases specifically indicated in this Pact, a majority vote of the Council shall be sufficient to make enforceable decisions on the following matters:

(A) Matters relating to personnel.

(B) Adoption of the budget of the League.

(C) Establishment of the administrative regulation for Council, the committee, and the Secretariat–General.

(D) Decisions to adjourn the sessions.

Article 17. Each member state of the League shall deposit with the Secretariat–General one copy of every treaty or agreement concluded in the future between itself and another member state of the League or a third state.

Article 18. If a member state contemplates withdrawal from the League, it shall inform the Council of its intention one year before such withdrawal is to go into effect.

The Council of the League may consider any state which fails to fulfill its obligations under this Pact as having become separated from the League, this to go into effect upon a unanimous decision of the states, not counting the state concerned.

Article 19. This Pact may be amended with the consent of two-thirds of the states belonging to the League, especially in order to make firmer and stronger the ties between the member states, to create an Arab Tribunal of Arbitration, and to regulate the relations of the League with any international bodies to be created in the future to guarantee security and peace.

Final action on an amendment cannot be taken prior to the session following the session in which the motion was initiated.

If a state does not accept such an amendment it may withdraw at such time as the amendment goes into effect, without being bound by the provisions of the preceding article.

* * *

1.5 CHARTER OF THE UNITED NATIONS. Done at San Francisco, June 26, 1945. Entered into force, Oct. 24, 1945; for the United States, Oct. 24, 1945. 59 Stat. 1031, T.S. No. 993, 3 Bevans 1153, 1976 Y.B.U.N. 1043

WE THE PEOPLES OF THE UNITED NATIONS DETERMINED

to save succeeding generations from the scourge of war, which twice in our lifetime has brought untold sorrow to mankind, and

to reaffirm faith in fundamental human rights, in the dignity and worth of the human person, in the equal rights of men and women and of nations large and small, and

to establish conditions under which justice and respect for the obligations arising from treaties and other sources of international law can be maintained, and

to promote social progress and better standards of life in larger freedom.

AND FOR THESE ENDS

to practice tolerance and live together in peace with one another as good neighbours, and

to unite our strength to maintain international peace and security, and

to ensure, by the acceptance of principles and the institution of methods, that armed force shall not be used, save in the common interest, and

to employ international machinery for the promotion of the economic and social advancement of all peoples.

HAVE RESOLVED TO COMBINE OUR EFFORTS TO ACCOMPLISH THESE AIMS

Accordingly, our respective Governments, through representatives assembled in the city of San Francisco, who have exhibited their full powers found to be in good and due form, have agreed to the present Charter of the United Nations and do hereby establish an international organization to be known as the United Nations.

CHAPTER I. PURPOSES AND PRINCIPLES

Article 1. The Purposes of the United Nations are:

(1) To maintain international peace and security, and to that end: to take effective collective measures for the prevention and removal of threats to the peace, and for the suppression of acts of aggression or other breaches of the peace, and to bring about by peaceful means, and in conformity with the principles of justice and international law, adjustment or settlement of international disputes or situations which might lead to a breach of the peace;

(2) To develop friendly relations among nations based on respect for the principle of equal rights and self-determination of peoples, and to take other appropriate measures to strengthen universal peace;

(3) To achieve international co-operation in solving international problems of an economic, social, cultural, or humanitarian character, and in promoting and encouraging respect for human rights and for fundamental freedoms for all without distinction as to race, sex, language, or religion; and

(4) To be a centre for harmonizing the actions of nations in the attainment of these common ends.

Article 2. The Organization and its Members, in pursuit of the Purposes stated in Article 1, shall act in accordance with the following Principles.

(1) The Organization is based on the principle of the sovereign equality of all its Members.

(2) All Members, in order to ensure to all of them the rights and benefits resulting from membership, shall fulfil in good faith the obligations assumed by them in accordance with the present Charter.

(3) All Members shall settle their international disputes by peaceful means in such a manner that international peace and security, and justice, are not endangered.

(4) All Members shall refrain in their international relations from the threat or use of force against the territorial integrity or political independence of any state, or in any other manner inconsistent with the Purposes of the United Nations.

(5) All Members shall give the United Nations every assistance in any action it takes in accordance with the present Charter, and shall refrain from giving assistance to any state against which the United Nations is taking preventive or enforcement action.

(6) The Organization shall ensure that states which are not Members of the United Nations act in accordance with these Principles so far as may be necessary for the maintenance of international peace and security.

(7) Nothing contained in the present Charter shall authorize the United Nations to intervene in matters which are essentially within the domestic jurisdiction of any state or shall require the Members to submit such matters to settlement under the present Charter; but this principle shall not prejudice the application of enforcement measures under Chapter VII.

CHAPTER II. MEMBERSHIP

Article 3. The original Members of the United Nations shall be the states which, having participated in the United Nations Conference on International Organization at San Francisco, or having previously signed the Declaration by United Nations of 1 January 1942, sign the present Charter and ratify it in accordance with Article 110.

Article 4. (1) Membership in the United Nations is open to all other peace-loving states which accept the obligations contained in the present Charter and, in the judgment of the Organization, are able and willing to carry out these obligations.

(2) The admission of any such state to membership in the United Nations will be effected by a decision of the General Assembly upon the recommendation of the Security Council.

Article 5. A Member of the United Nations against which preventive or enforcement action has been taken by the Security Council may be suspended from the exercise of the rights and privileges of membership by the General Assembly upon the recommendation of the Security Council. The exercise of these rights and privileges may be restored by the Security Council.

Article 6. A Member of the United Nations which has persistently violated the Principles contained in the present Charter may be expelled from the Organization by the General Assembly upon the recommendation of the Security Council.

CHAPTER III. ORGANS

Article 7. (1) There are established as the principal organs of the United Nations: a General Assembly, a Security Council, an Economic and Social Council, a Trusteeship Council, an International Court of Justice, and a Secretariat.

(2) Such subsidiary organs as may be found necessary may be established in accordance with the present Charter.

Article 8. The United Nations shall place no restrictions on the eligibility of men and women to participate in any capacity and under conditions of equality in its principal and subsidiary organs.

CHAPTER IV. THE GENERAL ASSEMBLY

Composition

Article 9. (1) The General Assembly shall consist of all the Members of the United Nations.

(2) Each Member shall have not more than five representatives in the General Assembly.

Functions and Powers

Article 10. The General Assembly may discuss any questions or any matters within the scope of the present Charter or relating to the powers and functions of any organs provided for in the present Charter, and, except as provided in Article 12, may make recommendations to the Members of the United Nations or to the Security Council or to both on any such questions or matters.

Article 11. (1) The General Assembly may consider the general principles of co-operation in the maintenance of international peace and security, including the principles governing disarmament and the regulation of armaments, and may make recommendations with regard to such principles to the Members or to the Security Council or to both.

(2) The General Assembly may discuss any questions relating to the maintenance of international peace and security brought before it by any Member of the United Nations, or by the Security Council, or by a state which is not a Member of the United Nations in accordance with Article 35, paragraph 2, and, except as provided in Article 12, may make recommendations with regard to any such questions to the state or states concerned or to the Security Council or to both. Any such question on which action is necessary shall be referred to the Security Council by the General Assembly either before or after discussion.

(3) The General Assembly may call the attention of the Security Council to situations which are likely to endanger international peace and security.

(4) The powers of the General Assembly set forth in this Article shall not limit the general scope of Article 10.

Article 12. (1) While the Security Council is exercising in respect of any dispute or situation the functions assigned to it in the present Charter, the General Assembly shall not make any recommendation with regard to that dispute or situation unless the Security Council so requests.

(2) The Secretary–General, with the consent of the Security Council, shall notify the General Assembly at each session of any matters relative to the maintenance of international peace and security which are being dealt with by the Security Council and shall similarly notify the General Assembly, or the Members of the United Nations if the General Assembly is not in session, immediately the Security Council ceases to deal with such matters.

Article 13. (1) The General Assembly shall initiate studies and make recommendations for the purpose of:

(a) promoting international co-operation in the political field and encouraging the progressive development of international law and its codification;

(b) promoting international co-operation in the economic, social, cultural, educational, and health fields, and assisting in the realization of human rights and fundamental freedoms for all without distinction as to race, sex, language, or religion.

(2) The further responsibilities, functions and powers of the General Assembly with respect to matters mentioned in paragraph (1)(b) above are set forth in Chapters IX and X.

Article 14. Subject to the provisions of Article 12, the General Assembly may recommend measures for the peaceful adjustment of any situation, regardless of origin, which it deems likely to impair the general welfare or friendly relations among nations, including situations resulting from a violation of the provisions of the present Charter setting forth the Purposes and Principles of the United Nations.

Article 15. (1) The General Assembly shall receive and consider annual and special reports from the Security Council; these reports shall include an account of the measures that the Security Council has decided upon or taken to maintain international peace and security.

(2) The General Assembly shall receive and consider reports from the other organs of the United Nations.

Article 16. The General Assembly shall perform such functions with respect to the international trusteeship system as are assigned to it under Chapters XII and XIII, including the approval of the trusteeship agreements for areas not designated as strategic.

Article 17. (1) The General Assembly shall consider and approve the budget of the Organization.

(2) The expenses of the Organization shall be borne by the Members as apportioned by the General Assembly.

(3) The General Assembly shall consider and approve any financial and budgetary arrangements with specialized agencies referred to in Article 57 and shall examine the administrative budgets of such specialized agencies with a view to making recommendations to the agencies concerned.

Voting

Article 18. (1) Each member of the General Assembly shall have one vote.

(2) Decisions of the General Assembly on important questions shall be made by a two-thirds majority of the members present and voting. These questions shall include: recommendations with respect to the maintenance of international peace and security, the election of the non-permanent members of the Security Council, the election of the members of the Economic and Social Council, the election of the members of the Trusteeship Council in accordance with paragraph 1(c) of Article 86, the admission of new Members to the United Nations, the suspension of the rights and privileges of membership, the expulsion of Members, questions relating to the operation of the trusteeship system, and budgetary questions.

(3) Decisions on other questions, including the determination of additional categories of questions to be decided by a two-thirds majority, shall be made by a majority of the members present and voting.

Article 19. A Member of the United Nations which is in arrears in the payment of its financial contributions to the Organization shall have no vote in the General Assembly if the amount of its arrears equals or exceeds the amount of the contributions due from it for the preceding two full years. The General Assembly may, nevertheless, permit such a Member to vote if it is satisfied that the failure to pay is due to conditions beyond the control of the Member.

Procedure

Article 20. The General Assembly shall meet in regular annual sessions and in such special sessions as occasion may require. Special sessions shall be convoked by the Secretary–General at the request of the Security Council or of a majority of the Members of the United Nations.

Article 21. The General Assembly shall adopt its own rules of procedure. It shall elect its President for each session.

Article 22. The General Assembly may establish such subsidiary organs as it deems necessary for the performance of its functions.

CHAPTER V. THE SECURITY COUNCIL

Composition

Article 23.[a] (1) The Security Council shall consist of fifteen Members of the United Nations. The Republic of China, France, the Union of Soviet Socialist Republics, the United Kingdom of Great Britain and Northern Ireland, and the United States of America shall be permanent members of the Security Council. The General Assembly shall elect ten other Members of the United Nations to be non-permanent members of the Security Council, due regard being specially paid, in the first instance to the contribution of Members of the United Nations to the maintenance of international peace and security and to the other purposes of the Organization, and also to equitable geographical distribution.

(2) The non-permanent members of the Security Council shall be elected for a term of two years. In the first election of the non-permanent members after the increase of the membership of the Security Council from eleven to fifteen, two of the four additional members shall be chosen for a term of one year. A retiring member shall not be eligible for immediate re-election.

(3) Each member of the Security Council shall have one representative.

Functions and Powers

Article 24. (1) In order to ensure prompt and effective action by the United Nations, its Members confer on the Security Council primary responsibility for the maintenance of international peace and security, and agree that in carrying out its duties under this responsibility the Security Council acts on their behalf.

(2) In discharging these duties the Security Council shall act in accordance with the Purposes and Principles of the United Nations. The specific powers granted to the Security Council for the discharge of these duties are laid down in Chapters VI, VII, VIII, and XII.

(3) The Security Council shall submit annual and, when necessary, special reports to the General Assembly for its consideration.

Article 25. The Members of the United Nations agree to accept and carry out the decisions of the Security Council in accordance with the present Charter.

Article 26. In order to promote the establishment and maintenance of international peace and security with the least diversion for armaments of the world's human and economic resources, the Security Council shall be responsible for formulating, with the assistance of the Military Staff Committee referred to in Article 47, plans to be submitted to the Members of the United Nations for the establishment of a system for the regulation of armaments.

Voting

Article 27.[b] (1) Each member of the Security Council shall have one vote.

(2) Decisions of the Security Council on procedural matters shall be made by an affirmative vote of nine members.

(3) Decisions of the Security Council on all other matters shall be made by an affirmative vote of nine members including the concurring votes of the permanent members; provided that, in decisions under Chapter VI, and under paragraph 3 of Article 52, a party to a dispute shall abstain from voting.

a. Amended text of Article 23 which came into force on August 31, 1965.

b. Amended text of Article 27 which came into force on August 31, 1965.

Procedure

Article 28. (1) The Security Council shall be so organized as to be able to function continuously. Each member of the Security Council shall for this purpose be represented at all times at the seat of the Organization.

(2) The Security Council shall hold periodic meetings at which each of its members may, if it so desires, be represented by a member of the government or by some other specially designated representative.

(3) The Security Council may hold meetings at such places other than the seat of the Organization as in its judgment will best facilitate its work.

Article 29. The Security Council may establish such subsidiary organs as it deems necessary for the performance of its functions.

Article 30. The Security Council shall adopt its own rules of procedure, including the method of selecting its President.

Article 31. Any Member of the United Nations which is not a member of the Security Council may participate, without vote, in the discussion of any question brought before the Security Council whenever the latter considers that the interests of that Member are specially affected.

Article 32. Any Member of the United Nations which is not a member of the Security Council or any state which is not a Member of the United Nations, if it is a party to a dispute under consideration by the Security Council, shall be invited to participate, without vote, in the discussion relating to the dispute. The Security Council shall lay down such conditions as it deems just for the participation of a state which is not a Member of the United Nations.

CHAPTER VI. PACIFIC SETTLEMENT OF DISPUTES

Article 33. (1) The parties to any dispute, the continuance of which is likely to endanger the maintenance of international peace and security, shall, first of all, seek a solution by negotiation, enquiry, mediation, conciliation, arbitration, judicial settlement, resort to regional agencies or arrangements, or other peaceful means of their own choice.

(2) The Security Council shall, when it deems necessary, call upon the parties to settle their dispute by such means.

Article 34. The Security Council may investigate any dispute, or any situation which might lead to international friction or give rise to a dispute, in order to determine whether the continuance of the dispute or situation is likely to endanger the maintenance of international peace and security.

Article 35. (1) Any Member of the United Nations may bring any dispute, or any situation of the nature referred to in Article 34, to the attention of the Security Council or of the General Assembly.

(2) A state which is not a Member of the United Nations may bring to the attention of the Security Council or of the General Assembly any dispute to which it is a party if it accepts in advance, for the purposes of the dispute, the obligations of pacific settlement provided in the present Charter.

(3) The proceedings of the General Assembly in respect of matters brought to its attention under this Article will be subject to the provisions of Articles 11 and 12.

Article 36. (1) The Security Council may, at any stage of a dispute of the nature referred to in Article 33 or of a situation of like nature, recommend appropriate procedures or methods of adjustment.

(2) The Security Council should take into consideration any procedures for the settlement of the dispute which have already been adopted by the parties.

(3) In making recommendations under this Article the Security Council should also take into consideration that legal disputes should as a general rule be referred by the parties to the International Court of Justice in accordance with the provisions of the Statute of the Court.

Article 37. (1) Should the parties to a dispute of the nature referred to in Article 33 fail to settle it by the means indicated in that Article, they shall refer it to the Security Council.

(2) If the Security Council deems that the continuance of the dispute is in fact likely to endanger the maintenance of international peace and security, it shall decide whether to take action under Article 36 or to recommend such terms of settlement as it may consider appropriate.

Article 38. Without prejudice to the provisions of Articles 33 to 37, the Security Council may, if all the parties to any dispute so request, make recommendations to the parties with a view to a pacific settlement of the dispute.

CHAPTER VII. ACTION WITH RESPECT TO THREATS TO THE PEACE, BREACHES OF THE PEACE, AND ACTS OF AGGRESSION

Article 39. The Security Council shall determine the existence of any threat to the peace, breach of the peace, or act of aggression and shall make recommendations, or decide what measures shall be taken in accordance with Articles 41 and 42, to maintain or restore international peace and security.

Article 40. In order to prevent an aggravation of the situation, the Security Council may, before making the recommendations or deciding upon the measures provided for in Article 39, call upon the parties concerned to comply with such provisional measures as it deems necessary or desirable. Such provisional measures shall be without prejudice to the rights, claims, or position of the parties concerned. The Security Council shall duly take account of failure to comply with such provisional measures.

Article 41. The Security Council may decide what measures not involving the use of armed force are to be employed to give effect to its decisions, and it may call upon the Members of the United Nations to apply such measures. These may include complete or partial interruption of economic relations and of rail, sea, air, postal, telegraphic, radio, and other means of communication, and the severance of diplomatic relations.

Article 42. Should the Security Council consider that measures provided for in Article 41 would be inadequate or have proved to be inadequate, it may take such action by air, sea, or land forces as may be necessary to maintain or restore international peace and security. Such action may include demonstrations, blockade, and other operations by air, sea, or land forces of Members of the United Nations.

Article 43. (1) All Members of the United Nations, in order to contribute to the maintenance of international peace and security, undertake to make available to the Security Council, on its call and in accordance with a special agreement or agreements, armed forces, assistance, and facilities, including rights of passage, necessary for the purpose of maintaining international peace and security.

(2) Such agreement or agreements shall govern the numbers and types of forces, their degree of readiness and general location, and the nature of the facilities and assistance to be provided.

(3) The agreement or agreements shall be negotiated as soon as possible on the initiative of the Security Council. They shall be concluded between the Security Council and Members or between the Security Council and groups of Members and shall be subject to ratification by the signatory states in accordance with their respective constitutional processes.

Article 44. When the Security Council has decided to use force it shall, before calling upon a Member not represented on it to provide armed forces in fulfilment of the obligations assumed under Article 43, invite that Member, if the Member so desires, to participate in the decisions of the Security Council concerning the employment of contingents of that Member's armed forces.

Article 45. In order to enable the United Nations to take urgent military measures, Members shall hold immediately available national air-force contingents for combined international enforcement action. The strength and degree of readiness of these contingents and plans for their combined action shall be determined, within the limits laid down in the special agreement or agreements referred to in Article 43, by the Security Council with the assistance of the Military Staff Committee.

Article 46. Plans for the application of armed force shall be made by the Security Council with the assistance of the Military Staff Committee.

Article 47. (1) There shall be established a Military Staff Committee to advise and assist the Security Council on all questions relating to the Security Council's military requirements for the maintenance of international peace and security, the employment and command of forces placed at its disposal, the regulation of armaments, and possible disarmament.

(2) The Military Staff Committee shall consist of the Chiefs of Staff of the permanent members of the Security Council or their representatives. Any Member of the United Nations not permanently represented on the Committee shall be invited by the Committee to be associated with it when the efficient discharge of the Committee's responsibilities requires the participation of that Member in its work.

(3) The Military Staff Committee shall be responsible under the Security Council for the strategic direction of any armed forces placed at the disposal of the Security Council. Questions relating to the command of such forces shall be worked out subsequently.

(4) The Military Staff Committee, with the authorization of the Security Council and after consultation with appropriate regional agencies, may establish regional subcommittees.

Article 48. (1) The action required to carry out the decisions of the Security Council for the maintenance of international peace and security shall be taken by all the Members of the United Nations or by some of them, as the Security Council may determine.

(2) Such decisions shall be carried out by the Members of the United Nations directly and through their action in the appropriate international agencies of which they are members.

Article 49. The Members of the United Nations shall join in affording mutual assistance in carrying out the measures decided upon by the Security Council.

Article 50. If preventive or enforcement measures against any state are taken by the Security Council, any other state, whether a Member of the United Nations or not, which finds itself confronted with special economic problems arising from the carrying out of those measures shall have the right to consult the Security Council with regard to a solution of those problems.

Article 51. Nothing in the present Charter shall impair the inherent right of individual or collective self-defence if an armed attack occurs against a Member of the United Nations, until the Security Council has taken measures necessary to maintain international peace and security. Measures taken by Members in the exercise of this right of self-defence shall be immediately reported to the Security Council and shall not in any way affect the authority and responsibility of the

Security Council under the present Charter to take at any time such action as it deems necessary in order to maintain or restore international peace and security.

CHAPTER VIII. REGIONAL ARRANGEMENTS

Article 52. (1) Nothing in the present Charter precludes the existence of regional arrangements or agencies for dealing with such matters relating to the maintenance of international peace and security as are appropriate for regional action, provided that such arrangements or agencies and their activities are consistent with the Purposes and Principles of the United Nations.

(2) The Members of the United Nations entering into such arrangements or constituting such agencies shall make every effort to achieve pacific settlement of local disputes through such regional arrangements or by such regional agencies before referring them to the Security Council.

(3) The Security Council shall encourage the development of pacific settlement of local disputes through such regional arrangements or by such regional agencies either on the initiative of the states concerned or by reference from the Security Council.

(4) This Article in no way impairs the application of Articles 34 and 35.

Article 53. (1) The Security Council shall, where appropriate, utilize such regional arrangements or agencies for enforcement action under its authority. But no enforcement action shall be taken under regional arrangements or by regional agencies without the authorization of the Security Council, with the exception of measures against any enemy state, as defined in paragraph 2 of this Article, provided for pursuant to Article 107 or in regional arrangements directed against renewal of aggressive policy on the part of any such state, until such time as the Organization may, on request of the Governments concerned, be charged with the responsibility for preventing further aggression by such a state.

(2) The term enemy state as used in paragraph 1 of this Article applies to any state which during the Second World War has been an enemy of any signatory of the present Charter.

Article 54. The Security Council shall at all times be kept fully informed of activities undertaken or in contemplation under regional arrangements or by regional agencies for the maintenance of international peace and security.

CHAPTER IX. INTERNATIONAL ECONOMIC AND SOCIAL CO-OPERATION

Article 55. With a view to the creation of conditions of stability and well-being which are necessary for peaceful and friendly relations among nations based on respect for the principle of equal rights and self-determination of peoples, the United Nations shall promote:

(a) higher standards of living, full employment, and conditions of economic and social progress and development;

(b) solutions of international economic, social, health, and related problems; and international cultural and educational co-operation; and

(c) universal respect for, and observance of, human rights and fundamental freedoms for all without distinction as to race, sex, language, or religion.

Article 56. All Members pledge themselves to take joint and separate action in co-operation with the Organization for the achievement of the purposes set forth in Article 55.

Article 57. (1) The various specialized agencies, established by intergovernmental agreement and having wide international responsibilities, as defined in their basic instruments, in economic, social, cultural, educational, health, and related fields, shall be brought into relationship with the United Nations in accordance with the provisions of Article 63.

(2) Such agencies thus brought into relationship with the United Nations are hereinafter referred to as specialized agencies.

Article 58. The Organization shall make recommendations for the co-ordination of the policies and activities of the specialized agencies.

Article 59. The Organization shall, where appropriate, initiate negotiations among the states concerned for the creation of any new specialized agencies required for the accomplishment of the purposes set forth in Article 55.

Article 60. Responsibility for the discharge of the functions of the Organization set forth in this Chapter shall be vested in the General Assembly and, under the authority of the General Assembly, in the Economic and Social Council, which shall have for this purpose the powers set forth in Chapter X.

CHAPTER X. THE ECONOMIC AND SOCIAL COUNCIL

Composition

Article 61.[c] (1) The Economic and Social Council shall consist of fifty-four Members of the United Nations elected by the General Assembly.

(2) Subject to the provisions of paragraph 3, eighteen members of the Economic and Social Council shall be elected each year for a term of three years. A retiring member shall be eligible for immediate re-election.

(3) At the first election after the increase in the membership of the Economic and Social Council from twenty-seven to fifty-four members, in addition to the members elected in place of the nine members whose term of office expires at the end of that year, twenty-seven additional members shall be elected. Of these twenty-seven additional members, the term of office of nine members so elected shall expire at the end of one year, and of nine other members at the end of two years, in accordance with arrangements made by the General Assembly.

(4) Each member of the Economic and Social Council shall have one representative.

Functions and Powers

Article 62. (1) The Economic and Social Council may make or initiate studies and reports with respect to international economic, social, cultural, educational, health, and related matters and may make recommendations with respect to any such matters to the General Assembly, to the Members of the United Nations, and to the specialized agencies concerned.

(2) It may make recommendations for the purpose of promoting respect for, and observance of, human rights and fundamental freedoms for all.

(3) It may prepare draft conventions for submission to the General Assembly, with respect to matters falling within its competence.

(4) It may call, in accordance with the rules prescribed by the United Nations, international conferences on matters falling within its competence.

Article 63. (1) The Economic and Social Council may enter into agreements with any of the agencies referred to in Article 57, defining the terms on which the agency concerned shall be brought into relationship with the United Nations. Such agreements shall be subject to approval by the General Assembly.

c. Amended text of Article 61, which came into force on September 24, 1973.

(2) It may co-ordinate the activities of the specialized agencies through consultation with and recommendations to such agencies and through recommendations to the General Assembly and to the Members of the United Nations.

Article 64. (1) The Economic and Social Council may take appropriate steps to obtain regular reports from the specialized agencies. It may make arrangements with the Members of the United Nations and with the specialized agencies to obtain reports on the steps taken to give effect to its own recommendations and to recommendations on matters falling within its competence made by the General Assembly.

(2) It may communicate its observations on these reports to the General Assembly.

Article 65. The Economic and Social Council may furnish information to the Security Council and shall assist the Security Council upon its request.

Article 66. (1) The Economic and Social Council shall perform such functions as fall within its competence in connexion with the carrying out of the recommendations of the General Assembly.

(2) It may, with the approval of the General Assembly, perform services at the request of Members of the United Nations and at the request of specialized agencies.

(3) It shall perform such other functions as are specified elsewhere in the present Charter or as may be assigned to it by the General Assembly.

Voting

Article 67. (1) Each member of the Economic and Social Council shall have one vote.

(2) Decisions of the Economic and Social Council shall be made by a majority of the members present and voting.

Procedure

Article 68. The Economic and Social Council shall set up commissions in economic and social fields and for the promotion of human rights, and such other commissions as may be required for the performance of its functions.

Article 69. The Economic and Social Council shall invite any Member of the United Nations to participate, without vote, in its deliberations on any matter of particular concern to that Member.

Article 70. The Economic and Social Council may make arrangements for representatives of the specialized agencies to participate, without vote, in its deliberations and in those of the commissions established by it, and for its representatives to participate in the deliberations of the specialized agencies.

Article 71. The Economic and Social Council may make suitable arrangements for consultation with non-governmental organizations which are concerned with matters within its competence. Such arrangements may be made with international organizations and, where appropriate, with national organizations after consultation with the Member of the United Nations concerned.

Article 72. (1) The Economic and Social Council shall adopt its own rules of procedure, including the method of selecting its President.

(2) The Economic and Social Council shall meet as required in accordance with its rules, which shall include provision for the convening of meetings on the request of a majority of its members.

CHAPTER XI. DECLARATION REGARDING NON–SELF–GOVERNING TERRITORIES

Article 73. Members of the United Nations which have or assume responsibilities for the administration of territories whose peoples have not yet attained a full measure of self-government recognize the principle that the interests of the inhabitants of these territories are paramount, and accept as a sacred trust the obligation to promote to the utmost, within the system of international peace and security established by the present Charter, the well-being of the inhabitants of these territories, and, to this end:

(a) to ensure, with due respect for the culture of the peoples concerned, their political, economic, social, and educational advancement, their just treatment, and their protection against abuses;

(b) to develop self-government, to take due account of the political aspirations of the peoples, and to assist them in the progressive development of their free political institutions, according to the particular circumstances of each territory and its peoples and their varying stages of advancement;

(c) to further international peace and security;

(d) to promote constructive measures of development, to encourage research, and to co-operate with one another and, when and where appropriate, with specialized international bodies with a view to the practical achievement of the social, economic, and scientific purposes set forth in this Article; and

(e) to transmit regularly to the Secretary–General for information purposes, subject to such limitation as security and constitutional considerations may require, statistical and other information of a technical nature relating to economic, social, and educational conditions in the territories for which they are respectively responsible other than those territories to which Chapters XII and XIII apply.

Article 74. Members of the United Nations also agree that their policy in respect of the territories to which this Chapter applies, no less than in respect of their metropolitan areas, must be based on the general principle of good neighbourliness, due account being taken of the interests and well-being of the rest of the world, in social, economic, and commercial matters.

CHAPTER XII. INTERNATIONAL TRUSTEESHIP SYSTEM

Article 75. The United Nations shall establish under its authority an international trusteeship system for the administration and supervision of such territories as may be placed thereunder by subsequent individual agreements. These territories are hereinafter referred to as trust territories.

Article 76. The basic objectives of the trusteeship system, in accordance with the Purposes of the United Nations laid down in Article 1 of the present Charter, shall be:

(a) to further international peace and security;

(b) to promote the political, economic, social, and educational advancement of the inhabitants of the trust territories, and their progressive development towards self-government or independence as may be appropriate to the particular circumstances of each territory and its peoples and the freely expressed wishes of the peoples concerned, and as may be provided by the terms of each trusteeship agreement;

(c) to encourage respect for human rights and for fundamental freedoms for all without distinction as to race, sex, language, or religion, and to encourage recognition of the interdependence of the peoples of the world; and

(d) to ensure equal treatment in social, economic, and commercial matters for all Members of the United Nations and their nationals, and also equal treatment for the latter in the administration of justice, without prejudice to the attainment of the foregoing objectives and subject to the provisions of Article 80.

Article 77. (1) The trusteeship system shall apply to such territories in the following categories as may be placed thereunder by means of trusteeship agreements:

(a) territories now held under mandate;

(b) territories which may be detached from enemy states as a result of the Second World War; and

(c) territories voluntarily placed under the system by states responsible for their administration.

(2) It will be a matter for subsequent agreement as to which territories in the foregoing categories will be brought under the trusteeship system and upon what terms.

Article 78. The trusteeship system shall not apply to territories which have become Members of the United Nations, relationship among which shall be based on respect for the principle of sovereign equality.

Article 79. The terms of trusteeship for each territory to be placed under the trusteeship system, including any alteration or amendment, shall be agreed upon by the states directly concerned, including the mandatory power in the case of territories held under mandate by a Member of the United Nations, and shall be approved as provided for in Articles 83 and 85.

Article 80. (1) Except as may be agreed upon in individual trusteeship agreements, made under Articles 77, 79, and 81, placing each territory under the trusteeship system, and until such agreements have been concluded, nothing in this Chapter shall be construed in or of itself to alter in any manner the rights whatsoever of any states or any peoples or the terms of existing international instruments to which Members of the United Nations may respectively be parties.

(2) Paragraph 1 of this Article shall not be interpreted as giving grounds for delay or postponement of the negotiation and conclusion of agreements for placing mandated and other territories under the trusteeship system as provided for in Article 77.

Article 81. The trusteeship agreement shall in each case include the terms under which the trust territory will be administered and designate the authority which will exercise the administration of the trust territory. Such authority, hereinafter called the administering authority, may be one or more states or the Organization itself.

Article 82. There may be designated, in any trusteeship agreement, a strategic area or areas which may include part or all of the trust territory to which the agreement applies, without prejudice to any special agreement or agreements made under Article 43.

Article 83. (1) All functions of the United Nations relating to strategic areas, including the approval of the terms of the trusteeship agreements and of their alteration or amendment, shall be exercised by the Security Council.

(2) The basic objectives set forth in Article 76 shall be applicable to the people of each strategic area.

(3) The Security Council shall, subject to the provisions of the trusteeship agreements and without prejudice to security considerations, avail itself of the assistance of the Trusteeship Council to perform those functions of the United

Nations under the trusteeship system relating to political, economic, social, and educational matters in the strategic areas.

Article 84. It shall be the duty of the administering authority to ensure that the trust territory shall play its part in the maintenance of international peace and security. To this end the administering authority may make use of volunteer forces, facilities, and assistance from the trust territory in carrying out the obligations towards the Security Council undertaken in this regard by the administering authority, as well as for local defence and the maintenance of law and order within the trust territory.

Article 85. (1) The functions of the United Nations with regard to trusteeship agreements for all areas not designated as strategic, including the approval of the terms of the trusteeship agreements and of their alteration or amendment, shall be exercised by the General Assembly.

(2) The Trusteeship Council, operating under the authority of the General Assembly, shall assist the General Assembly in carrying out these functions.

CHAPTER XIII. THE TRUSTEESHIP COUNCIL

Composition

Article 86. (1) The Trusteeship Council shall consist of the following Members of the United Nations:

(a) those Members administering trust territories;

(b) such of those Members mentioned by name in Article 23 as are not administering trust territories; and

(c) as many other Members elected for three-year terms by the General Assembly as may be necessary to ensure that the total number of members of the Trusteeship Council is equally divided between those Members of the United Nations which administer trust territories and those which do not.

(2) Each member of the Trusteeship Council shall designate one specially qualified person to represent it therein.

Functions and Powers

Article 87. The General Assembly and, under its authority, the Trusteeship Council, in carrying out their functions, may:

(a) consider reports submitted by the administering authority;

(b) accept petitions and examine them in consultation with the administering authority;

(c) provide for periodic visits to the respective trust territories at times agreed upon with the administering authority; and

(d) take these and other actions in conformity with the terms of the trusteeship agreements.

Article 88. The Trusteeship Council shall formulate a questionnaire on the political, economic, social, and educational advancement of the inhabitants of each trust territory, and the administering authority for each trust territory within the competence of the General Assembly shall make an annual report to the General Assembly upon the basis of such questionnaire.

Voting

Article 89. (1) Each member of the Trusteeship Council shall have one vote.

(2) Decisions of the Trusteeship Council shall be made by a majority of the members present and voting.

Procedure

Article 90. (1) The Trusteeship Council shall adopt its own rules of procedure, including the method of selecting its President.

(2) The Trusteeship Council shall meet as required in accordance with its rules, which shall include provision for the convening of meetings on the request of a majority of its members.

Article 91. The Trusteeship Council shall, when appropriate, avail itself of the assistance of the Economic and Social Council and of the specialized agencies in regard to matters with which they are respectively concerned.

CHAPTER XIV. THE INTERNATIONAL COURT OF JUSTICE

Article 92. The International Court of Justice shall be the principal judicial organ of the United Nations. It shall function in accordance with the annexed Statute, which is based upon the Statute of the Permanent Court of International Justice and forms an integral part of the present Charter.

Article 93. (1) All Members of the United Nations are *ipso facto* parties to the Statute of the International Court of Justice.

(2) A state which is not a Member of the United Nations may become a party to the Statute of the International Court of Justice on conditions to be determined in each case by the General Assembly upon the recommendation of the Security Council.

Article 94. (1) Each Member of the United Nations undertakes to comply with the decision of the International Court of Justice in any case to which it is a party.

(2) If any party to a case fails to perform the obligations incumbent upon it under a judgment rendered by the Court, the other party may have recourse to the Security Council, which may, if it deems necessary, make recommendations or decide upon measures to be taken to give effect to the judgment.

Article 95. Nothing in the present Charter shall prevent Members of the United Nations from entrusting the solution of their differences to other tribunals by virtue of agreements already in existence or which may be concluded in the future.

Article 96. (1) The General Assembly or the Security Council may request the International Court of Justice to give an advisory opinion on any legal question.

(2) Other organs of the United Nations and specialized agencies, which may at any time be so authorized by the General Assembly, may also request advisory opinions of the Court on legal questions arising within the scope of their activities.

CHAPTER XV. THE SECRETARIAT

Article 97. The Secretariat shall comprise a Secretary–General and such staff as the Organization may require. The Secretary–General shall be appointed by the General Assembly upon the recommendation of the Security Council. He shall be the chief administrative officer of the Organization.

Article 98. The Secretary–General shall act in that capacity in all meetings of the General Assembly, of the Security Council, of the Economic and Social Council, and of the Trusteeship Council, and shall perform such other functions as are entrusted to him by these organs. The Secretary–General shall make an annual report to the General Assembly on the work of the Organization.

Article 99. The Secretary–General may bring to the attention of the Security Council any matter which in his opinion may threaten the maintenance of international peace and security.

Article 100. (1) In the performance of their duties the Secretary–General and the staff shall not seek or receive instructions from any government or from any other authority external to the Organization. They shall refrain from any action which might reflect on their position as international officials responsible only to the Organization.

(2) Each Member of the United Nations undertakes to respect the exclusively international character of the responsibilities of the Secretary–General and the staff and not to seek to influence them in the discharge of their responsibilities.

Article 101. (1) The staff shall be appointed by the Secretary–General under regulations established by the General Assembly.

(2) Appropriate staffs shall be permanently assigned to the Economic and Social Council, the Trusteeship Council, and, as required, to other organs of the United Nations. These staffs shall form a part of the Secretariat.

(3) The paramount consideration in the employment of the staff and in the determination of the conditions of service shall be the necessity of securing the highest standards of efficiency, competence, and integrity. Due regard shall be paid to the importance of recruiting the staff on as wide a geographical basis as possible.

CHAPTER XVI. MISCELLANEOUS PROVISIONS

Article 102. (1) Every treaty and every international agreement entered into by any Member of the United Nations after the present Charter comes into force shall as soon as possible be registered with the Secretariat and published by it.

(2) No party to any such treaty or international agreement which has not been registered in accordance with the provisions of paragraph 1 of this Article may invoke that treaty or agreement before any organ of the United Nations.

Article 103. In the event of a conflict between the obligations of the Members of the United Nations under the present Charter and their obligations under any other international agreement, their obligations under the present Charter shall prevail.

Article 104. The Organization shall enjoy in the territory of each of its Members such legal capacity as may be necessary for the exercise of its functions and the fulfilment of its purposes.

Article 105. (1) The Organization shall enjoy in the territory of each of its Members such privileges and immunities as are necessary for the fulfilment of its purposes.

(2) Representatives of the Members of the United Nations and officials of the Organization shall similarly enjoy such privileges and immunities as are necessary for the independent exercise of their functions in connexion with the Organization.

(3) The General Assembly may make recommendations with a view to determining the details of the application of paragraphs 1 and 2 of this Article or may propose conventions to the Members of the United Nations for this purpose.

CHAPTER XVII. TRANSITIONAL SECURITY ARRANGEMENTS

Article 106. Pending the coming into force of such special agreements referred to in Article 43 as in the opinion of the Security Council enable it to begin the exercise of its responsibilities under Article 42, the parties to the Four–Nation Declaration, signed at Moscow, 30 October 1943, and France, shall, in accordance with the provisions of paragraph 5 of that Declaration, consult with one another and as occasion requires with other Members of the United Nations with a view to such joint action on behalf of the Organization as may be necessary for the purpose of maintaining international peace and security.

Article 107. Nothing in the present Charter shall invalidate or preclude action, in relation to any state which during the Second World War has been an enemy of any signatory to the present Charter, taken or authorized as a result of that war by the Governments having responsibility for such action.

CHAPTER XVIII. AMENDMENTS

Article 108. Amendments to the present Charter shall come into force for all Members of the United Nations when they have been adopted by a vote of two thirds of the members of the General Assembly and ratified in accordance with their respective constitutional processes by two thirds of the Members of the United Nations, including all the permanent members of the Security Council.

Article 109.[d] (1) A General Conference of the Members of the United Nations for the purpose of reviewing the present Charter may be held at a date and place to be fixed by a two-thirds vote of the members of the General Assembly and by a vote of any nine members of the Security Council. Each Member of the United Nations shall have one vote in the conference.

(2) Any alteration of the present Charter recommended by a two-thirds vote of the conference shall take effect when ratified in accordance with their respective constitutional processes by two thirds of the Members of the United Nations including all the permanent members of the Security Council.

(3) If such a conference has not been held before the tenth annual session of the General Assembly following the coming into force of the present Charter, the proposal to call such a conference shall be placed on the agenda of that session of the General Assembly, and the conference shall be held if so decided by a majority vote of the members of the General Assembly and by a vote of any seven members of the Security Council.

CHAPTER XIX. RATIFICATION AND SIGNATURE

Article 110. (1) The present Charter shall be ratified by the signatory states in accordance with their respective constitutional processes.

(2) The ratifications shall be deposited with the Government of the United States of America, which shall notify all the signatory states of each deposit as well as the Secretary–General of the Organization when he has been appointed.

(3) The present Charter shall come into force upon the deposit of ratifications by the Republic of China, France, the Union of Soviet Socialist Republics, the United Kingdom of Great Britain and Northern Ireland, and the United States of America, and by a majority of the other signatory states. A protocol of the ratifications deposited shall thereupon be drawn up by the Government of the United States of America which shall communicate copies thereof to all the signatory states.

(4) The states signatory to the present Charter which ratify if after it has come into force will become original Members of the United Nations on the date of the deposit of their respective ratifications.

Article 111. The present Charter, of which the Chinese, French, Russian, English, and Spanish texts are equally authentic, shall remain deposited in the archives of the Government of the United States of America. Duly certified copies thereof shall be transmitted by that Government to the Governments of the other signatory states.

d. Amended text of Article 109 which came into force on June 12, 1968.

1.6 STATUTE OF THE INTERNATIONAL COURT OF JUSTICE. Done at San Francisco, June 26, 1945. Entered into force, Oct. 24, 1945; for the United States, Oct. 24, 1945. 59 Stat. 1031, T.S. No. 993, 3 Bevans 1153, 1976 Y.B.U.N. 1052

Article 1. THE INTERNATIONAL COURT OF JUSTICE established by the Charter of the United Nations as the principal judicial organ of the United Nations shall be constituted and shall function in accordance with the provisions of the present Statute.

CHAPTER I. ORGANIZATION OF THE COURT

Article 2. The Court shall be composed of a body of independent judges, elected regardless of their nationality from among persons of high moral character, who possess the qualifications required in their respective countries for appointment to the highest judicial offices, or are jurisconsults of recognized competence in international law.

Article 3. (1) The Court shall consist of fifteen members, no two of whom may be nationals of the same state.

(2) A person who for the purposes of membership in the Court could be regarded as a national of more than one state shall be deemed to be a national of the one in which he ordinarily exercises civil and political rights.

Article 4. (1) The members of the Court shall be elected by the General Assembly and by the Security Council from a list of persons nominated by the national groups in the Permanent Court of Arbitration, in accordance with the following provisions.

(2) In the case of Members of the United Nations not represented in the Permanent Court of Arbitration, candidates shall be nominated by national groups appointed for this purpose by their governments under the same conditions as those prescribed for members of the Permanent Court of Arbitration by Article 44 of the Convention of The Hague of 1907 for the pacific settlement of international disputes.

(3) The conditions under which a state which is a party to the present Statute but is not a Member of the United Nations may participate in electing the members of the Court shall, in the absence of a special agreement, be laid down by the General Assembly upon recommendation of the Security Council.

* * *

Article 8. The General Assembly and the Security Council shall proceed independently of one another to elect the members of the Court.

Article 9. At every election, the electors shall bear in mind not only that the persons to be elected should individually possess the qualifications required, but also that in the body as a whole the representation of the main forms of civilization and of the principal legal systems of the world should be assured.

* * *

Article 13. (1) The members of the Court shall be elected for nine years and may be re-elected: provided, however, that of the judges elected at the first election, the terms of five judges shall expire at the end of three years and the terms of five more judges shall expire at the end of six years.

* * *

Article 16. (1) No member of the Court may exercise any political or administrative function, or engage in any other occupation of a professional nature.

(2) Any doubt on this point shall be settled by the decision of the Court.

Article 17. (1) No member of the Court may act as agent, counsel, or advocate in any case.

(2) No member may participate in the decision of any case in which he has previously taken part as agent, counsel, or advocate for one of the parties, or as a member of a national or international court, or of a commission of enquiry, or in any other capacity.

(3) Any doubt on this point shall be settled by the decision of the Court.

Article 18. (1) No member of the Court can be dismissed unless, in the unanimous opinion of the other members, he has ceased to fulfil the required conditions.

(2) Formal notification thereof shall be made to the Secretary-General by the Registrar.

(3) This notification makes the place vacant.

Article 19. The members of the Court, when engaged on the business of the Court, shall enjoy diplomatic privileges and immunities.

Article 20. Every member of the Court shall, before taking up his duties, make a solemn declaration in open court that he will exercise his powers impartially and conscientiously.

* * *

Article 22. (1) The seat of the Court shall be established at The Hague. This, however, shall not prevent the Court from sitting and exercising its functions elsewhere whenever the Court considers it desirable.

(2) The President and the Registrar shall reside at the seat of the Court.

Article 23. (1) The Court shall remain permanently in session, except during the judicial vacations, the dates and duration of which shall be fixed by the Court.

* * *

Article 24. (1) If, for some special reason, a member of the Court considers that he should not take part in the decision of a particular case, he shall so inform the President.

(2) If the President considers that for some special reason one of the members of the Court should not sit in a particular case, he shall give him notice accordingly.

(3) If in any such case the member of the Court and the President disagree, the matter shall be settled by the decision of the Court.

Article 25. (1) The full Court shall sit except when it is expressly provided otherwise in the present Statute.

(2) Subject to the condition that the number of judges available to constitute the Court is not thereby reduced below eleven, the Rules of the Court may provide for allowing one or more judges, according to circumstances and in rotation, to be dispensed from sitting.

(3) A quorum of nine judges shall suffice to constitute the Court.

Article 26. (1) The Court may from time to time form one or more chambers, composed of three or more judges as the Court may determine, for dealing with particular categories of cases; for example, labour cases and cases relating to transit and communications.

(2) The Court may at any time form a chamber for dealing with a particular case. The number of judges to constitute such a chamber shall be determined by the Court with the approval of the parties.

(3) Cases shall be heard and determined by the chambers provided for in this Article if the parties so request.

Article 27. A judgment given by any of the chambers provided for in Articles 26 and 29 shall be considered as rendered by the Court.

* * *

Article 29. With a view to the speedy dispatch of business, the Court shall form annually a chamber composed of five judges which, at the request of the parties, may hear and determine cases by summary procedure. In addition, two judges shall be selected for the purpose of replacing judges who find it impossible to sit.

Article 30. (1) The Court shall frame rules for carrying out its functions. In particular, it shall lay down rules of procedure.

(2) The Rules of the Court may provide for assessors to sit with the Court or with any of its chambers, without the right to vote.

Article 31. (1) Judges of the nationality of each of the parties shall retain their right to sit in the case before the Court.

* * *

Article 33. The expenses of the Court shall be borne by the United Nations in such a manner as shall be decided by the General Assembly.

CHAPTER II. COMPETENCE OF THE COURT

Article 34. (1) Only states may be parties in cases before the Court.

(2) The Court, subject to and in conformity with its Rules, may request of public international organizations information relevant to cases before it, and shall receive such information presented by such organizations on their own initiative.

(3) Whenever the construction of the constituent instrument of a public international organization or of an international convention adopted thereunder is in question in a case before the Court, the Registrar shall so notify the public international organization concerned and shall communicate to it copies of all the written proceedings.

Article 35. (1) The Court shall be open to the states parties to the present Statute.

(2) The conditions under which the Court shall be open to other states shall, subject to the special provisions contained in treaties in force, be laid down by the Security Council, but in no case shall such conditions place the parties in a position of inequality before the Court.

(3) When a state which is not a Member of the United Nations is a party to a case, the Court shall fix the amount which that party is to contribute towards the expenses of the Court. This provision shall not apply if such state is bearing a share of the expenses of the Court.

Article 36. (1) The jurisdiction of the Court comprises all cases which the parties refer to it and all matters specially provided for in the Charter of the United Nations or in treaties and conventions in force.

(2) The states parties to the present Statute may at any time declare that they recognize as compulsory *ipso facto* and without special agreement, in relation to any other state accepting the same obligation, the jurisdiction of the Court in all legal disputes concerning:

(a) the interpretation of a treaty;

(b) any question of international law;

(c) the existence of any fact which, if established, would constitute a breach of an international obligation;

(d) the nature or extent of the reparation to be made for the breach of an international obligation.

(3) The declarations referred to above may be made unconditionally or on condition of reciprocity on the part of several or certain states, or for a certain time.

(4) Such declarations shall be deposited with the Secretary-General of the United Nations, who shall transmit copies thereof to the parties to the Statute and to the Registrar of the Court.

(5) Declarations made under Article 36 of the Statute of the Permanent Court of International Justice and which are still in force shall be deemed, as between the parties to the present Statute, to be acceptances of the compulsory jurisdiction of the International Court of Justice for the period which they still have to run and in accordance with their terms.

(6) In the event of a dispute as to whether the Court has jurisdiction, the matter shall be settled by the decision of the Court.

Article 37. Whenever a treaty or convention in force provides for reference of a matter to a tribunal to have been instituted by the League of Nations, or to the Permanent Court of International Justice, the matter shall, as between the parties to the present Statute, be referred to the International Court of Justice.

Article 38. (1) The Court, whose function is to decide in accordance with international law such disputes as are submitted to it, shall apply:

(a) international conventions, whether general or particular, establishing rules expressly recognized by the contesting states;

(b) international custom, as evidence of a general practice accepted as law;

(c) the general principles of law recognized by civilized nations;

(d) subject to the provisions of Article 59, judicial decisions and the teachings of the most highly qualified publicists of the various nations, as subsidiary means for the determination of rules of law.

(2) This provision shall not prejudice the power of the Court to decide a case *ex aequo et bono,* if the parties agree thereto.

CHAPTER III. PROCEDURE

Article 39. (1) The official languages of the Court shall be French and English. If the parties agree that the case shall be conducted in French, the judgment shall be delivered in French. If the parties agree that the case shall be conducted in English, the judgment shall be delivered in English.

* * *

(3) The Court shall, at the request of any party, authorize a language other than French or English to be used by that party.

Article 40. (1) Cases are brought before the Court, as the case may be, either by the notification of the special agreement or by a written application addressed to the Registrar. In either case the subject of the dispute and the parties shall be indicated.

(2) The Registrar shall forthwith communicate the application to all concerned.

* * *

Article 41. (1) The Court shall have the power to indicate, if it considers that circumstances so require, any provisional measures which ought to be taken to preserve the respective rights of either party.

(2) Pending the final decision, notice of the measures suggested shall forthwith be given to the parties and to the Security Council.

Article 42. (1) The parties shall be represented by agents.

(2) They may have the assistance of counsel or advocates before the Court.

(3) The agents, counsel, and advocates of parties before the Court shall enjoy the privileges and immunities necessary to the independent exercise of their duties.

Article 43. (1) The procedure shall consist of two parts: written and oral.

(2) The written proceedings shall consist of the communication to the Court and to the parties of memorials, counter-memorials and, if necessary, replies; also all papers and documents in support.

* * *

(5) The oral proceedings shall consist of the hearing by the Court of witnesses, experts, agents, counsel, and advocates.

Article 44. (1) For the service of all notices upon persons other than the agents, counsel, and advocates, the Court shall apply direct to the government of the state upon whose territory the notice has to be served.

(2) The same provision shall apply whenever steps are to be taken to procure evidence on the spot.

* * *

Article 48. The Court shall make orders for the conduct of the case, shall decide the form and time in which each party must conclude its arguments, and make all arrangements connected with the taking of evidence.

* * *

Article 50. The Court may, at any time, entrust any individual, body, bureau, commission, or other organization that it may select, with the task of carrying out an enquiry or giving an expert opinion.

* * *

Article 53. (1) Whenever one of the parties does not appear before the Court, or fails to defend its case, the other party may call upon the Court to decide in favour of its claim.

(2) The Court must, before doing so, satisfy itself, not only that it has jurisdiction in accordance with Articles 36 and 37, but also that the claim is well founded in fact and law.

Article 54. (1) When, subject to the control of the Court, the agents, counsel, and advocates have completed their presentation of the case, the President shall declare the hearing closed.

(2) The Court shall withdraw to consider the judgment.

(3) The deliberations of the Court shall take place in private and remain secret.

Article 55. (1) All questions shall be decided by a majority of the judges present.

(2) In the event of an equality of votes, the President or the judge who acts in his place shall have a casting vote.

Article 56. (1) The judgment shall state the reasons on which it is based.

(2) It shall contain the names of the judges who have taken part in the decision.

Article 57. If the judgment does not represent in whole or in part the unanimous opinion of the judges, any judge shall be entitled to deliver a separate opinion.

Article 58. The judgment shall be signed by the President and by the Registrar. It shall be read in open court, due notice having been given to the agents.

Article 59. The decision of the Court has no binding force except between the parties and in respect of that particular case.

Article 60. The judgment is final and without appeal. In the event of dispute as to the meaning or scope of the judgment, the Court shall construe it upon the request of any party.

Article 61. (1) An application for revision of a judgment may be made only when it is based upon the discovery of some fact of such a nature as to be a decisive factor, which fact was, when the judgment was given, unknown to the Court and also to the party claiming revision, always provided that such ignorance was not due to negligence.

(2) The proceedings for revision shall be opened by a judgment of the Court expressly recording the existence of the new fact, recognizing that it has such a character as to lay the case open to revision, and declaring the application admissible on this ground.

(3) The Court may require previous compliance with the terms of the judgment before it admits proceedings in revision.

(4) The application for revision must be made at latest within six months of the discovery of the new fact.

(5) No application for revision may be made after the lapse of ten years from the date of the judgment.

Article 62. (1) Should a state consider that it has an interest of a legal nature which may be affected by the decision in the case, it may submit a request to the Court to be permitted to intervene.

(2) It shall be for the Court to decide upon this request.

Article 63. (1) Whenever the construction of a convention to which states other than those concerned in the case are parties is in question, the Registrar shall notify all such states forthwith.

(2) Every state so notified has the right to intervene in the proceedings; but if it uses this right, the construction given by the judgment will be equally binding upon it.

Article 64. Unless otherwise decided by the Court, each party shall bear its own costs.

CHAPTER IV. ADVISORY OPINIONS

Article 65. (1) The Court may give an advisory opinion on any legal question at the request of whatever body may be authorized by or in accordance with the Charter of the United Nations to make such a request.

(2) Questions upon which the advisory opinion of the Court is asked shall be laid before the Court by means of a written request containing an exact statement of the question upon which an opinion is required, and accompanied by all documents likely to throw light upon the question.

* * *

Article 67. The Court shall deliver its advisory opinions in open court, notice having been given to the Secretary–General and to the representatives of Members of the United Nations, of other states and of international organizations immediately concerned.

Article 68. In the exercise of its advisory functions the Court shall further be guided by the provisions of the present Statute which apply in contentious cases to the extent to which it recognizes them to be applicable.

* * *

1.7 CONVENTION ON THE PRIVILEGES AND IMMUNITIES OF THE UNITED NATIONS. Done at London, Feb. 13, 1946. Entered into force, Sept. 17, 1946; for the United States, Apr. 29, 1970. 21 U.S.T. 1418, T.I.A.S. No. 6900, 1 U.N.T.S. 15

Article I

JURIDICAL PERSONALITY

SECTION 1. The United Nations shall possess juridical personality. It shall have the capacity:

(*a*) To contract;

(*b*) To acquire and dispose of immovable and movable property;

(*c*) To institute legal proceedings.

Article II

PROPERTY, FUNDS AND ASSETS

SECTION 2. The United Nations, its property and assets wherever located and by whomsoever held, shall enjoy immunity from every form of legal process except insofar as in any particular case it has expressly waived its immunity. It is, however, understood that no waiver of immunity shall extend to any measure of execution.

SECTION 3. The premises of the United Nations shall be inviolable. The property and assets of the United Nations, wherever located and by whomsoever held, shall be immune from search, requisition, confiscation, expropriation and any other form of interference, whether by executive, administrative, judicial or legislative action.

SECTION 4. The archives of the United Nations, and in general all documents belonging to it or held by it, shall be inviolable wherever located.

SECTION 5. Without being restricted by financial controls, regulations or moratoria of any kind,

(*a*) The United Nations may hold funds, gold or currency of any kind and operate accounts in any currency;

(*b*) The United Nations shall be free to transfer its funds, gold or currency from one country to another or within any country and to convert any currency held by it into any other currency.

SECTION 6. In exercising its rights under Section 5 above, the United Nations shall pay due regard to any representations made by the Government of any Member insofar as it is considered that effect can be given to such representations without detriment to the interests of the United Nations.

SECTION 7. The United Nations, its assets, income and other property shall be:

(*a*) Exempt from all direct taxes; it is understood, however, that the United Nations will not claim exemption from taxes which are, in fact, no more than charges for public utility services;

(*b*) Exempt from customs duties and prohibitions and restrictions on imports and exports in respect of articles imported or exported by the United Nations for its official use. It is understood, however, that articles imported under such exemption will not be sold in the country into which they were imported except under conditions agreed with the Government of that country;

(*c*) Exempt from customs duties and prohibitions and restrictions on imports and exports in respect of its publications.

SECTION 8. While the United Nations will not, as a general rule, claim exemption from excise duties and from taxes on the sale of movable and immovable property which form part of the price to be paid, nevertheless when the United Nations is making important purchases for official use of property on which such duties and taxes have been charged or are chargeable, Members will, whenever possible, make appropriate administrative arrangements for the remission or return of the amount of duty or tax.

Article III

FACILITIES IN RESPECT OF COMMUNICATIONS

SECTION 9. The United Nations shall enjoy in the territory of each Member for its official communications treatment not less favourable than that accorded by the Government of that Member to any other Government including its diplomatic mission in the matter of priorities, rates and taxes on mails, cables, telegrams, radiograms, telephotos, telephone and other communications; and press rates for information to the press and radio. No censorship shall be applied to the official correspondence and other official communications of the United Nations.

SECTION 10. The United Nations shall have the right to use codes and to despatch and receive its correspondence by courier or in bags, which shall have the same immunities and privileges as diplomatic couriers and bags.

Article IV

THE REPRESENTATIVES OF MEMBERS

SECTION 11. Representatives of Members to the principal and subsidiary organs of the United Nations and to conferences convened by the United Nations, shall, while exercising their functions and during the journey to and from the place of meeting, enjoy the following privileges and immunities:

(*a*) Immunity from personal arrest or detention and from seizure of their personal baggage, and, in respect of words spoken or written and all acts done by them in their capacity as representatives, immunity from legal process of every kind;

(*b*) Inviolability for all papers and documents;

(*c*) The right to use codes and to receive papers or correspondence by courier or in sealed bags;

(*d*) Exemption in respect of themselves and their spouses from immigration restrictions, aliens registration or national service obligations in the state they are visiting or through which they are passing in the exercise of their functions;

(*e*) The same facilities in respect of currency or exchange restrictions as are accorded to representatives of foreign governments on temporary official missions;

(*f*) The same immunities and facilities in respect of their personal baggage as are accorded to diplomatic envoys, and also;

(*g*) Such other privileges, immunities and facilities not inconsistent with the foregoing as diplomatic envoys enjoy, except that they shall have no right to claim exemption from customs duties on goods imported (otherwise than as part of their personal baggage) or from excise duties or sales taxes.

SECTION 12. In order to secure, for the representatives of Members to the principal and subsidiary organs of the United Nations and to conferences convened by the United Nations, complete freedom of speech and independence in the discharge of their duties, the immunity from legal process in respect of words spoken or written and all acts done by them in discharging their duties shall continue to be accorded, notwithstanding that the persons concerned are no longer the representatives of Members.

SECTION 13. Where the incidence of any form of taxation depends upon residence, periods during which the representatives of Members to the principal and subsidiary organs of the United Nations and to conferences convened by the United Nations are present in a state for the discharge of their duties shall not be considered as periods of residence.

SECTION 14. Privileges and immunities are accorded to the representatives of Members not for the personal benefit of the individuals themselves, but in order to safeguard the independent exercise of their functions in connection with the United Nations. Consequently a Member not only has the right but is under a duty to waive the immunity of its representative in any case where in the opinion of the Member the immunity would impede the course of justice, and it can be waived without prejudice to the purpose for which the immunity is accorded.

SECTION 15. The provisions of Sections 11, 12 and 13 are not applicable as between a representative and the authorities of the state of which he is a national or of which he is or has been the representative.

SECTION 16. In this article the expression "representatives" shall be deemed to include all delegates, deputy delegates, advisers, technical experts and secretaries of delegations.

Article V

OFFICIALS

SECTION 17. The Secretary-General will specify the categories of officials to which the provisions of this Article and Article VII shall apply. He shall submit these categories to the General Assembly. Thereafter these categories shall be communicated to the Governments of all Members. The names of the officials included in these categories shall from time to time be made known to the Governments of Members.

SECTION 18. Officials of the United Nations shall:

(*a*) Be immune from legal process in respect of words spoken or written and all acts performed by them in their official capacity;

(*b*) Be exempt from taxation on the salaries and emoluments paid to them by the United Nations;

(*c*) Be immune from national service obligations;

(*d*) Be immune, together with their spouses and relatives dependent on them, from immigration restrictions and alien registration;

(*e*) Be accorded the same privileges in respect of exchange facilities as are accorded to the officials of comparable ranks forming part of diplomatic missions to the Government concerned;

(*f*) Be given, together with their spouses and relatives dependent on them, the same repatriation facilities in time of international crisis as diplomatic envoys;

(*g*) Have the right to import free of duty their furniture and effects at the time of first taking up their post in the country in question.

SECTION 19. In addition to the immunities and privileges specified in Section 18, the Secretary-General and all Assistant Secretaries-General shall be accorded in respect of themselves, their spouses and minor children, the privileges and immunities, exemptions and facilities accorded to diplomatic envoys, in accordance with international law.

SECTION 20. Privileges and immunities are granted to officials in the interests of the United Nations and not for the personal benefit of the individuals themselves. The Secretary-General shall have the right and the duty to waive the immunity of any official in any case where, in his opinion, the immunity would impede the course of justice and can be waived without prejudice to the interests of the United Nations. In the case of the Secretary-General, the Security Council shall have the right to waive immunity.

SECTION 21. The United Nations shall co-operate at all times with the appropriate authorities of Members to facilitate the proper administration of justice, secure the observance of police regulations and prevent the occurrence of any abuse in connection with the privileges, immunities and facilities mentioned in this Article.

Article VI

EXPERTS ON MISSIONS FOR THE UNITED NATIONS

SECTION 22. Experts (other than officials coming within the scope of Article V) performing missions for the United Nations shall be accorded such privileges and immunities as are necessary for the independent exercise of their functions during the period of their missions, including the time spent on journeys in connection with their missions. In particular they shall be accorded:

(*a*) Immunity from personal arrest or detention and from seizure of their personal baggage;

(*b*) In respect of words spoken or written and acts done by them in the course of the performance of their mission, immunity from legal process of every kind. This immunity from legal process shall continue to be accorded notwithstanding that the persons concerned are no longer employed on missions for the United Nations;

(*c*) Inviolability for all papers and documents;

(*d*) For the purpose of their communications with the United Nations, the right to use codes and to receive papers or correspondence by courier or in sealed bags;

(*e*) The same facilities in respect of currency or exchange restrictions as are accorded to representatives of foreign governments on temporary official missions;

(*f*) The same immunities and facilities in respect of their personal baggage as are accorded to diplomatic envoys.

SECTION 23. Privileges and immunities are granted to experts in the interests of the United Nations and not for the personal benefit of the individuals themselves. The Secretary-General shall have the right and the duty to waive the immunity of any expert in any case where, in his opinion, the immunity would impede the course of justice and it can be waived without prejudice to the interests of the United Nations.

Article VII

UNITED NATIONS LAISSEZ-PASSER

SECTION 24. The United Nations may issue United Nations laissez-passer to its officials. These laissez-passer shall be recognized and accepted as valid travel documents by the authorities of Members, taking into account the provisions of Section 25.

SECTION 25. Applications for visas (where required) from the holders of United Nations laissez-passer, when accompanied by a certificate that they are travelling on the business of the United Nations, shall be dealt with as speedily as possible. In addition, such persons shall be granted facilities for speedy travel.

SECTION 26. Similar facilities to those specified in Section 25 shall be accorded to experts and other persons who, though not the holders of United Nations laissez-passer, have a certificate that they are travelling on the business of the United Nations.

SECTION 27. The Secretary–General, Assistant Secretaries–General and Directors travelling on United Nations laissez-passer on the business of the United Nations shall be granted the same facilities as are accorded to diplomatic envoys.

SECTION 28. The provisions of this article may be applied to the comparable officials of specialized agencies if the agreements for relationship made under Article 63 of the Charter so provide.

Article VIII

SETTLEMENTS OF DISPUTES

SECTION 29. The United Nations shall make provisions for appropriate modes of settlement of:

(*a*) Disputes arising out of contracts or other disputes of a private law character to which the United Nations is a party;

(*b*) Disputes involving any official of the United Nations who by reason of his official position enjoys immunity, if immunity has not been waived by the Secretary–General.

SECTION 30. All differences arising out of the interpretation or application of the present convention shall be referred to the International Court of Justice, unless in any case it is agreed by the parties to have recourse to another mode of settlement. If a difference arises between the United Nations on the one hand and a Member on the other hand, a request shall be made for an advisory opinion on any legal question involved in accordance with Article 96 of the Charter and Article 65 of the Statute of the Court. The opinion given by the Court shall be accepted as decisive by the parties.

* * *

1.8 AGREEMENT BETWEEN THE UNITED NATIONS AND THE UNITED STATES OF AMERICA REGARDING THE HEADQUARTERS OF THE UNITED NATIONS. Done at Lake Success, June 26, 1947. Entered into force, Nov. 21, 1947. 61 Stat. 3416, T.I.A.S. No. 1676, 12 Bevans 956, 11(2) U.N.T.S. 11

Article I

DEFINITIONS

* * *

Article II

THE HEADQUARTERS DISTRICT

Section 2

The seat of the United Nations shall be the headquarters district.

Section 3

The appropriate American authorities shall take whatever action may be necessary to assure that the United Nations shall not be dispossessed of its property in the headquarters district, except as provided in section 22 in the event that the United Nations ceases to use the same, provided that the United Nations shall reimburse the appropriate American authorities for any costs incurred, after consultation with the United Nations, in liquidating by eminent domain proceedings or otherwise any adverse claims.

* * *

Article III

LAW AND AUTHORITY IN THE HEADQUARTERS DISTRICT

Section 7

(*a*) The headquarters district shall be under the control and authority of the United Nations as provided in this agreement.

(*b*) Except as otherwise provided in this agreement or in the General Convention, the federal, state and local law of the United States shall apply within the headquarters district.

(*c*) Except as otherwise provided in this agreement or in the General Convention, the federal, state and local courts of the United States shall have jurisdiction over acts done and transactions taking place in the headquarters district as provided in applicable federal, state and local laws.

(*d*) The federal, state and local courts of the United States, when dealing with cases arising out of or relating to acts done or transactions taking place in the headquarters district, shall take into account the regulations enacted by the United Nations under section 8.

Section 8

The United Nations shall have the power to make regulations, operative within the headquarters district, for the purpose of establishing therein conditions in all respects necessary for the full execution of its functions. No federal, state or local law or regulation of the United States which is inconsistent with a regulation of the United Nations authorized by this section shall, to the extent of such inconsistency, be applicable within the headquarters district. Any dispute, between the United Nations and the United States, as to whether a regulation of the United Nations is authorized by this section or as to whether a federal, state or local law or regulation is inconsistent with any regulation of the United Nations authorized by this section, shall be promptly settled as provided in Section 21. Pending such settlement, the regulation of the United Nations shall apply, and the federal, state or local law or regulation shall be inapplicable in the headquarters district to the extent that the United Nations claims it to be inconsistent with the regulation of the United Nations. This section shall not prevent the reasonable application of fire protection regulations of the appropriate American authorities.

Section 9

(*a*) The headquarters district shall be inviolable. Federal, state or local officers or officials of the United States, whether administrative, judicial, military or police, shall not enter the headquarters district to perform any official duties therein except with the consent of and under conditions agreed to by the Secretary–General. The service of legal process, including the seizure of private property, may take place within the headquarters district only with the consent of and under conditions approved by the Secretary–General.

(*b*) Without prejudice to the provisions of the General Convention or Article IV of this agreement, the United Nations shall prevent the headquarters district from becoming a refuge either for persons who are avoiding arrest under the federal, state, or local law of the United States or are required by the Government of the United States for extradition to another country, or for persons who are endeavoring to avoid service of legal process.

Section 10

The United Nations may expel or exclude persons from the headquarters district for violation of its regulations adopted under Section 8 or for other cause. Persons who violate such regulations shall be subject to other penalties or to detention under arrest only in accordance with the provisions of such laws or regulations as may be adopted by the appropriate American authorities.

Article IV

Communications and Transit

Section 11

The federal, state or local authorities of the United States shall not impose any impediments to transit to or from the headquarters district of: (1) representatives of Members or officials of the United Nations, or of specialized agencies as defined in Article 57, paragraph 2, of the Charter, or the families of such representatives or officials, (2) experts performing missions for the United Nations or for such specialized agencies, (3) representatives of the press, or of radio, film or other information agencies, who have been accredited by the United Nations (or by such a specialized agency) in its discretion after consultation with the United States, (4) representatives of non-governmental organizations recognized by the United Nations for the purpose of consultation under Article 71 of the Charter, or (5) other persons invited to the headquarters district by the United Nations or by such specialized agency on official business. The appropriate American authorities shall afford any necessary protection to such persons while in transit to or from the headquarters district. This section does not apply to general interruptions of transportation which are to be dealt with as provided in Section 17, and does not impair the effectiveness of generally applicable laws and regulations as to the operation of means of transportation.

Section 12

The provisions of Section 11 shall be applicable irrespective of the relations existing between the Governments of the persons referred to in that section and the Government of the United States.

Section 13

(*a*) Laws and regulations in force in the United States regarding the entry of aliens shall not be applied in such manner as to interfere with the privileges referred to in Section 11. When visas are required for persons referred to in that section, they shall be granted without charge and as promptly as possible.

(*b*) Laws and regulations in force in the United States regarding the residence of aliens shall not be applied in such manner as to interfere with the privileges referred to in Section 11 and, specifically, shall not be applied in such manner as to require any such person to leave the United States on account of any activities performed by him in his official capacity. In case of abuse of such privileges of residence by any such person in activities in the United States outside his official capacity, it is understood that the privileges referred to in Section 11 shall not be construed to grant him exemption from the laws and regulations of the United States regarding the continued residence of aliens, provided that:

(1) No proceedings shall be instituted under such laws or regulations to require any such person to leave the United States except with the prior approval of the Secretary of State of the United States. Such approval shall be given only after consultation with the appropriate Member in the case of a representative of a Member (or a member of his family) or with the Secretary–General or the principal executive officer of the appropriate specialized agency in the case of any other person referred to in Section 11;

(2) A representative of the Member concerned, the Secretary–General or the principal executive officer of the appropriate specialized agency, as the case may be, shall have the right to appear in any such proceedings on behalf of the person against whom they are instituted;

(3) Persons who are entitled to diplomatic privileges and immunities under Section 15 or under the General Convention shall not be required to leave the United States otherwise than in accordance with the customary procedure applicable to diplomatic envoys accredited to the United States.

(*c*) This section does not prevent the requirement of reasonable evidence to establish that persons claiming the rights granted by Section 11 come within the classes described in that section, or the reasonable application of quarantine and public health regulations.

(*d*) Except as provided above in this section and in the General Convention, the United States retains full control and authority over the entry of persons or property into the territory of the United States and the conditions under which persons may remain or reside there.

(*e*) The Secretary–General shall, at the request of the appropriate American authorities, enter into discussions with such authorities, with a view to making arrangements for registering the arrival and departure of persons who have been granted visas valid only for transit to and from the headquarters district and sojourn therein and in its immediate vicinity.

(*f*) The United Nations shall, subject to the foregoing provisions of this section, have the exclusive right to authorize or prohibit entry of persons and property into the headquarters district and to prescribe the conditions under which persons may remain or reside there.

Section 14

The Secretary–General and the appropriate American authorities shall, at the request of either of them, consult, as to methods of facilitating entrance into the United States, and the use of available means of transportation, by persons coming from abroad who wish to visit the headquarters district and do not enjoy the rights referred to in this Article.

Article V

RESIDENT REPRESENTATIVES TO THE UNITED NATIONS

Section 15

(1) Every person designated by a Member as the principal resident representative to the United Nations of such Member or as a resident representative with the rank of ambassador or minister plenipotentiary,

(2) such resident members of their staffs as may be agreed upon between the Secretary–General, the Government of the United States and the Government of the Member concerned;

(3) every person designated by a member of a specialized agency, as defined in Article 57, paragraph 2 of the Charter, as its principal permanent representative, with the rank of ambassador or minister plenipotentiary at the headquarters of such agency in the United States, and

(4) such other principal resident representatives of members of a specialized agency and such resident members of the staffs of representatives of a specialized agency as may be agreed upon between the principal executive officer of the specialized agency, the Government of the United States and the Government of the Member concerned,

shall, whether residing inside or outside the headquarters district, be entitled in the territory of the United States to the same privileges and immunities, subject to corresponding conditions and obligations, as it accords to diplomatic envoys accredited to it. In the case of Members whose governments are not recognized by the United States, such privileges and immunities need be extended to such representatives, or persons on the staffs of such representatives, only within the headquarters district, at their residences and offices outside the district, in transit between the district and such residences and offices, and in transit on official business to or from foreign countries.

Article VI

POLICE PROTECTION OF THE HEADQUARTERS DISTRICT

Section 16

(*a*) The appropriate American authorities shall exercise due diligence to ensure that the tranquility of the headquarters district is not disturbed by the unauthorized entry of groups of persons from outside or by disturbances in its immediate vicinity and shall cause to be provided on the boundaries of the headquarters district such police protection as is required for these purposes.

(*b*) If so requested by the Secretary–General, the appropriate American authorities shall provide a sufficient number of police for the preservation of law and order in the headquarters district, and for the removal therefrom of persons as requested under the authority of the United Nations. The United Nations shall, if requested, enter into arrangements with the appropriate American authorities to reimburse them for the reasonable cost of such services.

Article VII

PUBLIC SERVICES AND PROTECTION OF THE HEADQUARTERS DISTRICT

Section 17

(*a*) The appropriate American authorities will exercise, to the extent requested by the Secretary–General, the powers which they possess to ensure that the headquarters district shall be supplied on equitable terms with the necessary public services, including electricity, water, gas, post, telephone, telegraph, transportation, drainage, collection of refuse, fire protection, snow removal, *et cetera*. In case of any interruption or threatened interruption of any such services, the appropriate American authorities will consider the needs of the United Nations as being of equal importance with the similar needs of essential agencies of the Government of the United States, and will take steps accordingly to ensure that the work of the United Nations is not prejudiced.

(*b*) Special provision with reference to maintenance of utilities and underground construction are contained in Annex 2.

Section 18

The appropriate American authorities shall take all reasonable steps to ensure that the amenities of the headquarters district are not prejudiced and the purposes for which the district is required are not obstructed by any use made of the land in the vicinity of the district. The United Nations shall on its part take all reasonable steps to ensure that the amenities of the land in the vicinity of the headquarters district are not prejudiced by any use made of the land in the headquarters district by the United Nations.

Section 19

It is agreed that no form of racial or religious discrimination shall be permitted within the headquarters district.

Article VIII

MATTERS RELATING TO THE OPERATION OF THIS AGREEMENT

Section 20

The Secretary–General and the appropriate American authorities shall settle by agreement the channels through which they will communicate regarding the application of the provisions of this agreement and other questions affecting the headquarters district, and may enter into such supplemental agreements as may be necessary to fulfill the purposes of this agreement. In making supplemental agreements with the Secretary–General, the United States shall consult with the appropriate state and local authorities. If the Secretary–General so requests, the Secretary of State of the United States shall appoint a special representative for the purpose of liaison with the Secretary–General.

Section 21

(*a*) Any dispute between the United Nations and the United States concerning the interpretation or application of this agreement or of any supplemental agreement, which is not settled by negotiation or other agreed mode of settlement, shall be referred for final decision to a tribunal of three arbitrators, one to be named by the Secretary–General, one to be named by the Secretary of State of the United States, and the third to be chosen by the two, or, if they should fail to agree upon a third, then by the President of the International Court of Justice.

(*b*) The Secretary–General or the United States may ask the General Assembly to request of the International Court of Justice an advisory opinion on any legal question arising in the course of such proceedings. Pending the receipt of the opinion of the Court, an interim decision of the arbitral tribunal shall be observed by both parties. Thereafter, the arbitral tribunal shall render a final decision, having regard to the opinion of the Court.

Article IX

Miscellaneous Provisions

Section 22

(*a*) The United Nations shall not dispose of all or any part of the land owned by it in the headquarters district without the consent of the United States. If the United States is unwilling to consent it shall buy the land in question from the United Nations at a price to be determined as provided in paragraph (*d*) of this section.

(*b*) If the seat of the United Nations is removed from the headquarters district, all right, title and interest of the United Nations in and to real property in the headquarters district or any part of it shall, on request of either the United Nations or the United States, be assigned and conveyed to the United States. In the absence of such request, the same shall be assigned and conveyed to the sub-division of a state in which it is located or, if such sub-division shall not desire it, then to the state in which it is located. If none of the foregoing desire the same, it may be disposed of as provided in paragraph (*a*) of this section.

(*c*) If the United Nations disposes of all or any part of the headquarters district, the provisions of other sections of this agreement which apply to the headquarters district shall immediately cease to apply to the land and buildings so disposed of.

(*d*) The price to be paid for any conveyance under this section shall, in default of agreement, be the then fair value of the land, buildings and installations, to be determined under the procedure provided in Section 21.

Section 23

The seat of the United Nations shall not be removed from the headquarters district unless the United Nations should so decide.

Section 24

This agreement shall cease to be in force if the seat of the United Nations is removed from the territory of the United States, except for such provisions as may be applicable in connection with the orderly termination of the operations of the United Nations at its seat in the United States and the disposition of its property therein.

* * *

Section 27

This agreement shall be construed in the light of its primary purpose to enable the United Nations at its headquarters in the United States, fully and efficiently, to discharge its responsibilities and fulfill its purposes.

* * *

1.9 CHARTER OF THE ORGANIZATION OF AMERICAN STATES. Done at Bogota, April 30, 1948. Entered into force, Dec. 13, 1951; for the United States, Dec. 13, 1951. 2 U.S.T. 2394, T.I.A.S. No. 2361, 119 U.N.T.S. 3. PROTOCOL OF AMENDMENT. Done at Buenos Aires, Feb. 27, 1967. Entered into force, Feb. 27, 1970; for the United States, Feb. 27, 1970. 21 U.S.T. 607, T.I.A.S. No. 6847

PART ONE

CHAPTER I. NATURE AND PURPOSES

Article 1. The American States establish by this Charter the international organization that they have developed to achieve an order of peace and justice, to promote their solidarity, to strengthen their collaboration, and to defend their sovereignty, their territorial integrity, and their independence. Within the United Nations, the Organization of American States is a regional agency.

Article 2. The Organization of American States, in order to put into practice the principles on which it is founded and to fulfill its regional obligations under the Charter of the United Nations, proclaims the following essential purposes:

(a) To strengthen the peace and security of the continent;

(b) To prevent possible causes of difficulties and to ensure the pacific settlement of disputes that may arise among the Member States;

(c) To provide for common action on the part of those States in the event of aggression;

(d) To seek the solution of political, juridical, and economic problems that may arise among them; and

(e) To promote, by cooperative action, their economic, social, and cultural development.

CHAPTER II. PRINCIPLES

Article 3. The American States reaffirm the following principles:

(a) International law is the standard of conduct of States in their reciprocal relations;

(b) International order consists essentially of respect for the personality, sovereignty, and independence of States, and the faithful fulfillment of obligations derived from treaties and other sources of international law;

(c) Good faith shall govern the relations between States;

(d) The solidarity of the American States and the high aims which are sought through it require the political organization of those States on the basis of the effective exercise of representative democracy;

(e) The American States condemn war of aggression: victory does not give rights;

(f) An act of aggression against one American State is an act of aggression against all the other American States;

(g) Controversies of an international character arising between two or more American States shall be settled by peaceful procedures;

(h) Social justice and social security are bases of lasting peace;

(i) Economic cooperation is essential to the common welfare and prosperity of the peoples of the continent;

(j) The American States proclaim the fundamental rights of the individual without distinction as to race, nationality, creed, or sex;

(k) The spiritual unity of the continent is based on respect for the cultural values of the American countries and requires their close cooperation for the high purposes of civilization;

(*l*) The education of peoples should be directed toward justice, freedom, and peace.

CHAPTER III. MEMBERS

Article 4. All American States that ratify the present Charter are Members of the Organization.

* * *

CHAPTER IV. FUNDAMENTAL RIGHTS AND DUTIES OF STATES

Article 9. States are juridically equal, enjoy equal rights and equal capacity to exercise these rights, and have equal duties. The rights of each State depend not upon its power to ensure the exercise thereof, but upon the mere fact of its existence as a person under international law.

Article 10. Every American State has the duty to respect the rights enjoyed by every other State in accordance with international law.

Article 11. The fundamental rights of States may not be impaired in any manner whatsoever.

Article 12. The political existence of the State is independent of recognition by other States. Even before being recognized, the State has the right to defend its integrity and independence, to provide for its preservation and prosperity, and consequently to organize itself as it sees fit, to legislate concerning its interests, to administer its services, and to determine the jurisdiction and competence of its courts. The exercise of these rights is limited only by the exercise of the rights of other States in accordance with international law.

* * *

Article 14. The right of each State to protect itself and to live its own life does not authorize it to commit unjust acts against another State.

Article 15. The jurisdiction of States within the limits of their national territory is exercised equally over all the inhabitants, whether nationals or aliens.

Article 16. Each State has the right to develop its cultural, political, and economic life freely and naturally. In this free development, the State shall respect the rights of the individual and the principles of universal morality.

* * *

Article 18. No State or group of States has the right to intervene, directly or indirectly, for any reason whatever, in the internal or external affairs of any other State. The foregoing principle prohibits not only armed force but also any other form of interference or attempted threat against the personality of the State or against its political, economic, and cultural elements.

Article 19. No State may use or encourage the use of coercive measures of an economic or political character in order to force the sovereign will of another State and obtain from it advantages of any kind.

Article 20. The territory of a State is inviolable; it may not be the object, even temporarily, of military occupation or of other measures of force taken by another State, directly or indirectly, on any grounds whatever. No territorial acquisitions or special advantages obtained either by force or by other means of coercion shall be recognized.

Article 21. The American States bind themselves in their international relations not to have recourse to the use of force, except in the case of self-defense in accordance with existing treaties or in fulfillment thereof.

* * *

CHAPTER V. PACIFIC SETTLEMENT OF DISPUTES

Article 23. All international disputes that may arise between American States shall be submitted to the peaceful procedures set forth in this Charter, before being referred to the Security Council of the United Nations.

Article 24. The following are peaceful procedures: direct negotiation, good offices, mediation, investigation and conciliation, judicial settlement, arbitration, and those which the parties to the dispute may especially agree upon at any time.

Article 25. In the event that a dispute arises between two or more American States which, in the opinion of one of them, cannot be settled through the usual diplomatic channels, the parties shall agree on some other peaceful procedure that will enable them to reach a solution.

* * *

CHAPTER VI. COLLECTIVE SECURITY

Article 27. Every act of aggression by a State against the territorial integrity or the inviolability of the territory or against the sovereignty or political independence of an American State shall be considered an act of aggression against the other American States.

Article 28. If the inviolability or the integrity of the territory or the sovereignty or political independence of any American State should be affected by an armed attack or by an act of aggression that is not an armed attack, or by an extracontinental conflict, or by a conflict between two or more American States, or by any other fact or situation that might endanger the peace of America, the American States, in furtherance of the principles of continental solidarity or collective self-defense, shall apply the measures and procedures established in the special treaties on the subject.

CHAPTER VII. ECONOMIC STANDARDS

Article 29. The Member States, inspired by the principles of inter-American solidarity and cooperation, pledge themselves to a united effort to ensure social justice in the Hemisphere and dynamic and balanced economic development for their peoples, as conditions essential to peace and security.

Article 30. The Member States pledge themselves to mobilize their own national human and material resources through suitable programs, and recognize the importance of operating within an efficient domestic structure, as fundamental conditions for their economic and social progress and for assuring effective inter-American cooperation.

Article 31. To accelerate their economic and social development, in accordance with their own methods and procedures and within the framework of the democratic principles and the institutions of the inter-American system, the Member States agree to dedicate every effort to achieve the following basic goals:

(a) Substantial and self-sustained increase in the per capita national product;

(b) Equitable distribution of national income;

(c) Adequate and equitable systems of taxation;

(d) Modernization of rural life and reforms leading to equitable and efficient land-tenure systems, increased agricultural productivity, expanded use of undeveloped land, diversification of production; and improved processing and marketing systems for agricultural products; and the strengthening and expansion of facilities to attain these ends;

(e) Accelerated and diversified industrialization, especially of capital and intermediate goods;

(f) Stability in the domestic price levels, compatible with sustained economic development and the attainment of social justice;

(g) Fair wages, employment opportunities, and acceptable working conditions for all;

(h) Rapid eradication of illiteracy and expansion of educational opportunities for all;

(i) Protection of man's potential through the extension and application of modern medical science;

(j) Proper nutrition, especially through the acceleration of national efforts to increase the production and availability of food;

(k) Adequate housing for all sectors of the population;

(*l*) Urban conditions that offer the opportunity for a healthful, productive, and full life;

(m) Promotion of private initiative and investment in harmony with action in the public sector; and

(n) Expansion and diversification of exports.

Article 32. In order to attain the objectives set forth in this Chapter, the Member States agree to cooperate with one another, in the broadest spirit of inter-American solidarity, as far as their resources may permit and their laws may provide.

* * *

Article 34. The Member States should make every effort to avoid policies, actions, or measures that have serious adverse effects on the economic or social development of another Member State.

Article 35. The Member States agree to join together in seeking a solution to urgent or critical problems that may arise whenever the economic development or stability of any Member State is seriously affected by conditions that cannot be remedied through the efforts of that State.

Article 36. The Member States shall extend among themselves the benefits of science and technology by encouraging the exchange and utilization of scientific and technical knowledge in accordance with existing treaties and national laws.

Article 37. The Member States, recognizing the close interdependence between foreign trade and economic and social development, should make individual and united efforts to bring about the following:

(a) Reduction or elimination, by importing countries, of tariff and non-tariff barriers that affect the exports of the Members of the Organization, except when such barriers are applied in order to diversify the economic structure, to speed up the development of the less-developed Member States, or to intensify their process of economic integration, or when they are related to national security or to the needs for economic balance;

(b) Maintenance of continuity in their economic and social development by means of:

(i) Improved conditions for trade in basic commodities through international agreements, where appropriate; orderly marketing procedures that avoid the disruption of markets; and other measures designed to promote the expansion of markets, and to obtain dependable incomes for producers, adequate and dependable supplies for consumers, and stable prices that are both remunerative to producers and fair to consumers;

(ii) Improved international financial cooperation and the adoption of other means for lessening the adverse impact of sharp fluctuations in export earnings experienced by the countries exporting basic commodities; and

(iii) Diversification of exports and expansion of export opportunities for manufactured and semimanufactured products from the developing countries by promoting and strengthening national and multinational institutions and arrangements established for these purposes.

* * *

Article 40. The Member States recognize that integration of the developing countries of the Hemisphere is one of the objectives of the inter-American system and, therefore, shall orient their efforts and take the necessary measures to accelerate the integration process, with a view to establishing a Latin American common market in the shortest possible time.

* * *

Article 42. The Member States agree that technical and financial cooperation that seeks to promote regional economic integration should be based on the principle of harmonious, balanced, and efficient development, with particular attention to the relatively less-developed countries, so that it may be a decisive factor that will enable them to promote, with their own efforts, the improved development of their infrastructure programs, new lines of production, and export diversification.

CHAPTER VIII. SOCIAL STANDARDS

Article 43. The Member States, convinced that man can only achieve the full realization of his aspirations within a just social order, along with economic development and true peace, agree to dedicate every effort to the application of the following principles and mechanisms:

(a) All human beings, without distinction as to race, sex, nationality, creed, or social condition, have a right to material well-being and to their spiritual development, under circumstances of liberty, dignity, equality of opportunity, and economic security;

(b) Work is a right and a social duty, it gives dignity to the one who performs it, and it should be performed under conditions, including a system of fair wages, that ensure life, health, and a decent standard of living for the worker and his family, both during his working years and in his old age, or when any circumstance deprives him of the possibility of working;

(c) Employers and workers, both rural and urban, have the right to associate themselves freely for the defense and promotion of their interests, including the right to collective bargaining and the workers' right to strike, and recognition of the juridical personality of associations and the protection of their freedom and independence, all in accordance with applicable laws;

(d) Fair and efficient systems and procedures for consultation and collaboration among the sectors of production, with due regard for safeguarding the interests of the entire society;

(e) The operation of systems of public administration, banking and credit, enterprise, and distribution and sales, in such a way, in harmony with the private sector, as to meet the requirements and interests of the community;

(f) The incorporation and increasing participation of the marginal sectors of the population, in both rural and urban areas, in the economic, social, civic, cultural, and political life of the nation, in order to achieve the full integration of the national community, acceleration of the process of social mobility, and the consolidation of the democratic system. The encouragement of all efforts of popular promotion and cooperation that have as their purpose the development and progress of the community;

(g) Recognition of the importance of the contribution of organizations such as labor unions, cooperatives, and cultural, professional, business, neighborhood, and community associations to the life of the society and to the development process;

(h) Development of an efficient social security policy; and

(i) Adequate provision for all persons to have due legal aid in order to secure their rights.

Article 44. The Member States recognize that, in order to facilitate the process of Latin American regional integration, it is necessary to harmonize the social legislation of the developing countries, especially in the labor and social security fields, so that the rights of the workers shall be equally protected, and they agree to make the greatest efforts possible to achieve this goal.

CHAPTER IX. EDUCATIONAL, SCIENTIFIC, AND CULTURAL STANDARDS

Article 45. The Member States will give primary importance within their development plans to the encouragement of education, science, and culture, oriented toward the over-all improvement of the individual, and as a foundation for democracy, social justice, and progress.

Article 46. The Member States will cooperate with one another to meet their educational needs, to promote scientific research, and to encourage technological progress. They consider themselves individually and jointly bound to preserve and enrich the cultural heritage of the American peoples.

Article 47. The Member States will exert the greatest efforts, in accordance with their constitutional processes, to ensure the effective exercise of the right to education. . . .

Article 48. The Member States will give special attention to the eradication of illiteracy, will strengthen adult and vocational education systems, and will ensure that the benefits of culture will be available to the entire population. They will promote the use of all information media to fulfill these aims.

* * *

PART TWO

CHAPTER X. THE ORGANS

Article 51. The Organization of American States accomplishes its purposes by means of:

(a) The General Assembly;

(b) The Meeting of Consultation of Ministers of Foreign Affairs;

(c) The Councils;

(d) The Inter-American Juridical Committee;

(e) The Inter-American Commission on Human Rights;

(f) The General Secretariat;

(g) The Specialized Conferences; and

(h) The Specialized Organizations.

There may be established, in addition to those provided for in the Charter and in accordance with the provisions thereof, such subsidiary organs, agencies, and other entities as are considered necessary.

CHAPTER XI. THE GENERAL ASSEMBLY

Article 52. The General Assembly is the supreme organ of the Organization of American States. It has as its principal powers, in addition to such others as are assigned to it by the Charter, the following:

(a) To decide the general action and policy of the Organization, determine the structure and functions of its organs, and consider any matter relating to friendly relations among the American States;

(b) To establish measures for coordinating the activities of the organs, agencies, and entities of the Organization among themselves and such activities with those of the other institutions of the inter-American system;

(c) To strengthen and coordinate cooperation with the United Nations and its specialized agencies;

(d) To promote collaboration, especially in the economic, social, and cultural fields, with other international organizations whose purposes are similar to those of the Organization of American States;

(e) To approve the program-budget of the Organization and determine the quotas of the Member States;

(f) To consider the annual and special reports that shall be presented to it by the organs, agencies, and entities of the inter-American system;

(g) To adopt general standards to govern the operations of the General Secretariat; and

(h) To adopt its own rules of procedure and, by a two-thirds vote, its agenda.

The General Assembly shall exercise its powers in accordance with the provisions of the Charter and of other inter-American treaties.

* * *

Article 54. All Member States have the right to be represented in the General Assembly. Each State has the right to one vote.

Article 55. The General Assembly shall convene annually during the period determined by the rules of procedure and at a place selected in accordance with the principle of rotation. At each regular session the date and place of the next regular session shall be determined, in accordance with the rules of procedure.

* * *

Article 57. Decisions of the General Assembly shall be adopted by the affirmative vote of an absolute majority of the Member States, except in those cases that require a two-thirds vote as provided in the Charter or as may be provided by the General Assembly in its rules of procedure.

* * *

CHAPTER XII. THE MEETING OF CONSULTATION OF MINISTERS OF FOREIGN AFFAIRS

Article 59. The Meeting of Consultation of Ministers of Foreign Affairs shall be held in order to consider problems of an urgent nature and of common interest to the American States, and to serve as the Organ of Consultation.

Article 60. Any Member State may request that a Meeting of Consultation be called. The request shall be addressed to the Permanent Council of the Organization, which shall decide by an absolute majority whether a meeting should be held.

* * *

Article 63. In case of an armed attack within the territory of an American State or within the region of security delimited by treaties in force, a Meeting of Consultation shall be held without delay. Such Meeting shall be called immediately by the Chairman of the Permanent Council of the Organization, who shall at the same time call a meeting of the Council itself.

* * *

CHAPTER XIII. THE COUNCILS OF THE ORGANIZATION

Common Provisions

Article 68. The Permanent Council of the Organization, the Inter-American Economic and Social Council, and the Inter-American Council for Education, Science, and Culture are directly responsible to the General Assembly and each has the authority granted to it in the Charter and other inter-American instruments, as well as the functions assigned to it by the General Assembly and the Meeting of Consultation of Ministers of Foreign Affairs.

Article 69. All Member States have the right to be represented on each of the Councils. Each State has the right to one vote.

Article 70. The Councils may, within the limits of the Charter and other inter-American instruments, make recommendations on matters within their authority.

* * *

Article 73. The Councils, to the extent of their ability, and with the cooperation of the General Secretariat, shall render to the Governments such specialized services as the latter may request.

Article 74. Each Council has the authority to require the other Councils, as well as the subsidiary organs and agencies responsible to them, to provide it with information and advisory services on matters within their respective spheres of competence. The Councils may also request the same services from the other agencies of the inter-American system.

* * *

CHAPTER XIV. THE PERMANENT COUNCIL OF THE ORGANIZATION

Article 78. The Permanent Council of the Organization is composed of one representative of each Member State, especially appointed by the respective Government, with the rank of ambassador. Each Government may accredit an acting representative, as well as such alternates and advisers as it considers necessary.

* * *

Article 80. Within the limits of the Charter and of inter-American treaties and agreements, the Permanent Council takes cognizance of any matter referred to it by the General Assembly or the Meeting of Consultation of Ministers of Foreign Affairs.

Article 81. The Permanent Council shall serve provisionally as the Organ of Consultation when the circumstances contemplated in Article 63 of this Charter arise.

Article 82. The Permanent Council shall keep vigilance over the maintenance of friendly relations among the Member States, and for that purpose shall effectively assist them in the peaceful settlement of their disputes, in accordance with the following provisions.

Article 83. To assist the Permanent Council in the exercise of these powers, an Inter-American Committee on Peaceful Settlement shall be established, which shall function as a subsidiary organ of the Council. The statutes of the Committee shall be prepared by the Council and approved by the General Assembly.

Article 84. The parties to a dispute may resort to the Permanent Council to obtain its good offices. In such a case the Council shall have authority to assist the parties and to recommend the procedures it considers suitable for the peaceful settlement of the dispute.

If the parties so wish, the Chairman of the Council shall refer the dispute directly to the Inter-American Committee on Peaceful Settlement.

Article 85. In the exercise of these powers, the Permanent Council, through the Inter-American Committee on Peaceful Settlement or by any other means, may ascertain the facts in the dispute, and may do so in the territory of any of the parties with the consent of the Government concerned.

Article 86. Any party to a dispute in which none of the peaceful procedures set forth in Article 24 of the Charter is being followed may appeal to the Permanent Council to take cognizance of the dispute.

The Council shall immediately refer the request to the Inter-American Committee on Peaceful Settlement, which shall consider whether or not the matter is within its competence and, if it deems it appropriate, shall offer its good offices to the other party or parties. Once these are accepted, the Inter-American Committee on Peaceful Settlement may assist the parties and recommend the procedures that it considers suitable for the peaceful settlement of the dispute.

In the exercise of these powers, the Committee may carry out an investigation of the facts in the dispute, and may do so in the territory of any of the parties with the consent of the Government concerned.

Article 87. If one of the parties should refuse the offer, the Inter-American Committee on Peaceful Settlement shall limit itself to informing the Permanent Council, without prejudice to its taking steps to restore relations between the parties, if they were interrupted, or to reestablish harmony between them.

Article 88. Once such a report is received, the Permanent Council may make suggestions for bringing the parties together for the purpose of Article 87 and, if it considers it necessary, it may urge the parties to avoid any action that might aggravate the dispute.

If one of the parties should continue to refuse the good offices of the Inter-American Committee on Peaceful Settlement or of the Council, the Council shall limit itself to submitting a report to the General Assembly.

Article 89. The Permanent Council, in the exercise of these functions, shall take its decisions by an affirmative vote of two thirds of its members, excluding the parties to the dispute, except for such decisions as the rules of procedure provide shall be adopted by a simple majority.

* * *

CHAPTER XV. THE INTER-AMERICAN ECONOMIC AND SOCIAL COUNCIL

Article 93. The Inter-American Economic and Social Council is composed of one principal representative, of the highest rank, of each Member State, especially appointed by the respective Government.

Article 94. The purpose of the Inter-American Economic and Social Council is to promote cooperation among the American countries in order to attain accelerated economic and social development, in accordance with the standards set forth in Chapters VII and VIII.

* * *

CHAPTER XVI. THE INTER–AMERICAN COUNCIL FOR EDUCATION, SCIENCE, AND CULTURE

Article 99. The Inter–American Council for Education, Science, and Culture is composed of one principal representative, of the highest rank, of each Member State, especially appointed by the respective Government.

Article 100. The purpose of the Inter–American Council for Education, Science, and Culture is to promote friendly relations and mutual understanding between the peoples of the Americas through educational, scientific, and cultural cooperation and exchange between Member States, in order to raise the cultural level of the peoples, reaffirm their dignity as individuals, prepare them fully for the tasks of progress, and strengthen the devotion to peace, democracy, and social justice that has characterized their evolution.

* * *

CHAPTER XVII. THE INTER–AMERICAN JURIDICAL COMMITTEE

Article 105. The purpose of the Inter–American Juridical Committee is to serve the Organization as an advisory body on juridical matters; to promote the progressive development and the codification of international law; and to study juridical problems related to the integration of the developing countries of the Hemisphere and, insofar as may appear desirable, the possibility of attaining uniformity in their legislation.

Article 106. The Inter–American Juridical Committee shall undertake the studies and preparatory work assigned to it by the General Assembly, the Meeting of Consultation of Ministers of Foreign Affairs, or the Councils of the Organization. It may also, on its own initiative, undertake such studies and preparatory work as it considers advisable, and suggest the holding of specialized juridical conferences.

* * *

CHAPTER XVIII. THE INTER–AMERICAN COMMISSION ON HUMAN RIGHTS

Article 112. There shall be an Inter–American Commission on Human Rights, whose principal function shall be to promote the observance and protection of human rights and to serve as a consultative organ of the Organization in these matters.

An inter-American convention on human rights shall determine the structure, competence, and procedure of this Commission, as well as those of other organs responsible for these matters.

CHAPTER XIX. THE GENERAL SECRETARIAT

Article 113. The General Secretariat is the central and permanent organ of the Organization of American States. It shall perform the functions assigned to it in the Charter, in other inter-American treaties and agreements, and by the General Assembly, and shall carry out the duties entrusted to it by the General Assembly, the Meeting of Consultation of Ministers of Foreign Affairs, or the Councils.

Article 114. The Secretary General of the Organization shall be elected by the General Assembly for a five-year term and may not be reelected more than once or succeeded by a person of the same nationality. In the event that the office of Secretary General becomes vacant, the Assistant Secretary General shall assume his duties until the General Assembly shall elect a new Secretary General for a full term.

Article 115. The Secretary General shall direct the General Secretariat, be the legal representative thereof, and, notwithstanding the provisions of Article 91.b, be responsible to the General Assembly for the proper fulfillment of the obligations and functions of the General Secretariat.

Article 116. The Secretary General, or his representative, participates with voice but without vote in all meetings of the Organization.

Article 117. The General Secretariat shall promote economic, social, juridical, educational, scientific, and cultural relations among all the Member States of the Organization, in keeping with the actions and policies decided upon by the General Assembly and with the pertinent decisions of the Councils.

* * *

Article 127. The seat of the General Secretariat is the city of Washington.

CHAPTER XX. THE SPECIALIZED CONFERENCES

Article 128. The Specialized Conferences are inter-governmental meetings to deal with special technical matters or to develop specific aspects of inter-American cooperation. They shall be held when either the General Assembly or the Meeting of Consultation of Ministers of Foreign Affairs so decides, on its own initiative or at the request of one of the Councils or Specialized Organizations.

* * *

CHAPTER XXI. THE SPECIALIZED ORGANIZATIONS

Article 130. For the purposes of the present Charter, Inter-American Specialized Organizations are the intergovernmental organizations established by multilateral agreements and having specific functions with respect to technical matters of common interest to the American States.

* * *

PART THREE

CHAPTER XXII. THE UNITED NATIONS

Article 137. None of the provisions of this Charter shall be construed as impairing the rights and obligations of the Member States under the Charter of the United Nations.

CHAPTER XXIII. MISCELLANEOUS PROVISIONS

Article 138. Attendance at meetings of the permanent organs of the Organization of American States or at the conferences and meetings provided for in the Charter, or held under the auspices of the Organization, shall be in accordance with the multilateral character of the aforesaid organs, conferences, and meetings and shall not depend on the bilateral relations between the Government of any Member State and the Government of the host country.

Article 139. The Organization of American States shall enjoy in the territory of each Member such legal capacity, privileges, and immunities as are necessary for the exercise of its functions and the accomplishment of its purposes.

Article 140. The representatives of the Member States on the organs of the Organization, the personnel of their delegations, as well as the Secretary General and the Assistant Secretary General shall enjoy the privileges and immunities corresponding to their positions and necessary for the independent performance of their duties.

Article 141. The juridical status of the Specialized Organizations and the privileges and immunities that should be granted to them and to their personnel, as well as to the officials of the General Secretariat, shall be determined in a multilateral agreement. The foregoing shall not preclude, when it is considered necessary, the concluding of bilateral agreements.

* * *

Article 143. The Organization of American States does not allow any restriction based on race, creed, or sex, with respect to eligibility to participate in the activities of the Organization and to hold positions therein.

* * *

1.10 STATUTE OF THE COUNCIL OF EUROPE, Done at London, May 5, 1949. Entered into force, August 3, 1949. 87 U.N.T.S. 103 [a]

The Governments of the Kingdom of Belgium, the Kingdom of Denmark, the French Republic, the Irish Republic, the Italian Republic, the Grand Duchy of Luxembourg, the Kingdom of the Netherlands, the Kingdom of Norway, the Kingdom of Sweden and the United Kingdom of Great Britain and Northern Ireland:

Convinced that the pursuit of peace based upon justice and international co-operation is vital for the preservation of human society and civilisation;

Reaffirming their devotion to the spiritual and moral values which are the common heritage of their peoples and the true source of individual freedom, political liberty and the rule of law, principles which form the basis of all genuine democracy;

Believing that, for the maintenance and further realisation of these ideals and in the interests of economic and social progress, there is need of a closer unity between all like-minded countries of Europe;

Considering that, to respond to this need and to the expressed aspirations of their peoples in this regard, it is necessary forthwith to create an organisation which will bring European States into closer association;

Have in consequence decided to set up a Council of Europe consisting of a Committee of representatives of Governments and of a Consultative Assembly, and have for this purpose adopted the following Statute:—

CHAPTER I.—AIM OF THE COUNCIL OF EUROPE

Article 1

(*a*) The aim of the Council of Europe is to achieve a greater unity between its Members for the purpose of safeguarding and realising the ideals and principles which are their common heritage and facilitating their economic and social progress.

(*b*) This aim shall be pursued through the organs of the Council by discussion of questions of common concern and by agreements and common action in economic, social, cultural, scientific, legal and administrative matters and in the maintenance and further realisation of human rights and fundamental freedoms.

(*c*) Participation in the Council of Europe shall not affect the collaboration of its Members in the work of the United Nations and of other international organisations or unions to which they are parties.

(*d*) Matters relating to National Defence do not fall within the scope of the Council of Europe.

CHAPTER II.—MEMBERSHIP

Article 2

The Members of the Council of Europe are the Parties to this Statute.

Article 3

Every Member of the Council of Europe must accept the principles of the rule of law and of the enjoyment by all persons within its jurisdiction of human rights and

a. *See also* the Treaty Establishing the European Coal and Steel Community (ECSC), Apr. 18, 1951, 1 Eur.Y.B. 358, 261 U.N.T.S. 140; Treaty Establishing the European Economic Community (EEC), Mar. 25, 1957, 4 Eur.Y.B. 412, 298 U.N.T.S. 11; Treaty Establishing the European Atomic Energy Community (Euratom), Mar. 25, 1957, 5 Eur.Y.B. 454, 298 U.N.T.S.; and the Single European Act, Feb. 17, 1986 and Feb. 28, 1986, E.C. 12 (1986), reprinted in 25 I.L.M. 506 (1986). These additional European constitutive instruments are too lengthy to reproduce in this volume.

fundamental freedoms, and collaborate sincerely and effectively in the realisation of the aim of the Council as specified in Chapter I.

Article 4

Any European State, which is deemed to be able and willing to fulfil the provisions of Article 3, may be invited to become a Member of the Council of Europe by the Committee of Ministers. Any State so invited shall become a Member on the deposit on its behalf with the Secretary–General of an instrument of accession to the present Statute.

Article 5

(*a*) In special circumstances, a European country, which is deemed to be able and willing to fulfil the provisions of Article 3, may be invited by the Committee of Ministers to become an Associate Member of the Council of Europe. Any country so invited shall become an Associate Member on the deposit on its behalf with the Secretary–General of an instrument accepting the present Statute. An Associate Member shall be entitled to be represented in the Consultative Assembly only.

(*b*) The expression "Member" in this Statute includes an Associate Member except when used in connexion with representation on the Committee of Ministers.

Article 6

Before issuing invitations under Articles 4 or 5 above, the Committee of Ministers shall determine the number of representatives on the Consultative Assembly to which the proposed Member shall be entitled and its proportionate financial contribution.

Article 7

Any Member of the Council of Europe may withdraw by formally notifying the Secretary–General of its intention to do so. Such withdrawal shall take effect at the end of the financial year in which it is notified, if the notification is given during the first nine months of that financial year. If the notification is given in the last three months of the financial year, it shall take effect at the end of the next financial year.

Article 8

Any Member of the Council of Europe, which has seriously violated Article 3, may be suspended from its rights of representation and requested by the Committee of Ministers to withdraw under Article 7. If such Member does not comply with this request, the Committee may decide that it has ceased to be a Member of the Council as from such date as the Committee may determine.

Article 9

The Committee of Ministers may suspend the right of representation on the Committee and on the Consultative Assembly of a Member, which has failed to fulfil its financial obligation, during such period as the obligation remains unfulfilled.

CHAPTER III.—GENERAL

Article 10

The organs of the Council of Europe are:

(i) the Committee of Ministers;

(ii) the Consultative Assembly.

Both these organs shall be served by the Secretariat of the Council of Europe.

Article 11

The seat of the Council of Europe is at Strasbourg.

Article 12

The official languages of the Council of Europe are English and French. The rules of procedure of the Committee of Ministers and of the Consultative Assembly shall determine in what circumstances and under what conditions other languages may be used.

CHAPTER IV.—COMMITTEE OF MINISTERS

Article 13

The Committee of Ministers is the organ which acts on behalf of the Council of Europe in accordance with Articles 15 and 16.

Article 14

Each Member shall be entitled to one representative on the Committee of Ministers and each representative shall be entitled to one vote. Representatives on the Committee shall be the Ministers for Foreign Affairs. When a Minister for Foreign Affairs is unable to be present or in other circumstances where it may be desirable, an alternate may be nominated to act for him, who shall, whenever possible, be a member of his Government.

Article 15

(*a*) On the recommendation of the Consultative Assembly or on its own initiative, the Committee of Ministers shall consider the action required to further the aim of the Council of Europe, including the conclusion of conventions or agreements and the adoption by Governments of a common policy with regard to particular matters. Its conclusions shall be communicated to Members by the Secretary-General.

(*b*) In appropriate cases, the conclusions of the Committee may take the form of recommendations to the Governments of Members, and the Committee may request the Governments of Members to inform it of the action taken by them with regard to such recommendations.

Article 16

The Committee of Ministers shall, subject to the provisions of Articles 24, 28, 30, 32, 33 and 35, relating to the powers of the Consultative Assembly, decide with binding effect all matters relating to the internal organisation and arrangements of the Council of Europe. For this purpose the Committee of Ministers shall adopt such financial and administrative regulations as may be necessary.

Article 17

The Committee of Ministers may set up advisory and technical committees or commissions for such specific purposes as it may deem desirable.

Article 18

The Committee of Ministers shall adopt its rules of procedure which shall determine amongst other things:—

(i) the quorum;

(ii) the method of appointment and term of office of its President;

(iii) the procedure for the admission of items to its agenda, including the giving of notice of proposals for resolutions; and

(iv) the notifications required for the nomination of alternates under Article 14.

Article 19

At each session of the Consultative Assembly the Committee of Ministers shall furnish the Assembly with statements of its activities, accompanied by appropriate documentation.

Article 20

(*a*) Resolutions of the Committee of Ministers relating to the following important matters, namely:

(i) recommendations under Article 15(*b*);

(ii) questions under Article 19;

(iii) questions under Article 21(*a*)(i) and (*b*);

(iv) questions under Article 33;

(v) recommendations for the amendment of Articles 1(*d*), 7, 15, 20 and 22; and

(vi) any other question which the Committee may, by a resolution passed under (*d*) below, decide should be subject to a unanimous vote on account of its importance

require the unanimous vote of the representatives casting a vote, and of a majority of the representatives entitled to sit on the Committee.

(*b*) Questions arising under the rules of procedure or under the financial and administrative regulations may be decided by a simple majority vote of the representatives entitled to sit on the Committee.

(*c*) Resolutions of the Committee under Articles 4 and 5 require a two-thirds majority of all the representatives entitled to sit on the Committee.

(*d*) All other resolutions of the Committee, including the adoption of the Budget, of rules of procedure and of financial and administrative regulations, recommendations for the amendment of articles of this Statute, other than those mentioned in paragraph (*a*)(v) above, and deciding in case of doubt which paragraph of this Article applies, require a two-thirds majority of the representatives casting a vote and of a majority of the representatives entitled to sit on the Committee.

Article 21

(*a*) Unless the Committee decides otherwise, meetings of the Committee of Ministers shall be held—

(i) in private, and

(ii) at the seat of the Council.

(*b*) The Committee shall determine what information shall be published regarding the conclusions and discussions of a meeting held in private.

(*c*) The Committee shall meet before and during the beginning of every session of the Consultative Assembly and at such other times as it may decide.

CHAPTER V.—THE CONSULTATIVE ASSEMBLY

Article 22

The Consultative Assembly is the deliberative organ of the Council of Europe. It shall debate matters within its competence under this Statute and present its conclusions, in the form of recommendations, to the Committee of Ministers.

Article 23

(*a*) The Consultative Assembly shall discuss, and may make recommendations upon, any matter within the aim and scope of the Council of Europe as defined in Chapter 1, which (i) is referred to it by the Committee of Ministers with a request for its opinion, or (ii) has been approved by the Committee for inclusion in the Agenda of the Assembly on the proposal of the latter.

(*b*) In taking decisions under (*a*), the Committee shall have regard to the work of other European inter-governmental organisations to which some or all of the Members of the Council are parties.

(*c*) The President of the Assembly shall decide, in case of doubt, whether any question raised in the course of the Session is within the Agenda of the Assembly approved under (*a*) above.

Article 24

The Consultative Assembly may, with due regard to the provisions of Article 38(*d*), establish committees or commissions to consider and report to it on any matter which falls within its competence under Article 23, to examine and prepare questions on its agenda and to advise on all matters of procedure.

Article 25

(*a*) The Consultative Assembly shall consist of representatives of each Member appointed in such a manner as the Government of that Member shall decide. Each representative must be a national of the Member whom he represents, but shall not at the same time be a member of the Committee of Ministers.

(*b*) No representative shall be deprived of his position as such during a session of the Assembly without the agreement of the Assembly.

(*c*) Each representative may have a substitute who may, in the absence of the representative, sit, speak and vote in his place. The provisions of paragraph (*a*) above apply to the appointment of substitutes.

Article 26

The following States, on becoming Members, shall be entitled to the number of representatives given below:—

Belgium	6	Luxembourg	3
Denmark	4	Netherlands	6
France	18	Norway	4
Irish Republic	4	Sweden	6
Italy	18	United Kingdom	18

Article 27

The conditions under which the Committee of Ministers collectively may be represented in the debates of the Consultative Assembly, or individual representatives on the Committee may address the Assembly, shall be determined by such rules of procedure on this subject as may be drawn up by the Committee after consultation with the Assembly.

Article 28

(*a*) The Consultative Assembly shall adopt its rules of procedure and shall elect from its members its President, who shall remain in office until the next ordinary session.

(*b*) The President shall control the proceedings but shall not take part in the debate or vote. The substitute of the representative who is President may sit, speak and vote in his place.

(c) The rules of procedure shall determine *inter alia:*

(i) the quorum;

(ii) the manner of the election and terms of office of the President and other officers;

(iii) the manner in which the agenda shall be drawn up and be communicated to representatives; and

(iv) the time and manner in which the names of representatives and their substitutes shall be notified.

Article 29

Subject to the provisions of Article 30, all resolutions of the Consultative Assembly, including resolutions:

(i) embodying recommendations to the Committee of Ministers;

(ii) proposing to the Committee matters for discussion in the Assembly;

(iii) establishing committees or commissions;

(iv) determining the date of commencement of its sessions;

(v) determining what majority is required for resolutions in cases not covered by (i) to (iv) above or determining cases of doubt as to what majority is required

shall require a two-thirds majority of the representatives casting a vote.

Article 30

On matters relating to its internal procedure, which includes the election of officers, the nomination of persons to serve on committees and commissions and the adoption of rules of procedure, resolutions of the Consultative Assembly shall be carried by such majorities as the Assembly may determine in accordance with Article 29(v).

Article 31

Debates on proposals to be made to the Committee of Ministers that a matter should be placed on the Agenda of the Consultative Assembly shall be confined to an indication of the proposed subject-matter and the reasons for and against its inclusion in the Agenda.

Article 32

The Consultative Assembly shall meet in ordinary session once a year, the date and duration of which shall be determined by the Assembly so as to avoid as far as possible overlapping with parliamentary sessions of Members and with sessions of the General Assembly of the United Nations. In no circumstances shall the duration of an ordinary session exceed one month unless both the Assembly and the Committee of Ministers concur.

Article 33

Ordinary sessions of the Consultative Assembly shall be held at the seat of the Council unless both the Assembly and the Committee of Ministers concur that it should be held elsewhere.

Article 34

The Committee of Ministers may convoke an extraordinary session of the Consultative Assembly at such time and place as the Committee, with the concurrence of the President of the Assembly, shall decide.

Article 35

Unless the Consultative Assembly decides otherwise, its debates shall be conducted in public.

CHAPTER VI.—THE SECRETARIAT

Article 36

(*a*) The Secretariat shall consist of a Secretary–General, a Deputy Secretary–General and such other staff as may be required.

(*b*) The Secretary–General and Deputy Secretary–General shall be appointed by the Consultative Assembly on the recommendation of the Committee of Ministers.

(*c*) The remaining staff of the Secretariat shall be appointed by the Secretary–General, in accordance with the administrative regulations.

(*d*) No member of the Secretariat shall hold any salaried office from any Government or be a member of the Consultative Assembly or of any national legislature or engage in any occupation incompatible with his duties.

(*e*) Every member of the staff of the Secretariat shall make a solemn declaration affirming that his duty is to the Council of Europe and that he will perform his duties conscientiously, uninfluenced by any national considerations, and that he will not seek or receive instructions in connexion with the performance of his duties from any Government or any authority external to the Council and will refrain from any action which might reflect on his position as an international official responsible only to the Council. In the case of the Secretary–General and the Deputy Secretary–General this declaration shall be made before the Committee, and in the case of all other members of the staff, before the Secretary–General.

(*f*) Every Member shall respect the exclusively international character of the responsibilities of the Secretary–General and the staff of the Secretariat and not seek to influence them in the discharge of their responsibilities.

Article 37

(*a*) The Secretariat shall be located at the seat of the Council.

(*b*) The Secretary–General is responsible to the Committee of Ministers for the work of the Secretariat. Amongst other things, he shall, subject to Article 38(*d*), provide such secretarial and other assistance as the Consultative Assembly may require.

CHAPTER VII.—FINANCE

Article 38

(*a*) Each Member shall bear the expenses of its own representation in the Committee of Ministers and in the Consultative Assembly.

(*b*) The expenses of the Secretariat and all other common expenses shall be shared between all Members in such proportions as shall be determined by the Committee on the basis of the population of Members.

The contributions of an Associate Member shall be determined by the Committee.

(*c*) In accordance with the financial regulations, the budget of the Council shall be submitted annually by the Secretary–General for adoption by the Committee.

(*d*) The Secretary–General shall refer to the Committee requests from the Assembly which involve expenditure exceeding the amount already allocated in the Budget for the Assembly and its activities.

Article 39

The Secretary–General shall each year notify the Government of each Member of the amount of its contribution and each Member shall pay to the Secretary–General the amount of its contribution, which shall be deemed to be due on the date of its notification, not later than six months after that date.

CHAPTER VIII.—PRIVILEGES AND IMMUNITIES

Article 40

(*a*) The Council of Europe, representatives of Members and the Secretariat shall enjoy in the territories of its Members such privileges and immunities as are reasonably necessary for the fulfilment of their functions. These immunities shall include immunity for all representatives in the Consultative Assembly from arrest and all legal proceedings in the territories of all Members, in respect of words spoken and votes cast in the debates of the Assembly or its committees or commissions.

(*b*) The Members undertake as soon as possible to enter into an agreement for the purpose of fulfilling the provisions of paragraph (*a*) above. For this purpose the Committee of Ministers shall recommend to the Governments of Members the acceptance of an Agreement defining the privileges and immunities to be granted in the territories of all Members. In addition a special Agreement shall be concluded with the Government of the French Republic defining the privileges and immunities which the Council shall enjoy at its seat.

CHAPTER IX.—AMENDMENTS

Article 41

(*a*) Proposals for the amendment of this Statute may be made in the Committee of Ministers or, in the conditions provided for in Article 23, in the Consultative Assembly.

(*b*) The Committee shall recommend and cause to be embodied in a Protocol those amendments which it considers to be desirable.

(*c*) An amending Protocol shall come into force when it has been signed and ratified on behalf of two-thirds of the Members.

(*d*) Notwithstanding the provisions of the preceding paragraphs of this Article, amendments to Articles 23–35, 38 and 39 which have been approved by the Committee and by the Assembly, shall come into force on the date of the certificate of the Secretary–General, transmitted to the Governments of Members, certifying that they have been so approved. This paragraph shall not operate until the conclusion of the second ordinary session of the Assembly.

* * *

1.11 THE STATUTE OF THE ORGANIZATION OF THE PETROLEUM EXPORTING COUNTRIES (OPEC). Adopted as Resolution II.6 at the Second Conference of the Petroleum Exporting Countries, Caracas, Jan. 15–21, 1961, and amended through November, 1979. Composite text available through the Public Relations Department, Organization of the Petroleum Exporting Countries, Obere Donaustrasse 93, A–1020 Vienna, Austria

CHAPTER I. ORGANIZATION AND OBJECTIVES

Article 1. The Organization of the Petroleum Exporting Countries (OPEC), hereinafter referred to as "the Organization", created as a permanent intergovernmental organization in conformity with the Resolutions of the Conference of the Representatives of the Governments of Iran, Iraq, Kuwait, Saudi Arabia and Venezuela, held in Baghdad from September 10 to 14, 1960, shall carry out its functions in accordance with the provisions set forth hereunder.

Article 2. (A) The principal aim of the Organization shall be the coordination and unification of the petroleum policies of Member Countries and the determination of the best means for safeguarding their interests, individually and collectively.

(B) The Organization shall devise ways and means of ensuring the stabilization of prices in international oil markets with a view to eliminating harmful and unnecessary fluctuations.

(C) Due regard shall be given at all times to the interests of the producing nations and to the necessity of securing a steady income to the producing countries; an efficient, economic and regular supply of petroleum to consuming nations; and a fair return on their capital to those investing in the Petroleum industry.

Article 3. The Organization shall be guided by the principle of the sovereign equality of its Member Countries. Member Countries shall fulfil, in good faith, the obligations assumed by them in accordance with this Statute.

Article 4. If, as a result of the application of any decision of the Organization, sanctions are employed, directly or indirectly, by any interested company or companies against one or more Member Countries, no other Member shall accept any offer of a beneficial treatment, whether in the form of an increase in oil exports or in an improvement in prices, which may be made to it by such interested company or companies with the intention of discouraging the application of the decision of the Organization.

* * *

CHAPTER II. MEMBERSHIP

Article 7. (A) Founder Members of the Organization are those countries which were represented at the First Conference, held in Baghdad, and which signed the original agreement of the establishment of the Organization.

(B) Full Members shall be the Founder Members as well as those countries whose application for membership has been accepted by the Conference.

(C) Any other country with a substantial net export of crude petroleum, which has fundamentally similar interests to those of Member Countries, may become a full Member of the Organization, if accepted by a majority of three-fourths of Full Members, including the concurrent vote of all Founder Members.

(D) A net petroleum-exporting country which does not qualify for membership under paragraph C above may nevertheless be admitted as an Associate Member by the Conference under such special conditions as may be prescribed by the Conference, if accepted by a majority of three-fourths including the concurrent vote of all Founder Members.

No country may be admitted to Associate Membership which does not fundamentally have interests and aims similar to those of Member Countries.

(E) Associate Members may be invited by the Conference to attend any meeting of a Conference, the Board of Governors or Consultative Meetings, and to participate in their deliberations without the right to vote. They are, however, fully entitled to benefit from all general facilities of the Secretariat including its publications and library as any Full Member.

(F) Whenever the words "Members" or "Member Countries" occur in this Statute, they mean a Full Member of the Organization unless the context otherwise demonstrates to the contrary.

Article 8. (A) No Member of the Organization may withdraw from membership without giving notice of its intention to do so to the Conference. Such notice shall take effect at the beginning of the next calendar year after the date of its receipt by the Conference, subject to the Member having at that time fulfilled all financial obligations arising out of its membership.

(B) In the event of any country having ceased to be a Member of the Organization, its readmission to membership shall be made in accordance with Article 7, paragraph C.

CHAPTER III. ORGANS

Article 9. The Organization shall have three organs:

I. *The Conference;*

II. *The Board of Governors; and*

III. *The Secretariat.*

I. The Conference

Article 10. The Conference shall be the supreme authority of the Organization.

Article 11. (A) The Conference shall consist of delegations representing the Member Countries. A delegation may consist of one or more delegates, as well as advisers and observers. When a delegation consists of more than one person, the appointing country shall nominate one person as the Head of the Delegation.

(B) Each Member Country should be represented at all Conferences; however, a quorum of three-quarters of Member Countries shall be necessary for holding a Conference.

(C) Each Full Member Country shall have one vote. All decisions of the Conference, other than on procedural matters, shall require the unanimous agreement of all Full Members.

* * *

Article 15. The Conference shall:

(1) formulate the general policy of the Organization and determine the appropriate ways and means of its implementation;

(2) decide upon any application for membership of the Organization;

(3) confirm the appointment of Members of the Board of Governors;

(4) direct the Board of Governors to submit reports or make recommendations on any matters of interest to the Organization;

(5) consider, or decide upon, the reports and recommendations submitted by the Board of Governors on the affairs of the Organization;

(6) consider and decide upon the Budget of the Organization, as submitted by the Board of Governors;

(7) consider and decide upon the Statement of Accounts and the Auditor's Report, as submitted by the Board of Governors;

(8) call a Consultative Meeting for such Member Countries, for such purposes and in such places, when the Conference deems fit;

(9) approve any amendments to this Statute;

(10) appoint the Chairman of the Board of Governors and an Alternate Chairman;

(11) appoint the Secretary General;

(12) appoint the Deputy Secretary General; and

(13) appoint the Auditor of the Organization for a duration of one year.

Article 16. All matters that are not expressly assigned to other organs of the Organization shall fall within the competence of the Conference.

II. The Board of Governors

Article 17. (A) The Board of Governors shall be composed of Governors nominated by the Member Countries and confirmed by the Conference.

(B) Each Member of the Organization should be represented at all meetings of the Board of Governors; however, a quorum of two-thirds shall be necessary for the holding of a meeting.

* * *

(D) Each Governor shall have one vote. A simple majority vote of attending Governors shall be required for decisions of the Board of Governors.

(E) The term of office of each Governor shall be two years.

* * *

Article 20. The Board of Governors shall:

(1) direct the management of the affairs of the Organization and the implementation of the decisions of the Conference;

(2) consider and decide upon any reports submitted by the Secretary General;

(3) submit reports and make recommendations to the Conference on the affairs of the Organization;

(4) draw up the Budget of the Organization for each calendar year and submit it to the Conference for approval;

(5) nominate the Auditor of the Organization for a duration of one year;

(6) consider the Statement of Accounts and the Auditor's Report and submit them to the Conference for approval;

(7) approve the appointment of Directors of Divisions and Heads of Departments, upon nomination by the Member Countries, due consideration being given to the recommendations of the Secretary General;

(8) convene an extraordinary meeting of the Conference;

(9) nominate a Deputy Secretary General for appointment by the Conference; and

(10) prepare the Agenda for the Conference.

* * *

III. The Secretariat

Article 25. The Secretariat shall carry out the executive functions of the Organization in accordance with the provisions of this Statute under the direction of the Board of Governors.

Article 26. The Secretariat of the Organization shall consist of the Secretary General, the Deputy Secretary General and such staff as may be required. It shall function at the headquarters of the Organization.

Article 27. (A) The Secretary General shall be the legally authorized representative of the Organization.

(B) The Secretary General shall be the chief officer of the Secretariat, and in that capacity shall have the authority to direct the affairs of the Organization, in accordance with directions of the Board of Governors.

* * *

Article 29. The Secretary General shall:

(1) organize and administer the work of the Organization;

(2) ensure that the functions and duties assigned to the different departments of the Secretariat are carried out;

(3) prepare reports for submission to each meeting of the Board of Governors concerning matters which call for consideration and decision;

(4) inform the Chairman and other Members of the Board of Governors of all activities of the Secretariat, of all studies undertaken and of the progress of the implementation of the Resolutions of the Conference; and

(5) ensure the due performance of the duties which may be assigned to the Secretariat by the Conference or the Board of Governors.

* * *

CHAPTER IV. CONSULTATIVE MEETINGS AND SPECIALIZED ORGANS

Article 36. (A) A Consultative Meeting shall be composed of Heads of Delegations of Member Countries or their representatives.

(B) In case a Conference is not in session, a Consultative Meeting may be convened at any time at the request of the President of the Conference.

(C) The Agenda of each Consultative Meeting shall be prepared by the President of the Conference, unless it has been previously specified by the Conference itself.

(D) The Consultative Meeting may pass decisions or recommendations to be approved by the next Conference unless otherwise authorized by a previous Conference.

Article 37. (A) The Conference may establish specialized organs, as circumstances require, in order to assist in resolving certain problems of particular importance. The Specialized organs shall function in accordance with the Resolutions or Statutes prepared to that effect.

(B) The specialized organs shall operate within the general framework of the Secretariat of the Organization, both functionally and financially.

(C) The specialized organs shall act at all times in accordance with the principles of the Organization, as set out in the Resolutions of the Conference.

CHAPTER V. FINANCIAL PROVISIONS

Article 38. (A) The Budget of the Organization shall be drawn up for each calendar year.

(B) The Conference, in accepting any Associate Member to the Organization, shall ask it to pay a fixed annual subscription to be considered as its financial contribution to the Organization.

(C) Budget appropriations shall be apportioned on an equal basis among all Member Countries, after taking into consideration the annual subscriptions of the Associate Members.

Article 39. (A) Each Member Country shall bear all expenses incurred in sending delegations or representatives to Conferences, Consultative Meetings and Working Parties.

(B) The Organization shall bear the travelling expenses and remuneration of the Governors who attend the meetings of the Board of Governors.

* * *

1.12 VIENNA CONVENTION ON DIPLOMATIC RELATIONS.[a] Done at Vienna, Apr. 18, 1961. Entered into force, Apr. 24, 1964; for the United States, Dec. 13, 1972. 23 U.S.T. 3227, T.I.A.S. No. 7502, 500 U.N. T.S. 95

The States Parties to the present Convention,

Recalling that peoples of all nations from ancient times have recognized the status of diplomatic agents,

Having in mind the purposes and principles of the Charter of the United Nations concerning the sovereign equality of States, the maintenance of international peace and security, and the promotion of friendly relations among nations,

Believing that an international convention on diplomatic intercourse, privileges and immunities would contribute to the development of friendly relations among nations, irrespective of their differing constitutional and social systems,

Realizing that the purpose of such privileges and immunities is not to benefit individuals but to ensure the efficient performance of the functions of diplomatic missions as representing States,

Affirming that the rules of customary international law should continue to govern questions not expressly regulated by the provisions of the present Convention,

Have agreed as follows:

Article I

For the purpose of the present Convention, the following expressions shall have the meanings hereunder assigned to them:

(*a*) the "head of the mission" is the person charged by the sending State with the duty of acting in that capacity;

(*b*) the "members of the mission" are the head of the mission and the members of the staff of the mission;

(*c*) the "members of the staff of the mission" are the members of the diplomatic staff, of the administrative and technical staff and of the service staff of the mission;

(*d*) the "members of the diplomatic staff" are the members of the staff of the mission having diplomatic rank;

(*e*) a "diplomatic agent" is the head of the mission or a member of the diplomatic staff of the mission;

(*f*) the "members of the administrative and technical staff" are the members of the staff of the mission employed in the administrative and technical service of the mission;

(*g*) the "members of the service staff" are the members of the staff of the mission in the domestic service of the mission;

(*h*) a "private servant" is a person who is in the domestic service of a member of the mission and who is not an employee of the sending State;

a. *See also* Optional Protocol to the Vienna Convention on Diplomatic Relations Concerning the Compulsory Settlement of Disputes. Done at Vienna, Apr. 18, 1961. Entered into force, June 24, 1964; for the United States, Nov. 13, 1972. 23 U.S.T. 3374, 500 U.N.T.S. 241. *Also see* Vienna Convention on Consular Relations. Done at Vienna, Apr. 24, 1963. Entered into force, Mar. 19, 1967; for the United States, Nov. 24, 1969. 21 U.S.T. 77, T.I.A.S. No. 6820, 596 U.N.T.S. 261.

(*i*) the "premises of the mission" are the buildings or parts of buildings and the land ancillary thereto, irrespective of ownership, used for the purposes of the mission including the residence of the head of the mission.

Article 2

The establishment of diplomatic relations between States, and of permanent diplomatic missions, takes place by mutual consent.

Article 3

1. The functions of a diplomatic mission consist *inter alia* in:

(*a*) representing the sending State in the receiving State;

(*b*) protecting in the receiving State the interests of the sending State and of its nationals, within the limits permitted by international law;

(*c*) negotiating with the Government of the receiving State;

(*d*) ascertaining by all lawful means conditions and developments in the receiving State, and reporting thereon to the Government of the sending State;

(*e*) promoting friendly relations between the sending State and the receiving State, and developing their economic, cultural and scientific relations.

2. Nothing in the present Convention shall be construed as preventing the performance of consular functions by a diplomatic mission.

Article 4

1. The sending State must make certain that the *agrément* of the receiving State has been given for the person it proposes to accredit as head of the mission to that State.

2. The receiving State is not obliged to give reasons to the sending State for a refusal of *agrément.*

Article 5

1. The sending State may, after it has given due notification to the receiving States concerned, accredit a head of mission or assign any member of the diplomatic staff, as the case may be, to more than one State, unless there is express objection by any of the receiving States.

2. If the sending State accredits a head of mission to one or more other States it may establish a diplomatic mission headed by a chargé d'affaires ad interim in each State where the head of mission has not his permanent seat.

3. A head of mission or any member of the diplomatic staff of the mission may act as representative of the sending State to any international organization.

Article 6

Two or more States may accredit the same person as head of mission to another State, unless objection is offered by the receiving State.

Article 7

Subject to the provisions of Articles 5, 8, 9 and 11, the sending State may freely appoint the members of the staff of the mission. In the case of military, naval or air attachés, the receiving State may require their names to be submitted beforehand, for its approval.

Article 8

1. Members of the diplomatic staff of the mission should in principle be of the nationality of the sending State.

2. Members of the diplomatic staff of the mission may not be appointed from among persons having the nationality of the receiving State, except with the consent of that State which may be withdrawn at any time.

3. The receiving State may reserve the same right with regard to nationals of a third State who are not also nationals of the sending State.

Article 9

1. The receiving State may at any time and without having to explain its decision, notify the sending State that the head of the mission or any member of the diplomatic staff of the mission is *persona non grata* or that any other member of the staff of the mission is not acceptable. In any such case, the sending State shall, as appropriate, either recall the person concerned or terminate his functions with the mission. A person may be declared *non grata* or not acceptable before arriving in the territory of the receiving State.

2. If the sending State refuses or fails within a reasonable period to carry out its obligations under paragraph 1 of this Article, the receiving State may refuse to recognize the person concerned as a member of the mission.

Article 10

1. The Ministry for Foreign Affairs of the receiving State, or such other ministry as may be agreed, shall be notified of:

(*a*) the appointment of members of the mission, their arrival and their final departure or the termination of their functions with the mission;

(*b*) the arrival and final departure of a person belonging to the family of a member of the mission and, where appropriate, the fact that a person becomes or ceases to be a member of the family of a member of the mission;

(*c*) the arrival and final departure of private servants in the employ of persons referred to in sub-paragraph (*a*) of this paragraph and, where appropriate, the fact that they are leaving the employ of such persons;

(*d*) the engagement and discharge of persons resident in the receiving State as members of the mission or private servants entitled to privileges and immunities.

2. Where possible, prior notification of arrival and final departure shall also be given.

Article 11

1. In the absence of specific agreement as to the size of the mission, the receiving State may require that the size of a mission be kept within limits considered by it to be reasonable and normal, having regard to circumstances and conditions in the receiving State and to the needs of the particular mission.

2. The receiving State may equally, within similar bounds and on a non-discriminatory basis, refuse to accept officials of a particular category.

Article 12

The sending State may not, without the prior express consent of the receiving State, establish offices forming part of the mission in localities other than those in which the mission itself is established.

Article 13

1. The head of the mission is considered as having taken up his functions in the receiving State either when he has presented his credentials or when he has notified his arrival and a true copy of his credentials has been presented to the Ministry for Foreign Affairs of the receiving State, or such other ministry as may be agreed, in

accordance with the practice prevailing in the receiving State which shall be applied in a uniform manner.

2. The order of presentation of credentials or of a true copy thereof will be determined by the date and time of the arrival of the head of the mission.

Article 14

1. Heads of mission are divided into three classes, namely:

(*a*) that of ambassadors or nuncios accredited to Heads of State, and other heads of mission of equivalent rank;

(*b*) that of envoys, ministers and internuncios accredited to Heads of State;

(*c*) that of chargés d'affaires accredited to Ministers for Foreign Affairs.

2. Except as concerns precedence and etiquette, there shall be no differentiation between heads of mission by reason of their class.

* * *

Article 20

The mission and its head shall have the right to use the flag and emblem of the sending State on the premises of the mission, including the residence of the head of the mission, and on his means of transport.

Article 21

1. The receiving State shall either facilitate the acquisition on its territory, in accordance with its laws, by the sending State of premises necessary for its mission or assist the latter in obtaining accommodation in some other way.

2. It shall also, where necessary, assist missions in obtaining suitable accommodation for their members.

Article 22

1. The premises of the mission shall be inviolable. The agents of the receiving State may not enter them, except with the consent of the head of the mission.

2. The receiving State is under a special duty to take all appropriate steps to protect the premises of the mission against any intrusion or damage and to prevent any disturbance of the peace of the mission or impairment of its dignity.

3. The premises of the mission, their furnishings and other property thereon and the means of transport of the mission shall be immune from search, requisition, attachment or execution.

Article 23

1. The sending State and the head of the mission shall be exempt from all national, regional or municipal dues and taxes in respect of the premises of the mission, whether owned or leased, other than such as represent payment for specific services rendered.

2. The exemption from taxation referred to in this Article shall not apply to such dues and taxes payable under the law of the receiving State by persons contracting with the sending State or the head of the mission.

Article 24

The archives and documents of the mission shall be inviolable at any time and wherever they may be.

Article 25

The receiving State shall accord full facilities for the performance of the functions of the mission.

Article 26

Subject to its laws and regulations concerning zones entry into which is prohibited or regulated for reasons of national security, the receiving State shall ensure to all members of the mission freedom of movement and travel in its territory.

Article 27

1. The receiving State shall permit and protect free communication on the part of the mission for all official purposes. In communicating with the Government and the other missions and consulates of the sending State, wherever situated, the mission may employ all appropriate means, including diplomatic couriers and messages in code or cipher. However, the mission may install and use a wireless transmitter only with the consent of the receiving State.

2. The official correspondence of the mission shall be inviolable. Official correspondence means all correspondence relating to the mission and its functions.

3. The diplomatic bag shall not be opened or detained.

4. The packages constituting the diplomatic bag must bear visible external marks of their character and may contain only diplomatic documents or articles intended for official use.

5. The diplomatic courier, who shall be provided with an official document indicating his status and the number of packages constituting the diplomatic bag, shall be protected by the receiving State in the performance of his functions. He shall enjoy personal inviolability and shall not be liable to any form of arrest or detention.

6. The sending State or the mission may designate diplomatic couriers *ad hoc*. In such cases the provisions of paragraph 5 of this Article shall also apply, except that the immunities therein mentioned shall cease to apply when such a courier has delivered to the consignee the diplomatic bag in his charge.

7. A diplomatic bag may be entrusted to the captain of a commercial aircraft scheduled to land at an authorized port of entry. He shall be provided with an official document indicating the number of packages constituting the bag but he shall not be considered to be a diplomatic courier. The mission may send one of its members to take possession of the diplomatic bag directly and freely from the captain of the aircraft.

Article 28

The fees and charges levied by the mission in the course of its official duties shall be exempt from all dues and taxes.

Article 29

The person of a diplomatic agent shall be inviolable. He shall not be liable to any form of arrest or detention. The receiving State shall treat him with due respect and shall take all appropriate steps to prevent any attack on his person, freedom or dignity.

Article 30

1. The private residence of a diplomatic agent shall enjoy the same inviolability and protection as the premises of the mission.

2. His papers, correspondence and, except as provided in paragraph 3 of Article 31, his property, shall likewise enjoy inviolability.

Article 31

1. A diplomatic agent shall enjoy immunity from the criminal jurisdiction of the receiving State. He shall also enjoy immunity from its civil and administrative jurisdiction, except in the case of:

(*a*) a real action relating to private immovable property situated in the territory of the receiving State, unless he holds it on behalf of the sending State for the purposes of the mission;

(*b*) an action relating to succession in which the diplomatic agent is involved as executor, administrator, heir or legatee as a private person and not on behalf of the sending State;

(*c*) an action relating to any professional or commercial activity exercised by the diplomatic agent in the receiving State outside his official functions.

2. A diplomatic agent is not obliged to give evidence as a witness.

3. No measures of execution may be taken in respect of a diplomatic agent except in the cases coming under sub-paragraphs (*a*), (*b*) and (*c*) of paragraph 1 of this Article, and provided that the measures concerned can be taken without infringing the inviolability of his person or of his residence.

4. The immunity of a diplomatic agent from the jurisdiction of the receiving State does not exempt him from the jurisdiction of the sending State.

Article 32

1. The immunity from jurisdiction of diplomatic agents and of persons enjoying immunity under Article 37 may be waived by the sending State.

2. Waiver must always be express.

3. The initiation of proceedings by a diplomatic agent or by a person enjoying immunity from jurisdiction under Article 37 shall preclude him from invoking immunity from jurisdiction in respect of any counter-claim directly connected with the principal claim.

4. Waiver of immunity from jurisdiction in respect of civil or administrative proceedings shall not be held to imply waiver of immunity in respect of the execution of the judgment, for which a separate waiver shall be necessary.

Article 33

1. Subject to the provisions of paragraph 3 of this Article, a diplomatic agent shall with respect to services rendered for the sending State be exempt from social security provisions which may be in force in the receiving State.

2. The exemption provided for in paragraph 1 of this Article shall also apply to private servants who are in the sole employ of a diplomatic agent, on condition:

(*a*) that they are not nationals of or permanently resident in the receiving State; and

(*b*) that they are covered by the social security provisions which may be in force in the sending State or a third State.

3. A diplomatic agent who employs persons to whom the exemption provided for in paragraph 2 of this Article does not apply shall observe the obligations which the social security provisions of the receiving State impose upon employers.

4. The exemption provided for in paragraphs 1 and 2 of this Article shall not preclude voluntary participation in the social security system of the receiving State provided that such participation is permitted by that State.

5. The provisions of this Article shall not affect bilateral or multilateral agreements concerning social security concluded previously and shall not prevent the conclusion of such agreements in the future.

Article 34

A diplomatic agent shall be exempt from all dues and taxes, personal or real, national, regional or municipal, except:

(*a*) indirect taxes of a kind which are normally incorporated in the price of goods or services;

(*b*) dues and taxes on private immovable property situated in the territory of the receiving State, unless he holds it on behalf of the sending State for the purposes of the mission;

(*c*) estate, succession or inheritance duties levied by the receiving State, subject to the provisions of paragraph 4 of Article 39;

(*d*) dues and taxes on private income having its source in the receiving State and capital taxes on investments made in commercial undertakings in the receiving State;

(*e*) charges levied for specific services rendered;

(*f*) registration, court or record fees, mortgage dues and stamp duty, with respect to immovable property, subject to the provisions of Article 23.

Article 35

The receiving State shall exempt diplomatic agents from all personal services, from all public service of any kind whatsoever, and from military obligations such as those connected with requisitioning, military contributions and billeting.

Article 36

1. The receiving State shall, in accordance with such laws and regulations as it may adopt, permit entry of and grant exemption from all customs duties, taxes, and related charges other than charges for storage, cartage and similar services, on:

(*a*) articles for the official use of the mission;

(*b*) articles for the personal use of a diplomatic agent or members of his family forming part of his household, including articles intended for his establishment.

2. The personal baggage of a diplomatic agent shall be exempt from inspection, unless there are serious grounds for presuming that it contains articles not covered by the exemptions mentioned in paragraph 1 of this Article, or articles the import or export of which is prohibited by the law or controlled by the quarantine regulations of the receiving State. Such inspection shall be conducted only in the presence of the diplomatic agent or of his authorized representative.

Article 37

1. The members of the family of a diplomatic agent forming part of his household shall, if they are not nationals of the receiving State, enjoy the privileges and immunities specified in Articles 29 to 36.

2. Members of the administrative and technical staff of the mission, together with members of their families forming part of their respective households, shall, if they are not nationals of or permanently resident in the receiving State, enjoy the privileges and immunities specified in Articles 29 to 35, except that the immunity from civil and administrative jurisdiction of the receiving State specified in paragraph 1 of Article 31 shall not extend to acts performed outside the course of their duties. They shall also enjoy the privileges specified in Article 36, paragraph 1, in respect of articles imported at the time of first installation.

3. Members of the service staff of the mission who are not nationals of or permanently resident in the receiving State shall enjoy immunity in respect of acts performed in the course of their duties, exemption from dues and taxes on the emoluments they receive by reason of their employment and the exemption contained in Article 33.

4. Private servants of members of the mission shall, if they are not nationals of or permanently resident in the receiving State, be exempt from dues and taxes on the emoluments they receive by reason of their employment. In other respects, they may enjoy privileges and immunities only to the extent admitted by the receiving State. However, the receiving State must exercise its jurisdiction over those persons in such a manner as not to interfere unduly with the performance of the functions of the mission.

Article 38

1. Except insofar as additional privileges and immunities may be granted by the receiving State, a diplomatic agent who is a national of or permanently resident in that State shall enjoy only immunity from jurisdiction, and inviolability, in respect of official acts performed in the exercise of his functions.

2. Other members of the staff of the mission and private servants who are nationals of or permanently resident in the receiving State shall enjoy privileges and immunities only to the extent admitted by the receiving State. However, the receiving State must exercise its jurisdiction over those persons in such a manner as not to interfere unduly with the performance of the functions of the mission.

Article 39

1. Every person entitled to privileges and immunities shall enjoy them from the moment he enters the territory of the receiving State on proceeding to take up his post or, if already in its territory, from the moment when his appointment is notified to the Ministry for Foreign Affairs or such other ministry as may be agreed.

2. When the functions of a person enjoying privileges and immunities have come to an end, such privileges and immunities shall normally cease at the moment when he leaves the country, or on expiry of a reasonable period in which to do so, but shall subsist until that time, even in case of armed conflict. However, with respect to acts performed by such a person in the exercise of his functions as a member of the mission, immunity shall continue to subsist.

3. In case of the death of a member of the mission, the members of his family shall continue to enjoy the privileges and immunities to which they are entitled until the expiry of a reasonable period in which to leave the country.

4. In the event of the death of a member of the mission not a national of or permanently resident in the receiving State or a member of his family forming part of his household, the receiving State shall permit the withdrawal of the movable property of the deceased, with the exception of any property acquired in the country the export of which was prohibited at the time of his death. Estate, succession and inheritance duties shall not be levied on movable property the presence of which in the receiving State was due solely to the presence there of the deceased as a member of the mission or as a member of the family of a member of the mission.

Article 40

1. If a diplomatic agent passes through or is in the territory of a third State, which has granted him a passport visa if such visa was necessary, while proceeding to take up or to return to his post, or when returning to his own country, the third State shall accord him inviolability and such other immunities as may be required to ensure his transit or return. The same shall apply in the case of any members of his

family enjoying privileges or immunities who are accompanying the diplomatic agent, or travelling separately to join him or to return to their country.

2. In circumstances similar to those specified in paragraph 1 of this Article, third States shall not hinder the passage of members of the administrative and technical or service staff of a mission, and of members of their families, through their territories.

3. Third States shall accord to official correspondence and other official communications in transit, including messages in code or cipher, the same freedom and protection as is accorded by the receiving State. They shall accord to diplomatic couriers, who have been granted a passport visa if such visa was necessary, and diplomatic bags in transit the same inviolability and protection as the receiving State is bound to accord.

4. The obligations of third States under paragraphs 1, 2 and 3 of this Article shall also apply to the persons mentioned respectively in those paragraphs, and to official communications and diplomatic bags, whose presence in the territory of the third State is due to *force majeure.*

Article 41

1. Without prejudice to their privileges and immunities, it is the duty of all persons enjoying such privileges and immunities to respect the laws and regulations of the receiving State. They also have a duty not to interfere in the internal affairs of that State.

2. All official business with the receiving State entrusted to the mission by the sending State shall be conducted with or through the Ministry for Foreign Affairs of the receiving State or such other ministry as may be agreed.

3. The premises of the mission must not be used in any manner incompatible with the functions of the mission as laid down in the present Convention or by other rules of general international law or by any special agreements in force between the sending and the receiving State.

Article 42

A diplomatic agent shall not in the receiving State practise for personal profit any professional or commercial activity.

Article 43

The function of a diplomatic agent comes to an end, *inter alia:*

(*a*) on notification by the sending State to the receiving State that the function of the diplomatic agent has come to an end;

(*b*) on notification by the receiving State to the sending State that, in accordance with paragraph 2 of Article 9, it refuses to recognize the diplomatic agent as a member of the mission.

Article 44

The receiving State must, even in case of armed conflict, grant facilities in order to enable persons enjoying privileges and immunities, other than nationals of the receiving State, and members of the families of such persons irrespective of their nationality, to leave at the earliest possible moment. It must, in particular, in case of need, place at their disposal the necessary means of transport for themselves and their property.

Article 45

If diplomatic relations are broken off between two States, or if a mission is permanently or temporarily recalled:

(*a*) the receiving State must, even in case of armed conflict, respect and protect the premises of the mission, together with its property and archives;

(*b*) the sending State may entrust the custody of the premises of the mission, together with its property and archives, to a third State acceptable to the receiving State;

(*c*) the sending State may entrust the protection of its interests and those of its nationals to a third State acceptable to the receiving State.

Article 46

A sending State may with the prior consent of a receiving State, and at the request of a third State not represented in the receiving State, undertake the temporary protection of the interests of the third State and of its nationals.

Article 47

1. In the application of the provisions of the present Convention, the receiving State shall not discriminate as between States.

2. However, discrimination shall not be regarded as taking place:

(*a*) where the receiving State applies any of the provisions of the present Convention restrictively because of a restrictive application of that provision to its mission in the sending State;

(*b*) where by custom or agreement States extend to each other more favourable treatment than is required by the provisions of the present Convention.

* * *

1.13 CHARTER OF THE ORGANIZATION OF AFRICAN UNITY. Done at Addis Ababa, May 25, 1963. Entered into force, Sept. 13, 1963. 479 U.N.T.S. 39, *reprinted in* 2 I.L.M. 766 (1963)

We, the Heads of African States and Governments assembled in the City of Addis Ababa, Ethiopia;

CONVINCED that it is the inalienable right of all people to control their own destiny;

CONSCIOUS of the fact that freedom, equality, justice and dignity are essential objectives for the achievement of the legitimate aspirations of the African peoples;

CONSCIOUS of our responsibility to harness the natural and human resources of our continent for the total advancement of our peoples in spheres of human endeavour;

INSPIRED by a common determination to promote understanding among our peoples and co-operation among our States in response to the aspirations of our peoples for brotherhood and solidarity, in a larger unity transcending ethnic and national differences;

CONVINCED that, in order to translate this determination into a dynamic force in the cause of human progress, conditions for peace and security must be established and maintained;

DETERMINED to safeguard and consolidate the hard-won independence as well as the sovereignty and territorial integrity of our States, and to fight against neo-colonialism in all its forms;

DEDICATED to the general progress of Africa;

PERSUADED that the Charter of the United Nations and the Universal Declaration of Human Rights, to the principles of which we reaffirm our adherence, provide a solid foundation for peaceful and positive co-operation among States;

DESIROUS that all African States should henceforth unite so that the welfare and well-being of their peoples can be assured;

RESOLVED to reinforce the links between our states by establishing and strengthening common institutions;

HAVE agreed to the present Charter.

ESTABLISHMENT

Article I. (1) The High Contracting Parties do by the present Charter establish an Organization to be known as the ORGANIZATION OF AFRICAN UNITY.

(2) The Organization shall include the Continental African States, Madagascar and other Islands surrounding Africa.

PURPOSES

Article II. (1) The Organization shall have the following purposes;

(a) to promote the unity and solidarity of the African States;

(b) to co-ordinate and intensify their co-operation and efforts to achieve a better life for the peoples of Africa;

(c) to defend their sovereignty, their territorial integrity and independence;

(d) to eradicate all forms of colonialism from Africa; and

(e) to promote international co-operation, having due regard to the Charter of the United Nations and the Universal Declaration of Human Rights.

(2) To these ends, the Member States shall co-ordinate and harmonize their general policies, especially in the following fields;

(a) political and diplomatic co-operation;

(b) economic co-operation, including transport and communications;

(c) educational and cultural co-operation;

(d) health, sanitation, and nutritional co-operation;

(e) scientific and technical co-operation; and

(f) co-operation for defence and security.

PRINCIPLES

Article III. The Member States, in pursuit of the purposes stated in Article II, solemnly affirm and declare their adherence to the following principles:

(1) the sovereign equality of all Member States;

(2) non-interference in the internal affairs of States;

(3) respect for the sovereignty and territorial integrity of each State and for its inalienable right to independent existence;

(4) peaceful settlement of disputes by negotiation, mediation, conciliation or arbitration;

(5) unreserved condemnation, in all its forms, of political assassination as well as of subversive activities on the part of neighbouring States or any other States;

(6) absolute dedication to the total emancipation of the African territories which are still dependent;

(7) affirmation of a policy of non-alignment with regard to all blocs.

MEMBERSHIP

Article IV. Each independent sovereign African State shall be entitled to become a Member of the Organization.

RIGHTS AND DUTIES OF MEMBER STATES

Article V. All Member States shall enjoy equal rights and have equal duties.

Article VI. The Member States pledge themselves to observe scrupulously the principles enumerated in Article III of the present Charter.

INSTITUTIONS

Article VII. The Organization shall accomplish its purposes through the following principal institutions:

(1) the Assembly of Heads of State and Government;

(2) the Council of Ministers;

(3) the General Secretariat;

(4) the Commission of Mediation, Conciliation and Arbitration.

THE ASSEMBLY OF HEADS OF STATE AND GOVERNMENT

Article VIII. The Assembly of Heads of State and Government shall be the supreme organ of the Organization. It shall, subject to the provisions of this Charter, discuss matters of common concern to Africa with a view to co-ordinating and harmonizing the general policy of the Organization. It may in addition review the structure, functions and acts of all the organs and any specialized agencies which may be created in accordance with the present Charter.

Article IX. The Assembly shall be composed of the Heads of State and Government or their duly accredited representatives and it shall meet at least once a year. At the request of any Member State and on approval by a two-thirds majority of the Member States, the Assembly shall meet in extraordinary session.

Article X. (1) Each Member State shall have one vote.

(2) All resolutions shall be determined by a two-thirds majority of the Members of the Organization.

(3) Questions of procedure shall require a simple majority. Whether or not a question is one of procedure shall be determined by a simple majority of all Member States of the Organization.

(4) Two-thirds of the total membership of the Organization shall form a quorum at any meeting of the Assembly.

Article XI. The Assembly shall have the power to determine its own rules of procedure.

THE COUNCIL OF MINISTERS

Article XII. (1) The Council of Ministers shall consist of Foreign Ministers or such other Ministers as are designated by the Governments of Member States.

(2) The Council of Ministers shall meet at least twice a year. When requested by any Member State and approved by two-thirds of all Member States, it shall meet in extraordinary session.

Article XIII. (1) The Council of Ministers shall be responsible to the Assembly of Heads of State and Government. It shall be entrusted with the responsibility of preparing conferences of the Assembly.

(2) It shall take cognisance of any matter referred to it by the Assembly. It shall be entrusted with the implementation of the decision of the Assembly of Heads of State and Government. It shall co-ordinate inter-African co-operation in accordance with the instructions of the Assembly and in conformity with Article II(2) of the present Charter.

Article XIV. (1) Each Member State shall have one vote.

(2) All resolutions shall be determined by a simple majority of the members of the Council of Ministers.

(3) Two-thirds of the total membership of the Council of Ministers shall form a quorum for any meeting of the Council.

Article XV. The Council shall have the power to determine its own rules of procedure.

GENERAL SECRETARIAT

Article XVI. There shall be an Administrative Secretary–General of the Organization, who shall be appointed by the Assembly of Heads of State and Government. The Administrative Secretary–General shall direct the affairs of the Secretariat.

Article XVII. There shall be one or more Assistant Secretaries–General of the Organization, who shall be appointed by the Assembly of Heads of State and Government.

Article XVIII. The functions and conditions of services of the Secretary–General, of the Assistant Secretaries–General and other employees of the Secretariat shall be governed by the provisions of this Charter and the regulations approved by the Assembly of Heads of State and Government.

(1) In the performance of their duties the Administrative Secretary–General and the staff shall not seek or receive instructions from any government or from any other authority external to the Organization. They shall refrain from any

action which might reflect on their position as international officials responsible only to the Organization.

(2) Each member of the Organization undertakes to respect the exclusive character of the responsibilities of the Administrative Secretary–General and the staff and not to seek to influence them in the discharge of their responsibilities.

COMMISSION OF MEDIATION, CONCILIATION AND ARBITRATION

Article XIX. Member States pledge to settle all disputes among themselves by peaceful means and, to this end decide to establish a Commission of Mediation, Conciliation and Arbitration, the composition of which and conditions of service shall be defined by a separate Protocol to be approved by the Assembly of Heads of State and Government. Said Protocol shall be regarded as forming an integral part of the present Charter.

SPECIALIZED COMMISSIONS

Article XX. The Assembly shall establish such Specialized Commissions as it may deem necessary, including the following:

(1) Economic and Social Commission;

(2) Educational and Cultural Commission;

(3) Health, Sanitation and Nutrition Commission;

(4) Defence Commission;

(5) Scientific, Technical and Research Commission.

Article XXI. Each Specialized Commission referred to in Article XX shall be composed of the Ministers concerned or other Ministers or Plenipotentiaries designated by the Governments of the Member States.

Article XXII. The functions of the Specialized Commissions shall be carried out in accordance with the provisions of the present Charter and of the regulations approved by the Council of Ministers.

THE BUDGET

Article XXIII. The budget of the Organization prepared by the Administrative Secretary–General shall be approved by the Council of Ministers. The budget shall be provided by contributions from Member States in accordance with the scale of assessment of the United Nations: provided, however, that no Member States shall be assessed an amount exceeding twenty percent of the yearly regular budget of the Organization. The Member States agree to pay their respective contributions regularly.

* * *

INTERPRETATION OF THE CHARTER

Article XXVII. Any question which may arise concerning the interpretation of this Charter shall be decided by a vote of two-thirds of the Assembly of Heads of State and Government of the Organization.

* * *

MISCELLANEOUS

Article XXIX. The working languages of the Organization and all its institutions shall be, if possible African languages, English and French.

* * *

Article XXXI. The Council of Ministers shall decide on the privileges and immunities to be accorded to the personnel of the Secretariat in the respective territories of the Member States.

* * *

1.14 THE PALESTINIAN NATIONAL CHARTER OF 1968.[a] Done at Cairo, National Congress of the Palestine Liberation Organization, July 1–17, 1968 *reproduced in* 3 The Arab–Israeli Conflict 706 (J.N. Moore ed. 1974)

Article 1: Palestine is the homeland of the Arab Palestinian people; it is an indivisible part of the Arab homeland, and the Palestinian people are an integral part of the Arab nation.

Article 2: Palestine, with the boundaries it had during the British mandate, is an indivisible territorial unit.

Article 3: The Palestinian Arab people possess the legal right to their homeland and have the right to determine their destiny after achieving the liberation of their country in accordance with their wishes and entirely of their own accord and will.

Article 4: The Palestinian identity is a genuine, essential and inherent characteristic; it is transmitted from parents to children. The Zionist occupation and the dispersal of the Palestinian Arab people, through the disasters which befell them, do not make them lose their Palestinian identity and their membership of the Palestinian community, nor do they negate them.

Article 5: The Palestinians are those Arab nationals who, until 1947, normally resided in Palestine regardless of whether they were evicted from it or have stayed there. Anyone born, after that date, of a Palestinian father—whether inside Palestine or outside it—is also a Palestinian.

Article 6: The Jews who had normally resided in Palestine until the beginning of the Zionist invasion will be considered Palestinians.

Article 7: That there is a Palestinian community and that it has material, spiritual and historical connection with Palestine are indisputable facts. It is a national duty to bring up individual Palestinians in an Arab revolutionary manner. All means of information and education must be adopted in order to acquaint the Palestinian with his country in the most profound manner, both spiritual and material, that is possible. He must be prepared for the armed struggle and ready to sacrifice his wealth and his life in order to win back his homeland and bring about its liberation.

Article 8: The phase in their history, through which the Palestinian people are now living, is that of national struggle for the liberation of Palestine. Thus the conflicts among the Palestinian national forces are secondary, and should be ended for the sake of the basic conflict that exists between the forces of Zionism and of imperialism on the one hand, and the Palestinian Arab people on the other. On this basis the Palestinian masses, regardless of whether they are residing in the national homeland or in diaspora, constitute—both their organizations and the individuals—one national front working for the retrieval of Palestine and its liberation through armed struggle.

Article 9: Armed struggle is the only way to liberate Palestine. Thus it is the overall strategy, not merely a tactical phase. The Palestinian Arab people assert their absolute determination and firm resolution to continue their armed struggle and to work for an armed popular revolution for the liberation of their country and their return to it. They also assert their right to normal life in Palestine and to exercise their right to self-determination and sovereignty over it.

a. Includes all provisions of the Palestinian National Charter of May 1964, *reprinted in* 3 The Arab–Israeli Conflict 698 (J.N. Moore ed. 1974).

Article 10: Commando action constitutes the nucleus of the Palestinian popular liberation war. This requires its escalation, comprehensiveness and the mobilization of all the Palestinian popular and educational efforts and their organization and involvement in the armed Palestinian revolution. It also requires the achieving of unity for the national struggle among the different groupings of the Palestinian people, and between the Palestinian people and the Arab masses so as to secure the continuation of the revolution, its escalation and victory.

Article 11: The Palestinians will have three mottoes: national unity, national mobilization and liberation.

Article 12: The Palestinian people believe in Arab unity. In order to contribute their share towards the attainment of that objective, however, they must, at the present stage of their struggle, safeguard their Palestinian identity and develop their consciousness of that identity, and oppose any plan that may dissolve or impair it.

Article 13: Arab unity and the liberation of Palestine are two complementary objectives, the attainment of either of which facilitates the attainment of the other. Thus, Arab unity leads to the liberation of Palestine; the liberation of Palestine leads to Arab unity; and work towards the realization of one objective proceeds side by side with work towards the realization of the other.

Article 14: The destiny of the Arab nation, and indeed Arab existence itself, depends upon the destiny of the Palestine cause. From this interdependence springs the Arab nation's pursuit of, and striving for, the liberation of Palestine. The people of Palestine play the role of the vanguard in the realization of this sacred national goal.

Article 15: The liberation of Palestine, from an Arab viewpoint, is a national duty and it attempts to repel the Zionist and imperialist aggression against the Arab homeland, and aims at the elimination of Zionism in Palestine. Absolute responsibility for this falls upon the Arab nation—peoples and governments—with the Arab people of Palestine in the vanguard. Accordingly the Arab nation must mobilize all its military, human, moral and spiritual capabilities to participate actively with the Palestinian people in the liberation of Palestine. It must, particularly in the phase of the armed Palestinian revolution, offer and furnish the Palestinian people with all possible help, and material and human support, and make available to them the means and opportunities that will enable them to continue to carry out their leading role in the armed revolution, until they liberate their homeland.

Article 16: The liberation of Palestine, from a spiritual point of view, will provide the Holy Land with an atmosphere of safety and tranquillity, which in turn will safeguard the country's religious sanctuaries and guarantee freedom of worship and of visit to all, without discrimination of race, color, language, or religion. Accordingly, the people of Palestine look to all spiritual forces in the world for support.

Article 17: The liberation of Palestine, from a human point of view, will restore to the Palestinian individual his dignity, pride and freedom. Accordingly the Palestinian Arab people look forward to the support of all those who believe in the dignity of man and his freedom in the world.

Article 18: The liberation of Palestine, from an international point of view, is a defensive action necessitated by the demands of self-defence. Accordingly, the Palestinian people, desirous as they are of the friendship of all people, look to freedom-loving, justice-loving and peace-loving states for support in order to restore their legitimate rights in Palestine, to re-establish peace and security in the country, and to enable its people to exercise national sovereignty and freedom.

Article 19: The partition of Palestine in 1947 and the establishment of the state of Israel are entirely illegal, regardless of the passage of time, because they were contrary to the will of the Palestinian people and to their natural right in their homeland, and inconsistent with the principles embodied in the Charter of the United Nations, particularly the right to self-determination.

Article 20: The Balfour Declaration, the mandate for Palestine and everything that has been based upon them, are deemed null and void. Claims of historical or religious ties of Jews with Palestine are incompatible with the facts of history and the true conception of what constitutes statehood. Judaism, being a religion, is not an independent nationality. Nor do Jews constitute a single nation with an identity of its own; they are citizens of the states to which they belong.

Article 21: The Arab Palestinian people, expressing themselves by the armed Palestinian revolution, reject all solutions which are substitutes for the total liberation of Palestine and reject all proposals aiming at the liquidation of the Palestinian problem, or its internationalization.

Article 22: Zionism is a political movement organically associated with international imperialism and antagonistic to all action for liberation and to progressive movements in the world. It is racist and fanatic in its nature, aggressive, expansionist and colonial in its aims, and fascist in its methods. Israel is the instrument of the Zionist movement, and a geographical base for world imperialism placed strategically in the midst of the Arab homeland to combat the hopes of the Arab nation for liberation, unity and progress. Israel is a constant source of threat *vis-à-vis* peace in the Middle East and the whole world. Since the liberation of Palestine will destroy the Zionist and imperialist presence and will contribute to the establishment of peace in the Middle East, the Palestinian people look for the support of all the progressive and peaceful forces and urge them all, irrespective of their affiliations and beliefs, to offer the Palestinian people all aid and support in their just struggle for the liberation of their homeland.

Article 23: The demands of security and peace, as well as the demands of right and justice, require all states to consider Zionism an illegitimate movement, to outlaw its existence, and to ban its operations, in order that friendly relations among peoples may be preserved, and the loyalty of citizens to their respective homelands safeguarded.

Article 24: The Palestinian people believe in the principles of justice, freedom, sovereignty, self-determination, human dignity, and in the right of all peoples to exercise them.

Article 25: For the realization of the goals of this Charter and its principles, the Palestine Liberation Organization will perform its role in the liberation of Palestine in accordance with the Constitution of this Organization.

Article 26: The Palestine Liberation Organization, representative of the Palestinian revolutionary forces, is responsible for the Palestinian Arab people's movement in its struggle—to retrieve its homeland, liberate and return to it and exercise the right to self-determination in it—in all military, political and financial fields and also for whatever may be required by the Palestine case on the inter-Arab and international levels.

Article 27: The Palestine Liberation Organization shall cooperate with all Arab states, each according to its potentialities; and will adopt a neutral policy among them in the light of the requirements of the war of liberation; and on this basis it shall not interfere in the internal affairs of any Arab state.

Article 28: The Palestinian Arab people assert the genuineness and independence of their national revolution and reject all forms of intervention, trusteeship and subordination.

Article 29: The Palestinian people possess the fundamental and genuine legal right to liberate and retrieve their homeland. The Palestinian people determine their attitude towards all states and forces on the basis of the stands they adopt *vis-à-vis* the Palestinian case and the extent of the support they offer to the Palestinian revolution to fulfill the aims of the Palestinian people.

Article 30: Fighters and carriers of arms in the war of liberation are the nucleus of the popular army which will be the protective force for the gains of the Palestinian Arab people.

Article 31: The Organization shall have a flag, an oath of allegiance and an anthem. All this shall be decided upon in accordance with a special regulation.

Article 32: Regulations, which shall be known as the Constitution of the Palestine Liberation Organization, shall be annexed to this Charter. It shall lay down the manner in which the Organization, and its organs and institutions, shall be constituted; the respective competence of each; and the requirements of its obligations under the Charter.

Article 33: This Charter shall not be amended save by (vote of) a majority of two-thirds of the total membership of the National Congress of the Palestine Liberation Organization (taken) at a special session convened for that purpose.

1.15 VIENNA CONVENTION ON THE LAW OF TREATIES.[a] Done at Vienna, May 23, 1969. Entered into force, Jan. 27, 1980. U.N. Doc. A/CONF.39/27 at 289 (1969), 1155 U.N.T.S. 331, *reprinted in* 8 I.L.M. 679 (1969) [b]

PART I. INTRODUCTION

Article 1. Scope of the Present Convention

The present Convention applies to treaties between States.

Article 2. Use of Terms

(1) For the purposes of the present Convention:

(a) "treaty" means an international agreement concluded between States in written form and governed by international law, whether embodied in a single instrument or in two or more related instruments and whatever its particular designation;

(b) "ratification", "acceptance", "approval" and "accession" mean in each case the international act so named whereby a State establishes on the international plane its consent to be bound by a treaty;

(c) "full powers" means a document emanating from the competent authority of a State designating a person or persons to represent the State for negotiating, adopting or authenticating the text of a treaty, for expressing the consent of the State to be bound by a treaty, or for accomplishing any other act with respect to a treaty;

(d) "reservation" means a unilateral statement, however phrased or named, made by a State, when signing, ratifying, accepting, approving or acceding to a treaty, whereby it purports to exclude or to modify the legal effect of certain provisions of the treaty in their application to that State;

(e) "negotiating State" means a State which took part in the drawing up and adoption of the text of the treaty;

(f) "contracting State" means a State which has consented to be bound by the treaty, whether or not the treaty has entered into force;

(g) "party" means a State which has consented to be bound by the treaty and for which the treaty is in force;

(h) "third State" means a State not a party to the treaty;

(i) "international organization" means an intergovernmental organization.

(2) The provisions of paragraph 1 regarding the use of terms in the present Convention are without prejudice to the use of those terms or to the meanings which may be given to them in the internal law of any State.

Article 3. International Agreements Not Within the Scope of the Present Convention

The fact that the present Convention does not apply to international agreements concluded between States and other subjects of international law or between such

a. Also known as "the Treaty on Treaties."

b. *See also* Declaration on the Prohibition of Military, Political or Economic Coercion in the Conclusion of Treaties, adopted by U.N. Conference on the Law of Treaties, U.N. Conference on the Law of Treaties Off.Rec., First and Second Sessions Mar. 26–May 24 1968 and April 9–May 22 1969, Documents of the Conference (U.N.Doc.A/CONF.39/26), p. 285; Declaration of Universal Participation in the Vienna Convention on the Law of Treaties, id.

other subjects of international law, or to international agreements not in written form, shall not affect:

(a) the legal force of such agreements;

(b) the application to them of any of the rules set forth in the present Convention to which they would be subject under international law independently of the Convention;

(c) the application of the Convention to the relations of States as between themselves under international agreements to which other subjects of international law are also parties.

Article 4. Non-retroactivity of the Present Convention

Without prejudice to the application of any rules set forth in the present Convention to which treaties would be subject under international law independently of the Convention, the Convention applies only to treaties which are concluded by States after the entry into force of the present Convention with regard to such States.

Article 5. Treaties Constituting International Organizations and Treaties Adopted Within an International Organization

The present Convention applies to any treaty which is the constituent instrument of an international organization and to any treaty adopted within an international organization without prejudice to any relevant rules of the organization.

PART II. CONCLUSION AND ENTRY INTO FORCE OF TREATIES

SECTION 1. CONCLUSION OF TREATIES

Article 6. Capacity of States to Conclude Treaties

Every State possesses capacity to conclude treaties.

Article 7. Full Powers

(1) A person is considered as representing a State for the purpose of adopting or authenticating the text of a treaty or for the purpose of expressing the consent of the State to be bound by a treaty if:

(a) he produces appropriate full powers; or

(b) it appears from the practice of the States concerned or from other circumstances that their intention was to consider that person as representing the State for such purposes and to dispense with full powers.

(2) In virtue of their functions and without having to produce full powers, the following are considered as representing their State:

(a) Heads of State, Heads of Government and Ministers for Foreign Affairs, for the purpose of performing all acts relating to the conclusion of a treaty;

(b) heads of diplomatic missions, for the purpose of adopting the text of a treaty between the accrediting State and the State to which they are accredited;

(c) representatives accredited by States to an international conference or to an international organization or one of its organs, for the purpose of adopting the text of a treaty in that conference, organization or organ.

Article 8. Subsequent Confirmation of an Act Performed Without Authorization

An act relating to the conclusion of a treaty performed by a person who cannot be considered under article 7 as authorized to represent a State for that purpose is without legal effect unless afterwards confirmed by that State.

* * *

Article 11. Means of Expressing Consent to Be Bound by a Treaty

The consent of a State to be bound by a treaty may be expressed by signature, exchange of instruments constituting a treaty, ratification, acceptance, approval or accession, or by any other means if so agreed.

Article 12. Consent to Be Bound by a Treaty Expressed by Signature

(1) The consent of a State to be bound by a treaty is expressed by the signature of its representative when:

(a) the treaty provides that signature shall have that effect;

(b) it is otherwise established that the negotiating States were agreed that signature should have that effect; or

(c) the intention of the State to give that effect to the signature appears from the full powers of its representative or was expressed during the negotiation.

(2) For the purposes of paragraph 1:

(a) the initialling of a text constitutes a signature of the treaty when it is established that the negotiating States so agreed;

(b) the signature *ad referendum* of a treaty by a representative, if confirmed by his State, constitutes a full signature of the treaty.

Article 13. Consent to Be Bound by a Treaty Expressed by an Exchange of Instruments Constituting a Treaty

The consent of States to be bound by a treaty constituted by instruments exchanged between them is expressed by that exchange when:

(a) the instruments provide that their exchange shall have that effect; or

(b) it is otherwise established that those States were agreed that the exchange of instruments should have that effect.

Article 14. Consent to Be Bound by a Treaty Expressed by Ratification, Acceptance or Approval

(1) The consent of a State to be bound by a treaty is expressed by ratification when:

(a) the treaty provides for such consent to be expressed by means of ratification;

(b) it is otherwise established that the negotiating States were agreed that ratification should be required;

(c) the representative of the State has signed the treaty subject to ratification; or

(d) the intention of the State to sign the treaty subject to ratification appears from the full powers of its representative or was expressed during the negotiation.

(2) The consent of a State to be bound by a treaty is expressed by acceptance or approval under conditions similar to those which apply to ratification.

Article 15. Consent to Be Bound by a Treaty Expressed by Accession

The consent of a State to be bound by a treaty is expressed by accession when:

(a) the treaty provides that such consent may be expressed by that State by means of accession;

(b) it is otherwise established that the negotiating States were agreed that such consent may be expressed by that State by means of accession; or

(c) all the parties have subsequently agreed that such consent may be expressed by that State by means of accession.

Article 16. Exchange or Deposit of Instruments of Ratification, Acceptance, Approval or Accession

Unless the treaty otherwise provides, instruments of ratification, acceptance, approval or accession establish the consent of a State to be bound by a treaty upon:

(a) their exchange between the contracting States;

(b) their deposit with the depositary; or

(c) their notification to the contracting States or to the depositary, if so agreed.

Article 17. Consent to Be Bound by Part of a Treaty and Choice of Differing Provisions

(1) Without prejudice to articles 19 and 23, the consent of a State to be bound by part of a treaty is effective only if the treaty so permits or the other contracting States so agree.

(2) The consent of a State to be bound by a treaty which permits a choice between differing provisions is effective only if it is made clear to which of the provisions the consent relates.

Article 18. Obligation Not to Defeat the Object and Purpose of a Treaty Prior to Its Entry into Force

A State is obliged to refrain from acts which would defeat the object and purpose of a treaty when:

(a) it has signed the treaty or has exchanged instruments constituting the treaty subject to ratification, acceptance or approval, until it shall have made its intention clear not to become a party to the treaty; or

(b) it has expressed its consent to be bound by the treaty, pending the entry into force of the treaty and provided that such entry into force is not unduly delayed.

SECTION 2. RESERVATIONS

Article 19. Formulation of Reservations

A State may, when signing, ratifying, accepting, approving or acceding to a treaty, formulate a reservation unless:

(a) the reservation is prohibited by the treaty;

(b) the treaty provides that only specified reservations, which do not include the reservation in question, may be made; or

(c) in cases not falling under sub-paragraphs (*a*) and (*b*), the reservation is incompatible with the object and purpose of the treaty.

Article 20. Acceptance of and Objection to Reservations

(1) A reservation expressly authorized by a treaty does not require any subsequent acceptance by the other contracting States unless the treaty so provides.

(2) When it appears from the limited number of the negotiating States and the object and purpose of a treaty that the application of the treaty in its entirety between all the parties is an essential condition of the consent of each one to be bound by the treaty, a reservation requires acceptance by all the parties.

(3) When a treaty is a constituent instrument of an international organization and unless it otherwise provides, a reservation requires the acceptance of the competent organ of that organization.

(4) In cases not falling under the preceding paragraphs and unless the treaty otherwise provides:

(a) acceptance by another contracting State of a reservation constitutes the reserving State a party to the treaty in relation to that other State if or when the treaty is in force for those States;

(b) an objection by another contracting State to a reservation does not preclude the entry into force of the treaty as between the objecting and reserving States unless a contrary intention is definitely expressed by the objecting State;

(c) an act expressing a State's consent to be bound by the treaty and containing a reservation is effective as soon as at least one other contracting State has accepted the reservation.

(5) For the purposes of paragraphs 2 and 4 and unless the treaty otherwise provides, a reservation is considered to have been accepted by a State if it shall have raised no objection to the reservation by the end of a period of twelve months after it was notified of the reservation or by the date on which it expressed its consent to be bound by the treaty, whichever is later.

Article 21. Legal Effects of Reservations and of Objections to Reservations

(1) A reservation established with regard to another party in accordance with articles 19, 20 and 23:

(a) modifies for the reserving State in its relations with that other party the provisions of the treaty to which the reservation relates to the extent of the reservation; and

(b) modifies those provisions to the same extent for that other party in its relations with the reserving State.

(2) The reservation does not modify the provisions of the treaty for the other parties to the treaty inter se.

(3) When a State objecting to a reservation has not opposed the entry into force of the treaty between itself and the reserving State, the provisions to which the reservation relates do not apply as between the two States to the extent of the reservation.

* * *

Article 23. Procedure Regarding Reservations

(1) A reservation, an express acceptance of a reservation and an objection to a reservation must be formulated in writing and communicated to the contracting States and other States entitled to become parties to the treaty.

(2) If formulated when signing the treaty subject to ratification, acceptance or approval, a reservation must be formally confirmed by the reserving State when expressing its consent to be bound by the treaty. In such a case the reservation shall be considered as having been made on the date of its confirmation.

(3) An express acceptance of, or an objection to, a reservation made previously to confirmation of the reservation does not itself require confirmation.

(4) The withdrawal of a reservation or of an objection to a reservation must be formulated in writing.

SECTION 3. ENTRY INTO FORCE AND PROVISIONAL APPLICATION OF TREATIES

Article 24. Entry into Force

(1) A treaty enters into force in such manner and upon such date as it may provide or as the negotiating States may agree.

(2) Failing any such provision or agreement, a treaty enters into force as soon as consent to be bound by the treaty has been established for all the negotiating States.

(3) When the consent of a State to be bound by a treaty is established on a date after the treaty has come into force, the treaty enters into force for that State on that date, unless the treaty otherwise provides.

(4) The provisions of a treaty regulating the authentication of its text, the establishment of the consent of States to be bound by the treaty, the manner or date of its entry into force, reservations, the functions of the depositary and other matters arising necessarily before the entry into force of the treaty apply from the time of the adoption of its text.

Article 25. Provisional Application

(1) A treaty or a part of a treaty is applied provisionally pending its entry into force if:

(a) the treaty itself so provides; or

(b) the negotiating States have in some other manner so agreed.

(2) Unless the treaty otherwise provides or the negotiating States have otherwise agreed, the provisional application of a treaty or a part of a treaty with respect to a State shall be terminated if that State notifies the other States between which the treaty is being applied provisionally of its intention not to become a party to the treaty.

PART III. OBSERVANCE, APPLICATION AND INTERPRETATION OF TREATIES

SECTION 1. OBSERVANCE OF TREATIES

Article 26. Pacta Sunt Servanda

Every treaty in force is binding upon the parties to it and must be performed by them in good faith.

Article 27. Internal Law and Observance of Treaties

A party may not invoke the provisions of its internal law as justification for its failure to perform a treaty. This rule is without prejudice to article 46.

SECTION 2. APPLICATION OF TREATIES

Article 28. Non-retroactivity of Treaties

Unless a different intention appears from the treaty or is otherwise established, its provisions do not bind a party in relation to any act or fact which took place or any situation which ceased to exist before the date of the entry into force of the treaty with respect to that party.

* * *

SECTION 3. INTERPRETATION OF TREATIES

Article 31. General Rule of Interpretation

(1) A treaty shall be interpreted in good faith in accordance with the ordinary meaning to be given to the terms of the treaty in their context and in the light of its object and purpose.

(2) The context for the purpose of the interpretation of a treaty shall comprise, in addition to the text, including its preamble and annexes:

(a) any agreement relating to the treaty which was made between all the parties in connexion with the conclusion of the treaty;

(b) any instrument which was made by one or more parties in connexion with the conclusion of the treaty and accepted by the other parties as an instrument related to the treaty.

(3) There shall be taken into account, together with the context:

(a) any subsequent agreement between the parties regarding the interpretation of the treaty or the application of its provisions;

(b) any subsequent practice in the application of the treaty which establishes the agreement of the parties regarding its interpretation;

(c) any relevant rules of international law applicable in the relations between the parties.

(4) A special meaning shall be given to a term if it is established that the parties so intended.

Article 32. Supplementary Means of Interpretation

Recourse may be had to supplementary means of interpretation, including the preparatory work of the treaty and the circumstances of its conclusion, in order to confirm the meaning resulting from the application of article 31, or to determine the meaning when the interpretation according to article 31:

(a) leaves the meaning ambiguous or obscure; or

(b) leads to a result which is manifestly absurd or unreasonable.

* * *

SECTION 4. TREATIES AND THIRD STATES

Article 34. General Rule Regarding Third States

A treaty does not create either obligations or rights for a third State without its consent.

Article 35. Treaties Providing for Obligations for Third States

An obligation arises for a third State from a provision of a treaty if the parties to the treaty intend the provision to be the means of establishing the obligation and the third State expressly accepts that obligation in writing.

Article 36. Treaties Providing for Rights for Third States

(1) A right arises for a third State from a provision of a treaty if the parties to the treaty intend the provision to accord that right either to the third State, or to a group of States to which it belongs, or to all States, and the third State assents thereto. Its assent shall be presumed so long as the contrary is not indicated, unless the treaty otherwise provides.

(2) A State exercising a right in accordance with paragraph 1 shall comply with the conditions for its exercise provided for in the treaty or established in conformity with the treaty.

Article 37. Revocation or Modification of Obligations or Rights of Third States

(1) When an obligation has arisen for a third State in conformity with article 35, the obligation may be revoked or modified only with the consent of the parties to the treaty and of the third State, unless it is established that they had otherwise agreed.

(2) When a right has arisen for a third State in conformity with article 36, the right may not be revoked or modified by the parties if it is established that the right was intended not to be revocable or subject to modification without the consent of the third State.

Article 38. Rules in a Treaty Becoming Binding on Third States Through International Custom

Nothing in articles 34 and 37 precludes a rule set forth in a treaty from becoming binding upon a third State as a customary rule of international law, recognized as such.

PART IV. AMENDMENT AND MODIFICATION OF TREATIES

Article 39. General Rule Regarding the Amendment of Treaties

A treaty may be amended by agreement between the parties. The rules laid down in Part II apply to such an agreement except in so far as the treaty may otherwise provide.

* * *

Article 41. Agreements to Modify Multilateral Treaties Between Certain of the Parties Only

(1) Two or more of the parties to a multilateral treaty may conclude an agreement to modify the treaty as between themselves alone if:

(a) the possibility of such a modification is provided for by the treaty; or

(b) the modification in question is not prohibited by the treaty and:

(i) does not affect the enjoyment by the other parties of their rights under the treaty or the performance of their obligation;

(ii) does not relate to a provision, derogation from which is incompatible with the effective execution of the object and purpose of the treaty as a whole.

(2) Unless in a case falling under paragraph 1(a) the treaty otherwise provides, the parties in question shall notify the other parties of their intention to conclude the agreement and of the modification to the treaty for which it provides.

PART V. INVALIDITY, TERMINATION AND SUSPENSION OF THE OPERATION OF TREATIES

SECTION 1. GENERAL PROVISIONS

Article 42. Validity and Continuance in Force of Treaties

(1) The validity of a treaty or of the consent of a State to be bound by a treaty may be impeached only through the application of the present Convention.

(2) The termination of a treaty, its denunciation or the withdrawal of a party, may take place only as a result of the application of the provisions of the treaty or of the present Convention. The same rule applies to suspension of the operation of a treaty.

Article 43. Obligations Imposed by International Law Independently of a Treaty

The invalidity, termination or denunciation of a treaty, the withdrawal of a party from it, or the suspension of its operation, as a result of the application of the present Convention or of the provisions of the treaty, shall not in any way impair the duty of any State to fulfil any obligation embodied in the treaty to which it would be subject under international law independently of the treaty.

Article 44. Separability of Treaty Provisions

(1) A right of a party, provided for in a treaty or arising under article 56, to denounce, withdraw from or suspend the operation of the treaty may be exercised only with respect to the whole treaty unless the treaty otherwise provides or the parties otherwise agree.

(2) A ground for invalidating, terminating, withdrawing from or suspending the operation of a treaty recognized in the present Convention may be invoked only with respect to the whole treaty except as provided in the following paragraphs or in article 60.

(3) If the ground relates solely to particular clauses, it may be invoked only with respect to those clauses where:

(a) the said clauses are separable from the remainder of the treaty with regard to their application;

(b) it appears from the treaty or is otherwise established that acceptance of those clauses was not an essential basis of the consent of the other party or parties to be bound by the treaty as a whole; and

(c) continued performance of the remainder of the treaty would not be unjust.

(4) In cases falling under articles 49 and 50 the State entitled to invoke the fraud or corruption may do so with respect either to the whole treaty or, subject to paragraph 3, to the particular clauses alone.

(5) In cases falling under articles 51, 52 and 53, no separation of the provisions of the treaty is permitted.

Article 45. Loss of a Right to Invoke a Ground for Invalidating, Terminating, Withdrawing from or Suspending the Operation of a Treaty

A State may no longer invoke a ground for invalidating, terminating, withdrawing from or suspending the operation of a treaty under articles 46 to 50 or articles 60 and 62, if, after becoming aware of the facts:

(a) it shall have expressly agreed that the treaty is valid or remains in force or continues in operation, as the case may be; or

(b) it must by reason of its conduct be considered as having acquiesced in the validity of the treaty or in its maintenance in force or in operation, as the case may be.

SECTION 2. INVALIDITY OF TREATIES

Article 46. Provisions of Internal Law Regarding Competence to Conclude Treaties

(1) A State may not invoke the fact that its consent to be bound by a treaty has been expressed in violation of a provision of its internal law regarding competence to conclude treaties as invalidating its consent unless that violation was manifest and concerned a rule of its internal law of fundamental importance.

(2) A violation is manifest if it would be objectively evident to any State conducting itself in the matter in accordance with normal practice and in good faith.

Article 47. Specific Restrictions on Authority to Express the Consent of a State

If the authority of a representative to express the consent of a State to be bound by a particular treaty has been made subject to a specific restriction, his omission to observe that restriction may not be invoked as invalidating the consent expressed by him unless the restriction was notified to the other negotiating States prior to his expressing such consent.

Article 48. Error

(1) A State may invoke an error in a treaty as invalidating its consent to be bound by the treaty if the error relates to a fact or situation which was assumed by

that State to exist at the time when the treaty was concluded and formed an essential basis of its consent to be bound by the treaty.

(2) Paragraph 1 shall not apply if the State in question contributed by its own conduct to the error or if the circumstances were such as to put that State on notice of a possible error.

(3) An error relating only to the wording of the text of a treaty does not affect its validity; article 79 then applies.

Article 49. Fraud

If a State has been induced to conclude a treaty by the fraudulent conduct of another negotiating State, the State may invoke the fraud as invalidating its consent to be bound by the treaty.

Article 50. Corruption of a Representative of a State

If the expression of a State's consent to be bound by a treaty has been procured through the corruption of its representative directly or indirectly by another negotiating State, the State may invoke such corruption as invalidating its consent to be bound by the Treaty.

Article 51. Coercion of a Representative of a State

The expression of a State's consent to be bound by a treaty which has been procured by the coercion of its representative through acts or threats directed against him shall be without any legal effect.

Article 52. Coercion of a State by the Threat or Use of Force

A treaty is void if its conclusion has been procured by the threat or use of force in violation of the principles of international law embodied in the Charter of the United Nations.

Article 53. Treaties Conflicting with a Peremptory Norm of General International Law (Jus Cogens)

A treaty is void if, at the time of its conclusion, it conflicts with a peremptory norm of general international law. For the purposes of the present Convention, a peremptory norm of general international law is a norm accepted and recognized by the international community of States as a whole as a norm from which no derogation is permitted and which can be modified only by a subsequent norm of general international law having the same character.

SECTION 3. TERMINATION AND SUSPENSION OF THE OPERATION OF TREATIES

Article 54. Termination of or Withdrawal from a Treaty Under Its Provisions or by Consent of the Parties

The termination of a treaty or the withdrawal of a party may take place:

(a) in conformity with the provisions of the treaty; or

(b) at any time by consent of all the parties after consultation with the other contracting States.

Article 55. Reduction of the Parties to a Multilateral Treaty Below the Number Necessary for Its Entry into Force

Unless the treaty otherwise provides, a multilateral treaty does not terminate by reason only of the fact that the number of the parties falls below the number necessary for its entry into force.

Article 56. Denunciation of or Withdrawal from a Treaty Containing No Provision Regarding Termination, Denunciation or Withdrawal

(1) A treaty which contains no provision regarding its termination and which does not provide for denunciation or withdrawal is not subject to denunciation or withdrawal unless:

(a) it is established that the parties intended to admit the possibility of denunciation or withdrawal; or

(b) a right of denunciation or withdrawal may be implied by the nature of the treaty.

(2) A party shall give not less than twelve months' notice of its intention to denounce or withdraw from a treaty under paragraph 1.

Article 57. Suspension of the Operation of a Treaty Under its Provisions or by Consent of the Parties

The operation of a treaty in regard to all the parties or to a particular party may be suspended:

(a) in conformity with the provisions of the treaty; or

(b) at any time by consent of all the parties after consultation with the other contracting States.

Article 58. Suspension of the Operation of a Multilateral Treaty by Agreement between Certain of the Parties Only

(1) Two or more parties to a multilateral treaty may conclude an agreement to suspend the operation of provisions of the treaty, temporarily and as between themselves alone, if:

(a) the possibility of such a suspension is provided for by the treaty; or

(b) the suspension in question is not prohibited by the treaty and:

(i) does not affect the enjoyment by the other parties of their rights under the treaty or the performance of their obligations;

(ii) is not incompatible with the object and purpose of the treaty.

(2) Unless in a case falling under paragraph 1(a) the treaty otherwise provides, the parties in question shall notify the other parties of their intention to conclude the agreement and of those provisions of the treaty the operation of which they intend to suspend.

Article 59. Termination or Suspension of the Operation of a Treaty Implied by Conclusion of a Later Treaty

(1) A treaty shall be considered as terminated if all the parties to it conclude a later treaty relating to the same subject-matter and:

(a) it appears from the later treaty or is otherwise established that the parties intended that the matter should be governed by that treaty; or

(b) the provisions of the later treaty are so far incompatible with those of the earlier one that the two treaties are not capable of being applied at the same time.

(2) The earlier treaty shall be considered as only suspended in operation if it appears from the later treaty or is otherwise established that such was the intention of the parties.

Article 60. Termination or Suspension of the Operation of a Treaty as a Consequence of Its Breach

(1) A material breach of a bilateral treaty by one of the parties entitles the other to invoke the breach as a ground for terminating the treaty or suspending its operation in whole or in part.

(2) A material breach of a multilateral treaty by one of the parties entitles:

(a) the other parties by unanimous agreement to suspend the operation of the treaty in whole or in part or to terminate it either:

(i) in the relations between themselves and the defaulting State, or

(ii) as between all the parties;

(b) a party specially affected by the breach to invoke it as a ground for suspending the operation of the treaty in whole or in part in the relations between itself and the defaulting State;

(c) any party other than the defaulting State to invoke the breach as a ground for suspending the operation of the treaty in whole or in part with respect to itself if the treaty is of such a character that a material breach of its provisions by one party radically changes the position of every party with respect to the further performance of its obligations under the treaty.

(3) A material breach of a treaty, for the purposes of this article, consists in:

(a) a repudiation of the treaty not sanctioned by the present Convention; or

(b) the violation of a provision essential to the accomplishment of the object or purpose of the treaty.

(4) The foregoing paragraphs are without prejudice to any provision in the treaty applicable in the event of a breach.

(5) Paragraphs 1 to 3 do not apply to provisions relating to the protection of the human person contained in treaties of a humanitarian character, in particular to provisions prohibiting any form of reprisals against persons protected by such treaties.

Article 61. Supervening Impossibility of Performance

(1) A party may invoke the impossibility of performing a treaty as a ground for terminating or withdrawing from it if the impossibility results from the permanent disappearance or destruction of an object indispensable for the execution of the treaty. If the impossibility is temporary, it may be invoked only as a ground for suspending the operation of the treaty.

(2) Impossibility of performance may not be invoked by a party as a ground for terminating, withdrawing from or suspending the operation of a treaty if the impossibility is the result of a breach by that party either of an obligation under the treaty or of any other international obligation owed to any other party to the treaty.

Article 62. Fundamental Change of Circumstances

(1) A fundamental change of circumstances which has occurred with regard to those existing at the time of the conclusion of a treaty, and which was not foreseen by the parties, may not be invoked as a ground for terminating or withdrawing from the treaty unless:

(a) the existence of those circumstances constituted an essential basis of the consent of the parties to be bound by the treaty; and

(b) the effect of the change is radically to transform the extent of obligations still to be performed under the treaty.

(2) A fundamental change of circumstances may not be invoked as a ground for terminating or withdrawing from a treaty:

(a) if the treaty establishes a boundary; or

(b) if the fundamental change is the result of a breach by the party invoking it either of an obligation under the treaty or of any other international obligation owed to any other party to the treaty.

(3) If, under the foregoing paragraphs, a party may invoke a fundamental change of circumstances as a ground for terminating or withdrawing from a treaty it may also invoke the change as a ground for suspending the operation of the treaty.

Article 63. Severance of Diplomatic or Consular Relations

The severance of diplomatic or consular relations between parties to a treaty does not affect the legal relations established between them by the treaty except in so far as the existence of diplomatic or consular relations is indispensable for the application of the treaty.

Article 64. Emergence of a New Peremptory Norm of General International Law (Jus Cogens)

If a new peremptory norm of general international law emerges, any existing treaty which is in conflict with that norm becomes void and terminates.

SECTION 4. PROCEDURE

Article 65. Procedure to be Followed With Respect to Invalidity, Termination, Withdrawal From or Suspension of the Operation of a Treaty

(1) A party which, under the provisions of the present Convention, invokes either a defect in its consent to be bound by a treaty or a ground for impeaching the validity of a treaty, terminating it, withdrawing from it or suspending its operation, must notify the other parties of its claim. The notification shall indicate the measure proposed to be taken with respect to the treaty and the reasons therefor.

(2) If, after the expiry of a period which, except in cases of special urgency, shall not be less than three months after the receipt of the notification, no party has raised any objection, the party making the notification may carry out in the manner provided in article 67 the measure which it has proposed.

(3) If, however, objection has been raised by any other party, the parties shall seek a solution through the means indicated in Article 33 of the Charter of the United Nations.

(4) Nothing in the foregoing paragraphs shall affect the rights or obligations of the parties under any provisions in force binding the parties with regard to the settlement of disputes.

(5) Without prejudice to article 45, the fact that a State has not previously made the notification prescribed in paragraph 1 shall not prevent it from making such notification in answer to another party claiming performance of the treaty or alleging its violation.

Article 66. Procedures for Judicial Settlement, Arbitration and Conciliation

If, under paragraph 3 of article 65, no solution has been reached within a period of 12 months following the date on which the objection was raised, the following procedures shall be followed:

(a) any one of the parties to a dispute concerning the application or the interpretation of article 53 or 64 may, by a written application, submit it to the International Court of Justice for a decision unless the parties by common consent agree to submit the dispute to arbitration;

(b) any one of the parties to a dispute concerning the application or the interpretation of any of the other articles in Part V of the present Convention may set in motion the procedure specified in the Annex to the Convention by submitting a request to that effect to the Secretary-General of the United Nations.

Article 67. Instruments for Declaring Invalid, Terminating, Withdrawing From or Suspending the Operation of a Treaty

(1) The notification provided for under article 65, paragraph 1 must be made in writing.

(2) Any act declaring invalid, terminating, withdrawing from or suspending the operation of a treaty pursuant to the provisions of the treaty or of paragraphs 2 or 3 of article 65 shall be carried out through an instrument communicated to the other parties. If the instrument is not signed by the Head of State, Head of Government or Minister for Foreign Affairs, the representative of the State communicating it may be called upon to produce full powers.

Article 68. Revocation of Notifications and Instruments Provided for in Articles 65 and 67

A notification or instrument provided for in articles 65 or 67 may be revoked at any time before it takes effect.

SECTION 5. CONSEQUENCES OF THE INVALIDITY, TERMINATION OR SUSPENSION OF THE OPERATION OF A TREATY

Article 69. Consequences of the Invalidity of a Treaty

(1) A treaty the invalidity of which is established under the present Convention is void. The provisions of a void treaty have no legal force.

(2) If acts have nevertheless been performed in reliance on such a treaty:

(a) each party may require any other party to establish as far as possible in their mutual relations the position that would have existed if the acts had not been performed;

(b) acts performed in good faith before the invalidity was invoked are not rendered unlawful by reason only of the invalidity of the treaty.

(3) In cases falling under articles 49, 50, 51 or 52, paragraph 2 does not apply with respect to the party to which the fraud, the act of corruption or the coercion is imputable.

(4) In the case of the invalidity of a particular State's consent to be bound by a multilateral treaty, the foregoing rules apply in the relations between that State and the parties to the treaty.

Article 70. Consequences of the Termination of a Treaty

(1) Unless the treaty otherwise provides or the parties otherwise agree, the termination of a treaty under its provisions or in accordance with the present Convention:

(a) releases the parties from any obligation further to perform the treaty;

(b) does not affect any right, obligation or legal situation of the parties created through the execution of the treaty prior to its termination.

(2) If a State denounces or withdraws from a multilateral treaty, paragraph 1 applies in the relations between that State and each of the other parties to the treaty from the date when such denunciation or withdrawal takes effect.

Article 71. Consequences of the Invalidity of a Treaty Which Conflicts With a Peremptory Norm of General International Law

(1) In the case of a treaty which is void under article 53 the parties shall:

(a) eliminate as far as possible the consequences of any act performed in reliance on any provision which conflicts with the peremptory norm of general international law; and

(b) bring their mutual relations into conformity with the peremptory norm of general international law.

(2) In the case of a treaty which becomes void and terminates under article 64, the termination of the treaty:

(a) releases the parties from any obligation further to perform the treaty;

(b) does not affect any right, obligation or legal situation of the parties created through the execution of the treaty prior to its termination; provided that those rights, obligations or situations may thereafter be maintained only to the extent that their maintenance is not in itself in conflict with the new peremptory norm of general international law.

Article 72. Consequences of the Suspension of the Operation of a Treaty

(1) Unless the treaty otherwise provides or the parties otherwise agree, the suspension of the operation of a treaty under its provisions or in accordance with the present Convention:

(a) releases the parties between which the operation of the treaty is suspended from the obligation to perform the treaty in their mutual relations during the period of the suspension;

(b) does not otherwise affect the legal relations between the parties established by the treaty.

(2) During the period of the suspension the parties shall refrain from acts tending to obstruct the resumption of the operation of the treaty.

PART VI. MISCELLANEOUS PROVISIONS

Article 73. Cases of State Succession, State Responsibility and Outbreak of Hostilities

The provisions of the present Convention shall not prejudge any question that may arise in regard to a treaty from a succession of States or from the international responsibility of a State or from the outbreak of hostilities between States.

Article 74. Diplomatic and Consular Relations and the Conclusion of Treaties

The severance or absence of diplomatic or consular relations between two or more States does not prevent the conclusion of treaties between those States. The conclusion of a treaty does not in itself affect the situation in regard to diplomatic or consular relations.

Article 75. Case of an Aggressor State

The provisions of the present Convention are without prejudice to any obligation in relation to a treaty which may arise for an aggressor State in Consequence of measures taken in conformity with the Charter of the United Nations with reference to that State's aggression.

* * *

PART VIII. FINAL PROVISIONS

* * *

1.16 DECLARATION ON PRINCIPLES OF INTERNATIONAL LAW CONCERNING FRIENDLY RELATIONS AND CO-OPERATION AMONG STATES IN ACCORDANCE WITH THE CHARTER OF THE UNITED NATIONS. Adopted by the U.N. General Assembly, Oct. 24, 1970. U.N.G.A. Res. 2625 (XXV), 25 U.N. GAOR, Supp. (No. 28) 121, U.N. Doc. A/8028 (1971), *reprinted in* 9 I.L.M. 1292 (1970)

PREAMBLE

THE GENERAL ASSEMBLY,

Reaffirming in the terms of the Charter that the maintenance of international peace and security and the development of friendly relations and co-operation between nations are among the fundamental purposes of the United Nations,

Recalling that the peoples of the United Nations are determined to practise tolerance and live together in peace with one another as good neighbours,

Bearing in mind the importance of maintaining and strengthening international peace founded upon freedom, equality, justice and respect for fundamental human rights and of developing friendly relations among nations irrespective of their political, economic and social systems or the levels of their development,

Bearing in mind also the paramount importance of the Charter of the United Nations in the promotion of the rule of law among nations,

Considering that the faithful observance of the principles of international law concerning friendly relations and co-operation among States, and fulfilment in good faith of the obligations assumed by States, in accordance with the Charter, is of the greatest importance for the maintenance of international peace and security, and for the implementation of the other purposes of the United Nations,

Noting that the great political, economic and social changes and scientific progress which have taken place in the world since the adoption of the Charter of the United Nations give increased importance to these principles and to the need for their more effective application in the conduct of States wherever carried on,

Recalling the established principle that outer space, including the Moon and other celestial bodies, is not subject to national appropriation by claim of sovereignty by means of use or occupation or by any other means, and mindful of the fact that consideration is being given in the United Nations to the question of establishing other appropriate provisions similarly inspired,

Convinced that the strict observance by States of the obligation not to intervene in the affairs of any other State is an essential condition to ensure that nations live together in peace with one another since the practice of any form of intervention not only violates the spirit and letter of the Charter of the United Nations but also leads to the creation of situations which threaten international peace and security,

Recalling the duty of States to refrain in their international relations from military, political, economic or any other form of coercion aimed against the political independence or territorial integrity of any State,

Considering it essential that all States shall refrain in their international relations from the threat or use of force against the territorial integrity or political independence of any State, or in any other manner inconsistent with the purposes of the United Nations,

Considering it equally essential that all States shall settle their international disputes by peaceful means in accordance with the Charter,

Reaffirming, in accordance with the Charter, the basic importance of sovereign equality and stressing that the purposes of the United Nations can be implemented only if States enjoy sovereign equality and comply fully with the requirements of this principle in their international relations,

Convinced that the subjection of peoples to alien subjugation, domination and exploitation constitutes a major obstacle to the promotion of international peace and security,

Convinced that the principle of equal rights and self-determination of peoples constitutes a significant contribution to contemporary international law, and that its effective application is of paramount importance for the promotion of friendly relations among States, based on respect for the principle of sovereign equality,

Convinced in consequence that any attempt aimed at the partial or total disruption of the national unity and territorial integrity of a State or country or at its political independence is incompatible with the purposes and principles of the Charter,

Considering the provisions of the Charter as a whole and taking into account the role of relevant resolutions adopted by the competent organs of the United Nations relating to the content of the principles,

Considering the progressive development and codification of the following principles:

(a) The principle that States shall refrain in their international relations from the threat or use of force against the territorial integrity or political independence of any State, or in any other manner inconsistent with the purposes of the United Nations,

(b) The principle that States shall settle their international disputes by peaceful means in such a manner that international peace and security and justice are not endangered,

(c) The duty not to intervene in matters within the domestic jurisdiction of any State, in accordance with the Charter,

(d) The duty of States to co-operate with one another in accordance with the Charter,

(e) The principle of equal rights and self-determination of peoples,

(f) The principle of sovereign equality of States,

(g) The principle that States shall fulfil in good faith the obligations assumed by them in accordance with the Charter, so as to secure their more effective application within the international community would promote the realization of the purposes of the United Nations,

Having considered the principles of international law relating to friendly relations and co-operation among States,

All States shall comply in good faith with their obligations under the generally recognized principles and rules of international law with respect to the maintenance of international peace and security, and shall endeavour to make the United Nations security system based upon the Charter more effective.

Nothing in the foregoing paragraphs shall be construed as enlarging or diminishing in any way the scope of the provisions of the Charter concerning cases in which the use of force is lawful.

The principle that States shall settle their international disputes by peaceful means in such a manner that international peace and security and justice are not endangered

Every State shall settle its international disputes with other States by peaceful means, in such a manner that international peace and security, and justice, are not endangered.

States shall accordingly seek early and just settlement of their international disputes by negotiation, inquiry, mediation, conciliation, arbitration, judicial settlement, resort to regional agencies or arrangements or other peaceful means of their choice. In seeking such a settlement, the parties shall agree upon such peaceful means as may be appropriate to the circumstances and nature of the dispute.

The parties to a dispute have the duty, in the event of failure to reach a solution by any one of the above peaceful means, to continue to seek a settlement of the dispute by other peaceful means agreed upon by them.

States parties to an international dispute, as well as other States, shall refrain from any action which may aggravate the situation so as to endanger the maintenance of international peace and security, and shall act in accordance with the purposes and principles of the United Nations.

International disputes shall be settled on the basis of the sovereign equality of States and in accordance with the principle of free choice of means. Recourse to, or acceptance of, a settlement procedure freely agreed to by States with regard to existing or future disputes to which they are parties shall not be regarded as incompatible with sovereign equality.

Nothing in the foregoing paragraphs prejudices or derogates from the applicable provisions of the Charter, in particular those relating to the pacific settlement of international disputes.

The principle concerning the duty not to intervene in matters within the domestic jurisdiction of any State, in accordance with the Charter

No State or group of States has the right to intervene, directly or indirectly, for any reason whatever, in the internal or external affairs of any other State. Consequently, armed intervention and all other forms of interference or attempted threats against the personality of the State or against its political, economic and cultural elements, are in violation of international law.

No State may use or encourage the use of economic, political or any other type of measures to coerce another State in order to obtain from it the subordination of the exercise of its sovereign rights and to secure from it advantages of any kind. Also, no State shall organize, assist, foment, finance, incite or tolerate subversive, terrorist or armed activities directed towards the violent overthrow of the régime of another State, or interfere in civil strife in another State.

The use of force to deprive peoples of their national identity constitutes a violation of their inalienable rights and of the principle of non-intervention.

Every State has an inalienable right to choose its political, economic, social and cultural systems, without interference in any form by another State.

Nothing in the foregoing paragraphs shall be construed as affecting the relevant provisions of the Charter relating to the maintenance of international peace and security.

The duty of States to co-operate with one another in accordance with the Charter

States have the duty to co-operate with one another, irrespective of the differences in their political, economic and social systems, in the various spheres of international relations, in order to maintain international peace and security and to promote international economic stability and progress, the general welfare of nations and international co-operation free from discrimination based on such differences. To this end:

(a) States shall co-operate with other States in the maintenance of international peace and security;

(b) States shall co-operate in the promotion of universal respect for and observance of human rights and fundamental freedoms for all, and in the elimination of all forms of racial discrimination and all forms of religious intolerance;

(c) States shall conduct their international relations in the economic, social, cultural, technical and trade fields in accordance with the principles of sovereign equality and non-intervention;

(d) States Members of the United Nations have the duty to take joint and separate action in co-operation with the United Nations in accordance with the relevant provisions of the Charter.

States should co-operate in the economic, social and cultural fields as well as in the field of science and technology and for the promotion of international cultural and educational progress. States should co-operate in the promotion of economic growth throughout the world, especially that of the developing countries.

The principle of equal rights and self-determination of peoples

By virtue of the principle of equal rights and self-determination of peoples enshrined in the Charter, all peoples have the right freely to determine, without external interference, their political status and to pursue their economic, social and cultural development, and every State has the duty to respect this right in accordance with the provisions of the Charter.

Every State has the duty to promote, through joint and separate action, the realization of the principle of equal rights and self-determination of peoples, in accordance with the provisions of the Charter, and to render assistance to the United Nations in carrying out the responsibilities entrusted to it by the Charter regarding the implementation of the principle in order:

(a) To promote friendly relations and co-operation among States; and

(b) To bring a speedy end to colonialism, having due regard to the freely expressed will of the peoples concerned;

and bearing in mind that subjection of peoples to alien subjugation, domination and exploitation constitutes a violation of the principle, as well as a denial of fundamental human rights, and is contrary to the Charter of the United Nations.

Every State has the duty to promote through joint and separate action universal respect for and observance of human rights and fundamental freedoms in accordance with the Charter.

The establishment of a sovereign and independent State, the free association or integration with an independent State or the emergence into any other political status freely determined by a people constitute modes of implementing the right of self-determination by that people.

Every State has the duty to refrain from any forcible action which deprives peoples referred to above in the elaboration of the present principle of their right to self-determination and freedom and independence. In their actions against and resistance to such forcible action in pursuit of the exercise of their right to self-determination, such peoples are entitled to seek and to receive support in accordance with the purposes and principles of the Charter of the United Nations.

The territory of a colony or other non-self-governing territory has, under the Charter of the United Nations, a status separate and distinct from the territory of the State administering it; and such separate and distinct status under the Charter shall exist until the people of the colony or non-self-governing territory have exercised their right of self-determination in accordance with the Charter, and particularly its purposes and principles.

Nothing in the foregoing paragraphs shall be construed as authorizing or encouraging any action which would dismember or impair, totally or in part, the territorial integrity or political unity of sovereign and independent States conducting themselves in compliance with the principle of equal rights and self-determination of peoples as described above and thus possessed of a government representing the whole people belonging to the territory without distinction as to race, creed or colour.

Every state shall refrain from any action aimed at the partial or total disruption of the national unity and territorial integrity of any other State or country.

The principle of sovereign equality of States

All States enjoy sovereign equality. They have equal rights and duties and are equal members of the international community, notwithstanding differences of an economic, social, political or other nature.

In particular, sovereign equality includes the following elements:

(a) States are juridically equal;

(b) Each State enjoys the rights inherent in full sovereignty;

(c) Each State has the duty to respect the personality of other States;

(d) The territorial integrity and political independence of the State are inviolable;

(e) Each State has the right freely to choose and develop its political, social, economic and cultural systems;

(f) Each State has the duty to comply fully and in good faith with its international obligations and to live in peace with other States.

The principle that States shall fulfil in good faith the obligations assumed by them in accordance with the Charter

Every State has the duty to fulfil in good faith the obligations assumed by it in accordance with the Charter of the United Nations.

Every State has the duty to fulfil in good faith its obligations under the generally recognized principles and rules of international law.

Every State has the duty to fulfil in good faith its obligations under international agreements valid under the generally recognized principles and rules of international law.

Where obligations arising under international agreements are in conflict with the obligations of Members of the United Nations under the Charter of the United Nations, the obligations under the Charter shall prevail.

General part.

2. *Declares* that:

In their interpretation and application the above principles are interrelated and each principle should be construed in the context of the other principles,

Nothing in this Declaration shall be construed as prejudicing in any manner the provisions of the Charter or the rights and duties of Member States under the Charter or the rights of peoples under the Charter taking into account the elaboration of these rights in this Declaration,

3. ***Declares further*** **that:**

The principles of the Charter which are embodied in this Declaration constitute basic principles of international law, and consequently appeals to all States to be guided by these principles in their international conduct and to develop their mutual relations on the basis of their strict observance.

1.17 FINAL ACT OF THE CONFERENCE ON SECURITY AND CO-OPERATION IN EUROPE.[a] Adopted by the Conference on Security and Co-operation in Europe at Helsinki, Aug. 1, 1975. Dep't State Pub. No. 8826 (GEN'L FOR.SERV. 298), *reprinted in* 14 I.L.M. 1292 (1975)[b]

The States participating in the Conference on Security and Co-operation in Europe.

Reaffirming their objective of promoting better relations among themselves and ensuring conditions in which their people can live in true and lasting peace free from any threat to or attempt against their security:

Convinced of the need to exert efforts to make détente both a continuing and an increasingly viable and comprehensive process, universal in scope, and that the implementation of the results of the Conference on Security and Co-operation in Europe will be a major contribution to this process:

Considering that solidarity among peoples, as well as the common purpose of the participating States in achieving the aims as set forth by the Conference on Security and Co-operation in Europe, should lead to the development of better and closer relations among them in all fields and thus to overcoming the confrontation stemming from the character of their past relations, and to better mutual understanding:

Mindful of their common history and recognizing that the existence of elements common to their traditions and values can assist them in developing their relations, and desiring to search, fully taking into account the individuality and diversity of their positions and views, for possibilities of joining their efforts with a view to overcoming distrust and increasing confidence, solving the problems that separate them and co-operating in the interest of mankind:

Recognizing the indivisibility of security in Europe as well as their common interest in the development of co-operation throughout Europe and among themselves and expressing their intention to pursue efforts accordingly:

Recognizing the close link between peace and security in Europe and in the world as a whole and conscious of the need for each of them to make its contribution to the strengthening of world peace and security and to the promotion of fundamental rights, economic and social progress and well-being for all peoples:

Have adopted the following:

1.

(a) DECLARATION ON PRINCIPLES GUIDING RELATIONS BETWEEN PARTICIPATING STATES

The Participating States.

Reaffirming their commitment to peace, security and justice and the continuing development of friendly relations and co-operation:

Recognizing that this commitment, which reflects the interest and aspirations of peoples, constitutes for each participating State a present and future responsibility, heightened by experience of the past;

Reaffirming, in conformity with their membership in the United Nations and in accordance with the purposes and principles of the United Nations, their full and active support for the United Nations and for the enhancement of its role and

a. Also known as "the Helsinki Final Act" or "the Helsinki Accords."

b. *See also* Basic Document 1.18.

effectiveness in strengthening international peace, security and justice, and in promoting the solution of international problems, as well as the development of friendly relations and co-operation among States;

Expressing their common adherence to the principles which are set forth below and are in conformity with the Charter of the United Nations, as well as their common will to act, in the application of these principles, in conformity with the purposes and principles of the Charter of the United Nations;

Declare their determination to respect and put into practice, each of them in its relations with all other participating States, irrespective of their political, economic or social systems as well as of their size, geographical location or level of economic development, the following principles, which all are of primary significance, guiding their mutual relations:

I. Sovereign Equality, Respect for the Rights Inherent in Sovereignty

The participating States will respect each other's sovereign equality and individuality as well as all the rights inherent in and encompassed by its sovereignty, including in particular the right of every State to juridicial equality, to territorial integrity and to freedom and political independence. They will also respect each other's right freely to choose and develop its political, social, economic and cultural systems as well as its right to determine its laws and regulations.

Within the framework of international law, all the participating States have equal rights and duties. They will respect each other's right to define and conduct as it wishes its relations with other States in accordance with international law and in the spirit of the present Declaration. They consider that their frontiers can be changed, in accordance with international law, by peaceful means and by agreement. They also have the right to belong or not to belong to international organizations, to be or not to be a party to bilateral or multilateral treaties including the right to be or not to be a party to treaties of alliance; they also have the right to neutrality.

II. Refraining from the Threat or Use of Force

The participating States will refrain in their mutual relations, as well as in their international relations in general, from the threat or use of force against the territorial integrity or political independence of any State, or in any other manner inconsistent with the purposes of the United Nations and with the present Declaration. No consideration may be invoked to serve to warrant resort to the threat or use of force in contravention of this principle.

Accordingly, the participating States will refrain from any acts constituting a threat of force or direct or indirect use of force against another participating State. Likewise they will refrain from any manifestation of force for the purpose of inducing another participating State to renounce the full exercise of its sovereign rights. Likewise they will also refrain in their mutual relations from any act of reprisal by force.

No such threat or use of force will be employed as a means of settling disputes, or questions likely to give rise to disputes, between them.

III. Inviolability of Frontiers

The participating States regard as inviolable all one another's frontiers as well as the frontiers of all States in Europe and therefore they will refrain now and in the future from assaulting these frontiers.

Accordingly, they will also refrain from any demand for, or act of, seizure and usurpation of part or all of the territory of any participating State.

IV. Territorial Integrity of States

The participating States will respect the territorial integrity of each of the participating States.

Accordingly, they will refrain from any action inconsistent with the purposes and principles of the Charter of the United Nations against the territorial integrity, political independence or the unity of any participating State, and in particular from any such action constituting a threat or use of force.

The participating States will likewise refrain from making each other's territory the object of military occupation or other direct or indirect measures of force in contravention of international law, or the object of acquisition by means of such measures or the threat of them. No such occupation or acquisition will be recognized as legal.

V. Peaceful Settlement of Disputes

The participating States will settle disputes among them by peaceful means in such a manner as not to endanger international peace and security, and justice.

They will endeavour in good faith and a spirit of co-operation to reach a rapid and equitable solution on the basis of international law.

For this purpose they will use such means as negotiation, enquiry, mediation, conciliation, arbitration, judicial settlement or other peaceful means of their own choice including any settlement procedure agreed to in advance of disputes to which they are parties.

In the event of failure to reach a solution by any of the above peaceful means, the parties to a dispute will continue to seek a mutually agreed way to settle the dispute peacefully.

Participating States, parties to a dispute among them, as well as other participating States, will refrain from any action which might aggravate the situation to such a degree as to endanger the maintenance of international peace and security and thereby make a peaceful settlement of the dispute more difficult.

VI. Non-intervention in Internal Affairs

The participating States will refrain from any intervention, direct or indirect, individual or collective, in the internal or external affairs falling within the domestic jurisdiction of another participating State, regardless of their mutual relations.

They will accordingly refrain from any form of armed intervention or threat of such intervention against another participating State.

They will likewise in all circumstances refrain from any other act of military, or of political, economic or other coercion designed to subordinate to their own interest the exercise by another participating State of the rights inherent in its sovereignty and thus to secure advantages of any kind.

Accordingly, they will, inter alia, refrain from direct or indirect assistance to terrorist activities, or to subversive or other activities directed towards the violent overthrow of the regime of another participating State.

VII. Respect for Human Rights and Fundamental Freedoms, Including the Freedom of Thought, Conscience, Religion or Belief

The participating States will respect human rights and fundamental freedoms, including the freedom of thought, conscience, religion or belief, for all without distinction as to race, sex, language or religion.

They will promote and encourage the effective exercise of civil, political, economic, social, cultural and other rights and freedoms all of which derive from the inherent dignity of the human person and are essential for his free and full development.

Within this framework the participating States will recognize and respect the freedom of the individual to profess and practise, alone or in community with others, religion or belief acting in accordance with the dictates of his own conscience.

The participating States on whose territory national minorities exist will respect the right of persons belonging to such minorities to equality before the law, will afford them the full opportunity for the actual enjoyment of human rights and fundamental freedoms and will, in this manner, protect their legitimate interests in this sphere.

The participating States recognize the universal significance of human rights and fundamental freedoms, respect for which is an essential factor for the peace, justice and well-being necessary to ensure the development of friendly relations and co-operation among themselves as among all States.

They will constantly respect these rights and freedoms in their mutual relations and will endeavour jointly and separately, including in co-operation with the United Nations, to promote universal and effective respect for them.

They confirm the right of the individual to know and act upon his rights and duties in this field.

In the field of human rights and fundamental freedoms, the participating States will act in conformity with the purposes and principles of the Charter of the United Nations and with the Universal Declaration of Human Rights. They will also fulfil their obligations as set forth in the international declarations and agreements in this field, including inter alia the International Covenants on Human Rights, by which they may be bound.

VII. Equal Rights and Self-determination of Peoples

The participating States will respect the equal rights of peoples and their right to self-determination, acting at all times in conformity with the purposes and principles of the Charter of the United Nations and with the relevant norms of international law, including those relating to territorial integrity of States.

By virtue of the principle of equal rights and self-determination of peoples, all peoples always have the right, in full freedom, to determine, when and as they wish, their internal and external political status, without external interference, and to pursue as they wish their political, economic, social and cultural development.

The participating States reaffirm the universal significance of respect for and effective exercise of equal rights and self-determination of peoples for the development of friendly relations among themselves as among all States; they also recall the importance of the elimination of any form of violation of this principle.

IX. Co-operation Among States

The participating States will develop their co-operation with one another and with all States in all fields in accordance with the purposes and principles of the Charter of the United Nations. In developing their co-operation the participating States will place special emphasis on the fields as set forth within the framework of the Conference on Security and Co-operation in Europe, with each of them making its contribution in conditions of full equality.

They will endeavour, in developing their co-operation as equals, to promote mutual understanding and confidence, friendly and good-neighbourly relations among themselves, international peace, security and justice. They will equally endeavour, in developing their co-operation, to improve the well-being of peoples and contribute to the fulfilment of their aspirations through, inter alia, the benefits resulting from increased mutual knowledge and from progress and achievement in the economic, scientific, technological, social, cultural and humanitarian fields. They will take steps to promote conditions favourable to making these benefits available to all; they will take into account the interest of all in the narrowing of differences in the levels of economic development, and in particular the interest of developing countries throughout the world.

They confirm that governments, institutions, organizations and persons have a relevant and positive role to play in contributing toward the achievement of these aims of their co-operation.

They will strive, in increasing their co-operation as set forth above, to develop closer relations among themselves on an improved and more enduring basis for the benefit of peoples.

X. *Fulfilment in Good Faith of Obligations under International Law*

The participating States will fulfil in good faith their obligations under international law, both those obligations arising from the generally recognized principles and rules of international law and those obligations arising from treaties or other agreements, in conformity with international law, to which they are parties.

In exercising their sovereign rights, including the right to determine their laws and regulations, they will conform with their legal obligations under international law; they will furthermore pay due regard to and implement the provisions in the Final Act of the Conference on Security and Co-operation in Europe.

The participating States confirm that in the event of a conflict between the obligations of the members of the United Nations under the Charter of the United Nations and their obligations under any treaty or other international agreement, their obligations under the Charter will prevail, in accordance with Article 103 of the Charter of the United Nations.

All the principles set forth above are of primary significance and, accordingly, they will be equally and unreservedly applied, each of them being interpreted taking into account the others.

The participating States express their determination fully to respect and apply these principles, as set forth in the present Declaration, in all aspects, to their mutual relations and co-operation in order to ensure to each participating State the benefits resulting from the respect and application of these principles by all.

The participating States, paying due regard to the principles above and, in particular, to the first sentence of the tenth principle, "Fulfilment in good faith of obligations under international law", note that the present Declaration does not affect their rights and obligations, nor the corresponding treaties and other agreements and arrangements.

The participating States express the conviction that respect for these principles will encourage the development of normal and friendly relations and the progress of co-operation among them in all fields. They also express the conviction that respect for these principles will encourage the development of political contacts among them which in turn would contribute to better mutual understanding of their positions and views.

The participating States declare their intention to conduct their relations with all other States in the spirit of the principles contained in the present Declaration.

(b) MATTERS RELATED TO GIVING EFFECT TO CERTAIN OF THE ABOVE PRINCIPLES

(i) The participating States,

Reaffirming that they will respect and give effect to refraining from the threat or use of force and convinced of the necessity to make it an effective norm of international life.

Declare that they are resolved to respect and carry out, in their relations with one another, inter alia, the following provisions which are in conformity with the Declaration on Principles Guiding Relations between Participating States:

- To give effect and expression, by all the ways and forms which they consider appropriate, to the duty to refrain from the threat or use of force in their relations with one another.
- To refrain from any use of armed forces inconsistent with the purposes and principles of the Charter of the United Nations and the provisions of the Declaration on Principles Guiding Relations between Participating States, against another participating State, in particular from invasion of or attack on its territory.
- To refrain from any manifestation of force for the purpose of inducing another participating State to renounce the full exercise of its sovereign rights.
- To refrain from any act of economic coercion designed to subordinate to their own interest the exercise by another participating State of the rights inherent in its sovereignty and thus to secure advantages of any kind.
- To take effective measures which by their scope and by their nature constitute steps towards the ultimate achievement of general and complete disarmament under strict and effective international control.
- To promote, by all means which each of them considers appropriate, a climate of confidence and respect among peoples consonant with their duty to refrain from propaganda for wars of aggression or for any threat or use of force inconsistent with the purposes of the United Nations and with the Declaration on Principles Guiding Relations between Participating States, against another participating State.
- To make every effort to settle exclusively by peaceful means any dispute between them, the continuance of which is likely to endanger the maintenance of international peace and security in Europe, and to seek, first of all, a solution through the peaceful means set forth in Article 33 of the United Nations Charter.
- To refrain from any action which could hinder the peaceful settlement of disputes between the participating States.

(ii) The participating States,

Reaffirming their determination to settle their disputes as set forth in the Principle of Peaceful Settlement of Disputes;

Convinced that the peaceful settlement of disputes is a complement to refraining from the threat or use of force, both being essential though not exclusive factors for the maintenance and consolidation of peace and security;

Desiring to reinforce and to improve the methods at their disposal for the peaceful settlement of disputes;

(1) Are resolved to pursue the examination and elaboration of a generally acceptable method for the peaceful settlement of disputes aimed at complementing existing methods, and to continue to this end to work upon the "Draft Convention on a European System for the Peaceful Settlement of Disputes" submitted by Switzerland during the second stage of the Conference on Security and Co-operation in Europe, as well as other proposals relating to it and directed towards the elaboration of such a method.

(2) Decide that, on the invitation of Switzerland, a meeting of experts of all the participating States will be convoked in order to fulfil the mandate described in

paragraph 1 above within the framework and under the procedures of the follow-up to the Conference laid down in the chapter "Follow-up to the Conference".

(3) This meeting of experts will take place after the meeting of the representatives appointed by the Ministers of Foreign Affairs of the participating States, scheduled according to the chapter "Follow-up to the Conference" for 1977; the results of the work of this meeting of experts will be submitted to Governments.

[The remainder of the Helsinki Final Act details additional agreement in the following areas of mutual concern: "Confidence–Building Measures and Certain Aspects of Security and Disarmament;" "Co-operation in the Field of Economics, of Science and Technology and of the Environment;" "Questions Relating to Security and Co-operation in the Mediterranean;" and "Co-operation in Humanitarian and Other Fields."]

1.18 CONCLUDING DOCUMENT OF THE VIENNA MEETING 1986 OF REPRESENTATIVES OF THE PARTICIPATING STATES OF THE CONFERENCE ON SECURITY AND CO-OPERATION IN EUROPE.[a] Adopted by the Conference on Security and Co-operation in Europe at Vienna, Jan. 17, 1989. U.S. Dept. State, Bureau Pub.Aff., CSCE Vienna Follow-Up Meeting: A Framework for Europe's Future 4 (Selected Docs. No. 35, Jan. 1989), *reprinted in* 28 I.L.M. 527 (1989) [b]

* * *

PRINCIPLES

1. The participating States reaffirm their commitment to all ten principles of the Final Act's Declaration on Principles Guiding Relations between Participating States and their determination to respect them and put them into practice. The participating States reaffirm that all these Principles are of primary significance and, accordingly, will be equally and unreservedly applied, each of them being interpreted taking into account the others.

2. They stress that respect for and full application of these principles as well as strict compliance with all CSCE commitments deriving from them, are of great political importance and essential for building confidence and security as well as for the development of their friendly relations and of their cooperation in all fields.

3. In this context, they confirm that they will respect each other's right freely to choose and develop their political, social, economic and cultural systems as well as their right to determine their laws, regulations, practices and policies. In exercising these rights, they will ensure that their laws, regulations, practices and policies conform with their obligations under international law and are brought into harmony with the provisions of the Declaration on Principles and other CSCE commitments.

4. They also confirm that, by virtue of the principle of equal rights and self-determination of peoples and in conformity with the relevant provisions of the Final Act, all peoples always have the right, in full freedom, to determine, when and as they wish, their internal and external political status, without external interference, and to pursue as they wish their political, economic, social and cultural development.

5. They confirm their commitment strictly and effectively to observe the principle of the territorial integrity of States. They will refrain from any violation of this principle and thus from any action aimed by direct or indirect means, in contravention of the purposes and principles of the Charter of the United Nations, other obligations under international law or the provisions of the Final Act, at violating the territorial integrity, political independence or the unity of a State. No actions or situations in contravention of this principle will be recognized as legal by the participating States.

6. The participating States confirm their commitment to the principle of peaceful settlement of disputes, convinced that it is an essential complement to the duty of States to refrain from the threat or use of force, both being essential factors for the maintenance and consolidation of peace and security. They express their determination to pursue continuous efforts to examine and elaborate, on the basis of the relevant provisions of the Final Act and the Madrid Concluding Document, and

a. Also known as the "Vienna Concluding Document." *See also* Basic Document 1.17.

b. Eleven annexes omitted.

taking into account the reports of the meetings of experts in Montreux and Athens, a generally acceptable method for the peaceful settlement of disputes aimed at complementing existing methods. In this context they accept, in principle, the mandatory involvement of a third party when a dispute cannot be settled by other peaceful means.

7. In order to ensure the progressive implementation of this commitment, including, as a first step, the mandatory involvement of a third party in the settlement of certain categories of disputes, they decide to convene a Meeting of Experts in Valletta from 15 January to 8 February 1991 to establish a list of such categories and the related procedures and mechanisms. This list would be subject to subsequent gradual extension. The Meeting will also consider the possibility of establishing mechanisms for arriving at binding third-party decisions. The next CSCE Follow-up meeting will assess the progress achieved at the Meeting of Experts. The agenda, timetable and other organizational modalities are set out in Annex I.

8. The participating States unreservedly condemn, as criminal, all acts, methods and practices of terrorism, wherever and by whomever committed, including those which jeopardize friendly relations among States and their security, and agree that terrorism cannot be justified under any circumstances.

9. They express their determination to work for the eradication of terrorism both bilaterally and through multilateral co-operation, particularly in such international fora as the United Nations, the International Civil Aviation Organization and the International Maritime Organization and in accordance with the relevant provisions of the Final Act and the Madrid Concluding Document.

10. Convinced of the need to combine measures at a national level with reinforced international cooperation, the participating States express their intention

10a • to pursue a policy of firmness in response to terrorist demands;

10b • to reinforce and develop bilateral and multilateral co-operation among themselves in order to prevent and combat terrorism as well as to increase efficiency in existing co-operation at the bilateral level or in the framework of groups of States, including, as appropriate, through the exchange of information;

10c • to prevent on their territories illegal activities of persons, groups or organizations that instigate, organize or engage in the perpetration of acts of terrorism or subversive or other activities directed towards the violent overthrow of the regime of another participating State;

10d • to take effective measures for the prevention and suppression of acts of terrorism directed at diplomatic or consular representatives and against terrorism involving violations of the Vienna Conventions on Diplomatic and Consular Relations, in particular their provisions relating to diplomatic and consular privileges and immunities;

10e • to ensure the extradition or prosecution of persons implicated in terrorist acts and to cooperate closely in cases of conflict of jurisdiction where several States are concerned, acting in both respects in accordance with the relevant international agreements;

10f • to consider becoming parties, if they have not yet done so, to the relevant international conventions relating to the suppression of acts of terrorism;

10g • to continue to work in the appropriate international bodies in order to improve and extend measures against terrorism and to ensure that the relevant agreements are accepted and acted upon by as many States as possible.

11. They confirm that they will respect human rights and fundamental freedoms, including the freedom of thought, conscience, religion or belief, for all without

distinction as to race, sex, language or religion. They also confirm the universal significance of human rights and fundamental freedoms, respect for which is an essential factor for the peace, justice and security necessary to ensure the development of friendly relations and co-operation among themselves, as among all States.

12. They express their determination to guarantee the effective exercise of human rights and fundamental freedoms, all of which derive from the inherent dignity of the human person and are essential for his free and full development. They recognize that civil, political, economic, social, cultural and other rights and freedoms are all of paramount importance and must be fully realized by all appropriate means.

13. In this context they will

13a • develop their laws, regulations and policies in the field of civil, political, economic, social, cultural and other human rights and fundamental freedoms and put them into practice in order to guarantee the effective exercise of these rights and freedoms;

13b • consider acceding to the International Covenant on Civil and Political Rights, the International Covenant on Economic, Social and Cultural Rights, the Optional Protocol to the Covenant on Civil and Political Rights and other relevant international instruments, if they have not yet done so;

13c • publish and disseminate the text of the Final Act, of the Madrid Concluding Document, and of the present Document as well as those of any relevant international instruments in the field of human rights, in order to ensure the availability of these documents in their entirety, to make them known as widely as possible and to render them accessible to all individuals in their countries, in particular through public library systems;

13d • ensure effectively the right of the individual to know and act upon his rights and duties in this field, and to that end publish and make accessible all laws, regulations and procedures relating to human rights and fundamental freedoms;

13e • respect the right of their citizens to contribute actively, individually or in association with others, to the promotion and protection of human rights and fundamental freedoms;

13f • encourage in schools and other educational institutions consideration of the promotion and protection of human rights and fundamental freedoms;

13g • ensure human rights and fundamental freedoms to everyone within their territory and subject to their jurisdiction, without distinction of any kind such as race, colour, sex, language, religion, political or other opinion, national or social origin, property, birth or other status;

13h • ensure that no individual exercising, expressing the intention to exercise or seeking to exercise these rights and freedoms, or any member of his family, will as a consequence be discriminated against in any manner;

13i • ensure that effective remedies as well as full information about them are available to those who claim that their human rights and fundamental freedoms have been violated; they will, *inter alia,* effectively apply the following remedies:

• the right of the individual to appeal to executive, legislative, judicial or administrative organs;

• the right to a fair and public hearing within a reasonable time before an independent and impartial tribunal, including the right to present legal arguments and to be represented by legal counsel of one's choice;

• the right to be promptly and officially informed of the decision taken on any appeal, including the legal grounds on which this decision was based. This information will be provided as a rule in writing and, in any event, in a way that will enable the individual to make effective use of further available remedies.

14. The participating States recognize that the promotion of economic, social, cultural rights as well as of civil and political rights is of paramount importance for human dignity and for the attainment of the legitimate aspirations of every individual. They will therefore continue their efforts with a view to achieving progressively the full realization of economic, social and cultural rights by all appropriate means, including in particular by the adoption of legislative measures.

In this context they will pay special attention to problems in the areas of employment, housing, social security, health, education and culture. They will promote constant progress in the realization of all rights and freedoms within their countries, as well as in the development of their relations among themselves and with other States, so that everyone will actually enjoy to the full his economic, social and cultural rights as well as his civil and political rights.

15. The participating States confirm their determination to ensure equal rights of men and women. Accordingly, they will take all measures necessary, including legislative measures, to promote equally effective participation of men and women in political, economic, social and cultural life. They will consider the possibility of acceding, if they have not yet done so, to the Convention on the Elimination of All Forms of Discrimination Against Women.

16. In order to ensure the freedom of the individual to profess and practice religion or belief the participating States will, *inter alia,*

16a • take effective measures to prevent and eliminate discrimination against individuals or communities, on the grounds of religion or belief in the recognition, exercise and enjoyment of human rights and fundamental freedoms in all fields of civil, political, economic, social and cultural life, and ensure the effective equality between believers and non-believers;

16b • foster a climate of mutual tolerance and respect between believers of different communities as well as between believers and non-believers;

16c • grant upon their request to communities of believers, practising or prepared to practise their faith within the constitutional framework of their States, recognition of the status provided for them in their respective countries;

16d • respect the right of religious communities to

• establish and maintain freely accessible places of worship or assembly,

• organize themselves according to their own hierarchical and institutional structure,

• select, appoint and replace their personnel in accordance with their respective requirements and standards as well as with any freely accepted arrangement between them and their State,

• solicit and receive voluntary financial and other contributions;

16e • engage in consultations with religious faiths, institutions and organizations in order to achieve a better understanding of the requirements of religious freedom;

16f • respect the right of everyone to give and receive religious education in the language of his choice, individually or in association with others;

16g • in this context respect, *inter alia,* the liberty of parents to ensure the religious and moral education of their children in conformity with their own convictions;

16h • allow the training of religious personnel in appropriate institutions;

16i • respect the right of individual believers and communities of believers to acquire, possess, and use sacred books, religious publications in the language of their choice and other articles and materials related to the practice of religion or belief;

16j • allow religious faiths, institutions and organizations to produce and import and disseminate religious publications and materials;

16k • favorably consider the interest of religious communities in participating in public dialogue, inter alia, through mass media.

17. The participating States recognize that the exercise of the above-mentioned rights relating to the freedom of religion or belief may be subject only to such limitations as are provided by law and consistent with their obligations under international law and with their international commitments. They will ensure in their laws and regulations and in their application the full and effective implementation of the freedom of thought, conscience, religion or belief.

18. The participating States will exert sustained efforts to implement the provisions of the Final Act and of the Madrid Concluding Document pertaining to national minorities. They will take all the necessary legislative, administrative, judicial and other measures and apply the relevant international instruments by which they may be bound, to ensure the protection of human rights and fundamental freedoms of persons belonging to national minorities within their territory. They will refrain from any discrimination against such persons and contribute to the realization of their legitimate interests and aspirations in the field of human rights and fundamental freedoms.

19. They will protect and create conditions for the promotion of the ethnic, cultural, linguistic and religious identity of national minorities on their territory. They will respect the free exercise of rights by persons belonging to such minorities and ensure their full equality with others.

20. The participating States will respect fully, the right of everyone

• to freedom of movement and residence within the borders of each State, and

• to leave any country, including his own, and to return to his country.

21. The participating States will ensure that the exercise of the above-mentioned rights shall not be subject to any restrictions except to those which are provided by law and consistent with their obligations under international law, in particular the International Covenant on Civil and Political Rights and their international commitments, in particular the Universal Declaration of Human Rights. These restrictions have the character of exceptions. The participating States will ensure that these restrictions are not abused and are not applied in an arbitrary manner, but in such a way that the effective exercise of these rights is ensured.

22. In this context they will allow all refugees who so desire to return in safety to their homes.

23. The participating States will

23a • ensure that no one shall be subjected to arbitrary arrest, detention or exile;

23b • ensure that all individuals in detention or incarceration will be treated with humanity and with respect for the inherent dignity of the human person;

23c • observe the UN Standard Minimum Rules for the Treatment of Prisoners as well as the UN Code of Conduct for Law Enforcement Officials;

23d • prohibit torture and other cruel, inhuman or degrading treatment or punishment and take effective legislative, administrative, judicial and other measures to prevent and punish such practices;

23e • consider acceding to the Convention against Torture and other Cruel, Inhuman or Degrading Treatment or Punishment, if they have not yet done so;

23f • protect individuals from any psychiatric or other medical practices that violate human rights and fundamental freedoms and take effective measures to prevent and punish such practices.

24. With regard to the question of capital punishment, the participating States note that capital punishment has been abolished in a number of them. In participating States where capital punishment has not been abolished, sentence of death may be imposed only for the most serious crimes in accordance with the law in force at the time of the commission of the crime and not contrary to their international commitments. This question will be kept under consideration. In this context, the participating States will cooperate within relevant international organizations.

25. The participating States will, with the aim of developing mutual understanding and confidence, promoting friendly and good neighbourly relations, strengthening international peace, security and justice and of improving the implementation of their CSCE commitments, further develop co-operation and promote dialogue between them in all fields and at all levels on the basis of full equality. They agree that full respect for and application of the Principles and the fulfillment of the other CSCE provisions will improve their relations and advance the development of their co-operation. They will refrain from any action inconsistent with the provisions of the Final Act and other CSCE documents and recognize that any such action would impair relations between them and hinder the development of co-operation among them.

26. They confirm that governments, institutions, organizations and persons have a relevant and positive role to play in contributing to the achievement of the aims of their co-operation and to the full realization of the Final Act. To that end they will respect the right of persons to observe and promote the implementation of CSCE provisions and to associate with others for this purpose. They will facilitate direct contacts and communication among these persons, organizations and institutions within and between participating States and remove, where they exist, legal and administrative impediments inconsistent with the CSCE provisions. They will also take effective measures to facilitate access to information on the implementation of CSCE provisions and the free expression of views on these matters.

* * *

[The remainder of the Vienna Concluding Document details additional agreement in the following areas of mutual concern: "Confidence– and Security–Building Measures and Certain Aspects of Security and Disarmament in Europe"; "Co-operation in the Field of Economics, of Science and Technology and of the Environment"; "Questions Relating to Security and Co-operation in the Mediterranean"; and "Co-operation in Humanitarian and Other Fields." In addition, it addresses the topic of the "Human Dimension of the CSCE," as follows:]

HUMAN DIMENSION OF THE CSCE

The participating States,

Recalling the undertakings entered into in the Final Act and in other CSCE documents concerning respect for all human rights and fundamental freedoms, human contacts and other issues of a related humanitarian character,

Recognizing the need to improve the implementation of their CSCE commitments and their co-operation in these areas which are hereafter referred to as the human dimension of the CSCE,

Have, on the basis of the principles and provisions of the Final Act and of other relevant CSCE documents, decided:

1. to exchange information and respond to requests for information and to representations made to them by other participating States on questions relating to the human dimension of the CSCE. Such communications may be forwarded through diplomatic channels or be addressed to any agency designated for these purposes;

2. to hold bilateral meetings with other participating States that so request, in order to examine questions relating to the human dimension of the CSCE, including situations and specific cases with a view to resolving them. The date and place of such meetings will be arranged by mutual agreement through diplomatic channels;

3. that any participating State which deems it necessary may bring situations and cases in the human dimensions of the CSCE, including those which have been raised at the bilateral meetings described in paragraph 2, to the attention of other participating States though diplomatic channels;

4. that any participating State which deems it necessary may provide information on the exchange of information and the responses to its requests for information and to representations (paragraph 1) and on the results of the bilateral meetings (paragraph 2), including information concerning situations and specific cases, at the meetings of the Conference of the Human Dimension as well as at the main CSCE Follow-up Meetings.

The participating States decide further to convene a Conference on the Human Dimension of the CSCE in order to achieve further progress concerning respect for all human rights and fundamental freedoms, human contacts and other issues of a related humanitarian character. The Conference will hold three meetings before the next CSCE Follow-up Meeting.

The Conference will:

- review developments in the human dimension of the CSCE including the implementation of the relevant CSCE commitments;
- evaluate the functioning of the procedure described in paragraphs 1 to 4 and discuss the information provided according to paragraph 4;
- consider practical proposals for new measures aimed at improving the implementation of the commitments relating to the human dimension of the CSCE and enhancing the effectiveness of the procedures described in paragraphs 1 to 4.

On the basis of these proposals, the Conference will consider adopting new measures.

* * *

2. WAR/PEACE

2.1 DECLARATION RENOUNCING THE USE, IN TIME OF WAR, OF EXPLOSIVE PROJECTILES UNDER 400 GRAMMES WEIGHT. Adopted by the International Military Commission at St. Petersburg, Dec. 11, 1868. *Reproduced in* 1 A.J.I.L. Supp. 95 (1907) [a]

Upon the invitation of the Imperial Cabinet of Russia, an international military commission having been assembled at St. Petersburg in order to consider the desirability of forbidding the use of certain projectiles in time of war among civilized nations, and this commission having fixed by a common accord the technical limits within which the necessities of war ought to yield to the demands of humanity, the undersigned have been authorized by the orders of their Governments to declare as follows:

Considering that the progress of civilization should have the effect of alleviating, as much as possible the calamities of war:

That the only legitimate object which states should endeavor to accomplish during war is to weaken the military force of the enemy;

That for this purpose, it is sufficient to disable the greatest possible number of men;

That this object would be exceeded by the employment of arms which uselessly aggravate the sufferings of disabled men, or render their death inevitable;

That the employment of such arms would, therefore, be contrary to the laws of humanity;

The contracting parties engage, mutually, to renounce, in case of war among themselves, the employment, by their military or naval forces, of any projectile of less weight than four hundred grammes, which is explosive, or is charged with fulminating or inflammable substances.

They agree to invite all the states which have not taken part in the deliberations of the International Military Commission, assembled at St. Petersburg, by sending delegates thereto, to accede to the present engagement.

This engagement is obligatory only upon the contracting or acceding parties thereto, in case of war between two or more of themselves; it is not applicable with regard to non-contracting powers, or powers that shall not have acceded to it.

It will also cease to be obligatory from the moment when, in a war between contracting or acceding parties, a non-contracting party, or a non-acceding party, shall join one of the belligerents.

The contracting or acceding parties reserve to themselves the right to come to an understanding, hereafter, whenever a precise proposition shall be drawn up, in view of future improvements which may be effected in the armament of troops, in order to maintain the principles which they have established, and to reconcile the necessities of war with the laws of humanity.

a. Also known as "the St. Petersburg Declaration."

2.2 CONVENTION (NO. IV) RESPECTING THE LAWS AND CUSTOMS OF WAR ON LAND, WITH ANNEX OF REGULATIONS.[a] Done at The Hague, Oct. 18, 1907. Entered into force, Jan. 26, 1910; for the United States, Jan. 26, 1910. 36 Stat. 2277, T.S. No. 539, 1 Bevans 631

His Majesty the German Emperor, King of Prussia; the President of the United States of America; the President of the Argentine Republic; His Majesty the Emperor of Austria, King of Bohemia, &c., and Apostolic King of Hungary; His Majesty the King of the Belgians; the President of the Republic of Bolivia; the President of the Republic of the United States of Brazil; His Royal Highness the Prince of Bulgaria; the President of the Republic of Chile; the President of the Republic of Colombia; the Provisional Governor of the Republic of Cuba; His Majesty the King of Denmark; the President of the Dominican Republic; the President of the Republic of Ecuador; the President of the French Republic; His Majesty the King of the United Kingdom of Great Britain and Ireland and of the British Dominions beyond the Seas, Emperor of India; His Majesty the King of the Hellenes; the President of the Republic of Haiti; His Majesty the King of Italy; His Majesty the Emperor of Japan; His Royal Highness the Grand Duke of Luxemburg, Duke of Nassau; the President of the United States of Mexico; His Royal Highness the Prince of Montenegro; His Majesty the King of Norway; the President of the Republic of Panama; the President of the Republic of Paraguay; Her Majesty the Queen of the Netherlands; the President of the Republic of Peru; His Imperial Majesty the Shah of Persia; His Majesty the King of Portugal and of the Algarves, &c., His Majesty the King of Roumania; His Majesty the Emperor of All the Russias; the President of the Republic of Salvador; His Majesty the King of Servia; His Majesty the King of Siam; His Majesty the King of Sweden; the Swiss Federal Council; His Majesty the Emperor of the Ottomans; the President of the Oriental Republic of Uruguay; the President of the United States of Venezuela:

Seeing that, while seeking means to preserve peace and prevent armed conflicts between nations, it is likewise necessary to bear in mind the case where the appeal to arms has been brought about by events which their care was unable to avert;

Animated by the desire to serve, even in this extreme case, the interests of humanity and the ever progressive needs of civilization;

Thinking it important, with this object, to revise the general laws and customs of war, either with a view to defining them with greater precision or to confining them within such limits as would mitigate their severity as far as possible;

Have deemed it necessary to complete and explain in certain particulars the work of the First Peace Conference, which, following on the Brussels Conference of 1874, and inspired by the ideas dictated by a wise and generous forethought, adopted provisions intended to define and govern the usages of war on land.

Accordingly to the views of the High Contracting Parties, these provisions, the wording of which has been inspired by the desire to diminish the evils of war, as far as military requirements permit, are intended to serve as a general rule of conduct for the belligerents in their mutual relations and in their relations with the inhabitants.

It has not, however, been found possible at present to concert Regulations covering all the circumstances which arise in practice;

a. Also known as "Hague IV" and "the Hague Regulations."

On the other hand, the High Contracting Parties clearly do not intend that unforeseen cases should, in the absence of a written undertaking, be left to the arbitrary judgment of military commanders.

Until a more complete code of the laws of war has been issued, the High Contracting Parties deem it expedient to declare that, in cases not included in the Regulations adopted by them, the inhabitants and the belligerents remain under the protection and the rule of the principles of the law of nations, as they result from the usages established among civilized peoples, from the laws of humanity, and the dictates of the public conscience.

They declare that it is in this sense especially that Articles 1 and 2 of the Regulations adopted must be understood.

The High Contracting Parties, wishing to conclude a fresh Convention to this effect, have appointed the following as their Plenipotentiaries:—

[Here follow the names of Plenipotentiaries.]

Who, after having deposited their full powers, found in good and due form, have agreed upon the following:—

Article 1. The Contracting Powers shall issue instructions to their armed land forces which shall be in conformity with the Regulations respecting the Laws and Customs of War on Land, annexed to the present Convention.

Article 2. The provisions contained in the Regulations referred to in Article 1, as well as in the present Convention, do not apply except between Contracting Powers, and then only if all the belligerents are parties to the Convention.

Article 3. A belligerent party which violates the provisions of the said Regulations shall, if the case demands, be liable to pay compensation. It shall be responsible for all acts committed by persons forming part of its armed forces.

ARTICLE 4

The present Convention, duly ratified, shall as between the Contracting Powers, be substituted for the Convention of the 29th July, 1899, respecting the Laws and Customs of War on Land.

The Convention of 1899 remains in force as between the Powers which signed it, and which do not also ratify the present Convention.

ARTICLE 5

The present Convention shall be ratified as soon as possible.

The ratifications shall be deposited at The Hague.

The first deposit of ratifications shall be recorded in a *procès-verbal* signed by the Representatives of the Powers which take part therein and by the Netherland Minister for Foreign Affairs.

The subsequent deposits of ratifications shall be made by means of a written notification, addressed to the Netherland Government and accompanied by the instrument of ratification.

A duly certified copy of the *procès-verbal* relative to the first deposit of ratifications, of the notifications mentioned in the preceding paragraph, as well as of the instruments of ratification, shall be immediately sent by the Netherland Government, through the diplomatic channel, to the Powers invited to the Second Peace Conference, as well as to the other Powers which have adhered to the Convention. In the cases contemplated in the preceding paragraph the said Government shall at the same time inform them of the date on which it received the notification.

ARTICLE 6

Non-Signatory Powers may adhere to the present Convention.

The Power which desires to adhere notifies in writing its intention to the Netherland Government, forwarding to it the act of adhesion, which shall be deposited in the archives of the said Government.

This Government shall at once transmit to all the other Powers a duly certified copy of the notification as well as of the act of adhesion, mentioning the date on which it received the notification.

ARTICLE 7

The present Convention shall come into force, in the case of the Powers which were a party to the first deposit of ratifications, sixty days after the date of the *procès-verbal* of this deposit, and, in the case of the Powers which ratify subsequently or which adhere, sixty days after the notification of their ratification or of their adhesion has been received by the Netherland Government.

ARTICLE 8

In the event of one of the Contracting Powers wishing to denounce the present Convention, the denunciation shall be notified in writing to the Netherland Government, which shall at once communicate a duly certified copy of the notification to all the other Powers, informing them of the date on which it was received.

The denunciation shall only have effect in regard to the notifying Power, and one year after the notification has reached the Netherland Government.

ARTICLE 9

A register kept by the Netherland Ministry for Foreign Affairs shall give the date of the deposit of ratifications made in virtue of Article 5, paragraphs 3 and 4, as well as the date on which the notifications of adhesion (Article 6, paragraph 2) or of denunciation (Article 8, paragraph 1) were received.

Each Contracting Power is entitled to have access to this register and to be supplied with duly certified extracts.

In faith whereof the Plenipotentiaries have appended their signatories to the present Convention.

Done at The Hague, the 18th October, 1907, in a single copy, which shall remain deposited in the archives of the Netherland Government, and duly certified copies of which shall be sent, through the diplomatic channel, to the Powers which have been invited to the Second Peace Conference.

[Here follow signatures.]

* * *

ANNEX TO THE CONVENTION

REGULATIONS RESPECTING THE LAWS AND CUSTOMS OF WAR ON LAND

SECTION I. ON BELLIGERENTS

CHAPTER I. *The Qualifications of Belligerents*

Article 1. The laws, rights, and duties of war apply not only to armies, but also to militia and volunteer corps fulfilling the following conditions:—

(1) To be commanded by a person responsible for his subordinates;

(2) To have a fixed distinctive emblem recognizable at a distance;

(3) To carry arms openly; and

(4) To conduct their operations in accordance with the laws and customs of war. In countries where militia or volunteer corps constitute the army, or form part of it, they are included under the denomination "army."

* * *

CHAPTER II. *Prisoners of War* [b]

Article 4. Prisoners of war are in the power of the hostile Government, but not of the individuals or corps who capture them.

They must be humanely treated.

All their personal belongings, except arms, horses, and military papers, remain their property.

Article 5. Prisoners of war may be interned in a town, fortress, camp, or other place, and bound not to go beyond certain fixed limits; but they cannot be confined except as an indispensable measure of safety and only while the circumstances which necessitate the measure continue to exist.

Article 6. The State may utilize the labour of prisoners of war according to their rank and aptitude, officers excepted. The tasks shall not be excessive and shall have no connection with the operations of the war.

Prisoners may be authorized to work for the public service, for private persons, or on their own account.

Work done for the State is paid at the rates in force for work of a similar kind done by soldiers of the national army, or, if there are none in force, at a rate according to the work executed.

When the work is for other branches of the public service or for private persons the conditions are settled in agreement with the military authorities.

The wages of the prisoners shall go towards improving their position, and the balance shall be paid them on their release, after deducting the cost of their maintenance.

Article 7. The Government into whose hands prisoners of war have fallen is charged with their maintenance.

In the absence of a special agreement between the belligerents, prisoners of war shall be treated as regards board, lodging, and clothing on the same footing as the troops of the Government who captured them.

Article 8. Prisoners of war shall be subject to the laws, regulations, and orders in force in the army of the State in whose power they are. Any act of insubordination justifies the adoption towards them of such measures of severity as may be considered necessary.

Escaped prisoners who are retaken before being able to rejoin their own army or before leaving the territory occupied by the army which captured them are liable to disciplinary punishment.

Prisoners who, after succeeding in escaping, are again taken prisoners, are not liable to any punishment on account of the previous flight.

* * *

Article 17. Officers taken prisoners shall receive the same rate of pay as officers of corresponding rank in the country where they are detained, the amount to be ultimately refunded by their own Government.

Article 18. Prisoners of war shall enjoy complete liberty in the exercise of their religion, including attendance at the services of whatever Church they may belong to,

b. This Chapter is complemented by the 1949 Convention Relative to the Treatment of Prisoners of War (Basic Document 2.12, *infra*), as between parties to both conventions.

on the sole condition that they comply with the measures of order and police issued by the military authorities.

Article 19. The wills of prisoners of war are received or drawn up in the same way as for soldiers of the national army.

The same rules shall be observed regarding death certificates as well as for the burial of prisoners of war, due regard being paid to their grade and rank.

* * *

SECTION II. HOSTILITIES [c]

CHAPTER I. *Means of Injuring the Enemy, Sieges, and Bombardments.*

Article 22. The right of belligerents to adopt means of injuring the enemy is not unlimited.

Article 23. In addition to the prohibitions provided by special Conventions, it is especially forbidden:

(a) To employ poison or poisoned weapons;

(b) To kill or wound treacherously individuals belonging to the hostile nation or army;

(c) To kill or wound an enemy who, having laid down his arms, or having no longer means of defence, has surrendered at discretion;

(d) To declare that no quarter will be given;

(e) To employ arms, projectiles, or material calculated to cause unnecessary suffering;

(f) To make improper use of a flag of truce, of the national flag, or of the military insignia and uniform of the enemy, as well as the distinctive badges of the Geneva Convention;

(g) To destroy or seize the enemy's property, unless such destruction or seizure be imperatively demanded by the necessities of war;

(h) To declare abolished, suspended, or inadmissible in a court of law the rights and actions of the nationals of the hostile party.

A belligerent is likewise forbidden to compel the nationals of the hostile party to take part in the operations of war directed against their own country, even if they were in the belligerent's service before the commencement of the war.

* * *

Article 25. The attack or bombardment, by whatever means, of towns, villages, dwellings, or buildings which are undefended is prohibited.

* * *

Article 27. In sieges and bombardments all necessary steps must be taken to spare, as far as possible, buildings dedicated to religion, art, science, or charitable purposes, historic monuments, hospitals, and places where the sick and wounded are collected, provided they are not being used at the time for military purposes.

It is the duty of the besieged to indicate the presence of such buildings or places by distinctive and visible signs, which shall be notified to the enemy beforehand.

Article 28. The pillage of a town or place, even when taken by assault, is prohibited.

c. Sections II and III of these Regulations are supplemented by the 1949 Convention Relative to the Protection of Civilian Persons in Time of War (Basic Document 2.13, *infra*), as between parties to both conventions.

CHAPTER II. *Spies*

Article 29. A person can only be considered a spy when, acting clandestinely or on false pretences, he obtains or endeavours to obtain information in the zone of operations of a belligerent, with the intention of communicating it to the hostile party.

* * *

Article 30. A spy taken in the act shall not be punished without previous trial.

* * *

SECTION III. MILITARY AUTHORITY OVER THE TERRITORY OF THE HOSTILE STATE

Article 42. Territory is considered occupied when it is actually placed under the authority of the hostile army.

The occupation extends only to the territory where such authority has been established and can be exercised.

Article 43. The authority of the legitimate power having in fact passed into the hands of the occupant, the latter shall take all the measures in his power to restore, and ensure, as far as possible, public order and safety, while respecting, unless absolutely prevented, the laws in force in the country.

* * *

Article 45. It is forbidden to compel the inhabitants of occupied territory to swear allegiance to the hostile Power.

Article 46. Family honour and rights, the lives of persons, and private property, as well as religious convictions and practice, must be respected.

Private property cannot be confiscated.

Article 47. Pillage is formally forbidden.

* * *

Article 50. No general penalty, pecuniary or otherwise, shall be inflicted upon the population on account of the acts of individuals for which they cannot be regarded as jointly and severally responsible.

Article 51. No contribution shall be collected except under a written order, and on the responsibility of a Commander-in-chief.

The collection of the said contribution shall only be effected as far as possible in accordance with the rules of assessment and incidence of the taxes in force.

For every contribution a receipt shall be given to the contributors.

Article 52. Requisitions in kind and services shall not be demanded from municipalities or inhabitants except for the needs of the army of occupation. They shall be in proportion to the resources of the country, and of such a nature as not to involve the inhabitants in the obligation of taking part in military operations against their own country.

Such requisitions and services shall only be demanded on the authority of the commander in the locality occupied.

Contributions in kind shall as far as possible be paid for in cash; if not, a receipt shall be given and the payment of the amount due shall be made as soon as possible.

Article 53. An army of occupation can only take possession of cash, funds, and realizable securities which are strictly the property of the State, depôts of arms, means of transport, stores and supplies, and, generally, all movable property belonging to the State which may be used for military operations.

All appliances, whether on land, at sea, or in the air, adapted for the transmission of news, or for the transport of persons or things, exclusive of cases governed by naval law, depôts of arms, and, generally, all kinds of ammunition of war, may be seized, even if they belong to private individuals, but must be restored and compensation fixed when peace is made.

* * *

Article 56. The property of municipalities, that of institutions dedicated to religion, charity and education, the arts and sciences, even when State property, shall be treated as private property.

All seizure of, destruction or wilful damage done to institutions of this character, historic monuments, works of art and science, is forbidden, and should be made the subject of legal proceedings.

2.3 PROTOCOL FOR THE PROHIBITION OF THE USE IN WAR OF ASPHYXIATING, POISONOUS OR OTHER GASES, AND OF BACTERIOLOGICAL METHODS OF WARFARE.[a] Done at Geneva, June 17, 1925. Entered into force, Feb. 8, 1928; for the United States, April 10, 1975. 26 U.S.T. 571, T.I.A.S. No. 8061, 94 L.N.T.S. 65, *reprinted in* 14 I.L.M. 49 (1975) [b]

THE UNDERSIGNED PLENIPOTENTIARIES, in the name of their respective Governments:

WHEREAS the use in war of asphyxiating, poisonous or other gases, and of all analogous liquids, materials or devices, has been justly condemned by the general opinion of the civilised world; and

WHEREAS the prohibition of such use has been declared in Treaties to which the majority of Powers of the world are Parties; and

TO THE END that this prohibition shall be universally accepted as a part of International Law, binding alike the conscience and the practice of nations;

DECLARE:

> That the High Contracting Parties, so far as they are not already Parties to Treaties prohibiting such use, accept this prohibition, agree to extend this prohibition to the use of bacteriological methods of warfare and agree to be bound as between themselves according to the terms of this declaration.

The High Contracting Parties will exert every effort to induce other States to accede to the present Protocol. Such accession will be notified to the Government of the French Republic, and by the latter to all signatory and acceding Powers, and will take effect on the date of the notification by the Government of the French Republic.

* * *

a. Also known as "the 1925 Geneva Protocol."

b. *See also* Basic Documents 2.26 and 2.40, *infra*.

2.4 TREATY PROVIDING FOR THE RENUNCIATION OF WAR AS AN INSTRUMENT OF NATIONAL POLICY.[a] Done at Paris, Aug. 27, 1928. Entered into force, July 24, 1929; for the United States, July 24, 1929. 46 Stat. 2343, T.S. No. 796, 2 Bevans 732, L.N.T.S. 57

[The High Contracting Parties:]

Deeply sensible of their solemn duty to promote the welfare of mankind;

Persuaded that the time has come when a frank renunciation of war as an instrument of national policy should be made to the end that the peaceful and friendly relations now existing between their peoples may be perpetuated;

Convinced that all changes in their relations with one another should be sought only by pacific means and be the result of a peaceful and orderly process, and that any signatory Power which shall hereafter seek to promote its national interests by resort to war should be denied the benefits furnished by this Treaty;

Hopeful that, encouraged by their example, all the other nations of the world will join in this humane endeavor and by adhering to the present Treaty as soon as it comes into force bring their peoples within the scope of its beneficent provisions, thus uniting the civilized nations of the world in a common renunciation of war as an instrument of their national policy;

Have decided to conclude a Treaty and for that purpose have appointed as their respective Plenipotentiaries:

[Here follow the names of Plenipotentiaries.]

who, having communicated to one another their full powers found in good and due form have agreed upon the following articles:

Article I. The High Contracting Parties solemnly declare in the names of their respective peoples that they condemn recourse to war for the solution of international controversies, and renounce it as an instrument of national policy in their relations with one another.

Article II. The High Contracting Parties agree that the settlement or solution of all disputes or conflicts of whatever nature or of whatever origin they may be, which may arise among them, shall never be sought except by pacific means.

Article III. The present Treaty shall be ratified by the High Contracting Parties named in the Preamble in accordance with their respective constitutional requirements, and shall take effect as between them as soon as all their several instruments of ratification shall have been deposited at Washington.

This Treaty shall, when it has come into effect as prescribed in the preceding paragraph, remain open as long as may be necessary for adherence by all the other Powers of the world. Every instrument evidencing the adherence of a Power shall be deposited at Washington and the Treaty shall immediately upon such deposit become effective as between the Power thus adhering and the other Powers parties hereto.

* * *

a. Also known as "the Pact of Paris" or "Kellogg–Briand Pact."

2.5 AGREEMENT FOR THE PROSECUTION AND PUNISHMENT OF THE MAJOR WAR CRIMINALS OF THE EUROPEAN AXIS POWERS AND CHARTER OF THE INTERNATIONAL MILITARY TRIBUNAL.[a] Done at London, Aug. 8, 1945. Entered into force, Aug. 8, 1945; for the United States, Sept. 10, 1945. 59 Stat. 1544, 82 U.N.T.S. 279[b]

CHARTER OF THE INTERNATIONAL MILITARY TRIBUNAL

* * *

II. JURISDICTION AND GENERAL PRINCIPLES

Article 6.

The Tribunal established by the Agreement referred to in Article 1 hereof for the trial and punishment of the major war criminals of the European Axis countries shall have the power to try and punish persons who, acting in the interests of the European Axis countries, whether as individuals or as members of organizations, committed any of the following crimes.

The following acts, or any of them, are crimes coming within the jurisdiction of the Tribunal for which there shall be individual responsibility:

(a) CRIMES AGAINST PEACE: namely, planning, preparation, initiation or waging of a war of aggression, or a war in violation of international treaties, agreements or assurances, or participation in a common plan or conspiracy for the accomplishment of any of the foregoing;

(b) WAR CRIMES: namely, violations of the laws or customs of war. Such violations shall include, but not be limited to, murder, ill-treatment or deportation to slave labor or for any other purpose of civilian population of or in occupied territory, murder or ill-treatment of prisoners of war or persons on the seas, killing of hostages, plunder of public or private property, wanton destruction of cities, towns or villages, or devastation not justified by military necessity;

(c) CRIMES AGAINST HUMANITY: namely, murder, extermination, enslavement, deportation, and other inhumane acts committed against any civilian population, before or during the war; or persecutions on political, racial or religious grounds in execution of or in connection with any crime within the jurisdiction of the Tribunal, whether or not in violation of the domestic law of the country where perpetrated.

Leaders, organizers, instigators and accomplices participating in the formulation or execution of a common plan or conspiracy to commit any of the foregoing crimes are responsible for all acts performed by any persons in execution of such plan.

Article 8.

The fact that the Defendant acted pursuant to order of his Government or of a superior shall not free him from responsibility, but may be considered in mitigation of punishment if the Tribunal determines that justice so requires.

* * *

a. Also known as "the London Agreement" and "the Nuremberg Charter."

b. *See also* Basic Documents 2.6, 2.15, and 3.39, *infra.*

IV. Fair Trial for Defendants

Article 16.

In order to ensure fair trial for the Defendants, the following procedure shall be followed:

(a) The Indictment shall include full particulars specifying in detail the charges against the Defendants. A copy of the Indictment and of all the documents lodged with the Indictment, translated into a language which he understands, shall be furnished to the Defendant at a reasonable time before the Trial.

(b) During any preliminary examination or trial of a Defendant he shall have the right to give any explanation relevant to the charges made against him.

(c) A preliminary examination of a Defendant and his Trial shall be conducted in, or translated into, a language which the Defendant understands.

(d) A defendant shall have the right to conduct his own defense before the Tribunal or to have the assistance of Counsel.

(e) A defendant shall have the right through himself or through his Counsel to present evidence at the Trial in support of his defense, and to cross-examine any witness called by the Prosecution.

* * *

2.6 AFFIRMATION OF THE PRINCIPLES OF INTERNATIONAL LAW RECOGNIZED BY THE CHARTER OF NUREMBERG TRIBUNAL.[a] Adopted by the U.N. General Assembly, Dec. 11, 1946. U.N.G.A. Res. 95(I), U.N. Doc. A/236 (1946), at 1144

The General Assembly,

Recognizes the obligation laid upon it by Article 13, paragraph 1, sub-paragraph a, of the Charter, to initiate studies and make recommendations for the purpose of encouraging the progressive development of international law and its codification;

Takes note of the Agreement for the establishment of an International Military Tribunal for the prosecution and punishment of the major war criminals of the European Axis signed in London on 8 August 1945, and of the Charter annexed thereto, and of the fact that similar principles have been adopted in the Charter of the International Military Tribunal for the trial of the major war criminals in the Far East, proclaimed at Tokyo on 19 January 1946;

Therefore,

Affirms the principles of international law recognized by the Charter of the Nürnberg Tribunal and the judgment of the Tribunal;

Directs the Committee on the codification of international law established by the resolution of the General Assembly of 11 December 1946, to treat as a matter of primary importance plans for the formulation, in the context of a general codification of offences against the peace and security of mankind, or of an International Criminal Code, of the principles recognized in the Charter of the Nürnberg Tribunal and in the judgment of the Tribunal.

a. *See also* Basic Document 2.5 and 2.15 supra, and Basic Document 3.39, *infra*.

2.7 INTER-AMERICAN TREATY OF RECIPROCAL ASSISTANCE.[a] Done at Rio de Janeiro, Sept. 2, 1947. Entered into force, Dec. 3, 1948; for the United States, Dec. 3, 1948. 62 Stat. 1681, T.I.A.S. No. 1838, 121 U.N.T.S. 77

Article 1. The High Contracting Parties formally condemn war and undertake in their international relations not to resort to the threat or the use of force in any manner inconsistent with the provisions of the Charter of the United Nations or of this Treaty.

Article 2. As a consequence of the principle set forth in the preceding Article, the High Contracting Parties undertake to submit every controversy which may arise between them to methods of peaceful settlement and to endeavor to settle any such controversy among themselves by means of the procedures in force in the Inter-American System before referring it to the General Assembly or the Security Council of the United Nations.

Article 3. (1) The High Contracting Parties agree that an armed attack by any State against an American State shall be considered as an attack against all the American States and, consequently, each one of the said Contracting Parties undertakes to assist in meeting the attack in the exercise of the inherent right of individual or collective self-defense recognized by Article 51 of the Charter of the United Nations.

(2) On the request of the State or States directly attacked and until the decision of the Organ of Consultation of the Inter-American System, each one of the Contracting Parties may determine the immediate measures which it may individually take in fulfillment of the obligation contained in the preceding paragraph and in accordance with the principle of continental solidarity. The Organ of Consultation shall meet without delay for the purpose of examining those measures and agreeing upon the measures of a collective character that should be taken.

(3) The provisions of this Article shall be applied in case of any armed attack which takes place within the region described in Article 4 or within the territory of an American State. When the attack takes place outside of the said areas, the provisions of Article 6 shall be applied.

(4) Measures of self-defense provided for under this Article may be taken until the Security Council of the United Nations has taken the measures necessary to maintain international peace and security.

* * *

Article 5. The High Contracting Parties shall immediately send to the Security Council of the United Nations, in conformity with Articles 51 and 54 of the Charter of the United Nations, complete information concerning the activities undertaken or in contemplation in the exercise of the right of self-defense or for the purpose of maintaining inter-American peace and security.

Article 6. If the inviolability or the integrity of the territory or the sovereignty or political independence of any American State should be affected by an aggression which is not an armed attack or by an extra-continental or intra-continental conflict, or by any other fact or situation that might endanger the peace of America, the Organ of Consultation shall meet immediately in order to agree on the measures which must be taken in case of aggression to assist the victim of the aggression or, in any case, the measures which should be taken for the common defense and for the maintenance of the peace and security of the Continent.

a. Also known as "the Rio Pact."

Article 7. In the case of a conflict between two or more American States, without prejudice to the right of self-defense in conformity with Article 51 of the Charter of the United Nations, the High Contracting Parties, meeting in consultation shall call upon the contending States to suspend hostilities and restore matters to the *statu quo ante bellum,* and shall take in addition all other necessary measures to reestablish or maintain inter-American peace and security and for the solution of the conflict by peaceful means. The rejection of the pacifying action will be considered in the determination of the aggressor and in the application of the measures which the consultative meeting may agree upon.

Article 8. For the purpose of this Treaty, the measures on which the Organ of Consultation may agree will comprise one or more of the following: recall of chiefs of diplomatic missions; breaking of diplomatic relations; breaking of consular relations; partial or complete interruption of economic relations or of rail, sea, air, postal, telegraphic, telephonic, and radiotelephonic communications; and use of armed force.

Article 9. In addition to other acts which the Organ of Consultation may characterize as aggression, the following shall be considered as such:

(a) Unprovoked armed attack by a State against the territory, the people, or the land, sea or air forces of another State;

(b) Invasion, by the armed forces of a State, of the territory of an American State, through the trespassing of boundaries demarcated in accordance with a treaty, judicial decision, or arbitral award, or, in the absence of frontiers thus demarcated, invasion affecting a region which is under the effective jurisdiction of another State.

Article 10. None of the provisions of this Treaty shall be construed as impairing the rights and obligations of the High Contracting Parties under the Charter of the United Nations.

Article 11. The consultations to which this Treaty refers shall be carried out by means of the Meetings of Ministers of Foreign Affairs of the American Republics which have ratified the Treaty, or in the manner or by the organ which in the future may be agreed upon.

* * *

2.8 AMERICAN TREATY ON PACIFIC SETTLEMENT.[a] Done at Bogota, April 30, 1948. Entered into force, May 6, 1949. 30 U.N.T.S. 55

In the name of their peoples, the Governments represented at the Ninth International Conference of American States have resolved, in fulfillment of Article XXIII of the Charter of the Organization of American States, to conclude the following Treaty;

CHAPTER ONE

GENERAL OBLIGATION TO SETTLE DISPUTES BY PACIFIC MEANS

Article I. The High Contracting Parties, solemnly reaffirming their commitments made in earlier international conventions and declarations, as well as in the Charter of the United Nations, agree to refrain from the threat or the use of force, or from any other means of coercion for the settlement of their controversies, and to have recourse at all times to pacific procedures.

Article II. The High Contracting Parties recognize the obligation to settle international controversies by regional pacific procedures before referring them to the Security Council of the United Nations.

Consequently, in the event that a controversy arises between two or more signatory States which, in the opinion of the parties, cannot be settled by direct negotiations through the usual diplomatic channels, the parties bind themselves to use the procedures established in the present Treaty, in the manner and under the conditions provided for in the following articles, or, alternatively, such special procedures as, in their opinion, will permit them to arrive at a solution.

Article III. The order of the pacific procedures established in the present Treaty does not signify that the parties may not have recourse to the procedure which they consider most appropriate in each case, or that they should use all these procedures, or that any of them have preference over others except as expressly provided.

Article IV. Once any pacific procedure has been initiated, whether by agreement between the parties or in fulfillment of the present Treaty or a previous pact, no other procedure may be commenced until that procedure is concluded.

Article V. The aforesaid procedures may not be applied to matters which, by their nature, are within the domestic jurisdiction of the State. If the parties are not in agreement as to whether the controversy concerns a matter of domestic jurisdiction, this preliminary question shall be submitted to decision by the International Court of Justice, at the request of any of the parties.

Article VI. The aforesaid procedures, furthermore, may not be applied to matters already settled by arrangement between the parties, or by arbitral award or by decision of an international court, or which are governed by agreements or treaties in force on the date of the conclusion of the present Treaty.

Article VII. The High Contracting Parties bind themselves not to make diplomatic representations in order to protect their nationals, or to refer a controversy to a court of international jurisdiction for that purpose, when the said nationals have had available the means to place their case before competent domestic courts of the respective State.

Article VIII. Neither recourse to pacific means for the solution of controversies, nor the recommendation of their use, shall, in the case of an armed attack, be ground for delaying the exercise of the right of individual or collective self-defense, as provided for in the Charter of the United Nations.

a. Also known as "the Pact of Bogota."

[The remainder of this treaty details, *inter alia,* the specific procedures according to which the High Contracting Parties will fulfill their general obligation to settle disputes by pacific means: "Procedure of Good Offices and Mediation" (Chapter Two); "Procedure of Investigation and Conciliation" (Chapter Three); "Judicial Procedure" (Chapter Four); and "Procedure of Arbitration" (Chapter Five).]

2.9 NORTH ATLANTIC TREATY.[a] Done at Washington, D.C., April 4, 1949. Entered into force, Aug. 24, 1949; for the United States, Aug. 24, 1949. 63 Stat. 2241, T.I.A.S. No. 1964, 4 Bevans 828, 34 U.N.T.S. 243

The Parties to this Treaty reaffirm their faith in the purposes and principles of the Charter of the United Nations and their desire to live in peace with all peoples and all governments.

They are determined to safeguard the freedom, common heritage and civilization of their peoples, founded on the principles of democracy, individual liberty and the rule of law.

They seek to promote stability and well-being in the North Atlantic area.

They are resolved to unite their efforts for collective defense and for the preservation of peace and security.

They therefore agree to this North Atlantic Treaty:

Article 1. The Parties undertake, as set forth in the Charter of the United Nations, to settle any international disputes in which they may be involved by peaceful means in such a manner that international peace and security, and justice, are not endangered, and to refrain in their international relations from the threat or use of force in any manner inconsistent with the purposes of the United Nations.

Article 2. The Parties will contribute toward the further development of peaceful and friendly international relations by strengthening their free institutions, by bringing about a better understanding of the principles upon which these institutions are founded, and by promoting conditions of stability and well-being. They will seek to eliminate conflict in their international economic policies and will encourage economic collaboration between any or all of them.

Article 3. In order more effectively to achieve the objectives of this Treaty, the Parties, separately and jointly, by means of continuous and effective self-help and mutual aid, will maintain and develop their individual and collective capacity to resist armed attack.

Article 4. The Parties will consult together whenever, in the opinion of any of them, the territorial integrity, political independence or security of any of the Parties is threatened.

Article 5. The Parties agree that an armed attack against one or more of them in Europe or North America shall be considered an attack against them all; and consequently they agree that, if such an armed attack occurs, each of them, in exercise of the right of individual or collective self-defense recognized by Article 51 of the Charter of the United Nations, will assist the Party or Parties so attacked by taking forthwith, individually and in concert with the other Parties, such action as it deems necessary, including the use of armed force, to restore and maintain the security of the North Atlantic area.

Any such armed attack and all measures taken as a result thereof shall immediately be reported to the Security Council. Such measures shall be terminated when the Security Council has taken the measures necessary to restore and maintain international peace and security.

* * *

Article 7. This Treaty does not affect, and shall not be interpreted as affecting, in any way the rights and obligations under the Charter of the Parties which are

a. Also known as "the NATO Treaty" or "NATO Pact."

members of the United Nations, or the primary responsibility of the Security Council for the maintenance of international peace and security.

* * *

Article 9. **The Parties hereby establish a council, on which each of them shall be represented, to consider matters concerning the implementation of this Treaty. The council shall be so organized as to be able to meet promptly at any time. The council shall set up such subsidiary bodies as may be necessary; in particular it shall establish immediately a defense committee which shall recommend measures for the implementation of Articles 3 and 5.**

* * *

2.10 CONVENTION FOR THE AMELIORATION OF THE CONDITION OF THE WOUNDED AND SICK IN ARMED FORCES IN THE FIELD.[a] Done at Geneva, Aug. 12, 1949. Entered into force, Oct. 21, 1950; for the United States, Feb. 2, 1956. 6 U.S.T. 3114, T.I.A.S. No. 3362, 75 U.N.T.S. 31

CHAPTER I. GENERAL PROVISIONS

Article 1. The High Contracting Parties undertake to respect and to ensure respect for the present Convention in all circumstances.

Article 2. In addition to the provisions which shall be implemented in peacetime, the present Convention shall apply to all cases of declared war or of any other armed conflict which may arise between two or more of the High Contracting Parties, even if the state of war is not recognized by one of them.

The Convention shall also apply to all cases of partial or total occupation of the territory of a High Contracting Party, even if the said occupation meets with no armed resistance.

Although one of the Powers in conflict may not be a party to the present Convention, the Powers who are parties thereto shall remain bound by it in their mutual relations. They shall furthermore be bound by the Convention in relation to the said Power, if the latter accepts and applies the provisions thereof.

Article 3. In the case of armed conflict not of an international character occurring in the territory of one of the High Contracting Parties, each Party to the conflict shall be bound to apply, as a minimum, the following provisions:

(1) Persons taking no active part in the hostilities, including members of armed forces who have laid down their arms and those placed *hors de combat* by sickness, wounds, detention, or any other cause, shall in all circumstances be treated humanely, without any adverse distinction founded on race, colour, religion or faith, sex, birth or wealth, or any other similar criteria.

To this end, the following acts are and shall remain prohibited at any time and in any place whatsoever with respect to the above-mentioned persons:

(a) violence to life and person, in particular murder of all kinds, mutilation, cruel treatment and torture;

(b) taking of hostages;

(c) outrages upon personal dignity, in particular humiliating and degrading treatment;

(d) the passing of sentences and the carrying out of executions without previous judgment pronounced by a regularly constituted court, affording all the judicial guarantees which are recognized as indispensable by civilized peoples.

(2) The wounded and sick shall be collected and cared for.

An impartial humanitarian body, such as the International Committee of the Red Cross, may offer its services to the Parties to the conflict.

a. This Convention is supplemented and augmented by two additional protocols. *See* Basic Documents 2.33 and 2.34, *infra*.

The Parties to the conflict should further endeavour to bring into force, by means of special agreements, all or part of the other provisions of the present Convention.

The application of the preceding provisions shall not affect the legal status of the Parties to the conflict.

Article 4. Neutral Powers shall apply by analogy the provisions of the present Convention to the wounded and sick, and to members of the medical personnel and to chaplains of the armed forces of the Parties to the conflict, received or interned in their territory, as well as to dead persons found.

Article 5. For the protected persons who have fallen into the hands of the enemy, the present Convention shall apply until their final repatriation.

* * *

Article 8. The present Convention shall be applied with the cooperation and under the scrutiny of the Protecting Powers whose duty it is to safeguard the interests of the Parties to the conflict. For this purpose, the Protecting Powers may appoint, apart from their diplomatic or consular staff, delegates from amongst their own nationals or the nationals of other neutral Powers. The said delegates shall be subject to the approval of the Power with which they are to carry out their duties.

The Parties to the conflict shall facilitate to the greatest extent possible, the task of the representatives or delegates of the Protecting Powers.

The representatives or delegates of the Protecting Powers shall not in any case exceed their mission under the present Convention. They shall, in particular, take account of the imperative necessities of security of the State wherein they carry out their duties. Their activities shall only be restricted as an exceptional and temporary measure when this is rendered necessary by imperative military necessities.

Article 9. The provisions of the present Convention constitute no obstacle to the humanitarian activities which the International Committee of the Red Cross or any other impartial humanitarian organization may, subject to the consent of the Parties to the conflict concerned, undertake for the protection of wounded and sick, medical personnel and chaplains, and for their relief.

Article 10. The High Contracting Parties may at any time agree to entrust to an organization which offers all guarantees of impartiality and efficacy the duties incumbent on the Protecting Powers by virtue of the present Convention.

When wounded and sick, or medical personnel and chaplains do not benefit or cease to benefit, no matter for what reason, by the activities of a Protecting Power or of an organization provided for in the first paragraph above, the Detaining Power shall request a neutral State, or such an organization, to undertake the functions performed under the present Convention by a Protecting Power designated by the Parties to a conflict.

If protection cannot be arranged accordingly, the Detaining Power shall request or shall accept, subject to the provisions of this Article, the offer of the services of a humanitarian organization, such as the International Committee of the Red Cross, to assume the humanitarian functions performed by Protecting Powers under the present Convention.

* * *

Article 11. In cases where they deem it advisable in the interest of protected persons, particularly in cases of disagreement between the Parties to the conflict as to the application or interpretation of the provisions of the present Convention, the Protecting Powers shall lend their good offices with a view to settling the disagreement.

* * *

CHAPTER II. WOUNDED AND SICK

Article 12. Members of the armed forces and other persons mentioned in the following Article, who are wounded or sick, shall be respected and protected in all circumstances.

They shall be treated humanely and cared for by the Party to the conflict in whose power they may be, without any adverse distinction founded on sex, race, nationality, religion, political opinions, or any other similar criteria. Any attempts upon their lives, or violence to their persons, shall be strictly prohibited; in particular, they shall not be murdered or exterminated, subjected to torture or to biological experiments; they shall not wilfully be left without medical assistance and care, nor shall conditions exposing them to contagion or infection be created.

Only urgent medical reasons will authorize priority in the order of treatment to be administered.

Women shall be treated with all consideration due to their sex.

The Party to the conflict which is compelled to abandon wounded or sick to the enemy shall, as far as military considerations permit, leave with them a part of its medical personnel and material to assist in their care.

Article 13. The present Convention shall apply to the wounded and sick belonging to the following categories:

(1) Members of the armed forces of a Party to the conflict, as well as members of militias or volunteer corps forming part of such armed forces.

(2) Members of other militias and members of other volunteer corps, including those of organized resistance movements, belonging to a Party to the conflict and operating in or outside their own territory, even if this territory is occupied, provided that such militias or volunteer corps, including such organized resistance movements, fulfil the following conditions:

(a) that of being commanded by a person responsible for his subordinates;

(b) that of having a fixed distinctive sign recognizable at a distance;

(c) that of carrying arms openly;

(d) that of conducting their operations in accordance with the laws and customs of war.

(3) Members of regular armed forces who profess allegiance to a Government or an authority not recognized by the Detaining Power.

(4) Persons who accompany the armed forces without actually being members thereof, such as civil members of military aircraft crews, war correspondents, supply contractors, members of labour units or of services responsible for the welfare of the armed forces, provided that they have received authorization from the armed forces which they accompany.

(5) Members of crews, including masters, pilots and apprentices, of the merchant marine and the crews of civil aircraft of the Parties to the conflict, who do not benefit by more favourable treatment under any other provisions in international law.

(6) Inhabitants of a non-occupied territory who, on the approach of the enemy, spontaneously take up arms to resist the invading forces, without having had time to form themselves into regular armed units, provided they carry arms openly and respect the laws and customs of war.

Article 14. Subject to the provisions of Article 12, the wounded and sick of a belligerent who fall into enemy hands shall be prisoners of war, and the provisions of international law concerning prisoners of war shall apply to them.

Article 15. At all times, and particularly after an engagement, Parties to the conflict shall, without delay, take all possible measures to search for and collect the wounded and sick, to protect them against pillage and ill-treatment, to ensure their adequate care, and to search for the dead and prevent their being despoiled.

* * *

Article 16. Parties to the conflict shall record as soon as possible, in respect of each wounded, sick or dead person of the adverse Party falling into their hands, any particulars which may assist in his identification.

These records should if possible include:

(a) designation of the Power on which he depends;

(b) army, regimental, personal or serial number;

(c) surname;

(d) first name or names;

(e) date of birth;

(f) any other particulars shown on his identity card or disc;

(g) date and place of capture or death;

(h) particulars concerning wounds or illness, or cause of death.

As soon as possible the above mentioned information shall be forwarded to the Information Bureau described in Article 122 of the Geneva Convention relative to the Treatment of Prisoners of War of August 12, 1949, which shall transmit this information to the Power on which these persons depend through the intermediary of the Protecting Power and of the Central Prisoners of War Agency.

* * *

Article 17. Parties to the conflict shall ensure that burial or cremation of the dead, carried out individually as far as circumstances permit, is preceded by a careful examination, if possible by a medical examination, of the bodies, with a view to confirming death, establishing identity and enabling a report to be made. One half of the double identity disc, or the identity disc itself if it is a single disc, should remain on the body.

Bodies shall not be cremated except for imperative reasons of hygiene or for motives based on the religion of the deceased. In case of cremation, the circumstances and reasons for cremation shall be stated in detail in the death certificate or on the authenticated list of the dead.

They shall further ensure that the dead are honourably interred, if possible according to the rites of the religion to which they belonged, that their graves are respected, grouped if possible according to the nationality of the deceased, properly maintained and marked so that they may always be found. For this purpose, they shall organize at the commencement of hostilities an Official Graves Registration Service, to allow subsequent exhumations and to ensure the identification of bodies, whatever the site of the graves, and the possible transportation to the home country. These provisions shall likewise apply to the ashes, which shall be kept by the Graves Registration Service until proper disposal thereof in accordance with the wishes of the home country.

As soon as circumstances permit, and at latest at the end of hostilities, these Services shall exchange, through the Information Bureau mentioned in the second paragraph of Article 16, lists showing the exact location and markings of the graves, together with particulars of the dead interred therein.

Article 18. The military authorities may appeal to the charity of the inhabitants voluntarily to collect and care for, under their direction, the wounded and sick, granting persons who have responded to this appeal the necessary protection and facilities. Should the adverse Party take or retake control of the area, he shall likewise grant these persons the same protection and the same facilities.

The military authorities shall permit the inhabitants and relief societies, even in invaded or occupied areas, spontaneously to collect and care for wounded or sick of whatever nationality. The civilian population shall respect these wounded and sick, and in particular abstain from offering them violence.

No one may ever be molested or convicted for having nursed the wounded or sick.

The provisions of the present Article do not relieve the occupying Power of its obligation to give both physical and moral care to the wounded and sick.

CHAPTER III. MEDICAL UNITS AND ESTABLISHMENTS

Article 19. Fixed establishments and mobile medical units of the Medical Service may in no circumstances be attacked, but shall at all times be respected and protected by the Parties to the conflict. Should they fall into the hands of the adverse Party, their personnel shall be free to pursue their duties, as long as the capturing Power has not itself ensured the necessary care of the wounded and sick found in such establishments and units.

The responsible authorities shall ensure that the said medical establishments and units are, as far as possible, situated in such a manner that attacks against military objectives cannot imperil their safety.

Article 20. Hospital ships entitled to the protection of the Geneva Convention for the Amelioration of the Condition of Wounded, Sick and Shipwrecked Members of Armed Forces at Sea of August 12, 1949, shall not be attacked from the land.

Article 21. The protection to which fixed establishments and mobile medical units of the Medical Service are entitled shall not cease unless they are used to commit, outside their humanitarian duties, acts harmful to the enemy. Protection may, however, cease only after a due warning has been given, naming, in all appropriate cases, a reasonable time limit, and after such warning has remained unheeded.

Article 22. The following conditions shall not be considered as depriving a medical unit or establishment of the protection guaranteed by Article 19:

(1) That the personnel of the unit or establishment are armed, and that they use the arms in their own defence, or in that of the wounded and sick in their charge.

(2) That in the absence of armed orderlies, the unit or establishment is protected by a picket or by sentries or by an escort.

(3) That small arms and ammunition taken from the wounded and sick and not yet handed to the proper service, are found in the unit or establishment.

(4) That personnel and material of the veterinary service are found in the unit or establishment, without forming an integral part thereof.

(5) That the humanitarian activities of medical units and establishments or of their personnel extend to the care of civilian wounded or sick.

* * *

CHAPTER IV. PERSONNEL

Article 24. Medical personnel exclusively engaged in the search for, or the collection, transport or treatment of the wounded or sick, or in the prevention of disease, staff exclusively engaged in the administration of medical units and establishments, as well as chaplains attached to the armed forces, shall be respected and protected in all circumstances.

Article 25. Members of the armed forces specially trained for employment, should the need arise, as hospital orderlies, nurses or auxiliary stretcher-bearers, in the search for or the collection, transport or treatment of the wounded and sick shall likewise be respected and protected if they are carrying out these duties at the time when they come into contact with the enemy or fall into his hands.

Article 26. The staff of National Red Cross Societies and that of other Voluntary Aid Societies, duly recognized and authorized by their Governments, who may be employed on the same duties as the personnel named in Article 24, are placed on the same footing as the personnel named in the said Article, provided that the staff of such societies are subject to military laws and regulations.

* * *

Article 28. Personnel designated in Articles 24 and 26 who fall into the hands of the adverse Party, shall be retained only in so far as the state of health, the spiritual needs and the number of prisoners of war require.

Personnel thus retained shall not be deemed prisoners of war. Nevertheless they shall at least benefit by all the provisions of the Geneva Convention relative to the Treatment of Prisoners of War of August 12, 1949. Within the framework of the military laws and regulations of the Detaining Power, and under the authority of its competent service, they shall continue to carry out, in accordance with their professional ethics, their medical and spiritual duties on behalf of prisoners of war, preferably those of the armed forces to which they themselves belong. * * *

* * *

Article 29. Members of the personnel designated in Article 25 who have fallen into the hands of the enemy, shall be prisoners of war, but shall be employed on their medical duties in so far as the need arises.

Article 30. Personnel whose retention is not indispensable by virtue of the provisions of Article 28 shall be returned to the Party to the conflict to whom they belong, as soon as a road is open for their return and military requirements permit.

Pending their return, they shall not be deemed prisoners of war. Nevertheless they shall at least benefit by all the provisions of the Geneva Convention relative to the Treatment of Prisoners of War of August 12, 1949. They shall continue to fulfil their duties under the orders of the adverse Party and shall preferably be engaged in the care of the wounded and sick of the Party to the conflict to which they themselves belong.

On their departure, they shall take with them the effects, personal belongings, valuables and instruments belonging to them.

* * *

CHAPTER V. BUILDINGS AND MATERIAL

Article 33. The material of mobile medical units of the armed forces which fall into the hands of the enemy, shall be reserved for the care of wounded and sick.

The buildings, material and stores of fixed medical establishments of the armed forces shall remain subject to the laws of war, but may not be diverted from their purpose as long as they are required for the care of wounded and sick. Nevertheless, the commanders of forces in the field may make use of them, in case of urgent military necessity, provided that they make previous arrangements for the welfare of the wounded and sick who are nursed in them.

The material and stores defined in the present Article shall not be intentionally destroyed.

Article 34. The real and personal property of aid societies which are admitted to the privileges of the Convention shall be regarded as private property.

The right of requisition recognized for belligerents by the laws and customs of war shall not be exercised except in case of urgent necessity, and only after the welfare of the wounded and sick has been ensured.

CHAPTER VI. MEDICAL TRANSPORTS

Article 35. Transports of wounded and sick or of medical equipment shall be respected and protected in the same way as mobile medical units.

Should such transports or vehicles fall into the hands of the adverse Party, they shall be subject to the laws of war, on condition that the Party to the conflict who captures them shall in all cases ensure the care of the wounded and sick they contain.

The civilian personnel and all means of transport obtained by requisition shall be subject to the general rules of international law.

Article 36. Medical aircraft, that is to say, aircraft exclusively employed for the removal of wounded and sick and for the transport of medical personnel and equipment, shall not be attacked, but shall be respected by the belligerents, while flying at heights, times and on routes specifically agreed upon between the belligerents concerned.

They shall bear, clearly marked, the distinctive emblem prescribed in Article 38, together with their national colours, on their lower, upper and lateral surfaces. * * *

* * *

CHAPTER VII. THE DISTINCTIVE EMBLEM

Article 38. As a compliment to Switzerland, the heraldic emblem of the red cross on a white ground, formed by reversing the Federal colours, is retained as the emblem and distinctive sign of the Medical Service or armed forces.

Nevertheless, in the case of countries which already use as emblem, in place of the red cross, the red crescent or the red lion and sun on a white ground, those emblems are also recognized by the terms of the present Convention.

* * *

CHAPTER VIII. EXECUTION OF THE CONVENTION

Article 45. Each Party to the conflict, acting through its commanders-in-chief, shall ensure the detailed execution of the preceding Articles and provide for unforeseen cases, in conformity with the general principles of the present Convention.

Article 46. Reprisals against the wounded, sick, personnel, buildings or equipment protected by the Convention are prohibited.

Article 47. The High Contracting Parties undertake, in time of peace as in time of war, to disseminate the text of the present Convention as widely as possible in their respective countries, and, in particular, to include the study thereof in their programmes of military and, if possible, civil instruction, so that the principles thereof may become known to the entire population, in particular to the armed fighting forces, the medical personnel and the chaplains.

* * *

CHAPTER IX. REPRESSION OF ABUSES AND INFRACTIONS

Article 49. The High Contracting Parties undertake to enact any legislation necessary to provide effective penal sanctions for persons committing, or ordering to be committed, any of the grave breaches of the present Convention defined in the following Article.

* * *

In all circumstances, the accused persons shall benefit by safeguards of proper trial and defence, which shall not be less favourable than those provided by Article

105 and those following of the Geneva Convention relative to the Treatment of Prisoners of War of August 12, 1949.

Article 50. Grave breaches to which the preceding Article relates shall be those involving any of the following acts, if committed against persons or property protected by the Convention: wilful killing, torture or inhuman treatment, including biological experiments, wilfully causing great suffering or serious injury to body or health, and extensive destruction and appropriation of property, not justified by military necessity and carried out unlawfully and wantonly.

Article 51. No High Contracting Party shall be allowed to absolve itself or any other High Contracting Party of any liability incurred by itself or by another High Contracting Party in respect of breaches referred to in the preceding Article.

Article 52. At the request of a Party to the conflict, an enquiry shall be instituted, in a manner to be decided between the interested Parties, concerning any alleged violation of the Convention.

If agreement has not been reached concerning the procedure for the enquiry, the Parties should agree on the choice of an umpire who will decide upon the procedure to be followed.

Once the violation has been established, the Parties to the conflict shall put an end to it and shall repress it with the least possible delay.

* * *

[*Note: Omitted are the "Final Provisions" (Articles 55–64) which pertain mainly to the Convention's ratification and entry into force.*]

2.11 CONVENTION FOR THE AMELIORATION OF THE CONDITION OF WOUNDED, SICK AND SHIP-WRECKED MEMBERS OF ARMED FORCES AT SEA.[a] Done at Geneva, Aug. 12, 1949. Entered into force, Oct. 21, 1950; for the United States, Feb. 2, 1956. 6 U.S.T. 3217, T.I.A.S. No. 3363, 75 U.N.T.S. 85

CHAPTER I. GENERAL PROVISIONS

[*Note: Articles 1–3 of Chapter I of this Convention are identical to Articles 1–3 of Chapter I in Basic Document 2.10, supra.*]

Article 4. In case of hostilities between land and naval forces of Parties to the conflict, the provisions of the present Convention shall apply only to forces on board ship.

Forces put ashore shall immediately become subject to the provisions of the Geneva Convention for the Amelioration of the Condition of the Wounded and Sick in Armed Forces in the Field of August 12, 1949.

[*Note: Except for language pertaining to shipwrecked personnel, Articles 5–11 of this Convention are identical to Articles 4 and 6–11 in Basic Document 2.10, supra.*]

CHAPTER II. WOUNDED, SICK AND SHIPWRECKED

Article 12. Members of the armed forces and other persons mentioned in the following Article, who are at sea and who are wounded, sick or shipwrecked, shall be respected and protected in all circumstances, it being understood that the term "shipwreck" means shipwreck from any cause and includes forced landings at sea by or from aircraft.

Such persons shall be treated humanely and cared for by the Parties to the conflict in whose power they may be, without any adverse distinction founded on sex, race, nationality, religion, political opinions, or any other similar criteria. Any attempts upon their lives, or violence to their persons, shall be strictly prohibited; in particular, they shall not be murdered or exterminated, subjected to torture or to biological experiments; they shall not wilfully be left without medical assistance and care, nor shall conditions exposing them to contagion or infection be created.

Only urgent medical reasons will authorize priority in the order of treatment to be administered.

Women shall be treated with all consideration due to their sex.

[*Note: Except for language pertaining to shipwrecked personnel, Article 13 of this Convention is identical to Article 13 in Basic Document 2.10, supra.*]

Article 14. All warships of a belligerent Party shall have the right to demand that the wounded, sick or shipwrecked on board military hospital ships, and hospital ships belonging to relief societies or to private individuals, as well as merchant vessels, yachts and other craft shall be surrendered, whatever their nationality, provided that the wounded and sick are in a fit state to be moved and that the warship can provide adequate facilities for necessary medical treatment.

Article 15. If wounded, sick or shipwrecked persons are taken on board a neutral warship or a neutral military aircraft, it shall be ensured, where so required by international law, that they can take no further part in operations of war.

a. This Convention is supplemented and augmented by two additional protocols. *See* Basic Documents 2.33 and 2.34, *infra.*

Article 16. Subject to the provisions of Article 12, the wounded, sick and shipwrecked of a belligerent who fall into enemy hands shall be prisoners of war, and the provisions of international law concerning prisoners of war shall apply to them. The captor may decide, according to circumstances, whether it is expedient to hold them, or to convey them to a port in the captor's own country, to a neutral port or even to a port in enemy territory. In the last case, prisoners of war thus returned to their home country may not serve for the duration of the war.

Article 17. Wounded, sick or shipwrecked persons who are landed in neutral ports with the consent of the local authorities, shall, failing arrangements to the contrary between the neutral and the belligerent Powers, be so guarded by the neutral Power, where so required by international law, that the said persons cannot again take part in operations of war.

The costs of hospital accommodation and internment shall be borne by the Power on whom the wounded, sick or shipwrecked persons depend.

[*Note: Except for language pertaining to shipwrecked personnel, Articles 18 and 19 of this Convention are identical to Articles 15 and 16 in Basic Document 2.10, supra.*]

Article 20. Parties to the conflict shall ensure that burial at sea of the dead, carried out individually as far as circumstances permit, is preceded by a careful examination, if possible by a medical examination, of the bodies, with a view to confirming death, establishing identity and enabling a report to be made. Where a double identity disc is used, one half of the disc should remain on the body.

If dead persons are landed, the provisions of the Geneva Convention for the Amelioration of the Condition of the Wounded and Sick in Armed Forces in the Field of August 12, 1949, shall be applicable.

Article 21. The Parties to the conflict may appeal to the charity of commanders of neutral merchant vessels, yachts or other craft, to take on board and care for wounded, sick or shipwrecked persons, and to collect the dead.

Vessels of any kind responding to this appeal, and those having of their own accord collected wounded, sick or shipwrecked persons, shall enjoy special protection and facilities to carry out such assistance.

They may, in no case, be captured on account of any such transport; but, in the absence of any promise to the contrary, they shall remain liable to capture for any violations of neutrality they may have committed.

CHAPTER III. HOSPITAL SHIPS

Article 22. Military hospital ships, that is to say, ships built or equipped by the Powers specially and solely with a view to assisting the wounded, sick and shipwrecked, to treating them and to transporting them, may in no circumstances be attacked or captured, but shall at all times be respected and protected, on condition that their names and descriptions have been notified to the Parties to the conflict ten days before those ships are employed.

The characteristics which must appear in the notification shall include registered gross tonnage, the length from stem to stern and the number of masts and funnels.

Article 23. Establishments ashore entitled to the protection of the Geneva Convention for the Amelioration of the Condition of the Wounded and Sick in Armed Forces in the Field of August 12, 1949, shall be protected from bombardment or attack from the sea.

Article 24. Hospital ships utilized by National Red Cross Societies, by officially recognized relief societies or by private persons shall have the same protection as military hospital ships and shall be exempt from capture, if the Party to the conflict on which they depend has given them an official commission and in so far as the provisions of Article 22 concerning notification have been complied with.

These ships must be provided with certificates from the responsible authorities, stating that the vessels have been under their control while fitting out and on departure.

Article 25. Hospital ships utilized by National Red Cross Societies, officially recognized relief societies, or private persons of neutral countries shall have the same protection as military hospital ships and shall be exempt from capture, on condition that they have placed themselves under the control of one of the Parties to the conflict, with the previous consent of their own governments and with the authorization of the Party to the conflict concerned, in so far as the provisions of Article 22 concerning notification have been complied with.

* * *

Article 27. Under the same conditions as those provided for in Articles 22 and 24, small craft employed by the State or by the officially recognized lifeboat institutions for coastal rescue operations, shall also be respected and protected, so far as operational requirements permit.

The same shall apply so far as possible to fixed coastal installations used exclusively by these craft for their humanitarian missions.

Article 28. Should fighting occur on board a warship, the sick-bays shall be respected and spared as far as possible. Sick-bays and their equipment shall remain subject to the laws of warfare, but may not be diverted from their purpose so long as they are required for the wounded and sick. Nevertheless, the commander into whose power they have fallen may, after ensuring the proper care of the wounded and sick who are accommodated therein, apply them to other purposes in case of urgent military necessity.

Article 29. Any hospital ship in a port which falls into the hands of the enemy shall be authorized to leave the said port.

Article 30. The vessels described in Articles 22, 24, 25 and 27 shall afford relief and assistance to the wounded, sick and shipwrecked without distinction of nationality.

The High Contracting Parties undertake not to use these vessels for any military purpose. Such vessels shall in no wise hamper the movements of the combatants.

During and after an engagement, they will act at their own risk.

Article 31. The Parties to the conflict shall have the right to control and search the vessels mentioned in Articles 22, 24, 25 and 27. They can refuse assistance from these vessels, order them off, make them take a certain course, control the use of their wireless and other means of communication, and even detain them for a period not exceeding seven days from the time of interception, if the gravity of the circumstances so requires.

They may put a commissioner temporarily on board whose sole task shall be to see that orders given in virtue of the provisions of the preceding paragraph are carried out.

As far as possible, the Parties to the conflict shall enter in the log of the hospital ship, in a language he can understand, the orders they have given the captain of the vessel.

Parties to the conflict may, either unilaterally or by particular agreements, put on board their ships neutral observers who shall verify the strict observation of the provisions contained in the present Convention.

Article 32. Vessels described in Articles 22, 24, 25 and 27 are not classed as warships as regards their stay in a neutral port.

Article 33. Merchant vessels which have been transformed into hospital ships cannot be put to any other use throughout the duration of hostilities.

Article 34. The protection to which hospital ships and sick-bays are entitled shall not cease unless they are used to commit, outside their humanitarian duties, acts harmful to the enemy. Protection may, however, cease only after due warning has been given, naming in all appropriate cases a reasonable time limit, and after such warning has remained unheeded.

In particular, hospital ships may not possess or use a secret code for their wireless or other means of communication.

Article 35. The following conditions shall not be considered as depriving hospital ships or sick-bays of vessels of the protection due to them:

(1) The fact that the crews of ships or sick-bays are armed for the maintenance of order, for their own defence or that of the sick and wounded.

(2) The presence on board of apparatus exclusively intended to facilitate navigation or communication.

(3) The discovery on board hospital ships or in sick-bays of portable arms and ammunition taken from the wounded, sick and shipwrecked and not yet handed to the proper service.

(4) The fact that the humanitarian activities of hospital ships and sick-bays of vessels or of the crews extend to the care of wounded, sick or shipwrecked civilians.

(5) The transport of equipment and of personnel intended exclusively for medical duties, over and above the normal requirements.

CHAPTER IV. PERSONNEL

Article 36. The religious, medical and hospital personnel of hospital ships and their crews shall be respected and protected; they may not be captured during the time they are in the service of the hospital ship, whether or not there are wounded and sick on board.

Article 37. The religious, medical and hospital personnel assigned to the medical or spiritual care of the persons designated in Articles 12 and 13 shall, if they fall into the hands of the enemy, be respected and protected; they may continue to carry out their duties as long as this is necessary for the care of the wounded and sick. They shall afterwards be sent back as soon as the Commander-in-Chief, under whose authority they are, considers it practicable. They may take with them, on leaving the ship, their personal property.

If, however, it proves necessary to retain some of this personnel owing to the medical or spiritual needs of prisoners of war, everything possible shall be done for their earliest possible landing.

Retained personnel shall be subject, on landing, to the provisions of the Geneva Convention for the Amelioration of the Condition of the Wounded and Sick in Armed Forces in the Field of August 12, 1949.

CHAPTER V. MEDICAL TRANSPORTS

Article 38. Ships chartered for that purpose shall be authorized to transport equipment exclusively intended for the treatment of wounded and sick members of armed forces or for the prevention of disease, provided that the particulars regarding their voyage have been notified to the adverse Power and approved by the latter. The adverse Power shall preserve the right to board the carrier ships, but not to capture them or seize the equipment carried.

By agreement amongst the Parties to the conflict, neutral observers may be placed on board such ships to verify the equipment carried. For this purpose, free access to the equipment shall be given.

[*Note: Except for language pertaining to shipwrecked personnel, Articles 39 and 40 of this Convention are identical to Articles 36 and 37 in Basic Document 2.10, supra.*]

CHAPTER VI. THE DISTINCTIVE EMBLEM

Article 41. Under the direction of the competent military authority, the emblem of the red cross on a white ground shall be displayed on the flags, armlets and on all equipment employed in the Medical Service.

Nevertheless, in the case of countries which already use as emblem, in place of the red cross, the red crescent or the red lion and sun on a white ground, these emblems are also recognized by the terms of the present Convention.

[*Note: Except for language pertaining to markings on ships, the remainder of this Convention, embracing Articles 42–63, is in essential respects identical to Articles 40–64 in Basic Document 2.10, supra.*]

2.12 CONVENTION RELATIVE TO THE TREATMENT OF PRISONERS OF WAR.[a] Done at Geneva, Aug. 12, 1949. Entered into force, Oct. 21, 1950; for the United States, Feb. 2, 1956. 6 U.S.T. 3316, T.I.A.S. No. 3364, 75 U.N.T.S. 135

PART I. GENERAL PROVISIONS

[*Note: Articles 1–3 of Part I of this Convention are identical to Articles 1–3 of Chapter I in Basic Document 2.10, supra.*]

Article 4. (A) Prisoners of war, in the sense of the present Convention, are persons belonging to one of the following categories, who have fallen into the power of the enemy:

(1) Members of the armed forces of a Party to the conflict, as well as members of militias or volunteer corps forming part of such armed forces.

(2) Members of other militias and members of other volunteer corps, including those of organized resistance movements, belonging to a Party to the conflict and operating in or outside their own territory, even if this territory is occupied, provided that such militias or volunteer corps, including such organized resistance movements, fulfil the following conditions:

(a) that of being commanded by a person responsible for his subordinates;

(b) that of having a fixed distinctive sign recognizable at a distance;

(c) that of carrying arms openly;

(d) that of conducting their operations in accordance with the laws and customs of war.

(3) Members of regular armed forces who profess allegiance to a government or an authority not recognized by the Detaining Power.

(4) Persons who accompany the armed forces without actually being members thereof, such as civilian members of military aircraft crews, war correspondents, supply contractors, members of labour units or of services responsible for the welfare of the armed forces, provided that they have received authorization from the armed forces which they accompany, who shall provide them for that purpose with an identity card similar to the annexed model.

(5) Members of crews, including masters, pilots and apprentices, of the merchant marine and the crews of civil aircraft of the Parties to the conflict, who do not benefit by more favourable treatment under any other provisions of international law.

(6) Inhabitants of a non-occupied territory, who on the approach of the enemy spontaneously take up arms to resist the invading forces, without having had time to form themselves into regular armed units, provided they carry arms openly and respect the laws and customs of war.

(B) The following shall likewise be treated as prisoners of war under the present Convention:

(1) Persons belonging, or having belonged, to the armed forces of the occupied country, if the occupying Power considers it necessary by reason of such allegiance to intern them * * *.

a. This Convention is supplemented and augmented by two additional protocols. *See* Basic Documents 2.33 and 2.34, *infra*.

(2) The persons belonging to one of the categories enumerated in the present Article, who have been received by neutral or non-belligerent Powers on their territory and whom these Powers are required to intern under international law * * *.

* * *

Article 5. The present Convention shall apply to the persons referred to in Article 4 from the time they fall into the power of the enemy and until their final release and repatriation.

Should any doubt arise as to whether persons, having committed a belligerent act and having fallen into the hands of the enemy, belong to any of the categories enumerated in Article 4, such persons shall enjoy the protection of the present Convention until such time as their status has been determined by a competent tribunal.

[*Note: Except for language pertaining to prisoners of war, Articles 6–11 of this Convention are identical to Articles 6–11 in Basic Document 2.10, supra.*]

PART II. GENERAL PROTECTION OF PRISONERS OF WAR

Article 12. Prisoners of war are in the hands of the enemy Power, but not of the individuals or military units who have captured them. Irrespective of the individual responsibilities that may exist, the Detaining Power is responsible for the treatment given them.

Prisoners of war may only be transferred by the Detaining Power to a Power which is a party to the Convention and after the Detaining Power has satisfied itself of the willingness and ability of such transferee Power to apply the Convention. When prisoners of war are transferred under such circumstances, responsibility for the application of the Convention rests on the Power accepting them while they are in its custody.

Nevertheless, if that Power fails to carry out the provisions of the Convention in any important respect, the Power by whom the prisoners of war were transferred shall, upon being notified by the Protecting Power, take effective measures to correct the situation or shall request the return of the prisoners of war. Such requests must be complied with.

Article 13. Prisoners of war must at all times be humanely treated. Any unlawful act or omission by the Detaining Power causing death or seriously endangering the health of a prisoner of war in its custody is prohibited, and will be regarded as a serious breach of the present Convention. In particular, no prisoner of war may be subjected to physical mutilation or to medical or scientific experiments of any kind which are not justified by the medical, dental or hospital treatment of the prisoner concerned and carried out in his interest.

Likewise, prisoners of war must at all times be protected, particularly against acts of violence or intimidation and against insults and public curiosity.

Measures of reprisal against prisoners of war are prohibited.

Article 14. Prisoners of war are entitled in all circumstances to respect for their persons and their honour.

Women shall be treated with all the regard due to their sex and shall in all cases benefit by treatment as favourable as that granted to men.

Prisoners of war shall retain the full civil capacity which they enjoyed at the time of their capture. The Detaining Power may not restrict the exercise, either within or without its own territory, of the rights such capacity confers except in so far as the captivity requires.

Article 15. The Power detaining prisoners of war shall be bound to provide free of charge for their maintenance and for the medical attention required by their state of health.

Article 16. Taking into consideration the provisions of the present Convention relating to rank and sex, and subject to any privileged treatment which may be accorded to them by reason of their state of health, age or professional qualifications, all prisoners of war shall be treated alike by the Detaining Power, without any adverse distinction based on race, nationality, religious belief or political opinions, or any other distinction founded on similar criteria.

PART III. CAPTIVITY

SECTION I. BEGINNING OF CAPTIVITY

Article 17. Every prisoner of war, when questioned on the subject, is bound to give only his surname, first names and rank, date of birth, and army, regimental, personal or serial number, or failing this, equivalent information.

If he wilfully infringes this rule, he may render himself liable to a restriction of the privileges accorded to his rank or status.

Each Party to a conflict is required to furnish the persons under its jurisdiction who are liable to become prisoners of war, with an identity card showing the owner's surname, first names, rank, army, regimental, personal or serial number or equivalent information, and date of birth. The identity card may, furthermore, bear the signature or the fingerprints, or both, of the owner, and may bear, as well, any other information the Party to the conflict may wish to add concerning persons belonging to its armed forces. As far as possible the card shall measure 6.5 × 10 cm. and shall be issued in duplicate. The identity card shall be shown by the prisoner of war upon demand, but may in no case be taken away from him.

No physical or mental torture, nor any other form of coercion, may be inflicted on prisoners of war to secure from them information of any kind whatever. Prisoners of war who refuse to answer may not be threatened, insulted, or exposed to unpleasant or disadvantageous treatment of any kind.

Prisoners of war who, owing to their physical or mental condition, are unable to state their identity, shall be handed over to the medical service. The identity of such prisoners shall be established by all possible means, subject to the provisions of the preceding paragraph.

The questioning of prisoners of war shall be carried out in a language which they understand.

Article 18. All effects and articles of personal use, except arms, horses, military equipment and military documents, shall remain in the possession of prisoners of war, likewise their metal helmets and gas masks and like articles issued for personal protection. Effects and articles used for their clothing or feeding shall likewise remain in their possession, even if such effects and articles belong to their regulation military equipment.

At no time should prisoners of war be without identity documents. The Detaining Power shall supply such documents to prisoners of war who possess none.

Badges of rank and nationality, decorations and articles having above all a personal or sentimental value may not be taken from prisoners of war.

Sums of money carried by prisoners of war may not be taken away from them except by order of an officer, and after the amount and particulars of the owner have been recorded in a special register and an itemized receipt has been given, legibly inscribed with the name, rank and unit of the person issuing the said receipt. Sums in the currency of the Detaining Power, or which are changed into such currency at the prisoner's request, shall be placed to the credit of the prisoner's account as provided in Article 64.

The Detaining Power may withdraw articles of value from prisoners of war only for reasons of security; when such articles are withdrawn, the procedure laid down for sums of money impounded shall apply.

Such objects, likewise sums taken away in any currency other than that of the Detaining Power and the conversion of which has not been asked for by the owners, shall be kept in the custody of the Detaining Power and shall be returned in their initial shape to prisoners of war at the end of their captivity.

Article 19. Prisoners of war shall be evacuated, as soon as possible after their capture, to camps situated in an area far enough from the combat zone for them to be out of danger.

Only those prisoners of war who, owing to wounds or sickness, would run greater risks by being evacuated than by remaining where they are, may be temporarily kept back in a danger zone.

Prisoners of war shall not be unnecessarily exposed to danger while awaiting evacuation from a fighting zone.

Article 20. The evacuation of prisoners of war shall always be effected humanely and in conditions similar to those for the forces of the Detaining Power in their changes of station.

The Detaining Power shall supply prisoners of war who are being evacuated with sufficient food and potable water, and with the necessary clothing and medical attention. The Detaining Power shall take all suitable precautions to ensure their safety during evacuation, and shall establish as soon as possible a list of the prisoners of war who are evacuated.

If prisoners of war must, during evacuation, pass through transit camps, their stay in such camps shall be as brief as possible.

SECTION II. INTERNMENT OF PRISONERS OF WAR

CHAPTER I. *General Observations*

Article 21. The Detaining Power may subject prisoners of war to internment. It may impose on them the obligation of not leaving, beyond certain limits, the camp where they are interned, or if the said camp is fenced in, of not going outside its perimeter. Subject to the provisions of the present Convention relative to penal and disciplinary sanctions, prisoners of war may not be held in close confinement except where necessary to safeguard their health and then only during the continuation of the circumstances which make such confinement necessary.

* * *

CHAPTER II. *Quarters, Food and Clothing of Prisoners of War*

Article 25. Prisoners of war shall be quartered under conditions as favourable as those for the forces of the Detaining Power who are billeted in the same area. The said conditions shall make allowance for the habits and customs of the prisoners and shall in no case be prejudicial to their health.

* * *

Article 26. The basic daily food rations shall be sufficient in quantity, quality and variety to keep prisoners of war in good health and to prevent loss of weight or the development of nutritional deficiencies. Account shall also be taken of the habitual diet of the prisoners.

The Detaining Power shall supply prisoners of war who work with such additional rations as are necessary for the labour on which they are employed.

Sufficient drinking water shall be supplied to prisoners of war. The use of tobacco shall be permitted.

* * *

Article 27. Clothing, underwear and footwear shall be supplied to prisoners of war in sufficient quantities by the Detaining Power, which shall make allowance for the climate of the region where the prisoners are detained.

* * *

CHAPTER III. *Hygiene and Medical Attention*

Article 29. The Detaining Power shall be bound to take all sanitary measures necessary to ensure the cleanliness and heathfulness of camps and to prevent epidemics.

Prisoners of war shall have for their use, day and night, conveniences which conform to the rules of hygiene and are maintained in a constant state of cleanliness. In any camps in which women prisoners of war are accommodated, separate conveniences shall be provided for them.

* * *

Article 30. Every camp shall have an adequate infirmary where prisoners of war may have the attention they require, as well as appropriate diet. Isolation wards shall, if necessary, be set aside for cases of contagious or mental disease.

Prisoners of war suffering from serious disease, or whose condition necessitates special treatment, a surgical operation or hospital care, must be admitted to any military or civil medical unit where such treatment can be given, even if their repatriation is contemplated in the near future. Special facilities shall be afforded for the care to be given to the disabled, in particular to the blind, and for their rehabilitation, pending repatriation.

* * *

CHAPTER IV. *Medical Personnel and Chaplains Retained to Assist Prisoners of War*

* * *

CHAPTER V. *Religious, Intellectual and Physical Activities*

Article 34. Prisoners of war shall enjoy complete latitude in the exercise of their religious duties, including attendance at the service of their faith, on condition that they comply with the disciplinary routine prescribed by the military authorities.

Adequate premises shall be provided where religious services may be held.

* * *

Article 38. While respecting the individual preferences of every prisoner, the Detaining Power shall encourage the practice of intellectual, educational, and recreational pursuits, sports and games amongst prisoners, and shall take the measures necessary to ensure the exercise thereof by providing them with adequate premises and necessary equipment.

Prisoners shall have opportunities for taking physical exercise including sports and games and for being out of doors. Sufficient open spaces shall be provided for this purpose in all camps.

CHAPTER VI. *Discipline*

* * *

Article 41. In every camp the text of the present Convention and its Annexes and the contents of any special agreement provided for in Article 6, shall be posted, in the prisoners' own language, in places where all may read them. Copies shall be supplied, on request, to the prisoners who cannot have access to the copy which has been posted.

Regulations, orders, notices and publications of every kind relating to the conduct of prisoners of war shall be issued to them in a language which they understand. Such regulations, orders and publications shall be posted in the manner described above and copies shall be handed to the prisoners' representative. Every order and command addressed to prisoners of war individually must likewise be given in a language which they understand.

Article 42. The use of weapons against prisoners of war, especially against those who are escaping or attempting to escape, shall constitute an extreme measure, which shall always be preceded by warnings appropriate to the circumstances.

CHAPTER VII. *Rank of Prisoners of War*

* * *

CHAPTER VIII. *Transfer of Prisoners of War After Their Arrival in Camp*

* * *

SECTION III. LABOUR OF PRISONERS OF WAR

Article 49. The Detaining Power may utilize the labour of prisoners of war who are physically fit, taking into account their age, sex, rank and physical aptitude, and with a view particularly to maintaining them in a good state of physical and mental health.

Non-commissioned officers who are prisoners of war shall only be required to do supervisory work. Those not so required may ask for other suitable work which shall, so far as possible, be found for them.

If officers or persons of equivalent status ask for suitable work, it shall be found for them, so far as possible, but they may in no circumstances be compelled to work.

* * *

SECTION IV. FINANCIAL RESOURCES OF PRISONERS OF WAR

* * *

SECTION V. RELATIONS OF PRISONERS OF WAR WITH THE EXTERIOR

* * *

Article 70. Immediately upon capture, or not more than one week after arrival at a camp, even if it is a transit camp, likewise in case of sickness or transfer to hospital or to another camp, every prisoner of war shall be enabled to write direct to his family, on the one hand, and to the Central Prisoners of War Agency provided for in Article 123, on the other hand, a card similar, if possible, to the model annexed to the present Convention, informing his relatives of his capture, address and state of health. The said cards shall be forwarded as rapidly as possible and may not be delayed in any manner.

Article 71. Prisoners of war shall be allowed to send and receive letters and cards. If the Detaining Power deems it necessary to limit the number of letters and cards sent by each prisoner of war, the said number shall not be less than two letters and four cards monthly, exclusive of the capture cards provided for in Article 70, and conforming as closely as possible to the models annexed to the present Convention. Further limitations may be imposed only if the Protecting Power is satisfied that it would be in the interests of the prisoners of war concerned to do so owing to difficulties of translation caused by the Detaining Power's inability to find sufficient qualified linguists to carry out the necessary censorship. If limitations must be placed on the correspondence addressed to prisoners of war, they may be ordered only by the Power on which the prisoners depend, possibly at the request of the Detaining Power. Such letters and cards must be conveyed by the most rapid method at the disposal of the Detaining Power; they may not be delayed or retained for disciplinary reasons.

Prisoners of war who have been without news for a long period, or who are unable to receive news from their next of kin or to give them news by the ordinary postal route, as well as those who are at a great distance from their homes, shall be permitted to send telegrams, the fees being charged against the prisoners of war's accounts with the Detaining Power or paid in the currency at their disposal. They shall likewise benefit by this measure in cases of urgency.

* * *

Article 72. Prisoners of war shall be allowed to receive by post or by any other means individual parcels or collective shipments containing, in particular, foodstuffs, clothing, medical supplies and articles of a religious, educational or recreational character which may meet their needs, including books, devotional articles, scientific equipment, examination papers, musical instruments, sports outfits and materials allowing prisoners of war to pursue their studies or their cultural activities.

Such shipments shall in no way free the Detaining Power from the obligations imposed upon it by virtue of the present Convention.

The only limits which may be placed on these shipments shall be those proposed by the Protecting Power in the interest of the prisoners themselves, or by the International Committee of the Red Cross or any other organization giving assistance to the prisoners, in respect of their own shipments only, on account of exceptional strain on transport or communications.

The conditions for the sending of individual parcels and collective relief shall, if necessary, be the subject of special agreements between the Powers concerned, which may in no case delay the receipt by the prisoners of relief supplies. Books may not be included in parcels of clothing and foodstuffs. Medical supplies shall, as a rule, be sent in collective parcels.

* * *

Article 77. The Detaining Powers shall provide all facilities for the transmission, through the Protecting Power or the Central Prisoners of War Agency provided for in Article 123, of instruments, papers or documents intended for prisoners of war or despatched by them, especially powers of attorney and wills.

In all cases they shall facilitate the preparation and execution of such documents on behalf of prisoners of war; in particular, they shall allow them to consult a lawyer and shall take what measures are necessary for the authentication of their signatures.

SECTION VI. RELATIONS BETWEEN PRISONERS OF WAR AND THE AUTHORITIES

CHAPTER I. *Complaints of Prisoners of War Respecting the Conditions of Captivity*

Article 78. Prisoners of war shall have the right to make known to the military authorities in whose power they are, their requests regarding the conditions of captivity to which they are subjected.

* * *

CHAPTER II. *Prisoner of War Representatives*

Article 79. In all places where there are prisoners of war, except in those where there are officers, the prisoners shall freely elect by secret ballot, every six months, and also in case of vacancies, prisoners' representatives entrusted with representing them before the military authorities, the Protecting Powers, the International Committee of the Red Cross and any other organization which may assist them. These prisoners' representatives shall be eligible for re-election.

* * *

CHAPTER III. *Penal and Disciplinary Sanctions*

* * *

Article 82. A prisoner of war shall be subject to the laws, regulations and orders in force in the armed forces of the Detaining Power; the Detaining Power shall be justified in taking judicial or disciplinary measures in respect of any offence committed by a prisoner of war against such laws, regulations or orders. However, no proceedings or punishments contrary to the provisions of this Chapter shall be allowed.

If any law, regulation or order of the Detaining Power shall declare acts committed by a prisoner of war to be punishable, whereas the same acts would not be punishable if committed by a member of the forces of the Detaining Power, such acts shall entail disciplinary punishments only.

* * *

PART IV. TERMINATION OF CAPTIVITY

SECTION I. DIRECT REPATRIATION AND ACCOMMODATION IN NEUTRAL COUNTRIES

Article 109. Subject to the provisions of the third paragraph of this Article, Parties to the conflict are bound to send back to their own country, regardless of number or rank, seriously wounded and seriously sick prisoners of war, after having cared for them until they are fit to travel, in accordance with the first paragraph of the following Article.

Throughout the duration of hostilities, Parties to the conflict shall endeavour, with the cooperation of the neutral Powers concerned, to make arrangements for the accommodation in neutral countries of the sick and wounded prisoners of war referred to in the second paragraph of the following Article. They may, in addition, conclude agreements with a view to the direct repatriation or internment in a neutral country of able-bodied prisoners of war who have undergone a long period of captivity.

No sick or injured prisoner of war who is eligible for repatriation under the first paragraph of this Article, may be repatriated against his will during hostilities.

Article 110. The following shall be repatriated direct:

(1) Incurably wounded and sick whose mental or physical fitness seems to have been gravely diminished.

(2) Wounded and sick who, according to medical opinion, are not likely to recover within one year, whose condition requires treatment and whose mental or physical fitness seems to have been gravely diminished.

(3) Wounded and sick who have recovered, but whose mental or physical fitness seems to have been gravely and permanently diminished.

The following may be accommodated in a neutral country:

(1) Wounded and sick whose recovery may be expected within one year of the date of the wound or the beginning of the illness, if treatment in a neutral country might increase the prospects of a more certain and speedy recovery.

(2) Prisoners of war whose mental or physical health, according to medical opinion, is seriously threatened by continued captivity, but whose accommodation in a neutral country might remove such a threat.

The conditions which prisoners of war accommodated in a neutral country must fulfil in order to permit their repatriation shall be fixed, as shall likewise their status, by agreement between the Powers concerned. In general, prisoners of war who have been accommodated in a neutral country, and who belong to the following categories, should be repatriated:

(1) those whose state of health has deteriorated so as to fulfil the conditions laid down for direct repatriation;

(2) those whose mental or physical powers remain, even after treatment, considerably impaired.

If no special agreements are concluded between the Parties to the conflict concerned, to determine the cases of disablement or sickness entailing direct repatriation or accommodation in a neutral country, such cases shall be settled in accordance with the principles laid down in the Model Agreement concerning direct repatriation and accommodation in neutral countries of wounded and sick prisoners of war and in the Regulations concerning Mixed Medical Commissions annexed to the present Convention.

* * *

SECTION II. RELEASE AND REPATRIATION OF PRISONERS OF WAR AT THE CLOSE OF HOSTILITIES

Article 118. Prisoners of war shall be released and repatriated without delay after the cessation of active hostilities.

* * *

SECTION III. DEATH OF PRISONERS OF WAR

Article 120. Wills of prisoners of war shall be drawn up so as to satisfy the conditions of validity required by the legislation of their country of origin, which will take steps to inform the Detaining Power of its requirements in this respect. At the request of the prisoner of war and, in all cases, after death, the will shall be transmitted without delay to the Protecting Power; a certified copy shall be sent to the Central Agency.

* * *

PART V. INFORMATION BUREAUX AND RELIEF SOCIETIES FOR PRISONERS OF WAR

* * *

Article 123. A Central Prisoners of War Information Agency shall be created in a neutral country. The International Committee of the Red Cross shall, if it deems necessary, propose to the Powers concerned the organization of such an Agency.

The function of the Agency shall be to collect all the information it may obtain through official or private channels respecting prisoners of war, and to transmit it as rapidly as possible to the country of origin of the prisoners of war or to the Power on which they depend. It shall receive from the Parties to the conflict all facilities for effecting such transmissions.

The High Contracting Parties, and in particular those whose nationals benefit by the services of the Central Agency, are requested to give the said Agency the financial aid it may require.

The foregoing provisions shall in no way be interpreted as restricting the humanitarian activities of the International Committee of the Red Cross, or of the relief societies provided for in Article 125.

* * *

Article 125. Subject to the measures which the Detaining Powers may consider essential to ensure their security or to meet any other reasonable need, the representatives of religious organizations, relief societies, or any other organization assisting prisoners of war, shall receive from the said Powers, for themselves and their duly accredited agents, all necessary facilities for visiting the prisoners, for distributing relief supplies and material, from any source, intended for religious, educational or recreative purposes, and for assisting them in organizing their leisure time within the camps. Such societies or organizations may be constituted in the territory of the

Detaining Power or in any other country, or they may have an international character.

* * *

[The remaining articles pertain mainly to the Convention's execution, ratification, and entry into force.]

2.13 CONVENTION RELATIVE TO THE PROTECTION OF CIVILIAN PERSONS IN TIME OF WAR.[a] Done at Geneva, Aug. 12, 1949. Entered into force, Oct. 21, 1950; for the United States, Feb. 2, 1956. 6 U.S.T. 3516, T.I.A.S. No. 3365, 75 U.N.T.S. 287

PART I. GENERAL PROVISIONS

[Note: *Articles 1–3 of Part I of this Convention are identical to Articles 1–3 of Chapter I in Basic Document 2.10, supra.*]

Article 4. Persons protected by the Convention are those who, at a given moment and in any manner whatsoever, find themselves, in case of a conflict or occupation, in the hands of a Party to the conflict or Occupying Power of which they are not nationals.

Nationals of a State which is not bound by the Convention are not protected by it. Nationals of a neutral State who find themselves in the territory of a belligerent State, and nationals of a co-belligerent State, shall not be regarded as protected persons while the State of which they are nationals has normal diplomatic representation in the State in whose hands they are.

The provisions of Part II are, however, wider in application, as defined in Article 13.

Persons protected by the Geneva Convention for the Amelioration of the Condition of the Wounded and Sick in Armed Forces in the Field of August 12, 1949, or by the Geneva Convention for the Amelioration of the Condition of Wounded, Sick and Shipwrecked Members of Armed Forces at Sea of August 12, 1949, or by the Geneva Convention relative to the Treatment of Prisoners of War of August 12, 1949, shall not be considered as protected persons within the meaning of the present Convention.

Article 5. Where, in the territory of a Party to the conflict, the latter is satisfied that an individual protected person is definitely suspected of or engaged in activities hostile to the security of the State, such individual person shall not be entitled to claim such rights and privileges under the present Convention as would, if exercised in the favour of such individual person, be prejudicial to the security of such State.

Where in occupied territory an individual protected person is detained as a spy or saboteur, or as a person under definite suspicion of activity hostile to the security of the Occupying Power, such person shall, in those cases where absolute military security so requires, be regarded as having forfeited rights of communication under the present Convention.

In each case, such persons shall nevertheless be treated with humanity, and in case of trial, shall not be deprived of the rights of fair and regular trial prescribed by the present Convention. They shall also be granted the full rights and privileges of a protected person under the present Convention at the earliest date consistent with the security of the State or Occupying Power, as the case may be.

Article 6. The present Convention shall apply from the outset of any conflict or occupation mentioned in Article 2.

In the territory of Parties to the conflict, the application of the present Convention shall cease on the general close of military operations.

In the case of occupied territory, the application of the present Convention shall cease one year after the general close of military operations; however, the Occupying

a. This Convention is supplemented and augmented by two additional protocols. *See* Basic Documents 2.33 and 2.34, *infra.*

Power shall be bound, for the duration of the occupation, to the extent that such Power exercises the functions of government in such territory, by the provisions of the following Articles of the present Convention: *1 to 12, 27, 29 to 34, 47, 49, 51, 52, 53, 59, 61 to 77, 143.*

Protected persons whose release, repatriation or re-establishment may take place after such dates shall meanwhile continue to benefit by the present Convention.

[Note: Except for language pertaining to civilian persons in time of war, Articles 7–12 of this Convention are identical to Articles 6–11 in Basic Document 2.10, supra.]

PART II. GENERAL PROTECTION OF POPULATIONS AGAINST CERTAIN CONSEQUENCES OF WAR

Article 13. The provisions of Part II cover the whole of the populations of the countries in conflict, without any adverse distinction based, in particular, on race, nationality, religion or political opinion, and are intended to alleviate the sufferings caused by war.

* * *

Article 15. Any Party to the conflict may, either direct or through a neutral State or some humanitarian organization, propose to the adverse Party to establish, in the regions where fighting is taking place, neutralized zones intended to shelter from the effects of war the following persons, without distinction:

(a) wounded and sick combatants or non-combatants;

(b) civilian persons who take no part in hostilities, and who, while they reside in the zones, perform no work of a military character.

When the Parties concerned have agreed upon the geographical position, administration, food supply and supervision of the proposed neutralized zone, a written agreement shall be concluded and signed by the representatives of the Parties to the conflict. The agreement shall fix the beginning and the duration of the neutralization of the zone.

Article 16. The wounded and sick, as well as the infirm, and expectant mothers, shall be the object of particular protection and respect.

As far as military considerations allow, each Party to the conflict shall facilitate the steps taken to search for the killed and wounded, to assist the shipwrecked and other persons exposed to grave danger, and to protect them against pillage and ill-treatment.

* * *

Article 18. Civilian hospitals organized to give care to the wounded and sick, the infirm and maternity cases, may in no circumstances be the object of attack, but shall at all times be respected and protected by the Parties to the conflict.

States which are Parties to a conflict shall provide all civilian hospitals with certificates showing that they are civilian hospitals and that the buildings which they occupy are not used for any purpose which would deprive these hospitals of protection in accordance with Article 19.

Civilian hospitals shall be marked by means of the emblem provided for in Article 38 of the Geneva Convention for the Amelioration of the Condition of the Wounded and Sick in Armed Forces in the Field of August 12, 1949, but only if so authorized by the State.

* * *

In view of the dangers to which hospitals may be exposed by being close to military objectives, it is recommended that such hospitals be situated as far as possible from such objectives.

Article 19. The protection to which civilian hospitals are entitled shall not cease unless they are used to commit, outside their humanitarian duties, acts harmful to the enemy. Protection may, however, cease only after due warning has been given, naming, in all appropriate cases, a reasonable time limit, and after such warning has remained unheeded.

The fact that sick or wounded members of the armed forces are nursed in these hospitals, or the presence of small arms and ammunition taken from such combatants and not yet handed to the proper service, shall not be considered to be acts harmful to the enemy.

Article 20. Persons regularly and solely engaged in the operation and administration of civilian hospitals, including the personnel engaged in the search for, removal and transporting of and caring for wounded and sick civilians, the infirm and maternity cases, shall be respected and protected.

* * *

Article 21. Convoys of vehicles or hospital trains on land or specially provided vessels on sea, conveying wounded and sick civilians, the infirm and maternity cases, shall be respected and protected in the same manner as the hospitals provided for in Article 18, and shall be marked, with the consent of the State, by the display of the distinctive emblem provided for in Article 38 of the Geneva Convention for the Amelioration of the Condition of the Wounded and Sick in Armed Forces in the Field of August 12, 1949.

Article 22. Aircraft exclusively employed for the removal of wounded and sick civilians, the infirm and maternity cases, or for the transport of medical personnel and equipment, shall not be attacked, but shall be respected while flying at heights, times and on routes specifically agreed upon between all the Parties to the conflict concerned.

* * *

Article 23. Each High Contracting Party shall allow the free passage of all consignments of medical and hospital stores and objects necessary for religious worship intended only for civilians of another High Contracting Party, even if the latter is its adversary. It shall likewise permit the free passage of all consignments of essential foodstuffs, clothing and tonics intended for children under fifteen, expectant mothers and maternity cases.

* * *

Article 24. The Parties to the conflict shall take the necessary measures to ensure that children under fifteen, who are orphaned or are separated from their families as a result of the war, are not left to their own resources, and that their maintenance, and exercise of their religion and their education are facilitated in all circumstances. Their education shall, as far as possible, be entrusted to persons of a similar cultural tradition.

* * *

The Parties to the conflict shall facilitate the reception of such children in a neutral country for the duration of the conflict with the consent of the Protecting Power, if any, and under due safeguards for the observance of the principles stated in the first paragraph.

They shall, furthermore, endeavour to arrange for all children under twelve to be identified by the wearing of identity discs, or by some other means.

Article 25. All persons in the territory of a Party to the conflict, or in a territory occupied by it, shall be enabled to give news of a strictly personal nature to members of their families, wherever they may be, and to receive news from them. This correspondence shall be forwarded speedily and without undue delay.

If, as a result of circumstances, it becomes difficult or impossible to exchange family correspondence by the ordinary post, the Parties to the conflict concerned shall apply to a neutral intermediary, such as the Central Agency provided for in Article 140, and shall decide in consultation with it how to ensure the fulfilment of their obligations under the best possible conditions, in particular with the cooperation of the National Red Cross (Red Crescent, Red Lion and Sun) Societies.

If the Parties to the conflict deem it necessary to restrict family correspondence, such restrictions shall be confined to the compulsory use of standard forms containing twenty-five freely chosen words, and to the limitation of the number of these forms despatched to one each month.

Article 26. Each Party to the conflict shall facilitate enquiries made by members of families dispersed owing to the war, with the object of renewing contact with one another and of meeting, if possible. It shall encourage, in particular, the work of organizations engaged on this task provided they are acceptable to it and conform to its security regulations.

PART III. STATUS AND TREATMENT OF PROTECTED PERSONS

SECTION I. PROVISIONS COMMON TO THE TERRITORIES OF THE PARTIES TO THE CONFLICT AND TO OCCUPIED TERRITORIES

Article 27. Protected persons are entitled, in all circumstances, to respect for their persons, their honour, their family rights, their religious convictions and practices, and their manners and customs. They shall at all times be humanely treated, and shall be protected especially against all acts of violence or threats thereof and against insults and public curiosity.

Women shall be especially protected against any attack on their honour, in particular against rape, enforced prostitution, or any form of indecent assault.

Without prejudice to the provisions relating to their state of health, age and sex, all protected persons shall be treated with the same consideration by the Party to the conflict in whose power they are, without any adverse distinction based, in particular, on race, religion or political opinion.

However, the Parties to the conflict may take such measures of control and security in regard to protected persons as may be necessary as a result of the war.

Article 28. The presence of a protected person may not be used to render certain points or areas immune from military operations.

Article 29. The Party to the conflict in whose hands protected persons may be, is responsible for the treatment accorded to them by its agents, irrespective of any individual responsibility which may be incurred.

Article 30. Protected persons shall have every facility for making application to the Protecting Powers, the International Committee of the Red Cross, the National Red Cross (Red Crescent, Red Lion and Sun) Society of the country where they may be, as well as to any organization that might assist them.

These several organizations shall be granted all facilities for that purpose by the authorities, within the bounds set by military or security considerations.

Apart from the visits of the delegates of the Protecting Powers and of the International Committee of the Red Cross, provided for by Article 143, the Detaining or Occupying Powers shall facilitate as much as possible visits to protected persons by the representatives of other organizations whose object is to give spiritual aid or material relief to such persons.

Article 31. No physical or moral coercion shall be exercised against protected persons, in particular to obtain information from them or from third parties.

Article 32. The High Contracting Parties specifically agree that each of them is prohibited from taking any measure of such a character as to cause the physical suffering or extermination of protected persons in their hands. This prohibition applies not only to murder, torture, corporal punishment, mutilation and medical or scientific experiments not necessitated by the medical treatment of a protected person, but also to any other measures of brutality whether applied by civilian or military agents.

Article 33. No protected person may be punished for an offence he or she has not personally committed. Collective penalties and likewise all measures of intimidation or of terrorism are prohibited.

Pillage is prohibited.

Reprisals against protected persons and their property are prohibited.

Article 34. The taking of hostages is prohibited.

SECTION II. ALIENS IN THE TERRITORY OF A PARTY TO THE CONFLICT

Article 35. All protected persons who may desire to leave the territory at the outset of, or during a conflict, shall be entitled to do so, unless their departure is contrary to the national interests of the State. The applications of such persons to leave shall be decided in accordance with regularly established procedures and the decision shall be taken as rapidly as possible. Those persons permitted to leave may provide themselves with the necessary funds for their journey and take with them a reasonable amount of their effects and articles of personal use.

* * *

SECTION III. OCCUPIED TERRITORIES

Article 47. Protected persons who are in occupied territory shall not be deprived, in any case or in any manner whatsoever, of the benefits of the present Convention by any change introduced, as the result of the occupation of a territory, into the institutions or government of the said territory, nor by any agreement concluded between the authorities of the occupied territories and the Occupying Power, nor by any annexation by the latter of the whole or part of the occupied territory.

Article 49. Individual or mass forcible transfers, as well as deportations of protected persons from occupied territory to the territory of the Occupying Power or to that of any other country, occupied or not, are prohibited, regardless of their motive.

Nevertheless, the Occupying Power may undertake total or partial evacuation of a given area if the security of the population or imperative military reasons so demand. Such evacuations may not involve the displacement of protected persons outside the bounds of the occupied territory except when for material reasons it is impossible to avoid such displacement. Persons thus evacuated shall be transferred back to their homes as soon as hostilities in the area in question have ceased.

The Occupying Power undertaking such transfers or evacuations shall ensure, to the greatest practicable extent, that proper accommodation is provided to receive the protected persons, that the removals are effected in satisfactory conditions of hygiene, health, safety and nutrition, and that members of the same family are not separated.

The Protecting Power shall be informed of any transfers and evacuations as soon as they have taken place.

The Occupying Power shall not detain protected persons in an area particularly exposed to the dangers of war unless the security of the population or imperative military reasons so demand.

The Occupying Power shall not deport or transfer parts of its own civilian population into the territory it occupies.

Article 50. The Occupying Power shall, with the cooperation of the national and local authorities, facilitate the proper working of all institutions devoted to the care and education of children.

The Occupying Power shall take all necessary steps to facilitate the identification of children and the registration of their parentage. It may not, in any case, change their personal status, nor enlist them in formations or organizations subordinate to it.

Should the local institutions be inadequate for the purpose, the Occupying Power shall make arrangements for the maintenance and education, if possible by persons of their own nationality, language and religion, of children who are orphaned or separated from their parents as a result of the war and who cannot be adequately cared for by a near relative or friend.

A special section of the Bureau set up in accordance with Article 136 shall be responsible for taking all necessary steps to identify children whose identity is in doubt. Particulars of their parents or other near relatives should always be recorded if available.

The Occupying Power shall not hinder the application of any preferential measures in regard to food, medical care and protection against the effects of war, which may have been adopted prior to the occupation in favour of children under fifteen years, expectant mothers, and mothers of children under seven years.

Article 51. The Occupying Power may not compel protected persons to serve in its armed or auxiliary forces. No pressure or propaganda which aims at securing voluntary enlistment is permitted.

The Occupying Power may not compel protected persons to work unless they are over eighteen years of age, and then only on work which is necessary either for the needs of the army of occupation, or for the public utility services, or for the feeding, sheltering, clothing, transportation or health of the population of the occupied country. Protected persons may not be compelled to undertake any work which would involve them in the obligation of taking part in military operations. The Occupying Power may not compel protected persons to employ forcible means to ensure the security of the installations where they are performing compulsory labour.

The work shall be carried out only in the occupied territory where the persons whose services have been requisitioned are. Every such person shall, so far as possible, be kept in his usual place of employment. Workers shall be paid a fair wage and the work shall be proportionate to their physical and intellectual capacities. The legislation in force in the occupied country concerning working conditions, and safeguards as regards, in particular, such matters as wages, hours of work, equipment, preliminary training and compensation for occupational accidents and diseases, shall be applicable to the protected persons assigned to the work referred to in this Article.

In no case shall requisition of labour lead to a mobilization of workers in an organization of a military or semi-military character.

* * *

Article 53. Any destruction by the Occupying Power of real or personal property belonging individually or collectively to private persons, or to the State, or to other public authorities, or to social or cooperative organizations, is prohibited, except where such destruction is rendered absolutely necessary by military operations.

Article 54. The Occupying Power may not alter the status of public officials or judges in the occupied territories, or in any way apply sanctions to or take any measures of coercion or discrimination against them, should they abstain from fulfilling their functions for reasons of conscience.

This prohibition does not prejudice the application of the second paragraph of Article 51. It does not affect the right of the Occupying Power to remove public officials from their posts.

Article 55. To the fullest extent of the means available to it, the Occupying Power has the duty of ensuring the food and medical supplies of the population; it should, in particular, bring in the necessary foodstuffs, medical stores and other articles if the resources of the occupied territory are inadequate.

The Occupying Power may not requisition foodstuffs, articles or medical supplies available in the occupied territory, except for use by the occupation forces and administration personnel, and then only if the requirements of the civilian population have been taken into account. Subject to the provisions of other international Conventions, the Occupying Power shall make arrangements to ensure that fair value is paid for any requisitioned goods.

The Protecting Power shall, at any time, be at liberty to verify the state of the food and medical supplies in occupied territories, except where temporary restrictions are made necessary by imperative military requirements.

Article 56. To the fullest extent of the means available to it, the Occupying Power has the duty of ensuring and maintaining, with the cooperation of national and local authorities, the medical and hospital establishments and services, public health and hygiene in the occupied territory, with particular reference to the adoption and application of the prophylactic and preventive measures necessary to combat the spread of contagious diseases and epidemics. Medical personnel of all categories shall be allowed to carry out their duties.

If new hospitals are set up in occupied territory and if the competent organs of the occupied State are not operating there, the occupying authorities shall, if necessary, grant them the recognition provided for in Article 18. In similar circumstances, the occupying authorities shall also grant recognition to hospital personnel and transport vehicles under the provisions of Articles 20 and 21.

In adopting measures of health and hygiene and in their implementation, the Occupying Power shall take into consideration the moral and ethical susceptibilities of the population of the occupied territory.

* * *

Article 58. The Occupying Power shall permit ministers of religion to give spiritual assistance to the members of their religious communities.

The Occupying Power shall also accept consignments of books and articles required for religious needs and shall facilitate their distribution in occupied territory.

Article 59. If the whole or part of the population of an occupied territory is inadequately supplied, the Occupying Power shall agree to relief schemes on behalf of the said population, and shall facilitate them by all the means at its disposal.

* * *

Article 63. Subject to temporary and exceptional measures imposed for urgent reasons of security by the Occupying Power:

(a) recognized National Red Cross (Red Crescent, Red Lion and Sun) Societies shall be able to pursue their activities in accordance with Red Cross principles, as defined by the International Red Cross Conferences. Other relief societies shall be permitted to continue their humanitarian activities under similar conditions;

(b) the Occupying Power may not require any changes in the personnel or structure of these societies, which would prejudice the aforesaid activities.

The same principles shall apply to the activities and personnel of special organizations of a non-military character, which already exist or which may be established, for the purpose of ensuring the living conditions of the civilian population by the maintenance of the essential public utility services, by the distribution of relief and by the organization of rescues.

Article 64. The penal laws of the occupied territory shall remain in force, with the exception that they may be repealed or suspended by the Occupying Power in cases where they constitute a threat to its security or an obstacle to the application of the present Convention. Subject to the latter consideration and to the necessity for ensuring the effective administration of justice, the tribunals of the occupied territory shall continue to function in respect of all offences covered by the said laws.

The Occupying Power may, however, subject the population of the occupied territory to provisions which are essential to enable the Occupying Power to fulfil its obligations under the present Convention, to maintain the orderly government of the territory, and to ensure the security of the Occupying Power, of the members and property of the occupying forces or administration, and likewise of the establishments and lines of communication used by them.

Article 65. The penal provisions enacted by the Occupying Power shall not come into force before they have been published and brought to the knowledge of the inhabitants in their own language. The effect of these penal provisions shall not be retroactive.

Article 66. In case of a breach of the penal provisions promulgated by it by virtue of the second paragraph of Article 64, the Occupying Power may hand over the accused to its properly constituted, non-political military courts, on condition that the said courts sit in the occupied country. Courts of appeal shall preferably sit in the occupied country.

Article 67. The courts shall apply only those provisions of law which were applicable prior to the offence, and which are in accordance with general principles of law, in particular the principle that the penalty shall be proportioned to the offence. They shall take into consideration the fact that the accused is not a national of the Occupying Power.

Article 68. Protected persons who commit an offence which is solely intended to harm the Occupying Power, but which does not constitute an attempt on the life or limb of members of the occupying forces or administration, nor a grave collective danger, nor seriously damage the property of the occupying forces or administration or the installations used by them, shall be liable to internment or simple imprisonment, provided the duration of such internment or imprisonment is proportionate to the offence committed. Furthermore, internment or imprisonment shall, for such offences, be the only measure adopted for depriving protected persons of liberty. The courts provided for under Article 66 of the present Convention may at their discretion convert a sentence of imprisonment to one of internment for the same period.

The penal provisions promulgated by the Occupying Power in accordance with Articles 64 and 65 may impose the death penalty on a protected person only in cases where the person is guilty of espionage, of serious acts of sabotage against the military installations of the Occupying Power or of intentional offences which have caused the death of one or more persons, provided that such offences were punishable by death under the law of the occupied territory in force before the occupation began.

The death penalty may not be pronounced against a protected person unless the attention of the court has been particularly called to the fact that since the accused is not a national of the Occupying Power, he is not bound to it by any duty of allegiance.

In any case, the death penalty may not be pronounced against a protected person who was under eighteen years of age at the time of the offence.

* * *

Article 71. No sentence shall be pronounced by the competent courts of the Occupying Power except after a regular trial.

Accused persons who are prosecuted by the Occupying Power shall be promptly informed, in writing, in a language which they understand, of the particulars of the charges preferred against them, and shall be brought to trial as rapidly as possible. The Protecting Power shall be informed of all proceedings instituted by the Occupying Power against protected persons in respect of charges involving the death penalty or imprisonment for two years or more; it shall be enabled, at any time, to obtain information regarding the state of such proceedings. Furthermore, the Protecting Power shall be entitled, on request, to be furnished with all particulars of these and of any other proceedings instituted by the Occupying Power against protected persons.

* * *

Article 72. Accused persons shall have the right to present evidence necessary to their defence and may, in particular, call witnesses. They shall have the right to be assisted by a qualified advocate or counsel of their own choice, who shall be able to visit them freely and shall enjoy the necessary facilities for preparing the defence.

* * *

Article 74. Representatives of the Protecting Power shall have the right to attend the trial of any protected person, unless the hearing has, as an exceptional measure, to be held *in camera* in the interests of the security of the Occupying Power, which shall then notify the Protecting Power. A notification in respect of the date and place of trial shall be sent to the Protecting Power.

* * *

Article 75. In no case shall persons condemned to death be deprived of the right of petition for pardon or reprieve.

No death sentence shall be carried out before the expiration of a period of at least six months from the date of receipt by the Protecting Power of the notification of the final judgment confirming such death sentence, or of an order denying pardon or reprieve.

The six months period of suspension of the death sentence herein prescribed may be reduced in individual cases in circumstances of grave emergency involving an organized threat to the security of the Occupying Power or its forces, provided always that the Protecting Power is notified of such reduction and is given reasonable time and opportunity to make representations to the competent occupying authorities in respect of such death sentences.

Article 76. Protected persons accused of offences shall be detained in the occupied country, and if convicted they shall serve their sentences therein. They shall, if possible, be separated from other detainees and shall enjoy conditions of food and hygiene which will be sufficient to keep them in good health, and which will be at least equal to those obtaining in prisons in the occupied country.

* * *

Article 77. Protected persons who have been accused of offences or convicted by the courts in occupied territory, shall be handed over at the close of occupation, with the relevant records, to the authorities of the liberated territory.

Article 78. If the Occupying Power considers it necessary, for imperative reasons of security, to take safety measures concerning protected persons, it may, at the most, subject them to assigned residence or to internment.

* * *

SECTION IV. REGULATIONS FOR THE TREATMENT OF INTERNEES

CHAPTER I. *General Provisions*

Article 79. The Parties to the conflict shall not intern protected persons, except in accordance with the provisions of Articles 41, 42, 43, 68 and 78.

Article 80. Internees shall retain their full civil capacity and shall exercise such attendant rights as may be compatible with their status.

Article 81. Parties to the conflict who intern protected persons shall be bound to provide free of charge for their maintenance, and to grant them also the medical attention required by their state of health.

No deduction from the allowances, salaries or credits due to the internees shall be made for the repayment of these costs.

The Detaining Power shall provide for the support of those dependent on the internees, if such dependents are without adequate means of support or are unable to earn a living.

Article 82. The Detaining Power shall, as far as possible, accommodate the internees according to their nationality, language and customs. Internees who are nationals of the same country shall not be separated merely because they have different languages.

* * *

CHAPTER II. *Places of Internment*

Article 83. The Detaining Power shall not set up places of internment in areas particularly exposed to the dangers of war.

The Detaining Power shall give the enemy Powers, through the intermediary of the Protecting Powers, all useful information regarding the geographical location of places of internment.

* * *

[Section IV of the Convention further provides for the treatment of civilian internees according to, inter alia, *the following categories: Food and Clothing (Ch. III); Hygiene and Medical Attention (Ch. IV); Religious, Intellectual, and Physical Activities (Ch. V); Personal Property and Financial Resources (Ch. VI); Administration and Discipline (Ch. VII); Relations with the Exterior (Ch. VIII); Penal and Disciplinary Sanctions (Ch. IX); Transfers of Internees (Ch. X). In addition, Section IV provides for the treatment of civilian internees in relation to Deaths (Ch. XI) and Release, Repatriation, and Accommodation in Neutral Countries (Ch. XII):]*

CHAPTER XI. *Deaths*

Article 129. The wills of internees shall be received for safe-keeping by the responsible authorities; and in the event of the death of an internee his will shall be transmitted without delay to a person whom he has previously designated.

Deaths of internees shall be certified in every case by a doctor, and a death certificate shall be made out, showing the causes of death and the conditions under which it occurred.

An official record of the death, duly registered, shall be drawn up in accordance with the procedure relating thereto in force in the territory where the place of internment is situated, and a duly certified copy of such record shall be transmitted without delay to the Protecting Power as well as to the Central Agency referred to in Article 140.

* * *

CHAPTER XII. *Release, Repatriation and Accommodation in Neutral Countries*

Article 132. Each interned person shall be released by the Detaining Power as soon as the reasons which necessitated his internment no longer exist.

* * *

Article 133. Internment shall cease as soon as possible after the close of hostilities.

* * *

SECTION V. INFORMATION BUREAUX AND CENTRAL AGENCY

* * *

Article 140. A Central Information Agency for protected persons, in particular for internees, shall be created in a neutral country. The International Committee of the Red Cross shall, if it deems necessary, propose to the Powers concerned the organization of such an Agency, which may be the same as that provided for in Article 123 of the Geneva Convention relative to the Treatment of Prisoners of War of August 12, 1949.

The function of the Agency shall be to collect all information of the type set forth in Article 136 which it may obtain through official or private channels and to transmit it as rapidly as possible to the countries of origin or of residence of the persons concerned, except in cases where such transmissions might be detrimental to the persons whom the said information concerns, or to their relatives. It shall receive from the Parties to the conflict all reasonable facilities for effecting such transmissions.

The High Contracting Parties, and in particular those whose nationals benefit by the services of the Central Agency, are requested to give the said Agency the financial aid it may require.

The foregoing provisions shall in no way be interpreted as restricting the humanitarian activities of the International Committee of the Red Cross and of the relief Societies described in Article 142.

* * *

[The remaining articles pertain mainly to the Convention's execution, ratification, and entry into force.]

2.14 UNITING FOR PEACE RESOLUTION. Adopted by the U.N. General Assembly, Nov. 3, 1950, U.N.G.A. Res. 337A(V), 5 U.N. GAOR Supp. (No. 20) 10, U.N. Doc. A/1775 (1951)

THE GENERAL ASSEMBLY,

* * *

Finding that international tension exists on a dangerous scale.

* * *

Reaffirming the importance of the exercise by the Security Council of its primary responsibility for the maintenance of international peace and security, and the duty of the permanent members to seek unanimity and to exercise restraint in the use of veto.

Reaffirming that the initiative in negotiating the agreements for armed forces provided for in Article 43 of the Charter belongs to the Security Council, and desiring to ensure that, pending the conclusion of such agreements, the United Nations has at its disposal means for maintaining international peace and security.

Conscious that failure of the Security Council to discharge its responsibilities on behalf of all the Member States, particularly those responsibilities referred to in the two preceding paragraphs, does not relieve Member States of their obligations or the United Nations of its responsibility under the Charter to maintain international peace and security.

Recognizing in particular that such failure does not deprive the General Assembly of its rights or relieve it of its responsibilities under the Charter in regard to the maintenance of international peace and security.

Recognizing that discharge by the General Assembly of its responsibilities in these respects calls for possibilities of observation which would ascertain the facts and expose aggressors; for the existence of armed forces which could be used collectively; and for the possibility of timely recommendation by the General Assembly to Members of the United Nations for collective action which, to be effective, should be prompt.

A.

1. Resolves that if the Security Council, because of lack of unanimity of the permanent members, fails to exercise its primary responsibility for the maintenance of international peace and security in any case where there appears to be a threat to the peace, breach of the peace or act of aggression, the General Assembly shall consider the matter immediately with a view to making appropriate recommendations to Members for collective measures, including in the case of a breach of the peace or act of aggression the use of armed force when necessary, to maintain or restore international peace and security. If not in session at the time, the General Assembly may meet in an emergency special session within twenty-four hours of the request therefor. Such emergency special session shall be called if requested by the Security Council on the vote of any seven members, or by a majority of the Members of the United Nations:

* * *

C.

7. Invites each Member of the United Nations to survey its resources in order to determine the nature and scope of the assistance it may be in a position to render in support of any recommendations of the Security Council or of the General Assembly for the restoration of international peace and security;

8. Recommends to the Members of the United Nations that each Member maintain within its national armed forces elements so trained, organized and equipped that they could promptly be made available, in accordance with its constitutional processes, for service as a United Nations unit or units, upon recommendation by the Security Council or General Assembly, without prejudice to the use of such elements in exercise of the right of individual or collective self-defence recognized in Article 51 of the Charter. * * *

* * *

2.15 DRAFT CODE OF CRIMES AGAINST THE PEACE AND SECURITY OF MANKIND.[a] Adopted by the U.N. International Law Commission in 1954, 2 Y.B. Int'l L. Comm. 150 (1954); revised in 1987, 1988 and 1989, U.N. Doc. A/42/420 (1987), U.N.Doc. A/CN.4/404 (1987), U.N. Doc. A/43/539 (1988), U.N. Doc. A/CN.4/419 (1989), and U.N. Doc. A/44/150 (1989)[b]

CHAPTER I
INTRODUCTION

PART I. Definition and characterization

Article 1
Definition

The crimes [under international law] defined in this draft Code constitute crimes against the peace and security of mankind.

Article 2
Characterization

The characterization of an act or omission as a crime against the peace and security of mankind is independent of internal law. The fact that an act or omission is or is not punishable under internal law does not affect this characterization.

PART II. General principles

Article 3
Responsibility and punishment

1. Any individual who commits a crime against the peace and security of mankind is responsible for such crime irrespective of any motives invoked by the accused that are not covered by the definition of the offence and is liable to punishment therefor.

2. Prosecution of an individual for a crime against the peace and security of mankind does not relieve a State of any responsibility under international law for an act or omission attributable to it.

Article 4
Obligation to try or extradite

1. Any State in whose territory an individual alleged to have committed a crime against the peace and security of mankind is present shall either try or extradite him.

2. If extradition is requested by several States, special consideration shall be given to the request of the State in whose territory the crime was committed.

3. The provisions of paragraphs 1 and 2 of this article do not prejudge the establishment and the jurisdiction of an international criminal court.

a. At the request of the U.N. General Assembly, the Draft Code is the subject of continuing study and revision.

b. *See also* Basic Documents 2.5 and 2.6, *supra*, and Basic Document 3.39, *infra*.

Article 5

Non-applicability of statutory limitations

No statutory limitation shall apply to crimes against the peace and security of mankind.

Article 6

Judicial guarantees

Any individual charged with a crime against the peace and security of mankind shall be entitled without discrimination to the minimum guarantees due to all human beings with regard to the law and the facts. In particular:

1. He shall have the right to be presumed innocent until proved guilty;

2. He shall have the right:

(a) In the determination of any charge against him, to have a fair and public hearing by a competent, independent and impartial tribunal duly established by law or by treaty;

(b) To be informed promptly and in detail in a language which he understands of the nature and cause of the charge against him;

(c) To have adequate time and facilities for the preparation of his defence and to communicate with counsel of his own choosing;

(d) To be tried without undue delay;

(e) To be tried in his presence, and to defend himself in person or through legal assistance of his own choosing; to be informed, if he does not have legal assistance, of this right; and to have legal assistance assigned to him and without payment by him in any such case if he does not have sufficient means to pay for it;

(f) To examine, or have examined, the witnesses against him and to obtain the attendance and examination of witnesses on his behalf under the same conditions as witnesses against him;

(g) To have the free assistance of an interpreter if he cannot understand or speak the language used in court;

(h) Not to be compelled to testify against himself or to confess guilt.

Article 7

[1. No one shall be liable to be tried or punished for a crime under this Code for which he has already been finally convicted or acquitted by an international criminal court.]

2. Subject to paragraphs 3, 4 and 5 of this article, no one shall be liable to be tried or punished for a crime under this Code in respect of an act for which he has already been finally convicted or acquitted by a national court, provided that, if a punishment was imposed, it has been enforced or is in the process of being enforced.

3. Notwithstanding the provisions of paragraph 2, an individual may be tried and punished [by an international criminal court or] by a national court for a crime under this Code if the act which was the subject of a trial and judgement as an ordinary crime corresponds to one of the crimes characterized in this Code.

4. Notwithstanding the provisions of paragraph 2, an individual may be tried and punished by a national court of another State for a crime under this Code:

(a) If the act which was the subject of the previous judgement took place on the territory of that State;

(b) If that State has been the main victim of the crime.

5. In the case of a subsequent conviction under this Code, the court, in passing sentence, shall deduct any penalty imposed and implemented as a result of a previous conviction for the same act.

Article 8

Non-retroactivity

1. No one shall be convicted under this Code for acts committed before its entry into force.

2. Nothing in this article shall preclude the trial and punishment of anyone for any act which, at the time when it was committed, was criminal in accordance with international law or domestic law applicable in conformity with international law.

* * *

Article 9

Exceptions to the principle of responsibility

The following constitute exceptions to criminal responsibility:

(a) Self-defence;

(b) Coercion, state of necessity or *force majeure;*

(c) An error of law or of fact, provided, in the circumstances in which it was committed, it was unavoidable for the perpetrator;

(d) The order of a Government or of a superior, provided a moral choice was in fact not possible to the perpetrator.

Article 10

Responsibility of the superior

The fact that a crime against the peace and security of mankind was committed by a subordinate does not relieve his superiors of criminal responsibility, if they knew or had information enabling them to conclude, in the circumstances at the time, that the subordinate was committing or was going to commit such a crime and if they did not take all feasible measures within their power to prevent or repress the crime.

Article 11

Official position and criminal responsibility

The official position of the individual who commits a crime against the peace and security of mankind, and particularly the fact that he acts as Head of State or Government, does not relieve him of criminal responsibility.

CHAPTER II

ACTS CONSTITUTING CRIMES AGAINST THE PEACE AND SECURITY OF MANKIND

PART I. Crimes against peace

Article 12

Aggression

1. Any individual to whom responsibility for acts constituting aggression is attributed under this Code shall be liable to be tried and punished for a crime against peace.

2. Aggression is the use of armed force by a State against the sovereignty, territorial integrity or political independence of another State, or in any other manner inconsistent with the Charter of the United Nations.

3. The first use of armed force by a State in contravention of the Charter shall constitute *prima facie* evidence of an act of aggression although the Security Council may, in conformity with the Charter, conclude that a determination that an act of aggression has been committed would not be justified in the light of other relevant circumstances, including the fact that the acts concerned or their consequences are not of sufficient gravity.

4. [In particular] any of the following acts, regardless of a declaration of war, constitutes an act of aggression, due regard being paid to paragraphs 2 and 3 of this article:

(a) The invasion or attack by the armed forces of a State of the territory of another State, or any military occupation, however temporary, resulting from such invasion or attack, or any annexation by the use of force of the territory of another State or part thereof;

(b) Bombardment by the armed forces of a State against the territory of another State or the use of any weapons by a State against the territory of another State;

(c) The blockade of the ports or coasts of a State by the armed forces of another State;

(d) An attack by the armed forces of a State on the land, sea or air forces, or marine and air fleets of another State;

(e) The use of armed forces of one State which are within the territory of another State with the agreement of the receiving State, in contravention of the conditions provided for in the agreement, or any extension of their presence in such territory beyond the termination of the agreement;

(f) The action of a State in allowing its territory, which it has placed at the disposal of another State, to be used by that other State for perpetrating an act of aggression against a third State;

(g) The sending by or on behalf of a State of armed bands, groups, irregulars or mercenaries, which carry out acts of armed force against another State of such gravity as to amount to the acts listed above, or its substantial involvement therein;

(h) Any other acts determined by the Security Council as constituting acts of aggression under the provisions of the Charter.

[5. Any determination by the Security Council as to the existence of an act of aggression is binding on national courts.]

6. Nothing in this article shall be interpreted as in any way enlarging or diminishing the scope of the Charter of the United Nations including its provisions concerning cases in which the use of force is lawful.

7. Nothing in this article could in any way prejudice the right to self-determination, freedom and independence, as derived from the Charter, of peoples forcibly deprived of that right and referred to in the Declaration on Principles of International Law concerning Friendly Relations and Co-operation among States in accordance with the Charter of the United Nations, particularly peoples under colonial and racist régimes or other forms of alien domination; nor the right of these peoples to struggle to that end and to seek and receive support, in accordance with the principles of the Charter and in conformity with the above-mentioned Declaration.

Article 13

Threat of aggression

Threat of aggression consisting of declarations, communications, demonstrations of force or any other measures which would give good reason to the Government of a State to believe that aggression is being seriously contemplated against that State.

Article 14

Intervention

1. Intervention in the internal or external affairs of a State by fomenting [armed] subversive or terrorist activities or by organizing, assisting or financing such activities, or supplying arms for the purpose of such activities, thereby [seriously] undermining the free exercise by that State of its sovereign rights.

2. Nothing in this article shall in any way prejudice the right of peoples to self-determination as enshrined in the Charter of the United Nations.

Article 15

Colonial domination and other forms of alien domination

Establishment or maintenance by force of colonial domination or any other form of alien domination contrary to the right of peoples to self-determination as enshrined in the Charter of the United Nations.

2.16 TREATY OF FRIENDSHIP, COOPERATION AND MUTUAL ASSISTANCE.[a] Done at Warsaw, May 14, 1955. Entered into force, Oct. 10, 1955. 219 U.N. T.S. 3

The Contracting Parties, reaffirming their desire for the establishment of a system of European collective security based on the participation of all European states irrespective of their social and political systems, which would make it possible to unite their efforts in safeguarding the peace of Europe; mindful, at the same time, of the situation created in Europe by the ratification of the Paris agreements, which envisage the formation of a new military alignment in the shape of "Western European Union," with the participation of a remilitarized Western Germany and the integration of the latter in the North–Atlantic bloc, which increases the danger of another war and constitutes a threat to the national security of the peaceable states; being persuaded that in these circumstances the peaceable European states must take the necessary measures to safeguard their security and in the interests of preserving peace in Europe; guided by the objects and principles of the Charter of the United Nations Organization; being desirous of further promoting and developing friendship, co-operation and mutual assistance in accordance with the principles of respect for the independence and sovereignty of states and of noninterference in their internal affairs, have decided to conclude the present Treaty of Friendship, Cooperation and Mutual Assistance and have for that purpose appointed . . . their plenipotentiaries . . . who, having presented their full powers, found in good and due form, have agreed as follows:

Article 1. The Contracting Parties undertake, in accordance with the Charter of the United Nations Organization, to refrain in their international relations from the threat or use of force, and to settle their international disputes peacefully and in such manner as will not jeopardize international peace and security.

Article 2. The Contracting Parties declare their readiness to participate in a spirit of sincere cooperation in all international actions designed to safeguard international peace and security, and will fully devote their energies to the attainment of this end.

The Contracting Parties will furthermore strive for the adoption, in agreement with other states which may desire to cooperate in this, of effective measures for universal reduction of armaments and prohibition of atomic, hydrogen and other weapons of mass destruction.

Article 3. The Contracting Parties shall consult with one another on all important international issues affecting their common interests, guided by the desire to strengthen international peace and security.

They shall immediately consult with one another whenever, in the opinion of any one of them, a threat of armed attack on one or more of the Parties to the Treaty has arisen, in order to ensure joint defence and the maintenance of peace and security.

Article 4. In the event of armed attack in Europe on one or more of the Parties to the Treaty by any state or group of states, each of the Parties to the Treaty, in the exercise of its right to individual or collective self-defence in accordance with Article 51 of the Charter of the United Nations Organization, shall immediately, either individually or in agreement with other Parties to the Treaty, come to the assistance of the state or states attacked with all such means as it deems necessary, including armed force. The Parties to the Treaty shall immediately consult concerning the

a. Also known as "the Warsaw Pact".

necessary measures to be taken by them jointly in order to restore and maintain international peace and security.

Measures taken on the basis of this Article shall be reported to the Security Council in conformity with the provisions of the Charter of the United Nations Organization. These measures shall be discontinued immediately as the Security Council adopts the necessary measures to restore and maintain international peace and security.

Article 5. The Contracting Parties have agreed to establish a Joint Command of the armed forces that by agreement among the Parties shall be assigned to the Command, which shall function on the basis of jointly established principles. They shall likewise adopt other agreed measures necessary to strengthen their defensive power, in order to protect the peaceful labours of their peoples, guarantee the inviolability of their frontiers and territories, and provide defence against possible aggression.

Article 6. For the purpose of the consultations among the Parties envisaged in the present Treaty, and also for the purpose of examining questions which may arise in the operation of the Treaty, a Political Consultative Committee shall be set up, in which each of the Parties to the Treaty shall be represented by a member of its Government or by another specifically appointed representative.

The Committee may set up such auxiliary bodies as may prove necessary.

* * *

Article 8. The Contracting Parties declare that they will act in a spirit of friendship and cooperation with a view to further developing and fostering economic and cultural intercourse with one another, each adhering to the principle of respect for the independence and sovereignty of the others and non-interference in their internal affairs.

* * *

2.17 DECLARATION ON THE PROHIBITION OF THE USE OF NUCLEAR AND THERMO-NUCLEAR WEAPONS.[a] Adopted by the U.N. General Assembly, Nov. 24, 1961. U.N.G.A.Res. 1653 (XVI), 16 U.N. GAOR, Supp. (No. 17) at 4, U.N.Doc. A/5100 (1961).

The General Assembly,

Mindful of its responsibility under the Charter of the United Nations in the maintenance of international peace and security, as well as in the consideration of principles governing disarmament,

Gravely concerned that, while negotiations on disarmament have not so far achieved satisfactory results, the armaments race, particularly in the nuclear and thermo-nuclear fields, has reached a dangerous stage requiring all possible precautionary measures to protect humanity and civilization from the hazard of nuclear and thermo-nuclear catastrophe,

Recalling that the use of weapons of mass destruction, causing unnecessary human suffering, was in the past prohibited, as being contrary to the laws of humanity and to the principles of international law, by international declarations and binding agreements, such as the Declaration of St. Petersburg of 1868, the Declaration of the Brussels Conference of 1874, the Conventions of The Hague Peace Conferences of 1899 and 1907, and the Geneva Protocol of 1925, to which the majority of nations are still parties,

Considering that the use of nuclear and thermo-nuclear weapons would bring about indiscriminate suffering and destruction to mankind and civilization to an even greater extent than the use of those weapons declared by the aforementioned international declarations and agreements to be contrary to the laws of humanity and a crime under international law,

Believing that the use of weapons of mass destruction, such as nuclear and thermo-nuclear weapons, is a direct negation of the high ideals and objectives which the United Nations has been established to achieve through the protection of succeeding generations from the scourge of war and through the preservation and promotion of their cultures,

1. *Declares* that:

(a) The use of nuclear and thermo-nuclear weapons is contrary to the spirit, letter and aims of the United Nations and, as such, a direct violation of the Charter of the United Nations;

(b) The use of nuclear and thermo-nuclear weapons would exceed even the scope of war and cause indiscriminate suffering and destruction to mankind and civilization and, as such, is contrary to the rules of international law and to the laws of humanity;

(c) The use of nuclear and thermo-nuclear weapons is a war directed not against an enemy or enemies alone but also against mankind in general, since the peoples of the world not involved in such a war will be subjected to all the evils generated by the use of such weapons;

(d) Any State using nuclear and thermo-nuclear weapons is to be considered as violating the Charter of the United Nations, as acting contrary to the laws of humanity and as committing a crime against mankind and civilization.

a. *See also* Basic Documents 2.29 and 2.36, *infra.*

2. *Requests* the Secretary–General to consult the Governments of Member States to ascertain their views on the possibility of convening a special conference for signing a convention on the prohibition of the use of nuclear and thermo-nuclear weapons for war purposes and to report on the results of such consultation to the General Assembly at its seventeenth session.

2.18 TREATY BANNING NUCLEAR WEAPONS TESTS IN THE ATMOSPHERE, IN OUTER SPACE AND UNDER WATER.[a] Done at Moscow, Aug. 5, 1963. Entered into force, Oct. 10, 1963; for the United States, Oct. 10, 1963. 14 U.S.T. 1313, T.I.A.S. No. 5433, 480 U.N.T.S. 43, *reprinted in* 2 I.L.M. 889 (1963)

ARTICLE I

1. Each of the Parties to this Treaty undertakes to prohibit, to prevent, and not to carry out any nuclear weapon test explosion, or any other nuclear explosion, at any place under its jurisdiction or control:

(a) in the atmosphere; beyond its limits, including outer space; or underwater, including territorial waters or high seas; or

(b) in any other environment if such explosion causes radioactive debris to be present outside the territorial limits of the State under whose jurisdiction or control such explosion is conducted. It is understood in this connection that the provisions of this subparagraph are without prejudice to the conclusion of a treaty resulting in the permanent banning of all nuclear test explosions, including all such explosions underground, the conclusion of which, as the Parties have stated in the Preamble to this Treaty, they seek to achieve.

2. Each of the Parties to this Treaty undertakes furthermore to refrain from causing, encouraging, or in any way participating in, the carrying out of any nuclear weapon test explosion, or any other nuclear explosion, anywhere which would take place in any of the environments described, or have the effect referred to, in paragraph 1 of this Article.

ARTICLE II

1. Any Party may propose amendments to this Treaty. The text of any proposed amendment shall be submitted to the Depositary Governments which shall circulate it to all Parties to this Treaty. Thereafter, if requested to do so by one-third or more of the Parties, the Depositary Governments shall convene a conference, to which they shall invite all the Parties, to consider such amendment.

2. Any amendment to this Treaty must be approved by a majority of the votes of all the Parties to this Treaty, including the votes of all of the Original Parties. The amendment shall enter into force for all Parties upon the deposit of instruments of ratification by a majority of all the Parties, including the instruments of ratification of all of the Original Parties.

ARTICLE III

1. This Treaty shall be open to all States for signature. Any State which does not sign this Treaty before its entry into force in accordance with paragraph 3 of this Article may accede to it at any time.

2. This Treaty shall be subject to ratification by signatory States. Instruments of ratification and instruments of accession shall be deposited with the Governments of the Original Parties—the United States of America, the United Kingdom of Great Britain and Northern Ireland, and the Union of Soviet Socialist Republics—which are hereby designated the Depositary Governments.

a. Also known as "the Nuclear Test Ban Treaty" or "the Partial Test Ban (PTB) Treaty."

3. This Treaty shall enter into force after its ratification by all the Original Parties and the deposit of their instruments of ratification.

4. For States whose instruments of ratification or accession are deposited subsequent to the entry into force of this Treaty, it shall enter into force on the date of the deposit of their instruments of ratification or accession.

* * *

ARTICLE IV

This Treaty shall be of unlimited duration.

Each Party shall in exercising its national sovereignty have the right to withdraw from the Treaty if it decides that extraordinary events, related to the subject matter of this Treaty, have jeopardized the supreme interests of its country. It shall give notice of such withdrawal to all other Parties to the Treaty three months in advance.

* * *

2.19 RESOLUTION REGARDING WEAPONS OF MASS DESTRUCTION IN OUTER SPACE. Adopted by the U.N. General Assembly, Oct. 17, 1963. U.N.G.A. Res. 1884 (XVIII), 18 U.N. GAOR, Supp. (No. 15) 13, U.N.Doc. A/5515 (1964), *reprinted in* 2 I.L.M. 1192 (1963)

THE GENERAL ASSEMBLY,

Recalling its resolution 1721 A(XVI) of 20 December 1961, in which it expressed the belief that the exploration and use of outer space should be only for the betterment of mankind.

Determined to take steps to prevent the spread of the arms race to outer space.

1. *Welcomes* the expressions by the Union of Soviet Socialist Republics and the United States of America of their intention not to station in outer space any objects carrying nuclear weapons or other kinds of weapons of mass destruction:

2. *Solemnly calls upon* all States:

(a) To refrain from placing in orbit around the earth any objects carrying nuclear weapons or any other kinds of weapons of mass destruction, installing such weapons on celestial bodies, or stationing such weapons in outer space in any other manner;

(b) To refrain from causing, encouraging or in any way participating in the conduct of the foregoing activities.

2.20 DECLARATION ON THE INADMISSABILITY OF INTERVENTION IN THE DOMESTIC AFFAIRS OF THE STATES AND THE PROTECTION OF THEIR INDEPENDENCE AND SOVEREIGNTY. Adopted by the U.N. General Assembly, Dec. 21, 1965. U.N.G.A. Res. 2131 (XX), 20 U.N. GAOR, Supp. (No. 14) 11, U.N. Doc. A/6014, (1966), *reprinted in* 5 I.L.M. 374 (1966)

THE GENERAL ASSEMBLY,

Deeply concerned at the gravity of the international situation and the increasing threat to universal peace due to armed intervention and other direct or indirect forms of interference threatening the sovereign personality and the political independence of States,

Considering that the United Nations, in accordance with their aim to eliminate war, threats to the peace and acts of aggression, created an Organization, based on the sovereign equality of States, whose friendly relations would be based on respect for the principle of equal rights and self-determination of peoples and on the obligation of its Members to refrain from the threat or use of force against the territorial integrity or political independence of any State,

Recognizing that, in fulfilment of the principle of self-determination, the General Assembly, in the Declaration on the Granting of Independence to Colonial Countries and Peoples contained in resolution 1514 (XV) of 14 December 1960, stated its conviction that all peoples have an inalienable right to complete freedom, the exercise of their sovereignty and the integrity of their national territory, and that, by virtue of that right, they freely determine their political status and freely pursue their economic, social and cultural development,

Recalling that in the Universal Declaration of Human Rights the General Assembly proclaimed that recognition of the inherent dignity and of the equal and inalienable rights of all members of the human family is the foundation of freedom, justice and peace in the world, without distinction of any kind,

Reaffirming the principle of non-intervention, proclaimed in the charters of the Organization of American States, the League of Arab States and the Organization of African Unity and affirmed at the conferences held at Montevideo, Buenos Aires, Chapultepec and Bogotá, as well as in the decisions of the Asian–African Conference at Bandung, the First Conference of Heads of State or Government of Non–Aligned Countries at Belgrade, in the Programme for Peace and International Co-operation adopted at the end of the Second Conference of Heads of State or Government of Non–Aligned Countries at Cairo, and in the declaration on subversion adopted at Accra by the Heads of State and Government of the African States,

Recognizing that full observance of the principle of the non-intervention of States in the internal and external affairs of other States is essential to the fulfilment of the purposes and principles of the United Nations,

Considering that armed intervention is synonymous with aggression and, as such, is contrary to the basic principles on which peaceful international co-operation between States should be built,

Considering further that direct intervention, subversion and all forms of indirect intervention are contrary to these principles and, and, consequently, constitute a violation of the Charter of the United Nations,

Mindful that violation of the principle of non-intervention poses a threat to the independence, freedom and normal political, economic, social and cultural development of countries, particularly those which have freed themselves from colonialism, and can pose a serious threat to the maintenance of peace,

Fully aware of the imperative need to create appropriate conditions which would enable all States, and in particular the developing countries, to choose without duress or coercion their own political, economic and social institutions,

In the light of the foregoing considerations, solemnly declares:

1. No State has the right to intervene, directly or indirectly, for any reason whatever, in the internal or external affairs of any other State. Consequently, armed intervention and all other forms of interference or attempted threats against the personality of the State or against its political, economic and cultural elements, are condemned.

2. No State may use or encourage the use of economic, political or any other type of measures to coerce another State in order to obtain from it the subordination of the exercise of its sovereign rights or to secure from it advantages of any kind. Also, no State shall organize, assist, foment, finance, incite or tolerate subversive, terrorist or armed activities directed towards the violent overthrow of the régime of another State, or interfere in civil strife in another State.

3. The use of force to deprive peoples of their national identity constitutes a violation of their inalienable rights and of the principle of non-intervention.

4. The strict observance of these obligations is an essential condition to ensure that nations live together in peace with one another, since the practice of any form of intervention not only violates the spirit and letter of the Charter of the United Nations but also leads to the creation of situations which threaten international peace and security.

5. Every State has an inalienable right to choose its political, economic, social and cultural systems, without interference in any form by another State.

6. All States shall respect the right of self-determination and independence of peoples and nations, to be freely exercised without any foreign pressure, and with absolute respect to human rights and fundamental freedoms. Consequently, all States shall contribute to the complete elimination of racial discrimination and colonialism in all its forms and manifestations.

7. For the purpose of the present Declaration, the term "State" covers both individual States and groups of States.

8. Nothing in this Declaration shall be construed as affecting in any manner the relevant provisions of the Charter of the United Nations relating to the maintenance of international peace and security, in particular those contained in Chapters VI, VII and VIII.

2.21 TREATY FOR THE PROHIBITION OF NUCLEAR WEAPONS IN LATIN AMERICA.[a] Done at Mexico (Federal District), Feb. 14, 1967. Entered into force for twenty-two Latin American States as of Dec. 31, 1979, 634 U.N.T.S. 281, *reprinted in* 6 I.L.M. 521 (1967)[b]

ARTICLE 1. OBLIGATIONS

1. The Contracting Parties hereby undertake to use exclusively for peaceful purposes the nuclear material and facilities which are under their jurisdiction, and to prohibit and prevent in their respective territories:

(a) The testing, use, manufacture, production or acquisition by any means whatsoever of any nuclear weapons, by the Parties themselves, directly or indirectly, on behalf of anyone else or in any other way, and

(b) The receipt, storage, installation, deployment and any form of possession of any nuclear weapons, directly or indirectly, by the Parties themselves, by anyone on their behalf or in any other way.

2. The Contracting Parties also undertake to refrain from engaging in, encouraging or authorizing, directly or indirectly, or in any way participating in the testing, use, manufacture, production, possession or control of any nuclear weapon.

ARTICLE 2. DEFINITION OF THE CONTRACTING PARTIES

For the purposes of this Treaty, the Contracting Parties are those for whom the Treaty is in force.

ARTICLE 3. DEFINITION OF TERRITORY

For the purposes of this Treaty, the term "territory" shall include the territorial sea, air space and any other space over which the State exercises sovereignty in accordance with its own legislation.

ARTICLE 4. ZONE OF APPLICATION

1. The zone of application of this Treaty is the whole of the territories for which the Treaty is in force.

2. Upon fulfilment of the requirements of article 28, paragraph 1, the zone of application of this Treaty shall also be that which is situated in the western hemisphere within the following limits (except the continental part of the territory of the United States of America and its territorial waters): starting at a point located at 35° north latitude, 75° west longitude; from this point directly southward to a point at 30° north latitude, 75° west longitude; from there, directly eastward to a point at 30° north latitude, 50° west longitude; from there, along a loxodromic line to a point at 5° north latitude, 20° west longitude; from there, directly southward to a point at 60° south latitude, 20° west longitude; from there, directly westward to a point at 60°

a. This treaty, also known as "the Treaty of Tlatelolco", incorporates two protocols included here: Additional Protocol I, which is intended to commit States having territorial interests in the Americas (i.e., France, the Netherlands, the United Kingdom, and the United States); and Additional Protocol II, which is intended to commit nuclear-weapon States whether or not situated in the Americas. The United States has ratified Protocols I and II, subject to certain "understandings" and "declarations" also included here. *See* T.I.A.S. No. 10147, 637 U.N.T.S. 360, *reprinted in* 6 I.L.M. 533 (Protocol I) and 22 U.S.T. 754, T.I.A.S. No. 7137, 634 U.N.T.S. 364 (Protocol II), *reprinted in* 6 I.L.M. 534 (1967).

b. *See also* Basic Document 2.38, *infra.*

south latitude, 115° west longitude; from there, directly northward to a point at 0 latitude, 115° west longitude; from there, along a loxodromic line to a point at 35° north latitude, 150° west longitude; from there, directly eastward to a point at 35° north latitude, 75° west longitude.

ARTICLE 5. DEFINITION OF NUCLEAR WEAPONS

For the purposes of this Treaty, a nuclear weapon is any device which is capable of releasing nuclear energy in an uncontrolled manner and which has a group of characteristics that are appropriate for use for warlike purposes. An instrument that may be used for the transport or propulsion of the device is not included in this definition if it is separable from the device and not an indivisible part thereof.

ARTICLE 6. MEETING OF SIGNATORIES

At the request of any of the signatory States or if the Agency established by article 7 should so decide, a meeting of all the signatories may be convoked to consider in common questions which may affect the very essence of this instrument, including possible amendments to it. In either case, the meeting will be convoked by the General Secretary.

[*Note: Articles 7–11 provide for the establishment and operation of an international organization (the "Agency for the Prohibition of Nuclear Weapons in Latin America") designed to ensure compliance with the Treaty and composed of a General Conference, a Council, and a Secretariat.*]

ARTICLE 12. CONTROL SYSTEM

1. For the purpose of verifying compliance with the obligations entered into by the Contracting Parties in accordance with article 1, a control system shall be established which shall be put into effect in accordance with the provisions of articles 13–18 of this Treaty.

2. The control system shall be used in particular for the purpose of verifying:

(a) That devices, services and facilities intended for peaceful uses of nuclear energy are not used in the testing or manufacture of nuclear weapons;

(b) That none of the activities prohibited in article 1 of this Treaty are carried out in the territory of the Contracting Parties with nuclear materials or weapons introduced from abroad, and

(c) That explosions for peaceful purposes are compatible with article 18 of this Treaty.

ARTICLE 13. IAEA SAFEGUARDS

Each Contracting Party shall negotiate multilateral or bilateral agreements with the International Atomic Energy Agency for the application of its safeguards to its nuclear activities. Each Contracting Party shall initiate negotiations within a period of 180 days after the date of the deposit of its instrument of ratification of this Treaty. These agreements shall enter into force, for each Party, not later than eighteen months after the date of the initiation of such negotiations except in case of unforeseen circumstances or *force majeure.*

ARTICLE 14. REPORTS OF THE PARTIES

1. The Contracting Parties shall submit to the Agency and to the International Atomic Energy Agency, for their information, semi-annual reports stating that no activity prohibited under this Treaty has occurred in their respective territories.

2. The Contracting Parties shall simultaneously transmit to the Agency a copy of any report they may submit to the International Atomic Energy Agency which relates to matters that are the subject of this Treaty and to the application of safeguards.

3. The Contracting Parties shall also transmit to the Organization of American States, for its information, any reports that may be of interest to it, in accordance with the obligations established by the Inter-American System.

ARTICLE 15. SPECIAL REPORTS REQUESTED BY THE GENERAL SECRETARY

1. With the authorization of the Council, the General Secretary may request any of the Contracting Parties to provide the Agency with complementary or supplementary information regarding any event or circumstance connected with compliance with this Treaty, explaining his reasons. The Contracting Parties undertake to co-operate promptly and fully with the General Secretary.

2. The General Secretary shall inform the Council and the Contracting Parties forthwith of such requests and of the respective replies.

ARTICLE 16. SPECIAL INSPECTIONS

1. The International Atomic Energy Agency and the Council established by this Treaty have the power of carrying out special inspections in [certain] cases * * *.

* * *

4. The Contracting Parties undertake to grant the inspectors carrying out such special inspections full and free access to all places and all information which may be necessary for the performance of their duties and which are directly and intimately connected with the suspicion of violation of this Treaty. If so requested by the authorities of the Contracting Party in whose territory the inspection is carried out, the inspectors designated by the General Conference shall be accompanied by representatives of said authorities, provided that this does not in any way delay or hinder the work of the inspectors.

* * *

ARTICLE 17. USE OF NUCLEAR ENERGY FOR PEACEFUL PURPOSES

Nothing in the provisions of this Treaty shall prejudice the rights of the Contracting Parties, in conformity with this Treaty, to use nuclear energy for peaceful purposes, in particular for their economic development and social progress.

ARTICLE 18. EXPLOSIONS FOR PEACEFUL PURPOSES

1. The Contracting Parties may carry out explosions of nuclear devices for peaceful purposes—including explosions which involve devices similar to those used in nuclear weapons—or collaborate with third parties for the same purpose, provided that they do so in accordance with the provisions of this article and the other articles of the Treaty, particularly articles 1 and 5.

2. Contracting Parties intending to carry out, or to co-operate in carrying out, such an explosion shall notify the Agency and the International Atomic Energy Agency, as far in advance as the circumstances require, of the date of the explosion and shall at the same time provide the following information:

(a) The nature of the nuclear device and the source from which it was obtained;

(b) The place and purpose of the planned explosion;

(c) The procedures which will be followed in order to comply with paragraph 3 of this article;

(d) The expected force of the device, and

(e) The fullest possible information on any possible radioactive fall-out that may result from the explosion or explosions, and measures which will be taken to avoid danger to the population, flora, fauna and territories of any other Party or Parties.

3. The General Secretary and the technical personnel designated by the Council and the International Atomic Energy Agency may observe all the preparations, including the explosion of the device, and shall have unrestricted access to any area in the vicinity of the site of the explosion in order to ascertain whether the device and the procedures followed during the explosion are in conformity with the information supplied under paragraph 2 of this article and the other provisions of this Treaty.

4. The Contracting Party may accept the collaboration of third parties for the purpose set forth in paragraph 1 of the present article, in accordance with paragraphs 2 and 3 thereof.

* * *

ARTICLE 20. MEASURES IN THE EVENT OF VIOLATION OF THE TREATY

1. The General Conference shall take note of all cases in which, in its opinion, any Contracting Party is not complying fully with its obligations under this Treaty and shall draw the matter to the attention of the Party concerned, making such recommendations as it deems appropriate.

2. If, in its opinion, such non-compliance constitutes a violation of this Treaty which might endanger peace and security, the General Conference shall report thereon simultaneously to the United Nations Security Council and the General Assembly through the Secretary–General of the United Nations, and to the Council of the Organization of American States. The General Conference shall likewise report to the International Atomic Energy Agency for such purposes as are relevant in accordance with its Statute.

* * *

ARTICLE 22. PRIVILEGES AND IMMUNITIES

1. The Agency shall enjoy in the territory of each of the Contracting Parties such legal capacity and such privileges and immunities as may be necessary for the exercise of its functions and the fulfilment of its purposes.

2. Representatives of the Contracting Parties accredited to the Agency and officials of the Agency shall similarly enjoy such privileges and immunities as are necessary for the performance of their functions.

* * *

ARTICLE 25. SIGNATURE

1. This Treaty shall be open indefinitely for signature by:

(a) All the Latin American Republics, and

(b) All other sovereign States situated in their entirety south of latitude 35° north in the western hemisphere; and, except as provided in paragraph 2 of this article, all such States which become sovereign, when they have been admitted by the General Conference.

2. The General Conference shall not take any decision regarding the admission of a political entity part or all of whose territory is the subject, prior to the date when this Treaty is opened for signature, of a dispute or claim between an extra-continental country and one or more Latin American States, so long as the dispute has not been settled by peaceful means.

* * *

ARTICLE 27. RESERVATIONS

This Treaty shall not be subject to reservations.

ARTICLE 28. ENTRY INTO FORCE

1. Subject to the provisions of paragraph 2 of this article, this Treaty shall enter into force among the States that have ratified it as soon as the following requirements have been met:

(a) Deposit of the instruments of ratification of this Treaty with the Depositary Government by the Governments of the States mentioned in article 25 which are in existence on the date when this Treaty is opened for signature and which are not affected by the provisions of article 25, paragraph 2;

(b) Signature and ratification of Additional Protocol I annexed to this Treaty by all extra-continental or continental States have *de jure* or *de facto* international responsibility for territories situated in the zone of application of the Treaty;

(c) Signature and ratification of the Additional Protocol II annexed to this Treaty by all powers possessing nuclear weapons;

(d) Conclusion of bilateral or multilateral agreements on the application of the Safeguards System of the International Atomic Energy Agency in accordance with article 13 of this Treaty.

* * *

4. After the entry into force of this Treaty for all the countries of the zone, the rise of a new power possessing nuclear weapons shall have the effect of suspending the execution of this Treaty for those countries which have ratified it without waiving requirements of paragraph 1, sub-paragraph (*c*) of this article, and which request such suspension; the Treaty shall remain suspended until the new power, on its own initiative or upon request by the General Conference, ratifies the annexed Additional Protocol II.

* * *

ADDITIONAL PROTOCOL I

The undersigned Plenipotentiaries, furnished with full powers by their respective Governments, * * *

Have agreed as follows:

Article 1. To undertake to apply the status of denuclearization in respect of warlike purposes as defined in articles 1, 3, 5 and 13 of the Treaty for the Prohibition of Nuclear Weapons in Latin America in territories for which, *de jure* or *de facto,* they are internationally responsible and which lie within the limits of the geographical zone established in that Treaty.

Article 2. The duration of this Protocol shall be the same as that of the Treaty for the Prohibition of Nuclear Weapons in Latin America of which this Protocol is an annex, and the provisions regarding ratification and denunciation contained in the Treaty shall be applicable to it.

Article 3. This Protocol shall enter into force, for the States which have ratified it, on the date of the deposit of their respective instruments of ratification.

* * *

ADDITIONAL PROTOCOL II

The undersigned Plenipotentiaries, furnished with full powers by their respective Governments, * * *

Have agreed as follows:

Article 1. The status of denuclearization of Latin America in respect of warlike purposes, as defined, delimited and set forth in the Treaty for the Prohibition of Nuclear Weapons in Latin America of which this instrument is an annex, shall be fully respected by the Parties to this Protocol in all its express aims and provisions.

Article 2. The Governments represented by the undersigned Plenipotentiaries undertake, therefore, not to contribute in any way to the performance of acts involving a violation of the obligations of article 1 of the Treaty in the territories to which the Treaty applies in accordance with article 4 thereof.

Article 3. The Governments represented by the undersigned Plenipotentiaries also undertake not to use or threaten to use nuclear weapons against the Contracting Parties of the Treaty for the Prohibition of Nuclear Weapons in Latin America.

Article 4. The duration of this Protocol shall be the same as that of the Treaty for the Prohibition of Nuclear Weapons in Latin America of which this Protocol is an annex, and the definitions of territory and nuclear weapons set forth in articles 3 and 5 of the Treaty shall be applicable to the Protocol, as well as the provisions regarding ratification, reservations, denunciation, authentic texts and registration contained in articles 26, 27, 30 and 31 of the Treaty.

Article 5. This Protocol shall enter into force, for the States which have ratified it, on the date of the deposit of their respective instruments of ratification.

* * *

Understandings and Declarations Included in the U.S. Instrument at Ratification [c]

I

That the United States Government understands the reference in Article 3 of the treaty to "its own legislation" to relate only to such legislation as is compatible with the rules of international law and as involves an exercise of sovereignty consistent with those rules, and accordingly that ratification of Additional Protocol II by the United States Government could not be regarded as implying recognition, for the purposes of this treaty and its protocols or for any other purpose, of any legislation which did not, in the view of the United States, comply with the relevant rules of international law.

That the United States Government takes note of the Preparatory Commission's interpretation of the treaty, as set forth in the Final Act, that, governed by the principles and rules of international law, each of the Contracting Parties retains exclusive power and legal competence, unaffected by the terms of the treaty, to grant or deny non-Contracting Parties transit and transport privileges.

That as regards the undertaking in Article 3 of Protocol II not to use or threaten to use nuclear weapons against the Contracting Parties, the United States Government would have to consider that an armed attack by a Contracting Party, in which it was assisted by a nuclear-weapon state, would be incompatible with the Contracting Party's corresponding obligations under Article I of the treaty.

II

That the United States Government considers that the technology of making nuclear explosive devices for peaceful purposes is indistinguishable from the technology of making nuclear weapons, and that nuclear weapons and nuclear explosive devices for peaceful purposes are both capable of releasing nuclear energy in an uncontrolled manner and have the common group of characteristics of large amounts of energy generated instantaneously from a compact source. Therefore the United States Government understands the definition contained in Article 5 of the treaty as necessarily encompassing all nuclear explosive devices. It is also understood that Articles 1 and 5 restrict accordingly the activities of the Contracting Parties under paragraph 1 of Article 18.

c. 22 UST 760.

That the United States Government understands that paragraph 4 of Article 18 of the treaty permits, and that United States adherence to Protocol II will not prevent, collaboration by the United States with Contracting Parties for the purpose of carrying out explosions of nuclear devices for peaceful purposes in a manner consistent with a policy of not contributing to the proliferation of nuclear weapons capabilities. In this connection, the United States Government notes Article V of the Treaty on the Non–Proliferation of Nuclear Weapons, under which it joined in an undertaking to take appropriate measures to ensure that potential benefits of peaceful applications of nuclear explosions would be made available to non-nuclear-weapon states party to that treaty, and reaffirms its willingness to extend such undertaking, on the same basis, to states precluded by the present treaty from manufacturing or acquiring any nuclear explosive device.

III

That the United States Government also declares that, although not required by Protocol II, it will act with respect to such territories of Protocol I adherents as are within the geographical area defined in paragraph 2 of Article 4 of the treaty in the same manner as Protocol II requires it to act with respect to the territories of Contracting Parties.

The President ratified Additional Protocol II on May 8, 1971, with the above-recited understandings and declarations, in pursuance of the advice and consent of the Senate.

* * *

2.22 TREATY ON THE NON-PROLIFERATION OF NUCLEAR WEAPONS.[a] Done at London, Moscow and Washington, July 1, 1968. Entered into force, Mar. 5, 1970; for the United States, Mar. 5, 1970. 21 U.S.T. 483, T.I.A.S. No. 6839, 729 U.N.T.S. 161, *reprinted in* 7 I.L.M. 811 (1968)

Article I. Each nuclear-weapon State Party to the Treaty undertakes not to transfer to any recipient whatsoever nuclear weapons or other nuclear explosive devices or control over such weapons or explosive devices directly, or indirectly; and not in any way to assist, encourage, or induce any non-nuclear-weapon State to manufacture or otherwise acquire nuclear weapons or other nuclear explosive devices, or control over such weapons or explosive devices.

Article II. Each non-nuclear-weapon State Party to the Treaty undertakes not to receive the transfer from any transferor whatsoever of nuclear weapons or other nuclear explosive devices or of control over such weapons or explosive devices directly, or indirectly; not to manufacture or otherwise acquire nuclear weapons or other nuclear explosive devices; and not to seek or receive any assistance in the manufacture of nuclear weapons or other nuclear explosive devices.

Article III. (1) Each non-nuclear-weapon State Party to the Treaty undertakes to accept safeguards, as set forth in an agreement to be negotiated and concluded with the International Atomic Energy Agency in accordance with the Statute of the International Atomic Energy Agency and the Agency's safeguards system, for the exclusive purpose of verification of the fulfilment of its obligations assumed under this Treaty with a view to preventing diversion of nuclear energy from peaceful uses to nuclear weapons or other nuclear explosive devices. Procedures for the safeguards required by this Article shall be followed with respect to source or special fissionable material whether it is being produced, processed or used in any principal nuclear facility or is outside any such facility. The safeguards required by this Article shall be applied on all source or special fissionable material in all peaceful nuclear activities within the territory of such State, under its jurisdiction, or carried out under its control anywhere.

(2) Each State Party to the Treaty undertakes not to provide: (*a*) source or special fissionable material, or (*b*) equipment or material especially designed or prepared for the processing, use or production of special fissionable material, to any non-nuclear-weapon State for peaceful purposes, unless the source or special fissionable material shall be subject to the safeguards required by this Article.

(3) The safeguards required by this Article shall be implemented in a manner designed to comply with Article IV of this Treaty, and to avoid hampering the economic or technological development of the Parties or international co-operation in the field of peaceful nuclear activities, including the international exchange of nuclear material and equipment for the processing, use or production of nuclear material for peaceful purposes in accordance with the provisions of this Article and the principle of safeguarding set forth in the Preamble of the Treaty.

(4) Non-nuclear-weapon States Party to the Treaty shall conclude agreements with the International Atomic Energy Agency to meet the requirements of this Article either individually or together with other States in accordance with the Statute of the International Atomic Energy Agency. Negotiation of such agreements shall commence within 180 days from the original entry into force of this Treaty. For States depositing their instruments of ratification or accession after the 180-day period, negotiation of such agreements shall commence not later than the date of

a. Also known as "the NPT".

such deposit. Such agreements shall enter into force not later than eighteen months after the date of initiation of negotiations.

Article IV. (1) Nothing in this Treaty shall be interpreted as affecting the inalienable right of all the Parties to the Treaty to develop research, production and use of nuclear energy for peaceful purposes without discrimination and in conformity with Articles I and II of this Treaty.

(2) All the Parties to the Treaty undertake to facilitate, and have the right to participate in, the fullest possible exchange of equipment, materials and scientific and technological information for the peaceful uses of nuclear energy. Parties to the Treaty in a position to do so shall also co-operate in contributing alone or together with other States or international organizations to the further development of the applications of nuclear energy for peaceful purposes, especially in the territories of non-nuclear weapon States Party to the Treaty, with due consideration for the needs of the developing areas of the world.

Article V. Each Party to the Treaty undertakes to take appropriate measures to ensure that, in accordance with this Treaty, under appropriate international observation and through appropriate international procedures, potential benefits from any peaceful applications of nuclear explosions will be made available to non-nuclear-weapon States Party to the Treaty on a non-discriminatory basis and that the charge to such Parties for the explosive devices used will be as low as possible and exclude any charge for research and development. Non-nuclear-weapon States Party to the Treaty shall be able to obtain such benefits, pursuant to a special international agreement or agreements, through an appropriate international body with adequate representation of non-nuclear-weapon States. Negotiations on this subject shall commence as soon as possible after the Treaty enters into force. Non-nuclear-weapon States Party to the Treaty so desiring may also obtain such benefits pursuant to bilateral agreements.

Article VI. Each of the Parties to the Treaty undertakes to pursue negotiations in good faith on effective measures relating to cessation of the nuclear arms race at an early date and to nuclear disarmament, and on a treaty on general and complete disarmament under strict and effective international control.

Article VII. Nothing in this Treaty affects the right of any group of States to conclude regional treaties in order to assure the total absence of nuclear weapons in their respective territories.

Article VIII. (1) Any Party to the Treaty may propose amendments to this Treaty. The text of any proposed amendment shall be submitted to the Depositary Governments which shall circulate it to all Parties to the Treaty. Thereupon, if requested to do so by one-third or more of the Parties to the Treaty, the Depositary Governments shall convene a conference, to which they shall invite all the Parties to the Treaty, to consider such an amendment.

(2) Any amendment to this Treaty must be approved by a majority of the votes of all the Parties to the Treaty, including the votes of all nuclear-weapon States Party to the Treaty and all other Parties which on the date the amendment is circulated, are members of the Board of Governors of the International Atomic Energy Agency. The amendment shall enter into force for each Party that deposits its instrument of ratification by a majority of all the Parties, including the instruments of ratification of all nuclear-weapon States Party to the Treaty and all other Parties which, on the date the amendment is circulated, are members of the Board of Governors of the International Atomic Energy Agency. Thereafter, it shall enter into force for any other Party upon the deposit of its instrument of ratification of the amendment.

(3) Five years after the entry into force of this Treaty, a conference of Parties to the Treaty shall be held in Geneva, Switzerland, in order to review the operation of

this Treaty with a view of assuring that the purposes of the Preamble and the provisions of the Treaty are being realised. At intervals of five years thereafter, a majority of the Parties to the Treaty may obtain, by submitting a proposal to this effect to the Depositary Governments, the convening of further conferences with the same objectives of reviewing the operation of the Treaty.

Article IX. * * *

(3) * * * For the purposes of this Treaty, a nuclear-weapon State is one which has manufactured and exploded a nuclear weapon or other nuclear explosive device prior to 1 January, 1967.

Article X. (1) Each Party shall in exercising its national sovereignty have the right to withdraw from the Treaty if it decides that extraordinary events, related to the subject matter of this Treaty, have jeopardized the supreme interests of its country. It shall give notice of such withdrawal to all other Parties to the Treaty and to the United Nations Security Council three months in advance. Such notice shall include a statement of the extraordinary events it regards as having jeopardized its supreme interests.

(2) Twenty-five years after the entry into force of the Treaty, a conference shall be convened to decide whether the Treaty shall continue in force indefinitely, or shall be extended for an additional fixed period or periods. This decision shall be taken by a majority of the Parties of the Treaty.

* * *

2.23 TREATY ON THE PROHIBITION OF THE EMPLACEMENT OF NUCLEAR WEAPONS AND OTHER WEAPONS OF MASS DESTRUCTION ON THE SEABED AND THE OCEAN FLOOR AND IN THE SUBSOIL THEREOF.[a] Done at London, Moscow and Washington, Feb. 11, 1971. Entered into force, May 18, 1972; for the United States, May 18, 1972. 23 U.S.T. 701, T.I.A.S. No. 7337, *reprinted in* 10 I.L.M. 146 (1971)

Article I. (1) The States Parties to this Treaty undertake not to emplant or emplace on the seabed and the ocean floor and in the subsoil thereof beyond the outer limit of a seabed zone, as defined in article II, any nuclear weapons or any other types of weapons of mass destruction as well as structures, launching installations or any other facilities specifically designed for storing, testing or using such weapons.

(2) The undertakings of paragraph 1 of this article shall also apply to the seabed zone referred to in the same paragraph, except that within such seabed zone, they shall not apply either to the coastal State or to the seabed beneath its territorial waters.

(3) The States Parties to this Treaty undertake not to assist, encourage or induce any State to carry out activities referred to in paragraph 1 of this article and not to participate in any other way in such actions.

Article II. For the purpose of this Treaty, the outer limit of the seabed zone referred to in article I shall be coterminous with the twelve-mile outer limit of the zone referred to in part II of the Convention on the Territorial Sea and the Contiguous Zone, signed at Geneva on April 29, 1958, and shall be measured in accordance with the provisions of part I, section II, of that Convention and in accordance with international law.

Article III. (1) In order to promote the objectives of and insure compliance with the provisions of this Treaty, each State Party to the Treaty shall have the right to verify through observation the activities of other States Parties to the Treaty on the seabed and the ocean floor and in the subsoil thereof beyond the zone referred to in article I, provided that observation does not interfere with such activities.

(2) If after such observation reasonable doubts remain concerning the fulfilment of the obligations assumed under the Treaty, the State Party having such doubts and the State Party that is responsible for the activities giving rise to the doubts shall consult with a view to removing the doubts. If the doubts persist, the State Party having such doubts shall notify the other State Parties, and the Parties concerned shall cooperate on such further procedures for verification as may be agreed, including appropriate inspection of objects, structures, installations or other facilities that reasonably may be expected to be of a kind described in article I. The Parties in the region of the activities, including any coastal State, and any other Party so requesting, shall be entitled to participate in such consultation and cooperation. After completion of the further procedures for verification, an appropriate report shall be circulated to other Parties by the Party that initiated such procedures.

(3) If the State responsible for the activities giving rise to the reasonable doubts is not identifiable by observation of the object, structure, installation or other facility, the State Party having such doubts shall notify and make appropriate inquiries of

a. Also known as "the Seabed Arms Control Treaty".

States Parties in the region of the activities and of any other State Party. If it is ascertained through these inquiries that a particular State Party is responsible for the activities, that State Party shall consult and cooperate with other Parties as provided in paragraph 2 of this article. If the identity of the State responsible for the activities cannot be ascertained through these inquiries, then further verification procedures, including inspection, may be undertaken by the inquiring State Party, which shall invite the participation of the Parties in the region of the activities, including any coastal State, and of any other Party desiring to cooperate.

(4) If consultation and cooperation pursuant to paragraphs 2 and 3 of this article have not removed the doubts concerning the activities and there remains a serious question concerning fulfillment of the obligations assumed under this Treaty, a State Party may, in accordance with the provisions of the Charter of the United Nations, refer the matter to the Security Council, which may take action in accordance with the Charter.

(5) Verification pursuant to this article may be undertaken by any State Party using its own means, or with the full or partial assistance of any other State Party, or through appropriate international procedures within the framework of the United Nations and in accordance with its Charter.

(6) Verification activities pursuant to this Treaty shall not interfere with activities of other States Parties and shall be conducted with due regard for rights recognized under international law, including the freedoms of the high seas and the rights of coastal States with respect to the exploration and exploitation of their continental shelves.

Article IV. Nothing in this Treaty shall be interpreted as supporting or prejudicing the position of any State Party with respect to existing international conventions, including the 1958 Convention on the Territorial Sea and the Contiguous Zone, or with respect to rights or claims which such State Party may assert, or with respect to recognition or non-recognition of rights or claims asserted by any other State, related to waters off its coasts, including, *inter alia,* territorial seas and contiguous zones, or to the seabed and the ocean floor, including continental shelves.

Article V. The Parties to this Treaty undertake to continue negotiations in good faith concerning further measures in the field of disarmament for the prevention of an arms race on the seabed, the ocean floor and the subsoil thereof.

* * *

Article VII. Five years after the entry into force of this Treaty, a conference of Parties to the Treaty shall be held at Geneva, Switzerland, in order to review the operation of this Treaty with a view to assuring that the purposes of the preamble and the provisions of the Treaty are being realized. Such review shall take into account any relevant technological developments. The review conference shall determine, in accordance with the views of a majority of those Parties attending, whether and when an additional review conference shall be convened.

* * *

2.24 AGREEMENT ON MEASURES TO REDUCE THE RISK OF OUTBREAK OF NUCLEAR WAR BETWEEN THE UNITED STATES OF AMERICA AND THE UNION OF SOVIET SOCIALIST REPUBLICS.[a] Done at Washington, Sept. 30, 1971. Entered into force, Sept. 30, 1971. 22 U.S.T. 1590, T.I.A.S. No. 7186, 807 U.N.T.S. 57, *reprinted in* 10 I.L.M. 1173 (1971)

Article 1. Each Party undertakes to maintain and to improve, as it deems necessary, its existing organizational and technical arrangements to guard against the accidental or unauthorized use of nuclear weapons under its control.

Article 2. The Parties undertake to notify each other immediately in the event of an accidental, unauthorized or any other unexplained incident involving a possible detonation of a nuclear weapon which could create a risk of outbreak of nuclear war. In the event of such an incident, the Party whose nuclear weapon is involved will immediately make every effort to take necessary measures to render harmless or destroy such weapon without its causing damage.

Article 3. The Parties undertake to notify each other immediately in the event of detection by missile warning systems of unidentified objects, or in the event of signs of interference with these systems or with related communications facilities, if such occurrences could create a risk of outbreak of nuclear war between the two countries.

Article 4. Each Party undertakes to notify the other Party in advance of any planned missile launches if such launches will extend beyond its national territory in the direction of the other Party.

Article 5. Each Party, in other situations involving unexplained nuclear incidents, undertakes to act in such a manner as to reduce the possibility of its actions being misinterpreted by the other Party. In any such situation, each Party may inform the other Party or request information when, in its view, this is warranted by the interests of averting the risk of outbreak of nuclear war.

Article 6. For transmission of urgent information, notifications and requests for information in situations requiring prompt clarification, the Parties shall make primary use of the Direct Communications Link between the Governments of the United States of America and the Union of Soviet Socialist Republics.

For transmission of other information, notifications and request for information, the Parties, at their own discretion, may use any communications facilities, including diplomatic channels, depending on the degree of urgency.

Article 7. The Parties undertake to hold consultations, as mutually agreed, to consider questions relating to implementation of the provisions of this Agreement, as well as to discuss possible amendments thereto aimed at further implementation of the purposes of this Agreement.

Article 8. This Agreement shall be of unlimited duration.

* * *

a. This Agreement is one of the four agreements known collectively as "SALT I." *See also* Basic Documents 2.25, 2.27 and 2.28, *infra*.

2.25 AGREEMENT BETWEEN THE UNITED STATES OF AMERICA AND THE UNION OF SOVIET SOCIALIST REPUBLICS ON MEASURES TO IMPROVE THE USA–USSR DIRECT COMMUNICATIONS LINK.[a] Done at Washington, Sept. 30, 1971. Entered into force, Sept. 30, 1971. 22 U.S.T. 1598, T.I.A.S. No. 7187, 806 U.N.T.S. 402, *reprinted in* 10 I.L.M. 1174 (1971)

Article 1. (1) For the purpose of increasing the reliability of the Direct Communications Link, there shall be established and put into operation the following:

(a) two additional circuits between the United States of America and the Union of Soviet Socialist Republics each using a satellite communications system, with each Party selecting a satellite communications system of its own choice,

(b) a system of terminals (more than one) in the territory of each Party for the Direct Communications Link, with the locations and number of terminals in the United States of America to be determined by the United States side, and the locations and number of terminals in the Union of Soviet Socialist Republics to be determined by the Soviet side.

(2) Matters relating to the implementation of the aforementioned improvements of the Direct Communications Link are set forth in the Annex which is attached hereto and forms an integral part hereof.

Article 2. Each Party confirms its intention to take all possible measures to assure the continuous and reliable operation of the communications circuits and the system of terminals of the Direct Communications Link for which it is responsible in accordance with this Agreement and the Annex hereto, as well as to communicate to the head of its Government any messages received via the Direct Communications Link from the head of Government of the other Party.

Article 3. The Memorandum of Understanding Between the United States of America and the Union of Soviet Socialist Republics Regarding the Establishment of a Direct Communications Link, signed on June 20, 1963, with the Annex thereto, shall remain in force, except to the extent that its provisions are modified by this Agreement and Annex hereto.

* * *

a. This Agreement, popularly known as "the Hot Line Agreement", is one of the four agreements known collectively as "SALT I." *See also* Basic Document 2.24, *supra*, and Basic Documents 2.27 and 2.28, *infra*.

2.26 CONVENTION ON THE PROHIBITION OF THE DEVELOPMENT, PRODUCTION AND STOCKPILING OF BACTERIOLOGICAL (BIOLOGICAL) AND TOXIN WEAPONS AND ON THEIR DESTRUCTION.[a] Done at London, Moscow and Washington, Apr. 10, 1972. Entered into force, Mar. 26, 1975; for the United States, Mar. 26, 1975. 26 U.S.T. 583, T.I.A.S. No. 8062, *reprinted in* 11 I.L.M. 310 (1972)

Article I. Each State Party to this Convention undertakes never in any circumstances to develop, produce, stockpile or otherwise acquire or retain:

(1) Microbial or other biological agents, or toxins whatever their origin or method of production, of types and in quantities that have no justification for prophylactic, protective or other peaceful purposes;

(2) Weapons, equipment or means of delivery designed to use such agents or toxins for hostile purposes or in armed conflict.

Article II. Each State Party to this Convention undertakes to destroy, or to divert to peaceful purposes, as soon as possible but not later than nine months after the entry into force of the Convention, all agents, toxins, weapons, equipment and means of delivery specified in article I of the Convention, which are in its possession or under its jurisdiction or control. In implementing the provisions of this article all necessary safety precautions shall be observed to protect populations and the environment.

Article III. Each State Party to this Convention undertakes not to transfer to any recipient whatsoever, directly or indirectly, and not in any way to assist, encourage, or induce any State, group of States or international organizations to manufacture or otherwise acquire any of the agents, toxins, weapons, equipment or means of delivery specified in article I of the Convention.

Article IV. Each State Party to this Convention shall, in accordance with its constitutional processes, take any necessary measures to prohibit and prevent the development, production, stockpiling, acquisition or retention of the agents, toxins, weapons, equipment and means of delivery specified in article I of the Convention, within the territory of such State, under its jurisdiction or under its control anywhere.

Article V. The States Parties to this Convention undertake to consult one another and to cooperate in solving any problems which may arise in relation to the objective of, or in the application of the provisions of, the Convention. Consultation and cooperation pursuant to this article may also be undertaken through appropriate international procedures within the framework of the United Nations and in accordance with its Charter.

Article VI. (1) Any State Party to this Convention which finds that any other State Party is acting in breach of obligations deriving from the provisions of the Convention may lodge a complaint with the Security Council of the United Nations. Such a complaint should include all possible evidence confirming its validity, as well as a request for its consideration by the Security Council.

(2) Each State Party to this Convention undertakes to cooperate in carrying out any investigation which the Security Council may initiate, in accordance with the

a. *See also* Basic Document 2.3, *supra*, and Basic Document 2.40, *infra*.

provisions of the Charter of the United Nations, on the basis of the complaint received by the Council. The Security Council shall inform the States Parties to the Convention of the results of the investigation.

Article VII. Each State Party to this Convention undertakes to provide or support assistance, in accordance with the United Nations Charter, to any Party to the Convention which so requests, if the Security Council decides that such Party has been exposed to danger as a result of violation of the Convention.

Article VIII. Nothing in this Convention shall be interpreted as in any way limiting or detracting from the obligations assumed by any State under the Protocol for the Prohibition of the Use in War of Asphyxiating, Poisonous or Other Gases, and of Bacteriological Methods of Warfare, signed at Geneva on June 17, 1925.

Article IX. Each State Party to this Convention affirms the recognized objective of effective prohibition of chemical weapons and, to this end, undertakes to continue negotiations in good faith with a view to reaching early agreement on effective measures for the prohibition of their development, production and stockpiling and for their destruction, and on appropriate measures concerning equipment and means of delivery specifically designed for the production or use of chemical agents for weapons purposes.

Article X. (1) The States Parties to this Convention undertake to facilitate, and have the right to participate in, the fullest possible exchange of equipment, materials and scientific and technological information for the use of bacteriological (biological) agents and toxins for peaceful purposes. Parties to the Convention in a position to do so shall also cooperate in contributing individually or together with other States or international organizations to the further development and application of scientific discoveries in the field of bacteriology (biology) for prevention of disease, or for other peaceful purposes.

(2) This Convention shall be implemented in a manner designed to avoid hampering the economic or technological development of States Parties to the Convention or international cooperation in the field of peaceful bacteriological (biological) activities, including the international exchange of bacteriological (biological) agents and toxins and equipment for the processing, use or production of bacteriological (biological) agents and toxins for peaceful purposes in accordance with the provisions of the Convention.

* * *

Article XII. Five years after the entry into force of this Convention, or earlier if it is requested by a majority of Parties to the Convention by submitting a proposal to this effect to the Depositary Governments, a conference of States Parties to the Convention shall be held at Geneva, Switzerland, to review the operation of the Convention, with a view to assuring that the purposes of the preamble and the provisions of the Convention, including the provisions concerning negotiations on chemical weapons, are being realized. Such review shall take into account any new scientific and technological developments relevant to the Convention.

Article XIII. (1) This Convention shall be of unlimited duration.

* * *

2.27 TREATY BETWEEN THE UNITED STATES OF AMERICA AND THE UNION OF SOVIET SOCIALIST REPUBLICS ON THE LIMITATION OF ANTI-BALLISTIC MISSILE SYSTEMS.[a] Done at Moscow, May 26, 1972. Entered into force, Oct. 3, 1972. 23 U.S.T. 3435, T.I.A.S. No. 7503, *reprinted in* 11 I.L.M. 784 (1972)

Article I. (1) Each Party undertakes to limit anti-ballistic missile (ABM) systems and to adopt other measures in accordance with the provisions of this Treaty.

(2) Each Party undertakes not to deploy ABM systems for a defense of the territory of its country and not to provide a base for such a defense, and not to deploy ABM systems for defense of an individual region except as provided for in Article III of this Treaty.

Article II. (1) For the purposes of this Treaty an ABM system is a system to counter strategic ballistic missiles or their elements in flight trajectory, currently consisting of:

(a) ABM interceptor missiles, which are interceptor missiles constructed and deployed for an ABM role, or of a type tested in an ABM mode;

(b) ABM launchers, which are launchers constructed and deployed for launching ABM interceptor missiles; and

(c) ABM radars, which are radars constructed and deployed for an ABM role, or of a type tested in an ABM mode.

(2) The ABM system components listed in paragraph 1 of this Article include those which are:

(a) operational;

(b) under construction;

(c) undergoing testing;

(d) undergoing overhaul, repair or conversion; or

(e) mothballed.

Article III. Each Party undertakes not to deploy ABM systems or their components except that:

(a) within one ABM system deployment area having a radius of one hundred and fifty kilometers and centered on the Party's national capital, a Party may deploy: (1) no more than one hundred ABM launchers and no more than one hundred ABM interceptor missiles at launch sites, and (2) ABM radars within no more than six ABM radar complexes, the area of each complex being circular and having a diameter of no more than three kilometers; and

(b) within one ABM system deployment area having a radius of one hundred and fifty kilometers and containing ICBM silo launchers, a Party may deploy: (1) no more than one hundred ABM launchers and no more than one hundred ABM interceptor missiles at launch sites, (2) two large phased-array ABM radars comparable in potential to corresponding ABM radars operational or under construction on the date of signature of the Treaty in an ABM system deployment area containing ICBM silo launchers, and (3) no more than eighteen ABM

a. This Treaty, also known as "the ABM Treaty," is one of the four agreements known collectively as "SALT I." *See also* Basic Documents 2.24 and 2.25, *supra*, and Basic Document 2.28, *infra*. In addition, see Protocol to the Treaty of May 26, 1972 on the Limitation of Anti-Ballistic Missile Systems, 27 U.S.T. 1645, T.I.A.S. No. 8276, *reprinted in* 13 I.L.M. 904 (1974).

radars each having a potential less than the potential of the smaller of the above-mentioned two large phased-array ABM radars.

Article IV. The limitations provided for in Article III shall not apply to ABM systems or their components used for development or testing, and located within current or additionally agreed test ranges. Each Party may have no more than a total of fifteen ABM launchers at test ranges.

Article V. (1) Each Party undertakes not to develop, test, or deploy ABM systems or components which are sea-based, air-based, space-based, or mobile land-based.

(2) Each Party undertakes not to develop, test, or deploy ABM launchers for launching more than one ABM interceptor missile at a time from each launcher, nor to modify deployed launchers to provide them with such a capability, nor to develop, test, or deploy automatic or semi-automatic or other similar systems for rapid reload of ABM launchers.

Article VI. To enhance assurance of the effectiveness of the limitations on ABM systems and their components provided by this Treaty, each Party undertakes:

(a) not to give missiles, launchers, or radars, other than ABM interceptor missiles, ABM launchers, or ABM radars, capabilities to counter strategic ballistic missiles or their elements in flight trajectory, and not to test them in an ABM mode; and

(b) not to deploy in the future radars for early warning of strategic ballistic missile attack except at locations along the periphery of its national territory and oriented outward.

Article VII. Subject to the provisions of this Treaty, modernization and replacement of ABM systems or their components may be carried out.

Article VIII. ABM systems or their components in excess of the numbers or outside the areas specified in this Treaty, as well as ABM systems or their components prohibited by this Treaty, shall be destroyed or dismantled under agreed procedures within the shortest possible agreed period of time.

Article IX. To assure the viability and effectiveness of this Treaty, each Party undertakes not to transfer to other States, and not to deploy outside its national territory, ABM systems or their components limited by this Treaty.

Article X. Each Party undertakes not to assume any international obligations which would conflict with this Treaty.

Article XI. The Parties undertake to continue active negotiations for limitations on strategic offensive arms.

Article XII. (1) For the purpose of providing assurance of compliance with the provisions of this Treaty, each Party shall use national technical means of verification at its disposal in a manner consistent with generally recognized principles of international law.

(2) Each Party undertakes not to interfere with the national technical means of verification of the other Party operating in accordance with paragraph 1 of this Article.

(3) Each Party undertakes not to use deliberate concealment measures which impede verification by national technical means of compliance with the provisions of this Treaty. This obligation shall require changes in current construction, assembly, conversion, or overhaul practices.

Article XIII. (1) To promote the objectives and implementation of the provisions of this Treaty, the Parties shall establish promptly a Standing Consultative Commission, within the framework of which they will:

(a) consider questions concerning compliance with the obligations assumed and related situations which may be considered ambiguous;

(b) provide on a voluntary basis such information as either Party considers necessary to assure confidence in compliance with the obligations assumed;

(c) consider questions involving unintended interference with national technical means of verification;

(d) consider possible changes in the strategic situation which have a bearing on the provisions of this Treaty;

(e) agree upon procedures and dates for destruction or dismantling of ABM systems or their components in cases provided for by the provisions of this Treaty;

(f) consider, as appropriate, possible proposals for further increasing the viability of this Treaty, including proposals for amendments in accordance with the provisions of this Treaty;

(g) consider, as appropriate, proposals for further measures aimed at limiting strategic arms.

(2) The Parties through consultation shall establish, and may amend as appropriate, Regulations for the Standing Consultative Commission governing procedures, composition and other relevant matters.

* * *

2.28 INTERIM AGREEMENT BETWEEN THE UNITED STATES OF AMERICA AND THE UNION OF SOVIET SOCIALIST REPUBLICS OF CERTAIN MEASURES WITH RESPECT TO THE LIMITATION OF STRATEGIC OFFENSIVE ARMS.[a] Done at Moscow, May 26, 1972. Entered into force, Oct. 3, 1972. Expired, Oct. 3, 1977. 23 U.S.T. 3462, T.I.A.S. No. 7504, *reprinted in* 11 I.L.M. 791 (1972)

Article I. The Parties undertake not to start construction of additional fixed land-based intercontinental ballistic missile (ICBM) launchers after July 1, 1972.

Article II. The Parties undertake not to convert land-based launchers for light ICBMs or for ICBMs of older types deployed prior to 1964, into land-based launchers for heavy ICBMs of types deployed after that time.

Article III. The Parties undertake to limit submarine-launched ballistic missile (SLBM) launchers and modern ballistic missile submarines to the numbers operational and under construction on the date of signature of this Interim Agreement, and in addition to launchers and submarines constructed under procedures established by the Parties as replacements for an equal number of ICBM launchers of older types deployed prior to 1964 or for launchers on older submarines.

Article IV. Subject to the provisions of this Interim Agreement, modernization and replacement of strategic offensive ballistic missiles and launchers covered by this Interim Agreement may be undertaken.

Article V. (1) For the purpose of providing assurance of compliance with the provisions of this Interim Agreement, each Party shall use technical means of verification at its disposal in a manner consistent with generally recognized principles of international law.

(2) Each Party undertakes not to interfere with the national technical means of verification of the other Party operating in accordance with paragraph 1 of this Article.

(3) Each Party undertakes not to use deliberate concealment measures which impede verification by national technical means of compliance with the provisions of this Interim Agreement. This obligation shall not require changes in current construction, assembly, conversion, or overhaul practices.

Article VI. To promote the objectives and implementation of the provisions of this Interim Agreement, the Parties shall use the Standing Consultative Commission established under Article XIII of the Treaty on the Limitation of Anti–Ballistic Missile Systems in accordance with the provisions of that Article.

Article VII. The Parties undertake to continue active negotiations for limitations on strategic offensive arms. The obligations provided for in this Interim Agreement shall not prejudice the scope or terms of the limitations on strategic offensive arms which may be worked out in the course of further negotiations.

Article VIII. * * *

(2) This Interim Agreement shall remain in force for a period of five years unless replaced earlier by an agreement on more complete measures limiting

a. This Interim Agreement, one of four agreements known collectively as "SALT I" expired Oct. 3, 1977, as indicated above, pursuant to its Article 8(2). At the time, both the United States and the Soviet Union issued statements expressing their intention not to take any action inconsistent with this Interim Agreement pending the negotiation of a comprehensive agreement limiting strategic arms (SALT II) to replace it. For the other SALT I accords, see Basic Documents 2.24, 2.25, and 2.27 *supra*.

strategic offensive arms. It is the objective of the Parties to conduct active follow-on negotiations with the aim of concluding such an agreement as soon as possible.

* * *

2.29 RESOLUTION ON THE NON-USE OF FORCE IN INTERNATIONAL RELATIONS AND PERMANENT PROHIBITION OF THE USE OF NUCLEAR WEAPONS.[a] Adopted by the U.N. General Assembly, Nov. 29, 1972. U.N.G.A. Res. 2936, 27 U.N. GAOR Supp. (No. 30) 5, U.N.Doc. A/8730 (1972)

The General Assembly,

Noting that renunciation of the use or threat of force as proclaimed in the Charter of the United Nations and reaffirmed in the Declaration on the Strengthening of International Security, contained in General Assembly resolution 2734 (XXV) of 16 December 1970, and the Declaration on Principles of International Law concerning Friendly Relations and Co-operation among States in accordance with the Charter of the United Nations, contained in Assembly resolution 2625 (XXV) of 24 October 1970, is an obligation that all States should respect,

Noting with concern that the use of force in various forms is still occurring in violation of the Charter,

Bearing in mind that the threat of the use of nuclear weapons continues to exist,

Guided by the desire of all peoples to eliminate war and above all to prevent a nuclear disaster,

Reaffirming, in accordance with Article 51 of the Charter, the inalienable right of States to self-defence against armed attack,

Mindful of the principle of the inadmissibility of acquisition of territory by force and the inherent right of States to recover such territories by all the means at their disposal,

Reaffirming its recognition of the legitimacy of the struggle of colonial peoples for their freedom by all appropriate means at their disposal,

Recalling the Declaration on the Prohibition of the Use of Nuclear and Thermonuclear Weapons, contained in General Assembly resolution 1653 (XVI) of 24 November 1961,

Recalling further its resolution 2160 (XXI) of 30 November 1966 on the strict observance of the prohibition of the threat or use of force in international relations, and of the right of peoples to self-determination,

Believing that renunciation of the use or threat of force and prohibition of the use of nuclear weapons should be fully observed as a law of international life,

1. *Solemnly declares,* on behalf of the States Members of the Organization, their renunciation of the use or threat of force in all its forms and manifestations in international relations, in accordance with the Charter of the United Nations, and the permanent prohibition of the use of nuclear weapons;

2. *Recommends* that the Security Council should take, as soon as possible, appropriate measures for the full implementation of the present declaration of the General Assembly.

a. *See also* Basic Document 2.17, *supra,* and Basic Document 2.36, *infra.*

2.30 WAR POWERS RESOLUTION, Nov. 7, 1973, 87 Stat. 555, 50 U.S.C. §§ 1541–1548 (1976)

§ 1541. Purpose and policy

(a) Congressional declaration

It is the purpose of this chapter to fulfill the intent of the framers of the Constitution of the United States and insure that the collective judgment of both the Congress and the President will apply to the introduction of United States Armed Forces into hostilities, or into situations where imminent involvement in hostilities is clearly indicated by the circumstances, and to the continued use of such forces in hostilities or in such situations.

(b) Congressional legislative power under necessary and proper clause

Under article I, section 8, of the Constitution, it is specifically provided that the Congress shall have the power to make all laws necessary and proper for carrying into execution, not only its own powers but also all other powers vested by the Constitution in the Government of the United States, or in any department or officer hereof.

(c) Presidential executive power as Commander-in-Chief; limitation

The constitutional powers of the President as Commander-in-Chief to introduce United States Armed Forces into hostilities, or into situations where imminent involvement in hostilities is clearly indicated by the circumstances, are exercised only pursuant to (1) a declaration of war, (2) specific statutory authorization, or (3) a national emergency created by attack upon the United States, its territories or possessions, or its armed forces.

§ 1542. Consultation; initial and regular consultations

The President in every possible instance shall consult with Congress before introducing United States Armed Forces into hostilities or into situations where imminent involvement in hostilities is clearly indicated by the circumstances, and after every such introduction shall consult regularly with the Congress until United States Armed Forces are no longer engaged in hostilities or have been removed from such situations.

§ 1543. Reporting requirement

(a) Written report; time of submission; circumstances necessitating submission; information reported

In the absence of a declaration of war, in any case in which United States Armed Forces are introduced—

(1) into hostilities or into situations where imminent involvement in hostilities is clearly indicated by the circumstances;

(2) into the territory, airspace or waters of a foreign nation, while equipped for combat, except for deployments which relate solely to supply, replacement, repair, or training of such forces; or

(3) in numbers which substantially enlarge United States Armed Forces equipped for combat already located in a foreign nation;

the President shall submit within 48 hours to the Speaker of the House of Representatives and to the President pro tempore of the Senate a report, in writing, setting forth—

(A) the circumstances necessitating the introduction of United States Armed Forces;

(B) the constitutional and legislative authority under which such introduction took place; and

(C) the estimated scope and duration of the hostilities or involvement.

(b) Other information reported

The President shall provide such other information as the Congress may request in the fulfillment of its constitutional responsibilities with respect to committing the Nation to war and to the use of United States Armed Forces abroad.

(c) Periodic reports; semiannual requirement

Whenever United States Armed Forces are introduced into hostilities or into any situation described in subsection (a) of this section, the President shall, so long as such armed forces continue to be engaged in such hostilities or situation, report to the Congress periodically on the status of such hostilities or situation as well as on the scope and duration of such hostilities or situation, but in no event shall he report to the Congress less often than once every six months.

§ 1544. Congressional action

(a) Transmittal of report and referral to Congressional committees; joint request for convening Congress

Each report submitted pursuant to section 1543(a)(1) of this title shall be transmitted to the Speaker of the House of Representatives and to the President pro tempore of the Senate on the same calendar day. Each report so transmitted shall be referred to the Committee on Foreign Affairs of the House of Representatives and to the Committee on Foreign Relations of the Senate for appropriate action. If, when the report is transmitted, the Congress has adjourned sine die or has adjourned for any period in excess of three calendar days, the Speaker of the House of Representatives and the President pro tempore of the Senate, if they deem it advisable (or if petitioned by at least 30 percent of the membership of their respective Houses) shall jointly request the President to convene Congress in order that it may consider the report and take appropriate action pursuant to this section.

(b) Termination of use of United States Armed Forces; exceptions; extension period

Within sixty calendar days after a report is submitted or is required to be submitted pursuant to section 1543(a)(1) of this title, whichever is earlier, the President shall terminate any use of United States Armed Forces with respect to which such report was submitted (or required to be submitted), unless the Congress (1) has declared war or has enacted a specific authorization for such use of United States Armed Forces, (2) has extended by law such sixty-day period, or (3) is physically unable to meet as a result of an armed attack upon the United States. Such sixty-day period shall be extended for not more than an additional thirty days if the President determines and certifies to the Congress in writing that unavoidable military necessity respecting the safety of United States Armed Forces requires the continued use of such armed forces in the course of bringing about a prompt removal of such forces.

(c) Concurrent resolution for removal by President of United States Armed Forces

Notwithstanding subsection (b) of this section, at any time that United States Armed Forces are engaged in hostilities outside the territory of the United States, its possessions and territories without a declaration of war or specific statutory authorization, such forces shall be removed by the President if the Congress so directs by concurrent resolution.

§ 1545. Congressional priority procedures for joint resolution or bill

(a) Time requirement; referral to Congressional committee; single report

Any joint resolution or bill introduced pursuant to section 1544(b) of this title at least thirty calendar days before the expiration of the sixty-day period specified in such section shall be referred to the Committee on Foreign Affairs of the House of Representatives or the Committee on Foreign Relations of the Senate, as the case may be, and such committee shall report one such joint resolution or bill, together with its recommendations, not later than twenty-four calendar days before the expiration of the sixty-day period specified in such section, unless such House shall otherwise determine by the yeas and nays.

(b) Pending business; vote

Any joint resolution or bill so reported shall become the pending business of the House in question (in the case of the Senate the time for debate shall be equally divided between the proponents and the opponents), and shall be voted on within three calendar days thereafter, unless such House shall otherwise determine by yeas and nays.

(c) Referral to other House committee

Such a joint resolution or bill passed by one House shall be referred to the committee of the other House named in subsection (a) of this section and shall be reported out not later than fourteen calendar days before the expiration of the sixty-day period specified in section 1544(b) of this title. The joint resolution or bill so reported shall become the pending business of the House in question and shall be voted on within three calendar days after it has been reported, unless such House shall otherwise determine by yeas and nays.

(d) Disagreement between Houses

In the case of any disagreement between the two Houses of Congress with respect to a joint resolution or bill passed by both Houses, conferees shall be promptly appointed and the committee of conference shall make and file a report with respect to such resolution or bill not later than four calendar days before the expiration of the sixty-day period specified in section 1544(b) of this title. In the event the conferees are unable to agree within 48 hours, they shall report back to their respective Houses in disagreement. Notwithstanding any rule in either House concerning the printing of conference reports in the Record or concerning any delay in the consideration of such reports, such report shall be acted on by both Houses not later than the expiration of such sixty-day period.

§ 1546. Congressional priority procedures for concurrent resolution

(a) Referral to Congressional committee; single report

Any concurrent resolution introduced pursuant to section 1544(c) of this title shall be referred to the Committee on Foreign Affairs of the House of Representatives or the Committee on Foreign Relations of the Senate, as the case may be, and one such concurrent resolution shall be reported out by such committee together with its recommendations within fifteen calendar days, unless such House shall otherwise determine by the yeas and nays.

(b) Pending business; vote

Any concurrent resolution so reported shall become the pending business of the House in question (in the case of the Senate the time for debate shall be equally divided between the proponents and the opponents) and shall be voted on within three calendar days thereafter, unless such House shall otherwise determine by yeas and nays.

(c) Referral to other House committee

Such a concurrent resolution passed by one House shall be referred to the committee of the other House named in subsection (a) of this section and shall be reported out by such committee together with its recommendations within fifteen calendar days and shall thereupon become the pending business of such House and shall be voted upon within three calendar days, unless such House shall otherwise determine by yeas and nays.

(d) Disagreement between Houses

In the case of any disagreement between the two Houses of Congress with respect to a concurrent resolution passed by both Houses, conferees shall be promptly appointed and the committee of conference shall make and file a report with respect to such concurrent resolution within six calendar days after the legislation is referred to the committee of conference.

§ 1547. Interpretation of joint resolution

(a) Inferences from any law or treaty

Authority to introduce United States Armed Forces into hostilities or into situations wherein involvement in hostilities is clearly indicated by the circumstances shall not be inferred—

(1) from any provision of law (whether or not in effect before November 7, 1973), including any provision contained in any appropriation Act, unless such provision specifically authorizes the introduction of United States Armed Forces into hostilities or into such situations and states that it is intended to constitute specific statutory authorization within the meaning of this chapter; or

(2) from any treaty heretofore or hereafter ratified unless such treaty is implemented by legislation specifically authorizing the introduction of United States Armed Forces into hostilities or into such situations and stating that it is intended to constitute specific statutory authorization within the meaning of this chapter.

(b) Joint headquarters operations of high-level military commands

Nothing in this chapter shall be construed to require any further specific statutory authorization to permit members of United States Armed Forces to participate jointly with members of the armed forces of one or more foreign countries in the headquarters operations of high-level military commands which were established prior to November 7, 1973, and pursuant to the United Nations Charter or any treaty ratified by the United States prior to such date.

(c) Introduction of United States Armed Forces

For purposes of this chapter, the term "introduction of United States Armed Forces" includes the assignment of members of such armed forces to command, coordinate, participate in the movement of, or accompany the regular or irregular military forces of any foreign country or government when such military forces are engaged, or there exists an imminent threat that such forces will become engaged, in hostilities.

(d) Constitutional authorities or existing treaties unaffected; construction against grant of Presidential authority respecting use of United States Armed Forces

Nothing in this chapter—

(1) is intended to alter the constitutional authority of the Congress or of the President, or the provisions of existing treaties; or

(2) shall be construed as granting any authority to the President with respect to the introduction of United States Armed Forces into hostilities or into

situations wherein involvement in hostilities is clearly indicated by the circumstances which authority he would not have had in the absence of this chapter.

§ 1548. Separability of provisions

If any provision of this chapter or the application thereof to any person or circumstance is held invalid, the remainder of the chapter and the application of such provision to any other person or circumstance shall not be affected thereby.

Notwithstanding any rule in either House concerning the printing of conference reports in the Record or concerning any delay in the consideration of such reports, such report shall be acted on by both Houses not later than six calendar days after the conference report is filed. In the event the conferees are unable to agree within 48 hours, they shall report back to their respective Houses in disagreement.

2.31 RESOLUTION ON THE DEFINITION OF AGGRESSION. Adopted by the U.N. General Assembly, Dec. 14, 1974. U.N.G.A. Res. 3314 (XXIX), 29 U.N. GAOR, Supp. (No. 31) 142, U.N. Doc. A/9631 (1975), *reprinted in* 13 I.L.M. 710 (1974)

THE GENERAL ASSEMBLY,

Having considered the report of the Special Committee on the Question of Defining Aggression, established pursuant to its resolution 2330 (XXII) of 18 December 1967, covering the work of its seventh session held from 11 March to 12 April 1974, including the draft Definition of Aggression adopted by the Special Committee by consensus and recommended for adoption by the General Assembly,

Deeply convinced that the adoption of the Definition of Aggression would contribute to the strengthening of international peace and security,

1. *Approves* the Definition of Aggression, the text of which is annexed to the present resolution;

2. *Expresses its appreciation* to the Special Committee on the Question of Defining Aggression for its work which resulted in the elaboration of the Definition of Aggression;

3. *Calls upon* all States to refrain from all acts of aggression and other uses of force contrary to the Charter of the United Nations and the Declaration on Principles of International Law concerning Friendly Relations and Co-operation among States in accordance with the Charter of the United Nations;

4. *Calls the attention* of the Security Council to the Definition of Aggression, as set out below, and recommends that it should, as appropriate, take account of that Definition as guidance in determining, in accordance with the Charter, the existence of an act of aggression.

ANNEX. DEFINITION OF AGGRESSION

THE GENERAL ASSEMBLY

Basing itself on the fact that one of the fundamental purposes of the United Nations is to maintain international peace and security and to take effective collective measures for the prevention and removal of threats to the peace, and for the suppression of acts of aggression or other breaches of the peace,

Recalling that the Security Council, in accordance with Article 39 of the Charter of the United Nations, shall determine the existence of any threat to the peace, breach of the peace or act of aggression and shall make recommendations, or decide what measures shall be taken in accordance with Articles 41 and 42, to maintain or restore international peace and security,

Recalling also the duty of States under the Charter to settle their international disputes by peaceful means in order not to endanger international peace, security and justice,

Bearing in mind that nothing in this Definition shall be interpreted as in any way affecting the scope of the provisions of the Charter with respect to the functions and powers of the organs of the United Nations,

Considering also that, since aggression is the most serious and dangerous form of the illegal use of force, being fraught, in the conditions created by the existence of all types of weapons of mass destruction, with the possible threat of a world conflict and all its catastrophic consequences, aggression should be defined at the present stage,

Reaffirming the duty of States not to use armed force to deprive peoples of their right to self-determination, freedom and independence, or to disrupt territorial integrity,

Reaffirming also that the territory of a State shall not be violated by being the object, even temporarily, of military occupation or of other measures of force taken by another State in contravention of the Charter, and that it shall not be the object of acquisition by another State resulting from such measures or the threat thereof,

Reaffirming also the provisions of the Declaration on Principles of International Law concerning Friendly Relations and Co-operation among States in accordance with the Charter of the United Nations,

Convinced that the adoption of a definition of aggression ought to have the effect of deterring a potential aggressor, would simplify the determination of acts of aggression and also facilitate the protection of the rights and lawful interests of, and the rendering of assistance to, the victim,

Believing that, although the question whether an act of aggression has been committed must be considered in the light of all the circumstances of each particular case, it is nevertheless desirable to formulate basic principles as guidance for such determination,

Adopts the following Definition of Aggression:

Article 1. Aggression is the use of armed force by a State against the sovereignty, territorial integrity or political independence of another State, or in any other manner inconsistent with the Charter of the United Nations, as set out in this Definition.

Article 2. The first use of armed force by a State in contravention of the Charter shall constitute *prima facie* evidence of an act of aggression although the Security Council may, in conformity with the Charter, conclude that a determination that an act of aggression has been committed would not be justified in the light of other relevant circumstances, including the fact that the acts concerned or their consequences are not of sufficient gravity.

Article 3. Any of the following acts, regardless of a declaration of war, shall, subject to and in accordance with the provisions of article 2, qualify as an act of aggression:

(a) The invasion or attack by the armed forces of a State of the territory of another State, or any military occupation, however temporary, resulting from such invasion or attack, or any annexation by the use of force of the territory of another State or part thereof;

(b) Bombardment by the armed forces of a State against the territory of another State or the use of any weapons by a State against the territory of another State;

(c) The blockade of the ports or coasts of a State by the armed forces of another State;

(d) An attack by the armed forces of a State on the land, sea or air forces, or marine and air fleets of another State;

(e) The use of armed forces of one State which are within the territory of another State with the agreement of the receiving State, in contravention of the conditions provided for in the agreement or any extension of their presence in such territory beyond the termination of the agreement;

(f) The action of a State in allowing its territory, which it has placed at the disposal of another State, to be used by that other State for perpetrating an act of aggression against a third State;

(g) The sending by or on behalf of a State of armed bands, groups, irregulars or mercenaries, which carry out acts of armed force against another State of such gravity as to amount to the acts listed above, or its substantial involvement therein.

Article 4. The acts enumerated above are not exhaustive and the Security Council may determine that other acts constitute aggression under the provisions of the Charter.

Article 5. (1) No consideration of whatever nature, whether political, economic, military or otherwise, may serve as a justification for aggression.

(2) A war of aggression is a crime against international peace. Aggression gives rise to international responsibility.

(3) No territorial acquisition or special advantage resulting from aggression is or shall be recognized as lawful.

Article 6. Nothing in this Definition shall be construed as in any way enlarging or diminishing the scope of the Charter, including its provisions concerning cases in which the use of force is lawful.

Article 7. Nothing in this Definition, and in particular article 3, could in any way prejudice the right to self-determination, freedom and independence, as derived from the Charter, of peoples forcibly deprived of that right and referred to in the Declaration on Principles of International Law concerning Friendly Relations and Co-operation among States in accordance with the Charter of the United Nations, particularly peoples under colonial and racist régimes or other forms of alien domination; nor the right of these peoples to struggle to that end and to seek and receive support, in accordance with the principles of the Charter and in conformity with the above-mentioned Declaration.

Article 8. In their interpretation and application the above provisions are interrelated and each provision should be construed in the context of the other provisions.

2.32 CONVENTION ON THE PROHIBITION OF MILITARY OR ANY OTHER HOSTILE USE OF ENVIRONMENTAL MODIFICATION TECHNIQUES.[a] Done at New York, Dec. 10, 1976. Entered into force, Oct. 5, 1978; for the United States, Jan. 17, 1980. 31 U.S.T. 333, T.I.A.S. No. 9614, 1976 U.N.JURID. Y.B. 125, *reprinted in* 16 I.L.M. 88 (1977)

ARTICLE I

1. Each State Party to this Convention undertakes not to engage in military or any other hostile use of environmental modification techniques having widespread, long-lasting or severe effects as the means of destruction, damage or injury to any other State Party.

2. Each State Party to this Convention undertakes not to assist, encourage or induce any State, group of States or international organization to engage in activities contrary to the provisions of paragraph 1 of this article.

ARTICLE II

As used in article I, the term "environmental modification techniques" refers to any technique for changing—through the deliberate manipulation of natural processes—the dynamics, composition or structure of the earth, including its biota, lithosphere, hydrosphere, and atmosphere, or of outer space.

ARTICLE III

1. The provisions of this Convention shall not hinder the use of environmental modification techniques for peaceful purposes and shall be without prejudice to generally recognized principles and applicable rules of international law concerning such use.

2. The State Parties to this Convention undertake to facilitate, and have the right to participate in, the fullest possible exchange of scientific and technological information on the use of environmental modification techniques for peaceful purposes. States Parties in a position to do so shall contribute, alone or together with other States or international organizations, to international economic and scientific co-operation in the preservation, improvement, and peaceful utilization of the environment, with due consideration for the needs of the developing areas of the world.

ARTICLE IV

Each State Party to this Convention undertakes to take any measures it considers necessary in accordance with its constitutional processes to prohibit and prevent any activity in violation of the provisions of the Convention anywhere under its jurisdiction or control.

ARTICLE V

1. The States Parties to this Convention undertake to consult one another and to co-operate in solving any problems which may arise in relation to the objectives of, or in the application of the provisions of, the Convention. Consultation and co-operation pursuant to this article may also be undertaken through appropriate international procedures within the framework of the United Nations and in accordance with its Charter. These international procedures may include the services of

a. Annex omitted.

appropriate international organizations, as well as of a consultative committee of experts as provided for in paragraph 2 of this article.

2. For the purposes set forth in paragraph 1 of this article, the Depositary shall, within one month of the receipt of a request from any State Party, convene a consultative committee of experts. Any State Party may appoint an expert to this committee whose functions and rules of procedure are set out in the annex, which constitutes an integral part of this Convention. The committee shall transmit to the Depositary a summary of its findings of fact, incorporating all views and information presented to the committee during its proceedings. The Depositary shall distribute the summary to all States Parties.

3. Any State Party to this Convention which has reasons to believe that any other State Party is acting in breach of obligations deriving from the provisions of the Convention may lodge a complaint with the Security Council of the United Nations. Such a complaint should include all relevant information as well as all possible evidence supporting its validity.

4. Each State Party to this Convention undertakes to co-operate in carrying out any investigation which the Security Council may initiate, in accordance with the provisions of the Charter of the United Nations, on the basis of the complaint received by the Council. The Security Council shall inform the States Parties to the Convention of the results of the investigation.

5. Each State Party to this Convention undertakes to provide or support assistance, in accordance with the provisions of the Charter of the United Nations, to any Party to the Convention which so requests, if the Security Council decides that such Party has been harmed or is likely to be harmed as a result of violation of the Convention.

ARTICLE VI

1. Any State Party may propose amendments to this Convention. The text of any proposed amendment shall be submitted to the Depositary, who shall promptly circulate it to all States Parties.

2. An amendment shall enter into force for all States Parties which have accepted it, upon the deposit with the Depositary of instruments of acceptance by a majority of States Parties. Thereafter it shall enter into force for any remaining State Party on the date of deposit of its instrument of acceptance.

ARTICLE VII

This Convention shall be of unlimited duration.

ARTICLE VIII

1. Five years after the entry into force of this Convention, a conference of the States Parties to the Convention shall be convened by the Depositary at Geneva. The conference shall review the operation of the Convention with a view to ensuring that its purposes and provisions are being realized, and shall in particular examine the effectiveness of the provisions of article I, paragraph 1, in eliminating the dangers of military or any other hostile use of environmental modification techniques.

2. At intervals of not less than five years thereafter, a majority of the States Parties to this Convention may obtain, by submitting a proposal to this effect to the Depositary, the convening of a conference with the same objectives.

3. If no review conference has been convened pursuant to paragraph 2 of this article within 10 years following the conclusion of a previous review conference, the Depositary shall solicit the views of all States Parties to this Convention on the

holding of such a conference. If one third or 10 of the States Parties, whichever number is less, respond affirmatively, the Depositary shall take immediate steps to convene the conference.

* * *

2.33 PROTOCOL ADDITIONAL TO THE GENEVA CONVENTIONS OF AUGUST 12, 1949, AND RELATING TO THE PROTECTION OF VICTIMS OF INTERNATIONAL ARMED CONFLICTS.[a] Done at Geneva, June 8, 1977. Entered into force, Dec. 7, 1978. 1977 U.N. JURID. Y.B. 95, *reprinted in* 16 I.L.M. 1391 (1977)[b]

Part I

GENERAL PROVISIONS

Article I—General principles and scope of application

1. The High Contracting Parties undertake to respect and to ensure respect for this Protocol in all circumstances.

2. In cases not covered by this Protocol or by other international agreements, civilians and combatants remain under the protection and authority of the principles of international law derived from established custom, from the principles of humanity and from dictates of public conscience.

3. This Protocol, which supplements the Geneva Conventions of 12 August 1949 for the protection of war victims, shall apply in the situations referred to in Article 2 common to those Conventions.

4. The situations referred to in the preceding paragraph include armed conflicts in which peoples are fighting against colonial domination and alien occupation and against racist régimes in the exercise of their right of self-determination, as enshrined in the Charter of the United Nations and the Declaration on Principles of International Law concerning Friendly Relations and Co-operation among States in accordance with the Charter of the United Nations.

* * *

Article 4—Legal status of the Parties to the conflict

The application of the Conventions and of this Protocol, as well as the conclusion of the agreements provided for therein, shall not affect the legal status of the Parties to the conflict. Neither the occupation of a territory nor the application of the Conventions and this Protocol shall affect the legal status of the territory in question.

Part II

WOUNDED, SICK AND SHIPWRECKED

Section I

GENERAL PROTECTION

* * *

Article 10—Protection and care

1. All the wounded, sick and shipwrecked, to whichever Party they belong, shall be respected and protected.

2. In all circumstances they shall be treated humanely and shall receive, to the fullest extent practicable and with the least possible delay, the medical care and attention required by their condition. There shall be no distinction among them founded on any grounds other than medical ones.

a. Also known as "1977 Protocol I." *See also* Basic Documents 2.10, 2.11, 2.12, & 2.13, *supra*, and Basic Document 2.34, *infra*.

b. Annexes I and II to this Protocol are omitted.

Article 11—Protection of persons

1. The physical or mental health and integrity of persons who are in the power of the adverse Party or who are interned, detained or otherwise deprived of liberty as a result of a situation referred to in Article 1 shall not be endangered by any unjustified act or omission. Accordingly, it is prohibited to subject the persons described in this Article to any medical procedure which is not indicated by the state of health of the person concerned and which is not consistent with generally accepted medical standards which would be applied under similar medical circumstances to persons who are nationals of the Party conducting the procedure and who are in no way deprived of liberty.

2. It is, in particular, prohibited to carry out on such persons, even with their consent:

(*a*) physical mutilations;

(*b*) medical or scientific experiments;

(*c*) removal of tissue or organs for transplantation, except where these acts are justified in conformity with the conditions provided for in paragraph 1.

3. Exceptions to the prohibition in paragraph 2 (*c*) may be made only in the case of donations of blood for transfusion or of skin for grafting, provided that they are given voluntarily and without any coercion or inducement, and then only for therapeutic purposes, under conditions consistent with generally accepted medical standards and controls designed for the benefit of both the donor and the recipient.

4. Any wilful act or omission which seriously endangers the physical or mental health or integrity of any person who is in the power of a Party other than the one on which he depends and which either violates any of the prohibitions in paragraphs 1 and 2 or fails to comply with the requirements of paragraph 3 shall be a grave breach of this Protocol.

5. The persons described in paragraph 1 have the right to refuse any surgical operation. In case of refusal, medical personnel shall endeavour to obtain a written statement to that effect, signed or acknowledged by the patient.

* * *

Article 12—Protection of medical units

1. Medical units shall be respected and protected at all times and shall not be the object of attack.

* * *

Article 15—Protection of civilian medical and religious personnel

1. Civilian medical personnel shall be respected and protected.

2. If needed, all available help shall be afforded to civilian medical personnel in an area where civilian medical services are disrupted by reason of combat activity.

* * *

Article 17—Role of the civilian population and of aid societies

1. The civilian population shall respect the wounded, sick and shipwrecked, even if they belong to the adverse Party, and shall commit no act of violence against them. The civilian population and aid societies, such as national Red Cross (Red Crescent, Red Lion and Sun) Societies, shall be permitted, even on their own initiative, to collect and care for the wounded, sick and shipwrecked, even in invaded or occupied areas. No one shall be harmed, prosecuted, convicted or punished for such humanitarian acts.

* * *

Article 18—Identification

1. Each Party to the conflict shall endeavour to ensure that medical and religious personnel and medical units and transports are identifiable.

2. Each Party to the conflict shall also endeavour to adopt and to implement methods and procedures which will make it possible to recognize medical units and transports which use the distinctive emblem and distinctive signals.

3. In occupied territory and in areas where fighting is taking place or is likely to take place, civilian medical personnel and civilian religious personnel should be recognizable by the distinctive emblem and an identity card certifying their status.

* * *

Article 20—Prohibition of reprisals

Reprisals against the persons and objects protected by this Part are prohibited.

Section II

MEDICAL TRANSPORTATION

* * *

Section III

MISSING AND DEAD PERSONS

Article 32—General principle

In the implementation of this Section, the activities of the High Contracting Parties, of the Parties to the conflict and of the international humanitarian organizations mentioned in the Conventions and in this Protocol shall be prompted mainly by the right of families to know the fate of their relatives.

Article 33—Missing persons

1. As soon as circumstances permit, and at the latest from the end of active hostilities, each Party to the conflict shall search for the persons who have been reported missing by an adverse Party. Such adverse Party shall transmit all relevant information concerning such persons in order to facilitate such searches.

* * *

Article 34—Remains of deceased

1. The remains of persons who have died for reasons related to occupation or in detention resulting from occupation or hostilities and those of persons not nationals of the country in which they have died as a result of hostilities shall be respected, and the gravesites of all such persons shall be respected, maintained and marked as provided for in Article 130 of the Fourth Convention, where their remains or gravesites would not receive more favourable consideration under the Conventions and this Protocol.

* * *

Part III

METHODS AND MEANS OF WARFARE COMBATANT AND PRISONER-OF-WAR STATUS

Section I

METHODS AND MEANS OF WARFARE

Article 35—Basic rules

1. In any armed conflict, the right of the Parties to the conflict to choose methods or means of warfare is not unlimited.

2. It is prohibited to employ weapons, projectiles and material and methods of warfare of a nature to cause superfluous injury or unnecessary suffering.

3. It is prohibited to employ methods or means of warfare which are intended, or may be expected, to cause widespread, long-term and severe damage to the natural environment.

Article 36—New weapons

In the study, development, acquisition or adoption of a new weapon, means or method of warfare, a High Contracting Party is under an obligation to determine whether its employment would, in some or all circumstances, be prohibited by this Protocol or by any other rule of international law applicable to the High Contracting Party.

Article 37—Prohibition of perfidy

1. It is prohibited to kill, injure or capture an adversary by resort to perfidy. Acts inviting the confidence of an adversary to lead him to believe that he is entitled to, or is obliged to accord, protection under the rules of international law applicable in armed conflict, with intent to betray that confidence, shall constitute perfidy. The following acts are examples of perfidy:

(*a*) the feigning of an intent to negotiate under a flag of truce or of a surrender;

(*b*) the feigning of an incapacitation by wounds or sickness;

(*c*) the feigning of civilian, non-combatant status; and

(*d*) the feigning of protected status by the use of signs, emblems or uniforms of the United Nations or of neutral or other States not Parties to the conflict.

2. Ruses of war are not prohibited. Such ruses are acts which are intended to mislead an adversary or to induce him to act recklessly but which infringe no rule of international law applicable in armed conflict and which are not perfidious because they do not invite the confidence of an adversary with respect to protection under that law. The following are examples of such ruses: the use of camouflage, decoys, mock operations and misinformation.

Article 38—Recognized emblems

1. It is prohibited to make improper use of the distinctive emblem of the red cross, red crescent or red lion and sun or of other emblems, signs or signals provided for by the Conventions or by this Protocol. It is also prohibited to misuse deliberately in an armed conflict other internationally recognized protective emblems, signs or signals, including the flag of truce, and the protective emblem of cultural property.

2. It is prohibited to make use of the distinctive emblem of the United Nations, except as authorized by that Organization.

Article 39—Emblems of nationality

1. It is prohibited to make use in an armed conflict of the flags or military emblems, insignia or uniforms of neutral or other States not Parties to the conflict.

2. It is prohibited to make use of the flags or military emblems, insignia or uniforms of adverse Parties while engaging in attacks or in order to shield, favour, protect or impede military operations.

3. Nothing in this Article or in Article 37, paragraph 1 (*d*), shall affect the existing generally recognized rules of international law applicable to espionage or to the use of flags in the conduct of armed conflict at sea.

Article 40—Quarter

It is prohibited to order that there shall be no survivors, to threaten an adversary therewith or to conduct hostilities on this basis.

Article 41—Safeguard of an enemy hors de combat

1. A person who is recognized or who, in the circumstances should be recognized to be *hors de combat* shall not be made the object of attack.

2. A person is *hors de combat* if:

(*a*) he is in the power of an adverse Party;

(*b*) he clearly expresses an intention to surrender; or

(*c*) he has been rendered unconscious or is otherwise incapacitated by wounds or sickness, and therefore is incapable of defending himself;

provided that in any of these cases he abstains from any hostile act and does not attempt to escape.

3. When persons entitled to protection as prisoners of war have fallen into the power of an adverse Party under unusual conditions of combat which prevent their evacuation as provided for in Part III, Section I, of the Third Convention, they shall be released and all feasible precautions shall be taken to ensure their safety.

Article 42—Occupants of aircraft

1. No person parachuting from an aircraft in distress shall be made the object of attack during his descent.

2. Upon reaching the ground in territory controlled by an adverse Party, a person who has parachuted from an aircraft in distress shall be given an opportunity to surrender before being made the object of attack, unless it is apparent that he is engaging in a hostile act.

3. Airborne troops are not protected by this Article.

Section II

COMBATANT AND PRISONER–OF–WAR STATUS

Article 43—Armed forces

1. The armed forces of a Party to a conflict consist of all organized armed forces, groups and units which are under a command responsible to that Party for the conduct of its subordinates, even if that Party is represented by a government or an authority not recognized by an adverse Party. Such armed forces shall be subject to an internal disciplinary system which, *inter alia,* shall enforce compliance with the rules of international law applicable in armed conflict.

2. Members of the armed forces of a Party to a conflict (other than medical personnel and chaplains covered by Article 33 of the Third Convention) are combatants, that is to say, they have the right to participate directly in hostilities.

3. Whenever a Party to a conflict incorporates a paramilitary or armed law enforcement agency into its armed forces it shall so notify the other Parties to the conflict.

Article 44—Combatants and prisoners of war

1. Any combatant, as defined in Article 43, who falls into the power of an adverse Party shall be a prisoner of war.

2. While all combatants are obliged to comply with the rules of international law applicable in armed conflict, violations of these rules shall not deprive a combatant of his right to be a combatant or, if he falls into the power of an adverse Party, of his right to be a prisoner of war, except as provided in paragraphs 3 and 4.

3. In order to promote the protection of the civilian population from the effects of hostilities, combatants are obliged to distinguish themselves from the civilian population while they are engaged in an attack or in a military operation preparatory to an attack. Recognizing, however, that there are situations in armed conflicts where, owing to the nature of the hostilities an armed combatant cannot so distinguish himself, he shall retain his status as a combatant, provided that, in such situations, he carries his arms openly:

(*a*) during each military engagement, and

(*b*) during such time as he is visible to the adversary while he is engaged in a military deployment preceding the launching of an attack in which he is to participate.

Acts which comply with the requirements of this paragraph shall not be considered as perfidious within the meaning of Article 37, paragraph 1(*c*).

4. A combatant who falls into the power of an adverse Party while failing to meet the requirements set forth in the second sentence of paragraph 3 shall forfeit his right to be a prisoner of war, but he shall, nevertheless, be given protections equivalent in all respects to those accorded to prisoners of war by the Third Convention and by this Protocol. This protection includes protections equivalent to those accorded to prisoners of war by the Third Convention in the case where such a person is tried and punished for any offences he has committed.

5. Any combatant who falls into the power of an adverse Party while not engaged in an attack or in a military operation preparatory to an attack shall not forfeit his rights to be a combatant and a prisoner of war by virtue of his prior activities.

6. This Article is without prejudice to the right of any person to be a prisoner of war pursuant to Article 4 of the Third Convention.

7. This Article is not intended to change the generally accepted practice of States with respect to the wearing of the uniform by combatants assigned to the regular, uniformed armed units of a Party to the conflict.

8. In addition to the categories of persons mentioned in Article 13 of the First and Second Conventions, all members of the armed forces of a Party to the conflict, as defined in Article 43 of this Protocol, shall be entitled to protection under those Conventions if they are wounded or sick or, in the case of the Second Convention, shipwrecked at sea or in other waters.

* * *

Article 46—Spies

1. Notwithstanding any other provision of the Conventions or of this Protocol, any member of the armed forces of a Party to the conflict who falls into the power of an adverse Party while engaging in espionage shall not have the right to the status of prisoner of war and may be treated as a spy.

* * *

Article 47—Mercenaries

1. A mercenary shall not have the right to be a combatant or a prisoner of war.

2. A mercenary is any person who:

(*a*) is specially recruited locally or abroad in order to fight in an armed conflict;

(*b*) does, in fact, take a direct part in the hostilities;

(*c*) is motivated to take part in the hostilities essentially by the desire for private gain and, in fact, is promised, by or on behalf of a Party to the conflict, material compensation substantially in excess of that promised or paid to combatants of similar ranks and functions in the armed forces of that Party;

(*d*) is neither a national of a Party to the conflict nor a resident of territory controlled by a Party to the conflict;

(*e*) is not a member of the armed forces of a Party to the conflict; and

(*f*) has not been sent by a State which is not a Party to the conflict on official duty as a member of its armed forces.

Part IV

CIVILIAN POPULATION

Section I

GENERAL PROTECTION AGAINST EFFECTS OF HOSTILITIES

CHAPTER I

BASIC RULE AND FIELD OF APPLICATION

Article 48—Basic rule

In order to ensure respect for and protection of the civilian population and civilian objects, the Parties to the conflict shall at all times distinguish between the civilian population and combatants and between civilian objects and military objectives and accordingly shall direct their operations only against military objectives.

* * *

CHAPTER II

CIVILIANS AND CIVILIAN POPULATION

Article 50—Definition of civilians and civilian population

1. A civilian is any person who does not belong to one of the categories of persons referred to in Article 4(A)(1), (2), (3), and (6) of the Third Convention and in Article 43 of this Protocol. In case of doubt whether a person is a civilian, that person shall be considered to be a civilian.

2. The civilian population comprises all persons who are civilians.

3. The presence within the civilian population of individuals who do not come within the definition of civilians does not deprive the population of its civilian character.

Article 51—Protection of the civilian population

1. The civilian population and individual civilians shall enjoy general protection against dangers arising from military operations. To give effect to this protection, the following rules, which are additional to other applicable rules of international law, shall be observed in all circumstances.

2. The civilian population as such, as well as individual civilians, shall not be the object of attack. Acts or threats of violence the primary purpose of which is to spread terror among the civilian population are prohibited.

3. Civilians shall enjoy the protection afforded by this section, unless and for such time as they take a direct part in hostilities.

4. Indiscriminate attacks are prohibited. Indiscriminate attacks are:

(*a*) those which are not directed at a specific military objective;

(*b*) those which employ a method or means of combat which cannot be directed at a specific military objective; or (*c*) those which employ a method or means of combat the effects of which cannot be limited as required by this Protocol;

and consequently, in each such case, are of a nature to strike military objectives and civilians or civilian objects without distinction.

5. Among others, the following types of attacks are to be considered as indiscriminate:

(*a*) an attack by bombardment by any methods or means which treats as a single military objective a number of clearly separated and distinct military objectives located in a city, town, village or other area containing a similar concentration of civilians or civilian objects; and

(*b*) an attack which may be expected to cause incidental loss of civilian life, injury to civilians, damage to civilian objects, or a combination thereof, which would be excessive in relation to the concrete and direct military advantage anticipated.

6. Attacks against the civilian population or civilians by way of reprisals are prohibited.

7. The presence or movements of the civilian population or individual civilians shall not be used to render certain points or areas immune from military operations, in particular in attempts to shield military objectives from attacks or to shield, favour or impede military operations. The Parties to the conflict shall not direct the movement of the civilian population or individual civilians in order to attempt to shield military objectives from attacks or to shield military operations.

8. Any violation of these prohibitions shall not release the Parties to the conflict from their legal obligations with respect to the civilian population and civilians, including the obligations to take the precautionary measures provided for in Article 57.

CHAPTER III

CIVILIAN OBJECTS

Article 52—General protection of civilian objects

1. Civilian objects shall not be the object of attack or of reprisals. Civilian objects are all objects which are not military objectives as defined in paragraph 2.

2. Attacks shall be limited strictly to military objectives. In so far as objects are concerned, military objectives are limited to those objects which by their nature, location, purpose or use make an effective contribution to military action and whose total or partial destruction, capture or neutralization, in the circumstances ruling at the time, offers a definite military advantage.

3. In case of doubt whether an object which is normally dedicated to civilian purposes, such as a place of worship, a house or other dwelling or a school, is being used to make an effective contribution to military action, it shall be presumed not to be so used.

Article 53—Protection of cultural objects and of places of worship

Without prejudice to the provisions of the Hague Convention for the Protection of Cultural Property in the Event of Armed Conflict of 14 May 1954, and of other relevant international instruments, it is prohibited:

(a) to commit any acts of hostility directed against the historic monuments, works of art or places of worship which constitute the cultural or spiritual heritage of peoples;

(b) to use such objects in support of the military effort;

(c) to make such objects the object of reprisals.

Article 54—Protection of objects indispensable to the survival of the civilian population

1. Starvation of civilians as a method of warfare is prohibited.

2. It is prohibited to attack, destroy, remove or render useless objects indispensable to the survival of the civilian population, such as food-stuffs, agricultural areas for the production of food-stuffs, crops, livestock, drinking water installations and supplies and irrigation works, for the specific purpose of denying them for their sustenance value to the civilian population or to the adverse Party, whatever the motive, whether in order to starve out civilians, to cause them to move away, or for any other motive.

3. The prohibitions in paragraph 2 shall not apply to such of the objects covered by it as are used by an adverse Party:

(a) as sustenance solely for the members of its armed forces; or

(b) if not as sustenance, then in direct support of military action, provided, however, that in no event shall actions against these objects be taken which may be expected to leave the civilian population with such inadequate food or water as to cause its starvation or force its movement.

4. These objects shall not be made the object of reprisals.

5. In recognition of the vital requirements of any Party to the conflict in the deference of its national territory against invasion, derogation from the prohibitions contained in paragraph 2 may be made by a Party to the conflict within such territory under its own control where required by imperative military necessity.

Article 55—Protection of the natural environment

1. Care shall be taken in warfare to protect the natural environment against wide-spread, long-term and severe damage. This protection includes a prohibition of the use of methods or means of warfare which are intended or may be expected to cause such damage to the natural environment and thereby to prejudice the health or survival of the population.

2. Attacks against the natural environment by way of reprisals are prohibited.

Article 56—Protection of works and installations containing dangerous forces

1. Works or installations containing dangerous forces, namely dams, dykes and nuclear electrical generating stations, shall not be made the object of attack, even where these objects are military objectives, if such attack may cause the release of dangerous forces and consequent severe losses among the civilian population. Other military objectives located at or in the vicinity of these works or installations shall not be made the object of attack if such attack may cause the release of dangerous forces from the works or installations and consequent severe losses among the civilian population.

2. The special protection against attack provided by paragraph 1 shall cease:

(a) for a dam or a dyke only if it is used for other than its normal function and in regular, significant and direct support of military operations and if such attack is the only feasible way to terminate such support;

(b) for a nuclear electrical generating station only if it provides electric power in regular, significant and direct support of military operations and if such attack is the only feasible way to terminate such support;

(c) for other military objectives located at or in the vicinity of these works or installations only if they are used in regular, significant and direct support of military operations and if such attack is the only feasible way to terminate such support.

3. In all cases, the civilian population and individual civilians shall remain entitled to all the protection accorded them by international law, including the protection of the precautionary measures provided for in Article 57. If the protection ceases and any of the works, installations or military objectives mentioned in paragraph 1 is attacked, all practical precautions shall be taken to avoid the release of the dangerous forces.

4. It is prohibited to make any of the works, installations or military objectives mentioned in paragraph 1 the object of reprisals.

5. The Parties to the conflict shall endeavour to avoid locating any military objectives in the vicinity of the works or installations mentioned in paragraph 1. Nevertheless, installations erected for the sole purpose of defending the protected works or installations from attack are permissible and shall not themselves be made the object of attack, provided that they are not used in hostilities except for defensive actions necessary to respond to attacks against the protected works or installations and that their armament is limited to weapons capable only of repelling hostile action against the protected works or installations.

6. The High Contracting Parties and the Parties to the conflict are urged to conclude further agreements among themselves to provide additional protection for objects containing dangerous forces.

7. In order to facilitate the identification of the objects protected by this article, the Parties to the conflict may mark them with a special sign consisting of a group of three bright orange circles placed on the same axis, as specified in Article 16 of Annex I to this Protocol. The absence of such marking in no way relieves any Party to the conflict of its obligations under this Article.

CHAPTER IV

PRECAUTIONARY MEASURES

Article 57—Precautions in attack

1. In the conduct of military operations, constant care shall be taken to spare the civilian population, civilians and civilian objects.

2. With respect to attacks, the following precautions shall be taken:

(a) those who plan or decide upon attack shall:

(i) do everything feasible to verify that the objectives to be attacked are neither civilians nor civilian objects and are not subject to special protection but are military objectives within the meaning of paragraph 2 of Article 52 and that it is not prohibited by the provisions of this Protocol to attack them;

(ii) take all feasible precautions in the choice of means and methods of attack with a view to avoiding, and in any event to minimizing, incidental loss of civilian life, injury to civilians and damage to civilian objects;

(iii) refrain from deciding to launch any attacks which may be expected to cause incidental loss of civilian life, injury to civilians, damage to civilian objects, or a combination thereof, which would be excessive in relation to the concrete and direct military advantage anticipated;

(b) an attack shall be cancelled or suspended if it becomes apparent that the objective is not a military one or is subject to special protection or that the attack may be expected to cause incidental loss of civilian life, injury to civilians, damage to civilian objects, or a combination thereof, which would be excessive in relation to the concrete and direct military advantage anticipated;

(c) effective advance warning shall be given of attacks which may affect the civilian population, unless circumstances do not permit.

3. When a choice is possible between several military objectives for obtaining a similar military advantage, the objective to be selected shall be that the attack on which may be expected to cause the least danger to civilian lives and to civilian objects.

4. In the conduct of military operations at sea or in the air, each Party to the conflict shall, in conformity with its rights and duties under the rules of international law applicable in armed conflict, take all reasonable precautions to avoid losses of civilian lives and damage to civilian objects.

5. No provision of this article may be construed as authorizing any attacks against the civilian population, civilians or civilian objects.

Article 58—Precautions against the effects of attacks

The Parties to the conflict shall, to the maximum extent feasible:

(a) without prejudice to Article 49 of the Fourth Convention, endeavour to remove the civilian population, individual civilians and civilian objects under their control from the vicinity of military objectives;

(b) avoid locating military objectives within or near densely populated areas;

(c) take the other necessary precautions to protect the civilian population, individual civilians and civilian objects under their control against the dangers resulting from military operations.

CHAPTER V

LOCALITIES AND ZONES UNDER SPECIAL PROTECTION

Article 59—Non-defended localities

1. It is prohibited for the Parties to the conflict to attack, by any means whatsoever, non-defended localities.

* * *

Article 60—Demilitarized zones

1. It is prohibited for the Parties to the conflict to extend their military operations to zones on which they have conferred by agreement the status of demilitarized zone, if such extension is contrary to the terms of this agreement.

* * *

CHAPTER VI

CIVIL DEFENCE

* * *

Article 62—General protection

1. Civilian civil defence organizations and their personnel shall be respected and protected, subject to the provisions of this Protocol, particularly the provisions of this section. They shall be entitled to perform their civil defence tasks except in case of imperative military necessity.

Section II

RELIEF IN FAVOUR OF THE CIVILIAN POPULATION

* * *

Article 69—Basic needs in occupied territories

1. In addition to the duties specified in Article 55 of the Fourth Convention concerning food and medical supplies, the Occupying Power shall, to the fullest extent of the means available to it and without any adverse distinction, also ensure the provision of clothing, bedding, means of shelter, other supplies essential to the

survival of the civilian population of the occupied territory and objects necessary for religious worship.

2. Relief actions for the benefit of the civilian population of occupied territories are governed by Articles 59, 60, 61, 62, 108, 109, 110 and 111 of the Fourth Convention, and by Article 71 of this Protocol, and shall be implemented without delay.

Article 70—Relief actions

1. If the civilian population of any territory under the control of a Party to the conflict, other than occupied territory, is not adequately provided with the supplies mentioned in Article 69, relief actions which are humanitarian and impartial in character and conducted without any adverse distinction shall be undertaken, subject to the agreement of the Parties concerned in such relief actions. Offers of such relief shall not be regarded as interference in the armed conflict or as unfriendly acts. In the distribution of relief consignments, priority shall be given to those persons, such as children, expectant mothers, maternity cases and nursing mothers, who, under the Fourth Convention or under this Protocol, are to be accorded privileged treatment or special protection.

2. The Parties to the conflict and each High Contracting Party shall allow and facilitate rapid and unimpeded passage of all relief consignments, equipment and personnel provided in accordance with this Section, even if such assistance is destined for the civilian population of the adverse Party.

* * *

Section III

TREATMENT OF PERSONS IN THE POWER OF A PARTY TO THE CONFLICT

CHAPTER I

FIELD OF APPLICATION AND PROTECTION OF PERSONS AND OBJECTS

* * *

Article 73—Refugees and stateless persons

Persons who, before the beginning of hostilities, were considered as stateless persons or refugees under the relevant international instruments accepted by the Parties concerned or under the national legislation of the State of refuge or State of residence shall be protected persons within the meaning of Parts I and III of the Fourth Convention, in all circumstances and without any adverse distinction.

Article 74—Reunion of dispersed families

The High Contracting Parties and the Parties to the conflict shall facilitate in every possible way the reunion of families dispersed as a result of armed conflicts and shall encourage in particular the work of the humanitarian organizations engaged in this task in accordance with the provisions of the Conventions and of this Protocol and in conformity with their respective security regulations.

Article 75—Fundamental guarantees

1. In so far as they are affected by a situation referred to in Article 1 of this Protocol, persons who are in the power of a Party to the conflict and who do not benefit from more favourable treatment under the Conventions or under this Protocol shall be treated humanely in all circumstances and shall enjoy, as a minimum, the protection provided by this Article without any adverse distinction based upon race, colour, sex, language, religion or belief, political or other opinion, national or social origin, wealth, birth or other status, or on any other similar criteria. Each

Party shall respect the person, honour, convictions and religious practices of all such persons.

2. The following acts are and shall remain prohibited at any time and in any place whatsoever, whether committed by civilian or by military agents:

(*a*) violence to the life, health, or physical or mental well-being of persons, in particular:

(i) murder;

(ii) torture of all kinds, whether physical or mental;

(iii) corporal punishment; and

(iv) mutilation;

(*b*) outrages upon personal dignity, in particular humiliating and degrading treatment, enforced prostitution and any form of indecent assault;

(*c*) the taking of hostages;

(*d*) collective punishments; and

(*e*) threats to commit any of the foregoing acts.

3. Any person arrested, detained or interned for actions related to the armed conflict shall be informed promptly, in a language he understands, of the reasons why these measures have been taken. Except in cases of arrest or detention for penal offences, such persons shall be released with the minimum delay possible and in any event as soon as the circumstances justifying the arrest, detention or internment have ceased to exist.

4. No sentence may be passed and no penalty may be executed on a person found guilty of a penal offence related to the armed conflict except pursuant to a conviction pronounced by an impartial and regularly constituted court respecting the generally recognized principles of regular judicial procedure, which include the following:

(*a*) the procedure shall provide for an accused to be informed without delay of the particulars of the offence alleged against him and shall afford the accused before and during his trial all necessary rights and means of defence;

(*b*) no one shall be convicted of an offence except on the basis of individual penal responsibility;

(*c*) no one shall be accused or convicted of a criminal offence on account of any act or omission which did not constitute a criminal offence under the national or international law to which he was subject at the time when it was committed; nor shall a heavier penalty be imposed than that which was applicable at the time when the criminal offence was committed; if, after the commission of the offence, provision is made by law for the imposition of a lighter penalty, the offender shall benefit thereby;

(*d*) anyone charged with an offence is presumed innocent until proved guilty according to law;

(*e*) anyone charged with an offence shall have the right to be tried in his presence;

(*f*) no one shall be compelled to testify against himself or to confess guilt;

(*g*) anyone charged with an offence shall have the right to examine, or have examined, the witnesses against him and to obtain the attendance and examination of witnesses on his behalf under the same conditions as witnesses against him;

(*h*) no one shall be prosecuted or punished by the same Party for an offence in respect of which a final judgement acquitting or convicting that person has been previously pronounced under the same law and judicial procedure;

(*i*) anyone prosecuted for an offence shall have the right to have the judgement pronounced publicly; and

(*j*) a convicted person shall be advised on conviction of his judicial and other remedies and of the time-limits within which they may be exercised.

5. Women whose liberty has been restricted for reasons related to the armed conflict shall be held in quarters separated from men's quarters. They shall be under the immediate supervision of women. Nevertheless, in cases where families are detained or interned, they shall, whenever possible, be held in the same place and accommodated as family units.

6. Persons who are arrested, detained or interned for reasons related to the armed conflict shall enjoy the protection provided by this Article until their final release, repatriation or re-establishment, even after the end of the armed conflict.

7. In order to avoid any doubt concerning the prosecution and trial of persons accused of war crimes or crimes against humanity, the following principles shall apply:

(*a*) persons who are accused of such crimes should be submitted for the purpose of prosecution and trial in accordance with the applicable rules of international law; and

(*b*) any such persons who do not benefit from more favourable treatment under the Conventions or this Protocol shall be accorded the treatment provided by this Article, whether or not the crimes of which they are accused constitute grave breaches of the Conventions or of this Protocol.

8. No provision of this Article may be construed as limiting or infringing any other more favourable provision granting greater protection, under any applicable rules of international law, to persons covered by paragraph 1.

CHAPTER II

MEASURES IN FAVOUR OF WOMEN AND CHILDREN

Article 76—Protection of women

1. Women shall be the object of special respect and shall be protected in particular against rape, forced prostitution and any other form of indecent assault.

2. Pregnant women and mothers having dependent infants who are arrested, detained or interned for reasons related to the armed conflict, shall have their cases considered with the utmost priority.

3. To the maximum extent feasible, the Parties to the conflict shall endeavour to avoid the pronouncement of the death penalty on pregnant women or mothers having dependent infants, for an offence related to the armed conflict. The death penalty for such offences shall not be executed on such women.

Article 77—Protection of children

1. Children shall be the object of special respect and shall be protected against any form of indecent assault. The Parties to the conflict shall provide them with the care and aid they require, whether because of their age or for any other reason.

2. The Parties to the conflict shall take all feasible measures in order that children who have not attained the age of fifteen years do not take a direct part in hostilities and, in particular, they shall refrain from recruiting them into their armed forces. In recruiting among those persons who have attained the age of

fifteen years but who have not attained the age of eighteen years the Parties to the conflict shall endeavour to give priority to those who are oldest.

3. If, in exceptional cases, despite the provisions of paragraph 2, children who have not attained the age of fifteen years take a direct part in hostilities and fall into the power of an adverse Party, they shall continue to benefit from the special protection accorded by this Article, whether or not they are prisoners of war.

4. If arrested, detained or interned for reasons related to the armed conflict, children shall be held in quarters separate from the quarters of adults, except where families are accommodated as family units as provided in Article 75, paragraph 5.

5. The death penalty for an offence related to the armed conflict shall not be executed on persons who had not attained the age of eighteen years at the time the offence was committed.

Article 78—Evacuation of children

1. No Party to the conflict shall arrange for the evacuation of children, other than its own nationals, to a foreign country except for a temporary evacuation where compelling reasons of the health or medical treatment of the children or, except in occupied territory, their safety, so require. Where the parents or legal guardians can be found, their written consent to such evacuation is required. If these persons cannot be found, the written consent to such evacuation of the persons who by law or custom are primarily responsible for the care of the children is required. Any such evacuation shall be supervised by the Protecting Power in agreement with the Parties concerned, namely, the Party arranging for the evacuation, the Party receiving the children and any Parties whose nationals are being evacuated. In each case, all Parties to the conflict shall take all feasible precautions to avoid endangering the evacuation.

* * *

CHAPTER III

JOURNALISTS

Article 79—Measures of protection for journalists

1. Journalists engaged in dangerous professional missions in areas of armed conflict shall be considered as civilians within the meaning of Article 50, paragraph 1.

* * *

Part V

EXECUTION OF THE CONVENTIONS AND OF THIS PROTOCOL

Section I

GENERAL PROVISIONS

* * *

Section II

REPRESSION OF BREACHES OF THE CONVENTIONS AND OF THIS PROTOCOL

Article 85—Repression of breaches of this Protocol

1. The provisions of the Conventions relating to the repression of breaches and grave breaches, supplemented by this Section, shall apply to the repression of breaches and grave breaches of this Protocol.

2. Acts described as grave breaches in the Conventions are grave breaches of this Protocol if committed against persons in the power of an adverse Party protected

by Articles 44, 45 and 73 of this Protocol, or against the wounded, sick and shipwrecked of the adverse Party who are protected by this Protocol, or against those medical or religious personnel, medical units or medical transports which are under the control of the adverse Party and are protected by this Protocol.

3. In addition to the grave breaches defined in Article 11, the following acts shall be regarded as grave breaches of this Protocol, when committed wilfully, in violation of the relevant provisions of this Protocol, and causing death or serious injury to body or health:

(*a*) making the civilian population or individual civilians the object of attack;

(*b*) launching an indiscriminate attack affecting the civilian population or civilian objects in the knowledge that such attack will cause excessive loss of life, injury to civilians or damage to civilian objects, as defined in Article 57, paragraph 2(*a*)(iii);

(*c*) launching an attack against works or installations containing dangerous forces in the knowledge that such attack will cause excessive loss of life, injury to civilians or damage to civilian objects, as defined in Article 57, paragraph 2(*a*)(iii);

(*d*) making non-defended localities and demilitarized zones the object of attack;

(*e*) making a person the object of attack in the knowledge that he is *hors de combat*;

(*f*) the perfidious use, in violation of Article 37, of the distinctive emblem of the red cross, red crescent or red lion and sun or of other protective signs recognized by the Conventions or this Protocol.

4. In addition to the grave breaches defined in the preceding paragraphs and in the Conventions, the following shall be regarded as grave breaches of this Protocol, when committed wilfully and in violation of the Conventions or the Protocol:

(*a*) the transfer by the occupying Power of parts of its own civilian population into the territory it occupies, or the deportation or transfer of all or parts of the population of the occupied territory within or outside this territory, in violation of Article 49 of the Fourth Convention;

(*b*) unjustifiable delay in the repatriation of prisoners of war or civilians;

(*c*) practices of *apartheid* and other inhuman and degrading practices involving outrages upon personal dignity, based on racial discrimination;

(*d*) making the clearly-recognized historic monuments, works of art or places of worship which constitute the cultural or spiritual heritage of peoples and to which special protection has been given by special arrangement, for example, within the framework of a competent international organization, the object of attack, causing as a result extensive destruction thereof, where there is no evidence of the violation by the adverse Party of Article 53, subparagraph (*b*), and when such historic monuments, works of art and places of worship are not located in the immediate proximity of military objectives;

(*e*) depriving a person protected by the Conventions or referred to in paragraph 2 of this Article of the rights of fair and regular trial.

5. Without prejudice to the application of the Conventions and of this Protocol, grave breaches of these instruments shall be regarded as war crimes.

Article 86—Failure to act

1. The High Contracting Parties and the Parties to the conflict shall repress grave breaches, and take measures necessary to suppress all other breaches, of the

Conventions or of this Protocol which result from a failure to act when under a duty to do so.

2. The fact that a breach of the Conventions or of this Protocol was committed by a subordinate does not absolve his superiors from penal disciplinary responsibility, as the case may be, if they knew, or had information which should have enabled them to conclude in the circumstances at the time, that he was committing or was going to commit such a breach and if they did not take all feasible measures within their power to prevent or repress the breach.

* * *

Article 91—Responsibility

A Party to the conflict which violates the provisions of the Conventions or of this Protocol shall, if the case demands, be liable to pay compensation. It shall be responsible for all acts committed by persons forming part of its armed forces.

Part VI

FINAL PROVISIONS

* * *

2.34 PROTOCOL ADDITIONAL TO THE GENEVA CONVENTIONS OF AUGUST 12, 1949, AND RELATING TO THE PROTECTION OF VICTIMS OF NON-INTERNATIONAL ARMED CONFLICTS.[a] Done at Geneva, June 8, 1977. Entered into force, Dec. 7, 1978. 1977 U.N.JURID.Y.B. 135, *reprinted in* 16 I.L.M. 1442 (1977)

Part I

SCOPE OF THIS PROTOCOL

Article 1—Material field of application

1. This Protocol, which develops and supplements Article 3 common to the Geneva Conventions of 12 August 1949 without modifying its existing conditions of application, shall apply to all armed conflicts which are not covered by Article 1 of the Protocol Additional to the Geneva Conventions of 12 August 1949, and relating to the Protection of Victims of International Armed Conflicts (Protocol I) and which take place in the territory of a High Contracting Party between its armed forces and dissident armed forces or other organized armed groups which, under responsible command, exercise such control over a part of its territory as to enable them to carry out sustained and concerted military operations and to implement this Protocol.

2. This Protocol shall not apply to situations of internal disturbances and tensions, such as riots, isolated and sporadic acts of violence and other acts of a similar nature, as not being armed conflicts.

Article 2—Personal field of application

1. This Protocol shall be applied without any adverse distinction founded on race, colour, sex, language, religion or belief, political or other opinion, national or social origin, wealth, birth or other status, or on any other similar criteria (hereinafter referred to as "adverse distinction") to all persons affected by an armed conflict as defined in Article 1.

2. At the end of the armed conflict, all the persons who have been deprived of their liberty or whose liberty has been restricted for reasons related to such conflict, as well as those deprived of their liberty or whose liberty is restricted after the conflict for the same reasons, shall enjoy the protection of Articles 5 and 6 until the end of such deprivation or restriction of liberty.

Article 3—Non-intervention

1. Nothing in this Protocol shall be invoked for the purpose of affecting the sovereignty of a State or the responsibility of the government, by all legitimate means, to maintain or re-establish law and order in the State or to defend the national unity and territorial integrity of the State.

2. Nothing in this Protocol shall be invoked as a justification for intervening, directly or indirectly, for any reason whatever, in the armed conflict or in the internal or external affairs of the High Contracting Party in the territory of which that conflict occurs.

a. Also known as "1977 Protocol II." *See also* Basic Documents 2.10, 2.11, 2.12, 2.13, & 2.33, *supra.*

Part II

HUMANE TREATMENT

Article 4—Fundamental guarantees

1. All persons who do not take a direct part or who have ceased to take part in hostilities, whether or not their liberty has been restricted, are entitled to respect for their person, honour and convictions and religious practices. They shall in all circumstances be treated humanely, without any adverse distinction. It is prohibited to order that there shall be no survivors.

2. Without prejudice to the generality of the foregoing, the following acts against the persons referred to in paragraph I are and shall remain prohibited at any time and in any place whatsoever:

(*a*) violence to the life, health and physical or mental well-being of persons, in particular murder as well as cruel treatment such as torture, mutilation or any form of corporal punishment;

(*b*) collective punishments;

(*c*) taking of hostages;

(*d*) acts of terrorism;

(*e*) outrages upon personal dignity, in particular humiliating and degrading treatment, rape, enforced prostitution and any form of indecent assault;

(*f*) slavery and the slave trade in all their forms;

(*g*) pillage;

(*h*) threats to commit any of the foregoing acts.

3. Children shall be provided with the care and aid they require, and in particular:

(*a*) they shall receive an education, including religious and moral education, in keeping with the wishes of their parents, or in the absence of parents, of those responsible for their care;

(*b*) all appropriate steps shall be taken to facilitate the reunion of families temporarily separated;

(*c*) children who have not attained the age of fifteen years shall neither be recruited in the armed forces, or groups nor allowed to take part in hostilities;

(*d*) the special protection provided by this Article to children who have not attained the age of fifteen years shall remain applicable to them if they take a direct part in hostilities despite the provisions of subparagraph (*c*) and are captured;

(*e*) measures shall be taken, if necessary, and whenever possible with the consent of their parents or persons who by law or custom are primarily responsible for their care, to remove children temporarily from the area in which hostilities are taking place to a safer area within the country and ensure that they are accompanied by persons responsible for their safety and well-being.

Article 5—Persons whose liberty has been restricted

1. In addition to the provisions of Article 4 the following provisions shall be respected as a minimum with regard to persons deprived of their liberty for reasons related to the armed conflict, whether they are interned or detained:

(*a*) the wounded and the sick shall be treated in accordance with Article 7;

(*b*) the persons referred to in this paragraph shall, to the same extent as the local civilian population, be provided with food and drinking water and be afforded safeguards as regards health and hygiene and protection against the rigours of the climate and the dangers of the armed conflict;

(*c*) they shall be allowed to receive individual or collective relief;

(*d*) they shall be allowed to practise their religion and, if requested and appropriate, to receive spiritual assistance from persons, such as chaplains, performing religious functions;

(*e*) they shall, if made to work, have the benefit of working conditions and safeguards similar to those enjoyed by the local civilian population.

2. Those who are responsible for the internment or detention of the persons referred to in paragraph 1 shall also, within the limits of their capabilities, respect the following provisions relating to such persons:

(*a*) except when men and women of a family are accommodated together, women shall be held in quarters separated from those of men and shall be under the immediate supervision of women;

(*b*) they shall be allowed to send and receive letters and cards, the number of which may be limited by competent authority if it deems necessary;

(*c*) places of internment and detention shall not be located close to the combat zone. The persons referred to in paragraph 1 shall be evacuated when the places where they are interned or detained become particularly exposed to danger arising out of the armed conflict, if their evacuation can be carried out under adequate conditions of safety;

(*d*) they shall have the benefit of medical examinations;

(*e*) their physical or mental health and integrity shall not be endangered by any unjustified act or omission. Accordingly, it is prohibited to subject the persons described in this Article to any medical procedure which is not indicated by the state of health of the person concerned, and which is not consistent with the generally accepted medical standards applied to free persons under similar medical circumstances.

3. Persons who are not covered by paragraph 1 but whose liberty has been restricted in any way whatsoever for reasons related to the armed conflict shall be treated humanely in accordance with Article 4 and with paragraphs 1(*a*), (*c*) and (*d*), and 2(*b*) of this Article.

4. If it is decided to release persons deprived of their liberty, necessary measures to ensure their safety shall be taken by those so deciding.

Article 6—Penal prosecutions

1. This Article applies to the prosecution and punishment of criminal offences related to the armed conflict.

2. No sentence shall be passed and no penalty shall be executed on a person found guilty of an offence except pursuant to a conviction pronounced by a court offering the essential guarantees of independence and impartiality. In particular:

(*a*) the procedure shall provide for an accused to be informed without delay of the particulars of the offence alleged against him and shall afford the accused before and during his trial all necessary rights and means of defence;

(*b*) no one shall be convicted of an offence except on the basis of individual penal responsibility;

(*c*) no one shall be held guilty of any criminal offence on account of any act or omission which did not constitute a criminal offence, under the law, at the time when it was committed; nor shall a heavier penalty be imposed than that which was applicable at the time when the criminal offence was committed; if, after the commission of the offence, provision is made by law for the imposition of a lighter penalty, the offender shall benefit thereby;

(*d*) anyone charged with an offence is presumed innocent until proved guilty according to law;

(*e*) anyone charged with an offence shall have the right to be tried in his presence;

(*f*) no one shall be compelled to testify against himself or to confess guilt.

3. A convicted person shall be advised on conviction of his judicial and other remedies and of the time-limits within which they may be exercised.

4. The death penalty shall not be pronounced on persons who were under the age of eighteen years at the time of the offence and shall not be carried out on pregnant women or mothers of young children.

5. At the end of hostilities, the authorities in power shall endeavour to grant the broadest possible amnesty to persons who have participated in the armed conflict, or those deprived of their liberty for reasons related to the armed conflict, whether they are interned or detained.

Part III

WOUNDED, SICK AND SHIPWRECKED

Article 7—Protection and care

1. All the wounded, sick and shipwrecked, whether or not they have taken part in the armed conflict, shall be respected and protected.

2. In all circumstances they shall be treated humanely and shall receive to the fullest extent practicable and with the least possible delay, the medical care and attention required by their condition. There shall be no distinction among them founded on any grounds other than medical ones.

Article 8—Search

Whenever circumstances permit and particularly after an engagement, all possible measures shall be taken, without delay, to search for and collect the wounded, sick and shipwrecked, to protect them against pillage and ill-treatment, to ensure their adequate care, and to search for the dead, prevent their being despoiled, and decently dispose of them.

Article 9—Protection of medical and religious personnel

1. Medical and religious personnel shall be respected and protected and shall be granted all available help for the performance of their duties. They shall not be compelled to carry out tasks which are not compatible with their humanitarian mission.

2. In the performance of their duties medical personnel may not be required to give priority to any person except on medical grounds.

Article 10—General protection of medical duties

1. Under no circumstances shall any person be punished for having carried out medical activities compatible with medical ethics, regardless of the person benefiting therefrom.

2. Persons engaged in medical activities shall neither be compelled to perform acts or to carry out work contrary to, nor be compelled to refrain from acts required by, the rules of medical ethics or other rules designed for the benefit of the wounded and sick, or this Protocol.

3. The professional obligations of persons engaged in medical activities regarding information which they may acquire concerning the wounded and sick under their care shall, subject to national law, be respected.

4. Subject to national law, no person engaged in medical activities may be penalized in any way for refusing or failing to give information concerning the wounded and sick who are, or who have been, under his care.

Article 11—Protection of medical units and transports

1. Medical units and transports shall be respected and protected at all times and shall not be the object of attack.

2. The protection to which medical units and transports are entitled shall not cease unless they are used to commit hostile acts, outside their humanitarian function. Protection may, however, cease only after a warning has been given, setting, whenever appropriate, a reasonable time-limit, and after such warning has remained unheeded.

Article 12—The distinctive emblem

Under the direction of the competent authority concerned, the distinctive emblem of the red cross, red crescent or red lion and sun on a white ground shall be displayed by medical and religious personnel and medical units, and on medical transports. It shall be respected in all circumstances. It shall not be used improperly.

Part IV
CIVILIAN POPULATION

Article 13—Protection of the civilian population

1. The civilian population and individual civilians shall enjoy general protection against the dangers arising from military operations. To give effect to this protection, the following rules shall be observed in all circumstances.

2. The civilian population as such, as well as individual civilians, shall not be the object of attack. Acts or threats of violence the primary purpose of which is to spread terror among the civilian population are prohibited.

3. Civilians shall enjoy the protection afforded by this part, unless and for such time as they take a direct part in hostilities.

Article 14—Protection of objects indispensable to the survival of the civilian population

Starvation of civilians as a method of combat is prohibited. It is therefore prohibited to attack, destroy, or remove or render useless, for that purpose, objects indispensable to the survival of the civilian population such as food-stuffs, agricultural areas for the production of food-stuffs, crops, livestock, drinking water installations and supplies and irrigation works.

Article 15—Protection of works and installations containing dangerous forces

Works or installations containing dangerous forces, namely dams, dykes and nuclear electrical generating stations, shall not be made the object of attack, even where these objects are military objectives, if such attack may cause the release of dangerous forces and consequent severe losses among the civilian population.

Article 16—Protection of cultural objects and of places of worship

Without prejudice to the provisions of the Hague Convention for the Protection of Cultural Property in the Event of Armed Conflict of 14 May 1954, it is prohibited to commit any acts of hostility directly against historic monuments, works of art or places of worship which constitute the cultural or spiritual heritage of peoples, and to use them in support of the military effort.

Article 17—Prohibition of forced movement of civilians

1. The displacement of the civilian population shall not be ordered for reasons related to the conflict unless the security of the civilians involved or imperative military reasons so demand. Should such displacements have to be carried out, all possible measures shall be taken in order that the civilian population may be received under satisfactory conditions of shelter, hygiene, health, safety and nutrition.

2. Civilians shall not be compelled to leave their own territory for reasons connected with the conflict.

Article 18—Relief societies and relief actions

1. Relief societies located in the territory of the High Contracting Party, such as Red Cross (Red Crescent, Red Lion and Sun) organizations, may offer their services for the performance of their traditional functions in relation to the victims of the armed conflict. The civilian population may, even on its own initiative, offer to collect and care for the wounded, sick and shipwrecked.

2. If the civilian population is suffering undue hardship owing to a lack of the supplies essential for its survival, such as food-stuffs and medical supplies, relief actions for the civilian population which are of an exclusively humanitarian and impartial nature and which are conducted without any adverse distinction shall be undertaken subject to the consent of the High Contracting Party concerned.

Part V

FINAL PROVISIONS

* * *

2.35 FINAL ACT OF THE UNITED NATIONS GENERAL ASSEMBLY SPECIAL SESSION ON DISARMAMENT. Adopted by consensus of the U.N. General Assembly, June 30, 1978. U.N.G.A.Res. S–10/2 (S–X), 10 (Special) U.N. GAOR, Supp. (No. 4) 3, U.N. Doc. A/S–10/4 (1978), *reprinted in* 17 I.L.M. 1016 (1978)

THE GENERAL ASSEMBLY,

Alarmed by the threat to the very survival of mankind posed by the existence of nuclear weapons and the continuing arms race, and recalling the devastation inflicted by all wars.

Convinced that disarmament and arms limitation, particularly in the nuclear field, are essential for the prevention of the danger of nuclear war and the strengthening of international peace and security and for the economic and social advancement of all peoples, thus facilitating the achievement of the new international economic order.

Having resolved to lay the foundations of an international disarmament strategy which, through co-ordinated and persevering efforts in which the United Nations should play a more effective role, aims at general and complete disarmament under effective international control.

Adopts the following Final Document of this special session of the General Assembly devoted to disarmament:

I. INTRODUCTION

1. Attainment of the objective of security, which is an inseparable element of peace, has always been one of the most profound aspirations of humanity. States have for a long time sought to maintain their security through the possession of arms. Admittedly, their survival has, in certain cases, effectively depended on whether they could count on appropriate means of defence. Yet the accumulation of weapons, particularly nuclear weapons, today constitutes much more a threat than a protection for the future of mankind. The time has therefore come to put an end to this situation, to abandon the use of force in international relations and to seek security in disarmament, that is to say, through a gradual but effective process beginning with a reduction in the present level of armaments. The ending of the arms race and the achievement of real disarmament are tasks of primary importance and urgency. To meet this historic challenge is in the political and economic interests of all the nations and peoples of the world as well as in the interests of ensuring their genuine security and peaceful future.

2. Unless its avenues are closed, the continued arms race means a growing threat to international peace and security and even to the very survival of mankind. The nuclear and conventional arms build-up threatens to stall the efforts aimed at reaching the goals of development, to become an obstacle on the road of achieving the new international economic order and to hinder the solution of other vital problems facing mankind.

3. Dynamic development of detente, encompassing all spheres of international relations in all regions of the world, with the participation of all countries, would create conditions conducive to the efforts of States to end the arms race, which has engulfed the world, thus reducing the danger of war. Progress on detente and progress on disarmament mutually complement and strengthen each other.

4. The Disarmament Decade solemnly declared in 1969 by the United Nations is coming to an end. Unfortunately, the objectives established on that occasion by the General Assembly appear to be as far away today as they were then, or even further because the arms race is not diminishing but increasing and outstrips by far the efforts to curb it. While it is true that some limited agreements have been reached, "effective measures relating to the cessation of the nuclear arms race at an early date and to nuclear disarmament" continue to elude man's grasp. Yet the implementation of such measures is urgently required. There has not been any real progress either that might lead to the conclusion of a treaty on general and complete disarmament under effective international control. Furthermore, it has not been possible to free any amount, however modest, of the enormous resources, both material and human, which are wasted on the unproductive and spiralling arms race and which should be made available for the purpose of economic and social development, especially since such a race "places a great burden on both the developing and the developed countries."

5. The Members of the United Nations are fully aware of the conviction of their peoples that the question of general and complete disarmament is of utmost importance and that peace, security and economic and social development are indivisible, and they have therefore recognized that the corresponding obligations and responsibilities are universal.

6. Thus a powerful current of opinion has gradually formed, leading to the convening of what will go down in the annals of the United Nations as the first special session of the General Assembly devoted entirely to disarmament.

7. The outcome of this special session, whose deliberations have to a large extent been facilitated by the five sessions of the Preparatory Committee which preceded it, is the present Final Document. This introduction serves as a preface to the document which comprises also the following three sections: a Declaration, a Programme of Action and recommendations concerning the international machinery for disarmament negotiations.

8. While the final objective of the efforts of all States should continue to be general and complete disarmament under effective international control, the immediate goal is that of the elimination of the danger of a nuclear war and the implementation of measures to halt and reverse the arms race and clear the path towards lasting peace. Negotiations on the entire range of those issues should be based on the strict observance of the purposes and principles enshrined in the Charter of the United Nations, with full recognition of the role of the United Nations in the field of disarmament and reflecting the vital interest of all the peoples of the world in this sphere. The aim of the Declaration is to review and assess the existing situation, outline the objectives and the priority tasks and set forth fundamental principles for disarmament negotiations.

9. For disarmament—the aims and purposes of which the Declaration proclaims—to become a reality, it was essential to agree on a series of specific disarmament measures, selected by common accord as those on which there is a consensus to the effect that their subsequent realization in the short term appears to be feasible. There is also a need to prepare through agreed procedures a comprehensive disarmament programme. That programme, passing through all the necessary stages, should lead to general and complete disarmament under effective international control. Procedures for watching over the fulfilment of the obligations thus assumed had also to be agreed upon. That is the purpose of the Programme of Action.

10. Although the decisive factor for achieving real measures of disarmament is the "political will" of States, and especially of those possessing nuclear weapons, a significant role can also be played by the effective functioning of an appropriate international machinery designed to deal with the problems of disarmament in its

various aspects. Consequently, it would be necessary that the two kinds of organs required to that end, the deliberative and the negotiating organs, have the appropriate organization and procedures that would be most conducive to obtaining constructive results. The last section of the Final Document, section IV, has been prepared with that end in view.

II. DECLARATION

11. Mankind today is confronted with an unprecedented threat of self-extinction arising from the massive and competitive accumulation of the most destructive weapons ever produced. Existing arsenals of nuclear weapons alone are more than sufficient to destroy all life on earth. Failure of efforts to halt and reverse the arms race, in particular the nuclear arms race, increases the danger of the proliferation of nuclear weapons. Yet the arms race continues. Military budgets are constantly growing, with enormous consumption of human and material resources. The increase in weapons, especially nuclear weapons, far from helping to strengthen international security, on the contrary weakens it. The vast stockpiles and tremendous build-up of arms and armed forces and the competition for qualitative refinement of weapons of all kinds to which scientific resources and technological advances are diverted, pose incalculable threats to peace. This situation both reflects and aggravates international tensions, sharpens conflicts in various regions of the world, hinders the process of detente, exacerbates the differences between opposing military alliances, jeopardizes the security of all States, heightens the sense of insecurity among all States, including the non-nuclear-weapon States and increases the threat of nuclear war.

12. The arms race, particularly in its nuclear aspect, runs counter to efforts to achieve further relaxation of international tension, to establish international relations based on peaceful coexistence and trust between all States and to develop broad international co-operation and understanding. The arms race impedes the realization of the purposes, and is incompatible with the principles of the Charter of the United Nations, especially respect for sovereignty, refraining from the threat or use of force against the territorial integrity or political independence of any State, peaceful settlement of disputes and non-intervention and non-interference in the internal affairs of States. It also adversely affects the rights of peoples freely to determine their systems of social and economic development, and hinders the struggle for self-determination and the elimination of colonial rule, racial or foreign domination or occupation. Indeed, the massive accumulation of armaments and the acquisition of armaments technology by racist regimes, as well as their possible acquisition of nuclear weapons, present a challenging and increasingly dangerous obstacle to a world community faced with the urgent need to disarm. It is, therefore, essential for purposes of disarmament to prevent any further acquisitions of arms or arms technology by such regimes, especially through strict adherence by all States to relevant decisions of the Security Council.

13. Enduring international peace and security cannot be built on the accumulation of weaponry by military alliances nor be sustained by a precarious balance of deterrence or doctrines of strategic superiority. Genuine and lasting peace can only be created through the effective implementation of the security system provided for in the Charter of the United Nations and the speedy and substantial reduction of arms and armed forces, by international agreement and mutual example, leading ultimately to general and complete disarmament under effective international control. At the same time, the causes of the arms race and threats to peace must be reduced and to this end effective action should be taken to eliminate tensions and settle disputes by peaceful means.

14. Since the process of disarmament affects the vital security interests of all States, they must all be actively concerned with and contribute to the measures of

disarmament and arms limitation, which have an essential part to play in maintaining and strengthening international security. Therefore the role and responsibility of the United Nations in the sphere of disarmament, in accordance with its Charter, must be strengthened.

15. It is essential that not only Governments but also the peoples of the world recognize and understand the dangers in the present situation. In order that an international conscience may develop and that world public opinion may exercise a positive influence, the United Nations should increase the dissemination of information on the armaments race and disarmament with the full co-operation of Member States.

16. In a world of finite resources there is a close relationship between expenditure on armaments and economic and social development. Military expenditures are reaching ever higher levels, the highest percentage of which can be attributed to the nuclear-weapon States and most of their allies, with prospects of further expansion and the danger of further increases in the expenditures of other countries. The hundreds of billions of dollars spent annually on the manufacture or improvement of weapons are in sombre and dramatic contrast to the want and poverty in which two thirds of the world's population live. This colossal waste of resources is even more serious in that it diverts to military purposes not only material but also technical and human resources which are urgently needed for development in all countries, particularly in the developing countries. Thus, the economic and social consequences of the arms race are so detrimental that its continuation is obviously incompatible with the implementation of the new international economic order based on justice, equity and co-operation. Consequently, resources released as a result of the implementation of disarmament measures should be used in a manner which will help to promote the well-being of all peoples and to improve the economic conditions of the developing countries.

17. Disarmament has thus become an imperative and most urgent task facing the international community. No real progress has been made so far in the crucial field of reduction of armaments. However, certain positive changes in international relations in some areas of the world provide some encouragement. Agreements have been reached that have been important in limiting certain weapons or eliminating them altogether, as in the case of the Convention on the Prohibition of the Development, Production and Stockpiling of Bacteriological (Biological) and Toxin Weapons and on Their Destruction and excluding particular areas from the arms race. The fact remains that these agreements relate only to measures of limited restraint while the arms race continues. These partial measures have done little to bring the world closer to the goal of general and complete disarmament. For more than a decade there have been no negotiations leading to a treaty on general and complete disarmament. The pressing need now is to translate into practical terms the provisions of this Final Document and to proceed along the road of binding and effective international agreements in the field of disarmament.

18. Removing the threat of a world war—a nuclear war—is the most acute and urgent task of the present day. Mankind is confronted with a choice: we must halt the arms race and proceed to disarmament or face annihilation.

19. The ultimate objective of the efforts of States in the disarmament process is general and complete disarmament under effective international control. The principal goals of disarmament are to ensure the survival of mankind and to eliminate the danger of war, in particular nuclear war, to ensure that war is no longer an instrument for settling international disputes and that the use and the threat of force are eliminated from international life, as provided for in the Charter of the United Nations. Progress towards this objective requires the conclusion and implementation

of agreements on the cessation of the arms race and on genuine measures of disarmament, taking into account the need of States to protect their security.

20. Among such measures, effective measures of nuclear disarmament and the prevention of nuclear war have the highest priority. To this end, it is imperative to remove the threat of nuclear weapons, to halt and reverse the nuclear arms race until the total elimination of nuclear weapons and their delivery systems has been achieved and to prevent the proliferation of nuclear weapons. At the same time, other measures designed to prevent the outbreak of nuclear war and to lessen the danger of the threat or use of nuclear weapons should be taken.

21. Along with these measures, agreements or other effective measures should be adopted to prohibit or prevent the development, production or use of other weapons of mass destruction. In this context, an agreement on elimination of all chemical weapons should be concluded as a matter of high priority.

22. Together with negotiations on nuclear disarmament measures, negotiations should be carried out on the balanced reduction of armed forces and of conventional armaments, based on the principle of undiminished security of the parties with a view to promoting or enhancing stability at a lower military level, taking into account the need of all States to protect their security. These negotiations should be conducted with particular emphasis on armed forces and conventional weapons of nuclear-weapon States and other militarily significant countries. There should also be negotiations on the limitation of international transfer of conventional weapons, based in particular on the same principle, and taking into account the inalienable right to self-determination and independence of peoples under colonial or foreign domination and the obligations of States to respect that right, in accordance with the Charter of the United Nations and the Declaration on Principles of International Law concerning Friendly Relations and Co-operation among States, as well as the need of recipient States to protect their security.

23. Further international action should be taken to prohibit or restrict for humanitarian reasons the use of specific conventional weapons, including those which may be excessively injurious, cause unnecessary suffering or have indiscriminate effects.

24. Collateral measures in both the nuclear and conventional fields, together with other measures specifically designed to build confidence, should be undertaken in order to contribute to the creation of favourable conditions for the adoption of additional disarmament measures and to further the relaxation of international tension.

25. Negotiations and measures in the field of disarmament shall be guided by the fundamental principles set forth below.

26. All States Members of the United Nations reaffirm their full commitment to the purposes of the Charter of the United Nations and their obligation strictly to observe its principles as well as other relevant and generally accepted principles of international law relating to the maintenance of international peace and security. They stress the special importance of refraining from the threat or use of force against the sovereignty, territorial integrity or political independence of any State, or against peoples under colonial or foreign domination seeking to exercise their right to self-determination and to achieve independence; non-intervention and non-interference in the internal affairs of other States; the inviolability of international frontiers; and the peaceful settlement of disputes, having regard to the inherent right of States to individual and collective self-defence in accordance with the Charter.

27. In accordance with the Charter, the United Nations has a central role and primary responsibility in the sphere of disarmament. In order effectively to discharge this role and facilitate and encourage all measures in this field, the United

Nations should be kept appropriately informed of all steps in this field, whether unilateral, bilateral, regional or multilateral, without prejudice to the progress of negotiations.

28. All the peoples of the world have a vital interest in the success of disarmament negotiations. Consequently, all States have the duty to contribute to efforts in the field of disarmament. All States have the right to participate in disarmament negotiations. They have the right to participate on an equal footing in those multilateral disarmament negotiations which have a direct bearing on their national security. While disarmament is the responsibility of all States, the nuclear-weapon States have the primary responsibility for nuclear disarmament and, together with other militarily significant States, for halting and reversing the arms race. It is therefore important to secure their active participation.

29. The adoption of disarmament measures should take place in such an equitable and balanced manner as to ensure the right of each State to security and to ensure that no individual State or group of States may obtain advantages over others at any stage. At each stage the objective should be undiminished security at the lowest possible level of armaments and military forces.

30. An acceptable balance of mutual responsibilities and obligations for nuclear and non-nuclear-weapon States should be strictly observed.

31. Disarmament and arms limitation agreements should provide for adequate measures of verification satisfactory to all parties concerned in order to create the necessary confidence and ensure that they are being observed by all parties. The form and modalities of the verification to be provided for in any specific agreement depend upon and should be determined by the purposes, scope and nature of the agreement. Agreements should provide for the participation of parties directly or through the United Nations system in the verification process. Where appropriate, a combination of several methods of verification as well as other compliance procedures should be employed.

32. All States, and in particular nuclear-weapon States, should consider various proposals designed to secure the avoidance of the use of nuclear weapons, and the prevention of nuclear war. In this context, while noting the declarations made by nuclear-weapon States, effective arrangements, as appropriate, to assure non-nuclear-weapon States against the use or the threat of use of nuclear weapons could strengthen the security of those States and international peace and security.

33. The establishment of nuclear-weapon-free zones on the basis of agreements or arrangements freely arrived at among the States of the zone concerned, and the full compliance with those agreements or arrangements, thus ensuring that the zones are genuinely free from nuclear weapons, and respect for such zones by nuclear-weapon States, constitute an important disarmament measure.

34. Disarmament, relaxation of international tension, respect for the right to self-determination and national independence, and peaceful settlement of disputes in accordance with the Charter of the United Nations and the strengthening of international peace and security are directly related to each other. Progress in any of these spheres has a beneficial effect on all of them; in turn, failure in one sphere has negative effects on others.

35. There is also a close relationship between disarmament and development. Progress in the former would help greatly in the realization of the latter. Therefore resources released as a result of the implementation of disarmament measures should be devoted to the economic and social development of all nations and contribute to the bridging of the economic gap between developed and developing countries.

36. Non-proliferation of nuclear weapons is a matter of universal concern. Measures of disarmament must be consistent with the inalienable right of all States, without discrimination, to develop, acquire and use nuclear technology, equipment and materials for the peaceful use of nuclear energy and to determine their peaceful nuclear programmes in accordance with their national priorities, needs and interests, bearing in mind the need to prevent the proliferation of nuclear weapons. International co-operation in the peaceful uses of nuclear energy should be conducted under agreed and appropriate international safeguards applied on a non-discriminatory basis.

37. Significant progress in disarmament, including nuclear disarmament, would be facilitated by parallel measures to strengthen the security of States and to improve the international situation in general.

38. Negotiations on partial measures of disarmament should be conducted concurrently with negotiations on more comprehensive measures and should be followed by negotiations leading to a treaty on general and complete disarmament under effective international control.

39. Qualitative and quantitative disarmament measures are both important for halting the arms race. Efforts to that end must include negotiations on the limitation and cessation of the qualitative improvement of armaments, especially weapons of mass destruction and the development of new means of warfare so that ultimately scientific and technological achievements may be used solely for peaceful purposes.

40. Universality of disarmament agreements helps create confidence among States. When multilateral agreements in the field of disarmament are negotiated, every effort should be made to ensure that they are universally acceptable. The full compliance of all parties with the provisions contained in such agreements would also contribute to the attainment of that goal.

41. In order to create favourable conditions for success in the disarmament process, all States should strictly abide by the provisions of the Charter of the United Nations, refrain from actions which might adversely affect efforts in the field of disarmament and display a constructive approach to negotiations and the political will to reach agreements. There are certain negotiations on disarmament under way at different levels, the early and successful completion of which could contribute to limiting the arms race. Unilateral measures of arms limitation or reduction could also contribute to the attainment of that goal.

42. Since prompt measures should be taken in order to halt and reverse the arms race, Member States hereby declare that they will respect the objectives and principles stated above and make every effort faithfully to carry out the Programme of Action set forth in section III below.

III. PROGRAMME OF ACTION

43. Progress towards the goal of general and complete disarmament can be achieved through the implementation of a programme of action on disarmament, in accordance with the goals and principles established in the Declaration on disarmament. The present Programme of Action contains priorities and measures in the field of disarmament that States should undertake as a matter of urgency with a view to halting and reversing the arms race and to giving the necessary impetus to efforts designed to achieve genuine disarmament leading to general and complete disarmament under effective international control.

44. The present Programme of Action enumerates the specific measures of disarmament which should be implemented over the next few years, as well as other measures and studies to prepare the way for future negotiations and for progress towards general and complete disarmament.

45. Priorities in disarmament negotiations shall be: nuclear weapons; other weapons of mass destruction, including chemical weapons; conventional weapons, including any which may be deemed to be excessively injurious or to have indiscriminate effects; and reduction of armed forces.

46. Nothing should preclude States from conducting negotiations on all priority items concurrently.

47. Nuclear weapons pose the greatest danger to mankind and to the survival of civilization. It is essential to halt and reverse the nuclear arms race in all its aspects in order to avert the danger of war involving nuclear weapons. The ultimate goal in this context is the complete elimination of nuclear weapons.

48. In the task of achieving the goals of nuclear disarmament, all the nuclear-weapon States, in particular those among them which possess the most important nuclear arsenals, bear a special responsibility.

49. The process of nuclear disarmament should be carried out in such a way, and requires measures to ensure, that the security of all States is guaranteed at progressively lower levels of nuclear armaments, taking into account the relative qualitative and quantitative importance of the existing arsenals of the nuclear-weapon States and other States concerned.

50. The achievement of nuclear disarmament will require urgent negotiations of agreements at appropriate stages and with adequate measures of verification satisfactory to the State concerned for:

(a) Cessation of the qualitative improvement and development of nuclear-weapon systems;

(b) Cessation of the production of all types of nuclear weapons and their means of delivery, and of the production of fissionable material for weapons purposes;

(c) A comprehensive, phased programme with agreed time-frames, whenever feasible, for progressive and balanced reduction of stockpiles of nuclear weapons and their means of delivery, leading to their ultimate and complete elimination at the earliest possible time.

Consideration can be given in the course of the negotiations to mutual and agreed limitation or prohibition, without prejudice to the security of any State, or any types of nuclear armaments.

51. The cessation of nuclear-weapon testing by all States within the framework of an effective nuclear disarmament process would be in the interest of mankind. It would make a significant contribution to the above aim of ending the qualitative improvement of nuclear weapons and the development of new types of such weapons and of preventing the proliferation of nuclear weapons. In this context the negotiations now in progress on "a treaty prohibiting nuclear-weapon tests, and a protocol covering nuclear explosions for peaceful purposes, which would be an integral part of the treaty," should be concluded urgently and the result submitted for full consideration by the multilateral negotiating body with a view to the submission of a draft treaty to the General Assembly at the earliest possible date. All efforts should be made by the negotiating parties to achieve an agreement which, following endorsement by the General Assembly, could attract the widest possible adherence. In this context, various views were expressed by non-nuclear-weapon States that, pending the conclusion of this treaty, the world community would be encouraged if all the nuclear-weapon States refrained from testing nuclear weapons. In this connexion, some nuclear-weapon States expressed different views.

52. The Union of Soviet Socialist Republics and the United States of America should conclude at the earliest possible date the agreement they have been pursuing for several years in the second series of the strategic arms limitation talks (SALE II).

They are invited to transmit in good time the text of the agreement to the General Assembly. It should be followed promptly by further strategic arms limitation negotiations between the two parties, leading to agreed significant reductions of, and qualitative limitations on strategic arms. It should constitute an important step in the direction of nuclear disarmament and, ultimately of establishment of a world free of such weapons.

53. The process of nuclear disarmament described in the paragraph on this subject should be expedited by the urgent and vigorous pursuit to a successful conclusion of ongoing negotiations and the urgent initiation of further negotiations among the nuclear-weapon states.

54. Significant progress in nuclear disarmament would be facilitated both by parallel political or international legal measures to strengthen the security of States and by progress in the limitation and reduction of armed forces and conventional armaments of the nuclear-weapon States and other States in the regions concerned.

55. Real progress in the field of nuclear disarmament could create an atmosphere conducive to progress in conventional disarmament on a world-wide basis.

56. The most effective guarantee against the danger of nuclear war and the use of nuclear weapons is nuclear disarmament and the complete elimination of nuclear weapons.

57. Pending the achievement of this goal, for which negotiations should be vigorously pursued, and bearing in mind the devastating results which nuclear war would have on belligerents and non-belligerents alike, the nuclear-weapon States have special responsibilities to undertake measures aimed at preventing the outbreak of nuclear war, and of the use of force in international relations, subject to the provisions of the Charter of the United Nations, including the use of nuclear weapons.

58. In this context all States, and in particular nuclear-weapon States, should consider as soon as possible various proposals designed to secure the avoidance of the use of nuclear weapons, the prevention of nuclear war and related objectives, where possible through international agreement and thereby ensure that the survival of mankind is not endangered. All States should actively participate in efforts to bring about conditions in international relations among States in which a code of peaceful conduct of nations in international affairs could be agreed and which would preclude the use or threat of use of nuclear weapons.

59. In the same context, the nuclear-weapon States are called upon to take steps to assure the non-nuclear-weapon States against the use or threat of use of nuclear weapons. The General Assembly notes the declarations made by the nuclear-weapon States and urges them to pursue efforts to conclude, as appropriate, effective arrangements to assure non-nuclear-weapon States against the use or threat of use of nuclear weapons.

60. The establishment of nuclear-weapon-free zones on the basis of arrangements freely arrived at among the States of the region concerned constitutes an important disarmament measure.

61. The process of establishing such zones in different parts of the world should be encouraged with the ultimate objective of achieving a world entirely free of nuclear weapons. In the process of establishing such zones, the characteristics of each region should be taken into account. The States participating in such zones should undertake to comply fully with all the objectives, purposes and principles of the agreements or arrangements establishing the zones, thus ensuring that they are genuinely free from nuclear weapons.

62. With respect to such zones, the nuclear-weapon States in turn are called upon to give undertakings, the modalities of which are to be negotiated with the competent authority of each zone, in particular:

(a) To respect strictly the status of the nuclear-weapon-free zone:

(b) To refrain from the use or threat of nuclear weapons against the States of the zone.

63. In the light of existing conditions, and without prejudice to other measures which may be considered in other regions, the following measures are especially desirable:

(a) Adoption by the States concerned of all relevant measures to ensure the full application of the Treaty for the Prohibition of Nuclear Weapons in Latin America (Treaty of Tlatelolco), taking into account the views expressed at the tenth special session on the adherence to it:

(b) Signature and ratification of the Additional Protocols of the Treaty for the Prohibition of Nuclear Weapons in Latin America (Treaty of Tlatelolco) by the States entitled to become parties to those instruments which have not yet done so;

(c) In Africa, where the Organization of African Unity has affirmed a decision for the denuclearization of the region, the Security Council of the United Nations shall take appropriate effective steps whenever necessary to prevent the frustration of this objective;

(d) The serious consideration of the practical and urgent steps, as described in the paragraphs above, required for the implementation of the proposal to establish a nuclear-weapon-free zone in the Middle East, in accordance with the relevant General Assembly resolutions, where all parties directly concerned have expressed their support for the concept and where the danger of nuclear-weapon proliferation exists. The establishment of a nuclear-weapon-free zone in the Middle East would greatly enhance international peace and security. Pending the establishment of such a zone in the region, States of the region should solemnly declare that they will refrain on a reciprocal basis from producing, acquiring or in any other way possessing nuclear weapons and nuclear explosive devices, and from permitting the stationing of nuclear weapons on their territory by any third party and agree to place all their nuclear activities under International Atomic Energy Agency safeguards. Consideration should be given to a Security Council role in advancing the establishment of a nuclear-weapon-free zone in the Middle East;

(e) All States in the region of South Asia have expressed their determination to keep their countries free of nuclear weapons. No action should be taken by them which might deviate from that objective. In this context, the question of establishing a nuclear-weapon-free zone in South Asia has been dealt with in several resolutions of the General Assembly, which is keeping the subject under consideration.

64. The establishment of zones of peace in various regions of the world under appropriate conditions, to be clearly defined and determined freely by the States concerned in the zone, taking into account the characteristics of the zone and the principles of the Charter of the United Nations, and in conformity with international law, can contribute to strengthening the security of States within such zones and to international peace and security as a whole. In this regard, the General Assembly notes the proposals for the establishment of zones of peace, *inter alia,* in:

(a) South–East Asia where States in the region have expressed interest in the establishment of such a zone, in conformity with their views:

(b) The Indian Ocean, taking into account the deliberations of the General Assembly and its relevant resolutions and the need to ensure the maintenance of peace and security in the region.

65. It is imperative, as an integral part of the effort to halt and reverse the arms race, to prevent the proliferation of nuclear weapons. The goal of nuclear non-proliferation is on the one hand to prevent the emergence of any additional nuclear-weapon States besides the existing five nuclear-weapon States, and on the other progressively to reduce and eventually eliminate nuclear weapons altogether. This involves obligations and responsibilities on the part of both nuclear-weapon States and non-nuclear-weapon States, the former undertaking to stop the nuclear arms race and to achieve nuclear disarmament by urgent application of the measures outlined in the relevant paragraphs of this Final Document, and all States undertaking to prevent the spread of nuclear weapons.

66. Effective measures can and should be taken at the national level and through international agreements to minimize the danger of the proliferation of nuclear weapons without jeopardizing energy supplies or the development of nuclear energy for peaceful purposes. Therefore, the nuclear-weapon States and the non-nuclear-weapon States should jointly take further steps to develop an international consensus of ways and means, on a universal and non-discriminatory basis, to prevent the proliferation of nuclear weapons.

67. Full implementation of all the provisions of existing instruments on non-proliferation, such as the Treaty on the Non–Proliferation of Nuclear Weapons and/or the Treaty for the Prohibition of Nuclear Weapons in Latin America (Treaty of Tlatelolco) by States parties to those instruments will be an important contribution to this end. Adherence to such instruments has increased in recent years and the hope has been expressed by the parties that this trend might continue.

68. Non-proliferation measures should not jeopardize the full exercise of the inalienable rights of all States to apply and develop their programmes for the peaceful uses of nuclear energy for economic and social development in conformity with their priorities, interests and needs. All States should also have access to and be free to acquire technology, equipment and materials for peaceful uses of nuclear energy, taking into account the particular needs of the developing countries. International co-operation in this field should be under agreed and appropriate international safeguards applied through the International Atomic Energy Agency on a non-discriminatory basis in order to prevent effectively the proliferation of nuclear weapons.

69. Each country's choices and decisions in the field of the peaceful uses of nuclear energy should be respected without jeopardizing their respective fuel cycle policies or international co-operation, agreements and contracts for the peaceful use of nuclear energy, provided that the agreed safeguard measures mentioned above are applied.

70. In accordance with the principles and provisions of General Assembly resolution 32/50 of 8 December 1977, international co-operation for the promotion of the transfer and utilization of nuclear technology for economic and social development, especially in the developing countries, should be strengthened.

71. Efforts should be made to conclude the work of the International Nuclear Fuel Cycle Evaluation strictly in accordance with the objectives set out in the final communique of its Organizing Conference.

72. All States should adhere to the Protocol for the Prohibition of the Use in War of Asphyxiating, Poisonous or Other Gases, and of Bacteriological Methods of Warfare, signed at Geneva on 17 June 1925.

73. All States which have not yet done so should consider adhering to the Convention on the Prohibition of the Development, Production and Stockpiling of Bacteriological (Biological) and Toxin Weapons and on Their Destruction.

74. States should also consider the possibility of adhering to multilateral agreements concluded so far in the disarmament field which are mentioned below in this section.

75. The complete and effective prohibition of the development, production and stockpiling of all chemical weapons and their destruction represent one of the most urgent measures of disarmament. Consequently, conclusion of a convention to this end, on which negotiations have been going on for several years, is one of the most urgent tasks of multilateral negotiations. After its conclusion, all States should contribute to ensuring the broadest possible application of the convention through its early signature and ratification.

76. A convention should be concluded prohibiting the development, production, stockpiling and use of radiological weapons.

77. In order to help prevent a qualitative arms race and so that scientific and technological achievements may ultimately be used solely for peaceful purposes, effective measures should be taken to avoid the danger and prevent the emergence of new types of weapons of mass destruction based on new scientific principles and achievements. Efforts should be appropriately pursued aiming at the prohibition of such new types and new systems of weapons of mass destruction. Specific agreements could be concluded on particular types of new weapons of mass destruction which may be identified. This question should be kept under continuing review.

78. The Committee on Disarmament should keep under review the need for a further prohibition of military or any other hostile use of environmental modification techniques in order to eliminate the dangers to mankind from such use.

79. In order to promote the peaceful use of and to avoid an arms race on the sea-bed and the ocean floor and in the subsoil thereof, the Committee on Disarmament is requested—in consultation with the States parties to the Treaty on the Prohibition of the Emplacement of Nuclear Weapons and Other Weapons of Mass Destruction on the Sea–Bed and the Ocean Floor and in the Subsoil Thereof, and taking into account the proposals made during the 1977 Review Conference of the parties to that Treaty and any relevant technological developments—to proceed promptly with the consideration of further measures in the field of disarmament for the prevention of an arms race in that environment.

80. In order to prevent an arms race in outer space, further measures should be taken and appropriate international negotiations held in accordance with the spirit of the Treaty on Principles Governing the Activities of States in the Exploration and Use of Outer Space, including the Moon and Other Celestial Bodies.

81. Together with negotiations on nuclear disarmament measures, the limitation and gradual reduction of armed forces and conventional weapons should be resolutely pursued within the framework of progress towards general and complete disarmament. States with the largest military arsenals have a special responsibility in pursuing the process of conventional armaments reductions.

82. In particular the achievement of a more stable situation in Europe at a lower level of military potential on the basis of approximate equality and parity, as well as on the basis of undiminished security of all States with full respect for security interests and independence of States outside military alliances, by agreement on appropriate mutual reductions and limitations would contribute to the strengthening of security in Europe and constitute a significant step towards enhancing international peace and security. Current efforts to this end should be continued most energetically.

83. Agreements or other measures should be resolutely pursued on a bilateral, regional and multilateral basis with the aim of strengthening peace and security at a lower level of forces, by the limitation and reduction of armed forces and of conventional weapons, taking into account the need of States to protect their security, bearing in mind the inherent right of self-defence embodied in the Charter of the United Nations and without prejudice to the principle of equal rights and self-determination of peoples in accordance with the Charter, and the need to ensure balance at each stage and undiminished security of all States. Such measures might include those in the following two paragraphs.

84. Bilateral, regional and multilateral consultations and conferences where appropriate conditions exist with the participation of all the countries concerned for the consideration of different aspects of conventional disarmament, such as the initiative envisaged in the Declaration of Ayacucho subscribed to by eight Latin American countries on 9 December 1974.

85. Consultations should be carried out among major arms supplier and recipient countries on the limitation of all types of international transfer of conventional weapons, based in particular on the principle of undiminished security of the parties with a view to promoting or enhancing stability at a lower military level, taking into account the need of all States to protect their security as well as the inalienable right to self-determination and independence of peoples under colonial or foreign domination and the obligations of States to respect that right, in accordance with the Charter of the United Nations and the Declaration on Principles of International Law concerning Friendly Relations and Co-operation among States.

86. The United Nations Conference on Prohibitions or Restrictions of Use of Certain Conventional Weapons Which May Be Deemed to Be Excessively Injurious or to Have Indiscriminate Effects, to be held in 1979, should seek agreement, in the light of humanitarian and military considerations, on the prohibition or restriction of use of certain conventional weapons including those which may cause unnecessary suffering or have indiscriminate effects. The Conference should consider specific categories of such weapons, including those which were the subject-matter of previously conducted discussions.

87. All States are called upon to contribute towards carrying out this task.

88. The result of the Conferences should be considered by all States, and especially producer States, in regard to the question of the transfer of such weapons to other States.

89. Gradual reduction of military budgets on a mutually agreed basis, for example, in absolute figures or in terms of percentage points, particularly by nuclear-weapon States and other militarily significant States, would be a measure that would contribute to the curbing of the arms race and would increase the possibilities of reallocation of resources now being used for military purposes to economic and social development, particularly for the benefit of the developing countries. The basis for implementing this measure will have to be agreed by all participating States and will require ways and means of its implementation acceptable to all of them, taking account of the problems involved in assessing the relative significance of reductions as among different States and with due regard to the proposals of States on all the aspects of reduction of military budgets.

90. The General Assembly should continue to consider what concrete steps should be taken to facilitate the reduction of military budgets, bearing in mind the relevant proposals and documents of the United Nations on this question.

91. In order to facilitate the conclusion and effective implementation of disarmament agreements and to create confidence, States should accept appropriate provisions for verification in such agreements.

92. In the context of international disarmament negotiations, the problem of verification should be further examined and adequate methods and procedures in this field be considered. Every effort should be made to develop appropriate methods and procedures which are non-discriminatory and which do not unduly interfere with the internal affairs of other States or jeopardize their economic and social development.

93. In order to facilitate the process of disarmament, it is necessary to take measures and pursue policies to strengthen international peace and security and to build confidence among States. Commitment to confidence-building measures could significantly contribute to preparing for further progress in disarmament. For this purpose, measures such as the following, and other measures yet to be agreed upon, should be undertaken:

(a) The prevention of attacks which take place by accident, miscalculation or communications failure by taking steps to improve communications between Governments, particularly in areas of tension, by the establishment of "hot lines" and other methods of reducing the risk of conflict;

(b) States should assess the possible implications of their military research and development for existing agreements as well as for further efforts in the field of disarmament;

(c) The Secretary–General shall periodically submit reports to the General Assembly on the economic and social consequences of the arms race and its extremely harmful effects on world peace and security.

94. In view of the relationship between expenditure on armaments and economic and social development and the necessity to release real resources now being used for military purposes to economic and social development in the world, particularly for the benefit of the developing countries, the Secretary–General should, with the assistance of a group of qualified governmental experts appointed by him, initiate an expert study on the relationship between disarmament and development. The Secretary–General should submit an interim report on the subject to the General Assembly at its thirty-fourth session and submit the final results to the Assembly at its thirty-sixth session for subsequent action.

95. The expert study should have the terms of reference contained in the report of the *Ad Hoc* Group on the Relationship between Disarmament and Development appointed by the Secretary–General in accordance with General Assembly resolution 32/88A of 12 December 1977. It should investigate the three main areas listed in the report, bearing in mind the United Nations studies previously carried out. The study should be made in the context of how disarmament can contribute to the establishment of the new international economic order. The study should be forward-looking and policy-oriented and place special emphasis on both the desirability of a reallocation, following disarmament measures, of resources now being used for military purposes to economic and social development, particularly for the benefit of the developing countries and the substantive feasibility of such a reallocation. A principal aim should be to produce results that could effectively guide the formulation of practical measures to reallocate those resources at the local, national, regional and international levels.

96. Taking further steps in the field of disarmament and other measures aimed at promoting international peace and security would be facilitated by carrying out studies by the Secretary–General in this field with appropriate assistance from governmental or consultant experts.

97. The Secretary–General shall, with the assistance of consultant experts appointed by him, continue the study of the interrelationship between disarmament and international security requested in Assembly resolution 32/87C of 12 December 1977 and submit it to the thirty-fourth session of the General Assembly.

98. The thirty-third and subsequent sessions of the General Assembly should determine the specified guidelines for carrying out studies, taking into account the proposals already submitted including those made by individual countries at the special session, as well as other proposals which can be introduced later in this field. In doing so, the Assembly would take into consideration a report on these matters prepared by the Secretary-General.

99. In order to mobilize world public opinion on behalf of disarmament, the specific measures set forth below, designed to increase the dissemination of information about the armaments race and the efforts to halt and reverse it, should be adopted.

100. Governmental and non-governmental information organs and those of the United Nations and its specialized agencies should give priority to the preparation and distribution of printed and audio-visual material relating to the danger represented by the armaments race as well as to the disarmament efforts and negotiations on specific disarmament measures.

101. In particular, publicity should be given to the Final Document of the tenth special session.

102. The General Assembly proclaims the week starting 24 October, the day of the foundation of the United Nations, as a week devoted to fostering the objectives of disarmament.

103. To encourage study and research on disarmament, the United Nations Centre for Disarmament should intensify its activities in the presentation of information concerning the armaments race and disarmament. Also, the United Nations Educational, Scientific and Cultural Organization is urged to intensify its activities aimed at facilitating research and publications on disarmament, related to its fields of competence, especially in developing countries, and should disseminate the results of such research.

104. Throughout this process of disseminating information about developments in the disarmament field of all countries, there should be increased participation by non-governmental organizations concerned with the matter, through closer liaison between them and the United Nations.

105. Member States should be encouraged to ensure a better flow of information with regard to the various aspects of disarmament to avoid dissemination of false and tendentious information concerning armaments, and to concentrate on the danger of escalation of the armaments race and on the need for general and complete disarmament under effective international control.

106. With a view to contributing to a greater understanding and awareness of the problems created by the armaments race and of the need for disarmament, Governments and governmental and non-governmental international organizations are urged to take steps to develop programmes of education for disarmament and peace studies at all levels.

107. The General Assembly welcomes the initiative of the United Nations Educational, Scientific and Cultural Organization in planning to hold a world congress on disarmament education and, in this connexion, urges that Organization to step up its programme aimed at the development of disarmament education as a distinct field of study through the preparation, *inter alia,* of teachers' guides, textbooks, readers and audio-visual materials. Member States should take all possible measures to encourage the incorporation of such materials in the curricula of their educational institutes.

108. In order to promote expertise in disarmament in more Member States, particularly in the developing countries, a General Assembly decides to establish a programme of fellowships on disarmament. The Secretary-General, taking into

account the proposal submitted to the special session, should prepare guidelines for the programme. He should also submit the financial requirements of 20 fellowships to the General Assembly at its thirty-third session for inclusion in the regular budget of the United Nations, bearing in mind the savings that can be made within the existing budgetary appropriations.

109. Implementation of these priorities should lead to general and complete disarmament under effective international control, which remains the ultimate goal of all efforts exerted in the field of disarmament. Negotiations on general and complete disarmament shall be conducted concurrently with negotiations on partial measures of disarmament. With this purpose in mind, the Committee on Disarmament will undertake the elaboration of a comprehensive programme of disarmament encompassing all measures thought to be advisable in order to ensure that the goal of general and complete disarmament under effective international control becomes a reality in a world in which international peace and security prevail and in which the new international economic order is strengthened and consolidated. The comprehensive programme should contain appropriate procedures for ensuring that the General Assembly is kept fully informed of the progress of the negotiations including an appraisal of the situation when appropriate and, in particular, a continuing review of the implementation of the programme.

110. Progress in disarmament should be accompanied by measures to strengthen institutions for maintaining peace and the settlement of international disputes by peaceful means. During and after the implementation of the programme of general and complete disarmament, there should be taken, in accordance with the principles of the Charter of the United Nations, the necessary measures to maintain international peace and security, including the obligation of States to place at the disposal of the United Nations agreed manpower necessary for an international peace force to be equipped with agreed types of armaments. Arrangements for the use of this force should ensure that the United Nations can effectively deter or suppress any threat or use of arms in violation of the purposes and principles of the United Nations.

111. General and complete disarmament under strict and effective international control shall permit States to have at their disposal only those non-nuclear forces, armaments, facilities and establishments as are agreed to be necessary to maintain internal order and protect the personal security of citizens and in order that States shall support and provide agreed manpower for a United Nations peace force.

112. In addition to the several questions dealt with in this Programme of Action, there are a few others of fundamental importance, on which, because of the complexity of the issues involved and the short time at the disposal of the special session, it has proved impossible to reach satisfactory agreed conclusions. For those reasons they are treated only in very general terms and, in a few instances, not even treated at all in the Programme. It should be stressed, however, that a number of concrete approaches to deal with such questions emerged from the exchange of views carried out in the General Assembly which will undoubtedly facilitate the continuation of the study and negotiation of the problems involved in the competent disarmament organs.

IV. MACHINERY

113. While disarmament, particularly in the nuclear field, has become a necessity for the survival of mankind and for the elimination of the danger of nuclear war, little progress has been made since the end of the Second World War. In addition to the need to exercise political will, the international machinery should be utilized more effectively and also improved to enable implementation of the Programme of Action and help the United Nations to fulfil its role in the field of disarmament. In spite of the best efforts of the international community, adequate results have not been produced with the existing machinery. There is, therefore, an urgent need that

existing disarmament machinery be revitalized and forums appropriately constituted for disarmament deliberations and negotiations with a better representative character. For maximum effectiveness, two kinds of bodies are required in the field of disarmament—deliberative and negotiating. All Member States should be represented on the former, whereas the latter, for the sake of convenience, should have a relatively small membership.

114. The United Nations, in accordance with the Charter, has a central role and primary responsibility in the sphere of disarmament. Accordingly, it should play a more active role in this field and, in order to discharge its functions effectively, the United Nations should facilitate and encourage all disarmament measures—unilateral, bilateral, regional or multilateral—and be kept duly informed through the General Assembly, or any other appropriate United Nations channel reaching all Members of the Organization, of all disarmament efforts outside its aegis without prejudice to the progress of negotiations.

115. The General Assembly has been and should remain the main deliberative organ of the United Nations in the field of disarmament and should make every effort to facilitate the implementation of disarmament measures. An item entitled "Review of the implementation of the recommendations and decisions adopted by the General Assembly at its tenth special session" shall be included in the provisional agenda of the thirty-third and subsequent sessions of the General Assembly.

116. Draft multilateral disarmament conventions should be subjected to the normal procedures applicable in the law of treaties. Those submitted to the General Assembly for its commendation should be subject to full review by the Assembly.

117. The First Committee of the General Assembly should deal in the future only with questions of disarmament and related international security questions.

118. The General Assembly establishes, as successor to the Commission originally established by resolution 502(VI) of 11 January 1952 a Disarmament Commission, composed of all States Members of the United Nations, and decides that:

(a) The Disarmament Commission shall be a deliberative body, a subsidiary organ of the General Assembly, the function of which shall be to consider and make recommendations on various problems in the field of disarmament and to follow up the relevant decisions and recommendations of the special session devoted to disarmament. The Disarmament Commission should, *inter alia*, consider the elements of a comprehensive programme for disarmament to be submitted as recommendations to the General Assembly and, through it, to the negotiating body, the Committee on Disarmament;

(b) The Disarmament Commission shall function under the rules of procedure relating to the committees of the General Assembly with such modifications as the Commission may deem necessary and shall make every effort to ensure that, in so far as possible, decisions on substantive issues be adopted by consensus;

(c) The Disarmament Commission shall report annually to the General Assembly and will submit for consideration by the Assembly at its thirty-third session a report on organizational matters; in 1979, the Disarmament Commission will meet for a period not exceeding four weeks, the dates to be decided at the thirty-third session of the Assembly;

(d) The Secretary–General shall furnish such experts, staff and services as are necessary for the effective accomplishment of the Commission's functions.

119. A second special session of the General Assembly devoted to disarmament should be held on a date to be decided by the Assembly at its thirty-third session.

120. The General Assembly is conscious of the work that has been done by the international negotiating body that has been meeting since 14 March 1962 as well as

the considerable and urgent work that remains to be accomplished in the field of disarmament. The Assembly is deeply aware of the continuing requirement for a single multilateral disarmament negotiating forum of limited size taking decisions on the basis of consensus. It attaches great importance to the participation of all the nuclear-weapon States in an appropriately constituted negotiating body, the Committee on Disarmament. The Assembly welcomes the agreement reached following appropriate consultations among the Member States during the special session of the General Assembly devoted to disarmament that the Committee on Disarmament will be open to the nuclear-weapon States, and thirty-two to thirty-five other States to be chosen in consultation with the President of the thirty-second session of the Assembly; that the membership of the Committee on Disarmament will be reviewed at regular intervals; that the Committee on Disarmament will be convened in Geneva not later than January 1979 by the country whose name appears first in the alphabetical list of membership; and that the Committee on Disarmament will:

(a) Conduct its work by consensus;

(b) Adopt its own rules of procedure;

(c) Request the Secretary–General of the United Nations, following consultations with the Committee on Disarmament, to appoint the Secretary of the Committee, who shall also act as his personal representative, to assist the Committee and its chairman in organizing the business and time-tables of the Committee;

(d) Rotate the chairmanship of the Committee among all its members on a monthly basis;

(e) Adopt its own agenda taking into account the recommendations made to it by the General Assembly and the proposals presented by the members of the Committee;

(f) Submit a report to the General Assembly annually, or more frequently as appropriate, and provide its formal and other relevant documents to the States Members of the United Nations on a regular basis;

(g) Make arrangements for interested States, not members of the Committee, to submit to the Committee written proposals or working documents on measures of disarmament that are the subject of negotiation in the Committee and to participate in the discussion of the subject-matter of such proposals or working documents;

(h) Invite States not members of the Committee, upon their request, to express views in the Committee when the particular concerns of those States are under discussion;

(i) Open its plenary meetings to the public unless otherwise decided.

121. Bilateral and regional disarmament negotiations may also play an important role and could facilitate negotiations of multilateral agreements in the field of disarmament.

122. At the earliest appropriate time, a world disarmament conference should be convened with universal participation and with adequate preparation.

123. In order to enable the United Nations to continue to fulfil its role in the field of disarmament and to carry out the additional tasks assigned to it by this special session, the United Nations Centre for Disarmament should be adequately strengthened and its research and information functions accordingly extended. The Centre should also take account fully of the possibilities offered by specialized agencies and other institutions and programmes within the United Nations system with regard to studies and information on disarmament. The Centre should also increase contacts with non-governmental organizations and research institutions in

view of the valuable role they play in the field of disarmament. This role could be encouraged also in other ways that may be considered as appropriate.

124. The Secretary–General is requested to set up an advisory board of eminent persons, selected on the basis of their personal expertise and taking into account the principle of equitable geographical representation, to advise him on various aspects of studies to be made under the auspices of the United Nations in the field of disarmament and arms limitation, including a programme of such studies.

125. The General Assembly notes with satifaction that the active participation of the Member States in the consideration of the agenda items of the special session and the proposals and suggestions submitted by them and reflected to a considerable extent in the Final Document have made a valuable contribution to the work of the special session and to its positive conclusion. Since a number of those proposals and suggestions, which have become an integral part of the work of the special session of the General Assembly, deserve to be studied further and more thoroughly, taking into consideration the many relevant comments and observations made in both the general debate of the plenary and the deliberations of the *Ad Hoc* Committee of the Tenth Special Session, the Secretary–General is requested to transmit, together with this Final Document, to the appropriate deliberative and negotiating organs dealing with the questions of disarmament all the official records of the special session devoted to disarmament, in accordance with the recommendations which the Assembly may adopt at its thirty-third session. * * *

126. In adopting this Final Document, the States Members of the United Nations solemnly reaffirm their determination to work for general and complete disarmament and to make further collective efforts aimed at strengthening peace and international security; eliminating the threat of war, particularly nuclear war; implementing practical measures aimed at halting and reversing the arms race; strengthening the procedures for the peaceful settlement of disputes; and reducing military expenditures and utilizing the resources thus released in a manner which will help to promote the well-being of all peoples and to improve the economic conditions of the developing countries.

127. The General Assembly expresses its satisfaction that the proposals submitted to its special session devoted to disarmament and the deliberations thereon have made it possible to reaffirm and define in this Final Document fundamental principles, goals, priorities and procedures for the implementation of the above purposes, either in the Declaration or the Programme of Action or in both. The Assembly also welcomes the important decisions agreed upon regarding the deliberative and negotiating machinery and is confident that these organs will discharge their functions in an effective manner.

128. Finally, it should be borne in mind that the number of States that participated in the general debate, as well as the high level of representation and the depth and scope of that debate, are unprecedented in the history of disarmament efforts. Several Heads of State or Government addressed the General Assembly. In addition, other Heads of State or Government sent messages and expressed their good wishes for the success of the special session of the Assembly. Several high officials of specialized agencies and other institutions and programmes within the United Nations system and spokesmen of twenty-five non-governmental organizations and six research institutes also made valuable contributions to the proceedings of the session. It must be emphasized, moreover, that the special session marks not the end but rather the beginning of a new phase of the efforts of the United Nations in the field of disarmament.

129. The General Assembly is convinced that the discussions of the disarmament problems at the special session and its Final Document will attract the attention of all peoples, further mobilize world public opinion and provide a powerful impetus for the cause of disarmament.

2.36 RESOLUTION ON THE NON-USE OF NUCLEAR WEAPONS AND PREVENTION OF NUCLEAR WAR.[a] Adopted by the U.N. General Assembly, Dec. 12, 1980. U.N.G.A. Res. 35/152D, 35 U.N.GAOR Supp. (No. 48) 69, U.N.Doc. A/35/48 (1980)

The General Assembly,

Alarmed by the threat to the survival of mankind and to the life-sustaining system posed by nuclear weapons and by their use, inherent in concepts of deterrence,

Convinced that nuclear disarmament is essential for the prevention of nuclear war and for the strengthening of international peace and security,

Recalling its declaration, contained in the Final Document of the Tenth Special Session of the General Assembly, that all States should actively participate in efforts to bring about conditions in international relations among States in which a code of peaceful conduct of nations in international affairs could be agreed upon and which would preclude the use or threat of use of nuclear weapons,

Recalling its resolutions 1653 (XVI) of 24 November 1961, 33/71 B of 14 December 1978 and 34/83 G of 11 December 1979,

Taking note of the report of the Secretary–General, to which is annexed the Comprehensive Study on Nuclear Weapons, prepared with the assistance of a Group of Experts,

1. *Declares once again* that:

(*a*) The use of nuclear weapons would be a violation of the Charter of the United Nations and a crime against humanity;

(*b*) The use or threat of use of nuclear weapons should therefore be prohibited, pending nuclear disarmament;

2. *Requests* all States that have so far not submitted their proposals concerning the non-use of nuclear weapons, avoidance of nuclear war and related matters, to do so, in order that the question of an international convention or some other agreement on the subject may be further considered at the thirty-sixth session of the General Assembly;

3. *Decides* to include in the provisional agenda of its thirty-sixth session the item entitled "Non-use of nuclear weapons and prevention of nuclear war".

a. *See also* Basic Documents 2.17 and 2.29, *supra.*

2.37 DELHI DECLARATION.[a] Issued by Raúl Alfonsin (President of Argentina), Rajiu Gandhi (Prime Minister of India), Miguel De La Madrid (President of Mexico), Lucius Nyerere (President of the United Republic of Tanzania), Olof Palme (Prime Minister of Sweden), and Andreas Papandreou (Prime Minister of Greece), Jan. 28, 1985. Conference on Disarmament, U.N. Doc. CD/549 (Feb. 6, 1985)

Forty years ago, when atomic bombs were blasted over Hiroshima and Nagasaki, the human race became aware that it could destroy itself, and horror came to dwell among us. Forty years ago, also, the nations of the world gathered to organize the international community, and with the United Nations hope was born for all people.

Almost imperceptibly, over the last four decades, every nation and every human being has lost ultimate control over their own life and death. For all of us, it is a small group of men and machines in cities far away who can decide our fate. Every day we remain alive is a day of grace as if mankind as a whole were a prisoner in the death cell awaiting the uncertain moment of execution. And like every innocent defendant, we refuse to believe that the execution will ever take place.

We find ourselves in this situation because the nuclear weapon States have applied traditional doctrines of war in a world where new weapons have made them obsolete. What is the point of nuclear "superiority" or "balance" when each side already has enough weapons to devastate the earth dozens of times over? If the old doctrines are applied in the future, the holocaust will be inescapable sooner or later. But nuclear war can be prevented if our voices are joined in a universal demand in defence of our right to live.

As a result of recent atmospheric and biological studies, there have been new findings which indicate that in addition to blast, heat and radiation, nuclear war, even on a limited scale, would trigger an arctic nuclear winter which may transform the Earth into a darkened, frozen planet posing unprecedented peril to all nations, even those far removed from the nuclear explosions. We are convinced that this makes it still more pressing to take preventive action to exclude forever the use of nuclear weapons and the occurrence of a nuclear war.

In our Joint Statement of 22 May 1984 we called upon the nuclear weapon States to bring their arms race to a halt. We are encouraged by the world-wide response to our appeal. The international support we received, and the responses of the nuclear weapon States themselves, have been such that we deemed it our duty to meet here in New Delhi to consider ways to further our efforts.

The nuclear weapon States have a particular responsibility for the dangerous state of the arms race. We urge them to join us in the search for a new direction. We welcome the agreement in Geneva on 8 January 1985 between the Soviet Union and the United States to start bilateral negotiations on "a complex of questions concerning space and nuclear arms—both strategic and intermediate range—with all the questions considered and resolved in their inter-relationship". We attach great importance to the proclaimed objective of these negotiations: to prevent an arms race in space and to terminate it on earth, ultimately to eliminate nuclear arms everywhere. We expect the two major nuclear weapon powers to implement, in good faith, their undertaking and their negotiations to produce, at an early date, significant results. We will follow their work closely and we expect that they will keep the

a. Also known as "the Five Continent Initiative."

international community informed of its progress. We stress that the agenda for and the outcome of these negotiations is a matter of concern for all nations and all people.

We reiterate our appeal for an all-embracing halt to the testing, production and deployment of nuclear weapons and their delivery systems. Such a halt would greatly facilitate negotiations. Two specific steps today require special attention: the prevention of an arms race in outer space, and a comprehensive test ban treaty.

Outer space must be used for the benefit of mankind as a whole, not as a battleground of the future. We therefore call for the prohibition of the development, testing, production, deployment and use of all space weapons. An arms race in space would be enormously costly, and have grave destabilizing effects. It would also endanger a number of arms limitation and disarmament agreements.

We further urge the nuclear weapon States to immediately halt the testing of all kinds of nuclear weapons, and to conclude, at an early date, a treaty on a nuclear weapon test ban. Such a treaty would be a major step towards ending the continuous modernization of nuclear arsenals.

We are convinced that all such steps, in so far as necessary, can be accompanied by adequate and non-discriminatory measures of verification.

A halt to the nuclear arms race is at the present moment imperative. Only thus can it be ensured that nuclear arsenals do not grow while negotiations proceed. However, this halt should not be an end in itself. It must be immediately followed by substantial reductions in nuclear forces, leading to the complete elimination of nuclear weapons and the final goal of General and Complete Disarmament. Parallel to this process it is urgently necessary to transfer precious resources currently wasted in military expenditure to social and economic development. The strengthening of the United Nations must also be an essential part of this endeavour.

It is imperative to find a remedy to the existing situation where hundreds of billions of dollars, amounting to approximately one and a half million per minute, are spent annually on weapons. This stands in dramatic contrast to the poverty, and in some cases misery, in which two-thirds of the world population lives.

The future of all peoples is at stake. As representatives from non-nuclear weapon States, we will not cease to express our legitimate concern and make known our demands. We affirm our determination to facilitate agreement among the nuclear weapon States, so that the required steps can be taken. We will seek to work together with them for the common security of mankind and for peace.

We urge people, parliaments and governments the world over to lend forceful support to this appeal. Progress in disarmament can only be achieved with an informed public applying strong pressure on governments. Only then will governments summon the necessary political will to overcome the many obstacles which lie in the path of peace. The World Disarmament Campaign launched by the United Nations represents a very important element in generating that political will.

For centuries, men and women have fought for their rights and freedoms. We now face the greatest struggle of all—for the right to live, for ourselves and for future generations.

Forty years ago, in Hiroshima and San Francisco, the horror of nuclear war was matched by the hope for peace. We would like this year of 1985 to be the year when hope begins to prevail over terror. We dare to hope that by 24 October 1985, the Fortieth Anniversary of the United Nations, we might see the first concrete steps to avert the threat to the survival of humanity.

2.38 SOUTH PACIFIC NUCLEAR FREE ZONE TREATY.[a] Done at Rarotonga, Aug. 6, 1985. Entered into force Dec. 11, 1986. *Reproduced in* 24 I.L.M. 1442 (1985)[b]

* * *

ARTICLE 1

USAGE OF TERMS

For the purposes of this Treaty and its Protocols:

a) "South Pacific Nuclear Free Zone" means the areas described in Annex 1 as illustrated by the map attached to that Annex;

b) "territory" means internal waters, territorial sea and archipelagic waters, the seabed and subsoil beneath, the land territory and the airspace above them;

c) "nuclear explosive device" means any nuclear weapon or other explosive device capable of releasing nuclear energy, irrespective of the purpose for which it could be used. The term includes such a weapon or device in unassembled and partly assembled forms, but does not include the means of transport or delivery of such a weapon or device if separable from and not an indivisible part of it;

d) "stationing" means emplantation, emplacement, transportation on land or inland waters, stockpiling, storage, installation and deployment.

ARTICLE 2

APPLICATION OF THE TREATY

1. Except where otherwise specified, this Treaty and its Protocols shall apply to territory within the South Pacific Nuclear Free Zone.

2. Nothing in this Treaty shall prejudice or in any way affect the rights, or the exercise of the rights, of any State under international law with regard to freedom of the seas.

ARTICLE 3

RENUNCIATION OF NUCLEAR EXPLOSIVE DEVICES

Each Party undertakes:

(a) not to manufacture or otherwise acquire, possess or have control over any nuclear explosive device by any means anywhere inside or outside the South Pacific Nuclear Free Zone;

(b) not to seek or receive any assistance in the manufacture or acquisition of any nuclear explosive device;

(c) not to take any action to assist or encourage the manufacture or acquisition of any nuclear explosive device by any State.

a. This treaty, also known as "the Treaty of Rarotonga," incorporates two annexes and three protocols, none of which are included here. All three protocols are in force. *Protocol 1* (open to France, the U.K., and the U.S.) requires parties with dependent territories within the zone to comply with the relevant provisions of the Treaty. *Protocol 2* (open to China, France, the U.K., the U.S., and the U.S.S.R.) requires the parties not to assist a violation of the Treaty or its protocols and not to use or threaten to use nuclear weapons against parties to the Treaty or territories within the zone for which Protocol 1 parties are responsible. *Protocol 3* (open to China, France, the U.K., the U.S., and the U.S.S.R.) requires the parties not to test nuclear weapons within the zone.

b. *See also* Basic Document 2.21, *supra.*

ARTICLE 4

PEACEFUL NUCLEAR ACTIVITIES

Each Party undertakes:

(a) not to provide source or special fissionable material, or equipment or material especially designed or prepared for the processing, use or production of special fissionable material for peaceful purposes to:

(i) any non-nuclear-weapon State unless subject to the safeguards required by Article III.1 of the NPT, or

(ii) any nuclear-weapon State unless subject to applicable safeguards agreements with the International Atomic Energy Agency (IAEA).

Any such provision shall be in accordance with strict non-proliferation measures to provide assurance of exclusively peaceful non-explosive use;

(b) to support the continued effectiveness of the international non-proliferation system based on the NPT and the IAEA safeguards system.

ARTICLE 5

PREVENTION OF STATIONING OF NUCLEAR EXPLOSIVE DEVICES

1. Each Party undertakes to prevent in its territory the stationing of any nuclear explosive device.

2. Each Party in the exercise of its sovereign rights remains free to decide for itself whether to allow visits by foreign ships and aircraft to its ports and airfields, transit of its airspace by foreign aircraft, and navigation by foreign ships in its territorial sea or archipelagic waters in a manner not covered by the rights of innocent passage, archipelagic sea lane passage or transit passage of straits.

ARTICLE 6

PREVENTION OF TESTING OF NUCLEAR EXPLOSIVE DEVICES

Each Party undertakes:

(a) to prevent in its territory the testing of any nuclear explosive device;

(b) not to take any action to assist or encourage the testing of any nuclear explosive device by any State.

ARTICLE 7

PREVENTION OF DUMPING

1. Each Party undertakes:

(a) not to dump radioactive wastes and other radioactive matter at sea anywhere within the South Pacific Nuclear Free Zone;

(b) to prevent the dumping of radioactive wastes and other radioactive matter by anyone in its territorial sea;

(c) not to take any action to assist or encourage the dumping by anyone of radioactive wastes and other radioactive matter at sea anywhere within the South Pacific Nuclear Free Zone;

(d) to support the conclusion as soon as possible of the proposed Convention relating to the protection of the natural resources and environment of the South Pacific region and its Protocol for the prevention of pollution of the South Pacific region by dumping, with the aim of precluding dumping at sea of radioactive wastes and other radioactive matter by anyone anywhere in the region.

2. Paragraphs 1(a) and 1(b) of this Article shall not apply to areas of the South Pacific Nuclear Free Zone in respect of which such a Convention and Protocol have entered into force.

ARTICLE 8

CONTROL SYSTEM

1. The Parties hereby establish a control system for the purpose of verifying compliance with their obligations under this Treaty.

2. The control system shall comprise:

(a) reports and exchange of information as provided for in Article 9;

(b) consultations as provided for in Article 10 and Annex 4(1);

(c) the application to peaceful nuclear activities of safeguards by the IAEA as provided for in Annex 2;

(d) a complaints procedure as provided for in Annex 4.

ARTICLE 9

REPORTS AND EXCHANGES OF INFORMATION

1. Each Party shall report to the Director of the South Pacific Bureau for Economic Co-operation (the Director) as soon as possible any significant event within its jurisdiction affecting the implementation of this Treaty. The Director shall circulate such reports promptly to all Parties.

2. The Parties shall endeavour to keep each other informed on matters arising under or in relation to this Treaty. They may exchange information by communicating it to the Director, who shall circulate it to all Parties.

3. The Director shall report annually to the South Pacific Forum on the status of this Treaty and matters arising under or in relation to it, incorporating reports and communications made under paragraphs 1 and 2 of this Article and matters arising under Articles 8(2)(d) and 10 and Annex 2(4).

ARTICLE 10

CONSULTATIONS AND REVIEW

Without prejudice to the conduct of consultations among Parties by other means, the Director, at the request of any Party, shall convene a meeting of the Consultative Committee established by Annex 3 for consultation and co-operation on any matter arising in relation to this Treaty or for reviewing its operation.

ARTICLE 11

AMENDMENT

The Consultative Committee shall consider proposals for amendment of the provisions of this Treaty proposed by any Party and circulated by the Director to all Parties not less than three months prior to the convening of the Consultative Committee for this purpose. Any proposal agreed upon by consensus by the Consultative Committee shall be communicated to the Director who shall circulate it for acceptance to all Parties. An amendment shall enter into force thirty days after receipt by the depositary of acceptances from all Parties.

* * *

ARTICLE 13

WITHDRAWAL

1. This Treaty is of a permanent nature and shall remain in force indefinitely, provided that in the event of a violation by any Party of a provision of this Treaty

essential to the achievement of the objectives of the Treaty or of the spirit of the Treaty, every other Party shall have the right to withdraw from the Treaty.

2. Withdrawal shall be effected by giving notice twelve months in advance to the Director who shall circulate such notice to all other Parties.

ARTICLE 14

RESERVATIONS

This Treaty shall not be subject to reservations.

* * *

2.39 TREATY BETWEEN THE UNITED STATES OF AMERICA AND THE UNION OF SOVIET SOCIALIST REPUBLICS ON THE ELIMINATION OF THEIR INTERMEDIATE–RANGE AND SHORTER–RANGE MISSILES.[a] Done at Washington, Dec. 8, 1987. Entered into force, June 1, 1988. Dept. State Pub. 9555 (Dec. 1987), *reprinted in* 27 I.L.M. 90 (1988) [b]

Article I

In accordance with the provisions of this Treaty which includes the Memorandum of Understanding and Protocols which form an integral part thereof, each Party shall eliminate its intermediate-range and shorter-range missiles, not have such systems thereafter, and carry out the other obligations set forth in this Treaty.

Article II

For the purposes of this Treaty:

1. The term "ballistic missile" means a missile that has a ballistic trajectory over most of its flight path. The term "ground-launched ballistic missile (GLBM)" means a ground-launched ballistic missile that is a weapon-delivery vehicle.

2. The term "cruise missile" means an unmanned, self-propelled vehicle that sustains flight through the use of aerodynamic lift over most of its flight path. The term "ground-launched cruise missile (GLCM)" means a ground-launched cruise missile that is a weapon-delivery vehicle.

3. The term "GLBM launcher" means a fixed launcher or a mobile land-based transporter-erector-launcher mechanism for launching a GLBM.

4. The term "GLCM launcher" means a fixed launcher or a mobile land-based transporter-erector-launcher mechanism for launching a GLCM.

5. The term "intermediate-range missile" means a GLBM or a GLCM having a range capability in excess of 1000 kilometers but not in excess of 5500 kilometers.

6. The term "shorter-range missile" means a GLBM or a GLCM having a range capability equal to or in excess of 500 kilometers but not in excess of 1000 kilometers.

7. The term "deployment area" means a designated area within which intermediate-range missiles and launchers of such missiles may operate and within which one or more missile operating bases are located.

8. The term "missile operating base" means:

(a) in the case of intermediate-range missiles, a complex of facilities located within a deployment area at which intermediate-range missiles and launchers of such missiles normally operate, in which support structures associated with such

a. Also known as "the INF Treaty."

b. Omitted are the Memorandum of Understanding Regarding the Establishment of the Data Base for the [INF Treaty], 88 State Dep't Bull. 31 (Feb. 1988), Dec. 8, 1987, *reprinted in* 27 I.L.M. 98 (1988); Protocol on Procedures Governing the Elimination of the Missile Systems Subject to the [INF Treaty], Dec. 8, 1987, 88 State Dep't Bull. 64 (Feb. 1988), *reprinted in* 27 I.L.M. 183 (1988); Protocol Regarding Inspections Relating to the [INF Treaty], Dec. 8, 1987, 88 State Dep't Bull. 70 (Feb. 1988), *reprinted in* 27 I.L.M. 190 (1988); and Agreement Among the United States of America and the Kingdom of Belgium, the Federal Republic of Germany, the Republic of Italy, the Kingdom of the Netherlands, and the United Kingdom of Great Britain and Northern Ireland Relative to the [INF Treaty], Dec. 11, 1988, 88 State Dep't Bull. 78 (Feb. 1988).

missiles and launchers are also located and in which support equipment associated with such missiles and launchers is normally located; and

(b) in the case of shorter-range missiles, a complex of facilities located any place at which shorter-range missiles and launchers of such missiles normally operate and in which support equipment associated with such missiles and launchers is normally located.

9. The term "missile support facility," as regards intermediate-range or shorter-range missiles and launchers of such missiles, means a missile production facility or a launcher production facility, a missile repair facility or a launcher repair facility, a training facility, a missile storage facility or a launcher storage facility, a test range, or an elimination facility as those terms are defined in the Memorandum of Understanding.

10. The term "transit" means movement, notified in accordance with paragraph 5(f) of Article IX of this Treaty, of an intermediate-range missile or a launcher of such a missile between missile support facilities, between such a facility and a deployment area or between deployment areas, or of a shorter-range missile or a launcher of such a missile from a missle support facility or missile operating base to an elimination facility.

11. The term "deployed missile" means an intermediate-range missile located within a deployment area or a shorter-range missile located at a missile operating base.

12. The term "non-deployed missile" means an intermediate-range missile located outside a deployment area or a shorter-range missile located outside a missile operating base.

13. The term "deployed launcher" means a launcher of an intermediate-range missile located within a deployment area or a launcher of a shorter-range missile located at a missile operating base.

14. The term "non-deployed launcher" means a launcher of an intermediate-range missile located outside a deployment area or a launcher of a shorter-range missile located outside a missile operating base.

15. The term "basing country" means a country other than the United States of America or the Union of Soviet Socialist Republics on whose territory intermediate-range or shorter-range missiles of the Parties, launchers of such missiles or support structures associated with such missiles and launchers were located at any time after November 1, 1987. Missiles or launchers in transit are not considered to be "located."

Article III

1. For the purposes of this Treaty, existing types of intermediate-range missiles are:

(a) for the United States of America, missiles of the types designated by the United States of America as the Pershing II and the BGM–109G, which are known to the Union of Soviet Socialist Republics by the same designations; and

(b) for the Union of Soviet Socialist Republics, missiles of the types designated by the Union of Soviet Socialist Republics as the RSD–10, the R–12 and the R–14, which are known to the United States of America as the SS–20, the SS–4 and the SS–5, respectively.

2. For the purposes of this Treaty, existing types of shorter-range missiles are:

(a) for the United States of America, missiles of the type designated by the United States of America as the Pershing IA, which is known to the Union of Soviet Socialist Republics by the same designation; and

(b) for the Union of Soviet Socialist Republics, missiles of the types designated by the Union of Soviet Socialist Republics as the OTR-22 and the OTR-23, which are known to the United States of America as the SS-12 and the SS-23, respectively.

Article IV

1. Each Party shall eliminate all its intermediate-range missiles and launchers of such missiles, and all support structures and support equipment of the categories listed in the Memorandum of Understanding associated with such missiles and launchers, so that no later than three years after entry into force of this Treaty and thereafter no such missiles, launchers, support structures or support equipment shall be possessed by either Party.

2. To implement paragraph 1 of this Article, upon entry into force of this Treaty, both Parties shall begin and continue throughout the duration of each phase, the reduction of all types of their deployed and non-deployed intermediate-range missiles and deployed and non-deployed launchers of such missiles and support structures and support equipment associated with such missiles and launchers in accordance with the provisions of this Treaty. These reductions shall be implemented in two phases so that:

(a) by the end of the first phase, that is, no later than 29 months after entry into force of this Treaty:

(i) the number of deployed launchers of intermediate-range missiles for each Party shall not exceed the number of launchers that are capable of carrying or containing at one time missiles considered by the Parties to carry 171 warheads;

(ii) the number of deployed intermediate-range missiles for each Party shall not exceed the number of such missiles considered by the Parties to carry 180 warheads;

(iii) the aggregate number of deployed and non-deployed launchers of intermediate-range missiles for each Party shall not exceed the number of launchers that are capable of carrying or containing at one time missiles considered by the Parties to carry 200 warheads;

(iv) the aggregate number of deployed and non-deployed intermediate-range missiles for each Party shall not exceed the number of such missiles considered by the Parties to carry 200 warheads; and

(v) the ratio of the aggregate number of deployed and non-deployed intermediate-range GLBMs of existing types for each Party to the aggregate number of deployed and non-deployed intermediate-range missiles of existing types possessed by that Party shall not exceed the ratio of such intermediate-range GLBMs to such intermediate-range missiles for that Party as of November 1, 1987, as set forth in the Memorandum of Understanding; and

(b) by the end of the second phase, that is, no later than three years after entry into force of this Treaty, all intermediate-range missiles of each Party, launchers of such missiles and all support structures and support equipment of the categories listed in the Memorandum of Understanding associated with such missiles and launchers, shall be eliminated.

Article V

1. Each Party shall eliminate all its shorter-range missiles and launchers of such missiles, and all support equipment of the categories listed in the Memorandum of Understanding associated with such missiles and launchers, so that no later than 18 months after entry into force of this Treaty and thereafter no such missiles, launchers or support equipment shall be possessed by either Party.

2. No later than 90 days after entry into force of this Treaty, each Party shall complete the removal of all its deployed shorter-range missiles and deployed and non-deployed launchers of such missiles to elimination facilities and shall retain them at those locations until they are eliminated in accordance with the procedures set forth in the Protocol on Elimination. No later than 12 months after entry into force of this Treaty, each Party shall complete the removal of all its non-deployed shorter-range missiles to elimination facilities and shall retain them at those locations until they are eliminated in accordance with the procedures set forth in the Protocol on Elimination.

3. Shorter-range missiles and launchers of such missiles shall not be located at the same elimination facility. Such facilities shall be separated by no less than 1000 kilometers.

Article VI

1. Upon entry into force of this Treaty and thereafter, neither Party shall:

(a) produce or flight-test any intermediate-range missiles or produce any stages of such missiles or any launchers of such missiles; or

(b) produce, flight-test or launch any shorter-range missiles or produce any stages of such missiles or any launchers of such missiles.

2. Notwithstanding paragraph 1 of this Article, each Party shall have the right to produce a type of GLBM not limited by this Treaty which uses a stage which is outwardly similar to, but not interchangeable with, a stage of an existing type of intermediate-range GLBM having more than one stage, providing that that Party shall not produce any other stage which is outwardly similar to, but not interchangeable with, any other stage of an existing type of intermediate-range GLBM.

Article VII

For the purposes of this Treaty:

1. If a ballistic missile or a cruise missile has been flight-tested or deployed for weapon delivery, all missiles of that type shall be considered to be weapon-delivery vehicles.

2. If a GLBM or GLCM is an intermediate-range missile, all GLBMs or GLCMs of that type shall be considered to be intermediate-range missiles. If a GLBM or GLCM is a shorter-range missile, all GLBMs or GLCMs of that type shall be considered to be shorter-range missiles.

3. If a GLBM is of a type developed and tested solely to intercept and counter objects not located on the surface of the earth, it shall not be considered to be a missile to which the limitations of this Treaty apply.

4. The range capability of a GLBM not listed in Article III of this Treaty shall be considered to be the maximum range to which it has been tested. The range capability of a GLCM not listed in Article III of this Treaty shall be considered to be the maximum distance which can be covered by the missile in its standard design mode flying until fuel exhaustion, determined by projecting its flight path onto the earth's sphere from the point of launch to the point of impact. GLBMs or GLCMs that have a range capability equal to or in excess of 500 kilometers but not in excess of 1000 kilometers shall be considered to be shorter-range missiles. GLBMs or GLCMs that have a range capability in excess of 1000 kilometers but not in excess of 5500 kilometers shall be considered to be intermediate-range missiles.

5. The maximum number of warheads an existing type of intermediate-range missile or shorter-range missile carries shall be considered to be the number listed for missiles of that type in the Memorandum of Understanding.

6. Each GLBM or GLCM shall be considered to carry the maximum number of warheads listed for a GLBM or GLCM of that type in the Memorandum of Understanding.

7. If a launcher has been tested for launching a GLBM or a GLCM, all launchers of that type shall be considered to have been tested for launching GLBMs or GLCMs.

8. If a launcher has contained or launched a particular type of GLBM or GLCM, all launchers of that type shall be considered to be launchers of that type of GLBM or GLCM.

9. The number of missiles each launcher of an existing type of intermediate-range missile or shorter-range missile shall be considered to be capable of carrying or containing at one time is the number listed for launchers of missiles of that type in the Memorandum of Understanding.

10. Except in the case of elimination in accordance with the procedures set forth in the Protocol on Elimination, the following shall apply:

(a) for GLBMs which are stored or moved in separate stages, the longest stage of an intermediate-range or shorter-range GLBM shall be counted as a complete missile;

(b) for GLBMs which are not stored or moved in separate stages, a canister of the type used in the launch of an intermediate-range GLBM, unless a Party proves to the satisfaction of the other Party that it does not contain such a missile, or an assembled intermediate-range or shorter-range GLBM, shall be counted as a complete missile; and

(c) for GLCMs, the airframe of an intermediate-range or shorter-range GLCM shall be counted as a complete missile.

11. A ballistic missile which is not a missile to be used in a ground-based mode shall not be considered to be a GLBM if it is test-launched at a test site from a fixed land-based launcher which is used solely for test purposes and which is distinguishable from GLBM launchers. A cruise missile which is not a missile to be used in a ground-based mode shall not be considered to be a GLCM if it is test-launched at a test site from a fixed land-based launcher which is used solely for test purposes and which is distinguishable from GLCM launchers.

12. Each Party shall have the right to produce and use for booster systems, which might otherwise be considered to be intermediate-range or shorter-range missiles, only existing types of booster stages for such booster systems. Launches of such booster systems shall not be considered to be flight-testing of intermediate-range or shorter-range missiles provided that:

(a) stages used in such booster systems are different from stages used in those missiles listed as existing types of intermediate-range or shorter-range missiles in Article III of this Treaty;

(b) such booster systems are used only for research and development purposes to test objects other than the booster systems themselves;

(c) the aggregate number of launchers for such booster systems shall not exceed 35 for each Party at any one time; and

(d) the launchers for such booster systems are fixed, emplaced above ground and located only at research and development launch sites which are specified in the Memorandum of Understanding.

Research and development launch sites shall not be subject to inspection pursuant to Article XI of this Treaty.

Article VIII

1. All intermediate-range missiles and launchers of such missiles shall be located in deployment areas, at missile support facilities or shall be in transit. Intermediate-range missiles or launchers of such missiles shall not be located elsewhere.

2. Stages of intermediate-range missiles shall be located in deployment areas, at missile support facilities or moving between deployment areas, between missile support facilities or between missile support facilities and deployment areas.

3. Until their removal to elimination facilities as required by paragraph 2 of Article V of this Treaty, all shorter-range missiles and launchers of such missiles shall be located at missile operating bases, at missile support facilities or shall be in transit. Shorter-range missiles or launchers of such missiles shall not be located elsewhere.

4. Transit of a missile or launcher subject to the provisions of this Treaty shall be completed within 25 days.

5. All deployment areas, missile operating bases and missile support facilities are specified in the Memorandum of Understanding or in subsequent updates of data pursuant to paragraphs 3, 5(a) or 5(b) of Article IX of this Treaty. Neither Party shall increase the number of, or change the location or boundaries of, deployment areas, missile operating bases or missile support facilities, except for elimination facilities, from those set forth in the Memorandum of Understanding. A missile support facility shall not be considered to be part of a deployment area even though it may be located within the geographic boundaries of a deployment area.

6. Beginning 30 days after entry into force of this Treaty, neither Party shall locate intermediate-range or shorter-range missiles, including stages of such missiles, or launchers of such missiles at missile production facilities, launcher production facilities or test ranges listed in the Memorandum of Understanding.

7. Neither Party shall locate any intermediate-range or shorter-range missiles at training facilities.

8. A non-deployed intermediate-range or shorter-range missile shall not be carried on or contained within a launcher of such a type of missile, except as required for maintenance conducted at repair facilities or for elimination by means of launching conducted at elimination facilities.

9. Training missiles and training launchers for intermediate-range or shorter-range missiles shall be subject to the same locational restrictions as are set forth for intermediate-range and shorter-range missiles and launchers of such missiles in paragraphs 1 and 3 of this Article.

Article IX

1. The Memorandum of Understanding contains categories of data relevant to obligations undertaken with regard to this Treaty and lists all intermediate-range and shorter-range missiles, launchers of such missiles, and support structures and support equipment associated with such missiles and launchers, possessed by the Parties as of November 1, 1987. Updates of that data and notifications required by this Article shall be provided according to the categories of data contained in the Memorandum of Understanding.

2. The Parties shall update that data and provide the notifications required by this Treaty through the Nuclear Risk Reduction Centers, established pursuant to the Agreement Between the United States of America and the Union of Soviet Socialist Republics on the Establishment of Nuclear Risk Reduction Centers of September 15, 1987.

3. No later than 30 days after entry into force of this Treaty, each Party shall provide the other Party with updated data, as of the date of entry into force of this Treaty, for all categories of data contained in the Memorandum of Understanding.

4. No later than 30 days after the end of each six-month interval following the entry into force of this Treaty, each Party shall provide updated data for all categories of data contained in the Memorandum of Understanding by informing the other Party of all changes, completed and in process, in that data, which have occurred during the six-month interval since the preceding data exchange, and the net effect of those changes.

5. Upon entry into force of this Treaty and thereafter, each Party shall provide the following notifications to the other Party:

(a) notification, no less than 30 days in advance, of the scheduled date of the elimination of a specific deployment area, missile operating base or missile support facility;

(b) notification, no less than 30 days in advance, of changes in the number or location of elimination facilities, including the location and scheduled date of a change;

(c) notification, except with respect to launches of intermediate-range missiles for the purpose of their elimination, no less than 30 days in advance, of the scheduled date of the initiation of the elimination of intermediate-range and shorter-range missiles, and stages of such missiles, and launchers of such missiles and support structures and support equipment associated with such missiles and launchers, including:

(i) the number and type of items of missile systems to be eliminated;

(ii) the elimination site;

(iii) for intermediate-range missiles, the location from which such missiles, launchers of such missiles and support equipment associated with such missiles and launchers are moved to the elimination facility; and

(iv) except in the case of support structures, the point of entry to be used by an inspection team conducting an inspection pursuant to paragraph 7 of Article XI of this Treaty and the estimated time of departure of an inspection team from the point of entry to the elimination facility;

(d) notification, no less than ten days in advance, of the scheduled date of the launch, or the scheduled date of the initiation of a series of launches, of intermediate-range missiles for the purpose of their elimination, including:

(i) the type of missiles to be eliminated;

(ii) location of the launch, or, if elimination is by a series of launches, the location of such launches and number of launches in the series;

(iii) the point of entry to be used by an inspection team conducting an inspection pursuant to paragraph 7 of Article XI of this Treaty; and

(iv) the estimated time of departure of an inspection team from the point of entry to the elimination facility;

(e) notification, no later than 48 hours after they occur, of changes in the number of intermediate-range and shorter-range missiles, launchers of such missiles and support structures and support equipment associated with such missiles and launchers resulting from elimination as described in the Protocol on Elimination, including:

(i) the number and type of items of a missile system which were eliminated; and

(ii) the date and location of such elimination; and

(f) notification of transit of intermediate-range or shorter-range missiles or launchers of such missiles, or the movement of training missiles or training launchers for such intermediate-range and shorter-range missiles, no later than 48 hours after it has been completed, including:

(i) the number of missiles or launchers;

(ii) the points, dates and times of departure and arrival;

(iii) the mode of transport; and

(iv) the location and time at that location at least once every four days during the period of transit.

6. Upon entry into force of this Treaty and thereafter, each Party shall notify the other Party, no less than ten days in advance, of the scheduled date and location of the launch of a research and development booster system as described in paragraph 12 of Article VII of this Treaty.

Article X

1. Each Party shall eliminate its intermediate-range and shorter-range missiles and launchers of such missiles and support structures and support equipment associated with such missiles and launchers in accordance with the procedures set forth in the Protocol on Elimination.

2. Verification by on-site inspection of the elimination of items of missile systems specified in the Protocol on Elimination shall be carried out in accordance with Article XI of this Treaty, the Protocol on Elimination and the Protocol on Inspection.

3. When a Party removes its intermediate-range missiles, launchers of such missiles and support equipment associated with such missiles and launchers from deployment areas to elimination facilities for the purpose of their elimination, it shall do so in complete deployed organizational units. For the United States of America, these units shall be Pershing II batteries and BGM–109G flights. For the Union of Soviet Socialist Republics, these units shall be SS–20 regiments composed of two or three battalions.

4. Elimination of intermediate-range and shorter-range missiles and launchers of such missiles and support equipment associated with such missiles and launchers shall be carried out at the facilities that are specified in the Memorandum of Understanding or notified in accordance with paragraph 5(b) of Article IX of this Treaty, unless eliminated in accordance with Sections IV or V of the Protocol on Elimination. Support structures, associated with the missiles and launchers subject to this Treaty, that are subject to elimination shall be eliminated *in situ*.

5. Each Party shall have the right, during the first six months after entry into force of this Treaty, to eliminate by means of launching no more than 100 of its intermediate-range missiles.

6. Intermediate-range and shorter-range missiles which have been tested prior to entry into force of this Treaty, but never deployed, and which are not existing types of intermediate-range or shorter-range missiles listed in Article III of this Treaty, and launchers of such missiles, shall be eliminated within six months after entry into force of this Treaty in accordance with the procedures set forth in the Protocol on Elimination. Such missiles are:

(a) for the United States of America, missiles of the type designated by the United States of America as the Pershing IB, which is known to the Union of Soviet Socialist Republics by the same designation; and

(b) for the Union of Soviet Socialist Republics, missiles of the type designated by the Union of Soviet Socialist Republics as the RK–55, which is known to the United States of America as the SSC–X–4.

7. Intermediate-range and shorter-range missiles and launchers of such missiles and support structures and support equipment associated with such missiles and launchers shall be considered to be eliminated after completion of the procedures set forth in the Protocol on Elimination and upon the notification provided for in paragraph 5(e) of Article IX of this Treaty.

8. Each Party shall eliminate its deployment areas, missile operating bases and missile support facilities. A Party shall notify the other Party pursuant to paragraph 5(a) of Article IX of this Treaty once the conditions set forth below are fulfilled:

(a) all intermediate-range and shorter-range missiles, launchers of such missiles and support equipment associated with such missiles and launchers located there have been removed;

(b) all support structures associated with such missiles and launchers located there have been eliminated; and

(c) all activity related to production, flight-testing, training, repair, storage or deployment of such missiles and launchers has ceased there.

Such deployment areas, missile operating bases and missile support facilities shall be considered to be eliminated either when they have been inspected pursuant to paragraph 4 of Article XI of this Treaty or when 60 days have elapsed since the date of the scheduled elimination which was notified pursuant to paragraph 5(a) of Article IX of this Treaty. A deployment area, missile operating base or missile support facility listed in the Memorandum of Understanding that met the above conditions prior to entry into force of this Treaty, and is not included in the initial data exchange pursuant to paragraph 3 of Article IX of this Treaty, shall be considered to be eliminated.

9. If a Party intends to convert a missile operating base listed in the Memorandum of Understanding for use as a base associated with GLBM or GLCM systems not subject to this Treaty, then that Party shall notify the other Party, no less than 30 days in advance of the scheduled date of the initiation of the conversion, of the scheduled date and the purpose for which the base will be converted.

Article XI

1. For the purpose of ensuring verification of compliance with the provisions of this Treaty, each Party shall have the right to conduct on-site inspections. The Parties shall implement on-site inspections in accordance with this Article, the Protocol on Inspection and the Protocol on Elimination.

2. Each Party shall have the right to conduct inspections provided for by this Article both within the territory of the other Party and within the territories of basing countries.

3. Beginning 30 days after entry into force of this Treaty, each Party shall have the right to conduct inspections at all missile operating bases and missile support facilities specified in the Memorandum of Understanding other than missile production facilities, and at all elimination facilities included in the initial data update required by paragraph 3 of Article IX of this Treaty. These inspections shall be completed no later than 90 days after entry into force of this Treaty. The purpose of these inspections shall be to verify the number of missiles, launchers, support structures and support equipment and other data, as of the date of entry into force of this Treaty, provided pursuant to paragraph 3 of Article IX of this Treaty.

4. Each Party shall have the right to conduct inspections to verify the elimination, notified pursuant to paragraph 5(a) of Article IX of this Treaty, of missile operating bases and missile support facilities other than missile production facilities, which are thus no longer subject to inspections pursuant to paragraph 5(a) of this Article. Such an inspection shall be carried out within 60 days after the scheduled

date of the elimination of that facility. If a Party conducts an inspection at a particular facility pursuant to paragraph 3 of this Article after the scheduled date of the elimination of that facility, then no additional inspection of that facility pursuant to this paragraph shall be permitted.

5. Each Party shall have the right to conduct inspections pursuant to this paragraph for 13 years after entry into force of this Treaty. Each Party shall have the right to conduct 20 such inspections per calendar year during the first three years after entry into force of this Treaty, 15 such inspections per calendar year during the subsequent five years, and ten such inspections per calendar year during the last five years. Neither Party shall use more than half of its total number of these inspections per calendar year within the territory of any one basing country. Each Party shall have the right to conduct:

(a) inspections, beginning 90 days after entry into force of this Treaty, of missile operating bases, and missile support facilities other than elimination facilities and missile production facilities, to ascertain, according to the categories of data specified in the Memorandum of Understanding, the numbers of missiles, launchers, support structures and support equipment located at each missile operating base or missile support facility at the time of the inspection; and

(b) inspections of former missile operating bases and former missile support facilities eliminated pursuant to paragraph 8 of Article X of this Treaty other than former missile production facilities.

6. Beginning 30 days after entry into force of this Treaty, each Party shall have the right, for 13 years after entry into force of this Treaty, to inspect by means of continuous monitoring:

(a) the portals of any facility of the other Party at which the final assembly of a GLBM using stages, any of which is outwardly similar to a stage of a solid-propellant GLBM listed in Article III of this Treaty, is accomplished; or

(b) if a Party has no such facility, the portals of an agreed former missile production facility at which existing types of intermediate-range or shorter-range GLBMs were produced.

The Party whose facility is to be inspected pursuant to this paragraph shall ensure that the other Party is able to establish a permanent continuous monitoring system at that facility within six months after entry into force of this Treaty or within six months of initiation of the process of final assembly described in subparagraph (a). If, after the end of the second year after entry into force of this Treaty, neither Party conducts the process of final assembly described in subparagraph (a) for a period of 12 consecutive months, then neither Party shall have the right to inspect by means of continuous monitoring any missile production facility of the other Party unless the process of final assembly as described in subparagraph (a) is initiated again. Upon entry into force of this Treaty, the facilities to be inspected by continuous monitoring shall be: in accordance with subparagraph (b), for the United States of America, Hercules Plant Number 1, at Magna, Utah; in accordance with subparagraph (a), for the Union of Soviet Socialist Republics, the Votkinsk Machine Building Plant, Udmurt Autonomous Soviet Socialist Republic, Russian Soviet Federative Socialist Republic.

7. Each Party shall conduct inspections of the process of elimination, including elimination of intermediate-range missiles by means of launching, of intermediate-range and shorter-range missiles and launchers of such missiles and support equipment associated with such missiles and launchers carried out at elimination facilities in accordance with Article X of this Treaty and the Protocol on Elimination. Inspectors conducting inspections provided for in this paragraph shall determine that

the processes specified for the elimination of the missiles, launchers and support equipment have been completed.

8. Each Party shall have the right to conduct inspections to confirm the completion of the process of elimination of intermediate-range and shorter-range missiles and launchers of such missiles and support equipment associated with such missiles and launchers eliminated pursuant to Section V of the Protocol on Elimination, and of training missiles, training missile stages, training launch canisters and training launchers eliminated pursuant to Sections II, IV and V of the Protocol on Elimination.

Article XII

1. For the purpose of ensuring verification of compliance with the provisions of this Treaty, each Party shall use national technical means of verification at its disposal in a manner consistent with generally recognized principles of international law.

2. Neither Party shall:

(a) interfere with national technical means of verification of the other Party operating in accordance with paragraph 1 of this Article; or

(b) use concealment measures which impede verification of compliance with the provisions of this Treaty by national technical means of verification carried out in accordance with paragraph 1 of this Article. This obligation does not apply to cover or concealment practices, within a deployment area, associated with normal training, maintenance and operations, including the use of environmental shelters to protect missiles and launchers.

3. To enhance observation by national technical means of verification, each Party shall have the right until a treaty between the Parties reducing and limiting strategic offensive arms enters into force, but in any event for no more than three years after entry into force of this Treaty, to request the implementation of cooperative measures at deployment bases for road-mobile GLBMs with a range capability in excess of 5500 kilometers, which are not former missile operating bases eliminated pursuant to paragraph 8 of Article X of this Treaty. The Party making such a request shall inform the other Party of the deployment base at which cooperative measures shall be implemented. The Party whose base is to be observed shall carry out the following cooperative measures:

(a) No later than six hours after such a request, the Party shall have opened the roofs of all fixed structures for launchers located at the base, removed completely all missiles on launchers from such fixed structures for launchers and displayed such missiles on launchers in the open without using concealment measures; and

(b) The Party shall leave the roofs open and the missiles on launchers in place until twelve hours have elapsed from the time of the receipt of a request for such an observation.

Each Party shall have the right to make six such requests per calendar year. Only one deployment base shall be subject to these cooperative measures at any one time.

Article XIII

1. To promote the objectives and implementation of the provisions of this Treaty, the Parties hereby establish the Special Verification Commission. The Parties agree that, if either Party so requests, they shall meet within the framework of the Special Verification Commission to:

(a) resolve questions relating to compliance with the obligations assumed; and

(b) agree upon such measures as may be necessary to improve the viability and effectiveness of this Treaty.

2. The Parties shall use the Nuclear Risk Reduction Centers, which provide for continuous communication between the Parties, to:

(a) exchange data and provide notifications as required by paragraphs 3, 4, 5 and 6 of Article IX of this Treaty and the Protocol on Elimination;

(b) provide and receive the information required by paragraph 9 of Article X of this Treaty;

(c) provide and receive notifications of inspections as required by Article XI of this Treaty and the Protocol on Inspection; and

(d) provide and receive requests for cooperative measures as provided for in paragraph 3 of Article XII of this Treaty.

Article XIV

The Parties shall comply with this Treaty and shall not assume any international obligations or undertakings which would conflict with its provisions.

Article XV

1. This Treaty shall be of unlimited duration.

2. Each Party shall, in exercising its national sovereignty, have the right to withdraw from this Treaty if it decides that extraordinary events related to the subject matter of this Treaty have jeopardized its supreme interests. It shall give notice of its decision to withdraw to the other Party six months prior to withdrawal from this Treaty. Such notice shall include a statement of the extraordinary events the notifying Party regards as having jeopardized its supreme interests.

Article XVI

Each Party may propose amendments to this Treaty. Agreed amendments shall enter into force in accordance with the procedures set forth in Article XVII governing the entry into force of this Treaty.

Article XVII

1. This Treaty, including the Memorandum of Understanding and Protocols, which form an integral part thereof, shall be subject to ratification in accordance with the constitutional procedures of each Party. This Treaty shall enter into force on the date of the exchange of instruments of ratification.

2. This Treaty shall be registered pursuant to Article 102 of the Charter of the United Nations.

2.40 DECLARATION ON THE PROHIBITION OF CHEMICAL WEAPONS.[a] Adopted by the Conference on the Prohibition of Chemical Weapons at Paris, Jan. 11, 1989. 89 Dep't State Bull. 9 (Mar. 1989), *reprinted in* 28 I.L.M. 1020 (1989)

The representatives of States participating in the Conference on the Prohibition of Chemical Weapons, bringing together States Parties to the Geneva Protocol of 1925 and other interested States in Paris from 7 to 11 January 1989, solemnly declare the following:

1. The participating States are determined to promote international peace and security throughout the world in accordance with the Charter of the United Nations and to pursue effective disarmament measures. In this context, they are determined to prevent any recourse of chemical weapons by completely eliminating them. They solemnly affirm their commitments not to use chemical weapons and condemn such use. They recall their serious concern at recent violations as established and condemned by the competent organs of the United Nations. They support the humanitarian assistance given to the victims affected by chemical weapons.

2. The participating States recognize the importance and continuing validity of the Protocol for the prohibition of the use in war of asphyxiating, poisonous or other gases and bacteriological methods of warfare, signed on 17 June 1925 in Geneva. The States Parties to the Protocol solemnly reaffirm the prohibition as established in it. They call upon all States which have not yet done so to accede to the Protocol.

3. The participating States stress the necessity of concluding, at an early date, a convention on the prohibition of the development, production, stockpiling and use of all chemical weapons, and on their destruction. This convention shall be global and comprehensive and effectively verifiable. It should be of unlimited duration. To this end, they call on the Conference on Disarmament in Geneva to redouble its efforts, as a matter of urgency, to resolve expeditiously the remaining issues and to conclude the convention at the earliest date. All States are requested to make, in an appropriate way, a significant contribution to the negotiations in Geneva by undertaking efforts in the relevant fields. The participating States, therefore, believe that any State wishing to contribute to these negotiations should be able to do so. In addition, in order to achieve as soon as possible the indispensable universal character of the convention, they call upon all States to become parties thereto as soon as it is concluded.

4. The participating States are gravely concerned by the growing danger posed to international peace and security by the risk of the use of chemical weapons as long as such weapons remain and are spread. In this context, they stress the need for the early conclusion and entry into force of the convention, which will be established on a non-discriminatory basis. They deem it necessary, in the meantime, for each State to exercise restraint and to act responsibly in accordance with the purpose of the present declaration.

5. The participating States confirm their full support for the United Nations in the discharge of its indispensable role, in conformity with its Charter. They affirm that the United Nations provides a framework and an instrument enabling the international community to exercise vigilance with respect to the prohibition of the use of chemical weapons. They confirm their support for appropriate and effective steps taken by the United Nations in this respect in conformity with its Charter. They further reaffirm their full support for the Secretary-General in carrying out his

a. *See also* Basic Documents 2.3 and 2.26, *supra*.

responsibilities for investigations in the event of alleged violations of the Geneva Protocol. They express their wish for early completion of the work undertaken to strengthen the efficiency of existing procedures and call for the co-operation of all States, in order to facilitate the action of the Secretary-General.

6. The participating States, recalling the Final Document of the first Special Session of the United Nations General Assembly Devoted to Disarmament in 1978, underline the need to pursue with determination their efforts to secure general and complete disarmament under effective international control, so as to ensure the right of all States to peace and security.

3. HUMAN RIGHTS

3.1 AMERICAN DECLARATION OF THE RIGHTS AND DUTIES OF MAN. O.A.S. Res. XXX, adopted by the Ninth International Conference of American States (March 30–May 2, 1948), Bogota, O.A.S. Off. Rec. OEA/Ser. L/V/I.4 Rev. (1965)

PREAMBLE

All men are born free and equal, in dignity and in rights, and, being endowed by nature with reason and conscience, they should conduct themselves as brothers one to another.

The fulfillment of duty by each individual is a prerequisite to the rights of all. Rights and duties are interrelated in every social and political activity of man. While rights exalt individual liberty, duties express the dignity of that liberty.

Duties of a juridical nature presuppose others of a moral nature which support them in principle and constitute their basis.

Inasmuch as spiritual development is the supreme end of human existence and the highest expression thereof, it is the duty of man to serve that end with all his strength and resources.

Since culture is the highest social and historical expression of that spiritual development, it is the duty of man to preserve, practice and foster culture by every means within his power.

And, since moral conduct constitutes the noblest flowering of culture, it is the duty of every man always to hold it in high respect.

CHAPTER ONE. RIGHTS

Article I. Every human being has the right to life, liberty and the security of his person.

Article II. All persons are equal before the law and have the rights and duties established in this Declaration, without distinction as to race, sex, language, creed or any other factor.

Article III. Every person has the right freely to profess a religious faith, and to manifest and practice it both in public and in private.

Article IV. Every person has the right to freedom of investigation, of opinion, and of the expression and dissemination of ideas, by any medium whatsoever.

Article V. Every person has the right to the protection of the law against abusive attacks upon his honor, his reputation, and his private and family life.

Article VI. Every person has the right to establish a family, the basic element of society, and to receive protection therefor.

Article VII. All women, during pregnancy and the nursing period, and all children have the right to special protection, care and aid.

Article VIII. Every person has the right to fix his residence within the territory of the state of which he is a national, to move about freely within such territory, and not to leave it except by his own will.

Article IX. Every person has the right to the inviolability of his home.

Article X. Every person has the right to the inviolability and transmission of his correspondence.

Article XI. Every person has the right to the preservation of his health through sanitary and social measures relating to food, clothing, housing and medical care, to the extent permitted by public and community resources.

Article XII. Every person has the right to an education, which should be based on the principles of liberty, morality and human solidarity.

Likewise every person has the right to an education that will prepare him to attain a decent life, to raise his standard of living, and to be a useful member of society.

The right to an education includes the right to equality of opportunity in every case, in accordance with natural talents, merit and the desire to utilize the resources that the state or the community is in a position to provide.

Every person has the right to receive, free, at least a primary education.

Article XIII. Every person has the right to take part in the cultural life of the community, to enjoy the arts, and to participate in the benefits that result from intellectual progress, especially scientific discoveries.

He likewise has the right to the protection of his moral and material interests as regards his inventions or any literary, scientific or artistic works of which he is the author.

Article XIV. Every person has the right to work, under proper conditions, and to follow his vocation freely, in so far as existing conditions of employment permit.

Every person who works has the right to receive such remuneration as will, in proportion to his capacity and skill, assure him a standard of living suitable for himself and for his family.

Article XV. Every person has the right to leisure time, to wholesome recreation, and to the opportunity for advantageous use of his free time to his spiritual, cultural and physical benefit.

Article XVI. Every person has the right to social security which will protect him from the consequences of unemployment, old age, and any disabilities arising from causes beyond his control that make it physically or mentally impossible for him to earn a living.

Article XVII. Every person has the right to be recognized everywhere as a person having rights and obligations, and to enjoy the basic civil rights.

Article XVIII. Every person may resort to the courts to ensure respect for his legal rights. There should likewise be available to him a simple, brief procedure whereby the courts will protect him from acts of authority that, to his prejudice, violate any fundamental constitutional rights.

Article XIX. Every person has the right to the nationality to which he is entitled by law and to change it, if he so wishes, for the nationality of any other country that is willing to grant it to him.

Article XX. Every person having legal capacity is entitled to participate in the government of his country, directly or through his representatives, and to take part in popular elections, which shall be by secret ballot, and shall be honest, periodic and free.

Article XXI. Every person has the right to assemble peaceably with others in a formal public meeting or an informal gathering, in connection with matters of common interest of any nature.

Article XXII. Every person has the right to associate with others to promote, exercise and protect his legitimate interests of a political, economic, religious, social, cultural, professional, labor union or other nature.

Article XXIII. Every person has a right to own such private property as meets the essential needs of decent living and helps to maintain the dignity of the individual and of the home.

Article XXIV. Every person has the right to submit respectful petitions to any competent authority, for reasons of either general or private interest, and the right to obtain a prompt decision thereon.

Article XXV. No person may be deprived of his liberty except in the cases and according to the procedures established by pre-existing law.

No person may be deprived of liberty for nonfulfillment of obligations of a purely civil character.

Every individual who has been deprived of his liberty has the right to have the legality of his detention ascertained without delay by a court, and the right to be tried without undue delay, or otherwise, to be released. He also has the right to humane treatment during the time he is in custody.

Article XXVI. Every accused person is presumed to be innocent until proved guilty.

Every person accused of an offense has the right to be given an impartial and public hearing, and to be tried by courts previously established in accordance with pre-existing laws, and not to receive cruel, infamous or unusual punishment.

Article XXVII. Every person has the right, in case of pursuit not resulting from ordinary crimes, to seek and receive asylum in foreign territory, in accordance with the laws of each country and with international agreements.

Article XXVIII. The rights of man are limited by the rights of others, by the security of all, and by the just demands of the general welfare and the advancement of democracy.

CHAPTER TWO. DUTIES

Article XXIX. It is the duty of the individual so to conduct himself in relation to others that each and every one may fully form and develop his personality.

Article XXX. It is the duty of every person to aid, support, educate and protect his minor children, and it is the duty of children to honor their parents always and to aid, support and protect them when they need it.

Article XXXI. It is the duty of every person to acquire at least an elementary education.

Article XXXII. It is the duty of every person to vote in the popular elections of the country of which he is a national, when he is legally capable of doing so.

Article XXXIII. It is the duty of every person to obey the law and other legitimate commands of the authorities of his country and those of the country in which he may be.

Article XXXIV. It is the duty of every able-bodied person to render whatever civil and military service his country may require for its defense and preservation, and, in case of public disaster, to render such services as may be in his power.

It is likewise his duty to hold any public office to which he may be elected by popular vote in the state of which he is a national.

Article XXXV. It is the duty of every person to cooperate with the state and the community with respect to social security and welfare, in accordance with his ability and with existing circumstances.

Article XXXVI. It is the duty of every person to pay the taxes established by law for the support of public services.

Article XXXVII. It is the duty of every person to work, as far as his capacity and possibilities permit, in order to obtain the means of livelihood or to benefit his community.

Article XXXVIII. It is the duty of every person to refrain from taking part in political activities that, according to law, are reserved exclusively to the citizens of the state in which he is an alien.

3.2 CONVENTION ON THE PREVENTION AND PUNISHMENT OF THE CRIME OF GENOCIDE. Done at New York, Dec. 9, 1948. Entered into force, Jan. 12, 1951; for the United States, Feb. 23, 1989. ____ U.S.T. ____, T.I.A.S. No. ____, 78 U.N.T.S. 277

Article I. The Contracting Parties confirm that genocide, whether committed in time of peace or in time of war, is a crime under international law which they undertake to prevent and to punish.

Article II. In the present Convention, genocide means any of the following acts committed with intent to destroy, in whole or in part, a national, ethnical, racial or religious group, as such:

(a) Killing members of the group;

(b) Causing serious bodily or mental harm to members of the group;

(c) Deliberately inflicting on the group conditions of life calculated to bring about its physical destruction in whole or in part;

(d) Imposing measures intended to prevent births within the group;

(e) Forcibly transferring children of the group to another group.

Article III. The following acts shall be punishable:

(a) Genocide;

(b) Conspiracy to commit genocide;

(c) Direct and public incitement to commit genocide;

(d) Attempt to commit genocide;

(e) Complicity in genocide.

Article IV. Persons committing genocide or any of the other acts enumerated in Article III shall be punished, whether they are constitutionally responsible rulers, public officials or private individuals.

Article V. The Contracting Parties undertake to enact, in accordance with their respective Constitutions, the necessary legislation to give effect to the provisions of the present Convention and, in particular, to provide effective penalties for persons guilty of genocide or of any of the other acts enumerated in Article III.

Article VI. Persons charged with genocide or any of the other acts enumerated in Article III shall be tried by a competent tribunal of the State in the territory of which the act was committed, or by such international penal tribunal as may have jurisdiction with respect to those Contracting Parties which shall have accepted its jurisdiction.

Article VII. Genocide and the other acts enumerated in Article III shall not be considered as political crimes for the purpose of extradition.

The Contracting Parties pledge themselves in such cases to grant extradition in accordance with their laws and treaties in force.

Article VIII. Any Contracting Party may call upon the competent organs of the United Nations to take such action under the Charter of the United Nations as they consider appropriate for the prevention and suppression of acts of genocide or any of the other acts enumerated in Article III.

Article IX. Disputes between the Contracting Parties relating to the interpretation, application or fulfilment of the present Convention, including those relating to the responsibility of a State for genocide or for any of the other acts enumerated in Article III, shall be submitted to the International Court of Justice at the request of any of the parties to the dispute.

* * *

3.3 UNIVERSAL DECLARATION OF HUMAN RIGHTS. Adopted by the U.N. General Assembly, Dec. 10, 1948. U.N.G.A. Res. 217 A (III), U.N. Doc. A/810, at 71 (1948)

PREAMBLE

Whereas recognition of the inherent dignity and of the equal and inalienable rights of all members of the human family is the foundation of freedom, justice and peace in the world,

Whereas disregard and contempt for human rights have resulted in barbarous acts which have outraged the conscience of mankind, and the advent of a world in which human beings shall enjoy freedom of speech and belief and freedom from fear and want has been proclaimed as the highest aspiration of the common people,

Whereas it is essential, if man is not to be compelled to have recourse, as a last resort, to rebellion against tyranny and oppression, that human rights should be protected by the rule of law,

Whereas it is essential to promote the development of friendly relations between nations,

Whereas the peoples of the United Nations have in the Charter reaffirmed their faith in fundamental human rights, in the dignity and worth of the human person and in the equal rights of men and women and have determined to promote social progress and better standards of life in larger freedom,

Whereas Member States have pledged themselves to achieve, in co-operation with the United Nations, the promotion of universal respect for and observance of human rights and fundamental freedoms,

Whereas a common understanding of these rights and freedoms is of the greatest importance for the full realization of this pledge,

Now, therefore,

The General Assembly

Proclaims this Universal Declaration of Human Rights as a common standard of achievement for all peoples and all nations, to the end that every individual and every organ of society, keeping this Declaration constantly in mind, shall strive by teaching and education to promote respect for these rights and freedoms and by progressive measures, national and international, to secure their universal and effective recognition and observance, both among the peoples of Member States themselves and among the peoples of territories under their jurisdiction.

Article 1. All human beings are born free and equal in dignity and rights. They are endowed with reason and conscience and should act towards one another in a spirit of brotherhood.

Article 2. Everyone is entitled to all the rights and freedoms set forth in this Declaration, without distinction of any kind, such as race, colour, sex, language, religion, political or other opinion, national or social origin, property, birth or other status.

Furthermore, no distinction shall be made on the basis of the political, jurisdictional or international status of the country or territory to which a person belongs, whether it be independent, trust, non-self-governing or under any other limitation of sovereignty.

Article 3. Everyone has the right to life, liberty and the security of person.

Article 4. No one shall be held in slavery or servitude; slavery and the slave trade shall be prohibited in all their forms.

Article 5. No one shall be subjected to torture or to cruel, inhuman or degrading treatment or punishment.

Article 6. Everyone has the right to recognition everywhere as a person before the law.

Article 7. All are equal before the law and are entitled without any discrimination to equal protection of the law. All are entitled to equal protection against any discrimination in violation of this Declaration and against any incitement to such discrimination.

Article 8. Everyone has the right to an effective remedy by the competent national tribunals for acts violating the fundamental rights granted him by the constitution or by law.

Article 9. No one shall be subjected to arbitrary arrest, detention or exile.

Article 10. Everyone is entitled in full equality to a fair and public hearing by an independent and impartial tribunal, in the determination of his rights and obligations and of any criminal charge against him.

Article 11. (1) Everyone charged with a penal offence has the right to be presumed innocent until proved guilty according to law in a public trial at which he has had all the guarantees necessary for his defence.

(2) No one shall be held guilty of any penal offence on account of any act or omission which did not constitute a penal offence, under national or international law, at the time when it was committed. Nor shall a heavier penalty be imposed than the one that was applicable at the time the penal offence was committed.

Article 12. No one shall be subjected to arbitrary interference with his privacy, family, home or correspondence, nor to attacks upon his honour and reputation. Everyone has the right to the protection of the law against such interference or attacks.

Article 13. (1) Everyone has the right to freedom of movement and residence within the borders of each State.

(2) Everyone has the right to leave any country, including his own, and to return to his country.

Article 14. (1) Everyone has the right to seek and to enjoy in other countries asylum from persecution.

(2) This right may not be invoked in the case of prosecutions genuinely arising from nonpolitical crimes or from acts contrary to the purposes and principles of the United Nations.

Article 15. (1) Everyone has the right to a nationality.

(2) No one shall be arbitrarily deprived of his nationality nor denied the right to change his nationality.

Article 16. (1) Men and women of full age, without any limitation due to race, nationality or religion, have the right to marry and to found a family. They are entitled to equal rights as to marriage, during marriage and at its dissolution.

(2) Marriage shall be entered into only with the free and full consent of the intending spouses.

(3) The family is the natural and fundamental group unit of society and is entitled to protection by society and the State.

Article 17. (1) Everyone has the right to own property alone as well as in association with others.

(2) No one shall be arbitrarily deprived of his property.

Article 18. Everyone has the right to freedom of thought, conscience and religion; this right includes freedom to change his religion or belief, and freedom, either alone or in community with others and in public or private, to manifest his religion or belief in teaching, practice, worship and observance.

Article 19. Everyone has the right to freedom of opinion and expression; this right includes freedom to hold opinions without interference and to seek, receive and impart information and ideas through any media and regardless of frontiers.

Article 20. (1) Everyone has the right to freedom of peaceful assembly and association.

(2) No one may be compelled to belong to an association.

Article 21. (1) Everyone has the right to take part in the government of his country, directly or through freely chosen representatives.

(2) Everyone has the right of equal access to public service in his country.

(3) The will of the people shall be the basis of the authority of government; this will shall be expressed in periodic and genuine elections which shall be by universal and equal suffrage and shall be held by secret vote or by equivalent free voting procedures.

Article 22. Everyone, as a member of society, has the right to social security and is entitled to realization, through national effort and international co-operation and in accordance with the organization and resources of each State, of the economic, social and cultural rights indispensable for his dignity and the free development of his personality.

Article 23. (1) Everyone has the right to work, to free choice of employment, to just and favourable conditions of work and to protection against unemployment.

(2) Everyone, without any discrimination, has the right to equal pay for equal work.

(3) Everyone who works has the right to just and favourable remuneration ensuring for himself and his family an existence worthy of human dignity, and supplemented, if necessary, by other means of social protection.

(4) Everyone has the right to form and to join trade unions for the protection of his interests.

Article 24. Everyone has the right to rest and leisure, including reasonable limitation of working hours and periodic holidays with pay.

Article 25. (1) Everyone has the right to a standard of living adequate for the health and well-being of himself and of his family, including food, clothing, housing and medical care and necessary social services, and the right to security in the event of unemployment, sickness, disability, widowhood, old age or other lack of livelihood in circumstances beyond his control.

(2) Motherhood and childhood are entitled to special care and assistance. All children, whether born in or out of wedlock, shall enjoy the same social protection.

Article 26. (1) Everyone has the right to education. Education shall be free, at least in the elementary and fundamental stages. Elementary education shall be compulsory. Technical and professional education shall be made generally available and higher education shall be equally accessible to all on the basis of merit.

(2) Education shall be directed to the full development of the human personality and to the strengthening of respect for human rights and fundamental freedoms. It shall promote understanding, tolerance and friendship among all nations, racial or religious groups, and shall further the activities of the United Nations for the maintenance of peace.

(3) Parents have a prior right to choose the kind of education that shall be given to their children.

Article 27. (1) Everyone has the right freely to participate in the cultural life of the community, to enjoy the arts and to share in scientific advancement and its benefits.

(2) Everyone has the right to the protection of the moral and material interests resulting from any scientific, literary or artistic production of which he is the author.

Article 28. Everyone is entitled to a social and international order in which the rights and freedoms set forth in this Declaration can be fully realized.

Article 29. (1) Everyone has duties to the community in which alone the free and full development of his personality is possible.

(2) In the exercise of his rights and freedoms, everyone shall be subject only to such limitations as are determined by law solely for the purpose of securing due recognition and respect for the rights and freedoms of others and of meeting the just requirements of morality, public order and the general welfare in a democratic society.

(3) These rights and freedoms may in no case be exercised contrary to the purposes and principles of the United Nations.

Article 30. Nothing in this Declaration may be interpreted as implying for any State, group or person any right to engage in any activity or to perform any act aimed at the destruction of any of the rights and freedoms set forth herein.

3.4 EUROPEAN CONVENTION FOR THE PROTECTION OF HUMAN RIGHTS AND FUNDAMENTAL FREEDOMS.[a] Done at Rome, Nov. 4, 1950. Entered into force, Sept. 3, 1953. Euop. T.S. No. 5, 213 U.N.T.S. 221

Article 1. The High Contracting Parties shall secure to everyone within their jurisdiction the rights and freedoms defined in Section I of this Convention.

SECTION I

Article 2. (1) Everyone's right to life shall be protected by law. No one shall be deprived of his life intentionally save in the execution of a sentence of a court following his conviction of a crime for which this penalty is provided by law.

(2) Deprivation of life shall not be regarded as inflicted in contravention of this Article when it results from the use of force which is not more than absolutely necessary:

(a) in defence of any person from unlawful violence;

(b) in order to effect a lawful arrest or to prevent the escape of a person lawfully detained;

(c) in action lawfully taken for the purpose of quelling a riot or insurrection.

Article 3. No one shall be subjected to torture or to inhuman or degrading treatment or punishment.

Article 4. (1) No one shall be held in slavery or servitude.

(2) No one shall be required to perform forced or compulsory labour.

(3) For the purpose of this Article the term "forced or compulsory labour" shall not include:

(a) any work required to be done in the ordinary course of detention imposed according to the provisions of Article 5 of this Convention or during conditional release from such detention;

(b) any service of a military character or, in case of conscientious objectors in countries where they are recognized, service exacted instead of compulsory military service;

(c) any service exacted in case of an emergency or calamity threatening the life or well-being of the community;

(d) any work or service which forms part of normal civic obligations.

Article 5. (1) Everyone has the right to liberty and security of person.

No one shall be deprived of his liberty save in the following cases and in accordance with a procedure prescribed by law;

(a) the lawful detention of a person after conviction by a competent court;

(b) the lawful arrest or detention of a person for non-compliance with the lawful order of a court or in order to secure the fulfilment of any obligation prescribed by law;

(c) the lawful arrest or detention of a person effected for the purpose of bringing him before the competent legal authority on reasonable suspicion of

a. This Convention is supplemented by five protocols. Protocols I and IV are included in this volume as Basic Documents 3.6 and 3.15, *infra*. *See also* Basic Documents 3.13, 3.25, and 3.37, *infra*; and Draft Charter on Human and People's Rights in the Arab World (International Institute of Higher Studies in Criminal Sciences, Siracusa, Italy, 1987).

having committed an offence or when it is reasonably considered necessary to prevent his committing an offence of fleeing after having done so;

(d) the detention of a minor by lawful order for the purpose of educational supervision or his lawful detention for the purpose of bringing him before the competent legal authority;

(e) the lawful detention of persons for the prevention of the spreading of infectious diseases, of persons of unsound mind, alcoholics or drug addicts, or vagrants;

(f) the lawful arrest or detention of a person to prevent his effecting an unauthorized entry into the country or of a person against whom action is being taken with a view to deportation or extradition.

(2) Everyone who is arrested shall be informed promptly, in a language which he understands, of the reasons for his arrest and of any charge against him.

(3) Everyone arrested or detained in accordance with the provisions of paragraph I(c) of this Article shall be brought promptly before a judge or other officer authorized by law to exercise judicial power and shall be entitled to trial within a reasonable time or to release pending trial. Release may be conditioned by guarantees to appear for trial.

(4) Everyone who is deprived of his liberty by arrest or detention shall be entitled to take proceedings by which the lawfulness of his detention shall be decided speedily by a court and his release ordered if the detention is not lawful.

(5) Everyone who has been the victim of arrest or detention in contravention of the provisions of this Article shall have an enforceable right to compensation.

Article 6. (1) In the determination of his civil rights and obligations or of any criminal charge against him, everyone is entitled to a fair and public hearing within a reasonable time by an independent and impartial tribunal established by law. Judgment shall be pronounced publicly but the press and public may be excluded from all or part of the trial in the interest of morals, public order or national security in a democratic society, where the interests of juveniles or the protection of the private life of the parties so require, or to the extent strictly necessary in the opinion of the court in special circumstances where publicity would prejudice the interests of justice.

(2) Everyone charged with a criminal offence shall be presumed innocent until proved guilty according to law.

(3) Everyone charged with a criminal offence has the following minimum rights:

(a) to be informed promptly, in a language which he understands and in detail, of the nature and cause of the accusation against him;

(b) to have adequate time and facilities for the preparation of his defence;

(c) to defend himself in person or through legal assistance of his own choosing or, if he has not sufficient means to pay for legal assistance, to be given it free when the interests of justice so require;

(d) to examine or have examined witnesses against him and to obtain the attendance and examination of witnesses on his behalf under the same conditions as witnesses against him;

(e) to have the free assistance of an interpreter if he cannot understand or speak the language used in court.

Article 7. (1) No one shall be held guilty of any criminal offence on account of any act or omission which did not constitute a criminal offence under national or international law at the time when it was committed. Nor shall a heavier penalty be imposed than the one that was applicable at the time the criminal offence was committed.

(2) This Article shall not prejudice the trial and punishment of any person for any act or omission which, at the time when it was committed, was criminal according to the general principles of law recognized by civilized nations.

Article 8. (1) Everyone has the right to respect for his private and family life, his home and his correspondence.

(2) There shall be no interference by a public authority with the exercise of this right except such as is in accordance with the law and is necessary in a democratic society in the interests of national security, public safety or the economic well-being of the country, for the prevention of disorder or crime, for the protection of health or morals, or for the protection of the rights and freedoms of others.

Article 9. (1) Everyone has the right to freedom of thought, conscience and religion; this right includes freedom to change his religion or belief, and freedom, either alone or in community with others and in public or private, to manifest his religion or belief, in worship, teaching, practice and observance.

(2) Freedom to manifest one's religion or beliefs shall be subject only to such limitations as are prescribed by law and are necessary in a democratic society in the interests of public safety, for the protection of public order, health or morals, or for the protection of the rights and freedoms of others.

Article 10. (1) Everyone has the right to freedom of expression. This right shall include freedom to hold opinions and to receive and impart information and ideas without interference by public authority and regardless of frontiers. This Article shall not prevent States from requiring the licensing of broadcasting, television or cinema enterprises.

(2) The exercise of these freedoms, since it carries with it duties and responsibilities, may be subject to such formalities, conditions, restrictions or penalties as are prescribed by law and are necessary in a democratic society, in the interests of national security, territorial integrity or public safety, for the prevention of disorder or crime, for the protection of health or morals, for the protection of the reputation or rights of others, for preventing the disclosure of information received in confidence, or for maintaining the authority and impartiality of the judiciary.

Article 11. (1) Everyone has the right to freedom of peaceful assembly and to freedom of association with others, including the right to form and to join trade unions for the protection of his interests.

(2) No restrictions shall be placed on the exercise of these rights other than such as are prescribed by law and are necessary in a democratic society in the interests of national security or public safety, for the prevention of disorder or crime, for the protection of health or morals or for the protection of the rights and freedoms of others. This Article shall not prevent the imposition of lawful restrictions on the exercise of these rights by members of the armed forces, of the police or of the administration of the State.

Article 12. Men and women of marriageable age have the right to marry and to found a family, according to the national laws governing the exercise of this right.

Article 13. Everyone whose rights and freedoms as set forth in this Convention are violated shall have an effective remedy before a national authority notwithstanding that the violation has been committed by persons acting in an official capacity.

Article 14. The enjoyment of the rights and freedoms set forth in this Convention shall be secured without discrimination on any ground such as sex, race, colour, language, religion, political or other opinion, national or social origin, association with a national minority, property, birth or other status.

Article 15. (1) In time of war or other public emergency threatening the life of the nation any High Contracting Party may take measures derogating from its obligations under this Convention to the extent strictly required by the exigencies of the situation, provided that such measures are not inconsistent with its other obligations under international law.

(2) No derogation from Article 2, except in respect of deaths resulting from lawful acts of war, or from Articles 3, 4 (paragraph I) and 7 shall be made under this provision.

(3) Any High Contracting Party availing itself of this right of derogation shall keep the Secretary–General of the Council of Europe fully informed of the measures which it has taken and the reasons therefor. It shall also inform the Secretary–General of the Council of Europe when such measures have ceased to operate and the provisions of the Convention are again being fully executed.

Article 16. Nothing in Articles 10, 11, and 14 shall be regarded as preventing the High Contracting Parties from imposing restrictions on the political activity of aliens.

Article 17. Nothing in this Convention may be interpreted as implying for any State, group or person any right to engage in any activity or perform any act aimed at the destruction of any of the rights and freedoms set forth herein or at their limitation to a greater extent than is provided for in the Convention.

Article 18. The restrictions permitted under this Convention to the said rights and freedoms shall not be applied for any purpose other than those for which they have been prescribed.

SECTION II

Article 19. To ensure the observance of the engagements undertaken by the High Contracting Parties in the present Convention, there shall be set up:

(1) A European Commission of Human Rights hereinafter referred to as "the Commission";

(2) A European Court of Human Rights, hereinafter referred to as "the Court".

SECTION III

Article 20. The Commission shall consist of a number of members equal to that of the High Contracting Parties. No two members of the Commission may be nationals of the same State.

Article 21. (1) The members of the Commission shall be elected by the Committee of Ministers by an absolute majority of votes, from a list of names drawn up by the Bureau of the Consultative Assembly; each group of the Representatives of the High Contracting Parties in the Consultative Assembly shall put forward three candidates, of whom two at least shall be its nationals.

(2) As far as applicable, the same procedure shall be followed to complete the Commission in the event of other States subsequently becoming Parties to this Convention, and in filling casual vacancies.

Article 22. (1) The members of the Commission shall be elected for a period of six years. They may be re-elected. However, of the members elected at the first election, the terms of seven members shall expire at the end of three years.

(2) The members whose terms are to expire at the end of the initial period of three years shall be chosen by lot by the Secretary–General of the Council of Europe immediately after the first election has been completed.

(3) A member of the Commission elected to replace a member whose term of office has not expired shall hold office for the remainder of his predecessor's term.

(4) The members of the Commission shall hold office until replaced. After having been replaced, they shall continue to deal with such cases as they already have under consideration.

Article 23. The members of the Commission shall sit on the Commission in their individual capacity.

Article 24. Any High Contracting Party may refer to the Commission through the Secretary–General of the Council of Europe, any alleged breach of the provisions of the Convention by another High Contracting Party.

Article 25. (1) The Commission may receive petitions addressed to the Secretary–General of the Council of Europe from any person, non-governmental organization or group of individuals claiming to be the victim of a violation by one of the High Contracting Parties of the rights set forth in this Convention, provided that the High Contracting Party against which the complaint has been lodged has declared that it recognizes the competence of the Commission to receive such petitions. Those of the High Contracting Parties who have made such a declaration undertake not to hinder in any way the effective exercise of this right.

(2) Such declarations may be made for a specific period.

(3) The declarations shall be deposited with the Secretary–General of the Council of Europe who shall transmit copies thereof to the High Contracting Parties and publish them.

(4) The Commission shall only exercise the powers provided for in this Article when at least six High Contracting Parties are bound by declarations made in accordance with the preceding paragraphs.

Article 26. The Commission may only deal with the matter after all domestic remedies have been exhausted, according to the generally recognized rules of international law, and within a period of six months from the date on which the final decision was taken.

Article 27. (1) The Commission shall not deal with any petition submitted under Article 25 which

(a) is anonymous, or

(b) is substantially the same as a matter which has already been examined by the Commission or has already been submitted to another procedure of international investigation or settlement and if it contains no relevant new information.

(2) The Commission shall consider inadmissible any petition submitted under Article 25 which it considers incompatible with the provisions of the present Convention, manifestly illfounded, or an abuse of the right of petition.

(3) The Commission shall reject any petition referred to it which it considers inadmissible under Article 26.

Article 28. In the event of the Commission accepting a petition referred to it:

(a) it shall, with a view to ascertaining the facts undertake together with the representatives of the parties an examination of the petition and, if need be, an investigation, for the effective conduct of which the States concerned shall furnish all necessary facilities, after an exchange of views with the Commission:

(b) it shall place itself at the disposal of the parties concerned with a view to securing a friendly settlement of the matter on the basis of respect for Human Rights as defined in this Convention.

Article 29. (1) The Commission shall perform the functions set out in Article 28 by means of a Sub–Commission consisting of seven members of the Commission.

(2) Each of the parties concerned may appoint as members of this Sub–Commission a person of its choice.

(3) The remaining members shall be chosen by lot in accordance with arrangements prescribed in the Rules of Procedure of the Commission.

Article 30. If the Sub–Commission succeeds in effecting a friendly settlement in accordance with Article 28, it shall draw up a Report which shall be sent to the States concerned, to the Committee of Ministers and to the Secretary–General of the Council of Europe for publication. This Report shall be confined to a brief statement of the facts and of the solution reached.

Article 31. (1) If a solution is not reached, the Commission shall draw up a Report on the facts and state its opinion as to whether the facts found disclose a breach by the State concerned of its obligations under the Convention. The opinions of all the members of the Commission on this point may be stated in the Report.

(2) The Report shall be transmitted to the Committee of Ministers. It shall also be transmitted to the States concerned, who shall not be at liberty to publish it.

(3) In transmitting the Report to the Committee of Ministers the Commission may make such proposals as it thinks fit.

Article 32. (1) If the question is not referred to the Court in accordance with Article 48 of this Convention within a period of three months from the date of the transmission of the Report to the Committee of Ministers, the Committee of Ministers shall decide by a majority of two-thirds of the members entitled to sit on the Committee whether there has been a violation of the Convention.

(2) In the affirmative case the Committee of Ministers shall prescribe a period during which the Contracting Party concerned must take the measures required by the decision of the Committee of Ministers.

(3) If the High Contracting Party concerned has not taken satisfactory measures within the prescribed period, the Committee of Ministers shall decide by the majority provided for in paragraph I above what effect shall be given to its original decision and shall publish the Report.

(4) The High Contracting Parties undertake to regard as binding on them any decision which the Committee of Ministers may take in application of the preceding paragraphs.

Article 33. The Commission shall meet *in camera.*

Article 34. The Commission shall take its decisions by a majority of the Members present and voting; the Sub–Commission shall take its decisions by a majority of its members.

Article 35. The Commission shall meet as the circumstances require. The meetings shall be convened by the Secretary–General of the Council of Europe.

Article 36. The Commission shall draw up its own rules of procedure.

Article 37. The secretariat of the Commission shall be provided by the Secretary–General of the Council of Europe.

SECTION IV

Article 38. The European Court of Human Rights shall consist of a number of judges equal to that of the Members of the Council of Europe. No two judges may be nationals of the same State.

Article 39. (1) The members of the Court shall be elected by the Consultative Assembly by a majority of the votes cast from a list of persons nominated by the Members of the Council of Europe; each Member shall nominate three candidates, of whom two at least shall be its nationals.

(2) As far as applicable, the same procedure shall be followed to complete the Court in the event of the admission of new members of the Council of Europe, and in filling casual vacancies.

(3) The candidates shall be of high moral character and must either possess the qualifications required for appointment to high judicial office or be jurisconsults of recognized competence.

Article 40. (1) The members of the Court shall be elected for a period of nine years. They may be re-elected. However, of the members elected at the first election the terms of four members shall expire at the end of three years, and the terms of four more members shall expire at the end of six years.

(2) The members whose terms are to expire at the end of the initial periods of three and six years shall be chosen by lot by the Secretary–General immediately after the first election has been completed.

(3) A member of the Court elected to replace a member whose term of office has not expired shall hold office for the remainder of his predecessor's term.

(4) The members of the Court shall hold office until replaced. After having been replaced, they shall continue to deal with such cases as they already have under consideration.

Article 41. The Court shall elect its President and Vice–President for a period of three years. They may be re-elected.

Article 42. The members of the Court shall receive for each day of duty a compensation to be determined by the Committee of Ministers.

Article 43. For the consideration of each case brought before it the Court shall consist of a Chamber composed of seven judges. There shall sit as an *ex officio* member of the Chamber the judge who is a national of any State party concerned, or, if there is none, a person of its choice who shall sit in the capacity of judge; the names of the other judges shall be chosen by lot by the President before the opening of the case.

Article 44. Only the High Contracting Parties and the Commission shall have the right to bring a case before the Court.

Article 45. The jurisdiction of the Court shall extend to all cases concerning the interpretation and application of the present Convention which the High Contracting Parties or the Commission shall refer to it in accordance with Article 48.

Article 46. (1) Any of the High Contracting Parties may at any time declare that it recognizes as compulsory *ipso facto* and without special agreement the jurisdiction of the Court in all matters concerning the interpretation and application of the present Convention.

(2) The declarations referred to above may be made unconditionally or on condition of reciprocity on the part of several or certain other High Contracting Parties or for a specified period.

(3) These declarations shall be deposited with the Secretary–General of the Council of Europe who shall transmit copies thereof to the High Contracting Parties.

Article 47. The Court may deal with a case after the Commission has acknowledged the failure of efforts for a friendly settlement and within the period of three months provided for in Article 32.

Article 48. The following may bring a case before the Court, provided that the High Contracting Party concerned, if there is only one, or the High Contracting Parties concerned, if there is more than one, are subject to the compulsory jurisdiction of the Court or, failing that, with the consent of the High Contracting Party concerned, if there is only one, or of the High Contracting Parties concerned if there is more than one:

(a) the Commission;

(b) a High Contracting Party whose national is alleged to be a victim;

(c) a High Contracting Party which referred the case to the Commission;

(d) a High Contracting Party against which the complaint has been lodged.

Article 49. In the event of dispute as to whether the Court has jurisdiction, the matter shall be settled by the decision of the Court.

Article 50. If the Court finds that a decision or a measure taken by a legal authority or any other authority of a High Contracting Party, is completely or partially in conflict with the obligations arising from the present Convention, and if the internal law of the said Party allows only partial reparation to be made for the consequences of this decision or measure, the decision of the Court shall, if necessary, afford just satisfaction to the injured party.

Article 51. (1) Reasons shall be given for the judgment of the Court.

(2) If the judgment does not represent in whole or in part the unanimous opinion of the judges, any judge shall be entitled to deliver a separate opinion.

Article 52. The judgment of the Court shall be final.

Article 53. The High Contracting Parties undertake to abide by the decision of the Court in any case to which they are parties.

Article 54. The judgment of the Court shall be transmitted to the Committee of Ministers which shall supervise its execution.

Article 55. The Court shall draw up its own rules and shall determine its own procedure.

* * *

SECTION V

Article 57. On receipt of a request from the Secretary–General of the Council of Europe any High Contracting Party shall furnish an explanation of the manner in which its internal law ensures the effective implementation of any of the provisions of this Convention.

* * *

Article 60. Nothing in this Convention shall be construed as limiting or derogating from any of the human rights and fundamental freedoms which may be ensured under the laws of any High Contracting Party or under any other agreement to which it is a Party.

* * *

Article 64. (1) Any State may, when signing this Convention or when depositing its instrument of ratification, make a reservation in respect of any particular provision of the Convention to the extent that any law then in force in its territory is not in conformity with the provision. Reservations of a general character shall not be permitted under this Article.

(2) Any reservation made under this Article shall contain a brief statement of the law concerned.

* * *

3.5 CONVENTION RELATING TO THE STATUS OF REFUGEES.[a] Done at Geneva, July 28, 1951. Entered into force, Apr. 22, 1954. 189 U.N.T.S. 137

CHAPTER I. GENERAL PROVISIONS

Article 1. Definition of the Term "Refugee"

A. For the purposes of the present Convention, the term "refugee" shall apply to any person who:

(1) Has been considered a refugee under the Arrangements of 12 May 1926 and 30 June 1928 or under the Conventions of 28 October 1933 and 10 February 1938, the Protocol of 14 September 1939 or the Constitution of the International Refugee Organization;

Decisions of non-eligibility taken by the International Refugee Organization during the period of its activities shall not prevent the status of refugee being accorded to persons who fulfil the conditions of paragraph 2 of this section;

(2) As a result of events occurring before 1 January 1951 and owing to well-founded fear of being persecuted for reasons of race, religion, nationality, membership of a particular social group or political opinion, is outside the country of his nationality and is unable or, owing to such fear, is unwilling to avail himself of the protection of that country; or who, not having a nationality and being outside the country of his former habitual residence as a result of such events, is unable or, owing to such fear, is unwilling to return to it.

In the case of a person who has more than one nationality, the term "the country of his nationality" shall mean each of the countries of which he is a national and a person shall not be deemed to be lacking the protection of the country of his nationality if, without any valid reason based on wellfounded fear, he has not availed himself of the protection of one of the countries of which he is a national.

B. (1) For the purposes of this Convention, the words "events occurring before 1 January 1951" in article 1, section A, shall be understood to mean either

(a) "events occurring in Europe before 1 January 1951"; or

(b) "events occurring in Europe or elsewhere before 1 January 1951" and each Contracting State shall make a declaration at the time of signature ratification or accession, specifying which of these meanings it applies for the purpose of its obligations under this Convention.

(2) Any Contracting State which has adopted alternative (*a*) may at any time extend its obligations by adopting alternative (*b*) by means of a notification addressed to the Secretary–General of the United Nations.

C. This Convention shall cease to apply to any person falling under the term of section A if:

(1) He has voluntarily re-availed himself of the protection of the country of his nationality; or

(2) Having lost his nationality, he has voluntarily reacquired it; or

(3) He has acquired a new nationality, and enjoys the protection of the country of his new nationality; or

(4) He has voluntarily re-established himself in the country which he left or outside which he remained owing to fear of persecution; or

a. *See also* Basic Documents 3.8 and 3.21, *infra.*

(5) He can no longer, because the circumstances in connexion with which he has been recognized as a refugee have ceased to exist, continue to refuse to avail himself of the protection of the country of his nationality;

Provided that this paragraph shall not apply to a refugee falling under section A (1) of this article who is able to invoke compelling reasons arising out of previous persecution for refusing to avail himself of the protection of the country of nationality;

(6) Being a person who has no nationality he is, because the circumstances in connexion with which he has been recognized as a refugee have ceased to exist, able to return to the country of his former habitual residence;

Provided that this paragraph shall not apply to a refugee falling under section A (1) of this article who is able to invoke compelling reasons arising out of previous persecution for refusing to return to the country of his former habitual residence.

D. This Convention shall not apply to persons who are at present receiving from organs or agencies of the United Nations other than the United Nations High Commissioner for Refugees protection or assistance.

When such protection or assistance has ceased for any reason, without the position of such persons being definitively settled in accordance with the relevant resolutions adopted by the General Assembly of the United Nations, these persons shall *ipso facto* be entitled to the benefits of this Convention.

E. This Convention shall not apply to a person who is recognized by the competent authorities of the country in which he has taken residence as having the rights and obligations which are attached to the possession of the nationality of that country.

F. The provisions of this Convention shall not apply to any person with respect to whom there are serious reasons for considering that:

(a) he has committed a crime against peace, a war crime, or a crime against humanity, as defined in the international instruments drawn up to make provision in respect of such crimes;

(b) he has committed a serious non-political crime outside the country of refuge prior to his admission to that country as a refugee;

(c) he has been guilty of acts contrary to the purposes and principles of the United Nations.

Article 2. General Obligations

Every refugee has duties to the country in which he finds himself, which require in particular that he conform to its laws and regulations as well as to measures taken for the maintenance of public order.

Article 3. Non–discrimination

The Contracting States shall apply the provisions of this Convention to refugees without discrimination as to race, religion or country of origin.

Article 4. Religion

The Contracting States shall accord to refugees within their territories treatment at least as favorable as that accorded to their nationals with respect to freedom to practice their religion and freedom as regards the religious education of their children.

Article 5. Rights Granted Apart From this Convention

Nothing in this Convention shall be deemed to impair any rights and benefits granted by a Contracting State to refugees apart from this Convention.

* * *

Article 7. Exemption From Reciprocity

1. Except where this Convention contains more favourable provisions, a Contracting State shall accord to refugees the same treatment as is accorded to aliens generally.

2. After a period of three years' residence, all refugees shall enjoy exemption from legislative reciprocity in the territory of the Contracting States.

3. Each Contracting State shall continue to accord to refugees the rights and benefits to which they were already entitled, in the absence of reciprocity, at the date of entry into force of this Convention for that State.

4. The Contracting States shall consider favourably the possibility of according to refugees, in the absence of reciprocity, rights and benefits beyond those to which they are entitled according to paragraphs 2 and 3, and to extending exemption from reciprocity to refugees who do not fulfil the conditions provided for in paragraphs 2 and 3.

5. The provisions of paragraphs 2 and 3 apply both to the rights and benefits referred to in articles 13, 18, 19, 21 and 22 [b] of this Convention and to rights and benefits for which this Convention does not provide.

Article 8. Exemption From Exceptional Measures

With regard to exceptional measures which may be taken against the person, property or interests of nationals of a foreign State, the Contracting States shall not apply such measures to a refugee who is formally a national of the said State solely on account of such nationality. Contracting States which, under their legislation, are prevented from applying the general principle expressed in this article, shall, in appropriate cases, grant exemptions in favour of such refugees.

Article 9. Provisional Measures

Nothing in this Convention shall prevent a Contracting State, in time of war or other grave and exceptional circumstances, from taking provisionally measures which it considers to be essential to the national security in the case of a particular person, pending a determination by the Contracting State that that person is in fact a refugee and that the continuance of such measures is necessary in his case in the interests of national security.

Article 10. Continuity of Residence

1. Where a refugee has been forcibly displaced during the Second World War and removed to the territory of a Contracting State, and is resident there, the period of such enforced sojourn shall be considered to have been lawful residence within that territory.

2. Where a refugee has been forcibly displaced during the Second World War from the territory of a Contracting State and has, prior to the date of entry into force of this Convention, returned there for the purpose of taking up residence, the period of residence before and after such enforced displacement shall be regarded as one uninterrupted period for any purposes for which uninterrupted residence is required.

b. These articles are omitted here. *But see* page 313, *infra*.

Article 11. Refugee Seamen

In the case of refugees regularly serving as crew members on board a ship flying the flag of a Contracting State, that State shall give sympathetic consideration to their establishment on its territory and the issue of travel documents to them or their temporary admission to its territory particularly with a view to facilitating their establishment in another country.

[*Chapters II, III, IV, and V of this Convention, embracing Articles 12–34, detail the rights and duties of both refugees and the Contracting States under the following headings:*

CHAPTER II. JURIDICAL STATUS
- Article 12. Personal
- Article 13. Movable and Immovable Property
- Article 14. Artistic Rights and Industrial Property
- Article 15. Right of Association
- Article 16. Access to Courts

CHAPTER III. GAINFUL EMPLOYMENT
- Article 17. Wage–Earning Employment
- Article 18. Self–Employment
- Article 19. Liberal Professions

CHAPTER IV. WELFARE
- Article 20. Rationing
- Article 21. Housing
- Article 22. Public Education
- Article 23. Public Relief
- Article 24. Labour Legislation and Social Security

CHAPTER V. ADMINISTRATIVE MEASURES
- Article 25. Administrative Assistance
- Article 26. Freedom of Movement
- Article 27. Identity Papers
- Article 28. Travel Documents
- Article 29. Fiscal Charges
- Article 30. Transfer of Assets
- Article 31. Refugees Unlawfully in the Country of Refuge
- Article 32. Expulsion
- Article 33. Prohibition of Expulsion or Return ("Refoulement")
- Article 34. Naturalization

Chapters VI and VII of this Convention, embracing concluding Articles 35–46, pertain mainly to the Convention's execution, ratification, and entry into force.]

3.6 PROTOCOL (NO. 1) TO THE EUROPEAN CONVENTION FOR THE PROTECTION OF HUMAN RIGHTS AND FUNDAMENTAL FREEDOMS.[a] Done at Paris, Mar. 20, 1952. Entered into force, May 18, 1954. Europ.T.S. No. 9, 213 U.N.T.S. 262

Article 1. Every natural or legal person is entitled to the peaceful enjoyment of his possessions. No one shall be deprived of his possessions except in the public interest and subject to the conditions provided for by law and by the general principles of international law.

The preceding provisions shall not, however, in any way impair the right of a State to enforce such laws as it deems necessary to control the use of property in accordance with the general interest or to secure the payment of taxes or other contributions or penalties.

Article 2. No person shall be denied the right to education. In the exercise of any functions which it assumes in relation to education and to teaching, the State shall respect the right of parents to ensure such education and teaching in conformity with their own religious and philosophical convictions.

Article 3. The High Contracting Parties undertake to hold free elections at reasonable intervals by secret ballot, under conditions which will ensure the free expression of the opinion of the people in the choice of the legislature.

* * *

a. This Protocol is one of five protocols supplementing the European Convention for the Protection of Human Rights and Fundamental Freedoms (Basic Document 3.4). *See also* Basic Document 3.15, *infra*.

3.7 CONVENTION ON THE POLITICAL RIGHTS OF WOMEN.[a] Entered into force, July 7, 1954; for the United States, Apr. 8, 1976. 27 U.S.T. 1909, T.I.A.S. No. 8289, 193 U.N.T.S. 135

The Contracting Parties,

Desiring to implement the principle of equality of rights for men and women contained in the Charter of the United Nations,

Recognizing that everyone has the right to take part in the government of his country, directly or indirectly through freely chosen representatives, and has the right to equal access to public service in his country, and desiring to equalize the status of men and women in the enjoyment and exercise of political rights, in accordance with the provisions of the Charter of the United Nations and of the Universal Declaration of Human Rights,

Having resolved to conclude a Convention for this purpose,

Hereby agree as hereinafter provided:

ARTICLE I

Women shall be entitled to vote in all elections on equal terms with men, without any discrimination.

ARTICLE II

Women shall be eligible for election to all publicly elected bodies, established by national law, on equal terms with men, without any discrimination.

ARTICLE III

Women shall be entitled to hold public office and to exercise all public functions, established by national law, on equal terms with men, without any discrimination.

* * *

a. *See also* Basic Document 3.36, *infra.*

3.8 CONVENTION RELATING TO THE STATUS OF STATELESS PERSONS.[a] Done at New York, Sept. 28, 1954. Entered into force, June 6, 1960. 360 U.N. T.S. 117

The High Contracting Parties,

Considering that the Charter of the United Nations and the Universal Declaration of Human Rights approved on 10 December 1948 by the General Assembly of the United Nations have affirmed the principle that human beings shall enjoy fundamental rights and freedoms without discrimination,

Considering that the United Nations has, on various occasions, manifested its profound concern for stateless persons and endeavoured to assure stateless persons the widest possible exercise of these fundamental rights and freedoms,

Considering that only those stateless persons who are also refugees are covered by the Convention relating to the Status of Refugees of 28 July 1951, and that there are many stateless persons who are not covered by that Convention,

Considering that it is desirable to regulate and improve the status of stateless persons by an international agreement,

Have agreed as follows:

CHAPTER I

GENERAL PROVISIONS

Article 1

DEFINITION OF THE TERM "STATELESS PERSON"

1. For the purpose of this Convention, the term "stateless person" means a person who is not considered as a national by any State under the operation of its law.

2. This Convention shall not apply:

(i) To persons who are at present receiving from organs or agencies of the United Nations other than the United Nations High Commissioner for Refugees protection or assistance so long as they are receiving such protection or assistance;

(ii) To persons who are recognized by the competent authorities of the country in which they have taken residence as having the rights and obligations which are attached to the possession of the nationality of that country;

(iii) To persons with respect to whom there are serious reasons for considering that:

(*a*) They have committed a crime against peace, a war crime, or a crime against humanity, as defined in the international instruments drawn up to make provisions in respect of such crimes;

(*b*) They have committed a serious non-political crime outside the country of their residence prior to their admission to that country;

(*c*) They have been guilty of acts contrary to the purposes and principles of the United Nations.

a. *See also* Basic Document 3.5, *supra*, and Basic Document 3.21, *infra*.

Article 2

GENERAL OBLIGATIONS

Every stateless person has duties to the country in which he finds himself, which require in particular that he conform to its laws and regulations as well as to measures taken for the maintenance of public order.

Article 3

NON-DISCRIMINATION

The Contracting States shall apply the provisions of this Convention to stateless persons without discrimination as to race, religion or country of origin.

Article 4

RELIGION

The Contracting States shall accord to stateless persons within their territories treatment at least as favourable as that accorded to their nationals with respect to freedom to practise their religion and freedom as regards the religious education of their children.

Article 5

RIGHTS GRANTED APART FROM THIS CONVENTION

Nothing in this Convention shall be deemed to impair any rights and benefits granted by a Contracting State to stateless persons apart from this Convention.

Article 6

THE TERM "IN THE SAME CIRCUMSTANCES"

For the purpose of this Convention, the term "in the same circumstances" implies that any requirements (including requirements as to length and conditions of sojourn or residence) which the particular individual would have to fulfill for the enjoyment of the right in question, if he were not a stateless person, must be fulfilled by him, with the exception of requirements which by their nature a stateless person is incapable of fulfilling.

Article 7

EXEMPTION FROM RECIPROCITY

1. Except where this Convention contains more favourable provisions, a Contracting State shall accord to stateless persons the same treatment as is accorded to aliens generally.

2. After a period of three years' residence, all stateless persons shall enjoy exemption from legislative reciprocity in the territory of the Contracting States.

3. Each Contracting State shall continue to accord to stateless persons the rights and benefits to which they were already entitled, in the absence of reciprocity, at the date of entry into force of this Convention for that State.

4. The Contracting States shall consider favourably the possibility of according to stateless persons, in the absence of reciprocity, rights and benefits beyond those to which they are entitled according to paragraphs 2 and 3, and to extending exemption from reciprocity to stateless persons who do not fulfill the conditions provided for in paragraphs 2 and 3.

5. The provisions of paragraphs 2 and 3 apply both to the rights and benefits referred to in articles 13, 18, 19, 21 and 22 of this Convention and to rights and benefits for which this Convention does not provide.

Article 8

Exemption from exceptional measures

With regard to exceptional measures which may be taken against the person, property or interests of nationals or former nationals of a foreign State, the Contracting States shall not apply such measures to a stateless person solely on account of his having previously possessed the nationality of the foreign State in question. Contracting States which, under their legislation, are prevented from applying the general principle expressed in this article shall, in appropriate cases, grant exemptions in favour of such stateless persons.

Article 9

Provisional measures

Nothing in this Convention shall prevent a Contracting State, in time of war or other grave and exceptional circumstances, from taking provisionally measures which it considers to be essential to the national security in the case of a particular person, pending a determination by the Contracting State that that person is in fact a stateless person and that the continuance of such measures is necessary in his case in the interests of national security.

* * *

Article 11

Stateless seamen

In the case of stateless persons regularly serving as crew members on board a ship flying the flag of a Contracting State, that State shall give sympathetic consideration to their establishment on its territory and the issue of travel documents to them or their temporary admission to its territory particularly with a view to facilitating their establishment in another country.

CHAPTER II

JURIDICAL STATUS

Article 12

Personal status

1. The personal status of a stateless person shall be governed by the law of the country of his domicile or, if he has no domicile, by the law of the country of his residence.

2. Rights previously acquired by a stateless person and dependent on personal status, more particularly rights attaching to marriage, shall be respected by a Contracting State, subject to compliance, if this be necessary, with the formalities required by the law of that State, provided that the right in question is one which would have been recognized by the law of that State had he not become stateless.

Article 13

Movable and immovable property

The Contracting States shall accord to a stateless person treatment as favourable as possible and, in any event, not less favourable than that accorded to aliens generally in the same circumstances, as regards the acquisition of movable and immovable property and other rights pertaining thereto, and to leases and other contracts relating to movable and immovable property.

Article 14

ARTISTIC RIGHTS AND INDUSTRIAL PROPERTY

In respect of the protection of industrial property, such as inventions, designs or models, trade marks, trade names, and of rights in literary, artistic and scientific works, a stateless person shall be accorded in the country in which he has his habitual residence the same protection as is accorded to nationals of that country. In the territory of any other Contracting State, he shall be accorded the same protection as is accorded in that territory to nationals of the country in which he has his habitual residence.

Article 15

RIGHT OF ASSOCIATION

As regards non-political and non-profit-making associations and trade unions the Contracting States shall accord to stateless persons lawfully staying in their territory treatment as favourable as possible, and in any event, not less favourable than that accorded to aliens generally in the same circumstances.

Article 16

ACCESS TO COURTS

1. A stateless person shall have free access to the Courts of Law on the territory of all Contracting States.

2. A stateless person shall enjoy in the Contracting State in which he has his habitual residence the same treatment as a national in matters pertaining to access to the Courts, including legal assistance and exemption from *cautio judicatum solvi.*

3. A stateless person shall be accorded in the matters referred to in paragraph 2 in countries other than that in which he has his habitual residence the treatment granted to a national of the country of his habitual residence.

CHAPTER III

GAINFUL EMPLOYMENT

[This chapter guarantees to stateless persons the same treatment as "aliens generally in the same circumstances" relative to wage-earning employment (Art. 17), self-employment (Art. 18), and the liberal professions (Art. 19).]

CHAPTER IV

WELFARE

[This chapter guarantees stateless persons "the same treatment as nationals" relative to rationing (Art. 20), as "aliens generally in the same circumstances" relative to housing (Art. 21), and again as nationals relative to public education (Art. 22), relief (Art. 23), and, with some qualifications, labor legislation and social security (Art. 24).]

CHAPTER V

ADMINISTRATIVE MEASURES

Article 25

ADMINISTRATIVE ASSISTANCE

1. When the exercise of a right by a stateless person would normally require the assistance of authorities of a foreign country to whom he cannot have recourse, the Contracting State in whose territory he is residing shall arrange that such assistance be afforded to him by their own authorities.

2. The authority or authorities mentioned in paragraph 1 shall deliver or cause to be delivered under their supervision to stateless persons such documents or certifications as would normally be delivered to aliens by or through their national authorities.

3. Documents or certifications so delivered shall stand in the stead of the official instruments delivered to aliens by or through their national authorities, and shall be given credence in the absence of proof to the contrary.

4. Subject to such exceptional treatment as may be granted to indigent persons, fees may be charged for the services mentioned herein, but such fees shall be moderate and commensurate with those charged to nationals for similar services.

5. The provisions of this article shall be without prejudice to articles 27 and 28.

Article 26

FREEDOM OF MOVEMENT

Each Contracting State shall accord to stateless persons lawfully in its territory the right to choose their place of residence and to move freely within its territory, subject to any regulations applicable to aliens generally in the same circumstances.

Article 27

IDENTITY PAPERS

The Contracting States shall issue identity papers to any stateless person in their territory who does not possess a valid travel document.

Article 28

TRAVEL DOCUMENTS

The Contracting States shall issue to stateless persons lawfully staying in their territory travel documents for the purpose of travel outside their territory, unless compelling reasons of national security or public order otherwise require, and the provisions of the Schedule [b] to this Convention shall apply with respect to such documents. The Contracting States may issue such a travel document to any other stateless person in their territory; they shall in particular give sympathetic consideration to the issue of such a travel document to stateless persons in their territory who are unable to obtain a travel document from the country of their lawful residence.

Article 29

FISCAL CHARGES

1. The Contracting States shall not impose upon stateless persons duties, charges or taxes, of any description whatsoever, other or higher than those which are or may be levied on their nationals in similar situations.

2. Nothing in the above paragraph shall prevent the application to stateless persons of the laws and regulations concerning charges in respect of the issue to aliens of administrative documents including identity papers.

Article 30

TRANSFER OF ASSETS

1. A Contracting State shall, in conformity with its laws and regulations, permit stateless persons to transfer assets which they have brought into its territory, to another country where they have been admitted for the purposes of resettlement.

2. A Contracting State shall give sympathetic consideration to the application of stateless persons for permission to transfer assets wherever they may be and which

b. Omitted here.

are necessary for their resettlement in another country to which they have been admitted.

Article 31

EXPULSION

1. The Contracting States shall not expel a stateless person lawfully in their territory save on grounds of national security or public order.

2. The expulsion of such a stateless person shall be only in pursuance of a decision reached in accordance with due process of law. Except where compelling reasons of national security otherwise require, the stateless person shall be allowed to submit evidence to clear himself, and to appeal to and be represented for the purpose before competent authority or a person or persons specially designated by the competent authority.

3. The Contracting States shall allow such a stateless person a reasonable period within which to seek legal admission into another country. The Contracting States reserve the right to apply during that period such internal measures as they may deem necessary.

Article 32

NATURALIZATION

The Contracting States shall as far as possible facilitate the assimilation and naturalization of stateless persons. They shall in particular make every effort to expedite naturalization proceedings and to reduce as far as possible the charges and costs of such proceedings.

* * *

Article 37

FEDERAL CLAUSE

In the case of a Federal or non-unitary State, the following provisions shall apply:

(*a*) With respect to those articles of this Convention that come within the legislative jurisdiction of the federal legislative authority, the obligations of the Federal Government shall to this extent be the same as those of Parties which are not Federal States;

(*b*) With respect to those articles of this Convention that come within the legislative jurisdiction of constituent States, provinces or cantons which are not, under the constitutional system of the Federation, bound to take legislative action, the Federal Government shall bring such articles with a favourable recommendation to the notice of the appropriate authorities of states, provinces or cantons at the earliest possible moment.

(*c*) A Federal State Party to this Convention shall, at the request of any other Contracting State transmitted through the Secretary–General of the United Nations, supply a statement of the law and practice of the Federation and its constituent units in regard to any particular provision of the Convention showing the extent to which effect has been given to that provision by legislative or other action.

* * *

3.9 STANDARD MINIMUM RULES FOR THE TREATMENT OF PRISONERS. Adopted by the First United Nations Congress on the Prevention of Crime and the Treatment of Offenders, Aug. 30, 1955, U.N.Doc. A/CONF/6/1, Annex I, A (1956); adopted by the U.N. Economic and Social Council, July 1, 1957, E.S.C. Res. 663 (XXIV) C, 24 U.N. ESCOR, Supp. (No. 1) 11, U.N.Doc. E/3048 (1957)

PRELIMINARY OBSERVATIONS

1. The following rules are not intended to describe in detail a model system of penal institutions. They seek only, on the basis of the general consensus of contemporary thought and the essential elements of the most adequate systems of today, to set out what is generally accepted as being good principle and practice in the treatment of prisoners and the management of institutions.

2. In view of the great variety of legal, social, economic and geographical conditions of the world, it is evident that not all of the rules are capable of application in all places and at all times. They should, however, serve to stimulate a constant endeavour to overcome practical difficulties in the way of their application, in the knowledge that they represent, as a whole, the minimum conditions which are accepted as suitable by the United Nations.

3. On the other hand, the rules cover a field in which thought is constantly developing. They are not intended to preclude experiment and practices, provided these are in harmony with the principles and seek to further the purposes which derive from the text of the rules as a whole. It will always be justifiable for the central prison administration to authorize departures from the rules in this spirit.

4. (1) Part I of the rules covers the general management of institutions, and is applicable to all categories of prisoners, criminal or civil, untried or convicted, including prisoners subject to "security measures" or corrective measures ordered by the judge.

(2) Part II contains rules applicable only to the special categories dealt with in each section. Nevertheless, the rules under section A, applicable to prisoners under sentence, shall be equally applicable to categories of prisoners dealt with in sections B, C and D, provided they do not conflict with the rules governing those categories and are for their benefit.

5. (1) The rules do not seek to regulate the management of institutions set aside for young persons such as Borstal institutions or correctional schools, but in general part I would be equally applicable in such institutions.

(2) The category of young prisoners should include at least all young persons who come within the jurisdiction of juvenile courts. As a rule, such young persons should not be sentenced to imprisonment.

PART I. RULES OF GENERAL APPLICATION

Basic Principle

6. (1) The following rules shall be applied impartially. There shall be no discrimination on grounds of race, colour, sex, language, religion, political or other opinion, national or social origin, property, birth or other status.

(2) On the other hand, it is necessary to respect the religious beliefs and moral precepts of the group to which a prisoner belongs.

Register

7. (1) In every place where persons are imprisoned there shall be kept a bound registration book with numbered pages in which shall be entered in respect of each prisoner received:

(*a*) Information concerning his identity;

(*b*) The reasons for his commitment and the authority therefor;

(*c*) The day and hour of his admission and release.

(2) No person shall be received in an institution without a valid commitment order of which the details shall have been previously entered in the register.

Separation of Categories

8. The different categories of prisoners shall be kept in separate institutions or parts of institutions taking account of their sex, age, criminal record, the legal reason for their detention and the necessities of their treatment. Thus,

(*a*) Men and women shall so far as possible be detained in separate institutions; in an institution which receives both men and women the whole of the premises allocated to women shall be entirely separate;

(*b*) Untried prisoners shall be kept separate from convicted prisoners;

(*c*) Persons imprisoned for debt and other civil prisoners shall be kept separate from persons imprisoned by reason of a criminal offence;

(*d*) Young prisoners shall be kept separate from adults.

Accommodation

9. (1) Where sleeping accommodation is in individual cells or rooms, each prisoner shall occupy by night a cell or room by himself. If for special reasons, such as temporary overcrowding, it becomes necessary for the central prison administration to make an exception to this rule, it is not desirable to have two prisoners in a cell or room.

(2) Where dormitories are used, they shall be occupied by prisoners carefully selected as being suitable to associate with one another in those conditions. There shall be regular supervision by night, in keeping with the nature of the institution.

10. All accommodation provided for the use of prisoners and in particular all sleeping accommodation shall meet all requirements of health, due regard being paid to climatic conditions and particularly to cubic content of air, minimum floor space, lighting, heating and ventilation.

11. In all places where prisoners are required to live or work,

(*a*) The windows shall be large enough to enable the prisoners to read or work by natural light, and shall be so constructed that they can allow the entrance of fresh air whether or not there is artificial ventilation;

(*b*) Artificial light shall be provided sufficient for the prisoners to read or work without injury to eyesight.

12. The sanitary installations shall be adequate to enable every prisoner to comply with the needs of nature when necessary and in a clean and decent manner.

13. Adequate bathing and shower installations shall be provided so that every prisoner may be enabled and required to have a bath or shower, at a temperature suitable to the climate, as frequently as necessary for general hygiene according to season and geographical region, but at least once a week in a temperate climate.

14. All parts of an institution regularly used by prisoners shall be properly maintained and kept scrupulously clean at all times.

Personal Hygiene

15. Prisoners shall be required to keep their persons clean, and to this end they shall be provided with water and with such toilet articles as are necessary for health and cleanliness.

16. In order that prisoners may maintain a good appearance compatible with their self-respect, facilities shall be provided for the proper care of the hair and beard, and men shall be enabled to shave regularly.

Clothing and Bedding

17. (1) Every prisoner who is not allowed to wear his own clothing shall be provided with an outfit of clothing suitable for the climate and adequate to keep him in good health. Such clothing shall in no manner be degrading or humiliating.

(2) All clothing shall be clean and kept in proper condition. Underclothing shall be changed and washed as often as necessary for the maintenance of hygiene.

(3) In exceptional circumstances, whenever a prisoner is removed outside the institution for an authorized purpose, he shall be allowed to wear his own clothing or other inconspicuous clothing.

18. If prisoners are allowed to wear their own clothing, arrangements shall be made on their admission to the institution to ensure that it shall be clean and fit for use.

19. Every prisoner shall, in accordance with local or national standards, be provided with a separate bed, and with separate and sufficient bedding which shall be clean when issued, kept in good order and changed often enough to ensure its cleanliness.

Food

20. (1) Every prisoner shall be provided by the administration at the usual hours with food of nutritional value adequate for health and strength, of wholesome quality and well prepared and served.

(2) Drinking water shall be available to every prisoner whenever he needs it.

Exercise and Sport

21. (1) Every prisoner who is not employed in outdoor work shall have at least one hour of suitable exercise in the open air daily if the weather permits.

(2) Young prisoners, and others of suitable age and physique, shall receive physical and recreational training during the period of exercise. To this end space, installations and equipment should be provided.

Medical Services

22. (1) At every institution there shall be available the services of at least one qualified medical officer who should have some knowledge of psychiatry. The medical services should be organized in close relationship to the general health administration of the community or nation. They shall include a psychiatric service for the diagnosis and, in proper cases, the treatment of states of mental abnormality.

(2) Sick prisoners who require specialist treatment shall be transferred to specialized institutions or to civil hospitals. Where hospital facilities are provided in an institution, their equipment, furnishings and pharmaceutical supplies shall be proper for the medical care and treatment of sick prisoners, and there shall be a staff of suitably trained officers.

(3) The services of a qualified dental officer shall be available to every prisoner.

23. (1) In women's institutions there shall be special accommodation for all necessary pre-natal and post-natal care and treatment. Arrangements shall be made

wherever practicable for children to be born in a hospital outside the institution. If a child is born in prison, this fact shall not be mentioned in the birth certificate.

(2) Where nursing infants are allowed to remain in the institution with their mothers, provision shall be made for a nursery staffed by qualified persons, where the infants shall be placed when they are not in the care of their mothers.

24. The medical officer shall see and examine every prisoner as soon as possible after his admission and thereafter as necessary, with a view particularly to the discovery of physical or mental illness and the taking of all necessary measures; the segregation of prisoners suspected of infectious or contagious conditions; the noting of physical or mental defects which might hamper rehabilitation, and the determination of the physical capacity of every prisoner for work.

25. (1) The medical officer shall have the care of the physical and mental health of the prisoners and should daily see all sick prisoners, all who complain of illness, and any prisoner to whom his attention is specially directed.

(2) The medical officer shall report to the director whenever he considers that a prisoner's physical or mental health has been or will be injuriously affected by continued imprisonment or by any condition of imprisonment.

26. (1) The medical officer shall regularly inspect and advise the director upon:

(*a*) The quantity, quality, preparation and service of food;

(*b*) The hygiene and cleanliness of the institution and the prisoners;

(*c*) The sanitation, heating, lighting and ventilation of the institution;

(*d*) The suitability and cleanliness of the prisoners' clothing and bedding;

(*e*) The observance of the rules concerning physical education and sports, in cases where there is no technical personnel in charge of these activities.

(2) The director shall take into consideration the reports and advice that the medical officer submits according to rules 25(2) and 26 and, in case he concurs with the recommendations made, shall take immediate steps to give effect to those recommendations; if they are not within his competence or if he does not concur with them, he shall immediately submit his own report and the advice of the medical officer to higher authority.

Discipline and Punishment

27. Discipline and order shall be maintained with firmness, but with no more restriction than is necessary for safe custody and well-ordered community life.

28. (1) No prisoner shall be employed, in the service of the institution, in any disciplinary capacity.

(2) This rule shall not, however, impede the proper functioning of systems based on self-government, under which specified social, educational or sports activities or responsibilities are entrusted, under supervision, to prisoners who are formed into groups for the purposes of treatment.

29. The following shall always be determined by the law or by the regulation of the competent administrative authority:

(*a*) Conduct constituting a disciplinary offence;

(*b*) The types and duration of punishment which may be inflicted;

(*c*) The authority competent to impose such punishment.

30. (1) No prisoner shall be punished except in accordance with the terms of such law or regulation, and never twice for the same offence.

(2) No prisoner shall be punished unless he has been informed of the offence alleged against him and given a proper opportunity of presenting his defence. The competent authority shall conduct a thorough examination of the case.

(3) Where necessary and practicable the prisoner shall be allowed to make his defence through an interpreter.

31. Corporal punishment, punishment by placing in a dark cell, and all cruel, inhuman or degrading punishments shall be completely prohibited as punishments for disciplinary offences.

32. (1) Punishment by close confinement or reduction of diet shall never be inflicted unless the medical officer has examined the prisoner and certified in writing that he is fit to sustain it.

(2) The same shall apply to any other punishment that may be prejudicial to the physical or mental health of a prisoner. In no case may such punishment be contrary to or depart from the principle stated in rule 31.

(3) The medical officer shall visit daily prisoners undergoing such punishments and shall advise the director if he considers the termination or alteration of the punishment necessary on grounds of physical or mental health.

Instruments of Restraint

33. Instruments of restraint, such as handcuffs, chains, irons and strait-jackets, shall never be applied as a punishment. Furthermore, chains or irons shall not be used as restraints. Other instruments of restraint shall not be used except in the following circumstances:

(*a*) As a precaution against escape during a transfer, provided that they shall be removed when the prisoner appears before a judicial or administrative authority;

(*b*) On medical grounds by direction of the medical officer;

(*c*) By order of the director, if other methods of control fail, in order to prevent a prisoner from injuring himself or others or from damaging property; in such instances the director shall at once consult the medical officer and report to the higher administrative authority.

34. The patterns and manner of use of instruments of restraint shall be decided by the central prison administration. Such instruments must not be applied for any longer time than is strictly necessary.

Information To and Complaints by Prisoners

35. (1) Every prisoner on admission shall be provided with written information about the regulations governing the treatment of prisoners of his category, the disciplinary requirements of the institution, the authorized methods of seeking information and making complaints, and all such other matters as are necessary to enable him to understand both his rights and his obligations and to adapt himself to the life of the institution.

(2) If a prisoner is illiterate, the aforesaid information shall be conveyed to him orally.

36. (1) Every prisoner shall have the opportunity each week day of making requests or complaints to the director of the institution or the officer authorized to represent him.

(2) It shall be possible to make requests or complaints to the inspector of prisons during his inspection. The prisoner shall have the opportunity to talk to the inspector or to any other inspecting officer without the director or other members of the staff being present.

(3) Every prisoner shall be allowed to make a request or complaint, without censorship as to substance but in proper form, to the central prison administration, the judicial authority or other proper authorities through approved channels.

(4) Unless it is evidently frivolous or groundless, every request or complaint shall be promptly dealt with and replied to without undue delay.

Contact With the Outside World

37. Prisoners shall be allowed under necessary supervision to communicate with their family and reputable friends at regular intervals, both by correspondence and by receiving visits.

38. (1) Prisoners who are foreign nationals shall be allowed reasonable facilities to communicate with the diplomatic and consular representatives of the State to which they belong.

(2) Prisoners who are nationals of States without diplomatic or consular representation in the country and refugees or stateless persons shall be allowed similar facilities to communicate with the diplomatic representative of the State which takes charge of their interests or any national or international authority whose task it is to protect such persons.

39. Prisoners shall be kept informed regularly of the more important items of news by the reading of newspapers, periodicals or special institutional publications, by hearing wireless transmissions, by lectures or by any similar means as authorized or controlled by the administration.

Books

40. Every institution shall have a library for the use of all categories of prisoners, adequately stocked with both recreational and instructional books, and prisoners shall be encouraged to make full use of it.

Religion

41. (1) If the institution contains a sufficient number of prisoners of the same religion, a qualified representative of that religion shall be appointed or approved. If the number of prisoners justifies it and conditions permit, the arrangement should be on a full-time basis.

(2) A qualified representative appointed or approved under paragraph (1) shall be allowed to hold regular services and to pay pastoral visits in private to prisoners of his religion at proper times.

(3) Access to a qualified representative of any religion shall not be refused to any prisoner. On the other hand, if any prisoner should object to a visit of any religious representative, his attitude shall be fully respected.

42. So far as practicable, every prisoner shall be allowed to satisfy the needs of his religious life by attending the services provided in the institution and having in his possession the books of religious observance and institution of his denomination.

Retention of Prisoners' Property

43. (1) All money, valuables, clothing and other effects belonging to a prisoner which under the regulations of the institution he is not allowed to retain shall on his admission to the institution be placed in safe custody. An inventory thereof shall be signed by the prisoner. Steps shall be taken to keep them in good condition.

(2) On the release of the prisoner all such articles and money shall be returned to him except in so far as he has been authorized to spend money or send any such property out of the institution, or it has been found necessary on hygienic grounds to destroy any article of clothing. The prisoner shall sign a receipt for the articles and money returned to him.

(3) Any money or effects received for a prisoner from outside shall be treated in the same way.

(4) If a prisoner brings in any drugs or medicine, the medical officer shall decide what use shall be made of them.

Notification of Death, Illness, Transfer, etc.

44. (1) Upon the death or serious illness of, or serious injury to a prisoner, or his removal to an institution for the treatment of mental affections, the director shall at once inform the spouse, if the prisoner is married, or the nearest relative and shall in any event inform any other person previously designated by the prisoner.

(2) A prisoner shall be informed at once of the death or serious illness of any near relative. In case of the critical illness of a near relative, the prisoner should be authorized, whenever circumstances allow, to go to his bedside either under escort or alone.

(3) Every prisoner shall have the right to inform at once his family of his imprisonment or his transfer to another institution.

Removal of Prisoners

45. (1) When prisoners are being removed to or from an institution, they shall be exposed to public view as little as possible, and proper safeguards shall be adopted to protect them from insult, curiosity and publicity in any form.

(2) The transport of prisoners in conveyances with inadequate ventilation or light, or in any way which would subject them to unnecessary physical hardship, shall be prohibited.

(3) The transport of prisoners shall be carried out at the expense of the administration and equal conditions shall obtain for all of them.

Institutional Personnel

46. (1) The prison administration, shall provide for the careful selection of every grade of the personnel, since it is on their integrity, humanity, professional capacity and personal suitability for the work that the proper administration of the institutions depends.

* * *

47. (1) The personnel shall possess an adequate standard of education and intelligence.

* * *

48. All members of the personnel shall at all times so conduct themselves and perform their duties as to influence the prisoners for good by their example and to command their respect.

49. (1) So far as possible, the personnel shall include a sufficient number of specialists such as psychiatrists, psychologists, social workers, teachers and trade instructors.

* * *

50. (1) The director of an institution should be adequately qualified for his task by character, administrative ability, suitable training and experience.

* * *

51. (1) The director, his deputy, and the majority of the other personnel of the institution shall be able to speak the language of the greatest number of prisoners, or a language understood by the greatest number of them.

(2) Whenever necessary, the services of an interpreter shall be used.

52. (1) In institutions which are large enough to require the services of one or more full-time medical officers, at least one of them shall reside on the premises of the institution or in its immediate vicinity.

(2) In other institutions the medical officer shall visit daily and shall reside near enough to be able to attend without delay in cases of urgency.

53. (1) In an institution for both men and women, the part of the institution set aside for women shall be under the authority of a responsible woman officer who shall have the custody of the keys of all that part of the institution.

(2) No male member of the staff shall enter the part of the institution set aside for women unless accompanied by a woman officer.

(3) Women prisoners shall be attended and supervised only by women officers. This does not, however, preclude male members of the staff, particularly doctors and teachers, from carrying out their professional duties in institutions or parts of institutions set aside for women.

54. (1) Officers of the institutions shall not, in their relations with the prisoners, use force except in self-defence or in cases of attempted escape, or active or passive physical resistance to an order based on law or regulations. Officers who have recourse to force must use no more than is strictly necessary and must report the incident immediately to the director of the institution.

(2) Prison officers shall be given special physical training to enable them to restrain aggressive prisoners.

(3) Except in special circumstances, staff performing duties which bring them into direct contact with prisoners should not be armed. Furthermore, staff should in no circumstances be provided with arms unless they have been trained in their use.

Inspection

55. There shall be a regular inspection of penal institutions and services by qualified and experienced inspectors appointed by a competent authority. Their task shall be in particular to ensure that these institutions are administered in accordance with existing laws and regulations and with a view to bringing about the objectives of penal and correctional services.

PART II. RULES APPLICABLE TO SPECIAL CATEGORIES

A. PRISONERS UNDER SENTENCE

Guiding Principles

56. The guiding principles hereafter are intended to show the spirit in which penal institutions should be administered and the purposes at which they should aim, in accordance with the declaration made under Preliminary Observation 1 of the present text.

57. Imprisonment and other measures which result in cutting off an offender from the outside world are afflictive by the very fact of taking from the person the right of self-determination by depriving him of his liberty. Therefore the prison system shall not, except as incidental to justifiable segregation or the maintenance of discipline, aggravate the suffering inherent in such a situation.

58. The purpose and justification of a sentence of imprisonment or a similar measure deprivative of liberty is ultimately to protect society against crime. This end can only be achieved if the period of imprisonment is used to ensure, so far as possible, that upon his return to society the offender is not only willing but able to lead a law-abiding and self-supporting life.

59. To this end, the institution should utilize all the remedial, educational, moral, spiritual and other forces and forms of assistance which are appropriate and available, and should seek to apply them according to the individual treatment needs of the prisoners.

60. (1) The régime of the institution should seek to minimize any differences between prison life and life at liberty which tend to lessen the responsibility of the prisoners or the respect due to their dignity as human beings.

(2) Before the completion of the sentence, it is desirable that the necessary steps be taken to ensure for the prisoner a gradual return to life in society. This aim may be achieved, depending on the case, by a pre-release régime organized in the same institution or in another appropriate institution, or by release on trial under some kind of supervision which must not be entrusted to the police but should be combined with effective social aid.

61. The treatment of prisoners should emphasize not their exclusion from the community, but their continuing part in it. Community agencies should, therefore, be enlisted wherever possible to assist the staff of the institution in the task of social rehabilitation of the prisoners. There should be in connexion with every institution social workers charged with the duty of maintaining and improving all desirable relations of a prisoner with his family and with valuable social agencies. Steps should be taken to safeguard, to the maximum extent compatible with the law and the sentence, the rights relating to civil interests, social security rights and other social benefits of prisoners.

62. The medical services of the institution shall seek to detect and shall treat any physical or mental illnesses or defects which may hamper a prisoner's rehabilitation. All necessary medical, surgical and psychiatric services shall be provided to that end.

63. (1) The fulfilment of these principles requires individualization of treatment and for this purpose a flexible system of classifying prisoners in groups; it is therefore desirable that such groups should be distributed in separate institutions suitable for the treatment of each group.

(2) These institutions need not provide the same degree of security for every group. It is desirable to provide varying degrees of security according to the needs of different groups. Open institutions, by the very fact that they provide no physical security against escape but rely on the self-discipline of the inmates, provide the conditions most favourable to rehabilitation for carefully selected prisoners.

(3) It is desirable that the number of prisoners in closed institutions should not be so large that the individualization of treatment is hindered. In some countries it is considered that the population of such institutions should not exceed five hundred. In open institutions the population should be as small as possible.

(4) On the other hand, it is undesirable to maintain prisons which are so small that proper facilities cannot be provided.

64. The duty of society does not end with a prisoner's release. There should, therefore, be governmental or private agencies capable of lending the released prisoner efficient after-care directed towards the lessening of prejudice against him and towards his social rehabilitation.

Treatment

65. The treatment of persons sentenced to imprisonment or a similar measure shall have as its purpose, so far as the length of the sentence permits, to establish in them the will to lead law-abiding and self-supporting lives after their release and to fit them to do so. The treatment shall be such as will encourage their self-respect and develop their sense of responsibility.

66. (1) To these ends, all appropriate means shall be used, including religious care in the countries where this is possible, education, vocational guidance and training, social casework, employment counseling, physical development and strengthening of moral character, in accordance with the individual needs of his prisoner, taking account of his social and criminal history, his physical and mental capacities and aptitudes, his personal temperament, the length of his sentence and his prospects after release.

(2) For every prisoner with a sentence of suitable length, the director shall receive, as soon as possible after his admission, full reports on all the matters referred to in the foregoing paragraph. Such reports shall always include a report by a medical officer, wherever possible qualified in psychiatry, on the physical and mental condition of the prisoner.

(3) The reports and other relevant documents shall be placed in an individual file. This file shall be kept up to date and classified in such a way that it can be consulted by the responsible personnel whenever the need arises.

Classification and Individualization

67. The purposes of classification shall be:

(*a*) To separate from others those prisoners who, by reason of their criminal records or bad characters, are likely to exercise a bad influence;

(*b*) To divide the prisoners into classes in order to facilitate their treatment with a view to their social rehabilitation.

68. So far as possible separate institutions or separate sections of an institution shall be used for the treatment of the different classes of prisoners.

69. As soon as possible after admission and after a study of the personality of each prisoner with a sentence of suitable length, a programme of treatment shall be prepared for him in the light of the knowledge obtained about his individual needs, his capacities and dispositions.

Privileges

70. Systems of privileges appropriate for the different classes of prisoners and the different methods of treatment shall be established at every institution, in order to encourage good conduct, develop a sense of responsibility and secure the interest and co-operation of the prisoners in their treatment.

Work

71. (1) Prison labour must not be of an afflictive nature.

(2) All prisoners under sentence shall be required to work, subject to their physical and mental fitness as determined by the medical officer.

(3) Sufficient work of a useful nature shall be provided to keep prisoners actively employed for a normal working day.

(4) So far as possible the work provided shall be such as will maintain or increase the prisoners' ability to earn an honest living after release.

(5) Vocational training in useful trades shall be provided for prisoners able to profit thereby and especially for young prisoners.

(6) Within the limits compatible with proper vocational selection and with the requirements of institutional administration and discipline, the prisoners shall be able to choose the type of work they wish to perform.

72. (1) The organization and methods of work in the institutions shall resemble as closely as possible those of similar work outside institutions, so as to prepare prisoners for the conditions of normal occupational life.

(2) The interests of the prisoners and of their vocational training, however, must not be subordinated to the purpose of making a financial profit from an industry in the institution.

* * *

76. (1) There shall be a system of equitable remuneration of the work of prisoners.

(2) Under the system prisoners shall be allowed to spend at least a part of their earnings on approved articles for their own use and to send a part of their earnings to their family.

(3) The system should also provide that a part of the earnings should be set aside by the administration so as to constitute a savings fund to be handed over to the prisoner on his release.

Education and Recreation

77. (1) Provision shall be made for the further education of all prisoners capable of profiting thereby, including religious instruction in the countries where this is possible. The education of illiterates and young prisoners shall be compulsory and special attention shall be paid to it by the administration.

(2) So far as practicable, the education of prisoners shall be integrated with the educational system of the country so that after their release they may continue their education without difficulty.

78. Recreational and cultural activities shall be provided in all institutions for the benefit of the mental and physical health of prisoners.

Social Relations and After-Care

79. Special attention shall be paid to the maintenance and improvement of such relations between a prisoner and his family as are desirable in the best interests of both.

80. From the beginning of a prisoner's sentence consideration shall be given to his future after release and he shall be encouraged and assisted to maintain or establish such relations with persons or agencies outside the institution as may promote the best interests of his family and his own social rehabilitation.

81. (1) Services and agencies, governmental or otherwise, which assist released prisoners to re-establish themselves in society shall ensure, so far as is possible and necessary, that released prisoners be provided with appropriate documents and identification papers, have suitable homes and work to go to, are suitably and adequately clothed having regard to the climate and season, and have sufficient means to reach their destination and maintain themselves in the period immediately following their release.

(2) The approved representatives of such agencies shall have all necessary access to the institution and to prisoners and shall be taken into consultation as to the future of a prisoner from the beginning of his sentence.

(3) It is desirable that the activities of such agencies shall be centralized or co-ordinated as far as possible in order to secure the best use of their efforts.

B. INSANE AND MENTALLY ABNORMAL PRISONERS

82. (1) Persons who are found to be insane shall not be detained in prisons and arrangements shall be made to remove them to mental institutions as soon as possible.

(2) Prisoners who suffer from other mental diseases or abnormalities shall be observed and treated in specialized institutions under medical management.

(3) During their stay in a prison, such prisoners shall be placed under the special supervision of a medical officer.

(4) The medical or psychiatric service of the penal institutions shall provide for the psychiatric treatment of all other prisoners who are in need of such treatment.

83. It is desirable that steps should be taken, by arrangement with the appropriate agencies, to ensure if necessary the continuation of psychiatric treatment after release and the provision of social-psychiatric after-care.

C. PRISONERS UNDER ARREST OR AWAITING TRIAL

84. (1) Persons arrested or imprisoned by reason of a criminal charge against them, who are detained either in police custody or in prison custody (jail) but have not yet been tried and sentenced, will be referred to as "untried prisoners" hereinafter in these rules.

(2) Unconvicted prisoners are presumed to be innocent and shall be treated as such.

(3) Without prejudice to legal rules for the protection of individual liberty or prescribing the procedure to be observed in respect of untried prisoners, these prisoners shall benefit by a special régime which is described in the following rules in its essential requirements only.

85. (1) Untried prisoners shall be kept separate from convicted prisoners.

(2) Young untried prisoners shall be kept separate from adults and shall in principle be detained in separate institutions.

86. Untried prisoners shall sleep singly in separate rooms, with the reservation of different local custom in respect of the climate.

87. Within the limits compatible with the good order of the institution, untried prisoners may, if they so desire, have their food procured at their own expense from the outside, either through the administration or through their family or friends. Otherwise, the administration shall provide their food.

88. (1) An untried prisoner shall be allowed to wear his own clothing if it is clean and suitable.

(2) If he wears prison dress, it shall be different from that supplied to convicted prisoners.

89. An untried prisoner shall always be offered opportunity to work, but shall not be required to work. If he chooses to work, he shall be paid for it.

90. An untried prisoner shall be allowed to procure at his own expense or at the expense of a third party such books, newspapers, writing materials and other means of occupation as are compatible with the interests of the administration of justice and the security and good order of the institution.

91. An untried prisoner shall be allowed to be visited and treated by his own doctor or dentist if there is reasonable ground for his application and he is able to pay any expenses incurred.

92. An untried prisoner shall be allowed to inform immediately his family of his detention and shall be given all reasonable facilities for communicating with his family and friends, and for receiving visits from them, subject only to such restrictions and supervision as are necessary in the interests of the administration of justice and of the security and good order of the institution.

93. For the purposes of his defence, an untried prisoner shall be allowed to apply for free legal aid where such aid is available, and to receive visits from his legal adviser with a view to his defence and to prepare and hand to him confidential instructions. For these purposes, he shall if he so desires be supplied with writing material. Interviews between the prisoner and his legal adviser may be within sight but not within the hearing of a police or institution official.

D. CIVIL PRISONERS

94. In countries where the law permits imprisonment for debt, or by order of a court under any other non-criminal process, persons so imprisoned shall not be subjected to any greater restriction or severity than is necessary to ensure safe custody and good order. Their treatment shall be not less favourable than that of

untried prisoners, with the reservation, however, that they may possibly be required to work.

E. PERSONS ARRESTED OR DETAINED WITHOUT CHARGE

95. Without prejudice to the provisions of article 9 of the International Covenant on Civil and Political Rights, persons arrested or imprisoned without charge shall be accorded the same protection as that accorded under part I and part II, section C. Relevant provisions of part II, section A, shall likewise be applicable where their application may be conducive to the benefit of this special group of persons in custody, provided that no measures shall be taken implying that re-education or rehabilitation is in any way appropriate to persons not convicted of any criminal offence.

3.10 INTERNATIONAL LABOR ORGANIZATION CONVENTION (No. 107) CONCERNING THE PROTECTION AND INTEGRATION OF INDIGENOUS AND OTHER TRIBAL AND SEMI-TRIBAL POPULATIONS IN INDEPENDENT COUNTRIES.[a] Done at Geneva, June 26, 1957. Entered into force, June 2, 1959. 328 U.N.T.S. 247

PART I. GENERAL POLICY

Article 1

1. This Convention applies to—

(*a*) members of tribal or semi-tribal populations in independent countries whose social and economic conditions are at a less advanced stage than the stage reached by the other sections of the national community, and whose status is regulated wholly or partially by their own customs or traditions or by special laws or regulations;

(*b*) members of tribal or semi-tribal populations in independent countries which are regarded as indigenous on account of their descent from the populations which inhabited the country, or a geographical region to which the country belongs, at the time of conquest or colonisation and which, irrespective of their legal status, live more in conformity with the social, economic and cultural institutions of that time than with the institutions of the nation to which they belong.

2. For the purposes of this Convention, the term "semi-tribal" includes groups and persons who, although they are in the process of losing their tribal characteristics, are not yet integrated into the national community.

3. The indigenous and other tribal or semi-tribal populations mentioned in paragraphs 1 and 2 of this Article are referred to hereinafter as "the populations concerned."

Article 2

1. Governments shall have the primary responsibility for developing co-ordinated and systematic action for the protection of the populations concerned and their progressive integration into the life of their respective countries.

2. Such action shall include measures for—

(*a*) enabling the said populations to benefit on an equal footing from the rights and opportunities which national laws or regulations grant to the other elements of the population;

(*b*) promoting the social, economic and cultural development of these populations and raising their standard of living;

(*c*) creating possibilities of national integration to the exclusion of measures tending towards the artificial assimilation of these populations.

3. The primary objective of all such action shall be the fostering of individual dignity, and the advancement of individual usefulness and initiative.

4. Recourse to force or coercion as a means of promoting the integration of these populations into the national community shall be excluded.

a. *See also* Basic Document 3.46, *infra*.

Article 3

1. So long as the social, economic and cultural conditions of the populations concerned prevent them from enjoying the benefits of the general laws of the country to which they belong, special measures shall be adopted for the protection of the institutions, persons, property and labour of these populations.

2. Care shall be taken to ensure that such special measures of protection—

(*a*) are not used as a means of creating or prolonging a state of segregation; and

(*b*) will be continued only so long as there is need for special protection and only to the extent that such protection is necessary.

3. Enjoyment of the general rights of citizenship, without discrimination, shall not be prejudiced in any way by such special measures of protection.

Article 4

In applying the provisions of this Convention relating to the integration of the populations concerned—

(*a*) due account shall be taken of the cultural and religious values and of the forms of social control existing among these populations, and of the nature of the problems which face them both as groups and as individuals when they undergo social and economic change;

(*b*) the danger involved in disrupting the values and institutions of the said populations unless they can be replaced by appropriate substitutes which the groups concerned are willing to accept shall be recognised;

(*c*) policies aimed at mitigating the difficulties experienced by these populations in adjusting themselves to new conditions of life and work shall be adopted.

Article 5

In applying the provisions of this Convention relating to the protection and integration of the populations concerned, governments shall—

(*a*) seek the collaboration of these populations and of their representatives;

(*b*) provide these populations with opportunities for the full development of their initiative;

(*c*) stimulate by all possible means the development among these populations of civil liberties and the establishment of or participation in elective institutions.

Article 6

The improvement of the conditions of life and work and level of education of the populations concerned shall be given high priority in plans for the over-all economic development of areas inhabited by these populations. Special projects for economic development of the areas in question shall also be so designed as to promote such improvement.

Article 7

1. In defining the rights and duties of the populations concerned, regard shall be had to their customary laws.

2. These populations shall be allowed to retain their own customs and institutions where these are not incompatible with the national legal system or the objectives of integration programmes.

3. The application of the preceding paragraphs of this Article shall not prevent members of these populations from exercising, according to their individual capacity, the rights granted to all citizens and from assuming the corresponding duties.

Article 8

To the extent consistent with the interests of the national community and with the national legal system—

(*a*) the methods of social control practised by the populations concerned shall be used as far as possible for dealing with crimes or offences committed by members of these populations;

(*b*) where use of such methods of social control is not feasible, the customs of these populations in regard to penal matters shall be borne in mind by the authorities and courts dealing with such cases.

Article 9

Except in cases prescribed by law for all citizens the exaction from the members of the populations concerned of compulsory personal services in any form, whether paid or unpaid, shall be prohibited and punishable by law.

Article 10

1. Persons belonging to the populations concerned shall be specially safeguarded against the improper application of preventive detention and shall be able to take legal proceedings for the effective protection of their fundamental rights.

2. In imposing penalties laid down by general law on members of these populations account shall be taken of the degree of cultural development of the populations concerned.

3. Preference shall be given to methods of rehabilitation rather than confinement in prison.

PART II. LAND

Article 11

The right of ownership, collective or individual, of the members of the populations concerned over the lands which these populations traditionally occupy shall be recognised.

Article 12

1. The populations concerned shall not be removed without their free consent from their habitual territories except in accordance with national laws and regulations for reasons relating to national security, or in the interest of national economic development or of the health of the said populations.

2. When in such cases removal of these populations is necessary as an exceptional measure, they shall be provided with lands of quality at least equal to that of the lands previously occupied by them, suitable to provide for their present needs and future development. In cases where chances of alternative employment exist and where the populations concerned prefer to have compensation in money or in kind, they shall be so compensated under appropriate guarantees.

3. Persons thus removed shall be fully compensated for any resulting loss or injury.

Article 13

1. Procedures for the transmission of rights of ownership and use of land which are established by the customs of the populations concerned shall be respected, within the framework of national laws and regulations, in so far as they satisfy the needs of these populations and do not hinder their economic and social development.

2. Arrangements shall be made to prevent persons who are not members of the populations concerned from taking advantage of these customs or of lack of under-

standing of the laws on the part of the members of these populations to secure the ownership or use of the lands belonging to such members.

Article 14

National agrarian programmes shall secure to the populations concerned treatment equivalent to that accorded to other sections of the national community with regard to—

(*a*) the provision of more land for these populations when they have not the area necessary for providing the essentials of a normal existence, or for any possible increase in their numbers;

(*b*) the provision of the means required to promote the development of the lands which these populations already possess.

PART III. RECRUITMENT AND CONDITIONS OF EMPLOYMENT

Article 15

1. Each Member shall, within the framework of national laws and regulations, adopt special measures to ensure the effective protection with regard to recruitment and conditions of employment of workers belonging to the populations concerned so long as they are not in a position to enjoy the protection granted by law to workers in general.

2. Each Member shall do everything possible to prevent all discrimination between workers belonging to the populations concerned and other workers, in particular as regards—

(*a*) admission to employment, including skilled employment;

(*b*) equal remuneration for work of equal value;

(*c*) medical and social assistance, the prevention of employment injuries, workmen's compensation, industrial hygiene and housing;

(*d*) the right of association and freedom for all lawful trade union activities, and the right to conclude collective agreements with employers or employers' organisations.

PART IV. VOCATIONAL TRAINING, HANDICRAFTS AND RURAL INDUSTRIES

Article 16

Persons belonging to the populations concerned shall enjoy the same opportunities as other citizens in respect of vocational training facilities.

Article 17

1. Whenever programmes of vocational training of general application do not meet the special needs of persons belonging to the populations concerned governments shall provide special training facilities for such persons.

2. These special training facilities shall be based on a careful study of the economic environment, stage of cultural development and practical needs of the various occupational groups among the said populations; they shall, in particular, enable the persons concerned to receive the training necessary for occupations for which these populations have traditionally shown aptitude.

3. These special training facilities shall be provided only so long as the stage of cultural development of the populations concerned requires them; with the advance of the process of integration they shall be replaced by the facilities provided for other citizens.

Article 18

1. Handicrafts and rural industries shall be encouraged as factors in the economic development of the populations concerned in a manner which will enable these populations to raise their standard of living and adjust themselves to modern methods of production and marketing.

2. Handicrafts and rural industries shall be developed in a manner which preserves the cultural heritage of these populations and improves their artistic values and particular modes of cultural expression.

PART V. SOCIAL SECURITY AND HEALTH

Article 19

Existing social security schemes shall be extended progressively, where practicable, to cover—

(*a*) wage earners belonging to the populations concerned;

(*b*) other persons belonging to these populations.

Article 20

1. Governments shall assume the responsibility for providing adequate health services for the populations concerned.

2. The organisation of such services shall be based on systematic studies of the social, economic and cultural conditions of the populations concerned.

3. The development of such services shall be co-ordinated with general measures of social, economic and cultural development.

PART VI. EDUCATION AND MEANS OF COMMUNICATION

Article 21

Measures shall be taken to ensure that members of the populations concerned have the opportunity to acquire education at all levels on an equal footing with the rest of the national community.

Article 22

1. Education programmes for the populations concerned shall be adapted, as regards methods and techniques, to the stage these populations have reached in the process of social, economic and cultural integration into the national community.

2. The formulation of such programmes shall normally be preceded by ethnological surveys.

Article 23

1. Children belonging to the populations concerned shall be taught to read and write in their mother tongue or, where this is not practicable, in the language most commonly used by the group to which they belong.

2. Provision shall be made for a progressive transition from the mother tongue or the vernacular language to the national language or to one of the official languages of the country.

3. Appropriate measures shall, as far as possible, be taken to preserve the mother tongue or the vernacular language.

Article 24

The imparting of general knowledge and skills that will help children to become integrated into the national community shall be an aim of primary education for the populations concerned.

Article 25

Educational measures shall be taken among other sections of the national community and particularly among those that are in most direct contact with the populations concerned with the object of eliminating prejudices that they may harbour in respect of these populations.

Article 26

1. Governments shall adopt measures, appropriate to the social and cultural characteristics of the populations concerned, to make known to them their rights and duties, especially in regard to labour and social welfare.

2. If necessary this shall be done by means of written translations and through the use of media of mass communication in the languages of these populations.

PART VII. ADMINISTRATION

Article 27

1. The governmental authority responsible for the matters covered in this Convention shall create or develop agencies to administer the programmes involved.

* * *

PART VIII. GENERAL PROVISIONS

Article 28

The nature and the scope of the measures to be taken to give effect to this Convention shall be determined in a flexible manner, having regard to the conditions characteristic of each country.

Article 29

The application of the provisions of this Convention shall not affect benefits conferred on the populations concerned in pursuance of other Conventions and Recommendations.

* * *

Article 32

1. A Member which has ratified this Convention may denounce it after the expiration of ten years from the date on which the Convention first comes into force, by an act communicated to the Director-General of the International Labour Office for registration. Such denunciation shall not take effect until one year after the date on which it is registered.

* * *

3.11 COMMUNICATIONS CONCERNING HUMAN RIGHTS, E.S.C. RES. 728F (XXVIII).[a] Adopted by the U.N. Economic and Social Council, July 30, 1959. 28 U.N. ESCOR, Supp. (No. 1) 19, U.N. Doc. E/3290 (1959)

The Economic and Social Council,

Having considered chapter V of the report of the Commission on Human Rights on its first session, concerning communications, and chapter IX of the report of the Commission on its fifteenth session,

1. *Approves* the statement that the Commission on Human Rights recognizes that it has no power to take any action in regard to any complaints concerning human rights;

2. *Requests* the Secretary–General:

(*a*) To compile and distribute to members of the Commission on Human Rights before each session a non-confidential list containing a brief indication of the substance of each communication, however addressed, which deals with the principles involved in the promotion of universal respect for, and observance of, human rights and to divulge the identity of the authors of such communications unless they indicate that they wish their names to remain confidential;

(*b*) To compile before each session of the Commission a confidential list containing a brief indication of the substance of other communications concerning human rights, however addressed, and to furnish this list to members of the Commission, in private meeting, without divulging the identity of the authors of communications except in cases where the authors state that they have already divulged or intend to divulge their names or that they have no objection to their names being divulged;

(*c*) To enable the members of the Commission, upon request, to consult the originals of communications dealing with the principles, involved in the promotion of universal respect for, and observance of, human rights;

(*d*) To inform the writers of all communications concerning human rights, however addressed, that their communications will be handled in accordance with this resolution, indicating that the Commission has no power to take any action in regard to any complaint concerning human rights;

(*e*) To furnish each Member State concerned with a copy of any communication concerning human rights which refers explicitly to that State or to territories under its jurisdiction, without divulging the identity of the author, except as provided for in sub-paragraph (*b*) above;

(*f*) To ask Governments sending replies to communications brought to their attention in accordance with sub-paragraph (*e*) whether they wish their replies to be presented to the Commission in summary form or in full;

3. *Resolves* to give members of the Sub–Commission on Prevention of Discrimination and Protection of Minorities, with respect to communications dealing with discrimination and minorities, the same facilities as are enjoyed by members of the Commission on Human Rights under the present resolution;

4. *Suggests* to the Commission on Human Rights that it should at each session appoint an ad hoc committee to meet shortly before its next session for the purpose of

a. *See also* Basic Documents 3.20, 3.22 and 3.26, *infra.*

reviewing the list of communications prepared by the Secretary–General under paragraph 2(*a*) above and of recommending which of these communications, in original, should, in accordance with paragraph 2(*c*) above, be made available to members of the Commission on request.

3.12 DECLARATION ON THE GRANTING OF INDEPENDENCE TO COLONIAL COUNTRIES AND PEOPLES. Adopted by the U.N. General Assembly, Dec. 14, 1960. U.N.G.A. Res. 1514 (XV), 15 U.N. GAOR, Supp. (No. 16) 66, U.N. Doc. A/4684 (1961)

THE GENERAL ASSEMBLY.

Mindful of the determination proclaimed by the peoples of the world in the Charter of the United Nations to reaffirm faith in fundamental human rights, in the dignity and worth of the human person, in the equal rights of men and women and of nations large and small and to promote social progress and better standards of life in larger freedom.

Conscious of the need for the creation of conditions of stability and well-being and peaceful and friendly relations based on respect for the principles of equal rights and self-determination of all peoples, and of universal respect for, and observance of, human rights and fundamental freedoms for all without distinction as to race, sex, language or religion.

Recognizing the passionate yearning for freedom in all dependent peoples and the decisive role of the freedom of such peoples, which constitute a serious threat to world peace.

Aware of the increasing conflicts resulting from the denial of or impediments in the way of the freedom of such peoples, which constitute a serious threat to world peace.

Considering the important role of the United Nations in assisting the movement for independence in Trust and Non–Self–Governing Territories.

Recognizing that the peoples of the world ardently desire the end of colonialism in all its manifestations.

Convinced that the continued existence of colonialism prevents the development of international economic co-operation, impedes the social, cultural and economic development of dependent peoples and militates against the United Nations ideal of universal peace.

Affirming that peoples may, for their own ends, freely dispose of their natural wealth and resources without prejudice to any obligations arising out of international economic co-operation, based upon the principle of mutual benefit, and international law.

Believing that the process of liberation is irresistible and irreversible and that, in order to avoid serious crises, an end must be put to colonialism and all practices of segregation and discrimination associated therewith.

Welcoming the emergence in recent years of a large number of dependent territories into freedom and independence, and recognizing the increasingly powerful trends towards freedom in such territories which have not yet attained independence.

Convinced that all peoples have an inalienable right to complete freedom, the exercise of their sovereignty and the integrity of their national territory.

Solemnly proclaims the necessity of bringing to a speedy and unconditional end colonialism in all its forms and manifestations:

And to this end

Declares that:

1. The subjection of peoples to alien subjugation, domination and exploitation constitutes a denial of fundamental human rights, is contrary to the Charter of the

United Nations and is an impediment to the promotion of world peace and co-operation.

2. All peoples have the right to self-determination; by virtue of that right they freely determine their political status and freely pursue their economic, social and cultural development.

3. Inadequacy of political, economic, social or educational preparedness should never serve as a pretext for delaying independence.

4. All armed action or repressive measures of all kinds directed against dependent peoples shall cease in order to enable them to exercise peacefully and freely their right to complete independence, and the integrity of their national territory shall be respected.

5. Immediate steps shall be taken, in Trust and Non–Self–Governing Territories or all other territories which have not yet attained independence, to transfer all powers to the peoples of those territories, without any conditions or reservations, in accordance with their freely expressed will and desire, without any distinction as to race, creed or colour, in order to enable them to enjoy complete independence and freedom.

6. Any attempt aimed at the partial or total disruption of the national unity and the territorial integrity of a country is incompatible with the purposes and principles of the Charter of the United Nations.

7. All States shall observe faithfully and strictly the provisions of the Charter of the United Nations, the Universal Declaration of Human Rights and the present Declaration on the basis of equality, noninterference in the internal affairs of all States, and respect for the sovereign rights of all peoples and their territorial integrity.

3.13 EUROPEAN SOCIAL CHARTER.[a] Done at Turin, Oct. 18, 1961. Entered into force, Feb. 26, 1965. Europ. T.S. No. 35, 529 U.N.T.S. 89

PART I

The Contracting Parties accept as the aim of their policy, to be pursued by all appropriate means, both national and international in character, the attainment of conditions in which the following rights and principles may be effectively realized:

(1) Everyone shall have the opportunity to earn his living in an occupation freely entered upon.

(2) All workers have the right to just conditions of work.

(3) All workers have the right to safe and healthy working conditions.

(4) All workers have the right to a fair remuneration sufficient for a decent standard of living for themselves and their families.

(5) All workers and employers have the right to freedom of association in national or international organizations for the protection of their economic and social interests.

(6) All workers and employers have the right to bargain collectively.

(7) Children and young persons have the right to a special protection against the physical and moral hazards to which they are exposed.

(8) Employed women, in case of maternity, and other employed women as appropriate, have the right to a special protection in their work.

(9) Everyone has the right to appropriate facilities for vocational guidance with a view to helping him choose an occupation suited to his personal aptitude and interests.

(10) Everyone has the right to appropriate facilities for vocational training.

(11) Everyone has the right to benefit from any measures enabling him to enjoy the highest possible standard of health attainable.

(12) All workers and their dependents have the right to social security.

(13) Anyone without adequate resources has the right to social and medical assistance.

(14) Everyone has the right to benefit from social welfare services.

(15) Disabled persons have the right to vocational training, rehabilitation and resettlement, whatever the origin and nature of their disability.

(16) The family as a fundamental unit of society has the right to appropriate social, legal and economic protection to ensure its full development.

(17) Mothers and children, irrespective of marital status and family relations, have the right to appropriate social and economic protection.

(18) The nationals of any one of the Contracting Parties have the right to engage in any gainful occupation in the territory of any one of the others on a footing of equality with the nationals of the latter, subject to restrictions based on cogent economic or social reasons.

(19) Migrant workers who are nationals of a Contracting Party and their families have the right to protection and assistance in the territory of any other Contracting Party.

a. This Charter is intended to complement the European Convention for the Protection of Human Rights and Fundamental Freedoms (Basic Document 3.4).

PART II

The Contracting Parties undertake, as provided for in Part III, to consider themselves bound by the obligations laid down in the following Articles and paragraphs.

Article 1. The Right to Work

With a view to ensuring the effective exercise of the right to work, the Contracting Parties undertake:

(1) to accept as one of their primary aims and responsibilities the achievement and maintenance of as high and stable a level of employment as possible, with a view to the attainment of full employment;

(2) to protect effectively the right of the worker to earn his living in an occupation freely entered upon;

(3) to establish or maintain free employment services for all workers;

(4) to provide or promote appropriate vocational guidance, training and rehabilitation.

Article 2. The Right to Just Conditions of Work

With a view to ensuring the effective exercise of the right to just conditions of work, the Contracting Parties undertake:

(1) to provide for reasonable daily and weekly working hours, the working week to be progressively reduced to the extent that the increase of productivity and other relevant factors permit:

(2) to provide for public holidays with pay;

(3) to provide for a minimum of two weeks annual holiday with pay;

(4) to provide for additional paid holidays or reduced working hours for workers engaged in dangerous or unhealthy occupations as prescribed;

(5) to ensure a weekly rest period which shall, as far as possible, coincide with the day recognized by tradition or custom in the country or region concerned as a day of rest.

Article 3. The Right to Safe and Healthy Working Conditions

With a view to ensuring the effective exercise of the right to safe and healthy working conditions, the Contracting Parties undertake:

(1) to issue safety and health regulations;

(2) to provide for the enforcement of such regulations by measures of supervision;

(3) to consult, as appropriate, employers' and workers' organizations on measures intended to improve industrial safety and health.

Article 4. The Right to a Fair Remuneration

With a view to ensuring the effective exercise of the right to a fair remuneration, the Contracting Parties undertake:

(1) to recognize the right of workers to a remuneration such as will give them and their families a decent standard of living;

(2) to recognize the right of workers to an increased rate of remuneration for overtime work, subject to exceptions in particular cases;

(3) to recognize the right of men and women workers to equal pay for work of equal value;

(4) to recognize the right of all workers to a reasonable period of notice for termination of employment;

(5) to permit deductions from wages only under conditions and to the extent prescribed by national laws or regulations or fixed by collective agreements or arbitration awards.

The exercise of these rights shall be achieved by freely concluded collective agreements, by statutory wage-fixing machinery, or by other means appropriate to national conditions.

Article 5. The Right to Organize

With a view to ensuring or promoting the freedom of workers and employers to form local, national or international organizations for the protection of their economic and social interests and to join those organizations, the Contracting Parties undertake that national law shall not be such as to impair, nor shall it be so applied as to impair, this freedom. The extent to which the guarantees provided for in this Article shall apply to the police shall be determined by national laws or regulations. The principle governing the application to the members of the armed forces of these guarantees and the extent to which they shall apply to persons in this category shall equally be determined by national laws or regulations.

Article 6. The Right to Bargain Collectively

With a view to ensuring the effective exercise of the right to bargain collectively, the Contracting Parties undertake:

(1) to promote joint consultation between workers and employers;

(2) to promote, where necessary and appropriate, machinery for voluntary negotiations between employers or employers' organizations and workers' organizations, with a view to the regulation of terms and conditions of employment by means of collective agreements:

(3) to promote the establishment and use of appropriate machinery for conciliation and voluntary arbitration for the settlement of labour disputes;

and recognize:

(4) the right of workers and employers to collective action in cases of conflicts of interest, including the right to strike, subject to obligations that might arise out of collective agreements previously entered into.

Article 7. The Right of Children and Young Persons to Protection

With a view to ensuring the effective exercise of the right of children and young persons to protection, the Contracting Parties undertake:

(1) to provide that the maximum age of admission to employment shall be 15 years, subject to exceptions for children employed in prescribed light work without harm to their health, morals or education;

(2) to provide that a higher minimum age of admission to employment shall be fixed with respect to prescribed occupations regarded as dangerous or unhealthy;

(3) to provide that persons who are still subject to compulsory education shall not be employed in such work as would deprive them of the full benefit of their education;

(4) to provide that the working hours of persons under 16 years of age shall be limited in accordance with the needs of their development, and particularly with their need for vocational training;

(5) to recognize the right of young workers and apprentices to a fair wage or other appropriate allowances;

(6) to provide that the time spent by young persons in vocational training during the normal working hours with the consent of the employer shall be treated as forming part of the working day;

(7) to provide that employed persons of under 18 years of age shall be entitled to not less than three weeks' annual holiday with pay;

(8) to provide that persons under 18 years of age shall not be employed in night work with the exception of certain occupations provided for by national laws or regulations;

(9) to provide that persons under 18 years of age employed in occupations prescribed by national laws or regulations shall be subject to regular medical control;

(10) to ensure special protection against physical and moral dangers to which children and young persons are exposed, and particularly against those resulting directly or indirectly from their work.

Article 8. The Right of Employed Women to Protection

With a view to ensuring the effective exercise of the right of employed women to protection, the Contracting Parties undertake:

(1) to provide either by paid leave, by adequate social security benefits or by benefits from public funds for women to take leave before and after childbirth up to a total of at least 12 weeks;

(2) to consider it as unlawful for an employer to give a woman notice of dismissal during her absence on maternity leave or to give her notice of dismissal at such a time that the notice would expire during such absence;

(3) to provide that mothers who are nursing their infants shall be entitled to sufficient time off for this purpose;

(4)(a) to regulate the employment of women workers on night work in industrial employment;

(b) to prohibit the employment of women workers in underground mining, and, as appropriate, on all other work which is unsuitable for them by reason of its dangerous, unhealthy, or arduous nature.

Article 9. The Right to Vocational Guidance

With a view to ensuring the effective exercise of the right to vocational guidance, the Contracting Parties undertake to provide or promote, as necessary, a service which will assist all persons, including the handicapped, to solve problems related to occupational choice and progress, with due regard to the individual's characteristics and their relation to occupational opportunity: this assistance should be available free of charge, both to young persons, including school children, and to adults.

Article 10. The Right to Vocational Training

With a view to ensuring the effective exercise of the right to vocational training, the Contracting Parties undertake:

(1) to provide or promote, as necessary, the technical and vocational training of all persons, including the handicapped, in consultation with employers' and workers' organizations, and to grant facilities for access to higher technical and university education, based solely on individual aptitude;

(2) to provide or promote a system of apprenticeship and other systematic arrangements for training young boys and girls in their various employments;

(3) to provide or promote, as necessary:

(a) adequate and readily available training facilities for adult workers;

(b) special facilities for the re-training of adult workers needed as a result of technological development or new trends in employment;

(4) to encourage the full utilization of the facilities provided by appropriate measures such as:

(a) reducing or abolishing any fees or charges;

(b) granting financial assistance in appropriate cases;

(c) including in the normal working hours times spent on supplementary training taken by the worker, at the request of this employer, during employment;

(d) ensuring, through adequate supervision, in consultation with the employers' and workers' organizations, the efficiency of apprenticeship and other training arrangements for young workers, and the adequate protection of young workers generally.

Article 11. The Right to Protection of Health

With a view to ensuring the effective exercise of the right to protection of health, the Contracting Parties undertake, either directly or in co-operation with public or private organizations, to take appropriate measures designed inter alia:

(1) to remove as far as possible the causes of ill-health;

(2) to provide advisory and educational facilities for the promotion of health and the encouragement of individual responsibility in matters of health;

(3) to prevent as far as possible epidemic, endemic and other diseases.

Article 12. The Right to Social Security

With a view to ensuring the effective exercise of the right to social security, the Contracting Parties undertake:

(1) to establish or maintain a system of social security;

(2) to maintain the social security system at a satisfactory level at least equal to that required for ratification of International Labour Convention (No. 102) Concerning Minimum Standards of Social Security;

(3) to endeavour to raise progressively the system of social security to a higher level;

(4) to take steps, by the conclusion of appropriate bilateral and multilateral agreements, or by other means, and subject to the conditions laid down in such agreements, in order to ensure:

(a) equal treatment with their own nationals of the nationals of other Contracting Parties in respect of social security rights, including the retention of benefits arising out of social security legislation, whatever movements the persons protected may undertake between the territories of the Contracting Parties;

(b) the granting, maintenance and resumption of social security rights by such means as the accumulation of insurance or employment periods completed under the legislation of each of the Contracting Parties.

Article 13. The Right to Social and Medical Assistance

With a view to ensuring the effective exercise of the right to social and medical assistance, the Contracting Parties undertake:

(1) to ensure that any person who is without adequate resources and who is unable to secure such resources either by his own efforts or from other sources,

in particular by benefits under a social security scheme, be granted adequate assistance, and, in case of sickness, the care necessitated by his condition;

(2) to ensure that persons receiving such assistance shall not, for that reason, suffer from a diminution of their political or social rights;

(3) to provide that everyone may receive by appropriate public or private services such advice and personal help as may be required to prevent, to remove, or to alleviate personal or family want;

(4) to apply the provisions referred to in paragraphs 1, 2 and 3 of this Article on an equal footing with their nationals to nationals of other Contracting Parties lawfully within their territories, in accordance with their obligations under the European Convention on Social and Medical Assistance, signed at Paris on 11th December 1953.

Article 14. The Right to Benefit from Social Welfare Services

With a view to ensuring the effective exercise of the right to benefit from social welfare services, the Contracting Parties undertake:

(1) to promote or provide services which, by using methods of social work, would contribute to the welfare and development of both individuals and groups in the community, and to their adjustment to the social environment;

(2) to encourage the participation of individuals and voluntary or other organizations in the establishment and maintenance of such services.

Article 15. The Right of Physically or Mentally Disabled Persons to Vocational Training, Rehabilitation and Social Resettlement

With a view to ensuring the effective exercise of the right of the physically or mentally disabled to vocational training, rehabilitation and resettlement, the Contracting Parties undertake:

(1) to take adequate measures for the provision of training facilities, including, where necessary, specialized institutions, public or private;

(2) to take adequate measures for the placing of disabled persons in employment, such as specialized placing services, facilities for sheltered employment and measures to encourage employers to admit disabled persons to employment.

Article 16. The Right of the Family to Social, Legal and Economic Protection

With a view to ensuring the necessary conditions for the full development of the family, which is a fundamental unit of society, the Contracting Parties undertake to promote the economic, legal and social protection of family life by such means as social and family benefits, fiscal arrangements, provision of family housing, benefits for the newly married, and other appropriate means.

Article 17. The Right of Mothers and Children to Social and Economic Protection

With a view to ensuring the effective exercise of the right of mothers and children to social and economic protection, the Contracting Parties will take all appropriate and necessary measures to that end, including the establishment or maintenance of appropriate institutions or services.

Article 18. The Right to Engage in a Gainful Occupation in the Territory of Other Contracting Parties

With a view to ensuring the effective exercise of the right to engage in a gainful occupation in the territory of any other Contracting Party, the Contracting Parties undertake:

(1) to apply existing regulations in a spirit of liberality;

(2) to simplify existing formalities and to reduce or abolish chancery dues and other charges payable by foreign workers or their employers;

(3) to liberalize, individually or collectively, regulations governing the employment of foreign workers;

and recognize:

(4) the right of their nationals to leave the country to engage in a gainful occupation in the territories of the other Contracting Parties.

Article 19. The Right of Migrant Workers and their Families to Protection and Assistance

With a view to ensuring the effective exercise of the right of migrant workers and their families to protection and assistance in the territory of any other Contracting Party, the Contracting Parties undertake:

(1) to maintain or to satisfy themselves that there are maintained adequate and free services to assist such workers, particularly in obtaining accurate information, and to take all appropriate steps, so far as national laws and regulations permit, against misleading propaganda relating to emigration and immigration;

(2) to adopt appropriate measures within their own jurisdiction to facilitate the departure, journey and reception of such workers and their families, and to provide, within their own jurisdiction, appropriate services for health, medical attention and good hygienic conditions during the journey;

(3) to promote co-operation, as appropriate, between social services, public and private, in emigration and immigration countries;

(4) to secure for such workers lawfully within their territories, insofar as such matters are regulated by law or regulations or are subject to the control of administrative authorities, treatment not less favourable than that of their own nationals in respect of the following matters:

(a) remuneration and other employment and working conditions;

(b) membership of trade unions and enjoyment of the benefits of collective bargaining;

(c) accommodation;

(5) to secure for such workers lawfully within their territories treatment not less favourable than that of their own nationals with regard to employment taxes, dues or contributions payable in respect of employed persons;

(6) to facilitate as far as possible the reunion of the family of a foreign worker permitted to establish himself in the territory;

(7) to secure for such workers lawfully within their territories treatment not less favourable than that of their own nationals in respect of legal proceedings relating to matters referred to in this Article;

(8) to secure that such workers lawfully residing within their territories are not expelled unless they endanger national security or offend against public interest or morality;

(9) to permit, within legal limits, the transfer of such parts of the earnings and savings of such workers as they may desire;

(10) to extend the protection and assistance provided for in this Article to self-employed migrants insofar as such measures apply.

PART III

Article 20. Undertakings

1. Each of the Contracting Parties undertakes:

(a) to consider Part I of this Charter as a declaration of the aims which it will pursue by all appropriate means, as stated in the introductory paragraph of that Part;

(b) to consider itself bound by at least five of the following Articles of Part II of this Charter: Articles 1, 5, 6, 12, 13, 16 and 19;

(c) in addition to the Articles selected by it in accordance with the preceding sub-paragraph, to consider itself bound by such a number of Articles or numbered paragraphs of Part II of the Charter as it may select, provided that the total number of Articles or numbered paragraphs by which it is bound is not less than 10 Articles or 45 numbered paragraphs.

2. The Articles or paragraphs selected in accordance with sub-paragraphs (b) and (c) of paragraph 1 of this Article shall be notified to the Secretary–General of the Council of Europe at the time when the instrument of ratification or approval of the Contracting Party concerned is deposited.

3. Any Contracting Party may, at a later date, declare by notification to the Secretary–General that it considers itself bound by any Articles or any numbered paragraphs of Part II of the Charter which it has not already accepted under the terms of paragraph 1 of this Article. Such undertakings subsequently given shall be deemed to be an integral part of the ratification or approval, and shall have the same effect as from the thirtieth day after the date of the notification.

4. The Secretary–General shall communicate to all the signatory Governments and to the Director–General of the International Labour Office any notification which he shall have received pursuant to this Part of the Charter.

5. Each Contracting Party shall maintain a system of labour inspection appropriate to national conditions.

PART IV

Article 21. Reports concerning Accepted Provisions

The Contracting Parties shall send to the Secretary–General of the Council of Europe a report at two-yearly intervals, in a form to be determined by the Committee of Ministers, concerning the application of such provisions of Part II of the Charter as they have accepted.

Article 22. Reports concerning Provisions which are not accepted

The Contracting Parties shall send to the Secretary–General, at appropriate intervals as requested by the Committee of Ministers, reports relating to the provisions of Part II of the Charter which they did not accept at the time of their ratification or approval or in a subsequent notification. The Committee of Ministers shall determine from time to time in respect of which provisions such reports shall be requested and the form of the reports to be provided.

Article 23. Communication of Copies

1. Each Contracting Party shall communicate copies of its reports referred to in Articles 21 and 22 to such of its national organizations as are members of the

international organizations of employers and trade unions to be invited under Article 27, paragraph 2, to be represented at meetings of the Sub-committee of the Governmental Social Committee.

2. The Contracting Parties shall forward to the Secretary–General any comments on the said reports received from these national organizations, if so requested by them.

Article 24. Examination of the Reports

The reports sent to the Secretary–General in accordance with Articles 21 and 22 shall be examined by a Committee of Experts, who shall have also before them any comments forwarded to the Secretary–General in accordance with paragraph 2 of Article 23.

Article 25. Committee of Experts

1. The Committee of Experts shall consist of not more than seven members appointed by the Committee of Ministers from a list of independent experts of the highest integrity and of recognized competence in international social questions, nominated by the Contracting Parties.

2. The members of the Committee shall be appointed for a period of six years. They may be reappointed. However, of the members first appointed, the terms of office of two members shall expire at the end of four years.

3. The members whose terms of office are to expire at the end of the initial period of four years shall be chosen by lot by the Committee of Ministers immediately after the first appointment has been made.

4. A member of the Committee of Experts appointed to replace a member whose term of office has not expired shall hold office for the remainder of his predecessor's term.

Article 26. Participation of the International Labour Organization

The International Labour Organization shall be invited to nominate a representative to participate in a consultative capacity in the deliberations of the Committee of Experts.

Article 27. Sub–Committee of the Governmental Social Committee

1. The reports of the Contracting Parties and the conclusions of the Committee of Experts shall be submitted for examination to a Sub-committee of the Governmental Social Committee of the Council of Europe.

2. The Sub-committee shall be composed of one representative of each of the Contracting Parties. It shall invite no more than two international organizations of employers and no more than two international trade union organizations as it may designate to be represented as observers in a consultative capacity at its meetings. Moreover, it may consult no more than two representatives of international non-governmental organizations having consultative status with the Council of Europe, in respect of questions with which the organizations are particularly qualified to deal, such as social welfare, and the economic and social protection of the family.

3. The Sub-committee shall present to the Committee of Ministers a report containing its conclusions and append the report of the Committee of Experts.

Article 28. Consultative Assembly

The Secretary–General of the Council of Europe shall transmit to the Consultative Assembly the conclusions of the Committee of Experts. The Consultative Assembly shall communicate its views on these Conclusions to the Committee of Ministers.

Article 29. Committee of Ministers

By a majority of two-thirds of the members entitled to sit on the Committee, the Committee of Ministers may, on the basis of the report of the Sub-committee, and after consultation with the Consultative Assembly, make to each Contracting Party any necessary recommendations.

PART V

Article 30. Derogations in time of War or Public Emergency

1. In time of war or other public emergency threatening the life of the nation any Contracting Party may take measures derogating from its obligations under this Charter to the extent strictly required by the exigencies of the situation, provided that such measures are not inconsistent with its other obligations under international law.

2. Any Contracting Party which has availed itself of this right of derogation shall, within a reasonable lapse of time, keep the Secretary–General of the Council of Europe fully informed of the measures taken and of the reasons therefor. It shall likewise inform the Secretary–General when such measures have ceased to operate and the provisions of the Charter which it has accepted are again being fully executed.

3. The Secretary–General shall in turn inform other Contracting Parties and the Director–General of the International Labour Office of all communications received in accordance with paragraph 2 of this Article.

Article 31. Restrictions

1. The rights and principles set forth in Part I when effectively realized, and their effective exercise as provided for in Part II, shall not be subject to any restrictions or limitations not specified in those Parts, except such as are prescribed by law and are necessary in a democratic society for the protection of the rights and freedoms of others or for the protection of public interest, national security, public health, or morals.

2. The restrictions permitted under this Charter to the rights and obligations set forth herein shall not be applied for any purpose other than that for which they have been prescribed.

Article 32. Relations Between the Charter and Domestic Law or International Agreements

The provisions of this Charter shall not prejudice the provisions of domestic law or of any bilateral or multilateral treaties, conventions or agreements which are already in force, or may come into force, under which more favourable treatment would be accorded to the persons protected.

Article 33. Implementation by Collective Agreements

1. In member States where the provisions of paragraphs 1, 2, 3, 4 and 5 of Article 2, paragraphs 4, 6 and 7 of Article 7 and paragraphs 1, 2, 3, and 4 of Article 10 of Part II of this Charter are matters normally left to agreements between employers or employers' organizations and workers' organizations, or are normally carried out otherwise than by law, the undertakings of those paragraphs may be given and compliance with them shall be treated as effective if their provisions are applied through such agreements or other means to the great majority of the workers concerned.

2. In member States where these provisions are normally the subject of legislation, the undertakings concerned may likewise be given, and compliance with them

shall be regarded as effective if the provisions are applied by law to the great majority of the workers concerned.

* * *

Article 38. Appendix

The Appendix to this Charter shall form an integral part of it.

* * *

APPENDIX TO THE SOCIAL CHARTER

Scope of the Social Charter in Terms of Persons Protected

1. Without prejudice to Article 12, paragraph 4 and Article 13, paragraph 4, the persons covered by Articles 1 to 17 include foreigners only insofar as they are nationals of other Contracting Parties lawfully resident or working regularly within the territory of the Contracting Party concerned, subject to the understanding that these Articles are to be interpreted in the light of the provisions of Articles 18 and 19.

This interpretation would not prejudice the extension of similar facilities to other persons by any of the Contracting Parties.

2. Each Contracting Party will grant to refugees as defined in the Convention relating to the Status of Refugees, signed at Geneva on 28th July, 1951, and lawfully staying in its territory, treatment as favourable as possible, and in any case not less favourable than under the obligations accepted by the Contracting Party under the said Convention and under any other existing international instruments applicable to those refugees.

PART I AND PART II

Paragraph 18 and Article 18, Paragraph 1. It is understood that these provisions are not concerned with the question of entry into the territories of the Contracting Parties and do not prejudice the provisions of the European Convention on Establishment, signed at Paris on 13th December, 1955.

PART II

Article 1, Paragraph 2. This provision shall not be interpreted as prohibiting or authorizing any union security clause or practice.

Article 4, Paragraph 4. This provision shall be so understood as not to prohibit immediate dismissal for any serious offence.

Article 4, Paragraph 5. It is understood that a Contracting Party may give the undertaking required in this paragraph if the great majority of workers are not permitted to suffer deductions from wages either by law or through collective agreements or arbitration awards, the exceptions being those persons not so covered.

Article 6, Paragraph 4. It is understood that each Contracting Party may, insofar as it is concerned, regulate the exercise of the right to strike by law, provided that any further restriction than this might place on the right can be justified under the terms of Article 31.

Article 7, Paragraph 8. It is understood that a Contracting Party may give the undertaking required in this paragraph if it fulfills the spirit of the undertaking by providing by law that the great majority of persons under 18 years of age shall not be employed in night work.

* * *

Article 12, Paragraph 4. The words "and subject to the conditions laid down in such agreements" in the introduction to this paragraph are taken to imply *inter alia* that with regard to benefits which are available independently of any insurance contribution a Contracting Party may require the completion of a prescribed period of residence before granting such benefits to nationals of other Contracting Parties.

Article 13, Paragraph 4. Governments not Parties to the European Convention on Social and Medical Assistance may ratify the Social Charter in respect of this paragraph provided that they grant to nationals of other Contracting Parties a treatment which is in conformity with the provisions of the said Convention.

Article 19, Paragraph 6. For the purpose of this provision, the term "family of a foreign worker" is understood to mean at least his wife and dependent children under the age of 21 years.

PART III

It is understood that the Charter contains legal obligations of an international character, the application of which is submitted solely to the supervision provided for in Part IV thereof.

Article 20, Paragraph 1. It is understood that the "numbered paragraphs" may include Articles consisting of only one paragraph.

PART V

Article 30. The term "in time of war or other public emergency" shall be so understood as to cover also the *threat* of war.

3.14 CONVENTION ON OFFENSES AND CERTAIN OTHER ACTS COMMITTED ON BOARD AIRCRAFT.[a] Done at Tokyo, Sept. 14, 1963. Entered into force for the United States, Dec. 4, 1969. 20 U.T.S. 2941, T.I.A.S. No. 6768, 704 U.N.T.S. 219, *reprinted in 2 I.L.M. 1042 (1963)*

CHAPTER I

SCOPE OF THE CONVENTION

Article 1

1. This Convention shall apply in respect of:

(*a*) offences against penal law;

(*b*) acts which, whether or not they are offences, may or do jeopardize the safety of the aircraft or of persons or property therein or which jeopardize good order and discipline on board.

2. Except as provided in Chapter III, this Convention shall apply in respect of offences committed or acts done by a person on board any aircraft registered in a Contracting State, while that aircraft is in flight or on the surface of the high seas or of any other area outside the territory of any State.

3. For the purposes of this Convention, an aircraft is considered to be in flight from the moment when power is applied for the purpose of take-off until the moment when the landing run ends.

4. This Convention shall not apply to aircraft used in military, customs or police services.

Article 2

Without prejudice to the provisions of Article 4 and except when the safety of the aircraft or of persons or property on board so requires, no provision of this Convention shall be interpreted as authorizing or requiring any action in respect of offences against penal laws of a political nature or those based on racial or religious discrimination.

CHAPTER II

JURISDICTION

Article 3

1. The State of registration of the aircraft is competent to exercise jurisdiction over offences and acts committed on board.

2. Each Contracting State shall take such measures as may be necessary to establish its jurisdiction as the State of registration over offences committed on board aircraft registered in such State.

3. This Convention does not exclude any criminal jurisdiction exercised in accordance with national law.

a. *See also* Basic Documents 3.27, 3.28, 3.30, 3.32, 3.33, 3.35, 3.42, and 3.43, *infra*.

Article 4

A Contracting State which is not the State of registration may not interfere with an aircraft in flight in order to exercise its criminal jurisdiction over an offence committed on board except in the following cases:

(*a*) the offence has effect on the territory of such State;

(*b*) the offence has been committed by or against a national or permanent resident of such State;

(*c*) the offence is against the security of such State;

(*d*) the offence consists of a breach of any rules or regulations relating to the flight or manœuvre of aircraft in force in such State;

(*e*) the exercise of jurisdiction is necessary to ensure the observance of any obligation of such State under a multilateral international agreement.

CHAPTER III

POWERS OF THE AIRCRAFT COMMANDER

Article 5

1. The provisions of this Chapter shall not apply to offences and acts committed or about to be committed by a person on board an aircraft in flight in the airspace of the State of registration or over the high seas or any other area outside the territory of any State unless the last point of take-off or the next point of intended landing is situated in a State other than that of registration, or the aircraft subsequently flies in the airspace of a State other than that of registration with such person still on board.

2. Notwithstanding the provisions of Article 1, paragraph 3, an aircraft shall for the purposes of this Chapter, be considered to be in flight at any time from the moment when all its external doors are closed following embarkation until the moment when any such door is opened for disembarkation. In the case of a forced landing, the provisions of this Chapter shall continue to apply with respect to offences and acts committed on board until competent authorities of a State take over the responsibility for the aircraft and for the persons and property on board.

Article 6

1. The aircraft commander may, when he has reasonable grounds to believe that a person has committed, or is about to commit, on board the aircraft, an offence or act contemplated in Article 1, paragraph 1, impose upon such person reasonable measures including restraint which are necessary:

(*a*) to protect the safety of the aircraft, or of persons or property therein; or

(*b*) to maintain good order and discipline on board; or

(*c*) to enable him to deliver such person to competent authorities or to disembark him in accordance with the provisions of this Chapter.

2. The aircraft commander may require or authorize the assistance of other crew members and may request or authorize, but not require, the assistance of passengers to restrain any person whom he is entitled to restrain. Any crew member or passenger may also take reasonable preventive measures without such authorization when he has reasonable grounds to believe that such action is immediately necessary to protect the safety of the aircraft, or of persons or property therein.

Article 7

1. Measures of restraint imposed upon a person in accordance with Article 6 shall not be continued beyond any point at which the aircraft lands unless:

(*a*) such point is in the territory of a non-Contracting State and its authorities refuse to permit disembarkation of that person or those measures have been imposed in accordance with Article 6, paragraph 1(*c*) in order to enable his delivery to competent authorities;

(*b*) the aircraft makes a forced landing and the aircraft commander is unable to deliver that person to competent authorities; or

(*c*) that person agrees to onward carriage under restraint.

2. The aircraft commander shall as soon as practicable, and if possible before landing in the territory of a State with a person on board who has been placed under restraint in accordance with the provisions of Article 6, notify the authorities of such State of the fact that a person on board is under restraint and of the reasons for such restraint.

Article 8

1. The aircraft commander may, in so far as it is necessary for the purpose of subparagraph (*a*) or (*b*) of paragraph 1 of Article 6, disembark in the territory of any State in which the aircraft lands any person who he has reasonable grounds to believe has committed, or is about to commit, on board the aircraft an act contemplated in Article 1, paragraph 1(*b*).

2. The aircraft commander shall report to the authorities of the State in which he disembarks any person pursuant to this Article, the fact of, and the reasons for, such disembarkation.

Article 9

1. The aircraft commander may deliver to the competent authorities of any Contracting State in the territory of which the aircraft lands any person who he has reasonable grounds to believe has committed on board the aircraft an act which, in his opinion, is a serious offence according to the penal law of the State of registration of the aircraft.

2. The aircraft commander shall as soon as practicable and if possible before landing in the territory of a Contracting State with a person on board whom the aircraft commander intends to deliver in accordance with the preceding paragraph, notify the authorities of such State of his intention to deliver such person and the reasons therefor.

3. The aircraft commander shall furnish the authorities to whom any suspected offender is delivered in accordance with the provisions of this Article with evidence and information which, under the law of the State of registration of the aircraft, are lawfully in his possession.

Article 10

For actions taken in accordance with this Convention, neither the aircraft commander, any other member of the crew, any passenger, the owner or operator of the aircraft, nor the person on whose behalf the flight was performed shall be held responsible in any proceeding on account of the treatment undergone by the person against whom the actions were taken.

CHAPTER IV

UNLAWFUL SEIZURE OF AIRCRAFT

Article 11

1. When a person on board has unlawfully committed by force or threat thereof an act of interference, seizure, or other wrongful exercise of control of an aircraft in flight or when such an act is about to be committed, Contracting States shall take all

appropriate measures to restore control of the aircraft to its lawful commander or to preserve his control of the aircraft.

2. In the cases contemplated in the preceding paragraph, the Contracting State in which the aircraft lands shall permit its passengers and crew to continue their journey as soon as practicable, and shall return the aircraft and its cargo to the persons lawfully entitled to possession.

CHAPTER V

POWERS AND DUTIES OF STATES

Article 12

Any Contracting State shall allow the commander of an aircraft registered in another Contracting State to disembark any person pursuant to Article 8, paragraph 1.

Article 13

1. Any Contracting State shall take delivery of any person whom the aircraft commander delivers pursuant to Article 9, paragraph 1.

2. Upon being satisfied that the circumstances so warrant, any Contracting State shall take custody or other measures to ensure the presence of any person suspected of an act contemplated in Article 11, paragraph 1 and of any person of whom it has taken delivery. The custody and other measures shall be as provided in the law of that State but may only be continued for such time as is reasonably necessary to enable any criminal or extradition proceedings to be instituted.

3. Any person in custody pursuant to the previous paragraph shall be assisted in communicating immediately with the nearest appropriate representative of the State of which he is a national.

4. Any Contracting State, to which a person is delivered pursuant to Article 9, paragraph 1, or in whose territory an aircraft lands following the commission of an act contemplated in Article 11, paragraph 1, shall immediately make a preliminary enquiry into the facts.

5. When a State, pursuant to this Article, has taken a person into custody, it shall immediately notify the State of registration of the aircraft and the State of nationality of the detained person and, if it considers it advisable, any other interested State of the fact that such person is in custody and of the circumstances which warrant his detention. The State which makes the preliminary enquiry contemplated in paragraph 4 of this Article shall promptly report its findings to the said States and shall indicate whether it intends to exercise jurisdiction.

Article 14

1. When any person has been disembarked in accordance with Article 8, paragraph 1, or delivered in accordance with Article 9, paragraph 1, or has disembarked after committing an act contemplated in Article 11, paragraph 1, and when such person cannot or does not desire to continue his journey and the State of landing refuses to admit him, that State may, if the person in question is not a national or permanent resident of that State, return him to the territory of the State of which he is a national or permanent resident or to the territory of the State in which he began his journey by air.

2. Neither disembarkation, nor delivery, nor the taking of custody or other measures contemplated in Article 13, paragraph 2, nor return of the person concerned, shall be considered as admission to the territory of the Contracting State concerned for the purpose of its law relating to entry or admission of persons and

nothing in this Convention shall affect the law of a Contracting State relating to the expulsion of persons from its territory.

Article 15

1. Without prejudice to Article 14, any person who has been disembarked in accordance with Article 8, paragraph 1, or delivered in accordance with Article 9, paragraph 1, or has disembarked after committing an act contemplated in Article 11, paragraph 1, and who desires to continue his journey shall be at liberty as soon as practicable to proceed to any destination of his choice unless his presence is required by the law of the State of landing for the purpose of extradition or criminal proceedings.

2. Without prejudice to its law as to entry and admission to, and extradition and expulsion from its territory, a Contracting State in whose territory a person has been disembarked in accordance with Article 8, paragraph 1, or delivered in accordance with Article 9, paragraph 1 or has disembarked and is suspected of having committed an act contemplated in Article 11, paragraph 1, shall accord to such person treatment which is no less favourable for his protection and security than that accorded to nationals of such Contracting State in like circumstances.

CHAPTER VI

OTHER PROVISIONS

Article 16

1. Offences committed on aircraft registered in a Contracting State shall be treated, for the purpose of extradition, as if they had been committed not only in the place in which they have occurred but also in the territory of the State of registration of the aircraft.

2. Without prejudice to the provisions of the preceding paragraph, nothing in this Convention shall be deemed to create an obligation to grant extradition.

Article 17

In taking any measures for investigation or arrest or otherwise exercising jurisdiction in connection with any offence committed on board an aircraft the Contracting States shall pay due regard to the safety and other interests of air navigation and shall so act as to avoid unnecessary delay of the aircraft, passengers, crew or cargo.

Article 18

If Contracting States establish joint air transport operating organizations or international operating agencies, which operate aircraft not registered in any one State those States shall, according to the circumstances of the case, designate the State among them which, for the purposes of this Convention, shall be considered as the State of registration and shall give notice thereof to the International Civil Aviation Organization which shall communicate the notice to all States Parties to this Convention.

* * *

Article 23

1. Any Contracting State may denounce this Convention by notification addressed to the International Civil Aviation Organization.

2. Denunciation shall take effect six months after the date of receipt by the International Civil Aviation Organization of the notification of denunciation.

Article 24

1. Any dispute between two or more Contracting States concerning the interpretation or application of this Convention which cannot be settled through negotiation, shall, at the request of one of them, be submitted to arbitration. If within six months from the date of the request for arbitration the Parties are unable to agree on the organization of the arbitration, any one of those Parties may refer the dispute to the International Court of Justice by request in conformity with the Statute of the Court.

2. Each State may at the time of signature or ratification of this Convention or accession thereto, declare that it does not consider itself bound by the preceding paragraph. The other Contracting States shall not be bound by the preceding paragraph with respect to any Contracting State having made such a reservation.

3. Any Contracting State having made a reservation in accordance with the preceding paragraph may at any time withdraw this reservation by notification to the International Civil Aviation Organization.

Article 25

Except as provided in Article 24 no reservation may be made to this Convention.

3.15 PROTOCOL (NO. IV) TO THE EUROPEAN CONVENTION FOR THE PROTECTION OF HUMAN RIGHTS AND FREEDOMS.[a] Done at Strasbourg, Sept. 16, 1963. Entered into force, May 2, 1968. Europ.T.S. No. 46

Article 1. No one shall be deprived of his liberty merely on the ground of inability to fulfil a contractual obligation.

Article 2. (1) Everyone lawfully within the territory of a State shall, within that territory, have the right to liberty of movement and freedom to choose his residence.

(2) Everyone shall be free to leave any country, including his own.

(3) No restrictions shall be placed on the exercise of these rights other than such as are in accordance with law and are necessary in a democratic society in the interests of national security or public safety for the maintenance of "ordre public," for the prevention of crime, for the protection of the rights and freedoms of others.

(4) The rights set forth in paragraph 1 may also be subject, in particular areas, to restrictions imposed in accordance with law and justified by the public interest in a democratic society.

Article 3. (1) No one shall be expelled, by means either of an individual or of a collective measure, from the territory of the State of which he is a national.

(2) No one shall be deprived of the right to enter the territory of the State of which he is a national.

Article 4. Collective expulsion of aliens is prohibited.

* * *

a. This Protocol is one of five protocols supplementing the European Convention for the Protection of Human Rights and Fundamental Freedoms (Basic Document 3.4). *See also* Basic Document 3.6, *supra.*

3.16 INTERNATIONAL CONVENTION ON THE ELIMINATION OF ALL FORMS OF RACIAL DISCRIMINATION. Done at New York, Mar. 7, 1966. Entered into force, Jan. 4, 1969. 660 U.N.T.S. 195, *reprinted in* 5 I.L.M. 352 (1966)

PART I

Article 1. (1) In this Convention, the term "racial discrimination" shall mean any distinction, exclusion, restriction or preference based on race, colour, descent, or national or ethnic origin which has the purpose or effect of nullifying or impairing the recognition, enjoyment or exercise, on an equal footing, of human rights and fundamental freedoms in the political, economic, social, cultural or any other field of public life.

(2) This Convention shall not apply to distinctions, exclusions, restrictions or preferences made by a State Party to this Convention between citizens and noncitizens.

(3) Nothing in this Convention may be interpreted as affecting in any way the legal provisions of States Parties concerning nationality, citizenship or naturalization, provided that such provisions do not discriminate against any particular nationality.

(4) Special measures taken for the sole purpose of securing adequate advancement of certain racial or ethnic groups or individuals requiring such protection as may be necessary in order to ensure such groups or individuals equal enjoyment or exercise of human rights and fundamental freedoms shall not be deemed racial discrimination, provided, however, that such measures do not, as a consequence, lead to the maintenance of separate rights for different racial groups and that they shall not be continued after the objectives for which they were taken have been achieved.

Article 2. (1) States Parties condemn racial discrimination and undertake to pursue by all appropriate means and without delay a policy of eliminating racial discrimination in all its forms and promoting understanding among all races, and, to this end:

(a) Each State Party undertakes to engage in no act or practice of racial discrimination against persons, groups of persons or institutions and to ensure that all public authorities and public institutions, national and local, shall act in conformity with this obligation;

(b) Each State Party undertakes not to sponsor, defend or support racial discrimination by any persons or organizations;

(c) Each State Party shall take effective measures to review governmental, national and local policies, and to amend, rescind or nullify any laws and regulations which have the effect of creating or perpetuating racial discrimination wherever it exists;

(d) Each State Party shall prohibit and bring to an end, by all appropriate means, including legislation as required by circumstances, racial discrimination by any persons, group or organization;

(e) Each State Party undertakes to encourage, where appropriate, integrationist multi-racial organizations and movements and other means of eliminating barriers between races, and to discourage anything which tends to strengthen racial division.

(2) States Parties shall, when the circumstances so warrant, take, in the social, economic, cultural and other fields, special and concrete measures to ensure the

adequate development and protection of certain racial groups or individuals belonging to them, for the purpose of guaranteeing them the full and equal enjoyment of human rights and fundamental freedoms. These measures shall in no case entail as a consequence the maintenance of unequal or separate rights for different racial groups after the objectives for which they were taken have been achieved.

Article 3. States Parties particularly condemn racial segregation and *apartheid* and undertake to prevent, prohibit and eradicate all practices of this nature in territories under their jurisdiction.

Article 4. States Parties condemn all propaganda and all organizations which are based on ideas or theories of superiority of one race or group of persons of one colour or ethnic origin, or which attempt to justify or promote racial hatred and discrimination in any form, and undertake to adopt immediate and positive measures designed to eradicate all incitement to, or acts of, such discrimination and, to this end, with due regard to the principles embodied in the Universal Declaration of Human Rights and the rights expressly set forth in article 5 of this Convention, *inter alia:*

(a) Shall declare an offence punishable by law all dissemination of ideas based on racial superiority or hatred, incitement to racial discrimination, as well as all acts of violence or incitement to such acts against any race or group of persons of another colour or ethnic origin, and also the provision of any assistance to racist activities, including the financing thereof;

(b) Shall declare illegal and prohibit organizations, and also organized and all other propaganda activities, which promote and incite racial discrimination, and shall recognize participation in such organizations or activities as an offence punishable by law;

(c) Shall not permit public authorities or public institutions, national or local, to promote or incite racial discrimination.

Article 5. In compliance with the fundamental obligations laid down in article 2 of this Convention, States Parties undertake to prohibit and to eliminate racial discrimination in all its forms and to guarantee the right of everyone, without distinction as to race, colour, or national or ethnic origin, to equality before the law, notably in the enjoyment of the following rights:

(a) The right to equal treatment before the tribunals and all other organs administering justice;

(b) The right to security of person and protection by the State against violence or bodily harm, whether inflicted by government officials or by any individual, group or institution;

(c) Political rights, in particular the rights to participate in elections—to vote and to stand for election—on the basis of universal and equal suffrage, to take part in the Government as well as in the conduct of public affairs at any level and to have equal access to public service;

(d) Other civil rights, in particular:

(i) The right to freedom of movement and residence within the border of the State;

(ii) The right to leave any country, including one's own, and to return to one's own country;

(iii) The right to nationality;

(iv) The right to marriage and choice of spouse;

(v) The right to own property alone as well as in association with others;

(vi) The right to inherit;

(vii) The right to freedom of thought, conscience and religion;

(viii) The right to freedom of opinion and expression;

(ix) The right to freedom of peaceful assembly and association;

(e) Economic, social and cultural rights, in particular:

(i) The rights to work, to free choice of employment, to just and favourable conditions of work, to protection against unemployment, to equal pay for equal work, to just and favourable remuneration;

(ii) The right to form and join trade unions;

(iii) The right to housing;

(iv) The right to public health, medical care, social security and social services;

(v) The right to education and training;

(vi) The right to equal participation in cultural activities;

(f) The right of access to any place or service intended for use by the general public, such as transport, hotels, restaurants, cafés, theatres and parks.

Article 6. States Parties shall assure to everyone within their jurisdiction effective protection and remedies, through the competent national tribunals and other State institutions, against any acts of racial discrimination which violate his human rights and fundamental freedoms contrary to this Convention, as well as the right to seek from such tribunals just and adequate reparation or satisfaction for any damage suffered as a result of such discrimination.

Article 7. States Parties undertake to adopt immediate and effective measures, particularly in the fields of teaching, education, culture and information, with a view to combating prejudices which lead to racial discrimination and to promoting understanding, tolerance and friendship among nations and racial or ethnical groups, as well as to propagating the purposes and principles of the Charter of the United Nations, the Universal Declaration of Human Rights, the United Nations Declaration on the Elimination of All Forms of Racial Discrimination, and this Convention.

PART II

Article 8. (1) There shall be established a Committee on the Elimination of Racial Discrimination (hereinafter referred to as the Committee) consisting of eighteen experts of high moral standing and acknowledged impartiality elected by States Parties from among their nationals, who shall serve in their personal capacity, consideration being given to equitable geographical distribution and to the representation of the different forms of civilization as well as of the principal legal systems.

(2) The members of the Committee shall be elected by secret ballot from a list of persons nominated by the States Parties. Each State Party may nominate one person from among its own nationals.

* * *

Article 9. (1) States Parties undertake to submit to the Secretary–General of the United Nations, for consideration by the Committee, a report on the legislative, judicial, administrative or other measures which they have adopted and which give effect to the provisions of this Convention: (a) within one year after the entry into force of the Convention for the State concerned; and (b) thereafter every two years and whenever the Committee so requests. The Committee may request further information from the States Parties.

(2) The Committee shall report annually, through the Secretary–General, to the General Assembly of the United Nations on its activities and may make suggestions and general recommendations based on the examination of the reports and information received from the States Parties. Such suggestions and general recommenda-

tions shall be recorded to the General Assembly together with comments, if any, from States Parties.

* * *

Article 11. (1) If a State Party considers that another State Party is not giving effect to the provisions of this Convention, it may bring the matter to the attention of the Committee. The Committee shall then transmit the communication to the State Party concerned. Within three months, the receiving State shall submit to the Committee written explanations or statements clarifying the matter and the remedy, if any, that may have been taken by that State.

(2) If the matter is not adjusted to the satisfaction of both parties, either by bilateral negotiations or by any other procedure open to them, within six months after the receipt by the receiving State of the initial communication, either State shall have the right to refer the matter again to the Committee by notifying the Committee and also the other State.

(3) The Committee shall deal with a matter referred to it in accordance with paragraph 2 of this article after it has ascertained that all available domestic remedies have been invoked and exhausted in the case, in conformity with the generally recognized principles of international law. This shall not be the rule where the application of the remedies is unreasonably prolonged.

(4) In any matter referred to it, the Committee may call upon the States Parties concerned to supply any other relevant information.

(5) When any matter arising out of this article is being considered by the Committee, the States Parties concerned shall be entitled to send a representative to take part in the proceedings of the Committee, without voting rights, while the matter is under consideration.

Article 12. (1)(a) After the Committee has obtained and collated all the information it deems necessary, the Chairman shall appoint an *ad hoc* Conciliation Commission (hereinafter referred to as the Commission) comprising five persons who may or may not be members of the Committee. The members of the Commission shall be appointed with the unanimous consent of the parties to the dispute, and its good offices shall be made available to the States concerned with a view to an amicable solution of the matter on the basis of respect for this Convention.

(b) If the States Parties to the dispute fail to reach agreement within three months on all or part of the composition of the Commission, the members of the Commission not agreed upon by the States Parties to the dispute shall be elected by secret ballot by a two-thirds majority vote of the Committee from among its own members.

(2) The members of the Commission shall serve in their personal capacity. They shall not be nationals of the States Parties to the dispute or of a State not Party to this Convention.

* * *

Article 13. (1) When the Commission has fully considered the matter, it shall prepare and submit to the Chairman of the Committee a report embodying its findings on all questions of fact relevant to the issue between the parties and containing such recommendations as it may think proper for the amicable solution of the dispute.

* * *

Article 14. (1) A State Party may at any time declare that it recognizes the competence of the Committee to receive and consider communications from individuals or groups of individuals within its jurisdiction claiming to be victims of a violation by that State Party of any of the rights set forth in this Convention. No communication shall be received by the Committee if it concerns a State Party which has not made such a declaration.

(2) Any State Party which makes a declaration as provided for in paragraph 1 of this article may establish or indicate a body within its national legal order which shall be competent to receive and consider petitions from individuals and groups of individuals within its jurisdiction who claim to be victims of a violation of any of the rights set forth in this Convention and who have exhausted other available local remedies.

* * *

(5) In the event of failure to obtain satisfaction from the body established or indicated in accordance with paragraph 2 of this article, the petitioner shall have the right to communicate the matter to the Committee within six months.

(6)(a) The Committee shall confidentially bring any communication referred to it to the attention of the State Party alleged to be violating any provision of this Convention, but the identity of the individual or groups of individuals concerned shall not be revealed without his or their express consent. The Committee shall not receive anonymous communications.

(b) Within three months, the receiving State shall submit to the Committee written explanations or statements clarifying the matter and the remedy, if any, that may have been taken by that State.

(7)(a) The Committee shall consider communications in the light of all information made available to it by the State Party concerned and by the petitioner. The Committee shall not consider any communication from a petitioner unless it has ascertained that the petitioner has exhausted all available domestic remedies. However, this shall not be the rule where the application of the remedies is unreasonably prolonged.

(b) The Committee shall forward its suggestions and recommendations, if any, to the State Party concerned and to the petitioner.

(8) The Committee shall include in its annual report a summary of such communications and, where appropriate, a summary of the explanations and statements of the States Parties concerned and of its own suggestions and recommendations.

* * *

3.17 U.N. SECURITY COUNCIL RESOLUTION 232,[a] Dec. 16, 1966, U.N. SCOR (1340th Mtg.) 7, U.N.Doc. S/INF/21/Rev. 1 (1966), *reprinted in* 6 I.L.M. 141 (1967)

THE SECURITY COUNCIL,

Reaffirming its resolutions 216 (1965) of 12 November 1965, 217 (1965) of 20 November 1965 and 221 (1966) of 9 April 1966, and in particular its appeal to all States to do their utmost in order to break off economic relations with Southern Rhodesia.

Deeply concerned that the Council's efforts so far and the measures taken by the administering Power have failed to bring the rebellion in Southern Rhodesia to an end.

Reaffirming that to the extent not superseded in this resolution, the measures provided for in resolution 217 (1965) of 20 November 1965, as well as those initiated by Member States in implementation of that resolution, shall continue in effect,

Acting in accordance with Articles 39 and 41 of the United Nations Charter.

1. *Determines* that the present situation in Southern Rhodesia constitutes a threat to international peace and security;

2. *Decides* that all States Members of the United Nations shall prevent:

(a) the import into their territories of asbestos, iron ore, chrome, pig-iron, sugar, tobacco, copper, meat and meat products and hides, skins and leather originating in Southern Rhodesia and exported therefrom after the date of this resolution;

(b) any activities by their nationals or in their territories which promote or are calculated to promote the export of these commodities from Southern Rhodesia and any dealings by their nationals or in their territories in any of these commodities originating in Southern Rhodesia and exported therefrom after the date of this resolution, including in particular any transfer of funds to Southern Rhodesia for the purposes of such activities or dealings;

(c) shipment in vessels or aircraft of their registration of any of these commodities originating in Southern Rhodesia and exported therefrom after the date of this resolution;

(d) any activities by their nationals or in their territories which promote or are calculated to promote the sale or shipment to Southern Rhodesia of arms, ammunition of all types, military aircraft, military vehicles, and equipment and materials for the manufacture and maintenance of arms and ammunition in Southern Rhodesia;

(e) any activities by their nationals or in their territories which promote or are calculated to promote the supply to Southern Rhodesia of all other aircraft and motor vehicles and of equipment and materials for the manufacture, assembly or maintenance of aircraft and motor vehicles in Southern Rhodesia: the shipment in vessels and aircraft of their registration of any such goods destined for Southern Rhodesia: and any activities by their nationals or in their territories which promote or are calculated to promote the manufacture or assembly of aircraft or motor vehicles in Southern Rhodesia;

a. *See also* Basic Document 3.24, *infra.*

(f) participation in their territories or territories under their administration or in land or air transport facilities or by their nationals or vessels of their registration in the supply of oil or oil products to Southern Rhodesia;

notwithstanding any contracts entered into or licenses granted before the date of this resolution;

3. *Reminds* Member States that the failure or refusal by any of them to implement the present resolution shall constitute a violation of Article 25 of the Charter;

4. *Reaffirms* the inalienable rights of the people of Southern Rhodesia to freedom and independence in accordance with the Declaration on the Granting of Independence to Colonial Countries and Peoples contained in General Assembly resolution 1514(XV); and recognizes the legitimacy of their struggle to secure the enjoyment of their rights as set forth in the Charter of the United Nations;

5. *Calls upon* all States not to render financial or other economic aid to the illegal racist régime in Southern Rhodesia;

6. *Calls upon* all States Members of the United Nations to carry out this decision of the Security Council in accordance with Article 25 of the United Nations Charter;

7. *Urges,* having regard to the principles stated in Article 2 of the United Nations Charter, States not Members of the United Nations to act in accordance with the provisions of paragraph 2 of the present resolution;

8. *Calls upon* States Members of the United Nations or of the specialized agencies to report to the Secretary–General the measures each has taken in accordance with the provisions of paragraph 2 of the present resolution;

9. *Requests* the Secretary–General to report to the Council on the progress of the implementation of the present resolution, the first report to be submitted not later than 1 March 1967;

10. *Decides* to keep this item on its agenda for further action as appropriate in the light of developments.

3.18 INTERNATIONAL COVENANT ON ECONOMIC, SOCIAL AND CULTURAL RIGHTS. Done at New York, Dec. 16, 1966. Entered into force, Jan. 3, 1976. U.N.G.A. Res. 2200 (XXI), 21 U.N. GAOR, Supp. (No. 16) 49, U.N. Doc. A/6316 (1967), *reprinted in* 6 I.L.M. 360 (1967)

PART I

Article 1. (1) All peoples have the right of self-determination. By virtue of that right they freely determine their political status and freely pursue their economic, social and cultural development.

(2) All peoples may, for their own ends, freely dispose of their natural wealth and resources without prejudice to any obligations arising out of international economic co-operation, based upon the principle of mutual benefit, and international law. In no case may a people be deprived of its own means of subsistence.

(3) The States Parties to the present Covenant, including those having responsibility for the administration of Non–Self–Governing and Trust Territories, shall promote the realization of the right of self-determination, and shall respect that right, in conformity with the provisions of the Charter of the United Nations.

PART II

Article 2. (1) Each State Party to the present Covenant undertakes to take steps, individually and through international assistance and co-operation, especially economic and technical, to the maximum of its available resources, with a view to achieving progressively the full realization of the rights recognized in the present Covenant by all appropriate means, including particularly the adoption of legislative measures.

(2) The States Parties to the present Covenant undertake to guarantee that the rights enunciated in the present Covenant will be exercised without discrimination of any kind as to race, colour, sex, language, religion, political or other opinion, national or social origin, property, birth or other status.

(3) Developing countries, with due regard to human rights and their national economy, may determine to what extent they would guarantee the economic rights recognized in the present Covenant to non-nationals.

Article 3. The States Parties to the present Covenant undertake to ensure the equal right of men and women to the enjoyment of all economic, social and cultural rights set forth in the present Covenant.

Article 4. The States Parties to the present Covenant recognize that, in the enjoyment of those rights provided by the State in conformity with the present Covenant, the State may subject such rights only to such limitations as are determined by law only in so far as this may be compatible with the nature of these rights and solely for the purpose of promoting the general welfare in a democratic society.

Article 5. (1) Nothing in the present Covenant may be interpreted as implying for any State, group or person any right to engage in any activity or to perform any act aimed at the destruction of any of the rights or freedoms recognized herein, or at their limitation to a greater extent than is provided for in the present Covenant.

(2) No restriction upon or derogation from any of the fundamental human rights recognized or existing in any country in virtue of law, conventions, regulations or custom shall be admitted on the pretext that the present Covenant does not recognize such rights or that it recognizes them to a lesser extent.

PART III

Article 6. (1) The States Parties to the present Covenant recognize the right to work, which includes the right of everyone to the opportunity to gain his living by work which he freely chooses or accepts, and will take appropriate steps to safeguard this right.

(2) The steps to be taken by a State Party to the present Covenant to achieve the full realization of this right shall include technical and vocational guidance and training programmes, policies and techniques to achieve steady economic, social and cultural development and full and productive employment under conditions safeguarding fundamental political and economic freedoms to the individual.

Article 7. The States Parties to the present Covenant recognize the right of everyone to the enjoyment of just and favourable conditions of work which ensure, in particular:

(a) Remuneration which provides all workers, as a minimum, with:

(i) Fair wages and equal remuneration for work of equal value without distinction of any kind, in particular women being guaranteed conditions of work not inferior to those enjoyed by men, with equal pay for equal work;

(ii) A decent living for themselves and their families in accordance with the provisions of the present Covenant;

(b) Safe and healthy working conditions;

(c) Equal opportunity for everyone to be promoted in his employment to an appropriate higher level, subject to no considerations other than those of seniority and competence;

(d) Rest, leisure and reasonable limitation of working hours and periodic holidays with pay, as well as remuneration for public holidays.

Article 8. (1) The States Parties to the present Covenant undertake to ensure:

(a) The right of everyone to form trade unions and join the trade union of his choice, subject only to the rules of the organization concerned, for the promotion and protection of his economic and social interests. No restrictions may be placed on the exercise of this right other than those prescribed by law and which are necessary in a democratic society in the interests of national security or public order or for the protection of the rights and freedoms of others;

(b) The right of trade unions to establish national federations or confederations and the right of the latter to form or join international trade-union organizations;

(c) The right of trade unions to function freely subject to no limitations other than those prescribed by law and which are necessary in a democratic society in the interests of national security or public order or for the protection of the rights and freedoms of others;

(d) The right to strike, provided that it is exercised in conformity with the laws of the particular country.

(2) This article shall not prevent the imposition of lawful restrictions on the exercise of these rights by members of the armed forces or of the police or of the administration of the State.

(3) Nothing in this article shall authorize States Parties to the International Labour Organisation Convention of 1948 concerning Freedom of Association and Protection of the Right to Organize to take legislative measures which would prejudice, or apply the law in such a manner as would prejudice, the guarantees provided for in that Convention.

Article 9. The States Parties to the present Covenant recognize the right of everyone to social security, including social insurance.

Article 10. The States Parties to the present Covenant recognize that:

(1) The widest possible protection and assistance should be accorded to the family, which is the natural and fundamental group unit of society, particularly for its establishment and while it is responsible for the care and education of dependent children. Marriage must be entered into with the free consent of the intending spouses.

(2) Special protection should be accorded to mothers during a reasonable period before and after childbirth. During such period working mothers should be accorded paid leave or leave with adequate social security benefits.

(3) Special measures of protection and assistance should be taken on behalf of all children and young persons without any discrimination for reasons of parentage or other conditions. Children and young persons should be protected from economic and social exploitation. Their employment in work harmful to their morals or health or dangerous to life or likely to hamper their normal development should be punishable by law. States should also set age limits below which the paid employment of child labour should be prohibited and punishable by law.

Article 11. (1) The States Parties to the present Covenant recognize the right of everyone to an adequate standard of living for himself and his family, including adequate food, clothing and housing, and to the continuous improvement of living conditions. The States Parties will take appropriate steps to ensure the realization of this right, recognizing to this effect the essential importance of international co-operation based on free consent.

(2) The States Parties to the present Covenant, recognizing the fundamental right of everyone to be free from hunger, shall take, individually and through international co-operation, the measures, including specific programmes, which are needed:

(a) To improve methods of production, conservation and distribution of food by making full use of technical and scientific knowledge, by disseminating knowledge of the principles of nutrition and by developing or reforming agrarian systems in such a way as to achieve the most efficient development and utilization of natural resources;

(b) Taking into account the problems of both food-importing and food-exporting countries, to ensure an equitable distribution of world food supplies in relation to need.

Article 12. (1) The States Parties to the present Covenant recognize the right of everyone to the enjoyment of the highest attainable standard of physical and mental health.

(2) The steps to be taken by the States Parties to the present Covenant to achieve the full realization of this right shall include those necessary for:

(a) The provision for the reduction of the stillbirth-rate and of infant mortality and for the healthy development of the child;

(b) The improvement of all aspects of environmental and industrial hygiene;

(c) The prevention, treatment and control of epidemic, endemic, occupational and other diseases;

(d) The creation of conditions which would assure to all medical service and medical attention in the event of sickness.

Article 13. (1) The States Parties to the present Covenant recognize the right of everyone to education. They agree that education shall be directed to the full development of the human personality and the sense of its dignity, and shall strengthen the respect for human rights and fundamental freedoms. They further agree that education shall enable all persons to participate effectively in a free society, promote understanding, tolerance and friendship among all nations and all racial, ethnic or religious groups, and further the activities of the United Nations for the maintenance of peace.

(2) The States Parties to the present Covenant recognize that, with a view to achieving the full realization of this right:

(a) Primary education shall be compulsory and available free to all;

(b) Secondary education in its different forms, including technical and vocational secondary education, shall be made generally available and accessible to all by every appropriate means, and in particular by the progressive introduction of free education;

(c) Higher education shall be made equally accessible to all, on the basis of capacity, by every appropriate means, and in particular by the progressive introduction of free education;

(d) Fundamental education shall be encouraged or intensified as far as possible for those persons who have not received or completed the whole period of their primary education;

(e) The development of a system of schools at all levels shall be actively pursued, an adequate fellowship system shall be established, and the material conditions of teaching staff shall be continuously improved.

(3) The States Parties to the present Covenant undertake to have respect for the liberty of parents and, when applicable, legal guardians to choose for their children schools, other than those established by the public authorities, which conform to such minimum educational standards as may be laid down or approved by the State and to ensure the religious and moral education of their children in conformity with their own convictions.

(4) No part of this article shall be construed so as to interfere with the liberty of individuals and bodies to establish and direct educational institutions, subject always to the observance of the principles set forth in paragraph 1 of this article and to the requirement that the education given in such institutions shall conform to such minimum standards as may be laid down by the State.

Article 14. Each State Party to the present Covenant which, at the time of becoming a Party, has not been able to secure in its metropolitan territory or other territories under its jurisdiction compulsory primary education, free of charge, undertakes, within two years, to work out and adopt a detailed plan of action for the progressive implementation, within a reasonable number of years, to be fixed in the plan, of the principle of compulsory education free of charge for all.

Article 15. (1) The States Parties to the present Covenant recognize the right of everyone:

(a) To take part in cultural life;

(b) To enjoy the benefits of scientific progress and its applications;

(c) To benefit from the protection of the moral and material interests resulting from any scientific, literary or artistic production of which he is the author.

(2) The steps to be taken by the States Parties to the present Covenant to achieve the full realization of this right shall include those necessary for the conservation, the development and the diffusion of science and culture.

(3) The States Parties to the present Covenant undertake to respect the freedom indispensable for scientific research and creative activity.

(4) The States Parties to the present Covenant recognize the benefits to be derived from the encouragement and development of international contacts and co-operation in the scientific and cultural fields.

PART IV

Article 16. (1) The States Parties to the present Covenant undertake to submit in conformity with this part of the Covenant reports on the measures which they have adopted and the progress made in achieving the observance of the rights recognized herein.

(2)(a) All reports shall be submitted to the Secretary–General of the United Nations, who shall transmit copies to the Economic and Social Council for consideration in accordance with the provisions of the present Covenant.

(b) The Secretary–General of the United Nations shall also transmit to the specialized agencies copies of the reports, or any relevant parts therefrom, from States Parties to the present Covenant which are also members of these specialized agencies in so far as these reports, or parts therefrom, relate to any matters which fall within the responsibilities of the said agencies in accordance with their constitutional instruments.

* * *

Article 19. The Economic and Social Council may transmit to the Commission on Human Rights for study and general recommendation or, as appropriate, for information the reports concerning human rights submitted by States in accordance with articles 16 and 17, and those concerning human rights submitted by the specialized agencies in accordance with article 18.[a]

* * *

Article 21. The Economic and Social Council may submit from time to time to the General Assembly reports with recommendations of a general nature and a summary of the information received from the States Parties to the present Covenant and the specialized agencies on the measures taken and the progress made in achieving general observance of the rights recognized in the present Covenant.

Article 22. The Economic and Social Council may bring to the attention of other organs of the United Nations, their subsidiary organs and specialized agencies concerned with furnishing technical assistance any matters arising out of the reports referred to in this part of the present Covenant which may assist such bodies in deciding, each within its field of competence, on the advisability of international measures likely to contribute to the effective progressive implementation of the present Covenant.

Article 23. The State Parties to the present Covenant agree that international action for the achievement of the rights recognized in the present Covenant includes such methods as the conclusion of conventions, the adoption of recommendations, the furnishing of technical assistance and the holding of regional meetings and technical meetings for the purpose of consultation and study organized in conjunction with the Governments concerned.

Article 24. Nothing in the present Covenant shall be interpreted as impairing the provisions of the Charter of the United Nations and of the constitutions of the specialized agencies which define the respective responsibilities of the various organs of the United Nations and of the specialized agencies in regard to the matters dealt with in the present Covenant.

Article 25. Nothing in the present Covenant shall be interpreted as impairing the inherent right of all peoples to enjoy and utilize fully and freely their natural wealth and resources.

* * *

a. Omitted here.

3.19 INTERNATIONAL COVENANT ON CIVIL AND POLITICAL RIGHTS.[a] Done at New York, Dec. 16, 1966. Entered into force, Mar. 23, 1976. U.N.G.A. Res. 2200 (XXI), 21 U.N. GAOR, Supp. (No. 16) 52, U.N.Doc. A/6316 (1967), *reprinted in* 6 I.L.M. 368 (1967)

PART I

Article 1. (1) All peoples have the right of self-determination. By virtue of that right they freely determine their political status and freely pursue their economic, social and cultural development.

(2) All peoples may, for their own ends, freely dispose of their natural wealth and resources without prejudice to any obligations arising out of international economic co-operation, based upon the principle of mutual benefit, and international law. In no case may a people be deprived of its own means of subsistence.

(3) The States Parties to the present Covenant, including those having responsibility for the administration of Non-Self-Governing and Trust Territories, shall promote the realization of the right of self-determination, and shall respect that right, in conformity with the provisions of the Charter of the United Nations.

PART II

Article 2. (1) Each State Party to the present Covenant undertakes to respect and to ensure to all individuals within its territory and subject to its jurisdiction the rights recognized in the present Covenant, without distinction of any kind, such as race, colour, sex, language, religion, political or other opinion, national or social origin, property, birth or other status.

(2) Where not already provided for by existing legislative or other measures, each State Party to the present Covenant undertakes to take the necessary steps, in accordance with its constitutional processes and with the provisions of the present Covenant, to adopt such legislative or other measures as may be necessary to give effect to the rights recognized in the present Covenant.

(3) Each State Party to the present Covenant undertakes:

(a) To ensure that any person whose rights or freedoms as herein recognized are violated shall have an effective remedy, notwithstanding that the violation has been committed by persons acting in an official capacity;

(b) To ensure that any person claiming such a remedy shall have his right thereto determined by competent judicial, administrative or legislative authorities, or by any other competent authority provided for by the legal system of the State, and to develop the possibilities of judicial remedy;

(c) To ensure that the competent authorities shall enforce such remedies when granted.

Article 3. The States Parties to the present Covenant undertake to ensure the equal right of men and women to the enjoyment of all civil and political rights set forth in the present Covenant.

Article 4. (1) In time of public emergency which threatens the life of the nation and the existence of which is officially proclaimed, the State Parties to the present Covenant may take measures derogating from their obligations under the present Covenant to the extent strictly required by the exigencies of the situation, provided that such measures are not inconsistent with their other obligations under interna-

a. *See also* Basic Document 3.20, *infra.*

tional law and do not involve discrimination solely on the ground of race, colour, sex, language, religion or social origin.

(2) No derogation from articles 6, 7, 8 (paragraphs 1 and 2), 11, 15, 16 and 18 may be made under this provision.

(3) Any State Party to the present Covenant availing itself of the right of derogation shall immediately inform the other States Parties to the present Covenant, through the intermediary of the Secretary–General of the United Nations, of the provisions from which it has derogated and of the reasons by which it was actuated. A further communication shall be made, through the same intermediary, on the date on which it terminates such derogation.

Article 5. (1) Nothing in the present Covenant may be interpreted as implying for any State, group or person any right to engage in any activity or perform any act aimed at the destruction of any of the rights and freedoms recognized herein or at their limitation to a greater extent than is provided for in the present Covenant.

(2) There shall be no restriction upon or derogation from any of the fundamental human rights recognized or existing in any State Party to the present Covenant pursuant to law, conventions, regulations or custom on the pretext that the present Covenant does not recognize such rights or that it recognizes them to a lesser extent.

PART III

Article 6. (1) Every human being has the inherent right to life. This right shall be protected by law. No one shall be arbitrarily deprived of his life.

(2) In countries which have not abolished the death penalty, sentence of death may be imposed only for the most serious crimes in accordance with the law in force at the time of the commission of the crime and not contrary to the provisions of the present Covenant and to the Convention on the Prevention and Punishment of the Crime of Genocide. This penalty can only be carried out pursuant to a final judgment rendered by a competent court.

(3) When deprivation of life constitutes the crime of genocide, it is understood that nothing in this article shall authorize any State Party to the present Covenant to derogate in any way from any obligation assumed under the provisions of the Convention on the Prevention and Punishment of the Crime of Genocide.

(4) Anyone sentenced to death shall have the right to seek pardon or commutation of the sentence. Amnesty, pardon or commutation of the sentence of death may be granted in all cases.

(5) Sentence of death shall not be imposed for crimes committed by persons below eighteen years of age and shall not be carried out on pregnant women.

(6) Nothing in this article shall be invoked to delay or to prevent the abolition of capital punishment by any State Party to the present Covenant.

Article 7. No one shall be subjected to torture or to cruel, inhuman or degrading treatment or punishment. In particular, no one shall be subjected without his free consent to medical or scientific experimentation.

Article 8. (1) No one shall be held in slavery; slavery and slave-trade in all their forms shall be prohibited.

(2) No one shall be held in servitude.

(3)(a) No one shall be required to perform forced or compulsory labour;

(b) Paragraph 3(a) shall not be held to preclude, in countries where imprisonment with hard labour may be imposed as a punishment for a crime, the performance of hard labour in pursuance of a sentence to such punishment by a competent court;

(c) For the purpose of this paragraph the term "forced or compulsory labour" shall not include:

(i) Any work or service, not referred to in sub-paragraph (b), normally required of a person who is under detention in consequence of a lawful order of a court, or of a person during conditional release from such detention;

(ii) Any service of a military character and, in countries where conscientious objection is recognized, any national service required by law of conscientious objectors;

(iii) Any service exacted in cases of emergency or calamity threatening the life or well-being of the community;

(iv) Any work or service which forms part of normal civil obligations.

Article 9. (1) Everyone has the right to liberty and security of person. No one shall be subjected to arbitrary arrest or detention. No one shall be deprived of his liberty except on such grounds and in accordance with such procedure as are established by law.

(2) Anyone who is arrested shall be informed, at the time of arrest, of the reasons for his arrest and shall be promptly informed of any charges against him.

(3) Anyone arrested or detained on a criminal charge shall be brought promptly before a judge or other officer authorized by law to exercise judicial power and shall be entitled to trial within a reasonable time or to release. It shall not be the general rule that persons awaiting trial shall be detained in custody, but release may be subject to guarantees to appear for trial, at any other stage of the judicial proceedings, and, should occasion arise, for execution of the judgment.

(4) Anyone who is deprived of his liberty by arrest or detention shall be entitled to take proceedings before a court, in order that that court may decide without delay on the lawfulness of his detention and order his release if the detention is not lawful.

(5) Anyone who has been the victim of unlawful arrest or detention shall have an enforceable right to compensation.

Article 10. (1) All persons deprived of their liberty shall be treated with humanity and with respect for the inherent dignity of the human person.

(2)(a) Accused persons shall, save in exceptional circumstances, be segregated from convicted persons and shall be subject to separate treatment appropriate to their status as unconvicted persons;

(b) Accused juvenile persons shall be separated from adults and brought as speedily as possible for adjudication.

(3) The penitentiary system shall comprise treatment of prisoners the essential aim of which shall be their reformation and social rehabilitation. Juvenile offenders shall be segregated from adults and be accorded treatment appropriate to their age and legal status.

Article 11. No one shall be imprisoned merely on the ground of inability to fulfill a contractual obligation.

Article 12. (1) Everyone lawfully within the territory of a State shall, within that territory, have the right to liberty of movement and freedom to choose his residence.

(2) Everyone shall be free to leave any country, including his own.

(3) The above-mentioned rights shall not be subject to any restrictions except those which are provided by law, are necessary to protect national security, public order (*ordre public*), public health or morals or the rights and freedoms of others, and are consistent with the other rights recognized in the present Covenant.

(4) No one shall be arbitrarily deprived of the right to enter his own country.

Article 13. An alien lawfully in the territory of a State Party to the present Covenant may be expelled therefrom only in pursuance of a decision reached in accordance with law and shall, except where compelling reasons of national security otherwise require, be allowed to submit the reasons against his expulsion and to have his case reviewed by, and be represented for the purpose before, the competent authority or a person or persons especially designated by the competent authority.

Article 14. (1) All persons shall be equal before the courts and tribunals. In the determination of any criminal charge against him, or of his rights and obligations in a suit at law, everyone shall be entitled to a fair and public hearing by a competent, independent and impartial tribunal established by law. The Press and the public may be excluded from all or part of a trial for reasons of morals, public order (*ordre public*) or national security in a democratic society, or when the interest of the private lives of the parties so requires, or to the extent strictly necessary in the opinion of the court in special circumstances where publicity would prejudice the interests of justice; but any judgment rendered in a criminal case or in a suit at law shall be made public except where the interest of juvenile persons otherwise requires or the proceedings concern matrimonial disputes or the guardianship of children.

(2) Everyone charged with a criminal offence shall have the right to be presumed innocent until proved guilty according to law.

(3) In the determination of any criminal charge against him, everyone shall be entitled to the following minimum guarantees, in full equality:

(a) To be informed promptly and in detail in a language which he understands of the nature and cause of the charge against him;

(b) To have adequate time and facilities for the preparation of his defence and to communicate with counsel of his own choosing;

(c) To be tried without undue delay;

(d) To be tried in his presence, and to defend himself in person or through legal assistance of his own choosing; to be informed, if he does not have legal assistance, of this right; and to have legal assistance assigned to him, in any case where the interests of justice so require, and without payment by him in any such case if he does not have sufficient means to pay for it;

(e) To examine, or have examined, the witnesses against him and to obtain the attendance and examination of witnesses on his behalf under the same conditions as witnesses against him;

(f) To have the free assistance of an interpreter if he cannot understand or speak the language used in court;

(g) Not to be compelled to testify against himself or to confess guilt.

(4) In the case of juvenile persons, the procedure shall be such as will take account of their age and the desirability of promoting their rehabilitation.

(5) Everyone convicted of a crime shall have the right to his conviction and sentence being reviewed by a higher tribunal according to law.

(6) When a person has by a final decision been convicted of a criminal offence and when subsequently his conviction has been reversed or he has been pardoned on the ground that a new or newly discovered fact shows conclusively that there has been a miscarriage of justice, the person who has suffered punishment as a result of such conviction shall be compensated according to law, unless it is proved that the non-disclosure of the unknown fact in time is wholly or partly attributable to him.

(7) No one shall be liable to be tried or punished again for an offence for which he has already been finally convicted or acquitted in accordance with the law and penal procedure of each country.

Article 15. (1) No one shall be held guilty of any criminal offence on account of any act of omission which did not constitute a criminal offence, under national or international law, at the time when it was committed. Nor shall a heavier penalty be imposed than the one that was applicable at the time when the criminal offence was committed. If, subsequent to the commission of the offence, provision is made by law for the imposition of a lighter penalty, the offender shall benefit thereby.

(2) Nothing in this article shall prejudice the trial and punishment of any person for any act or omission which, at the time when it was committed, was criminal according to the general principles of law recognized by the community of nations.

Article 16. Everyone shall have the right to recognition everywhere as a person before the law.

Article 17. (1) No one shall be subjected to arbitrary or unlawful interference with his privacy, family, home or correspondence, nor to unlawful attacks on his honour and reputation.

(2) Everyone has the right to the protection of the law against such interference or attacks.

Article 18. (1) Everyone shall have the right to freedom of thought, conscience and religion. This right shall include freedom to have or to adopt a religion or belief of his choice, and freedom, either individually or in community with others and in public or private, to manifest his religion or belief in worship, observance, practice and teaching.

(2) No one shall be subject to coercion which would impair his freedom to have or to adopt a religion or belief of his choice.

(3) Freedom to manifest one's religion or beliefs may be subject only to such limitations as are prescribed by law and are necessary to protect public safety, order, health, or morals or the fundamental rights and freedoms of others.

(4) The States Parties to the present Covenant undertake to have respect for the liberty of parents and, when applicable, legal guardians to ensure the religious and moral education of their children in conformity with their own convictions.

Article 19. (1) Everyone shall have the right to hold opinions without interference.

(2) Everyone shall have the right to freedom of expression; this right shall include freedom to seek, receive and impart information and ideas of all kinds, regardless of frontiers, either orally, in writing or in print, in the form of art, or through any other media of his choice.

(3) The exercise of the rights provided for in paragraph 2 of this article carries with it special duties and responsibilities. It may therefore be subject to certain restrictions, but these shall only be such as are provided by law and are necessary:

(a) For respect of the rights or reputations of others;

(b) For the protection of national security or of public order *(ordre public)*, or of public health or morals.

Article 20. (1) Any propaganda for war shall be prohibited by law.

(2) Any advocacy of national, racial or religious hatred that constitutes incitement to discrimination, hostility or violence shall be prohibited by law.

Article 21. The right of peaceful assembly shall be recognized. No restrictions may be placed on the exercise of this right other than those imposed in conformity with the law and which are necessary in a democratic society in the interests of national security or public safety, public order *(ordre public)*, the protection of public health or morals or the protection of the rights and freedoms of others.

Article 22. (1) Everyone shall have the right to freedom of association with others, including the right to form and join trade unions for the protection of his interests.

(2) No restrictions may be placed on the exercise of this right other than those which are prescribed by law and which are necessary in a democratic society in the interests of national security or public safety, public order *(ordre public),* the protection of public health or morals or the protection of the rights and freedoms of others. This article shall not prevent the imposition of lawful restrictions on members of the armed forces and of the police in their exercise of this right.

(3) Nothing in this article shall authorize States Parties to the International Labour Organization Convention of 1948 concerning Freedom of Association and Protection of the Right to Organize to take legislative measures which would prejudice, or to apply the law in such a manner as to prejudice, the guarantees provided for in that Convention.

Article 23. (1) The family is the natural and fundamental group unit of society and is entitled to protection by society and the State.

(2) The right of men and women of marriageable age to marry and to found a family shall be recognized.

(3) No marriage shall be entered into without the free and full consent of the intending spouses.

(4) States Parties to the present Covenant shall take appropriate steps to ensure equality of rights and responsibilities of spouses as to marriage, during marriage and at its dissolution. In the case of dissolution, provision shall be made for the necessary protection of any children.

Article 24. (1) Every child shall have, without any discrimination as to race, colour, sex, language, religion, national or social origin, property or birth, the right to such measures of protection as are required by his status as a minor, on the part of his family, society and the State.

(2) Every child shall be registered immediately after birth and shall have a name.

(3) Every child has the right to acquire a nationality.

Article 25. Every citizen shall have the right and the opportunity, without any of the distinctions mentioned in article 2 and without unreasonable restrictions:

(a) To take part in the conduct of public affairs, directly or through freely chosen representatives;

(b) To vote and to be elected at genuine periodic elections which shall be by universal and equal suffrage and shall be held by secret ballot, guaranteeing the free expression of the will of the electors;

(c) To have access, on general terms of equality, to public service in his country.

Article 26. All persons are equal before the law and are entitled without any discrimination to the equal protection of the law. In this respect, the law shall prohibit any discrimination and guarantee to all persons equal and effective protection against discrimination on any ground such as race, colour, sex, language, religion, political or other opinion, national or social origin, property, birth or other status.

Article 27. In those States in which ethnic, religious or linguistic minorities exist, persons belonging to such minorities shall not be denied the right, in community with the other members of their group, to enjoy their own culture, to profess and practise their own religion, or to use their own language.

PART IV

Article 28. (1) There shall be established a Human Rights Committee (hereafter referred to in the present Covenant as the Committee). It shall consist of eighteen members and shall carry out the functions hereinafter provided.

(2) The Committee shall be composed of nationals of the States Parties to the present Covenant who shall be persons of high moral character and recognized competence in the field of human rights, consideration being given to the usefulness of the participation of some persons having legal experience.

(3) The members of the Committee shall be elected and shall serve in their personal capacity.

* * *

Article 40. (1) The States Parties to the present Covenant undertake to submit reports on the measures they have adopted which give effect to the rights recognized herein and on the progress made in the enjoyment of those rights:

(a) Within one year of the entry into force of the present Covenant for the States Parties concerned;

(b) Thereafter whenever the Committee so requests.

(2) All reports shall be submitted to the Secretary-General of the United Nations, who shall transmit them to the Committee for consideration. Reports shall indicate the factors and difficulties, if any, affecting the implementation of the present Covenant.

(3) The Secretary-General of the United Nations may, after consultation with the Committee, transmit to the specialized agencies concerned copies of such parts of the reports as may fall within their field of competence.

(4) The Committee shall study the reports submitted by the States Parties to the present Covenant. It shall transmit its reports, and such general comments as it may consider appropriate, to the States Parties. The Committee may also transmit to the Economic and Social Council these comments along with the copies of the reports it has received from States Parties to the present Covenant.

(5) The States Parties to the present Covenant may submit to the Committee observations on any comments that may be made in accordance with paragraph 4 of this article.

Article 41. (1) A State Party to the present Covenant may at any time declare under this article that it recognizes the competence of the Committee to receive and consider communications to the effect that a State Party claims that another State Party is not fulfilling its obligations under the present Covenant. Communications under this article may be received and considered only if submitted by a State Party which has made a declaration recognizing in regard to itself the competence of the Committee. No communication shall be received by the Committee if it concerns a State Party which has not made such a declaration. Communications received under this article shall be dealt with in accordance with the following procedure:

(a) If a State Party to the present Covenant considers that another State Party is not giving effect to the provisions of the present Covenant, it may, by written communication, bring the matter to the attention of that State Party. Within three months after the receipt of the communication, the receiving State shall afford the State which sent the communication an explanation or any other statement in writing clarifying the matter, which should include, to the extent possible and pertinent, reference to domestic procedures and remedies taken, pending, or available in the matter.

(b) If the matter is not adjusted to the satisfaction of both States Parties concerned within six months after the receipt by the receiving State of the initial communication, either State shall have the right to refer the matter to the Committee, by notice given to the Committee and to the other State.

(c) The Committee shall deal with a matter referred to it only after it has ascertained that all available domestic remedies have been invoked and exhausted in the matter, in conformity with the generally recognized principles of international law. This shall not be the rule where the application of the remedies is unreasonably prolonged.

(d) The Committee shall hold closed meetings when examining communications under this article.

(e) Subject to the provisions of sub-paragraph (c), the Committee shall make available its good offices to the States Parties concerned with a view to a friendly solution of the matter on the basis of respect for human rights and fundamental freedoms as recognized in the present Covenant.

(f) In any matter referred to it, the Committee may call upon the States Parties concerned, referred to in sub-paragraph (b), to supply any relevant information.

(g) The States Parties concerned, referred to in sub-paragraph (b), shall have the right to be represented when the matter is being considered in the Committee and to make submissions orally and/or in writing.

(h) The Committee shall, within twelve months after the date of receipt of notice under sub-paragraph (b), submit a report:

(i) If a solution within the terms of sub-paragraph (e) is reached, the Committee shall confine its report to a brief statement of the facts and of the solution reached;

(ii) If a solution within the terms of sub-paragraph (e) is not reached, the Committee shall confine its report to a brief statement of the facts; the written submissions and record of the oral submissions made by the States Parties concerned shall be attached to the report.

In every matter, the report shall be communicated to the States Parties concerned.

(2) The provisions of this article shall come into force when ten States Parties to the present Covenant have made declarations under paragraph 1 of this article. Such declarations shall be deposited by the States Parties with the Secretary-General of the United Nations, who shall transmit copies thereof to the other States Parties. A declaration may be withdrawn at any time by notification to the Secretary-General. Such a withdrawal shall not prejudice the consideration of any matter which is the subject of a communication already transmitted under this article; no further communication by any State Party shall be received after the notification of withdrawal of the declaration has been received by the Secretary-General, unless the State Party concerned had made a new declaration.

Article 42. (1) (a) If a matter referred to the Committee in accordance with article 41 is not resolved to the satisfaction of the States Parties concerned, the Committee may, with the prior consent of the States Parties concerned, appoint an *ad hoc* Conciliation Commission (hereinafter referred to as the Commission). The good offices of the Commission shall be made available to the States Parties concerned with a view to an amicable solution of the matter on the basis of respect for the present Covenant;

(b) The Commission shall consist of five persons acceptable to the States Parties concerned. If the States Parties concerned fail to reach agreement within three months on all or part of the composition of the Commission, the members of the Commission concerning whom no agreement has been reached shall be elected by secret ballot by a two-thirds majority vote of the Committee from among its members.

(2) The members of the Commission shall serve in their personal capacity. They shall not be nationals of the States Parties concerned, or of a State not party to the present Covenant, or of a State Party which has not made a declaration under article 41.

(3) The Commission shall elect its own Chairman and adopt its own rules of procedure.

(4) The meetings of the Commission shall normally be held at the Headquarters of the United Nations or at the United Nations Office at Geneva. However, they may be held at such other convenient places as the Commission may determine in consultation with the Secretary-General of the United Nations and the States Parties concerned.

(5) The secretariat provided in accordance with article 36 shall also service the commissions appointed under this article.

(6) The information received and collated by the Committee shall be made available to the Commission and the Commission may call upon the States Parties concerned to supply any other relevant information.

(7) When the Commission has fully considered the matter, but in any event not later than twelve months after having been seized of the matter, it shall submit to the Chairman of the Committee a report for communication to the States Parties concerned:

(a) If the Commission is unable to complete its consideration of the matter within twelve months, it shall confine its report to a brief statement of the status of its consideration of the matter;

(b) If an amicable solution to the matter on the basis of respect for human rights as recognized in the present Covenant is reached, the Commission shall confine its report to a brief statement of the facts and of the solution reached;

(c) If a solution within the terms of sub-paragraph (b) is not reached, the Commission's report shall embody its findings on all questions of fact relevant to the issues between the States Parties concerned, and its views on the possibilities of an amicable solution of the matter. This report shall also contain the written submissions and a record of the oral submissions made by the States Parties concerned;

(d) If the Commission's report is submitted under sub-paragraph (c), the States Parties concerned shall, within three months of the receipt of the report, notify the Chairman of the Committee whether or not they accept the contents of the report of the Commission.

(8) The provisions of this article are without prejudice to the responsibilities of the Committee under article 41.

(9) The States Parties concerned shall share equally all the expenses of the members of the Commission in accordance with estimates to be provided by the Secretary-General of the United Nations.

(10) The Secretary-General of the United Nations shall be empowered to pay the expenses of the members of the Commission, if necessary, before reimbursement by the States Parties concerned, in accordance with paragraph 9 of this article.

* * *

Article 44. The provisions for the implementation of the present Covenant shall apply without prejudice to the procedures prescribed in the field of human rights by or under the constituent instruments and the conventions of the United Nations and of the specialized agencies and shall not prevent the States Parties to the present

Covenant from having recourse to other procedures for settling a dispute in accordance with general or special international agreements in force between them.

Article 45. The Committee shall submit to the General Assembly of the United Nations, through the Economic and Social Council, an annual report on its activities.

PART V

Article 46. Nothing in the present Covenant shall be interpreted as impairing the provisions of the Charter of the United Nations and of the constitutions of the specialized agencies which define the respective responsibilities of the various organs of the United Nations and of the specialized agencies in regard to the matters dealt with in the present Covenant.

Article 47. Nothing in the present Covenant shall be interpreted as impairing the inherent right of all peoples to enjoy and utilize fully and freely their natural wealth and resources.

* * *

3.20 OPTIONAL PROTOCOL TO THE INTERNATIONAL COVENANT ON CIVIL AND POLITICAL RIGHTS.[a] Done at New York, Dec. 16, 1966. Entered into force, Mar. 23, 1976. U.N.G.A. Res. 2200 (XXI), 21 U.N. GAOR, Supp. (No. 16) 59, U.N. Doc. A/6316 (1967), *reprinted in* 6 I.L.M. 383 (1967)

THE STATES PARTIES TO THE PRESENT PROTOCOL.

Considering that in order further to achieve the purposes of the Covenant on Civil and Political Rights (hereinafter referred to as the Covenant) and the implementation of its provisions it would be appropriate to enable the Human Rights Committee set up in part IV of the Covenant (hereinafter referred to as the Committee) to receive and consider, as provided in the present Protocol, communications from individuals claiming to be victims of violations of any of the rights set forth in the Covenant.

Have agreed as follows:

Article 1. A State Party to the Covenant that becomes a party to the present Protocol recognizes the competence of the Committee to receive and consider communications from individuals subject to its jurisdiction who claim to be victims of a violation by that State Party of any of the rights set forth in the Covenant. No communication shall be received by the Committee if it concerns a State Party to the Covenant which is not a party to the present Protocol.

Article 2. Subject to the provisions of article 1, individuals who claim that any of their rights enumerated in the Covenant have been violated and who have exhausted all available domestic remedies may submit a written communication to the Committee for consideration.

Article 3. The Committee shall consider inadmissible any communication under the present Protocol which is anonymous, or which it considers to be an abuse of the rights of submission of such communications or to be incompatible with the provisions of the Covenant.

Article 4. (1) Subject to the provisions of article 3, the Committee shall bring any communications submitted to it under the present Protocol to the attention of the State Party to the present Protocol alleged to be violating any provisions of the Covenant.

(2) Within six months, the receiving State shall submit to the Committee written explanations or statements clarifying the matter and the remedy, if any, that may have been taken by that State.

Article 5. (1) The Committee shall consider communications received under the present Protocol in the light of all written information made available to it by the individual and by the State Party concerned.

(2) The Committee shall not consider any communication from an individual unless it has ascertained that:

(a) The same matter is not being examined under another procedure of international investigation or settlement;

(b) The individual has exhausted all available domestic remedies. This shall not be the rule where the application of the remedies is unreasonably prolonged.

(3) The Committee shall hold closed meetings when examining communications under the present Protocol.

a. *See also* Basic Documents 3.11 and 3.19, *supra*, and 3.22 and 3.26, *infra*.

(4) The Committee shall forward its views to the State Party concerned and to the individual.

Article 6. The Committee shall include in its annual report under article 45 of the Covenant a summary of its activities under the present Protocol.

* * *

3.21 PROTOCOL RELATING TO THE STATUS OF REFUGEES.[a] Done at New York, Jan. 31, 1967. Entered into force, Oct. 4, 1967; for the United States, Nov. 1, 1968. 19 U.S.T. 6223, T.I.A.S. No. 6577, 606 U.N.T.S. 267, *reprinted in* 6 I.L.M. 78 (1967)

PROTOCOL RELATING TO THE STATUS OF REFUGEES

The States Parties to the present Protocol,

Considering that the Convention relating to the Status of Refugees done at Geneva on 28 July 1951 (hereinafter referred to as the Convention) covers only those persons who have become refugees as a result of events occurring before 1 January 1951,

Considering that new refugee situations have arisen since the Convention was adopted and that the refugees concerned may therefore not fall within the scope of the Convention,

Considering that it is desirable that equal status should be enjoyed by all refugees covered by the definition in the Convention irrespective of the dateline 1 January 1951,

Have agreed as follows:

Article I

GENERAL PROVISION

1. The States Parties to the present Protocol undertake to apply articles 2 to 34 inclusive of the Convention to refugees as hereinafter defined.

2. For the purpose of the present Protocol, the term "refugee" shall, except as regards the application of paragraph 3 of this article, mean any person within the definition of article 1 of the Convention as if the words "As a result of events occurring before 1 January 1951 and * * *" and the words "* * * as a result of such events", in article 1A(2) were omitted.

3. The present Protocol shall be applied by the States Parties hereto without any geographic limitation, save that existing declarations made by States already Parties to the Convention in accordance with article 1B(1)(*a*) of the Convention, shall, unless extended under article 1B(2) thereof, apply also under the present Protocol.

Article II

CO–OPERATION OF THE NATIONAL AUTHORITIES WITH THE UNITED NATIONS

1. The States Parties to the present Protocol undertake to co-operate with the Office of the United Nations High Commissioner for Refugees, or any other agency of the United Nations which may succeed it, in the exercise of its functions, and shall in particular facilitate its duty of supervising the application of the provisions of the present Protocol.

2. In order to enable the Office of the High Commissioner, or any other agency of the United Nations which may succeed it, to make reports to the competent organs of the United Nations, the States Parties to the present Protocol undertake to provide

a. *See also* Basic Documents 3.5 and 3.8, *supra*.

them with the information and statistical data requested, in the appropriate form, concerning:

(*a*) The condition of refugees;

(*b*) The implementation of the present Protocol;

(*c*) Laws, regulations and decrees which are, or may hereafter be, in force relating to refugees.

Article III

INFORMATION ON NATIONAL LEGISLATION

The States Parties to the present Protocol shall communicate to the Secretary-General of the United Nations the laws and regulations which they may adopt to ensure the application of the present Protocol.

Article IV

SETTLEMENT OF DISPUTES

Any dispute between States Parties to the present Protocol which relates to its interpretation or application and which cannot be settled by other means shall be referred to the International Court of Justice at the request of any one of the parties to the dispute.

* * *

Article VI

FEDERAL CLAUSE

In the case of a Federal or non-unitary State, the following provisions shall apply:

(*a*) With respect to those articles of the Convention to be applied in accordance with article I, paragraph 1, of the present Protocol that come within the legislative jurisdiction of the federal legislative authority, the obligations of the Federal Government shall to this extent be the same as those of States Parties which are not Federal States;

(*b*) With respect to those articles of the Convention to be applied in accordance with article I, paragraph 1, of the present Protocol that come within the legislative jurisdiction of constituent States, provinces or cantons which are not, under the constitutional system of the federation, bound to take legislative action, the Federal Government shall bring such articles with a favourable recommendation to the notice of the appropriate authorities of States, provinces or cantons at the earliest possible moment;

(*c*) A Federal State Party to the present Protocol shall, at the request of any other State Party hereto transmitted through the Secretary-General of the United Nations, supply a statement of the law and practice of the Federation and its constituent units in regard to any particular provision of the Convention to be applied in accordance with article I, paragraph 1, of the present Protocol, showing the extent to which effect has been given to that provision by legislative or other action.

Article VII

RESERVATIONS AND DECLARATIONS

1. At the time of accession, any State may make reservations in respect of article IV of the present Protocol and in respect of the application in accordance with article I of the present Protocol of any provisions of the Convention other than those contained in articles 1, 3, 4, 16(1) and 33 thereof, provided that in the case of a State

Party to the Convention reservations made under this article shall not extend to refugees in respect of whom the Convention applies.

2. Reservations made by States Parties to the Convention in accordance with article 42 thereof shall, unless withdrawn, be applicable in relation to their obligations under the present Protocol.

3. Any State making a reservation in accordance with paragraph 1 of this article may at any time withdraw such reservation by a communication to that effect addressed to the Secretary–General of the United Nations.

4. Declaration made under article 40, paragraphs 1 and 2, of the Convention by a State Party thereto which accedes to the present Protocol shall be deemed to apply in respect of the present Protocol, unless upon accession a notification to the contrary is addressed by the State Party concerned to the Secretary–General of the United Nations. The provisions of article 40, paragraphs 2 and 3, and of article 44, paragraph 3, of the Convention shall be deemed to apply *mutatis mutandis* to the present Protocol.

* * *

Article IX

DENUNCIATION

1. Any State Party hereto may denounce this Protocol at any time by a notification addressed to the Secretary–General of the United Nations.

2. Such denunciation shall take effect for the State Party concerned one year from the date on which it is received by the Secretary–General of the United Nations.

* * *

3.22 ECONOMIC AND SOCIAL COUNCIL RESOLUTION 1235 (XLII).[a] Adopted by the U.N. Economic and Social Council, June 6, 1967. 42 U.N. ESCOR, Supp. (No. 1) 17, U.N.Doc. E/4393 (1967)

The Economic and Social Council,

Noting resolutions 8 (XXIII) and 9 (XXIII) of the Commission on Human Rights,

1. *Welcomes* the decision of the Commission on Human Rights to give annual consideration to the item entitled "Question of the violation of human rights and fundamental freedoms, including policies of racial discrimination and segregation and of apartheid, in all countries, with particular reference to colonial and other dependent countries and territories," without prejudice to the functions and powers of organs already in existence or which may be established within the framework of measures of implementation included in international covenants and conventions on the protection of human rights and fundamental freedoms; and concurs with the requests for assistance addressed to the Sub–Commission on Prevention of Discrimination and Protection of Minorities and to the Secretary–General;

2. *Authorizes* the Commission on Human Rights and the Sub–Commission on Prevention of Discrimination and Protection of Minorities, in conformity with the provisions of paragraph 1 of the Commission's resolution 8 (XXIII); to examine information relevant to gross violations of human rights and fundamental freedoms, as exemplified by the policy of apartheid as practised in the Republic of South Africa and in the Territory of South West Africa under the direct responsibility of the United Nations and now illegally occupied by the Government of the Republic of South Africa, and to racial discrimination as practised notably in Southern Rhodesia, contained in the communications listed by the Secretary–General pursuant to Economic and Social Council resolution 728 F (XXVIII) of 30 July 1959;

3. *Decides* that the Commission on Human Rights may, in appropriate cases, and after careful consideration of the information thus made available to it, in conformity with the provisions of paragraph 1 above, make a thorough study of situations which reveal a consistent pattern of violations of human rights, as exemplified by the policy of apartheid as practised in the Republic of South Africa in the Territory of South West Africa under the direct responsibility of the United Nations and now illegally occupied by the Government of the Republic of South Africa, and racial discrimination as practised notably in Southern Rhodesia, and report, with recommendations thereon, to the Economic and Social Council;

4. *Decides* to review the provisions of paragraphs 2 and 3 of the present resolution after the entry into force of the International Covenants on Human Rights;

5. *Takes note* of the fact that the Commission on Human Rights, in its resolution 6 (XXIII), has instructed an ad hoc study group to study in all its aspects the question of the ways and means by which the Commission might be enabled or assisted to discharge functions in relation to violations of human rights and fundamental freedoms, whilst maintaining and fulfilling its other functions;

6. *Requests* the Commission on Human Rights to report to it on the result of this study after having given consideration to the conclusions of the ad hoc study group referred to in paragraph 5 above.

a. *See also* Basic Documents 3.11 and 3.20, *supra*, and Basic Document 3.26, *infra*.

3.23 DECLARATION ON TERRITORIAL ASYLUM.[a] Adopted by the U.N. General Assembly on Dec. 14, 1967. U.N.G.A. Res. 2312 (XXII), 22 U.N. GAOR, Supp. (No. 16) 81, U.N. Doc. A/6716 (1968)

THE GENERAL ASSEMBLY,

Noting that the purposes proclaimed in the Charter of the United Nations are to maintain international peace and security, to develop friendly relations among all nations and to achieve international co-operation in solving international problems of an economic, social, cultural or humanitarian character and in promoting and encouraging respect for human rights and for fundamental freedoms for all without distinction as to race, sex, language or religion.

Mindful of the Universal Declaration of Human Rights, which declares in article 14 that:

"1. Everyone has the right to seek and to enjoy in other countries asylum from persecution.

"2. This right may not be invoked in the case of prosecutions genuinely arising from non-political crimes or from acts contrary to the purpose and principles of the United Nations".

Recalling also article 13, paragraph 2, of the Universal Declaration of Human Rights, which states:

"Everyone has the right to leave any country, including his own, and to return to his country".

Recognizing that the grant of asylum by a State to persons entitled to invoke article 14 of the Universal Declaration of Human Rights is a peaceful and humanitarian act and that, as such, it cannot be regarded as unfriendly by any other State.

Recommends that, without prejudice to existing instruments dealing with asylum and the status of refugees and stateless persons. States should base themselves in their practices relating to territorial asylum on the following principles:

Article 1. (1) Asylum granted by a State, in the exercise of its sovereignty, to persons entitled to invoke article 14 of the Universal Declaration of Human Rights, including persons struggling against colonialism, shall be respected by all other States.

(2) The right to seek and to enjoy asylum may not be invoked by any person with respect to whom there are serious reasons for considering that he has committed a crime against peace, a war crime or a crime against humanity, as defined in the international instruments drawn up to make provision in respect of such crimes.

(3) It shall rest with the State granting asylum to evaluate the grounds for the grant of asylum.

Article 2. (1) The situation of persons referred to in article 1, paragraph 1, is, without prejudice to the sovereignty of States and the purposes and principles of the United Nations, of concern to the international community.

a. For noteworthy regional instruments on asylum, see in particular: Convention on Asylum, done at Havana, Feb. 20, 1928, entered into force, May 23, 1929, 4 M. Hudson, Int'l Legis. 2412 (1931); Convention on Political Asylum, done at Montevideo, Dec. 26, 1933, entered into force, Mar. 28, 1935, 6 M. Hudson, Int'l Legis. 607 (1937); Convention on Diplomatic Asylum, done at Caracas, Mar. 28, 1954, entered into force, Dec. 29, 1954, O.A.S. Treaty Series No. 18, O.A.S. Off.Rec. OEA/Ser. A/9; Convention on Territorial Asylum, done at Caracas, Mar. 28, 1954, entered into force, Dec. 29, 1954, O.A.S. Treaty Series No. 19, O.A.S. Off.Rec. OEA/Ser. A/10.

(2) Where a State finds difficulty in granting or continuing to grant asylum. States individually or jointly or through the United Nations shall consider, in a spirit of international solidarity, appropriate measures to lighten the burden on that State.

Article 3. (1) No person referred to in article 1, paragraph 1, shall be subjected to measures such as rejection at the frontier or, if he has already entered the territory in which he seeks asylum, expulsion or compulsory return to any State where he may be subjected to persecution.

(2) Exception may be made to the foregoing principle only for overriding reasons of national security or in order to safeguard the population, as in the case of a mass influx of persons.

(3) Should a State decide in any case that exception to the principle stated in paragraph 1 of this article would be justified, it shall consider the possibility of granting to the person concerned, under such conditions as it may deem appropriate, an opportunity, whether by way of provisional asylum or otherwise, of going to another State.

Article 4. States granting asylum shall not permit persons who have received asylum to engage in activities contrary to the purposes and principles of the United Nations.

3.24 UNITED NATIONS SECURITY COUNCIL RESOLUTION 253.[a] Adopted by the U.N. Security Council, May 29, 1968. 23 U.N. SCOR (1428th Mtg.) 5, U.N. Doc. S/INF/23/Rev. 1 (1969), *reprinted in* 7 I.L.M. 897 (1968)

THE SECURITY COUNCIL,

Recalling and reaffirming its resolutions 216 (1965) of 12 November 1965, 217 (1965) of 20 November 1965, 221 (1966) of 9 April 1966, and 232 (1966) of 16 December 1966.

Taking note of resolution 2262 (XXII) adopted by the General Assembly on 3 November 1967.

Noting with great concern that the measures taken so far have failed to bring the rebellion in Southern Rhodesia to an end.

Reaffirming that, to the extent not superseded in this resolution, the measures provided for in resolutions 217 (1965) of 20 November 1965, and 232 (1966) of 16 December 1966, as well as those initiated by Member States in implementation of those resolutions, shall continue in effect.

Gravely concerned that the measures taken by the Security Council have not been complied with by all States and that some States, contrary to resolution 232 (1966) of the Security Council and to their obligations under Article 25 of the Charter, have failed to prevent trade with the illegal régime in Southern Rhodesia.

Condemning the recent inhuman executions carried out by the illegal régime in Southern Rhodesia which have flagrantly affronted the conscience of mankind and have been universally condemned.

Affirming the primary responsibility of the Government of the United Kingdom to enable the people of Southern Rhodesia to achieve self-determination and independence, and in particular their responsibility for dealing with the prevailing situation.

Recognizing the legitimacy of the struggle of the people of Southern Rhodesia to secure the enjoyment of their rights as set forth in the Charter of the United Nations and in conformity with the objectives of General Assembly resolution 1514 (XV).

Reaffirming its determination that the present situation in Southern Rhodesia constitutes a threat to international peace and security.

Acting under Chapter VII of the United Nations Charter.

1. *Condemns* all measures of political repression, including arrests, detentions, trials and executions which violate fundamental freedoms and rights of the people of Southern Rhodesia, and calls upon the Government of the United Kingdom to take all possible measures to put an end to such actions;

2. *Calls upon* the United Kingdom as the administering Power in the discharge of its responsibility to take urgently all effective measures to bring to an end the rebellion in Southern Rhodesia, and enable the people to secure the enjoyment of their rights as set forth in the Charter of the United Nations and in conformity with the objectives of General Assembly resolution 1514 (XV);

3. *Decides* that, in furtherance of the objective of ending the rebellion, all States Members of the United Nations shall prevent:

(a) The import into their territories of all commodities and products originating in Southern Rhodesia and exported therefrom after the date of this resolution (whether or not the commodities or products are for consumption or

a. *See also* Basic Document 3.17, *supra*.

processing in their territories, whether or not they are imported in bond and whether or not any special legal status with respect to the import of goods is enjoyed by the port or other place where they are imported or stored);

(b) Any activities by their nationals or in their territories which would promote or are calculated to promote the export of any commodities or products from Southern Rhodesia; and any dealings by their nationals or in their territories in any commodities or products originating in Southern Rhodesia and exported therefrom after the date of this resolution, including in particular any transfer of funds to Southern Rhodesia for the purpose of such activities or dealings;

(c) The shipment in vessels or aircraft of their registration or under charter to their nationals, or the carriage (whether or not in bond) by land transport facilities across their territories of any commodities or products originating in Southern Rhodesia and exported therefrom after the date of this resolution;

(d) The sale or supply by their nationals or from their territories of any commodities or products (whether or not originating in their territories, but not including supplies intended strictly for medical purposes, educational equipment and material for use in schools and other educational institutions, publications, news material and, in special humanitarian circumstances, food-stuffs) to any person or body in Southern Rhodesia or to any other person or body for the purposes of any business carried on in or operated from Southern Rhodesia, and any activities by their nationals or in their territories which promote or are calculated to promote such sale or supply;

(e) The shipment in vessels or aircraft of their registration, or under charter to their nationals, or the carriage (whether or not in bond) by land transport facilities across their territories of any such commodities or products which are consigned to any person or body in Southern Rhodesia, or to any other person or body for the purposes of any business carried on in or operated from Southern Rhodesia;

4. *Decides* that all States Members of the United Nations shall not make available to the illegal régime in Southern Rhodesia or to any commercial, industrial or public utility undertaking, including tourist enterprises, in Southern Rhodesia any funds for investment or any other financial or economic resources and shall prevent their nationals and any other financial or economic resources and shall prevent their nationals and any persons within their territories from making available to the régime or to any such undertaking any such funds or resources and from remitting any other funds to persons or bodies within Southern Rhodesia except payments exclusively for pensions or for strictly medical, humanitarian or educational purposes or for the provision of news material and in special humanitarian circumstances, food-stuffs;

5. *Decides* that all States Members of the United Nations shall:

(a) Prevent the entry into their territories, save on exceptional humanitarian grounds, of any person travelling on a Southern Rhodesian passport, regardless of its date of issue, or on a purported passport issued by or on behalf of the illegal régime in Southern Rhodesia; and

(b) Take all possible measures to prevent the entry into their territories of persons whom they have reason to believe to be ordinarily resident in Southern Rhodesia and whom they have reason to believe to have furthered or encouraged, or to be likely to further or encourage, the unlawful actions of the illegal régime in Southern Rhodesia or any activities which are calculated to evade any measure decided upon in this resolution or resolution 232 (1966) of 16 December 1966;

6. *Decides* that all States Members of the United Nations shall prevent airline companies constituted in their territories and aircraft of their registration or under charter to their nationals from operating to or from Southern Rhodesia and from linking up with any airline company constituted or aircraft registered in Southern Rhodesia;

7. *Decides* that all States Members of the United Nations shall give effect to the decisions set out in operative paragraphs 3, 4, 5 and 6 of this resolution notwithstanding any contract entered into or license granted before the date of this resolution;

8. *Calls upon* all States Members of the United Nations or of the specialized agencies to take all possible measures to prevent activities by their nationals and persons in their territories promoting, assisting or encouraging emigration to Southern Rhodesia, with a view to stopping such emigration;

9. *Requests* all States Members of the United Nations or of the specialized agencies to take all possible further action under Article 41 of the Charter to deal with the situation in Southern Rhodesia, not excluding any of the measures provided in that Article;

10. *Emphasizes* the need for the withdrawal of all consular and trade representation in Southern Rhodesia, in addition to the provisions of operative paragraph 6 of resolution 217 (1965);

11. *Calls upon* all States Members of the United Nations to carry out these decisions of the Security Council in accordance with Article 25 of the United Nations Charter and reminds them that failure or refusal by any one of them to do so would constitute a violation of that Article;

12. *Deplores* the attitude of States that have not complied with their obligations under Article 25 of the Charter, and censures in particular those States which have persisted in trading with the illegal régime in defiance of the resolutions of the Security Council, and which have given active assistance to the régime;

13. *Urges* all States Members of the United Nations to render moral and material assistance to the people of Southern Rhodesia in their struggle to achieve their freedom and independence;

14. *Urges,* having regard to the principles stated in Article 2 of the United Nations Charter, States not Members of the United Nations to act in accordance with the provisions of the present resolution;

15. *Requests* States Members of the United Nations, the United Nations Organization, the specialized agencies, and other international organizations in the United Nations system to extend assistance to Zambia as a matter of priority with a view to helping her solve such special economic problems as she may be confronted with arising from the carrying out of these decisions of the Security Council;

16. *Calls upon* all States Members of the United Nations, and in particular those with primary responsibility under the Charter for the maintenance of international peace and security, to assist effectively in the implementation of the measures called for by the present resolution;

17. *Considers* that the United Kingdom as the administering Power should ensure that no settlement is reached without taking into account the views of the people of Southern Rhodesia, and in particular the political parties favouring majority rule, and that it is acceptable to the people of Southern Rhodesia as a whole;

18. *Calls upon* all States Members of the United Nations or of the specialized agencies to report to the Secretary–General by 1 August 1968 on measures taken to implement the present resolution;

19. *Requests* the Secretary–General to report to the Security Council on the progress of the implementation of this resolution, the first report to be made not later than 1 September 1968;

20. *Decides* to establish, in accordance with rule 28 of the provisional rules of procedure of the Security Council, a committee of the Security Council to undertake the following tasks and to report to it with its observations:

(a) To examine such reports on the implementation of the present resolution as are submitted by the Secretary–General;

(b) To seek from any States Members of the United Nations or of the specialized agencies such further information regarding the trade of that State (including information regarding the commodities and products exempted from the prohibition contained in operative paragraph 3(d) above) or regarding any activities by any nationals of that State or in its territories that may constitute an evasion of the measures decided upon in this resolution as it may consider necessary for the proper discharge of its duty to report to the Security Council;

21. *Requests* the United Kingdom, as the administering Power, to give maximum assistance to the committee, and to provide the committee with any information which it may receive in order that the measures envisaged in this resolution and resolution 232 (1966) may be rendered fully effective;

22. *Calls upon* all States Members of the United Nations, or of the specialized agencies, as well as the specialized agencies themselves, to supply such further information as may be sought by the Committee in pursuance of this resolution;

23. *Decides* to maintain this item on its agenda for further action as appropriate in the light of developments.

3.25 AMERICAN CONVENTION ON HUMAN RIGHTS. Done at San José, Nov. 22, 1969.[a] Entered into force, July 18, 1978. O.A.S. Treaty Ser. No. 36, O.A.S. Off Rec. OEA/Ser. L/V/II.23 doc. 21 rev. 6 (1979), *reprinted in* 9 I.L.M. 673 (1970)

PART I. STATE OBLIGATIONS AND RIGHTS PROTECTED

CHAPTER I. GENERAL OBLIGATIONS

Article 1. Obligation to Respect Rights

1. The States Parties to this Convention undertake to respect the rights and freedoms recognized herein and to ensure to all persons subject to their jurisdiction the free and full exercise of those rights and freedoms, without any discrimination for reasons of race, color, sex, language, religion, political or other opinion, national or social origin, economic status, birth, or any other social condition.

2. For the purposes of this Convention, "person" means every human being.

Article 2. Domestic Legal Effects

Where the exercise of any of the rights or freedoms referred to in Article 1 is not already ensured by legislative or other provisions, the States Parties undertake to adopt, in accordance with their constitutional processes and the provisions of this Convention, such legislative or other measures as may be necessary to give effect to those rights or freedoms.

CHAPTER II. CIVIL AND POLITICAL RIGHTS

Article 3. Right to Juridical Personality

Every person has the right to recognition as a person before the law.

Article 4. Right to Life

1. Every person has the right to have his life respected. This right shall be protected by law and, in general, from the moment of conception. No one shall be arbitrarily deprived of his life.

2. In countries that have not abolished the death penalty, it may be imposed only for the most serious crimes and pursuant to a final judgment rendered by a competent court and in accordance with a law establishing such punishment, enacted prior to the commission of the crime. The application of such punishment shall not be extended to crimes to which it does not presently apply.

3. The death penalty shall not be reestablished in states that have abolished it.

4. In no case shall capital punishment be inflicted for political offenses or related common crimes.

5. Capital punishment shall not be imposed upon persons who, at the time the crime was committed, were under 18 years of age or over 70 years of age; nor shall it be applied to pregnant women.

6. Every person condemned to death shall have the right to apply for amnesty, pardon, or commutation of sentence, which may be granted in all cases. Capital punishment shall not be imposed while such a petition is a pending decision by the competent authority.

a. *See also* Basic Documents 3.4 and 3.13, *supra*, and 3.37, *infra*; and Draft Charter on Human and People's Rights in the Arab World (International Institute of Higher Studies in Criminal Sciences, Siracusa, Italy, 1987).

Article 5. Right to Humane Treatment

1. Every person has the right to have his physical, mental, and moral integrity respected.

2. No one shall be subjected to torture or to cruel, inhuman, or degrading punishment or treatment. All persons deprived of their liberty shall be treated with respect for the inherent dignity of the human person.

3. Punishment shall not be extended to any person other than the criminal.

4. Accused persons shall, save in exceptional circumstances, be segregated from convicted persons, and shall be subject to separate treatment appropriate to their status as unconvicted persons.

5. Minors while subject to criminal proceedings shall be separated from adults and brought before specialized tribunals, as speedily as possible, so that they may be treated in accordance with their status as minors.

6. Punishments consisting of deprivation of liberty shall have as an essential aim the reform and social readaptation of the prisoners.

Article 6. Freedom from Slavery

1. No one shall be subject to slavery or to involuntary servitude, which are prohibited in all their forms, as are the slave trade and traffic in women.

2. No one shall be required to perform forced or compulsory labor. This provision shall not be interpreted to mean that, in those countries in which the penalty established for certain crimes is deprivation of liberty at forced labor, the carrying out of such a sentence imposed by a competent court is prohibited. Forced labor shall not adversely affect the dignity or the physical or intellectual capacity of the prisoner.

3. For the purposes of this article, the following do not constitute forced or compulsory labor:

a. work or service normally required of a person imprisoned in execution of a sentence or formal decision passed by the competent judicial authority. Such work or service shall be carried out under the supervision and control of public authorities, and any persons performing such work or service shall not be placed at the disposal of any private party, company, or juridical person;

b. military service and, in countries in which conscientious objectors are recognized, national service that the law may provide for in lieu of military service;

c. service exacted in time of danger or calamity that threatens the existence or the well-being of the community; or

d. work or service that forms part of normal civic obligations.

Article 7. Right to Personal Liberty

1. Every person has the right to personal liberty and security.

2. No one shall be deprived of his physical liberty except for the reasons and under the conditions established beforehand by the constitution of the State Party concerned or by a law established pursuant thereto.

3. No one shall be subject to arbitrary arrest or imprisonment.

4. Anyone who is detained shall be informed of the reasons for his detention and shall be promptly notified of the charge or charges against him.

5. Any person detained shall be brought promptly before a judge or other officer authorized by law to exercise judicial power and shall be entitled to trial within a reasonable time or to be released without prejudice to the continuation of

the proceedings. His release may be subject to guarantees to assure his appearance for trial.

6. Anyone who is deprived of his liberty shall be entitled to recourse to a competent court, in order that the court may decide without delay on the lawfulness of his arrest or detention and order his release if the arrest or detention is unlawful. In States Parties whose laws provide that anyone who believes himself to be threatened with deprivation of his liberty is entitled to recourse to a competent court in order that it may decide on the lawfulness of such threat, this remedy may not be restricted or abolished. The interested party or another person in his behalf is entitled to seek these remedies.

7. No one shall be detained for debt. This principle shall not limit the orders of a complete judicial authority issued for nonfulfillment of duties of support.

Article 8. Right to a Fair Trial

1. Every person has the right to a hearing, with due guarantees and within a reasonable time, by a competent, independent, and impartial tribunal, previously established by law, in the substantiation of any accusation of a criminal nature made against him or for the determination of his rights and obligations of a civil, labor, fiscal, or any other nature.

2. Every person accused of a criminal offense has the right to be presumed innocent so long as his guilt has not been proven according to law. During the proceedings, every person is entitled, with full equality, to the following minimum guarantees:

a. the right of the accused to be assisted without charge by a translator or interpreter, if he does not understand or does not speak the language of the tribunal or court;

b. prior notification in detail to the accused of the charges against him;

c. adequate time and means for the preparation of his defense;

d. the right of the accused to defend himself personally or to be assisted by legal counsel of his own choosing, and to communicate freely and privately with his counsel;

e. the inalienable right to be assisted by counsel provided by the state, paid or not as the domestic law provides, if the accused does not defend himself personally or engage his own counsel within the time period established by law;

f. the right of the defense to examine witnesses present in the court and to obtain the appearance, as witnesses, of experts or other persons who may throw light on the facts;

g. the right not to be compelled to be a witness against himself or to plead guilty; and

h. the right to appeal the judgment to a higher court.

3. A confession of guilt by the accused shall be valid only if it is made without coercion of any kind.

4. An accused person acquitted by a nonappealable judgment shall not be subjected to a new trial for the same cause.

5. Criminal proceedings shall be public, except insofar as may be necessary to protect the interests of justice.

Article 9. Freedom from Ex Post Facto Laws

No one shall be convicted of any act or omission that did not constitute a criminal offense, under the applicable law, at the time it was committed. A heavier penalty shall not be imposed than the one that was applicable at the time the criminal offense was committed. If subsequent to the commission of the offense the law provides for the imposition of a lighter punishment, the guilty person shall benefit therefrom.

Article 10. Right to Compensation

Every person has the right to be compensated in accordance with the law in the event he has been sentenced by a final judgment through a miscarriage of justice.

Article 11. Right to Privacy

1. Everyone has the right to have his honor respected and his dignity recognized.

2. No one may be the object of arbitrary or abusive interference with his private life, his family, his home, or his correspondence, or of unlawful attacks on his honor or reputation.

3. Everyone has the right to the protection of the law against such interference or attacks.

Article 12. Freedom of Conscience and Religion

1. Everyone has the right to freedom of conscience and of religion. This right includes freedom to maintain or to change one's religion or beliefs, and freedom to profess or disseminate one's religion or beliefs, either individually or together with others, in public or in private.

2. No one shall be subject to restrictions that might impair his freedom to maintain or to change his religion or beliefs.

3. Freedom to manifest one's religion and beliefs may be subject only to the limitations prescribed by law that are necessary to protect public safety, order, health, or morals, or the rights or freedoms of others.

4. Parents or guardians, as the case may be, have the right to provide for the religious and moral education of their children or wards that is in accord with their own convictions.

Article 13. Freedom of Thought and Expression

1. Everyone has the right to freedom of thought and expression. This right includes freedom to seek, receive, and impart information and ideas of all kinds, regardless of frontiers, either orally, in writing, in print, in the form of art, or through any other medium of one's choice.

2. The exercise of the right provided for in the foregoing paragraph shall not be subject to prior censorship but shall be subject to subsequent imposition of liability, which shall be expressly established by law to the extent necessary to ensure:

a. respect for the rights or reputations of others; or

b. the protection of national security, public order, or public health or morals.

3. The right of expression may not be restricted by indirect methods or means, such as the abuse of government or private controls over newsprint, radio broadcasting frequencies, or equipment used in the dissemination of information, or by any other means tending to impede the communication and circulation of ideas and opinions.

4. Notwithstanding the provisions of paragraph 2 above, public entertainments may be subject by law to prior censorship for the sole purpose of regulating access to them for the moral protection of childhood and adolescence.

5. Any propaganda for war and any advocacy of national, racial, or religious hatred that constitute incitements to lawless violence or to any other including those

of race, color, religion, language, or national origin shall be considered as offenses punishable by law.

Article 14. Right of Reply

1. Anyone injured by inaccurate or offensive statements or ideas disseminated to the public in general by a legally regulated medium of communication has the right to reply or to make a correction using the same communications outlet, under such conditions as the law may establish.

2. The correction or reply shall not in any case remit other legal liabilities that may have been incurred.

3. For the effective protection of honor and reputation, every publisher, and every newspaper, motion picture, radio, and television company, shall have a person responsible who is not protected by immunities or special privileges.

Article 15. Right of Assembly

The right of peaceful assembly, without arms, is recognized. No restrictions may be placed on the exercise of this right other than those imposed in conformity with the law and necessary in a democratic society in the interest of national security, public safety or public order, or to protect public health or morals or the rights or freedoms of others.

Article 16. Freedom of Association

1. Everyone has the right to associate freely for ideological, religious, political, economic, labor, social, cultural, sports, or other purposes.

2. The exercise of this right shall be subject only to such restrictions established by law as may be necessary in a democratic society, in the interest of national security, public safety or public order, or to protect public health or morals or the rights and freedoms of others.

3. The provisions of this article do not bar the imposition of legal restrictions, including even deprivation of the exercise of the right of association, on members of the armed forces and the police.

Article 17. Rights of the Family

1. The family is the natural and fundamental group unit of society and is entitled to protection by society and the state.

2. The right of men and women of marriageable age to marry and to raise a family shall be recognized, if they meet the conditions required by domestic laws, insofar as such conditions do not affect the principle of nondiscrimination established in this Convention.

3. No marriage shall be entered into without the free and full consent of the intending spouses.

4. The States Parties shall take appropriate steps to ensure the quality of rights and the adequate balancing of responsibilities of the spouses as to marriage, during marriage, and in the event of its dissolution. In case of dissolution, provision shall be made for the necessary protection of any children solely on the basis of their own best interests.

5. The law shall recognize equal rights for children born out of wedlock and those born in wedlock.

Article 18. Right to a Name

Every person has the right to a given name and to the surnames of his parents or that of one of them. The law shall regulate the manner in which this right shall be ensured for all, by the use of assumed names if necessary.

Article 19. Rights of the Child

Every minor child has the right to the measures of protection required by his condition as a minor on the part of his family, society, and the state.

Article 20. Right to Nationality

1. Every person has the right to a nationality.

2. Every person has the right to the nationality of the state in whose territory he was born if he does not have the right to any other nationality.

3. No one shall be arbitrarily deprived of his nationality or of the right to change it.

Article 21. Right to Property

1. Everyone has the right to the use and enjoyment of his property. The law may subordinate such use and enjoyment to the interest of society.

2. No one shall be deprived of his property except upon payment of just compensation, for reasons of public utility or social interest, and in the cases and according to the forms established by law.

3. Usury and any other form of exploitation of man by man shall be prohibited by law.

Article 22. Freedom of Movement and Residence

1. Every person lawfully in the territory of a State Party has the right to move about in it, and to reside in it subject to the provisions of the law.

2. Every person has the right to leave any country freely, including his own.

3. The exercise of the foregoing rights may be restricted only pursuant to a law to the extent necessary in a democratic society to prevent crime or to protect national security, public safety, public order, public morals, public health, or the rights or freedoms of others.

4. The exercise of the rights recognized in paragraph 1 may also be restricted by law in designated zones for reasons of public interest.

5. No one can be expelled from the territory of the state of which he is a national or be deprived of the right to enter it.

6. An alien lawfully in the territory of a State Party to this Convention may be expelled from it only pursuant to a decision reached in accordance with law.

7. Every person has the right to seek and be granted asylum in a foreign territory, in accordance with the legislation of the state and international conventions, in the event he is being pursued for political offenses or related common crimes.

8. In no case may an alien be deported or returned to a country, regardless of whether or not it is his country of origin, if in that country his right to life or personal freedom is in danger of being violated because of his race, nationality, religion, social status, or political opinions.

9. The collective expulsion of aliens is prohibited.

Article 23. Right to Participate in Government

1. Every citizen shall enjoy the following rights and opportunities:

a. to take part in the conduct of public affairs, directly or through freely chosen representatives;

b. to vote and to be elected in genuine periodic elections, which shall be by universal and equal suffrage and by secret ballot that guarantees the free expression of the will of the voters; and

c. to have access, under general conditions of equality, to the public service of his country.

2. The law may regulate the exercise of the rights and opportunities referred to in the preceding paragraph only on the basis of age, nationality, residence, language, education, civil and mental capacity, or sentencing by a competent court in criminal proceedings.

Article 24. Right to Equal Protection

All persons are equal before the law. Consequently, they are entitled, without discrimination, to equal protection of the law.

Article 25. Right to Judicial Protection

1. Everyone has the right to simple and prompt recourse, or any other effective recourse, to a competent court or tribunal for protection against acts that violate his fundamental rights recognized by the constitution or laws of the state concerned or by this Convention, even though such violation may have been committed by persons acting in the course of their official duties.

2. The States Parties undertake:

a. to ensure that any person claiming such remedy shall have his rights determined by the competent authority provided for by the legal system of the state;

b. to develop the possibilities of judicial remedy; and

c. to ensure that the competent authorities shall enforce such remedies when granted.

CHAPTER III. ECONOMIC, SOCIAL, AND CULTURAL RIGHTS

Article 26. Progressive Development

The States Parties undertake to adopt measures, both internally and through international cooperation, especially those of an economic and technical nature, with a view to achieving progressively, by legislation or other appropriate means, the full realization of the rights implicit in the economic, social, educational, scientific, and cultural standards set forth in the Charter of the Organization of American States as amended by the Protocol of Buenos Aires.

CHAPTER IV. SUSPENSION OF GUARANTEES, INTERPRETATION, AND APPLICATION

Article 27. Suspension of Guarantees

1. In time of war, public danger, or other emergency that threatens the independence or security of a State Party, it may take measures derogating from its obligations under the present Convention to the extent and for the period of time strictly required by the exigencies of the situation, provided that such measures are not inconsistent with its other obligations under international law and do not involve discrimination on the ground of race, color, sex, language, religion, or social origin.

2. The foregoing provision does not authorize any suspension of the following articles: Article 3 (Right to Juridical Personality), Article 4 (Right to Life), Article 5 (Right to Humane Treatment), Article 6 (Freedom from Slavery), Article 9 (Freedom from Ex Post Facto Laws), Article 12 (Freedom of Conscience and Religion), Article 17 (Rights of the Family), Article 18 (Right to a Name), Article 19 (Rights of the Child), Article 20 (Right to Nationality), and Article 23 (Right to Participate in Government), or of the judicial guarantees essential for the protection of such rights.

3. Any State Party availing itself of the right of suspension shall immediately inform the other States Parties, through the Secretary General of the Organization of

American States, of the provisions the application of which it has suspended, the reasons that gave rise to the suspension, and the date set for the termination of such suspension.

Article 28. Federal Clause

1. Where a State Party is constituted as a federal state, the national government of such State Party shall implement all the provisions of the Convention over whose subject matter it exercises legislative and judicial jurisdiction.

2. With respect to the provisions over whose subject matter the constituent units of the federal state have jurisdiction, the national government shall immediately take suitable measures, in accordance with its constitution and its laws, to the end that the competent authorities of the constituent units may adopt appropriate provisions for the fulfillment of this Convention.

3. Whenever two or more States Parties agree to form a federation or other type of association, they shall take care that the resulting federal or other compact contains the provisions necessary for continuing and rendering effective the standards of this Convention in the new state that is organized.

Article 29. Restrictions Regarding Interpretation

No provision of this Convention shall be interpreted as:

a. permitting any State Party, group, or person to suppress the enjoyment or exercise of the rights and freedoms recognized in this Convention or to restrict them to a greater extent than is provided for herein;

b. restricting the enjoyment or exercise of any right or freedom recognized by virtue of the laws of any State Party or by virtue of another convention to which one of the said states is a party;

c. precluding other rights or guarantees that are inherent in the human personality or derived from representative democracy as a form of government; or

d. excluding or limiting the effect that the American Declaration of the Rights and Duties of Man and other international acts of the same nature may have.

Article 30. Scope of Restrictions

The restrictions that, pursuant to this Convention, may be placed on the enjoyment of exercise of the rights or freedoms recognized herein may not be applied except in accordance with laws enacted for reasons of general interest and in accordance with the purpose for which such restrictions have been established.

* * *

CHAPTER V. PERSONAL RESPONSIBILITIES

Article 32. Relationship Between Duties and Rights

1. Every person has responsibilities to his family, his community, and mankind.

2. The rights of each person are limited by the rights of others, by the security of all, and by the just demands of the general welfare, in a democratic society.

PART II. MEANS OF PROTECTION

CHAPTER VI. COMPETENT ORGANS

Article 33

The following organs shall have competence with respect to matters relating to the fulfillment of the commitments made by the States Parties to this Convention:

a. the Inter-American Commission on Human Rights, referred to as "The Commission"; and

b. the Inter-American Court of Human Rights, referred to as "The Court."

CHAPTER VII. INTER-AMERICAN COMMISSION ON HUMAN RIGHTS

SECTION 1. ORGANIZATION

Article 34

The Inter-American Commission on Human Rights shall be composed of seven members, who shall be persons of high moral character and recognized competence in the field of human rights.

Article 35

The Commission shall represent all the member countries of the Organization of American States.

Article 36

1. The members of the Commission shall be elected in a personal capacity by the General Assembly of the Organization from a list of candidates proposed by the governments of the member states.

* * *

Article 37

1. The members of the Commission shall be elected for a term of four years and may be reelected only once, but the terms of three of the members chosen in the first election shall expire at the end of two years. Immediately following that election the General Assembly shall determine the names of those three members by lot.

2. No two nationals of the same state may be members of the Commission.

* * *

SECTION 2. FUNCTIONS

Article 41

The main function of the Commission shall be to promote respect for and defense of human rights. In the exercise of its mandate, it shall have the following functions and powers:

a. to develop an awareness of human rights among the peoples of America;

b. to make recommendations to the governments of the member states, when it considers such action advisable, for the adoption of progressive measures in favor of human rights within the framework of their domestic law and constitutional provisions as well as appropriate measures to further the observance of those rights;

c. to prepare such studies or reports as it considers advisable in the performance of its duties;

d. to request the governments of the member states to supply it with information on the measures adopted by them in matters of human rights;

e. to respond, through the General Secretariat of the Organization of American States, to inquiries made by the member states on matters related to human rights and, within the limits of its possibilities, to provide those states with the advisory services they request;

f. to take action on petitions and other communications pursuant to its authority under the provisions of Articles 44 through 51 of this Convention; and

g. to submit an annual report to the General Assembly of the Organization of American States.

Article 42

The States Parties shall transmit to the Commission a copy of each of the reports and studies that they submit annually to the Executive Committees of the Inter-American Economic and Social Council and the Inter-American Council for Education, Science, and Culture, in their respective fields, so that the Commission may watch over the promotion of the rights implicit in the economic, social, educational, scientific, and cultural standards set forth in the Charter of the Organization of American States as amended by the Protocol of Buenos Aires.

Article 43

The States Parties undertake to provide the Commission with such information as it may request of them as to the manner in which their domestic law ensures the effective application of any provisions of this Convention.

SECTION 3. COMPETENCE

Article 44

Any person or group of persons, or any nongovernmental entity legally recognized in one or more member states of the Organization, may lodge petitions with the Commission containing denunciations or complaints of violation of this Convention by a State Party.

Article 45

1. Any State Party may, when it deposits its instrument of ratification of or adherence to this Convention, or at any later time, declare that it recognizes the competence of the Commission to receive and examine communications in which a State Party alleges that another State Party has committed a violation of a human right set forth in this Convention.

2. Communications presented by virtue of this article may be admitted and examined only if they are presented by a State Party that has made a declaration recognizing the aforementioned competence of the Commission. The Commission shall not admit any communication against a State Party that has not made such a declaration.

3. A declaration concerning recognition of competence may be made to be valid for an indefinite time, for a specified period, or for a specific case.

* * *

Article 46

1. Admission by the Commission of a petition or communication lodged in accordance with Articles 44 or 45 shall be subject to the following requirements:

a. that the remedies under domestic law have been pursued and exhausted in accordance with generally recognized principles of international law;

b. that the petition or communication is lodged within a period of six months from the date on which the party alleging violation of his rights was notified of the final judgment;

c. that the subject of the petition or communication is not pending in another international proceeding for settlement; and

d. that, in the case of Article 44, the petition contains the name, nationality, profession, domicile, and signature of the person or persons or of the legal representative of the entity lodging the petition.

2. The provisions of paragraphs 1.a and 1.b of this article shall not be applicable when:

a. the domestic legislation of the state concerned does not afford due process of law for the protection of the right or rights that have allegedly been violated;

b. the party alleging violation of his rights has been denied access to the remedies under domestic law or has been prevented from exhausting them; or

c. there has been unwarranted delay in rendering a final judgment under the aforementioned remedies.

Article 47

The Commission shall consider inadmissible any petition or communication submitted under Articles 44 or 45 if:

a. any of the requirements indicated in Article 46 has not been met;

b. the petition or communication does not state facts that tend to establish a violation of the rights guaranteed by this Convention;

c. the statements of the petitioner or of the state indicate that the petition or communication is manifestly groundless or obviously out of order; or

d. the petition or communication is substantially the same as one previously studied by the Commission or by another international organization.

SECTION 4. PROCEDURE

Article 48

1. When the Commission receives a petition or communication alleging violation of any of the rights protected by this Convention, it shall proceed as follows:

a. If it considers the petition or communication admissible, it shall request information from the government of the state indicated as being responsible for the alleged violations and shall furnish that government a transcript of the pertinent portions of the petition or communication. This information shall be submitted within a reasonable period to be determined by the Commission in accordance with the circumstances of each case.

b. After the information has been received, or after the period established has elapsed and the information has not been received, the Commission shall ascertain whether the grounds for the petition or communication still exist. If they do not, the Commission shall order the record to be closed.

c. The Commission may also declare the petition or communication inadmissible or out of order on the basis of information or evidence subsequently received.

d. If the record has not been closed, the Commission shall, with the knowledge of the parties, examine the matter set forth in the petition or communication in order to verify the facts. If necessary and advisable, the Commission shall carry out an investigation, for the effective conduct of which it shall request, and the states concerned shall furnish to it, all necessary facilities.

e. The Commission may request the states concerned to furnish any pertinent information and, if so requested, shall hear oral statements or receive written statements from the parties concerned.

f. The Commission shall place itself at the disposal of the parties concerned with a view to reaching a friendly settlement of the matter on the basis of respect for the human rights recognized in this Convention.

2. However, in serious and urgent cases, only the presentation of a petition or communication that fulfills all the formal requirements of admissibility shall be

necessary in order for the Commission to conduct an investigation with the prior consent of the state in whose territory a violation has allegedly been committed.

Article 49

If a friendly settlement has been reached in accordance with paragraph 1.f of Article 48, the Commission shall draw up a report, which shall be transmitted to the petitioner and to the States Parties to this Convention, and shall then be communicated to the Secretary General of the Organization of American States for publication. This report shall contain a brief statement of the facts and of the solution reached. If any party in the case so requests, the fullest possible information shall be provided to it.

Article 50

1. If a settlement is not reached, the Commission shall, within the time limit established by its Statute, draw up a report setting forth the facts and stating its conclusions. If the report, in whole or in part, does not represent the unanimous agreement of the members of the Commission, any member may attach to it a separate opinion. The written and oral statements made by the parties in accordance with paragraph 1.e of Article 48 shall also be attached to the report.

2. The report shall be transmitted to the states concerned, which shall not be at liberty to publish it.

3. In transmitting the report, the Committee may make such proposals and recommendations as it sees fit.

Article 51

1. If, within a period of three months from the date of the transmittal of the report of the Commission to the states concerned, the matter has not either been settled or submitted by the Commission or by the state concerned to the Court and its jurisdiction accepted, the Commission may, by the vote of an absolute majority of its members, set forth its opinion and conclusions concerning the question submitted for its consideration.

2. Where appropriate, the Commission shall make pertinent recommendations and shall prescribe a period within which the state is to take the measures that are incumbent upon it to remedy the situation examined.

3. When the prescribed period has expired, the Commission shall decide by the vote of an absolute majority of its members whether the state has taken adequate measures and whether to publish its report.

CHAPTER VIII. INTER-AMERICAN COURT OF HUMAN RIGHTS

SECTION 1. ORGANIZATION

Article 52

1. The Court shall consist of seven judges, nationals of the member states of the Organization, elected in an individual capacity from among jurists of the highest moral authority and of recognized competence in the field of human rights, who possess the qualifications required for the exercise of the highest judicial functions in conformity with the law of the state of which they are nationals or of the state that proposes them as candidates.

2. No two judges may be nationals of the same state.

Article 53

1. The judges of the Court shall be elected by secret ballot by an absolute majority vote of the States Parties to the Convention, in the General Assembly of the Organization, from a panel of candidates proposed by those states.

* * *

Article 54

1. The judges of the Court shall be elected for a term of six years and may be reelected only once. The term of three of the judges chosen in the first election shall expire at the end of three years. Immediately after the election, the names of the three judges shall be determined by lot in the General Assembly.

* * *

Article 55

1. If a judge is a national of any of the States Parties to a case submitted to the Court, he shall retain his right to hear that case.

2. If one of the judges called upon to hear a case should be a national of one of the States Parties to the case, any other State Party in the case may appoint a person of its choice to serve on the Court as an *ad hoc* judge.

3. If among the judges called upon to hear a case none is a national of any of the States Parties to the case, each of the latter may appoint an *ad hoc* judge.

4. An *ad hoc* judge shall possess the qualifications indicated in Article 52.

5. If several States Parties to the Convention should have the same interest in a case, they shall be considered as a single party for purposes of the above provisions. In case of doubt, the Court shall decide.

* * *

Article 57

The Commission shall appear in all cases before the Court.

* * *

Article 60

The Court shall draw up its Statute which it shall submit to the General Assembly for approval. It shall adopt its own Rules of Procedure.

SECTION 2. JURISDICTION AND FUNCTIONS

Article 61

1. Only the States Parties and the Commission shall have the right to submit a case to the Court.

2. In order for the Court to hear a case, it is necessary that the procedures set forth in Articles 48 to 50 shall have been completed.

Article 62

1. A State Party may, upon depositing its instrument of ratification or adherence to this Convention, or at any subsequent time, declare that it recognizes as binding, *ipso facto,* and not requiring special agreement, the jurisdiction of the Court on all matters relating to the interpretation or application of this Convention.

2. Such declaration may be made unconditionally, on the condition of reciprocity, for a specified period, or for specific cases. It shall be presented to the Secretary General of the Organization, who shall transmit copies thereof to the other member states of the Organization and to the Secretary of the Court.

3. The jurisdiction of the Court shall comprise all cases concerning the interpretation and application of the provisions of this Convention that are submitted to it, provided that the States Parties to the case recognize or have recognized such

jurisdiction, whether by special declaration pursuant to the preceding paragraphs, or by a special agreement.

Article 63

1. If the Court finds that there has been a violation of a right or freedom protected by this Convention, the Court shall rule that the injured party be ensured the enjoyment of his right or freedom that was violated. It shall also rule, if appropriate, that the consequences of the measure or situation that constituted the breach of such right or freedom be remedied and that fair compensation be paid to the injured party.

2. In cases of extreme gravity and urgency, and when necessary to avoid irreparable damage to persons, the Court shall adopt such provisional measures as it deems pertinent in matters it has under consideration. With respect to a case not yet submitted to the Court, it may act at the request of the Commission.

Article 64

1. The member states of the Organization may consult the Court regarding the interpretation of this Convention or of other treaties concerning the protection of human rights in the American states. Within their spheres of competence, the organs listed in Chapter X of the Charter of the Organization of American States, as amended by the Protocol of Buenos Aires, may in like manner consult the Court.

2. The Court, at the request of a member state of the Organization, may provide that state with opinions regarding the compatibility of any of its domestic laws with the aforesaid international instruments.

Article 65

To each regular session of the General Assembly of the Organization of American States the Court shall submit, for the Assembly's consideration, a report on its work during the previous year. It shall specify, in particular, the cases in which a state has not complied with its judgments, making any pertinent recommendations.

SECTION 3. PROCEDURE

Article 66

1. Reasons shall be given for the judgment of the Court.

2. If the judgment does not represent in whole or in part the unanimous opinion of the judges, any judge shall be entitled to have his dissenting or separate opinion attached to the judgment.

Article 67

The judgment of the Court shall be final and not subject to appeal. In case of disagreement as to the meaning or scope of the judgment, the Court shall interpret it at the request of any of the parties, provided the request is made within ninety days from the date of notification of the judgment.

Article 68

1. The States Parties to the Convention undertake to comply with the judgment of the Court in any case to which they are parties.

2. That part of a judgment that stipulates compensatory damages may be executed in the country concerned in accordance with domestic procedure governing the execution of judgments against the state.

Article 69

The parties to the case shall be notified of the judgment of the Court and it shall be transmitted to the States Parties to the Convention.

CHAPTER IX. COMMON PROVISIONS

Article 70

1. The judges of the Court and the members of the Commission shall enjoy, from the moment of their election and throughout their term of office, the immunities extended to diplomatic agents in accordance with international law. During the exercise of their official function they shall, in addition, enjoy the diplomatic privileges necessary for the performance of their duties.

2. At no time shall the judges of the Court or the members of the Commission be held liable for any decisions or opinions issued in the exercise of their functions.

Article 71

The position of judge of the Court or member of the Commission is incompatible with any other activity that might affect the independence or impartiality of such judge or member, as determined in the respective statutes.

* * *

3.26 PROCEDURE FOR DEALING WITH COMMUNICATIONS RELATING TO VIOLATIONS OF HUMAN RIGHTS AND FUNDAMENTAL FREEDOMS.[a] Adopted by the U.N. Economic and Social Council, May 27, 1970. E.S.C. Res. 1503 (XLVIII), 48 U.N. ESCOR, Supp. (No. 1A) 8, U.N. Doc. E/4832/Add. 1 (1970)

The Economic and Social Council,

Noting resolutions 7 (XXVI) and 17 (XXV) of the Commission on Human Rights and resolution 2 (XXI) of the Sub–Commission on Prevention of Discrimination and Protection of Minorities,

1. *Authorizes* the Sub–Commission on Prevention of Discrimination and Protection of Minorities to appoint a working group consisting of not more than five of its members, with due regard to geographical distribution, to meet once a year in private meetings for a period not exceeding ten days immediately before the sessions of the Sub–Commission to consider all communications, including replies of Governments thereon, received by the Secretary–General under Council resolution 728 F (XXVIII) of 30 July 1959 with a view to bringing to the attention of the Sub–Commission those communications, together with replies of Governments, if any, which appear to reveal a consistent pattern of gross and reliably attested violations of human rights and fundamental freedoms within the terms of reference of the Sub–Commission;

2. *Decides* that the Sub–Commission on Prevention of Discrimination and Protection of Minorities should, as the first stage in the implementation of the present resolution, devise at its twenty-third session appropriate procedures for dealing with the question of admissibility of communications received by the Secretary–General under Council resolution 728 F (XXVIII) and in accordance with Council resolution 1235 (XLII) of 6 June 1967;

3. *Requests* the Secretary–General to prepare a document on the question of admissibility of communications for the Sub–Commission's consideration at its twenty-third session;

4. *Further requests* the Secretary–General:

(*a*) To furnish to the members of the Sub–Commission every month a list of communications prepared by him in accordance with Council resolution 728 F (XXVIII) and a brief description of them, together with the text of any replies received from Governments;

(*b*) To make available to the members of the working group at their meetings the originals of such communications listed as they may request, having due regard to the provisions of paragraph 2(*b*) of Council resolution 728 F (XXVIII) concerning the divulging of the identity of the authors of communications;

(*c*) To circulate to the members of the Sub–Commission, in the working languages, the originals of such communications as are referred to the Sub–Commission by the working group;

5. *Requests* the Sub–Commission on Prevention of Discrimination and Protection of Minorities to consider in private meetings, in accordance with paragraph 1 above, the communications brought before it in accordance with the decision of a majority of the members of the working group and any replies of Governments

a. *See also* Basic Documents 3.11, 3.20 and 3.22, *supra*.

relating thereto and other relevant information, with a view to determining whether to refer to the Commission on Human Rights particular situations which appear to reveal a consistent pattern of gross and reliably attested violations of human rights requiring consideration by the Commission;

6. *Requests* the Commission on Human Rights after it has examined any situation referred to it by the Sub-Commission to determine:

(*a*) Whether it requires a thorough study by the Commission and a report and recommendations thereon to the Council in accordance with paragraph 3 of Council resolution 1235 (XLII);

(*b*) Whether it may be a subject of an investigation by an *ad hoc* committee to be appointed by the Commission which shall be undertaken only with the express consent of the State concerned and shall be conducted in constant co-operation with that State and under conditions determined by agreement with it. In any event, the investigation may be undertaken only if:

(i) All available means at the national level have been resorted to and exhausted;

(ii) The situation does not relate to a matter which is being dealt with under other procedures prescribed in the constituent instruments of, or conventions adopted by, the United Nations and the specialized agencies, or in regional conventions, or which the State concerned wishes to submit to other procedures in accordance with general or special international agreements to which it is a party.

7. *Decides* that if the Commission on Human Rights appoints an *ad hoc* committee to carry on an investigation with the consent of the State concerned:

(*a*) The composition of the committee shall be determined by the Commission. The members of the committee shall be independent persons whose competence and impartiality is beyond question. Their appointment shall be subject to the consent of the Government concerned;

(*b*) The committee shall establish its own rules of procedure. It shall be subject to the quorum rule. It shall have authority to receive communications and hear witnesses, as necessary. The investigation shall be conducted in co-operation with the Government concerned;

(*c*) The committee's procedure shall be confidential, its proceedings shall be conducted in private meetings and its communications shall not be publicized in any way;

(*d*) The committee shall strive for friendly solutions before, during and even after the investigation;

(*e*) The committee shall report to the Commission on Human Rights with such observations and suggestions as it may deem appropriate;

8. *Decides* that all actions envisaged in the implementation of the present resolution by the Sub-Commission on Prevention of Discrimination and Protection of Minorities or the Commission on Human Rights shall remain confidential until such time as the Commission may decide to make recommendations to the Economic and Social Council;

* * *

10. *Decides* that the procedure set out in the present resolution for dealing with communications relating to violations of human rights and fundamental freedoms should be reviewed if any new organ entitled to deal with such communications should be established within the United Nations or by international agreement.

3.27 CONVENTION FOR THE SUPPRESSION OF UNLAWFUL SEIZURE OF AIRCRAFT.[a] Done at The Hague, Dec. 16, 1970. Entered into force, Oct. 14, 1971; for the United States, Oct. 14, 1971. 22 U.S.T. 1641, T.I.A.S. 7192, 860 U.N.T.S. 105, *reprinted in* 10 I.L.M. 133 (1971)

Article 1

Any person who on board an aircraft in flight:

(*a*) unlawfully, by force or threat thereof, or by any other form of intimidation, seizes, or exercises control of, that aircraft, or attempts to perform any such act, or

(*b*) is an accomplice of a person who performs or attempts to perform any such act

commits an offence (hereinafter referred to as "the offence").

Article 2

Each Contracting State undertakes to make the offence punishable by severe penalties.

Article 3

1. For the purposes of this Convention, an aircraft is considered to be in flight at any time from the moment when all its external doors are closed following embarkation until the moment when any such door is opened for disembarkation. In the case of a forced landing, the flight shall be deemed to continue until the competent authorities take over the responsibility for the aircraft and for persons and property on board.

2. This Convention shall not apply to aircraft used in military, customs or police services.

3. This Convention shall apply only if the place of take-off or the place of actual landing of the aircraft on board which the offence is committed is situated outside the territory of the State of registration of that aircraft; it shall be immaterial whether the aircraft is engaged in an international or domestic flight.

4. In the cases mentioned in Article 5, this Convention shall not apply if the place of take-off and the place of actual landing of the aircraft on board which the offence is committed are situated within the territory of the same State where that State is one of those referred to in that Article.

5. Notwithstanding paragraphs 3 and 4 of this Article, Articles 6, 7, 8 and 10 shall apply whatever the place of take-off or the place of actual landing of the aircraft, if the offender or the alleged offender is found in the territory of a State other than the State of registration of that aircraft.

Article 4

1. Each Contracting State shall take such measures as may be necessary to establish its jurisdiction over the offence and any other act of violence against passengers or crew committed by the alleged offender in connection with the offence, in the following cases:

a. *See also* Basic Document 3.14, *supra*, and Basic Documents 3.28, 3.30, 3.32, 3.33, 3.35, 3.42, and 3.43, *infra*.

(*a*) when the offence is committed on board an aircraft registered in that State;

(*b*) when the aircraft on board which the offence is committed lands in its territory with the alleged offender still on board;

(*c*) when the offence is committed on board an aircraft leased without crew to a lessee who has his principal place of business or, if the lessee has no such place of business, his permanent residence, in that State.

2. Each Contracting State shall likewise take such measures as may be necessary to establish its jurisdiction over the offence in the case where the alleged offender is present in its territory and it does not extradite him pursuant to Article 8 to any of the States mentioned in paragraph 1 of this Article.

3. This Convention does not exclude any criminal jurisdiction exercised in accordance with national law.

Article 5

The Contracting States which establish joint air transport operating organizations or international operating agencies, which operate aircraft which are subject to joint or international registration shall, by appropriate means, designate for each aircraft the State among them which shall exercise the jurisdiction and have the attributes of the State of registration for the purpose of this Convention and shall give notice thereof to the International Civil Aviation Organization which shall communicate the notice to all States Parties to this Convention.

Article 6

1. Upon being satisfied that the circumstances so warrant, any Contracting State in the territory of which the offender or the alleged offender is present, shall take him into custody or take other measures to ensure his presence. The custody and other measures shall be as provided in the law of that State but may only be continued for such time as is necessary to enable any criminal or extradition proceedings to be instituted.

2. Such State shall immediately make a preliminary enquiry into the facts.

3. Any person in custody pursuant to paragraph 1 of this Article shall be assisted in communicating immediately with the nearest appropriate representative of the State of which he is a national.

4. When a State, pursuant to this Article, has taken a person into custody, it shall immediately notify the State of registration of the aircraft, the State mentioned in Article 4, paragraph 1(*c*), the State of nationality of the detained person and, if it considers it advisable, any other interested States of the fact that such person is in custody and of the circumstances which warrant his detention. The State which makes the preliminary enquiry contemplated in paragraph 2 of this Article shall promptly report its findings to the said States and shall indicate whether it intends to exercise jurisdiction.

Article 7

The Contracting State in the territory of which the alleged offender is found shall, if it does not extradite him, be obliged, without exception whatsoever and whether or not the offence was committed in its territory, to submit the case to its competent authorities for the purpose of prosecution. Those authorities shall take their decision in the same manner as in the case of any ordinary offence of a serious nature under the law of that State.

Article 8

1. The offence shall be deemed to be included as an extraditable offence in any extradition treaty existing between Contracting States. Contracting States undertake to include the offence as an extraditable offence in every extradition treaty to be concluded between them.

2. If a Contracting State which makes extradition conditional on the existence of a treaty receives a request for extradition from another Contracting State with which it has no extradition treaty, it may at its option consider this Convention as the legal basis for extradition in respect of the offence. Extradition shall be subject to the other conditions provided by the law of the requested State.

3. Contracting States which do not make extradition conditional on the existence of a treaty shall recognize the offence as an extraditable offence between themselves subject to the conditions provided by the law of the requested State.

4. The offence shall be treated, for the purpose of extradition between Contracting States, as if it had been committed not only in the place in which it occurred but also in the territories of the States required to establish their jurisdiction in accordance with Article 4, paragraph 1.

Article 9

1. When any of the acts mentioned in Article 1(*a*) has occurred or is about to occur, Contracting States shall take all appropriate measures to restore control of the aircraft to its lawful commander or to preserve his control of the aircraft.

2. In the cases contemplated by the preceding paragraph, any Contracting State in which the aircraft or its passengers or crew are present shall facilitate the continuation of the journey of the passengers and crew as soon as practicable, and shall without delay return the aircraft and its cargo to the persons lawfully entitled to possession.

Article 10

1. Contracting States shall afford one another the greatest measure of assistance in connection with criminal proceedings brought in respect of the offence and other acts mentioned in Article 4. The law of the State requested shall apply in all cases.

2. The provisions of paragraph 1 of this Article shall not affect obligations under any other treaty, bilateral or multilateral, which governs or will govern, in whole or in part, mutual assistance in criminal matters.

Article 11

Each Contracting State shall in accordance with its national law report to the Council of the International Civil Aviation Organization as promptly as possible any relevant information in its possession concerning:

(*a*) the circumstances of the offence;

(*b*) the action taken pursuant to Article 9;

(*c*) the measures taken in relation to the offender or the alleged offender, and, in particular, the results of any extradition proceedings or other legal proceedings.

Article 12

1. Any dispute between two or more Contracting States concerning the interpretation or application of this Convention which cannot be settled through negotiation, shall, at the request of one of them, be submitted to arbitration. If within six months from the date of the request for arbitration the Parties are unable to agree on the organization of the arbitration, any one of those Parties may refer the dispute

to the International Court of Justice by request in conformity with the Statute of the Court.

2. Each State may at the time of signature or ratification of this Convention or accession thereto, declare that it does not consider itself bound by the preceding paragraph. The other Contracting States shall not be bound by the preceding paragraph with respect to any Contracting State having made such a reservation.

3. Any Contracting State having made a reservation in accordance with the preceding paragraph may at any time withdraw this reservation by notification to the Depositary Governments.

* * *

3.28 CONVENTION FOR THE SUPPRESSION OF UNLAWFUL ACTS AGAINST THE SAFETY OF CIVIL AVIATION..[a] Done at Montreal, Sept. 23, 1971. Entered into force, Jan. 26, 1973; for the United States, Jan. 26, 1973. 24 U.S.T. 564, T.I.A.S. 7570, 1971 U.N. JURID. Y.B. 143, *reprinted in* 10 I.L.M. 1151 (1971)

ARTICLE 1

1. Any person commits an offence if he unlawfully and intentionally:

(a) performs an act of violence against a person on board an aircraft in flight if that act is likely to endanger the safety of that aircraft; or

(b) destroys an aircraft in service or causes damage to such an aircraft which renders it incapable of flight or which is likely to endanger its safety in flight; or

(c) places or causes to be placed on an aircraft in service, by any means whatsoever, a device or substance which is likely to destroy that aircraft, or to cause damage to it which renders it incapable of flight, or to cause damage to it which is likely to endanger its safety in flight; or

(d) destroys or damages air navigation facilities or interferes with their operation, if any such act is likely to endanger the safety of aircraft in flight; or

(e) communicates information which he knows to be false, thereby endangering the safety of an aircraft in flight.

2. Any person also commits an offence if he:

(a) attempts to commit any of the offences mentioned in paragraph 1 of this Article; or

(b) is an accomplice of a person who commits or attempts to commit any such offence.

ARTICLE 2

For the purposes of this Convention:

(a) an aircraft is considered to be in flight at any time from the moment when all its external doors are closed following embarkation until the moment when any such door is opened for disembarkation; in the case of a forced landing, the flight shall be deemed to continue until the competent authorities take over the responsibility for the aircraft and for persons and property on board;

(b) an aircraft is considered to be in service from the beginning of the preflight preparation of the aircraft by ground personnel or by the crew for a specific flight until twenty-four hours after any landing; the period of service shall, in any event, extend for the entire period during which the aircraft is in flight as defined in paragraph (a) of this Article.

ARTICLE 3

Each Contracting State undertakes to make the offences mentioned in Article 1 punishable by severe penalties.

a. *See also* Basic Documents 3.14 and 3.27, *supra*, and Basic Documents 3.30, 3.32, 3.33, 3.35, 3.42, and 3.43, *infra*.

ARTICLE 4

1. This Convention shall not apply to aircraft used in military, customs or police services.

2. In the cases contemplated in subparagraphs (a), (b), (c) and (e) of paragraph 1 of Article 1, this Convention shall apply, irrespective of whether the aircraft is engaged in an international or domestic flight, only if:

(a) the place of take-off or landing, actual or intended, of the aircraft is situated outside the territory of the State of registration of that aircraft; or

(b) the offence is committed in the territory of a State other than the State of registration of the aircraft.

3. Notwithstanding paragraph 2 of this Article, in the cases contemplated in subparagraphs (a), (b), (c) and (e) of paragraph 1 of Article 1, this Convention shall also apply if the offender or the alleged offender is found in the territory of a State other than the State of registration of the aircraft.

4. With respect to the States mentioned in Article 9 and in the cases mentioned in subparagraphs (a), (b), (c) and (e) of paragraph 1 of Article 1, this Convention shall not apply if the places referred to in subparagraph (a) of paragraph 2 of this Article are situated within the territory of the same State where that State is one of those referred to in Article 9, unless the offence is committed or the offender or alleged offender is found in the territory of a State other than that State.

5. In the cases contemplated in subparagraph (d) of paragraph 1 of Article 1, this Convention shall apply only if the air navigation facilities are used in international air navigation.

6. The provisions of paragraphs 2, 3, 4 and 5 of this Article shall also apply in the cases contemplated in paragraph 2 of Article 1.

ARTICLE 5

1. Each Contracting State shall take such measures as may be necessary to establish its jurisdiction over the offences in the following cases:

(a) when the offence is committed in the territory of that State;

(b) when the offence is committed against or on board an aircraft registered in that State;

(c) when the aircraft on board which the offence is committed lands in its territory with the alleged offender still on board;

(d) when the offence is committed against or on board an aircraft leased without crew to a lessee who has his principal place of business or, if the lessee has no such place of business, his permanent residence, in that State.

2. Each Contracting State shall likewise take such measures as may be necessary to establish its jurisdiction over the offences mentioned in Article 1, paragraph 1(a), (b) and (c), and in Article 1, paragraph 2, in so far as that paragraph relates to those offences, in the case where the alleged offender is present in its territory and it does not extradite him pursuant to Article 8 to any of the States mentioned in paragraph 1 of this Article.

3. This Convention does not exclude any criminal jurisdiction exercised in accordance with national law.

ARTICLE 6

1. Upon being satisfied that the circumstances so warrant, any Contracting State in the territory of which the offender or the alleged offender is present, shall take him into custody or take other measures to ensure his presence. The custody and other measures shall be as provided in the law of that State but may only be

continued for such time as is necessary to enable any criminal or extradition proceedings to be instituted.

2. Such State shall immediately make a preliminary enquiry into the facts.

3. Any person in custody pursuant to paragraph 1 of this Article shall be assisted in communicating immediately with the nearest appropriate representative of the State of which he is a national.

4. When a State, pursuant to this Article, has taken a person into custody, it shall immediately notify the States mentioned in Article 5, paragraph 1, the State of nationality of the detained person and, if it considers it advisable, any other interested States of the fact that such person is in custody and of the circumstances which warrant his detention. The State which makes the preliminary enquiry contemplated in paragraph 2 of this Article shall promptly report its findings to the said States and shall indicate whether it intends to exercise jurisdiction.

ARTICLE 7

The Contracting State in the territory of which the alleged offender is found shall, if it does not extradite him, be obliged, without exception whatsoever and whether or not the offence was committed in its territory, to submit the case to its competent authorities for the purpose of prosecution. Those authorities shall take their decision in the same manner as in the case of any ordinary offence of a serious nature under the law of that State.

ARTICLE 8

1. The offences shall be deemed to be included as extraditable offences in any extradition treaty existing between Contracting States. Contracting States undertake to include the offences as extraditable offences in every extradition treaty to be concluded between them.

2. If a Contracting State which makes extradition conditional on the existence of a treaty receives a request for extradition from another Contracting State with which it has no extradition treaty, it may at its option consider this Convention as the legal basis for extradition in respect of the offences. Extradition shall be subject to the other conditions provided by the law of the requested State.

3. Contracting States which do not make extradition conditional on the existence of a treaty shall recognize the offences as extraditable offences between themselves subject to the conditions provided by the law of the requested State.

4. Each of the offences shall be treated, for the purpose of extradition between Contracting States, as if it had been committed not only in the place in which it occurred but also in the territories of the States required to establish their jurisdiction in accordance with Article 5, paragraph 1(b), (c) and (d).

ARTICLE 9

The Contracting States which establish joint air transport operating organizations or international operating agencies, which operate aircraft which are subject to joint or international registration shall, by appropriate means, designate for each aircraft the State among them which shall exercise the jurisdiction and have the attributes of the State of registration for the purpose of this Convention and shall give notice thereof to the International Civil Aviation Organization which shall communicate the notice to all States Parties to this Convention.

ARTICLE 10

1. Contracting States shall, in accordance with international and national law, endeavour to take all practicable measures for the purpose of preventing the offences mentioned in Article 1.

2. When, due to the commission of one of the offences mentioned in Article 1, a flight has been delayed or interrupted, any Contracting State in whose territory the aircraft or passengers or crew are present shall facilitate the continuation of the journey of the passengers and crew as soon as practicable, and shall without delay return the aircraft and its cargo to the persons lawfully entitled to possession.

Article 11

1. Contracting States shall afford one another the greatest measure of assistance in connection with criminal proceedings brought in respect of the offences. The law of the State requested shall apply in all cases.

2. The provisions of paragraph 1 of this Article shall not affect obligations under any other treaty, bilateral or multilateral, which governs or will govern, in whole or in part, mutual assistance in criminal matters.

Article 12

Any Contracting State having reason to believe that one of the offences mentioned in Article 1 will be committed shall, in accordance with its national law, furnish any relevant information in its possession to those States which it believes would be the States mentioned in Article 5, paragraph 1.

Article 13

Each Contracting State shall in accordance with its national law report to the Council of the International Civil Aviation Organization as promptly as possible any relevant information in its possession concerning:

(a) the circumstances of the offence;

(b) the action taken pursuant to Article 10, paragraph 2;

(c) the measures taken in relation to the offender or the alleged offender and, in particular, the results of any extradition proceedings or other legal proceedings.

Article 14

1. Any dispute between two or more Contracting States concerning the interpretation or application of this Convention which cannot be settled through negotiation, shall, at the request of one of them, be submitted to arbitration. If within six months from the date of the request for arbitration the Parties are unable to agree on the organization of the arbitration, any one of those Parties may refer the dispute to the International Court of Justice by request in conformity with the Statute of the Court.

2. Each State may at the time of signature or ratification of this Convention or accession thereto, declare that it does not consider itself bound by the preceding paragraph. The other Contracting States shall not be bound by the preceding paragraph with respect to any Contracting State having made such a reservation.

3. Any Contracting State having made a reservation in accordance with the preceding paragraph may at any time withdraw this reservation by notification to the Depositary Governments.

* * *

3.29 INTERNATIONAL CONVENTION ON THE SUPPRESSION AND PUNISHMENT OF THE CRIME OF "APARTHEID." Done at New York, Nov. 30, 1973. Entered into force, July 18, 1976. U.N.G.A. Res. 3068 (XXVIII), 28 U.N. GAOR, Supp. (No. 30) 75, U.N. Doc. A/9030 (1974), *reprinted in* 13 I.L.M. 50 (1974)

Article I. (1) The States Parties to the present Convention declare that *apartheid* is a crime against humanity and that inhuman acts resulting from the policies and practices of *apartheid* and similar policies and practices of racial segregation and discrimination, as defined in article II of the Convention, are crimes violating the principles of international law, in particular the purposes and principles of the Charter of the United Nations, and constituting a serious threat to international peace and security.

(2) The States Parties to the present Convention declare criminal those organizations, institutions and individuals committing the crime of *apartheid.*

Article II. For the purpose of the present Convention, the term "the crime of *apartheid*" which shall include similar policies and practices of racial segregation and discrimination as practised in southern Africa, shall apply to the following inhuman acts committed for the purpose of establishing and maintaining domination by one racial group of persons over any other racial group of persons and systematically oppressing them:

(a) Denial to a member or members of a racial group or groups of the right to life and liberty of person:

(i) By murder of members of a racial group or groups;

(ii) By the infliction upon the members of a racial group or groups of serious bodily or mental harm by the infringement of their freedom or dignity, or by subjecting them to torture or to cruel, inhuman or degrading treatment or punishment;

(iii) By arbitrary arrest and illegal imprisonment of the members of a racial group or groups;

(b) Deliberate imposition on a racial group or groups of living conditions calculated to cause its or their physical destruction in whole or in part;

(c) Any legislative measures and other measures calculated to prevent a racial group or groups from participation in the political, social, economic and cultural life of the country and the deliberate creation of conditions preventing the full development of such a group or groups, in particular by denying to members of a racial group or groups basic human rights and freedoms, including the right to work, the right to form recognized trade unions, the right to education, the right to leave and to return to their country, the right to freedom of opinion and expression, and the right to freedom of peaceful assembly and association;

(d) Any measures, including legislative measures, designed to divide the population along racial lines by the creation of separate reserves and ghettos for the members of a racial group or groups, the prohibition of mixed marriages among members of various racial groups, the expropriation of landed property belonging to a racial group or groups or to members thereof;

(e) Exploitation of the labour of the members of a racial group or groups, in particular by submitting them to forced labour;

(f) Persecution of organizations and persons, by depriving them of fundamental rights and freedoms, because they oppose *apartheid.*

Article III. International criminal responsibility shall apply, irrespective of the motive involved, to individuals, members of organizations and institutions and representatives of the State, whether residing in the territory of the State in which the acts are perpetrated or in some other State, whenever they:

(a) Commit, participate in, directly incite or conspire in the commission of the acts mentioned in Article II of the present Convention;

(b) Directly abet, encourage or co-operate in the commission of the crime of *apartheid.*

Article IV. The States Parties to the present Convention undertake:

(a) To adopt any legislative or other measure necessary to suppress as well as to prevent any encouragement of the crime of *apartheid* and similar segregationist policies or their manifestations and to punish persons guilty of that crime;

(b) To adopt legislative, judicial and administrative measures to prosecute, bring to trial and punish in accordance with their jurisdiction persons responsible for, or accused of, the acts defined in article II of the present Convention, whether or not such persons reside in the territory of the State in which the acts are committed or are nationals of that State or of some other State or are stateless persons.

Article V. Persons charged with the acts enumerated in article II of the present Convention may be tried by a competent tribunal of any State Party to the Convention which may acquire jurisdiction with respect to those State Parties which shall have accepted its jurisdiction.

Article VI. The States Parties to the present Convention undertake to accept and carry out in accordance with the Charter of the United Nations the decisions taken by the Security Council aimed at the prevention, suppression and punishment of the crime of *apartheid,* and to co-operate in the implementation of decisions adopted by other competent organs of the United Nations with a view to achieving the purposes of the Convention.

Article VII. (1) The States Parties to the present Convention undertake to submit periodic reports to the group established under article IX on the legislative, judicial, administrative or other measures that they have adopted and that give effect to the provisions of the Convention.

(2) Copies of the reports shall be transmitted through the Secretary–General of the United Nations to the Special Committee on *Apartheid.*

Article VIII. Any State Party to the present Convention may call upon any competent organ of the United Nations to take such action under the Charter of the United Nations as it considers appropriate for the prevention and suppression of the crime of *apartheid.*

Article IX. (1) The Chairman of the Commission on Human Rights shall appoint a group consisting of three members of the Commission on Human Rights, who are also representatives of States Parties to the present Convention, to consider reports submitted by States Parties in accordance with article VII.

(2) If, among the members of the Commission on Human Rights, there are no representatives of States Parties to the present Convention or if there are fewer than three such representatives, the Secretary–General of the United Nations shall, after consulting all States Parties to the Convention, designate a representative of the State Party or representatives of the States Parties which are not members of the Commission on Human Rights to take part in the work of the group established in accordance with paragraph 1 of this article, until such time as representatives of the States Parties to the Convention are elected to the Commission on Human Rights.

(3) The group may meet for a period of not more than five days, either before the opening or after the closing of the session of the Commission on Human Rights, to consider the reports submitted in accordance with article VII.

Article X. (1) The States Parties to the present Convention empower the Commission on Human Rights:

(a) To request United Nations organs, when transmitting copies of petitions under article 15 of the International Convention on the Elimination of All Forms of Racial Discrimination, to draw its attention to complaints concerning acts which are enumerated in article II of the present Convention;

(b) To prepare, on the basis of reports from competent organs of the United Nations and periodic reports from States Parties to the present Convention, a list of individuals, organizations, institutions and representatives of States which are alleged to be responsible for the crimes enumerated in article II of the Convention, as well as those against whom legal proceedings have been undertaken by States Parties to the Convention;

(c) To request information for the competent United Nations organs concerning measures taken by the authorities responsible for the administration of Trust and Non-Self-Governing Territories, and all other Territories to which General Assembly resolution 1514(XV) of 14 December 1960 applies, with regard to such individuals alleged to be responsible for crimes under article II of the Convention who are believed to be under their territorial and administrative jurisdiction.

(2) Pending the achievement of the objectives of the Declaration on the Granting of Independence to Colonial Countries and Peoples, contained in General Assembly resolution 1514(XV), the provisions of the present Convention shall in no way limit the right of petition granted to those peoples by other international instruments or by the United Nations and its specialized agencies.

Article XI. (1) Acts enumerated in article II of the present Convention shall not be considered political crimes for the purpose of extradition.

(2) The States Parties to the present Convention undertake in such cases to grant extradition with their legislation and with the treaties in force.

* * *

3.30 CONVENTION ON THE PREVENTION AND PUNISHMENT OF CRIMES AGAINST INTERNATIONALLY PROTECTED PERSONS, INCLUDING DIPLOMATIC AGENTS.[a] Done at New York, Dec. 14, 1973. Entered into force, Feb. 20, 1977; for the United States, Feb. 20, 1977. 28 U.S.T. 1975, T.I.A.S. No. 8532, *reprinted in* 13 I.L.M. 43 (1974)

Article 1. For the purposes of this Convention:

(1) "internationally protected person" means:

(a) a Head of State, including any member of a collegial body performing the functions of a Head of State under the constitution of the State concerned, a Head of Government or a Minister for Foreign Affairs, whenever any such person is in a foreign State, as well as members of his family who accompany him;

(b) any representative or official of a State or any official or other agent of an international organization of an intergovernmental character who, at the time when and in the place where a crime against him, his official premises, his private accommodation or his means of transport is committed, is entitled pursuant to international law to special protection from any attack on his person, freedom or dignity, as well as members of his family forming part of his household;

(2) "alleged offender" means a person as to whom there is sufficient evidence to determine *prima facie* that he has committed or participated in one or more of the crimes set forth in article 2.

Article 2. (1) The international commission of:

(a) a murder, kidnapping or other attack upon the person or liberty of an internationally protected person;

(b) a violent attack upon the official premises, the private accommodation or the means of transport of an internationally protected person likely to endanger his person or liberty;

(c) a threat to commit any such attack;

(d) an attempt to commit any such attack; and

(e) an act constituting participation as an accomplice in any such attack shall be made by each State Party a crime under its internal law.

(2) Each State Party shall make these crimes punishable by appropriate penalties which take into account their grave nature.

(3) Paragraphs 1 and 2 of this article in no way derogate from the obligation of States Parties under international law to take all appropriate measures to prevent other attacks on the person, freedom or dignity of an internationally protected person.

Article 3. (1) Each State Party shall take such measures as may be necessary to establish its jurisdiction over the crimes set forth in article 2 in the following cases:

(a) when the crime is committed in the territory of that State or on board a ship or aircraft registered in that State;

(b) when the alleged offender is a national of that State;

a. *See also* Basic Documents 3.14, 3.27, and 3.28, *supra*, and Basic Documents 3.32, 3.33, 3.35, 3.42, and 3.43, *infra*.

(c) when the crime is committed against an internationally protected person as defined in article 1 who enjoys his status as such by virtue of functions which he exercises on behalf of that State.

(2) Each State Party shall likewise take such measures as may be necessary to establish its jurisdiction over these crimes in cases where the alleged offender is present in its territory and it does not extradite him pursuant to article 8 to any of the States mentioned in paragraph 1 of this article.

(3) This Convention does not exclude any criminal jurisdiction exercised in accordance with internal law.

Article 4. States Parties shall co-operate in the prevention of the crimes set forth in article 2, particularly by:

(a) taking all practicable measures to prevent preparations in their respective territories for the commission of those crimes within or outside their territories;

(b) exchanging information and co-ordinating the taking of administrative and other measures as appropriate to prevent the commission of those crimes.

Article 5. (1) The State Party in which any of the crimes set forth in article 2 has been committed shall, if it has reason to believe that an alleged offender has fled from its territory, communicate to all other States concerned, directly or through the Secretary-General of the United Nations, all the pertinent facts regarding the crime committed and all available information regarding the identity of the alleged offender.

(2) Whenever any of the crimes set forth in article 2 has been committed against an internationally protected person, any State Party which has information concerning the victim and the circumstances of the crime shall endeavour to transmit it, under the conditions provided for in its internal law, fully and promptly to the State Party on whose behalf he was exercising his functions.

Article 6. (1) Upon being satisfied that the circumstances so warrant, the State Party in whose territory the alleged offender is present shall take the appropriate measures under its internal law so as to ensure his presence for the purpose of prosecution or extradition. . . .

(2) Any person regarding whom the measures referred to in paragraph 1 of this article are being taken shall be entitled:

(a) to communicate without delay with the nearest appropriate representative of the State of which he is a national or which is otherwise entitled to protect his rights or, if he is a stateless person, which he requests and which is willing to protect his rights; and

(b) to be visited by a representative of that State.

Article 7. The State Party in whose territory the alleged offender is present shall, if it does not extradite him, submit, without exception whatsoever and without undue delay, the case to its competent authorities for the purpose of prosecution, through proceedings in accordance with the laws of that State.

Article 8. (1) To the extent that the crimes set forth in article 2 are not listed as extraditable offences in any extradition treaty existing between States Parties, they shall be deemed to be included as such therein. States Parties undertake to include those crimes as extraditable offences in every future extradition treaty to be concluded between them.

(2) If a State Party which makes extradition conditional on the existence of a treaty receives a request for extradition from another State Party with which it has no extradition treaty, it may, if it decides to extradite, consider this Convention as the legal basis for extradition in respect of those crimes. Extradition shall be subject

to the procedural provisions and the other conditions of the law of the requested State.

(3) States Parties which do not make extradition conditional on the existence of a treaty shall recognize those crimes as extraditable offences between themselves subject to the procedural provisions and the other conditions of the law of the requested State.

(4) Each of the crimes shall be treated, for the purpose of extradition between States Parties, as if it had been committed not only in the place in which it occurred but also in the territories of the States required to establish their jurisdiction in accordance with paragraph 1 of article 3.

Article 9. Any person regarding whom proceedings are being carried out in connexion with any of the crimes set forth in article 2 shall be guaranteed fair treatment at all stages of the proceedings.

Article 10. (1) States Parties shall afford one another the greatest measure of assistance in connexion with criminal proceedings brought in respect of the crimes set forth in article 2, including the supply of all evidence at their disposal necessary for the proceedings.

(2) The provisions of paragraph 1 of this article shall not affect obligations concerning mutual judicial assistance embodied in any other treaty.

Article 11. The State Party where an alleged offender is prosecuted shall communicate the final outcome of the proceedings to the Secretary-General of the United Nations, who shall transmit the information to the other States Parties.

Article 12. The provisions of this Convention shall not affect the application of the Treaties on Asylum, in force at the date of the adoption of this Convention, as between the States which are parties to those Treaties; but a State Party to this Convention may not invoke those Treaties with respect to another State Party to this Convention which is not a party to those Treaties.

* * *

3.31 UNIVERSAL DECLARATION ON THE ERADICATION OF HUNGER AND MALNUTRITION.[a] Adopted by the U.N. World Food Conference, Nov. 16, 1974. Report of the World Food Conference, Rome, U.N.Doc. E/Conf. 65/20, Ch. IV (1974), *reprinted in* The Right to Food 3–7 (K. Tomasewski ed. 1987)

The World Food Conference,

Convened by the General Assembly of the United Nations and entrusted with developing ways and means whereby the international community, as a whole, could take specific action to resolve the world food problem within the broader context of development and international economic co-operation,

Adopts the following Declaration:

UNIVERSAL DECLARATION ON THE ERADICATION OF HUNGER AND MALNUTRITION

Recognizing that:

(*a*) The grave food crisis that is afflicting the peoples of the developing countries where most of the world's hungry and ill-nourished live and where more than two thirds of the world's population produce about one third of the world's food—an imbalance which threatens to increase in the next 10 years—is not only fraught with grave economic and social implications, but also acutely jeopardizes the most fundamental principles and values associated with the right to life and human dignity as enshrined in the Universal Declaration of Human Rights;

(*b*) The elimination of hunger and malnutrition, included as one of the objectives in the United Nations Declaration on Social Progress and Development, and the elimination of the causes that determine this situation are the common objectives of all nations;

(*c*) The situation of the peoples afflicted by hunger and malnutrition arises from their historical circumstances, especially social inequalities, including in many cases alien and colonial domination, foreign occupation, racial discrimination, *apartheid* and neo-colonialism in all its forms, which continue to be among the greatest obstacles to the full emancipation and progress of the developing countries and all the peoples involved;

(*d*) This situation has been aggravated in recent years by a series of crises to which the world economy has been subjected, such as the deterioration in the international monetary system, the inflationary increase in import costs, the heavy burdens imposed by external debt on the balance of payments of many developing countries, a rising food demand partly due to demographic pressure, speculation, and a shortage of, and increased costs for, essential agricultural inputs;

(*e*) These phenomena should be considered within the framework of the on-going negotiations on the Charter of Economic Rights and Duties of States, and the General Assembly of the United Nations should be urged unanimously to agree upon, and to adopt, a Charter that will be an effective instrument for the establishment of new international economic relations based on principles of equity and justice;

(*f*) All countries, big or small, rich or poor, are equal. All countries have the full right to participate in the decisions on the food problem;

(*g*) The well-being of the peoples of the world largely depends on the adequate production and distribution of food as well as the establishment of a world food

a. *See also* Basic Document 3.44, *infra.*

security system which would ensure adequate availability of, and reasonable prices for, food at all times, irrespective of periodic fluctuations and vagaries of weather and free of political and economic pressures, and should thus facilitate, amongst other things, the development process of developing countries;

(*h*) Peace and justice encompass an economic dimension helping the solution of the world economic problems, the liquidation of under-development, offering a lasting and definitive solution of the food problem for all peoples and guaranteeing to all countries the right to implement freely and effectively their development programmes. To this effect, it is necessary to eliminate threats and resort to force and to promote peaceful co-operation between States to the fullest extent possible, to apply the principles of non-interference in the internal affairs of other States, full equality of rights and respect of national independence and sovereignty, as well as to encourage the peaceful co-operation between all States, irrespective of their political, social and economic systems. The further improvement of international relations will create better conditions for international co-operation in all fields which should make possible large financial and material resources to be used, *inter alia,* for developing agricultural production and substantially improving world food security;

(*i*) For a lasting solution of the food problem all efforts should be made to eliminate the widening gaps which today separate developed and developing countries and to bring about a new international economic order. It should be possible for all countries to participate actively and effectively in the new international economic relations by the establishment of suitable international systems, where appropriate, capable of producing adequate action in order to establish just and equitable relations in international economic co-operation;

(*j*) Developing countries reaffirm their belief that the primary responsibility for ensuring their own rapid development rests with themselves. They declare, therefore, their readiness to continue to intensify their individual and collective efforts with a view to expanding their mutual co-operation in the field of agricultural development and food production, including the eradication of hunger and malnutrition;

(*k*) Since, for various reasons, many developing countries are not yet always able to meet their own food needs, urgent and effective international action should be taken to assist them, free of political pressures.

Consistent with the aims and objectives of the Declaration on the Establishment of a New International Economic Order and the Programme of Action adopted by the General Assembly at its sixth special session,

The Conference consequently solemnly proclaims:

1. Every man, woman and child has the inalienable right to be free from hunger and malnutrition in order to develop fully and maintain their physical and mental faculties. Society today already possesses sufficient resources, organizational ability and technology and hence the competence to achieve this objective. Accordingly, the eradication of hunger is a common objective of all the countries of the international community, especially of the developed countries and others in a position to help.

2. It is a fundamental responsibility of Governments to work together for higher food production and a more equitable and efficient distribution of food between countries and within countries. Governments should initiate immediately a greater concerted attack on chronic malnutrition and deficiency diseases among the vulnerable and lower income groups. In order to ensure adequate nutrition for all, Governments should formulate appropriate food and nutrition policies integrated in over-all socio-economic and agricultural development plans based on adequate knowl-

edge of available as well as potential food resources. The importance of human milk in this connexion should be stressed on nutritional grounds.

3. Food problems must be tackled during the preparation and implementation of national plans and programmes for economic and social development, with emphasis on their humanitarian aspects.

4. It is a responsibility of each State concerned, in accordance with its sovereign judgement and internal legislation, to remove the obstacles to food production and to provide proper incentives to agricultural producers. Of prime importance for the attainment of these objectives are effective measures of socio-economic transformation by agrarian, tax, credit and investment policy reform and the reorganization of rural structures, such as the reform of the conditions of ownership, the encouragement of producer and consumer co-operatives, the mobilization of the full potential of human resources, both male and female, in the developing countries for an integrated rural development and the involvement of small farmers, fishermen and landless workers in attaining the required food production and employment targets. Moreover, it is necessary to recognize the key role of women in agricultural production and rural economy in many countries, and to ensure that appropriate education, extension programmes and financial facilities are made available to women on equal terms with men.

5. Marine and inland water resources are today becoming more important than ever as a source of food and economic prosperity. Accordingly, action should be taken to promote a rational exploitation of these resources, preferably for direct human consumption, in order to contribute to meeting the food requirements of all peoples.

6. The efforts to increase food production should be complemented by every endeavour to prevent wastage of food in all its forms.

7. To give impetus to food production in developing countries and in particular in the least developed and most seriously affected among them, urgent and effective international action should be taken, by the developed countries and other countries in a position to do so, to provide them with sustained additional technical and financial assistance on favourable terms and in a volume sufficient to their needs on the basis of bilateral and multilateral arrangements. This assistance must be free of conditions inconsistent with the sovereignty of the receiving States.

8. All countries, and primarily the highly industrialized countries, should promote the advancement of food production technology and should make all efforts to promote the transfer, adaptation and dissemination of appropriate food production technology for the benefit of the developing countries and, to that end, they should *inter alia* make all efforts to disseminate the results of their research work to Governments and scientific institutions of developing countries in order to enable them to promote a sustained agricultural development.

9. To assure the proper conservation of natural resources being utilized, or which might be utilized, for food production, all countries must collaborate in order to facilitate the preservation of the environment, including the marine environment.

10. All developed countries and others able to do so should collaborate technically and financially with the developing countries in their efforts to expand land and water resources for agricultural production and to assure a rapid increase in the availability, at fair costs, of agricultural inputs such as fertilizers and other chemicals, high-quality seeds, credit and technology. Co-operation among developing countries, in this connexion, is also important.

11. All States should strive to the utmost to readjust, where appropriate, their agricultural policies to give priority to food production, recognizing, in this connexion, the interrelationship between the world food problem and international trade.

In the determination of attitudes towards farm support programmes for domestic food production, developed countries should take into account, as far as possible, the interest of the food-exporting developing countries, in order to avoid detrimental effect on their exports. Moreover, all countries should co-operate to devise effective steps to deal with the problem of stabilizing world markets and promoting equitable and remunerative prices, where appropriate through international arrangements, to improve access to markets through reduction or elimination of tariff and non-tariff barriers on the products of interest to the developing countries, to substantially increase the export earnings of these countries, to contribute to the diversification of their exports, and apply to them, in the multilateral trade negotiations, the principles as agreed upon in the Tokyo Declaration, including the concept of non-reciprocity and more favourable treatment.

12. As it is the common responsibility of the entire international community to ensure the availability at all times of adequate world supplies of basic food-stuffs by way of appropriate reserves, including emergency reserves, all countries should co-operate in the establishment of an effective system of world food security by:

Participating in and supporting the operation of the Global Information and Early Warning System on Food and Agriculture;

Adhering to the objectives, policies and guidelines of the proposed International Undertaking on World Food Security as endorsed by the World Food Conference;

Earmarking, where possible, stocks or funds for meeting international emergency food requirements as envisaged in the proposed International Undertaking on World Food Security and developing international guidelines to provide for the co-ordination and the utilization of such stocks;

Co-operating in the provision of food aid for meeting emergency and nutritional needs as well as for stimulating rural employment through development projects.

All donor countries should accept and implement the concept of forward planning of food aid and make all efforts to provide commodities and/or financial assistance that will ensure adequate quantities of grains and other food commodities.

Time is short. Urgent and sustained action is vital. The Conference, therefore, calls upon all peoples expressing their will as individuals, and through their Governments and non-governmental organizations, to work together to bring about the end of the age-old scourge of hunger.

The Conference affirms:

The determination of the participating States to make full use of the United Nations system in the implementation of this Declaration and the other decisions adopted by the Conference.

3.32 ANTIHIJACKING ACT OF 1974, 49 U.S.C.A. §§ 1301, 1472, 1514 (Supp.1989).[a]

* * *

§ 1301. Definitions

As used in this chapter, unless the context otherwise requires—

* * *

(38) The term "special aircraft jurisdiction of the United States" includes—

(a) civil aircraft of the United States;

(b) aircraft of the national defense forces of the United States;

(c) any other aircraft within the United States;

(d) any other aircraft outside the United States—

(i) that has its next scheduled destination or last point of departure in the United States, if that aircraft next actually lands in the United States;

(ii) having "an offense", as defined in the Convention for the Suppression of Unlawful Seizure of Aircraft, committed aboard, if that aircraft lands in the United States with the alleged offender still aboard; or;

(iii) regarding which an offense as defined in subsection (d) or (e) of article I, section I of the Convention for the Suppression of Unlawful Acts against the Safety of Civil Aviation (Montreal, September 23, 1971) is committed if the aircraft lands in the United States with an alleged offender still on board; and

(e) other aircraft leased without crew to a lessee who has his principal place of business in the United States, or if none, who has his permanent residence in the United States;

while that aircraft is in flight, which is from the moment when all external doors are closed following embarkation until the moment when one such door is opened for disembarkation or in the case of a forced landing, until the competent authorities take over the responsibility for the aircraft and for the persons and property aboard.

* * *

§ 1472. Criminal penalties

(i) Aircraft piracy

(1) Whoever commits or attempts to commit aircraft piracy, as herein defined, shall be punished—

(A) by imprisonment for not less than 20 years; or

(B) if notwithstanding the provisions of section 3559(b) of Title 18, the death of another person results from the commission or attempted commission of the offense, by death or by imprisonment for life.

(2) As used in this subsection, the term "aircraft piracy" means any seizure or exercise of control, by force or violence or threat of force or violence, or by any other form of intimidation, and with wrongful intent, of an aircraft within the special aircraft jurisdiction of the United States.

(3) An attempt to commit aircraft piracy shall be within the special aircraft jurisdiction of the United States even though the aircraft is not in flight at the time of such attempt if the aircraft would have been within the special aircraft jurisdiction of the United States had the offense of aircraft piracy been completed.

* * *

a. *See also* Basic Documents 3.14, 3.27, 3.28 and 3.30, *supra*, and Basic Documents 3.33, 3.35, 3.42, and 3.43, *infra*.

(n) Aircraft piracy outside special aircraft jurisdiction of United States

(1) Whoever aboard an aircraft in flight outside the special aircraft jurisdiction of the United States commits "an offense", as defined in the Convention for the Suppression of Unlawful Seizure of Aircraft, and is afterward found in the United States shall be punished—

(A) by imprisonment for not less than 20 years; or

(B) if notwithstanding the provisions of section 3559(b) of Title 18, the death of another person results from the commission or attempted commission of the offense, by death or by imprisonment for life.

(2) A person commits "an offense", as defined in the Convention for the Suppression of Unlawful Seizure of Aircraft when, while aboard an aircraft in flight, he—

(A) unlawfully, by force or threat thereof, or by any other form of intimidation, seizes, or exercises control of, that aircraft, or attempts to perform any such act; or

(B) is an accomplice of a person who performs or attempts to perform any such act.

(3) This subsection shall only be applicable if the place of takeoff or the place of actual landing of the aircraft on board which the offense, as defined in paragraph (2) of this subsection, is committed is situated outside the territory of the State of registration of that aircraft.

(4) For purposes of this subsection an aircraft is considered to be in flight from the moment when all the external doors are closed following embarkation until the moment when one such door is opened for disembarkation, or in the case of a forced landing, until the competent authorities take over responsibility for the aircraft and for the persons and property aboard.

* * *

§ 1514. Suspension of air services by President; grounds; authority of President deemed condition to issuance of certificate of public convenience and necessity, etc.; unlawful activities

(a) Whenever the President determines that a foreign nation is acting in a manner inconsistent with the Convention for the Suppression of Unlawful Seizure of Aircraft, or if he determines that a foreign nation permits the use of territory under its jurisdiction as a base of operations or training or as a sanctuary for, or in any way arms, aids, or abets, any terrorist organization which knowingly uses the illegal seizure of aircraft or the threat thereof as an instrument of policy, he may, without notice or hearing and for as long as he determines necessary to assure the security of aircraft against unlawful seizure, suspend (1) the right of any air carrier or foreign air carrier to engage in foreign air transportation, and the right of any person to operate aircraft in foreign air commerce, to and from that foreign nation, and (2) the right of any foreign air carrier to engage in foreign air transportation, and the right of any foreign person to operate aircraft in foreign air commerce, between the United States and any foreign nation which maintains air service between itself and that foreign nation. Notwithstanding section 1502 of this title, the President's authority to suspend rights under this section shall be deemed to be a condition to any certificate of public convenience and necessity or foreign air carrier or foreign aircraft permit issued by the Civil Aeronautics Board and any air carrier operating certificate or foreign air carrier operating specification issued by the Secretary of Transportation.

(b) It shall be unlawful for any air carrier or foreign air carrier to engage in foreign air transportation, or for any person to operate aircraft in foreign air commerce, in violation of the suspension of rights by the President under this section.

3.33 EUROPEAN CONVENTION ON THE SUPPRESSION OF TERRORISM.[a] Done at Strasbourg, Nov. 10, 1976. Entered into force, Aug. 4, 1978. Europ. T.S. No. 90, *reprinted in* 15 I.L.M. 1272 (1976)

Article 1. For the purposes of extradition between Contracting States, none of the following offences shall be regarded as a political offence or as an offence connected with a political offence or as an offence inspired by political motives:

(a) an offence within the scope of the Convention for the Suppression of Unlawful Seizure of Aircraft, signed at The Hague on 16 December 1970;

(b) an offence within the scope of the Convention for the Suppression of Unlawful Acts against the Safety of Civil Aviation, signed at Montreal on 23 September 1971;

(c) a serious offence involving an attack against the life, physical integrity or liberty of internationally protected persons, including diplomatic agents;

(d) an offence involving kidnapping, the taking of a hostage or serious unlawful detention;

(e) an offence involving the use of a bomb, grenade, rocket, automatic firearm or letter or parcel bomb if this use endangers persons;

(f) an attempt to commit any of the foregoing offences or participation as an accomplice of a person who commits or attempts to commit such an offence.

Article 2. (1) For the purposes of extradition between Contracting States, a Contracting State may decide not to regard as a political offence or as an offence connected with a political offence or as an offence inspired by political motives a serious offence involving an act of violence, other than one covered by Article 1, against the life, physical integrity or liberty of a person.

(2) The same shall apply to a serious offence involving an act against property, other than one covered by Article 1, if the act created a collective danger for persons.

(3) The same shall apply to an attempt to commit any of the foregoing offences or participation as an accomplice of a person who commits or attempts to commit such an offence.

Article 3. The provisions of all extradition treaties and arrangements applicable between Contracting States, including the European Convention on Extradition, are modified as between Contracting States to the extent that they are incompatible with this Convention.

Article 4. For the purposes of this Convention and to the extent that any offence mentioned in Article 1 or 2 is not listed as an extraditable offence in any extradition convention or treaty existing between Contracting States, it shall be deemed to be included as such therein.

Article 5. Nothing in this Convention shall be interpreted as imposing an obligation to extradite if the requested State has substantial grounds for believing that the request for extradition for an offence on account of his race, religion, nationality or political opinion, or that that person's position may be prejudiced for any of these reasons.

Article 6. (1) Each Contracting State shall take such measures as may be necessary to establish its jurisdiction over an offence mentioned in Article 1 in the case where the suspected offender is present in its territory and it does not extradite

a. *See also* Basic Documents 3.14, 3.27, 3.28, 3.30, and 3.32, *supra*, and Basic Documents 3.35, 3.42, and 3.43, *infra*.

him after receiving a request for extradition from a Contracting State whose jurisdiction is based on a rule of jurisdiction existing equally in the law of the requested State.

(2) This Convention does not exclude any criminal jurisdiction exercised in accordance with national law.

Article 7. A Contracting State in whose territory a person suspected to have committed an offence mentioned in Article 1 is found and which has received a request for extradition under the conditions mentioned in Article 6, paragraph 1, shall, if it does not extradite that person, submit the case, without exception whatsoever and without undue delay, to its competent authorities for the purpose of prosecution. Those authorities shall take their decision in the same manner as in the case of any offence of a serious nature under the law of that State.

Article 8. (1) Contracting States shall afford one another the widest measure of mutual assistance in criminal matters in connection with proceedings brought in respect of the offences mentioned in Article 1 or 2. The law of the requested State concerning mutual assistance in criminal matters shall apply in all cases. Nevertheless this assistance may not be refused on the sole ground that it concerns a political offence or an offence connected with a political offence or an offence inspired by political motives.

(2) Nothing in this Convention shall be interpreted as imposing an obligation to afford mutual assistance if the requested State has substantial grounds for believing that the request for mutual assistance in respect of an offence mentioned in Article 1 or 2 has been made for the purpose of prosecuting or punishing a person on account of his race, religion, nationality or political opinion or that the person's position may prejudiced for any of these reasons.

(3) The provisions of all treaties and arrangements concerning mutual assistance in criminal matters applicable between Contracting States, including the European Convention on Mutual Assistance in Criminal Matters, are modified as between Contracting States to the extent that they are incompatible with this Convention.

Article 9. (1) The European Committee on Crime Problems of the Council of Europe shall be kept informed regarding the application of this Convention.

(2) It shall do whatever is needful to facilitate a friendly settlement of any difficulty which may arise out of its execution.

Article 10. (1) Any dispute between Contracting States concerning the interpretation or application of this Convention, which has not been settled in the framework of Article 9, paragraph 2, shall, at the request of any Party to the dispute, be referred to arbitration. Each Party shall nominate an arbitrator and the two arbitrators shall nominate a referee. If any Party has not nominated its arbitrator within the three months following the request for arbitration, he shall be nominated at the request of the other Party by the President of the European Court of Human Rights. If the latter should be a national of one of the Parties to the dispute, this duty shall be carried out by the Vice–President of the Court or, if the Vice–President is a national of one of the Parties to the dispute, by the most senior judge of the Court not being a national of one of the Parties to the dispute. The same procedure shall be observed if the arbitrators cannot agree on the choice of referee.

(2) The arbitration tribunal shall lay down its own procedure. Its decisions shall be taken by majority vote. Its award shall be final.

* * *

Article 13. (1) Any State may, at the time of signature or when depositing its instrument of ratification, acceptance or approval, declare that it reserves the right to refuse extradition in respect of any offence mentioned in Article 1 which it considers to be a political offence, an offence connected with a political offence or an offence inspired by political motives, provided that it undertakes to take into due consideration, when evaluating the character of the offence, any particularly serious aspects of the offence, including:

(a) that it created a collective danger to the life, physical integrity or liberty of persons; or

(b) that it affected persons foreign to the motives behind it; or

(c) that cruel or vicious means have been used in the commission of the offence.

(2) Any State may wholly or partly withdraw a reservation it has made in accordance with the foregoing paragraph by means of a declaration addressed to the Secretary General of the Council of Europe which shall become effective as from the date of its receipt.

(3) A State which has made a reservation in accordance with paragraph 1 of this article may not claim the application of Article 1 by any other State; it may, however, if its reservation is partial or conditional, claim the application of that article in so far as it has itself accepted it.

* * *

3.34 RESOLUTION ON DISAPPEARED PERSONS. Adopted by the U.N. General Assembly, Dec. 20, 1978. U.N.G.A. Res. 33/173, 33 U.N. GAOR, Supp. (No. 45) 158, U.N. Doc. A/33/509 (1978)

The General Assembly,

Recalling the provisions of the Universal Declaration of Human Rights, in particular articles 3, 5, 9, 10 and 11 concerning, *inter alia,* the right to life, liberty and security of person, freedom from torture, freedom from arbitrary arrest and detention, and the right to a fair and public trial, and the provisions of articles 6, 7, 9 and 10 of the International Covenant on Civil and Political Rights, which define and establish safeguards for certain of these rights,

Deeply concerned by reports from various parts of the world relating to enforced or involuntary disappearances of persons as a result of excesses on the part of law enforcement or security authorities or similar organizations, often while such persons are subject to detention or imprisonment, as well as of unlawful actions or widespread violence,

Concerned also at reports of difficulties in obtaining reliable information from competent authorities as to the circumstances of such persons, including reports of the persistent refusal of such authorities or organizations to acknowledge that they hold such persons in their custody or otherwise to account for them,

Mindful of the danger to the life, liberty and physical security of such persons arising from the persistent failure of these authorities or organizations to acknowledge that such persons are held in custody or otherwise to account for them,

Deeply moved by the anguish and sorrow which such circumstances cause to the relatives of disappeared persons, especially to spouses, children and parents,

1. *Calls upon* Governments:

(*a*) In the event of reports of enforced or involuntary disappearances, to devote appropriate resources to searching for such persons and to undertake speedy and impartial investigations;

(*b*) To ensure that law enforcement and security authorities or organizations are fully accountable, especially in law, in the discharge of their duties, such accountability to include legal responsibility for unjustifiable excesses which might lead to enforced or involuntary disappearances and to other violations of human rights;

(*c*) To ensure that the human rights of all persons, including those subjected to any form of detention and imprisonment, are fully respected;

(*d*) To co-operate with other Governments, relevant United Nations organs, specialized agencies, intergovernmental organizations and humanitarian bodies in a common effort to search for, locate or account for such persons in the event of reports of enforced or involuntary disappearances;

2. *Requests* the Commission on Human Rights to consider the question of disappeared persons with a view to making appropriate recommendations;

3. *Urges* the Secretary–General to continue to use his good offices in cases of enforced or involuntary disappearances of persons, drawing, as appropriate, upon the relevant experience of the International Committee of the Red Cross and of other humanitarian organizations;

4. *Requests* the Secretary–General to draw the concerns expressed in the present resolution to the attention of all Governments, regional and interregional organizations and specialized agencies for the purpose of conveying on an urgent basis the need for disinterested humanitarian action to respond to the situation of persons who have disappeared.

3.35 INTERNATIONAL CONVENTION AGAINST THE TAKING OF HOSTAGES.[a] Entered into force, June 4, 1983; for the United States, June 4, 1983. U.N.G.A. Res. 34/146 (XXXIV), 34 U.N. GAOR, Supp. (No. 46) 245, U.N. Doc. A/34/786 (1979), *reprinted in* 18 I.L.M. 1456 (1979)

Article 1. (1) Any person who seizes or detains and threatens to kill, to injure or to continue to detain another person (hereinafter referred to as the "hostage") in order to compel a third party, namely, a State, an international intergovernmental organization, a natural or juridical person, or a group of persons, to do or abstain from doing any act as an explicit or implicit condition for the release of the hostage commits the offence of taking of hostages ("hostage-taking") within the meaning of this Convention.

(2) Any person who:

(a) Attempts to commit an act of hostage-taking, or

(b) Participates as an accomplice of anyone who commits or attempts to commit an act of hostage-taking

likewise commits an offence for the purpose of this Convention.

Article 2. Each State Party shall make the offences set forth in article 1 punishable by appropriate penalties which take into account the grave nature of those offences.

Article 3. (1) The State Party in the territory of which the hostage is held by the offender shall take all measures it considers appropriate to ease the situation of the hostage, in particular, to secure his release and, after his release, to facilitate, when relevant, his departure.

(2) If any object which the offender has obtained as a result of the taking of hostages comes into the custody of a State Party, that State Party shall return it as soon as possible to the hostage or the third party referred to in article 1, as the case may be, or to the appropriate authorities thereof.

Article 4. State Parties shall co-operate in the prevention of the offences set forth in article 1, particularly by:

(a) Taking all practicable measures to prevent preparations in their respective territories for the commission of those offences within or outside their territories, including measures to prohibit in their territories illegal activities of persons, groups and organizations that encourage, instigate, organize or engage in the perpetration of acts of hostages:

(b) Exchanging information and co-ordinating the taking of administrative and other measures as appropriate to prevent the commission of those offences.

Article 5. Each State Party shall take such measures as may be necessary to establish its jurisdiction over any of the offences set forth in article 1 which are committed:

(a) In its territory or on board a ship or aircraft registered in that State:

(b) By any of its nationals or, if that State considers it appropriate, by those stateless persons who have their habitual residence in its territory;

(c) In order to compel that State to do or abstain from doing any act; or

a. *See also* Basic Documents 3.14, 3.27, 3.28, 3.30, 3.32, and 3.33, *supra*, and Basic Documents 3.42 and 3.43, *infra*.

(d) With respect to a hostage who is a national of that State, if that State considers it appropriate.

(2) Each State Party shall likewise take such measures as may be necessary to establish its jurisdiction over the offences set forth in article 1 in cases where the alleged offender is present in its territory and it does not extradite him to any of the States mentioned in paragraph 1 of this article.

(3) This Convention does not exclude any criminal jurisdiction exercised in accordance with internal law.

Article 6. (1) Upon being satisfied that the circumstances so warrant, any State Party in the territory of which the alleged offender is present shall, in accordance with its laws, take him into custody or take other measures to ensure his presence for such time as is necessary to enable any criminal or extradition proceedings to be instituted. That State Party shall immediately make a preliminary inquiry into the facts.

(2) The custody or other measures referred to in paragraph 1 of this article shall be notified without delay directly or through the Secretary–General of the United Nations to:

(a) The State where the offence was committed;

(b) The State against which compulsion has been directed or attempted:

(c) The State of which the natural or juridical person against whom compulsion has been directed or attempted is a national;

(d) The State of which the hostage is a national or in the territory of which he has his habitual residence;

(e) The State of which the alleged offender is a national or, if he is a stateless person, in the territory of which he has his habitual residence;

(f) The international intergovernmental organization against which compulsion has been directed or attempted;

(g) All other States concerned.

(3) Any person regarding whom the measures referred to in paragraph 1 of this article are being taken shall be entitled:

(a) To communicate without delay with the nearest appropriate representative of the State of which he is a national or which is otherwise entitled to establish such communication or, if he is a stateless person, the State in the territory of which he has his habitual residence;

(b) To be visited by a representative of that State.

(4) The rights referred to in paragraph 3 of this article shall be exercised in conformity with the laws and regulations of the State in the territory of which the alleged offender is present, subject to the proviso, however, that the said laws and regulations must enable full effect to be given to the purpose for which the rights accorded under paragraph 3 of this article are intended.

(5) The provisions of paragraphs 3 and 4 of this article shall be without prejudice to the right of any State Party having a claim to jurisdiction in accordance with paragraph 1(b) of article 5 to invite the International Committee of the Red Cross to communicate with and visit the alleged offender.

(6) The State which makes the preliminary inquiry contemplated in paragraph 1 of this article shall promptly report its findings to the States or organization referred to in paragraph 2 of this article and indicate whether it intends to exercise jurisdiction.

Article 7. The State Party where the alleged offender is prosecuted shall, in accordance with its laws, communicate the final outcome of the proceedings to the

Secretary–General of the United Nations, who shall transmit the information to the other States concerned and the international intergovernmental organizations concerned.

Article 8. The State Party in the territory of which the alleged offender is found shall, if it does not extradite him, be obliged, without exception whatsoever and whether or not the offence was committed in its territory, to submit the case to its competent authorities for the purpose of prosecution, through proceedings in accordance with the laws of that State. Those authorities shall take their decision in the same manner as in the case of any ordinary offence of a grave nature under the law of that State.

(2) Any person regarding whom proceedings are being carried out in connexion with any of the offences set forth in article 1 shall be guaranteed fair treatment at all stages of the proceedings, including enjoyment of all the rights and guarantees provided by the law of the State in the territory of which he is present.

Article 9. (1) A request for the extradition of an alleged offender, pursuant to this Convention, shall not be granted if the requested State Party has substantial grounds for believing:

(a) That the request for extradition for an offence set forth in article 1 has been made for the purpose of prosecuting or punishing a person on account of his race, religion, nationality, ethnic origin or political opinion; or

(b) That the person's position may be prejudiced.

(i) For any of the reasons mentioned in subparagraph (*a*) of this paragraph, or

(ii) For the reason that communication with him by the appropriate authorities of the State entitled to exercise rights of protection cannot be effected.

(2) With respect to the offences as defined in this Convention, the provisions of all extradition treaties and arrangements applicable between States Parties are modified as between States Parties to the extent that they are incompatible with this Convention.

Article 10. (1) The offences set forth in article 1 shall be deemed to be included as extraditable offences in any extradition treaty existing between States Parties. States Parties undertake to include such offences as extraditable offences in every extradition treaty to be concluded between them.

(2) If a State Party which makes extradition conditional on the existence of a treaty receives a request for extradition from another State Party with which it has no extradition treaty, the requested State may at its option consider this Convention as the legal basis for extradition in respect of the offences set forth in article 1. Extradition shall be subject to the other conditions provided by the law of the requested State.

(3) States Parties which do not make extradition conditional on the existence of a treaty shall recognize the offences set forth in article 1 as extraditable offences between themselves, subject to the conditions provided by the law of the requested State.

(4) The offences set forth in article 1 shall be treated, for the purpose of extradition between States Parties, as if they had been committed not only in the place in which they occurred but also in the territories of the States required to establish their jurisdiction in accordance with paragraph 1 of article 5.

Article 11. (1) States Parties shall afford one another the greatest measure of assistance in connexion with criminal proceedings brought in respect of the offences set forth in article 1, including the supply of all evidence at their disposal necessary for the proceedings.

(2) The provisions of paragraph 1 of this article shall not affect obligations concerning mutual judicial assistance embodied in any other treaty.

Article 12. In so far as the Geneva Conventions of 1949 for the protection of war victims or the Protocols Additional to those Conventions are applicable to a particular act of hostage-taking, and in so far as States Parties to this Convention are bound under those Conventions to prosecute or hand over the hostage-taker, the present Convention shall not apply to an act of hostage-taking committed in the course of armed conflicts as defined in the Geneva Conventions of 1949 and the Protocols thereto, including armed conflicts, mentioned in article 1, paragraph 4, of Protocol I of 1977, in which peoples are fighting against colonial domination and alien occupation and against racist régimes in the exercise of their right of self-determination, as enshrined in the Charter of the United Nations and the Declaration on Principles of International Law concerning Friendly Relations and Co-operation among States in accordance with the Charter of the United nations.

Article 13. This Convention shall not apply where the offence is committed within a single State, the hostage and the alleged offender are nationals of that State and the alleged offender is found in the territory of that State.

Article 14. Nothing in this Convention shall be construed as justifying the violation of the territorial integrity or political independence of a State in contravention of the Charter of the United Nations.

Article 15. The provisions of this Convention shall not affect the application of the Treaties on Asylum, in force at the date of the adoption of this Convention, as between the States which are parties to those treaties; but a State Party to this Convention may not invoke those treaties with respect to another State Party to this Convention which is not a party to those treaties.

* * *

3.36 CONVENTION ON THE ELIMINATION OF ALL FORMS OF DISCRIMINATION AGAINST WOMEN.[a] Done at New York, Dec. 18, 1979. Entered into force, Sept. 3, 1981. U.N.G.A. Res. 34/180 (XXXIV), 34 U.N. GAOR, Supp. (No. 46) 194, U.N. Doc. A/34/830 (1979), *reprinted in* 19 I.L.M. 33 (1980)

Part I

Article 1. For the purposes of the present Convention, the term "discrimination against women" shall mean any distinction, exclusion or restriction made on the basis of sex which has the effect or purpose of impairing or nullifying the recognition, enjoyment or exercise by women, irrespective of their marital status, on a basis of equality of men and women, of human rights and fundamental freedoms in the political, economic, social, cultural, civil or any other field.

* * *

Article 3. States Parties shall take in all fields, in particular in the political, social, economic and cultural fields, all appropriate measures, including legislation, to ensure the full development and advancement of women, for the purpose of guaranteeing them the exercise and enjoyment of human rights and fundamental freedoms on a basis of equality with men.

Article 4. (1) Adoption by States Parties of temporary special measures aimed at accelerating *de facto* equality between men and women shall not be considered discrimination as defined in this Convention, but shall in no way entail, as a consequence, the maintenance of unequal or separate standards. These measures shall be discontinued when the objectives of equality of opportunity and treatment have been achieved.

(2) Adoption by States Parties of special measures, including those measures contained in the present Convention, aimed at protecting maternity, shall not be considered discriminatory.

Article 5. States Parties shall take all appropriate measures:

(a) To modify the social and cultural patterns of conduct of men and women, with a view to achieving the elimination of prejudices and customary and all other practices which are based on the idea of the inferiority or the superiority of either of the sexes or on stereotyped roles for men and women.

(b) To ensure that family education includes a proper understanding of maternity as a social function and the recognition of the common responsibility of men and women in the upbringing and development of their children.

Article 6. States Parties shall take all appropriate measures, including legislation, to suppress all forms of traffic in women and exploitation of prostitution of women.

Part II

Article 7. States Parties shall take all appropriate measures to eliminate discrimination against women in the political and public life of the country and, in particular, shall ensure, on equal terms with men, the right:

(a) To vote in all elections and public referenda and to be eligible for election to all publicly elected bodies;

a. *See also* Basic Document 3.7, *supra.*

(b) To participate in the formulation of government policy and the implementation thereof and to hold public office and perform all public functions at all levels of government;

(c) To participate in non-governmental organizations and associations concerned with the public and political life of the country.

Article 8. States Parties shall take all appropriate measures to ensure to women on equal terms with men and, without any discrimination, the opportunity to represent their Governments at the international level and to participate in the work of international organizations.

Article 9. (1) States Parties shall grant women equal rights with men to acquire, change or retain their nationality. They shall ensure in particular that neither marriage to an alien nor change of nationality by the husband during marriage shall automatically change the nationality of the wife, render her stateless or force upon her the nationality of the husband.

(2) States Parties shall grant women equal rights with men with respect to the nationality of their children.

Part III

Article 10. States Parties shall take all appropriate measures to eliminate discrimination against women in order to ensure to them equal rights with men in the field of education and in particular to ensure, on a basis of equality of men and women:

(a) The same conditions for career and vocational guidance, for access to studies and for the achievement of diplomas in educational establishments of all categories in rural as well as in urban areas; this equality shall be ensured in pre-school, general, technical, professional and higher technical education, as well as in all types of vocational training;

(b) Access to the same curricula, the same examinations, teaching staff with qualifications of the same standard and school premises and equipment of the same quality;

(c) The elimination of any stereotyped concept of the roles of men and women at all levels and in all forms of education by encouraging coeducation and other types of education which will help to achieve this aim and, in particular, by the revision of textbooks and school programmes and the adaptation of teaching methods;

(d) The same opportunities to benefit from scholarships and other study grants;

(e) The same opportunities for access to programmes of continuing education, including adult and functional literacy programmes, particularly those aimed at reducing, at the earliest possible time, any gap in education existing between men and women;

(f) The reduction of female student drop-out rates and the organization of programmes for girls and women who have left school prematurely;

(g) The same opportunities to participate actively in sports and physical education;

(h) Access to specific educational information to help to ensure the health and well-being of families, including information and advice on family planning.

Article 11. (1) States Parties shall take all appropriate measures to eliminate discrimination against women in the field of employment in order to ensure, on a basis of equality of men and women, the same rights, in particular:

(a) The right to work as an inalienable right of all human beings;

(b) The right to the same employment opportunities, including the application of the same criteria for selection in matters of employment;

(c) The right to free choice of profession and employment, the right to promotion, job security and all benefits and conditions of service and the right to receive vocational training and retraining, including apprenticeships, advanced vocational training and recurrent training;

(d) The right to equal remuneration, including benefits, and to equal treatment in respect of work of equal value, as well as equality of treatment in the evaluation of the quality of work;

(e) The right to social security, particularly in cases of retirement, unemployment, sickness, invalidity and old age and other incapacity to work, as well as the right to paid leave;

(f) The right to protection of health and to safety in working conditions, including the safeguarding of the function of reproduction.

(2) In order to prevent discrimination against women on the grounds of marriage or maternity and to ensure their effective right to work, States Parties shall take appropriate measures:

(a) To prohibit, subject to the imposition of sanctions, dismissal on the grounds of pregnancy or of maternity leave and discrimination in dismissals on the basis of marital status;

(b) To introduce maternity leave with pay or with comparable social benefits without loss of former employment, seniority or social allowances;

(c) To encourage the provision of the necessary supporting social services to enable parents to combine family obligations with work responsibilities and participation in public life, in particular through promoting the establishment and development of a network of child-care facilities;

(d) To provide special protection to women during pregnancy in types of work proved to be harmful to them.

(3) Protective legislation relating to matters covered in this article shall be reviewed periodically in the light of scientific and technological knowledge and shall be revised, repealed or extended as necessary.

Article 12. (1) States Parties shall take all appropriate measures to eliminate discrimination against women in the field of health care in order to ensure, on a basis of equality of men and women, access to health care services, including those related to family planning.

(2) Notwithstanding the provisions of paragraph 1 above, States Parties shall ensure to women appropriate services in connexion with pregnancy, confinement and the post-natal period, granting free services where necessary, as well as adequate nutrition during pregnancy and lactation.

Article 13. States Parties shall take all appropriate measures to eliminate discrimination against women in other areas of economic and social life in order to ensure, on a basis of equality of men and women, the same rights, in particular:

(a) The right to family benefits;

(b) The right to bank loans, mortgages and other forms of financial credit;

(c) The right to participate in recreational activities, sports and in all aspects of cultural life.

Article 14. (1) States Parties shall take into account the particular problems faced by rural women and the significant roles which they play in the economic survival of their families, including their work in the non-monetized sectors of the economy, and shall take all appropriate measures to ensure the application of the provisions of this Convention to women in rural areas.

(2) States Parties shall take all appropriate measures to eliminate discrimination against women in rural areas in order to ensure, on a basis of equality of men and women, that they participate in and benefit from rural development and, in particular, shall ensure to such women the right:

(a) To participate in the elaboration and implementation of development planning at all levels;

(b) To have access to adequate health care facilities, including information, counselling and services in family planning;

(c) To benefit directly from social security programmes;

(d) To obtain all types of training and education, formal and non-formal, including that relating to functional literacy, as well as the benefit of all community and extension services, *inter alia,* in order to increase their technical proficiency;

(e) To organize self-help groups and co-operatives in order to obtain equal access to economic opportunities through employment or self-employment;

(f) To participate in all community activities;

(g) To have access to agricultural credit and loans, marketing facilities, appropriate technology and equal treatment in land and agrarian reform as well as in land resettlement schemes;

(h) To enjoy adequate living conditions, particularly in relation to housing, sanitation, electricity and water supply, transport and communications.

Part IV

Article 15. (1) States Parties shall accord to women equality with men before the law.

(2) States Parties shall accord to women, in civil matters, a legal capacity identical to that of men and the same opportunities to exercise that capacity. They shall in particular give women equal rights to conclude contracts and to administer property and treat them equally in all stages of procedure in courts and tribunals.

(3) States Parties agree that all contract and all other private instruments of any kind with a legal effect which is directed at restricting the legal capacity of women shall be deemed null and void.

(4) States Parties shall accord to men and women the same rights with regard to the law relating to the movement of persons and the freedom to choose their residence and domicile.

Article 16. (1) States Parties shall take all appropriate measures to eliminate discrimination against women in all matters relating to marriage and family relations and in particular shall ensure, on a basis of equality of men and women:

(a) The same right to enter into marriage;

(b) The same right freely to choose a spouse and to enter into marriage only with their free and full consent;

(c) The same rights and responsibilities during marriage and at its dissolution;

(d) The same rights and responsibilities as parents, irrespective of their marital status, in matters relating to their children. In all cases the interests of the children shall be paramount;

(e) The same rights to decide freely and responsibly on the number and spacing of their children and to have access to the information, education and means to enable them to exercise these rights;

(f) The same rights and responsibilities with regard to guardianship, wardship, trusteeship and adoption of children, or similar institutions where these concepts exist in national legislation. In all cases the interest of the children shall be paramount;

(g) The same personal rights as husband and wife, including the right to choose a family name, a profession and an occupation;

(h) The same rights for both spouses in respect of the ownership, acquisition, management, administration, enjoyment and disposition of property, whether free of charge or for a valuable consideration.

(2) The betrothal and the marriage of a child shall have no legal effect and all necessary action including legislation, shall be taken to specify a minimum age for marriage and to make the registration of marriages in an official registry compulsory.

* * *

3.37 AFRICAN CHARTER ON HUMAN AND PEOPLES' RIGHTS.[a] Done at Banjul, June 26, 1981. Entered into force, Oct. 21, 1986. O.A.U. Doc. CAB/LEG/67/3 Rev. 5, *reproduced in* 21 I.L.M. 59 (1982)

PREAMBLE

The African States members of the Organization of African Unity, parties to the present convention entitled "African Charter on Human and Peoples' Rights",

Recalling Decision 115 (XVI) of the Assembly of Heads of State and Government at its Sixteenth Ordinary Session held in Monrovia, Liberia, from 17 to 20 July 1979 on the preparation of a "preliminary draft on an African Charter on Human and Peoples' Rights providing *inter alia* for the establishment of bodies to promote and protect human and peoples' rights";

Considering the Charter of the Organization of African Unity, which stipulates that "freedom, equality, justice and dignity are essential objectives for the achievement of the legitimate aspirations of the African peoples";

Reaffirming the pledge they solemnly made in Article 2 of the said Charter to eradicate all forms of colonialism from Africa, to coordinate and intensify their cooperation and efforts to achieve a better life for the peoples of Africa and to promote international cooperation having due regard to the Charter of the United Nations and the Universal Declaration of Human Rights;

Taking into consideration the virtues of their historical tradition and the values of African civilization which should inspire and characterize their reflection on the concept of human and peoples' rights;

Recognizing on the one hand, that fundamental human rights stem from the attributes of human beings, which justifies their national and international protection and on the other hand that the reality and respect of peoples rights should necessarily guarantee human rights;

Considering that the enjoyment of rights and freedoms also implies the performance of duties on the part of everyone;

Convinced that it is henceforth essential to pay a particular attention to the right to development and that civil and political rights cannot be dissociated from economic, social and cultural rights in their conception as well as universality and that the satisfaction of economic, social and cultural rights is a guarantee for the enjoyment of civil and political rights;

Conscious of their duty to achieve the total liberation of Africa, the peoples of which are still struggling for their dignity and genuine independence, and undertaking to eliminate colonialism, neo-colonialism, apartheid, zionism and to dismantle aggressive foreign military bases and all forms of discrimination, particularly those based on race, ethnic group, color, sex, language, religion or political opinions;

Reaffirming their adherence to the principles of human and peoples' rights and freedoms contained in the declarations, conventions and other instruments adopted by the Organization of African Unity, the Movement of Non–Aligned Countries and the United Nations;

Firmly convinced of their duty to promote and protect human and peoples' rights and freedoms taking into account the importance traditionally attached to these rights and freedoms in Africa;

a. *See also* Basic Documents 3.4, 3.13, and 3.25, *supra*; and Draft Charter on Human and People's Rights in the Arab World (International Institute of Higher Studies in Criminal Sciences, Siracusa, Italy, 1987).

HAVE AGREED AS FOLLOWS:

PART I: RIGHTS AND DUTIES

CHAPTER I

HUMAN AND PEOPLES' RIGHTS

ARTICLE 1

The Member States of the Organization of African Unity parties to the present Charter shall recognize the rights, duties and freedoms enshrined in this Charter and shall undertake to adopt legislative or other measures to give effect to them.

ARTICLE 2

Every individual shall be entitled to the enjoyment of the rights and freedoms recognized and guaranteed in the present Charter without distinction of any kind such as race, ethnic group, color, sex, language, religion, political or any other opinion, national and social origin, fortune, birth or other status.

ARTICLE 3

1. Every individual shall be equal before the law.

2. Every individual shall be entitled to equal protection of the law.

ARTICLE 4

Human beings are inviolable. Every human being shall be entitled to respect for his life and the integrity of his person. No one may be arbitrarily deprived of this right.

ARTICLE 5

Every individual shall have the right to the respect of the dignity inherent in a human being and to the recognition of his legal status. All forms of exploitation and degredation of man particularly slavery, slave trade, torture, cruel, inhuman or degrading punishment and treatment shall be prohibited.

ARTICLE 6

Every individual shall have the right to liberty and to the security of his person. No one may be deprived of his freedom except for reasons and conditions previously laid down by law. In particular, no one may be arbitrarily arrested or detained.

ARTICLE 7

1. Every individual shall have the right to have his cause heard. This comprises:

a) the right to an appeal to competent national organs against acts of violating his fundamental rights as recognized and guaranteed by conventions, laws, regulations and customs in force;

b) the right to be presumed innocent until proved guilty by a competent court or tribunal;

c) the right to defence, including the right to be defended by counsel of his choice;

d) the right to be tried within a reasonable time by an impartial court or tribunal.

2. No one may be condemned for an act or omission which did not constitute a legally punishable offence at the time it was committed. No penalty may be inflicted for an offence for which no provision was made at the time it was committed. Punishment is personal and can be imposed only on the offender.

ARTICLE 8

Freedom of conscience, the profession and free practice of religion shall be guaranteed. No one may, subject to law and order, be submitted to measures restricting the exercise of these freedoms.

ARTICLE 9

1. Every individual shall have the right to receive information.

2. Every individual shall have the right to express and disseminate his opinions within the law.

ARTICLE 10

1. Every individual shall have the right to free association provided that he abides by the law.

2. Subject to the obligation of solidarity provided for in Article 29 no one may be compelled to join an association.

ARTICLE 11

Every individual shall have the right to assemble freely with others. The exercise of this right shall be subject only to necessary restrictions provided for by law in particular those enacted in the interest of national security, the safety, health, ethics and rights and freedoms of others.

ARTICLE 12

1. Every individual shall have the right to freedom of movement and residence within the borders of a State provided he abides by the law.

2. Every individual shall have the right to leave any country including his own, and to return to his country. This right may only be subject to restrictions, provided for by law for the protection of national security, law and order, public health or morality.

3. Every individual shall have the right, when persecuted, to seek and obtain asylum in other countries in accordance with laws of those countries and international conventions.

4. A non-national legally admitted in a territory of a State Party to the present Charter, may only be expelled from it by virtue of a decision taken in accordance with the law.

5. The mass expulsion of non-nationals shall be prohibited. Mass expulsion shall be that which is aimed at national, racial, ethnic or religious groups.

ARTICLE 13

1. Every citizen shall have the right to participate freely in the government of his country, either directly or through freely chosen representatives in accordance with the provisions of the law.

2. Every citizen shall have the right of equal access to the public service of his country.

3. Every individual shall have the right of access to public property and services in strict equality of all persons before the law.

ARTICLE 14

The right to property shall be guaranteed. It may only be encroached upon in the interest of public need or in the general interest of the community and in accordance with the provisions of appropriate laws.

ARTICLE 15

Every individual shall have the right to work under equitable and satisfactory conditions, and shall receive equal pay for equal work.

ARTICLE 16

1. Every individual shall have the right to enjoy the best attainable state of physical and mental health.

2. States parties to the present Charter shall take the necessary measures to protect the health of their people and to ensure that they receive medical attention when they are sick.

ARTICLE 17

1. Every individual shall have the right to education.

2. Every individual may freely, take part in the cultural life of his community.

3. The promotion and protection of morals and traditional values recognized by the community shall be the duty of the State.

ARTICLE 18

1. The family shall be the natural unit and basis of society. It shall be protected by the State which shall take care of its physical health and moral.

2. The State shall have the duty to assist the family which is the custodian of morals and traditional values recognized by the community.

3. The State shall ensure the elimination of every discrimination against women and also censure the protection of the rights of the woman and the child as stipulated in international declarations and conventions.

4. The aged and the disabled shall also have the right to special measures of protection in keeping with their physical or moral needs.

ARTICLE 19

All peoples shall be equal; they shall enjoy the same respect and shall have the same rights. Nothing shall justify the domination of a people by another.

ARTICLE 20

1. All peoples shall have the right to existence. They shall have the unquestionable and inalienable right to self-determination. They shall freely determine their political status and shall pursue their economic and social development according to the policy they have freely chosen.

2. Colonized or oppressed peoples shall have the right to free themselves from the bonds of domination by resorting to any means recognized by the international community.

3. All peoples shall have the right to the assistance of the States parties to the present Charter in their liberation struggle against foreign domination, be it political, economic or cultural.

ARTICLE 21

1. All peoples shall freely dispose of their wealth and natural resources. This right shall be exercised in the exclusive interest of the people. In no case shall a people be deprived of it.

2. In case of spoliation the dispossessed people shall have the right to the lawful recovery of its property as well as to an adequate compensation.

3. The free disposal of wealth and natural resources shall be exercised without prejudice to the obligation of promoting international economic cooperation based on mutual respect, equitable exchange and the principles of international law.

4. States parties to the present Charter shall individually and collectively exercise the right to free disposal of their wealth and natural resources with a view to strengthening African unity and solidarity.

5. States parties to the present Charter shall undertake to eliminate all forms of foreign economic exploitation particularly that practiced by international monopolies so as to enable their peoples to fully benefit from the advantages derived from their national resources.

ARTICLE 22

1. All peoples shall have the right to their economic, social and cultural development with due regard to their freedom and identity and in the equal enjoyment of the common heritage of mankind.

2. States shall have the duty, individually or collectively, to ensure the exercise of the right to development.

ARTICLE 23

1. All peoples shall have the right to national and international peace and security. The principles of solidarity and friendly relations implicitly affirmed by the Charter of the United Nations and reaffirmed by that of the Organization of African Unity shall govern relations between States.

2. For the purpose of strengthening peace, solidarity and friendly relations, States parties to the present Charter shall ensure that:

(a) any individual enjoying the right of asylum under Article 12 of the present Charter shall not engage in subversive activities against his country of origin or any other State party to the present Charter;

(b) their territories shall not be used as bases for subversive or terrorist activities against the people of any other State party to the present Charter.

ARTICLE 24

All peoples shall have the right to a general satisfactory environment favorable to their development.

ARTICLE 25

States parties to the present Charter shall have the duty to promote and ensure through teaching, education and publication, the respect of the rights and freedoms contained in the present Charter and to see to it that these freedoms and rights as well as corresponding obligations and duties are understood.

ARTICLE 26

States parties to the present Charter shall have the duty to guarantee the independence of the Courts and shall allow the establishment and improvement of appropriate national institutions entrusted with the promotion and protection of the rights and freedoms guaranteed by the present Charter.

CHAPTER II

DUTIES

ARTICLE 27

1. Every individual shall have duties towards his family and society, the State and other legally recognized communities and the international community.

2. The rights and freedoms of each individual shall be exercised with due regard to the rights of others, collective security, morality and common interest.

ARTICLE 28

Every individual shall have the duty to respect and consider his fellow beings without discrimination, and to maintain relations aimed at promoting, safeguarding and reinforcing mutual respect and tolerance.

ARTICLE 29

The individual shall also have the duty:

1. To preserve the harmonious development of the family and to work for the cohesion and respect of the family; to respect his parents at all times, to maintain them in case of need;

2. To serve his national community by placing his physical and intellectual abilities at its service;

3. Not to compromise the security of the State whose national or resident he is;

4. To preserve and strengthen social and national solidarity, particularly when the latter is threatened;

5. To preserve and strengthen the national independence and the territorial integrity of his country and to contribute to its defence in accordance with the law;

6. To work to the best of his abilities and competence, and to pay taxes imposed by law in the interest of the society;

7. To preserve and strengthen positive African cultural values in his relations with other members of the society, in the spirit of tolerance, dialogue and consultation and, in general, to contribute to the promotion of the moral well being of society;

8. To contribute to the best of his abilities, at all times and at all levels, to the promotion and achievement of African unity.

PART II: MEASURES OF SAFEGUARD

CHAPTER I

ESTABLISHMENT AND ORGANIZATION OF THE AFRICAN COMMISSION ON HUMAN AND PEOPLES' RIGHTS

ARTICLE 30

An African Commission on Human and Peoples' Rights, hereinafter called "the Commission", shall be established within the Organization of African Unity to promote human and peoples' rights and ensure their protection in Africa.

ARTICLE 31

1. The Commission shall consist of eleven members chosen from amongst African personalities of the highest reputation, known for their high morality, integrity, impartiality and competence in matters of human and peoples' rights; particular consideration being given to persons having legal experience.

2. The members of the Commission shall serve in their personal capacity.

ARTICLE 32

The Commission shall not include more than one national of the same State.

ARTICLE 33

The members of the Commission shall be elected by secret ballot by the Assembly of Heads of State and Government, from a list of persons nominated by the States parties to the present Charter.

ARTICLE 34

Each State party to the present Charter may not nominate more than two candidates. The candidates must have the nationality of one of the States parties to the present Charter. When two candidates are nominated by a State, one of them may not be a national of that State.

ARTICLE 35

1. The Secretary General of the Organization of African Unity shall invite States parties to the present Charter at least four months before the elections to nominate candidates;

2. The Secretary General of the Organization of African Unity shall make an alphabetical list of the persons thus nominated and communicate it to the Heads of State and Government at least one month before the elections.

ARTICLE 36

The members of the Commission shall be elected for a six year period and shall be eligible for re-election. However, the term of office of four of the members elected at the first election shall terminate after two years and the term of office of the three others, at the end of four years.

ARTICLE 37

Immediately after the first election, the Chairman of the Assembly of Heads of State and Government of the Organization of African Unity shall draw lots to decide the names of those members referred to in Article 36.

ARTICLE 38

After their election, the members of the Commission shall make a solemn declaration to discharge their duties impartially and faithfully.

ARTICLE 39

1. In case of death or resignation of a member of the Commission, the Chairman of the Commission shall immediately inform the Secretary General of the Organization of African Unity, who shall declare the seat vacant from the date of death or from the date on which the resignation takes effect.

2. If, in the unanimous opinion of other members of the Commission, a member has stopped discharging his duties for any reason other than a temporary absence, the Chairman of the Commission shall inform the Secretary General of the Organization of African Unity, who shall then declare the seat vacant.

3. In each of the cases anticipated above, the Assembly of Heads of State and Government shall replace the member whose seat became vacant for the remaining period of his term unless the period is less than six months.

ARTICLE 40

Every member of the Commission shall be in office until the date his successor assumes office.

ARTICLE 41

The Secretary General of the Organization of African Unity shall appoint the Secretary of the Commission. He shall also provide the staff and services necessary for the effective discharge of the duties of the Commission. The Organization of African Unity shall bear the costs of the staff and services.

ARTICLE 42

1. The Commission shall elect its Chairman and Vice Chairman for a two year period. They shall be eligible for re-election.

2. The Commission shall lay down its rules of procedure.

3. Seven members shall form a quorum.

4. In case of an equality of votes, the Chairman shall have a casting vote.

5. The Secretary General may attend the meetings of the Commission. He shall neither participate in deliberations nor shall he be entitled to vote. The Chairman of the Commission may, however, invite him to speak.

ARTICLE 43

In discharging their duties, members of the Commission shall enjoy diplomatic privileges and immunities provided for in the General Convention on the Privileges and Immunities of the Organization of African Unity.

ARTICLE 44

Provision shall be made for the emoluments and allowances of the members of the Commission in the Regular Budget of the Organization of African Unity.

CHAPTER II

MANDATE OF THE COMMISSION

ARTICLE 45

The functions of the Commission shall be:

1. To promote Human and Peoples' Rights and in particular:

a) to collect documents, undertake studies and researches on African problems in the field of human and peoples' rights, organize seminars, symposia and conferences, disseminate information, encourage national and local institutions concerned with human and peoples' rights, and should the case arise, give its views or make recommendations to Governments.

b) to formulate and lay down, principles and rules aimed at solving legal problems relating to human and peoples' rights and fundamental freedoms upon which African Governments may base their legislations.

c) co-operate with other African and international institutions concerned with the promotion and protection of human and peoples' rights.

2. Ensure the protection of human and peoples' rights under conditions laid down by the present Charter.

3. Interpret all the provisions of the present Charter at the request of a State party, an institution of the OAU or an African Organization recognized by the OAU.

4. Perform any other tasks which may be entrusted to it by the Assembly of Heads of State and Government.

CHAPTER III

PROCEDURE OF THE COMMISSION

ARTICLE 46

The Commission may resort to any appropriate method of investigation; it may hear from the Secretary General of the Organization of African Unity or any other person capable of enlightening it.

COMMUNICATION FROM STATES

ARTICLE 47

If a State party to the present Charter has good reason to believe that another State party to this Charter has violated the provisions of the Charter, it may draw, by written communication, the attention of that State to the matter. This communication shall also be addressed to the Secretary General of the OAU and to the Chairman of the Commission. Within three months of the receipt of the communication, the State to which the communication is addressed shall give the enquiring State, written explanation or statement elucidating the matter. This should include as much as possible relevant information relating to the laws and rules of procedure applied and applicable, and the redress already given or course of action available.

ARTICLE 48

If within three months from the date on which the original communication is received by the State to which it is addressed, the issue is not settled to the satisfaction of the two States involved through bilateral negotiation or by any other peaceful procedure, either State shall have the right to submit the matter to the Commission through the Chairman and shall notify the other States involved.

ARTICLE 49

Notwithstanding the provisions of Article 47, if a State party to the present Charter considers that another State party has violated the provisions of the Charter, it may refer the matter directly to the Commission by addressing a communication to the Chairman, to the Secretary General of the Organization of African Unity and the State concerned.

ARTICLE 50

The Commission can only deal with a matter submitted to it after making sure that all local remedies, if they exist, have been exhausted, unless it is obvious to the Commission that the procedure of achieving these remedies would be unduly prolonged.

ARTICLE 51

1. The Commission may ask the States concerned to provide it with all relevant information.

2. When the Commission is considering the matter, States concerned may be represented before it and submit written or oral representation.

ARTICLE 52

After having obtained from the States concerned and from other sources all the information it deems necessary and after having tried all appropriate means to reach an amicable solution based on the respect of Human and Peoples' Rights, the Commission shall prepare, within a reasonable period of time from the notification referred to in Article 48, a report stating the facts and its findings. This report shall be sent to the States concerned and communicated to the Assembly of Heads of State and Government.

ARTICLE 53

While transmitting its report, the Commission may make to the Assembly of Heads of State and Government such recommendations as it deems useful.

ARTICLE 54

The Commission shall submit to each ordinary Session of the Assembly of Heads of State and Government a report on its activities.

OTHER COMMUNICATIONS

ARTICLE 55

1. Before each Session, the Secretary of the Commission shall make a list of the communications other than those of States parties to the present Charter and transmit them to the members of the Commission, who shall indicate which communications should be considered by the Commission.

2. A communication shall be considered by the Commission if a simple majority of its members so decide.

ARTICLE 56

Communications relating to human and peoples' rights referred to in Article 55 received by the Commission, shall be considered if they:

1. Indicate their authors even if the latter request anonymity,

2. Are compatible with the Charter of the Organization of African Unity or with the present Charter,

3. Are not written in disparaging or insulting language directed against the State concerned and its institutions or to the Organization of African Unity,

4. Are not based exclusively on news discriminated through the mass media,

5. Are sent after exhausting local remedies, if any, unless it is obvious that this procedure is unduly prolonged,

6. Are submitted within a reasonable period from the time local remedies are exhausted or from the date the Commission is seized of the matter, and

7. Do not deal with cases which have been settled by these States involved in accordance with the principles of the Charter of the United Nations, or the Charter of the Organization of African Unity or the provisions of the present Charter.

ARTICLE 57

Prior to any substantive consideration, all communications shall be brought to the knowledge of the State concerned by the Chairman of the Commission.

ARTICLE 58

1. When it appears after deliberations of the Commission that one or more communications apparently relate to special cases which reveal the existence of a series of serious or massive violations of human and peoples' rights, the Commission shall draw the attention of the Assembly of Heads of State and Government to these special cases.

2. The Assembly of Heads of State and Government may then request the Commission to undertake an in-depth study of these cases and make a factual report, accompanied by its findings and recommendations.

3. A case of emergency duly noticed by the Commission shall be submitted by the latter to the Chairman of the Assembly of Heads of State and Government who may request an in-depth study.

ARTICLE 59

1. All measures taken within the provisions of the present Chapter shall remain confidential until such a time as the Assembly of Heads of State and Government shall otherwise decide.

2. However, the report shall be published by the Chairman of the Commission upon the decision of the Assembly of Heads of State and Government.

3. The report on the activities of the Commission shall be published by its Chairman after it has been considered by the Assembly of Heads of State and Government.

CHAPTER IV

APPLICABLE PRINCIPLES

ARTICLE 60

The Commission shall draw inspiration from international law on human and peoples' rights, particularly from the provisions of various African instruments on human and peoples' rights, the Charter of the United Nations, the Charter of the Organization of African Unity, the Universal Declaration of Human Rights, other instruments adopted by the United Nations and by African countries in the field of human and peoples' rights as well as from the provisions of various instruments adopted within the Specialized Agencies of the United Nations of which the parties to the present Charter are members.

ARTICLE 61

The Commission shall also take into consideration, as subsidiary measures to determine the principles of law, other general or special international conventions, laying down rules expressly recognized by member states of the Organization of African Unity, African practices consistent with international norms on human and peoples' rights, customs generally accepted as law, general principles of law recognized by African states as well as legal precedents and doctrine.

ARTICLE 62

Each state party shall undertake to submit every two years, from the date the present Charter comes into force, a report on the legislative or other measures taken with a view to giving effect to the rights and freedoms recognized and guaranteed by the present Charter.

* * *

3.38 DECLARATION ON THE ELIMINATION OF ALL FORMS OF INTOLERANCE AND OF DISCRIMINATION BASED ON RELIGION OR BELIEF. Adopted by the U.N. General Assembly, Nov. 25, 1981. U.N.G.A. Res. 36/55, 36 U.N. GAOR, Supp. (No. 51) 171, U.N. Doc. A/36/684 (1981), *reprinted in* 21 I.L.M. 205 (1982)

The General Assembly,

Considering that one of the basic principles of the Charter of the United Nations is that of the dignity and equality inherent in all human beings, and that all Member States have pledged themselves to take joint and separate action in co-operation with the Organization to promote and encourage universal respect for and observance of human rights and fundamental freedoms for all, without distinction as to race, sex, language or religion,

Considering that the Universal Declaration on Human Rights and the International Covenants on Human Rights proclaim the principles of non-discrimination and equality before the law and the right to freedom of thought, conscience, religion and belief,

Considering that the disregard and infringement of human rights and fundamental freedoms, in particular of the right to freedom of thought, conscience, religion or whatever belief, have brought, directly or indirectly, wars and great suffering to mankind, especially where they serve as a means of foreign interference in the internal affairs of other States and amount to kindling hatred between peoples and nations,

Considering that religion or belief, for anyone who professes either, is one of the fundamental elements in his conception of life and that freedom of religion or belief should be fully respected and guaranteed,

Considering that it is essential to promote understanding, tolerance and respect in matters relating to freedom of religion and belief and to ensure that the use of religion or belief for ends inconsistent with the Charter, other relevant instruments of the United Nations and the purposes and principles of the present Declaration is inadmissible,

Convinced that freedom of religion and belief should also contribute to the attainment of the goals of world peace, social justice and friendship among peoples and to the elimination of ideologies or practices of colonialism and racial discrimination,

Noting with satisfaction the adoption of several, and the coming into force of some, conventions, under the aegis of the United Nations and of the specialized agencies, for the elimination of various forms of discrimination,

Concerned by manifestations of intolerance and by the existence of discrimination in matters of religion or belief still in evidence in some areas of the world,

Resolved to adopt all necessary measures for the speedy elimination of such intolerance in all its forms and manifestations and to prevent and combat discrimination on the grounds of religion or belief,

Proclaims this Declaration on the Elimination of All Forms of Intolerance and of Discrimination Based on Religion or Belief:

Article 1

1. Everyone shall have the right to freedom of thought, conscience and religion. This right shall include freedom to have a religion or whatever belief of his choice,

and freedom, either individually or in community with others and in public or private, to manifest his religion or belief in worship, observance, practice and teaching.

2. No one shall be subject to coercion which would impair his freedom to have a religion or belief of his choice.

3. Freedom to manifest one's religion or beliefs may be subject only to such limitations as are prescribed by law and are necessary to protect public safety, order, health or morals or the fundamental rights and freedoms of others.

Article 2

1. No one shall be subject to discrimination by any State, institution, group of persons or person on the grounds of religion or other beliefs.

2. For the purposes of the present Declaration, the expression "intolerance and discrimination based on religion or belief" means any distinction, exclusion, restriction or preference based on religion or belief and having as its purpose or as its effect nullification or impairment of the recognition, enjoyment or exercise of human rights and fundamental freedoms on an equal basis.

Article 3

Discrimination between human beings on the grounds of religion or belief constitutes an affront to human dignity and a disavowal of the principles of the Charter of the United Nations, and shall be condemned as a violation of the human rights and fundamental freedoms proclaimed in the Universal Declaration on Human Rights and enunciated in detail in the International Covenants on Human Rights, and as an obstacle to friendly and peaceful relations between nations.

Article 4

1. All States shall take effective measures to prevent and eliminate discrimination on the grounds of religion or belief in the recognition, exercise and enjoyment of human rights and fundamental freedoms in all fields of civil, economic, political, social and cultural life.

2. All States shall make all efforts to enact or rescind legislation where necessary to prohibit any such discrimination, and to take all appropriate measures to combat intolerance on the grounds of religion or other beliefs in this matter.

Article 5

1. The parents or, as the case may be, the legal guardians of the child have the right to organize the life within the family in accordance with their religion or belief and bearing in mind the moral education in which they believe the child should be brought up.

2. Every child shall enjoy the right to have access to education in the matter of religion or belief in accordance with the wishes of his parents or, as the case may be, legal guardians, and shall not be compelled to receive teaching on religion or belief against the wishes of his parents or legal guardians, the best interests of the child being the guiding principle.

3. The child shall be protected from any form of discrimination on the grounds of religion or belief. He shall be brought up in a spirit of understanding, tolerance, friendship among peoples, peace and universal brotherhood, respect for freedom of religion or belief of others, and in full consciousness that his energy and talents should be devoted to the service of his fellow men.

4. In the case of a child who is not under the care either of his parents or of legal guardians, due account shall be taken of their expressed wishes or of any other

proof of their wishes in the matter of religion or belief, the best interests of the child being the guiding principle.

5. Practices of a religion or beliefs in which a child is brought up must not be injurious to his physical or mental health or to his full development, taking into account article 1, paragraph 3, of the present Declaration.

Article 6

In accordance with article 1 of the present Declaration, and subject to the provisions of article 1, paragraph 3, the right to freedom of thought, conscience, religion or belief shall include, *inter alia,* the following freedoms:

(*a*) To worship or assemble in connexion with a religion or belief, and to establish and maintain places for these purposes;

(*b*) To establish and maintain appropriate charitable or humanitarian institutions;

(*c*) To make, acquire and use to an adequate extent the necessary articles and materials related to the rites or customs of a religion or belief;

(*d*) To write, issue and disseminate relevant publications in these areas;

(*e*) To teach a religion or belief in places suitable for these purposes;

(*f*) To solicit and receive voluntary financial and other contributions from individuals and institutions;

(*g*) To train, appoint, elect or designate by succession appropriate leaders called for by the requirements and standards of any religion or belief;

(*h*) To observe days of rest and to celebrate holidays and ceremonies in accordance with the precepts of one's religion or belief;

(*i*) To establish and maintain communications with individuals and communities in matters of religion and belief at the national and international levels.

Article 7

The rights and freedoms set forth in the present Declaration shall be accorded in national legislations in such a manner that everyone shall be able to avail himself of such rights and freedoms in practice.

Article 8

Nothing in the present Declaration shall be construed as restricting or derogating from any right defined in the Universal Declaration on Human Rights and the International Covenants on Human Rights.

3.39 DECLARATION ON THE RIGHT OF PEOPLES TO PEACE.[a] Adopted by the U.N. General Assembly, Nov. 12, 1984. U.N.G.A. Res. 39/11/Annex, 39 U.N. GAOR, Supp. (No. 51) 22, U.N. Doc. A/39/L.14 (1984)

* * *

The General Assembly,

Reaffirming that the principal aim of the United Nations is the maintenance of international peace and security,

Bearing in mind the fundamental principles of international law set forth in the Charter of the United Nations,

Expressing the will and the aspirations of all peoples to eradicate war from the life of mankind and, above all, to avert a world-wide nuclear catastrophe,

Convinced that life without war serves as the primary international prerequisite for the material well-being, development and progress of countries, and for the full implementation of the rights and fundamental human freedoms proclaimed by the United Nations,

Aware that in the nuclear age the establishment of a lasting peace on Earth represents the primary condition for the preservation of human civilization and the survival of mankind,

Recognizing that the maintenance of a peaceful life for peoples is the sacred duty of each State,

1. *Solemnly proclaims* that the peoples of our planet have a sacred right to peace;

2. *Solemnly declares* that the preservation of the right of peoples to peace and the promotion of its implementation constitute a fundamental obligation of each State;

3. *Emphasizes* that ensuring the exercise of the right of peoples to peace demands that the policies of States be directed towards the elimination of the threat of war, particularly nuclear war, the renunciation of the use of force in international relations and the settlement of international disputes by peaceful means on the basis of the Charter of the United Nations;

4. *Appeals* to all States and international organizations to do their utmost to assist in implementing the right of peoples to peace through the adoption of appropriate measures at both the national and the international level.

a. *See also* Basic Documents 2.5 and 2.15, *supra.*

3.40 CONVENTION AGAINST TORTURE AND OTHER CRUEL INHUMAN OR DEGRADING TREATMENT OR PUNISHMENT.[a] Done at New York, Dec. 10, 1984. Entered into force, June 26, 1987. U.N. G.A. Res. 39/46 Annex, 39 U.N. GAOR, Supp. (No. 51) 197, U.N. Doc. E/CN.4/1984/72, Annex (1984), *reprinted in* 23 I.L.M. 1027 (1984)

PART I

Article 1

1. For the purposes of this Convention, the term "torture" means any act by which severe pain or suffering, whether physical or mental, is intentionally inflicted on a person for such purposes as obtaining from him or a third person information or a confession, punishing him for an act he or a third person has committed or is suspected of having committed, or intimidating or coercing him or a third person, or for any reason based on discrimination of any kind, when such pain or suffering is inflicted by or at the instigation of or with the consent or acquiescence of a public official or other person acting in an official capacity. It does not include pain or suffering arising only from, inherent in or incidental to lawful sanctions.

2. This article is without prejudice to any international instrument or national legislation which does or may contain provisions of wider application.

Article 2

1. Each State Party shall take effective legislative, administrative, judicial or other measures to prevent acts of torture in any territory under its jurisdiction.

2. No exceptional circumstances whatsoever, whether a state of war or a threat of war, internal political instability or any other public emergency, may be invoked as a justification of torture.

3. An order from a superior officer or a public authority may not be invoked as a justification of torture.

Article 3

1. No State Party shall expel, return ("*refouler*") or extradite a person to another State where there are substantial grounds for believing that he would be in danger of being subjected to torture.

2. For the purpose of determining whether there are such grounds, the competent authorities shall take into account all relevant considerations including, where applicable, the existence in the State concerned of a consistent pattern of gross, flagrant or mass violations of human rights.

Article 4

1. Each State Party shall ensure that all acts of torture are offences under its criminal law. The same shall apply to an attempt to commit torture and to an act by any person which constitutes complicity or participation in torture.

2. Each State Party shall make these offences punishable by appropriate penalties which take into account their grave nature.

a. *See also* Basic Documents 3.25 and 3.34, *supra.*

Article 5

1. Each State Party shall take such measures as may be necessary to establish its jurisdiction over the offences referred to in article 4 in the following cases:

(a) When the offences are committed in any territory under its jurisdiction or on board a ship or aircraft registered in that State;

(b) When the alleged offender is a national of that State;

(c) When the victim is a national of that State if that State considers it appropriate.

2. Each State Party shall likewise take such measures as may be necessary to establish its jurisdiction over such offences in cases where the alleged offender is present in any territory under its jurisdiction and it does not extradite him pursuant to article 8 to any of the States mentioned in paragraph 1 of this article.

3. This Convention does not exclude any criminal jurisdiction exercised in accordance with internal law.

Article 6

1. Upon being satisfied, after an examination of information available to it, that the circumstances so warrant, any State Party in whose territory a person alleged to have committed any offence referred to in article 4 is present shall take him into custody or take other legal measures to ensure his presence. The custody and other legal measures shall be as provided in the law of that State but may be continued only for such time as is necessary to enable any criminal or extradition proceedings to be instituted.

2. Such State shall immediately make a preliminary inquiry into the facts.

3. Any person in custody pursuant to paragraph 1 of this article shall be assisted in communicating immediately with the nearest appropriate representative of the State of which he is a national, or, if he is a stateless person, with the representative of the State where he usually resides.

4. When a State, pursuant to this article, has taken a person into custody, it shall immediately notify the States referred to in article 5, paragraph 1, of the fact that such person is in custody and of the circumstances which warrant his detention. The State which makes the preliminary inquiry contemplated in paragraph 2 of this article shall promptly report its findings to the said States and shall indicate whether it intends to exercise jurisdiction.

Article 7

1. The State Party in the territory under whose jurisdiction a person alleged to have committed any offence referred to in article 4 is found shall in the cases contemplated in article 5, if it does not extradite him, submit the case to its competent authorities for the purpose of prosecution.

2. These authorities shall take their decision in the same manner as in the case of any ordinary offence of a serious nature under the law of that State. In the cases referred to in article 5, paragraph 2, the standards of evidence required for prosecution and conviction shall in no way be less stringent than those which apply in the cases referred to in article 5, paragraph 1.

3. Any person regarding whom proceedings are brought in connection with any of the offences referred to in article 4 shall be guaranteed fair treatment at all stages of the proceedings.

Article 8

1. The offences referred to in article 4 shall be deemed to be included as extraditable offences in any extradition treaty existing between State Parties. States

Parties undertake to include such offences as extraditable offences in every extradition treaty to be concluded between them.

2. If a State Party which makes extradition conditional on the existence of a treaty receives a request for extradition from another State Party with which it has no extradition treaty, it may consider this Convention as the legal basis for extradition in respect of such offences. Extradition shall be subject to the other conditions provided by the law of the requested State.

3. States Parties which do not make extradition conditional on the existence of a treaty shall recognize such offences as extraditable offences between themselves subject to the conditions provided by the law of the requested State.

4. Such offences shall be treated, for the purpose of extradition between States Parties, as if they had been committed not only in the place in which they occurred but also in the territories of the States required to establish their jurisdiction in accordance with article 5, paragraph 1.

Article 9

1. States Parties shall afford one another the greatest measure of assistance in connection with criminal proceedings brought in respect of any of the offences referred to in article 4, including the supply of all evidence at their disposal necessary for the proceedings.

2. States Parties shall carry out their obligations under paragraph 1 of this article in conformity with any treaties on mutual judicial assistance that may exist between them.

Article 10

1. Each State Party shall ensure that education and information regarding the prohibition against torture are fully included in the training of law enforcement personnel, civil or military, medical personnel, public officials and other persons who may be involved in the custody, interrogation or treatment of any individual subjected to any form of arrest, detention or imprisonment.

2. Each State Party shall include this prohibition in the rules or instructions issued in regard to the duties and functions of any such persons.

Article 11

Each State Party shall keep under systematic review interrogation rules, instructions, methods and practices as well as arrangements for the custody and treatment of persons subjected to any form of arrest, detention or imprisonment in any territory under its jurisdiction, with a view to preventing any cases of torture.

Article 12

Each State Party shall ensure that its competent authorities proceed to a prompt and impartial investigation, wherever there is reasonable ground to believe that an act of torture has been committed in any territory under its jurisdiction.

Article 13

Each State Party shall ensure that any individual who alleges he has been subjected to torture in any territory under its jurisdiction has the right to complain to, and to have his case promptly and impartially examined by, its competent authorities. Steps shall be taken to ensure that the complainant and witnesses are protected against all ill-treatment or intimidation as a consequence of his complaint or any evidence given.

Article 14

1. Each State Party shall ensure in its legal system that the victim of an act of torture obtains redress and has an enforceable right to fair and adequate compensation, including the means for as full rehabilitation as possible. In the event of the death of the victim as a result of an act of torture, his dependents shall be entitled to compensation.

2. Nothing in this article shall affect any right of the victim or other persons to compensation which may exist under national law.

Article 15

Each State Party shall ensure that any statement which is established to have been made as a result of torture shall not be invoked as evidence in any proceedings, except against a person accused of torture as evidence that the statement was made.

Article 16

1. Each State Party shall undertake to prevent in any territory under its jurisdiction other acts of cruel, inhuman or degrading treatment or punishment which do not amount to torture as defined in article 1, when such acts are committed by or at the instigation of or with the consent or acquiescence of a public official or other person acting in an official capacity. In particular, the obligations contained in articles 10, 11, 12 and 13 shall apply with the substitution for references to torture of references to other forms of cruel, inhuman or degrading treatment or punishment.

2. The provisions of this Convention are without prejudice to the provisions of any other international instrument or national law which prohibits cruel, inhuman or degrading treatment or punishment or which relates to extradition or expulsion.

PART II

Article 17

1. There shall be established a Committee against Torture (hereinafter referred to as the Committee) which shall carry out the functions hereinafter provided. The Committee shall consist of ten experts of high moral standing and recognized competence in the field of human rights, who shall serve in their personal capacity. The experts shall be elected by the States Parties, consideration being given to equitable geographical distribution and to the usefulness of the participation of some persons having legal experience.

2. The members of the Committee shall be elected by secret ballot from a list of persons nominated by States Parties. Each State Party may nominate one person from among its own nationals. States Parties shall bear in mind the usefulness of nominating persons who are also members of the Human Rights Committee established under the International Covenant on Civil and Political Rights and who are willing to serve on the Committee against Torture.

3. Elections of the members of the Committee shall be held at biennial meetings of States Parties convened by the Secretary–General of the United Nations. At those meetings, for which two thirds of the States Parties shall constitute a quorum, the persons elected to the Committee shall be those who obtain the largest number of votes and an absolute majority of the votes of the representatives of States Parties present and voting.

4. The initial election shall be held no later than six months after the date of the entry into force of this Convention. At least four months before the date of each election, the Secretary–General of the United Nations shall address a letter to the States Parties inviting them to submit their nominations within three months. The Secretary–General shall prepare a list in alphabetical order of all persons thus

nominated, indicating the States Parties which have nominated them, and shall submit it to the States Parties.

5. The members of the Committee shall be elected for a term of four years. They shall be eligible for re-election if renominated. However, the term of five of the members elected at the first election shall expire at the end of two years; immediately after the first election the names of these five members shall be chosen by lot by the chairman of the meeting referred to in paragraph 3 of this article.

6. If a member of the Committee dies or resigns or for any other cause can no longer perform his Committee duties, the State Party which nominated him shall appoint another expert from among its nationals to serve for the remainder of his term, subject to the approval of the majority of the States Parties. The approval shall be considered given unless half or more of the States Parties respond negatively within six weeks after having been informed by the Secretary–General of the United Nations of the proposed appointment.

7. States Parties shall be responsible for the expenses of the members of the Committee while they are in performance of Committee duties.

Article 18

1. The Committee shall elect its officers for a term of two years. They may be re-elected.

2. The Committee shall establish its own rules of procedure, but these rules shall provide, *inter alia,* that:

(a) Six members shall constitute a quorum;

(b) Decisions of the Committee shall be made by a majority vote of the members present.

3. The Secretary–General of the United Nations shall provide the necessary staff and facilities for the effective performance of the functions of the Committee under this Convention.

4. The Secretary–General of the United Nations shall convene the initial meeting of the Committee. After its initial meeting, the Committee shall meet at such times as shall be provided in its rules of procedure.

5. The States Parties shall be responsible for expenses incurred in connection with the holding of meetings of the States Parties and of the Committee, including reimbursement to the United Nations for any expenses, such as the cost of staff and facilities, incurred by the United Nations pursuant to paragraph 3 of this article.

Article 19

1. The States Parties shall submit to the Committee, through the Secretary–General of the United Nations, reports on the measures they have taken to give effect to their undertakings under this Convention, within one year after the entry into force of the Convention for the State Party concerned. Thereafter the States Parties shall submit supplementary reports every four years on any new measures taken and such other reports as the Committee may request.

2. The Secretary–General of the United Nations shall transmit the reports to all States Parties.

3. Each report shall be considered by the Committee which may make such general comments on the report as it may consider appropriate and shall forward these to the State Party concerned. That State Party may respond with any observations it chooses to the Committee.

4. The Committee may, at its discretion, decide to include any comments made by it in accordance with paragraph 3 of this article, together with the observations thereon received from the State Party concerned, in its annual report made in

accordance with article 24. If so requested by the State Party concerned, the Committee may also include a copy of the report submitted under paragraph 1 of this article.

Article 20

1. If the Committee receives reliable information which appears to it to contain well-founded indications that torture is being systematically practised in the territory of a State Party, the Committee shall invite that State Party to co-operate in the examination of the information and to this end to submit observations with regard to the information concerned.

2. Taking into account any observations which may have been submitted by the State Party concerned, as well as any other relevant information available to it, the Committee may, if it decides that this is warranted, designate one or more of its members to make a confidential inquiry and to report to the Committee urgently.

3. If an inquiry is made in accordance with paragraph 2 of this article, the Committee shall seek the co-operation of the State Party concerned. In agreement with that State Party, such an inquiry may include a visit to its territory.

4. After examining the findings of its member or members submitted in accordance with paragraph 2 of this article, the Committee shall transmit these findings to the State Party concerned together with any comments or suggestions which seem appropriate in view of the situation.

5. All the proceedings of the Committee referred to in paragraphs 1 to 4 of this article shall be confidential, and at all stages of the proceedings the co-operation of the State Party shall be sought. After such proceedings have been completed with regard to an inquiry made in accordance with paragraph 2, the Committee may, after consultations with the State Party concerned, decide to include a summary account of the results of the proceedings in its annual report made in accordance with article 24.

Article 21

1. A State Party to this Convention may at any time declare under this article that it recognizes the competence of the Committee to receive and consider communications to the effect that a State Party claims that another State Party is not fulfilling its obligations under this Convention. Such communications may be received and considered according to the procedures laid down in this article only if submitted by a State Party which has made a declaration recognizing in regard to itself the competence of the Committee. No communication shall be dealt with by the Committee under this article if it concerns a State Party which has not made such a declaration. Communications received under this article shall be dealt with in accordance with the following procedure:

(a) If a State Party considers that another State Party is not giving effect to the provisions of this Convention, it may, by written communication, bring the matter to the attention of that State Party. Within three months after the receipt of the communication the receiving State shall afford the State which sent the communication an explanation or any other statement in writing clarifying the matter, which should include, to the extent possible and pertinent, reference to domestic procedures and remedies taken, pending or available in the matter;

(b) If the matter is not adjusted to the satisfaction of both States Parties concerned within six months after the receipt by the receiving State of the initial communication, either State shall have the right to refer the matter to the Committee, by notice given to the Committee and to the other State;

(c) The Committee shall deal with a matter referred to it under this article only after it has ascertained that all domestic remedies have been invoked and

exhausted in the matter, in conformity with the generally recognized principles of international law. This shall not be the rule where the application of the remedies is unreasonably prolonged or is unlikely to bring effective relief to the person who is the victim of the violation of this Convention;

(d) The Committee shall hold closed meetings when examining communications under this article;

(e) Subject to the provisions of subparagraph *(c)*, the Committee shall make available its good offices to the States Parties concerned with a view to a friendly solution of the matter on the basis of respect for the obligations provided for in this Convention. For this purpose, the Committee may, when appropriate, set up an *ad hoc* conciliation commission;

(f) In any matter referred to it under this article, the Committee may call upon the States Parties concerned, referred to in subparagraph *(b)*, to supply any relevant information;

(g) The States Parties concerned, referred to in subparagraph *(b)*, shall have the right to be represented when the matter is being considered by the Committee and to make submissions orally and/or in writing;

(h) The Committee shall, within twelve months after the date of receipt of notice under subparagraph *(b)*, submit a report:

(i) If a solution within the terms of subparagraph *(e)* is reached, the Committee shall confine its report to a brief statement of the facts and of the solution reached;

(ii) If a solution within the terms of subparagraph *(e)* is not reached, the Committee shall confine its report to a brief statement of the facts; the written submissions and record of the oral submissions made by the States Parties concerned shall be attached to the report.

In every matter, the report shall be communicated to the States Parties concerned.

2. The provisions of this article shall come into force when five States Parties to this Convention have made declarations under paragraph 1 of this article. Such declarations shall be deposited by the States Parties with the Secretary–General of the United Nations, who shall transmit copies thereof to the other States Parties. A declaration may be withdrawn at any time by notification to the Secretary–General. Such a withdrawal shall not prejudice the consideration of any matter which is the subject of a communication already transmitted under this article; no further communication by any State Party shall be received under this article after the notification of withdrawal of the declaration has been received by the Secretary–General, unless the State Party concerned has made a new declaration.

Article 22

1. A State Party to this Convention may at any time declare under this article that it recognizes the competence of the Committee to receive and consider communications from or on behalf of individuals subject to its jurisdiction who claim to be victims of a violation by a State Party of the provisions of the Convention. No communication shall be received by the Committee if it concerns a State Party which has not made such a declaration.

2. The Committee shall consider inadmissible any communication under this article which is anonymous or which it considers to be an abuse of the right of submission of such communications or to be incompatible with the provisions of this Convention.

3. Subject to the provisions of paragraph 2, the Committee shall bring any communications submitted to it under this article to the attention of the State Party

to this Convention which has made a declaration under paragraph 1 and is alleged to be violating any provisions of the Convention. Within six months, the receiving State shall submit to the Committee written explanations or statements clarifying the matter and the remedy, if any, that may have been taken by that State.

4. The Committee shall consider communications received under this article in the light of all information made available to it by or on behalf of the individual and by the State Party concerned.

5. The Committee shall not consider any communications from an individual under this article unless it has ascertained that:

(a) The same matter has not been, and is not being, examined under another procedure of international investigation or settlement;

(b) The individual has exhausted all available domestic remedies; this shall not be the rule where the application of the remedies is unreasonably prolonged or is unlikely to bring effective relief to the person who is the victim of the violation of this Convention.

6. The Committee shall hold closed meetings when examining communications under this article.

7. The Committee shall forward its views to the State Party concerned and to the individual.

8. The provisions of this article shall come into force when five States Parties to this Convention have made declarations under paragraph 1 of this article. Such declarations shall be deposited by the States Parties with the Secretary–General of the United Nations, who shall transmit copies thereof to the other States Parties. A declaration may be withdrawn at any time by notification to the Secretary–General. Such a withdrawal shall not prejudice the consideration of any matter which is the subject of a communication already transmitted under this article; no further communication by or on behalf of an individual shall be received under this article after the notification of withdrawal of the declaration has been received by the Secretary–General, unless the State Party has made a new declaration.

Article 23

The members of the Committee and of the *ad hoc* conciliation commissions which may be appointed under article 21, paragraph 1*(e)*, shall be entitled to the facilities, privileges and immunities of experts on mission for the United Nations as laid down in the relevant sections of the Convention on the Privileges and Immunities of the United Nations.

Article 24

The Committee shall submit an annual report on its activities under this Convention to the States Parties and to the General Assembly of the United Nations.

* * *

Article 28

1. Each State may, at the time of signature or ratification of this Convention or accession thereto, declare that it does not recognize the competence of the Committee provided for in article 20.

2. Any State Party having made a reservation in accordance with paragraph 1 of this article may, at any time, withdraw this reservation by notification to the Secretary–General of the United Nations.

* * *

Article 30

1. Any dispute between two or more States Parties concerning the interpretation or application of this Convention which cannot be settled through negotiation

shall, at the request of one of them, be submitted to arbitration. If within six months from the date of the request for arbitration the Parties are unable to agree on the organization of the arbitration, any one of those Parties may refer the dispute to the International Court of Justice by request in conformity with the Statute of the Court.

2. Each State may, at the time of signature or ratification of this Convention or accession thereto, declare that it does not consider itself bound by paragraph 1 of this article. The other States Parties shall not be bound by paragraph 1 of this article with respect to any State Party having made such a reservation.

3. Any State Party having made a reservation in accordance with paragraph 2 of this article may at any time withdraw this reservation by notification to the Secretary–General of the United Nations.

Article 31

1. A State Party may denounce this Convention by written notification to the Secretary–General of the United Nations. Denunciation becomes effective one year after the date of receipt of the notification by the Secretary–General.

2. Such a denunciation shall not have the effect of releasing the State Party from its obligations under this Convention in regard to any act or omission which occurs prior to the date at which the denunciation becomes effective, nor shall denunciation prejudice in any way the continued consideration of any matter which is already under consideration by the Committee prior to the date at which the denunciation becomes effective.

3. Following the date at which the denunciation of a State Party becomes effective, the Committee shall not commence consideration of any new matter regarding that State.

* * *

3.41 INTER–AMERICAN CONVENTION TO PREVENT AND PUNISH TORTURE.[a] Done at Cartegena de Indias, Dec. 9, 1985. Entered into force, Feb. 28, 1987. O.A.S. Treaty Ser. No. 67, O.A.S. Doc. OEA/Ser. P, AG/doc. 2023/85 rev. 1, at 46, *reprinted in* 25 I.L.M. 519 (1986)

The American States signatory to the present Convention,

Aware of the provision of the American Convention on Human Rights that no one shall be subjected to torture or to cruel, inhuman, or degrading punishment or treatment;

Reaffirming that all acts of torture or any other cruel, inhuman, or degrading treatment or punishment constitute an offense against human dignity and a denial of the principles set forth in the Charter of the Organization of American States and in the Charter of the United Nations and are violations of the fundamental human rights and freedoms proclaimed in the American Declaration of the Rights and Duties of Man and the Universal Declaration of Human Rights;

Noting that, in order for the pertinent rules contained in the aforementioned global and regional instruments to take effect, it is necessary to draft an Inter–American Convention that prevents and punishes torture;

Reaffirming their purpose of consolidating in this hemisphere the conditions that allow for recognition of and respect for the inherent dignity of man, and ensure the full exercise of his fundamental rights and freedoms,

Have agreed upon the following:

Article 1

The States Parties shall prevent and punish torture in accordance with the terms of this Convention.

Article 2

For the purposes of this Convention, torture shall be understood to be any act intentionally performed whereby physical or mental pain or suffering is inflicted upon a person for purposes of criminal investigation, as a means of intimidation, as personal punishment, as a preventive measure, as a penalty, or for any other purpose. Torture shall also be understood to be the use of methods upon a person intended to obliterate the personality of the victim or to diminish his physical or mental capacities, even if they do not cause physical pain or mental anguish.

The concept of torture shall not include physical or mental pain or suffering that is inherent in or solely the consequence of lawful measures, provided that they do not include the performance of the acts or use of the methods referred to in this article.

Article 3

The following shall be held guilty of the crime of torture:

a. A public servant or employee who acting in that capacity orders, instigates or induces the use of torture, or who directly commits it or who, being able to prevent it, fails to do so.

b. A person who at the instigation of a public servant or employee mentioned in subparagraph (a) orders, instigates or induces the use of torture, directly commits it or is an accomplice thereto.

a. See also Basic Document 3.25, supra, and Basic Document 3.40, infra.

Article 4

The fact of having acted under orders of a superior shall not provide exemption from the corresponding criminal liability.

Article 5

The existence of circumstances such as a state of war, threat of war, state of siege or of emergency, domestic disturbance or strife, suspension of constitutional guarantees, domestic political instability, or other public emergencies or disasters shall not be invoked or admitted as justification for the crime of torture.

Neither the dangerous character of the detainee or prisoner, nor the lack of security of the prison establishment or penitentiary shall justify torture.

Article 6

In accordance with the terms of Article 1, the States Parties shall take effective measures to prevent and punish torture within their jurisdiction.

The States Parties shall ensure that all acts of torture and attempts to commit torture are offenses under their criminal law and shall make such acts punishable by severe penalties that take into account their serious nature.

The States Parties likewise shall take effective measures to prevent and punish other cruel, inhuman, or degrading treatment or punishment within their jurisdiction.

Article 7

The States Parties shall take measures so that, in the training of police officers and other public officials responsible for the custody of persons temporarily or definitively deprived of their freedom, special emphasis shall be put on the prohibition of the use of torture in interrogation, detention, or arrest.

The States Parties likewise shall take similar measures to prevent other cruel, inhuman, or degrading treatment or punishment.

Article 8

The States Parties shall guarantee that any person making an accusation of having been subjected to torture within their jurisdiction shall have the right to an impartial examination of his case.

Likewise, if there is an accusation or well-grounded reason to believe that an act of torture has been committed within their jurisdiction, the States Parties shall guarantee that their respective authorities will proceed ex officio and immediately to conduct an investigation into the case and to initiate, whenever appropriate, the corresponding criminal process.

After all the domestic legal procedures of the respective State and the corresponding appeals have been exhausted, the case may be submitted to the international fora whose competence has been recognized by that State.

Article 9

The States Parties undertake to incorporate into their national laws regulations guaranteeing adequate compensation for victims of torture.

None of the provisions of this article shall affect the right to receive compensation that the victim or other persons may have by virtue of existing national legislation.

Article 10

No statement that is verified as having been obtained through torture shall be admissible as evidence in a legal proceeding, except in a legal action taken against a person or persons accused of having elicited it through acts of torture, and only as evidence that the accused obtained such statement by such means.

Article 11

The States Parties shall take the necessary steps to extradite anyone accused of having committed the crime of torture or sentenced for commission of that crime, in accordance with their respective national laws on extradition and their international commitments on this matter.

Article 12

Every State Party shall take the necessary measures to establish its jurisdiction over the crime described in this Convention in the following cases:

a. When torture has been committed within its jurisdiction;

b. When the alleged criminal is a national of that State; or

c. When the victim is a national of that State and it so deems appropriate.

Every State Party shall also take the necessary measures to establish its jurisdiction over the crime described in this Convention when the alleged criminal is within the area under its jurisdiction and it does not proceed to extradite him in accordance with Article 11.

This Convention does not exclude criminal jurisdiction exercised in accordance with domestic law.

Article 13

The crime referred to in Article 2 shall be deemed to be included among the extraditable crimes in every extradition treaty entered into between States Parties. The States Parties undertake to include the crime of torture as an extraditable offence in every extradition treaty to be concluded between them.

Every State Party that makes extradition conditional on the existence of a treaty may, if it receives a request for extradition from another State Party with which it has no extradition treaty, consider this Convention as the legal basis for extradition in respect of the crime of torture. Extradition shall be subject to the other conditions that may be required by the law of the requested State.

States Parties which do not make extradition conditional on the existence of a treaty shall recognize such crimes as extraditable offences between themselves, subject to the conditions required by the law of the requested State.

Extradition shall not be granted nor shall the person sought be returned when there are grounds to believe that his life is in danger, that he will be subjected to torture or to cruel, inhuman or degrading treatment, or that he will be tried by special or ad hoc courts in the requesting State.

Article 14

When a State Party does not grant the extradition, the case shall be submitted to its competent authorities as if the crime had been committed within its jurisdiction, for the purposes of investigation, and when appropriate, for criminal action, in accordance with its national law. Any decision adopted by these authorities shall be communicated to the State that has requested the extradition.

Article 15

No provision of this Convention may be interpreted as limiting the right of asylum, when appropriate, nor as altering the obligations of the States Parties in the matter of extradition.

Article 16

This Convention shall not affect the provisions of the American Convention on Human Rights, other conventions on the subject, or the Statutes of the Inter-American Commission on Human Rights, with respect to the crime of torture.

Article 17

The States Parties shall inform the Inter-American Commission on Human Rights of any legislative, judicial, administrative, or other measures they adopt in application of this Convention.

In keeping with its duties and responsibilities, the Inter-American Commission on Human Rights will endeavor in its annual report to analyze the existing situation in the member states of the Organization of American States in regard to the prevention and elimination of torture.

Article 18

This Convention is open to signature by the member states of the Organization of American States.

* * *

Article 21

The States Parties may, at the time of approval, signature, ratification, or accession, make reservations to this Convention, provided that such reservations are not incompatible with the object and purpose of the Convention and concern one or more specific provisions.

* * *

Article 23

This Convention shall remain in force indefinitely, but may be denounced by any State Party. The instrument of denunciation shall be deposited with the General Secretariat of the Organization of American States. After one year from the date of deposit of the instrument of denunciation, this Convention shall cease to be in effect for the denouncing State but shall remain in force for the remaining States Parties.

* * *

3.42 RESOLUTION ON MEASURES TO PREVENT INTERNATIONAL TERRORISM.[a] Adopted by the U.N. General Assembly, Dec. 9, 1985. U.N.G.A. Res 40/61, 40 U.N. GAOR, Supp. (No. 53) 301, U.N. Doc. A/40/1003 (1985)

The General Assembly,

Recalling its resolutions 3034 (XXVII) of 18 December 1972, 31/102 of 15 December 1976, 32/147 of 16 December 1977, 34/145 of 17 December 1979, 36/109 of 10 December 1981 and 38/130 of 19 December 1983,

Recalling also the Declaration on Principles of International Law concerning Friendly Relations and Co-operation among States in accordance with the Charter of the United Nations, the Declaration on the Strengthening of International Security, the Definition of Aggression and relevant instruments on international humanitarian law applicable in armed conflict,

Further recalling the existing international conventions relating to various aspects of the problem of international terrorism, *inter alia,* the Convention on Offences and Certain Other Acts Committed on Board Aircraft, signed at Tokyo on 14 September 1963, the Convention for the Suppression of Unlawful Seizure of Aircraft, signed at The Hague on 16 December 1970, the Convention for the Suppression of Unlawful Acts against the Safety of Civil Aviation, signed at Montreal on 23 September 1971, the Convention on the Prevention and Punishment of Crimes against Internationally Protected Persons, including Diplomatic Agents, signed at New York on 14 December 1973, and the International Convention against the Taking of Hostages, adopted at New York on 17 December 1979,

Deeply concerned about the world-wide escalation of acts of terrorism in all its forms, which endanger or take innocent human lives, jeopardize fundamental freedoms and seriously impair the dignity of human beings,

Taking note of the deep concern and condemnation of all acts of international terrorism expressed by the Security Council and the Secretary–General,

Convinced of the importance of expanding and improving international co-operation among States, on a bilateral and multilateral basis, which will contribute to the elimination of acts of international terrorism and their underlying causes and to the prevention and elimination of this criminal scourge,

Reaffirming the principle of self-determination of peoples enshrined in the Charter of the United Nations,

Reaffirming also the inalienable right to self-determination and independence of all peoples under colonial and racist régimes and other forms of alien domination, and upholding the legitimacy of their struggle, in particular the struggle of national liberation movements, in accordance with the purposes and principles of the Charter and of the Declaration on Principles of International Law concerning Friendly Relations and Co-operation among States in accordance with the Charter of the United Nations,

Mindful of the necessity of maintaining and safeguarding the basic rights of the individual in accordance with the relevant international human rights instruments and generally accepted international standards,

Convinced of the importance of the observance by States of their obligations under the relevant international conventions to ensure that appropriate law enforce-

a. *See also* Basic Documents 3.14, 3.27, 3.28, 3.30, 3.32, 3.33, and 3.35, *supra*, and Basic Document 3.43, *infra*.

ment measures are taken in connection with the offences addressed in those Conventions,

Expressing its concern that in recent years terrorism has taken on forms that have an increasingly deleterious effect on international relations, which may jeopardize the very territorial integrity and security of States,

Taking note of the report of the Secretary–General,

1. *Unequivocally condemns,* as criminal, all acts, methods and practices of terrorism wherever and by whomever committed, including those which jeopardize friendly relations among States and their security;

2. *Deeply deplores* the loss of innocent human lives which results from such acts of terrorism;

3. *Also deplores* the pernicious impact of acts of international terrorism on relations of co-operation among States, including co-operation for development;

4. *Appeals* to all States that have not yet done so to consider becoming party to the existing international conventions relating to various aspects of international terrorism;

5. *Invites* all States to take all appropriate measures at the national level with a view to the speedy and final elimination of the problem of international terrorism, such as the harmonization of domestic legislation with existing international conventions, the fulfilment of assumed international obligations, and the prevention of the preparation and organization in their respective territories of acts directed against other States;

6. *Calls upon* all States to fulfil their obligations under international law to refrain from organizing, instigating, assisting or participating in terrorist acts in other States, or acquiescing in activities within their territory directed towards the commission of such acts;

7. *Urges* all States not to allow any circumstances to obstruct the application of appropriate law enforcement measures provided for in the relevant conventions to which they are party to persons who commit acts of international terrorism covered by those conventions;

8. *Also urges* all States to co-operate with one another more closely, especially through the exchange of relevant information concerning the prevention and combating of terrorism, the apprehension and prosecution or extradition of the perpetrators of such acts, the conclusion of special treaties and/or the incorporation into appropriate bilateral treaties of special clauses, in particular regarding the extradition or prosecution of terrorists;

9. *Further urges* all States, unilaterally and in co-operation with other States, as well as relevant United Nations organs, to contribute to the progressive elimination of the causes underlying international terrorism and to pay special attention to all situations, including colonialism, racism and situations involving mass and flagrant violations of human rights and fundamental freedoms and those involving alien occupation, that may give rise to international terrorism and may endanger international peace and security;

10. *Calls upon* all States to observe and implement the recommendations of the *Ad Hoc* Committee on International Terrorism contained in its report to the General Assembly at its thirty-fourth session;

11. *Also calls upon* all States to take all appropriate measures as recommended by the International Civil Aviation Organization and as set forth in relevant international conventions to prevent terrorist attacks against civil aviation transport and other forms of public transport;

12. *Encourages* the International Civil Aviation Organization to continue its efforts aimed at promoting universal acceptance of and strict compliance with the international air security conventions;

13. *Requests* the International Maritime Organization to study the problem of terrorism aboard or against ships with a view to making recommendations on appropriate measures;

* * *

3.43 SECURITY COUNCIL RESOLUTION CONDEMNING HOSTAGE TAKING.[a] Adopted by the U.N. Security Council, Dec. 18, 1985. U.N.S.C.Res. 579, 40 U.N. SCOR 24. U.N.Doc. S/Res/579 (1985)

The Security Council,

Deeply disturbed at the prevalence of incidents of hostage-taking and abduction, several of which are of protracted duration and have included loss of life,

Considering that the taking of hostages and abductions are offences of grave concern to the international community, having severe adverse consequences for the rights of the victims and for the promotion of friendly relations and co-operation among States,

Recalling the statement of 9 October 1985 by the President of the Security Council, resolutely condemning all acts of terrorism, including hostage-taking,

Recalling also resolution 40/61 of 9 December 1985 of the General Assembly,

Bearing in mind the International Convention against the Taking of Hostages, adopted on 17 December 1979, the Convention on the Prevention and Punishment of Crimes against Internationally Protected Persons, including Diplomatic Agents, adopted on 14 December 1973, the Convention for the Suppression of Unlawful Acts against the Safety of Civil Aviation, signed on 23 September 1971, the Convention for the Suppression of Unlawful Seizure of Aircraft, signed on 16 December 1970, and other relevant conventions,

1. *Condemns unequivocally* all acts of hostage-taking and abduction;

2. *Calls for* the immediate safe release of all hostages and abducted persons wherever and by whomever they are being held;

3. *Affirms* the obligation of all States in whose territory hostages or abducted persons are held urgently to take all appropriate measures to secure their safe release and to prevent the commission of acts of hostage-taking and abduction in the future;

4. *Appeals* to all States that have not yet done so to consider the possibility of becoming parties to the International Convention against the Taking of Hostages, the Convention on the Prevention and Punishment of Crimes against Internationally Protected Persons, including Diplomatic Agents, the Convention for the Suppression of Unlawful Acts against the Safety of Civil Aviation, the Convention for the Suppression of Unlawful Seizure of Aircraft and other relevant conventions;

5. *Urges* the further development of international co-operation among States in devising and adopting effective measures which are in accordance with the rules of international law to facilitate the prevention, prosecution and punishment of all acts of hostage-taking and abduction as manifestations of international terrorism.

a. *See also* Basic Documents 3.14, 3.27, 3.28, 3.30. 3.32, 3.33, 3.35, and 3.42, *supra.*

3.44 FOOD AID CONVENTION.[a] Done at London, Mar. 13, 1986. Entered into force, July 1, 1986; for the United States, Jan. 27, 1988. S. Treaty Doc. No. 1, 100th Cong. 1st Sess., at 16 (1987)[b]

PART I—OBJECTIVE AND DEFINITIONS

ARTICLE I—OBJECTIVE

The objective of this Convention is to secure, through a joint effort by the international community, the achievement of the World Food Conference target of at least 10 million tonnes of food aid annually to developing countries in the form of grain suitable for human consumption, and as determined by the provisions of this Convention.

ARTICLE II—DEFINITIONS

(1) For the purposes of this Convention:

(a) "Committee" means the Food Aid Committee referred to in Article IX;

(b) "member" means a party to this Convention;

(c) "Executive Director" means the Executive Director of the International Wheat Council;

(d) "Secretariat" means the secretariat of the International Wheat Council;

(e) "grain" or "grains" means wheat, barley, maize, millet, oats, rye, sorghum and rice, and any other type of grain suitable for human consumption that the Committee may decide, or products derived therefrom, including products of secondary processing, as defined in the Rules of Procedure, subject to the provisions of paragraph (1) of Article III;

(f) "f.o.b." means free on board;

(g) "c.i.f." means cost, insurance and freight;

(h) "tonne" means 1,000 kilogrammes;

(i) "year" means the period from 1 July to 30 June, unless otherwise stated.

(2) Any reference in this Convention to a "Government" or "Governments" shall be construed as including a reference to the European Economic Community (hereinafter referred to as the EEC). Accordingly, any reference in this Convention to "signature" or to the "deposit of instruments of ratification, acceptance or approval" or "an instrument of accession" or to a "declaration of provisional application" by a Government shall, in the case of the EEC, be construed as including signature or declaration of provisional application on behalf of the EEC by its competent authority, and the deposit of the instrument required by the institutional procedures of the EEC to be deposited for the conclusion of an international agreement.

PART II—MAIN PROVISIONS

ARTICLE III—CONTRIBUTIONS OF MEMBERS

(1) The members of this Convention agree to contribute to developing countries grains as food aid, as defined in Article II, paragraph (1)(e), suitable for human consumption and of an acceptable type and quality, or the cash equivalent thereof, in the minimum annual amounts specified in paragraph (3) below.

(2) To the maximum extent possible, contributions shall be made by members on a forward planning basis, so that recipient countries may be able to take account, in

a. This convention supersedes and replaces the Food Aid Convention of Mar. 6, 1980.

b. *See also* Basic Document 3.31, *supra*.

their development programmes, of the likely flow of food aid they will receive during each year of this Convention. Furthermore, members should, to the extent possible, indicate the amount of their contributions to be made in the form of gifts, and the grant element of any aid which is not in the form of gifts.

(3) The minimum annual contribution, in wheat equivalent, of each member towards the achievement of the objective of Article I is as follows:

Member	*Tonnes*
Argentina	35,000
Australia	400,000
Austria	20,000
Canada	600,000
European Economic Community and its member States	1,670,000
Finland	25,000
Japan	300,000
Norway	30,000
Sweden	40,000
Switzerland	27,000
United States of America	4,470,000

(4) For the purposes of the operation of this Convention, any member which has acceded to this Convention pursuant to paragraph (2) of Article XX shall be deemed to be listed in paragraph (3) of this Article together with its minimum contribution as determined under the provisions of Article XX.

(5) In the case of the inability of a member to fulfill its obligations under this Convention in any one year, the obligations of that member shall be increased in the following year by the residual amount remaining from the preceding year.

(6) Contributions in the form of grains shall be placed in a f.o.b. forward position by members. However, donors are encouraged, as appropriate, to bear the costs of transporting their grain contributions under this Convention beyond the f.o.b. stage, especially in emergency situations or in the case of shipments to low-income, food deficit countries. Due reference to the payment of such contributions shall be made in any reviews of the performance of members under this Convention.

(7) Grain purchases under paragraph (1)(a) of Article IV shall be made from members of the Food Aid Convention, 1986, and the Wheat Trade Convention in force, with preference accorded to developing members of both Conventions, with a view to facilitating exports of, or processing by, developing members of both Conventions. In making purchases it shall be the general aim that the major part of such purchases shall come from developing countries, with priority being given to developing members of the Food Aid Convention. These provisions shall not however exclude the purchase of grain from a developing country, not a member of this Convention or the Wheat Trade Convention. In all purchases under this paragraph, special regard shall be given to the quality, the c.i.f. price advantages and the possibilities of speedy delivery to the recipient country and the specific requirements of the recipient countries themselves. Cash contributions shall not normally be used in any year to purchase grain from a country which is the same type of grain as that country has received as bilateral or multilateral food aid during the same year, or during previous years, if the grain so provided is still being used.

ARTICLE IV—TERMS OF FOOD AID CONTRIBUTIONS

Food aid under this Convention may be supplied on any of the following terms:

(a) gifts of grain or gifts of cash to be used to purchase grain for the recipient country;

(b) sales for the currency of the recipient country which is not transferable and is not convertible into currency or goods and services for use by the donor members; [1]

(c) sales on credit, with payment to be made in reasonable annual amounts over periods of 20 years or more and with interest at rates which are below commercial rates prevailing in world markets; [2]

on the understanding that such aid shall be supplied to the maximum extent possible by way of gifts, especially in the case of least developed countries, low *per capita* income countries and other developing countries in serious economic difficulties.

ARTICLE V—CHANNELLING OF CONTRIBUTIONS

(1) Members may, in respect of their contributions under this Convention, specify a recipient country or countries.

(2) Members may make their contributions bilaterally or through intergovernmental organizations and/or non-governmental organizations.

(3) Members shall give full consideration to the advantages of directing a greater proportion of food aid through multilateral channels, in particular the World Food Programme.

ARTICLE VI—WHEAT EQUIVALENTS

(1) The Committee shall establish Rules of Procedure for the purposes of evaluating a member's contribution shipped in grain other than wheat, or in grain products, taking into account, where appropriate, the grain content of products and the commercial value of the grain or product relative to wheat.

* * *

ARTICLE VII—IMPACT ON TRADE AND AGRICULTURAL PRODUCTION AND CONDUCT OF AID TRANSACTIONS

(1) All aid transactions under this Convention shall be carried out in a way consistent with the concerns expressed in the current FAO Principles of Surplus Disposal and Guiding Lines. Members undertake to conduct all aid transactions under this Convention in such a way as to avoid harmful interference with normal patterns of production and international commercial trade.

(2) Members shall, as appropriate, act in accordance with the Guidelines and Criteria for Food Aid, approved by the Committee on Food Aid Policies and Programmes of the World Food Programme.

ARTICLE VIII—SPECIAL PROVISION FOR EMERGENCY NEEDS

If in any year there is a substantial food grain production shortfall in low-income developing countries in a particular region or regions, the Chairman of the Committee, after considering information received from the Executive Director, may call a session of the Committee to consider the seriousness of the production shortfall. The Committee may recommend that members should respond to the situation by increasing the amount of food aid available.

ARTICLE IX—FOOD AID COMMITTEE

There shall be established a Food Aid Committee whose membership shall consist of all parties to this Convention. The Committee shall appoint a Chairman and a Vice–Chairman.

1. Under exceptional circumstances an exemption of not more than 10 per cent may be granted. This limitation may be waived for transactions which are to be used for the expansion of economic development activity in the recipient country, provided that the currency of the recipient country is not transferable or convertible in less than 10 years.

2. The credit sales agreement may provide for payment of up to 15 per cent of principal upon delivery of the grain.

ARTICLE X—POWERS AND FUNCTIONS OF THE COMMITTEE

(1) The Committee shall:

(a) receive from members, and members shall provide, regular reports on the amount, content, channelling and terms of their contributions under this Convention;

(b) keep under review the purchase of grains financed by cash contributions with particular reference to purchases of grain from developing countries under paragraph (7) of Article III;

(c) examine the way in which the obligations undertaken under this Convention have been fulfilled; and

(d) exchange information on a regular basis on the functioning of the food aid arrangements under this Convention.

* * *

(5) In addition to the powers and functions specified in this Article, the Committee shall have such other powers and perform such other functions as are necessary to carry out the provisions of this Convention.

ARTICLE XI—SEAT, SESSIONS AND QUORUM

(1) The seat of the Committee shall be in London.

(2) The Committee shall meet at least twice a year in conjunction with the statutory sessions of the International Wheat Council. The Committee shall meet also at such other times as the Chairman shall decide; or at the request of three members; or as otherwise required by this Convention.

(3) The presence of delegates representing two thirds of the membership of the Committee shall be necessary to constitute a quorum at any session of the Committee.

ARTICLE XII—DECISIONS

The decisions of the Committee shall be reached by consensus.

* * *

ARTICLE XV—DEFAULTS AND DISPUTES

In the case of a dispute concerning the interpretation or application of this Convention, or of a default in obligations under this Convention, the Committee shall meet and take appropriate action.

* * *

ARTICLE XXII—DURATION, EXTENSION AND TERMINATION

(1) This Convention shall remain in force until and including 30 June 1989, unless extended under paragraph (2) of this Article or terminated earlier under paragraph (4) of this Article, provided that the Wheat Trade Convention, 1986, or a new Wheat Trade Convention replacing it, remains in force until and including that date.

(2) The Committee may extend the Convention beyond 30 June 1989 for successive periods not exceeding two years on each occasion, provided always that the Wheat Trade Convention, 1986, or a new Wheat Trade Convention replacing it, remains in force during the period of the extension.

(3) If the Convention is extended under paragraph (2) of this Article, the annual contributions of members under paragraph (3) of Article III may be subject to review by members before the entry into force of each extension. Their respective obligations, as reviewed, shall remain unchanged for the duration of each extension.

(4) In the event of this Convention being terminated, the Committee shall continue in being for such time as may be required to carry out its liquidation, and

shall have such powers, and exercise such functions, as may be necessary for that purpose.

ARTICLE XXIII—WITHDRAWAL AND REJOINING

(1) Any member may withdraw from this Convention at the end of any year by giving written notice of withdrawal to the depositary at least ninety days prior to the end of that year, but shall not thereby be released from any obligations incurred under this Convention which have not been discharged by the end of that year. The member shall simultaneously inform the Committee of the action it has taken.

(2) Any member which withdraws from this Convention may thereafter rejoin by giving notice to the Committee. It shall be a condition of rejoining the Convention that the member shall be responsible for fulfilling its full annual obligations with effect from the year in which it rejoins.

ARTICLE XXIV—RELATIONSHIP OF THIS CONVENTION TO THE INTERNATIONAL WHEAT AGREEMENT, 1986

This Convention shall replace the Food Aid Convention, 1980, as extended, and shall be one of the constituent instruments of the International Wheat Agreement, 1986.

* * *

3.45 DECLARATION ON THE RIGHT TO DEVELOPMENT. Adopted by the U.N. General Assembly, Dec. 4, 1986. U.N.G.A. Res. 41/128, 41 U.N. GAOR, Supp. (No. 53) U.N. Doc. A/41/925 (1986)

The General Assembly,

Bearing in mind the purposes and principles of the Charter of the United Nations relating to the achievement of international co-operation in solving international problems of an economic, social, cultural or humanitarian nature, and in promoting and encouraging respect for human rights and fundamental freedoms for all without distinction as to race, sex, language or religion,

Recognizing that development is a comprehensive economic, social, cultural and political process, which aims at the constant improvement of the well-being of the entire population and of all individuals on the basis of their active, free and meaningful participation in development and in the fair distribution of benefits resulting therefrom,

Considering that under the provisions of the Universal Declaration of Human Rights everyone is entitled to a social and international order in which the rights and freedoms set forth in that Declaration can be fully realized,

Recalling the provisions of the International Covenant on Economic, Social and Cultural Rights and the International Covenant on Civil and Political Rights,

Recalling further the relevant agreements, conventions, resolutions, recommendations and other instruments of the United Nations and its specialized agencies concerning the integral development of the human being, economic and social progress and development of all peoples, including those instruments concerning decolonization, the prevention of discrimination, respect for, and observance of, human rights and fundamental freedoms, the maintenance of international peace and security and the further promotion of friendly relations and co-operation among States in accordance with the Charter,

Recalling the right of peoples to self-determination, by virtue of which they have the right freely to determine their political status and to pursue their economic, social and cultural development,

Recalling further the right of peoples to exercise, subject to relevant provisions of both International Covenants on Human Rights, their full and complete sovereignty over all their natural wealth and resources,

Mindful of the obligation of States under the Charter to promote universal respect for and observance of human rights and fundamental freedoms for all without distinction of any kind such as race, colour, sex, language, religion, political or other opinion, national or social origin, property, birth or other status,

Considering that the elimination of the massive and flagrant violations of the human rights of the peoples and individuals affected by situations such as those resulting from colonialism, neo-colonialism, *apartheid,* all forms of racism and racial discrimination, foreign domination and occupation, aggression and threats against national sovereignty, national unity and territorial integrity and threats of war would contribute to the establishment of circumstances propitious to the development of a great part of mankind,

Concerned at the existence of serious obstacles to development, as well as to the complete fulfilment of human beings and of peoples, constituted, *inter alia,* by the denial of civil, political, economic, social and cultural rights, and considering that all human rights and fundamental freedoms are indivisible and interdependent and that, in order to promote development, equal attention and urgent consideration should be given to the implementation, promotion and protection of civil, political, economic, social and cultural rights and that, accordingly, the promotion of, respect for, and enjoyment of certain human rights and fundamental freedoms cannot justify the denial of other human rights and fundamental freedoms,

Considering that international peace and security are essential elements for the realization of the right to development,

Reaffirming that there is a close relationship between disarmament and development and that progress in the field of disarmament would considerably promote progress in the field of development and that resources released through disarmament measures should be devoted to the economic and social development and well-being of all peoples and, in particular, those of the developing countries,

Recognizing that the human person is the central subject of the development process and that development policy should therefore make the human being the main participant and beneficiary of development,

Recognizing that the creation of conditions favourable to the development of peoples and individuals is the primary responsibility of their States,

Aware that efforts to promote and protect human rights at the international level should be accompanied by efforts to establish a new international economic order,

Confirming that the right to development is an inalienable human right and that equality of opportunity for development is a prerogative both of nations and of individuals who make up nations,

Proclaims the following Declaration on the right to development:

Article 1

1. The right to development is an inalienable human right by virtue of which every human person and all peoples are entitled to participate in, contribute to, and enjoy economic, social, cultural and political development, in which all human rights and fundamental freedoms can be fully realized.

2. The human right to development also implies the full realization of the right of peoples to self-determination, which includes, subject to relevant provisions of both International Covenants on Human Rights, the exercise of their inalienable right to full sovereignty over all their natural wealth and resources.

Article 2

1. The human person is the central subject of development and should be the active participant and beneficiary of the right to development.

2. All human beings have a responsibility for development, individually and collectively, taking into account the need for full respect of their human rights and fundamental freedoms as well as their duties to the community, which alone can ensure the free and complete fulfilment of the human being, and they should therefore promote and protect an appropriate political, social and economic order for development.

3. States have the right and the duty to formulate appropriate national development policies that aim at the constant improvement of the well-being of the entire population and of all individuals, on the basis of their active, free and meaningful participation in development and in the fair distribution of the benefits resulting therefrom.

Article 3

1. States have the primary responsibility for the creation of national and international conditions favourable to the realization of the right to development.

2. The realization of the right to development requires full respect for the principles of international law concerning friendly relations and co-operation among States in accordance with the Charter of the United Nations.

3. States have the duty to co-operate with each other in ensuring development and eliminating obstacles to development. States should fulfil their rights and duties in such a manner as to promote a new international economic order based on sovereign equality, interdependence, mutual interest and co-operation among all States, as well as to encourage the observance and realization of human rights.

Article 4

1. States have the duty to take steps, individually and collectively, to formulate international development policies with a view to facilitating the full realization of the right to development.

2. Sustained action is required to promote more rapid development of developing countries. As a complement to the efforts of developing countries effective international co-operation is essential in providing these countries with appropriate means and facilities to foster their comprehensive development.

Article 5

States shall take resolute steps to eliminate the massive and flagrant violations of the human rights of peoples and human beings affected by situations such as those resulting from *apartheid,* all forms of racism and racial discrimination, colonialism, foreign domination and occupation, aggression, foreign interference and threats against national sovereignty, national unity and territorial integrity, threats of war and refusal to recognize the fundamental right of peoples to self-determination.

Article 6

1. All States should co-operate with a view to promoting, encouraging and strengthening universal respect for and observance of all human rights and fundamental freedoms for all without any distinction as to race, sex, language and religion.

2. All human rights and fundamental freedoms are indivisible and interdependent, equal attention and urgent consideration should be given to the implementation, promotion and protection of civil, political, economic, social and cultural rights.

3. States should take steps to eliminate obstacles to development resulting from failure to observe civil and political rights as well as economic, social and cultural rights.

Article 7

All States should promote the establishment, maintenance and strengthening of international peace and security and, to that end, should do their utmost to achieve general and complete disarmament under effective international control as well as to ensure that the resources released by effective disarmament measures are used for comprehensive development, in particular that of the developing countries.

Article 8

1. States should undertake, at the national level, all necessary measures for the realization of the right to development and shall ensure, *inter alia,* equality of opportunity for all in their access to basic resources, education, health services, food, housing, employment and the fair distribution of income. Effective measures should be undertaken to ensure that women have an active role in the development process. Appropriate economic and social reforms should be made with a view to eradicating all social injustices.

2. States should encourage popular participation in all spheres as an important factor in development and in the full realization of all human rights.

Article 9

1. All the aspects of the right to development set forth in this Declaration are indivisible and interdependent and each of them should be considered in the context of the whole.

2. Nothing in this Declaration shall be construed as being contrary to the purposes and principles of the United Nations, or as implying that any State, group or person has a right to engage in any activity or to perform any act aimed at the violation of the rights set forth in the Universal Declaration of Human Rights and in the International Covenants on Human Rights.

Article 10

Steps should be taken to ensure the full exercise and progressive enhancement of the right to development, including the formulation, adoption and implementation of policy, legislative and other measures at the national and international levels.

3.46 INTERNATIONAL LABOR ORGANIZATION CONVENTION (NO. 169) CONCERNING INDIGENOUS AND TRIBAL PEOPLES IN INDEPENDENT COUNTRIES.[a] Done at Geneva, June 27, 1989. Opened for signature June 27, 1989. International Labor Conference, Draft Report of the Committee on Convention No. 107, Appendix I, C.C. 107/D. 303 (June 1989)

The General Conference of the International Labour Organisation,

Having been convened at Geneva by the Governing Body of the International Labour Office, and having met in its 76th Session on 7 June 1989, and

Noting the international standards contained in the Indigenous and Tribal Populations Convention and Recommendation, 1957, and

Recalling the terms of the Universal Declaration of Human Rights, the International Covenant on Economic, Social and Cultural Rights, the International Covenant on Civil and Political Rights, and the many international instruments on the prevention of discrimination, and

Considering that the developments which have taken place in international law since 1957, as well as developments in the situation of indigenous and tribal peoples in all regions of the world, have made it appropriate to adopt new international standards on the subject with a view to removing the assimilationist orientation of the earlier standards, and

Recognising the aspirations of these peoples to exercise control over their own institutions, ways of life and economic development and to maintain and develop their identities, languages and religions, within the framework of the States in which they live, and

Noting that in many parts of the world these peoples are unable to enjoy their fundamental human rights to the same degree as the rest of the population of the States within which they live, and that their laws, values, customs and perspectives have often been eroded, and

Calling attention to the distinctive contributions of indigenous and tribal peoples to the cultural diversity and social and ecological harmony of humankind and to international co-operation and understanding, and

Noting that the following provisions have been framed with the co-operation of the United Nations, the Food and Agriculture Organisation of the United Nations, the United Nations Educational, Scientific and Cultural Organisation and the World Health Organisation, as well as of the Inter-American Indian Institute, at appropriate levels and in their respective fields, and that it is proposed to continue this co-operation in promoting and securing the application of these provisions, and

Having decided upon the adoption of certain proposals with regard to the partial revision of the Indigenous and Tribal Populations Convention, 1957 (No. 107), which is the fourth item on the agenda of the session, and

Having determined that these proposals shall take the form of an international Convention revising the Indigenous and Tribal Populations Convention, 1957; adopts this 27 day of June of the year one thousand nine hundred and eighty-nine the following Convention, which may be cited as the Indigenous and Tribal Peoples Convention, 1989:

a. *See also* Basic Document 3.10, *supra.*

PART I. GENERAL POLICY

Article 1

1. This Convention applies to:

(a) tribal peoples in independent countries whose social, cultural and economic conditions distinguish them from other sections of the national community, and whose status is regulated wholly or partially by their own customs or traditions or by special laws or regulations;

(b) peoples in independent countries who are regarded as indigenous on account of their descent from the populations which inhabited the country, or a geographical region to which the country belongs, at the time of conquest or colonisation or the establishment of present state boundaries and who, irrespective of their legal status, retain some or all of their own social, economic, cultural and political institutions.

2. Self-identification as indigenous or tribal shall be regarded as a fundamental criterion for determining the groups to which the provisions of this Convention apply.

3. The use of the term "peoples" in this Convention shall not be construed as having any implications as regards the rights which may attach to the term under international law.

Article 2

1. Governments shall have the responsibility for developing, with the participation of the peoples concerned, co-ordinated and systematic action to protect the rights of these peoples and to guarantee respect for their integrity.

2. Such action shall include measures for:

(a) ensuring that members of these peoples benefit on an equal footing from the rights and opportunities which national laws and regulations grant to other members of the population;

(b) promoting the full realisation of the social, economic and cultural rights of these peoples with respect for their social and cultural identity, their customs and traditions and their institutions;

(c) assisting the members of the peoples concerned to eliminate socio-economic gaps that may exist between indigenous and other members of the national community, in a manner compatible with their aspirations and ways of life.

Article 3

1. Indigenous and tribal peoples shall enjoy the full measure of human rights and fundamental freedoms without hindrance or discrimination. The provisions of the Convention shall be applied without discrimination to male and female members of these peoples.

2. No form of force or coercion shall be used in violation of the human rights and fundamental freedoms of the peoples concerned, including the rights contained in this Convention.

Article 4

1. Special measures shall be adopted as appropriate for safeguarding the persons, institutions, property, labour, cultures and environment of the peoples concerned.

2. Such special measures shall not be contrary to the freely-expressed wishes of the peoples concerned.

3. Enjoyment of the general rights of citizenship, without discrimination, shall not be prejudiced in any way by such special measures.

Article 5

In applying the provisions of this Convention:

(a) the social, cultural, religious and spiritual values and practices of these peoples shall be recognised and protected, and due account shall be taken of the nature of the problems which face them both as groups and as individuals;

(b) the integrity of the values, practices and institutions of these peoples shall be respected;

(c) policies aimed at mitigating the difficulties experienced by these peoples in facing new conditions of life and work shall be adopted, with the participation and co-operation of the peoples affected.

Article 6

1. In applying the provisions of this Convention, governments shall:

(a) consult the peoples concerned, through appropriate procedures and in particular through their representative institutions, whenever consideration is being given to legislative or administrative measures which may affect them directly;

(b) establish means by which these peoples can freely participate, to at least the same extent as other sectors of the population, at all levels of decision-making in elective institutions and administrative and other bodies responsible for policies and programmes which concern them;

(c) establish means for the full development of these peoples' own institutions and initiatives, and in appropriate cases provide the resources necessary for this purpose.

2. The consultations carried out in application of this Convention shall be undertaken, in good faith and in a form appropriate to the circumstances, with the objective of achieving agreement or consent to the proposed measures.

Article 7

1. The peoples concerned shall have the right to decide their own priorities for the process of development as it affects their lives, beliefs, [territories] [lands], institutions and spiritual well-being and to exercise control, to the extent possible, over their own economic, social and cultural development. In addition, they shall participate in the formulation, implementation and evaluation of plans and programmes for national and regional development which may affect them directly.

2. The improvement of the conditions of life and work and levels of health and education of the peoples concerned, with their participation and co-operation, shall be a matter of priority in plans for the overall economic development of areas they inhabit. Special projects for development of the areas in question shall also be so designed as to promote such improvement.

3. Governments shall ensure that, whenever appropriate, studies are carried out, in co-operation with the peoples concerned, to assess the social, spiritual, cultural and environmental impact on them of planned development activities. The results of these studies shall be considered as fundamental criteria for the implementation of these activities.

4. Governments shall take measures, in co-operation with the peoples concerned, to protect and preserve the environment of the territories they inhabit.

Article 8

1. In the application of national laws and regulations to the peoples concerned, due regard shall be had to their customs or customary laws.

2. These peoples shall have the right to retain their own customs and institutions, where these are not incompatible with fundamental rights defined by the national legal system and with internationally recognised human rights. Procedures shall be established, whenever necessary, to resolve conflicts which may arise in the application of this principle.

3. The application of paragraphs 1 and 2 of this Article shall not prevent members of these peoples from exercising the rights granted to all citizens and from assuming the corresponding duties.

Article 9

1. To the extent compatible with the national legal system and internationally recognised human rights, the methods customarily practised by the peoples concerned for dealing with offences committed by their members shall be respected.

2. The customs of these peoples in regard to penal matters shall be taken into consideration by the authorities and courts dealing with such cases.

Article 10

1. In imposing penalties laid down by general law on members of these peoples account shall be taken of their economic, social and cultural characteristics.

2. Preference shall be given to methods of punishment other than confinement in prison.

Article 11

The exaction from members of the peoples concerned of compulsory personal services in any form, whether paid or unpaid, shall be prohibited and punishable by law, except in cases prescribed by law for all citizens.

Article 12

The peoples concerned shall be safeguarded against the abuse of their rights and shall be able to take legal proceedings, either individually or through their representative bodies, for the effective protection of these rights. Measures shall be taken to ensure that members of these peoples can understand and be understood in legal proceedings, where necessary through the provision of interpretation or by other effective means.

PART II. LAND

Article 13

1. In applying the provisions of this Part of the Convention governments shall respect the special importance for the cultures and spiritual values of the peoples concerned of their relationship with the lands or territories, or both as applicable, which they occupy or otherwise use, and in particular the collective aspects of this relationship.

2. The use of the term "lands" in Articles 15 and 16 shall include the concept of territories, which covers the total environment of the areas which the peoples concerned occupy or otherwise use.

Article 14

1. The rights of ownership and possession of the peoples concerned over the lands which they traditionally occupy shall be recognised. In addition, measures shall be taken in appropriate cases to safeguard the right of the peoples concerned to

use lands not exclusively occupied by them, but to which they have traditionally had access for their subsistence and traditional activities. Particular attention shall be paid to the situation of nomadic peoples and shifting cultivators in this respect.

2. Governments shall take steps as necessary to identify the lands which the peoples concerned traditionally occupy, and to guarantee effective protection of their rights of ownership and possession.

3. Adequate procedures shall be established within the national legal system to resolve land claims by the peoples concerned.

Article 15

1. The rights of the peoples concerned to the natural resources pertaining to their lands shall be specially safeguarded. These rights include the right of these peoples to participate in the use, management and conservation of these resources.

2. In cases in which the State retains the ownership of mineral or sub-surface resources or rights to other resources pertaining to lands, governments shall establish or maintain procedures through which they shall consult these peoples, with a view to ascertaining whether and to what degree their interests would be prejudiced, before undertaking or permitting any programmes for the exploration or exploitation of such resources pertaining to their lands. The peoples concerned shall wherever possible participate in the benefits of such activities, and shall receive fair compensation for any damages which they may sustain as a result of such activities.

Article 16

1. Subject to the following paragraphs of this Article, the peoples concerned shall not be removed from the lands which they occupy.

2. Where the relocation of these peoples is considered necessary as an exceptional measure, such relocation shall take place only with their free and informed consent. Where their consent cannot be obtained, such relocation shall take place only following appropriate procedures established by national laws and regulations, including public inquiries where appropriate, which provide the opportunity for effective representation of the peoples concerned.

3. Whenever possible, these peoples shall have the right to return to their traditional lands, as soon as the grounds for relocation cease to exist.

4. When such return is not possible, as determined by agreement or, in the absence of such agreement, through appropriate procedures, these peoples shall be provided in all possible cases with lands of quality and legal status at least equal to that of the lands previously occupied by them, suitable to provide for their present needs and future development. Where the peoples concerned express a preference for compensation in money or in kind, they shall be so compensated under appropriate guarantees.

5. Persons thus relocated shall be fully compensated for any resulting loss or injury.

Article 17

1. Procedures established by the peoples concerned for the transmission of land rights among members of these peoples shall be respected.

2. The peoples concerned shall be consulted whenever consideration is being given to their capacity to alienate their lands or otherwise transmit their rights outside their own community.

3. Persons who are not members of these peoples shall be prevented from taking advantage of their customs or of lack of understanding of the laws on the part of their members to secure the ownership, possession or use of land belonging to them.

Article 18

Adequate penalties shall be established by law for unauthorised intrusion upon, or use of, the lands of the peoples concerned, and governments shall take measures to prevent such offences.

Article 19

National agrarian programmes shall secure to the peoples concerned treatment equivalent to that accorded to other sectors of the population with regard to:

(a) the provision of more land for these peoples when they have not the area necessary for providing the essentials of a normal existence, or for any possible increase in their numbers;

(b) the provision of the means required to promote the development of the lands which these peoples already possess.

PART III. RECRUITMENT AND CONDITIONS OF EMPLOYMENT

Article 20

1. Governments shall, within the framework of national laws and regulations, and in co-operation with the peoples concerned, adopt special measures to ensure the effective protection with regard to recruitment and conditions of employment of workers belonging to these peoples, to the extent that they are not effectively protected by laws applicable to workers in general.

2. Governments shall do everything possible to prevent any discrimination between workers belonging to the peoples concerned and other workers, in particular as regards:

(a) admission to employment, including skilled employment, as well as measures for promotion and advancement;

(b) equal remuneration for work of equal value;

(c) medical and social assistance, occupational safety and health, all social security benefits and any other occupationally related benefits, and housing;

(d) the right of association and freedom for all lawful trade union activities, and the right to conclude collective agreements with employers or employers' organisations.

3. The measures taken shall include measures to ensure:

(a) that workers belonging to the peoples concerned, including seasonal, casual and migrant workers in agricultural and other employment, as well as those employed by labour contractors, enjoy the protection afforded by national law and practice to other such workers in the same sectors, and that they are fully informed of their rights under labour legislation and of the means of redress available to them;

(b) that workers belonging to these peoples are not subjected to working conditions hazardous to their health, in particular through exposure to pesticides or other toxic substances;

(c) that workers belonging to these peoples are not subjected to coercive recruitment systems, including bonded labour and other forms of debt servitude;

(d) that workers belonging to these peoples enjoy equal opportunities and equal treatment in employment for men and women, and protection from sexual harassment.

4. Particular attention shall be paid to the establishment of adequate labour inspection services in areas where workers belonging to the peoples concerned

undertake wage employment, in order to ensure compliance with the provisions of this Part of this Convention.

PART IV. VOCATIONAL TRAINING, HANDICRAFTS AND RURAL INDUSTRIES

Article 21

Members of the peoples concerned shall enjoy opportunities at least equal to those of other citizens in respect of vocational training measures.

Article 22

1. Measures shall be taken to promote the voluntary participation of members of the peoples concerned in vocational training programmes of general application.

2. Whenever existing programmes of vocational training of general application do not meet the special needs of the peoples concerned, governments shall, with the participation of these peoples, ensure the provision of special training programmes and facilities.

3. Any special training programmes shall be based on the economic environment, social and cultural conditions and practical needs of the peoples concerned. Any studies made in this connection shall be carried out in co-operation with these peoples, who shall be consulted on the organisation and operation of such programmes. Where feasible, these peoples shall progressively assume responsibility for the organisation and operation of such special training programmes, if they so decide.

Article 23

1. Handicrafts, rural and community-based industries, and subsistence economy and traditional activities of the peoples concerned, such as hunting, fishing, trapping and gathering, shall be recognised as important factors in the maintenance of their cultures and in their economic self-reliance and development. Governments shall, with the participation of these peoples and whenever appropriate, ensure that these activities are strengthened and promoted.

2. Upon the request of the peoples concerned, appropriate technical and financial assistance shall be provided wherever possible, taking into account the traditional technologies and cultural characteristics of these peoples, as well as the importance of sustainable and equitable development.

PART V. SOCIAL SECURITY AND HEALTH

Article 24

Social security schemes shall be extended progressively to cover the peoples concerned, and applied without discrimination against them.

Article 25

1. Governments shall ensure that adequate health services are made available to the peoples concerned, or shall provide them with resources to allow them to design and deliver such services under their own responsibility and control, so that they may enjoy the highest attainable standard of physical and mental health.

2. Health services shall, to the extent possible, be community-based. These services shall be planned and administered in co-operation with the peoples concerned and take into account their economic, geographic, social and cultural conditions as well as their traditional preventive care, healing practices and medicines.

3. The health care system shall give preference to the training and employment of local community health workers, and focus on primary health care while maintaining strong links with other levels of health care services.

4. The provision of such health services shall be co-ordinated with other social, economic and cultural measures in the country.

PART VI. EDUCATION AND MEANS OF COMMUNICATION

Article 26

Measures shall be taken to ensure that members of the peoples concerned have the opportunity to acquire education at all levels on at least an equal footing with the rest of the national community.

Article 27

1. Education programmes and services for the peoples concerned shall be developed and implemented in co-operation with them to address their special needs, and shall incorporate their histories, their knowledge and technologies, their value systems and their further social, economic and cultural aspirations.

2. The competent authority shall ensure the training of members of these peoples and their involvement in the formulation and implementation of education programmes, with a view to the progressive transfer of responsibility for the conduct of these programmes to these peoples as appropriate.

3. In addition, governments shall recognise the right of these peoples to establish their own educational institutions and facilities, provided that such institutions meet minimum standards established by the competent authority in consultation with these peoples. Appropriate resources shall be provided for this purpose.

Article 28

1. Children belonging to the peoples concerned shall, wherever practicable, be taught to read and write in their own indigenous language or in the language most commonly used by the group to which they belong. When this is not practicable, the competent authorities shall undertake consultations with these peoples with a view to the adoption of measures to achieve this objective.

2. Adequate measures shall be taken to ensure that these peoples have the opportunity to attain fluency in the national language or in one of the official languages of the country.

3. Measures shall be taken to preserve and promote the development and practice of the indigenous languages of the peoples concerned.

Article 29

The imparting of general knowledge and skills that will help children belonging to the peoples concerned to participate fully and on an equal footing in their own community and in the national community shall be an aim of education for these peoples.

Article 30

1. Governments shall adopt measures appropriate to the traditions and cultures of the peoples concerned, to make known to them their rights and duties, especially in regard to labour, economic opportunities, education and health matters, social welfare and their rights deriving from this Convention.

2. If necessary, this shall be done by means of written translations and through the use of mass communications in the languages of these peoples.

Article 31

Educational measures shall be taken among all sections of the national community, and particularly among those that are in most direct contact with the peoples concerned, with the object of eliminating prejudices that they may harbour in respect of these peoples. To this end, efforts shall be made to ensure that history textbooks and other educational materials provide a fair, accurate and informative portrayal of the societies and cultures of these peoples.

PART VII. MIGRATION ACROSS BORDERS

Article 32

Governments shall take appropriate measures, including by means of international agreements, to facilitate contacts and co-operation between indigenous and tribal peoples across borders, including activities in the economic, social, cultural, spiritual and environmental fields.

PART VIII. ADMINISTRATION

Article 33

1. The governmental authority responsible for the matters covered in this Convention shall ensure that agencies or other appropriate mechanisms exist to administer the programmes affecting the peoples concerned, and shall ensure that they have the means necessary for the proper fulfilment of the functions assigned to them.

2. These programmes shall include:

(a) the planning, co-ordination, execution and evaluation, in co-operation with the peoples concerned, of the measures provided for in this Convention;

(b) the proposing of legislative and other measures to the competent authorities and supervision of the application of the measures taken, in co-operation with the peoples concerned.

PART IX. GENERAL PROVISIONS

Article 34

The nature and scope of the measures to be taken to give effect to this Convention shall be determined in a flexible manner, having regard to the conditions characteristic of each country.

Article 35

The application of the provisions of this Convention shall not adversely affect rights and benefits of the peoples concerned pursuant to other Conventions and Recommendations, international instruments, treaties, or national laws, awards, custom or agreements.

PART X. FINAL PROVISIONS

Article 36

This Convention revises the Indigenous and Tribal Populations Convention, 1957.

3.47 CONVENTION ON THE RIGHTS OF THE CHILD. Done at New York, Nov. 20, 1989. Opened for signature, Jan. 26, 1990. U.N.G.A. Res. 25 (XLIV), 44 U.N. GAOR, Supp. (No. ___) ___, U.N. Doc. A/RES/44/25 (1989) *reprinted in* 28 I.L.M. 1457 (1989)

PREAMBLE

The States Parties to the present Convention,

Considering that, in accordance with the principles proclaimed in the Charter of the United Nations, recognition of the inherent dignity and of the equal and inalienable rights of all members of the human family is the foundation of freedom, justice and peace in the world,

Bearing in mind that the peoples of the United Nations have, in the Charter, reaffirmed their faith in fundamental human rights and in the dignity and worth of the human person, and have determined to promote social progress and better standards of life in larger freedom,

Recognizing that the United Nations has, in the Universal Declaration of Human Rights and in the International Covenants on Human Rights, proclaimed and agreed that everyone is entitled to all the rights and freedoms set forth therein, without distinction of any kind, such as race, colour, sex, language, religion, political or other opinion, national or social origin, property, birth or other status,

Recalling that, in the Universal Declaration of Human Rights, the United Nations has proclaimed that childhood is entitled to special care and assistance,

Convinced that the family, as the fundamental group of society and the natural environment for the growth and well-being of all its members and particularly children, should be afforded the necessary protection and assistance so that it can fully assume its responsibilities within the community,

Recognizing that the child, for the full and harmonious development of his or her personality, should grow up in a family environment, in an atmosphere of happiness, love and understanding,

Considering that the child should be fully prepared to live an individual life in society, and brought up in the spirit of the ideals proclaimed in the Charter of the United Nations, and in particular in the spirit of peace, dignity, tolerance, freedom, equality and solidarity,

Bearing in mind that the need to extend particular care to the child has been stated in the Geneva Declaration of the Rights of the Child of 1924 and in the Declaration of the Rights of the Child adopted by the General Assembly on 20 November 1959 and recognized in the Universal Declaration of Human Rights, in the International Covenant on Civil and Political Rights (in particular in articles 23 and 24), in the International Covenant on Economic, Social and Cultural Rights (in particular in article 10) and in the statutes and relevant instruments of specialized agencies and international organizations concerned with the welfare of children,

Bearing in mind that, as indicated in the Declaration of the Rights of the Child, "the child, by reason of his physical and mental immaturity, needs special safeguards and care, including appropriate legal protection, before as well as after birth,"

Recalling the provisions of the Declaration on Social and Legal Principles relating to the Protection and Welfare of Children, with Special Reference to Foster Placement and Adoption Nationally and Internationally; the United Nations Standard Minimum Rules for the Administration of Juvenile Justice (The Beijing Rules);

and the Declaration on the Protection of Women and Children in Emergency and Armed Conflict,

Recognizing that, in all countries in the world, there are children living in exceptionally difficult conditions, and that such children need special consideration,

Taking due account of the importance of the traditions and cultural values of each people for the protection and harmonious development of the child,

Recognizing the importance of international co-operation for improving the living conditions of children in every country, in particular in the developing countries,

Have agreed as follows:

PART I

Article 1

For the purposes of the present Convention, a child means every human being below the age of eighteen years unless, under the law applicable to the child, majority is attained earlier.

Article 2

1. States Parties shall respect and ensure the rights set forth in the present Convention to each child within their jurisdiction without discrimination of any kind, irrespective of the child's or his or her parent's or legal guardian's race, colour, sex, language, religion, political or other opinion, national, ethnic or social origin, property, disability, birth or other status.

2. States Parties shall take all appropriate measures to ensure that the child is protected against all forms of discrimination or punishment on the basis of the status, activities, expressed opinions, or beliefs of the child's parents, legal guardians, or family members.

Article 3

1. In all actions concerning children, whether undertaken by public or private social welfare institutions, courts of law, administrative authorities or legislative bodies, the best interests of the child shall be a primary consideration.

2. States Parties undertake to ensure the child such protection and care as is necessary for his or her well-being, taking into account the rights and duties of his or her parents, legal guardians, or other individuals legally responsible for him or her, and, to this end, shall take all appropriate legislative and administrative measures.

3. States Parties shall ensure that the institutions, services and facilities responsible for the care or protection of children shall conform with the standards established by competent authorities, particularly in the areas of safety, health, in the number and suitability of their staff, as well as competent supervision.

Article 4

States Parties shall undertake all appropriate legislative, administrative, and other measures for the implementation of the rights recognized in the present Convention. With regard to economic, social and cultural rights, States Parties shall undertake such measures to the maximum extent of their available resources and, where needed, within the framework of international co-operation.

Article 5

States Parties shall respect the responsibilities, rights and duties of parents or, where applicable, the members of the extended family or community as provided for by the local custom, legal guardians or other persons legally responsible for the child, to provide, in a manner consistent with the evolving capacities of the child, appropriate direction and guidance in the exercise by the child of the rights recognized in the present Convention.

Article 6

1. States Parties recognize that every child has the inherent right to life.

2. States Parties shall ensure to the maximum extent possible the survival and development of the child.

Article 7

1. The child shall be registered immediately after birth and shall have the right from birth to a name, the right to acquire a nationality and, as far as possible, the right to know and be cared for by his or her parents.

2. States Parties shall ensure the implementation of these rights in accordance with their national law and their obligations under the relevant international instruments in this field, in particular where the child would otherwise be stateless.

Article 8

1. States Parties undertake to respect the right of the child to preserve his or her identity, including nationality, name and family relations as recognized by law without unlawful interference.

2. Where a child is illegally deprived of some or all of the elements of his or her identity, States Parties shall provide appropriate assistance and protection, with a view to speedily re-establishing his or her identity.

Article 9

1. States Parties shall ensure that a child shall not be separated from his or her parents against their will, except when competent authorities subject to judicial review determine, in accordance with applicable law and procedures, that such separation is necessary for the best interests of the child. Such determination may be necessary in a particular case such as one involving abuse or neglect of the child by the parents, or one where the parents are living separately and a decision must be made as to the child's place of residence.

2. In any proceedings pursuant to paragraph 1 of the present article, all interested parties shall be given an opportunity to participate in the proceedings and make their views known.

3. States Parties shall respect the right of the child who is separated from one or both parents to maintain personal relations and direct contact with both parents on a regular basis, except if it is contrary to the child's best interests.

4. Where such separation results from any action initiated by a State Party, such as the detention, imprisonment, exile, deportation or death (including death arising from any cause while the person is in the custody of the State) of one or both parents or of the child, that State Party shall, upon request, provide the parents, the child or, if appropriate, another member of the family with the essential information concerning the whereabouts of the absent member(s) of the family unless the provision of the information would be detrimental to the well-being of the child. States Parties shall further ensure that the submission of such a request shall of itself entail no adverse consequences for the person(s) concerned.

Article 10

1. In accordance with the obligation of States Parties under article 9, paragraph 1, applications by a child or his or her parents to enter or leave a State Party for the purpose of family reunification shall be dealt with by States Parties in a positive, humane and expeditious manner. States Parties shall further ensure that the

submission of such a request shall entail no adverse consequences for the applicants and for the members of their family.

2. A child whose parents reside in different States shall have the right to maintain on a regular basis, save in exceptional circumstances, personal relations and direct contacts with both parents. Towards that end and in accordance with the obligation of States Parties under article 9, paragraph 1, States Parties shall respect the right of the child and his or her parents to leave any country, including their own, and to enter their own country. The right to leave any country shall be subject only to such restrictions as are prescribed by law and which are necessary to protect the national security, public order *(ordre public)*, public health or morals or the rights and freedoms of others and are consistent with the other rights recognized in the present Convention.

Article 11

1. States Parties shall take measures to combat the illicit transfer and non-return of children abroad.

2. To this end, States Parties shall promote the conclusion of bilateral or multilateral agreements or accession to existing agreements.

Article 12

1. States Parties shall assure to the child who is capable of forming his or her own views the right to express those views freely in all matters affecting the child, the views of the child being given due weight in accordance with the age and maturity of the child.

2. For this purpose, the child shall in particular be provided the opportunity to be heard in any judicial and administrative proceedings affecting the child, either directly, or through a representative or an appropriate body, in a manner consistent with the procedural rules of national law.

Article 13

1. The child shall have the right to freedom of expression; this right shall include freedom to seek, receive and impart information and ideas of all kinds, regardless of frontiers, either orally, in writing or in print, in the form of art, or through any other media of the child's choice.

2. The exercise of this right may be subject to certain restrictions, but these shall only be such as are provided by law and are necessary:

(a) for respect of the rights or reputations of others; or

(b) for the protection of national security or of public order *(ordre public)*, or of public health or morals.

Article 14

1. States Parties shall respect the right of the child to freedom of thought, conscience and religion.

2. States Parties shall respect the rights and duties of the parents and, when applicable, legal guardians, to provide direction to the child in the exercise of his or her right in a manner consistent with the evolving capacities of the child.

3. Freedom to manifest one's religion or beliefs may be subject only to such limitations as are prescribed by law and are necessary to protect public safety, order, health, or morals or the fundamental rights and freedoms of others.

Article 15

1. States Parties recognize the rights of the child to freedom of association and to freedom of peaceful assembly.

2. No restrictions may be placed on the exercise of these rights other than those imposed in conformity with the law and which are necessary in a democratic society in the interests of national security or public safety, public order *(ordre public)*, the protection of public health or morals or the protection of the rights and freedoms of others.

Article 16

1. No child shall be subjected to arbitrary or unlawful interference with his or her privacy, family, home or correspondence, nor to unlawful attacks on his or her honour and reputation.

2. The child has the right to the protection of the law against such interference or attacks.

Article 17

States Parties recognize the important function performed by the mass media and shall ensure that the child has access to information and material from a diversity of national and international sources, especially those aimed at the promotion of his or her social, spiritual and moral well-being and physical and mental health. To this end, States Parties shall:

(a) Encourage the mass media to disseminate information and material of social and cultural benefit to the child and in accordance with the spirit of article 29;

(b) Encourage international co-operation in the production, exchange and dissemination of such information and material from a diversity of cultural, national and international sources;

(c) Encourage the production and dissemination of children's books;

(d) Encourage the mass media to have particular regard to the linguistic needs of the child who belongs to a minority group or who is indigenous;

(e) Encourage the development of appropriate guidelines for the protection of the child from information and material injurious to his or her well-being, bearing in mind the provisions of articles 13 and 18.

Article 18

1. States Parties shall use their best efforts to ensure recognition of the principle that both parents have common responsibilities for the upbringing and development of the child. Parents or, as the case may be, legal guardians, have the primary responsibility for the upbringing and development of the child. The best interests of the child will be their basic concern.

2. For the purpose of guaranteeing and promoting the rights set forth in this Convention, States Parties shall render appropriate assistance to parents and legal guardians in the performance of their child-rearing responsibilities and shall ensure the development of institutions, facilities and services for the care of children.

3. States Parties shall take all appropriate measures to ensure that children of working parents have the right to benefit from child-care services and facilities for which they are eligible.

Article 19

1. States Parties shall take all appropriate legislative, administrative, social and educational measures to protect the child from all forms of physical or mental violence, injury or abuse, neglect or negligent treatment, maltreatment or exploitation, including sexual abuse, while in the care of parent(s), legal guardian(s) or any other person who has the care of the child.

2. Such protective measures should, as appropriate, include effective procedures for the establishment of social programmes to provide necessary support for the child and for those who have the care of the child, as well as for other forms of prevention and for identification, reporting, referral, investigation, treatment and follow-up of instances of child maltreatment described heretofore, and, as appropriate, for judicial involvement.

Article 20

1. A child temporarily or permanently deprived of his or her family environment, or in whose own best interests cannot be allowed to remain in that environment, shall be entitled to special protection and assistance provided by the State.

2. States Parties shall in accordance with their national laws ensure alternative care for such a child.

3. Such care could include, *inter alia,* foster placement, *kafalah* of Islamic law, adoption, or if necessary placement in suitable institutions for the care of children. When considering solutions, due regard shall be paid to the desirability of continuity in a child's upbringing and to the child's ethnic, religious, cultural and linguistic background.

Article 21

States Parties that recognize and/or permit the system of adoption shall ensure that the best interests of the child shall be the paramount consideration and they shall:

(a) Ensure that the adoption of a child is authorized only by competent authorities who determine, in accordance with applicable law and procedures and on the basis of all pertinent and reliable information, that the adoption is permissible in view of the child's status concerning parents, relatives and legal guardians and that, if required, the persons concerned have given their informed consent to the adoption on the basis of such counselling as may be necessary;

(b) Recognize that inter-country adoption may be considered as an alternative means of child's care, if the child cannot be placed in a foster or an adoptive family or cannot in any suitable manner be cared for in the child's country of origin;

(c) Ensure that the child concerned by inter-country adoption enjoys safeguards and standards equivalent to those existing in the case of national adoption;

(d) Take all appropriate measures to ensure that, in inter-country adoption, the placement does not result in improper financial gain for those involved in it;

(e) Promote, where appropriate, the objectives of the present article by concluding bilateral or multilateral arrangements or agreements, and endeavour, within this framework, to ensure that the placement of the child in another country is carried out by competent authorities or organs.

Article 22

1. States Parties shall take appropriate measures to ensure that a child who is seeking refugee status or who is considered a refugee in accordance with applicable international or domestic law and procedures shall, whether unaccompanied or accompanied by his or her parents or by any other person, receive appropriate protection and humanitarian assistance in the enjoyment of applicable rights set forth in the present Convention and in other international human rights or humanitarian instruments to which the said States are Parties.

2. For this purpose, States Parties shall provide, as they consider appropriate, co-operation in any efforts by the United Nations and other competent intergovern-

mental organizations or non-governmental organizations co-operating with the United Nations to protect and assist such a child and to trace the parents or other members of the family of any refugee child in order to obtain information necessary for reunification with his or her family. In cases where no parents or other members of the family can be found, the child shall be accorded the same protection as any other child permanently or temporarily deprived of his or her family environment for any reason, as set forth in the present Convention.

Article 23

1. States Parties recognize that a mentally or physically disabled child should enjoy a full and decent life, in conditions which ensure dignity, promote self-reliance and facilitate the child's active participation in the community.

2. States Parties recognize the right of the disabled child to special care and shall encourage and ensure the extension, subject to available resources, to the eligible child and those responsible for his or her care, of assistance for which application is made and which is appropriate to the child's condition and to the circumstances of the parents or others caring for the child.

3. Recognizing the special needs of a disabled child, assistance extended in accordance with paragraph 2 of the present article shall be provided free of charge, whenever possible, taking into account the financial resources of the parents or others caring for the child, and shall be designed to ensure that the disabled child has effective access to and receives education, training, health care services, rehabilitation services, preparation for employment and recreation opportunities in a manner conducive to the child's achieving the fullest possible social integration and individual development, including his or her cultural and spiritual development.

4. States Parties shall promote, in the spirit of international co-operation, the exchange of appropriate information in the field of preventive health care and of medical, psychological and functional treatment of disabled children, including dissemination of and access to information concerning methods of rehabilitation, education and vocational services, with the aim of enabling States Parties to improve their capabilities and skills and to widen their experience in these areas. In this regard, particular account shall be taken of the needs of developing countries.

Article 24

1. States Parties recognize the right of the child to the enjoyment of the highest attainable standard of health and to facilities for the treatment of illness and rehabilitation of health. States Parties shall strive to ensure that no child is deprived of his or her right of access to such health care services.

2. States Parties shall pursue full implementation of this right and, in particular, shall take appropriate measures:

(a) To diminish infant and child mortality;

(b) To ensure the provision of necessary medical assistance and health care to all children with emphasis on the development of primary health care;

(c) To combat disease and malnutrition, including within the framework of primary health care, through, *inter alia*, the application of readily available technology and through the provision of adequate nutritious foods and clean drinking water, taking into consideration the dangers and risks of environmental pollution;

(d) To ensure appropriate pre- and post-natal health care for mothers;

(e) To ensure that all segments of society, in particular parents and children, are informed, have access to education and are supported in the use of basic knowledge of child health and nutrition, the advantages of breast-feeding, hygiene and environmental sanitation and the prevention of accidents;

(f) To develop preventive health care, guidance for parents, and family planning education and services.

3. States Parties shall take all effective and appropriate measures with a view to abolishing traditional practices prejudicial to the health of children.

4. States Parties undertake to promote and encourage international co-operation with a view to achieving progressively the full realization of the right recognized in the present article. In this regard, particular account shall be taken of the needs of developing countries.

Article 25

States Parties recognize the right of a child who has been placed by the competent authorities for the purposes of care, protection or treatment of his or her physical or mental health, to a periodic review of the treatment provided to the child and all other circumstances relevant to his or her placement.

Article 26

1. States Parties shall recognize for every child the right to benefit from social security, including social insurance, and shall take the necessary measures to achieve the full realization of this right in accordance with their national law.

2. The benefits should, where appropriate, be granted, taking into account the resources and the circumstances of the child and persons having responsibility for the maintenance of the child, as well as any other consideration relevant to an application for benefits made by or on behalf of the child.

Article 27

1. States Parties recognize the right of every child to a standard of living adequate for the child's physical, mental, spiritual, moral and social development.

2. The parent(s) or others responsible for the child have the primary responsibility to secure, within their abilities and financial capacities, the conditions of living necessary for the child's development.

3. States Parties, in accordance with national conditions and within their means, shall take appropriate measures to assist parents and others responsible for the child to implement this right and shall in case of need provide material assistance and support programmes, particularly with regard to nutrition, clothing and housing.

4. States Parties shall take all appropriate measures to secure the recovery of maintenance for the child from the parents or other persons having financial responsibility for the child, both within the State Party and from abroad. In particular, where the person having financial responsibility for the child lives in a State different from that of the child, States Parties shall promote the accession to international agreements or the conclusion of such agreements, as well as the making of other appropriate arrangements.

Article 28

1. States Parties recognize the right of the child to education, and with a view to achieving this right progressively and on the basis of equal opportunity, they shall, in particular:

(a) Make primary education compulsory and available free to all;

(b) Encourage the development of different forms of secondary education, including general and vocational education, make them available and accessible to every child, and take appropriate measures such as the introduction of free education and offering financial assistance in case of need;

(c) Make higher education accessible to all on the basis of capacity by every appropriate means;

(d) Make educational and vocational information and guidance available and accessible to all children;

(e) Take measures to encourage regular attendance at schools and the reduction of drop-out rates.

2. States Parties shall take all appropriate measures to ensure that school discipline is administered in a manner consistent with the child's human dignity and in conformity with the present Convention.

3. States Parties shall promote and encourage international co-operation in matters relating to education, in particular with a view to contributing to the elimination of ignorance and illiteracy throughout the world and facilitating access to scientific and technical knowledge and modern teaching methods. In this regard, particular account shall be taken of the needs of developing countries.

Article 29

1. States Parties agree that the education of the child shall be directed to:

(a) The development of the child's personality, talents and mental and physical abilities to their fullest potential;

(b) The development of respect for human rights and fundamental freedoms, and for the principles enshrined in the Charter of the United Nations;

(c) The development of respect for the child's parents, his or her own cultural identity, language and values, for the national values of the country in which the child is living, the country from which he or she may originate, and for civilizations different from his or her own;

(d) The preparation of the child for responsible life in a free society, in the spirit of understanding, peace, tolerance, equality of sexes, and friendship among all peoples, ethnic, national and religious groups and persons of indigenous origin;

(e) The development of respect for the natural environment.

2. No part of the present article or article 28 shall be construed so as to interfere with the liberty of individuals and bodies to establish and direct educational institutions, subject always to the observance of the principles set forth in paragraph 1 of the present article and to the requirements that the education given in such institutions shall conform to such minimum standards as may be laid down by the State.

Article 30

In those States in which ethnic, religious or linguistic minorities or persons of indigenous origin exist, a child belonging to such a minority or who is indigenous shall not be denied the right, in community with other members of his or her group, to enjoy his or her own culture, to profess and practice his or her own religion, or to use his or her own language.

Article 31

1. States Parties recognize the right of the child to rest and leisure, to engage in play and recreational activities appropriate to the age of the child and to participate freely in cultural life and the arts.

2. States Parties shall respect and promote the right of the child to participate fully in cultural and artistic life and shall encourage the provision of appropriate and equal opportunities for cultural, artistic, recreational and leisure activity.

Article 32

1. States Parties recognize the right of the child to be protected from economic exploitation and from performing any work that is likely to be hazardous or to interfere with the child's education, or to be harmful to the child's health or physical, mental, spiritual, moral or social development.

2. States Parties shall take legislative, administrative, social and educational measures to ensure the implementation of the present article. To this end, and having regard to the relevant provisions of other international instruments, States Parties shall in particular:

(a) Provide for a minimum age or minimum ages for admission to employment;

(b) Provide for appropriate regulation of the hours and conditions of employment;

(c) Provide for appropriate penalties or other sanctions to ensure the effective enforcement of the present article.

Article 33

States Parties shall take all appropriate measures, including legislative, administrative, social and educational measures, to protect children from the illicit use of narcotic drugs and psychotropic substances as defined in the relevant international treaties, and to prevent the use of children in the illicit production and trafficking of such substances.

Article 34

States Parties undertake to protect the child from all forms of sexual exploitation and sexual abuse. For these purposes, States Parties shall in particular take all appropriate national, bilateral and multilateral measures to prevent:

(a) The inducement or coercion of a child to engage in any unlawful sexual activity;

(b) The exploitative use of children in prostitution or other unlawful sexual practices;

(c) The exploitative use of children in pornographic performances and materials.

Article 35

States Parties shall take all appropriate national, bilateral and multilateral measures to prevent the abduction of, the sale of or traffic in children for any purpose or in any form.

Article 36

States Parties shall protect the child against all other forms of exploitation prejudicial to any aspects of the child's welfare.

Article 37

States Parties shall ensure that:

(a) No child shall be subjected to torture or other cruel, inhuman or degrading treatment or punishment. Neither capital punishment nor life imprisonment without possibility of release shall be imposed for offences committed by persons below eighteen years of age;

(b) No child shall be deprived of his or her liberty unlawfully or arbitrarily. The arrest, detention or imprisonment of a child shall be in conformity with the law and shall be used only as a measure of last resort and for the shortest appropriate period of time;

(c) Every child deprived of liberty shall be treated with humanity and respect for the inherent dignity of the human person, and in a manner which takes into account the needs of persons of his or her age. In particular, every child deprived of liberty shall be separated from adults unless it is considered in the child's best interest not to do so and shall have the right to maintain contact with his or her family through correspondence and visits, save in exceptional circumstances;

(d) Every child deprived of his or her liberty shall have the right to prompt access to legal and other appropriate assistance, as well as the right to challenge the legality of the deprivation of his or her liberty before a court or other competent, independent and impartial authority, and to a prompt decision on any such action.

Article 38

1. States Parties undertake to respect and to ensure respect for rules of international humanitarian law applicable to them in armed conflicts which are relevant to the child.

2. States Parties shall take all feasible measures to ensure that persons who have not attained the age of fifteen years do not take a direct part in hostilities.

3. States Parties shall refrain from recruiting any person who has not attained the age of fifteen years into their armed forces. In recruiting among those persons who have attained the age of fifteen years but who have not attained the age of eighteen years, States Parties shall endeavour to give priority to those who are oldest.

4. In accordance with their obligations under international humanitarian law to protect the civilian population in armed conflicts, States Parties shall take all feasible measures to ensure protection and care of children who are affected by an armed conflict.

Article 39

States Parties shall take all appropriate measures to promote physical and psychological recovery and social reintegration of a child victim of: any form of neglect, exploitation, or abuse; torture or any other form of cruel, inhuman or degrading treatment or punishment; or armed conflicts. Such recovery and reintegration shall take place in an environment which fosters the health, self-respect and dignity of the child.

Article 40

1. States Parties recognize the right of every child alleged as, accused of, or recognized as having infringed the penal law to be treated in a manner consistent with the promotion of the child's sense of dignity and worth, which reinforces the child's respect for the human rights and fundamental freedoms of others and which takes into account the child's age and the desirability of promoting the child's reintegration and the child's assuming a constructive role in society.

2. To this end, and having regard to the relevant provisions of international instruments, States Parties shall, in particular, ensure that:

(a) No child shall be alleged as, be accused of, or recognized as having infringed the penal law by reason of acts or omissions which were not prohibited by national or international law at the time they were committed;

(b) Every child alleged as or accused of having infringed the penal law has at least the following guarantees:

(i) To be presumed innocent until proven guilty according to law;

(ii) To be informed promptly and directly of the charges against him or her, and, if appropriate through his or her parents or legal guardian, and to have legal or other appropriate assistance in the preparation and presentation of his or her defence;

(iii) To have the matter determined without delay by a competent, independent and impartial authority or judicial body in a fair hearing according to law, in the presence of legal or other appropriate assistance and, unless it is considered not to be in the best interest of the child, in particular, taking into account his or her age or situation, his or her parents or legal guardians;

(iv) Not to be compelled to give testimony or to confess guilt; to examine or have examined adverse witnesses and to obtain the participation and examination of witnesses on his or her behalf under conditions of equality;

(v) If considered to have infringed the penal law, to have this decision and any measures imposed in consequence thereof reviewed by a higher competent, independent and impartial authority or judicial body according to law;

(vi) To have the free assistance of an interpreter if the child cannot understand or speak the language used;

(vii) To have his or her privacy fully respected at all stages of the proceedings.

3. States Parties shall seek to promote the establishment of laws, procedures, authorities and institutions specifically applicable to children alleged as, accused of, or recognized as having infringed the penal law, and, in particular:

(a) The establishment of a minimum age below which children shall be presumed not to have the capacity to infringe the penal law;

(b) Whenever appropriate and desirable, measures for dealing with such children without resorting to judicial proceedings, providing that human rights and legal safeguards are fully respected.

4. A variety of dispositions, such as care, guidance and supervision orders; counselling; probation; foster care; education and vocational training programmes and other alternatives to institutional care shall be available to ensure that children are dealt with in a manner appropriate to their well-being and proportionate both to their circumstances and the offence.

Article 41

Nothing in the present Convention shall affect any provisions that are more conducive to the realization of the rights of the child and which may be contained in:

(a) the law of a State Party; or

(b) international law in force for that State.

PART II

Article 42

States Parties undertake to make the principles and provisions of the Convention widely known, by appropriate and active means, to adults and children alike.

Article 43

1. For the purpose of examining the progress made by States Parties in achieving the realization of the obligations undertaken in the present Convention, there shall be established a Committee on the Rights of the Child, which shall carry out the functions hereinafter provided.

2. The Committee shall consist of ten experts of high moral standing and recognized competence in the field covered by the present Convention. The members of the Committee shall be elected by States Parties from among their nationals and shall serve in their personal capacity, consideration being given to equitable geographical distribution, as well as to the principal legal systems.

3. The members of the Committee shall be elected by secret ballot from a list of persons nominated by States Parties. Each State Party may nominate one person from among its own nationals.

4. The initial election to the Committee shall be held no later than six months after the date of the entry into force of the present Convention and thereafter every second year. At least four months before the date of each election, the Secretary-General of the United Nations shall address a letter to States Parties inviting them to submit their nominations within two months. The Secretary-General shall subsequently prepare a list in alphabetical order of all persons thus nominated, indicating States Parties which have nominated them, and shall submit it to the States Parties to the present Convention.

5. The elections shall be held at meetings of States Parties convened by the Secretary-General at United Nations Headquarters. At those meetings, for which two-thirds of States Parties shall constitute a quorum, the persons elected to the Committee shall be those who obtain the largest number of votes and an absolute majority of the votes of the representatives of States Parties present and voting.

6. The members of the Committee shall be elected for a term of four years. They shall be eligible for re-election if renominated. The term of five of the members elected at the first election shall expire at the end of two years; immediately after the first election, the names of these five members shall be chosen by lot by the Chairman of the meeting.

7. If a member of the Committee dies or resigns or declares that for any other cause he or she can no longer perform the duties of the Committee, the State Party which nominated the member shall appoint another expert from among its nationals to serve for the remainder of the term, subject to the approval of the Committee.

8. The Committee shall establish its own rules of procedure.

9. The Committee shall elect its officers for a period of two years.

10. The meetings of the Committee shall normally be held at the United Nations Headquarters or at any other convenient place as determined by the Committee. The Committee shall normally meet annually. The duration of the meetings of the Committee shall be determined, and reviewed, if necessary, by a meeting of the States Parties to the present Convention, subject to the approval of the General Assembly.

11. The Secretary-General of the United Nations shall provide the necessary staff and facilities for the effective performance of the functions of the Committee under the present Convention.

12. With the approval of the General Assembly, the members of the Committee established under the present Convention shall receive emoluments from the United Nations resources on such terms and conditions as the Assembly may decide.

Article 44

1. States Parties undertake to submit to the Committee, through the Secretary-General of the United Nations, reports on the measures they have adopted which give effect to the rights recognized herein and on the progress made on the enjoyment of those rights:

(a) Within two years of the entry into force of the Convention for the State Party concerned;

(b) Thereafter every five years.

2. Reports made under the present article shall indicate factors and difficulties, if any, affecting the degree of fulfilment of the obligations under the present Convention. Reports shall also contain sufficient information to provide the Committee with a comprehensive understanding of the implementation of the Convention in the country concerned.

3. A State Party which has submitted a comprehensive initial report to the Committee need not, in its subsequent reports submitted in accordance with paragraph 1*(b)* of the present article, repeat basic information previously provided.

4. The Committee may request from States Parties further information relevant to the implementation of the Convention.

5. The Committee shall submit to the General Assembly, through the Economic and Social Council, every two years, reports on its activities.

6. States Parties shall make their reports widely available to the public in their own countries.

Article 45

In order to foster the effective implementation of the Convention and to encourage international co-operation in the field covered by the Convention:

(a) The specialized agencies, the United Nations Children's Fund, and other United Nations organs shall be entitled to be represented at the consideration of the implementation of such provisions of the present Convention as fall within the scope of their mandate. The Committee may invite the specialized agencies, the United Nations Children's Fund, and other competent bodies as it may consider appropriate to provide expert advice on the implementation of the Convention in areas falling within the scope of their respective mandates. The Committee may invite the specialized agencies, the United Nations Children's Fund, and other United Nations organs to submit reports on the implementation of the Convention in areas falling within the scope of their activities;

(b) The Committee shall transmit, as it may consider appropriate, to the specialized agencies, the United Nations Children's Fund, and other competent bodies, any reports from States Parties that contain a request, or indicate a need, for technical advice or assistance, along with the Committee's observations and suggestions, if any, on these requests or indications;

(c) The Committee may recommend to the General Assembly to request the Secretary–General to undertake on its behalf studies on specific issues relating to the rights of the child;

(d) The Committee may make suggestions and general recommendations based on information received pursuant to articles 44 and 45 of the present Convention. Such suggestions and general recommendations shall be transmitted to any State Party concerned and reported to the General Assembly, together with comments, if any, from States Parties.

* * *

Article 49

1. The present Convention shall enter into force on the thirtieth day following the date of deposit with the Secretary–General of the United Nations of the twentieth instrument of ratification or accession.

2. For each State ratifying or acceding to the Convention after the deposit of the twentieth instrument of ratification or accession, the Convention shall enter into

force on the thirtieth day after the deposit by such State of its instrument of ratification or accession.

* * *

Article 52

A State Party may denounce the present Convention by written notification to the Secretary–General of the United Nations. Denunciation becomes effective one year after the date of receipt of the notification by the Secretary–General.

* * *

4. ECONOMIC DEVELOPMENT

4.1 ARTICLES OF AGREEMENT OF THE INTERNATIONAL MONETARY FUND.[a] Done at Washington, Dec. 27, 1945. Entered into force, Dec. 27, 1945; for the United States, Dec. 27, 1945. 60 Stat. 1401, T.I.A.S. No. 1501, 3 Bevans 1351, 1 UNTS 39. AMENDMENT TO THE ARTICLES OF AGREEMENT. Done at Washington, May 31, 1968. Entered into force, July 28, 1969; for the United States, July 28, 1969. 20 U.S.T. 2775, T.I.A.S. No. 6748. AMENDMENT TO THE ARTICLES OF AGREEMENT. Done at Washington, Apr. 30, 1976. Entered into force, Apr. 1, 1978; for the United States, Apr. 1, 1978. 29 U.S.T. 2203, T.I.A.S. No. 8937

The Governments on whose behalf the present Agreement is signed agree as follows:

Introductory Article

(i) The International Monetary Fund is established and shall operate in accordance with the provisions of this Agreement as originally adopted and subsequently amended.

(ii) To enable the Fund to conduct its operations and transactions, the Fund shall maintain a General Department and a Special Drawing Rights Department. Membership in the Fund shall give the right to participation in the Special Drawing Rights Department.

(iii) Operations and transactions authorized by this Agreement shall be conducted through the General Department, consisting in accordance with the provisions of this Agreement of the General Resources Account, the Special Disbursement Account, and the Investment Account; except that operations and transactions involving special drawing rights shall be conducted through the Special Drawing Rights Department.

Article I

Purposes

The purposes of the International Monetary Fund are:

(i) To promote international monetary cooperation through a permanent institution which provides the machinery for consultation and collaboration on international monetary problems.

(ii) To facilitate the expansion and balanced growth of international trade, and to contribute thereby to the promotion and maintenance of high levels of employment and real income and to the development of the productive resources of all members as primary objectives of economic policy.

a. All schedules are omitted.

(iii) To promote exchange stability, to maintain orderly exchange arrangements among members, and to avoid competitive exchange depreciation.

(iv) To assist in the establishment of a multilateral system of payments in respect of current transactions between members and in the elimination of foreign exchange restrictions which hamper the growth of world trade.

(v) To give confidence to members by making the general resources of the Fund temporarily available to them under adequate safeguards, thus providing them with opportunity to correct maladjustments in their balance of payments without resorting to measures destructive of national or international prosperity.

(vi) In accordance with the above, to shorten the duration and lessen the degree of disequilibrium in the international balances of payments of members.

The Fund shall be guided in all its policies and decisions by the purposes set forth in this Article.

Article II

Membership

Section 1. *Original members*

The original members of the Fund shall be those of the countries represented at the United Nations Monetary and Financial Conference whose governments accept membership before December 31, 1945.

Section 2. *Other members*

Membership shall be open to other countries at such times and in accordance with such terms as may be prescribed by the Board of Governors. These terms, including the terms for subscriptions, shall be based on principles consistent with those applied to other countries that are already members.

Article III

Quotas and Subscriptions

Section 1. *Quotas and payment of subscriptions*

Each member shall be assigned a quota expressed in special drawing rights. The quotas of the members represented at the United Nations Monetary and Financial Conference which accept membership before December 31, 1945 shall be those set forth in Schedule A. The quotas of other members shall be determined by the Board of Governors. The subscription of each member shall be equal to its quota and shall be paid in full to the Fund at the appropriate depository.

Section 2. *Adjustment of quotas*

(*a*) The Board of Governors shall at intervals of not more than five years conduct a general review, and if it deems it appropriate propose an adjustment, of the quotas of the members. It may also, if it thinks fit, consider at any other time the adjustment of any particular quota at the request of the member concerned.

(*b*) The Fund may at any time propose an increase in the quotas of those members of the Fund that were members on August 31, 1975 in proportion to their quotas on that date in a cumulative amount not in excess of amounts transferred under Article V, Section 12(*f*), (*i*), and (*j*) from the Special Disbursement Account to the General Resources Account.

(*c*) An eighty-five percent majority of the total voting power shall be required for any change in quotas.

(*d*) The quota of a member shall not be changed until the member has consented and until payment has been made unless payment is deemed to have been made in accordance with Section 3(*b*) of this Article.

Section 3. *Payments when quotas are changed*

* * *

Section 4. *Substitution of securities for currency*

* * *

Article IV

Obligations Regarding Exchange Arrangements

Section 1. *General obligations of members*

Recognizing that the essential purpose of the international monetary system is to provide a framework that facilitates the exchange of goods, services, and capital among countries, and that sustains sound economic growth, and that a principal objective is the continuing development of the orderly underlying conditions that are necessary for financial and economic stability, each member undertakes to collaborate with the Fund and other members to assure orderly exchange arrangements and to promote a stable system of exchange rates. In particular, each member shall:

(i) endeavor to direct its economic and financial policies toward the objective of fostering orderly economic growth with reasonable price stability, with due regard to its circumstances;

(ii) seek to promote stability by fostering orderly underlying economic and financial conditions and a monetary system that does not tend to produce erratic disruptions;

(iii) avoid manipulating exchange rates or the international monetary system in order to prevent effective balance of payments adjustment or to gain an unfair competitive advantage over other members; and

(iv) follow exchange policies compatible with the undertakings under this Section.

Section 2. *General exchange arrangements*

(*a*) Each member shall notify the Fund, within thirty days after the date of the second amendment of this Agreement, of the exchange arrangements it intends to apply in fulfillment of its obligations under Section 1 of this Article, and shall notify the Fund promptly of any changes in its exchange arrangements.

(*b*) Under an international monetary system of the kind prevailing on January 1, 1976, exchange arrangements may include (i) the maintenance by a member of a value for its currency in terms of the special drawing right or another denominator, other than gold, selected by the member, or (ii) cooperative arrangements by which members maintain the value of their currencies in relation to the value of the currency or currencies of other members, or (iii) other exchange arrangements of a member's choice.

(*c*) To accord with the development of the international monetary system, the Fund, by an eighty-five percent majority of the total voting power, may make provision for general exchange arrangements without limiting the right of members to have exchange arrangements of their choice consistent with the purposes of the Fund and the obligations under Section 1 of this Article.

Section 3. *Surveillance over exchange arrangements*

(*a*) The Fund shall oversee the international monetary system in order to ensure its effective operation, and shall oversee the compliance of each member with its obligations under Section 1 of this Article.

(*b*) In order to fulfill its functions under (*a*) above, the Fund shall exercise firm surveillance over the exchange rate policies of members, and shall adopt specific principles for the guidance of all members with respect to those policies. Each member shall provide the Fund with the information necessary for such surveillance, and, when requested by the Fund, shall consult with it on the member's exchange rate policies. The principles adopted by the Fund shall be consistent with cooperative arrangements by which members maintain the value of their currencies in relation to the value of the currency or currencies of other members, as well as with other exchange arrangements of a member's choice consistent with the purposes of the Fund and Section 1 of this Article. These principles shall respect the domestic social and political policies of members, and in applying these principles the Fund shall pay due regard to the circumstances of members.

Section 4. *Par values*

The Fund may determine, by an eight-five percent majority of the total voting power, that international economic conditions permit the introduction of a widespread system of exchange arrangements based on stable but adjustable par values. The Fund shall make the determination on the basis of the underlying stability of the world economy, and for this purpose shall take into account price movements and rates of expansion in the economies of members. The determination shall be made in light of the evolution of the international monetary system, with particular reference to sources of liquidity, and, in order to ensure the effective operation of a system of par values, to arrangements under which both members in surplus and members in deficit in their balances of payments take prompt, effective, and symmetrical action to achieve adjustment, as well as to arrangements for intervention and the treatment of imbalances. Upon making such determination, the Fund shall notify members that the provisions of Schedule C apply.

* * *

Article V

Operations and Transactions of the Fund

Section 1. *Agencies dealing with the Fund*

Each member shall deal with the Fund only through its Treasury, central bank, stabilization fund, or other similar fiscal agency, and the Fund shall deal only with or through the same agencies.

Section 2. *Limitation on the Fund's operations and transactions*

(*a*) Except as otherwise provided in this Agreement, transactions on the account of the Fund shall be limited to transactions for the purpose of supplying a member, on the initiative of such member, with special drawing rights or the currencies of other members from the general resources of the Fund, which shall be held in the General Resources Account, in exchange for the currency of the member desiring to make the purchase.

(*b*) If requested, the Fund may decide to perform financial and technical services, including the administration of resources contributed by members, that are consistent with the purposes of the Fund. Operations involved in the performance of such financial services shall not be on the account of the Fund. Services under this subsection shall not impose any obligation on a member without its consent.

Section 3. *Conditions governing use of the Fund's general resources*

(*a*) The Fund shall adopt policies on the use of its general resources, including policies on stand-by or similar arrangements, and may adopt special policies for special balance of payments problems, that will assist members to solve their balance of payments problems in a manner consistent with the provisions of this Agreement and that will establish adequate safeguards for the temporary use of the general resources of the Fund.

(*b*) A member shall be entitled to purchase the currencies of other members from the Fund in exchange for an equivalent amount of its own currency subject to the following conditions:

(i) the member's use of the general resources of the Fund would be in accordance with the provisions of this Agreement and the policies adopted under them;

(ii) the member represents that it has a need to make the purchase because of its balance of payments or its reserve position or developments in its reserves;

(iii) the proposed purchase would be a reserve tranche purchase, or would not cause the Fund's holdings of the purchasing member's currency to exceed two hundred percent of its quota;

(iv) the Fund has not previously declared under Section 5 of this Article, Article VI, Section 1, or Article XXVI, Section 2(*a*) that the member desiring to purchase is ineligible to use the general resources of the Fund.

(*c*) The Fund shall examine a request for a purchase to determine whether the proposed purchase would be consistent with the provisions of this Agreement and the policies adopted under them, provided that requests for reserve tranche purchases shall not be subject to challenge.

(*d*) The Fund shall adopt policies and procedures on the selection of currencies to be sold that take into account, in consultation with members, the balance of payments and reserve position of members and developments in the exchange markets, as well as the desirability of promoting over time balanced positions in the Fund, provided that if a member represents that it is proposing to purchase the currency of another member because the purchasing member wishes to obtain an equivalent amount of its own currency offered by the other member, it shall be entitled to purchase the currency of the other member unless the Fund has given notice under Article VII, Section 3 that its holdings of the currency have become scarce.

(*e*) (i) Each member shall ensure that balances of its currency purchased from the Fund are balances of a freely usable currency or can be exchanged at the time of purchase for a freely usable currency of its choice at an exchange rate between the two currencies equivalent to the exchange rate between them on the basis of Article XIX, Section 7(*a*).

(ii) Each member whose currency is purchased from the Fund or is obtained in exchange for currency purchased from the Fund shall collaborate with the Fund and other members to enable such balances of its currency to be exchanged, at the time of purchase, for the freely usable currencies of other members.

(iii) An exchange under (i) above of a currency that is not freely usable shall be made by the member whose currency is purchased unless that member and the purchasing member agree on another procedure.

(iv) A member purchasing from the Fund the freely usable currency of another member and wishing to exchange it at the time of purchase for another freely usable currency shall make the exchange with the other member if requested by that member. The exchange shall be made for a freely usable currency selected by the other member at the rate of exchange referred to in (i) above.

(*f*) Under policies and procedures which it shall adopt, the Fund may agree to provide a participant making a purchase in accordance with this Section with special drawing rights instead of the currencies of other members.

Section 4. *Waiver of conditions*

The Fund may in its discretion, and on terms which safeguard its interests, waive any of the conditions prescribed in Section 3(*b*)(iii) and (iv) of this Article, especially in the case of members with a record of avoiding large or continuous use of the Fund's general resources. In making a waiver it shall take into consideration periodic or exceptional requirements of the member requesting the waiver. The

Fund shall also take into consideration a member's willingness to pledge as collateral security acceptable assets having a value sufficient in the opinion of the Fund to protect its interests and may require as a condition of waiver the pledge of such collateral security.

Section 5. *Ineligibility to use the Fund's general resources*

Whenever the Fund is of the opinion that any member is using the general resources of the Fund in a manner contrary to the purposes of the Fund, it shall present to the member a report setting forth the views of the Fund and prescribing a suitable time for reply. After presenting such a report to a member, the Fund may limit the use of its general resources by the member. If no reply to the report is received from the member within the prescribed time, or if the reply received is unsatisfactory, the Fund may continue to limit the member's use of the general resources of the Fund or may, after giving reasonable notice to the member, declare it ineligible to use the general resources of the Fund.

[Sections 6–12 address the following items: "Other purchases and sales of special drawing rights by the Fund," "Repurchase by a member of its currency held by the Fund," "Charges," "Remuneration," "Computations," "Maintenance of value," and "Other operations and transactions."]

* * *

Article VI

Capital Transfers

Section 1. *Use of the Fund's general resources for capital transfers*

(*a*) A member may not use the Fund's general resources to meet a large or sustained outflow of capital except as provided in Section 2 of this Article, and the Fund may request a member to exercise controls to prevent such use of the general resources of the Fund. If, after receiving such a request, a member fails to exercise appropriate controls, the Fund may declare the member ineligible to use the general resources of the Fund.

(*b*) Nothing in this Section shall be deemed:

(i) to prevent the use of the general resources of the Fund for capital transactions of reasonable amount required for the expansion of exports or in the ordinary course of trade, banking, or other business; or

(ii) to affect capital movements which are met out of a member's own resources, but members undertake that such capital movements will be in accordance with the purposes of the Fund.

Section 2. *Special provisions for capital transfers*

A member shall be entitled to make reserve tranche purchases to meet capital transfers.

Section 3. *Controls of capital transfers*

Members may exercise such controls as are necessary to regulate international capital movements, but no member may exercise these controls in a manner which will restrict payments for current transactions or which will unduly delay transfers of funds in settlement of commitments, except as provided in Article VII, Section 3(*b*) and in Article XIV, Section 2.

Article VII

Replenishment and Scarce Currencies

* * *

Article VIII

General Obligations of Members

Section 1. *Introduction*

In addition to the obligations assumed under other articles of this Agreement, each member undertakes the obligations set out in this Article.

Section 2. *Avoidance of restrictions on current payments*

(*a*) Subject to the provisions of Article VII, Section 3(*b*) and Article XIV, Section 2, no member shall, without the approval of the Fund, impose restrictions on the making of payments and transfers for current international transactions.

(*b*) Exchange contracts which involve the currency of any member and which are contrary to the exchange control regulations of that member maintained or imposed consistently with this Agreement shall be unenforceable in the territories of any member. In addition, members may, by mutual accord, cooperate in measures for the purpose of making the exchange control regulations of either member more effective, provided that such measures and regulations are consistent with this Agreement.

Section 3. *Avoidance of discriminatory currency practices*

No member shall engage in, or permit any of its fiscal agencies referred to in Article V, Section 1 to engage in, any discriminatory currency arrangements or multiple currency practices, whether within or outside margins under Article IV or prescribed by or under Schedule C, except as authorized under this Agreement or approved by the Fund. If such arrangements and practices are engaged in at the date when this Agreement enters into force, the member concerned shall consult with the Fund as to their progressive removal unless they are maintained or imposed under Article XIV, Section 2, in which case the provisions of Section 3 of that Article shall apply.

Section 4. *Convertibility of foreign-held balances*

(*a*) Each member shall buy balances of its currency held by another member if the latter, in requesting the purchase, represents:

(i) that the balances to be bought have been recently acquired as a result of current transactions; or

(ii) that their conversion is needed for making payments for current transactions.

The buying member shall have the option to pay either in special drawing rights, subject to Article XIX, Section 4, or in the currency of the member making the request.

(*b*) The obligation in (*a*) above shall not apply when:

(i) the convertibility of the balances has been restricted consistently with Section 2 of this Article or Article VI, Section 3;

(ii) the balances have accumulated as a result of transactions effected before the removal by a member of restrictions maintained or imposed under Article XIV, Section 2;

(iii) the balances have been acquired contrary to the exchange regulations of the member which is asked to buy them;

(iv) the currency of the member requesting the purchase has been declared scarce under Article VII, Section 3(*a*); or

(v) the member requested to make the purchase is for any reason not entitled to buy currencies of other members from the Fund for its own currency.

Section 5. *Furnishing of information*

(*a*) The Fund may require members to furnish it with such information as it deems necessary for its activities, including, as the minimum necessary for the effective discharge of the Fund's duties, national data on the following matters:

(i) official holdings at home and abroad of (1) gold, (2) foreign exchange;

(ii) holdings at home and abroad by banking and financial agencies, other than official agencies, of (1) gold, (2) foreign exchange;

(iii) production of gold;

(iv) gold exports and imports according to countries of destination and origin;

(v) total exports and imports of merchandise, in terms of local currency values, according to countries of destination and origin;

(vi) international balance of payments, including (1) trade in goods and services, (2) gold transactions, (3) known capital transactions, and (4) other items;

(vii) international investment position, i.e., investments within the territories of the member owned abroad and investments abroad owned by persons in its territories so far as it is possible to furnish this information;

(viii) national income;

(ix) price indices, i.e., indices of commodity prices in wholesale and retail markets and of export and import prices;

(x) buying and selling rates for foreign currencies;

(xi) exchange controls, i.e., a comprehensive statement of exchange controls in effect at the time of assuming membership in the Fund and details of subsequent changes as they occur; and

(xii) where official clearing arrangements exist, details of amounts awaiting clearance in respect of commercial and financial transactions, and of the length of time during which such arrears have been outstanding.

(*b*) In requesting information the Fund shall take into consideration the varying ability of members to furnish the data requested. Members shall be under no obligation to furnish information in such detail that the affairs of individuals or corporations are disclosed. Members undertake, however, to furnish the desired information in as detailed and accurate a manner as is practicable and, so far as possible, to avoid mere estimates.

(*c*) The Fund may arrange to obtain further information by agreement with members. It shall act as a centre for the collection and exchange of information on monetary and financial problems, thus facilitating the preparation of studies designed to assist members in developing policies which further the purposes of the Fund.

Section 6. *Consultation between members regarding existing international agreements*

Where under this Agreement a member is authorized in the special or temporary circumstances specified in the Agreement to maintain or establish restrictions on exchange transactions, and there are other engagements between members entered into prior to this Agreement which conflict with the application of such restrictions, the parties to such engagements shall consult with one another with a view to making such mutually acceptable adjustments as may be necessary. The provisions of this Article shall be without prejudice to the operation of Article VII, Section 5.

Section 7. *Obligation to collaborate regarding policies on reserve assets*

Each member undertakes to collaborate with the Fund and with other members in order to ensure that the policies of the member with respect to reserve assets shall be consistent with the objectives of promoting better international surveillance of international liquidity and making the special drawing right the principal reserve asset in the international monetary system.

Article IX

Status, Immunities, and Privileges

Section 1. *Purposes of Article*

To enable the Fund to fulfill the functions with which it is entrusted, the status, immunities, and privileges set forth in this Article shall be accorded to the Fund in the territories of each member.

Section 2. *Status of the Fund*

The Fund shall possess full juridical personality, and in particular, the capacity:

(i) to contract;

(ii) to acquire and dispose of immovable and movable property; and

(iii) to institute legal proceedings.

Section 3. *Immunity from judicial process*

The Fund, its property and its assets, wherever located and by whomsoever held, shall enjoy immunity from every form of judicial process except to the extent that it expressly waives its immunity for the purpose of any proceedings or by the terms of any contract.

Section 4. *Immunity from other action*

Property and assets of the Fund, wherever located and by whomsoever held, shall be immune from search, requisition, confiscation, expropriation, or any other form of seizure by executive or legislative action.

Section 5. *Immunity of archives*

The archives of the Fund shall be inviolable.

Section 6. *Freedom of assets from restrictions*

To the extent necessary to carry out the activities provided for in this Agreement, all property and assets of the Fund shall be free from restrictions, regulations, controls, and moratoria of any nature.

Section 7. *Privilege for communications*

The official communications of the Fund shall be accorded by members the same treatment as the official communications of other members.

Section 8. *Immunities and privileges of officers and employees*

All Governors, Executive Directors, Alternates, members of committees, representatives appointed under Article XII, Section 3(*j*), advisors of any of the foregoing persons, officers, and employees of the Fund:

(i) shall be immune from legal process with respect to acts performed by them in their official capacity except when the Fund waives this immunity;

(ii) not being local nationals, shall be granted the same immunities from immigration restrictions, alien registration requirements, and national service obligations and the same facilities as regards exchange restrictions as are accorded by members to the representatives, officials, and employees of comparable rank of other members; and

(iii) shall be granted the same treatment in respect of traveling facilities as is accorded by members to representatives, officials, and employees of comparable rank of other members.

Section 9. *Immunities from taxation*

(*a*) The Fund, its assets, property, income, and its operations and transactions authorized by this Agreement shall be immune from all taxation and from all customs duties. The Fund shall also be immune from liability for the collection or payment of any tax or duty.

(*b*) No tax shall be levied on or in respect of salaries and emoluments paid by the Fund to Executive Directors, Alternates, officers, or employees of the Fund who are not local citizens, local subjects, or other local nationals.

(*c*) No taxation of any kind shall be levied on any obligation or security issued by the Fund, including any dividend or interest thereon, by whomsoever held:

(i) which discriminates against such obligation or security solely because of its origin; or

(ii) if the sole jurisdictional basis for such taxation is the place or currency in which it is issued, made payable or paid, or the location of any office or place of business maintained by the Fund.

Section 10. *Application of Article*

Each member shall take such action as is necessary in its own territories for the purpose of making effective in terms of its own law the principles set forth in this Article and shall inform the Fund of the detailed action which it has taken.

Article X

Relations With Other International Organizations

The Fund shall cooperate within the terms of this Agreement with any general international organization and with public international organizations having specialized responsibilities in related fields. Any arrangements for such cooperation which would involve a modification of any provision of this Agreement may be effected only after amendment to this Agreement under Article XXVIII.

Article XI

Relations With Non-member Countries

* * *

Article XII

Organization and Management

Section 1. *Structure of the Fund*

The Fund shall have a Board of Governors, an Executive Board, a Managing Director, and a staff, and a Council if the Board of Governors decides, by an eighty-five percent majority of the total voting power, that the provisions of Schedule D shall be applied.

* * *

Section 5. *Voting*

(*a*) Each member shall have two hundred fifty votes plus one additional vote for each part of its quota equivalent to one hundred thousand special drawing rights.

(*b*) Whenever voting is required under Article V, Section 4 or 5, each member shall have the number of votes to which it is entitled under (*a*) above adjusted

(i) by the addition of one vote for the equivalent of each four hundred thousand special drawing rights of net sales of its currency from the general resources of the Fund up to the date when the vote is taken, or

(ii) by the subtraction of one vote for the equivalent of each four hundred thousand special drawing rights of its net purchases under Article V, Section 3(*b*) and (*f*) up to the date when the vote is taken,

provided that neither net purchases nor net sales shall be deemed at any time to exceed an amount equal to the quota of the member involved.

(*c*) Except as otherwise specifically provided, all decisions of the Fund shall be made by a majority of the votes cast.

Section 6. *Reserves, distribution of net income, and investment*

* * *

Article XIII

Offices and Depositories

Section 1. *Location of offices*

The principal office of the Fund shall be located in the territory of the member having the largest quota, and agencies or branch offices may be established in the territories of other members.

* * *

Article XV

Special Drawing Rights

Section 1. *Authority to allocate special drawing rights*

To meet the need, as and when it arises, for a supplement to existing reserve assets, the Fund is authorized to allocate special drawing rights to members that are participants in the Special Drawing Rights Department.

Section 2. *Valuation of the special drawing right*

The method of valuation of the special drawing right shall be determined by the Fund by a seventy percent majority of the total voting power, provided, however, that an eighty-five percent majority of the total voting power shall be required for a change in the principle of valuation or a fundamental change in the application of the principle in effect.

[*Articles XVI–XXV deal with various aspects of the Special Drawing Rights under the Fund.*]

Article XXVI

Withdrawal From Membership

Section 1. *Right of members to withdraw*

Any member may withdraw from the Fund at any time by transmitting a notice in writing to the Fund at its principal office. Withdrawal shall become effective on the date such notice is received.

Section 2. *Compulsory withdrawal*

(*a*) If a member fails to fulfill any of its obligations under this Agreement, the Fund may declare the member ineligible to use the general resources of the Fund. Nothing in this Section shall be deemed to limit the provisions of Article V, Section 5 or Article VI, Section 1.

(*b*) If, after the expiration of a reasonable period the member persists in its failure to fulfill any of its obligations under this Agreement, that member may be required to withdraw from membership in the Fund by a decision of the Board of

Governors carried by a majority of the Governors having eighty-five percent of the total voting power.

(*c*) Regulations shall be adopted to ensure that before action is taken against any member under (*a*) or (*b*) above, the member shall be informed in reasonable time of the complaint against it and given an adequate opportunity for stating its case, both orally and in writing.

Section 3. *Settlement of accounts with members withdrawing*

When a member withdraws from the Fund, normal operations and transactions of the Fund in its currency shall cease and settlement of all accounts between it and the Fund shall be made with reasonable despatch by agreement between it and the Fund. If agreement is not reached promptly, the provisions of Schedule J shall apply to the settlement of accounts.

* * *

Article XXIX

Interpretation

(*a*) Any question of interpretation of the provisions of this Agreement arising between any member and the Fund or between any members of the Fund shall be submitted to the Executive Board for its decision. If the question particularly affects any member not entitled to appoint an Executive Director, it shall be entitled to representation in accordance with Article XII, Section 3(*j*).

(*b*) In any case where the Executive Board has given a decision under (*a*) above, any member may require, within three months from the date of the decision, that the question be referred to the Board of Governors, whose decision shall be final. Any question referred to the Board of Governors shall be considered by a Committee on Interpretation of the Board of Governors. Each Committee member shall have one vote. The Board of Governors shall establish the membership, procedures, and voting majorities of the Committee. A decision of the Committee shall be the decision of the Board of Governors unless the Board of Governors, by an eighty-five percent majority of the total voting power, decides otherwise. Pending the result of the reference to the Board of Governors the Fund may, so far as it deems necessary, act on the basis of the decision of the Executive Board.

(*c*) Whenever a disagreement arises between the Fund and a member which has withdrawn, or between the Fund and any member during liquidation of the Fund, such disagreement shall be submitted to arbitration by a tribunal of three arbitrators, one appointed by the Fund, another by the member or withdrawing member, and an umpire who, unless the parties otherwise agree, shall be appointed by the President of the International Court of Justice or such other authority as may have been prescribed by regulation adopted by the Fund. The umpire shall have full power to settle all questions of procedure in any case where the parties are in disagreement with respect thereto.

Article XXX

Explanation of Terms

In interpreting the provisions of this Agreement the Fund and its members shall be guided by the following provisions:

(*a*) The Fund's holdings of a member's currency in the General Resources Account shall include any securities accepted by the Fund under Article III, Section 4.

(*b*) Stand-by arrangement means a decision of the Fund by which a member is assured that it will be able to make purchases from the General Resources Account in accordance with the terms of the decision during a specified period and up to a specified amount.

(*c*) Reserve tranche purchase means a purchase by a member of special drawing rights or the currency of another member in exchange for its own currency which does not cause the Fund's holdings of the member's currency in the General Resources Account to exceed its quota, provided that for the purposes of this definition the Fund may exclude purchases and holdings under:

(i) policies on the use of its general resources for compensatory financing of export fluctuations;

(ii) policies on the use of its general resources in connection with the financing of contributions to international buffer stocks of primary products; and

(iii) other policies on the use of its general resources in respect of which the Fund decides, by an eighty-five percent majority of the total voting power, that an exclusion shall be made.

(*d*) Payments for current transactions means payments which are not for the purpose of transferring capital, and includes, without limitation:

(1) all payments due in connection with foreign trade, other current business, including services, and normal short-term banking and credit facilities;

(2) payments due as interest on loans and as net income from other investments;

(3) payments of moderate amount for amortization of loans or for depreciation of direct investments; and

(4) moderate remittances for family living expenses.

The Fund may, after consultation with the members concerned, determine whether certain specific transactions are to be considered current transactions or capital transactions.

(*e*) Net cumulative allocation of special drawing rights means the total amount of special drawing rights allocated to a participant less its share of special drawing rights that have been cancelled under Article XVIII, Section 2(*a*).

(*f*) A freely usable currency means a member's currency that the Fund determines (i) is, in fact, widely used to make payments for international transactions, and (ii) is widely traded in the principal exchange markets.

(*g*) Members that were members on August 31, 1975 shall be deemed to include a member that accepted membership after that date pursuant to a resolution of the Board of Governors adopted before that date.

(*h*) Transactions of the Fund means exchanges of monetary assets by the Fund for other monetary assets. Operations of the Fund means other uses or receipts of monetary assets by the Fund.

(*i*) Transactions in special drawing rights means exchanges of special drawing rights for other monetary assets. Operations in special drawing rights means other uses of special drawing rights.

* * *

4.2 ARTICLES OF AGREEMENT OF THE INTERNATIONAL BANK FOR RECONSTRUCTION AND DEVELOPMENT.[a] Done at Washington, Dec. 27, 1945. Entered into force, Dec. 27, 1945; for the United States, Dec. 27, 1945. 60 Stat. 1440, T.I.A.S. No. 1502, 3 Bevans 1390, 2 U.N.T.S. 134. AMENDMENT TO THE ARTICLES OF AGREEMENT. Done at Washington, Dec. 16, 1965. Entered into force, Dec. 17, 1965; for the United States, Dec. 17, 1965. 16 U.S.T. 1942, T.I.A.S. No. 5959

The Governments on whose behalf the present Agreement is signed agree as follows:

INTRODUCTORY ARTICLE

The International Bank for Reconstruction and Development is established and shall operate in accordance with the following provisions:

ARTICLE I. PURPOSES

The purposes of the Bank are:

(i) To assist in the reconstruction and development of territories of members by facilitating the investment of capital for productive purposes, including the restoration of economies destroyed or disrupted by war, the reconversion of productive facilities to peacetime needs and the encouragement of the development of productive facilities and resources in less developed countries.

(ii) To promote private foreign investment by means of guarantees or participations in loans and other investments made by private investors; and when private capital is not available on reasonable terms, to supplement private investment by providing, on suitable conditions, finance for productive purposes out of its own capital, funds raised by it and its other resources.

(iii) To promote the long-range balanced growth of international trade and the maintenance of equilibrium in balances by payments of encouraging international investment for the development of the productive resources of members, thereby assisting in raising productivity, the standard of living and conditions of labor in their territories.

(iv) To arrange the loans made or guaranteed by it in relation to international loans through other channels so that the more useful and urgent projects, large and small alike, will be dealt with first.

(v) To conduct its operations with due regard to the effect of international investment on business conditions in the territories of members and, in the immediate postwar years, to assist in bringing about a smooth transition from a wartime to a peacetime economy.

The Bank shall be guided in all its decisions by the purposes set forth above.

a. For other notable instruments pertaining to "the World Bank Group," see: Articles of Agreement of the International Finance Corporation, done at London, May 25, 1955, entered into force for the United States and others, July 20, 1956, 7 U.S.T. 2197, T.I.A.S. No. 3620, 264 U.N.T.S. 117, as amended on Sept. 1, 1961, 12 U.S.T. 2945, T.I.A.S. No. 4894, 439 U.N.T.S. 318, amended on Aug. 25, 1965, 24 U.S.T. 1760, T.I.A.S. No. 7683; Articles of Agreement of the International Development Association, done at Washington, Jan. 26, 1960, entered into force for the United States and others, Sept. 24, 1960, 11 U.S.T. 2284, T.I.A.S. No. 4607, 439 U.N.T.S. 249. *See also* Basic Document 4.1, *supra.*

ARTICLE II. MEMBERSHIP IN AND CAPITAL OF THE BANK

Section 1. Membership

(a) The original members of the Bank shall be those members of the International Monetary Fund which accept membership in the Bank before the date specified in Article XI, Section 2(e).

(b) Membership shall be open to other members of the Fund, at such times and in accordance with such terms as may be prescribed by the Bank.

Section 2. Authorized Capital

(a) The authorized capital stock of the Bank shall be $10,000,000,000,[b] in terms of United States dollars of the weight and fineness in effect on July 1, 1944. The capital stock shall be divided into 100,000 shares having a par value of $100,000 each, which shall be available for subscription only by members.

(b) The capital stock may be increased when the Bank deems it advisable by a three-fourths majority of the total voting power.

Section 3. Subscription of Shares

(a) Each member shall subscribe shares of the capital stock of the Bank. The minimum number of shares to be subscribed by the original members shall be those set forth in Schedule A.[c] The minimum number of shares to be subscribed by other members shall be determined by the Bank, which shall reserve a sufficient portion of its capital stock for subscription by such members.

(b) The Bank shall prescribe rules laying down the conditions under which members may subscribe shares of the authorized capital stock of the Bank in addition to their minimum subscriptions.

(c) If the authorized capital stock of the Bank is increased, each member shall have a reasonable opportunity to subscribe, under such conditions as the Bank shall decide, a proportion of the increase of stock equivalent to the proportion which its stock theretofore subscribed bears to the total capital stock of the Bank, but no member shall be obligated to subscribe any part of the increased capital.

* * *

Section 6. Limitation on Liability

Liability on shares shall be limited to the unpaid portion of the issue price of the shares.

Section 7. Method of Payment of Subscriptions for Shares

Payment of subscriptions for shares shall be made in gold or United States dollars and in the currencies of the members as follows:

(i) under Section 5(i) of this Article, two percent of the price of each share shall be payable in gold or United States dollars, and, when calls are made, the remaining eighteen percent shall be paid in the currency of the member;

(ii) when a call is made under Section 5(ii) of this Article, payment may be made at the option of the member either in gold, in United States dollars or in the currency required to discharge the obligations of the Bank for the purpose for which the call is made;

(iii) when a member makes payments in any currency under (i) and (ii) above, such payments shall be made in amounts equal in value to the member's liability under the call. This liability shall be a proportionate part of the

b. The amount of authorized capital stock of the Bank has been increased from time to time.

c. This Schedule is omitted here.

subscribed capital stock of the Bank as authorized and defined in Section 2 of this Article.

* * *

Section 9. Maintenance of Value of Certain Currency Holdings of the Bank

(a) Whenever (i) the par value of a member's currency is reduced, or (ii) the foreign exchange value of a member's currency has, in the opinion of the Bank, depreciated to a significant extent within that member's territories, the member shall pay to the Bank within a reasonable time an additional amount of its own currency sufficient to maintain the value, as of the time of initial subscription, of the amount of the currency of such member which is held by the Bank and derived from currency originally paid in to the Bank by the member under Article II, Section 7(i), from currency referred to in Article IV, Section 2(b), or from any additional currency furnished under the provisions of the present paragraph, and which has not been repurchased by the member for gold or for the currency of any member which is acceptable to the Bank.

(b) Whenever the par value of a member's currency is increased, the Bank shall return to such member within a reasonable time an amount of that member's currency equal to the increase in the value of the amount of such currency described in (a) above.

(c) The provisions of the preceding paragraphs may be waived by the Bank when a uniform proportionate change in the par values of the currencies of all its members is made by the International Monetary Fund.

Section 10. Restriction on Disposal of Shares

Shares shall not be pledged or encumbered in any manner whatever and they shall be transferable only to the Bank.

ARTICLE III. GENERAL PROVISIONS RELATING TO LOANS AND GUARANTEES

Section 1. Use of Resources

(a) The resources and the facilities of the Bank shall be used exclusively for the benefit of members with equitable consideration to projects for development and projects for reconstruction alike.

(b) For the purpose of facilitating the restoration and reconstruction of the economy of members whose metropolitan territories have suffered great devastation from enemy occupation or hostilities, the Bank, in determining the conditions and terms of loans made to such members, shall pay special regard to lightening the financial burden and expediting the completion of such restoration and reconstruction.

Section 2. Dealings Between Members and the Bank

Each member shall deal with the Bank only through its Treasury, central bank, stabilization fund or other similar fiscal agency, and the Bank shall deal with members only by or through the same agencies.

Section 3. Limitations on Guarantees and Borrowings of the Bank

The total amount outstanding of guarantees, participations in loans and direct loans made by the Bank shall not be increased at any time, if by such increase the total would exceed one hundred percent of the unimpaired subscribed capital, reserves and surplus of the Bank.

Section 4. Conditions on Which the Bank May Guarantee or Make Loans

The Bank may guarantee, participate in, or make loans to any member of any political sub-division thereof and any business, industrial, and agricultural enterprise in the territories of a member, subject to the following conditions:

(i) When the member in whose territories the project is located is not itself the borrower, the member of the central bank or some comparable agency of the member which is acceptable to the Bank, fully guarantees the repayment of the principal and the payment of interest and other charges on the loan.

(ii) The Bank is satisfied that in the prevailing market conditions the borrower would be unable otherwise to obtain the loan under conditions which in the opinion of the Bank are reasonable for the borrower.

(iii) A competent committee, as provided for in Article V, Section 7, has submitted a written report recommending the project after a careful study of the merits of the proposal.

(iv) In the opinion of the Bank the rate of interest and other charges are reasonable and such rate, charges and the schedule for repayment of principal are appropriate to the project.

(v) In making or guaranteeing a loan, the Bank shall pay due regard to the prospects that the borrower, and, if the borrower is not a member, that the guarantor, will be in position to meet its obligations under the loan; and the Bank shall act prudently in the interests both of the particular member in whose territories the project is located and of the members as a whole.

(vi) In guaranteeing a loan made by other investors, the Bank receives suitable compensation for its risk.

(vii) Loans made or guaranteed by the Bank shall, except in special circumstances, be for the purpose of specific projects of reconstruction or development.

Section 5. Use of Loans Guaranteed, Participated in or Made by the Bank

(a) The Bank shall impose no conditions that the proceeds of a loan shall be spent in the territories of any particular member or members.

(b) The Bank shall make arrangements to ensure that the proceeds of any loan are used only for the purposes for which the loan was granted, with due attention to considerations of economy and efficiency and without regard to political or other non-economic influences or considerations.

(c) In the case of loans made by the Bank, it shall open an account in the name of the borrower and the amount of the loan shall be credited to this account in the currency or currencies in which the loan is made. The borrower shall be permitted by the Bank to draw on this account only to meet expenses in connection with the project as they are actually incurred.

Section 6. Loans to the International Finance Corporation

(a) The Bank may make, participate in, or guarantee loans to the International Finance Corporation, an affiliate of the Bank, for use in its lending operations. The total amount outstanding of such loans, participations and guarantees shall not be increased if, at the time or as a result thereof, the aggregate amount of debt (including the guarantee of any debt) incurred by the said Corporation from any source and then outstanding shall exceed an amount equal to four times its unimpaired subscribed capital and surplus.

(b) The provisions of Article III, Sections 4 and 5(c) and of Article IV, Section 3 shall not apply to loans, participations and guarantees authorized by this Section.

ARTICLE IV. OPERATIONS

Section 1. Methods of Making or Facilitating Loans

(a) The Bank may make or facilitate loans which satisfy the general conditions of Article III in any of the following ways:

(i) By making or participating in direct loans out of its own funds corresponding to its unimpaired paid-up capital and surplus and, subject to Section 6 of this Article, to its reserves.

(ii) By making or participating in direct loans out of funds raised in the market of a member, or otherwise borrowed by the Bank.

(iii) By guaranteeing in whole or in part loans made by private investors through the usual investment channels.

(b) The Bank may borrow funds under (a)(ii) above or guarantee loans under (a)(iii) above only with the approval of the member in whose markets the funds are raised and the member in whose currency the loan is denominated, and only if those members agree that the proceeds may be exchanged for the currency of any other member without restriction.

Section 2. Availability and Transferability of Currencies

(a) Currencies paid into the Bank under Article II, Section 7(i), shall be loaned only with the approval in each case of the member whose currency is involved; provided, however, that if necessary, after the Bank's subscribed capital has been entirely called, such currencies shall, without restriction by the members whose currencies are offered, be used or exchanged for the currencies required to meet contractual payments of interest, other charges or amortization on the Bank's own borrowings, or to meet the Bank's liabilities with respect to such contractual payments on loans guaranteed by the Bank.

(b) Currencies received by the Bank from borrowers or guarantors in payment on account of principal of direct loans made with currencies referred to in (a) above shall be exchanged for the currencies of other members or reloaned only with the approval in each case of the members whose currencies are involved; provided, however, that if necessary, after the Bank's subscribed capital has been entirely called, such currencies shall, without restriction by the members whose currencies are offered, be used or exchanged for the currencies required to meet contractual payments of interest, other charges or amortization on the Bank's own borrowings, or to meet the Bank's liabilities with respect to such contractual payments on loans guaranteed by the Bank.

(c) Currencies received by the Bank from borrowers or guarantors in payment on account of principal of direct loans made by the Bank under Section (a)(ii) of this Article, shall be held and used, without restriction by the members, to make amortization payments, or to anticipate payment of or repurchase part or all of the Bank's own obligations.

(d) All other currencies available to the Bank, including those raised in the market or otherwise borrowed under Section 1(a)(ii) of this Article, those obtained by the sale of gold, those received as payments of interest and other charges for direct loans made under Sections 1(a)(i) and (ii), and those received as payments of commissions and other charges under Section 1(a)(iii), shall be used or exchanged for other currencies or gold required in the operations of the Bank without restriction by the members whose currencies are offered.

(e) Currencies raised in the markets of members by borrowers on loans guaranteed by the Bank under Section 1(a)(iii) of this Article, shall also be used or exchanged for other currencies without restriction by such members.

Section 3. Provision of Currencies for Direct Loans

The following provisions shall apply to direct loans under Sections 1(a)(i) and (ii) of this Article:

(a) The Bank shall furnish the borrower with such currencies of members, other than the member in whose territories the project is located, as are needed by the borrower for expenditures to be made in the territories of such other members to carry out the purposes of the loan.

(b) The Bank may, in exceptional circumstances when local currency required for the purpose of the loan cannot be raised by the borrower on reasonable terms, provide the borrower as part of the loan with an appropriate amount of that currency.

(c) The Bank, if the project gives rise indirectly to an increased need for foreign exchange by the member in whose territories the project is located, may in exceptional circumstances provide the borrower as part of the loan with an appropriate amount of gold or foreign exchange not in excess of the borrower's local expenditure in connection with the purposes of the loan.

(d) The Bank may, in exceptional circumstances, at the request of a member in whose territories a portion of the loan is spent, repurchase with gold or foreign exchange a part of that member's currency thus spent but in no case shall the part so repurchased exceed the amount by which the expenditure of the loan in those territories gives rise to an increased need for foreign exchange.

Section 4. Payment Provisions for Direct Loans

Loan contracts under Section 1(a)(i) or (ii) of this Article shall be made in accordance with the following payment provisions:

(a) The terms and conditions of interest and amortization payments, maturity and dates of payment of each loan shall be determined by the Bank. The Bank shall also determine the rate and any other terms and conditions of commission to be charged in connection with such loan.

In the case of loans made under Section 1(a)(ii) of this Article during the first ten years of the Bank's operations, this rate of commission shall be not less than one percent per annum and not greater than one and one-half percent per annum, and shall be charged on the outstanding portion of any such loan. At the end of this period of ten years, the rate of commission may be reduced by the Bank with respect both to the outstanding portions of loans already made and to future loans, if the reserves accumulated by the Bank under Section 6 of this Article and out of other earnings are considered by it sufficient to justify a reduction. In the case of future loans the Bank shall also have discretion to increase the rate of commission beyond the above limit, if experience indicates that an increase is advisable.

(b) All loan contracts shall stipulate the currency or currencies in which payments under the contract shall be made to the Bank. At the option of the borrower, however, such payments may be made in gold, or subject to the agreement of the Bank, in the currency of a member other than that prescribed in the contract.

(i) In the case of loans made under Section 1(a)(i) of this Article, the loan contracts shall provide that payments to the Bank of interest, other charges and amortization shall be made in the currency loaned, unless the member whose currency is loaned agrees that such payments shall be made in some other specified currency or currencies. These payments, subject to the provisions of Article II, Section 9(c), shall be equivalent to the value of such contractual payments at the time the loans were made, in terms of a currency specified for the purpose by the Bank by a three-fourths majority of the total voting power.

(ii) In the case of loans made under Section 1(a)(ii) of this Article, the total amount outstanding and payable to the Bank in any one currency shall at no time exceed the total amount of the outstanding borrowings made by the Bank under Section 1(a)(ii) and payable in the same currency.

(c) If a member suffers from an acute exchange stringency, so that the service of any loan contracted by that member or guaranteed by it or by one of its agencies cannot be provided in the stipulated manner, the member concerned may apply to the Bank for a relaxation of the conditions of payment. If the Bank is satisfied that some relaxation is in the interests of the particular member and of the operations of the Bank and of its members as a whole, it may take action under either, or both, of the following paragraphs with respect to the whole, or part, of the annual service:

(i) The Bank may, in its discretion, make arrangements with the member concerned to accept service payments on the loan in the member's currency for periods not to exceed three years upon appropriate terms regarding the use of such currency and the maintenance of its foreign exchange value; and for the repurchase of such currency on appropriate terms.

(ii) The Bank may modify the terms of amortization or extend the life of the loan, or both.

Section 5. Guarantees

(a) In guaranteeing a loan placed through the usual investment channels, the Bank shall charge a guarantee commission payable periodically on the amount of the loan outstanding at a rate determined by the Bank. During the first ten years of the Bank's operations, this rate shall be not less than one percent per annum and not greater than one and one-half percent per annum. At the end of this period of ten years, the rate of commission may be reduced by the Bank with respect both to the outstanding portions of loans already guaranteed and to future loans if the reserves accumulated by the Bank under Section 6 of this Article and out of other earnings are considered by it sufficient to justify a reduction. In the case of future loans the Bank shall also have discretion to increase the rate of commission beyond the above limit, if experience indicates that an increase is advisable.

(b) Guarantee commissions shall be paid directly to the Bank by the borrower.

(c) Guarantees by the Bank shall provide that the Bank may terminate its liability with respect to interest if, upon default by the borrower and by the guarantor, if any, the Bank offers to purchase, at par and interest accrued to a date designated in the offer, the bonds or other obligations guaranteed.

(d) The Bank shall have power to determine any other terms and conditions of the guarantee.

Section 6. Special Reserve

The amount of commissions received by the Bank under Sections 4 and 5 of this Article shall be set aside as a special reserve, which shall be kept available for meeting liabilities of the Bank in accordance with Section 7 of this Article. The special reserve shall be held in such liquid form, permitted under this Agreement, as the Executive Directors may decide.

Section 7. Methods of Meeting Liabilities of the Bank in Case of Defaults

In cases of default on loans made, participated in, or guaranteed by the Bank:

(a) The Bank shall make such arrangements as may be feasible to adjust the obligations under the loans, including arrangements under or analogous to those provided in Section 4(c) of this Article.

(b) The payments in discharge of the Bank's liabilities on borrowings or guarantees under Section 1(a)(ii) and (iii) of this Article shall be charged:

(i) first, against the special reserve provided in Section 6 of this Article.

(ii) then, to the extent necessary and at the discretion of the Bank, against the other reserves, surplus and capital available to the Bank.

(c) Whenever necessary to meet contractual payments of interest, other charges or amortization on the Bank's own borrowings, or to meet the Bank's liabilities with respect to similar payments on loans guaranteed by it, the Bank may call an appropriate amount of the unpaid subscriptions of members in accordance with Article II, Sections 5 and 7. Moreover, if it believes that a default may be of long duration, the Bank may call an additional amount of such unpaid subscriptions not to exceed in any one year one percent of the total subscriptions of the members for the following purposes:

(i) To redeem prior to maturity, or otherwise discharge its liability on, all or part of the outstanding principal of any loan guaranteed by it in respect of which the debtor is in default.

(ii) To repurchase, or otherwise discharge its liability on, all or part of its own outstanding borrowings.

Section 8. Miscellaneous Operations

In addition to the operations specified elsewhere in this Agreement, the Bank shall have the power:

(i) To buy and sell securities it has issued and to buy and sell securities which it has guaranteed or in which it has invested, provided that the Bank shall obtain the approval of the member in whose territories the securities are to be bought or sold.

(ii) To guarantee securities in which it has invested for the purpose of facilitating their sale.

(iii) To borrow the currency of any member with the approval of that member.

(iv) To buy and sell such other securities as the Directors by a three-fourths majority of the total voting power may deem proper for the investment of all or part of the special reserve under Section 6 of this Article.

In exercising the powers conferred by this Section, the Bank may deal with any person, partnership, association, corporation or other legal entity in the territories of any member.

Section 9. Warning to be Placed on Securities

Every security guaranteed or issued by the Bank shall bear on its face a conspicuous statement to the effect that it is not an obligation of any government unless expressly stated on the security.

Section 10. Political Activity Prohibited

The Bank and its officers shall not interfere in the political affairs of any member; nor shall they be influenced in their decisions by the political character of the member or members concerned. Only economic considerations shall be relevant to their decisions, and these considerations shall be weighed impartially in order to achieve the purposes stated in Article I.

ARTICLE V. ORGANIZATION AND MANAGEMENT

Section 1. Structure of the Bank

The Bank shall have a Board of Governors, Executive Directors, a President and such other officers and staff to perform such duties as the Bank may determine.

* * *

Section 6. Advisory Council

(a) There shall be an Advisory Council of not less than seven persons selected by the Board of Governors including representatives of banking, commercial, industrial, labor, and agricultural interests, and with as wide a national representation as possible. In those fields where specialized international organizations exist, the members of the Council representative of those fields shall be selected in agreement with such organizations. The Council shall advise the Bank on matters of general policy. The Council shall meet annually and on such other occasions as the Bank may request.

(b) Councillors shall serve for two years and may be reappointed. They shall be paid their reasonable expenses incurred on behalf of the Bank.

Section 7. Loan Committees

The committees required to report on loans under Article III, Section 4, shall be appointed by the Bank. Each such committee shall include an expert selected by the governor representing the member in whose territories the project is located and one or more members of the technical staff of the Bank.

Section 8. Relationship to Other International Organizations

(a) The Bank, within the terms of this Agreement, shall cooperate with any general international organization and with public international organizations having specialized responsibilities in related fields. Any arrangements for such cooperation which would involve a modification of any provision of this Agreement may be effected only after amendment to this Agreement under Article VIII.

(b) In making decisions on applications for loans or guarantees relating to matters directly within the competence of any international organization of the types specified in the preceding paragraph and participated in primarily by members of the Bank, the Bank shall give consideration to the views and recommendations of such organization.

Section 9. Location of Offices

(a) The principal office of the Bank shall be located in the territory of the member holding the greatest number of shares.

(b) The Bank may establish agencies or branch offices in the territories of any member of the Bank.

* * *

ARTICLE VI. WITHDRAWAL AND SUSPENSION OF MEMBERSHIP: SUSPENSION OF OPERATIONS

Section 1. Right of Members to Withdraw

Any member may withdraw from the Bank at any time by transmitting a notice in writing to the Bank at its principal office. Withdrawal shall become effective on the date such notice is received.

Section 2. Suspension of Membership

If a member fails to fulfill any of its obligations to the Bank, the Bank may suspend its membership by decision of a majority of the Governors, exercising a majority of the total voting power. The member so suspended shall automatically cease to be a member one year from the date of its suspension unless a decision is taken by the same majority to restore the member to good standing.

While under suspension, a member shall not be entitled to exercise any rights under this Agreement, except the right of withdrawal, but shall remain subject to all obligations.

Section 3. Cessation of Membership in International Monetary Fund

Any member which ceases to be a member of the International Monetary Fund shall automatically cease after three months to be a member of the Bank unless the Bank by three-fourths of the total voting power has agreed to allow it to remain a member.

Section 4. Settlement of Accounts with Governments Ceasing to Be Members

(a) When a government ceases to be a member, it shall remain liable for its direct obligations to the Bank and for its contingent liabilities to the Bank so long as any part of the loans or guarantees contracted before it ceased to be a member are outstanding; but it shall cease to incur liabilities with respect to loans and guarantees entered into thereafter by the Bank and to share either in the income or the expenses of the Bank.

* * *

Section 5. Suspension of Operations and Settlement of Obligations

(a) In an emergency the Executive Directors may suspend temporarily operations in respect of new loans and guarantees pending an opportunity for further consideration and action by the Board of Governors.

* * *

ARTICLE VII. STATUS, IMMUNITIES AND PRIVILEGES

Section 1. Purposes of Article

To enable the Bank to fulfill the functions with which it is entrusted, the status, immunities and privileges set forth in this Article shall be accorded to the Bank in the territories of each member.

Section 2. Status of the Bank

The Bank shall possess full juridical personality, and, in particular, the capacity:

(i) to contract;

(ii) to acquire and dispose of immovable and movable property;

(iii) to institute legal proceedings.

Section 3. Position of the Bank with Regard to Judicial Process

Actions may be brought against the Bank only in a court of competent jurisdiction in the territories of a member in which the Bank has an office, has appointed an agent for the purpose of accepting service or notice of process, or has issued or guaranteed securities. No actions shall, however, be brought by members or persons acting for or deriving claims from members. The property and assets of the Bank shall, wheresoever located and by whomsoever held, be immune from all forms of seizure, attachment or execution before the delivery of final judgment against the Bank.

Section 4. Immunity of Assets from Seizure

Property and assets of the Bank, wherever located and by whomsoever held, shall be immune from search, requisition, confiscation, expropriation or any other form of seizure by executive or legislative action.

Section 5. Immunity of Archives

The archives of the Bank shall be inviolable.

Section 6. Freedom of Assets from Restrictions

To the extent necessary to carry out the operations provided for in this Agreement and subject to the provisions of this Agreement, all property and assets of the Bank shall be free from restrictions, regulations, controls and moratoria of any nature.

Section 7. Privilege for Communications

The official communications of the Bank shall be accorded by each member the same treatment that it accords to the official communications of other members.

Section 8. Immunities and Privileges of Officers and Employees

All governors, executive directors, alternates, officers and employees of the Bank:

(i) shall be immune from legal process with respect to acts performed by them in their official capacity except when the Bank waives this immunity;

(ii) not being local nationals, shall be accorded the same immunities from immigration restrictions, alien registration requirements and national service obligations and the same facilities as regards exchange restrictions as are accorded by members to the representatives, officials, and employees of comparable rank of other members;

(iii) shall be granted the same treatment in respect of travelling facilities as is accorded by members to representatives, officials and employees of comparable rank of other members.

* * *

ARTICLE IX. INTERPRETATION

(a) Any question of interpretation of the provisions of this Agreement arising between any member and the Bank or between any members of the Bank shall be submitted to the Executive Directors for their decision. If the question particularly affects any member not entitled to appoint an executive director, it shall be entitled to representation in accordance with Article V, Section 4(h).

(b) In any case where the Executive Directors have given a decision under (a) above, any member may require that the question be referred to the Board of Governors, whose decision shall be final. Pending the result of the reference to the Board, the Bank may, so far as it deems necessary, act on the basis of the decision of the Executive Directors.

(c) Whenever a disagreement arises between the Bank and a country which has ceased to be a member, or between the Bank and any member during the permanent suspension of the Bank, such disagreement shall be submitted to arbitration by a tribunal of three arbitrators, one appointed by the Bank, another by the country involved and an umpire who, unless the parties otherwise agree, shall be appointed by the President of the Permanent Court of International Justice or such other authority as may have been prescribed by regulation adopted by the Bank. The umpire shall have full power to settle all questions of procedure in any case where the parties are in disagreement with respect thereto.

* * *

4.3 RESOLUTION ON PERMANENT SOVEREIGNTY OVER NATURAL RESOURCES.[a] Adopted by the U.N. General Assembly, Dec. 14, 1962. U.N.G.A. Res. 1803 (XVII), 17 U.N. GAOR. Supp. (No. 17) 15, U.N. Doc. A/5217 (1963), *reprinted in* 2 I.L.M. 223 (1963)

The General Assembly,

Recalling its resolutions 523(VI) of 12 January 1952 and 626(VII) of 21 December 1952.

Bearing in mind its resolution 1314(XIII) of 12 December 1958, by which it established the Commission on Permanent Sovereignty over Natural Resources and instructed it to conduct a full survey of the status of permanent sovereignty over natural wealth and resources as a basic constituent of the right to self-determination, with recommendations, where necessary, for its strengthening, and decided further that, in the conduct of the full survey of the status of the permanent sovereignty of peoples and nations over their natural wealth and resources, due regard should be paid to the rights and duties of States under international law and to the importance of encouraging international co-operation in the economic development of developing countries.

Bearing in mind its resolution 1515(XV) of 15 December 1960, in which it recommended that the sovereign right of every State to dispose of its wealth and its natural resources should be respected.

Considering that any measure in this respect must be based on the recognition of the inalienable right of all States freely to dispose of their natural wealth and resources in accordance with their national interests, and on respect for the economic independence of States.

Considering that nothing in paragraph 4 below in any way prejudices the position of any Member State on any aspect of the question of the rights and obligations of successor States and Governments in respect of property acquired before the accession to complete sovereignty of countries formerly under colonial rule.

Noting that the subject of succession of States and Governments is being examined as a matter of priority by the International Law Commission.

Considering that it is desirable to promote international co-operation for the economic development of developing countries, and that economic and financial agreements between the developed and the developing countries must be based on the principles of equality and of the right of peoples and nations to self-determination.

Considering that the provision of economic and technical assistance, loans and increased foreign investment must not be subject to conditions which conflict with the interests of the recipient State.

Considering the benefits to be derived from exchanges of technical and scientific information likely to promote the development and use of such resources and wealth, and the important part which the United Nations and other international organizations are called upon to play in that connexion.

Attaching particular importance to the question of promoting the economic development of developing countries and securing their economic independence.

a. *See also* Basic Documents 4.5 and 4.8, *infra*.

Noting that the creation and strengthening of the inalienable sovereignty of States over their natural wealth and resources reinforces their economic independence.

Desiring that there should be further consideration by the United Nations of the subject of permanent sovereignty over natural resources in the spirit of international co-operation in the field of economic development, particularly that of the developing countries.

I

Declares that:

1. The right of peoples and nations to permanent sovereignty over their natural wealth and resources must be exercised in the interest of their national development and of the well-being of the people of the State concerned.

2. The exploration, development and disposition of such resources, as well as the import of the foreign capital required for these purposes, should be in conformity with the rules and conditions which the peoples and nations freely consider to be necessary or desirable with regard to the authorization, restriction or prohibition of such activities.

3. In cases where authorization is granted, the capital imported and the earnings on that capital shall be governed by the terms thereof, by the national legislation in force, and by international law. The profits derived must be shared in the proportions freely agreed upon, in each case, between the investors and the recipient State, due care being taken to ensure that there is no impairment, for any reason, of that State's sovereignty over its natural wealth and resources.

4. Nationalization, expropriation or requisitioning shall be based on grounds or reasons of public utility, security or the national interest which are recognized as overriding purely individual or private interests, both domestic and foreign. In such cases the owner shall be paid appropriate compensation, in accordance with the rules in force in the State taking such measures in the exercise of its sovereignty and in accordance with international law. In any case, where the question of compensation gives rise to a controversy, the national jurisdiction of the State taking such measures shall be exhausted. However, upon agreement by sovereign States and other parties concerned, settlement of the dispute should be made through arbitration or international adjudication.

5. The free and beneficial exercise of the sovereignty of peoples and nations over their natural resources must be furthered by the mutual respect of States based on their sovereign equality.

6. International co-operation for the economic development of developing countries, whether in the form of public or private capital investments, exchange of goods and services, technical assistance, or exchange of scientific information, shall be such as to further their independent national development and shall be based upon respect for their sovereignty over their natural wealth and resources.

7. Violation of the rights of peoples and nations to sovereignty over their natural wealth and resources is contrary to the spirit and principles of the Charter of the United Nations and hinders the development of international co-operation and the maintenance of peace.

8. Foreign investment agreements freely entered into by, or between, sovereign States shall be observed in good faith: States and international organizations shall strictly and conscientiously respect the sovereignty of peoples and nations over their natural wealth and resources in accordance with the Charter and the principles set forth in the present resolution.

* * *

4.4 CONVENTION ON THE SETTLEMENT OF INVESTMENT DISPUTES BETWEEN STATES AND NATIONALS OF OTHER STATES. Done at Washington, Mar. 18, 1965. Entered into force, Oct. 14, 1966; for the United States, Oct. 14, 1966. 17 U.S.T. 1270, T.I.A.S. No. 6090, 575 U.N.T.S. 159, *reprinted in* 4 I.L.M. 532 (1965)

CHAPTER I. INTERNATIONAL CENTRE FOR SETTLEMENT OF INVESTMENT DISPUTES

SECTION 1. ESTABLISHMENT AND ORGANIZATION

Article 1. (1) There is hereby established the International Centre for Settlement of Investment Disputes (hereinafter called the Centre).

(2) The purpose of the Centre shall be to provide facilities for conciliation and arbitration of investment disputes between Contracting States and nationals of other Contracting States in accordance with the provisions of this Convention.

Article 2. The seat of the Centre shall be at the principal office of the International Bank for Reconstruction and Development (hereinafter called the Bank). The seat may be moved to another place by decision of the Administrative Council adopted by a majority of two-thirds of its members.

Article 3. The Centre shall have an Administrative Council and a Secretariat and shall maintain a Panel of Conciliators and a Panel of Arbitrators.

SECTION 2. THE ADMINISTRATIVE COUNCIL

Article 4. (1) The Administrative Council shall be composed of one representative of each Contracting State. An alternate may act as representative in case of his principal's absence from a meeting or inability to act.

* * *

Article 6. (1) Without prejudice to the powers and functions vested in it by other provisions of this Convention, the Administrative Council shall

(a) adopt the administrative and financial regulations of the Centre;

(b) adopt the rules of procedure for the institution of conciliation and arbitration proceedings;

(c) adopt the rules of procedure for conciliation and arbitration proceedings (hereinafter called the Conciliation Rules and the Arbitration Rules);

(d) approve arrangements with the Bank for the use of the Bank's administrative facilities and services; * * *.

* * *

(2) The Administrative Council may appoint such committees as it considers necessary.

(3) The Administrative Council shall also exercise such other powers and perform such other functions as it shall determine to be necessary for the implementation of the provisions of this Convention.

* * *

Article 8. Members of the Administrative Council and the Chairman shall serve without remuneration from the Centre.

SECTION 3. THE SECRETARIAT

Article 9. The Secretariat shall consist of a Secretary–General, one or more Deputy Secretaries–General and staff.

Article 10. (1) The Secretary–General and any Deputy Secretary–General shall be elected by the Administrative Council by a majority of two-thirds of its members upon the nomination of the Chairman for a term of service not exceeding six years and shall be eligible for reelection. After consulting the members of the Administrative Council, the Chairman shall propose one or more candidates for each such office.

(2) The offices of Secretary–General and Deputy Secretary–General shall be incompatible with the exercise of any political function. Neither the Secretary–General nor any Deputy Secretary–General may hold any other employment or engage in any other occupation except with the approval of the Administrative Council.

* * *

Article 11. The Secretary–General shall be the legal representative and the principal officer of the Centre and shall be responsible for its administration, including the appointment of staff, in accordance with the provisions of this Convention and the rules adopted by the Administrative Council. He shall perform the function of registrar and shall have the power to authenticate arbitral awards rendered pursuant to this Convention, and to certify copies thereof.

SECTION 4. THE PANELS

Article 12. The Panel of Conciliators and the Panel of Arbitrators shall each consist of qualified persons, designated as hereinafter provided, who are willing to serve thereon.

Article 13. (1) Each Contracting State may designate to each Panel four persons who may but need not be its nationals.

(2) The Chairman may designate ten persons to each Panel. The persons so designated to a Panel shall each have a different nationality.

Article 14. (1) Persons designated to serve on the Panels shall be persons of high moral character and recognized competence in the fields of law, commerce, industry or finance, who may be relied upon to exercise independent judgment. Competence in the field of law shall be of particular importance in the case of persons on the Panel of Arbitrators.

(2) The Chairman, in designating persons to serve on the Panels, shall in addition pay due regard to the importance of assuring representation on the Panels of the principal legal systems of the world and of the main forms of economic activity.

SECTION 5. FINANCING THE CENTRE

Article 17. If the expenditure of the Centre cannot be met out of charges for the use of its facilities, or out of other receipts, the excess shall be borne by Contracting States which are members of the Bank in proportion to their respective subscriptions to the capital stock of the Bank, and by Contracting States which are not members of the Bank in accordance with rules adopted by the Administrative Council.

SECTION 6. STATUS, IMMUNITIES AND PRIVILEGES

Article 18. The Centre shall have full international legal personality. The legal capacity of the Centre shall include the capacity

(a) to contract;

(b) to acquire and dispose of movable and immovable property;

(c) to institute legal proceedings.

Article 19. To enable the Centre to fulfil its functions, it shall enjoy in the territories of each Contracting State the immunities and privileges set forth in this Section.

Article 20. The Centre, its property and assets shall enjoy immunity from all legal process, except when the Centre waives this immunity.

Article 21. The Chairman, the members of the Administrative Council, persons acting as conciliators or arbitrators or members of a Committee appointed pursuant to paragraph (3) of Article 52, and the officers and employees of the Secretariat

(a) shall enjoy immunity from legal process with respect to acts performed by them in the exercise of their functions, except when the Centre waives this immunity;

(b) not being local nationals, shall enjoy the same immunities from immigration restrictions, alien registration requirements and national service obligations, the same facilities as regards exchange restrictions and the same treatment in respect of travelling facilities as are accorded by Contracting States to the representatives, officials and employees of comparable rank of other Contracting States.

Article 22. The provisions of Article 21 shall apply to persons appearing in proceedings under this Convention as parties, agents, counsel, advocates, witnesses or experts; provided, however, that sub-paragraph (b) thereof shall apply only in connection with their travel to and from, and their stay at, the place where the proceedings are held.

Article 23. (1) The archives of the Centre shall be inviolable, wherever they may be.

(2) With regard to its official communications, the Centre shall be accorded by each Contracting State treatment not less favourable than that accorded to other international organizations.

* * *

Article 25. (1) The jurisdiction of the Centre shall extend to any legal dispute arising directly out of an investment, between a Contracting State (or any constituent subdivision or agency of a Contracting State designated to the Centre by that State) and a national of another Contracting State, which the parties to the dispute consent in writing to submit to the Centre. When the parties have given their consent, no party may withdraw its consent unilaterally.

(2) "National of another Contracting State" means:

(a) any natural person who had the nationality of a Contracting State other than the State party to the dispute on the date on which the parties consented to submit such dispute to conciliation or arbitration as well as on the date on which the request was registered pursuant to paragraph (3) of Article 28 or paragraph (3) of Article 36, but does not include any person who on either date also had the nationality of the Contracting State party to the dispute; and

(b) any juridical person which had the nationality of a Contracting State other than the State party to the dispute on the date on which the parties consented to submit such dispute to conciliation or arbitration and any juridical person which had the nationality of the Contracting State party to the dispute on that date and which, because of foreign control, the parties have agreed should be treated as a national of another Contracting State for the purposes of this Convention.

(3) Consent by a constituent subdivision or agency of a Contracting State shall require the approval of that State unless that State notifies the Centre that no such approval is required.

(4) Any Contracting State may, at the time of ratification, acceptance or approval of this Convention or at any time thereafter, notify the Centre of the class or classes of disputes which it would or would not consider submitting to the jurisdiction of the Centre. The Secretary–General shall forthwith transmit such notification to

all Contracting States. Such notification shall not constitute the consent required by paragraph (1).

Article 26. Consent of the parties to arbitration under this Convention shall, unless otherwise stated, be deemed consent to such arbitration to the exclusion of any other remedy. A Contracting State may require the exhaustion of local administrative or judicial remedies as a condition of its consent to arbitration under the Convention.

Article 27. (1) No Contracting State shall give diplomatic protection, or bring an international claim, in respect of a dispute which one of its nationals and another Contracting State shall have consented to submit or shall have submitted to arbitration under this Convention, unless such other Contracting State shall have failed to abide by and comply with the award rendered in such dispute.

(2) Diplomatic protection, for the purposes of paragraph (1), shall not include informal diplomatic exchanges for the sole purpose of facilitating a settlement of the dispute.

CHAPTER III. CONCILIATION

SECTION 1. REQUEST FOR CONCILIATION

Article 28. (1) Any Contracting State or any national of a Contracting State wishing to institute conciliation proceedings shall address a request to that effect in writing to the Secretary–General who shall send a copy of the request to the other party.

(2) The request shall contain information concerning the issues in dispute, the identity of the parties and their consent to conciliation in accordance with the rules of procedure for the institution of conciliation and arbitration proceedings.

(3) The Secretary–General shall register the request unless he finds, on the basis of the information contained in the request, that the dispute is manifestly outside the jurisdiction of the Centre. He shall forthwith notify the parties of registration or refusal to register.

SECTION 2. CONSTITUTION OF THE CONCILIATION COMMISSION

Article 29. (1) The Conciliation Commission (hereinafter called the Commission) shall be constituted as soon as possible after registration of a request pursuant to Article 28.

(2)(a) The Commission shall consist of a sole conciliator or any uneven number of conciliators appointed as the parties shall agree.

(b) Where the parties do not agree upon the number of conciliators and the method of their appointment, the Commission shall consist of three conciliators, one conciliator appointed by each party and the third, who shall be the president of the Commission, appointed by agreement of the parties.

Article 30. If the Commission shall not have been constituted within 90 days after notice of registration of the request has been dispatched by the Secretary–General in accordance with paragraph (3) of Article 28, or such other period as the parties may agree, the Chairman shall, at the request of either party and after consulting both parties as far as possible, appoint the conciliator or conciliators not yet appointed.

Article 31. (1) Conciliators may be appointed from outside the Panel of Conciliators, except in the case of appointments by the Chairman pursuant to Article 30.

(2) Conciliators appointed from outside the Panel of Conciliators shall possess the qualities stated in paragraph (1) of Article 14.

SECTION 3. CONCILIATION PROCEEDINGS

Article 32. (1) The Commission shall be the judge of its own competence.

(2) Any objection by a party to the dispute that that dispute is not within the jurisdiction of the Centre, or for other reasons is not within the competence of the Commission, shall be considered by the Commission which shall determine whether to deal with it as a preliminary question or to join it to the merits of the dispute.

Article 33. Any conciliation proceeding shall be conducted in accordance with the provisions of this Section and, except as the parties otherwise agree, in accordance with the Conciliation Rules in effect on the date on which the parties consented to conciliation. If any question of procedure arises which is not covered by this Section or the Conciliation Rules or any rules agreed by the parties, the Commission shall decide the question.

Article 34. (1) It shall be the duty of the Commission to clarify the issues in dispute between the parties and to endeavour to bring about agreement between them upon mutually acceptable terms. To that end, the Commission may at any stage of the proceedings and from time to time recommend terms of settlement to the parties. The parties shall cooperate in good faith with the Commission in order to enable the Commission to carry out its functions, and shall give their most serious consideration to its recommendations.

(2) If the parties reach agreement, the Commission shall draw up a report noting the issues in dispute and recording that the parties have reached agreement. If, at any stage of the proceedings, it appears to the Commission that there is no likelihood of agreement between the parties it shall close the proceedings and shall draw up a report noting the submission of the dispute and recording the failure of the parties to reach agreement. If one party fails to appear to participate in the proceedings, the Commission shall close the proceedings and shall draw up a report noting that party's failure to appear or participate.

Article 35. Except as the parties to the dispute shall otherwise agree, neither party to a conciliation proceeding shall be entitled in any other proceeding, whether before arbitrators or in a court of law or otherwise, to invoke or rely on any views expressed or statements or admissions or offers of settlement made by the other party in the conciliation proceedings, or the report or any recommendations made by the Commission.

CHAPTER IV. ARBITRATION

[*Note: Except for language pertaining to arbitration and as otherwise noted herein, the provisions of Chapter IV relating to arbitration procedures and proceedings are identical to those of Chapter III relating to conciliation procedures and proceedings.*]

SECTION 1. REQUEST FOR ARBITRATION

Article 36. (1) Any Contracting State or any national of a Contracting State wishing to institute arbitration proceedings shall address a request to that effect in writing to the Secretary–General who shall send a copy of the request to the other party.

(2) The request shall contain information concerning the issues in dispute, the identity of the parties and their consent to arbitration in accordance with the rules of procedure for the institution of conciliation and arbitration proceedings.

(3) The Secretary–General shall register the request unless he finds, on the basis of the information contained in the request, that the dispute is manifestly outside the jurisdiction of the Centre. He shall forthwith notify the parties of registration or refusal to register.

SECTION 2. CONSTITUTION OF THE TRIBUNAL

Article 37. (1) The Arbitral Tribunal (hereinafter called the Tribunal) shall be constituted as soon as possible after registration of a request pursuant to Article 36.

(2)(a) The Tribunal shall consist of a sole arbitrator or any uneven number of arbitrators appointed as the parties shall agree.

(b) Where the parties do not agree upon the number of arbitrators and the method of their appointment, the Tribunal shall consist of three arbitrators, one arbitrator appointed by each party and the third, who shall be the president of the Tribunal, appointed by agreement of the parties.

Article 38. If the Tribunal shall not have been constituted within 90 days after notice of registration of the request has been dispatched by the Secretary–General in accordance with paragraph (3) of Article 36, or such other period as the parties may agree, the Chairman shall, at the request of either party and after consulting both parties as far as possible, appoint the arbitrator or arbitrators not yet appointed. Arbitrators appointed by the Chairman pursuant to this Article shall not be nationals of the Contracting State party to the dispute or of the Contracting State whose national is a party to the dispute.

Article 39. The majority of the arbitrators shall be nationals of States other than the Contracting State party to the dispute and the Contracting State whose national is a party to the dispute; provided, however, that the foregoing provisions of this Article shall not apply if the sole arbitrator or each individual member of the Tribunal has been appointed by agreement of the parties.

* * *

Article 42. (1) The Tribunal shall decide a dispute in accordance with such rules of law as may be agreed by the parties. In the absence of such agreement, the Tribunal shall apply the law of the Contracting State party to the dispute (including its rules on the conflict of laws) and such rules of international law as may be applicable.

(2) The Tribunal may not bring in a finding of *non liquet* on the ground of silence or obscurity of the law.

(3) The provisions of paragraphs (1) and (2) shall not prejudice the power of the Tribunal to decide a dispute *ex aequo et bono* if the parties so agree.

Article 43. Except as the parties otherwise agree, the Tribunal may, if it deems it necessary at any stage of the proceedings,

(a) call upon the parties to produce documents or other evidence, and

(b) visit the scene connected with the dispute, and conduct such inquiries there as it may deem appropriate.

* * *

Article 45. (1) Failure of a party to appear or to present his case shall not be deemed an admission of the other party's assertions.

(2) If a party fails to appear or to present his case at any stage of the proceedings the other party may request the Tribunal to deal with the questions submitted to it and to render an award. Before rendering an award, the Tribunal shall notify, and grant a period of grace to, the party failing to appear or to present its case, unless it is satisfied that that party does not intend to do so.

Article 46. Except as the parties otherwise agree, the Tribunal shall, if requested by a party, determine any incidental or additional claims or counter-claims arising directly out of the subject-matter of the dispute provided that they are within the scope of the consent of the parties and are otherwise within the jurisdiction of the Centre.

Article 47. Except as the parties otherwise agree, the Tribunal may, if it considers that the circumstances so require, recommend any provisional measures which should be taken to preserve the respective rights of either party.

SECTION 4. THE AWARD

Article 48. (1) The Tribunal shall decide questions by a majority of the votes of all its members.

(2) The award of the Tribunal shall be in writing and shall be signed by the members of the Tribunal who voted for it.

(3) The award shall deal with every question submitted to the Tribunal, and shall state the reasons upon which it is based.

(4) Any member of the Tribunal may attach his individual opinion to the award, whether he dissents from the majority or not, or a statement of his dissent.

(5) The Centre shall not publish the award without the consent of the parties.

Article 49. (1) The Secretary–General shall promptly dispatch certified copies of the award to the parties. The award shall be deemed to have been rendered on the date on which the certified copies were dispatched.

(2) The Tribunal upon the request of a party made within 45 days after the date on which the award was rendered may after notice to the other party decide any question which it had omitted to decide in the award, and shall rectify any clerical, arithmetical or similar error in the award. Its decision shall become part of the award and shall be notified to the parties in the same manner as the award. The periods of time provided for under paragraph (2) of Article 51 and paragraph (2) of Article 52 shall run from the date on which the decision was rendered.

SECTION 5. INTERPRETATION, REVISION AND ANNULMENT OF THE AWARD

Article 50. (1) If any dispute shall arise between the parties as to the meaning or scope of an award, either party may request interpretation of the award by an application in writing addressed to the Secretary–General.

* * *

Article 51. (1) Either party may request revision of the award by an application in writing addressed to the Secretary–General on the ground of discovery of some fact of such a nature as decisively to affect the award, provided that when the award was rendered that fact was unknown to the Tribunal and to the applicant and that the applicant's ignorance of that fact was not due to negligence.

* * *

Article 52. (1) Either party may request annulment of the award by an application in writing addressed to the Secretary–General on one or more of the following grounds:

(a) that the Tribunal was not properly constituted;

(b) that the Tribunal has manifestly exceeded its powers;

(c) that there was corruption on the part of a member of the Tribunal;

(d) that there has been a serious departure from a fundamental rule of procedure; or

(e) that the award has failed to state the reasons on which it is based.

(2) The application shall be made within 120 days after the date on which the award was rendered except that when annulment is requested on the ground of corruption such application shall be made within 120 days after discovery of the corruption and in any event within three years after the date on which the award was rendered.

(3) On receipt of the request the Chairman shall forthwith appoint from the Panel of Arbitrators an *ad hoc* Committee of three persons. None of the members of the Committee shall have been a member of the Tribunal which rendered the award, shall be of the same nationality as any such member, shall be a national of the State party to the dispute or of the State whose national is a party to the dispute, shall have been designated to the Panel of Arbitrators by either of those States, or shall have acted as a conciliator in the same dispute. The Committee shall have the authority to annul the award or any part thereof on any of the grounds set forth in paragraph (1).

(4) The provisions of Articles 41–45, 48, 49, 53 and 54, and of Chapters VI and VII shall apply *mutatis mutandis* to proceedings before the Committee.

(5) The Committee may, if it considers that the circumstances so require, stay enforcement of the award pending its decision. If the applicant requests a stay of enforcement of the award in his application, enforcement shall be stayed provisionally until the Committee rules on such request.

(6) If the award is annulled the dispute shall, at the request of either party, be submitted to a new Tribunal constituted in accordance with Section 2 of this Chapter.

SECTION 6. RECOGNITION AND ENFORCEMENT OF THE AWARD

Article 53. (1) The award shall be binding on the parties and shall not be subject to any appeal or to any other remedy except those provided for in this Convention. Each party shall abide by and comply with the terms of the award except to the extent that enforcement shall have been stayed pursuant to the relevant provisions of this Convention.

(2) For the purposes of this Section, "award" shall include any decision interpreting, revising or annulling such award pursuant to Articles 50, 51 or 52.

Article 54. (1) Each Contracting State shall recognize an award rendered pursuant to this Convention as binding and enforce the pecuniary obligations imposed by that award within its territories as if it were a final judgment of a court in that State. A Contracting State with a federal constitution may enforce such an award in or through its federal courts and may provide that such courts shall treat the award as if it were a final judgment of the courts of a constituent state.

(2) A party seeking recognition or enforcement in the territories of a Contracting State shall furnish to a competent court or other authority which such State shall have designated for this purpose a copy of the award certified by the Secretary-General. Each Contracting State shall notify the Secretary-General of the designation of the competent court or other authority for this purpose and of any subsequent change in such designation.

(3) Execution of the award shall be governed by the laws concerning the execution of judgments in force in the State in whose territories such execution is sought.

Article 55. Nothing in Article 54 shall be construed as derogating from the law in force in any Contracting State relating to immunity of that State or of any foreign State from execution.

CHAPTER V. REPLACEMENT AND DISQUALIFICATION OF CONCILIATORS AND ARBITRATORS.

Article 56. (1) After a Commission or a Tribunal has been constituted and proceedings have begun, its composition shall remain unchanged; provided, however, that if a conciliator or an arbitrator should die, become incapacitated, or resign, the resulting vacancy shall be filled in accordance with the provisions of Section 2 of Chapter III or Section 2 of Chapter IV.

* * *

Article 57. A party may propose to a Commission or Tribunal the disqualification of any of its members on account of any fact indicating a manifest lack of the qualities required by paragraph (1) of Article 14. A party to arbitration proceedings may, in addition, propose the disqualification of an arbitrator on the ground that he was ineligible for appointment to the Tribunal under Section 2 of Chapter IV.

* * *

4.5 RESOLUTION ON PERMANENT SOVEREIGNTY OVER NATURAL RESOURCES.[a] Adopted by the U.N. General Assembly, Dec. 17, 1973. U.N.G.A. Res. 3171 (XXVIII); 28 U.N. GAOR. Supp. (No. 30) 52, U.N. Doc. A/9400 (1973)

The General Assembly,

Reiterating that the inalienable right of each State to the full exercise of national sovereignty over its natural resources has been repeatedly recognized by the international community in numerous resolutions of various organs of the United Nations,

Reiterating also that an intrinsic condition of the exercise of the sovereignty of every State is that it be exercised fully and effectively over all the natural resources of the State, whether found on land or in the sea,

Reaffirming the inviolable principle that every country has the right to adopt the economic and social system which it deems most favourable to its development,

Recalling its resolutions 1803 (XVII) of 14 December 1962, 2158 (XXI) of 25 November 1966, 2386 (XXIII) of 19 November 1968, 2625 (XXV) of 24 October 1970, 2692 (XXV) of 11 December 1970 and 3016 (XXVII) of 18 December 1972, and Security Council resolution 330 (1973) of 21 March 1973, which relate to permanent sovereignty over natural resources,

Recalling, in particular, the Declaration on Principles of International Law concerning Friendly Relations and Co-operation among States in accordance with the Charter of the United Nations, which proclaims that no State may use or encourage the use of economic, political or any other type of measures to coerce another State in order to obtain from it the subordination of the exercise of its sovereign rights and to secure from it advantages of any kind,

Considering that the full exercise by each State of sovereignty over its natural resources is an essential condition for achieving the objectives and targets of the Second United Nations Development Decade, and that this exercise requires that action by States aimed at achieving a better utilization and use of those resources must cover all stages, from exploration to marketing,

Taking note of section VII of the Economic Declaration adopted by the Fourth Conference of Heads of State or Government of Non–Aligned Countries, held at Algiers from 5 to 9 September 1973,

Taking note also of the report of the Secretary–General on permanent sovereignty over natural resources,

1. *Strongly reaffirms* the inalienable rights of States to permanent sovereignty over all their natural resources, on land within their international boundaries as well as those in the sea-bed and the subsoil thereof within their national jurisdiction and in the superjacent waters;

2. *Supports resolutely* the efforts of the developing countries and of the peoples of the territories under colonial and racial domination and foreign occupation in their struggle to regain effective control over their natural resources;

3. *Affirms* that the application of the principle of nationalization carried out by States, as an expression of their sovereignty in order to safeguard their natural resources, implies that each State is entitled to determine the amount of possible compensation and the mode of payment, and that any disputes which might arise

a. *See also* Basic Document 4.3, *supra*, and Basic Document 4.8, *infra*.

should be settled in accordance with the national legislation of each State carrying out such measures;

4. *Deplores* acts of States which use force, armed aggression, economic coercion or any other illegal or improper means in resolving disputes concerning the exercise of the sovereign rights mentioned in paragraphs ?? to 3 above;

5. *Re-emphasizes* that actions, measures or legislative regulations by States aimed at coercing, directly or indirectly, other States or peoples engaged in the reorganization of their internal structure or in the exercise of their sovereign rights over their natural resources, both on land and in their coastal waters, are in violation of the Charter of the United Nations and of the Declaration contained in General Assembly resolution 2625 (XXV) and contradict the targets, objectives and policy measures of the International Development Strategy for the Second United Nations Development Decade, and that to persist therein could constitute a threat to international peace and security;

6. *Emphasizes* the duty of all States to refrain in their international relations from military, political, economic or any other form of coercion aimed against the territorial integrity of any State and the exercise of its national jurisdiction;

7. *Recognizes* that, as stressed in Economic and Social Council resolution 1737 (LIV) of 4 May 1973, one of the most effective ways in which the developing countries can protect their natural resources is to establish, promote or strengthen machinery for co-operation among them which has as its main purpose to concert pricing policies, to improve conditions of access to markets, to co-ordinate production policies and, thus, to guarantee the full exercise of sovereignty by developing countries over their natural resources;

* * *

4.6 DECLARATION ON THE ESTABLISHMENT OF A NEW ECONOMIC ORDER.[a] Adopted by the U.N. General Assembly, May 1, 1974. U.N.G.A. Res. 3201 (S–VI), 6 (Special) U.N. GAOR, Supp. (No. 1) 3, U.N. Doc. A/9559 (1974), *reprinted in* 13 I.L.M. 715 (1974)

We, the Members of the United Nations,

Having convened a special session of the General Assembly to study for the first time the problems of raw materials and development, devoted to the consideration of the most important economic problems facing the world community,

Bearing in mind the spirit, purposes and principles of the Charter of the United Nations to promote the economic advancement and social progress of all peoples,

Solemnly proclaim our united determination to work urgently for the establishment of a new international economic order based on equity, sovereign equality, interdependence, common interest and co-operation among all States, irrespective of their economic and social systems which shall correct inequalities and redress existing injustices, make it possible to eliminate the widening gap between the developed and the developing countries and ensure steadily accelerating economic and social development and peace and justice for present and future generations, and, to that end, declare:

1. The greatest and most significant achievement during the last decades has been the independence from colonial and alien domination of a large number of peoples and nations which has enabled them to become members of the community of free peoples. Technological progress has also been made in all spheres of economic activities in the last three decades, thus providing a solid potential for improving the well-being of all peoples. However, the remaining vestiges of alien and colonial domination, foreign occupation, racial discrimination, *apartheid* and neo-colonialism in all its forms continue to be among the greatest obstacles to the full emancipation and progress of the developing countries and all the peoples involved. The benefits of technological progress are not shared equitably by all members of the international community. The developing countries, which constitute 70 per cent of the world's population, account for only 30 per cent of the world's income. It has proved impossible to achieve an even and balanced development of the international community under the existing international economic order. The gap between the developed and the developing countries continues to widen in a system which was established at a time when most of the developing countries did not even exist as independent States and which perpetuates inequality.

2. The present international economic order is in direct conflict with current developments in international political and economic relations. Since 1970, the world economy has experienced a series of grave crises which have had severe repercussions, especially on the developing countries because of their generally greater vulnerability to external economic impulses. The developing world has become a powerful factor that makes its influence felt in all fields of international activity. These irreversible changes in the relationship of forces in the world necessitate the active, full and equal participation of the developing countries in the formulation and application of all decisions that concern the international community.

3. All these changes have thrust into prominence the reality of interdependence of all the members of the world community. Current events have brought

a. *See also* Basic Documents 4.7 and 4.8, *infra*.

into sharp focus the realization that the interests of the developed countries and those of the developing countries can no longer be isolated from each other, that there is a close interrelationship between the prosperity of the developed countries and the growth and development of the developing countries, and that the prosperity of the international community as a whole depends upon the prosperity of its constituent parts. International co-operation for development is the shared goal and common duty of all countries. Thus the political, economic and social well-being of present and future generations depends more than ever on co-operation between all the members of the international community on the basis of sovereign equality and the removal of the disequilibrium that exists between them.

4. The new international economic order should be founded on full respect for the following principles:

(a) Sovereign equality of States, self-determination of all peoples, inadmissibility of the acquisition of territories by force, territorial integrity and non-interference in the internal affairs of other States;

(b) The broadest co-operation of all the States members of the international community, based on equity, whereby the prevailing disparities in the world may be banished and prosperity secured for all;

(c) Full and effective participation on the basis of equality of all countries in the solving of world economic problems in the common interest of all countries, bearing in mind the necessity to ensure the accelerated development of all the developing countries, while devoting particular attention to the adoption of special measures in favour of the least developed, land-locked and island developing countries as well as those developing countries most seriously affected by economic crises and natural calamities, without losing sight of the interests of other developing countries;

(d) The right of every country to adopt the economic and social system that it deems the most appropriate for its own development and not to be subjected to discrimination of any kind as a result;

(e) Full permanent sovereignty of every State over its natural resources and all economic activities. In order to safeguard these resources, each State is entitled to exercise effective control over them and their exploitation with means suitable to its own situation, including the right to nationalization or transfer of ownership to its nationals, this right being an expression of the full permanent sovereignty of the State. No State may be subjected to economic, political or any other type of coercion to prevent the free and full exercise of this inalienable right;

(f) The right of all States, territories and peoples under foreign occupation, alien and colonial domination or *apartheid* to restitution and full compensation for the exploitation and depletion of, and damages to, the natural resources and all other resources of those States, territories and peoples;

(g) Regulation and supervision of the activities of transnational corporations by taking measures in the interest of the national economies of the countries where such transnational corporations operate on the basis of the full sovereignty of those countries;

(h) The right of the developing countries and the peoples of territories under colonial and racial domination and foreign occupation to achieve their liberation and to regain effective control over their natural resources and economic activities;

(i) The extending of assistance to developing countries, peoples and territories which are under colonial and alien domination, foreign occupation, racial discrimination or *apartheid* or are subjected to economic, political or any other type of coercive measures to obtain from them the subordination of the exercise of their sovereign rights and to secure from them advantages of any kind, and to neocolonialism in all its forms, and which have established or are endeavouring to establish effective control over their natural resources and economic activities that have been or are still under foreign control;

(j) Just and equitable relationship between the prices of raw materials, primary commodities, manufactured and semi-manufactured goods exported by developing countries and the prices of raw materials, primary commodities, manufactures, capital goods and equipment imported by them with the aim of bringing about sustained improvement in their unsatisfactory terms of trade and the expansion of the world economy;

(k) Extension of active assistance to developing countries by the whole international community, free of any political or military conditions;

(*l*) Ensuring that one of the main aims of the reformed international monetary system shall be the promotion of the development of the developing countries and the adequate flow of real resources to them;

(m) Improving the competitiveness of natural materials facing competition from synthetic substitutes;

(n) Preferential and non-reciprocal treatment for developing countries, wherever feasible, in all fields of international economic co-operation whenever possible;

(*o*) Securing favourable conditions for the transfer of financial resources to developing countries;

(p) Giving to the developing countries access to the achievements of modern science and technology, and promoting the transfer of technology and the creation of indigenous technology for the benefit of the developing countries in forms and in accordance with procedures which are suited to their economies;

(q) The need for all States to put an end to the waste of natural resources, including food products;

(r) The need for developing countries to concentrate all their resources for the cause of development;

(s) The strengthening, through individual and collective actions, of mutual economic, trade, financial and technical co-operation among the developing countries, mainly on a preferential basis;

(t) Facilitating the role which producers' associations may play within the framework of international co-operation and, in pursuance of their aims, *inter alia* assisting in the promotion of sustained growth of the world economy and accelerating the development of developing countries.

5. The unanimous adoption of the International Development Strategy for the Second United Nations Development Decade was an important step in the promotion of international economic co-operation on a just and equitable basis. The accelerated implementation of obligations and commitments assumed by the international community within the framework of the Strategy, particularly those concerning imperative development needs of developing countries, would contribute significantly to the fulfilment of the aims and objectives of the present Declaration.

6. The United Nations as a universal organization should be capable of dealing with problems of international economic co-operation in a comprehensive manner and ensuring equally the interests of all countries. It must have an even greater role in the establishment of a new international economic order. The Charter of Economic Rights and Duties of States, for the preparation of which the present Declaration will provide an additional source of inspiration, will constitute a significant contribution in this respect. All the States Members of the United Nations are therefore called upon to exert maximum efforts with a view to securing the implementation of the present Declaration, which is one of the principal guarantees for the creation of better conditions for all peoples to reach a life worthy of human dignity.

7. The present Declaration on the Establishment of a New International Economic Order shall be one of the most important bases of economic relations between all peoples and all nations.

4.7 PROGRAMME OF ACTION ON THE ESTABLISHMENT OF A NEW INTERNATIONAL ECONOMIC ORDER.[a] Adopted by the U.N. General Assembly, May 1, 1974. U.N.G.A. Res. 3202 (S–VI), 6 (Special) U.N. GAOR, Supp. (No. 1) 5, U.N. Doc. A/9559 (1974), *reprinted in* 13 I.L.M. 720 (1974)

INTRODUCTION

1. In view of the continuing severe economic imbalance in the relations between developed and developing countries, and in the context of the constant and continuing aggravation of the imbalance of the economies of the developing countries and the consequent need for the mitigation of their current economic difficulties, urgent and effective measures need to be taken by the international community to assist the developing countries, while devoting particular attention to the least developed, land-locked and island developing countries and those developing countries most seriously affected by economic crises and natural calamities leading to serious retardation of development processes.

2. With a view to ensuring the application of the Declaration on the Establishment of a New International Economic Order, it will be necessary to adopt and implement within a specified period a programme of action of unprecedented scope and to bring about maximum economic co-operation and understanding among all States, particularly between developed and developing countries, based on the principles of dignity and sovereign equality.

I. FUNDAMENTAL PROBLEMS OF RAW MATERIALS AND PRIMARY COMMODITIES AS RELATED TO TRADE AND DEVELOPMENT

1. Raw Materials

All efforts should be made:

(a) To put an end to all forms of foreign occupation, racial discrimination, *apartheid,* colonial, neocolonial and alien domination and exploitation through the exercise of permanent sovereignty over natural resources;

(b) To take measures for the recovery, exploitation, development, marketing and distribution of natural resources, particularly of developing countries, to serve their national interests, to promote collective self-reliance among them and to strengthen mutually beneficial international economic co-operation with a view to bringing about the accelerated development of developing countries;

(c) To facilitate the functioning and to further the aims of producers' associations, including their joint marketing arrangements, orderly commodity trading, improvement in the export income of producing developing countries and in their terms of trade, and sustained growth of the world economy for the benefit of all;

(d) To evolve a just and equitable relationship between the prices of raw materials, primary commodities, manufactured and semi-manufactured goods exported by developing countries and the prices of raw materials, primary commodities, food, manufactured and semi-manufactured goods and capital equipment imported by them, and to work for a link between the prices of exports of developing countries and the prices of their imports from developed countries;

a. *See also* Basic Document 4.6, *supra*, and Basic Document 4.8, *infra*.

(e) To take measures to reverse the continued trend of stagnation or decline in the real price of several commodities exported by developing countries, despite a general rise in commodity prices, resulting in a decline in the export earnings of these developing countries;

(f) To take measures to expand the markets for natural products in relation to synthetics, taking into account the interests of the developing countries, and to utilize fully the ecological advantages of these products;

(g) To take measures to promote the processing of raw materials in the producer developing countries.

2. *Food*

All efforts should be made:

(a) To take full account of specific problems of developing countries, particularly in times of food shortages, in the international efforts connected with the food problem;

(b) To take into account that, owing to lack of means, some developing countries have vast potentialities of unexploited or underexploited land which, if reclaimed and put into practical use, would contribute considerably to the solution of the food crisis;

(c) By the international community to undertake concrete and speedy measures with a view to arresting desertification, salination and damage by locusts or any other similar phenomenon involving several developing countries, particularly in Africa, and gravely affecting the agricultural production capacity of these countries, and also to assist the developing countries affected by such phenomenon to develop the affected zones with a view to contributing to the solution of their food problems;

(d) To refrain from damaging or deteriorating natural resources and food resources, especially those derived from the sea, by preventing pollution and taking appropriate steps to protect and reconstitute those resources;

(e) By developed countries, in evolving their policies relating to production, stocks, imports and exports of food, to take full account of the interests of:

(i) Developing importing countries which cannot afford high prices for their imports;

(ii) Developing exporting countries which need increased market opportunities for their exports;

(f) To ensure that developing countries can import the necessary quantity of food without undue strain on their foreign exchange resources and without unpredictable deterioration in their balance of payments, and, in this context, that special measures are taken in respect of the least developed, land-locked and island developing countries as well as those developing countries most seriously affected by economic crises and natural calamities;

(g) To ensure that concrete measures to increase food production and storage facilities in developing countries are introduced, *inter alia,* by ensuring an increase in all available essential inputs, including fertilizers, from developed countries on favorable terms;

(h) To promote exports of food products of developing countries through just and equitable arrangements, *inter alia,* by the progressive elimination of such protective and other measures as constitute unfair competition.

3. *General Trade*

All efforts should be made:

(a) To take the following measures for the amelioration of terms of trade of developing countries and concrete steps to eliminate chronic trade deficits of developing countries:

(i) Fulfilment of relevant commitments already undertaken in the United Nations Conference on Trade and Development and in the International Development Strategy for the Second United Nations Development Decade;

(ii) Improved access to markets in developed countries through the progressive removal of tariff and non-tariff barriers and of restrictive business practices;

(iii) Expeditious formulation of commodity agreements where appropriate, in order to regulate as necessary and to stabilize the world markets for raw materials and primary commodities;

(iv) Preparation of an over-all integrated programme, setting out guidelines and taking into account the current work in this field, for a comprehensive range of commodities of export interest to developing countries;

(v) Where products of developing countries compete with the domestic production in developed countries, each developed country should facilitate the expansion of imports from developing countries and provide a fair and reasonable opportunity to the developing countries to share in the growth of the market;

(vi) When the importing developed countries derive receipts from customs duties, taxes and other protective measures applied to imports of these products, consideration should be given to the claim of the developing countries that these receipts should be reimbursed in full to the exporting developing countries or devoted to providing additional resources to meet their development needs;

(vii) Developed countries should make appropriate adjustments in their economies so as to facilitate the expansion and diversification of imports from developing countries and thereby permit a rational, just and equitable international division of labour;

(viii) Setting up general principles for pricing policy for exports of commodities of developing countries, with a view to rectifying and achieving satisfactory terms of trade for them;

(ix) Until satisfactory terms of trade are achieved for all developing countries, consideration should be given to alternative means, including improved compensatory financing schemes for meeting the development needs of the developing countries concerned;

(x) Implementation, improvement and enlargement of the generalized system of preferences for exports of agricultural primary commodities, manufactures and semi-manufactures from developing to developed countries and consideration of its extension to commodities, including those which are processed or semi-processed; developing countries which are or will be sharing their existing tariff advantages in some developed countries as the result of the introduction and eventual enlargement of the generalized system of preferences should, as a matter of urgency, be granted new openings in the markets of other developed countries which should offer them export opportunities that at least compensate for the sharing of those advantages;

(xi) The setting up of buffer stocks within the framework of commodity arrangements and their financing by international financial institutions, wherever necessary, by the developed countries and, when they are able to do so, by the developing countries, with the aim of favouring the producer developing and consumer developing countries and of contributing to the expansion of world trade as a whole;

(xii) In cases where natural materials can satisfy the requirements of the market, new investment for the expansion of the capacity to produce synthetic materials and substitutes should not be made;

(b) To be guided by the principles of non-reciprocity and preferential treatment of developing countries in multilateral trade negotiations between developed and developing countries, and to seek sustained and additional benefits for the international trade of developing countries, so as to achieve a substantial increase in their foreign exchange earnings, diversification of their exports and acceleration of the rate of their economic growth.

4. *Transportation and Insurance*

All efforts should be made:

(a) To promote an increasing and equitable participation of developing countries in the world shipping tonnage;

(b) To arrest and reduce the ever-increasing freight rates in order to reduce the costs of imports to, and exports from, the developing countries;

(c) To minimize the cost of insurance and reinsurance for developing countries and to assist the growth of domestic insurance and reinsurance markets in developing countries and the establishment to this end, where appropriate, of institutions in these countries or at the regional level;

(d) To ensure the early implementation of the code of conduct for liner conferences;

(e) To take urgent measures to increase the import and export capability of the least developed countries and to offset the disadvantages of the adverse geographic situation of land-locked countries, particularly with regard to their transportation and transit costs, as well as developing island countries in order to increase their trading ability;

(f) By the developed countries to refrain from imposing measures or implementing policies designed to prevent the importation, at equitable prices, of commodities from the developing countries or from frustrating the implementation of legitimate measures and policies adopted by the developing countries in order to improve prices and encourage the export of such commodities.

II. International Monetary System and Financing of the Development of Developing Countries

1. *Objectives*

All efforts should be made to reform the international monetary system with, *inter alia,* the following objectives:

(a) Measures to check the inflation already experienced by the developed countries, to prevent it from being transferred to developing countries and to study and devise possible arrangements within the International Monetary Fund to mitigate the effects of inflation in developed countries on the economies of developing countries;

(b) Measures to eliminate the instability of the international monetary system, in particular the uncertainty of the exchange rates, especially as it affects adversely the trade in commodities;

(c) Maintenance of the real value of the currency reserves of the developing countries by preventing their erosion from inflation and exchange rate depreciation of reserve currencies;

(d) Full and effective participation of developing countries in all phases of decision-making for the formulation of an equitable and durable monetary system and adequate participation of developing countries in all bodies entrusted with this reform and, particularly, in the proposed Council of Governors of the International Monetary Fund;

(e) Adequate and orderly creation of additional liquidity with particular regard to the needs of the developing countries through the additional allocation of special drawing rights based on the concept of world liquidity needs to be appropriately revised in the light of the new international environment; any creation of international liquidity should be made through international multilateral mechanisms;

(f) Early establishment of a link between special drawing rights and additional development financing in the interest of developing countries, consistent with the monetary characteristics of special drawing rights;

(g) Review by the International Monetary Fund of the relevant provisions in order to ensure effective participation by developing countries in the decision-making process;

(h) Arrangements to promote an increasing net transfer of real resources from the developed to the developing countries;

(i) Review of the methods of operation of the International Monetary Fund, in particular the terms for both credit repayments and "stand-by" arrangements, the system of compensatory financing, and the terms of the financing of commodity buffer stocks, so as to enable the developing countries to make more effective use of them.

2. Measures

All efforts should be made to take the following urgent measures to finance the development of developing countries and to meet the balance-of-payment crises in the developing world:

(a) Implementation at an accelerated pace by the developed countries of the time-bound programme, as already laid down in the International Development Strategy for the Second United Nations Development Decade, for the net amount of financial resource transfers to developing countries; increase in the official component of the net amount of financial resource transfers to developing countries so as to meet and even to exceed the target of the Strategy;

(b) International financing institutions should effectively play their role as development financing banks without discrimination on account of the political or economic system of any member country, assistance being untied;

(c) More effective participation by developing countries, whether recipients or contributors, in the decision-making process in the competent organs of the International Bank for Reconstruction and Development and the International Development Association, through the establishment of a more equitable pattern of voting rights;

(d) Exemption, wherever possible, of the developing countries from all import and capital outflow controls imposed by the developed countries;

(e) Promotion of foreign investment, both public and private, from developed to developing countries in accordance with the needs and requirements in sectors of their economics as determined by the recipient countries;

(f) Appropriate urgent measures, including international action, should be taken to mitigate adverse consequences for the current and future development of developing countries arising from the burden of external debt contracted on hard terms;

(g) Debt renegotiation on a case-by-case basis with a view to concluding agreements on debt cancellation, moratorium, rescheduling or interest subsidization;

(h) International financial institutions should take into account the special situation of each developing country in reorienting their lending policies to suit these urgent needs; there is also need for improvement in practices of international financial institutions in regard to, *inter alia,* development financing and international monetary problems;

(i) Appropriate steps should be taken to give priority to the least developed, land-locked and island developing countries and to the countries most seriously affected by economic crises and natural calamities, in the availability of loans for development purposes which should include more favourable terms and conditions.

III. Industrialization

All efforts should be made by the international community to take measures to encourage the industrialization of the developing countries, and to this end:

(a) The developed countries should respond favourably, within the framework of their official aid as well as international financial institutions, to the requests of developing countries for the financing of industrial projects;

(b) The developed countries should encourage investors to finance industrial production projects, particularly export-oriented production, in developing countries, in agreement with the latter and within the context of their laws and regulations;

(c) With a view to bringing about a new international economic structure which should increase the share of the developing countries in world industrial production, the developed countries and the agencies of the United Nations system, in co-operation with the developing countries, should contribute to setting up new industrial capacities including raw materials and commodity-transforming facilities as a matter of priority in the developing countries that produce those raw materials and commodities;

(d) The international community should continue and expand, with the aid of the developed countries and the international institutions, the operational and instruction-oriented technical assistance programmes, including vocational training and management development of national personnel of the developing countries, in the light of their special development requirements.

IV. Transfer of Technology

All efforts should be made:

(a) To formulate an international code of conduct for the transfer of technology corresponding to needs and conditions prevalent in developing countries;

(b) To give access on improved terms to modern technology and to adapt that technology, as appropriate, to specific economic, social and ecological conditions and varying stages of development in developing countries;

(c) To expand significantly the assistance from developed to developing countries in research and development programmes and in the creation of suitable indigenous technology;

(d) To adapt commercial practices governing transfer of technology to the requirements of the developing countries and to prevent abuse of the rights of sellers;

(e) To promote international co-operation in research and development in exploration and exploitation, conservation and the legitimate utilization of natural resources and all sources of energy.

In taking the above measures, the special needs of the least developed and land-locked countries should be borne in mind.

V. Regulation and Control Over the Activities of Transnational Corporations

All efforts should be made to formulate, adopt and implement an international code of conduct for transnational corporations:

(a) To prevent interference in the internal affairs of the countries where they operate and their collaboration with racist régimes and colonial administrations;

(b) To regulate their activities in host countries, to eliminate restrictive business practices and to conform to the national development plans and objectives of developing countries, and in this context facilitate, as necessary, the review and revision of previously concluded arrangements;

(c) To bring about assistance, transfer of technology and management skills to developing countries on equitable and favourable terms;

(d) To regulate the repatriation of the profits accruing from their operations, taking into account the legitimate interests of all parties concerned;

(e) To promote reinvestment of their profits in developing countries.

VI. Charter of Economic Rights and Duties of States

The Charter of Economic Rights and Duties of States, the draft of which is being prepared by a working group of the United Nations and which the General Assembly has already expressed the intention of adopting at its twenty-ninth regular session, shall constitute an effective instrument towards the establishment of a new system of international economic relations based on equity, sovereign equality, and interdependence of the interests of developed and developing countries. It is therefore of vital importance that the aforementioned Charter be adopted by the General Assembly at its twenty-ninth session.

VII. Promotion of Co-operation Among Developing Countries

1. Collective self-reliance and growing co-operation among developing countries will further strengthen their role in the new international economic order. Developing countries, with a view to expanding co-operation at the regional, subregional and interregional levels, should take further steps, *inter alia:*

(a) To support the establishment and/or improvement of an appropriate mechanism to defend the prices of their exportable commodities and to improve access to and stabilize markets for them. In this context the increasingly effective mobilization by the whole group of oil-exporting countries of their natural resources for the benefit of their economic development is to be welcomed. At the same time there is the paramount need for co-operation among the developing countries in evolving urgently and in a spirit of solidarity all possible means to assist developing countries to cope with the immediate problems resulting from this legitimate and perfectly justified action. The measures already taken in this regard are a positive indication of the evolving co-operation between developing countries;

(b) To protect their inalienable right to permanent sovereignty over their natural resources;

(c) To promote, establish or strengthen economic integration at the regional and subregional levels;

(d) To increase considerably their imports from other developing countries;

(e) To ensure that no developing country accords to imports from developed countries more favourable treatment than that accorded to imports from developing countries. Taking into account the existing international agreements, current limitations and possibilities and also their future evolution, preferential treatment should be given to the procurement of import requirements from other developing countries. Wherever possible, preferential treatment should be given to imports from developing countries and the exports of those countries;

(f) To promote close co-operation in the fields of finance, credit relations and monetary issues, including the development of credit relations on a preferential basis and on favourable terms;

(g) To strengthen efforts which are already being made by developing countries to utilize available financial resources for financing development in the developing countries through investment, financing of export-oriented and emergency projects and other long-term assistance;

(h) To promote and establish effective instruments of co-operation in the fields of industry, science and technology, transport, shipping and mass communication media.

2. Developed countries should support initiatives in the regional, subregional and interregional co-operation of developing countries through the extension of financial and technical assistance by more effective and concrete actions, particularly in the field of commercial policy.

VIII. Assistance in the Exercise of Permanent Sovereignty of States Over Natural Resources

All efforts should be made:

(a) To defeat attempts to prevent the free and effective exercise of the rights of every State to full and permanent sovereignty over its natural resources;

(b) To ensure that competent agencies of the United Nations system meet requests for assistance from developing countries in connexion with the operation of nationalized means of production.

IX. Strengthening the Role of the United Nations System in the Field of International Economic Co-operation

1. In furtherance of the objectives of the International Development Strategy for the Second United Nations Development Decade and in accordance with the aims and objectives of the Declaration on the Establishment of a New International Economic Order, all Member States pledge to make full use of the United Nations system in the implementation of the present Programme of Action, jointly adopted by them, in working for the establishment of a new international economic order and thereby strengthening the role of the United Nations in the field of world-wide co-operation for economic and social development.

2. The General Assembly of the United Nations shall conduct an over-all review of the implementation of the Programme of Action as a priority item. All the activities of the United Nations system to be undertaken under the Programme of Action as well as those already planned, such as the World Population Conference, 1974, the World Food Conference, the Second General Conference of the United Nations Industrial Development Organization and the mid-term review and appraisal

of the International Development Strategy for the Second United Nations Development Decade should be so directed as to enable the special session of the General Assembly on development, called for under Assembly resolution 3172 (XXVIII) of 17 December 1973, to make its full contribution to the establishment of the new international economic order. All Member States are urged, jointly and individually, to direct their efforts and policies towards the success of that special session.

3. The Economic and Social Council shall define the policy framework and co-ordinate the activities of all organizations, institutions and subsidiary bodies within the United Nations system which shall be entrusted with the task of implementing the present Programme of Action. In order to enable the Economic and Social Council to carry out its tasks effectively:

(a) All organizations, institutions and subsidiary bodies concerned within the United Nations system shall submit to the Economic and Social Council progress reports on the implementation of the Programme of Action within their respective fields of competence as often as necessary, but not less than once a year;

(b) The Economic and Social Council shall examine the progress reports as a matter of urgency, to which end it may be convened, as necessary, in special session or, if need be, may function continuously. It shall draw the attention of the General Assembly to the problems and difficulties arising in connexion with the implementation of the Programme of Action.

4. All organizations, institutions, subsidiary bodies and conferences of the United Nations system are entrusted with the implementation of the Programme of Action. The activities of the United Nations Conference on Trade and Development, as set forth in General Assembly resolution 1995 (XIX) of 30 December 1964, should be strengthened for the purpose of following in collaboration with other competent organizations the development of international trade in raw materials throughout the world.

5. Urgent and effective measures should be taken to review the lending policies of international financial institutions, taking into account the special situation of each developing country, to suit urgent needs, to improve the practices of these institutions in regard to, *inter alia,* development financing and international monetary problems, and to ensure more effective participation by developing countries—whether recipients or contributors—in the decision-making process through appropriate revision of the pattern of voting rights.

6. The developed countries and others in a position to do so should contribute substantially to the various organizations, programmes and funds established within the United Nations system for the purpose of accelerating economic and social development in developing countries.

* * *

X. SPECIAL PROGRAMME

The General Assembly adopts the following Special Programme, including particularly emergency measures to mitigate the difficulties of the developing countries most seriously affected by economic crisis, bearing in mind the particular problem of the least developed and land-locked countries:

The General Assembly,

Taking into account the following considerations:

(a) The sharp increase in the prices of their essential imports such as food, fertilizers, energy products, capital goods, equipment and services, including transportation and transit costs, has gravely exacerbated the increasingly adverse terms of trade of a number of developing countries, added to the burden of their foreign debt and, cumulatively, created a situation which, if left untended, will make it impossible for them to finance their essential imports and development and result in a further deterioration in the levels and conditions of life in these countries. The present crisis is the outcome of all the problems that have accumulated over the years: in the field of trade, in monetary reform, the world-wide inflationary situation, inadequacy and delay in provision of financial assistance and many other similar problems in the economic and developmental fields. In facing the crisis, this complex situation must be borne in mind so as to ensure that the Special Programme adopted by the international community provides emergency relief and timely assistance to the most seriously affected countries. Simultaneously, steps are being taken to resolve these outstanding problems through a fundamental restructuring of the world economic system, in order to allow these countries while solving the present difficulties to reach an acceptable level of development.

(b) The special measures adopted to assist the most seriously affected countries must encompass not only the relief which they require on an emergency basis to maintain their import requirements, but also, beyond that, steps to consciously promote the capacity of these countries to produce and earn more. Unless such a comprehensive approach is adopted, there is every likelihood that the difficulties of the most seriously affected countries may be perpetuated. Nevertheless, the first and most pressing task of the international community is to enable these countries to meet the shortfall in their balance-of-payments positions. But this must be simultaneously supplemented by additional development assistance to maintain and thereafter accelerate their rate of economic development.

(c) The countries which have been most seriously affected are precisely those which are at the greatest disadvantage in the world economy: the least developed, the land-locked and other low-income developing countries as well as other developing countries whose economies have been seriously dislocated as a result of the present economic crisis, natural calamities, and foreign aggression and occupation. An indication of the countries thus affected, the level of the impact on their economies and the kind of relief and assistance they require can be assessed on the basis, *inter alia,* of the following criteria:

(i) Low *per capita* income as a reflection of relative poverty, low productivity, low level of technology and development;

(ii) Sharp increase in their import cost of essentials relative to export earnings;

(iii) High ratio of debt servicing to export earnings;

(iv) Insufficiency in export earnings, comparative inelasticity of export incomes and unavailability of exportable surplus;

(v) Low level of foreign exchange reserves or their inadequacy for requirements;

(vi) Adverse impact of higher transportation and transit costs;

(vii) Relative importance of foreign trade in the development process.

(d) The assessment of the extent and nature of the impact on the economies of the most seriously affected countries must be made flexible, keeping in mind the present uncertainty in the world economy, the adjustment policies that may be adopted by the developed countries and the flow of capital and investment. Estimates of the payments situation and needs of these countries can be assessed and projected reliably only on the basis of their average performance over a number of years. Long-term projections, at this time, cannot but be uncertain.

(e) It is important that, in the special measures to mitigate the difficulties of the most seriously affected countries, all the developed countries as well as the developing countries, should contribute according to their level of development and the capacity and strength of their economies. It is notable that some developing countries, despite their own difficulties and development needs, have shown a willingness to play a concrete and helpful role in ameliorating the difficulties faced by the poorer developing countries. The various initiatives and measures taken recently by certain developing countries with adequate resources on a bilateral and multilateral basis to contribute to alleviating the difficulties of other developing countries are a reflection of their commitment to the principle of effective economic co-operation among developing countries.

(f) The response of the developed countries which have by far the greater capacity to assist the affected countries in overcoming their present difficulties must be commensurate with their responsibilities. Their assistance should be in addition to the presently available levels of aid. They should fulfil and if possible exceed the targets of the International Development Strategy for the Second United Nations Development Decade on financial assistance to the developing countries, especially that relating to official development assistance. They should also give serious consideration to the cancellation of the external debts of the most seriously affected countries. This would provide the simplest and quickest relief to the affected countries. Favourable consideration should also be given to debt moratorium and rescheduling. The current situation should not lead the industrialized countries to adopt what will ultimately prove to be a self-defeating policy aggravating the present crisis.

Recalling the constructive proposals made by His Imperial Majesty the Shahanshah of Iran and His Excellency Mr. Houari Boumediene, President of the People's Democratic Republic of Algeria.

1. *Decides* to launch a Special Programme to provide emergency relief and development assistance to the developing countries most seriously affected, as a matter of urgency, and for the period of time necessary, at least until the end of the Second United Nations Development Decade, to help them overcome their present difficulties and to achieve self-sustaining economic development;

2. *Decides* as a first step in the Special Programme to request the Secretary–General to launch an emergency operation to provide timely relief to the most seriously affected developing countries, as defined in subparagraph (*c*) above, with the aim of maintaining unimpaired essential imports for the duration of the coming twelve months and to invite the industrialized countries and other potential contributors to announce their contributions for emergency assistance, or intimate their intention to do so, by 15 June 1974 to be provided through bilateral or multilateral channels, taking into account the commitments and measures of assistance announced or already taken by some countries, and further requests the Secretary–General to report the progress of the emergency operation to the General Assembly at its twenty-ninth session, through the Economic and Social Council at its fifty-seventh session;

3. *Calls upon* the industrialized countries and other potential contributors to extend to the most seriously affected countries immediate relief and assistance which must be of an order of magnitude that is commensurate with the needs of these countries. Such assistance should be in addition to the existing level of aid and provided at a very early date to the maximum possible extent on a grant basis and, where not possible, on soft terms. The disbursement and relevant operational procedures and terms must reflect this exceptional situation. The assistance could be provided either through bilateral or multilateral channels, including such new institutions and facilities that have been or are to be set up. The special measures may include the following:

(a) Special arrangements on particularly favourable terms and conditions including possible subsidies for and assured supplies of essential commodities and goods;

(b) Deferred payments for all or part of imports of essential commodities and goods;

(c) Commodity assistance, including food aid, on a grant basis or deferred payments in local currencies, bearing in mind that this should not adversely affect the exports of developing countries;

(d) Long-term suppliers' credits on easy terms;

(e) Long-term financial assistance on concessionary terms;

(f) Drawings from special International Monetary Fund facilities on concessional terms;

(g) Establishment of a link between the creation of special drawing rights and development assistance, taking into account the additional financial requirements of the most seriously affected countries;

(h) Subsidies, provided bilaterally or multilaterally, for interest on funds available on commercial terms borrowed by the most seriously affected countries;

(i) Debt renegotiation on a case-by-case basis with a view to concluding agreements on debt cancellation, moratorium or rescheduling;

(j) Provision on more favourable terms of capital goods and technical assistance to accelerate the industrialization of the affected countries;

(k) Investment in industrial and development projects on favourable terms;

(*l*) Subsidizing the additional transit and transport costs, especially of the land-locked countries;

4. *Appeals* to the developed countries to consider favourably the cancellation, moratorium or rescheduling of the debts of the most seriously affected developing countries, on their request, as an important contribution to mitigating the grave and urgent difficulties of these countries;

5. *Decides* to establish a Special Fund under the auspices of the United Nations, through voluntary contributions from industrialized countries and other potential contributors, as a part of the Special Programme, to provide emergency relief and development assistance, which will commence its operations at the latest by 1 January 1975;

6. *Establishes* an *Ad Hoc* Committee on the Special Programme, composed of thirty-six Member States appointed by the President of the General Assembly, after appropriate consultations, bearing in mind the purposes of the Special Fund and its terms of reference:

(a) To make recommendations, *inter alia,* on the scope, machinery and modes of operation of the Special Fund, taking into account the need for:

(i) Equitable representation on its governing body;

(ii) Equitable distribution of its resources;

(iii) Full utilization of the services and facilities of existing international organizations;

(iv) The possibility of merging the United Nations Capital Development Fund with the operations of the Special Fund;

(v) A central monitoring body to oversee the various measures being taken both bilaterally and multilaterally;

and, to this end, bearing in mind the different ideas and proposals submitted at the sixth special session, including those put forward by Iran and those made at the 2208th plenary meeting, and the comments thereon, and the possibility of utilizing the Special Fund to provide an alternative channel for normal development assistance after the emergency period;

(b) To monitor, pending commencement of the operations of the Special Fund, the various measures being taken both bilaterally and multilaterally to assist the most seriously affected countries;

(c) To prepare, on the basis of information provided by the countries concerned and by appropriate agencies of the United Nations system, a broad assessment of:

(i) The magnitude of the difficulties facing the most seriously affected countries;

(ii) The kind and quantities of the commodities and goods essentially required by them;

(iii) Their need for financial assistance;

(iv) Their technical assistance requirements, including especially access to technology;

7. *Requests* the Secretary–General of the United Nations, the Secretary–General of the United Nations Conference on Trade and Development, the President of the International Bank for Reconstruction and Development, the Managing Director of the International Monetary Fund, the Administrator of the United Nations Development Programme and the heads of the other competent international organizations to assist the *Ad Hoc* Committee on the Special Programme in performing the functions assigned to it under paragraph 6 above, and to help, as appropriate, in the operations of the Special Fund;

8. *Requests* the International Monetary Fund to expedite decisions on:

(a) The establishment of an extended special facility with a view to enabling the most seriously affected developing countries to participate in it on favourable terms;

(b) The creation of special drawing rights and the early establishment of the link between their allocation and development financing;

(c) The establishment and operation of the proposed new special facility to extend credits and subsidize interest charges on commercial funds borrowed by Member States, bearing in mind the interests of the developing countries and especially the additional financial requirements of the most seriously affected countries;

9. *Requests* the World Bank Group and the International Monetary Fund to place their managerial, financial and technical services at the disposal of Governments contributing to emergency financial relief so as to enable them to assist without delay in channelling funds to the recipients, making such institutional and procedural changes as may be required;

10. *Invites* the United Nations Development Programme to take the necessary steps, particularly at the country level, to respond on an emergency basis to requests for additional assistance which it may be called upon to render within the framework of the Special Programme;

11. *Requests* the *Ad Hoc* Committee on the Special Programme to submit its report and recommendations to the Economic and Social Council at its fifty-seventh session and invites the Council, on the basis of its consideration of that report, to submit suitable recommendations to the General Assembly at its twenty-ninth session;

12. *Decides* to consider as a matter of high priority at its twenty-ninth session, within the framework of a new international economic order, the question of special measures for the most seriously affected countries.

4.8 CHARTER OF ECONOMIC RIGHTS AND DUTIES OF STATES.[a] Adopted by the U.N. General Assembly, Dec. 12, 1974. U.N.G.A.Res. 3281 (XXIX), 29 U.N. GAOR, Supp. (No. 31) 50, U.N.Doc. A/9631 (1975), *reprinted in* 14 I.L.M. 251 (1975)

PREAMBLE

THE GENERAL ASSEMBLY,

Reaffirming the fundamental purposes of the United Nations, in particular the maintenance of international peace and security, the development of friendly relations among nations and the achievement of international co-operation in solving international problems in the economic and social fields.

Affirming the need for strengthening international co-operation in these fields.

Reaffirming further the need for strengthening international co-operation for development.

Declaring that it is a fundamental purpose of the present Charter to promote the establishment of the new international economic order, based on equity, sovereign equality, interdependence, common interest and co-operation among all States, irrespective of their economic and social systems.

Desirous of contributing to the creation of conditions for:

(a) The attainment of wider prosperity among all countries and of higher standards of living for all peoples.

(b) The promotion by the entire international community of the economic and social progress of all countries, especially developing countries.

(c) The encouragement of co-operation, on the basis of mutual advantage and equitable benefits for all peace-loving States which are willing to carry out the provisions of the present Charter, in the economic, trade, scientific and technical fields, regardless of political, economic or social systems.

(d) The overcoming of main obstacles in the way of the economic development of the developing countries.

(e) The acceleration of the economic growth of developing countries with a view to bridging the economic gap between developing and developed countries.

(f) The protection, preservation and enhancement of the environment.

Mindful of the need to establish and maintain a just and equitable economic and social order through:

(a) The achievement of more rational and equitable international economic relations and the encouragement of structural changes in the world economy.

(b) The creation of conditions which permit the further expansion of trade and intensification of economic co-operation among all nations.

(c) The strengthening of the economic independence of developing countries.

(d) The establishment and promotion of international economic relations, taking into account the agreed differences in development of the developing countries and their specific needs.

Determined to promote collective economic security for development, in particular of the developing countries, with strict respect for the sovereign equality of each State and through the co-operation of the entire international community,

a. *See also* Basic Documents 4.6 and 4.7, *supra.*

Considering that genuine co-operation among States, based on joint consideration of and concerted action regarding international economic problems, is essential for fulfilling the international community's common desire to achieve a just and rational development of all parts of the world,

Stressing the importance of ensuring appropriate conditions for the conduct of normal economic relations among all States, irrespective of differences in social and economic systems, and for the full respect of the rights of all peoples, as well as strengthening instruments of international economic co-operation as means for the consolidation of peace for the benefit of all,

Convinced of the need to develop a system of international economic relations on the basis of sovereign equality, mutual and equitable benefit and the close interrelationship of the interests of all States,

Reiterating that the responsibility for the development of every country rests primarily upon itself but that concomitant and effective international co-operation is an essential factor for the full achievement of its own development goals,

Firmly convinced of the urgent need to evolve a substantially improved system of international economic relations,

Solemnly adopts the present Charter of Economic Rights and Duties of States.

CHAPTER I. FUNDAMENTALS OF INTERNATIONAL ECONOMIC RELATIONS

Economic as well as political and other relations among States shall be governed, *inter alia,* by the following principles:

(a) Sovereignty, territorial integrity and political independence of States;

(b) Sovereign equality of all States;

(c) Non-aggression;

(d) Non-intervention;

(e) Mutual and equitable benefit;

(f) Peaceful coexistence;

(g) Equal rights and self-determination of peoples;

(h) Peaceful settlement of disputes;

(i) Remedying of injustices which have been brought about by force and which deprive a nation of the natural means necessary for its normal development;

(j) Fulfilment in good faith of international obligations;

(k) Respect for human rights and fundamental freedoms;

(*l*) No attempt to seek hegemony and spheres of influence;

(m) Promotion of international social justice;

(n) International co-operation for development;

(*o*) Free access to and from the sea by land-locked countries within the framework of the above principles.

CHAPTER II. ECONOMIC RIGHTS AND DUTIES OF STATES

Article 1. Every State has the sovereign and inalienable right to choose its economic system as well as its political, social and cultural systems in accordance with the will of its people, without outside interference, coercion or threat in any form whatsoever.

Article 2. (1) Every State has and shall freely exercise full permanent sovereignty, including possession, use and disposal, over all its wealth, natural resources and economic activities.

(2) Each State has the right:

(a) To regulate and exercise authority over foreign investment within its national jurisdiction in accordance with its laws and regulations and in conformity with its national objectives and priorities. No State shall be compelled to grant preferential treatment to foreign investment;

(b) To regulate and supervise the activities of transnational corporations within its national jurisdiction and take measures to ensure that such activities comply with its laws, rules and regulations and conform with its economic and social policies. Transnational corporations shall not intervene in the internal affairs of a host State. Every State should, with full regard for its sovereign rights, co-operate with other States in the exercise of the right set forth in this subparagraph;

(c) To nationalize, expropriate or transfer ownership of foreign property, in which case appropriate compensation should be paid by the State adopting such measures, taking into account its relevant laws and regulations and all circumstances that the State considers pertinent. In any case where the question of compensation gives rise to a controversy, it shall be settled under the domestic law of the nationalizing State and by its tribunals, unless it is freely and mutually agreed by all States concerned that other peaceful means be sought on the basis of the sovereign equality of States and in accordance with the principle of free choice of means.

Article 3. In the exploitation of natural resources shared by two or more countries, each State must co-operate on the basis of a system of information and prior consultations in order to achieve optimum use of such resources without causing damage to the legitimate interest of others.

Article 4. Every State has the right to engage in international trade and other forms of economic co-operation irrespective of any differences in political, economic and social systems. No State shall be subjected to discrimination of any kind based solely on such differences. In the pursuit of international trade and other forms of economic co-operation, every State is free to choose the forms of organization of its foreign economic relations and to enter into bilateral and multilateral arrangements consistent with its international obligations and with the needs of international economic co-operation.

Article 5. All States have the right to associate in organizations of primary commodity producers in order to develop their national economies, to achieve stable financing for their development and, in pursuance of their aims, to assist in the promotion of sustained growth of the world economy, in particular accelerating the development of developing countries. Correspondingly all States have the duty to respect that right by refraining from applying economic and political measures that would limit it.

Article 6. It is the duty of States to contribute to the development of international trade of goods, particularly by means of arrangements and by the conclusion of long-term multilateral commodity agreements, where appropriate, and taking into account the interests of producers and consumers. All States share the responsibility to promote the regular flow and access of all commercial goods traded at stable, remunerative and equitable prices, thus contributing to the equitable development of the world economy, taking into account, in particular, the interests of developing countries.

Article 7. Every State has the primary responsibility to promote the economic, social and cultural development of its people. To this end, each State has the right and the responsibility to choose its means and goals of development, fully to mobilize and use its resources, to implement progressive economic and social reforms and to ensure the full participation of its people in the process and benefits of development. All States have the duty, individually and collectively, to co-operate in order to eliminate obstacles that hinder such mobilization and use.

Article 8. States should co-operate in facilitating more rational and equitable international economic relations and in encouraging structural changes in the context of a balanced world economy in harmony with the needs and interests of all countries, especially developing countries, and should take appropriate measures to this end.

Article 9. All States have the responsibility to co-operate in the economic, social, cultural, scientific and technological fields for the promotion of economic and social progress throughout the world, especially that of the developing countries.

Article 10. All States are juridically equal and, as equal members of the international community, have the right to participate fully and effectively in the international decisionmaking process in the solution of world economic, financial and monetary problems, *inter alia,* through the appropriate international organizations in accordance with their existing and evolving rules, and to share equitably in the benefits resulting therefrom.

Article 11. All States should co-operate to strengthen and continuously improve the efficiency of international organizations in implementing measures to stimulate the general economic progress of all countries, particularly of developing countries, and therefore should co-operate to adapt them, when appropriate, to the changing needs of international economic co-operation.

Article 12. (1) States have the right, in agreement with the parties concerned, to participate in subregional, regional and interregional co-operation in the pursuit of their economic and social development. All States engaged in such co-operation have the duty to ensure that the policies of those groupings to which they belong correspond to the provisions of the present Charter and are outward-looking, consistent with their international obligations and with the needs of international economic co-operation, and have full regard for the legitimate interests of third countries, especially developing countries.

(2) In the case of groupings to which the States concerned have transferred or may transfer certain competences as regards matters that come within the scope of the present Charter, its provisions shall also apply to those groupings, in regard to such matters, consistent with the responsibilities of such States as members of such groupings. Those States shall co-operate in the observance by the groupings of the provisions of this Charter.

Article 13. (1) Every State has the right to benefit from the advances and developments in science and technology for the acceleration of its economic and social development.

(2) All States should promote international scientific and technological co-operation and the transfer of technology, with proper regard for all legitimate interests including, *inter alia,* the rights and duties of holders, suppliers and recipients of technology. In particular, all States should facilitate the access of developing countries to the achievements of modern science and technology, the transfer of technology and the creation of indigenous technology for the benefit of the developing countries in forms and in accordance with procedures which are suited to their economies and their needs.

(3) Accordingly, developed countries should co-operate with the developing countries in the establishment, strengthening and development of their scientific and technological infrastructures and their scientific research and technological activities so as to help to expand and transform the economies of developing countries.

(4) All States should co-operate in research with a view to evolving further internationally accepted guidelines or regulations for the transfer of technology, taking fully into account the interests of developing countries.

Article 14. Every State has the duty to co-operate in promoting a steady and increasing expansion and liberalization of world trade and an improvement in the welfare and living standards of all peoples, in particular those of developing countries. Accordingly, all States should co-operate, *inter alia,* towards the progressive dismantling of obstacles to trade and the improvement of the international framework for the conduct of world trade and, to these ends, co-ordinated efforts shall be made to solve in an equitable way the trade problems of all countries, taking into account the specific trade problems of the developing countries. In this connexion, States shall take measures aimed at securing additional benefits for the international trade of developing countries so as to achieve a substantial increase in their foreign exchange earnings, the diversification of their exports, the acceleration of the rate of growth of their trade, taking into account their development needs, an improvement in the possibilities for these countries to participate in the expansion of world trade and a balance more favourable to developing countries in the sharing of the advantages resulting from this expansion, through, in the largest possible measure, a substantial improvement in the conditions of access for the products of interest to the developing countries and, wherever appropriate, measures designed to attain stable, equitable and remunerative prices for primary products.

Article 15. All States have the duty to promote the achievement of general and complete disarmament under effective international control and to utilize the resources released by effective disarmament measures for the economic and social development of countries, allocating a substantial portion of such resources as additional means for the development needs of developing countries.

Article 16. (1) It is the right and duty of all States, individually and collectively, to eliminate colonialism, *apartheid,* racial discrimination, neo-colonialism and social consequences thereof, as a prerequisite for development. States which practise such coercive policies are econonomically responsible to the countries, territories and peoples affected for the restitution and full compensation for the exploitation and depletion of, and damages to, the natural and all other resources of those countries, territories and peoples. It is the duty of all States to extend assistance to them.

(2) No State has the right to promote or encourage investments that may constitute an obstacle to the liberation of a territory occupied by force.

Article 17. International co-operation for development is the shared goal and common duty of all States. Every State should co-operate with the efforts of developing countries to accelerate their economic and social development by providing favourable external conditions and by extending active assistance to them, consistent with their development needs and objectives, with strict respect for the sovereign equality of States and free of any conditions derogating from their sovereignty.

Article 18. Developed countries should extend, improve and enlarge the system of generalized non-reciprocal and non-discriminatory tariff preferences to the developing countries consistent with the relevant agreed conclusions and relevant decisions as adopted on this subject, in the framework of the competent international organizations. Developed countries should also give serious consideration to the adoption of other differential measures, in areas where this is feasible and appropriate and in ways which will provide special and more favourable treatment, in order to meet the trade and development needs of the developing countries. In the conduct of international economic relations the developed countries should endeavour to avoid measures having a negative effect on the development of the national economics or the developing countries, as promoted by generalized tariff preferences and other generally agreed differential measures in their favour.

Article 19. With a view to accelerating the economic growth of developing countries and bridging the economic gap between developed and developing countries, developed countries should grant generalized preferential, non-reciprocal and non-discriminatory treatment to developing countries in those fields of international economic cooperation where it may be feasible.

Article 20. Developing countries should, in their efforts to increase their overall trade, give due attention to the possibility of expanding their trade with socialist countries, by granting to these countries conditions for trade not inferior to those granted normally to the developed market economy countries.

Article 21. Developing countries should endeavour to promote the expansion of their mutual trade and to this end may, in accordance with the existing and evolving provisions and procedures of international agreements where applicable, grant trade preferences to other developing countries without being obliged to extend such preferences to developed countries, provided these arrangements do not constitute an impediment to general trade liberalization and expansion.

Article 22. (1) All States should respond to the generally recognized or mutually agreed development needs and objectives of developing countries by promoting increased net flows of real resources to the developing countries from all sources, taking into account any obligations and commitments undertaken by the States concerned, in order to reinforce the efforts of developing countries to accelerate their economic and social development.

(2) In this context, consistent with the aims and objectives mentioned above and taking into account any obligations and commitments undertaken in this regard, it should be their endeavour to increase the net amount of financial flows from official sources to developing countries and to improve the terms and conditions thereof.

(3) The flow of development assistance resources should include economic and technical assistance.

Article 23. To enhance the effective mobilization of their own resources, the developing countries should strengthen their economic co-operation and expand their mutual trade so as to accelerate their economic and social development. All countries, especially developed countries, individually as well as through the competent international organizations of which they are members, should provide appropriate and effective support and co-operation.

Article 24. All States have the duty to conduct their mutual economic relations in a manner which takes into account the interests of other countries. In particular, all States should avoid prejudicing the interests of developing countries.

Article 25. In furtherance of world economic development, the international community, especially its developed members, shall pay special attention to the particular needs and problems of the least developed among the developing countries, of land-locked developing countries and also island developing countries, with a view to helping them to overcome their particular difficulties and thus contribute to their economic and social development.

Article 26. All States have the duty to coexist in tolerance and live together in peace, irrespective of differences in political, economic, social and cultural systems, and to facilitate trade between States having different economic and social systems. International trade should be conducted without prejudice to generalized non-discriminatory and non-reciprocal preferences in favour of developing countries, on the basis of mutual advantage, equitable benefits and the exchange of most-favoured-nation treatment.

Article 27. (1) Every State has the right to enjoy fully the benefits of world invisible trade and to engage in the expansion of such trade.

(2) World invisible trade, based on efficiency and mutual and equitable benefit, furthering the expansion of the world economy, is the common goal of all States. The role of developing countries in world invisible trade should be enhanced and strengthened consistent with the above objectives, particular attention being paid to the special needs of developing countries.

(3) All States should co-operate with developing countries in their endeavours to increase their capacity to earn foreign exchange with invisible transactions, in accordance with the potential and needs of each developing country and consistent with the objectives mentioned above.

Article 28. All States have the duty to co-operate in achieving adjustments in the prices of exports of developing countries in relation to prices of their imports so as to promote just and equitable terms of trade for them, in a manner which is remunerative for producers and equitable for producers and consumers.

CHAPTER III. COMMON RESPONSIBILITIES TOWARDS THE INTERNATIONAL COMMUNITY

Article 29. The sea-bed and ocean floor and the subsoil thereof, beyond the limits of national jurisdiction, as well as the resources of the area, are the common heritage of mankind. On the basis of the principles adopted by the General Assembly in resolution 2749 (XXV) of 17 December 1970, all States shall ensure that the exploration of the area and exploitation of its resources are carried out exclusively for peaceful purposes and that the benefits derived therefrom are shared equitably by all States, taking into account the particular interests and needs of developing countries; an international régime applying to the area and its resources and including appropriate international machinery to give effect to its provisions shall be established by an international treaty of a universal character, generally agreed upon.

Article 30. The protection, preservation and enhancement of the environment for the present and future generations is the responsibility of all States. All States shall endeavour to establish their own environmental and developmental policies in conformity with such responsibility. The environmental policies of all States shall enhance and not adversely affect the present and future development potential of developing countries. All States have the responsibility to ensure that activities within their jurisdiction or control do not cause damage to the environment of other States or of areas beyond the limits of national jurisdiction. All States should co-operate in evolving international norms and regulations in the field of the environment.

CHAPTER IV. FINAL PROVISIONS

Article 31. All States have the duty to contribute to the balanced expansion of the world economy, taking duly into account the close interrelationship between the well-being of the developed countries and the growth and development of the developing countries, and the fact that the prosperity of the international community as a whole depends upon the prosperity of its constituent parts.

Article 32. No State may use or encourage the use of economic, political or any other type of measures to coerce another State in order to obtain from it the subordination of the exercise of its sovereign rights.

Article 33. (1) Nothing in the present Charter shall be construed as impairing or derogating from the provisions of the Charter of the United Nations or actions taken in pursuance thereof.

(2) In their interpretation and application, the provisions of the present Charter are interrelated and each provision should be construed in the context of the other provisions.

Article 34. An item on the Charter of Economic Rights and Duties of State shall be included in the agenda of the General Assembly at its thirtieth session, and thereafter on the agenda of every fifth session. In this way a systematic and comprehensive consideration of the implementation of the Charter, covering both progress achieved and any improvements and additions which might become necessary, would be carried out and appropriate measures recommended. Such consideration should take into account the evolution of all the economic, social, legal and other factors related to the principles upon which the present Charter is based and on its purpose.

4.9 DECLARATION ON INTERNATIONAL INVESTMENT AND MULTINATIONAL ENTERPRISES.[a] Adopted by the Organisation for Economic Co-operation and Development Council, June 21, 1976. OECD, THE OECD GUIDELINES FOR MULTINATIONAL ENTERPRISES 9 (1986), *reprinted in* 15 I.L.M. 967 (1976)

THE GOVERNMENTS OF OECD MEMBER COUNTRIES

CONSIDERING

That international investment has assumed increased importance in the world economy and has considerably contributed to the development of their countries;

That multinational enterprises play an important role in this investment process;

That co-operation by Member countries can improve the foreign investment climate, encourage the positive contribution which multinational enterprises can make to economic and social progress, and minimise and resolve difficulties which may arise from their various operations;

That, while continuing endeavours within the OECD may lead to further international arrangements and agreements in this field, it seems appropriate at this stage to intensify their co-operation and consultation on issues relating to international investment and multinational enterprises through inter-related instruments each of which deals with a different aspect of the matter and together constitute a framework within which the OECD will consider these issues:

DECLARE:

I. that they jointly recommend to multinational enterprises operating in their territories the observance of the Guidelines as set forth in the Annex hereto having regard to the considerations and understandings which introduce the Guidelines and are an integral part of them.

II. 1. that Member countries should, consistent with their needs to maintain public order, to protect their essential security interests and to fulfil commitments relating to international peace and security, accord to enterprises operating in their territories and owned or controlled directly or indirectly by nationals of another Member country (hereinafter referred to as "Foreign–Controlled Enterprises") treatment under their laws, regulations and administrative practices, consistent with international law and no less favourable than that accorded in like situations to domestic enterprises (hereinafter referred to as "National Treatment").

2. that Member countries will consider applying "National Treatment" in respect of countries other than Member countries.

3. that Member countries will endeavour to ensure that their territorial subdivisions apply "National Treatment".

4. that this Declaration does not deal with the right of Member countries to regulate the entry of foreign investment or the conditions of establishment of foreign enterprises.

III. 1. that they recognise the need to strengthen their co-operation in the field of international direct investment.

a. *See also* the OECD "Guidelines for Multinational Enterprises" as amended in 1979 and 1984 (Basic Document 4.13).

2. that they thus recognise the need to give due weight to the interests of Member countries affected by specific laws, regulations and administrative practices in this field (hereinafter called "measures") providing official incentives and disincentives to international direct investment.

3. that Member countries will endeavour to make such measures as transparent as possible, so that their importance and purpose can be ascertained and that information on them can be readily available.

IV. that they are prepared to consult one another on the above matters in conformity with the Decisions of the Council relating to Inter–Governmental Consultation Procedures on the Guidelines for Multinational Enterprises, on National Treatment and on International Investment Incentives and Disincentives.

V. that they will review the above matters within three years with a view to improving the effectiveness of international economic co-operation among Member countries on issues relating to international investment and multinational enterprises.

4.10 CONSTITUTION OF THE UNITED NATIONS INDUSTRIAL DEVELOPMENT ORGANIZATION.[a] Adopted by the U.N. Conference on the Establishment of the United Nations Industrial Development Organization as a Specialized Agency, Apr. 8, 1979, U.N.Doc. A/CONF. 90/19 (1979), *reprinted in* 18 I.L.M. 667 (1979)

CHAPTER I. OBJECTIVES AND FUNCTIONS

Article 1. Objectives

The primary objective of the Organization shall be the promotion and acceleration of industrial development in the developing countries with a view to assisting in the establishment of a new international economic order. The Organization shall also promote industrial development and co-operation on global, regional and national, as well as on sectoral levels.

Article 2. Functions

In fulfillment of its foregoing objectives, the Organization shall generally take all necessary and appropriate action, and in particular shall:

(a) Encourage and extend, as appropriate, assistance to the developing countries in the promotion and acceleration of their industrialization, in particular in the development, expansion and modernization of their industries;

(b) In accordance with the Charter of the United Nations, initiate, co-ordinate and follow up the activities of the United Nations system with a view to enabling the Organization to play the central co-ordinating role in the field of industrial development;

(c) Create new and develop existing concepts and approaches in respect of industrial development on global, regional and national, as well as on sectoral levels, and carry out studies and surveys with a view to formulating new lines of action directed towards harmonious and balanced industrial development, with due consideration for the methods employed by countries with different socio-economic systems for solving industrialization problems;

(d) Promote and encourage the development and use of planning techniques, and assist in the formulation of development, scientific and technological programmes and plans for industrialization in the public, co-operative and private sectors;

(e) Encourage and assist in the development of an integrated and interdisciplinary approach towards the accelerated industrialization of the developing countries;

(f) Provide a forum and act as an instrument to serve the developing countries and industrialized countries in their contacts, consultations and, at the request of the countries concerned, negotiations directed towards the industrialization of the developing countries;

(g) Assist the developing countries in the establishment and operation of industries, including agro-related as well as basic industries, to achieve the full utilization of locally available natural and human resources and the production of goods for domestic and export markets, as well as contribute to the self-reliance of these countries;

a. Annexes are omitted.

(h) Serve as a clearing-house for industrial information and accordingly collect and monitor on a selective basis, analyse and generate for the purpose of dissemination information on all aspects of industrial development on global, regional and national, as well as on sectoral levels including the exchange of experience and technological achievements of the industrially developed and the developing countries with different social and economic systems;

(i) Devote particular attention to the adoption of special measures aimed at assisting the least-developed, land-locked, and island developing countries, as well as those developing countries most seriously affected by economic crises and natural calamities, without losing sight of the interest of the other developing countries;

(j) Promote, encourage and assist in the development, selection, adaptation, transfer and use of industrial technology, with due regard for the socio-economic conditions and the specific requirements of the industry concerned, with special reference to the transfer of technology from the industrialized to the developing countries as well as among the developing countries themselves;

(k) Organize and support industrial training programmes aimed at assisting the developing countries in the training of technical and other appropriate categories of personnel needed at various phases for their accelerated industrial development;

(*l*) Advise on and assist, in close co-operation with the appropriate bodies of the United Nations, specialized agencies and the International Atomic Energy Agency, the developing countries in the exploitation, conservation and local transformation of their natural resources for the purpose of furthering the industrialization of developing countries;

(m) Provide pilot and demonstration plans for accelerating industrialization in particular sectors;

(n) Develop special measures designed to promote co-operation in the industrial field among developing countries and between the developed and developing countries;

(*o*) Assist, in co-operation with other appropriate bodies, the regional planning of industrial development of the developing countries within the framework of regional and subregional groupings among those countries;

(p) Encourage and promote the establishment and strengthening of industrial, business and professional associations, and similar organizations which would contribute to the full utilization of the internal resources of the developing countries with a view to developing their national industries;

(q) Assist in the establishment and operation of institutional infra-structure for the provision of regulatory, advisory and developmental services to industry;

(r) Assist, at the request of Governments of the developing countries, in obtaining external financing for specific industrial projects on fair, equitable and mutually acceptable terms.

CHAPTER II. PARTICIPATION

Article 3. Members

Membership in the Organization is open to all States which associate themselves with the objectives and principles of the Organization * * *

* * *

CHAPTER III. ORGANS

Article 7. Principal and Subsidiary Organs

1. The principal organs of the Organization shall be:

(a) The General Conference (referred to as the "Conference");

(b) The Industrial Development Board (referred to as the "Board");

(c) The Secretariat.

2. There shall be established a Programme and Budget Committee to assist the Board in the preparation and examination of the programme of work, the regular budget and operational budget of the Organization and other financial matters pertaining to the Organization.

3. Other subsidiary organs, including technical committees, may be established by the Conference or the Board, which shall give due regard to the principle of equitable geographical representation.

Article 8. General Conference

1. The Conference shall consist of representatives of all Members.

2. (a) The Conference shall hold a regular session every two years, unless it decides otherwise. Special sessions shall be convened by the Director–General at the request of the Board or of a majority of all Members.

* * *

3. In addition to exercising other functions specified in this Constitution, the Conference shall:

(a) Determine the guiding principles and the policies of the Organization;

(b) Consider reports of the Board, of the Director–General and of the subsidiary organs of the Conference;

(c) Approve the programme of work, the regular budget and the operational budget of the Organization in accordance with Article 14, establish the scale of assessments in accordance with Article 15, approve the financial regulations of the Organization and supervise the effective utilization of the financial resources of the Organization;

(d) Have the authority to adopt, by a two-thirds majority of the Members present and voting, conventions or agreements with respect to any matter within the competence of the Organization and to make recommendations to the Members concerning such conventions or agreements;

(e) Make recommendations to Members and to international organizations with respect to matters within the competence of the Organization;

(f) Take any other appropriate action to enable the Organization to further its objectives and carry out its functions.

4. The Conference may delegate to the Board such of its powers and functions as it may consider desirable, except for those provided for in: Article 3, subparagraph (b); Article 4; Article 8, subparagraphs 3(a), (b), (c) and (d); Article 9, paragraph 1; Article 10, paragraph 1; Article 11, paragraph 2; Article 14, paragraphs 4 and 6; Article 15; Article 18; Article 23, subparagraphs 2(b) and 3(b); and Annex I.

5. The Conference shall adopt its own rules of procedure.

6. Each Member shall have one vote in the Conference. Decisions shall be made by a majority of the Members present and voting unless otherwise specified in this Constitution or in the rules of procedure of the Conference.

Article 9. Industrial Development Board

1. The Board shall consist of 53 Members of the Organization elected by the Conference, which shall give due regard to the principle of equitable geographical distribution. * * *

* * *

3. (a) The Board shall hold at least one regular session each year at such times as it may determine. Special sessions shall be convened by the Director–General at the request of a majority of all members of the Board.

* * *

4. In addition to exercising other functions specified in this Constitution or delegated to it by the Conference, the Board shall:

(a) Acting under the authority of the Conference, review the implementation of the approved programme of work and of the corresponding regular budget and operational budget, as well as of other decisions of the Conference;

(b) Recommend to the Conference a scale of assessments for regular budget expenditures;

(c) Report to the Conference at each regular session on the activities of the Board;

(d) Request Members to furnish information on their activities related to the work of the Organization;

(e) In accordance with the decisions of the Conference and having regard to circumstances arising between sessions of the Board or the Conference, authorize the Director–General to take such measures as the Board deems necessary to meet unforeseen events with due regard to the functions and financial resources of the Organization;

(f) If the office of Director–General becomes vacant between sessions of the Conference, appoint an Acting Director–General to serve until the next regular or special session of the Conference;

(g) Prepare the provisional agenda for the Conference;

(h) Undertake such other functions as may be required to further the objectives of the Organization subject to the limitations stipulated in this Constitution.

5. The Board shall adopt its own rules of procedure.

6. Each member of the Board shall have one vote. Decisions shall be made by a majority of the members present and voting unless otherwise specified in this Constitution or in the rules of procedure of the Board.

7. The Board shall invite any Member not represented on the Board to participate without vote in its deliberations on any matter of particular concern to that Member.

Article 10. Programme and Budget Committee

1. The Programme and Budget Committee shall consist of 27 Members of the Organization elected by the Conference, which shall give due regard to the principle of equitable geographical distribution. * * *

2. Members of the Committee shall hold office from the close of the regular session of the Conference at which they were elected until the close of the regular session of the Conference two years thereafter. Members of the Committee may be re-elected.

3. (a) The Committee shall hold at least one session each year. Additional sessions shall be convened by the Director–General at the request of the Board or the Committee.

* * *

4. The Committee shall:

(a) Perform the functions assigned to it in Article 14;

(b) Prepare the draft scale of assessments for regular budget expenditures, for submission to the Board;

(c) Exercise such other functions with respect to financial matters as may be assigned to it by the Conference or the Board;

(d) Report to the Board at each regular session on all activities of the Committee and submit advice or proposals on financial matters to the Board on its own initiative.

5. The Committee shall adopt its own rules of procedure.

6. Each member of the Committee shall have one vote. Decisions shall be made by a two-thirds majority of the members present and voting.

Article 11. Secretariat

1. The Secretariat shall comprise a Director–General, as well as such Deputy Directors–General and other staff as the Organization may require.

2. The Director–General shall be appointed by the Conference upon recommendation of the Board for a period of four years. He may be reappointed for a further term of four years, after which he shall not be eligible for reappointment.

3. The Director–General shall be the chief administrative officer of the Organization. Subject to general or specific directives of the Conference or the Board, the Director–General shall have the over-all responsibility and authority to direct the work of the Organization. Under the authority of and subject to the control of the Board, the Director–General shall be responsible for the appointment, organization and functioning of the staff.

4. In the performance of their duties the Director–General and the staff shall not seek or receive instructions from any government or from any authority external to the Organization. They shall refrain from any action that might reflect on their position as international officials responsible only to the Organization. Each Member undertakes to respect the exclusively international character of the responsibilities of the Director–General and the staff and not to seek to influence them in the discharge of their responsibilities.

* * *

CHAPTER IV. PROGRAMME OF WORK AND FINANCIAL MATTERS

Article 12. Expenses of Delegations

Each Member and observer shall bear the expenses of its own delegation to the Conference, to the Board or to any other organ in which it may participate.

Article 13. Composition of Budgets

1. The activities of the Organization shall be carried out in accordance with its approved programme of work and budgets.

2. The expenditures of the Organization shall be divided into the following categories:

(a) Expenditures to be met from assessed contributions (referred to as the "regular budget"); and

(b) Expenditures to be met from voluntary contributions to the Organization, and such other income as may be provided for in the financial regulations (referred to as the "optional budget").

3. The regular budget shall provide for expenditures for administration, research, other regular expenses of the Organization and for other activities, as provided for in Annex II.[b]

4. The operational budget shall provide for expenditures for technical assistance and other related activities.

* * *

Article 15. Assessed Contributions

1. Regular budget expenditures shall be borne by the Members, as apportioned in accordance with a scale of assessment established by the Conference by a two-thirds majority of the Members present and voting, upon the recommendation of the Board adopted by a two-thirds majority of the members present and voting, on the basis of a draft prepared by the Programme and Budget Committee.

2. The scale of assessments shall be based to the extent possible on the scale most recently employed by the United Nations. No Member shall be assessed more than twenty-five per cent of the regular budget of the Organization.

Article 16. Voluntary Contributions to the Organization

Subject to the financial regulations of the Organization, the Director–General, on behalf of the Organization, may accept voluntary contributions to the Organization, including gifts, bequests and subventions, made to the Organization by governments, intergovernmental or non-governmental organizations or other non-governmental sources, provided that the conditions attached to such voluntary contributions are consistent with the objectives and policies of the Organization.

Article 17. Industrial Development Fund

In order to increase the resources of the Organization and to enhance its ability to meet promptly and flexibly the needs of the developing countries, the Organization shall have an Industrial Development Fund which will be financed through the voluntary contributions to the Organization provided for in Article 16, and other income as may be provided for in the financial regulations of the Organization. The Director–General shall administer the Industrial Development Fund in accordance with the general policy guidelines governing the operations of the Fund that are established by the Conference, or by the Board acting on behalf of the Conference, and in accordance with the financial regulations of the Organization.

CHAPTER V. CO–OPERATION AND CO–ORDINATION

Article 18. Relations with the United Nations

The Organization shall be brought into relationship with the United Nations as one of the specialized agencies referred to in Article 57 of the Charter of the United Nations. Any agreement concluded in accordance with Article 63 of the Charter shall require the approval of the Conference, by a two-thirds majority of the Members present and voting, upon the recommendation of the Board.

Article 19. Relations With Other Organizations

1. The Director–General may, with the approval of the Board and subject to guidelines established by the Conference:

(a) Enter into agreements establishing appropriate relationships with other organizations of the United Nations system and with other intergovernmental and governmental organizations,

(b) Establish appropriate relations with non-governmental and other organizations the work of which is related to that of the Organization. When

b. This Annex is omitted here.

establishing such relations with national organizations the Director–General shall consult with the governments concerned.

2. Subject to such agreements and relations, the Director–General may establish working arrangements with such organizations.

CHAPTER VI. LEGAL MATTERS

Article 20. Seat

1. The seat of the Organization shall be Vienna. The Conference may change the seat by a two-thirds majority of all Members.

2. The Organization shall conclude a headquarters agreement with the Host Government.

Article 21. Legal Capacity, Privileges and Immunities

1. The Organization shall enjoy in the territory of each of its Members such legal capacity and such privileges and immunities as are necessary for the exercise of its functions and for the fulfilment of its objectives. Representatives of Members and officials of the Organization shall enjoy such privileges and immunities as are necessary for the independent exercise of their functions in connection with the Organization.

* * *

4.11 DRAFT INTERNATIONAL CODE OF CONDUCT ON THE TRANSFER OF TECHNOLOGY.[a] As at the close of the Sixth Session of the U.N. Conference on Trade and Development (UNCTAD), June 5, 1985. U.N.Doc. TD/CODE TOT/47 (1985)[b]

Chapter 1

Definitions and Scope of Application

1.1 For the purposes of the present Code of Conduct:

(a) "Party" means any person, either natural or juridical, of public or private law, either individual or collective, such as corporations, companies, firms, partnerships and other associations, or any combination thereof, whether created, owned or controlled by States, Government agencies, juridical persons, or individuals, wherever they operate, as well as States, Government agencies and international, regional and subregional organizations, when they engage in an international transfer of technology transaction which is usually considered to be of a commercial nature. The term "party" includes, among the entities enumerated above, incorporated branches, subsidiaries and affiliates, joint ventures or other legal entities regardless of the economic and other relationships between and among them.

(b) "Acquiring party" means the party which obtains a licence to use or to exploit, purchases or otherwise acquires technology of a proprietary or non-proprietary nature and/or rights related thereto in a transfer of technology.

(c) "Supplying party" means the party which licenses, sells, assigns or otherwise provides technology of a proprietary or non-proprietary nature and/or rights related thereto in a transfer of technology.

1.2 Transfer of technology under this Code is the transfer of systematic knowledge for the manufacture of a product, for the application of a process or for the rendering of a service and does not extend to the transactions involving the mere sale or mere lease of goods.

1.3 Transfer of technology transactions are arrangements between parties involving transfer of technology, as defined in paragraph 1.2 above, particularly in each of the following cases:

(a) The assignment, sale and licensing of all forms of industrial property, except for trade marks, service marks and trade names when they are not part of transfer of technology transactions;

(b) The provision of know-how and technical expertise in the form of feasibility studies, plans, diagrams, models, instructions, guides, formulae, basic or detailed engineering designs, specifications and equipment for training, services involving technical advisory and managerial personnel, and personnel training;

(c) The provision of technological knowledge necessary for the installation, operation and functioning of plant and equipment, and turnkey projects;

(d) The provision of technological knowledge necessary to acquire, install and use machinery, equipment, intermediate goods and/or raw materials which have been acquired by purchase, lease or other means;

(e) The provision of technological contents of industrial and technical co-operation arrangements.

a. Most footnotes and all appendices are omitted.

b. An asterisk [*] denotes a text under consideration.

1.4 International transfer of technology transactions.*

1.5 The Code of Conduct is universally applicable in scope and is addressed to all parties to transfer of technology transactions and to all countries and groups of countries, irrespective of their economic and political systems and their levels of development.

1.6 Regional groupings of States.*

Chapter 2

Objectives and Principles

2. The Code of Conduct is based on the following objectives and principles:

2.1 *Objectives*

(i) To establish general and equitable standards on which to base the relationships among parties to transfer of technology transactions and governments concerned, taking into consideration their legitimate interests, and giving due recognition to special needs of developing countries for the fulfilment of their economic and social development objectives.

(ii) To promote mutual confidence between parties as well as their governments.

(iii) To encourage transfer of technology transactions, particularly those involving developing countries, under conditions where bargaining positions of the parties to the transactions are balanced in such a way as to avoid abuses of a stronger position and thereby to achieve mutually satisfactory agreements.

(iv) To facilitate and increase the international flow of technological information, particularly on the availability of alternative technologies, as a prerequisite for the assessment, selection, adaptation, development and use of technologies in all countries, particularly in developing countries.

(v) To facilitate and increase the international flow of proprietary and non-proprietary technology for strengthening the growth of the scientific and technological capabilities of all countries, in particular developing countries, so as to increase their participation in world production and trade.

(vi) To increase the contributions of technology to the identification and solution of social and economic problems of all countries, particularly the developing countries, including the development of basic sectors of their national economies.

(vii) To facilitate the formulation, adoption and implementation of national policies, laws and regulations on the subject of transfer of technology by setting forth international norms.

(viii) To promote adequate arrangements as regards unpackaging in terms of information concerning the various elements of the technology to be transferred, such as that required for technical, institutional and financial evaluation of the transaction, thus avoiding undue or unnecessary packaging.

(ix) To specify restrictive [business] practices from which parties to technology transfer transactions [shall] [should] refrain.

(x) To set forth an appropriate set of responsibilities and obligations of parties to transfer of technology transactions, taking into consideration their legitimate interests as well as differences in their bargaining positions.

2.2 *Principles*

(i) The Code of Conduct is universally applicable in scope.

(ii) States have the right to adopt all appropriate measures for facilitating and regulating the transfer of technology, in a manner consistent with their international obligations, taking into consideration the legitimate interests of all parties concerned, and encouraging transfers of technology under mutually agreed, fair and reasonable terms and conditions.

(iii) The principles of sovereignty and political independence of States (covering, *inter alia,* the requirements of foreign policy and national security), and sovereign equality of States, should be recognized in facilitating and regulating transfer of technology transactions.

(iv) States should co-operate in the international transfer of technology in order to promote economic growth throughout the world, especially that of the developing countries. Co-operation in such transfer should be irrespective of any differences in political, economic and social systems; this is one of the important elements in maintaining international peace and security and promoting international economic stability and progress, the general welfare of nations and international co-operation free from discrimination based on such differences. Nothing in this Code may be construed as impairing or derogating from the provisions of the Charter of the United Nations or actions taken in pursuance thereof. It is understood that special treatment in transfer of technology should be accorded to developing countries in accordance with the provisions in this Code on the subject.

(v) The separate responsibilities of parties to transfer of technology transactions, on the one hand, and those of governments when not acting as parties, on the other, should be clearly distinguished.

(vi) Mutual benefits should accrue to technology supplying and recipient parties in order to maintain and increase the international flow of technology.

(vii) Facilitating and increasing the access to technology, particularly for developing countries, under mutually agreed fair and reasonable terms and conditions, are fundamental elements in the process of technology transfer and development.

(viii) Recognition of the protection of industrial property rights granted under national law.

(ix) Technology supplying parties when operating in an acquiring country should respect the sovereignty and the laws of that country, act with proper regard for that country's declared development policies and priorities and endeavour to contribute substantially to the development of the acquiring country. The freedom of parties to negotiate, conclude and perform agreements for the transfer of technology on mutually acceptable terms and conditions should be based on respect for the foregoing and other principles set forth in this Code.

Chapter 3

National Regulation of Transfer of Technology Transactions

3.1 In adopting, and in the light of evolving circumstances making necessary changes in laws, regulations and rules, and policies with respect to transfer of technology transactions, States have the right to adopt measures such as those listed in paragraph 3.4 of this chapter and should act on the basis that these measures should:

(i) Recognize that a close relationship exists between technology flows the conditions under which such flows are admitted and treated;

[and]

(ii) Promote a favourable and beneficial climate for the international transfer of technology;

(iii) Take into consideration in an equitable manner the legitimate interests of all parties;

(iv) Encourage and facilitate transfers of technology to take place under mutually agreed, fair and reasonable terms and conditions having regard to the principles and objectives of the Code;

(v) Take into account the differing factors characterizing the transactions such as local conditions, the nature of the technology and the scope of the undertaking;

(vi) Be consistent with their international obligations.

3.2 Measures adopted by States including decisions of competent administrative bodies should be applied fairly, equitably, and on the same basis to all parties in accordance with established procedures of law and the principles and objectives of the Code. Laws and regulations should be clearly defined and publicly and readily available. To the extent appropriate, relevant information regarding decisions of competent administrative bodies should be disseminated.

3.3 Each country adopting legislation on the protection of industrial property should have regard to its national needs of economic and social development, and should ensure an effective protection of industrial property rights granted under its national law and other related rights recognized by its national law.

3.4 Measures on regulation of the flow and effects of transfer of technology, finance and technical aspects of technology transactions and on organizational forms and mechanisms may deal with:

Finance

(a) Currency regulations of foreign exchange payments and remittances;

(b) Conditions of domestic credit and financing facilities;

(c) Transferability of payments;

(d) Tax treatment;

(e) Pricing policies;

Renegotiation

(f) Terms, conditions and objective criteria for the renegotiation of transfer of technology transactions;

Technical aspects

(g) Technology specifications and standards for the various components of the transfer of technology transactions and their payments;

(h) Analysis and evaluation of transfer of technology transactions to assist parties in their negotiations;

(i) Use of local and imported components;

Organizational forms and mechanisms

(j) Evaluation, negotiation, and registration of transfer of technology transactions;

(k) Terms, conditions, duration, of transfer of technology transactions;

(*l*) Loss of ownership and/or control of domestic acquiring enterprises;

(m) Regulation of foreign collaboration arrangements and agreements that could displace national enterprises from the domestic market;

(n) The definition of fields of activity of foreign enterprises and the choice of channels, mechanisms, organizational forms for the transfer of technology and the prior or subsequent approval of transfer of technology transactions and their registration in these fields;

(*o*) The determination of the legal effect of transactions which are not in conformity with national laws, regulations and administrative decisions on the transfer of technology;

(p) The establishment or strengthening of national administrative mechanisms for the implementation and application of the Code of Conduct and of national laws, regulations and policies on the transfer of technology;

(q) Promotion of appropriate channels for the international exchange of information and experience in the field of the transfer of technology.

Chapter 4 [1]

The Regulation of Practices and Arrangements Involving the Transfer of Technology. Restrictive Business Practices. Exclusion of Political Discrimination and Restrictive Business Practices

Section A: (Chapeau) *

Section B: (List of practices) *

1. [Exclusive] *Grant-back provisions* *

Requiring the acquiring party to transfer or grant back to the supplying party, or to any other enterprise designated by the supplying party, improvements arising from the acquired technology, on an exclusive basis [or] * without offsetting consideration or reciprocal obligations from the supplying party, or when the practice will constitute an abuse of a dominant market position of the supplying party.

2. *Challenges to validity* *

[Unreasonably] requiring the acquiring party to refrain from challenging the validity of patents and other types of protection for inventions involved in the transfer or the validity of other such grants claimed or obtained by the supplying party, recognizing that any issues concerning the mutual rights and obligations of the parties following such a challenge will be determined by the appropriate applicable law and the terms of the agreement to the extent consistent with that law.

3. *Exclusive dealing*

Restrictions on the freedom of the acquiring party to enter into sales, representation or manufacturing agreements relating to similar or competing technologies or products or to obtain competing technology, when such restrictions are not needed for ensuring the achievement of legitimate interests, particularly including securing the confidentiality of the technology transferred or best effort distribution or promotional obligations.

4. *Restrictions on research* *

[Unreasonably] **/*** restricting the acquiring party either in undertaking research and development directed to absorb and adapt the transferred technology to local conditions or in initiating research and development programmes in connection with new products, processes or equipment.

5. *Restrictions on use of personnel* *

[Unreasonably] ** requiring the acquiring party to use personnel designated by the supplying party, except to the extent necessary to ensure the efficient transmission phase for the transfer of technology and putting it to use or thereafter continuing such requirement beyond the time when adequately trained local personnel are available or have been trained; or prejudicing the use of personnel of the technology acquiring country.

1. In view of continuing negotiations on the chapter, no attempt has been made to number the provisions of this chapter consistently with the other chapters.

6. *Price fixing* *

[Unjustifiably] ** imposing regulation of prices to be charged by acquiring parties in the relevant market to which the technology was transferred for products manufactured or services produced using the technology supplied.

7. *Restrictions on adaptations* *

Restrictions which [unreasonably] ** prevent the acquiring party from adapting the imported technology to local conditions or introducing innovations in it, or which oblige the acquiring party to introduce unwanted or unnecessary design or specification changes, if the acquiring party makes adaptations on his own responsibility and without using the technology supplying party's name, trade or service marks or trade names, and except to the extent that this adaptation unsuitably affects those products, or the process for their manufacture, to be supplied to the supplying party, his designates, or his other licensees, or to be used as a component or spare part in a product to be supplied to his customers.

8. *Exclusive sales or representation agreements*

Requiring the acquiring party to grant exclusive sales or representation rights to the supplying party or any person designated by the supplying party, except as to subcontracting or manufacturing arrangements wherein the parties have agreed that all or part of the production under the technology transfer arrangement will be distributed by the supplying party or any person designated by him.

9. *Tying arrangements* *

[Unduly] ** imposing acceptance of additional technology, future inventions and improvements, goods or services not wanted by the acquiring party or [unduly] ** restricting sources of technology, goods or services, as a condition for obtaining the technology required when not required to maintain the quality of the product or service when the supplier's trade or service mark or other identifying item is used by the acquiring party, or to fulfil a specific performance obligation which has been guaranteed, provided further that adequate specification of the ingredients is not feasible or would involve the disclosure of additional technology not covered by the arrangement.

10. *Export restrictions* *

11. *Patent pool or cross-licensing agreements and other arrangements*

Restrictions on territories, quantities, prices, customers or markets arising out of patent pool or cross-licensing agreements or other international transfer of technology interchange arrangements among technology suppliers which unduly limit access to new technological developments or which would result in an abusive domination of an industry or market with adverse effects on the transfer of technology, except for those restrictions appropriate and ancillary to co-operative arrangements such as co-operative research arrangements.

12. *Restrictions on publicity* *

Restrictions [unreasonably] ** regulating the advertising or publicity by the acquiring party except where restrictions of such publicity may be required to prevent injury to the supplying party's goodwill or reputation where the advertising or publicity makes reference to the supplying party's name, trade or service marks, trade names or other identifying items, or for legitimate reasons of avoiding product liability when the supplying party may be subject to such liability, or where appropriate for safety purposes or to protect consumers, or when needed to secure the confidentiality of the technology transferred.

13. *Payments and other obligations after expiration of industrial property rights*

Requiring payments or imposing other obligations for continuing the use of industrial property rights which have been invalidated, cancelled or have expired recognizing that any other issue, including other payment obligations for technology, shall be dealt with by the appropriate applicable law and the terms of the agreement to the extent consistent with that law.

14. *Restrictions after expiration of arrangement* *

Chapter 5

Responsibilities and Obligations of Parties

Common provision on negotiating as well as contractual phase

5.1 When negotiating and concluding a technology transfer agreement, the parties should, in accordance with this chapter, be responsive to the economic and social development objectives of the respective countries of the parties and particularly of the technology acquiring country, and when negotiating, concluding and performing a technology transfer agreement, the parties should observe fair and honest business practices and take into account the specific circumstances of the individual case and recognition should be given to certain circumstances, mainly the stage of development of technology, the economic and technical capabilities of the parties, the nature and type of the transaction such as any ongoing or continuous flow of technology between the parties.

Negotiating phase

5.2 In being responsive to the economic and social development objectives mentioned in this chapter each party should take into account the other's request to include in the agreements, to the extent technically and commercially practicable and for adequate consideration, when appropriate, such as the case in which the supplying party incurs additional costs or efforts, items clearly related to the official economic and social development objectives of the country of the requesting party as enunciated by its government. * * *

* * *

(b) *Rendering of technical services*

Specific provisions for the rendering of technical services in the introduction and operation of the technology to be transferred;

(c) *Unpackaging*

Upon request of the potential acquiring party, the potential supplying party should, to the extent practicable, make adequate arrangements as regards unpackaging in terms of information concerning the various elements of the technology to be transferred, such as that required for technical, institutional and financial evaluation of the potential supplying party's offer.

5.3 *Business negotiating practices*

When negotiating a technology transfer agreement, the parties should observe fair and honest business practices and therefore:

(a) *Both potential parties*

(i) *Fair and reasonable terms and conditions*

(i) Should negotiate in good faith with the aim of reaching, in a timely manner, an agreement containing fair and reasonable commercial terms and conditions, including agreement on payments such as license fees, royalties and other considerations;

(ii) The price or consideration to be charged should be fair and reasonable, it should be clearly indicated and, to the extent practicable, specified in such a manner that the acquiring party would be able to appreciate its reasonableness and fairness by comparing it to the price or consideration for other comparable technologies transferred under similar conditions, which may be known to him;

(ii) *Relevant information*

Should consider requests to inform each other, to the extent appropriate, about their prior arrangements which may affect the contemplated technology transfer;

(iii) *Confidential information*

Should keep secret, in accordance with any obligation, either legal or contractual, all confidential information received from the other party and make use of the confidential information received from a potential party only for the purpose of evaluating this party's offer or request or for other purposes agreed upon by the parties;

(iv) *Termination of negotiations*

May cease negotiations if, during the negotiations, either party determines that a satisfactory agreement cannot be reached;

(b) *The potential acquiring party*

Relevant information

Should provide the potential technology supplier in a timely manner with the available specific information concerning the technical conditions and official economic and social development objectives as well as legislation of the acquiring country relevant to the particular transfer and use of the technology under negotiation as far as such information is needed for the supplying party's responsiveness under this chapter;

(c) *The potential supplying party*

Relevant information

(i) Should disclose, in a timely manner, to the potential technology acquiring party any reason actually known to him, on account of which the technology to be supplied, when used in accordance with the terms and conditions of the proposed agreement, would not meet particular health, safety and environmental requirements in the technology acquiring country, already known to him as being relevant in the specific case or which have been specifically drawn to his attention, as well as any serious health, safety and environmental risks known by the supplier associated with the use of the technology and of products to be produced by it;

(ii) Should disclose to the potential technology acquiring party, to the actual extent known to him, any limitation, including any pending official procedures or litigation which adversely concerns, in a direct manner, the existence or validity of the rights to be transferred, on his entitlement to grant the rights or render the assistance and services specified in the proposed agreement;

Provision of accessories, spare parts and components

(iii) Should to the extent feasible, take into account the request of the acquiring party to provide it for a period to be specified with accessories, spare parts and components produced by the supplying party and necessary for using the technology to be transferred, particularly where alternative sources are unavailable.

Contractual phase—Chapeau

5.4 The technology transfer agreement should, in accordance with 5.1, provide for mutually acceptable contractual obligations, including those relating to payments and, where appropriate, *inter alia,* the following:

(i) *Access to improvements*

Access for a specified period or for the lifetime of the agreement to improvements to the technology transferred under the agreement;

(ii) *Confidentiality* *

(iii) *Dispute settlement and applicable law* *

(iv) *Description of the technology*

The technology supplier's guarantee that the technology meets the description contained in the technology transfer agreement;

(v) *Suitability for use*

The technology supplier's guarantee that the technology, if used in accordance with the supplier's specific instructions given pursuant to the agreement, is suitable for manufacturing of goods or production of services as agreed upon by the parties and stipulated in the agreement;

(vi) *Rights to the technology transferred*

The technology supplier's representation that on the date of the signing of the agreement, it is, to the best of its knowledge, not aware of third parties' valid patent rights or similar protection for inventions which would be infringed by the use of the technology when used as specified in the agreement;

(vii) *Quality levels and goodwill*

The technology recipient's commitment to observe quality levels agreed upon in cases where the agreement includes the use of the supplier's trade marks, trade names or similar identification of goodwill, and both parties' commitment to avoid taking actions primarily or deliberately intended to injure the other's goodwill or reputation;

(viii) *Performance guarantees*

Specification to technical performance parameters which the supplying party has agreed to guarantee, including specification of requirements for the achievement of such parameters, details of the manner of determining whether the performance has been met and the consequences of failure to meet that performance;

(ix) *Transmission of documentation*

The supplying party's commitment that relevant technical documentation and other data required from him for a particular purpose defined in terms directly specified in the agreement will be transferred in a timely manner and as correctly and completely for such purpose as agreed upon;

(x) *Training of personnel and provision of accessories, spare parts and components*

Where negotiations under paragraphs 5.2(a)(i) and 5.5(c)(iii) have taken place, suitable provisions for training of personnel and supply of accessories, spare parts and components would be made, consistent with the results of the negotiations;

(xi) *Liability*

Disposition concerning liability for the non-fulfilment by either party of its responsibilities under the technology transfer agreement including questions of loss, damage or injury.

Chapter 6

Special Treatment for Developing Countries

6.1 Taking into consideration the needs and problems of developing countries, particularly of the least developed countries, governments of developed countries, directly or through appropriate international organizations, in order to facilitate and encourage the initiation and strengthening of the scientific and technological capabilities of developing countries so as to assist and co-operate with them in their efforts to fulfil their economic and social objectives, should take adequate specific measures, *inter alia,* to:

(i) facilitate access by developing countries to available information regarding the availabilities, description, location and, as far as possible, approximate cost of technologies which might help those countries to attain their economic and social development objectives;

(ii) give developing countries the freest and fullest possible access to technologies whose transfer is not subject to private decisions;

(iii) facilitate access by developing countries, to the extent practicable, to technologies whose transfer is subject to private decisions;

(iv) assist and co-operate with developing countries in the assessment and adaptation of existing technologies and in the development of national technologies by facilitating access, as far as possible, to available scientific and industrial research data;

(v) co-operate in the development of scientific and technological resources in developing countries, including the creation and growth of innovative capacities;

(vi) assist developing countries in strengthening their technological capacity, especially in the basic sectors of their national economy, through creation of and support for laboratories, experimental facilities and institutes for training and research;

(vii) co-operate in the establishment or strengthening of national, regional and/or international institutions, including technology transfer centres, to help developing countries to develop and obtain the technology and skills required for the establishment, development and enhancement of their technological capabilities including the design, construction and operation of plants;

(viii) encourage the adaptation of research and development, engineering and design to conditions and factor endowments prevailing in developing countries;

(ix) co-operate in measures leading to greater utilization of the managerial, engineering, design and technical experience of the personnel and the institutions of developing countries in specific economic and other development projects undertaken at the bilateral and multilateral levels;

(x) encourage the training of personnel from developing countries.

6.2 Governments of developed countries, directly or through appropriate international organizations, in assisting in the promotion of transfer of technology to developing countries—particularly to the least developed countries—should, as a part of programmes for development assistance and co-operation, take into account requests from developing countries to:

(i) contribute to the development of national technologies in developing countries by providing experts under development assistance and research exchange programmes;

(ii) provide training for research, engineering, design and other personnel from developing countries engaged in the development of national technologies or in the adaptation and use of technologies transferred;

(iii) provide assistance and co-operation in the development and administration of laws and regulations with a view to facilitating the transfer of technology;

(iv) provide support for projects in developing countries for the development and adaptation of new and existing technologies suitable to the particular needs of developing countries;

(v) grant credits on terms more favourable than the usual commercial terms for financing the acquisition of capital and intermediate goods in the context of approved development projects involving transfer of technology transactions so as to reduce the cost of projects and improve the quality of technology received by the developing countries;

(vi) provide assistance and co-operation in the development and administration of laws and regulations designed to avoid health, safety and environmental risks associated with technology or the products produced by it.

6.3 Governments of developed countries should take measures in accordance with national policies, laws and regulations to encourage and to endeavour to give incentive to enterprises and institutions in their countries, either individually or in collaboration with enterprises and institutions in developing countries, particularly those in the least developed countries, to make special efforts, *inter alia,* to:

(i) assist in the development of technological capabilities of the enterprises in developing countries, including special training as required by the recipients;

(ii) undertake the development of technology appropriate to the needs of developing countries;

(iii) undertake R and D activity in developing countries of interest to such countries, as well as to improve co-operation between enterprises and scientific and technological institutions of developed and developing countries;

(iv) assist in projects by enterprises and institutions in developing countries for the development and adaptation of new and existing technologies suitable to the particular needs and conditions of developing countries.

6.4 The special treatment accorded to developing countries should be responsive to their economic and social objectives vis-à-vis their relative stage of economic and social development and with particular attention to the special problems and conditions of the least developed countries.

Chapter 7

International Collaboration

7.1 The States recognize the need for appropriate international collaboration among governments, intergovernmental bodies, and organs and agencies of the United Nations system, including the international institutional machinery provided for in this Code, with a view to facilitating an expanded international flow of technology for strengthening the technological capabilities of all countries, taking into account the objectives and principles of this Code, and to promoting the effective implementation of its provisions.

7.2 Such international collaboration between governments at the bilateral or multilateral, subregional, regional or interregional levels may include, *inter alia,* the following measures:

(i) Exchange of available information on the availability and description of technologies and technological alternatives;

(ii) Exchange of available information on experience in seeking solutions to problems relating to the transfer of technology, particularly restrictive [business]** practices in the transfer of technology;*

(iii) Exchange of information on development of national legislation with respect to the transfer of technology;

(iv) Promotion of the conclusion of international agreements which should provide equitable treatment for both technology supplying and recipient parties and governments;

(v) Consultations which may lead to greater harmonization, where appropriate, of national legislation and policies with respect to the transfer of technology;

(vi) Promotion, where appropriate, of common programmes for searching for, acquiring and disseminating technologies;

(vii) Promotion of programmes for the adaptation and development of technology in the context of development objectives;

(viii) Promotion of the development of scientific and technological resources and capabilities stimulating the development of indigenous technologies;

(ix) Action through international agreements to avoid, as far as possible, imposition of double taxation on earnings and payments arising out of transfer of technology transactions.

Chapter 8

International Institutional Machinery

8.1 *Institutional arrangements*

(a) *

(b) *

(c) States which have accepted the Code of Conduct on the Transfer of Technology should take appropriate steps at the national level to meet their commitment to the Code.

8.2 *Functions of the International Institutional Machinery*

8.2.1 The International Institutional Machinery shall have the following functions:

(a) To provide a forum and modalities for consultations, discussion, and exchange of views between States on matters related to the Code, in particular its application and its greater harmonization, and the experience gained in its operations;

(b) To undertake and disseminate periodically studies and research on transfer of technology related to the provisions of the Code, with a view to increasing exchange of experience and giving greater effect to the application and implementation of the Code;

(c) To invite and consider relevant studies, documentation and reports from within the United Nations system, particularly from UNIDO and WIPO;

(d) To study matters relating to the Code and which might be characterized by data covering transfer of technology transactions and other relevant information obtained upon request addressed to all States;

(e) To collect and disseminate information on matters relating to the Code, to the over-all attainment of its goals and to the appropriate steps States have taken at the national level to promote an effective Code, including its objective and principles;

(f) To make appropriate reports and recommendations to States on matters within its competence including the application and implementation of the Code;

(g) To organize symposia, workshops and similar meetings concerning the application of the provisions of the Code, subject to the approval of the Trade and Development Board where financing from the regular budget is involved;

(h) To submit reports at least once a year on its work to the Trade and Development Board.

8.2.2 In the performance of its functions, the International Institutional Machinery may not act like a tribunal or otherwise pass judgement on the activities or conduct of individual Governments or of individual parties in connection with a specific transfer of technology transaction. The International Institutional Machinery should avoid becoming involved when parties in a specific transfer of technology transaction are in dispute.

8.2.3 The International Institutional Machinery shall establish such procedures as may be necessary to deal with issues related to confidentiality.

8.3 *Review procedure* *

8.4 *Secretariat*

The secretariat for the International Institutional Machinery shall be the UNCTAD secretariat. At the request of the International Institutional Machinery the secretariat shall submit relevant studies, documentation and other information to the International Institutional Machinery. It shall consult with and render assistance, by the relevant services, to States, particularly the developing countries, at their request, in the application of the Code at the national level, to the extent that resources are available.

8.5 *General provisions* *

Chapter 9
Applicable Law and Settlement of Disputes *

4.12 CONVENTION ESTABLISHING THE MULTILATERAL INVESTMENT GUARANTEE AGENCY.[a] Done at Seoul, Oct. 11, 1985. *Reproduced in* 24 I.L.M. 1605 (1985)

CHAPTER I

Establishment, Status, Purposes and Definitions

Article 1. Establishment and Status of the Agency

(a) There is hereby established the Multilateral Investment Guarantee Agency (hereinafter called the Agency).

(b) The Agency shall possess full juridical personality and, in particular, the capacity to:

(i) contract;

(ii) acquire and dispose of movable and immovable property; and

(iii) institute legal proceedings.

Article 2. Objective and Purposes

The objective of the Agency shall be to encourage the flow of investments for productive purposes among member countries, and in particular to developing member countries, thus supplementing the activities of the International Bank for Reconstruction and Development (hereinafter referred to as the Bank), the International Finance Corporation and other international development finance institutions.

To serve its objective, the Agency shall:

(a) issue guarantees, including coinsurance and reinsurance, against non-commercial risks in respect of investments in a member country which flow from other member countries;

(b) carry out appropriate complementary activities to promote the flow of investments to and among developing member countries; and

(c) exercise such other incidental powers as shall be necessary or desirable in the furtherance of its objective.

The Agency shall be guided in all its decisions by the provisions of this Article.

Article 3. Definitions

For the purposes of this Convention:

(a) "Member" means a State with respect to which this Convention has entered into force in accordance with Article 61.

(b) "Host country" or "host government" means a member, its government, or any public authority of a member in whose territories, as defined in Article 66, an investment which has been guaranteed or reinsured, or is considered for guarantee or reinsurance, by the Agency is to be located.

(c) A "developing member country" means a member which is listed as such in Schedule A hereto as this Schedule may be amended from time to time by the Council of Governors referred to in Article 30 (hereinafter called the Council).

(d) A "special majority" means an affirmative vote of not less than two-thirds of the total voting power representing not less than fifty-five percent of the subscribed shares of the capital stock of the Agency.

a. Annexes I and II and Schedules A and B are omitted.

(e) A "freely usable currency" means (i) any currency designated as such by the International Monetary Fund from time to time and (ii) any other freely available and effectively usable currency which the Board of Directors referred to in Article 30 (hereinafter called the Board) may designate for the purposes of this Convention after consultation with the International Monetary Fund and with the approval of the country of such currency.

CHAPTER II

Membership and Capital

Article 4. Membership

(a) Membership in the Agency shall be open to all members of the Bank and to Switzerland.

(b) Original members shall be the States which are listed in Schedule A hereto and become parties to this Convention on or before October 30, 1987.

Article 5. Capital

(a) The authorized capital stock of the Agency shall be one billion Special Drawing Rights (SDR 1,000,000,000). The capital stock shall be divided into 100,000 shares having a par value of SDR 10,000 each, which shall be available for subscription by members. All payment obligations of members with respect to capital stock shall be settled on the basis of the average value of the SDR in terms of United States dollars for the period January 1, 1981 to June 30, 1985, such value being 1.082 United States dollars per SDR.

(b) The capital stock shall increase on the admission of a new member to the extent that the then authorized shares are insufficient to provide the shares to be subscribed by such member pursuant to Article 6.

(c) The Council, by special majority, may at any time increase the capital stock of the Agency.

Article 6. Subscription of Shares

Each original member of the Agency shall subscribe at par to the number of shares of capital stock set forth opposite its name in Schedule A hereto. Each other member shall subscribe to such number of shares of capital stock on such terms and conditions as may be determined by the Council, but in no event at an issue price of less than par. No member shall subscribe to less than fifty shares. The Council may prescribe rules by which members may subscribe to additional shares of the authorized capital stock.

Article 7. Division and Calls of Subscribed Capital

The initial subscription of each member shall be paid as follows:

(i) Within ninety days from the date on which this Convention enters into force with respect to such member, ten percent of the price of each share shall be paid in cash as stipulated in Section (a) of Article 8 and an additional ten percent in the form of non-negotiable, non-interest-bearing promissory notes or similar obligations to be encashed pursuant to a decision of the Board in order to meet the Agency's obligations.

(ii) The remainder shall be subject to call by the Agency when required to meet its obligations.

Article 8. Payment of Subscription of Shares

(a) Payments of subscriptions shall be made in freely usable currencies except that payments by developing member countries may be made in their own currencies up to twenty-five percent of the paid-in cash portion of their subscriptions payable under Article 7(i).

(b) Calls on any portion of unpaid subscriptions shall be uniform on all shares.

(c) If the amount received by the Agency on a call shall be insufficient to meet the obligations which have necessitated the call, the Agency may make further successive calls on unpaid subscriptions until the aggregate amount received by it shall be sufficient to meet such obligations.

(d) Liability on shares shall be limited to the unpaid portion of the issue price.

Article 9. Valuation of Currencies

Whenever it shall be necessary for the purposes of this Convention to determine the value of one currency in terms of another, such value shall be as reasonably determined by the Agency, after consultation with the International Monetary Fund.

Article 10. Refunds

(a) The Agency shall, as soon as practicable, return to members amounts paid on calls on subscribed capital if and to the extent that:

(i) the call shall have been made to pay a claim resulting from a guarantee or reinsurance contract and thereafter the Agency shall have recovered its payment, in whole or in part, in a freely usable currency; or

(ii) the call shall have been made because of a default in payment by a member and thereafter such member shall have made good such default in whole or in part; or

(iii) the Council, by special majority, determines that the financial position of the Agency permits all or part of such amounts to be returned out of the Agency's revenues.

(b) Any refund effected under this Article to a member shall be made in freely usable currency in the proportion of the payments made by that member to the total amount paid pursuant to calls made prior to such refund.

(c) The equivalent of amounts refunded under this Article to a member shall become part of the callable capital obligations of the member under Article 7(ii).

CHAPTER III

Operations

Article 11. Covered Risks

(a) Subject to the provisions of Sections (b) and (c) below, the Agency may guarantee eligible investments against a loss resulting from one or more of the following types of risk:

(i) *Currency Transfer.* any introduction attributable to the host government of restrictions on the transfer outside the host country of its currency into a freely usable currency or another currency acceptable to the holder of the guarantee, including a failure of the host government to act within a reasonable period of time on an application by such holder for such transfer;

(ii) *Expropriation and Similar Measures.* any legislative action or administrative action or omission attributable to the host government which has the effect of depriving the holder of a guarantee of his ownership or control of, or a substantial benefit from, his investment, with the exception of non-discriminatory measures of general application which governments normally take for the purpose of regulating economic activity in their territories;

(iii) *Breach of Contract.* any repudiation or breach by the host government of a contract with the holder of a guarantee, when (a) the holder of a guarantee does not have recourse to a judicial or arbitral forum to determine the claim of repudiation or breach, or (b) a decision by such forum is not rendered within such reasonable period of time as shall be prescribed in the contracts of guarantee pursuant to the Agency's regulations, or (c) such a decision cannot be enforced; and

(iv) *War and Civil Disturbance.* any military action or civil disturbance in any territory of the host country to which this Convention shall be applicable as provided in Article 66.

(b) Upon the joint application of the investor and the host country, the Board, by special majority, may approve the extension of coverage under this Article to specific non-commercial risks other than those referred to in Section (a) above, but in no case to the risk of devaluation or depreciation of currency.

(c) Losses resulting from the following shall not be covered:

(i) any host government action or omission to which the holder of the guarantee has agreed or for which he has been responsible; and

(ii) any host government action or omission or any other event occurring before the conclusion of the contract of guarantee.

Article 12. Eligible Investments

(a) Eligible investments shall include equity interests, including medium- or long-term loans made or guaranteed by holders of equity in the enterprise concerned, and such forms of direct investment as may be determined by the Board.

(b) The Board, by special majority, may extend eligibility to any other medium- or long-term form of investment, except that loans other than those mentioned in Section (a) above may be eligible only if they are related to a specific investment covered or to be covered by the Agency.

(c) Guarantees shall be restricted to investments the implementation of which begins subsequent to the registration of the application for the guarantee by the Agency. Such investments may include:

(i) any transfer of foreign exchange made to modernize, expand, or develop an existing investment; and

(ii) the use of earnings from existing investments which could otherwise be transferred outside the host country.

(d) In guaranteeing an investment, the Agency shall satisfy itself as to:

(i) the economic soundness of the investment and its contribution to the development of the host country;

(ii) compliance of the investment with the host country's laws and regulations;

(iii) consistency of the investment with the declared development objectives and priorities of the host country; and

(iv) the investment conditions in the host country, including the availability of fair and equitable treatment and legal protection for the investment.

Article 13. Eligible Investors

(a) Any natural person and any juridical person may be eligible to receive the Agency's guarantee provided that:

(i) such natural person is a national of a member other than the host country;

(ii) such juridical person is incorporated and has its principal place of business in a member or the majority of its capital is owned by a member or members or nationals thereof, provided that such member is not the host country in any of the above cases; and

(iii) such juridical person, whether or not it is privately owned, operates on a commercial basis.

(b) In case the investor has more than one nationality, for the purposes of Section (a) above the nationality of a member shall prevail over the nationality of a non-member, and the nationality of the host country shall prevail over the nationality of any other member.

(c) Upon the joint application of the investor and the host country, the Board, by special majority, may extend eligibility to a natural person who is a national of the host country or a juridical person which is incorporated in the host country or the majority of whose capital is owned by its nationals, provided that the assets invested are transferred from outside the host country.

Article 14. Eligible Host Countries

Investments shall be guaranteed under this Chapter only if they are to be made in the territory of a developing member country.

Article 15. Host Country Approval

The Agency shall not conclude any contract of guarantee before the host government has approved the issuance of the guarantee by the Agency against the risks designated for cover.

Article 16. Terms and Conditions

The terms and conditions of each contract of guarantee shall be determined by the Agency subject to such rules and regulations as the Board shall issue, provided that the Agency shall not cover the total loss of the guaranteed investment. Contracts of guarantee shall be approved by the President under the direction of the Board.

Article 17. Payment of Claims

The President under the direction of the Board shall decide on the payment of claims to a holder of a guarantee in accordance with the contract of guarantee and such policies as the Board may adopt. Contracts of guarantee shall require holders of guarantees to seek, before a payment is made by the Agency, such administrative remedies as may be appropriate under the circumstances, provided that they are readily available to them under the laws of the host country. Such contracts may require the lapse of certain reasonable periods between the occurrence of events giving rise to claims and payments of claims.

Article 18. Subrogation

(a) Upon paying or agreeing to pay compensation to a holder of a guarantee, the Agency shall be subrogated to such rights or claims related to the guaranteed investment as the holder of a guarantee may have had against the host country and other obligors. The contract of guarantee shall provide the terms and conditions of such subrogation.

(b) The rights of the Agency pursuant to Section (a) above shall be recognized by all members.

(c) Amounts in the currency of the host country acquired by the Agency as subrogee pursuant to Section (a) above shall be accorded, with respect to use and conversion, treatment by the host country as favorable as the treatment to which such funds would be entitled in the hands of the holder of the guarantee. In any case, such amounts may be used by the Agency for the payment of its administrative expenditures and other costs. The Agency shall also seek to enter into arrangements with host countries on other uses of such currencies to the extent that they are not freely usable.

Article 19. Relationship to National and Regional Entities

The Agency shall cooperate with, and seek to complement the operations of, national entities of members and regional entities the majority of whose capital is owned by members, which carry out activities similar to those of the Agency, with a view to maximizing both the efficiency of their respective services and their contribution to increased flows of foreign investment. To this end, the Agency may enter into arrangements with such entities on the details of such cooperation, including in particular the modalities of reinsurance and coinsurance.

Article 20. Reinsurance of National and Regional Entities

(a) The Agency may issue reinsurance in respect of a specific investment against a loss resulting from one or more of the non-commercial risks underwritten by a member or agency thereof or by a regional investment guarantee agency the majority of whose capital is owned by members. The Board, by special majority, shall from time to time prescribe maximum amounts of contingent liability which may be assumed by the Agency with respect to reinsurance contracts. In respect of specific investments which have been completed more than twelve months prior to receipt of the application for reinsurance by the Agency, the maximum amount shall initially be set at ten percent of the aggregate contingent liability of the Agency under this Chapter. The conditions of eligibility specified in Articles 11 to 14 shall apply to reinsurance operations, except that the reinsured investments need not be implemented subsequent to the application for reinsurance.

(b) The mutual rights and obligations of the Agency and a reinsured member or agency shall be stated in contracts of reinsurance subject to such rules and regulations as the Board shall issue. The Board shall approve each contract for reinsurance covering an investment which has been made prior to receipt of the application for reinsurance by the Agency, with a view to minimizing risks, assuring that the Agency receives premiums commensurate with its risk, and assuring that the reinsured entity is appropriately committed toward promoting new investment in developing member countries.

(c) The Agency shall, to the extent possible, assure that it or the reinsured entity shall have the rights of subrogation and arbitration equivalent to those the Agency would have if it were the primary guarantor. The terms and conditions of reinsurance shall require that administrative remedies are sought in accordance with Article 17 before a payment is made by the Agency. Subrogation shall be effective with respect to the host country concerned only after its approval of the reinsurance by the Agency. The Agency shall include in the contracts of reinsurance provisions requiring the reinsured to pursue with due diligence the rights or claims related to the reinsured investment.

Article 21. Cooperation with Private Insurers and with Reinsurers

(a) The Agency may enter into arrangements with private insurers in member countries to enhance its own operations and encourage such insurers to provide coverage of non-commercial risks in developing member countries on conditions similar to those applied by the Agency. Such arrangements may include the provision of reinsurance by the Agency under the conditions and procedures specified in Article 20.

(b) The Agency may reinsure with any appropriate reinsurance entity, in whole or in part, any guarantee or guarantees issued by it.

(c) The Agency will in particular seek to guarantee investments for which comparable coverage on reasonable terms is not available from private insurers and reinsurers.

Article 22. Limits of Guarantee

(a) Unless determined otherwise by the Council by special majority, the aggregate amount of contingent liabilities which may be assumed by the Agency under this Chapter shall not exceed one hundred and fifty percent of the amount of the Agency's unimpaired subscribed capital and its reserves plus such portion of its reinsurance cover as the Board may determine. The Board shall from time to time review the risk profile of the Agency's portfolio in the light of its experience with claims, degree of risk diversification, reinsurance cover and other relevant factors with a view to ascertaining whether changes in the maximum aggregate amount of contingent liabilities should be recommended to the Council. The maximum amount determined by the Council shall not under any circumstances exceed five times the amount of the Agency's unimpaired subscribed capital, its reserves and such portion of its reinsurance cover as may be deemed appropriate.

(b) Without prejudice to the general limit of guarantee referred to in Section (a) above, the Board may prescribe:

(i) maximum aggregate amounts of contingent liability which may be assumed by the Agency under this Chapter for all guarantees issued to investors of each individual member. In determining such maximum amounts, the Board shall give due consideration to the share of the respective member in the capital of the Agency and the need to apply more liberal limitations in respect of investments originating in developing member countries; and

(ii) maximum aggregate amounts of contingent liability which may be assumed by the Agency with respect to such risk diversification factors as individual projects, individual host countries and types of investment or risk.

Article 23. Investment Promotion

(a) The Agency shall carry out research, undertake activities to promote investment flows and disseminate information on investment opportunities in developing member countries, with a view to improving the environment for foreign investment flows to such countries. The Agency may, upon the request of a member, provide technical advice and assistance to improve the investment conditions in the territories of that member. In performing these activities, the Agency shall:

(i) be guided by relevant investment agreements among member countries;

(ii) seek to remove impediments, in both developed and developing member countries, to the flow of investment to developing member countries; and

(iii) coordinate with other agencies concerned with the promotion of foreign investment, and in particular the International Finance Corporation.

(b) The Agency also shall:

(i) encourage the amicable settlement of disputes between investors and host countries;

(ii) endeavor to conclude agreements with developing member countries, and in particular with prospective host countries, which will assure that the Agency, with respect to investment guaranteed by it, has treatment at least as favorable as that agreed by the member concerned for the most favored investment guarantee agency or State in an agreement relating to investment, such agreements to be approved by special majority of the Board; and

(iii) promote and facilitate the conclusion of agreements, among its members, on the promotion and protection of investments.

(c) The Agency shall give particular attention in its promotional efforts to the importance of increasing the flow of investments among developing member countries.

Article 24. Guarantees of Sponsored Investments

In addition to the guarantee operations undertaken by the Agency under this Chapter, the Agency may guarantee investments under the sponsorship arrangements provided for in Annex I to this Convention.

CHAPTER IV

Financial Provisions

* * *

CHAPTER V

Organization and Management

Article 30. Structure of the Agency

The Agency shall have a Council of Governors, a Board of Directors, a President and staff to perform such duties as the Agency may determine.

* * *

Article 34. Political Activity Prohibited

The Agency, its President and staff shall not interfere in the political affairs of any member. Without prejudice to the right of the Agency to take into account all the circumstances surrounding an investment, they shall not be influenced in their decisions by the political character of the member or members concerned. Considerations relevant to their decisions shall be weighed impartially in order to achieve the purposes stated in Article 2.

Article 35. Relations With International Organizations

The Agency shall, within the terms of this Convention, cooperate with the United Nations and with other inter-governmental organizations having specialized responsibilities in related fields, including in particular the Bank and the International Finance Corporation.

Article 36. Location of Principal Office

(a) The principal office of the Agency shall be located in Washington, D.C., unless the Council, by special majority, decides to establish it in another location.

(b) The Agency may establish other offices as may be necessary for its work.

* * *

CHAPTER VI

Voting, Adjustments of Subscriptions and Representation

* * *

CHAPTER VII

Privileges and Immunities

Article 43. Purposes of Chapter

To enable the Agency to fulfill its functions, the immunities and privileges set forth in this Chapter shall be accorded to the Agency in the territories of each member.

Article 44. Legal Process

Actions other than those within the scope of Articles 57 and 58 may be brought against the Agency only in a court of competent jurisdiction in the territories of a member in which the Agency has an office or has appointed an agent for the purpose of accepting service or notice of process. No such action against the Agency shall be brought (i) by members or persons acting for or deriving claims from members or (ii) in respect of personnel matters. The property and assets of the Agency shall, wherever located and by whomsoever held, be immune from all forms of seizure, attachment or execution before the delivery of the final judgment or award against the Agency.

Article 45. Assets

(a) The property and assets of the Agency, wherever located and by whomsoever held, shall be immune from search, requisition, confiscation, expropriation or any other form of seizure by executive or legislative action.

(b) To the extent necessary to carry out its operations under this Convention, all property and assets of the Agency shall be free from restrictions, regulations, controls and moratoria of any nature; provided that property and assets acquired by the Agency as successor to or subrogee of a holder of a guarantee, a reinsured entity or an investor insured by a reinsured entity shall be free from applicable foreign exchange restrictions, regulations and controls in force in the territories of the member concerned to the extent that the holder, entity or investor to whom the Agency was subrogated was entitled to such treatment.

(c) For purposes of this Chapter, the term "assets" shall include the assets of the Sponsorship Trust Fund referred to in Annex I to this Convention and other assets administered by the Agency in furtherance of its objective.

Article 46. Archives and Communications

(a) The archives of the Agency shall be inviolable, wherever they may be.

(b) The official communications of the Agency shall be accorded by each member the same treatment that is accorded to the official communications of the Bank.

Article 47. Taxes

(a) The Agency, its assets, property and income, and its operations and transactions authorized by this Convention, shall be immune from all taxes and customs duties. The Agency shall also be immune from liability for the collection or payment of any tax or duty.

(b) Except in the case of local nationals, no tax shall be levied on or in respect of expense allowances paid by the Agency to Governors and their Alternates or on or in respect of salaries, expense allowances or other emoluments paid by the Agency to the Chairman of the Board, Directors, their Alternates, the President or staff of the Agency.

(c) No taxation of any kind shall be levied on any investment guaranteed or reinsured by the Agency (including any earnings therefrom) or any insurance policies reinsured by the Agency (including any premiums and other revenues therefrom) by whomsoever held: (i) which discriminates against such investment or insurance policy solely because it is guaranteed or reinsured by the Agency; or (ii) if the sole jurisdictional basis for such taxation is the location of any office or place of business maintained by the Agency.

Article 48. Officials of the Agency

All Governors, Directors, Alternates, the President and staff of the Agency:

(i) shall be immune from legal process with respect to acts performed by them in their official capacity;

(ii) not being local nationals, shall be accorded the same immunities from immigration restrictions, alien registration requirements and national service obligations, and the same facilities as regards exchange restrictions as are accorded by the members concerned to the representatives, officials and employees of comparable rank of other members; and

(iii) shall be granted the same treatment in respect of travelling facilities as is accorded by the members concerned to representatives, officials and employees of comparable rank of other members.

* * *

CHAPTER VIII

Withdrawal, Suspension of Membership and Cessation of Operations

Article 51. Withdrawal

Any member may, after the expiration of three years following the date upon which this Convention has entered into force with respect to such member, withdraw from the Agency at any time by giving notice in writing to the Agency at its principal office. The Agency shall notify the Bank, as depository of this Convention, of the receipt of such notice. Any withdrawal shall become effective ninety days following the date of the receipt of such notice by the Agency. A member may revoke such notice as long as it has not become effective.

Article 52. Suspension of Membership

(a) If a member fails to fulfill any of its obligations under this Convention, the Council may, by a majority of its members exercising a majority of the total voting power, suspend its membership.

(b) While under suspension a member shall have no rights under this Convention, except for the right of withdrawal and other rights provided in this Chapter and Chapter IX, but shall remain subject to all its obligations.

(c) For purposes of determining eligibility for a guarantee or reinsurance to be issued under Chapter III or Annex I to this Convention, a suspended member shall not be treated as a member of the Agency.

(d) The suspended member shall automatically cease to be a member one year from the date of its suspension unless the Council decides to extend the period of suspension or to restore the member to good standing.

Article 53. Rights and Duties of States Ceasing to be Members

(a) When a State ceases to be a member, it shall remain liable for all its obligations, including its contingent obligations, under this Convention which shall have been in effect before the cessation of its membership.

(b) Without prejudice to Section (a) above, the Agency shall enter into an arrangement with such State for the settlement of their respective claims and obligations. Any such arrangement shall be approved by the Board.

Article 54. Suspension of Operations

(a) The Board may, whenever it deems it justified, suspend the issuance of new guarantees for a specified period.

(b) In an emergency, the Board may suspend all activities of the Agency for a period not exceeding the duration of such emergency, provided that necessary arrangements shall be made for the protection of the interests of the Agency and of third parties.

(c) The decision to suspend operations shall have no effect on the obligations of the members under this Convention or on the obligations of the Agency towards holders of a guarantee or reinsurance policy or towards third parties.

Article 55. Liquidation

(a) The Council, by special majority, may decide to cease operations and to liquidate the Agency. Thereupon the Agency shall forthwith cease all activities, except those incident to the orderly realization, conservation and preservation of assets and settlement of obligations. Until final settlement and distribution of assets, the Agency shall remain in existence and all rights and obligations of members under this Convention shall continue unimpaired.

(b) No distribution of assets shall be made to members until all liabilities to holders of guarantees and other creditors shall have been discharged or provided for and until the Council shall have decided to make such distribution.

(c) Subject to the foregoing, the Agency shall distribute its remaining assets to members in proportion to each member's share in the subscribed capital. The Agency shall also distribute any remaining assets of the Sponsorship Trust Fund referred to in Annex I to this Convention to sponsoring members in the proportion which the investments sponsored by each bears to the total of sponsored investments. No member shall be entitled to its share in the assets of the Agency or the Sponsorship Trust Fund unless that member has settled all outstanding claims by the Agency against it. Every distribution of assets shall be made at such times as the Council shall determine and in such manner as it shall deem fair and equitable.

CHAPTER IX

Settlement of Disputes

Article 56. Interpretation and Application of the Convention

(a) Any question of interpretation or application of the provisions of this Convention arising between any member of the Agency and the Agency or among members of the Agency shall be submitted to the Board for its decision. Any member which is particularly affected by the question and which is not otherwise represented by a national in the Board may send a representative to attend any meeting of the Board at which such question is considered.

(b) In any case where the Board has given a decision under Section (a) above, any member may require that the question be referred to the Council, whose decision shall be final. Pending the result of the referral to the Council, the Agency may, so far as it deems necessary, act on the basis of the decision of the Board.

Article 57. Disputes between the Agency and Members

(a) Without prejudice to the provisions of Article 56 and of Section (b) of this Article, any dispute between the Agency and a member or an agency thereof and any dispute between the Agency and a country (or agency thereof) which has ceased to be a member, shall be settled in accordance with the procedure set out in Annex II to this Convention.

(b) Disputes concerning claims of the Agency acting as subrogee of an investor shall be settled in accordance with either (i) the procedure set out in Annex II to this Convention, or (ii) an agreement to be entered into between the Agency and the member concerned on an alternative method or methods for the settlement of such disputes. In the latter case, Annex II to this Convention shall serve as a basis for such an agreement which shall, in each case, be approved by the Board by special majority prior to the undertaking by the Agency of operations in the territories of the member concerned.

Article 58. Disputes Involving Holders of a Guarantee or Reinsurance

Any dispute arising under a contract of guarantee or reinsurance between the parties thereto shall be submitted to arbitration for final determination in accordance with such rules as shall be provided for or referred to in the contract of guarantee or reinsurance.

CHAPTER X

Amendments

* * *

4.13 OECD GUIDELINES FOR MULTINATIONAL ENTERPRISES.[a] Annexed to the Declaration of June 21, 1976 by Governments of OECD Member Countries on International Investment and Multinational Enterprises, as amended in 1979 and 1984. OECD, The Guidelines For Multinational Enterprises 11 (1986)

1. Multinational enterprises now play an important part in the economies of Member countries and in international economic relations, which is of increasing interest to governments. Through international direct investment, such enterprises can bring substantial benefits to home and host countries by contributing to the efficient utilisation of capital, technology and human resources between countries and can thus fulfil an important role in the promotion of economic and social welfare. But the advances made by multinational enterprises in organising their operations beyond the national framework may lead to abuse of concentrations of economic power and to conflicts with national policy objectives. In addition, the complexity of these multinational enterprises and the difficulty of clearly perceiving their diverse structures, operations and policies sometimes give rise to concern.

2. The common aim of the Member countries is to encourage the positive contributions which multinational enterprises can make to economic and social progress and to minimise and resolve the difficulties to which their various operations may give rise. In view of the transnational structure of such enterprises, this aim will be furthered by co-operation among the OECD countries where the headquarters of most of the multinational enterprises are established and which are the location of a substantial part of their operations. The Guidelines set out hereafter are designed to assist in the achievement of this common aim and to contribute to improving the foreign investment climate.

3. Since the operations of multinational enterprises extend throughout the world, including countries that are not Members of the Organisation, international co-operation in this field should extend to all States. Member countries will give their full support to efforts undertaken in co-operation with non-member countries, and in particular with developing countries, with a view to improving the welfare and living standards of all people both by encouraging the positive contributions which multinational enterprises can make and by minimising and resolving the problems which may arise in connection with their activities.

4. Within the Organisation, the programme of co-operation to attain these ends will be a continuing, pragmatic and balanced one. It comes within the general aims of the Convention on the Organisation for Economic Co-operation and Development (OECD) and makes full use of the various specialised bodies of the Organisation, whose terms of reference already cover many aspects of the role of multinational enterprises, notably in matters of international trade and payments. competition, taxation, manpower, industrial development, science and technology. In these bodies, work is being carried out on the identification of issues, the improvement of relevant qualitative and statistical information and the elaboration of proposals for action designed to strengthen inter-governmental co-operation. In some of these areas procedures already exist through which issues related to the operations of multinational enterprises can be taken up. This work could result in the conclusion of further and complementary agreements and arrangements between governments.

5. The initial phase of the co-operation programme is composed of a Declaration and three Decisions promulgated simultaneously as they are complementary and

a. *See also* Basic Document 4.9, *supra*.

inter-connected, in respect of Guidelines for multinational enterprises, National Treatment for foreign-controlled enterprises and international investment incentives and disincentives.

6. The Guidelines set out below are recommendations jointly addressed by Member countries to multinational enterprises operating in their territories. These Guidelines, which take into account the problems which can arise because of the international structure of these enterprises, lay down standards for the activities of these enterprises in the different Member countries. Observance of the Guidelines is voluntary and not legally enforceable. However, they should help to ensure that the operations of these enterprises are in harmony with national policies of the countries where they operate and to strengthen the basis of mutual confidence between enterprises and States.

7. Every State has the right to prescribe the conditions under which multinational enterprises operate within its national jurisdiction, subject to international law and to the international agreements to which it has subscribed. The entities of a multinational enterprise located in various countries are subject to the laws of these countries.

8. A precise legal definition of multinational enterprises is not required for the purposes of the Guidelines. These usually comprise companies or other entities whose ownership is private, state or mixed, established in different countries and so linked that one or more of them may be able to exercise a significant influence over the activities of others and, in particular, to share knowledge and resources with the others. The degree of autonomy of each entity in relation to the others varies widely from one multinational enterprise to another, depending on the nature of the links between such entities and the fields of activity concerned. For these reasons, the Guidelines are addressed to the various entities within the multinational enterprise (parent companies and/or local entities) according to the actual distribution of responsibilities among them on the understanding that they will co-operate and provide assistance to one another as necessary to facilitate observance of the Guidelines. The word "enterprise" as used in these Guidelines refers to these various entities in accordance with their responsibilities.

9. The Guidelines are not aimed at introducing differences of treatment between multinational and domestic enterprises; wherever relevant they reflect good practice for all. Accordingly, multinational and domestic enterprises are subject to the same expectations in respect of their conduct wherever the Guidelines are relevant to both.

10. The use of appropriate international dispute settlement mechanisms, including arbitration, should be encouraged as a means of facilitating the resolution of problems arising between enterprises and Member countries.

11. Member countries have agreed to establish appropriate review and consultation procedures concerning issues arising in respect of the Guidelines. When multinational enterprises are made subject to conflicting requirements by Member countries, the governments concerned will co-operate in good faith with a view to resolving such problems either within the Committee on International Investment and Multinational Enterprises established by the OECD Council on 21st January 1975 or through other mutually acceptable arrangements.

Having regard to the foregoing considerations, the Member countries set forth the following Guidelines for multinational enterprises with the understanding that Member countries will fulfil their responsibilities to treat enterprises equitably and in accordance with international law and international agreements, as well as contractual obligations to which they have subscribed.

GENERAL POLICIES

Enterprises should:

1. Take fully into account established general policy objectives of the Member countries in which they operate;

2. In particular, give due consideration to those countries' aims and priorities with regard to economic and social progress, including industrial and regional development, the protection of the environment and consumer interests, the creation of employment opportunities, the promotion of innovation and the transfer of technology;

3. While observing their legal obligations concerning information, supply their entities with supplementary information the latter may need in order to meet requests by the authorities of the countries in which those entities are located for information relevant to the activities of those entities, taking into account legitimate requirements of business confidentiality;

4. Favour close co-operation with the local community and business interests;

5. Allow their component entities freedom to develop their activities and to exploit their competitive advantage in domestic and foreign markets, consistent with the need for specialisation and sound commercial practice;

6. When filling responsible posts in each country of operation, take due account of individual qualifications without discrimination as to nationality, subject to particular national requirements in this respect;

7. Not render—and they should not be solicited or expected to render—any bribe or other improper benefit, direct or indirect, to any public servant or holder of public office;

8. Unless legally permissible, not make contributions to candidates for public office or to political parties or other political organisations;

9. Abstain from any improper involvement in local political activities.

DISCLOSURE OF INFORMATION

Enterprises should, having due regard to their nature and relative size in the economic context of their operations and to requirements of business confidentiality and to cost, publish in a form suited to improve public understanding a sufficient body of factual information on the structure, activities and policies of the enterprise as a whole, as a supplement, in so far as necessary for this purpose, to information to be disclosed under the national law of the individual countries in which they operate. To this end, they should publish within reasonable time limits, on a regular basis, but at least annually, financial statements and other pertinent information relating to the enterprise as a whole, comprising in particular:

i) The structure of the enterprise, showing the name and location of the parent company, its main affiliates, its percentage ownership, direct and indirect, in these affiliates, including shareholdings between them;

ii) The geographical areas where operations are carried out and the principal activities carried on therein by the parent company and the main affiliates;

iii) The operating results and sales by geographical area and the sales in the major lines of business for the enterprise as a whole;

iv) Significant new capital investment by geographical area and, as far as practicable, by major lines of business for the enterprise as a whole;

v) A statement of the sources and uses of funds by the enterprise as a whole;

vi) The average number of employees in each geographical area;

vii) Research and development expenditure for the enterprise as a whole;

viii) The policies followed in respect of intra-group pricing;

ix) The accounting policies, including those on consolidation, observed in compiling the published information.

COMPETITION

Enterprises should, while conforming to official competition rules and established policies of the countries in which they operate:

1. Refrain from actions which would adversely affect competition in the relevant market by abusing a dominant position of market power, by means of, for example:

a) Anti-competitive acquisitions;

b) Predatory behaviour toward competitors;

c) Unreasonable refusal to deal;

d) Anti-competitive abuse of industrial property rights;

e) Discriminatory (i.e. unreasonably differentiated) pricing and using such pricing transactions between affiliated enterprises as a means of affecting adversely competition outside these enterprises;

2. Allow purchasers, distributors and licensees freedom to resell, export, purchase and develop their operations consistent with law, trade conditions, the need for specialisation and sound commercial practice;

3. Refrain from participating in or otherwise purposely strengthening the restrictive effects of international or domestic cartels or restrictive agreements which adversely affect or eliminate competition and which are not generally or specifically accepted under applicable national or international legislation;

4. Be ready to consult and co-operate, including the provision of information, with competent authorities of countries whose interests are directly affected in regard to competition issues or investigations. Provision of information should be in accordance with safeguards normally applicable in this field.

FINANCING

Enterprises should, in managing the financial and commercial operations of their activities, and especially their liquid foreign assets and liabilities, take into consideration the established objectives of the countries in which they operate regarding balance of payments and credit policies.

TAXATION

Enterprises should:

1. Upon request of the taxation authorities of the countries in which they operate, provide, in accordance with the safeguards and relevant procedures of the national laws of these countries, the information necessary to determine correctly the taxes to be assessed in connection with their operations, including relevant information concerning their operations in other countries;

2. Refrain from making use of the particular facilities available to them, such as transfer pricing which does not conform to an arm's length standard, for modifying in ways contrary to national laws the tax base on which members of the group are assessed.

EMPLOYMENT AND INDUSTRIAL RELATIONS

Enterprises should, within the framework of law, regulations and prevailing labour relations and employment practices, in each of the countries in which they operate:

1. Respect the right of their employees to be represented by trade unions and other bona fide organisations of employees, and engage in constructive negotiations, either individually or through employers' associations, with such

employee organisations with a view to reaching agreements on employment conditions, which should include provisions for dealing with disputes arising over the interpretation of such agreements, and for ensuring mutually respected rights and responsibilities;

2. *a)* Provide such facilities to representatives of the employees as may be necessary to assist in the development of effective collective agreements;

b) Provide to representatives of employees information which is needed for meaningful negotiations on conditions of employment;

3. Provide to representatives of employees where this accords with local law and practice, information which enables them to obtain a true and fair view of the performance of the entity or, where appropriate, the enterprise as a whole;

4. Observe standards of employment and industrial relations not less favourable than those observed by comparable employers in the host country;

5. In their operations, to the greatest extent practicable, utilise, train and prepare for upgrading members of the local labour force in co-operation with representatives of their employees and, where appropriate, the relevant governmental authorities;

6. In considering changes in their operations which would have major effects upon the livelihood of their employees, in particular in the case of the closure of an entity involving collective lay-offs or dismissals, provide reasonable notice of such changes to representatives of their employees, and where appropriate to the relevant governmental authorities, and co-operate with the employee representatives and appropriate governmental authorities so as to mitigate to the maximum extent practicable adverse effects;

7. Implement their employment policies including hiring, discharge, pay, promotion and training without discrimination unless selectivity in respect of employee characteristics is in furtherance of established governmental policies which specifically promote greater equality of employment opportunity;

8. In the context of bona fide negotiations with representatives of employees on conditions of employment, or while employees are exercising a right to organise, not threaten to utilise a capacity to transfer the whole or part of an operating unit from the country concerned nor transfer employees from the enterprises' component entities in other countries in order to influence unfairly those negotiations or to hinder the exercise of a right to organise;

9. Enable authorised representatives of their employees to conduct negotiations on collective bargaining or labour management relations issues with representatives of management who are authorised to take decisions on the matters under negotiation.

SCIENCE AND TECHNOLOGY

Enterprises should:

1. Endeavour to ensure that their activities fit satisfactorily into the scientific and technological policies and plans of the countries in which they operate, and contribute to the development of national scientific and technological capacities, including as far as appropriate the establishment and improvement in host countries of their capacity to innovate;

2. To the fullest extent practicable, adopt in the course of their business activities practices which permit the rapid diffusion of technologies with due regard to the protection of industrial and intellectual property rights;

3. When granting licences for the use of industrial property rights or when otherwise transferring technology, do so on reasonable terms and conditions.

4.14 DRAFT CODE OF CONDUCT ON TRANSNATIONAL CORPORATIONS. Adopted by the U.N. Economic and Social Council, Feb. 1, 1988. U.N. Doc. E/1988/39/Add.1 (1988)

PREAMBLE

The General Assembly,

Recalling Economic and Social Council resolutions 1908 (LVII) of 2 August 1974 and 1913 (LVII) of 5 December 1974, establishing the Commission on Transnational Corporations and the United Nations Centre on Transnational Corporations with the mandate, as their highest priority of work, of concluding a Code of Conduct on Transnational Corporations,

Convinced that a universally accepted, comprehensive and effective Code of Conduct on Transnational Corporations is an essential element in the strengthening of international economic and social co-operation and, in particular, in achieving one of the main goals and objectives in that co-operation, namely, to maximize the contributions of transnational corporations to economic development and growth and to minimize the negative effects of the activities of these corporations.

Decides to adopt the following Code of Conduct on Transnational Corporations:

DEFINITIONS AND SCOPE OF APPLICATION

1. (a) This Code is universally applicable to enterprises, irrespective of their country of origin and their ownership, including private, public or mixed, comprising entities in two or more countries, regardless of the legal form and fields of activity of these entities, which operate under a system of decision-making, permitting coherent policies and a common strategy through one or more decision-making centres, in which the entities are so linked, by ownership or otherwise, that one or more of them may be able to exercise a significant influence over the activities of others and, in particular, to share knowledge, resources and responsibilities with the others. Such enterprises are referred to in this Code as transnational corporations.

(b) The term "entities" in the Code refers to both parent entities—that is, entities which are the main source of influence over others—and other entities, unless otherwise specified in the Code.

(c) The term "transnational corporation" in the Code refers to the enterprise as a whole or its various entities.

(d) The term "home country" means the country in which the parent entity is located. The term "host country" means a country other than the home country in which an entity other than the parent entity is located.

(e) The term "country in which a transnational corporation operates" refers to a home or host country in which an entity of a transnational corporation conducts operations.

2. For the application of this Code, it is irrelevant whether or not enterprises as described in paragraph 1(a) above are referred to in any country as transnational corporations.

3. The Code is universally applicable in all States, regardless of their political and economic systems or their level of development.

4. The provisions of the Code addressed to transnational corporations reflect good practice for all enterprises. Subject to the provisions of paragraph 52, wherever the provisions of the Code are relevant to both, transnational corporations and domestic enterprises shall be subject to the same expectations with regard to their conduct.

5. Subject to the relevant constitutions, charters or other fundamental laws of the regional groupings of States concerned, any reference in this Code to States, countries or Governments, also includes regional groupings of States, to the extent that the provisions of this Code relate to matters within these groupings' own competence, with respect to such competence.

6. In their interpretation and application the provisions of this Code are interrelated and each provision should be construed in the context of the other provisions.

ACTIVITIES OF TRANSNATIONAL CORPORATIONS

A. *General*

Respect for national sovereignty and observance of domestic laws, regulations and administrative practices

7. Transnational corporations shall respect the national sovereignty of the countries in which they operate and the right of each State to exercise its permanent sovereignty over its natural wealth and resources.

8. An entity of a transnational corporation is subject to the laws, regulations and established administrative practices of the country in which it operates.

9. Transnational corporations shall respect the right of each State to regulate and monitor accordingly the activities of their entities operating within its territory.

Adherence to economic goals and development objectives, policies and priorities

10. Transnational corporations should carry out their activities in conformity with the development policies, objectives and priorities set out by the Governments of the countries in which they operate and work seriously towards making a positive contribution to the achievement of such goals at the national and, as appropriate, the regional level, within the framework of regional integration programmes. Transnational corporations should co-operate with the Governments of the countries in which they operate with a view to contributing to the development process and should be responsive to requests for consultation in this respect, thereby establishing mutually beneficial relations with these countries.

11. Transnational corporations should carry out their operations in conformity with applicable intergovernmental co-operative arrangements concluded by the countries in which they operate.

Review and renegotiation of contracts and agreements

12. (a) Contracts or agreements between Governments and transnational corporations should be negotiated and implemented in good faith. In such contracts or agreements, especially long-term ones, review or renegotiation clauses should normally be included.

(b) In the absence of such clauses and where there has been a fundamental change of the circumstances on which the contract or agreement was based, transnational corporations, acting in good faith, should co-operate with Governments for the review or renegotiation of such contract or agreement.

Adherence to socio-cultural objectives and values

13. Transnational corporations should respect the social and cultural objectives, values and traditions of the countries in which they operate. While economic and technological development is normally accompanied by social change, transnational corporations should avoid practices, products or services which cause detrimental effects on cultural patterns and socio-cultural objectives as determined by Governments. For this purpose, transnational corporations should respond positively to requests for consultations from Governments concerned.

Respect for human rights and fundamental freedoms

14. Transnational corporations shall respect human rights and fundamental freedoms in the countries in which they operate. In their social and industrial relations, transnational corporations shall not discriminate on the basis of race, colour, sex, religion, language, social, national and ethnic origin or political or other opinion. Transnational corporations shall conform to government policies designed to extend equality of opportunity and treatment.

Non-collaboration by transnational corporations with racist minority régimes in Southern Africa

15. In accordance with the efforts of the international community towards the elimination of *apartheid* in South Africa and its continued illegal occupation of Namibia,

(a) Transnational corporations shall refrain from operations and activities supporting and sustaining the racist minority régime of South Africa in maintaining the system of *apartheid* and the illegal occupation of Namibia;

(b) Transnational corporations shall engage in appropriate activities within their competence with a view to eliminating racial discrimination and all other aspects of the system of *apartheid;*

(c) Transnational corporations shall comply strictly with obligations resulting from Security Council decisions and shall fully respect those resulting from all relevant United Nations resolutions;

(d) With regard to investment in Namibia, transnational corporations shall comply strictly with obligations resulting from Security Council resolution 283 (1970) and other relevant Security Council decisions and shall fully respect those resulting from all relevant United Nations resolutions.

Non-interference in internal affairs of host countries

16. Transnational corporations shall not interfere in the internal affairs of host countries, without prejudice to their participation in activities that are permitted by the laws, regulations or established administrative practices of host countries.

17. Transnational corporations shall not engage in activities of a political nature which are not permitted by the laws and established policies and administrative practices of the countries in which they operate.

Non-interference in intergovernmental relations

18. Transnational corporations shall not interfere in intergovernmental relations provided that this provision shall not preclude such activities as are sanctioned within the framework of bilateral or multilateral co-operation.

19. Transnational corporations should not request Governments acting on their behalf to take the measures referred to in the second sentence of paragraph 67.

20. With respect to the exhaustion of local remedies, transnational corporations should not request Governments to act on their behalf in any manner inconsistent with paragraph 67.

Abstention from corrupt practices

21. (a) Transnational corporations shall refrain, in their transactions, from the offering, promising or giving or any payment, gift or other advantage to or for the benefit of a public official as consideration for performing or refraining from the performance of his duties in connection with those transactions.

(b) Transnational corporations shall maintain accurate records of any payments made by them to any public official or intermediary. They shall make available these records to the competent authorities of the countries in which they operate, upon request, for investigations and proceedings concerning those payments.

B. *Economic, financial and social*

Ownership and control

22. Transnational corporations should make every effort so to allocate their decision-making powers among their entities as to enable them to contribute to the economic and social development of the countries in which they operate.

23. To the extent permitted by national laws, policies and established administrative practices of the country in which it operates, each entity of a transnational corporation should co-operate with the other entities, in accordance with the actual distribution of responsibilities among them and consistent with paragraph 22, so as to enable each entity to meet effectively the requirements established by the laws, policies and regulations of the country in which it operates.

24. Transnational corporations should co-operate with Governments and nationals of the countries in which they operate in the implementation of national objectives for local equity participation and for the effective exercise of control by local partners as determined by equity, contractual terms in non-equity arrangements or the laws of such countries.

25. Transnational corporations should carry out their personnel policies in accordance with the national policies of each of the countries in which they operate which give priority to the employment and promotion of its nationals at all levels of management and direction of the affairs of each entity so as to enhance the effective participation of its nationals in the decision-making process.

26. Transnational corporations should contribute to the managerial and technical training of nationals of the countries in which they operate and facilitate their employment at all levels of management of the entities and enterprises as a whole.

Employment conditions and industrial relations

27. For the purposes of this Code, the principles set out in the Tripartite Declaration of Principles concerning Multinational Enterprises and Social Policy, adopted by the Governing Body of the International Labour Office, should apply in the field of employment, training, conditions of work and life and industrial relations.

Balance of payments and financing

28. Transnational corporations shall carry out their operations in conformity with laws and regulations and with full regard to the policy objectives set out by the countries in which they operate, particularly developing countries, relating to balance of payments, financial transactions and other issues dealt with in the subsequent paragraphs of this section.

29. Transnational corporations should respond positively to requests for consultation on their activities from the Governments of the countries in which they operate, with a view to contributing to the alleviation of pressing problems of balance of payments and finance of such countries.

30. As required by government regulations and in furtherance of government policies, and consistent with the purpose, nature and extent of their operations, transnational corporations should contribute to the promotion of exports and the diversification of exports and, where appropriate, imports in the countries in which they operate and to an increased utilization of goods, services and other resources which are available in these countries.

31. Transnational corporations should be responsive to requests by Governments of the countries in which they operate, particularly developing countries, concerning the phasing over a limited period of time of the repatriation of capital in case of disinvestment or remittances of accumulated profits, when the size and timing of such transfers would cause serious balance-of-payments difficulties for such countries.

32. Transnational corporations should not, contrary to generally accepted financial practices prevailing in the countries in which they operate, engage in short-term financial operations or transfers or defer or advance foreign exchange payments, including intra-corporate payments, in a manner which would increase currency instability and thereby cause serious balance-of-payments difficulties for the countries concerned.

33. Transnational corporations should not impose restrictions on their entities, beyond generally accepted commercial practices prevailing in the countries in which they operate, regarding the transfer of goods, services and funds which would cause serious balance-of-payments difficulties for the countries in which they operate.

34. When having recourse to the money and capital markets of the countries in which they operate, transnational corporations should not, beyond generally accepted financial practices prevailing in such countries, engage in activities which would have a significant adverse impact on the working of local markets, particularly by restricting the availability of funds to other enterprises. When issuing shares with the objective of increasing local equity participation in an entity operating in such a country, or engaging in long-term borrowing in the local market, transnational corporations should consult with the Government of the country concerned upon its request on the effects of such transactions on the local money and capital markets.

Transfer pricing

35. In respect of their intra-corporate transactions, transnational corporations should not use pricing policies that are not based on relevant market prices, or, in the absence of such prices, the arm's length principle, which have the effect of adversely affecting the tax revenues, the foreign exchange resources or other aspects of the economy of the countries in which they operate.

Taxation

36. Transnational corporations shall not, contrary to the laws and regulations of the countries in which they operate, use their corporate structure and modes of operation, such as the use of intra-corporate pricing which is not based on the arm's length principle, or other means, to modify the tax base on which their entities are assessed.

Competition and restrictive business practices

37. For the purposes of this Code, the relevant provisions of the Set of Multilaterally Agreed Equitable Principles and Rules for the Control of Restrictive Business Practices adopted by the General Assembly in its resolution 35/63 of 5 December 1980 shall also apply in the field of restrictive business practices.

Transfer of technology

38. (a) Transnational corporations shall conform to the transfer of technology laws and regulations of the countries in which they operate. They shall co-operate with the competent authorities of those countries in assessing the impact of international transfers of technology in their economies and consult with them regarding the various technological options which might help those countries, particularly developing countries, to attain their economic and social development.

(b) Transnational corporations in their transfer of technology transactions, including intra-corporate transactions, should avoid practices which adversely affect the international flow of technology, or otherwise hinder the economic and technological development of countries, particularly developing countries.

(c) Transnational corporations should contribute to the strengthening of the scientific and technological capacities of developing countries, in accordance with the science and technology established policies and priorities of those countries. Transnational corporations should undertake substantial research and development activities in developing countries and should make full use of local resources and personnel in this process.

Consumer protection

39. Transnational corporations shall carry out their operations, in particular production and marketing, in accordance with national laws, regulations, administrative practices and policies concerning consumer protection of the countries in which they operate. Transnational corporations shall also perform their activities with due regard to relevant international standards, so that they do not cause injury to the health or endanger the safety of consumers or bring about variations in the quality of products in each market which would have detrimental effects on consumers.

40. Transnational corporations shall, in respect of the products and services which they produce or market or propose to produce or market in any country, supply to the competent authorities of that country on request or on a regular basis, as specified by these authorities, all relevant information concerning:

> Characteristics of these products or services which may be injurious to the health and safety of consumers including experimental uses and related aspects;
>
> Prohibitions, restrictions, warnings and other public regulatory measures imposed in other countries on grounds of health and safety protection on these products or services.

41. Transnational corporations should disclose to the public in the countries in which they operate all appropriate information on the contents and, to the extent known, on possible hazardous effects of the products they produce or market in the countries concerned by means of proper labelling, informative and accurate advertising or other appropriate methods. Packaging of their products should be safe and the contents of the product should not be misrepresented.

42. Transnational corporations should be responsive to requests from Governments of the countries in which they operate and be prepared to co-operate with international organizations in their efforts to develop and promote national and international standards for the protection of the health and safety of consumers and to meet the basic needs of consumers.

Environmental protection

43. Transnational corporations shall carry out their activities in accordance with national laws, regulations, established administrative practices and policies relating to the preservation of the environment of the countries in which they operate and with due regard to relevant international standards. Transnational corporations should, in performing their activities, take steps to protect the environment and where damaged to rehabilitate it and should make efforts to develop and apply adequate technologies for this purpose.

44. Transnational corporations shall, in respect of the products, processes and services they have introduced or propose to introduce in any country, supply to the competent authorities of that country on request or on a regular basis, as specified by these authorities, all relevant information concerning:

> Characteristics of these products, processes and other activities including experimental uses and related aspects which may harm the environment and the measures and costs necessary to avoid or at least to mitigate their harmful effects;
>
> Prohibitions, restrictions, warnings and other public regulatory measures imposed in other countries on grounds of protection of the environment on these products, processes and services.

45. Transnational corporations should be responsive to requests from Governments of the countries in which they operate and be prepared where appropriate to

co-operate with international organizations in their efforts to develop and promote national and international standards for the protection of the environment.

C. *Disclosure of information*

46. Transnational corporations should disclose to the public in the countries in which they operate, by appropriate means of communication, clear, full and comprehensible information on the structure, policies, activities and operations of the transnational corporations as a whole. The information should include financial as well as non-financial items and should be made available on a regular annual basis, normally within six months and in any case not later than 12 months from the end of the financial year of the corporation. In addition, during the financial year, transnational corporations should wherever appropriate make available a semi-annual summary of financial information.

The financial information to be disclosed annually should be provided where appropriate on a consolidated basis, together with suitable explanatory notes and should include, *inter alia,* the following:

(a) A balance sheet;

(b) An income statement, including operating results and sales;

(c) A statement of allocation of net profits or net income;

(d) A statement of the sources and uses of funds;

(e) Significant new long-term capital investment;

(f) Research and development expenditure.

The non-financial information referred to in the first subparagraph should include, *inter alia:*

(a) The structure of the transnational corporation, showing the name and location of the parent company, its main entities, its percentage ownership, direct and indirect, in these entities, including shareholdings between them;

(b) The main activity of its entities;

(c) Employment information including average number of employees;

(d) Accounting policies used in compiling and consolidating the information published;

(e) Policies applied in respect of transfer pricing.

The information provided for the transnational corporation as a whole should as far as practicable be broken down:

By geographical area or country, as appropriate, with regard to the activities of its main entities, sales, operating results, significant new investments and number of employees;

By major line of business as regards sales and significant new investment.

The method of breakdown as well as details of information provided shall be determined by the nature, scale and interrelationships of the transnational corporation's operations, with due regard to their significance for the areas or countries concerned.

The extent, detail and frequency of the information provided should take into account the nature and size of the transnational corporation as a whole, the requirements of confidentiality and effects on the transnational corporation's competitive position as well as the cost involved in producing the information.

The information herein required should, as necessary, be in addition to information required by national laws, regulations and established administrative practices of the countries in which transnational corporations operate.

47. (a) Transnational corporations shall supply to the competent authorities in each of the countries in which they operate, upon request or on a regular basis as specified by those authorities, and in accordance with national legislation, all information required for legislative and administrative purposes relevant to the activities and policies of their entities in the country concerned.

(b) Transnational corporations shall, to the extent permitted by the provisions of the relevant national laws, regulations, established administrative practices and policies of the countries concerned, supply to competent authorities in the countries in which they operate information held in other countries needed to enable them to obtain a true and fair view of the operations of the transnational corporation concerned as a whole in so far as the information requested relates to the activities of the entities in the countries seeking such information.

(c) The provisions of paragraph 54 concerning confidentiality shall apply to information supplied under the provisions of this paragraph.

48. (a) With due regard to the relevant provisions of the ILO Tripartite Declaration of Principles concerning Multinational Enterprises and Social Policy and in accordance with national laws, regulations and practices in the field of labour relations, transnational corporations shall provide to trade unions or other representatives of employees in their entities in each of the countries in which they operate, by appropriate means of communication, the necessary information on the activities dealt with in this Code to enable them to obtain a true and fair view of the performance of the local entity and, where appropriate, the corporation as a whole. Such information shall include, where provided for by national law and practices, *inter alia,* prospects or plans for future development having major economic and social effects on the employees concerned.

(b) Procedures for consultation on matters of mutual concern should be worked out by mutual agreement between entities of transnational corporations and trade unions or other representatives of employees in accordance with national law and practice.

(c) Information made available pursuant to the provisions of this paragraph should be subject to appropriate safeguards for confidentiality so that no damage is caused to the parties concerned.

TREATMENT OF TRANSNATIONAL CORPORATIONS

A. *General provisions relating to the treatment of transnational corporations*

49. In all matters relating to the Code, States shall fulfil, in good faith, their international obligations, including generally recognized and accepted international legal rules and principles.

50. States have the right to regulate the entry and establishment of transnational corporations including determining the role that such corporations may play in economic and social development and prohibiting or limiting the extent of their presence in specific sectors.

51. Transnational corporations should receive fair and equitable treatment in the countries in which they operate.

52. Subject to national requirements for maintaining public order and protecting national security and consistent with national constitutions and laws, and without prejudice to measures specified in legislation relating to the declared development objectives of the developing countries, entities of transnational corporations should be given treatment accorded to domestic enterprises in similar circumstances. Nothing in this paragraph should be construed as excluding the right of the host

country to grant such special incentives and facilities to transnational corporations as may be considered necessary in its national interest.

53. The importance of endeavouring to assure the clarity and stability of national policies, laws, regulations and established administrative practices is acknowledged. Laws and regulations affecting transnational corporations should be publicly and readily available. To the extent appropriate, relevant information regarding decisions of competent administrative bodies relating to transnational corporations should be disseminated.

54. Information furnished by transnational corporations to the authorities in each of the countries in which they operate containing confidential business information shall be accorded reasonable safeguards normally applicable in the area in which the information is provided, particularly to protect its confidentiality.

55. In order to achieve the purposes of paragraph 26 relating to managerial and technical training and employment of nationals of the countries in which transnational corporations operate, the transfer of those nationals between the entities of a transnational corporation should, subject to the laws and regulations of the countries concerned, be facilitated.

56. Transnational corporations are entitled to transfer all payments legally due. Such transfers are subject to the relevant legislation of host countries, such as foreign exchange laws, and to restrictions emanating from exceptional balance of payment difficulties.

B. *Nationalization and compensation*

57. It is acknowledged that States have the right to nationalize or expropriate the assets of a transnational corporation operating in their territory, and that appropriate compensation is to be paid by the State concerned, in accordance with the applicable legal rules and principles.

C. *Jurisdiction*

58. An entity of a transnational corporation is subject to the jurisdiction of the country in which it operates.

D. *Dispute settlement*

59. Disputes between States and entities of transnational corporations, which are not amicably settled between the parties, shall be submitted to competent national courts or authorities. Where the parties so agree, or have agreed, such disputes may be referred to other mutually acceptable dispute settlement procedures.

60. Where the exercise of jurisdiction over transnational corporations and their entities by more than one State may lead to conflicts of jurisdiction, States concerned should endeavour to avoid such conflicts, in particular by seeking to avoid the exercise of jurisdiction by one State where jurisdiction more properly appertains to another State, and should endeavour to adopt mutually acceptable principles and procedures, bilaterally and multilaterally, for the settlement of such conflicts on the basis of respect for the principle of sovereign equality and for their mutual interests.

INTERGOVERNMENTAL CO-OPERATION

61. States agree that intergovernmental co-operation is essential in accomplishing the objectives of the Code.

62. States agree that intergovernmental co-operation should be established or strengthened at the international level and, where appropriate, at the bilateral, regional and interregional levels.

63. States agree to exchange information on the measures they have taken to give effect to the Code and on their experience with the Code.

64. States agree to consult on a bilateral or multilateral basis, as appropriate, on matters relating to the Code and its application and with respect to the development of international agreements and arrangements on issues related to the Code.

65. States agree to take into consideration the objectives of the Code as reflected in its provisions when negotiating bilateral or multilateral agreements concerning transnational corporations.

66. States agree not to use transnational corporations as instruments to intervene in the internal or external affairs of other States and agree to take appropriate action within their jurisdiction to prevent transnational corporations from engaging in activities referred to in paragraphs 16 to 18 of this Code.

67. Government action on behalf of a transnational corporation operating in another country shall be subject to the principle of exhaustion of local remedies provided in such a country and, when agreed among the Governments concerned, to procedures for dealing with international legal claims. Such action should not in any event amount to the use of any type of coercive measures not consistent with the Charter of the United Nations and the Declaration on Principles of International Law concerning Friendly Relations and Co-operation among States in accordance with the Charter of the United Nations.

IMPLEMENTATION OF THE CODE OF CONDUCT

A. *Action at the national level*

68. In order to ensure and promote the implementation of the Code at the national level, States should, *inter alia:*

(a) Publicize and disseminate the Code;

(b) Follow the implementation of the Code within their territories;

(c) Report to the United Nations Commission on Transnational Corporations on the action taken at the national level to promote the Code and on the experience gained from its implementation;

(d) Take action to reflect their support for the Code and take into account the objectives of the Code as reflected in its provisions when introducing, implementing and reviewing laws, regulations and administrative practices on matters dealt with in the Code.

B. *International institutional machinery*

69. The United Nations Commission on Transnational Corporations shall assume the functions of the international institutional machinery for the implementation of the Code. In this capacity, the Commission shall be open to the participation of all States. It may establish the subsidiary bodies and specific procedures it deems necessary for the effective discharge of its functions. The United Nations Centre on Transnational Corporations shall act as the secretariat to the Commission.

70. The Commission shall act as the international body within the United Nations system for all matters related to the Code. It shall establish and maintain close contacts with other United Nations organizations and specialized agencies dealing with matters related to the Code and its implementation with a view to co-ordinating work related to the Code. When matters covered by international agreements or arrangements, specifically referred to in the Code, which have been worked out in other United Nations forums, arise, the Commission shall forward such matters to the competent bodies concerned with such agreements or arrangements.

71. The Commission shall have the following functions:

(a) To discuss at its annual sessions matters related to the Code. If agreed by the Governments engaged in consultations on specific issues related to the

Code, the Commission shall facilitate such intergovernmental consultations to the extent possible. Representatives of trade unions, business, consumer and other relevant groups may express their views on matters related to the Code through the non-governmental organizations represented in the Commission.

(b) Periodically to assess the implementation of the Code, such assessments being based on reports submitted by Governments and, as appropriate, on documentation from United Nations organizations and specialized agencies performing work relevant to the Code and non-governmental organizations represented in the Commission. The first assessment shall take place not earlier than two years and not later than three years after the adoption of the Code. The second assessment shall take place two years after the first one. The Commission shall determine whether a periodicity of two years is to be maintained or modified for subsequent assessments. The format of assessments shall be determined by the Commission.

(c) To provide, upon the request of a Government, clarification of the provisions of the Code in the light of actual situations in which the applicability and implications of the Code have been the subject of intergovernmental consultations. In clarifying the provisions of the Code, the Commission shall not draw conclusions concerning the conduct of the parties involved in the situation which led to the request for clarification. The clarification is to be restricted to issues illustrated by such a situation. The detailed procedures regarding clarification are to be determined by the Commission.

(d) To report annually to the General Assembly through the Economic and Social Council on its activities regarding the implementation of the Code.

(e) To facilitate intergovernmental arrangements or agreements on specific aspects relating to transnational corporations upon request of the Governments concerned.

72. The United Nations Centre on Transnational Corporations shall provide assistance relating to the implementation of the Code, *inter alia,* by collecting, analysing and disseminating information and conducting research and surveys, as required and specified by the Commission.

C. *Review procedure*

73. The Commission shall make recommendations to the General Assembly through the Economic and Social Council for the purpose of reviewing the Code. The first review shall take place not later than six years after the adoption of the Code. The General Assembly shall establish, as appropriate, the modalities for reviewing the Code.

4.15 RESOLUTION ON CONSUMER PROTECTION, WITH ANNEX. Adopted by the U.N. General Assembly, Apr. 9, 1985. U.N.G.A. Res. 39/248, 39 U.N. GAOR Supp. (No. 51) 179, U.N.Doc. A/39/789/Add.2 (1985)

The General Assembly,

Recalling Economic and Social Council resolution 1981/62 of 23 July 1981, in which the Council requested the Secretary–General to continue consultations on consumer protection with a view to elaborating a set of general guidelines for consumer protection, taking particularly into account the needs of the developing countries,

Recalling further General Assembly resolution 38/147 of 19 December 1983,

Noting Economic and Social Council resolution 1984/63 of 26 July 1984,

1. *Decides* to adopt the guidelines for consumer protection annexed to the present resolution;

2. *Requests* the Secretary–General to disseminate the guidelines to Governments and other interested parties;

3. *Requests* all organizations of the United Nations system that elaborate guidelines and related documents on specific areas relevant to consumer protection to distribute them to the appropriate bodies of individual States.

Annex

GUIDELINES FOR CONSUMER PROTECTION

I. *Objectives*

1. Taking into account the interests and needs of consumers in all countries, particularly those in developing countries; recognizing that consumers often face imbalances in economic terms, educational levels, and bargaining power; and bearing in mind that consumers should have the right of access to non-hazardous products, as well as the right to promote just, equitable and sustainable economic and social development, these guidelines for consumer protection have the following objectives:

(*a*) To assist countries in achieving or maintaining adequate protection for their population as consumers;

(*b*) To facilitate production and distribution patterns responsive to the needs and desires of consumers;

(*c*) To encourage high levels of ethical conduct for those engaged in the production and distribution of goods and services to consumers;

(*d*) To assist countries in curbing abusive business practices by all enterprises at the national and international levels which adversely affect consumers;

(*e*) To facilitate the development of independent consumer groups;

(*f*) To further international co-operation in the field of consumer protection;

(*g*) To encourage the development of market conditions which provide consumers with greater choice at lower prices.

II. *General principles*

2. Governments should develop, strengthen or maintain a strong consumer protection policy, taking into account the guidelines set out below. In so doing, each Government must set its own priorities for the protection of consumers in accordance

with the economic and social circumstances of the country, and the needs of its population, and bearing in mind the costs and benefits of proposed measures.

3. The legitimate needs which the guidelines are intended to meet are the following:

(*a*) The protection of consumers from hazards to their health and safety;

(*b*) The promotion and protection of the economic interests of consumers;

(*c*) Access of consumers to adequate information to enable them to make informed choices according to individual wishes and needs;

(*d*) Consumer education;

(*e*) Availability of effective consumer redress;

(*f*) Freedom to form consumer and other relevant groups or organizations and the opportunity of such organizations to present their views in decision-making processes affecting them.

4. Governments should provide or maintain adequate infrastructure to develop, implement and monitor consumer protection policies. Special care should be taken to ensure that measures for consumer protection are implemented for the benefit of all sectors of the population, particularly the rural population.

5. All enterprises should obey the relevant laws and regulations of the countries in which they do business. They should also conform to the appropriate provisions of international standards for consumer protection to which the competent authorities of the country in question have agreed. (Hereinafter references to international standards in the guidelines should be viewed in the context of this paragraph.)

6. The potential positive role of universities and public and private enterprises in research should be considered when developing consumer protection policies.

III. *Guidelines*

7. The following guidelines should apply both to home-produced goods and services and to imports.

8. In applying any procedures or regulations for consumer protection, due regard should be given to ensuring that they do not become barriers to international trade and that they are consistent with international trade obligations.

A. *Physical safety*

9. Governments should adopt or encourage the adoption of appropriate measures, including legal systems, safety regulations, national or international standards, voluntary standards and the maintenance of safety records to ensure that products are safe for either intended or normally foreseeable use.

10. Appropriate policies should ensure that goods produced by manufacturers are safe for either intended or normally foreseeable use. Those responsible for bringing goods to the market, in particular suppliers, exporters, importers, retailers and the like (hereinafter referred to as "distributors"), should ensure that while in their care these goods are not rendered unsafe through improper handling or storage and that while in their care they do not become hazardous through improper handling or storage. Consumers should be instructed in the proper use of goods and should be informed of the risks involved in intended or normally foreseeable use. Vital safety information should be conveyed to consumers by internationally understandable symbols wherever possible.

11. Appropriate policies should ensure that if manufacturers or distributors become aware of unforeseen hazards after products are placed on the market, they should notify the relevant authorities and, as appropriate, the public without delay.

Governments should also consider ways of ensuring that consumers are properly informed of such hazards.

12. Governments should, where appropriate, adopt policies under which, if a product is found to be seriously defective and/or to constitute a substantial and severe hazard even when properly used, manufacturers and/or distributors should recall it and replace or modify it, or substitute another product for it; if it is not possible to do this within a reasonable period of time, the consumer should be adequately compensated.

B. *Promotion and protection of consumers' economic interests*

13. Government policies should seek to enable consumers to obtain optimum benefit from their economic resources. They should also seek to achieve the goals of satisfactory production and performance standards, adequate distribution methods, fair business practices, informative marketing and effective protection against practices which could adversely affect the economic interests of consumers and the exercise of choice in the market-place.

14. Governments should intensify their efforts to prevent practices which are damaging to the economic interests of consumers through ensuring that manufacturers, distributors and others involved in the provision of goods and services adhere to established laws and mandatory standards. Consumer organizations should be encouraged to monitor adverse practices, such as the adulteration of foods, false or misleading claims in marketing and service frauds.

15. Governments should develop, strengthen or maintain, as the case may be, measures relating to the control of restrictive and other abusive business practices which may be harmful to consumers, including means for the enforcement of such measures. In this connection, Governments should be guided by their commitment to the Set of Multilaterally Agreed Equitable Principles and Rules for the Control of Restrictive Business Practices adopted by the General Assembly in resolution 35/63 of 5 December 1980.

16. Governments should adopt or maintain policies that make clear the responsibility of the producer to ensure that goods meet reasonable demands of durability, utility and reliability, and are suited to the purpose for which they are intended, and that the seller should see that these requirements are met. Similar policies should apply to the provision of services.

17. Governments should encourage fair and effective competition in order to provide consumers with the greatest range of choice among products and services at the lowest cost.

18. Governments should, where appropriate, see to it that manufacturers and/ or retailers ensure adequate availability of reliable after-sales service and spare parts.

19. Consumers should be protected from such contractual abuses as one-sided standard contracts, exclusion of essential rights in contracts, and unconscionable conditions of credit by sellers.

20. Promotional marketing and sales practices should be guided by the principle of fair treatment of consumers and should meet legal requirements. This requires the provision of the information necessary to enable consumers to take informed and independent decisions, as well as measures to ensure that the information provided is accurate.

21. Governments should encourage all concerned to participate in the free flow of accurate information on all aspects of consumer products.

22. Governments should, within their own national context, encourage the formulation and implementation by business, in co-operation with consumer organi-

zations, of codes of marketing and other business practices to ensure adequate consumer protection. Voluntary agreements may also be established jointly by business, consumer organizations and other interested parties. These codes should receive adequate publicity.

23. Governments should regularly review legislation pertaining to weights and measures and assess the adequacy of the machinery for its enforcement.

C. *Standards for the safety and quality of consumer goods and services*

24. Governments should, as appropriate, formulate or promote the elaboration and implementation of standards, voluntary and other, at the national and international levels for the safety and quality of goods and services and give them appropriate publicity. National standards and regulations for product safety and quality should be reviewed from time to time, in order to ensure that they conform, where possible, to generally accepted international standards.

25. Where a standard lower than the generally accepted international standard is being applied because of local economic conditions, every effort should be made to raise that standard as soon as possible.

26. Governments should encourage and ensure the availability of facilities to test and certify the safety, quality and performance of essential consumer goods and services.

D. *Distribution facilities for essential consumer goods and services*

27. Governments should, where appropriate, consider:

(*a*) Adopting or maintaining policies to ensure the efficient distribution of goods and services to consumers; where appropriate, specific policies should be considered to ensure the distribution of essential goods and services where this distribution is endangered, as could be the case particularly in rural areas. Such policies could include assistance for the creation of adequate storage and retail facilities in rural centres, incentives for consumer self-help and better control of the conditions under which essential goods and services are provided in rural areas;

(*b*) Encouraging the establishment of consumer co-operatives and related trading activities, as well as information about them, especially in rural areas.

E. *Measures enabling consumers to obtain redress*

28. Governments should establish or maintain legal and/or administrative measures to enable consumers or, as appropriate, relevant organizations to obtain redress through formal or informal procedures that are expeditious, fair, inexpensive and accessible. Such procedures should take particular account of the needs of low-income consumers.

29. Governments should encourage all enterprises to resolve consumer disputes in a fair, expeditious and informal manner, and to establish voluntary mechanisms, including advisory services and informal complaints procedures, which can provide assistance to consumers.

30. Information on available redress and other dispute-resolving procedures should be made available to consumers.

F. *Education and information programmes*

31. Governments should develop or encourage the development of general consumer education and information programmes, bearing in mind the cultural traditions of the people concerned. The aim of such programmes should be to enable people to act as discriminating consumers, capable of making an informed choice of goods and services, and conscious of their rights and responsibilities. In developing

such programmes, special attention should be given to the needs of disadvantaged consumers, in both rural and urban areas, including low-income consumers and those with low or non-existent literacy levels.

32. Consumer education should, where appropriate, become an integral part of the basic curriculum of the educational system, preferably as a component of existing subjects.

33. Consumer education and information programmes should cover such important aspects of consumer protection as the following:

(*a*) Health, nutrition, prevention of food-borne diseases and food adulteration;

(*b*) Product hazards;

(*c*) Product labelling;

(*d*) Relevant legislation, how to obtain redress, and agencies and organizations for consumer protection;

(*e*) Information on weights and measures, prices, quality, credit conditions and availability of basic necessities; and

(*f*) As appropriate, pollution and environment.

34. Governments should encourage consumer organizations and other interested groups, including the media, to undertake education and information programmes, particularly for the benefit of low-income consumer groups in rural and urban areas.

35. Business should, where appropriate, undertake or participate in factual and relevant consumer education and information programmes.

36. Bearing in mind the need to reach rural consumers and illiterate consumers, Governments should, as appropriate, develop or encourage the development of consumer information programmes in the mass media.

37. Governments should organize or encourage training programmes for educators, mass media professionals and consumer advisers, to enable them to participate in carrying out consumer information and education programmes.

G. *Measures relating to specific areas*

38. In advancing consumer interests, particularly in developing countries, Governments should, where appropriate, give priority to areas of essential concern for the health of the consumer, such as food, water and pharmaceuticals. Policies should be adopted or maintained for product quality control, adequate and secure distribution facilities, standardized international labelling and information, as well as education and research programmes in these areas. Government guidelines in regard to specific areas should be developed in the context of the provisions of this document.

39. *Food.* When formulating national policies and plans with regard to food, Governments should take into account the need of all consumers for food security and should support and, as far as possible, adopt standards from the Food and Agriculture Organization of the United Nations and the World Health Organization Codex Alimentarius or, in their absence, other generally accepted international food standards. Governments should maintain, develop or improve food safety measures, including, *inter alia,* safety criteria, food standards and dietary requirements and effective monitoring, inspection and evaluation mechanisms.

40. *Water.* Governments should, within the goals and targets set for the International Drinking Water Supply and Sanitation Decade, formulate, maintain or strengthen national policies to improve the supply, distribution and quality of water for drinking. Due regard should be paid to the choice of appropriate levels of service, quality and technology, the need for education programmes and the importance of community participation.

41. *Pharmaceuticals.* Governments should develop or maintain adequate standards, provisions and appropriate regulatory systems for ensuring the quality and appropriate use of pharmaceuticals through integrated national drug policies which could address, *inter alia,* procurement, distribution, production, licensing arrangements, registration systems and the availability of reliable information on pharmaceuticals. In so doing, Governments should take special account of the work and recommendations of the World Health Organization on pharmaceuticals. For relevant products, the use of that organization's Certification Scheme on the Quality of Pharmaceutical Products Moving in International Commerce and other international information systems on pharmaceuticals should be encouraged. Measures should also be taken, as appropriate, to promote the use of international non-proprietary names (INNs) for drugs, drawing on the work done by the World Health Organization.

42. In addition to the priority areas indicated above, Governments should adopt appropriate measures in other areas, such as pesticides and chemicals in regard, where relevant, to their use, production and storage, taking into account such relevant health and environmental information as Governments may require producers to provide and include in the labelling of products.

IV. *International co-operation*

43. Governments should, especially in a regional or subregional context:

(*a*) Develop, review, maintain or strengthen, as appropriate, mechanisms for the exchange of information on national policies and measures in the field of consumer protection;

(*b*) Co-operate or encourage co-operation in the implementation of consumer protection policies to achieve greater results within existing resources. Examples of such co-operation could be collaboration in the setting up or joint use of testing facilities, common testing procedures, exchange of consumer information and education programmes, joint training programmes and joint elaboration of regulations;

(*c*) Co-operate to improve the conditions under which essential goods are offered to consumers, giving due regard to both price and quality. Such co-operation could include joint procurement of essential goods, exchange of information on different procurement possibilities and agreements on regional product specifications.

44. Governments should develop or strengthen information links regarding products which have been banned, withdrawn or severely restricted in order to enable other importing countries to protect themselves adequately against the harmful effects of such products.

45. Governments should work to ensure that the quality of products, and information relating to such products, does not vary from country to country in a way that would have detrimental effects on consumers.

46. Governments should work to ensure that policies and measures for consumer protection are implemented with due regard to their not becoming barriers to international trade, and that they are consistent with international trade obligations.

5. EARTH–SPACE ENVIRONMENT

5.1 CONVENTION AND STATUTE ON THE REGIME OF NAVIGABLE WATERWAYS OF INTERNATIONAL CONCERN.[a] Done at Barcelona, April 20, 1921. Entered into force, Oct. 31, 1922. 7 L.N.T.S. 35

Article 1. The High Contracting Parties declare that they accept the Statute on the Regime of Navigable Waterways of International Concern annexed hereto, adopted by the Barcelona Conference on April 19th, 1921.

This Statute will be deemed to constitute an integral part of the present Convention. Consequently, they hereby declare that they accept the obligations and undertakings of the said Statute in conformity with the terms and in accordance with the conditions set out therein.

* * *

STATUTE ON THE REGIME OF NAVIGABLE WATERWAYS OF INTERNATIONAL CONCERN

Article 1. In the application of the Statute, the following are declared to be navigable waterways of international concern:

(1) All parts which are naturally navigable to and from the sea of a waterway which in its course, naturally navigable to and from the sea, separates or traverses different States, and also any part of any other waterway naturally navigable to and from the sea, which connects with the sea a waterway naturally navigable which separates or traverses different States.

It is understood that:

(a) Transhipment from one vessel to another is not excluded by the words "navigable to and from the sea";

(b) Any natural waterway or part of a natural waterway is termed "naturally navigable" if now used for ordinary commercial navigation, or capable by reason of its natural conditions of being so used; by "ordinary commercial navigation" is to be understood navigation which, in view of the economic condition of the riparian countries, is commercial and normally practicable;

(c) Tributaries are to be considered as separate waterways;

(d) Lateral canals constructed in order to remedy the defects of a waterway included in the above definition are assimilated thereto; and

(e) The different States separated or traversed by a navigable waterway of international concern, including its tributaries of international concern, are deemed to be "riparian States".

(2) Waterways, or parts of waterways, whether natural or artificial, expressly declared to be placed under the regime of the General Convention regarding navigable waterways of international concern either in unilateral Acts of the States under whose sovereignty or authority these waterways or parts of water-

a. Also known as "the Barcelona Convention."

ways are situated, or in agreements made with the consent, in particular, of such States.

Article 2. For the purpose of Articles 5, 10, 12 and 14 of this Statute, the following shall form a special category of navigable waterways of international concern:

(a) Navigable waterways for which there are international Commissions upon which nonriparian States are represented;

(b) Navigable waterways which may hereafter be placed in this category, either in pursuance of unilateral Acts of the States under whose sovereignty or authority they are situated, or in pursuance of agreements made with the consent, in particular, of such States.

Article 3. Subject to the provisions contained in Articles 5 and 17, each of the Contracting States shall accord free exercise of navigation to the vessels flying the flag of any one of the other contracting States on those parts of navigable waterways specified above which may be situated under its sovereignty or authority.

Article 4. In the exercise of navigation referred to above, the nationals, property and flags of all Contracting States shall be treated in all respects on a footing of perfect equality. No distinction shall be made between the nationals, the property and the flags of the different riparian States, including the riparian State exercising sovereignty or authority over the portion of the navigable waterway in question: similarly, no distinction shall be made between the nationals, the property and the flags of riparian and non-riparian States. It is understood, in consequence, that no exclusive right of navigation shall be accorded on such navigable waterways to companies or to private persons.

No distinction shall be made in the said exercise, by reason of the point of departure or of destination, or of the direction of the traffic.

Article 5. As an exception to the two preceding Articles, and in the absence of any Convention or obligation to the contrary:

(1) A riparian State has the right of reserving for its own flag the transport of passengers and goods loaded at one port situated under its sovereignty or authority and unloaded at another port also situated under its sovereignty or authority. A State which does not reserve the above-mentioned transport to its own flag may, nevertheless, refuse the benefit of equality of treatment with regard to such transport to a co-riparian which does reserve it.

On the navigable waterways referred to in Article 2, the Act of Navigation shall only allow to riparian States the right of reserving the local transport of passengers or of goods which are of national origin or are nationalised. In every case, however, in which greater freedom of navigation may have been already established, in a previous Act of Navigation, this freedom shall not be reduced.

(2) When a natural system of navigable waterways of international concern which does not include waterways of the kind referred to in Article 2 separates or traverses two States only, the latter have the right to reserve to their flags by mutual agreement the transport of passengers and goods loaded at one port of this system and unloaded at another port of the same system, unless this transport takes place between two ports which are not situated under the sovereignty or authority of the same State in the course of a voyage, effected without transshipment on the territory of either of the said States, involving a sea-passage or passage over a navigable waterway of international concern which does not belong to the said system.

Article 6. Each of the Contracting States maintains its existing right, on the navigable waterways or parts of navigable waterways referred to in Article 1 and situated under its sovereignty or authority, to enact the stipulations and to take the measures necessary for policing the territory and for applying the laws and regulations relating to customs, public health, precautions against the diseases of animals and plants, emigration or immigration, and to the import or export of prohibited goods, it being understood that such stipulations and measures must be reasonable, must be applied on a footing of absolute equality between the nationals, property and flags of any one of the Contracting States, including the State which is their author, and must not without good reason impede the freedom of navigation.

Article 7. No dues of any kind may be levied anywhere on the course or at the mouth of a navigable waterway of international concern, other than dues in the nature of payment for services rendered and intended solely to cover in an equitable manner the expenses of maintaining and improving the navigability of the waterway and its approaches, or to meet expenditures incurred in the interest of navigation. These dues shall be fixed in accordance with such expenses, and the tariff of dues shall be posted in the ports. These dues shall be levied in such a manner as to render unnecessary a detailed examination of the cargo, except in cases of suspected fraud or infringement of regulations, and so as to facilitate international traffic as much as possible, both as regards their rates and the method of their application.

* * *

Article 9. Subject to the provisions of Articles 5 and 17, the nationals, property and flags of all the Contracting States shall, in all ports situated on a navigable waterway of international concern, enjoy, in all that concerns the use of the port, including port dues and charges, a treatment equal to that accorded to the nationals, property and flag of the riparian State under whose sovereignty or authority the port is situated. It is understood that the property to which the present paragraph relates its property originating in, coming from or destined for, one or other of the Contracting States.

The equipment of ports situated on a navigable waterway of international concern, and the facilities afforded in these ports to navigation, must not be withheld from public use to an extent beyond what is reasonable and fully compatible with the free exercise of navigation.

In the application of customs or other analogous duties, local octroi or consumption duties, or incidental charges, levied on the occasion of the importation or exportation of goods through the aforesaid ports, no difference shall be made by reason of the flag of the vessel on which the transport has been or is to be accomplished, whether this flag be the national flag or that of any of the Contracting States.

The State under whose sovereignty or authority a port is situated may withdraw the benefits of the preceding paragraph from any vessel if it is proved that the owner of the vessel discriminates systematically against the nationals of that State, including companies controlled by such nationals.

In the absence of special circumstances justifying an exception on the ground of economic necessities, the customs duties must not be higher than those levied on the other customs frontiers of the State interested, on good of the same kind, source and destination. All facilities accorded by the Contracting States to the importation or exportation of goods by other land or water routes, or in other ports, shall be equally accorded to importation or exportation under the same conditions over the navigable waterway and through the ports referred to above.

Article 10. (1) Each riparian State is bound, on the one hand, to refrain from all measures likely to prejudice the navigability of the waterway, or to reduce the facilities for navigation, and, on the other hand, to take as rapidly as possible all necessary steps for removing any obstacles and dangers which may occur to navigation.

(2) If such navigation necessitates regular upkeep of the waterway, each of the riparian States is bound as towards the others to take such steps and to execute such works on its territory as are necessary for the purpose as quickly as possible, taking account at all times of the conditions of navigation, as well as of the economic state of the regions served by the navigable waterway.

In the absence of an agreement to the contrary, any riparian State will have the right, on valid reason being shown, to demand from the other riparians a reasonable contribution towards the cost of upkeep.

(3) In the absence of legitimate grounds for opposition by one of the riparian States, including the State territorially interested, based either on the actual conditions of navigability in its territory, or on other interests such as, *inter alia,* the maintenance of the normal water conditions, requirements for irrigation, the use of water-power, or the necessity for constructing other and more advantageous ways of communication, a riparian State may not refuse to carry out works necessary for the improvement of the navigability which are asked for by another riparian State, if the latter State offers to pay the cost of the works and a fair share of the additional cost of upkeep. It is understood, however, that such works cannot be undertaken so long as the State of the territory on which they are to be carried out objects on the ground of vital interests.

* * *

(6) Notwithstanding the provisions of paragraph 1 of this Article, a riparian State may, in the absence of any agreement to the contrary, close a waterway wholly or in part to navigation, with the consent of all the riparian States or of all the States represented on the International Commission in the case of navigable waterways referred to in Article 2.

As an exceptional case one of the riparian States of a navigable waterway of international concern not referred to in Article 2 may close the waterway to navigation, if the navigation on it is of very small importance, and if the State in question can justify its action on the ground of an economic interest clearly greater than that of navigation. In this case the closing to navigation may only take place after a year's notice and subject to an appeal on the part of any other riparian State under the conditions laid down in Article 22. If necessary, the judgment shall prescribe the conditions under which the closing to navigation may be carried into effect.

* * *

Article 12. In the absence of contrary stipulations contained in a special agreement or treaty, for example, existing Conventions concerning customs and police measures and sanitary precautions, the administration of navigable waterways of international concern is exercised by each of the riparian States under whose sovereignty or authority the navigable waterway is situated. Each of such riparian States has, *inter alia,* the power and duty of publishing regulations for the navigation of such waterway and of seeing to their execution. These regulations must be framed and applied in such a way as to facilitate the free exercise of navigation under the conditions laid down in this Statute.

* * *

Article 14. If any of the special agreements or treaties referred to in Article 12 has entrusted or shall hereafter entrust certain functions to an international Commission which includes representatives of States other than the riparian States, it shall be the duty of such Commission, subject to the provisions of Article 10, to have exclusive regard to the interests of navigation, and it shall be deemed to be one of the organisations referred to in Article 24 of the Covenant of the League of Nations. Consequently, it will exchange all useful information directly with the League and its organisations, and will submit an annual report to the League.

The powers and duties of the Commissions referred to in the preceding paragraph shall be laid down in the Act of Navigation of each navigable waterway and shall at least include the following:

(a) The Commission shall be entitled to draw up such navigation regulations as it thinks necessary itself to draw up, and all other navigation regulations shall be communicated to it;

(b) It shall indicate to the riparian States the action advisable for the upkeep of works and the maintenance of navigability;

(c) It shall be furnished by each of the riparian States with official information as to all schemes for the improvement of the waterway;

(d) It shall be entitled, in cases in which the Act of Navigation does not include a special regulation with regard to the levying of dues, to approve of the levying of such dues and charges in accordance with the provisions of Article 7 of this Statute.

Article 15. This Statute does not prescribe the rights and duties of belligerents and neutrals in time of war. The Statute shall, however, continue in force in time of war so far as such rights and duties permit.

* * *

Article 17. In the absence of any agreement to the contrary to which the State territorially interested is or may be a party, this Statute has no reference to the navigation of vessels of war or of vessels performing police or administrative functions, or, in general, exercising any kind of public authority.

* * *

Article 19. The measures of a general or particular character which a Contracting State is obliged to take in case of an emergency affecting the safety of the State or the vital interests of the country may, in exceptional cases and for a period as short as possible, involve a deviation from the provisions of the above Articles; it being understood that the principle of the freedom of navigation, and especially communication between the riparian States and the sea, must be maintained to the utmost possible extent.

* * *

Article 20. This Statute does not entail in any way the withdrawal of existing greater facilities granted to the free exercise of navigation on any navigable waterway of international concern, under conditions consistent with the principle of equality laid down in this Statute, as regards the nationals, the goods and the flags of all the Contracting States; nor does it entail the prohibition of such grant of greater facilities in the future.

* * *

Article 23. A navigable waterway shall not be considered as of international concern on the sole ground that it traverses or delimits zones or enclaves, the extent and population of which are small as compared with those of the territories which it traverses, and which form detached portions or establishments belonging to a State other than that to which the said river belongs, with this exception, throughout its navigable course.

* * *

5.2 INTERNATIONAL CONVENTION FOR THE REGULATION OF WHALING.[a] Done at Washington, Dec. 2, 1946. Entered into force, Nov. 10, 1948; for the United States, Nov. 10, 1947. 62 Stat (2) 1716, T.I.A.S. No. 1849, 4 Bevans 248, 161 U.N.T.S. 72

The Governments whose duly authorized representatives have subscribed hereto,

Recognizing the interest of the nations of the world in safeguarding for future generations the great natural resources represented by the whale stocks;

Considering that the history of whaling has seen overfishing of one area after another and of one species of whale after another to such a degree that it is essential to protect all species of whales from further overfishing;

Recognizing that the whale stocks are susceptible of natural increases if whaling is properly regulated, and that increases in the size of whale stocks will permit increases in the numbers of whales which may be captured without endangering these natural resources;

Recognizing that it is in the common interest to achieve the optimum level of whale stocks as rapidly as possible without causing wide-spread economic and nutritional distress;

Recognizing that in the course of achieving these objectives, whaling operations should be confined to those species best able to sustain exploitation in order to give an interval for recovery to certain species of whales now depleted in numbers;

Desiring to establish a system of international regulation for the whale fisheries to ensure proper and effective conservation and development of whale stocks on the basis of the principles embodied in the provisions of the International Agreement for the Regulation of Whaling signed in London on June 8, 1937 and the protocols to that Agreement signed in London on June 24, 1938 and November 26, 1945; and

Having decided to conclude a convention to provide for the proper conservation of whale stocks and thus make possible the orderly development of the whaling industry;

Have agreed as follows:

Article I

1. This Convention includes the Schedule attached thereto which forms an integral part thereof. All references to "Convention" shall be understood as including the said Schedule either in its present terms or as amended in accordance with the provisions of Article V.

2. This Convention applies to factory ships, land stations, and whale catchers under the jurisdiction of the Contracting Governments, and to all waters in which whaling is prosecuted by such factory ships, land stations, and whale catchers.

* * *

Article III

1. The Contracting Governments agree to establish an International Whaling Commission, hereinafter referred to as the Commission, to be composed of one member from each Contracting Government. Each member shall have one vote and may be accompanied by one or more experts and advisers.

* * *

a. Amendments to Schedule are omitted.

Article IV

1. The Commission may either in collaboration with or through independent agencies of the Contracting Governments or other public or private agencies, establishments, or organizations, or independently

(*a*) encourage, recommend, or if necessary, organize studies and investigations relating to whales and whaling;

(*b*) collect and analyze statistical information concerning the current condition and trend of the whale stocks and the effects of whaling activities thereon;

(*c*) study, appraise, and disseminate information concerning methods of maintaining and increasing the populations of whale stocks.

2. The Commission shall arrange for the publication of reports of its activities, and it may publish independently or in collaboration with the International Bureau for Whaling Statistics at Sandefjord in Norway and other organizations and agencies such reports as it deems appropriate, as well as statistical, scientific, and other pertinent information relating to whales and whaling.

Article V

1. The Commission may amend from time to time the provisions of the Schedule by adopting regulations with respect to the conservation and utilization of whale resources, fixing (*a*) protected and unprotected species; (*b*) open and closed seasons; (*c*) open and closed waters, including the designation of sanctuary areas; (*d*) size limits for each species; (*e*) time, methods, and intensity of whaling (including the maximum catch of whales to be taken in any one season); (*f*) types and specifications of gear and apparatus and appliances which may be used; (*g*) methods of measurement; and (*h*) catch returns and other statistical and biological records.

2. These amendments of the Schedule (*a*) shall be such as are necessary to carry out the objectives and purposes of this Convention and to provide for the conservation, development, and optimum utilization of the whale resources; (*b*) shall be based on scientific findings; (*c*) shall not involve restrictions on the number or nationality of factory ships or land stations, nor allocate specific quotas to any factory ship or land station or to any group of factory ships or land stations; and (*d*) shall take into consideration the interests of the consumers of whale products and the whaling industry.

3. Each of such amendments shall become effective with respect to the Contracting Governments ninety days following notification of the amendment by the Commission to each of the Contracting Governments, except that (*a*) if any Government presents to the Commission objection to any amendment prior to the expiration of this ninety-day period, the amendment shall not become effective with respect to any of the Governments for an additional ninety days; (*b*) thereupon, any other Contracting Government may present objection to the amendment at any time prior to the expiration of the additional ninety-day period, or before the expiration of thirty days from the date of receipt of the last objection received during such additional ninety-day period, whichever date shall be the later; and (*c*) thereafter, the amendment shall become effective with respect to all Contracting Governments which have not presented objection but shall not become effective with respect to any Government which has so objected until such date as the objection is withdrawn. The Commission shall notify each Contracting Government immediately upon receipt of each objection and withdrawal and each Contracting Government shall acknowledge receipt of all notifications of amendments, objections, and withdrawals.

* * *

Article VI

The Commission may from time to time make recommendations to any or all Contracting Governments on any matters which relate to whales or whaling and to the objectives and purposes of this Convention.

Article VII

The Contracting Governments shall ensure prompt transmission to the International Bureau for Whaling Statistics at Sandefjord in Norway, or to such other body as the Commission may designate, of notifications and statistical and other information required by this Convention in such form and manner as may be prescribed by the Commission.

Article VIII

1. Notwithstanding anything contained in this Convention, any Contracting Government may grant to any of its nationals a special permit authorizing that national to kill, take, and treat whales for purposes of scientific research subject to such restrictions as to number and subject to such other conditions as the Contracting Government thinks fit, and the killing, taking, and treating of whales in accordance with the provisions of this Article shall be exempt from the operation of this Convention. Each Contracting Government shall report at once to the Commission all such authorizations which it has granted. Each Contracting Government may at any time revoke any such special permit which it has granted.

2. Any whales taken under these special permits shall so far as practicable be processed and the proceeds shall be dealt with in accordance with directions issued by the Government by which the permit was granted.

3. Each Contracting Government shall transmit to such body as may be designated by the Commission, in so far as practicable, and at intervals of not more than one year, scientific information available to that Government with respect to whales and whaling, including the results of research conducted pursuant to paragraph 1 of this Article and to Article IV.

4. Recognizing that continuous collection and analysis of biological data in connection with the operations of factory ships and land stations are indispensable to sound and constructive management of the whale fisheries, the Contracting Governments will take all practicable measures to obtain such data.

Article IX

1. Each Contracting Government shall take appropriate measures to ensure the application of the provisions of this Convention and the punishment of infractions against the said provisions in operations carried out by persons or by vessels under its jurisdiction.

2. No bonus or other remuneration calculated with relation to the results of their work shall be paid to the gunners and crews of whale catchers in respect of any whales the taking of which is forbidden by this Convention.

3. Prosecution for infractions against or contraventions of this Convention shall be instituted by the Government having jurisdiction over the offense.

4. Each Contracting Government shall transmit to the Commission full details of each infraction of the provisions of this Convention by persons or vessels under the jurisdiction of that Government as reported by its inspectors. This information shall include a statement of measures taken for dealing with the infraction and of penalties imposed.

* * *

Article XI

Any Contracting Government may withdraw from this Convention on June thirtieth of any year by giving notice on or before January first of the same year to the depositary Government, which upon receipt of such a notice shall at once communicate it to the other Contracting Governments. Any other Contracting Government may, in like manner, within one month of the receipt of a copy of such a notice from the depositary Government, give notice of withdrawal, so that the Convention shall cease to be in force on June thirtieth of the same year with respect to the Government giving such notice of withdrawal.

5.3 INTERNATIONAL CONVENTION FOR THE PREVENTION OF POLLUTION OF THE SEA BY OIL.[a] Done at London, May 12, 1954. Entered into force, July 26, 1958; for the United States, Dec. 8, 1961. 12 U.S.T. 2989, T.I.A.S. No. 4900, 327 U.N.T.S. 3. AMENDMENTS ADOPTED BY THE CONFERENCE OF CONTRACTING GOVERNMENTS TO THE CONVENTION OF 1954. Done at London, April 11, 1962. Entered into force, June 28, 1967 (Art. 14), May 18, 1967 (remainder); for the United States, May 18, 1967 (Arts. 1–9, 16, 18), June 28, 1967, (Art. 14). 17 U.S.T. 1523, T.I.A.S. No. 6109, 600 U.N.T.S. 332. AMENDMENTS ADOPTED BY THE ASSEMBLY OF THE INTER-GOVERNMENTAL MARITIME CONSULTATIVE ORGANIZATION. Done at London, Oct. 21, 1969. Entered into force, Jan. 20, 1978; for the United States, Jan. 20, 1978. 28 U.S.T. 1205, T.I.A.S. No. 8505. *Reprinted in composite form* in 9 I.L.M. 1 (1970)

Article I. (1) For the purposes of the present Convention, the following expression shall (unless the context otherwise requires) have the meanings hereby respectively assigned to them that is to say:

"The Bureau" has the meaning assigned to it by Article XXI;

"Discharge" in relation to oil or to oily mixture means any discharge or escape howsoever caused;

"Heavy diesel oil" means diesel oil, other than those distillates of which more than 50 per cent by volume distills at a temperature not exceeding 340° C. when tested by A.S.T.M. Standard Method D.86/59;

"Instantaneous rate of discharge of oil content" means the rate of discharge of oil in litres per hour at any instant divided by the speed of the ship in knots at the same instant;

"Mile" means a nautical mile of 6,080 feet or 1,852 metres;

"Nearest Land". The term "from the nearest land" means "from the baseline from which the territorial sea of the territory in question is established in accordance with the Geneva Convention on the Territorial Sea and the Contiguous Zone, 1958";

a. For other notable instruments pertaining to marine pollution, see International Convention on Civil Liability for Oil Pollution Damage, done at Brussels, Nov. 29, 1969, entered into force, June 19, 1975, 1969 U.N. JURID. Y.B. 174, *reprinted in* 9 I.L.M. 45 (1970); International Convention on the Establishment of an International Fund for Compensation for Oil Pollution Damage, done at Brussels, Dec. 18, 1971, entered into force, Oct. 16, 1978, 1971 U.N. JURID. Y.B. 103, *reprinted in* 11 I.L.M. 284 (1972); Convention for the Prevention of Marine Pollution from Land-Based Sources, done at Paris, June 4, 1974, entered into force, May 6, 1978, *reproduced in* 13 I.L.M. 352 (1974); Convention on Civil Liability for Oil Pollution Damage Resulting from the Exploration and Exploitation of the Seabed Mineral Resources, done at London, Apr. 30, 1978. This last convention had not entered into force as of Dec. 31, 1989. *See also* Basic Documents 5.13, 5.18, 5.20, and 5.22, *infra.*

"Oil" means crude oil, fuel oil, heavy diesel oil and lubricating oil, and "oily" shall be construed accordingly;

"Oily mixture" means a mixture with any oil content;

"Organization" means the Inter–Governmental Maritime Consultative Organization;

"Ship" means any sea-going vessel of any type whatsoever, including floating craft, whether self-propelled or towed by another vessel, making a sea voyage; and "tanker" means a ship in which the greater part of the cargo space is constructed or adapted for the carriage of liquid cargoes in bulk and which is not, for the time being, carrying a cargo other than oil in that part of its cargo space.

(2) For the purposes of the present Convention, the territories of a Contracting Government mean the territory of the country of which it is the Government and any other territory for the international relations of which it is responsible and to which the Convention shall have been extended under Article XVIII.

Article II. (1) The present Convention shall apply to ships registered in any of the territories of a Contracting Government and to unregistered ships having the nationality of a Contracting Party, except:

(a) tankers of under 150 tons gross tonnage and other ships of under 500 tons gross tonnage, provided that each Contracting Government will take the necessary steps, so far as is reasonable and practicable, to apply the requirements of the Convention to such ships also, having regard to their size, service and the type of fuel used for their propulsion;

(b) ships for the time being engaged in the whaling industry when actually employed on whaling operations;

(c) ships for the time being navigating the Great Lakes of North America and their connecting and tributary waters as far east as the lower exit of St. Lambert Lock at Montreal in the Province of Quebec, Canada;

(d) naval ships and ships for the time being used as naval auxiliaries.

(2) Each Contracting Government undertakes to adopt appropriate measures ensuring that requirements equivalent to those of the present Convention are, so far as is reasonable and practicable, applied to the ships referred to in subparagraph (d) of paragraph (1) of this Article.

Article III. Subject to the provisions of Articles IV and V:

(a) the discharge from a ship to which the present Convention applies, other than a tanker, of oil or oily mixture shall be prohibited except when the following conditions are all satisfied:

(i) the ship is proceeding en route;

(ii) the instantaneous rate of discharge of oil content does not exceed 60 litres per mile;

(iii) the oil content of the discharge is less than 100 parts per 1,000,000 parts of the mixture;

(iv) the discharge is made as far as practicable from land;

(b) the discharge from a tanker to which the present Convention applies of oil or oily mixture shall be prohibited except when the following conditions are all satisfied:

(i) the tanker is proceeding en route;

(ii) the instantaneous rate of discharge of oil content does not exceed 60 litres per mile;

(iii) the total quantity of oil discharged on a ballast voyage does not exceed

$\frac{1}{15,000}$ of the total cargo-carrying capacity;

(iv) the tanker is more than 50 miles from the nearest land;

(c) the provisions of sub-paragraph (b) of this Article shall not apply to:

(i) the discharge of ballast from a cargo tank which, since the cargo was last carried therein, has been so cleaned that any effluent therefrom, if it were discharged from a stationary tanker into clean calm water on a clear day, would produce no visible traces of oil on the surface of the water; or

(ii) the discharge of oil or oily mixture from machinery space bilges, which shall be governed by the provisions of sub-paragraph (a) of this Article.

Article IV. Article III shall not apply to:

(a) the discharge of oil or of oily mixture from a ship for the purpose of securing the safety of a ship, preventing damage to a ship or cargo, or saving life at sea;

(b) the escape of oil or of oily mixture resulting from damage to a ship or unavoidable leakage, if all reasonable precautions have been taken after the occurrence of the damage or discovery of the leakage for the purpose of preventing or minimizing the escape;

* * *

Article VI. (1) Any contravention of Articles III and IX shall be an offence punishable under the law of the relevant territory in respect of the ship in accordance with paragraph (1) of Article II.

(2) The penalties which may be imposed under the law of any of the territories of a Contracting Government in respect of the unlawful discharge from a ship of oil or oily mixture outside the territorial sea of that territory shall be adequate in severity to discourage any such unlawful discharge and shall not be less than the penalties which may be imposed under the law of that territory in respect of the same infringements within the territorial sea.

(3) Each Contracting Government shall report to the Organization the penalties actually imposed for each infringement.

Article VII. (1) As from a date twelve months after the present Convention comes into force for the relevant territory in respect of a ship in accordance with paragraph (1) of Article II, such a ship shall be required to be so fitted as to prevent, as far as reasonable and practicable, the escape of oil into bilges, unless effective means are provided to ensure that the oil in the bilges is not discharged in contravention of this Convention.

(2) Carrying water ballast in oil fuel tanks shall be avoided if possible.

Article VIII. (1) Each Contracting Government shall take all appropriate steps to promote the provision of facilities as follows:

(a) according to the needs of ships using them, ports shall be provided with facilities adequate for the reception, without causing undue delay to ships, of such residues and oily mixtures as would remain for disposal from ships other than tankers if the bulk of the water had been separated from the mixture;

(b) oil loading terminals shall be provided with facilities adequate for the reception of such residues and oily mixtures as would similarly remain for disposal by tankers;

(c) ship repair shall be provided with facilities adequate for the reception of such residues and oily mixtures as would similarly remain for disposal by all ships entering for repairs.

(2) Each Contracting Government shall determine which are the ports and oil loading terminals in its territories suitable for the purposes of sub-paragraphs (a), (b) and (c) of paragraph (1) of this Article.

(3) As regards paragraph (1) of this Article, each Contracting Government shall report to the Organization, for transmission to the Contracting Government concerned, all cases where the facilities are alleged to be inadequate.

* * *

Article X. (1) Any Contracting Government may furnish to the Government of the relevant territory in respect of the ship in accordance with paragraph (1) of Article II particulars in writing of evidence that any provision of the present Convention has been contravened in respect of that ship, wheresoever the alleged contravention may have taken place. If it is practicable to do so, the competent authorities of the former Government shall notify the master of the ship of the alleged contravention.

(2) Upon receiving such particulars, the Government so informed shall investigate the matter, and may request the other Government to furnish further or better particulars of the alleged contravention. If the Government so informed is satisfied that sufficient evidence is available in the form required by its law to enable proceedings against the owner or master of the ship to be taken in respect of the alleged contravention, it shall cause such proceedings to be taken as soon as possible. That Government shall promptly inform the Government whose official has reported the alleged contravention, as well as the Organization, of the action taken as a consequence of the information communicated.

Article XI. Nothing in the present Convention shall be construed as derogating from the powers of any Contracting Government to take measures within its jurisdiction in respect of any matter to which the Convention relates or as extending the jurisdiction of any Contracting Government.

Article XII. Each Contracting Government shall send to the Bureau and to the appropriate organ of the United Nations:

(a) the text of laws, decrees, orders and regulations in force in its territories which give effect to present Convention;

(b) all official reports or summaries of official reports in so far as they show the results of the application of the provisions of the Convention, provided always that such reports or summaries are not, in the opinion of that Government, of a confidential nature.

* * *

Article XIX. (1) In case of war or other hostilities, a Contracting Government which considers that it is affected, whether as a belligerent or as a neutral, may suspend the operation of the whole or any part of the present Convention in respect of all or any of its territories. The suspending Government shall immediately give notice of any such suspension to the Bureau.

(2) The suspending Government may at any time terminate such suspension and shall in any event terminate it as soon as it ceases to be justified under paragraph (1) of this Article. Notice of such termination shall be given immediately to the Bureau by the Government concerned.

(3) The Bureau shall notify all Contracting Governments of any suspension or termination of suspension under this Article.

* * *

5.4 CONVENTION ON THE HIGH SEAS.[a] Done at Geneva, Apr. 29, 1958. Entered into force, Sept. 30, 1962; for the United States, Sept. 30, 1962. 13 U.S.T. 2312, T.I.A.S. No. 5200, 450 U.N.T.S. 82

Article 1. The term "high seas" means all parts of the sea that are not included in the territorial sea or in the internal waters of a State.

Article 2. The high seas being open to all nations, no State may validly purport to subject any part of them to its sovereignty. Freedom of the high seas is exercised under the conditions laid down by these articles and by the other rules of international law. It comprises, *inter alia,* both for coastal and non-coastal States:

(1) Freedom of navigation;

(2) Freedom of fishing;

(3) Freedom to lay submarine cables and pipelines;

(4) Freedom to fly over the high seas.

These freedoms, and others which are recognized by the general principles of international law, shall be exercised by all States with reasonable regard to the interests of other States in their exercise of the freedom of the high seas.

Article 3. (1) In order to enjoy the freedom of the seas on equal terms with coastal States, States having no sea-coast should have free access to the sea. To this end States situated between the sea and a State having no sea-coast shall by common agreement with the latter and in conformity with existing international convention accord:

(a) To the State having no sea-coast, on a basis of reciprocity, free transit through their territory; and

(b) To ships flying the flag of that State treatment equal to that accorded to their own ships, or to the ships of any other States, as regards access to seaports and the use of such ports.

(2) States situated between the sea and a State having no sea-coast shall settle, by mutual agreement with the latter, and taking into account the rights of the coastal State or State of transit and the special conditions of the State having no sea-coast, all matters relating to freedom of transit and equal treatment in ports, in case such States are not already parties to existing international conventions.

Article 4. Every State, whether coastal or not, has the right to sail ships under its flag on the high seas.

Article 5. (1) Each State shall fix the conditions for the grant of its nationality to ships, for the registration of ships in its territory, and for the right to fly its flag. Ships have the nationality of the State whose flag they are entitled to fly. There must exist a genuine link between the State and the ship; in particular, the State must effectively exercise its jurisdiction and control in administrative, technical and social matters over ships flying its flag.

(2) Each State shall issue to ships to which it has granted the right to fly its flag documents to that effect.

Article 6. (1) Ships shall sail under the flag of one State only and, save in exceptional cases expressly provided for in international treaties or in these articles, shall be subject to its exclusive jurisdiction on the high seas. A ship may not change its flag during a voyage or while in a port of call, save in the case of a real transfer of ownership or change of registry.

a. *See also* Basic Documents 5.5, 5.6, 5.7, and 5.27, *infra.*

(2) A ship which sails under the flags of two or more States, using them according to convenience, may not claim any of the nationalities in question with respect to any other State, and may be assimilated to a ship without nationality.

Article 7. The provisions of the preceding articles do not prejudice the question of ships employed on the official service of an inter-governmental organization flying the flag of the organization.

Article 8. (1) Warships on the high seas have complete immunity from the jurisdiction of any State other than the flag State.

(2) For the purposes of these articles, the term "warship" means a ship belonging to the naval forces of a State and bearing the external marks distinguishing warships of its nationality, under the command of an officer duly commissioned by the government and whose name appears in the Navy List, and manned by a crew who are under regular naval discipline.

Article 9. Ships owned or operated by a State and used only on government noncommercial service shall, on the high seas, have complete immunity from the jurisdiction of any State other than the flag State.

Article 10. (1) Every State shall take such measures for ships under its flag as are necessary to ensure safety at sea with regard *inter alia* to:

(a) The use of signals, the maintenance of communications and the prevention of collisions;

(b) The manning of ships and labour conditions for crews taking into account the applicable international labour instruments;

(c) The construction, equipment and seaworthiness of ships.

(2) In taking such measures each State is required to conform to generally accepted international standards and to take any steps which may be necessary to ensure their observance.

Article 11. (1) In the event of a collision or of any other incident of navigation concerning a ship on the high seas, involving the penal or disciplinary responsibility of the master or of any other person in the service of the ship, no penal or disciplinary proceedings may be instituted against such persons except before the judicial or administrative authorities either of the flag State or of the State of which such person is a national.

(2) In disciplinary matters, the State which has issued a master's certificate or a certificate of competence or license shall alone be competent, after due legal process, to pronounce the withdrawal of such certificates, even if the holder is not a national of the State which issued them.

(3) No arrest or detention of the ship, even as a measure of investigation, shall be ordered by any authorities other than those of the flag State.

Article 12. (1) Every State shall require the master of a ship sailing under its flag, in so far as he can do so without serious danger to the ship, the crew or the passengers,

(a) To render assistance to any person found at sea in danger of being lost;

(b) To proceed with all possible speed to the rescue of persons in distress if informed of their need of assistance, in so far as such action may reasonably be expected of him;

(c) After a collision, to render assistance to the other ship, her crew and her passengers and, where possible, to inform the other ship of the name of his own ship, her port of registry and the nearest port at which she will call.

(2) Every coastal State shall promote the establishment and maintenance of an adequate and effective search and rescue service regarding safety on and over the sea

and—where circumstances so require—by way of mutual regional arrangements co-operate with neighbouring States for this purpose.

Article 13. Every State shall adopt effective measures to prevent and punish the transport of slaves in ships authorized to fly its flag, and to prevent the unlawful use of its flag for that purpose. Any slave taking refuge on board any ship, whatever its flag, shall *ipso facto* be free.

Article 14. All States shall co-operate to the fullest possible extent in the repression of piracy on the high seas or in any other place outside the jurisdiction of any State.

Article 15. Piracy consists of any of the following acts:

(1) Any illegal acts of violence, detention or any act of depredation, committed for private ends by the crew or the passengers of a private ship or a private aircraft, and directed:

(a) On the high seas, against another ship or aircraft, or against persons or property on board such ship or aircraft;

(b) Against a ship, aircraft, persons or property in a place outside the jurisdiction of any State;

(2) Any act of voluntary participation in the operation of a ship or of an aircraft with knowledge of facts making it a pirate ship or aircraft;

(3) Any act of inciting or of intentionally facilitating an act described in sub-paragraph 1 or sub-paragraph 2 of this article.

Article 16. The acts of piracy, as defined in article 15, committed by a warship, government ship or government aircraft whose crew has mutinied and taken control of the ship or aircraft are assimilated to acts committed by a private ship.

Article 17. A ship or aircraft is considered a pirate ship or aircraft if it is intended by the persons in dominant control to be used for the purpose of committing one of the acts referred to in article 15. The same applies if the ship or aircraft has been used to commit any such act, so long as it remains under the control of the persons guilty of that act.

Article 18. A ship or aircraft may retain its nationality although it has become a pirate ship or aircraft. The retention or loss of nationality is determined by the law of the State from which such nationality was derived.

Article 19. On the high seas, or in any other place outside the jurisdiction of any State, every State may seize a pirate ship or aircraft, or a ship taken by piracy and under the control of pirates, and arrest the persons and seize the property on board. The courts of the State which carried out the seizure may decide upon the penalties to be imposed, and may also determine the action to be taken with regard to the ships, aircraft or property, subject to the rights of third parties acting in good faith.

Article 20. Where the seizure of a ship or aircraft on suspicion of piracy has been effected without adequate grounds, the State making the seizure shall be liable to the State the nationality of which is possessed by the ship or aircraft, for any loss or damage caused by the seizure.

Article 21. A seizure on account of piracy may only be carried out by warships or military aircraft, or other ships or aircraft on government service authorized to that effect.

Article 22. (1) Except where acts of interference derive from powers conferred by treaty, a warship which encounters a foreign merchant ship on the high seas is not justified in boarding her unless there is reasonable ground for suspecting:

(a) That the ship is engaged in piracy; or

(b) That the ship is engaged in the slave trade; or

(c) That, though flying a foreign flag or refusing to show its flag, the ship is, in reality, of the same nationality as the warship.

(2) In the cases provided for in sub-paragraphs (a), (b) and (c) above, the warship may proceed to verify the ship's right to fly its flag. To this end, it may send a boat under the command of an officer to the suspected ship. If suspicion remains after the documents have been checked, it may proceed to a further examination on board the ship, which must be carried out with all possible consideration.

(3) If the suspicions prove to be unfounded, and provided that the ship boarded has not committed any act justifying them, it shall be compensated for any loss or damage that may have been sustained.

Article 23. (1) The hot pursuit of a foreign ship may be undertaken when the competent authorities of the coastal State have good reason to believe that the ship has violated the laws and regulations of that State. Such pursuit must be commenced when the foreign ship or one of its boats is within the internal waters or the territorial sea or the contiguous zone of the pursuing State, and may only be continued outside the territorial sea or the contiguous zone if the pursuit has not been interrupted. It is not necessary that, at the time when the foreign ship within the territorial sea or the contiguous zone receives the order to stop, the ship giving the order should likewise be within the territorial sea or the contiguous zone. If the foreign ship is within a contiguous zone, as defined in article 24 of the Convention on the Territorial Sea and the Contiguous Zone, the pursuit may only be undertaken if there has been a violation of the rights for the protection of which the zone was established.

(2) The right of hot pursuit ceases as soon as the ship pursued enters the territorial sea of its own country or of a third State.

(3) Hot pursuit is not deemed to have begun unless the pursuing ship has satisfied itself by such practicable means as may be available that the ship pursued or one of its boats or other craft working as a team and using the ship pursued as a mother ship are within the limits of the territorial sea, or as the case may be within the contiguous zone. The pursuit may only be commenced after a visual or auditory signal to stop has been given at a distance which enables it to be seen or heard by the foreign ship.

(4) The right of hot pursuit may be exercised only by warships or military aircraft, or other ships or aircraft on government service specially authorized to that effect.

(5) Where hot pursuit is effected by an aircraft:

(a) The provisions of paragraphs 1 to 3 of this article shall apply *mutatis mutandis;*

(b) The aircraft giving the order to stop must itself actively pursue the ship until a ship or aircraft of the coastal State, summoned by the aircraft, arrives to take over the pursuit, unless the aircraft is itself able to arrest the ship. It does not suffice to justify an arrest on the high seas that the ship was merely sighted by the aircraft as an offender or suspected offender, if it was not both ordered to stop and pursued by the aircraft itself or other aircraft or ships which continue the pursuit without interruption.

(6) The release of a ship arrested within the jurisdiction of a State and escorted to a port of that State for the purposes of an enquiry before the competent authorities may not be claimed solely on the ground that the ship, in the course of its voyage, was escorted across a portion of the high seas, if the circumstances rendered this necessary.

(7) Where a ship has been stopped or arrested on the high seas in circumstances which do not justify the exercise of the right of hot pursuit, it shall be compensated for any loss or damage that may have been thereby sustained.

Article 24. Every State shall draw up regulations to prevent pollution of the seas by the discharge of oil from ships or pipelines or resulting from the exploitation and exploration of the seabed and its subsoil, taking account of existing treaty provisions on the subject.

Article 25. (1) Every State shall take measures to prevent pollution of the seas from the dumping of radio-active waste, taking into account any standards and regulations which may be formulated by the competent international organizations.

(2) All States shall co-operate with the competent international organizations in taking measures for the prevention of pollution of the seas or air space above, resulting from any activities with radio-active materials or other harmful agents.

Article 26. (1) All States shall be entitled to lay submarine cables and pipelines on the bed of the high seas.

(2) Subject to its right to take reasonable measures for the exploration of the continental shelf and the exploitation of its natural resources, the coastal State may not impede the laying or maintenance of such cables or pipelines.

(3) When laying such cables or pipelines the State in question shall pay due regard to cables or pipelines already in position on the seabed. In particular, possibilities of repairing existing cables or pipelines shall not be prejudiced.

Article 27. Every State shall take the necessary legislative measures to provide that the breaking or injury by a ship flying its flag or by a person subject to its jurisdiction of a submarine cable beneath the high seas done wilfully or through culpable negligence, in such a manner as to be liable to interrupt or obstruct telegraphic or telephonic communications, and similarly the breaking or injury of a submarine pipeline or high-voltage power cable shall be a punishable offence. This provision shall not apply to any break or injury caused by persons who acted merely with the legitimate object of saving their lives or their ships, after having taken all necessary precautions to avoid such break or injury.

Article 28. Every State shall take the necessary legislative measures to provide that, if persons subject to its jurisdiction who are the owners of a cable or pipeline beneath the high seas, in laying or repairing that cable or pipeline, cause a break in or injury to another cable or pipeline, they shall bear the cost of the repairs.

Article 29. Every State shall take the necessary legislative measures to ensure that the owners of ships who can prove that they have sacrificed an anchor, a net or any other fishing gear, in order to avoid injuring a submarine cable or pipeline, shall be indemnified by the owner of the cable or pipeline, provided that the owner of the ship has taken all reasonable precautionary measures beforehand.

* * *

5.5 CONVENTION ON THE CONTINENTAL SHELF.[a] Done at Geneva, Apr. 29, 1958. Entered into force, June 10, 1964; for the United States, June 10, 1964. 15 U.S.T. 471, T.I.A.S. No. 5578, 449 U.N.T.S. 311

Article 1. For the purpose of these articles, the term "continental shelf" is used as referring (a) to the seabed and subsoil of the submarine areas adjacent to the coast but outside the area of the territorial sea, to a depth of 200 metres or, beyond that limit, to where the depth of the superjacent waters admits of the exploitation of the natural resources of the said areas; (b) to the seabed and subsoil of similar submarine areas adjacent to the coasts of islands.

Article 2. (1) The coastal State exercises over the continental shelf sovereign rights for the purpose of exploring it and exploiting its natural resources.

(2) The rights referred to in paragraph 1 of this article are exclusive in the sense that if the coastal State does not explore the continental shelf or exploit its natural resources, no one may undertake these activities, or make a claim to the continental shelf, without the express consent of the coastal State.

(3) The rights of the coastal State over the continental shelf do not depend on occupation, effective or notional, or on any express proclamation.

(4) The natural resources referred to in these articles consist of the mineral and other non-living resources of the seabed and subsoil together with living organisms belonging to sedentary species, that is to say, organisms which, at the harvestable stage, either are immobile on or under the seabed or are unable to move except in constant physical contact with the seabed or the subsoil.

Article 3. The rights of the coastal State over the continental shelf do not affect the legal status of the superjacent waters as high seas, or that of the airspace above those waters.

Article 4. Subject to its right to take reasonable measures for the exploration of the continental shelf and the exploitation of its natural resources, the coastal State may not impede the laying or maintenance of submarine cables or pipe lines on the continental shelf.

Article 5. (1) The exploration of the continental shelf and the exploitation of its natural resources must not result in any unjustifiable interference with navigation, fishing or the conservation of the living resources of the sea, nor result in any interference with fundamental oceanographic or other scientific research carried out with the intention of open publication.

(2) Subject to the provisions of paragraphs 1 and 6 of this article, the coastal State is entitled to construct and maintain or operate on the continental shelf installations and other devices necessary for its exploration and the exploitation of its natural resources, and to establish safety zones around such installations and devices and to take in those zones measures necessary for their protection.

(3) The safety zones referred to in paragraph 2 of this article may extend to a distance of 500 metres around the installations and other devices which have been erected, measured from each point of their outer edge. Ships of all nationalities must respect these safety zones.

(4) Such installations and devices, though under the jurisdiction of the coastal State, do not possess the status of islands. They have no territorial sea of their own, and their presence does not affect the delimitation of the territorial sea of the coastal State.

a. *See also* Basic Document 5.4, *supra,* and Basic Documents 5.6, 5.7, and 5.27, *infra.*

(5) Due notice must be given of the construction of any such installations, and permanent means for giving warning of their presence must be maintained. Any installations which are abandoned or disused must be entirely removed.

(6) Neither the installations or devices, nor the safety zones around them, may be established where interference may be caused to the use of recognized sea lanes essential to international navigation.

(7) The coastal State is obliged to undertake, in the safety zones, all appropriate measures for the protection of the living resources of the sea from harmful agents.

(8) The consent of the coastal State shall be obtained in respect of any research concerning the continental shelf and undertaken there. Nevertheless the coastal State shall not normally withhold its consent if the request is submitted by a qualified institution with a view to purely scientific research into the physical or biological characteristics of the continental shelf, subject to the proviso that the coastal State shall have the right, if it so desires, to participate or to be represented in the research, and that in any event the results shall be published.

Article 6. (1) Where the same continental shelf is adjacent to the territories of two or more States whose coasts are opposite each other, the boundary of the continental shelf appertaining to such States shall be determined by agreement between them. In the absence of agreement, and unless another boundary line is justified by special circumstances, the boundary is the median line, every point of which is equidistant from the nearest points of the baselines from which the breadth of the territorial sea of each State is measured.

(2) Where the same continental shelf is adjacent to the territories of two adjacent States, the boundary of the continental shelf shall be determined by agreement between them. In the absence of agreement, and unless another boundary line is justified by special circumstances, the boundary shall be determined by application of the principle of equidistance from the nearest points of the baselines from which the breadth of the territorial sea of each State is measured.

(3) In delimiting the boundaries of the continental shelf, any lines which are drawn in accordance with the principles set out in paragraphs 1 and 2 of this article should be defined with reference to charts and geographical features as they exist at a particular date, and reference should be made to fixed permanent identifiable points on the land.

Article 7. The provisions of these articles shall not prejudice the right of the coastal State to exploit the subsoil by means of tunnelling irrespective of the depth of water above the subsoil.

* * *

5.6 CONVENTION ON THE TERRITORIAL SEA AND CONTIGUOUS ZONE.[a] Done at Geneva, Apr. 29, 1958. Entered into force, Sept. 10, 1964; for the United States, Sept. 10, 1964. 15 U.S.T. 1606, T.I.A.S. No. 5639, 516 U.N.T.S. 205

PART I. TERRITORIAL SEA

SECTION I. GENERAL

Article 1. (1) The sovereignty of a State extends, beyond its land territory and its internal waters, to a belt of sea adjacent to its coast, described as the territorial sea.

(2) This sovereignty is exercised subject to the provisions of these articles and to other rules of international law.

Article 2. The sovereignty of a coast State extends to the air space over the territorial sea as well as to its bed and subsoil.

SECTION II. LIMITS OF THE TERRITORIAL SEA

Article 3. Except where otherwise provided in these articles, the normal baseline for measuring the breadth of the territorial sea is the low-water line along the coast as marked on large-scale charts officially recognized by the coastal State.

Article 4. (1) In localities where the coast line is deeply indented and cut into, or if there is a fringe of islands along the coast in its immediate vicinity, the method of straight baselines joining appropriate points may be employed in drawing the baseline from which the breadth of the territorial sea is measured.

(2) The drawing of such baselines must not depart to any appreciable extent from the general direction of the coast, and the sea areas lying within the lines must be sufficiently closely linked to the land domain to be subject to the régime of internal waters.

(3) Baselines shall not be drawn to and from low-tide elevations, unless lighthouses or similar installations which are permanently above sea level have been built on them.

(4) Where the method of straight baselines is applicable under the provisions of paragraph 1, account may be taken, in determining particular baselines, of economic interests peculiar to the region concerned, the reality and the importance of which are clearly evidenced by a long usage.

(5) The system of straight baselines may not be applied by a State in such a manner as to cut off from the high seas the territorial sea of another State.

(6) The coastal State must clearly indicate straight baselines on charts, to which due publicity must be given.

Article 5. (1) Waters on the landward side of the baseline of the territorial sea form part of the internal waters of the State.

(2) Where the establishment of a straight baseline in accordance with article 4 has the effect of enclosing as internal waters areas which previously had been considered as part of the territorial sea or of the high seas, a right of innocent passage, as provided in articles 14 to 23, shall exist in those waters.

a. *See also* Basic Documents 5.4 and 5.5, *supra*, and Basic Documents 5.7 and 5.27, *infra*.

Article 6. The outer line of the territorial sea is the line every point of which is at a distance from the nearest point of the baseline equal to the breadth of the territorial sea.

Article 7. (1) This article relates only to bays, the coasts of which belong to a single State.

(2) For the purposes of these articles, a bay is a well-marked indentation whose penetration is in such proportion to the width of its mouth as to contain landlocked waters and constitute more than a mere curvature of the coast. An indentation shall not, however, be regarded as a bay unless its area is as large as, or larger than, that of the semi-circle whose diameter is a line drawn across the mouth of that indentation.

(3) For the purpose of measurement, the area of an indentation is that lying between the low-water mark around the shore of the indentation and a line joining the low-water marks of its natural entrance points. Where, because of the presence of islands, an indentation has more than one mouth, the semi-circle shall be drawn on a line as long as the sum total of the lengths of the lines across the different mouths. Islands within an indentation shall be included as if they were part of the water areas of the indentation.

(4) If the distance between the low-water marks of the natural entrance points of a bay does not exceed twenty-four miles, a closing line may be drawn between these two low-water marks, and the waters enclosed thereby shall be considered as internal waters.

(5) Where the distance between the low-water marks of the natural entrance points of a bay exceeds twenty-four miles, a straight baseline of twenty-four miles shall be drawn within the bay in such a manner as to enclose the maximum area of water that is possible with a line of that length.

(6) The foregoing provisions shall not apply to so-called "historic" bays, or in any cases where the straight baseline system provided for in article 4 is applied.

Article 8. For the purpose of delimiting the territorial sea, the outermost permanent harbour works which form an integral part of the harbour system shall be regarded as forming part of the coast.

Article 9. Roadsteads which are normally used for the loading, unloading and anchoring of ships, and which would otherwise be situated wholly or partly outside the outer limit of the territorial sea, are included in the territorial sea. The coastal State must clearly demarcate such roadsteads and indicate them on charts together with their boundaries, to which due publicity must be given.

Article 10. (1) An island is a naturally-formed area of land, surrounded by water, which is above water at high-tide.

(2) The territorial sea of an island is measured in accordance with the provisions of these articles.

Article 11. (1) A low-tide elevation is a naturally-formed area of land which is surrounded by and above water at low-tide but submerged at high-tide. Where a low-tide elevation is situated wholly or partly at a distance not exceeding the breadth of the territorial sea from the mainland or an island, the low-water line on that elevation may be used as the baseline for measuring the breadth of the territorial sea.

(2) Where a low-tide elevation is wholly situated at a distance exceeding the breadth of the territorial sea from the mainland or an island, it has no territorial sea of its own.

Article 12. (1) Where the coasts of two States are opposite or adjacent to each other, neither of the two States is entitled, failing agreement between them to the contrary, to extend its territorial sea beyond the median line every point of which is equidistant from the nearest points on the baselines from which the breadth of the territorial seas of each of the two States is measured. The provisions of this paragraph shall not apply, however, where it is necessary by reason of historic title or other special circumstances to delimit the territorial seas of the two States in a way which is at variance with this provision.

(2) The line of delimitation between the territorial seas of two States lying opposite to each other or adjacent to each other shall be marked on large-scale charts officially recognized by the coastal States.

Article 13. If a river flows directly into the sea, the baseline shall be a straight line across the mouth of the river between points on the low-tide line of its banks.

SECTION III. RIGHT OF INNOCENT PASSAGE

Sub-section A. Rules Applicable to All Ships

Article 14. (1) Subject to the provisions of these articles, ships of all States, whether coastal or not, shall enjoy the right of innocent passage through the territorial sea.

(2) Passage means navigation through the territorial sea for the purpose either of traversing that sea without entering internal waters, or of proceeding to internal waters, or of making for the high seas from internal waters.

(3) Passage includes stopping and anchoring, but only in so far as the same are incidental to ordinary navigation or are rendered necessary by *force majeure* or by distress.

(4) Passage is innocent so long as it is not prejudicial to the peace, good order or security of the coastal State. Such passage shall take place in conformity with these articles and with other rules of international law.

(5) Passage of foreign fishing vessels shall not be considered innocent if they do not observe such laws and regulations as the coastal State may make and publish in order to prevent these vessels from fishing in the territorial sea.

(6) Submarines are required to navigate on the surface and to show their flag.

Article 15. (1) The coastal State must not hamper innocent passage through the territorial sea.

(2) The coastal State is required to give appropriate publicity to any dangers to navigation, of which it has knowledge, within its territorial sea.

Article 16. (1) The coastal State may take the necessary steps in its territorial sea to prevent passage which is not innocent.

(2) In the case of ships proceeding to internal waters, the coastal State shall also have the right to take the necessary steps to prevent any breach of the conditions to which admission of those ships to those waters is subject.

(3) Subject to the provisions of paragraph 4, the coastal State may, without discrimination amongst foreign ships, suspend temporarily in specified areas of its territorial sea the innocent passage of foreign ships if such suspension is essential for the protection of its security. Such suspension shall take effect only after having been duly published.

(4) There shall be no suspension of the innocent passage of foreign ships through straits which are used for international navigation between one part of the high seas and another part of the high seas or the territorial sea of a foreign State.

Article 17. Foreign ships exercising the right of innocent passage shall comply with the laws and regulations enacted by the coastal State in conformity with these articles and other rules of international law and, in particular, with such laws and regulations relating to transport and navigation.

Sub-section B. Rules Applicable to Merchant Ships

Article 18. (1) No charge may be levied upon foreign ships by reason only of their passage through the territorial sea.

(2) Charges may be levied upon a foreign ship passing through the territorial sea as payment only for specific services rendered to the ship. These charges shall be levied without discrimination.

Article 19. (1) The criminal jurisdiction of the coastal State should not be exercised on board a foreign ship passing through the territorial sea to arrest any person or to conduct any investigation in connexion with any crime committed on board the ship during its passage, save only in the following cases:

(a) If the consequences of the crime extend to the coastal State; or

(b) If the crime is of a kind to disturb the peace of the country or the good order of the territorial sea; or

(c) If the assistance of the local authorities has been requested by the captain of the ship or by the consul of the country whose flag the ship flies; or

(d) If it is necessary for the suppression of illicit traffic in narcotic drugs.

(2) The above provisions do not affect the right of the coastal State to take any steps authorized by its laws for the purpose of an arrest or investigation on board a foreign ship passing through the territorial sea after leaving internal waters.

(3) In the cases provided for in paragraphs 1 and 2 of this article, the coastal State shall, if the captain so requests, advise the consular authority of the flag State before taking any steps, and shall facilitate contact between such authority and the ship's crew. In cases of emergency this notification may be communicated while the measures are being taken.

(4) In considering whether or how an arrest should be made, the local authorities shall pay due regard to the interests of navigation.

(5) The coastal State may not take any steps on board a foreign ship passing through the territorial sea to arrest any person or to conduct any investigation in connexion with any crime committed before the ship entered the territorial sea, if the ship, proceeding from a foreign port, is only passing through the territorial sea without entering internal waters.

Article 20. (1) The coastal State should not stop or divert a foreign ship passing through the territorial sea for the purpose of exercising civil jurisdiction in relation to a person on board the ship.

(2) The coastal State may not levy execution against or arrest the ship for the purpose of any civil proceedings, save only in respect of obligations or liabilities assumed or incurred by the ship itself in the course or for the purpose of its voyage through the waters of the coastal State.

(3) The provisions of the previous paragraph are without prejudice to the right of the coastal State, in accordance with its laws, to levy execution against or to arrest, for the purpose of any civil proceedings, a foreign ship lying in the territorial sea, or passing through the territorial sea after leaving internal waters.

Sub-section C. Rules Applicable to Government Ships Other Than Warships

Article 21. The rules contained in sub-sections A and B shall also apply to government ships operated for commercial purposes.

Article 22. (1) The rules contained in sub-section A and in article 18 shall apply to government ships operated for non-commercial purposes.

(2) With such exceptions as are contained in the provisions referred to in the preceding paragraph, nothing in these articles affects the immunities which such ships enjoy under these articles or other rules of international law.

Sub-section D. Rule Applicable to Warships

Article 23. If any warship does not comply with the regulations of the coastal State concerning passage through the territorial sea and disregards any request for compliance which is made to it, the coastal State may require the warship to leave the territorial sea.

PART II. CONTIGUOUS ZONE

Article 24. (1) In a zone of the high seas contiguous to its territorial sea, the coastal State may exercise the control necessary to:

(a) Prevent infringement of its customs, fiscal, immigration or sanitary regulations within its territory or territorial sea;

(b) Punish infringement of the above regulations committed within its territory or territorial sea.

(2) The contiguous zone may not extend beyond twelve miles from the baseline from which the breadth of the territorial sea is measured.

(3) Where the coasts of two States are opposite or adjacent to each other, neither of the two States is entitled, failing agreement between them to the contrary, to extend its contiguous zone beyond the median line every point of which is equidistant from the nearest points on the baselines from which the breadth of the territorial seas of the two States is measured.

* * *

5.7 CONVENTION ON FISHING AND CONSERVATION OF LIVING RESOURCES OF HIGH SEAS.[a] Done at Geneva, Apr. 29, 1958. Entered into force, Mar. 20, 1966; for the United States, Mar. 20, 1966. 17 U.S.T. 138, T.I.A.S. No. 5969, 559 U.N.T.S. 285

Article 1. (1) All States have the right for their nationals to engage in fishing on the high seas, subject (a) to their treaty obligations, (b) to the interests and rights of coastal States as provided for in this Convention, and (c) to the provisions contained in the following articles concerning conservation of the living resources of the high seas.

(2) All States have the duty to adopt, or to co-operate with other States in adopting, such measures for their respective nationals as may be necessary for the conservation of the living resources of the high seas.

Article 2. As employed in this Convention, the expression "conservation of the living resources of the high seas" means the aggregate of the measures rendering possible the optimum sustainable yield from those resources so as to secure a maximum supply of food and other marine products. Conservation programmes should be formulated with a view to securing in the first place a supply of food for human consumption.

Article 3. A State whose nationals are engaged in fishing any stock or stocks of fish or other living marine resources in any area of the high seas where the nationals of other States are not thus engaged shall adopt, for its own nationals, measures in that area when necessary for the purpose of the conservation of the living resources affected.

Article 4. (1) If the nationals of two or more States are engaged in fishing the same stock or stocks of fish or other living marine resources in any area or areas of the high seas, these States shall, at the request of any of them, enter into negotiations with a view to prescribing by agreement for their nationals the necessary measures for the conservation of the living resources affected.

(2) If the States concerned do not reach agreement within twelve months, any of the parties may initiate the procedure contemplated by article 9.

* * *

Article 6. (1) A coastal State has a special interest in the maintenance of the productivity of the living resources in any area of the high seas adjacent to its territorial sea.

(2) A coastal State is entitled to take part on an equal footing in any system of research and regulation for purposes of conservation of the living resources of the high seas in that area, even though its nationals do not carry on fishing there.

(3) A State whose nationals are engaged in fishing in any area of the high seas adjacent to the territorial sea of a coastal State shall, at the request of that coastal State, enter into negotiations with a view to prescribing by agreement the measures necessary for the conservation of the living resources of the high seas in that area.

(4) A State whose nationals are engaged in fishing in any area of the high seas adjacent to the territorial sea of a coastal State shall not enforce conservation measures in that area which are opposed to those which have been adopted by the coastal State, but may enter into negotiations with the coastal State with a view to prescribing by agreement the measures necessary for the conservation of the living resources of the high seas in that area.

a. *See also* Basic Documents 5.4, 5.5 and 5.6, *supra*, and 5.27, *infra*.

(5) If the States concerned do not reach agreement with respect to conservation measures within twelve months, any of the parties may initiate the procedure contemplated by article 9.

Article 7. (1) Having regard to the provisions of paragraph 1 of article 6, any coastal State may, with a view to the maintenance of the productivity of the living resources of the sea, adopt unilateral measures of conservation appropriate to any stock of fish or other marine resources in any area of the high seas adjacent to its territorial sea, provided that negotiations to that effect with the other States concerned have not led to an agreement within six months.

(2) The measures which the coastal State adopts under the previous paragraph shall be valid as to other States only if the following requirements are fulfilled:

(a) That there is a need for urgent application of conservation measures in the light of the existing knowledge of the fishery;

(b) That the measures adopted are based on appropriate scientific findings;

(c) That such measures do not discriminate in form or in fact against foreign fishermen.

(3) These measures shall remain in force pending the settlement, in accordance with the relevant provisions of this Convention, of any disagreement as to their validity.

(4) If the measures are not accepted by the other States concerned, any of the parties may initiate the procedure contemplated by article 9. Subject to paragraph 2 of article 10, the measure adopted shall remain obligatory pending the decision of the special commission.

(5) The principles of geographical demarcation as defined in article 12 of the Convention on the Territorial Sea and the Contiguous Zone shall be adopted when coasts of different States are involved.

Article 8. (1) Any State which, even if its nationals are not engaged in fishing in an area of the high seas not adjacent to its coast, has a special interest in the conservation of the living resources of the high seas in that area, may request the State or States whose nationals are engaged in fishing there to take the necessary measures of conservation under articles 3 and 4 respectively, at the same time mentioning the scientific reasons which in its opinion make such measures necessary, and indicating its special interest.

(2) If no agreement is reached within twelve months, such State may initiate the procedure contemplated by article 9.

Article 9. (1) Any dispute which may arise between States under articles 4, 5, 6, 7 and 8 shall, at the request of any of the parties, be submitted for settlement to a special commission of five members, unless the parties agree to seek a solution by another method of peaceful settlement, as provided for in Article 33 of the Charter of the United Nations.

* * *

(7) Decisions of the commission shall be by majority vote.

* * *

Article 11. The decisions of the special commission shall be binding on the States concerned and the provisions of paragraph 2 of Article 94 of the Charter of the United Nations shall be applicable to those decisions. If the decisions are accompanied by any recommendations, they shall receive the greatest possible consideration.

Article 12. (1) If the factual basis of the award of the special commission is altered by substantial changes in the conditions of the stock or stocks of fish or other living marine resources or in methods of fishing, any of the States concerned may request the other States to enter into negotiations with a view to prescribing by agreement the necessary modifications in the measures of conservation.

* * *

Article 14. In articles 1, 3, 4, 5, 6 and 8, the term "nationals" means fishing boats or craft of any size having the nationality of the State concerned, according to the law of that State, irrespective of the nationality of the members of their crews.

* * *

5.8 THE ANTARCTIC TREATY. Done at Washington, Dec. 1, 1959. Entered into force, June 23, 1961; for the United States, June 23, 1961. 12 U.S.T. 794, T.I.A.S. No. 4780, 402 U.N.T.S. 71

The Governments of Argentina, Australia, Belgium, Chile, the French Republic, Japan, New Zealand, Norway, the Union of South Africa, the Union of Soviet Socialist Republics, the United Kingdom of Great Britain and Northern Ireland, and the United States of America,

Recognizing that it is in the best interest of all mankind that Antarctica shall continue forever to be used exclusively for peaceful purposes and shall not become the scene or object of international discord;

Acknowledging the substantial contributions to scientific knowledge resulting from international cooperation in scientific investigation in Antarctica;

Convinced that the establishment of a firm foundation for the continuation and development of such cooperation on the basis of freedom of scientific investigation in Antarctica as applied during the International Geophysical Year accords with the interests of science and progress of all mankind;

Convinced also that a treaty ensuring the use of Antarctica for peaceful purposes only and the continuance of international harmony in Antarctica will further the purposes and principles embodied in the Charter of the United Nations;

Have agreed as follows:

Article I. (1) Antarctica shall be used for peaceful purposes only. There shall be prohibited, *inter alia,* any measures of a military nature, such as the establishment of military bases and fortifications, the carrying out of military maneuvers, as well as the testing of any type of weapons.

(2) The present Treaty shall not prevent the use of military personnel or equipment for scientific research or for any other peaceful purpose.

Article II. Freedom of scientific investigation in Antarctica and cooperation toward that end, as applied during the International Geophysical Year, shall continue, subject to the provisions of the present Treaty.

Article III. (1) In order to promote international cooperation in scientific investigation in Antarctica, as provided for in Article II of the present Treaty, the Contracting Parties agree that, to the greatest extent feasible and practicable:

(a) information regarding plans for scientific programs in Antarctica shall be exchanged to permit maximum economy and efficiency of operations;

(b) scientific personnel shall be exchanged in Antarctica between expeditions and stations;

(c) scientific observations and results from Antarctica shall be exchanged and made freely available.

(2) In implementing this Article, every encouragement shall be given to the establishment of cooperative working relations with those Specialized Agencies of the United Nations and other international organizations having a scientific or technical interest in Antarctica.

Article IV. (1) Nothing contained in the present Treaty shall be interpreted as:

(a) a renunciation by any Contracting Party of previously asserted rights of or claims to territorial sovereignty in Antarctica;

(b) a renunciation or diminution by any Contracting Party of any basis of claim to territorial sovereignty in Antarctica which it may have whether as a result of its activities or those of its nationals in Antarctica, or otherwise;

(c) prejudicing the position of any Contracting Party as regards its recognition or nonrecognition of any other State's right of or claim or basis of claim to territorial sovereignty in Antarctica.

(2) No acts or activities taking place while the present Treaty is in force shall constitute a basis for asserting, supporting or denying a claim to territorial sovereignty in Antarctica or create any rights of sovereignty in Antarctica. No new claim, or enlargement of an existing claim, to territorial sovereignty in Antarctica shall be asserted while the present Treaty is in force.

Article V. (1) Any nuclear explosions in Antarctica and the disposal there of radioactive waste material shall be prohibited.

(2) In the event of the conclusion of international agreements concerning the use of nuclear energy, including nuclear explosions and the disposal of radioactive waste material, to which all of the Contracting Parties whose representatives are entitled to participate in the meetings provided for under Article IX are parties, the rules established under such agreements shall apply in Antarctica.

Article VI. The provisions of the present Treaty shall apply to the area south of 60° South Latitude, including all ice shelves, but nothing in the present Treaty shall prejudice or in any way affect the rights, or the exercise of the rights, of any State under international law with regard to the high seas within that area.

Article VII. (1) In order to promote the objectives and ensure the observance of the provisions of the present Treaty, each Contracting Party whose representatives are entitled to participate in the meetings referred to in Article IX of the Treaty shall have the right to designate observers to carry out any inspection provided for by the present Article. Observers shall be nationals of the Contracting Parties which designate them. The names of observers shall be communicated to every other Contracting Party having the right to designate observers, and like notice shall be given of the termination of their appointment.

(2) Each observer designated in accordance with the provisions of paragraph 1 of this Article shall have complete freedom of access at any time to any or all areas of Antarctica.

(3) All areas of Antarctica, including all stations, installations and equipment within those areas, and all ships and aircraft at points of discharging or embarking cargoes or personnel in Antarctica, shall be open at all times to inspection by any observers designated in accordance with paragraph 1 of this Article.

(4) Aerial observation may be carried out at any time over any or all areas of Antarctica by any of the Contracting Parties having the right to designate observers.

(5) Each Contracting Party shall, at the time when the present Treaty enters into force for it, inform the other Contracting Parties, and thereafter shall give them notice in advance, of

(a) all expeditions to and within Antarctica, on the part of its ships or nationals, and all expeditions to Antarctica organized in or proceeding from its territory;

(b) all stations in Antarctica occupied by its nationals; and

(c) any military personnel or equipment intended to be introduced by it into Antarctica subject to the conditions prescribed in paragraph 2 of Article I of the present Treaty.

* * *

Article IX. (1) Representatives of the Contracting Parties named in the preamble to the present Treaty shall meet at the City of Canberra within two months after the date of entry into force of the Treaty, and thereafter at suitable intervals and places, for the purpose of exchanging information, consulting together on matters of common interest pertaining to Antarctica, and formulating and considering, and recommending to their Governments, measures in furtherance of the principles and objectives of the Treaty, including measures regarding:

(a) use of Antarctica for peaceful purposes only;

(b) facilitation of scientific research in Antarctica;

(c) facilitation of international scientific cooperation in Antarctica;

(d) facilitation of the exercise of the rights of inspection provided for in Article VII of the Treaty;

(e) questions relating to the exercise of jurisdiction in Antarctica;

(f) preservation and conservation of living resources in Antarctica.

* * *

Article X. Each of the Contracting Parties undertakes to exert appropriate efforts, consistent with the Charter of the United Nations, to the end that no one engages in any activity in Antarctica contrary to the principles or purposes of the present Treaty.

* * *

Article XII. (1)(a) The present Treaty may be modified or amended at any time by unanimous agreement of the Contracting Parties whose representatives are entitled to participate in the meetings provided for under Article IX. Any such modification or amendment shall enter into force when the depositary Government has received notice from all such Contracting Parties that they have ratified it.

* * *

5.9 CONVENTION ON CIVIL LIABILITY FOR NUCLEAR DAMAGE.[a] Done at Vienna, May 21, 1963. Entered into force Nov. 12, 1977. 1963 U.N. Jurid. Y.B. 148, *reprinted in* 2 I.L.M. 727 (1963)

Article I

1. For the purposes of this Convention—

(*a*) "Person" means any individual, partnership, any private or public body whether corporate or not, any international organization enjoying legal personality under the law of the Installation State, and any State or any of its constituent sub-divisions.

(*b*) "National of a Contracting Party" includes a Contracting Party or any of its constituent sub-divisions, a partnership, or any private or public body whether corporate or not established within the territory of a Contracting Party.

(*c*) "Operator", in relation to a nuclear installation, means the person designated or recognized by the Installation State as the operator of that installation.

(*d*) "Installation State", in relation to a nuclear installation, means the Contracting Party within whose territory that installation is situated or, if it is not situated within the territory of any State, the Contracting Party by which or under the authority of which the nuclear installation is operated.

(*e*) "Law of the competent court" means the law of the court having jurisdiction under this Convention, including any rules of such law relating to conflict of laws.

(*f*) "Nuclear fuel" means any material which is capable of producing energy by a self-sustaining chain process of nuclear fission.

(*g*) "Radioactive products or waste" means any radioactive material produced in, or any material made radioactive by exposure to the radiation incidental to, the production or utilization of nuclear fuel, but does not include radioisotopes which have reached the final stage of fabrication so as to be usable for any scientific, medical, agricultural, commercial or industrial purpose.

(*h*) "Nuclear material" means—

(i) nuclear fuel, other than natural uranium and depleted uranium, capable of producing energy by a self-sustaining chain process of nuclear fission outside a nuclear reactor, either alone or in combination with some other material; and

(ii) radioactive products or waste.

(*i*) "Nuclear reactor" means any structure containing nuclear fuel in such an arrangement that a self-sustaining chain process of nuclear fission can occur therein without an additional source of neutrons.

(*j*) "Nuclear installation" means—

(i) any nuclear reactor other than one with which a means of sea or air transport is equipped for use as a source of power, whether for propulsion thereof or for any other purpose;

(ii) any factory using nuclear fuel for the production of nuclear material, or any factory for the processing of nuclear material, including any factory for the re-processing of irradiated nuclear fuel; and

(iii) any facility where nuclear material is stored, other than storage incidental to the carriage of such material;

a. The Optional Protocol is omitted.

provided that the Installation State may determine that several nuclear installations of one operator which are located at the same site shall be considered as a single nuclear installation.

(*k*) "Nuclear damage" means—

(i) loss of life, any personal injury or any loss of, or damage to, property which arises out of or results from the radioactive properties or a combination of radioactive properties with toxic, explosive or other hazardous properties of nuclear fuel or radioactive products or waste in, or of nuclear material coming from, originating in, or sent to, a nuclear installation;

(ii) any other loss or damage so arising or resulting if and to the extent that the law of the competent court so provides; and

(iii) if the law of the Installation State so provides, loss of life, any personal injury or any loss of, or damage to, property which arises out of or results from other ionizing radiation emitted by any other source of radiation inside a nuclear installation.

(*l*) "Nuclear incident" means any occurrence or series of occurrences having the same origin which causes nuclear damage.

2. An Installation State may, if the small extent of the risks involved so warrants, exclude any small quantities of nuclear material from the application of this Convention, provided that—

(*a*) maximum limits for the exclusion of such quantities have been established by the Board of Governors of the International Atomic Energy Agency; and

(*b*) any exclusion by an Installation State is within such established limits.

The maximum limits shall be reviewed periodically by the Board of Governors.

Article II

1. The operator of a nuclear installation shall be liable for nuclear damage upon proof that such damage has been caused by a nuclear incident—

(*a*) in his nuclear installation; or

(*b*) involving nuclear material coming from or originating in his nuclear installation, and occurring—

(i) before liability with regard to nuclear incidents involving the nuclear material has been assumed, pursuant to the express terms of a contract in writing, by the operator of another nuclear installation;

(ii) in the absence of such express terms, before the operator of another nuclear installation has taken charge of the nuclear material; or

(iii) where the nuclear material is intended to be used in a nuclear reactor with which a means of transport is equipped for use as a source of power, whether for propulsion thereof or for any other purpose, before the person duly authorized to operate such reactor has taken charge of the nuclear material; but

(iv) where the nuclear material has been sent to a person within the territory of a non-Contracting State, before it has been unloaded from the means of transport by which it has arrived in the territory of that non-Contracting State;

(*c*) involving nuclear material sent to his nuclear installation, and occurring—

(i) after liability with regard to nuclear incidents involving the nuclear material has been assumed by him, pursuant to the express terms of a contract in writing, from the operator of another nuclear installation;

(ii) in the absence of such express terms, after he has taken charge of the nuclear material; or

(iii) after he has taken charge of the nuclear material from a person operating a nuclear reactor with which a means of transport is equipped for use as a source of power, whether for propulsion thereof or for any other purpose; but

(iv) where the nuclear material has, with the written consent of the operator, been sent from a person within the territory of a non-Contracting State, only after it has been loaded on the means of transport by which it is to be carried from the territory of that State;

provided that, if nuclear damage is caused by a nuclear incident occurring in a nuclear installation and involving nuclear material stored therein incidentally to the carriage of such material, the provisions of sub-paragraph (*a*) of this paragraph shall not apply where another operator or person is solely liable pursuant to the provisions of sub-paragraph (*b*) or (*c*) of this paragraph.

2. The Installation State may provide by legislation that, in accordance with such terms as may be specified therein, a carrier of nuclear material or a person handling radioactive waste may, at his request and with the consent of the operator concerned, be designated or recognized as operator in the place of that operator in respect of such nuclear material or radioactive waste respectively. In this case such carrier or such person shall be considered, for all the purposes of this Convention, as an operator of a nuclear installation situated within the territory of that State.

3. (*a*) Where nuclear damage engages the liability of more than one operator, the operators involved shall, in so far as the damage attributable to each operator is not reasonably separable, be jointly and severally liable.

(*b*) Where a nuclear incident occurs in the course of carriage of nuclear material, either in one and the same means of transport, or, in the case of storage incidental to the carriage, in one and the same nuclear installation, and causes nuclear damage which engages the liability of more than one operator, the total liability shall not exceed the highest amount applicable with respect to any one of them pursuant to Article V.

(*c*) In neither of the cases referred to in sub-paragraphs (*a*) and (*b*) of this paragraph shall the liability of any one operator exceed the amount applicable with respect to him pursuant to Article V.

4. Subject to the provisions of paragraph 3 of this Article, where several nuclear installations of one and the same operator are involved in one nuclear incident, such operator shall be liable in respect of each nuclear installation involved up to the amount applicable with respect to him pursuant to Article V.

5. Except as otherwise provided in this Convention, no person other than the operator shall be liable for nuclear damage. This, however, shall not affect the application of any international convention in the field of transport in force or open for signature, ratification or accession at the date on which this Convention is opened for signature.

6. No person shall be liable for any loss or damage which is not nuclear damage pursuant to sub-paragraph (*k*) of paragraph 1 of Article I but which could have been included as such pursuant to sub-paragraph (*k*)(ii) of that paragraph.

7. Direct action shall lie against the person furnishing financial security pursuant to Article VII, if the law of the competent court so provides.

Article III

The operator liable in accordance with this Convention shall provide the carrier with a certificate issued by or on behalf of the insurer or other financial guarantor furnishing the financial security required pursuant to Article VII. The certificate shall state the name and address of that operator and the amount, type and duration of the security, and these statements may not be disputed by the person by whom or on whose behalf the certificate was issued. The certificate shall also indicate the nuclear material in respect of which the security applies and shall include a statement by the competent public authority of the Installation State that the person named is an operator within the meaning of this Convention.

Article IV

1. The liability of the operator for nuclear damage under this Convention shall be absolute.

2. If the operator proves that the nuclear damage resulted wholly or partly either from the gross negligence of the person suffering the damage or from an act or omission of such person done with intent to cause damage, the competent court may, if its law so provides, relieve the operator wholly or partly from his obligation to pay compensation in respect of the damage suffered by such person.

3. (*a*) No liability under this Convention shall attach to an operator for nuclear damage caused by a nuclear incident directly due to an act of armed conflict, hostilities, civil war or insurrection.

(*b*) Except in so far as the law of the Installation State may provide to the contrary, the operator shall not be liable for nuclear damage caused by a nuclear incident directly due to a grave natural disaster of an exceptional character.

4. Whenever both nuclear damage and damage other than nuclear damage have been caused by a nuclear incident or jointly by a nuclear incident and one or more other occurrences, such other damage shall, to the extent that it is not reasonably separable from the nuclear damage, be deemed, for the purposes of this Convention, to be nuclear damage caused by that nuclear incident. Where, however, damage is caused jointly by a nuclear incident covered by this Convention and by an emission of ionizing radiation not covered by it, nothing in this Convention shall limit or otherwise affect the liability, either as regards any person suffering nuclear damage or by way of recourse or contribution, of any person who may be held liable in connexion with that emission of ionizing radiation.

5. The operator shall not be liable under this Convention for nuclear damage—

(*a*) to the nuclear installation itself or to any property on the site of that installation which is used or to be used in connexion with that installation; or

(*b*) to the means of transport upon which the nuclear material involved was at the time of the nuclear incident.

6. Any Installation State may provide by legislation that sub-paragraph (*b*) of paragraph 5 of this Article shall not apply, provided that in no case shall the liability of the operator in respect of nuclear damage, other than nuclear damage to the means of transport, be reduced to less than US $5 million for any one nuclear incident.

7. Nothing in this Convention shall affect—

(*a*) the liability of any individual for nuclear damage for which the operator, by virtue of paragraph 3 or 5 of this Article, is not liable under this Convention and which that individual caused by an act or omission done with intent to cause damage; or

(*b*) the liability outside this Convention of the operator for nuclear damage for which, by virtue of sub-paragraph (*b*) of paragraph 5 of this Article, he is not liable under this Convention.

Article V

1. The liability of the operator may be limited by the Installation State to not less than US $5 million for any one nuclear incident.

2. Any limits of liability which may be established pursuant to this Article shall not include any interest or costs awarded by a court in actions for compensation of nuclear damage.

3. The United States dollar referred to in this Convention is a unit of account equivalent to the value of the United States dollar in terms of gold on 29 April 1963, that is to say US $35 per one troy ounce of fine gold.

4. The sum mentioned in paragraph 6 of Article IV and in paragraph 1 of this Article may be converted into national currency in round figures.

Article VI

1. Rights of compensation under this Convention shall be extinguished if an action is not brought within ten years from the date of the nuclear incident. If, however, under the law of the Installation State the liability of the operator is covered by insurance or other financial security or by State funds for a period longer than ten years, the law of the competent court may provide that rights of compensation against the operator shall only be extinguished after a period which may be longer than ten years, but shall not be longer than the period for which his liability is so covered under the law of the Installation State. Such extension of the extinction period shall in no case affect rights of compensation under this Convention of any person who has brought an action for loss of life or personal injury against the operator before the expiry of the aforesaid period of ten years.

2. Where nuclear damage is caused by a nuclear incident involving nuclear material which at the time of the nuclear incident was stolen, lost, jettisoned or abandoned, the period established pursuant to paragraph 1 of this Article shall be computed from the date of that nuclear incident, but the period shall in no case exceed a period of twenty years from the date of the theft, loss, jettison or abandonment.

3. The law of the competent court may establish a period of extinction or prescription of not less than three years from the date on which the person suffering nuclear damage had knowledge or should have had knowledge of the damage and of the operator liable for the damage, provided that the period established pursuant to paragraphs 1 and 2 of this Article shall not be exceeded.

4. Unless the law of the competent court otherwise provides, any person who claims to have suffered nuclear damage and who has brought an action for compensation within the period applicable pursuant to this Article may amend his claim to take into account any aggravation of the damage, even after the expiry of that period, provided that final judgment has not been entered.

5. Where jurisdiction is to be determined pursuant to sub-paragraph (*b*) of paragraph 3 of Article XI and a request has been made within the period applicable pursuant to this Article to any one of the Contracting Parties empowered so to determine, but the time remaining after such determination is less than six months, the period within which an action may be brought shall be six months, reckoned from the date of such determination.

Article VII

1. The operator shall be required to maintain insurance or other financial security covering his liability for nuclear damage in such amount, of such type and in such terms as the Installation State shall specify. The Installation State shall ensure the payment of claims for compensation for nuclear damage which have been established against the operator by providing the necessary funds to the extent that the yield of insurance or other financial security is inadequate to satisfy such claims, but not in excess of the limit, if any, established pursuant to Article V.

2. Nothing in paragraph 1 of this Article shall require a Contracting Party or any of its constituent sub-divisions, such as States or Republics, to maintain insurance or other financial security to cover their liability as operators.

3. The funds provided by insurance, by other financial security or by the Installation State pursuant to paragraph 1 of this Article shall be exclusively available for compensation due under this Convention.

4. No insurer or other financial guarantor shall suspend or cancel the insurance or other financial security provided pursuant to paragraph 1 of this Article without giving notice in writing of at least two months to the competent public authority or, in so far as such insurance or other financial security relates to the carriage of nuclear material, during the period of the carriage in question.

Article VIII

Subject to the provisions of this Convention, the nature, form and extent of the compensation, as well as the equitable distribution thereof, shall be governed by the law of the competent court.

Article IX

1. Where provisions of national or public health insurance, social insurance, social security, workmen's compensation or occupational disease compensation systems include compensation for nuclear damage, rights of beneficiaries of such systems to obtain compensation under this Convention and rights of recourse by virtue of such systems against the operator liable shall be determined, subject to the provisions of this Convention, by the law of the Contracting Party in which such systems have been established, or by the regulations of the inter-governmental organization which has established such systems.

2. *(a)* If a person who is a national of a Contracting Party, other than the operator, has paid compensation for nuclear damage under an international convention or under the law of a non-Contracting State, such person shall, up to the amount which he has paid, acquire by subrogation the rights under this Convention of the person so compensated. No rights shall be so acquired by any person to the extent that the operator has a right of recourse against such person under this Convention.

(b) Nothing in this Convention shall preclude an operator who has paid compensation for nuclear damage out of funds other than those provided pursuant to paragraph 1 of Article VII from recovering from the person providing financial security pursuant to that paragraph or from the Installation State, up to the amount he has paid, the sum which the person so compensated would have obtained under this Convention.

Article X

The operator shall have a right of recourse only—

(a) if this is expressly provided for by a contract in writing; or

(b) if the nuclear incident results from an act or omission done with intent to cause damage, against the individual who has acted or omitted to act with such intent.

Article XI

1. Except as otherwise provided in this Article, jurisdiction over actions under Article II shall lie only with the courts of the Contracting Party within whose territory the nuclear incident occurred.

2. Where the nuclear incident occurred outside the territory of any Contracting Party, or where the place of the nuclear incident cannot be determined with

certainty, jurisdiction over such actions shall lie with the courts of the Installation State of the operator liable.

3. Where under paragraph 1 or 2 of this Article, jurisdiction would lie with the courts of more than one Contracting Party, jurisdiction shall lie—

(*a*) if the nuclear incident occurred partly outside the territory of any Contracting Party, and partly within the territory of a single Contracting Party, with the courts of the latter; and

(*b*) in any other case, with the courts of that Contracting Party which is determined by agreement between the Contracting Parties whose courts would be competent under paragraph 1 or 2 of this Article.

Article XII

1. A final judgment entered by a court having jurisdiction under Article XI shall be recognized within the territory of any other Contracting Party, except—

(*a*) where the judgment was obtained by fraud;

(*b*) where the party against whom the judgment was pronounced was not given a fair opportunity to present his case; or

(*c*) where the judgment is contrary to the public policy of the Contracting Party within the territory of which recognition is sought, or is not in accord with fundamental standards of justice.

2. A final judgment which is recognized shall, upon being presented for enforcement in accordance with the formalities required by the law of the Contracting Party where enforcement is sought, be enforceable as if it were a judgment of a court of that Contracting Party.

3. The merits of a claim on which the judgment has been given shall not be subject to further proceedings.

Article XIII

This Convention and the national law applicable thereunder shall be applied without any discrimination based upon nationality, domicile or residence.

Article XIV

Except in respect of measures of execution, jurisdictional immunities under rules of national or international law shall not be invoked in actions under this Convention before the courts competent pursuant to Article XI.

Article XV

The Contracting Parties shall take appropriate measures to ensure that compensation for nuclear damage, interest and costs awarded by a court in connexion therewith, insurance and reinsurance premiums and funds provided by insurance, reinsurance or other financial security, or funds provided by the Installation State, pursuant to this Convention, shall be freely transferable into the currency of the Contracting Party within whose territory the damage is suffered, and of the Contracting Party within whose territory the claimant is habitually resident, and, as regards insurance or reinsurance premiums and payments, into the currencies specified in the insurance or reinsurance contract.

Article XVI

No person shall be entitled to recover compensation under this Convention to the extent that he has recovered compensation in respect of the same nuclear damage under another international convention on civil liability in the field of nuclear energy.

Article XVII

This Convention shall not, as between the parties to them, affect the application of any international agreements or international conventions on civil liability in the field of nuclear energy in force, or open for signature, ratification or accession at the date on which this Convention is opened for signature.

Article XVIII

This Convention shall not be construed as affecting the rights, if any, of a Contracting Party under the general rules of public international law in respect of nuclear damage.

Article XIX

1. Any Contracting Party entering into an agreement pursuant to sub-paragraph (*b*) of paragraph 3 of Article XI shall furnish without delay to the Director–General of the International Atomic Energy Agency for information and dissemination to the other Contracting Parties a copy of such agreement.

2. The Contracting Parties shall furnish to the Director–General for information and dissemination to the other Contracting Parties copies of their respective laws and regulations relating to matters covered by this Convention.

Article XX

Notwithstanding the termination of the application of this Convention to any Contracting Party, either by termination pursuant to Article XXV or by denunciation pursuant to Article XXVI, the provisions of this Convention shall continue to apply to any nuclear damage caused by a nuclear incident occurring before such termination.

* * *

Article XXV

1. This Convention shall remain in force for a period of ten years from the date of its entry into force. Any Contracting Party may, by giving before the end of that period at least twelve months' notice to that effect to the Director–General of the International Atomic Energy Agency, terminate the application of this Convention to itself at the end of that period of ten years.

2. This Convention shall, after that period of ten years, remain in force for a further period of five years for such Contracting Parties as have not terminated its application pursuant to paragraph 1 of this Article, and thereafter for successive periods of five years each for those Contracting Parties which have not terminated its application at the end of one of such periods, by giving, before the end of one of such periods, at least twelve months' notice to that effect to the Director–General of the International Atomic Energy Agency.

Article XXVI

1. A conference shall be convened by the Director–General of the International Atomic Energy Agency at any time after the expiry of a period of five years from the date of the entry into force of this Convention in order to consider the revision thereof, if one-third of the Contracting Parties express a desire to that effect.

2. Any Contracting Party may denounce this Convention by notification to the Director–General of the International Atomic Energy Agency within a period of twelve months following the first revision conference held pursuant to paragraph 1 of this Article.

3. Denunciation shall take effect one year after the date on which notification to that effect has been received by the Director–General of the International Atomic Energy Agency.

* * *

5.10 RESOLUTION REGARDING WEAPONS OF MASS DESTRUCTION IN OUTER SPACE. Adopted by the U.N. General Assembly, Oct. 17, 1963. U.N.G.A. Res. 1884 (XVIII), 18 U.N. GAOR, Supp. (No. 15) 13, U.N. Doc. A/5571 Annex II (1963), *reprinted in* 2 I.L.M. 1192 (1963)

The General Assembly,

Recalling its resolution 1721A(XVI) of 20 December 1961, in which it expressed the belief that the exploration and use of outer space should be only for the betterment of mankind,

Determined to take steps to prevent the spread of the arms race to outer space,

1. *Welcomes* the expressions by the Union of Soviet Socialist Republics and the United States of America of their intention not to station in outer space any objects carrying nuclear weapons or other kinds of weapons of mass destruction;

2. *Solemnly calls upon* all States:

(*a*) To refrain from placing in orbit around the earth any objects carrying nuclear weapons or any other kinds of weapons of mass destruction, installing such weapons on celestial bodies, or stationing such weapons in outer space in any other manner;

(*b*) To refrain from causing, encouraging or in any way participating in the conduct of the foregoing activities.

5.11 HELSINKI RULES ON THE USES OF THE WATERS OF INTERNATIONAL RIVERS.[a] International Law Association, Report of the Fifty-Second Conference, Helsinki, 1966, at 484 (1966)

CHAPTER 1. GENERAL

Article I. The general rules of international law as set forth in these chapters are applicable to the use of the waters of an international drainage basin except as may be provided otherwise by convention, agreement or binding custom among the basin States.

Article II. An international drainage basin is a geographical area extending over two or more States determined by the watershed limits of the system of waters, including surface and underground waters, flowing into a common terminus.

Article III. A "basin State" is a state the territory of which includes a portion of an international drainage basin.

CHAPTER 2. EQUITABLE UTILIZATION OF THE WATERS OF AN INTERNATIONAL DRAINAGE BASIN

Article IV. Each basin State is entitled, within its territory, to a reasonable and equitable share in the beneficial uses of the waters of an international drainage basin.

Article V. (1) What is a reasonable and equitable share within the meaning of Article IV is to be determined in the light of all the relevant factors in each particular case.

(2) Relevant factors which are to be considered include, but are not limited to:

(a) the geography of the basin, including in particular the extent of the drainage area in the territory of each basin State;

(b) the hydrology of the basin, including in particular the contribution of water by each basin State;

(c) the climate affecting the basin;

(d) the past utilization of the waters of the basin, including in particular existing utilization;

(e) the economic and social needs of each basin State;

(f) the population dependent on the waters of the basin in each basin State;

(g) the comparative costs of alternative means of satisfying the economic and social needs of each basin State;

(h) the availability of other resources;

(i) the avoidance of unnecessary waste in the utilization of waters of the basin;

(j) the practicability of compensation to one or more of the co-basin States as a means of adjusting conflicts among uses; and

(k) the degree to which the needs of a basin State may be satisfied, without causing substantial injury to a co-basin State.

(3) The weight to be given to each factor is to be determined by its importance in comparison with that of other relevant factors. In determining what is a reasonable

a. The Comments accompanying the Rules (also known as the "Helsinki Rules") are omitted.

and equitable share, all relevant factors are to be considered together and a conclusion reached on the basis of the whole.

Article VI. A use or category of uses is not entitled to any inherent preference over any other use or category of uses.

Article VII. A basin State may not be denied the present reasonable use of the waters of an international drainage basin to reserve for a co-basin State a future use of such waters.

Article VIII. (1) An existing reasonable use may continue in operation unless the factors justifying its continuance are outweighed by other factors leading to the conclusion that it be modified or terminated so as to accommodate a competing incompatible use.

(2)(a) A use that is in fact operational is deemed to have been an existing use from the time of the initiation of construction directly related to the use or, where such construction is not required, the undertaking of comparable acts of actual implementation.

(b) Such a use continues to be an existing use until such time as it is discontinued with the intention that it be abandoned.

(3) A use will not be deemed an existing use if at the time of becoming operational it is incompatible with an already existing reasonable use.

CHAPTER 3. POLLUTION

Article IX. As used in this Chapter, the term "water pollution" refers to any detrimental change resulting from human conduct in the natural composition, content, or quality of the waters of an international drainage basin.

Article X. (1) Consistent with the principle of equitable utilization of the waters of an international drainage basin, a State

(a) must prevent any new form of water pollution or any increase in the degree of existing water pollution in an international drainage basin which would cause substantial injury in the territory of a co-basin State, and

(b) should take all reasonable measures to abate existing water pollution in an international drainage basin to such an extent that no substantial damage is caused in the territory of a co-basin State.

(2) The rule stated in paragraph 1 of this Article applies to water pollution originating:

(a) within a territory of the State, or

(b) outside the territory of the State, if it is caused by the State's conduct.

Article XI. (1) In the case of a violation of the rule stated in paragraph 1(a) of Article X of this Chapter, the State responsible shall be required to cease the wrongful conduct and compensate the injured co-basin State for the injury that has been caused to it.

(2) In a case falling under the rule stated in paragraph 1(b) of Article X, if a State fails to take reasonable measures, it shall be required promptly to enter into negotiations with the injured State with a view toward reaching a settlement equitable under the circumstances.

CHAPTER 4. NAVIGATION

Article XII. (1) This Chapter refers to those rivers and lakes, portions of which are both navigable and separate or traverse the territories of two or more States.

(2) Rivers or lakes are "navigable" if in their natural or canalized state they are currently used for commercial navigation or are capable by reason of their natural condition of being so used.

(3) In this Chapter the term "riparian State" refers to a State through or along which the navigable portion of a river flows or a lake lies.

Article XIII. Subject to any limitations or qualifications referred to in these Chapters, each riparian State is entitled to enjoy rights of free navigation on the entire course of a river or lake.

Article XIV. "Free navigation", as the term is used in this Chapter, includes the following freedom for vessels of a riparian State on a basis of equality:

(a) freedom of movement on the entire navigable course of the river or lake;

(b) freedom to enter ports and to make use of plants and docks; and

(c) freedom to transport goods and passengers, either directly or through trans-shipment, between the territory of one riparian State and the territory of another riparian State and between the territory of a riparian State and the open sea.

Article XV. A riparian State may exercise rights of police, including but not limited to the protection of public safety and health, over that portion of the river or lake subject to its jurisdiction, provided the exercise of such rights does not unreasonably interfere with the enjoyment of the rights of free navigation defined in Articles XIII and XIV.

Article XVI. Each riparian State may restrict or prohibit the loading by vessels of a foreign State of goods and passengers in its territory for discharge in such territory.

Article XVII. A riparian State may grant rights of navigation to non-riparian States on rivers or lakes within its territory.

Article XVIII. Each riparian State is, to the extent of the means available or made available to it, required to maintain in good order that portion of the navigable course of a river or lake within its jurisdiction.

Article XIX. The rules stated in this Chapter are not applicable to the navigation of vessels of war or of vessels performing police or administrative functions, or, in general, exercising any other form of public authority.

Article XX. In time of war, other armed conflict, or public emergency constituting a threat to the life of the State, a riparian State may take measures derogating from its obligations under this Chapter to the extent strictly required by the exigencies of the situation, provided that such measures are not inconsistent with its other obligations under international law. The riparian State shall in any case facilitate navigation for humanitarian purposes.

CHAPTER 5. TIMBER FLOATING

Article XXI. The floating of timber on a watercourse which flows through or between the territories of two or more States is governed by the following Articles except in cases in which floating is governed by rules of navigation according to applicable law or custom binding upon the riparians.

Article XXII. The States riparian to an international watercourse utilized for navigation may determine by common consent whether and under what conditions timber floating may be permitted upon the watercourse.

Article XXIII. (1) It is recommended that each State riparian to an international watercourse not used for navigation should, with due regard to other uses of the watercourse, authorise the co-riparian States to use the watercourse and its banks within the territory of each riparian State for the floating of timber.

(2) This authorization should extend to all necessary work along the banks by the floating crew and to the installation of such facilities as may be required for the timber floating.

Article XXIV. If a riparian State requires permanent installation for floating inside a territory of a co-riparian State or if it is necessary to regulate the flow of the watercourse, all questions connected with these installations and measures should be determined by agreement between the States concerned.

Article XXV. Co-riparian States of a watercourse which is, or is to be used for floating timber should negotiate in order to come to an agreement governing the administrative regime of floating, and if necessary to establish a joint agency or commission in order to facilitate the regulation of floating in all aspects.

CHAPTER 6. PROCEDURES FOR THE PREVENTION AND SETTLEMENT OF DISPUTES

Article XXVI. This Chapter relates to procedures for the prevention and settlement of international disputes as to the legal rights or other interests of basin States and of other States in the waters of an international drainage basin.

Article XXVII. (1) Consistently with the Charter of the United Nations, States are under an obligation to settle international disputes as to their legal rights or other interests by peaceful means in such a manner that international peace and security, and justice are not endangered.

(2) It is recommended that States resort progressively to the means of prevention and settlement of disputes stipulated in Articles XXIX to XXXIV of this Chapter.

Article XXVIII. (1) States are under a primary obligation to resort to means of prevention and settlement of disputes stipulated in the applicable treaties binding upon them.

(2) States are limited to the means of prevention and settlement of disputes stipulated in treaties binding upon them only to the extent provided by the applicable treaties.

Article XXIX. (1) With a view to preventing disputes from arising between basin States as to their legal rights or other interest, it is recommended that each basin State furnish relevant and reasonably available information to the other basin States concerning the waters of the drainage basin within its territory and its use of, and activities with respect to such waters.

(2) A State, regardless of its location in a drainage basin, should in particular furnish to any other basin State, the interests of which may be substantially affected, notice of any proposed construction or installation which would alter the regime of the basin in a way which might give rise to a dispute as defined in Article XXVI. The notice should include such essential facts as will permit the recipient to make an assessment of the probable effect of the proposed alteration.

(3) A State providing the notice referred to in paragraph 2 of this Article should afford to the recipient a reasonable period of time to make an assessment of the probable effect of the proposed construction or installation and to submit its views thereon to the State furnishing the notice.

(4) If a State has failed to give the notice referred to in paragraph 2 of this Article, the alteration by the State in the regime of the drainage basin shall not be given the weight normally accorded to temporal priority in use in the event of a determination of what is a reasonable and equitable share of the waters of the basin.

Article XXX. In case of a dispute between States as to their legal rights or other interests, as defined in Article XXVI, they should seek a solution by negotiation.

Article XXXI. (1) If a question of dispute arises which relates to the present or future utilization of the waters of an international drainage basin, it is recommended that the basin States refer the question or dispute to a joint agency and that they request the agency to survey the international drainage basin and to formulate plans or recommendations for the fullest and most efficient use thereof in the interests of all such States.

(2) It is recommended that the joint agency be instructed to submit reports on all matters within its competence to the appropriate authorities of the member States concerned.

(3) It is recommended that the member States of the joint agency in appropriate cases invite non-basin States which by treaty enjoy a right in the use of the waters as an international drainage basin to associate themselves with the work of the joint agency or that they be permitted to appear before the agency.

Article XXXII. If a question or a dispute is one which is considered by the States concerned to be incapable of resolution in the manner set forth in Article XXXI, it is recommended that they seek the good offices, or jointly request the mediation of a third State, of a qualified international organization or of a qualified person.

Article XXXIII. (1) If the States concerned have not been able to resolve their dispute through negotiation or have been unable to agree on the measures described in Article XXXI and XXXII, it is recommended that they form a commission of inquiry or an ad hoc conciliation commission, which shall endeavour to find a solution, likely to be accepted by the States concerned, of any dispute as to their legal rights.

(2) It is recommended that the conciliation commission be constituted in the manner set forth in the Annex.[b]

Article XXXIV. It is recommended that the States concerned agree to submit their legal disputes to an *ad hoc* arbitral tribunal to a permanent arbitral tribunal or to the International Court of Justice if:

(a) A commission has not been formed as provided in Article XXXIII, or

(b) The commission has not been able to find a solution to be recommended, or

(c) A solution recommended has not been accepted by the States concerned, and

(d) An agreement has not been otherwise arrived at.

Article XXXV. It is recommended that in the event of arbitration the States concerned have recourse to the Model Rules on Arbitral Procedure prepared by the International Law Commission of the United Nations at its tenth session in 1958.

Article XXXVI. Recourse to arbitration implies the undertaking by the States concerned to consider the award to be given as final and to submit in good faith to its execution.

Article XXXVII. The means of settlement referred to in the preceding Articles of this Chapter are without prejudice to the utilization of means of settlement recommended to, or required of, members of regional arrangements or agencies and of other international organizations.

b. The Annex is omitted.

5.12 TREATY ON PRINCIPLES GOVERNING THE ACTIVITIES OF STATES IN THE EXPLORATION AND USE OF OUTER SPACE, INCLUDING THE MOON AND OTHER CELESTIAL BODIES.[a] Done at Washington, London, and Moscow, Jan. 27, 1967. Entered into force, Oct. 10, 1967; for the United States, Oct. 10, 1967. 18 U.S.T. 2410, T.I.A.S. No. 6347, 610 U.N.T.S. 205, *reprinted in* 6 I.L.M. 386 (1967)

Article I. The exploration and use of outer space, including the moon and other celestial bodies, shall be carried out for the benefit and in the interests of all countries, irrespective of their degree of economic or scientific development, and shall be the province of all mankind.

Outer space, including the moon and other celestial bodies, shall be free for exploration and use by all States without discrimination of any kind, on a basis of equality and in accordance with international law, and there shall be free access to all areas of celestial bodies.

There shall be freedom of scientific investigation in outer space, including the moon and other celestial bodies, and States shall facilitate and encourage international co-operation in such investigation.

Article II. Outer space, including the moon and other celestial bodies, is not subject to national appropriation by claim of sovereignty, by means of use or occupation, or by any other means.

Article III. States Parties to the Treaty shall carry on activities in the exploration and use of outer space, including the moon and other celestial bodies, in accordance with international law, including the Charter of the United Nations, in the interest of maintaining international peace and security and promoting international co-operation and understanding.

Article IV. States Parties to the Treaty undertake not to place in orbit around the Earth any objects carrying nuclear weapons or any other kinds of weapons of mass destruction, install such weapons on celestial bodies, or station such weapons in outer space in any other manner.

The moon and other celestial bodies shall be used by all States Parties to the Treaty exclusively for peaceful purposes. The establishment of military bases, installations and fortifications, the testing of any type of weapons and the conduct of military maneuvers on celestial bodies shall be forbidden. The use of military personnel for scientific research or for any other peaceful purposes shall not be prohibited. The use of any equipment or facility necessary for peaceful exploration of the moon and other celestial bodies shall also not be prohibited.

Article V. States Parties to the Treaty shall regard astronauts as envoys of mankind in outer space and shall render to them all possible assistance in the event of accident, distress, or emergency landing on the territory of another State Party or

a. Also known as "the Outer Space Treaty." For other basic documents pertaining to activities in outer space, see: Agreement on the Rescue of Astronauts, the Return of Astronauts, and the Return of Objects Launched into Outer Space, done at Washington, London, and Moscow on April 22, 1968, entered into force, Dec. 3, 1968, 19 U.S.T. 7570, T.I.A.S. No. 6599, 672 U.N.T.S. 119; Convention on the International Liability for Damage Caused by Space Objects, done at Washington, London, and Moscow on Mar. 29, 1972, entered into force, Oct. 9, 1973, 24 U.S.T. 2389, T.I.A.S. No. 7762; Convention on Registration of Objects Launched into Outer Space, done at New York on Jan. 14, 1975, entered into force, Sept. 15, 1976, T.I.A.S. No. 8480. See also Basic Document 5.25, *infra*

on the high seas. When astronauts make such a landing, they shall be safely and promptly returned to the State of registry of their space vehicle.

In carrying on activities in outer space and on celestial bodies, the astronauts of one State Party shall render all possible assistance to the astronauts of other States Parties.

States Parties to the Treaty shall immediately inform the other States Parties to the Treaty or the Secretary–General of the United Nations of any phenomena they discover in outer space, including the moon and other celestial bodies, which could constitute a danger to the life or health of astronauts.

Article VI. States Parties to the Treaty shall bear international responsibility for national activities in outer space, including the moon and other celestial bodies, whether such activities are carried on by governmental agencies or by non-governmental entities, and for assuring that national activities are carried out in conformity with the provisions set forth in the present Treaty. The activities of non-governmental entities in outer space, including the moon and other celestial bodies, shall require authorization and continuing supervision by the appropriate State Party to the Treaty. When activities are carried on in outer space, including the moon and other celestial bodies, by an international organization, responsibility for compliance with this Treaty shall be borne both by the international organization and by the States Parties to the Treaty participating in such organization.

Article VII. Each State Party to the Treaty that launches or procures the launching of an object into outer space, including the moon and other celestial bodies, and each State Party from whose territory or facility an object is launched, is internationally liable for damage to another State Party to the Treaty or to its natural or juridical persons by such object or its component parts on the Earth, in air space or in outer space, including the moon and other celestial bodies.

Article VIII. A State Party to the Treaty on whose registry an object launched into outer space is carried shall retain jurisdiction and control over such object, and over any personnel thereof, while in outer space or on a celestial body. Ownership of objects launched into outer space, including objects landed or constructed on a celestial body, and of their component parts, is not affected by their presence in outer space or on a celestial body or by their return to the Earth. Such objects or component parts found beyond the limits of the State Party to the Treaty on whose registry they are carried shall be returned to that State Party, which shall, upon request, furnish identifying data prior to their return.

Article IX. In the exploration and use of outer space, including the moon and other celestial bodies, States Parties to the Treaty shall be guided by the principle of co-operation and mutual assistance and shall conduct all their activities in outer space, including the moon and other celestial bodies, with due regard to the corresponding interests of all other States Parties to the Treaty. States Parties to the Treaty shall pursue studies of outer space, including the moon and other celestial bodies, and conduct exploration of them so as to avoid their harmful contamination and also adverse changes in the environment of the Earth resulting from the introduction of extraterrestrial matter and, where necessary, shall adopt appropriate measures for this purpose. If a State Party to the Treaty has reason to believe that an activity or experiment planned by it or its nationals in outer space, including the moon and other celestial bodies, would cause potentially harmful interference with activities of other States Parties in the peaceful exploration and use of outer space, including the moon and other celestial bodies, it shall undertake appropriate international consultations before proceeding with any such activity or experiment. A State Party to the Treaty which has reason to believe that an activity or experiment planned by another State Party in outer space, including the moon and other celestial bodies, would cause potentially harmful interference with activities in the peaceful exploration and use of outer space, including the moon and other celestial bodies, may request consultation concerning the activity or experiment.

Article X. In order to promote international co-operation in the exploration and use of outer space, including the moon and other celestial bodies, in conformity with the purposes of this Treaty, the States Parties to the Treaty shall consider on a basis of equality any requests by other States Parties to the Treaty to be afforded an opportunity to observe the flight of space objects launched by those States.

The nature of such an opportunity for observation and the conditions under which it could be afforded shall be determined by agreement between the States concerned.

Article XI. In order to promote international co-operation in the peaceful exploration and use of outer space, States Parties to the Treaty conducting activities in outer space, including the moon and other celestial bodies, agree to inform the Secretary–General of the United Nations as well as the public and the international scientific community, to the greatest extent feasible and practicable, of the nature, conduct, locations and results of such activities. On receiving the said information, the Secretary–General of the United Nations should be prepared to disseminate it immediately and effectively.

Article XII. All stations, installations, equipment and space vehicles on the moon and other celestial bodies shall be open to representatives of other States Parties to the Treaty on a basis of reciprocity. Such representatives shall give reasonable advance notice of a projected visit, in order that appropriate consultations may be held and that maximum precautions may be taken to assure safety and to avoid interference with normal operations in the facility to be visited.

Article XIII. The provisions of this Treaty shall apply to the activities of States Parties to the Treaty in the exploration and use of outer space, including the moon and other celestial bodies, whether such activities are carried on by a single State Party to the Treaty or jointly with other States, including cases where they are carried on within the framework of international intergovernmental organizations.

Any practical questions arising in connection with activities carried on by international inter-governmental organizations in the exploration and use of outer space, including the moon and other celestial bodies, shall be resolved by the States Parties to the Treaty either with the appropriate international organization or with one or more States members of that international organization, which are Parties to this Treaty.

* * *

5.13 INTERNATIONAL CONVENTION RELATING TO INTERVENTION ON THE HIGH SEAS IN CASES OF OIL POLLUTION CASUALTIES.[a] Done at Brussels, Nov. 29, 1969. Entered into force, May 6, 1975; for the United States, May 6, 1975. 26 U.S.T. 765, T.I.A.S. No. 8068, 1969 U.N. JURID. Y.B. 166, *reprinted in* 9 I.L.M. 25 (1970)

Article I. (1) Parties to the present Convention may take such measures on the high seas as may be necessary to prevent, mitigate or eliminate grave and imminent danger to their coastline or related interests from pollution or threat of pollution of the sea by oil, following upon a maritime casualty or acts related to such a casualty, which may reasonably be expected to result in major harmful consequences.

(2) However, no measures shall be taken under the present Convention against any warship or other ship owned or operated by a State and used, for the time being, only on government non-commercial service.

Article II. For the purpose of the present Convention:

(1) "maritime casualty" means a collision of ships, stranding or other incident of navigation, or other occurrence on board a ship or external to it resulting in material damage or imminent threat of material damage to a ship or cargo;

(2) "ship" means;

(a) any sea-going vessel of any type whatsoever, and

(b) any floating craft, with the exception of an installation or device engaged in the exploration and exploitation of the resources of the sea-bed and the ocean floor and the subsoil thereof;

(3) "oil" means crude oil, fuel oil, deisel oil and lubricating oil;

(4) "related interests" means the interests of a coastal State directly affected or threatened by the maritime casualty, such as;

(a) maritime coastal, port or estuarine activities, including fisheries activities, constituting an essential means of livelihood of the persons concerned;

(b) tourist attractions of the area concerned;

(c) the health of the coastal population and the well-being of the area concerned, including conservation of living marine resources and of wildlife;

(5) "Organization" means the Inter–Governmental Maritime Consultative Organization.

Article III. When a coastal State is exercising the right to take measures in accordance with Article I, the following provisions shall apply:

a. For other notable instruments pertaining to marine pollution, see International Convention on Civil Liability for Oil Pollution Damage, done at Brussels, Nov. 29, 1969, entered into force, June 19, 1975, 1969 U.N. JURID. Y.B. 174, *reprinted in* 9 I.L.M. 45 (1970); International Convention on the Establishment of an International Fund for Compensation for Oil Pollution Damage, done at Brussels, Dec. 18, 1971, entered into force, Oct. 16, 1978, 1971 U.N. JURID. Y.B. 103, *reprinted in* 11 I.L.M. 284 (1972); Convention for the Prevention of Marine Pollution from Land–Based Sources, done at Paris, June 4, 1974, entered into force, May 6, 1978, *reproduced in* 13 I.L.M. 352 (1974); Convention on Civil Liability for Oil Pollution Damage Resulting from the Exploration and Exploitation of the Seabed Mineral Resources, done at London, Apr. 30, 1978. This last convention had not entered into force as of Dec. 31, 1989. *See also* Basic Document 5.3, *supra*, and Basic Documents 5.18, 5.20, and 5.22, *infra*.

(a) before taking any measures, a coastal State shall proceed to consultations with other States affected by the maritime casualty, particularly with the flag State or States;

(b) the coastal State shall notify without delay the proposed measures to any persons physical or corporate known to the coastal State, or made known to it during the consultations, to have interests which can reasonably be expected to be affected by those measures. The coastal State shall take into account any views they may submit;

(c) before any measure is taken, the coastal State may proceed to a consultation with independent experts, whose names shall be chosen from a list maintained by the Organization;

(d) in cases of extreme urgency requiring measures to be taken immediately, the coastal State may take measures rendered necessary by the urgency of the situation, without prior notification or consultation or without continuing consultations already begun;

(e) a coastal State shall, before taking such measures and during their course, use its best endeavours to avoid any risk to human life, and to afford persons in distress any assistance of which they may stand in need, and in appropriate cases to facilitate the repatriation of ships' crews, and to raise no obstacle thereto;

(f) measures which have been taken in application of Article I shall be notified without delay to the States and to the known physical or corporate persons concerned, as well as to the Secretary-General of the Organization.

* * *

Article V. (1) Measures taken by the coastal State in accordance with Article I shall be proportionate to the damage actual or threatened to it.

(2) Such measures shall not go beyond what is reasonably necessary to achieve the end mentioned in Article I and shall cease as soon as that end has been achieved; they shall not unnecessarily interfere with the rights and interests of the flag State, third States and of any persons, physical or corporate, concerned.

(3) In considering whether the measures are proportionate to the damage, account shall be taken of:

(a) the extent and probability of imminent damage if those measures are not taken; and

(b) the likelihood of those measures being effective; and

(c) the extent of the damage which may be caused by such measures.

Article VI. Any Party which has taken measures in contravention of the provisions of the present Convention causing damage to others, shall be obliged to pay compensation to the extent of the damage caused by measures which exceed those reasonably necessary to achieve the end mentioned in Article I.

Article VII. Except as specifically provided, nothing in the present Convention shall prejudice any otherwise applicable right, duty, privilege or immunity or deprive any of the Parties or any interested physical or corporate person of any remedy otherwise applicable.

* * *

5.14 RESOLUTION ON THE QUESTION OF THE RESERVATION EXCLUSIVELY FOR PEACEFUL PURPOSES OF THE SEA–BED AND THE OCEAN FLOOR, AND THE SUBSOIL THEREOF, UNDERLYING THE HIGH SEAS BEYOND THE LIMITS OF THE PRESENT NATIONAL JURISDICTION, AND THE USE OF THEIR RESOURCES IN THE INTERESTS OF MANKIND.[a] Adopted by the U.N. General Assembly, Dec. 15, 1969. U.N.G.A. Res. 2574 D (XXIV), 24 U.N. GAOR, Supp. (No. 30) 11, U.N.Doc. A/7630 (1970), *reprinted in* 9 I.L.M. 422 (1970)

THE GENERAL ASSEMBLY,

Recalling its resolution 2467 A (XXIII) of 21 December 1968 to the effect that the exploitation of the resources of the sea-bed and the ocean floor, and the subsoil thereof, beyond the limits of national jurisdiction, should be carried out for the benefit of mankind as a whole, irrespective of the geographical location of States, taking into account the special interests and needs of the developing countries.

Convinced that it is essential, for the achievement of this purpose, that such activities be carried out under an international régime, including appropriate international machinery.

Noting that this matter is under consideration by the Committee on the Peaceful Uses of the Sea–Bed and the Ocean Floor beyond the Limits of National Jurisdiction.

Recalling its resolution 2540 (XXII) of 18 December 1967 on the importance of preserving the sea-bed and the ocean floor, and the subsoil thereof, beyond the limits of national jurisdiction, from actions and uses which might be detrimental to the common interests of mankind.

Declares that, pending the establishment of the aforementioned international régime:

(a) State and persons, physical or juridical, are bound to refrain from all activities of exploitation of the resources of the area of the sea-bed and ocean floor, and the subsoil thereof, beyond the limits of national jurisdiction;

(b) No claim to any part of that area or its resources shall be recognized.

a. Also known as "the Moratorium Resolution".

5.15 DECLARATION OF THE PRINCIPLES GOVERNING THE SEA–BED AND OCEAN FLOOR, AND THE SUBSOIL THEREOF, BEYOND THE LIMITS OF NATIONAL JURISDICTION. Adopted by the U.N. General Assembly, Dec. 17, 1970. U.N.G.A.Res. 2749 (XXV), 25 U.N. GAOR, Supp. (No. 28) 24, U.N. Doc. A/8028 (1971), *reprinted in* 10 I.L.M. 220 (1971)

THE GENERAL ASSEMBLY,

Recalling its resolutions 2340 (XXII) of 18 December 1967, 2467 (XXIII) of 21 December 1968 and 2574 (XXIV) of 15 December 1969, concerning the area to which the title of the item refers.

Affirming that there is an area of the sea-bed and the ocean floor, and the subsoil thereof, beyond the limits of national jurisdiction, the precise limits of which are yet to be determined.

Recognizing that the existing legal régime of the high seas does not provide substantive rules for regulating the exploration of the aforesaid area and the exploitation of its resources.

Convinced that the area shall be reserved exclusively for peaceful purposes and that the exploration of the area and the exploitation of its resources shall be carried out for the benefit of mankind as a whole.

Believing it essential that an international régime applying to the area and its resources and including appropriate international machinery should be established as soon as possible.

Bearing in mind that the development and use of the area and its resources shall be undertaken in such a manner as to foster healthy development of the world economy and balanced growth of international trade, and to minimize any adverse economic effects caused by fluctuation of prices of raw materials resulting from such activities.

Solemnly declares that:

1. The sea-bed and ocean floor, and the subsoil thereof, beyond the limits of national jurisdiction (hereinafter referred to as the area), as well as the resources of the area, are the common heritage of mankind.

2. The area shall not be subject to appropriation by any means by States or persons, natural or juridical, and no State shall claim or exercise sovereignty or sovereign rights over any part thereof.

3. No State or person, natural or juridical, shall claim, exercise or acquire rights with respect to the area or its resources incompatible with the international régime to be established and the principles of this Declaration.

4. All activities regarding the exploration and exploitation of the resources of the area and other related activities shall be governed by the international régime to be established.

5. The area shall be open to use exclusively for peaceful purposes by all States whether coastal or land-locked, without discrimination, in accordance with international régime to be established.

6. States shall act in the area in accordance with the applicable principles and rules of international law including the Charter of the United Nations and the Declaration on Principles of International Law concerning Friendly Relations and

Co-operation among States in accordance with the Charter of the United Nations, adopted by the General Assembly on 24 October 1970, in the interests of maintaining international peace and security and promoting international co-operation and mutual understanding.

7. The exploration of the area and the exploitation of its resources shall be carried out for the benefit of mankind as a whole, irrespective of the geographical location of States, whether land-locked or coastal, and taking into particular consideration the interests and needs of the developing countries.

8. The area shall be reserved exclusively for peaceful purposes, without prejudice to any measures which have been or may be agreed upon in the context of international negotiations undertaken in the field of disarmament and which may be applicable to a broader area. One or more international agreements shall be concluded as soon as possible in order to implement effectively this principle and to constitute a step towards the exclusion of the sea-bed, the ocean floor and the subsoil thereof from the arms race.

9. On the basis of the principles of this Declaration, an international régime applying to the area and its resources and including appropriate international machinery to give effect to its provisions shall be established by an international treaty of a universal character, generally agreed upon. The régime shall, *inter alia,* provide for the orderly and safe development and rational management of the area and its resources and for expanding opportunities in the use thereof and ensure the equitable sharing by States in the benefits derived therefrom, taking into particular consideration the interests and needs of the developing countries, whether land-locked or coastal.

10. States shall promote international co-operation in scientific research exclusively for peaceful purposes:

(a) By participation in international programmes and by encouraging co-operation in scientific research by personnel of different countries;

(b) Through effective publication of research programmes and dissemination of the results of research through international channels;

(c) By co-operation in measures to strengthen research capabilities of developing countries, including the participation of their nationals in research programmes. No such activity shall form the legal basis for any claims with respect to any part of the area or its resources.

11. With respect to activities in the area and acting in conformity with the international régime to be established, States shall take appropriate measures for and shall co-operate in the adoption and implementation of international rules, standards and procedures for, *inter alia:*

(a) Prevention of pollution and contamination, and other hazards to the marine environment, including the coastline, and of interference with the ecological balance of the marine environment;

(b) Protection and conservation of the natural resources of the area and prevention of damage to the flora and fauna of the marine environment.

12. In their activities in the area, including those relating to its resources, States shall pay due regard to the rights and legitimate interests of coastal States in the region of such activities, as well as of all other States which may be affected by such activities. Consultations shall be maintained with the coastal States concerned with respect to activities relating to the exploration of the area and the exploitation of its resources with a view to avoiding infringement of such rights and interests.

13. Nothing herein shall affect:

(a) The legal status of the waters superjacent to the area or that of the air space above those waters;

(b) The rights of coastal States with respect to measures to prevent, mitigate or eliminate grave and imminent danger to their coastline or related interests from pollution or threat thereof resulting from, or from other hazardous occurrences caused by, any activities in the area, subject to the international régime to be established.

14. Every State shall have the responsibility to ensure that activities in the area, including those relating to its resources, whether undertaken by governmental agencies, or nongovernmental entities or persons under its jurisdiction, or acting on its behalf, shall be carried out in conformity with the international régime to be established. The same responsibility applies to international organizations and their members for activities undertaken by such organizations or on their behalf. Damage caused by such activities shall entail liability.

15. The parties to any dispute relating to activities in the area and its resources shall resolve such dispute by the measures mentioned in Article 33 of the Charter of the United Nations and such procedures for settling disputes as may be agreed upon in the international régime to be established.

5.16 CONVENTION ON THE INTERNATIONAL LIABILITY FOR DAMAGE CAUSED BY SPACE OBJECTS.[a] Done at Washington, London, and Moscow, Mar. 29, 1972. Entered into force, Sept. 1, 1972; for the United States, Oct. 9, 1973. 24 U.S.T. 2389, T.I.A.S. No. 7762, 1971 U.N. JURID. Y.B. 111

ARTICLE I

For the purposes of this Convention:

(a) The term "damage" means loss of life, personal injury or other impairment of health; or loss of or damage to property of States or of persons, natural or juridical, or property of international intergovernmental organizations;

(b) The term "launching" includes attempted launching;

(c) The term "launching State" means:

(i) A State which launches or procures the launching of a space object;

(ii) A State from whose territory or facility a space object is launched;

(d) The term "space object" includes component parts of a space object as well as its launch vehicle and parts thereof.

ARTICLE II

A launching State shall be absolutely liable to pay compensation for damage caused by its space object on the surface of the earth or to aircraft in flight.

ARTICLE III

In the event of damage being caused elsewhere than on the surface of the earth to a space object of one launching State or to persons or property on board such a space object by a space object of another launching State, the latter shall be liable only if the damage is due to its fault or the fault of persons for whom it is responsible.

ARTICLE IV

1. In the event of damage being caused elsewhere than on the surface of the earth to a space object of one launching State or to persons or property on board such a space object by a space object of another launching State, and of damage thereby being caused to a third State or to its natural or juridical persons, the first two States shall be jointly and severally liable to the third State, to the extent indicated by the following:

(a) If the damage has been caused to the third State on the surface of the earth or to aircraft in flight, their liability to the third State shall be absolute;

(b) If the damage has been caused to a space object of the third State or to persons or property on board that space object elsewhere than on the surface of the earth, their liability to the third State shall be based on the fault of either of the first two States or on the fault of persons for whom either is responsible.

2. In all cases of joint and several liability referred to in paragraph 1 of this article, the burden of compensation for the damage shall be apportioned between the first two States in accordance with the extent to which they were at fault; if the extent of the fault of each of these States cannot be established, the burden of compensation shall be apportioned equally between them. Such apportionment shall

a. This Convention supplements the Outer Space Convention, Basic Document 5.12, *supra*.

be without prejudice to the right of the third State to seek the entire compensation due under this Convention from any or all of the launching States which are jointly and severally liable.

ARTICLE V

1. Whenever two or more States jointly launch a space object, they shall be jointly and severally liable for any damage caused.

2. A launching State which has paid compensation for damage shall have the right to present a claim for indemnification to other participants in the joint launching. The participants in a joint launching may conclude agreements regarding the apportioning among themselves of the financial obligation in respect of which they are jointly and severally liable. Such agreements shall be without prejudice to the right of a State sustaining damage to seek the entire compensation due under this Convention from any or all of the launching States which are jointly and severally liable.

3. A State from whose territory or facility a space object is launched shall be regarded as a participant in a joint launching.

ARTICLE VI

1. Subject to the provisions of paragraph 2 of this article, exoneration from absolute liability shall be granted to the extent that a launching State establishes that the damage has resulted either wholly or partially from gross negligence or from an act or omission done with intent to cause damage on the part of a claimant State or of natural or juridical persons it represents.

2. No exoneration whatever shall be granted in cases where the damage has resulted from activities conducted by a launching State which are not in conformity with international law including, in particular, the Charter of the United Nations and the Treaty on Principles Governing the Activities of States in the Exploration and Use of Outer Space, including the Moon and Other Celestial Bodies.

ARTICLE VII

The provisions of this Convention shall not apply to damage caused by a space object of a launching State to:

(a) Nationals of that launching State;

(b) Foreign nationals during such time as they are participating in the operation of that space object from the time of its launching or at any stage thereafter until its descent, or during such time as they are in the immediate vicinity of a planned launching or recovery area as the result of an invitation by that launching State.

ARTICLE VIII

1. A State which suffers damage, or whose natural or juridical persons suffer damage, may present to a launching State a claim for compensation for such damage.

2. If the State of nationality has not presented a claim, another State may, in respect of damage sustained in its territory by any natural or juridical person, present a claim to a launching State.

3. If neither the State of nationality nor the State in whose territory the damage was sustained has presented a claim or notified its intention of presenting a claim, another State may, in respect of damage sustained by its permanent residents, present a claim to a launching State.

ARTICLE IX

A claim for compensation for damage shall be presented to a launching State through diplomatic channels. If a State does not maintain diplomatic relations with the launching State concerned, it may request another State to present its claim to that launching State or otherwise represent its interests under this Convention. It may also present its claim through the Secretary–General of the United Nations, provided the claimant State and the launching State are both Members of the United Nations.

ARTICLE X

1. A claim for compensation for damage may be presented to a launching State not later than one year following the date of the occurrence of the damage or the identification of the launching State which is liable.

2. If, however, a State does not know of the occurrence of the damage or has not been able to identify the launching State which is liable, it may present a claim within one year following the date on which it learned of the aforementioned facts; however, this period shall in no event exceed one year following the date on which the State could reasonably be expected to have learned of the facts through the exercise of due diligence.

3. The time-limits specified in paragraphs 1 and 2 of this article shall apply even if the full extent of the damage may not be known. In this event, however, the claimant State shall be entitled to revise the claim and submit additional documentation after the expiration of such time-limits until one year after the full extent of the damage is known.

ARTICLE XI

1. Presentation of a claim to a launching State for compensation for damage under this Convention shall not require the prior exhaustion of any local remedies which may be available to a claimant State or to natural or juridical persons it represents.

2. Nothing in this Convention shall prevent a State, or natural or juridical persons it might represent, from pursuing a claim in the courts or administrative tribunals or agencies of a launching State. A State shall not, however, be entitled to present a claim under this Convention in respect of the same damage for which a claim is being pursued in the courts or administrative tribunals or agencies of a launching State or under another international agreement which is binding on the States concerned.

ARTICLE XII

The compensation which the launching State shall be liable to pay for damage under this Convention shall be determined in accordance with international law and the principles of justice and equity, in order to provide such reparation in respect of the damage as will restore the person, natural or juridical, State or international organization on whose behalf the claim is presented to the condition which would have existed if the damage had not occurred.

ARTICLE XIII

Unless the claimant State and the State from which compensation is due under this Convention agree on another form of compensation, the compensation shall be paid in the currency of the claimant State or, if that State so requests, in the currency of the State from which compensation is due.

ARTICLE XIV

If no settlement of a claim is arrived at through diplomatic negotiations as provided for in article IX, within one year from the date on which the claimant State notifies the launching State that it has submitted the documentation of its claim, the parties concerned shall establish a Claims Commission at the request of either party.

ARTICLE XV

1. The Claims Commission shall be composed of three members: one appointed by the claimant State, one appointed by the launching State and the third member, the Chairman, to be chosen by both parties jointly. Each party shall make its appointment within two months of the request for the establishment of the Claims Commission.

2. If no agreement is reached on the choice of the Chairman within four months of the request for the establishment of the Commission, either party may request the Secretary–General of the United Nations to appoint the Chairman within a further period of two months.

* * *

ARTICLE XVIII

The Claims Commission shall decide the merits of the claim for compensation and determine the amount of compensation payable, if any.

ARTICLE XIX

1. The Claims Commission shall act in accordance with the provisions of article XII.

2. The decision of the Commission shall be final and binding if the parties have so agreed; otherwise the Commission shall render a final and recommendatory award, which the parties shall consider in good faith. The Commission shall state the reasons for its decision or award.

3. The Commission shall give its decision or award as promptly as possible and no later than one year from the date of its establishment, unless an extension of this period is found necessary by the Commission.

4. The Commission shall make its decision or award public. It shall deliver a certified copy of its decision or award to each of the parties and to the Secretary–General of the United Nations.

ARTICLE XX

The expenses in regard to the Claims Commission shall be borne equally by the parties, unless otherwise decided by the Commission.

ARTICLE XXI

If the damage caused by a space object presents a large-scale danger to human life or seriously interferes with the living conditions of the population or the functioning of vital centers, the States Parties, and in particular the launching State, shall examine the possibility of rendering appropriate and rapid assistance to the State which has suffered the damage, when it so requests. However, nothing in this article shall affect the rights or obligations of the States Parties under this Convention.

ARTICLE XXII

1. In this Convention, with the exception of articles XXIV to XXVII, references to States shall be deemed to apply to any international intergovernmental organization which conducts space activities if the organization declares its acceptance of the rights and obligations provided for in this Convention and if a majority of the States members of the organization are States Parties to this Convention and to the Treaty on Principles Governing the Activities of States in the Exploration and Use of Outer Space, including the Moon and Other Celestial Bodies.

2. States members of any such organization which are States Parties to this Convention shall take all appropriate steps to ensure that the organization makes a declaration in accordance with the preceding paragraph.

3. If an international intergovernmental organization is liable for damage by virtue of the provisions of this Convention, that organization and those of its members which are States Parties to this Convention shall be jointly and severally liable; provided, however, that:

(a) Any claim for compensation in respect of such damage shall be first presented to the organization;

(b) Only where the organization has not paid, within a period of six months, any sum agreed or determined to be due as compensation for such damage, may the claimant State invoke the liability of the members which are States Parties to this Convention for the payment of that sum.

4. Any claim, pursuant to the provisions of this Convention, for compensation in respect of damage caused to an organization which has made a declaration in accordance with paragraph 1 of this article shall be presented by a State member of the organization which is a State Party to this Convention.

* * *

5.17 STOCKHOLM DECLARATION OF THE UNITED NATIONS CONFERENCE ON THE HUMAN ENVIRONMENT. Adopted by the U.N. Conference on the Human Environment at Stockholm, June 16, 1972. Report of the U.N. Conference on the Human Environment, Stockholm, June 5–16, 1972, U.N. Doc. A/CONF. 48/14 (1972), *reprinted in* 11 I.L.M. 1416 (1972)

The United Nations Conference on the Human Environment.

Having met at Stockholm from 5 to 16 June 1972.

Having considered the need for a common outlook and for common principles to inspire and guide the peoples of the world in the preservation and enhancement of the human environment.

I

Proclaims that:

1. Man is both creature and moulder of his environment, which gives him physical sustenance and affords him the opportunity for intellectual, moral, social and spiritual growth. In the long and tortuous evolution of the human race on this planet a stage has been reached when, through the rapid acceleration of science and technology, man has acquired the power to transform his environment in countless ways and on an unprecedented scale. Both aspects of man's environment, the natural and the man-made, are essential to his well-being and to the enjoyment of basic human rights—even the right to life itself.

2. The protection and improvement of the human environment is a major issue which affects the well-being of peoples and economic development throughout the world: it is the urgent desire of the peoples of the whole world and the duty of all Governments.

3. Man has constantly to sum up experience and go on discovering, inventing, creating and advancing. In our time, man's capability to transform his surroundings, if used wisely, can bring to all peoples the benefits of development and the opportunity to enhance the quality of life. Wrongly or heedlessly applied, the same power can do incalculable harm to human beings and the human environment. We see around us growing evidence of man-made harm in many regions of the earth: dangerous levels of pollution in water, air, earth and living beings; major and undesirable disturbances to the ecological balance of the biosphere; destruction and depletion of irreplaceable resources; and gross deficiencies, harmful to the physical, mental and social health of man, in the man-made environment, particularly in the living and working environment.

4. In the developing countries most of the environmental problems are caused by under-development. Millions continue to live far below the minimum levels required for a decent human existence, deprived of adequate food and clothing, shelter and education, health and sanitation. Therefore, the developing countries must direct their efforts to development, bearing in mind their priorities and the need to safeguard and improve the environment. For the same purpose, the industrialized countries should make efforts to reduce the gap between themselves and the developing countries. In the industrialized countries, environmental problems are generally related to industrialization and technological development.

5. The natural growth of population continuously presents problems for the preservation of the environment, and adequate policies and measures should be

adopted, as appropriate, to face these problems. Of all things in the world, people are the most precious. It is the people that propel social progress, create social wealth, develop science and technology and, through their hard work, continuously transform the human environment. Along with social progress and the advance of production, science and technology, the capability of man to improve the environment increases with each passing day.

6. A point has been reached in history when we must shape our actions throughout the world with a more prudent care for their environmental consequences. Through ignorance or indifference we can do massive and irreversible harm to the earthly environment on which our life and well-being depend. Conversely, through fuller knowledge and wiser action, we can achieve for ourselves and our posterity a better life in an environment more in keeping with human needs and hopes. There are broad vistas for the enhancement of environmental quality and the creation of a good life. What is needed is an enthusiastic but calm state of mind and intense but orderly work. For the purpose of attaining freedom in the world of nature, man must use knowledge to build, in collaboration with nature, a better environment. To defend and improve the human environment for present and future generations has become an imperative goal for mankind—a goal to be pursued together with, and in harmony with, the established and fundamental goals of peace and of worldwide economic and social development.

7. To achieve this environmental goal will demand the acceptance of responsibility by citizens and communities and by enterprises and institutions at every level, all sharing equitably in common efforts. Individuals in all walks of life as well as organizations in many fields, by their values and the sum of their actions, will shape the world environment of the future. Local and national governments will bear the greatest burden for large-scale environmental policy and action within their jurisdictions. International co-operation is also needed in order to raise resources to support the developing countries in carrying out their responsibilities in this field. A growing class of environmental problems, because they are regional or global in extent or because they affect the common international realm, will require extensive co-operation among nations and action by international organizations in the common interest. The Conference calls upon Governments and peoples to exert common efforts for the preservation and improvement of the human environment, for the benefit of all the people and for their posterity.

II. PRINCIPLES

States the common conviction that:

Principle 1. Man has the fundamental right to freedom, equality and adequate conditions of life, in an environment of a quality that permits a life of dignity and well-being, and he bears a solemn responsibility to protect and improve the environment for present and future generations. In this respect, policies promoting or perpetuating *apartheid,* racial segregation, discrimination, colonial and other forms of oppression and foreign domination stand condemned and must be eliminated.

Principle 2. The natural resources of the earth, including the air, water, land, flora and fauna and especially representative samples of natural ecosystems, must be safeguarded for the benefit of present and future generations through careful planning or management, as appropriate.

Principle 3. The capacity of the earth to produce vital renewable resources must be maintained and, wherever practicable, restored or improved.

Principle 4. Man has a special responsibility to safeguard and wisely manage the heritage of wildlife and its habitat, which are now gravely imperilled by a combination of adverse factors. Nature conservation, including wildlife, must therefore receive importance in planning for economic development.

Principle 5. The non-renewable resources of the earth must be employed in such a way as to guard against the danger of their future exhaustion and to ensure that benefits from such employment are shared by all mankind.

Principle 6. The discharge of toxic substances or of other substances and the release of heat, in such quantities or concentrations as to exceed the capacity of the environment to render them harmless, must be halted in order to ensure that serious or irreversible damage is not inflicted upon ecosystems. The just struggle of the problems of all countries against pollution should be supported.

Principle 7. States shall take all possible steps to prevent pollution of the seas by substances that are liable to create hazards to human health, to harm living resources and marine life, to damage amenities or to interfere with other legitimate uses of the sea.

Principle 8. Economic and social development is essential for ensuring a favourable living and working environment for man and for creating conditions on earth that are necessary for the improvement of the quality of life.

Principle 9. Environmental deficiencies generated by the conditions of under-development and natural disasters pose grave problems and can best be remedied by accelerated development through the transfer of substantial quantities of financial and technological assistance as a supplement to the domestic effort of the developing countries and such timely assistance as may be required.

Principle 10. For the developing countries, stability of prices and adequate earnings for primary commodities and raw materials are essential to environmental management since economic factors as well as ecological processes must be taken into account.

Principle 11. The environmental policies of all States should enhance and not adversely affect the present or future development potential of developing countries, nor should they hamper the attainment of better living conditions for all, and appropriate steps should be taken by States and international organizations with a view to reaching agreement on meeting the possible national and international economic consequences resulting from the application of environmental measures.

Principle 12. Resources should be made available to preserve and improve the environment, taking into account the circumstances and particular requirements of developing countries and any costs which may emanate from their incorporating environmental safeguards into their development planning and the need for making available to them, upon their request, additional international technical and financial assistance for this purpose.

Principle 13. In order to achieve a more rational management of resources and thus to improve the environment, States should adopt an integrated and co-ordinated approach to their development planning so as to ensure that development is compatible with the need to protect and improve the environment for the benefit of their population.

Principle 14. Rational planning constitutes an essential tool for reconciling any conflict between the needs of development and the need to protect and improve the environment.

Principle 15. Planning must be applied to human settlements and urbanization with a view to avoiding adverse effects on the environment and obtaining maximum social, economic and environmental benefits for all. In this respect, projects which are designed for colonialist and racist domination must be abandoned.

Principle 16. Demographic policies which are without prejudice to basic human rights and which are deemed appropriate by Governments concerned should be applied in those regions where the rate of population growth or excessive population concentrations are likely to have adverse effects on the environment of the human environment and impede development.

Principle 17. Appropriate national institutions must be entrusted with the task of planning, managing or controlling the environmental resources of States with a view to enhancing environmental quality.

Principle 18. Science and technology, as part of their contribution to economic and social development, must be applied to the identification, avoidance and control of environmental risks and the solution of environmental problems and for the common good of mankind.

Principle 19. Education in environmental matters, for the younger generation as well as adults, giving due consideration to the underprivileged, is essential in order to broaden the basis for an enlightened opinion and responsible conduct by individuals, enterprises and communities in protecting and improving the environment in its full human dimension. It is also essential that mass media of communications avoid contributing to the deterioration of the environment, but, on the contrary, disseminate information of an educational nature on the need to protect and improve the environment in order to enable man to develop in every respect.

Principle 20. Scientific research and development in the context of environmental problems, both national and multinational, must be promoted in all countries, especially the developing countries. In this connexion, the free flow of up-to-date scientific information and transfer of experience must be supported and assisted, to facilitate the solution of environmental problems; environmental technologies should be made available to developing countries on terms which would encourage their wide dissemination without constituting an economic burden on the developing countries.

Principle 21. States have, in accordance with the Charter of the United Nations and the principles of international law, the sovereign right to exploit their own resources pursuant to their own environmental policies, and the responsibility to ensure that activities within their jurisdiction or control do not cause damage to the environment of other States or of areas beyond the limits of national jurisdiction.

Principle 22. States shall co-operate to develop further the international law regarding liability and compensation for the victims of pollution and other environmental damage caused by activities within the jurisdiction or control of such States to areas beyond their jurisdiction.

Principle 23. Without prejudice to such criteria as may be agreed upon by the international community, or to standards which will have to be determined nationally, it will be essential in all cases to consider the systems of values prevailing in each country, and the extent of the applicability of standards which are valid for the most advanced countries but which may be inappropriate and of unwarranted social cost for the developing countries.

Principle 24. International matters concerning the protection and improvement of the environment should be handled in a co-operative spirit by all countries, big and small, on an equal footing. Co-operation through multilateral or bilateral arrangements or other appropriate means is essential to effectively control, prevent, reduce and eliminate adverse environmental effects resulting from activities conducted in all spheres, in such a way that due account is taken of the sovereignty and interests of all States.

Principle 25. States shall ensure that international organizations play a co-ordinated, efficient and dynamic role for the protection and improvement of the environment.

Principle 26. Man and his environment must be spared the effects of nuclear weapons and all other means of mass destruction. States must strive to reach prompt agreement, in the relevant international organs, on the elimination and complete destruction of such weapons.

5.18 CONVENTION ON THE PREVENTION OF MARINE POLLUTIONS BY DUMPING OF WASTES AND OTHER MATTER, WITH ANNEXES I AND II.[a] Done at Washington, London, Mexico City, and Moscow, Dec. 29, 1972. Entered into force, Aug. 30, 1975; for the United States, Aug. 30, 1975. 26 U.S.T. 2403, T.I.A.S. No. 8165, *reprinted in* I.L.M. 1294 (1972)

Article I. Contracting Parties shall individually and collectively promote the effective control of all sources of pollution of the marine environment, and pledge themselves especially to take all practicable steps to prevent the pollution of the sea by the dumping of waste and other matter that is liable to create hazards to human health, to harm living resources and marine life, to damage amenities or to interfere with other legitimate uses of the sea.

Article II. Contracting Parties shall, as provided for in the following Articles, take effective measures individually, according to their scientific, technical and economic capabilities, and collectively, to prevent marine pollution caused by dumping and shall harmonize their policies in this regard.

Article III. For the purposes of this Convention:

(1) (a) "Dumping" means:

(i) any deliberate disposal at sea of wastes or other matter from vessels, aircraft, platforms or other man-made structures at sea;

(ii) any deliberate disposal at sea of vessels, aircraft, platforms or other man-made structures at sea.

(b) "Dumping" does not include:

(i) the disposal at sea of wastes or other matter incidental to, or derived from the normal operations of vessels, aircraft, platforms or other man-made structures at sea and their equipment, other than wastes or other matter transported by or to vessels, aircraft, platforms or other man-made structures at sea, operating for the purpose of disposal of such matter or derived from the treatment of such wastes or other matter on such vessels, aircraft, platforms or structures;

(ii) placement of matter for a purpose other than the mere disposal thereof, provided that such placement is not contrary to the aims of this Convention.

(c) The disposal of wastes or other matter directly arising from, or related to the exploration, exploitation and associated off-shore processing of sea-bed mineral resources will not be covered by the provisions of this Convention.

a. For other notable instruments pertaining to marine pollution, see International Convention on Civil Liability for Oil Pollution Damage, done at Brussels, Nov. 29, 1969, entered into force, June 19, 1975, 1969 U.N. JURID.Y.B. 174, *reprinted in* 9 I.L.M. 45 (1970); International Convention on the Establishment of an International Fund for Compensation for Oil Pollution Damage, done at Brussels, Dec. 18, 1971, entered into force, Oct. 16, 1978, 1971 U.N. JURID.Y.B. 103, *reprinted in* 11 I.L.M. 284 (1972); Convention for the Prevention of Marine Pollution from Land–Based Sources, done at Paris, June 4, 1974, entered into force, May 6, 1978, *reprinted in* 13 I.L.M. 352 (1974); Convention on Civil Liability for Oil Pollution Damage Resulting from the Exploration and Exploitation of the Seabed Mineral Resources, done at London, Apr. 30, 1978. This last convention had not entered into force as of Dec. 31, 1989. *See also* Basic Documents 5.3 and 5.13, *supra*, and Basic Documents 5.20 and 5.22, *infra*.

(2) "Vessels and aircraft" means waterborne or airborne craft of any type whatsoever. This expression includes air cushioned craft and floating craft, whether self-propelled or not.

(3) "Sea" means all marine waters other than the internal waters of States.

(4) "Wastes or other matter" means material and substance of any kind, form or description.

(5) "Special permit" means permission granted specifically on application in advance and in accordance with Annex II and Annex III.[b]

(6) "General permit" means permission granted in advance and in accordance with Annex III.[b]

(7) "The Organisation" means the Organisation designated by the Contracting Parties in accordance with Article XIV(2).

Article IV. (1) In accordance with the provisions of this Convention Contracting Parties shall prohibit the dumping of any wastes or other matter in whatever form or condition except as otherwise specified below:

(a) the dumping of wastes or other matter listed in Annex I is prohibited;

(b) the dumping of wastes or other matter listed in Annex II requires a prior special permit;

(c) the dumping of all other wastes or matter requires a prior general permit.

* * *

(3) No provision of this Convention is to be interpreted as preventing a Contracting Party from prohibiting, insofar as that Party is concerned, the dumping of wastes or other matter not mentioned in Annex I. That Party shall notify such measures to the Organisation.

Article V. (1) The provisions of Article IV shall not apply when it is necessary to secure the safety of human life or of vessels, aircraft, platforms or other man-made structures at sea in cases of *force majeure* caused by stress of weather, or in any case which constitutes a danger to human life or a real threat to vessels, aircraft, platforms or other man-made structures at sea, if dumping appears to be the only way of averting the threat and if there is every probability that the damage consequent upon such dumping will be less than would otherwise occur. Such dumping shall be so conducted as to minimise the likelihood of damage to human or marine life and shall be reported forthwith to the Organisation.

2. A Contracting Party may issue a special permit as an exception to Article IV(1)(*a*), in emergencies, posing unacceptable risk relating to human health and admitting no other feasible solution. Before doing so the Party shall consult any other country or countries that are likely to be affected and the Organisation which, after consulting other Parties, and international organisations as appropriate, shall, in accordance with Article XIV promptly recommend to the Party the most appropriate procedures to adopt. The Party shall follow these recommendations to the maximum extent feasible consistent with the time within which action must be taken and with the general obligation to avoid damage to the marine environment and shall inform the Organisation of the action it takes. The Parties pledge themselves to assist one another in such situations.

b. Annex III is omitted.

Article VII. (1) Each Contracting Party shall apply the measures required to implement the present Convention to all:

(a) vessels and aircraft registered in its territory or flying its flag;

(b) vessels and aircraft loading in its territory or territorial seas matter which is to be dumped;

(c) vessels and aircraft and fixed or floating platforms under its jurisdiction believed to be engaged in dumping.

(2) Each Party shall take in its territory appropriate measures to prevent and punish conduct in contravention of the provisions of this Convention.

(3) The Parties agree to co-operate in the development of procedures for the effective application of this Convention particularly on the high seas, including procedures for the reporting of vessels and aircraft observed dumping in contravention of the Convention.

(4) This Convention shall not apply to those vessels and aircraft entitled to sovereign immunity under international law. However each Party shall ensure by the adoption of appropriate measures that such vessels and aircraft owned or operated by it act in a manner consistent with the object and purpose of this Convention, and shall inform the Organisation accordingly.

(5) Nothing in this Convention shall affect the right of each Party to adopt other measures, in accordance with the principles of international law, to prevent dumping at sea.

Article VIII. In order to further the objectives of this Convention, the Contracting Parties with common interests to protect in the marine environment in a given geographical area shall endeavor, taking into account characteristic regional features, to enter into regional agreements consistent with this Convention for the prevention of pollution, especially by dumping. The Contracting Parties to the present Convention shall endeavour to act consistently with the objectives and provisions of such regional agreements, which shall be notified to them by the Organisation. Contracting Parties shall seek to co-operate with the Parties to regional agreements in order to develop harmonized procedures to be followed by Contracting Parties to the different conventions concerned. Special attention shall be given to co-operation in the field of monitoring and scientific research.

Article IX. The Contracting Parties shall promote, through collaboration within the Organisation and other international bodies, support for those Parties which request it for:

(a) the training of scientific and technical personnel;

(b) the supply of necessary equipment and facilities for research and monitoring;

(c) the disposal and treatment of waste and other measures to prevent or mitigate pollution caused by dumping;

preferably within the countries concerned, so furthering the aims and purposes of this Convention.

Article X. In accordance with the principles of international law regarding State responsibility for damage to the environment of other States or to any other area of the environment, caused by dumping of wastes and other matter of all kinds, the Contracting Parties undertake to develop procedures for the assessment of liability and the settlement of disputes regarding dumping.

* * *

Article XII. The Contracting Parties pledge themselves to promote, within the competent specialised agencies and other international bodies, measures to protect the marine environment against pollution caused by:

(a) hydrocarbons, including oil, and their wastes;

(b) other noxious or hazardous matter transported by vessels for purposes other than dumping;

(c) wastes generated in the course of operation of vessels, aircraft, platforms and other man-made structures at sea;

(d) radio-active pollutants from all sources, including vessels;

(e) agents of chemical and biological warfare;

(f) wastes or other matter directly arising from, or related to the exploration, exploitation and associated off-shore processing of sea-bed mineral resources.

The Parties will also promote, within the appropriate international organisation, the codification of signals to be used by vessels engaged in dumping.

Article XIII. Nothing in this Convention shall prejudice the codification and development of the law of the sea by the United Nations Conference on the Law of the Sea convened pursuant to Resolution 2750 C (XXV) of the General Assembly of the United Nations nor the present or future claims and legal views of any State concerning the law of the sea and the nature and extent of coastal and flag State jurisdiction. * * *

Article XIV. (1) The Government of the United Kingdom of Great Britain and Northern Ireland as a depositary shall call a meeting of the Contracting Parties not later than three months after the entry into force of this Convention to decide on organisational matters.

(2) The Contracting Parties shall designate a competent Organisation existing at the time of that meeting to be responsible for Secretariat duties in relation to this Convention. Any Party to this Convention not being a member of this Organisation shall make an appropriate contribution to the expenses incurred by the Organisation in performing these duties.

(3) The Secretariat duties of the Organisation shall include:

(a) the convening of consultative meetings of the Contracting Parties not less frequently than once very two years and of special meetings of the Parties at any time on the request of two-thirds of the Parties;

(b) preparing and assisting, in consultation with the Contracting Parties and appropriate International Organisations, in the development and implementation of procedures referred to in sub-paragraph (4)(*e*) of this Article;

(c) considering enquiries by, and information from the Contracting Parties, consulting with them and with the appropriate International Organisations, and providing recommendations to the Parties on questions related to, but not specifically covered by the Convention;

(d) conveying to the Parties concerned all notifications received by the Organisation in accordance with Articles IV(3), V(1) and (2), VI(4), XV, XX and XXI.

Prior to the designation of the Organisation these functions shall, as necessary, be performed by the depositary, who for this purpose shall be the Government of the United Kingdom of Great Britain and Northern Ireland.

* * *

ANNEX I

1. Organohalogen compounds.

2. Mercury and mercury compounds.

3. Cadmium and cadmium compounds.

4. Persistant plastics and other persistent synthetic materials, for example, netting and ropes, which may float or may remain in suspension in the sea in such a manner as to interfere materially with fishing, navigation or other legitimate uses of the sea.

5. Crude oil, fuel oil, heavy diesel oil, and lubricating oils, hydraulic fluids, and any mixtures containing any of these, taken on board for the purpose of dumping.

6. High-level radio-active wastes or other high-level radio-active matter, defined on public health, biological or other grounds, by the competent international body in this field, at present the International Atomic Energy Agency, as unsuitable for dumping at sea.

7. Materials in whatever form (e.g. solids, liquids, semi-liquids, gases or in a living state) produced for biological and chemical warfare.

8. The preceding paragraphs of this Annex do not apply to substances which are rapidly rendered harmless by physical, chemical or biological processes in the sea provided they do not:

(i) make edible marine organisms unpalatable, or

(ii) endanger human health or that of domestic animals.

The consultative procedure provided for under Article XIV should be followed by a Party if there is doubt about the harmlessness of the substances.

9. This Annex does not apply to wastes or other materials (e.g. sewage sludges and dredged spoils) containing the matter referred to in paragraphs 1–5 above as trace contaminants. Such wastes shall be subject to the provisions of Annexes II and III as appropriate.

ANNEX II

The following substances and materials requiring special care are listed for the purposes of Article VI(1)(a).

A. Wastes containing significant amounts of the matters listed below:

arsenic
lead
copper
zinc

} and their compounds

organosilicon compounds
cyanides
fluorides
pesticides and their by-products not covered in Annex I.

B. In the issue of permits for the dumping of large quantities of acids and alkalis, consideration shall be given to the possible presence in such wastes of the substances listed in paragraph A and to the following additional substances:

beryllium
chromium
nickel
vanadium } and their compounds

C. Containers, scrap metal and other bulky wastes liable to sink to the sea bottom which may present a serious obstacle to fishing or navigation.

D. Radio-active wastes or other radio-active matter not included in Annex I. In the issue of permits for the dumping of this matter, the Contracting Parties should take full account of the recommendations of the competent international body in this field, at present the International Atomic Energy Agency.

5.19 CONVENTION ON INTERNATIONAL TRADE IN ENDANGERED SPECIES OF WILD FAUNA AND FLORA. Done at Washington, Mar. 3, 1973. Entered into force, July 1, 1975; for the United States, July 1, 1975. 27 U.S.T. 1087, T.I.A.S. No. 8249, *reprinted in* 12 I.L.M. 1085 (1973)

The Contracting States,

RECOGNIZING that wild fauna and flora in their many beautiful and varied forms are an irreplaceable part of the natural systems of the earth which must be protected for this and the generations to come;

CONSCIOUS of the ever-growing value of wild fauna and flora from aesthetic, scientific, cultural, recreational and economic points of view;

RECOGNIZING that peoples and States are and should be the best protectors of their own wild fauna and flora;

RECOGNIZING, in addition, that international cooperation is essential for the protection of certain species of wild fauna and flora against over-exploitation through international trade;

CONVINCED of the urgency of taking appropriate measures to this end;

HAVE AGREED as follows:

ARTICLE I

Definitions

For the purpose of the present Convention, unless the context otherwise requires:

(a) "Species" means any species, subspecies, or geographically separate population thereof;

(b) "Specimen" means:

(i) any animal or plant, whether alive or dead;

(ii) in the case of an animal: for species included in Appendices I and II, any readily recognizable part or derivative thereof; and for species included in Appendix III, any readily recognizable part or derivative thereof specified in Appendix III in relation to the species; and

(iii) in the case of a plant: for species included in Appendix I, any readily recognizable part or derivative thereof; and for species included in Appendices II and III, any readily recognizable part or derivative thereof specified in Appendices II and III in relation to the species;

(c) "Trade" means export, re-export, import and introduction from the sea;

(d) "Re-export" means export of any specimen that has previously been imported;

(e) "Introduction from the sea" means transportation into a State of specimens of any species which were taken in the marine environment not under the jurisdiction of any State;

(f) "Scientific Authority" means a national scientific authority designated in accordance with Article IX;

(g) "Management Authority" means a national management authority designated in accordance with Article IX;

(h) "Party" means a State for which the present Convention has entered into force.

ARTICLE II

Fundamental Principles

1. Appendix I shall include all species threatened with extinction which are or may be affected by trade. Trade in specimens of these species must be subject to particularly strict regulation in order not to endanger further their survival and must only be authorized in exceptional circumstances.

2. Appendix II shall include:

(a) all species which although not necessarily now threatened with extinction may become so unless trade in specimens of such species is subject to strict regulation in order to avoid utilization incompatible with their survival; and

(b) other species which must be subject to regulation in order that trade in specimens of certain species referred to in sub-paragraph (a) of this paragraph may be brought under effective control.

3. Appendix III shall include all species which any Party identifies as being subject to regulation within its jurisdiction for the purpose of preventing or restricting exploitation, and as needing the cooperation of other parties in the control of trade.

4. The Parties shall not allow trade in specimens of species included in Appendices I, II and III except in accordance with the provisions of the present Convention.

ARTICLE III

Regulation of Trade in Specimens of Species included in Appendix I

1. All trade in specimens of species included in Appendix I shall be in accordance with the provisions of this Article.

2. The export of any specimen of a species included in Appendix I shall require the prior grant and presentation of an export permit. An export permit shall only be granted when the following conditions have been met:

(a) a Scientific Authority of the State of export has advised that such export will not be detrimental to the survival of that species;

(b) a Management Authority of the State of export is satisfied that the specimen was not obtained in contravention of the laws of that State for the protection of fauna and flora;

(c) a Management Authority of the State of export is satisfied that any living specimen will be so prepared and shipped as to minimize the risk of injury, damage to health or cruel treatment; and

(d) a Management Authority of the State of export is satisfied that an import permit has been granted for the specimen.

3. The import of any specimen of a species included in Appendix I shall require the prior grant and presentation of an import permit and either an export permit or a re-export certificate. An import permit shall only be granted when the following conditions have been met:

(a) a Scientific Authority of the State of import has advised that the import will be for purposes which are not detrimental to the survival of the species involved;

(b) a Scientific Authority of the State of import is satisfied that the proposed recipient of a living specimen is suitably equipped to house and care for it; and

(c) a Management Authority of the State of import is satisfied that the specimen is not to be used for primarily commercial purposes.

4. The re-export of any specimen of a species included in Appendix I shall require the prior grant and presentation of a re-export certificate. A re-export certificate shall only be granted when the following conditions have been met:

(a) a Management Authority of the State of re-export is satisfied that the specimen was imported into that State in accordance with the provisions of the present Convention;

(b) a Management Authority of the State of re-export is satisfied that any living specimen will be so prepared and shipped as to minimize the risk of injury, damage to health or cruel treatment; and

(c) a Management Authority of the State of re-export is satisfied that an import permit has been granted for any living specimen.

5. The introduction from the sea of any specimen of a species included in Appendix I shall require the prior grant of a certificate from a Management Authority of the State of introduction. A certificate shall only be granted when the following conditions have been met:

(a) a Scientific Authority of the State of introduction advises that the introduction will not be detrimental to the survival of the species involved;

(b) a Management Authority of the State of introduction is satisfied that the proposed recipient of a living specimen is suitably equipped to house and care for it; and

(c) a Management Authority of the State of introduction is satisfied that the specimen is not to be used for primarily commercial purposes.

ARTICLE IV

Regulation of Trade in Specimens of Species included in Appendix II

1. All trade in specimens of species included in Appendix II shall be in accordance with the provisions of this Article.

2. The export of any specimen of a species included in Appendix II shall require the prior grant and presentation of an export permit. An export permit shall only be granted when the following conditions have been met:

(a) a Scientific Authority of the State of export has advised that such export will not be detrimental to the survival of that species;

(b) a Management Authority of the State of export is satisfied that the specimen was not obtained in contravention of the laws of that State for the protection of fauna and flora; and

(c) a Management Authority of the State of export is satisfied that any living specimen will be so prepared and shipped as to minimize the risk of injury, damage to health or cruel treatment.

3. A Scientific Authority in each Party shall monitor both the export permits granted by that State for specimens of species included in Appendix II and the actual exports of such specimens. Whenever a Scientific Authority determines that the export of specimens of any such species should be limited in order to maintain that species throughout its range at a level consistent with its role in the ecosystems in which it occurs and well above the level at which that species might become eligible for inclusion in Appendix I, the Scientific Authority shall advise the appropriate Management Authority of suitable measures to be taken to limit the grant of export permits for specimens of that species.

4. The import of any specimen of a species included in Appendix II shall require the prior presentation of either an export permit or a re-export certificate.

5. The re-export of any specimen of a species included in Appendix II shall require the prior grant and presentation of a re-export certificate. A re-export certificate shall only be granted when the following conditions have been met:

(a) a Management Authority of the State of re-export is satisfied that the specimen was imported into that State in accordance with the provisions of the present Convention; and

(b) a Management Authority of the State of re-export is satisfied that any living specimen will be so prepared and shipped as to minimize the risk of injury, damage to health or cruel treatment.

6. The introduction from the sea of any specimen of a species included in Appendix II shall require the prior grant of a certificate from a Management Authority of the State of introduction. A certificate shall only be granted when the following conditions have been met:

(a) a Scientific Authority of the State of introduction advises that the introduction will not be detrimental to the survival of the species involved; and

(b) a Management Authority of the State of introduction is satisfied that any living specimen will be so handled as to minimize the risk of injury, damage to health or cruel treatment.

7. Certificates referred to in paragraph 6 of this Article may be granted on the advice of a Scientific Authority, in consultation with other national scientific authorities or, when appropriate, international scientific authorities, in respect of periods not exceeding one year for total numbers of specimens to be introduced in such periods.

ARTICLE V

Regulation of Trade in Specimens of Species included in Appendix III

1. All trade in specimens of species included in Appendix III shall be in accordance with the provisions of this Article.

2. The export of any specimen of a species included in Appendix III from any State which has included that species in Appendix III shall require the prior grant and presentation of an export permit. An export permit shall only be granted when the following conditions have been met:

(a) a Management Authority of the State of export is satisfied that the specimen was not obtained in contravention of the laws of that State for the protection of fauna and flora; and

(b) a Management Authority of the State of export is satisfied that any living specimen will be so prepared and shipped as to minimize the risk of injury, damage to health or cruel treatment.

3. The import of any specimen of a species included in Appendix III shall require, except in circumstances to which paragraph 4 of this Article applies, the prior presentation of a certificate of origin and, where the import is from a State which has included that species in Appendix III, an export permit.

4. In the case of re-export, a certificate granted by the Management Authority of the State of re-export that the specimen was processed in that State or is being re-exported shall be accepted by the State of import as evidence that the provisions of the present Convention have been complied with in respect of the specimen concerned.

ARTICLE VI

Permits and Certificates

1. Permits and certificates granted under the provisions of Articles III, IV, and V shall be in accordance with the provisions of this Article.

2. An export permit shall contain the information specified in the model set forth in Appendix IV, and may only be used for export within a period of six months from the date on which it was granted.

3. Each permit or certificate shall contain the title of the present Convention, the name and any identifying stamp of the Management Authority granting it and a control number assigned by the Management Authority.

4. Any copies of a permit or certificate issued by a Management Authority shall be clearly marked as copies only and no such copy may be used in place of the original, except to the extent endorsed thereon.

5. A separate permit or certificate shall be required for each consignment of specimens.

6. A Management Authority of the State of import of any specimen shall cancel and retain the export permit or re-export certificate and any corresponding import permit presented in respect of the import of that specimen.

7. Where appropriate and feasible a Management Authority may affix a mark upon any specimen to assist in identifying the specimen. For these purposes "mark" means any indelible imprint, lead seal or other suitable means of identifying a specimen, designed in such a way as to render its imitation by unauthorized persons as difficult as possible.

ARTICLE VII

Exemptions and Other Special Provisions Relating to Trade

1. The provisions of Articles III, IV and V shall not apply to the transit or trans-shipment of specimens through or in the territory of a Party while the specimens remain in Customs control.

2. Where a Management Authority of the State of export or re-export is satisfied that a specimen was acquired before the provisions of the present Convention applied to that specimen, the provisions of Articles III, IV and V shall not apply to that specimen where the Management Authority issues a certificate to that effect.

3. The provisions of Articles III, IV and V shall not apply to specimens that are personal or household effects. This exemption shall not apply where:

(a) in the case of specimens of a species included in Appendix I, they were acquired by the owner outside his State of usual residence, and are being imported into that State; or

(b) in the case of specimens of species included in Appendix II:

(i) they were acquired by the owner outside his State of usual residence and in a State where removal from the wild occurred;

(ii) they are being imported into the owner's State of usual residence; and

(iii) the State where removal from the wild occurred requires the prior grant of export permits before any export of such specimens;

unless a Management Authority is satisfied that the specimens were acquired before the provisions of the present Convention applied to such specimens.

4. Specimens of an animal species included in Appendix I bred in captivity for commercial purposes, or of a plant species included in Appendix I artificially

propagated for commercial purposes, shall be deemed to be specimens of species included in Appendix II.

5. Where a Management Authority of the State of export is satisfied that any specimen of an animal species was bred in captivity or any specimen of a plant species was artificially propagated, or is a part of such an animal or plant or was derived therefrom, a certificate by that Management Authority to that effect shall be accepted in lieu of any of the permits or certificates required under the provisions of Articles III, IV or V.

6. The provisions of Articles III, IV and V shall not apply to the non-commercial loan, donation or exchange between scientists or scientific institutions registered by a Management Authority of their State, of herbarium specimens, other preserved, dried or embedded museum specimens, and live plant material which carry a label issued or approved by a Management Authority.

7. A Management Authority of any State may waive the requirements of Articles III, IV and V and allow the movement without permits or certificates of specimens which form part of a travelling zoo, circus, menagerie, plant exhibition or other travelling exhibition provided that:

(a) the exporter or importer registers full details of such specimens with that Management Authority;

(b) the specimens are in either of the categories specified in paragraphs 2 or 5 of this Article; and

(c) the Management Authority is satisfied that any living specimen will be so transported and cared for as to minimize the risk of injury, damage to health or cruel treatment.

ARTICLE VIII

Measures to be Taken by the Parties

1. The Parties shall take appropriate measures to enforce the provisions of the present Convention and to prohibit trade in specimens in violation thereof. These shall include measures:

(a) to penalize trade in, or possession of, such specimens, or both; and

(b) to provide for the confiscation or return to the State of export of such specimens.

2. In addition to the measures taken under paragraph 1 of this Article, a Party may, when it deems it necessary, provide for any method of internal reimbursement for expenses incurred as a result of the confiscation of a specimen traded in violation of the measures taken in the application of the provisions of the present Convention.

3. As far as possible, the Parties shall ensure that specimens shall pass through any formalities required for trade with a minimum of delay. To facilitate such passage, a Party may designate ports of exit and ports of entry at which specimens must be presented for clearance. The Parties shall ensure further that all living specimens, during any period of transit, holding or shipment, are properly cared for so as to minimize the risk of injury, damage to health or cruel treatment.

4. Where a living specimen is confiscated as a result of measures referred to in paragraph 1 of this Article:

(a) the specimen shall be entrusted to a Management Authority of the State of confiscation;

(b) the Management Authority shall, after consultation with the State of export, return the specimen to that State at the expense of that State, or to a rescue centre or such other place as the Management Authority deems appropriate and consistent with the purposes of the present Convention; and

(c) the Management Authority may obtain the advice of a Scientific Authority, or may, whenever it considers it desirable, consult the Secretariat in order to facilitate the decision under subparagraph (b) of this paragraph, including the choice of a rescue centre or other place.

5. A rescue centre as referred to in paragraph 4 of this Article means an institution designated by a Management Authority to look after the welfare of living specimens, particularly those that have been confiscated.

6. Each Party shall maintain records of trade in specimens of species included in Appendices I, II and III which shall cover:

(a) the names and addresses of exporters and importers; and

(b) the number and type of permits and certificates granted; the States with which such trade occurred; the numbers or quantities and types of specimens, names of species as included in Appendices I, II and III and, where applicable, the size and sex of the specimens in question.

7. Each Party shall prepare periodic reports on its implementation of the present Convention and shall transmit to the Secretariat:

(a) an annual report containing a summary of the information specified in sub-paragraph (b) of paragraph 6 of this Article; and

(b) a biennial report on legislative, regulatory and administrative measures taken to enforce the provisions of the present Convention.

8. The information referred to in paragraph 7 of this Article shall be available to the public where this is not inconsistent with the law of the Party concerned.

ARTICLE IX

Management and Scientific Authorities

1. Each Party shall designate for the purposes of the present Convention:

(a) one or more Management Authorities competent to grant permits or certificates on behalf of that Party; and

(b) one or more Scientific Authorities.

2. A State depositing an instrument of ratification, acceptance, approval or accession shall at that time inform the Depositary Government of the name and address of the Management Authority authorized to communicate with other Parties and with the Secretariat.

3. Any changes in the designations or authorizations under the provisions of this Article shall be communicated by the Party concerned to the Secretariat for transmission to all other Parties.

4. Any Management Authority referred to in paragraph 2 of this Article shall if so requested by the Secretariat or the Management Authority of another Party, communicate to it impression of stamps, seals or other devices used to authenticate permits or certificates.

ARTICLE X

Trade With States Not Party to the Convention

Where export or re-export is to, or import is from, a State not a party to the present Convention, comparable documentation issued by the competent authorities in that State which substantially conforms with the requirements of the present Convention for permits and certificates may be accepted in lieu thereof by any Party.

ARTICLE XI

Conference of the Parties

1. The Secretariat shall call a meeting of the Conference of the Parties not later than two years after the entry into force of the present Convention.

2. Thereafter the Secretariat shall convene regular meetings at least once every two years, unless the Conference decides otherwise, and extraordinary meetings at any time on the written request of at least one-third of the Parties.

3. At meetings, whether regular or extraordinary, the Parties shall review the implementation of the present Convention and may:

(a) make such provision as may be necessary to enable the Secretariat to carry out its duties;

(b) consider and adopt amendments to Appendices I and II in accordance with Article XV;

(c) review the progress made towards the restoration and conservation of the species included in Appendices I, II and III;

(d) receive and consider any reports presented by the Secretariat or by any Party; and

(e) where appropriate, make recommendations for improving the effectiveness of the present Convention.

* * *

ARTICLE XII

The Secretariat

1. Upon entry into force of the present Convention, a Secretariat shall be provided by the Executive Director of the United Nations Environment Programme. To the extent and in the manner he considers appropriate, he may be assisted by suitable inter-governmental or non-governmental international or national agencies and bodies technically qualified in protection, conservation and management of wild fauna and flora.

* * *

ARTICLE XIII

International Measures

1. When the Secretariat in the light of information received is satisfied that any species included in Appendices I or II is being affected adversely by trade in specimens of that species or that the provisions of the present Convention are not being effectively implemented, it shall communicate such information to the authorized Management Authority of the Party or Parties concerned.

2. When any Party receives a communication as indicated in paragraph 1 of this Article, it shall, as soon as possible, inform the Secretariat of any relevant facts insofar as its laws permit and, where appropriate, propose remedial action. Where the Party considers that an inquiry is desirable, such inquiry may be carried out by one or more persons expressly authorized by the Party.

3. The information provided by the Party or resulting from any inquiry as specified in paragraph 2 of this Article shall be reviewed by the next Conference of the Parties which may make whatever recommendations it deems appropriate.

ARTICLE XIV

Effect on Domestic Legislation and International Conventions

1. The provisions of the present Convention shall in no way affect the right of Parties to adopt:

(a) stricter domestic measures regarding the conditions for trade, taking possession or transport of specimens of species included in Appendices I, II and III, or the complete prohibition thereof; or

(b) domestic measures restricting or prohibiting trade, taking possession, or transport of species not included in Appendices I, II or III.

2. The provisions of the present Convention shall in no way affect the provisions of any domestic measures or the obligations of Parties deriving from any treaty, convention, or international agreement relating to other aspects of trade, taking possession, or transport of specimens which is in force or subsequently may enter into force for any Party including any measure pertaining to the Customs, public health, veterinary or plant quarantine fields.

3. The provisions of the present Convention shall in no way affect the provisions of, or the obligations deriving from, any treaty, convention or international agreement concluded or which may be concluded between States creating a union or regional trade agreement establishing or maintaining a common external customs control and removing customs control between the parties thereto insofar as they relate to trade among the States members of that union or agreement.

4. A State party to the present Convention, which is also a party to any other treaty, convention or international agreement which is in force at the time of the coming into force of the present Convention and under the provisions of which protection is afforded to marine species included in Appendix II, shall be relieved of the obligations imposed on it under the provisions of the present Convention with respect to trade in specimens of species included in Appendix II that are taken by ships registered in that State and in accordance with the provisions of such other treaty, convention or international agreement.

5. Notwithstanding the provisions of Articles III, IV and V, any export of a specimen taken in accordance with paragraph 4 of this Article shall only require a certificate from a Management Authority of the State of introduction to the effect that the specimen was taken in accordance with the provisions of the other treaty, convention or international agreement in question.

6. Nothing in the present Convention shall prejudice the codification and development of the law of the sea by the United Nations Conference on the Law of the Sea convened pursuant to Resolution 2750 C (XXV) of the General Assembly of the United Nations nor the present or future claims and legal views of any State concerning the law of the sea and the nature and extent of coastal and flag State jurisdiction.

* * *

ARTICLE XVIII

Resolution of Disputes

1. Any dispute which may arise between two or more Parties with respect to the interpretation or application of the provisions of the present Convention shall be subject to negotiation between the Parties involved in the dispute.

2. If the dispute cannot be resolved in accordance with paragraph 1 of this Article, the Parties may, by mutual consent, submit the dispute to arbitration, in

particular that of the Permanent Court of Arbitration at The Hague, and the Parties submitting the dispute shall be bound by the arbitral decision.

* * *

ARTICLE XXIV

Denunciation

Any Party may denounce the present Convention by written notification to the Depositary Government at any time. The denunciation shall take effect twelve months after the Depositary Government has received the notification.

5.20 INTERNATIONAL CONVENTION FOR THE PREVENTION OF POLLUTION FROM SHIPS, WITH ANNEX I.[a] Done at London, Nov. 2, 1973. I.N.C.O. Doc. MP/CONF/WP. 35 (1973), *reproduced in* 12 I.L.M. 1319 (1973)[b]

ARTICLE 1

General Obligations under the Convention

(1) The Parties to the Convention undertake to give effect to the provisions of the present Convention and those Annexes thereto by which they are bound, in order to prevent the pollution of the marine environment by the discharge of harmful substances or effluents containing such substances in contravention of the Convention.

(2) Unless expressly provided otherwise, a reference to the present Convention constitutes at the same time a reference to its Protocols and to the Annexes.

ARTICLE 2

Definitions

For the purposes of the present Convention, unless expressly provided otherwise:

(1) "Regulations" means the Regulations contained in the Annexes to the present Convention.

(2) "Harmful substance" means any substance which, if introduced into the sea, is liable to create hazards to human health, to harm living resources and marine life, to damage amenities or to interfere with other legitimate uses of the sea, and includes any substance subject to control by the present Convention.

(3)(a) "Discharge", in relation to harmful substances or effluents containing such substances, means any release howsoever caused from a ship and includes any escape, disposal, spilling, leaking, pumping, emitting or emptying.

(b) "Discharge" does not include:

(i) dumping within the meaning of the Convention on the Prevention of Marine Pollution by Dumping of Wastes and Other Matter done at London on 13 November 1972; or

(ii) release of harmful substances directly arising from the exploration, exploitation and associated off-shore processing of sea-bed mineral resources; or

a. Annex I here includes only limited excerpts. Annex II ("Regulations for the Control of Pollution by Noxious Liquid Substances [e.g., chemicals] in Bulk") is omitted, as are also Annexes III–V ("Optional Annexes") and Protocols I ("Provisions Concerning Reports on Incidents Involving Harmful Substances") and II ("Arbitration").

b. This Convention is not intended to enter into force and be applied on its own. Accordingly, as of Oct. 2, 1983, the regime applied by the States Parties to the Protocol of Feb. 17, 1978 (Basic Document 5.22) is the regime contained in this 1973 Convention as modified by the 1978 Protocol. For other notable instruments pertaining to marine pollution, see International Convention on Civil Liberty for Oil Pollution Damage, done at Brussels, Nov. 29, 1969, entered into force, June 19, 1975, 1969 U.N. JURID.Y.B. 174, *reprinted in* 9 I.L.M. 45 (1970); International Convention on the Establishment of an International Fund for Compensation for Oil Pollution Damage, done at Brussels, Dec. 18, 1971, entered into force, Oct. 16, 1978, 1971 U.N. JURID.Y.B. 103, *reprinted in* 11 I.L.M. 284 (1972); Convention for the Prevention of Marine Pollution from Land–Based Sources, done at Paris, June 4, 1974, entered into force, May 6, 1978, *reproduced in* 13 I.L.M. 352 (1974); Convention on Civil Liability for Oil Pollution Damage Resulting from the Exploration and Exploitation of the Seabed Mineral Resources, done at London, Apr. 30, 1978. This last convention had not entered into force as of Dec. 31, 1989. *See also* Basic Documents 5.3, 5.13 and 5.18, *supra*.

(iii) release of harmful substances for purposes of legitimate scientific research into pollution abatement or control.

(4) "Ship" means a vessel of any type whatsoever operating in the marine environment and includes hydrofoil boats, air-cushion vehicles, submersibles, floating craft and fixed or floating platforms.

(5) "Administration" means the Government of the State under whose authority the ship is operating. With respect to a ship entitled to fly a flag of any State, the Administration is the Government of that State. With respect to fixed or floating platforms engaged in exploration and exploitation of the sea-bed and subsoil thereof adjacent to the coast over which the coastal State exercises sovereign rights for the purposes of exploration and exploitation of their natural resources, the Administration is the Government of the coastal State concerned.

(6) "Incident" means an event involving the actual or probable discharge into the sea of a harmful substance, or effluents containing such a substance.

(7) "Organization" means the Inter-governmental Maritime Consultative Organization.

ARTICLE 3

Application

(1) The present Convention shall apply to:

(a) ships entitled to fly the flag of a Party to the Convention; and

(b) ships not entitled to fly the flag of a Party but which operate under the authority of a Party.

(2) Nothing in the present Article shall be construed as derogating from or extending the sovereign rights of the Parties under international law over the sea-bed and subsoil thereof adjacent to their coasts for the purposes of exploration and exploitation of their natural resources.

(3) The present Convention shall not apply to any warship, naval auxiliary or other ship owned or operated by a State and used, for the time being, only on government non-commercial service. However, each Party shall ensure by the adoption of appropriate measures not impairing the operations or operational capabilities of such ships owned or operated by it, that such ships act in a manner consistent, so far as is reasonable and practicable, with the present Convention.

ARTICLE 4

Violation

(1) Any violation of the requirements of the present Convention shall be prohibited and sanctions shall be established therefor under the law of the Administration of the ship concerned wherever the violation occurs. If the Administration is informed of such a violation and is satisfied that sufficient evidence is available to enable proceedings to be brought in respect of the alleged violation, it shall cause such proceedings to be taken as soon as possible, in accordance with its law.

(2) Any violation of the requirements of the present Convention within the jurisdiction of any Party to the Convention shall be prohibited and sanctions shall be established therefor under the law of that Party. Whenever such a violation occurs, that Party shall either:

(a) cause proceedings to be taken in accordance with its law; or

(b) furnish to the Administration of the ship such information and evidence as may be in its possession that a violation has occurred.

(3) Where information or evidence with respect to any violation of the present Convention by a ship is furnished to the Administration of that ship, the Administra-

tion shall promptly inform the Party which has furnished the information or evidence, and the Organization, of the action taken.

(4) The penalties specified under the law of a Party pursuant to the present Article shall be adequate in severity to discourage violations of the present Convention and shall be equally severe irrespective of where the violations occur.

ARTICLE 5

Certificates and Special Rules on Inspection of Ships

(1) Subject to the provisions of paragraph (2) of the present Article a certificate issued under the authority of a Party to the Convention in accordance with the provisions of the Regulations shall be accepted by the other Parties and regarded for all purposes covered by the present Convention as having the same validity as a certificate issued by them.

(2) A ship required to hold a certificate in accordance with the provisions of the Regulations is subject while in the ports or off-shore terminals under the jurisdiction of a Party to inspection by officers duly authorized by that Party. Any such inspection shall be limited to verifying that there is on board a valid certificate, unless there are clear grounds for believing that the condition of the ship or its equipment does not correspond substantially with the particulars of that certificate. In that case, or if the ship does not carry a valid certificate, the Party carrying out the inspection shall take such steps as will ensure that the ship shall not sail until it can proceed to sea without presenting an unreasonable threat of harm to the marine environment. That Party may, however, grant such a ship permission to leave the port or off-shore terminal for the purpose of proceeding to the nearest appropriate repair yard available.

(3) If a Party denies a foreign ship entry to the ports or off-shore terminals under its jurisdiction or takes any action against such a ship for the reason that the ship does not comply with the provisions of the present Convention, the Party shall immediately inform the consul or diplomatic representative of the Party whose flag the ship is entitled to fly, or if this is not possible, the Administration of the ship concerned. Before denying entry or taking such action the Party may request consultation with the Administration of the ship concerned. Information shall also be given to the Administration when a ship does not carry a valid certificate in accordance with the provisions of the Regulations.

(4) With respect to the ships of non-Parties to the Convention, Parties shall apply the requirements of the present Convention as may be necessary to ensure that no more favourable treatment is given to such ships.

ARTICLE 6

Detection of Violations and Enforcement of the Convention

(1) Parties to the Convention shall co-operate in the detection of violations and the enforcement of the provisions of the present Convention, using all appropriate and practicable measures of detection and environmental monitoring, adequate procedures for reporting and accumulation of evidence.

(2) A ship to which the present Convention applies may, in any port or off-shore terminal of a Party, be subject to inspection by officers appointed or authorized by that Party for the purpose of verifying whether the ship has discharged any harmful substances in violation of the provisions of the Regulations. If an inspection indicates a violation of the Convention, a report shall be forwarded to the Administration for any appropriate action.

(3) Any Party shall furnish to the Administration evidence, if any, that the ship has discharged harmful substances or effluents containing such substances in viola-

tion of the provisions of the Regulations. If it is practicable to do so, the competent authority of the former Party shall notify the master of the ship of the alleged violation.

(4) Upon receiving such evidence, the Administration so informed shall investigate the matter, and may request the other Party to furnish further or better evidence of the alleged contravention. If the Administration is satisfied that sufficient evidence is available to enable proceedings to be brought in respect of the alleged violation, it shall cause such proceedings to be taken in accordance with its law as soon as possible. The Administration shall promptly inform the Party which has reported the alleged violation, as well as the Organization, of the action taken.

(5) A Party may also inspect a ship to which the present Convention applies when it enters the ports or off-shore terminals under its jurisdiction, if a request for an investigation is received from any Party together with sufficient evidence that the ship has discharged harmful substances or effluents containing such substances in any place. The report of such investigation shall be sent to the Party requesting it and to the Administration so that the appropriate action may be taken under the present Convention.

ARTICLE 7

Undue Delay to Ships

(1) All possible efforts shall be made to avoid a ship being unduly detained or delayed under Articles 4, 5 and 6 of the present Convention.

(2) When a ship is unduly detained or delayed under Articles 4, 5 and 6 of the present Convention, it shall be entitled to compensation for any loss or damage suffered.

ARTICLE 8

Reports on Incidents Involving Harmful Substances

(1) A report of an incident shall be made without delay to the fullest extent possible in accordance with the provisions of Protocol I to the present Convention.

(2) Each Party to the Convention shall:

(a) make all arrangements necessary for an appropriate officer or agency to receive and process all reports on incidents; and

(b) notify the Organization with complete details of such arrangements for circulation to other Parties and Member States of the Organization.

(3) Whenever a Party receives a report under the provisions of the present Article, that Party shall relay the report without delay to:

(a) the Administration of the ship involved; and

(b) any other State which may be affected.

(4) Each Party to the Convention undertakes to issue instructions to its maritime inspection vessels and aircraft and to other appropriate services, to report to its authorities any incident referred to in Protocol I to the present Convention. That Party shall, if it considers it appropriate, report accordingly to the Organization and to any other party concerned.

ARTICLE 9

Other Treaties and Interpretation

(1) Upon its entry into force, the present Convention supersedes the International Convention for the Prevention of Pollution of the Sea by Oil, 1954, as amended, as between Parties to that Convention.

(2) Nothing in the present Convention shall prejudice the codification and development of the law of the sea by the United Nations Conference on the Law of the Sea convened pursuant to Resolution 2750 C(XXV) of the General Assembly of the United Nations nor the present or future claims and legal views of any State concerning the law of the sea and the nature and extent of coastal and flag State jurisdiction.

(3) The term "jurisdiction" in the present Convention shall be construed in the light of international law in force at the time of application or interpretation of the present Convention.

ARTICLE 10

Settlement of Disputes

Any dispute between two or more Parties to the Convention concerning the interpretation or application of the present Convention shall, if settlement by negotiation between the Parties involved has not been possible, and if these Parties do not otherwise agree, be submitted upon request of any of them to arbitration as set out in Protocol II to the present Convention.

ARTICLE 11

Communication of Information

(1) The Parties to the Convention undertake to communicate to the Organization:

(a) the text of laws, orders, decrees and regulations and other instruments which have been promulgated on the various matters within the scope of the present Convention;

(b) a list of non-governmental agencies which are authorized to act on their behalf in matters relating to the design, construction and equipment of ships carrying harmful substances in accordance with the provisions of the Regulations;

(c) a sufficient number of specimens of their certificates issued under the provisions of the Regulations;

(d) a list of reception facilities including their location, capacity and available facilities and other characteristics;

(e) official reports or summaries of official reports in so far as they show the results of the application of the present Convention; and

(f) an annual statistical report, in a form standardised by the Organization, of penalties actually imposed for infringement of the present Convention.

(2) The Organization shall notify Parties of the receipt of any communications under the present Article and circulate to all Parties any information communicated to it under sub-paragraphs (1)(b) to (f) of the present Article.

ARTICLE 12

Casualties to Ships

(1) Each Administration undertakes to conduct an investigation of any casualty occurring to any of its ships subject to the provisions of the Regulations if such casualty has produced a major deleterious effect upon the marine environment.

(2) Each Party to the Convention undertakes to supply the Organization with information concerning the findings of such investigation, when it judges that such information may assist in determining what changes in the present Convention might be desirable.

* * *

ARTICLE 14

Optional Annexes

(1) A State may at the time of signing, ratifying, accepting, approving or acceding to the present Convention declare that it does not accept any one or all of Annexes III, IV and V (hereinafter referred to as "Optional Annexes") of the present Convention. Subject to the above, Parties to the Convention shall be bound by any Annex in its entirety.

* * *

ARTICLE 17

Promotion of Technical Co-operation

The Parties to the Convention shall promote, in consultation with the Organization and other international bodies, with assistance and co-ordination by the Executive Director of the United Nations Environment Programme, support for those Parties which request technical assistance for:

(a) the training of scientific and technical personnel;

(b) the supply of necessary equipment and facilities for reception and monitoring;

(c) the facilitation of other measures and arrangements to prevent or mitigate pollution of the marine environment by ships; and

(d) the encouragement of research;

preferably within the countries concerned, so furthering the aims and purposes of the present Convention.

ARTICLE 18

Denunciation

(1) The present Convention or any Optional Annex may be denounced by any Parties to the Convention at any time after the expiry of five years from the date on which the Convention or such Annex enters into force for that Party.

(2) Denunciation shall be effected by notification in writing to the Secretary-General of the Organization who shall inform all the other Parties of any such notification received and of the date of its receipt as well as the date on which such denunciation takes effect.

(3) A denunciation shall take effect twelve months after receipt of the notification of denunciation by the Secretary-General of the Organization or after the expiry of any other longer period which may be indicated in the notification.

* * *

ANNEX I

REGULATIONS FOR THE PREVENTION OF POLLUTION BY OIL

CHAPTER I

GENERAL

Regulation 1

Definitions

For the purposes of this Annex:

(1) "Oil" means petroleum in any form including crude oil, fuel oil, sludge, oil refuse and refined products (other than petrochemicals which are subject to the provisions of Annex II of the present Convention) and, without limiting the generality of the foregoing, includes the substances listed in Appendix I to this Annex.

(2) "Oily mixture" means a mixture with any oil content.

(3) "Oil fuel" means any oil used as fuel in connexion with the propulsion and auxiliary machinery of the ship in which such oil is carried.

(4) "Oil tanker" means a ship constructed or adapted primarily to carry oil in bulk in its cargo spaces and includes combination carriers and any "chemical tanker" as defined in Annex II of the present Convention when it is carrying a cargo or part cargo of oil in bulk.

(5) "Combination carrier" means a ship designed to carry either oil or solid cargoes in bulk.

(6) "New ship" means a ship:

(a) for which the building contract is placed after 31 December 1975; or

(b) in the absence of a building contract, the keel of which is laid or which is at a similar stage of construction after 30 June 1976; or

(c) the delivery of which is after 31 December 1979; or

(d) which has undergone a major conversion:

(i) for which the contract is placed after 31 December 1975; or

(ii) in the absence of a contract, the construction work of which is begun after 30 June 1976; or

(iii) which is completed after 31 December 1979.

(7) "Existing ship" means a ship which is not a new ship.

* * *

(9) "Nearest land". The term "from the nearest land" means from the baseline from which the territorial sea of the territory in question is established in accordance with international law, except [in the case of the northeastern coast of Australia, which involves special calculations].

(10) "Special area" means a sea area where for recognized technical reasons in relation to its oceanographical and ecological condition and to the particular character of its traffic the adoption of special mandatory methods for the prevention of sea pollution by oil is required. Special areas shall include those listed in Regulation 10 of this Annex.

(11) "Instantaneous rate of discharge of oil content" means the rate of discharge of oil in litres per hour at any instant divided by the speed of the ship in knots at the same instant.

(12) "Tank" means an enclosed space which is formed by the permanent structure of a ship and which is designed for the carriage of liquid in bulk.

(13) "Wing tank" means any tank adjacent to the side shell plating.

(14) "Centre tank" means any tank inboard of a longitudinal bulkhead.

(15) "Slop tank" means a tank specifically designated for the collection of tank drainings, tank washings and other oily mixtures.

(16) "Clean ballast" means the ballast in a tank which since oil was last carried therein, has been so cleaned that effluent therefrom if it were discharged from a ship which is stationary into clean calm water on a clear day would not produce visible traces of oil on the surface of the water or on adjoining shore lines or cause a sludge or emulsion to be deposited beneath the surface of the water or upon adjoining shore lines. If the ballast is discharged through an oil discharge monitoring and control system approved by the Administration, evidence based on such a system to the effect that the oil content of the effluent did not exceed 15 parts per million shall be determinative that the ballast was clean, notwithstanding the presence of visible traces.

(17) "Segregated ballast" means the ballast water introduced into a tank which is completely separated from the cargo oil and oil fuel system and which is permanently allocated to the carriage of ballast or to the carriage of ballast or cargoes other than oil or noxious substances as variously defined in the Annexes of the present Convention.

(18) "Length" (L) means 96 per cent of the total length on a waterline at 85 per cent of the least moulded depth measured from the top of the keel, or the length from the foreside of the stem to the axis of the rudder stock on that waterline, if that be greater. In ships designed with a rake of keel the waterline on which this length is measured shall be parallel to the designed waterline. The length (L) shall be measured in metres.

(19) "Forward and after perpendiculars" shall be taken at the forward and after ends of the length (L). The forward perpendicular shall coincide with the foreside of the stem on the waterline on which the length is measured.

(20) "Amidships" is at the middle of the length (L).

(21) "Breadth" (B) means the maximum breadth of the ship, measured amidships to the moulded line of the frame in a ship with a metal shell and to the outer surface of the hull in a ship with a shell of any other material. The breadth (B) shall be measured in metres.

(22) "Deadweight" (DW) means the difference in metric tons between the displacement of a ship in water of a specific gravity of 1.025 at the load waterline corresponding to the assigned summer freeboard and the lightweight of the ship.

* * *

(24) "Permeability" of a space means the ratio of the volume within that space which is assumed to be occupied by water to the total volume of that space.

(25) "Volumes" and "areas" in a ship shall be calculated in all cases to moulded lines.

Regulation 2

Application

(1) Unless expressly provided otherwise, the provisions of this Annex shall apply to all ships.

(2) In ships other than oil tankers fitted with cargo spaces which are constructed and utilized to carry oil in bulk or an aggregate capacity of 200 cubic metres or more, the requirements of Regulations 9, 10, 14, 15(1), (2) and (3), 18, 20 and 24(4) of this Annex for oil tankers shall also apply to the construction and operation of those spaces, except that where such aggregate capacity is less than 1,000 cubic metres the requirements of Regulation 15(4) of this Annex may apply in lieu of Regulation 15(1), (2) and (3).

(3) Where a cargo subject to the provisions of Annex II of the present Convention is carried in a cargo space of an oil tanker, the appropriate requirements of Annex II of the present Convention shall also apply.

(4)(a) Any hydrofoil, air-cushion vehicle and other new type of vessel (near-surface craft, submarine craft, etc.) whose constructional features are such as to render the application of any of the provisions of Chapters II and III of this Annex relating to construction and equipment unreasonable or impracticable may be exempted by the Administration from such provisions, provided that the construction and equipment of that ship provides equivalent protection against pollution by oil, having regard to the service for which it is intended.

(b) Particulars of any such exemption granted by the Administration shall be indicated in the Certificate referred to in Regulation 5 of this Annex.

(c) The Administration which allows any such exemption shall, as soon as possible, but not more than ninety days thereafter, communicate to the Organization particulars of same and the reasons therefor, which the Organization shall circulate to the Parties to the Convention for their information and appropriate action, if any.

* * *

CHAPTER II

REQUIREMENTS FOR CONTROL OF OPERATIONAL POLLUTION

Regulation 9

Control of Discharge of Oil

(1) Subject to the provisions of Regulations 10 and 11 of this Annex and paragraph (2) of this Regulation, any discharge into the sea of oil or oily mixtures from ships to which this Annex applies shall be prohibited except when all the following conditions are satisfied:

(a) for an oil tanker, except as provided for in sub-paragraph (b) of this paragraph:

(i) the tanker is not within a special area;

(ii) the tanker is more than 50 nautical miles from the nearest land;

(iii) the tanker is proceeding en route;

(iv) the instantaneous rate of discharge of oil content does not exceed 60 litres per nautical mile;

(v) the total quantity of oil discharged into the sea does not exceed for existing tankers 1/15,000 of the total quantity of the particular cargo of which the residue formed a part, and for new tankers 1/30,000 of the total quantity of the particular cargo of which the residue formed a part; and

(vi) the tanker has in operation, except as provided for in Regulation 15(3) of this Annex, an oil discharge monitoring and control system and a slop tank arrangement as required by Regulation 15 of this Annex;

(b) from a ship of 400 tons gross tonnage and above other than an oil tanker and from machinery space bilges excluding cargo pump room bilges of an oil tanker unless mixed with oil cargo residue:

(i) the ship is not within a special area;

(ii) the ship is more than 12 nautical miles from the nearest land;

(iii) the ship is proceeding en route;

(iv) the oil content of the effluent is less than 100 parts per million; and

(v) the ship has in operation an oil discharge monitoring and control system, oily water separating equipment, oil filtering system or other installation as required by Regulation 16 of this Annex.

(2) In the case of a ship of less than 400 tons gross tonnage other than an oil tanker whilst outside the special area, the Administration shall ensure that it is equipped as far as practicable and reasonable with installations to ensure the storage of oil residues on board and their discharge to reception facilities or into the sea in compliance with the requirements of paragraph (1)(b) of this Regulation.

(3) Whenever visible traces of oil are observed on or below the surface of the water in the immediate vicinity of a ship or its wake, Governments of Parties to the Convention should, to the extent they are reasonably able to do so, promptly investigate the facts bearing on the issue of whether there has been a violation of the provisions of this Regulation or Regulation 10 of this Annex. The investigation should include, in particular, the wind and sea conditions, the track and speed of the

ship, other possible sources of the visible traces in the vicinity, and any relevant oil discharge records.

(4) The provisions of paragraph (1) of this Regulation shall not apply to the discharge of clean or segregated ballast. The provisions of sub-paragraph (1)(b) of this Regulation shall not apply to the discharge of oily mixture which without dilution has an oil content not exceeding 15 parts per million.

(5) No discharge into the sea shall contain chemicals or other substances in quantities or concentrations which are hazardous to the marine environment or chemicals or other substances introduced for the purpose of circumventing the conditions of discharge specified in this Regulation.

(6) The oil residues which cannot be discharged into the sea in compliance with paragraphs (1), (2) and (4) of this Regulation shall be retained on board or discharged to reception facilities.

* * *

Regulation 11

Exception

Regulations 9 and 10 of this Annex shall not apply to:

(a) the discharge into the sea of oil or oily mixture necessary for the purpose of securing the safety of a ship or saving life at sea; or

(b) the discharge into the sea of oil or oily mixture resulting from damage to a ship or its equipment;

(i) provided that all reasonable precautions have been taken after the occurrence of the damage or discovery of the discharge for the purpose of preventing or minimizing the discharge; and

(ii) except if the owner or the Master acted either with intent to cause damage, or recklessly and with knowledge that damage would probably result; or

(c) the discharge into the sea of substances containing oil, approved by the Administration, when being used for the purpose of combating specific pollution incidents in order to minimize the damage from pollution. Any such discharge shall be subject to the approval of any Government in whose jurisdiction it is contemplated the discharge will occur.

* * *

5.21 DRAFT PRINCIPLES OF CONDUCT IN THE FIELD OF THE ENVIRONMENT FOR THE GUIDANCE OF STATES IN THE CONSERVATION AND HARMONIOUS UTILIZATION OF NATURAL RESOURCES SHARED BY TWO OR MORE STATES. Report on the Work of the Fifth Session of the United Nations Environment Programme Intergovernmental Working Group of Experts on Natural Resources Shared by Two or More States, Nairobi, Jan. 23–Feb. 7, 1978. *Reproduced in* 17 I.L.M. 1098 (1978)

Principle 1

It is necessary for States to co-operate in the field of the environment concerning the conservation and harmonious utilization of natural resources shared by two or more States. Accordingly, it is necessary that consistent with the concept of equitable utilization of shared natural resources, States co-operate with a view to controlling, preventing, reducing or eliminating adverse environmental effects which may result from the utilization of such resources. Such co-operation is to take place on an equal footing and taking into account the sovereignty, rights and interests of the States concerned.

Principle 2

In order to ensure effective international co-operation in the field of the environment concerning the conservation and harmonious utilization of natural resources shared by two or more States, States sharing such natural resources should endeavor to conclude bilateral or multilateral agreements between or among themselves in order to secure specific regulation of their conduct in this respect, applying as necessary the present principles in a legally binding manner or should endeavor to enter into other arrangements, as appropriate, for this purpose. In entering into such agreements or arrangements, States should consider the establishment of institutional structures, such as joint international commissions, for consultations on environmental problems relating to the protection and use of shared natural resources.

Principle 3

1. States have, in accordance with the Charter of the United Nations and the principles of international law, the sovereign right to exploit their own resources pursuant to their own environmental policies, and the responsibility to ensure that activities within their jurisdiction or control do not cause damage to the environment of other States or of areas beyond the limits of national jurisdiction.

2. The principles set forth in paragraph 1, as well as the other principles contained in this document, apply to shared natural resources.

3. Accordingly, it is necessary for each State to avoid the maximum extent possible and to reduce to the minimum extent possible the adverse environmental effects beyond its jurisdiction of the utilization of a shared natural resource so as to protect the environment, in particular when such utilization might:

(*a*) cause damage to the environment which could have repercussions on the utilization of the resource by another sharing State;

(*b*) threaten the conservation of a shared renewable resource;

(*c*) endanger the health of the population of another State.

Without prejudice to the generality of the above principle, it should be interpreted, taking into account, where appropriate, the practical capabilities of States sharing the natural resource.

Principle 4

States should make environmental assessments before engaging in any activity with respect to a shared natural resource which may create a risk of significantly affecting the environment of another State or States sharing that resource.

Principle 5

States sharing a natural resource should, to the extent practicable, exchange information and engage in consultations on a regular basis on its environmental aspects.

Principle 6

1. It is necessary for every State sharing a natural resource with one or more other States:

(*a*) to notify in advance the other State or States of the pertinent details of plans to initiate, or make a change in, the conservation or utilization of the resource which can reasonably be expected to affect significantly the environment in the territory of the other State or States; and

(*b*) upon request of the other State or States, to enter into consultations concerning the above-mentioned plans; and

(*c*) to provide, upon request to that effect by the other State or States, specific additional pertinent information concerning such plans; and

(*d*) if there has been no advance notification as envisaged in sub-paragraph (a) above, to enter into consultations about such plans upon request of the other State or States.

2. In cases where the transmission of certain information is prevented by national legislation or international conventions, the State or States withholding such information shall nevertheless, on the basis, in particular, of the principle of good faith and in the spirit of good neighbourliness, co-operate with the other interested State or States with the aim of finding a satisfactory solution.

Principle 7

Exchange of information, notification, consultations and other forms of co-operation regarding shared natural resources are carried out on the basis of the principle of good faith and in the spirit of good neighbourliness and in such a way as to avoid any unreasonable delays either in the forms of co-operation or in carrying out development or conservation projects.

Principle 8

When it would be useful to clarify environmental problems relating to a shared natural resource, States should engage in joint scientific studies and assessments, with a view to facilitating the finding of appropriate and satisfactory solutions to such problems on the basis of agreed data.

Principle 9

1. States have a duty urgently to inform other States which may be affected:

(*a*) Of any emergency situation arising from the utilization of a shared natural resource which might cause sudden harmful effects on their environment;

(*b*) Of any sudden grave natural events related to a shared natural resource which may affect the environment of such States.

2. States should also, when appropriate, inform the competent international organizations of any such situation or event.

3. States concerned should co-operate, in particular by means of agreed contingency plans, when appropriate, and mutual assistance, in order to avert grave situations, and to eliminate, reduce or correct, as far as possible, the effects of such situations or events.

Principle 10

States sharing a natural resource should, when appropriate, consider the possibility of jointly seeking the services of any competent international organization in clarifying the environmental problems relating to the conservation or utilization of such natural resource.

Principle 11

1. The relevant provisions of the Charter of the United Nations and of the Declaration of Principles of International Law concerning Friendly Relations and Co-operation among States in accordance with the Charter of the United Nations apply to the settlement of environmental disputes arising out of the conservation or utilization of shared natural resources.

2. In case negotiations or other non-binding means have failed to settle a dispute within a reasonable time, it is necessary for States to submit the dispute to an appropriate settlement procedure which is mutually agreed by them, preferably in advance. The procedure should be speedy, effective and binding.

3. It is necessary for the States parties to such a dispute to refrain from any action which may aggravate the situation with respect to the environment to the extent of creating an obstacle to the amicable settlement of the dispute.

Principle 12

1. States are responsible for the fulfillment of their international obligations in the field of the environment concerning the conservation and utilization of shared natural resources. They are subject to liability in accordance with applicable international law for environmental damage resulting from violations of these obligations caused to areas beyond their jurisdiction.

2. States should co-operate to develop further international law regarding liability and compensation for the victims of environmental damage arising out of the utilization of a shared natural resource and caused to areas beyond their jurisdiction.

Principle 13

It is necessary for States, when considering, under their domestic environmental policy, the permissibility of domestic activities, to take into account the potential adverse environmental effects arising out of the utilization of shared natural resources, without discrimination as to whether the effects would occur within their jurisdiction or outside it.

Principle 14

States should endeavour, in accordance with their legal systems and, where appropriate, on a basis agreed by them, to provide persons in other States who have been or may be adversely affected by environmental damage resulting from the utilization of shared natural resources with equivalent access to and treatment in the same administrative and judicial proceedings, and make available to them the same remedies as are available to persons within their own jurisdictions who have been or may be similarly affected.

Principle 15

The present principles should be interpreted and applied in such a way as to enhance and not to affect adversely development and the interests of all countries, and in particular of the developing countries.

DEFINITION

In the present text, the expression "significantly affect" refers to any appreciable effects on a shared natural resource and excludes "*de minimis*" effects.

5.22 PROTOCOL OF 1978 RELATING TO THE INTERNATIONAL CONVENTION FOR THE PREVENTION OF POLLUTION FROM SHIPS, 1973, WITH ANNEX.[a] Done at London, Feb. 17, 1978. Entered into force, Oct. 2, 1983; for the United States, Oct. 2, 1983. I.M.C.O. Doc. TSPP/CONF/11 (1978), *reproduced in* 17 I.L.M. 546 (1978)[b]

ARTICLE I

General Obligations

1. The Parties to the present Protocol undertake to give effect to the provisions of:

(a) the present Protocol and the Annex hereto which shall constitute an integral part of the present Protocol; and

(b) the International Convention for the Prevention of Pollution from Ships, 1973 (hereinafter referred to as "the Convention"), subject to the modifications and additions set out in the present Protocol.

2. The provisions of the Convention and the present Protocol shall be read and interpreted together as one single instrument.

3. Every reference to the present Protocol constitutes at the same time a reference to the Annex hereto.

ARTICLE II

Implementation of Annex II of the Convention

1. Notwithstanding the provisions of Article 14(1) of the Convention, the Parties to the present Protocol agree that they shall not be bound by the provisions of Annex II of the Convention for a period of three years from the date of entry into force of the present Protocol or for such longer period as may be decided by a two-thirds majority of the Parties to the present Protocol in the Marine Environment Protection Committee (hereinafter referred to as "the Committee") of the Inter–Governmental Maritime Consultative Organization (hereinafter referred to as "the Organization").

2. During the period specified in paragraph 1 of this Article, the Parties to the present Protocol shall not be under any obligations nor entitled to claim any privileges under the Convention in respect of matters related to Annex II of the Convention and all reference to Parties in the Convention shall not include the Parties to the present Protocol in so far as matters related to that Annex are concerned.

a. The Annex here includes only limited excerpts.

b. This Protocol modifies the 1973 International Convention for the Prevention of Pollution from Ships (Basic Document 5.20) and is intended to be applied in conjunction therewith. For other notable instruments pertaining to marine pollution, see International Convention on Civil Liberty for Oil Pollution Damage, done at Brussels, Nov. 29, 1969, entered into force, June 19, 1975, 1969 U.N. JURID. Y.B. 174, *reprinted in* 9 I.L.M. 45 (1970); International Convention on the Establishment of an International Fund for Compensation for Oil Pollution Damage, done at Brussels, Dec. 18, 1971, entered into force, Oct. 16, 1978, 1971 U.N. JURID. Y.B. 103, *reprinted in* 11 I.L.M. 284 (1972); Convention for the Prevention of Marine Pollution from Land–Based Sources, done at Paris, June 4, 1974, entered into force, May 6, 1978, *reproduced in* 13 I.L.M. 352 (1974); Convention on Civil Liability for Oil Pollution Damage Resulting from the Exploration and Exploitation of the Seabed Mineral Resources, done at London, Apr. 30, 1978. This last convention had not entered into force as of Dec. 31, 1989. *See also* Basic Documents 5.3, 5.13 and 5.18, *supra*.

ARTICLE III

Communication of Information

The text of Article 11(1)(b) of the Convention is replaced by the following:

"a list of nominated surveyors or recognized organizations which are authorized to act on their behalf in the administration of matters relating to the design, construction, operation and equipment of ships carrying harmful substances in accordance with the provisions of the Regulations for circulation to the Parties for information of their officers. The Administration shall therefore notify the Organization of the specific responsibilities and conditions of the authority delegated to nominated surveyors or recognized organizations."

* * *

ARTICLE VII

Denunciation

1. The present Protocol may be denounced by any Party to the present Protocol at any time after the expiry of five years from the date on which the Protocol enters into force for that Party.

2. Denunciation shall be effected by the deposit of an instrument of denunciation with the Secretary–General of the Organization.

3. A denunciation shall take effect twelve months after receipt of the notification by the Secretary–General of the Organization or after the expiry of any other longer period which may be indicated in the notification.

* * *

ANNEX

MODIFICATIONS AND ADDITIONS TO THE INTERNATIONAL CONVENTION FOR THE PREVENTION OF POLLUTION FROM SHIPS, 1973

ANNEX I

REGULATIONS FOR THE PREVENTION OF POLLUTION BY OIL

Regulation 1

Definitions

Paragraphs (1) to (7), (9) to (22) and (24) to (25)—*No change*

The existing text of paragraph (8) is replaced by the following:

(8)(a) "Major conversion" means a conversion of an existing ship:

(i) which substantially alters the dimensions or carrying capacity of the ship; or

(ii) which changes the type of the ship; or

(iii) the intent of which in the opinion of the Administration is substantially to prolong its life; or

(iv) which otherwise so alters the ship that if it were a new ship, it would become subject to relevant provisions of the present Protocol not applicable to it as an existing ship.

(b) Notwithstanding the provisions of sub-paragraph (a) of this paragraph, conversion of an existing oil tanker of 20,000 tons deadweight and above to meet the requirements of Regulation 13 of this Annex shall not be deemed to constitute a major conversion for the purposes of this Annex.

The existing text of paragraph (23) is replaced by the following:

(23) "Lightweight" means the displacement of a ship in metric tons without cargo, fuel, lubricating oil, ballast water, fresh water and feed water in tanks, consumable stores, and passengers and crew and their effects.

The following paragraphs are added to the existing text:

(26) Notwithstanding the provisions of paragraph (6) of this Regulation, for the purposes of Regulations 13, 13B, 13E and 18(5) of this Annex, "new oil tanker" means an oil tanker:

(a) for which the building contract is placed after 1 June 1979; or

(b) in the absence of a building contract, the keel of which is laid, or which is at a similar stage of construction after 1 January 1980; or

(c) the delivery of which is after 1 June 1982; or

(d) which has undergone a major conversion:

(i) for which the contract is placed after 1 June 1979; or

(ii) in the absence of a contract, the construction work of which is begun after 1 January 1980; or

(iii) which is completed after 1 June 1982,

except that for oil tankers of 70,000 tons deadweight and above the definition in paragraph (6) of this Regulation shall apply for the purposes of Regulation 13(1) of this Annex.

(27) Notwithstanding the provisions of paragraph (7) of this Regulation, for the purposes of Regulations 13, 13A, 13B, 13C, 13D and 18(6) of this Annex, "existing oil tanker" means an oil tanker which is not a new oil tanker as defined in paragraph (26) of this Regulation.

(28) "Crude oil" means any oil occurring naturally in the earth whether or not treated to render it suitable for transportation and includes:

(a) crude oil from which certain distillate fractions may have been removed; and

(b) crude oil to which certain distillate fractions may have been added.

(29) "Crude oil tanker" means an oil tanker engaged in the trade of carrying crude oil.

(30) "Product carrier" means an oil tanker engaged in the trade of carrying oil other than crude oil.

Regulations 2 and 3—*No change*

* * *

Regulations 9–12—*No change*

* * *

5.23 TREATY FOR AMAZONIAN COOPERATION. Done at Brasilia, July 3, 1978. Not entered into force as of Dec. 31, 1989. *Reproduced in* 17 I.L.M. 1045 (1978) (English translation provided by the Embassy of the Republic of Brazil, Washington, D.C.)

The Republics of Bolivia, Brazil, Colombia, Ecuador, Guyana, Peru, Suriname and Venezuela,

CONSCIOUS of the importance to each one of the Parties of their respective Amazonian regions as an integral part of their respective territories,

INSPIRED by the common aim of pooling the efforts being made, both within their respective territories as well as among themselves, to promote the harmonious development of the Amazon region, to permit an equitable distribution of the benefits of said development among the Contracting Parties so as to raise the standard of living of their peoples and so as to achieve total incorporation of their Amazonian territories into their respective national economies,

CONSCIOUS of the usefulness of sharing national experiences in matters pertaining to the promotion of regional development,

CONSIDERING that, so as to achieve overall development of their respective Amazonian territories, it is necessary to maintain a balance between economic growth and conservation of the environment,

CONSCIOUS that both socio-economic development as well as conservation of the environment are responsibilities inherent in the sovereignty of each State, and that cooperation among the Contracting Parties shall facilitate fulfillment of these responsibilities, by continuing and expanding the joint efforts being made for the ecological conservation of the Amazon region,

CONFIDENT that cooperation among the Latin American nations on specific matters which they have in common shall contribute to progress on the road towards the integration and solidarity of all Latin America,

CONVINCED that this Treaty represents the beginning of a process of cooperation which shall benefit their respective countries and the Amazon region as a whole,

RESOLVE to sign the following Treaty:

Article I. The Contracting Parties agree to undertake joint actions and efforts to promote the harmonious development of their respective Amazonian territories in such a way that these joint actions produce equitable and mutually beneficial results and achieve also the preservation of the environment, and the conservation and rational utilization of the natural resources of those territories.

* * *

Article II. This Treaty shall be in force in the territories of the Contracting Parties in the Amazonian Basin as well as in any territory of a Contracting Party which, by virtue of its geographical, ecological or economic characteristics is considered closely connected with that Basin.

Article III. In accordance with and without prejudice to the rights granted by unilateral acts, to the provisions of bilateral treaties among the Parties and to the principles and rules of International Law, the Contracting Parties mutually guarantee on a reciprocal basis that there shall be complete freedom of commercial navigation on the Amazon and other international Amazonian rivers, observing the fiscal and police regulations in force now or in the future within the territory of each. Such regulations should, insofar as possible, be uniform and favour said navigation and trade.

Paragraph: This article shall not apply to cabotage.

Article IV. The Contracting Parties declare that the exclusive use and utilization of natural resources within their respective territories is a right inherent in the sovereignty of each state and that the exercise of this right shall not be subject to any restrictions other than those arising from International Law.

Article V. Taking account of the importance and multiplicity of the functions which the Amazonian rivers have in the process of economic and social development of the region, the Contracting Parties shall make efforts aimed at achieving rational utilization of the hydro resources.

Article VI. In order to enable the Amazonian rivers to become an effective communication link among the Contracting Parties and with the Atlantic Ocean, the riparian states interested in any specific problem affecting free and unimpeded navigation shall, as circumstances may warrant, undertake national, bilateral or multilateral measures aimed at improving and making the said rivers navigable.

* * *

Article VII. Taking into account the need for the exploitation of the flora and fauna of the Amazon region to be rationally planned so as to maintain the ecological balance within the region and preserve the species, the Contracting Parties decide to:

(a) Promote scientific research and exchange information and technical personnel among the competent agencies within the respective countries so as to increase their knowledge of the flora and fauna of their Amazon territories and prevent and control diseases in said territories.

(b) Establish a regular system for the proper exchange of information on the conservationist measures adopted or to be adopted by each State in its Amazonian territories; these shall be the subject of an annual report to be presented by each country.

Article VIII. The Contracting Parties decide to promote coordination of the present health services in their respective Amazonian territories and to take other appropriate measures to improve the sanitary conditions in the region and perfect methods for preventing and combating epidemics.

Article IX. The Contracting Parties agree to establish close cooperation in the fields of scientific and technological research, for the purpose of creating more suitable conditions for the acceleration of the economic and social development of the region.

Paragraph One: For purposes of this Treaty, the technical and scientific cooperation among the Contracting Parties may be as follows:

(a) Joint or coordinated implementation of research and development programmes;

(b) Creation and operation of research institutions or centres for improvement and experimental production;

(c) Organization of seminars and conferences, exchange of information and documentation, and organization of means for their dissemination.

Paragraph Two: The Contracting Parties may, whensoever they deem it necessary and convenient, request the participation of international agencies in the execution of studies, programmes and projects resulting from the forms of technical and scientific cooperation defined in Paragraph One of this Article.

Article X. The Contracting Parties agree on the advisability of creating a suitable physical infrastructure among their respective countries, especially in relation to transportation and communications. They therefore undertake to study the most harmonious ways of establishing or improving road, river, air and telecommunication links bearing in mind the plans and programmes of each country aimed at attaining the priority goal of fully incorporating those respective Amazonian territories into their respective national economies.

Article XI. In order to increase the rational utilisation of the human and natural resources of their respective Amazonian territories, the Contracting Parties agree to encourage joint studies and measures aimed at promoting the economic and social development of said territories and generating complementary methods for reinforcing the actions envisaged in the national plans of their respective territories.

Article XII. The Contracting Parties recognise the benefit to be derived by developing, under equitable and mutually beneficial conditions, retail trade of products for local consumption among the respective Amazonian border populations, by means of suitable bilateral or multilateral agreements.

Article XIII. The Contracting Parties shall cooperate to increase the flow of tourists, both national and from third countries, in their respective Amazonian territories, without prejudice to national regulations for the protection of indigenous cultures and natural resources.

Article XIV. The Contracting Parties shall cooperate in ensuring that measures adopted for the conservation of ethnological, and archeological wealth of the Amazon region are effective.

Article XV. The Contracting Parties shall seek to maintain a permanent exchange of information and cooperation among themselves and with the agencies for Latin American cooperation in the areas pertaining to matters covered by this Treaty.

Article XVI. The decisions and commitments adopted by the Contracting Parties under this Treaty shall not be to the detriment of projects and undertakings executed within their respective territories, according to International Law and fair practice between neighboring and friendly countries.

* * *

Article XX. Notwithstanding the fact that more adequate frequency for meetings can be established at a later date, the Ministers of Foreign Affairs of the Contracting Parties shall convene meetings when deemed opportune or advisable, in order to establish the basic guidelines for common policies, for assessing and evaluating the general development or the process of Amazonian cooperation and for taking decisions designed to carry out the aims set out in this document.

* * *

Article XXI. The Amazonian Cooperation Council comprising of top level diplomatic representatives shall meet once a year. Its duties shall be as follows:

(1) To ensure that the aims and objectives of the Treaty are complied with.

(2) To be responsible for carrying out the decisions taken at meetings of Foreign Affairs Ministers.

(3) To recommend to the Parties the advisibility and the appropriateness of convening meetings of Foreign Affairs Ministers and of drawing-up the corresponding Agenda.

(4) To take under consideration initiatives and plans presented by the Parties as well as to adopt decisions for undertaking bilateral or multilateral studies and plans, the execution of which as the case may be, shall be the duty of the Permanent National Commissions.

(5) To evaluate the implementation of plans of bilateral or multilateral interest.

(6) To draw-up the Rules and Regulations for its proper functioning.

* * *

Article XXII. The functions of the Secretariat shall be performed *pro-tempore* by the Contracting Party in whose territory the next regular meeting of the Amazonian Cooperation Council is scheduled to be held.

* * *

Article XXIII. The Contracting Parties shall create Permanent National Commissions charged with enforcing in their respective territories the provisions set out in this Treaty, as well as carrying out the decisions taken at meetings of Foreign Affairs Ministers and by the Amazonian Cooperation Council, without jeopardizing other tasks assigned them by the State.

Article XXIV. Whenever necessary, the Contracting Parties may set up special Commissions to study specific problems or matters related to the aims of this Treaty.

Article XXV. Decisions at meetings held in accordance with Articles XX and XXI shall always require the unanimous vote of the Member Countries of this Treaty. Decisions made at meetings held in accordance with Article XXIV shall always require the unanimous vote of the participating countries.

Article XXVI. The Contracting Parties agree that the present Treaty shall not be susceptible to interpretative reservation or statements.

5.24 CONVENTION ON LONG-RANGE TRANSBOUNDARY AIR POLLUTION. Done at Geneva, Nov. 13, 1979. Entered into force, Mar. 16, 1983, *reproduced in* 18 I.L.M. 1442 (1979)

* * *

DEFINITIONS

Article 1

For the purposes of the present Convention:

(a) "*air pollution*" means the introduction by man, directly or indirectly, of substances or energy into the air resulting in deleterious effects of such a nature as to endanger human health, harm living resources and ecosystems and material property and impair or interfere with amenities and other legitimate uses of the environment, and "air pollutants" shall be construed accordingly;

(b) "*long-range transboundary air pollution*" means air pollution whose physical origin is situated wholly or in part within the area under the national jurisdiction of one State and which has adverse effects in the area under the jurisdiction of another State at such a distance that it is not generally possible to distinguish the contribution of individual emission sources or groups of sources.

FUNDAMENTAL PRINCIPLES

Article 2

The Contracting Parties, taking due account of the facts and problems involved, are determined to protect man and his environment against air pollution and shall endeavour to limit and, as far as possible, gradually reduce and prevent air pollution including long-range transboundary air pollution.

Article 3

The Contracting Parties, within the framework of the present Convention, shall by means of exchanges of information, consultation, research and monitoring, develop without undue delay policies and strategies which shall serve as a means of combating the discharge of air pollutants, taking into account efforts already made at national and international levels.

Article 4

The Contracting Parties shall exchange information on and review their policies, scientific activities and technical measures aimed at combating, as far as possible, the discharge of air pollutants which may have adverse effects, thereby contributing to the reduction of air pollution including long-range transboundary air pollution.

Article 5

Consultations shll be held, upon request, at an early stage between, on the one hand, Contracting Parties which are actually affected by or exposed to a significant risk of long-range transboundary air pollution and, on the other hand, Contracting Parties within which and subject to whose jurisdiction a significant contribution to long-range transboundary air pollution originates, or could originate, in connexion with activities carried on or contemplated therein.

AIR QUALITY MANAGEMENT

Article 6

Taking into account articles 2 to 5, the ongoing research, exchange of information and monitoring and the results thereof, the cost and effectiveness of local and other remedies and, in order to combat air pollution, in particular that originating from new or rebuilt installations, each Contracting Party undertakes to develop the best policies and strategies including air quality management systems and, as part of them, control measures compatible with balanced development, in particular by using the best available technology which is economically feasible and low- and non-waste technology.

RESEARCH AND DEVELOPMENT

Article 7

The Contracting Parties, as appropriate to their needs, shall initiate and co-operate in the conduct of research into and/or development of:

(a) existing and proposed technologies for reducing emissions of sulphur compounds and other major air pollutants, including technical and economic feasibility, and environmental consequences;

(b) instrumentation and other techniques for monitoring and measuring emission rates and ambient concentrations of air pollutants;

(c) improved models for a better understanding of the transmission of long-range transboundary air pollutants;

(d) the effects of sulphur compounds and other major air pollutants on human health and the environment, including agriculture, forestry, materials, aquatic and other natural ecosystems and visibility, with a view to establishing a scientific basis for dose/effect relationships designed to protect the environment;

(e) the economic, social and environmental assessment of alternative measures for attaining environmental objectives including the reduction of long-range transboundary air pollution;

(f) education and training programmes related to the environmental aspects of pollution by sulphur compounds and other major air pollutants.

EXCHANGE OF INFORMATION

Article 8

The Contracting Parties, within the framework of the Executive Body referred to in article 10 and bilaterally, shall, in their common interests, exchange available information on:

(a) data on emissions at periods of time to be agreed upon, of agreed air pollutants, starting with sulphur dioxide, coming from grid-units of agreed size; or on the fluxes of agreed air pollutants, starting with sulphur dioxide, across national borders, at distances and at periods of time to be agreed upon;

(b) major changes in national policies and in general industrial development, and their potential impact, which would be likely to cause significant changes in long-range transboundary air pollution;

(c) control technologies for reducing air pollution relevant to long-range transboundary air pollution;

(d) the projected cost of the emission control of sulphur compounds and other major air pollutants on a national scale;

(e) meteorological and physico-chemical data relating to the processes during transmission;

(f) physico-chemical and biological data relating to the effects of long-range transboundary air pollution and the extent of the damage [1] which these data indicate can be attributed to long-range transboundary air pollution;

(g) national, subregional and regional policies and strategies for the control of sulphur compounds and other major air pollutants.

IMPLEMENTATION AND FURTHER DEVELOPMENT OF THE CO-OPERATIVE PROGRAMME FOR THE MONITORING AND EVALUATION OF THE LONG-RANGE TRANSMISSION OF AIR POLLUTANTS IN EUROPE

Article 9

The Contracting Parties stress the need for the implementation of the existing "Co-operative programme for the monitoring and evaluation of the long-range transmission of air pollutants in Europe" (hereinafter referred to as EMEP) and, with regard to the further development of this programme, agree to emphasize:

(a) the desirability of Contracting Parties joining in and fully implementing EMEP which, as a first step, is based on the monitoring of sulphur dioxide and related substances;

(b) the need to use comparable or standardized procedures for monitoring whenever possible;

(c) the desirability of basing the monitoring programme on the framework of both national and international programmes. The establishment of monitoring stations and the collection of data shall be carried out under the national jurisdiction of the country in which the monitoring stations are located;

(d) the desirability of establishing a framework for a co-operative environmenal monitoring programme, based on and taking into account present and future national, subregional, regional and other international programmes;

(e) the need to exchange data on emissions at periods of time to be agreed upon, of agreed air pollutants, starting with sulphur dioxide, coming from grid-units of agreed size; or on the fluxes of agreed air pollutants, starting with sulphur dioxide, across national borders, at distances and at periods of time to be agreed upon. The method, including the model, used to determine the fluxes, as well as the method, including the model, used to determine the transmission of air pollutants based on the emissions per grid-unit, shall be made available and periodically reviewed, in order to improve the methods and the models;

(f) their willingness to continue the exchange and periodic updating of national data on total emissions of agreed air pollutants, starting with sulphur dioxide;

(g) the need to provide meteorological and physico-chemical data relating to processes during transmission;

(h) the need to monitor chemical components in other media such as water, soil and vegetation, as well as a similar monitoring programme to record effects on health and environment;

(i) the desirability of extending the national EMEP networks to make them operational for control and surveillance purposes.

EXECUTIVE BODY

Article 10

1. The representatives of the Contracting Parties shall, within the framework of the Senior Advisers to ECE Governments on Environmental Problems, constitute the

1. The present Convention does not contain a rule on State liability as to damage.

Executive Body of the present Convention, and shall meet at least annually in that capacity.

2. The Executive Body shall:

(a) review the implementation of the present Convention;

(b) establish, as appropriate, working groups to consider matters related to the implementation and development of the present Convention and to this end to prepare appropriate studies and other documentation and to submit recommendations to be considered by the Executive Body;

(c) fulfil such other functions as may be appropriate under the provisions of the present Convention.

3. The Executive Body shall utilize the Steering Body for the EMEP to play an integral part in the operation of the present Convention, in particular with regard to data collection and scientific co-operation.

4. The Executive Body, in discharging its functions, shall, when it deems appropriate, also make use of information from other relevant international organizations.

SECRETARIAT

Article 11

The Executive Secretary of the Economic Commission for Europe shall carry out, for the Executive Body, the following secretariat functions:

(a) to convene and prepare the meetings of the Executive Body;

(b) to transmit to the Contracting Parties reports and other information received in accordance with the provisions of the present Convention;

(c) to discharge the functions assigned by the Executive Body.

AMENDMENTS TO THE CONVENTION

Article 12

1. Any Contracting Party may propose amendments to the present Convention.

2. The text of proposed amendments shall be submitted in writing to the Executive Secretary of the Economic Commission for Europe, who shall communicate them to all Contracting Parties. The Executive Body shall discuss proposed amendments at its next annual meeting provided that such proposals have been circulated by the Executive Secretary of the Economic Commission for Europe to the Contracting Parties at least ninety days in advance.

3. An amendment to the present Convention shall be adopted by consensus of the representatives of the Contracting Parties, and shall enter into force for the Contracting Parties which have accepted it on the ninetieth day after the date on which two-thirds of the Contracting Parties have deposited their instruments of acceptance with the depositary. Thereafter, the amendment shall enter into force for any other Contracting Party on the ninetieth day after the date on which that Contracting Party deposits its instrument of acceptance of the amendment.

SETTLEMENT OF DISPUTES

Article 13

If a dispute arises between two or more Contracting Parties to the present Convention as to the interpretation or application of the Convention, they shall seek a solution by negotiation or by any other method of dispute settlement acceptable to the parties to the dispute.

* * *

ENTRY INTO FORCE

Article 16

1. The present Convention shall enter into force on the ninetieth day after the date of deposit of the twenty-fourth instrument of ratification, acceptance, approval or accession.

2. For each Contracting Party which ratifies, accepts or approves the present Convention or accedes thereto after the deposit of the twenty-fourth instrument of ratification, acceptance, approval or accession, the Convention shall enter into force on the ninetieth day after the date of deposit by such Contracting Party of its instrument of ratification, acceptance, approval or accession.

WITHDRAWAL

Article 17

At any time after five years from the date on which the present Convention has come into force with respect to a Contracting Party, that Contracting Party may withdraw from the Convention by giving written notification to the depositary. Any such withdrawal shall take effect on the ninetieth day after the date of its receipt by the depositary.

* * *

5.25 AGREEMENT GOVERNING THE ACTIVITIES OF STATES ON THE MOON AND OTHER CELESTIAL BODIES.[a] Done at New York, Dec. 5, 1979. Entered into force, July 11, 1984. U.N.G.A. Res. 34/68 (XXXIV), 34 U.N. GAOR, Supp. (No. 46) 77, U.N. Doc. A/34/664 ANNEXES (1979), *reprinted in* 18 I.L.M. 1434 (1979)

Article I. (1) The provisions of this Agreement relating to the moon shall also apply to other celestial bodies within the solar system, other than the earth, except in so far as specific legal norms enter into force with respect to any of these celestial bodies.

(2) For the purposes of this Agreement reference to the moon shall include orbits around or other trajectories to or around it.

(3) This Agreement does not apply to extraterrestrial materials which reach the surface of the earth by natural means.

Article II. All activities on the moon, including its exploration and use, shall be carried out in accordance with international law, in particular the Charter of the United Nations, and taking into account the Declaration on Principles of International Law concerning Friendly Relations and Co-operation among States in accordance with the Charter of the United Nations, adopted by the General Assembly on 24 October 1970, in the interest of maintaining international peace and security and promoting international co-operation and mutual understanding, and with due regard to the corresponding interests of all other States Parties.

Article III. (1) The moon shall be used by all States Parties exclusively for peaceful purposes.

(2) Any threat or use of force or any other hostile act or threat of hostile act on the moon is prohibited. It is likewise prohibited to use the moon in order to commit any such act or to engage in any such threat in relation to the earth, the moon, spacecraft, the personnel of spacecraft or man-made space objects.

(3) States Parties shall not place in orbit around or other trajectory to or around the moon objects carrying nuclear weapons or any other kinds of weapons of mass destruction or place or use such weapons on or in the moon.

(4) The establishment of military bases, installations and fortifications, the testing of any type of weapons and the conduct of military manoeuvres on the moon shall be forbidden. The use of military personnel for scientific research or for any other peaceful purposes shall not be prohibited. The use of any equipment or facility necessary for peaceful exploration and use of the moon shall also not be prohibited.

Article IV. (1) The exploration and use of the moon shall be the province of all mankind and shall be carried out for the benefit and in the interests of all countries, irrespective of their degree of economic or scientific development. Due regard shall

a. Also known as "the Moon Treaty." For other notable instruments pertaining to activities in outer space, see Agreement on the Rescue of Astronauts, the Return of Astronauts, and the Return of Objects Launched into Outer Space, done at Washington, London, and Moscow, Apr. 22, 1968, entered into force, Dec. 3, 1968, for the United States, Dec. 3, 1968, 19 U.S.T. 7570, T.I.A.S. No. 6599, 672 U.N.T.S. 119; Convention on the International Liability for Damage for Damage Caused by Space Objects, done at Washington, London, and Moscow on Mar. 29, 1972, entered into force, Sept. 1, 1972, for the United States, Oct. 9, 1973, 24 U.S.T. 2389, T.I.A.S. No. 7762; Convention on Registration of Objects Launched into Outer Space, done at New York, Nov. 12, 1974, entered into force, Sept. 15, 1976, for the United States, Sept. 15, 1976, T.I.A.S. No. 8480. *See also* Basic Documents 5.12 and 5.16, *supra*.

be paid to the interests of present and future generations as well as to the need to promote higher standards of living conditions of economic and social progress and development in accordance with the Charter of the United Nations.

(2) States Parties shall be guided by the principle of co-operation and mutual assistance in all their activities concerning the exploration and use of the moon. International cooperation in pursuance of this Agreement should be as wide as possible and may take place on a multilateral basis, on a bilateral basis, or through international intergovernmental organizations.

Article V. (1) States Parties shall inform the Secretary-General of the United Nations as well as the public and the international scientific community, to the greatest extent feasible and practicable, of their activities concerned with the exploration and use of the moon. Information on the time, purposes, locations, orbital parameters and duration shall be given in respect of each mission to the moon as soon as possible after launching, while information on the results of each mission, including scientific results, shall be furnished upon completion of the mission. In case of a mission lasting more than 60 days, information on conduct of the mission including any scientific results shall be given periodically at 30 days' intervals. For missions lasting more than six months, only significant additions to such information need be reported thereafter.

(2) If a State Party becomes aware that another State Party plans to operate simultaneously in the same area of or in the same orbit around or trajectory to or around the moon, it shall promptly inform the other State of the timing of and plans for its own operations.

(3) In carrying out activities under this Agreement, States Parties shall promptly inform the Secretary-General, as well as the public and the international scientific community, of any phenomena they discover in outer space, including the moon, which could endanger human life or health, as well as of any indication of organic life.

Article VI. (1) There shall be freedom of scientific investigation on the moon by all States Parties without discrimination of any kind, on the basis of equality and in accordance with international law.

(2) In carrying out scientific investigations and in furtherance of the provisions of this Agreement, the States Parties shall have the right to collect on and remove from the moon samples of its mineral and other substances. Such samples shall remain at the disposal of those States Parties which caused them to be collected and may be used by them for scientific purposes. States Parties shall have regard to the desirability of making a portion of such samples available to other interested States Parties and the international scientific community for scientific investigation. States Parties may in the course of scientific investigations also use mineral and other substances of the moon in quantities appropriate for the support of their missions.

(3) States Parties agree on the desirability of exchanging scientific and other personnel on expeditions to or installations on the moon to the greatest extent feasible and practicable.

Article VII. (1) In exploring and using the moon, States Parties shall take measures to prevent the disruption of the existing balance of its environment whether by introducing adverse changes in such environment, its harmful contamination through the introduction of extra-environmental matter or otherwise. States Parties shall also take measures to prevent harmfully affecting the environment of the earth through the introduction of extraterrestrial matter or otherwise.

(2) States Parties shall inform the Secretary-General of the United Nations of the measures being adopted by them in accordance with paragraph 1 of this article

and shall also to the maximum extent feasible notify him in advance of all placements by them of radioactive materials on the moon and of the purposes of such placements.

(3) States Parties shall report to other States Parties and to the Secretary–General concerning areas of the moon having special scientific interest in other that, without prejudice to the rights of other States Parties, consideration may be given to the designation of such areas as international scientific preserves for which special protective arrangements are to be agreed in consultation with the competent organs of the United Nations.

Article VIII. (1) States Parties may pursue their activities in the exploration and use of the moon anywhere on or below its surface, subject to the provisions of this Agreement.

(2) For these purposes States Parties may, in particular:

(a) Land their space objects on the moon and launch them from the moon;

(b) Place their personnel, space vehicles, equipment, facilities, stations and installations anywhere on or below the surface of the moon.

Personnel, space vehicles, equipment, facilities, stations and installations may move or be moved freely over or below the surface of the moon.

(3) Activities of States Parties in accordance with paragraphs 1 and 2 of this article shall not interfere with the activities of other States Parties on the moon. Where such interference may occur, the States Parties concerned shall undertake consultations in accordance with article XV, paragraphs 2 and 3.

Article IX. (1) States Parties may establish manned and unmanned stations on the moon. A State Party establishing a station shall use only that area which is required for the needs of the station and shall immediately inform the Secretary–General of the United Nations of the location and purposes of that station. Subsequently, at annual intervals that State shall likewise inform the Secretary–General whether the station continues in use and whether its purposes have changed.

(2) Stations shall be installed in such a manner that they do not impede the free access to all areas of the moon of personnel, vehicles and equipment of other States Parties conducting activities on the moon in accordance with the provisions of this Agreement or of article I of the Treaty on Principles Governing the Activities of States in the Exploration and Use of Outer Space, including the Moon and Other Celestial Bodies.

Article X. (1) States Parties shall adopt all practicable measures to safeguard the life and health of persons on the moon. For this purpose they shall regard any person on the moon as an astronaut within the meaning of article V of the Treaty on Principles Governing the Activities of States on the Exploration and Use of Outer Space, including the Moon and Other Celestial Bodies and as part of the personnel of a spacecraft within the meaning of the Agreement on the Rescue of Astronauts, the Return of Astronauts and the Return of Objects Launched into Outer Space.

(2) States Parties shall offer shelter in their stations, installations, vehicles and other facilities to persons in distress on the moon.

Article XI. (1) The moon and its natural resources are the common heritage of mankind, which finds its expression in the provisions of this Agreement and in particular in paragraph 5 of this article.

(2) The moon is not subject to national appropriation by any claim of sovereignty, by means of use or occupation, or by any other means.

(3) Neither the surface nor the subsurface of the moon, nor any part thereof or natural resources in place, shall become property of any State, international intergovernmental or non-governmental organization, national organization or non-gov-

ernmental entity or of any natural person. The placement of personnel, space vehicles, equipment facilities, stations and installations on or below the surface of the moon, including structures connected with their surface or subsurface, shall not create a right of ownership over the surface or the subsurface of the moon or any areas thereof. The foregoing provisions are without prejudice to the international régime referred to in paragraph 5 of this article.

(4) States Parties have the right to exploration and use of the moon without discrimination of any kind on a basis of equality, and in accordance with international law and the terms of this Agreement.

(5) States Parties to this Agreement hereby undertake to establish an international régime, including appropriate procedures, to govern the exploitation of the natural resources of the moon as such exploitation is about to become feasible. This provision shall be implemented in accordance with article XVIII of this Agreement.

(6) In order to facilitate the establishment of the international régime referred to in paragraph 5 of this article, States Parties shall inform the Secretary–General of the United Nations as well as the public and the international scientific community to the greatest extent feasible and practicable of any natural resources they may discover on the moon.

(7) The main purposes of the international régime to be established shall include:

(a) The orderly and safe development of the natural resources of the moon;

(b) The rational management of those resources;

(c) The expansion of opportunities in the use of those resources;

(d) An equitable sharing by all States Parties in the benefits derived from those resources, whereby the interests and needs of the developing countries as well as the efforts of those countries which have contributed either directly or indirectly to the exploration of the moon shall be given special consideration.

(8) All the activities with respect to the natural resources of the moon shall be carried out in a manner compatible with the purposes specified in paragraph 7 of this article and the provisions of article VI, paragraph 2, of this Agreement.

Article XII. (1) States Parties shall retain jurisdiction and control over their personnel, vehicles, equipment, facilities, stations and installations on the moon. The ownership of space vehicles, equipment, facilities, stations and installations shall not be affected by their presence on the moon.

(2) Vehicles, installations and equipment or their component parts found in places other than their intended location shall be dealt with in accordance with article V of the Agreement on Assistance to Astronauts, the Return of Astronauts and the Return of Objects Launched into Outer Space.

(3) In the event of an emergency involving a threat to human life, States Parties may use the equipment, vehicles, installations, facilities or supplies of other States Parties on the moon. Prompt notification of such use shall be made to the Secretary–General of the United Nations or State Party concerned.

Article XIII. A State Party which learns of the crash landing, forced landing or other unintended landing on the moon of a space object, or its component parts, that were not launched by it, shall promptly inform the launching State Party and the Secretary–General of the United Nations.

Article XIV. (1) States Parties to this Agreement shall bear international responsibility for national activities on the moon whether such activities are carried on by governmental agencies or by non-governmental entities, and for assuring that national activities are carried out in conformity with the provisions set forth in the present Agreement. States Parties shall ensure that non-governmental entities under their jurisdiction shall engage in activities on the moon only under the authority and continuing supervision of the appropriate State Party.

(2) States Parties recognize that detailed arrangements concerning liability for damage caused on the moon, in addition to the provisions of the Treaty on Principles Governing the Activities of States in the Exploration and Use of Outer Space, including the Moon and Other Celestial Bodies and the Convention on International Liability for Damage Caused by Space Objects, may become necessary as a result of more extensive activities on the moon. Any such arrangements shall be elaborated in accordance with the procedure provided for in article XVIII of this Agreement.

Article XV. (1) Each State Party may assure itself that the activities of other States Parties in the exploration and use of the moon are compatible with the provisions of this Agreement. To this end, all space vehicles, equipment, facilities, stations and installations on the moon shall be open to other States Parties. Such States Parties shall give reasonable advance notice of a projected visit, in order that appropriate consultations may be held and that maximum precautions may be taken to assure safety and to avoid interference with normal operations in the facility to be visited. In pursuance of this article, any State Party may act on its own behalf or with the full or partial assistance of any other State Party or through appropriate international procedures within the framework of the United Nations and in accordance with the Charter.

(2) A State Party which has reason to believe that another State Party is not fulfilling the obligations incumbent upon it pursuant to this Agreement or that another State Party is interfering with the rights which the former State has under this Agreement may request consultations with that Party. A State Party receiving such a request shall enter into such consultations without delay. Any other State Party which requests to do so shall be entitled to take part in the consultations. Each State Party participating in such consultations shall seek a mutually acceptable resolution of any controversy and shall bear in mind the rights and interests of all States Parties. The Secretary–General of the United Nations shall be informed of the results of the consultations and transmit the information received to all States Parties concerned.

(3) If the consultations do not lead to a mutually acceptable settlement which has due regard for the rights and interests of all the States Parties, the parties concerned shall take all measures to settle the dispute by other peaceful means of their choice and appropriate to the circumstances and the nature of the dispute. If difficulties arise in connection with the opening of consultations or if consultations do not lead to a mutually acceptable settlement, any State Party may seek the assistance of the Secretary–General without seeking the consent of any other State Party concerned, in order to resolve the controversy. A State Party which does not maintain diplomatic relations with another State Party concerned shall participate in such consultations, at its choice, either itself or through another State Party or the Secretary–General, as intermediary.

Article XVI. With the exception of articles XVII to XXI, references in this Agreement to States shall be deemed to apply to any international intergovernmental organization which conducts space activities if the organization declares its acceptance of the rights and obligations provided for in this Agreement and if a majority of the States members of the organization are States Parties to this Agreement and to the Treaty on Principles Governing the Activities of States in the Exploration and Use of Outer Space, including the Moon and Other Celestial Bodies. States members of any such organization which are States Parties to this Agreement shall take all appropriate steps to ensure that the organization makes a declaration in accordance with the foregoing.

5.26 WORLD CHARTER FOR NATURE. Adopted by the U.N. General Assembly, Oct. 28, 1982. U.N.G.A. Res. 37/7, U.N. GAOR Supp. (No. 51) 21, U.N. Doc. A/37/L.4 and Add. 1 (1982)

The General Assembly,

Reaffirming the fundamental purposes of the United Nations, in particular the maintenance of international peace and security, the development of friendly relations among nations and the achievement of international co-operation in solving international problems of an economic, social, cultural, technical, intellectual or humanitarian character.

Aware that:

(*a*) Mankind is a part of nature and life depends on the uninterrupted functioning of natural systems which ensure the supply of energy and nutrients,

(*b*) Civilization is rooted in nature, which has shaped human culture and influenced all artistic and scientific achievement, and living in harmony with nature gives man the best opportunities for the development of his creativity, and for rest and recreation,

Convinced that:

(*a*) Every form of life is unique, warranting respect regardless of its worth to man, and, to accord other organisms such recognition, man must be guided by a moral code of action,

(*b*) Man can alter nature and exhaust natural resources by his action or its consequences and, therefore, must fully recognize the urgency of maintaining the stability and quality of nature and of conserving natural resources,

Persuaded that:

(*a*) Lasting benefits from nature depend upon the maintenance of essential ecological processes and life support systems, and upon the diversity of life forms, which are jeopardized through excessive exploitation and habitat destruction by man,

(*b*) The degradation of natural systems owing to excessive consumption and misuse of natural resources, as well as the failure to establish an appropriate economic order among peoples and among States, leads to the breakdown of the economic, social and political framework of civilization,

(*c*) Competition for scarce resources creates conflicts, whereas the conservation of nature and natural resources contributes to justice and the maintenance of peace and cannot be achieved until mankind learns to live in peace and to forsake war and armaments,

Reaffirming that man must acquire the knowledge to maintain and enhance his ability to use natural resources in a manner which ensures the preservation of the species and ecosystems for the benefit of present and future generations,

Firmly convinced of the need for appropriate measures, at the national and international, individual and collective, and private and public levels, to protect nature and promote international co-operation in this field,

Adopts, to these ends, the present World Charter for Nature, which proclaims the following principles of conservation by which all human conduct affecting nature is to be guided and judged.

I. General Principles

1. Nature shall be respected and its essential processes shall not be impaired.

2. The genetic viability on the earth shall not be compromised; the population levels of all life forms, wild and domesticated, must be at least sufficient for their survival, and to this end necessary habitats shall be safeguarded.

3. All areas of the earth, both land and sea, shall be subject to these principles of conservation; special protection shall be given to unique areas, to representative samples of all the different types of ecosystems and to the habitats of rare or endangered species.

4. Ecosystems and organisms, as well as the land, marine and atmospheric resources that are utilized by man, shall be managed to achieve and maintain optimum sustainable productivity, but not in such a way as to endanger the integrity of those other ecosystems or species with which they coexist.

5. Nature shall be secured against degradation caused by warfare or other hostile activities.

II. FUNCTIONS

6. In the decision-making process it shall be recognized that man's needs can be met only by ensuring the proper functioning of natural systems and by respecting the principles set forth in the present Charter.

7. In the planning and implementation of social and economic development activities, due account shall be taken of the fact that the conservation of nature is an integral part of those activities.

8. In formulating long-term plans for economic development, population growth and the improvement of standards of living, due account shall be taken of the long-term capacity of natural systems to ensure the subsistence and settlement of the populations concerned, recognizing that this capacity may be enhanced through science and technology.

9. The allocation of areas of the earth to various uses shall be planned and due account shall be taken of the physical constraints, the biological productivity and diversity and the natural beauty of the areas concerned.

10. Natural resources shall not be wasted, but used with a restraint appropriate to the principles set forth in the present Charter, in accordance with the following rules:

(*a*) Living resources shall not be utilized in excess of their natural capacity for regeneration;

(*b*) The productivity of soils shall be maintained or enhanced through measures which safeguard their long-term fertility and the process of organic decomposition, and prevent erosion and all other forms of degradation;

(*c*) Resources, including water, which are not consumed as they are used shall be reused or recycled;

(*d*) Non-renewable resources which are consumed as they are used shall be exploited with restraint, taking into account their abundance, the rational possibilities of converting them for consumption, and the compatibility of their exploitation with the functioning of natural systems.

11. Activities which might have an impact on nature shall be controlled, and the best available technologies that minimize significant risks to nature or other adverse effects shall be used; in particular:

(*a*) Activities which are likely to cause irreversible damage to nature shall be avoided;

(*b*) Activities which are likely to pose a significant risk to nature shall be preceded by an exhaustive examination; their proponents shall demonstrate that expected benefits outweigh potential damage to nature, and where potential adverse effects are not fully understood, the activities should not proceed;

(*c*) Activities which may disturb nature shall be preceded by assessment of their consequences, and environmental impact studies of development projects shall be conducted sufficiently in advance, and if they are to be undertaken, such activities shall be planned and carried out so as to minimize potential adverse effects;

(*d*) Agriculture, grazing, forestry and fisheries practices shall be adapted to the natural characteristics and constraints of given areas;

(*e*) Areas degraded by human activities shall be rehabilitated for purposes in accord with their natural potential and compatible with the well-being of affected populations.

12. Discharge of pollutants into natural systems shall be avoided and:

(*a*) Where this is not feasible, such pollutants shall be treated at the source, using the best practicable means available;

(*b*) Special precautions shall be taken to prevent discharge of radioactive or toxic wastes.

13. Measures intended to prevent, control or limit natural disasters, infestations and diseases shall be specifically directed to the causes of these scourges and shall avoid adverse side-effects on nature.

III. Implementation

14. The principles set forth in the present Charter shall be reflected in the law and practice of each State, as well as at the international level.

15. Knowledge of nature shall be broadly disseminated by all possible means, particularly by ecological education as an integral part of general education.

16. All planning shall include, among its essential elements, the formulation of strategies for the conservation of nature, the establishment of inventories of ecosystems and assessments of the effects on nature of proposed policies and activities; all of these elements shall be disclosed to the public by appropriate means in time to permit effective consultation and participation.

17. Funds, programmes and administrative structures necessary to achieve the objective of the conservation of nature shall be provided.

18. Constant efforts shall be made to increase knowledge of nature by scientific research and to disseminate such knowledge unimpeded by restrictions of any kind.

19. The status of natural processes, ecosystems and species shall be closely monitored to enable early detection of degradation or threat, ensure timely intervention and facilitate the evaluation of conservation policies and methods.

20. Military activities damaging to nature shall be avoided.

21. States and, to the extent they are able, other public authorities, international organizations, individuals, groups and corporations shall:

(*a*) Co-operate in the task of conserving nature through common activities and other relevant actions, including information exchange and consultations;

(*b*) Establish standards for products and manufacturing processes that may have adverse effects on nature, as well as agreed methodologies for assessing these effects;

(*c*) Implement the applicable international legal provisions for the conservation of nature and the protection of the environment;

(*d*) Ensure that activities within their jurisdictions or control do not cause damage to the natural systems located within other States or in the areas beyond the limits of national jurisdiction;

(*e*) Safeguard and conserve nature in areas beyond national jurisdiction.

22. Taking fully into account the sovereignty of States over their natural resources, each State shall give effect to the provisions of the present Charter through its competent organs and in co-operation with other States.

23. All persons, in accordance with their national legislation, shall have the opportunity to participate, individually or with others, in the formulation of decisions of direct concern to their environment, and shall have access to means of redress when their environment has suffered damage or degradation.

24. Each person has a duty to act in accordance with the provisions of the present Charter; acting individually, in association with others or through participation in the political process, each person shall strive to ensure that the objectives and requirements of the present Charter are met.

* * *

Life on earth is part of nature. Mankind has evolved from the same origins as other forms of life, and lives in constant interaction with them and the physical elements of the environment.

Life depends on the uninterrupted functioning of natural systems which ensure the supply of energy and nutrients.

Civilization is rooted in nature; nature has shaped human culture and influences all artistic and scientific achievement. Living in harmony with nature gives man his best opportunities for creativity, rest and recreation.

Every form of life is unique and warrants respect regardless of its present worth to man. To accord other organisms such recognition, man requires a moral code of action, which takes into account the control of deleterious organisms.

Man can alter nature and exhaust natural resources by willful action or its consequences. Therefore man must fully recognize the urgency of maintaining the stability and quality of nature and of conserving natural resources.

Benefits from nature depend upon the maintenance of natural processes and the diversity of life forms, which are jeopardized through excessive exploitation and habitat destruction by man.

Failure to conserve natural systems due to excessive consumption and misuse of resources leads to the breakdown of the economic, social and political framework of civilization. Competition for scarce resources creates conflicts among States. Thus, the conservation of nature and natural resources contributes to the maintenance of peace.

Man must acquire the knowledge to maintain and enhance his ability to use resources in a manner benefiting present and future generations without lasting injury to nature. Man can be in harmony with nature if the human community acts as a steward for nature in the interests of future generations.

To this end, this World Charter for Nature is proclaimed and the following principles of conservation established as the common standard by which all human conduct affecting nature is to be guided and judged.

I. General principles

1. Nature shall be respected and its essential processes shall not be disrupted.

2. The continued existence of all forms of life shall not be compromised; the population levels of all species must be at least sufficient for their survival and to this end necessary habitats shall be maintained.

3. All areas shall be subject to the principles of conservation; special protection shall be given to unique areas, representative samples of all ecosystems and the habitats of rare and endangered species.

4. Ecosystems and organisms which are utilized by man shall be managed to achieve and maintain optimum sustainable productivity, but not in such a way as to endanger the integrity of the ecosystems and organisms with which they coexist.

5. Nature shall be secured against degradation caused by warfare or other hostile activities.

II. Responsibilities

6. In the decision-making process it shall be recognized that man's needs can be met only by ensuring the proper functioning of natural systems, and by acting in accordance with the principles of this Charter.

7. The growth and concentrations of human populations shall be correlated with the capacity of natural systems to sustain them.

8. Natural resources shall not be wasted, but used with a restraint appropriate to the principles of conservation.

9. Allocation of areas by man to various uses shall be planned, paying regard to their physical constraints, their biological productivity and diversity and their natural beauty.

10. The use of natural resources shall be as follows:

(*a*) Living resources shall not be utilized in excess of their natural powers of regeneration;

(*b*) Resources, including water, which are not consumed as they are used, shall be reused or recycled;

(*c*) Non-renewable resources which are consumed as they are used shall be exploited with restraint according to their abundance, the efficiency with which they can be converted to use, and the compatibility of their development with the functioning of natural systems; and

(*d*) The productivity of soils shall be maintained or enhanced through measures which safeguard their continuing fertility and the processes of organic decomposition, and prevent erosion and other forms of degradation.

11. Activities which might have an impact on nature shall be controlled and in particular:

(*a*) Activities which may cause irreversible damage to nature shall be avoided;

(*b*) Activities which pose a high risk to nature shall be preceded by an exhaustive examination of that risk; their proponents shall demonstrate that expected benefits outweigh potential damage to nature, and where potential adverse effects are not fully understood, the activities should not proceed;

(*c*) Activities which may disturb nature shall be preceded by an assessment of their consequences, and, if to be undertaken, such activities shall be planned and carried out so as to minimize adverse effects; and

(*d*) Areas degraded by human activities shall be rehabilitated for purposes compatible with their natural potential and with human well-being in nearby settlements.

12. All discharge of pollutants into natural systems shall be avoided:

(*a*) Where this is not possible, such discharge shall be treated at the source using the best methods available; and (*b*) Special precautions shall be taken to prevent discharge of radioactive or other toxic wastes.

13. Measures intended to prevent, control and mitigate natural disasters, infestations and diseases shall be specifically directed to the causes of these scourges and shall avoid producing secondary effects in nature.

III. REQUIREMENTS FOR IMPLEMENTATION

14. The principles set forth in this Charter shall be reflected in the law of each State.

15. Knowledge of nature shall be broadly disseminated by all possible means, particularly by conservation education as an integral part of general education.

16. Conservation strategies, inventories of ecosystems and assessments of the effects on nature of proposed policies and developments shall be essential elements of planning; all of these should be disclosed to the public in time to permit effective consultation.

17. The funds, programmes and administrative structures necessary to achieve conservation objectives shall be provided.

18. Knowledge of nature shall be constantly increased by research and extended by the wide dissemination of information unimpeded by restrictions of any kind.

19. The status of habitats and species shall be monitored to enable early detection of degradation or threat and evaluation of conservation policies and methods.

20. Military activity damaging to nature shall be avoided, and in particular:

(*a*) Further development, testing and use of nuclear, biological, chemical or environmental modification methods of warfare shall be prohibited; and

(*b*) Protected areas, the Antarctic region and outer space shall be free of military activity.

21. States, governments, and all other public authorities and, as they are able, individuals, groups, and corporations shall:

(*a*) Co-operate in the conservation of nature and exchange relevant information;

(*b*) Ensure that activities within their jurisdictions or control do not cause damage to natural systems located within other States or in areas beyond the limits of national jurisdiction;

(*c*) Implement the international legal provisions for conservation of nature and environmental protection;

(*d*) Establish standards for products and processes that may adversely affect nature; and

(*e*) Safeguard and conserve nature in areas beyond natural jurisdiction.

22. Each State shall give effect to the requirements of this Charter through all of its competent organs and in co-operation with other States.

23. All persons shall have the right to participate, singly or with others, in the formulation of decisions which directly concern their environment and shall have access to means of redress when their environment has suffered damage or deterioration.

24. Each person has a duty to act in accordance with the requirements set forth in this Charter; acting alone or in groups or through the political process, each person shall strive to ensure that these principles, responsibilities and requirements are met.

5.27 UNITED NATIONS CONVENTION ON THE LAW OF THE SEA.[a] Done at Montego Bay, Dec. 10, 1982. Opened for signature, Dec. 10, 1982. U.N. Doc. A/CONF 62/122, *reprinted in* 21 I.L.M. 1261 (1982)[b]

The States Parties to this Convention,

Prompted by the desire to settle, in a spirit of mutual understanding and co-operation, all issues relating to the law of the sea and aware of the historic significance of this Convention as an important contribution to the maintenance of peace, justice and progress for all peoples of the world,

Noting that developments since the United Nations Conferences on the Law of the Sea held at Geneva in 1958 and 1960 have accentuated the need for a new and generally acceptable Convention on the law of the sea,

Conscious that the problems of ocean space are closely interrelated and need to be considered as a whole,

Recognizing the desirability of establishing through this Convention, with due regard for the sovereignty of all States, a legal order for the seas and oceans which will facilitate international communication, and will promote the peaceful uses of the seas and oceans, the equitable and efficient utilization of their resources, the conservation of their living resources, and the study, protection and preservation of the marine environment,

Bearing in mind that the achievement of these goals will contribute to the realization of a just and equitable international economic order which takes into account the interests and needs of mankind as a whole and, in particular, the special interests and needs of developing countries, whether coastal or land-locked,

Desiring by this Convention to develop the principles embodied in resolution 2749 (XXV) of 17 December 1970 in which the General Assembly of the United Nations solemnly declared *inter alia* that the area of the sea-bed and ocean floor and the subsoil thereof, beyond the limits of national jurisdiction, as well as its resources, are the common heritage of mankind, the exploration and exploitation of which shall be carried out for the benefit of mankind as a whole, irrespective of the geographical location of States,

Believing that the codification and progressive development of the law of the sea achieved in this Convention will contribute to the strengthening of peace, security, co-operation and friendly relations among all nations in conformity with the principles of justice and equal rights and will promote the economic and social advancement of all peoples of the world, in accordance with the Purposes and Principles of the United Nations as set forth in the Charter,

Affirming that matters not regulated by this Convention continue to be governed by the rules and principles of general international law,

Have agreed as follows:

a. The Convention will replace the 1958 Geneva Law of the Sea Conventions (Basic Documents 5.4, 5.5, 5.6 and 5.7) upon entry into force (12 months after the sixtieth acceptance) for the parties.

b. Seven of nine annexes are omitted: "Basic Conditions of Prospecting, Exploration and Exploitation" (Annex III); "Statute of the Enterprise" (Annex IV); "Conciliation" (Annex V); "Statute of the International Tribunal for the Law of the Sea" (Annex VI); "Arbitration (Annex VII); "Special Arbitration" (Annex VIII); "Participation By International Organizations" (Annex IX).

PART I

INTRODUCTION

Article 1

Use of terms and scope

1. For the purposes of this Convention:

(1) "Area" means the sea-bed and ocean floor and subsoil thereof, beyond the limits of national jurisdiction;

(2) "Authority" means the International Sea-Bed Authority;

(3) "activities in the Area" means all activities of exploration for, and exploitation of, the resources of the Area;

(4) "pollution of the marine environment" means the introduction by man, directly or indirectly, of substances or energy into the marine environment, including estuaries, which results or is likely to result in such deleterious effects as harm to living resources and marine life, hazards to human health, hindrance to marine activities, including fishing and other legitimate uses of the sea, impairment of quality for use of sea water and reduction of amenities;

(5) (a) "dumping" means:

(i) any deliberate disposal of wastes or other matter from vessels, aircraft, platforms or other man-made structures at sea;

(ii) any deliberate disposal of vessels, aircraft, platforms or other man-made structures at sea;

(b) "dumping" does not include:

(i) the disposal of wastes or other matter incidental to, or derived from the normal operations of vessels, aircraft, platforms or other man-made structures at sea and their equipment, other than wastes or other matter transported by or to vessels, aircraft, platforms or other man-made structures at sea, operating for the purpose of disposal of such matter or derived from the treatment of such wastes or other matter on such vessels, aircraft, platforms or structures;

(ii) placement of matter for a purpose other than the mere disposal thereof, provided that such placement is not contrary to the aims of this Convention.

2. (1) "States Parties" means States which have consented to be bound by this Convention and for which this Convention is in force.

(2) This Convention applies *mutatis mutandis* to the entities referred to in article 305, paragraph 1(b), (c), (d), (e) and (f), which become Parties to this Convention in accordance with the conditions relevant to each, and to that extent "States Parties" refers to those entities.

PART II

TERRITORIAL SEA AND CONTIGUOUS ZONE

SECTION 1. GENERAL PROVISIONS

Article 2

Legal status of the territorial sea, of the air space over the territorial sea and of its bed and subsoil

1. The sovereignty of a coastal State extends, beyond its land territory and internal waters and, in the case of an archipelagic State, its archipelagic waters, to an adjacent belt of sea, described as the territorial sea.

2. This sovereignty extends to the air space over the territorial sea as well as to its bed and subsoil.

3. The sovereignty over the territorial sea is exercised subject to this Convention and to other rules of international law.

SECTION 2. LIMITS OF THE TERRITORIAL SEA

Article 3

Breadth of the territorial sea

Every State has the right to establish the breadth of its territorial sea up to a limit not exceeding 12 nautical miles, measured from baselines determined in accordance with this Convention.

Article 4

Outer limit of the territorial sea

The outer limit of the territorial sea is the line every point of which is at a distance from the nearest point of the baseline equal to the breadth of the territorial sea.

Article 5

Normal baseline

Except where otherwise provided in this Convention, the normal baseline for measuring the breadth of the territorial sea is the low-water line along the coast as marked on large-scale charts officially recognized by the coastal State.

Article 6

Reefs

In the case of islands situated on atolls or of islands having fringing reefs, the baseline for measuring the breadth of the territorial sea is the seaward low-water line of the reef, as shown by the appropriate symbol on charts officially recognized by the coastal State.

Article 7

Straight baselines

1. [*See* Basic Document 5.6, Art. 4(1).]

2. Where because of the presence of a delta and other natural conditions the coastline is highly unstable, the appropriate points may be selected along the furthest seaward extent of the low-water line and, notwithstanding subsequent regression of the low-water line, the straight baselines shall remain effective until changed by the coastal State in accordance with this Convention.

3. [*See* Basic Document 5.6, Art. 4(2).]

4. Straight baselines shall not be drawn to and from low-tide elevations, unless lighthouses or similar installations which are permanently above sea level have been built on them or except in instances where the drawing of baselines to and from such elevations has received general international recognition.

5. [*See* Basic Document 5.6, Art. 4(4).]

6. The system of straight baselines may not be applied by a State in such a manner as to cut off the territorial sea of another State from the high seas or an exclusive economic zone.

Article 8

Internal waters

1. Except as provided in Part IV, waters on the landward side of the baseline of the territorial sea form part of the internal waters of the State.

2. Where the establishment of a straight baseline in accordance with the method set forth in article 7 has the effect of enclosing as internal waters areas which had not previously been considered as such, a right of innocent passage as provided in this Convention shall exist in those waters.

Article 9

Mouths of rivers

[*See* Basic Document 5.6, Art. 13.]

Article 10

Bays

1. [*See* Basic Document 5.6, Art. 7(1).]

2. [*See* Basic Document 5.6, Art. 7(2).]

3. [*See* Basic Document 5.6, Art. 7(3).]

4. [*See* Basic Document 5.6, Art. 7(4).]

5. [*See* Basic Document 5.6, Art. 7(5).]

6. The foregoing provisions do not apply to so-called "historic" bays, or in any case where the system of straight baselines provided for in article 7 is applied.

Article 11

Ports

For the purpose of delimiting the territorial sea, the outermost permanent harbour works which form an integral part of the harbour system are regarded as forming part of the coast. Off-shore installations and artificial islands shall not be considered as permanent harbour works.

Article 12

Roadsteads

Roadsteads which are normally used for the loading, unloading and anchoring of ships, and which would otherwise be situated wholly or partly outside the outer limit of the territorial sea, are included in the territorial sea.

Article 13

Low-tide elevations

[*See* Basic Document 5.6, Art. 11.]

Article 14

Combination of methods for determining baselines

The coastal State may determine baselines in turn by any of the methods provided for in the foregoing articles to suit different conditions.

Article 15

Delimitation of the territorial sea between States with opposite or adjacent coasts

[*See* Basic Document 5.6, Art. 12(1).]

Article 16

Charts and lists of geographical co-ordinates

1. The baselines for measuring the breadth of the territorial sea determined in accordance with articles 7, 9 and 10, or the limits derived therefrom, and the lines of delimitation drawn in accordance with articles 12 and 15 shall be shown on charts of a scale or scales adequate for ascertaining their position. Alternatively, a list of geographical co-ordinates of points, specifying the geodetic datum, may be substituted.

2. The coastal State shall give due publicity to such charts or lists of geographical co-ordinates and shall deposit a copy of each such chart or list with the Secretary-General of the United Nations.

SECTION 3. INNOCENT PASSAGE IN THE TERRITORIAL SEA

SUBSECTION A. RULES APPLICABLE TO ALL SHIPS

Article 17

Right of innocent passage

[*See* Basic Document 5.6, Art. 14(1).]

Article 18

Meaning of passage

1. Passage means navigation through the territorial sea for the purpose of:

(a) traversing that sea without entering internal waters or calling at a roadstead or port facility outside internal waters; or

(b) proceeding to or from internal waters or a call at such roadstead or port facility.

2. Passage shall be continuous and expeditious. However, passage includes stopping and anchoring, but only in so far as the same are incidental to ordinary navigation or are rendered necessary by *force majeure* or distress or for the purpose of rendering assistance to persons, ships or aircraft in danger or distress.

Article 19

Meaning of innocent passage

1. [*See* Basic Document 5.6, Art. 14(4).]

2. Passage of a foreign ship shall be considered to be prejudicial to the peace, good order or security of the coastal State if in the territorial sea it engages in any of the following activities:

(a) any threat or use of force against the sovereignty, territorial integrity or political independence of the coastal State, or in any other manner in violation of the principles of international law embodied in the Charter of the United Nations;

(b) any exercise or practice with weapons of any kind;

(c) any act aimed at collecting information to the prejudice of the defence or security of the coastal State;

(d) any act of propaganda aimed at affecting the defence or security of the coastal State;

(e) the launching, landing or taking on board of any aircraft;

(f) the launching, landing or taking on board of any military device;

(g) the loading or unloading of any commodity, currency or person contrary to the customs, fiscal, immigration or sanitary laws and regulations of the coastal State;

(h) any act of wilful and serious pollution contrary to this Convention;

(i) any fishing activities;

(j) the carrying out of research or survey activities;

(k) any act aimed at interfering with any systems of communication or any other facilities or installations of the coastal State;

(*l*) any other activity not having a direct bearing on passage.

Article 20

Submarines and other underwater vehicles

In the territorial sea, submarines and other underwater vehicles are required to navigate on the surface and to show their flag.

Article 21

Laws and regulations of the coastal State relating to innocent passage

1. The coastal State may adopt laws and regulations, in conformity with the provisions of this Convention and other rules of international law, relating to innocent passage through the territorial sea, in respect of all or any of the following:

(a) the safety of navigation and the regulation of maritime traffic;

(b) the protection of navigational aids and facilities and other facilities or installations;

(c) the protection of cables and pipelines;

(d) the conservation of the living resources of the sea;

(e) the prevention of infringement of the fisheries laws and regulations of the coastal State;

(f) the preservation of the environment of the coastal State and the prevention, reduction and control of pollution thereof;

(g) marine scientific research and hydrographic surveys;

(h) the prevention of infringement of the customs, fiscal, immigration or sanitary laws and regulations of the coastal State.

2. Such laws and regulations shall not apply to the design, construction, manning or equipment of foreign ships unless they are giving effect to generally accepted international rules or standards.

3. The coastal State shall give due publicity to all such laws and regulations.

4. Foreign ships exercising the right of innocent passage through the territorial sea shall comply with all such laws and regulations and all generally accepted international regulations relating to the prevention of collisions at sea.

Article 22

Sea lanes and traffic separation schemes in the territorial sea

1. The coastal State may, where necessary having regard to the safety of navigation, require foreign ships exercising the right of innocent passage through its territorial sea to use such sea lanes and traffic separation schemes as it may designate or prescribe for the regulation of the passage of ships.

2. In particular, tankers, nuclear-powered ships and ships carrying nuclear or other inherently dangerous or noxious substances or materials may be required to confine their passage to such sea lanes.

3. In the designation of sea lanes and the prescription of traffic separation schemes under this article, the coastal State shall take into account:

(a) the recommendations of the competent international organization;

(b) any channels customarily used for international navigation;

(c) the special characteristics of particular ships and channels; and

(d) the density of traffic.

4. The coastal State shall clearly indicate such sea lanes and traffic separation schemes on charts to which due publicity shall be given.

Article 23

Foreign nuclear-powered ships and ships carrying nuclear or other inherently dangerous or noxious substances

Foreign nuclear-powered ships and ships carrying nuclear or other inherently dangerous or noxious substances shall, when exercising the right of innocent passage through the territorial sea, carry documents and observe special precautionary measures established for such ships by international agreements.

Article 24

Duties of the coastal State

1. The coastal State shall not hamper the innocent passage of foreign ships through the territorial sea except in accordance with this Convention. In particular, in the application of this Convention or of any laws or regulations adopted in conformity with this Convention, the coastal State shall not:

(a) impose requirements on foreign ships which have the practical effect of denying or impairing the right of innocent passage; or

(b) discriminate in form or in fact against the ships of any State or against ships carrying cargoes to, from or on behalf of any State.

2. [*See* Basic Document 5.6, Art. 15(2).]

Article 25

Rights of protection of the coastal State

1. [*See* Basic Document 5.6, Art. 16(1).]

2. In the case of ships proceeding to internal waters or a call at a port facility outside internal waters, the coastal State also has the right to take the necessary steps to prevent any breach of the conditions to which admission of those ships to internal waters or such a call is subject.

3. The coastal State may, without discrimination in form or in fact among foreign ships, suspend temporarily in specified areas of its territorial sea the innocent passage of foreign ships if such suspension is essential for the protection of its

security, including weapons exercises. Such suspension shall take effect only after having been duly published.

Article 26

Charges which may be levied upon foreign ships

[*See* Basic Document 5.6, Art. 18.]

SUBSECTION B. RULES APPLICABLE TO MERCHANT SHIPS AND GOVERNMENT SHIPS OPERATED FOR COMMERCIAL PURPOSES

Article 27

Criminal jurisdiction on board a foreign ship

1. The criminal jurisdiction of the coastal State should not be exercised on board a foreign ship passing through the territorial sea to arrest any person or to conduct any investigation in connection with any crime committed on board the ship during its passage, save only in the following cases:

(a) if the consequences of the crime extend to the coastal State;

(b) if the crime is of a kind to disturb the peace of the country or the good order of the territorial sea;

(c) if the assistance of the local authorities has been requested by the master of the ship or by a diplomatic agent or consular officer of the flag State; or

(d) if such measures are necessary for the suppression of illicit traffic in narcotic drugs or psychotropic substances.

2. [*See* Basic Document 5.6, Art. 19(2).]

3. [*See* Basic Document 5.6, Art. 19(3).]

4. [*See* Basic Document 5.6, Art. 19(4).]

5. Except as provided in Part XII or with respect to violations of laws and regulations adopted in accordance with Part V, the coastal State may not take any steps on board a foreign ship passing through the territorial sea to arrest any person or to conduct any investigation in connection with any crime committed before the ship entered the territorial sea, if the ship, proceeding from a foreign port, is only passing through the territorial sea without entering internal waters

Article 28

Civil jurisdiction in relation to foreign ships

[*See* Basic Document 5.6, Art. 20.]

SUBSECTION C. RULES APPLICABLE TO WARSHIPS AND OTHER GOVERNMENT SHIPS OPERATED FOR NON–COMMERCIAL PURPOSES

Article 29

Definition of warships

For the purposes of this Convention, "warship" means a ship belonging to the armed forces of a State bearing the external marks distinguishing such ships of its nationality, under the command of an officer duly commissioned by the government of the State and whose name appears in the appropriate service list or its equivalent, and manned by a crew which is under regular armed forces discipline.

Article 30

Non-compliance by warships with the laws and regulations of the coastal State

If any warship does not comply with the laws and regulations of the coastal State concerning passage through the territorial sea and disregards any request for compliance therewith which is made to it, the coastal State may require it to leave the territorial sea immediately.

Article 31

Responsibility of the flag State for damage caused by a warship or other government ship operated for non-commercial purposes

The flag State shall bear international responsibility for any loss or damage to the coastal State resulting from the non-compliance by a warship or other government ship operated for non-commercial purposes with the laws and regulations of the coastal State concerning passage through the territorial sea or with the provisions of this Convention or other rules of international law.

Article 32

Immunities of warships and other government ships operated for non-commercial purposes

With such exceptions as are contained in subsection A and in articles 30 and 31, nothing in this Convention affects the immunities of warships and other government ships operated for non-commercial purposes.

SECTION 4. CONTIGUOUS ZONE

Article 33

Contiguous zone

1. [*See* Basic Document 5.6, Art. 24(1).]

2. The contiguous zone may not extend beyond 24 nautical miles from the baselines from which the breadth of the territorial sea is measured.

PART III

STRAITS USED FOR INTERNATIONAL NAVIGATION

SECTION 1. GENERAL PROVISIONS

Article 34

Legal status of waters forming straits used for international navigation

1. The régime of passage through straits used for international navigation established in this Part shall not in other respects affect the legal status of the waters forming such straits or the exercise by the States bordering the straits of their sovereignty or jurisdiction over such waters and their air space, bed and subsoil.

2. The sovereignty or jurisdiction of the States bordering the straits is exercised subject to this Part and to other rules of international law.

Article 35

Scope of this Part

Nothing in this Part affects:

(a) any areas of internal waters within a strait, except where the establishment of a straight baseline in accordance with the method set forth in article 7 has the effect of enclosing as internal waters areas which had not previously been considered as such;

(b) the legal status of the waters beyond the territorial seas of States bordering straits as exclusive economic zones or high seas; or

(c) the legal régime in straits in which passage is regulated in whole or in part by long-standing international conventions in force specifically relating to such straits.

Article 36

High seas routes or routes through exclusive economic zones through straits used for international navigation

This Part does not apply to a strait used for international navigation if there exists through the strait a route through the high seas or through an exclusive economic zone of similar convenience with respect to navigational and hydrographical characteristics; in such routes, the other relevant Parts of this Convention, including the provisions regarding the freedoms of navigation and overflight, apply.

SECTION 2. TRANSIT PASSAGE

Article 37

Scope of this section

This section applies to straits which are used for international navigation between one part of the high seas or an exclusive economic zone and another part of the high seas or an exclusive economic zone.

Article 38

Right of transit passage

1. In straits referred to in article 37, all ships and aircraft enjoy the right of transit passage, which shall not be impeded; except that, if the strait is formed by an island of a State bordering the strait and its mainland, transit passage shall not apply if there exists seaward of the island a route through the high seas or through an exclusive economic zone of similar convenience with respect to navigational and hydrographical characteristics.

2. Transit passage means the exercise in accordance with this Part of the freedom of navigation and overflight solely for the purpose of continuous and expeditious transit of the strait between one part of the high seas or an exclusive economic zone and another part of the high seas or an exclusive economic zone. However, the requirement of continuous and expeditious transit does not preclude passage through the strait for the purpose of entering, leaving or returning from a State bordering the strait, subject to the conditions of entry to that State.

3. Any activity which is not an exercise of the right of transit passage through a strait remains subject to the other applicable provisions of this Convention.

Article 39

Duties of ships and aircraft during transit passage

1. Ships and aircraft, while exercising the right of transit passage, shall:

(a) proceed without delay through or over the strait;

(b) refrain from any threat or use of force against the sovereignty, territorial integrity or political independence of States bordering the strait, or in any other manner in violation of the principles of international law embodied in the Charter of the United Nations;

(c) refrain from any activities other than those incident to their normal modes of continuous and expeditious transit unless rendered necessary by *force majeure* or by distress;

(d) comply with other relevant provisions of this Part.

* * *

Article 40

Research and survey activities

During transit passage, foreign ships, including marine scientific research and hydrographic survey ships, may not carry out any research or survey activities without the prior authorization of the States bordering straits.

Article 41

Sea lanes and traffic separation schemes in straits used for international navigation

1. In conformity with this Part, States bordering straits may designate sea lanes and prescribe traffic separation schemes for navigation in straits where necessary to promote the safe passage of ships.

2. Such States may, when circumstances require, and after giving due publicity thereto, substitute other sea lanes or traffic separation schemes for any sea lanes or traffic separation schemes previously designated or prescribed by them.

3. Such sea lanes and traffic separation schemes shall conform to generally accepted international regulations.

4. Before designating or substituting sea lanes or prescribing or substituting traffic separation schemes, States bordering straits shall refer proposals to the competent international organization with a view to their adoption. The organization may adopt only such sea lanes and traffic separation schemes as may be agreed with the States bordering the straits, after which the States may designate, prescribe or substitute them.

5. In respect of a strait where sea lanes or traffic separation schemes through the waters of two or more States bordering the strait are being proposed, the States concerned shall co-operate in formulating proposals in consultation with the competent international organization.

6. States bordering straits shall clearly indicate all sea lanes and traffic separation schemes designated or prescribed by them on charts to which due publicity shall be given.

7. Ships in transit passage shall respect applicable sea lanes and traffic separation schemes established in accordance with this article.

Article 42

Laws and regulations of States bordering straits relating to transit passage

1. Subject to the provisions of this section, States bordering straits may adopt laws and regulations relating to transit passage through straits, in respect of all or any of the following:

(a) the safety of navigation and the regulation of maritime traffic, as provided in article 41;

(b) the prevention, reduction and control of pollution, by giving effect to applicable international regulations regarding the discharge of oil, oily wastes and other noxious substances in the strait;

(c) with respect to fishing vessels, the prevention of fishing, including the stowage of fishing gear;

(d) the loading or unloading of any commodity, currency or person in contravention of the customs, fiscal, immigration or sanitary laws and regulations of States bordering straits.

2. Such laws and regulations shall not discriminate in form or in fact among foreign ships or in their application have the practical effect of denying, hampering or impairing the right of transit passage as defined in this section.

3. States bordering straits shall give due publicity to all such laws and regulations.

4. Foreign ships exercising the right of transit passage shall comply with such laws and regulations.

5. The flag State of a ship or the State of registry of an aircraft entitled to sovereign immunity which acts in a manner contrary to such laws and regulations or other provisions of this Part shall bear international responsibility for any loss or damage which results to States bordering straits.

Article 43

Navigational and safety aids and other improvements and the prevention, reduction and control of pollution

User States and States bordering a strait should by agreement co-operate:

(a) in the establishment and maintenance in a strait of necessary navigational and safety aids or other improvements in aid of international navigation; and

(b) for the prevention, reduction and control of pollution from ships.

Article 44

Duties of States bordering straits

States bordering straits shall not hamper transit passage and shall give appropriate publicity to any danger to navigation or overflight within or over the strait of which they have knowledge. There shall be no suspension of transit passage.

SECTION 3. INNOCENT PASSAGE

Article 45

Innocent passage

1. The régime of innocent passage, in accordance with Part II, section 3, shall apply in straits used for international navigation:

(a) excluded from the application of the régime of transit passage under article 38, paragraph 1; or

(b) between a part of the high seas or an exclusive economic zone and the territorial sea of a foreign State.

2. There shall be no suspension of innocent passage through such straits.

PART IV
ARCHIPELAGIC STATES

Article 46

Use of terms

For the purposes of this Convention:

(a) "archipelagic State" means a State constituted wholly by one or more archipelagos and may include other islands;

(b) "archipelago" means a group of islands, including parts of islands, interconnecting waters and other natural features which are so closely interrelated that such islands, waters and other natural features form an intrinsic geographical, economic and political entity, or which historically have been regarded as such.

Article 47

Archipelagic baselines

1. An archipelagic State may draw straight archipelagic baselines joining the outermost points of the outermost islands and drying reefs of the archipelago provided that within such baselines are included the main islands and an area in which the ratio of the area of the water to the area of the land, including atolls, is between 1 to 1 and 9 to 1.

2. The length of such baselines shall not exceed 100 nautical miles, except that up to 3 per cent of the total number of baselines enclosing any archipelago may exceed that length, up to a maximum length of 125 nautical miles.

3. The drawing of such baselines shall not depart to any appreciable extent from the general configuration of the archipelago.

4. Such baselines shall not be drawn to and from low-tide elevations, unless lighthouses or similar installations which are permanently above sea level have been built on them or where a low-tide elevation is situated wholly or partly at a distance not exceeding the breadth of the territorial sea from the nearest island.

5. The system of such baselines shall not be applied by an archipelagic State in such a manner as to cut off from the high seas or the exclusive economic zone the territorial sea of another State.

6. If a part of the archipelagic waters of an archipelagic State lies between two parts of an immediately adjacent neighbouring State, existing rights and all other legitimate interests which the latter State has traditionally exercised in such waters and all rights stipulated by agreement between those States shall continue and be respected.

* * *

Article 48

Measurement of the breadth of the territorial sea, the contiguous zone, the exclusive economic zone and the continental shelf

The breadth of the territorial sea, the contiguous zone, the exclusive economic zone and the continental shelf shall be measured from archipelagic baselines drawn in accordance with article 47.

Article 49

Legal status of archipelagic waters, of the air space over archipelagic waters and of their bed and subsoil

1. The sovereignty of an archipelagic State extends to the waters enclosed by the archipelagic baselines drawn in accordance with article 47, described as archipelagic waters, regardless of their depth or distance from the coast.

2. This sovereignty extends to the air space over the archipelagic waters, as well as to their bed and subsoil, and the resources contained therein.

* * *

Article 50

Delimitation of internal waters

Within its archipelagic waters, the archipelagic State may draw closing lines for the delimitation of internal waters, in accordance with articles 9, 10 and 11.

Article 51

Existing agreements, traditional fishing rights and existing submarine cables

1. Without prejudice to article 49, an archipelagic State shall respect existing agreements with other States and shall recognize traditional fishing rights and other legitimate activities of the immediately adjacent neighbouring States in certain areas falling within archipelagic waters. The terms and conditions for the exercise of such rights and activities, including the nature, the extent and the areas to which they apply, shall, at the request of any of the States concerned, be regulated by bilateral agreements between them. Such rights shall not be transferred to or shared with third States or their nationals.

2. An archipelagic State shall respect existing submarine cables laid by other States and passing through its waters without making a landfall. An archipelagic State shall permit the maintenance and replacement of such cables upon receiving due notice of their location and the intention to repair or replace them.

Article 52

Right of innocent passage

1. Subject to article 53 and without prejudice to article 50, ships of all States enjoy the right of innocent passage through archipelagic waters, in accordance with Part II, section 3.

2. The archipelagic State may, without discrimination in form or in fact among foreign ships, suspend temporarily in specified areas of its archipelagic waters the innocent passage of foreign ships if such suspension is essential for the protection of its security. Such suspension shall take effect only after having been duly published.

Article 53

Right of archipelagic sea lanes passage

1. An archipelagic State may designate sea lanes and air routes thereabove, suitable for the continuous and expeditious passage of foreign ships and aircraft through or over its archipelagic waters and the adjacent territorial sea.

2. All ships and aircraft enjoy the right of archipelagic sea lanes passage in such sea lanes and air routes.

* * *

6. An archipelagic State which designates sea lanes under this article may also prescribe traffic separation schemes for the safe passage of ships through narrow channels in such sea lanes.

* * *

8. Such sea lanes and traffic separation schemes shall conform to generally accepted international regulations.

Article 54

Duties of ships and aircraft during their passage, research and survey activities, duties of the archipelagic State and laws and regulations of the archipelagic State relating to archipelagic sea lanes passage

Articles 39, 40, 42 and 44 apply *mutatis mutandis* to archipelagic sea lanes passage.

PART V

EXCLUSIVE ECONOMIC ZONE

Article 55

Specific legal régime of the exclusive economic zone

The exclusive economic zone is an area beyond and adjacent to the territorial sea, subject to the specific legal régime established in this Part, under which the rights and jurisdiction of the coastal State and the rights and freedoms of other States are governed by the relevant provisions of this Convention.

Article 56

Rights, jurisdiction and duties of the coastal State in the exclusive economic zone

1. In the exclusive economic zone, the coastal State has:

(a) sovereign rights for the purpose of exploring and exploiting, conserving and managing the natural resources, whether living or non-living, of the waters superjacent to the sea-bed and of the sea-bed and its subsoil, and with regard to other activities for the economic exploitation and exploration of the zone, such as the production of energy from the water, currents and winds;

(b) jurisdiction as provided for in the relevant provisions of this Convention with regard to:

(i) the establishment and use of artificial islands, installations and structures;

(ii) marine scientific research;

(iii) the protection and preservation of the marine environment;

(c) other rights and duties provided for in this Convention.

2. In exercising its rights and performing its duties under this Convention in the exclusive economic zone, the coastal State shall have due regard to the rights and duties of other States and shall act in a manner compatible with the provisions of this Convention.

3. The rights set out in this article with respect to the sea-bed and subsoil shall be exercised in accordance with Part VI.

Article 57

Breadth of the exclusive economic zone

The exclusive economic zone shall not extend beyond 200 nautical miles from the baselines from which the breadth of the territorial sea is measured.

Article 58

Rights and duties of other States in the exclusive economic zone

1. In the exclusive economic zone, all States, whether coastal or land-locked, enjoy, subject to the relevant provisions of this Convention, the freedoms referred to in article 87 of navigation and overflight and of the laying of submarine cables and pipelines, and other internationally lawful uses of the sea related to these freedoms, such as those associated with the operation of ships, aircraft and submarine cables and pipelines, and compatible with the other provisions of this Convention.

2. Articles 88 to 115 and other pertinent rules of international law apply to the exclusive economic zone in so far as they are not incompatible with this Part.

3. In exercising their rights and performing their duties under this Convention in the exclusive economic zone, States shall have due regard to the rights and duties

of the coastal State and shall comply with the laws and regulations adopted by the coastal State in accordance with the provisions of this Convention and other rules of international law in so far as they are not incompatible with this Part.

Article 59

Basis for the resolution of conflicts regarding the attribution of rights and jurisdiction in the exclusive economic zone

In cases where this Convention does not attribute rights or jurisdiction to the coastal State or to other States within the exclusive economic zone, and a conflict arises between the interests of the coastal State and any other State or States, the conflict should be resolved on the basis of equity and in the light of all the relevant circumstances, taking into account the respective importance of the interests involved to the parties as well as to the international community as a whole.

Article 60

Artificial islands, installations and structures in the exclusive economic zone

1. In the exclusive economic zone, the coastal State shall have the exclusive right to construct and to authorize and regulate the construction, operation and use of:

(a) artificial islands;

(b) installations and structures for the purposes provided for in article 56 and other economic purposes;

(c) installations and structures which may interfere with the exercise of the rights of the coastal State in the zone.

2. The coastal State shall have exclusive jurisdiction over such artificial islands, installations and structures, including jurisdiction with regard to customs, fiscal, health, safety and immigration laws and regulations.

3. Due notice must be given of the construction of such artificial islands, installations or structures, and permanent means for giving warning of their presence must be maintained. * * *

* * *

7. Artificial islands, installations and structures and the safety zones around them may not be established where interference may be caused to the use of recognized sea lanes essential to international navigation.

8. Artificial islands, installations and structures do not possess the status of islands. They have no territorial sea of their own, and their presence does not affect the delimitation of the territorial sea, the exclusive economic zone or the continental shelf.

Article 61

Conservation of the living resources

1. The coastal State shall determine the allowable catch of the living resources in its exclusive economic zone.

2. The coastal State, taking into account the best scientific evidence available to it, shall ensure through proper conservation and management measures that the maintenance of the living resources in the exclusive economic zone is not endangered by over-exploitation. As appropriate, the coastal State and competent international organizations, whether subregional, regional or global, shall co-operate to this end.

3. Such measures shall also be designed to maintain or restore populations of harvested species at levels which can produce the maximum sustainable yield, as

qualified by relevant environmental and economic factors, including the economic needs of coastal fishing communities and the special requirements of developing States, and taking into account fishing patterns, the interdependence of stocks and any generally recommended international minimum standards, whether subregional, regional or global.

4. In taking such measures the coastal State shall take into consideration the effects on species associated with or dependent upon harvested species with a view to maintaining or restoring populations of such associated or dependent species above levels at which their reproduction may become seriously threatened.

5. Available scientific information, catch and fishing effort statistics, and other data relevant to the conservation of fish stocks shall be contributed and exchanged on a regular basis through competent international organizations, whether subregional, regional or global, where appropriate and with participation by all States concerned, including States whose nationals are allowed to fish in the exclusive economic zone.

Article 62

Utilization of the living resources

1. The coastal State shall promote the objective of optimum utilization of the living resources in the exclusive economic zone without prejudice to article 61.

2. The coastal State shall determine its capacity to harvest the living resources of the exclusive economic zone. Where the coastal State does not have the capacity to harvest the entire allowable catch, it shall, through agreements or other arrangements and pursuant to the terms, conditions, laws and regulations referred to in paragraph 4, give other States access to the surplus of the allowable catch, having particular regard to the provisions of articles 69 and 70, especially in relation to the developing States mentioned therein.

3. In giving access to other States to its exclusive economic zone under this article, the coastal State shall take into account all relevant factors, including, *inter alia,* the significance of the living resources of the area to the economy of the coastal State concerned and its other national interests, the provisions of articles 69 and 70, the requirements of developing States in the subregion or region in harvesting part of the surplus and the need to minimize economic dislocation in States whose nationals have habitually fished in the zone or which have made substantial efforts in research and identification of stocks.

4. Nationals of other States fishing in the exclusive economic zone shall comply with the conservation measures and with the other terms and conditions established in the laws and regulations of the coastal State. These laws and regulations shall be consistent with this Convention. * * *

5. Coastal States shall give due notice of conservation and management laws and regulations.

Article 63

Stocks occurring within the exclusive economic zones of two or more coastal States or both within the exclusive economic zone and in an area beyond and adjacent to it

1. Where the same stock or stocks of associated species occur within the exclusive economic zones of two or more coastal States, these States shall seek, either directly or through appropriate subregional or regional organizations, to agree upon the measures necessary to co-ordinate and ensure the conservation and development of such stocks without prejudice to the other provisions of this Part.

2. Where the same stock or stocks of associated species occur both within the exclusive economic zone and in an area beyond and adjacent to the zone, the coastal

State and the States fishing for such stocks in the adjacent area shall seek, either directly or through appropriate subregional or regional organizations, to agree upon the measures necessary for the conservation of these stocks in the adjacent area.

Article 64

Highly migratory species

1. The coastal State and other States whose nationals fish in the region for the highly migratory species listed in Annex I shall co-operate directly or through appropriate international organizations with a view to ensuring conservation and promoting the objective of optimum utilization of such species throughout the region, both within and beyond the exclusive economic zone. In regions for which no appropriate international organization exists, the coastal State and other States whose nationals harvest these species in the region shall co-operate to establish such an organization and participate in its work.

2. The provisions of paragraph 1 apply in addition to the other provisions of this Part.

Article 65

Marine mammals

Nothing in this Part restricts the right of a coastal State or the competence of an international organization, as appropriate, to prohibit, limit or regulate the exploitation of marine mammals more strictly than provided for in this Part. States shall co-operate with a view to the conservation of marine mammals and in the case of cetaceans shall in particular work through the appropriate international organizations for their conservation, management and study.

Article 66

Anadromous stocks

1. States in whose rivers anadromous stocks originate shall have the primary interest in and responsibility for such stocks.

* * *

Article 67

Catadromous species

1. A coastal State in whose waters catadromous species spend the greater part of their life cycle shall have responsibility for the management of these species and shall ensure the ingress and egress of migrating fish.

* * *

Article 68

Sedentary species

This Part does not apply to sedentary species as defined in article 77, paragraph 4.

Article 69

Right of land-locked States

1. Land-locked States shall have the right to participate, on an equitable basis, in the exploitation of an appropriate part of the surplus of the living resources of the exclusive economic zones of coastal States of the same subregion or region, taking into account the relevant economic and geographical circumstances of all the States concerned and in conformity with the provisions of this article and of articles 61 and 62.

2. The terms and modalities of such participation shall be established by the States concerned through bilateral, subregional or regional agreements taking into account, *inter alia:*

(a) the need to avoid effects detrimental to fishing communities or fishing industries of the coastal State;

(b) the extent to which the land-locked State, in accordance with the provisions of this article, is participating or is entitled to participate under existing bilateral, subregional or regional agreements in the exploitation of living resources of the exclusive economic zones of other coastal States;

(c) the extent to which other land-locked States and geographically disadvantaged States are participating in the exploitation of the living resources of the exclusive economic zone of the coastal State and the consequent need to avoid a particular burden for any single coastal State or a part of it;

(d) the nutritional needs of the populations of the respective States.

3. When the harvesting capacity of a coastal State approaches a point which would enable it to harvest the entire allowable catch of the living resources in its exclusive economic zone, the coastal State and other States concerned shall co-operate in the establishment of equitable arrangements on a bilateral, subregional or regional basis to allow for participation of developing land-locked States of the same subregion or region in the exploitation of the living resources of the exclusive economic zones of coastal States of the subregion or region, as may be appropriate in the circumstances and on terms satisfactory to all parties. In the implementation of this provision the factors mentioned in paragraph 2 shall also be taken into account.

4. Developed land-locked States shall, under the provisions of this article, be entitled to participate in the exploitation of living resources only in the exclusive economic zones of developed coastal States of the same subregion or region having regard to the extent to which the coastal State, in giving access to other States to the living resources of its exclusive economic zone, has taken into account the need to minimize detrimental effects on fishing communities and economic dislocation in States whose nationals have habitually fished in the zone.

5. The above provisions are without prejudice to arrangements agreed upon in subregions or regions where the coastal States may grant to land-locked States of the same subregion or region equal or preferential rights for the exploitation of the living resources in the exclusive economic zones.

Article 70

Right of geographically disadvantaged States

[This article is in all essential respects identical to Article 69, supra.]

Article 71

Non-applicability of articles 69 and 70

The provisions of articles 69 and 70 do not apply in the case of a coastal State whose economy is overwhelmingly dependent on the exploitation of the living resources of its exclusive economic zone.

Article 72

Restrictions on transfer of rights

* * *

Article 73

Enforcement of laws and regulations of the coastal State

1. The coastal State may, in the exercise of its sovereign rights to explore, exploit, conserve and manage the living resources in the exclusive economic zone, take such measures, including boarding, inspection, arrest and judicial proceedings, as may be necessary to ensure compliance with the laws and regulations adopted by it in conformity with this Convention.

2. Arrested vessels and their crews shall be promptly released upon the posting of reasonable bond or other security.

3. Coastal State penalties for violations of fisheries laws and regulations in the exclusive economic zone may not include imprisonment, in the absence of agreements to the contrary by the States concerned, or any other form of corporal punishment.

4. In cases of arrest or detention of foreign vessels the coastal State shall promptly notify the flag State, through appropriate channels, of the action taken and of any penalties subsequently imposed.

Article 74

Delimitation of the exclusive economic zone between States with opposite or adjacent coasts

1. The delimitation of the exclusive economic zone between States with opposite or adjacent coasts shall be effected by agreement on the basis of international law, as referred to in Article 38 of the Statute of the International Court of Justice, in order to achieve an equitable solution.

2. If no agreement can be reached within a reasonable period of time, the States concerned shall resort to the procedures provided for in Part XV.

* * *

Article 75

Charts and lists of geographical co-ordinates

* * *

PART VI

CONTINENTAL SHELF

Article 76

Definition of the continental shelf

1. The continental shelf of a coastal State comprises the sea-bed and subsoil of the submarine areas that extend beyond its territorial sea throughout the natural prolongation of its land territory to the outer edge of the continental margin, or to a distance of 200 nautical miles from the baselines from which the breadth of the territorial sea is measured where the outer edge of the continental margin does not extend up to that distance.

2. The continental shelf of a coastal State shall not extend beyond the limits provided for in paragraphs 4 to 6.

3. The continental margin comprises the submerged prolongation of the land mass of the coastal State, and consists of the sea-bed and subsoil of the shelf, the slope and the rise. It does not include the deep ocean floor with its oceanic ridges or the subsoil thereof.

4. (a) For the purposes of this Convention, the coastal State shall establish the outer edge of the continental margin wherever the margin extends beyond 200

nautical miles from the baselines from which the breadth of the territorial sea is measured, by either:

(i) a line delineated in accordance with paragraph 7 by reference to the outermost fixed points at each of which the thickness of sedimentary rocks is at least 1 per cent of the shortest distance from such point to the foot of the continental slope; or

(ii) a line delineated in accordance with paragraph 7 by reference to fixed points not more than 60 nautical miles from the foot of the continental slope.

(b) In the absence of evidence to the contrary, the foot of the continental slope shall be determined as the point of maximum change in the gradient at its base.

5. The fixed points comprising the line of the outer limits of the continental shelf on the sea-bed, drawn in accordance with paragraph 4(a)(i) and (ii), either shall not exceed 350 nautical miles from the baselines from which the breadth of the territorial sea is measured or shall not exceed 100 nautical miles from the 2,500 metre isobath, which is a line connecting the depths of 2,500 metres.

6. Notwithstanding the provisions of paragraph 5, on submarine ridges, the outer limit of the continental shelf shall not exceed 350 nautical miles from the baselines from which the breadth of the territorial sea is measured. This paragraph does not apply to submarine elevations that are natural components of the continental margin, such as its plateaux, rises, caps, banks and spurs.

7. The coastal State shall delineate the outer limits of its continental shelf, where that shelf extends beyond 200 nautical miles from the baselines from which the breadth of the territorial sea is measured, by straight lines not exceeding 60 nautical miles in length, connecting fixed points, defined by coordinates of latitude and longitude.

* * *

Article 77

Rights of the coastal State over the continental shelf

1. [*See* Basic Document 5.5, Art. 2(1).]

2. The rights referred to in paragraph 1 are exclusive in the sense that if the coastal State does not explore the continental shelf or exploit its natural resources, no one may undertake these activities without the express consent of the coastal State.

3. [*See* Basic Document 5.5, Art. 2(3).]

4. [*See* Basic Document 5.5, Art. 2(4).]

Article 78

Legal status of the superjacent waters and air space and the rights and freedoms of other States

1. The rights of the coastal State over the continental shelf do not affect the legal status of the superjacent waters or of the air space above those waters.

2. The exercise of the rights of the coastal State over the continental shelf must not infringe or result in any unjustifiable interference with navigation and other rights and freedoms of other States as provided for in this Convention.

Article 79

Submarine cables and pipelines on the continental shelf

1. All States are entitled to lay submarine cables and pipelines on the continental shelf, in accordance with the provisions of this article.

2. Subject to its right to take reasonable measures for the exploration of the continental shelf, the exploitation of its natural resources and the prevention, reduction and control of pollution from pipelines, the coastal State may not impede the laying or maintenance of such cables or pipelines.

3. The delineation of the course for the laying of such pipelines on the continental shelf is subject to the consent of the coastal State.

4. Nothing in this Part affects the right of the coastal State to establish conditions for cables or pipelines entering its territory or territorial sea, or its jurisdiction over cables and pipelines constructed or used in connection with the exploration of its continental shelf or exploitation of its resources or the operations of artificial islands, installations and structures under its jurisdiction.

5. When laying submarine cables or pipelines, States shall have due regard to cables or pipelines already in position. In particular, possibilities of repairing existing cables or pipelines shall not be prejudiced.

Article 80

Artificial islands, installations and structures on the continental shelf

Article 60 applies *mutatis mutandis* to artificial islands, installations and structures on the continental shelf.

Article 81

Drilling on the continental shelf

The coastal State shall have the exclusive right to authorize and regulate drilling on the continental shelf for all purposes.

Article 82

Payments and contributions with respect to the exploitation of the continental shelf beyond 200 nautical miles

1. The coastal State shall make payments or contributions in kind in respect of the exploitation of the non-living resources of the continental shelf beyond 200 nautical miles from the baselines from which the breadth of the territorial sea is measured.

2. The payments and contributions shall be made annually with respect to all production at a site after the first five years of production at that site. For the sixth year, the rate of payment or contribution shall be 1 per cent of the value or volume of production at the site. The rate shall increase by 1 per cent for each subsequent year until the twelfth year and shall remain at 7 per cent thereafter. Production does not include resources used in connection with exploitation.

3. A developing State which is a net importer of a mineral resource produced from its continental shelf is exempt from making such payments or contributions in respect of that mineral resource.

4. The payments or contributions shall be made through the Authority, which shall distribute them to States Parties to this Convention, on the basis of equitable sharing criteria, taking into account the interests and needs of developing States, particularly the least developed and the land-locked among them.

Article 83

Delimitation of the continental shelf between States with opposite or adjacent coasts

1. The delimitation of the continental shelf between States with opposite or adjacent coasts shall be effected by agreement on the basis of international law, as

referred to in Article 38 of the Statute of the International Court of Justice, in order to achieve an equitable solution.

2. If no agreement can be reached within a reasonable period of time, the States concerned shall resort to the procedures provided for in Part XV.

Article 84

Charts and lists of geographical co-ordinates

* * *

Article 85

Tunnelling

This Part does not prejudice the right of the coastal State to exploit the subsoil by means of tunnelling, irrespective of the depth of water above the subsoil.

PART VII

HIGH SEAS

SECTION 1. GENERAL PROVISIONS

Article 86

Application of the provisions of this Part

The provisions of this Part apply to all parts of the sea that are not included in the exclusive economic zone, in the territorial sea or in the internal waters of a State, or in the archipelagic waters of an archipelagic State. This article does not entail any abridgement of the freedoms enjoyed by all States in the exclusive economic zone in accordance with article 58.

Article 87

Freedom of the high seas

1. The high seas are open to all States, whether coastal or land-locked. Freedom of the high seas is exercised under the conditions laid down by this Convention and by other rules of international law. It comprises, *inter alia,* both for coastal and land-locked States:

(a) freedom of navigation;

(b) freedom of overflight;

(c) freedom to lay submarine cables and pipelines, subject to Part VI;

(d) freedom to construct artificial islands and other installations permitted under international law, subject to Part VI;

(e) freedom of fishing, subject to the conditions laid down in section 2;

(f) freedom of scientific research, subject to Parts VI and XIII.

2. These freedoms shall be exercised by all States with due regard for the interests of other States in their exercise of the freedom of the high seas, and also with due regard for the rights under this Convention with respect to activities in the Area.

Article 88

Reservation of the high seas for peaceful purposes

The high seas shall be reserved for peaceful purposes.

Article 89

Invalidity of claims of sovereignty over the high seas

No State may validly purport to subject any part of the high seas to its sovereignty.

Article 90

Right of navigation

[*See* Basic Document 5.4, Art. 4.]

Article 91

Nationality of Ships

[*See* Basic Document 5.4, Art. 5.]

Article 92

Status of ships

[*See* Basic Document 5.4, Art. 6.]

Article 93

Ships flying the flag of the United Nations, its specialized agencies and the International Atomic Energy Agency

The preceding articles do not prejudice the question of ships employed on the official service of the United Nations, its specialized agencies or the International Atomic Energy Agency, flying the flag of the organization.

Article 94

Duties of the flag State

1. Every State shall effectively exercise its jurisdiction and control in administrative, technical and social matters over ships flying its flag.

2. In particular every State shall:

(a) maintain a register of ships containing the names and particulars of ships flying its flag, except those which are excluded from generally accepted international regulations on account of their small size; and

(b) assume jurisdiction under its internal law over each ship flying its flag and its master, officers and crew in respect of administrative, technical and social matters concerning the ship.

3. Every State shall take such measures for ships flying its flag as are necessary to ensure safety at sea with regard, *inter alia,* to:

(a) the construction, equipment and seaworthiness of ships;

(b) the manning of ships, labour conditions and the training of crews, taking into account the applicable international instruments;

(c) the use of signals, the maintenance of communications and the prevention of collisions.

4. Such measures shall include those necessary to ensure:

(a) that each ship, before registration and thereafter at appropriate intervals, is surveyed by a qualified surveyor of ships, and has on board such charts, nautical publications and navigational equipment and instruments as are appropriate for the safe navigation of the ship;

(b) that each ship is in the charge of a master and officers who possess appropriate qualifications, in particular in seamanship, navigation, communications and marine engineering, and that the crew is appropriate in qualification and numbers for the type, size, machinery and equipment of the ship;

(c) that the master, officers and, to the extent appropriate, the crew are fully conversant with and required to observe the applicable international regulations concerning the safety of life at sea, the prevention of collisions, the prevention, reduction and control of marine pollution, and the maintenance of communications by radio.

5. In taking the measures called for in paragraphs 3 and 4 each State is required to conform to generally accepted international regulations, procedures and practices and to take any steps which may be necessary to secure their observance.

6. A State which has clear grounds to believe that proper jurisdiction and control with respect to a ship have not been exercised may report the facts to the flag State. Upon receiving such a report, the flag State shall investigate the matter and, if appropriate, take any action necessary to remedy the situation.

7. Each State shall cause an inquiry to be held by or before a suitably qualified person or persons into every marine casualty or incident of navigation on the high seas involving a ship flying its flag and causing loss of life or serious injury to nationals of another State or serious damage to ships or installations of another State or to the marine environment. The flag State and the other State shall co-operate in the conduct of any inquiry held by that other State into any such marine casualty or incident of navigation.

Article 95

Immunity of warships on the high seas

[*See* Basic Document 5.4, Art. 8(1).]

Article 96

Immunity of ships used only on government non-commercial service

[*See* Basic Document 5.4, Art. 9.]

Article 97

Penal jurisdiction in matters of collision or in any other incident of navigation

[*See* Basic Document 5.4, Art. 11.]

Article 98

Duty to render assistance

[*See* Basic Document 5.4, Art. 12.]

Article 99

Prohibition of the transport of slaves

[*See* Basic Document 5.4, Art. 13.]

Article 100

Duty to co-operate in the repression of piracy

[*See* Basic Document 5.4, Art. 14.]

Article 101

Definition of piracy

[*See* Basic Document 5.4, Art. 15.]

Article 102

Piracy by a warship, government ship or government aircraft whose crew has mutinied

The acts of piracy, as defined in article 101, committed by a warship, government ship or government aircraft whose crew has mutinied and taken control of the ship or aircraft are assimilated to acts committed by a private ship or aircraft.

Article 103

Definition of a pirate ship or aircraft

A ship or aircraft is considered a pirate ship or aircraft if it is intended by the persons in dominant control to be used for the purpose of committing one of the acts referred to in article 101. The same applies if the ship or aircraft has been used to commit any such act, so long as it remains under the control of the persons guilty of that act.

Article 104

Retention or loss of the nationality of a pirate ship or aircraft

[*See* Basic Document 5.4, Art. 18.]

Article 105

Seizure of a pirate ship or aircraft

[*See* Basic Document 5.4, Art. 19.]

Article 106

Liability for seizure without adequate grounds

[*See* Basic Document 5.4, Art. 20.]

Article 107

Ships and aircraft which are entitled to seize on account of piracy

[*See* Basic Document 5.4, Art. 21.]

Article 108

Illicit traffic in narcotic drugs or psychotropic substances

1. All States shall co-operate in the suppression of illicit traffic in narcotic drugs and psychotropic substances engaged in by ships on the high seas contrary to international conventions.

2. Any State which has reasonable grounds for believing that a ship flying its flag is engaged in illicit traffic in narcotic drugs or psychotropic substances may request the co-operation of other States to suppress such traffic.

Article 109

Unauthorized broadcasting from the high seas

1. All States shall co-operate in the suppression of unauthorized broadcasting from the high seas.

2. For the purposes of this Convention, "unauthorized broadcasting" means the transmission of sound radio or television broadcasts from a ship or installation on the high seas intended for reception by the general public contrary to international regulations, but excluding the transmission of distress calls.

3. Any person engaged in unauthorized broadcasting may be prosecuted before the court of:

(a) the flag State of the ship;

(b) the State of registry of the installation;

(c) the State of which the person is a national;

(d) any State where the transmissions can be received; or

(e) any State where authorized radio communication is suffering interference.

4. On the high seas, a State having jurisdiction in accordance with paragraph 3 may, in conformity with article 110, arrest any person or ship engaged in unauthorized broadcasting and seize the broadcasting apparatus.

Article 110

Right of visit

1. Except where acts of interference derive from powers conferred by treaty, a warship which encounters on the high seas a foreign ship, other than a ship entitled to complete immunity in accordance with articles 95 and 96, is not justified in boarding it unless there is reasonable ground for suspecting that:

(a) the ship is engaged in piracy;

(b) the ship is engaged in the slave trade;

(c) the ship is engaged in unauthorized broadcasting and the flag State of the warship has jurisdiction under article 109;

(d) the ship is without nationality; or

(e) though flying a foreign flag or refusing to show its flag, the ship is, in reality, of the same nationality as the warship.

2. In the cases provided for in paragraph 1, the warship may proceed to verify the ship's right to fly its flag. To this end, it may send a boat under the command of an officer to the suspected ship. If suspicion remains after the documents have been checked, it may proceed to a further examination on board the ship, which must be carried out with all possible consideration.

3. If the suspicions prove to be unfounded, and provided that the ship boarded has not committed any act justifying them, it shall be compensated for any loss or damage that may have been sustained.

4. These provisions apply *mutatis mutandis* to military aircraft.

5. These provisions also apply to any other duly authorized ships or aircraft clearly marked and identifiable as being on government service.

Article 111

Right of hot pursuit

1. The hot pursuit of a foreign ship may be undertaken when the competent authorities of the coastal State have good reason to believe that the ship has violated the laws and regulations of that State. Such pursuit must be commenced when the foreign ship or one of its boats is within the internal waters, the archipelagic waters, the territorial sea or the contiguous zone of the pursuing State, and may only be continued outside the territorial sea or the contiguous zone if the pursuit has not been interrupted. It is not necessary that, at the time when the foreign ship within the territorial sea or the contiguous zone receives the order to stop, the ship giving the order should likewise be within the territorial sea or the contiguous zone. If the foreign ship is within a contiguous zone, as defined in article 33, the pursuit may only

be undertaken if there has been a violation of the rights for the protection of which the zone was established.

2. The right of hot pursuit shall apply *mutatis mutandis* to violations in the exclusive economic zone or on the continental shelf, including safety zones around continental shelf installations, of the laws and regulations of the coastal State applicable in accordance with this Convention to the exclusive economic zone or the continental shelf, including such safety zones.

3. [*See* Basic Document 5.4, Art. 23(2).]

4. Hot pursuit is not deemed to have begun unless the pursuing ship has satisfied itself by such practicable means as may be available that the ship pursued or one of its boats or other craft working as a team and using the ship pursued as a mother ship is within the limits of the territorial sea, or, as the case may be, within the contiguous zone or the exclusive economic zone or above the continental shelf. The pursuit may only be commenced after a visual or auditory signal to stop has been given at a distance which enables it to be seen or heard by the foreign ship.

5. The right of hot pursuit may be exercised only by warships or military aircraft, or other ships or aircraft clearly marked and identifiable as being on government service and authorized to that effect.

6. Where hot pursuit is effected by an aircraft:

(a) the provisions of paragraphs 1 to 4 shall apply *mutatis mutandis;*

(b) [See Basic Document 5.4, Art. 23(5)(b).]

7. The release of a ship arrested within the jurisdiction of a State and escorted to a port of that State for the purposes of an inquiry before the competent authorities may not be claimed solely on the ground that the ship, in the course of its voyage, was escorted across a portion of the exclusive economic zone or the high seas, if the circumstances rendered this necessary.

8. Where a ship has been stopped or arrested outside the territorial sea in circumstances which do not justify the exercise of the right of hot pursuit, it shall be compensated for any loss or damage that may have been thereby sustained.

Article 112

Right to lay submarine cables and pipelines

1. All States are entitled to lay submarine cables and pipelines on the bed of the high seas beyond the continental shelf.

2. Article 79, paragraph 5, applies to such cables and pipelines.

Article 113

Breaking or injury of a submarine cable or pipeline

[*See* Basic Document 5.4, Art. 27.]

Article 114

Breaking or injury by owners of a submarine cable or pipeline of another submarine cable or pipeline

[*See* Basic Document 5.4, Art. 28.]

Article 115

Indemnity for loss incurred in avoiding injury to a submarine cable or pipeline

[*See* Basic Document 5.4, Art. 29.]

SECTION 2. CONSERVATION AND MANAGEMENT OF THE LIVING RESOURCES OF THE HIGH SEAS

Article 116

Right to fish on the high seas

All States have the right for their nationals to engage in fishing on the high seas subject to:

(a) their treaty obligations;

(b) the rights and duties as well as the interests of coastal States provided for, *inter alia,* in article 63, paragraph 2, and articles 64 to 67; and

(c) the provisions of this section.

Article 117

Duty of States to adopt with respect to their nationals measures for the conservation of the living resources of the high seas

[*See* Basic Document 5.7, Art. 1(2).]

Article 118

Co-operation of States in the conservation and management of living resources

States shall co-operate with each other in the conservation and management of living resources in the areas of the high seas. States whose nationals exploit identical living resources, or different living resources in the same area, shall enter into negotiations with a view to taking the measures necessary for the conservation of the living resources concerned. They shall, as appropriate, co-operate to establish subregional or regional fisheries organizations to this end.

Article 119

Conservation of the living resources of the high seas

1. In determining the allowable catch and establishing other conservation measures for the living resources in the high seas, States shall:

(a) take measures which are designed, on the best scientific evidence available to the States concerned, to maintain or restore populations of harvested species at levels which can produce the maximum sustainable yield, as qualified by relevant environmental and economic factors, including the special requirements of developing States, and taking into account fishing patterns, the interdependence of stocks and any generally recommended international minimum standards, whether subregional, regional or global;

(b) take into consideration the effects on species associated with or dependent upon harvested species with a view to maintaining or restoring populations of such associated or dependent species above levels at which their reproduction may become seriously threatened.

2. Available scientific information, catch and fishing effort statistics, and other data relevant to the conservation of fish stocks shall be contributed and exchanged on a regular basis through competent international organizations, whether subregional, regional or global, where appropriate and with participation by all States concerned.

3. States concerned shall ensure that conservation measures and their implementation do not discriminate in form or in fact against the fishermen of any State.

Article 120

Marine mammals

Article 65 also applies to the conservation and management of marine mammals in the high seas.

PART VIII

REGIME OF ISLANDS

Article 121

Régime of islands

1. An island is a naturally formed area of land, surrounded by water, which is above water at high tide.

2. Except as provided for in paragraph 3, the territorial sea, the contiguous zone, the exclusive economic zone and the continental shelf of an island are determined in accordance with the provisions of this Convention applicable to other land territory.

3. Rocks which cannot sustain human habitation or economic life of their own shall have no exclusive economic zone or continental shelf.

PART IX

ENCLOSED OR SEMI-ENCLOSED SEAS

Article 122

Definition

For the purposes of this Convention, "enclosed or semi-enclosed sea" means a gulf, basin or sea surrounded by two or more States and connected to another sea or the ocean by a narrow outlet or consisting entirely or primarily of the territorial seas and exclusive economic zones of two or more coastal States.

Article 123

Co-operation of States bordering enclosed or semi-enclosed seas

States bordering an enclosed or semi-enclosed sea should co-operate with each other in the exercise of their rights and in the performance of their duties under this Convention. * * *

PART X

RIGHT OF ACCESS OF LAND-LOCKED STATES TO AND FROM THE SEA AND FREEDOM OF TRANSIT

Article 124

Use of terms

1. For the purposes of this Convention:

(a) "land-locked State" means a State which has no sea-coast;

(b) "transit State" means a State, with or without a sea-coast, situated between a land-locked State and the sea, through whose territory traffic in transit passes;

(c) "traffic in transit" means transit of persons, baggage, goods and means of transport across the territory of one or more transit States, when the passage across such territory, with or without trans-shipment, warehousing, breaking bulk or change in the mode of transport, is only a portion of a complete journey which begins or terminates within the territory of the land-locked State;

(d) "means of transport" means:

(i) railway rolling stock, sea, lake and river craft and road vehicles;

(ii) where local conditions so require, porters and pack animals.

2. Land-locked States and transit States may, by agreement between them, include as means of transport pipelines and gas lines and means of transport other than those included in paragraph 1.

Article 125

Right of access to and from the sea and freedom of transit

1. Land-locked States shall have the right of access to and from the sea for the purpose of exercising the rights provided for in this Convention including those relating to the freedom of the high seas and the common heritage of mankind. To this end, land-locked States shall enjoy freedom of transit through the territory of transit States by all means of transport.

2. The terms and modalities for exercising freedom of transit shall be agreed between the land-locked States and transit States concerned through bilateral, subregional or regional agreements.

3. Transit States, in the exercise of their full sovereignty over their territory, shall have the right to take all measures necessary to ensure that the rights and facilities provided for in this Part for land-locked States shall in no way infringe their legitimate interests.

Article 126

Exclusion of application of the most-favoured-nation clause

* * *

Article 127

Customs duties, taxes and other charges

1. Traffic in transit shall not be subject to any customs duties, taxes or other charges except charges levied for specific services rendered in connection with such traffic.

2. Means of transport in transit and other facilities provided for and used by land-locked States shall not be subject to taxes or charges higher than those levied for the use of means of transport of the transit State.

Article 128

Free zones and other customs facilities

* * *

Article 129

Co-operation in the construction and improvement of means of transport

* * *

Article 130

Measures to avoid or eliminate delays or other difficulties of a technical nature in traffic in transit

* * *

Article 131

Equal treatment in maritime ports

* * *

Article 132

Grant of greater transit facilities

* * *

PART XI

THE AREA

SECTION 1. GENERAL PROVISIONS

Article 133

Use of terms

For the purposes of this Part:

(a) "resources" means all solid, liquid or gaseous mineral resources *in situ* in the Area at or beneath the sea-bed, including polymetallic nodules;

(b) resources, when recovered from the Area, are referred to as "minerals".

Article 134

Scope of this Part

1. This Part applies to the Area.

2. Activities in the Area shall be governed by the provisions of this Part.

3. The requirements concerning deposit of, and publicity to be given to, the charts or lists of geographical co-ordinates showing the limits referred to in article 1, paragraph 1(1), are set forth in Part VI.

4. Nothing in this article affects the establishment of the outer limits of the continental shelf in accordance with Part VI or the validity of agreements relating to delimitation between States with opposite or adjacent coasts.

Article 135

Legal status of the superjacent waters and air space

Neither this Part nor any rights granted or exercised pursuant thereto shall affect the legal status of the waters superjacent to the Area or that of the air space above those waters.

SECTION 2. PRINCIPLES GOVERNING THE AREA

Article 136

Common heritage of mankind

The Area and its resources are the common heritage of mankind.

Article 137

Legal status of the Area and its resources

1. No State shall claim or exercise sovereignty or sovereign rights over any part of the Area or its resources, nor shall any State or natural or juridical person appropriate any part thereof. No such claim or exercise of sovereignty or sovereign rights nor such appropriation shall be recognized.

2. All rights in the resources of the Area are vested in mankind as a whole, on whose behalf the Authority shall act. These resources are not subject to alienation. The minerals recovered from the Area, however, may only be alienated in accordance with this Part and the rules, regulations and procedures of the Authority.

3. No State or natural or juridical person shall claim, acquire or exercise rights with respect to the minerals recovered from the Area except in accordance with this

Part. Otherwise, no such claim, acquisition or exercise of such rights shall be recognized.

Article 138

General conduct of States in relation to the Area

The general conduct of States in relation to the Area shall be in accordance with the provisions of this Part, the principles embodied in the Charter of the United Nations and other rules of international law in the interests of maintaining peace and security and promoting international co-operation and mutual understanding.

Article 139

Responsibility to ensure compliance and liability for damage

1. States Parties shall have the responsibility to ensure that activities in the Area, whether carried out by States Parties, or state enterprises or natural or juridical persons which possess the nationality of States Parties or are effectively controlled by them or their nationals, shall be carried out in conformity with this Part. The same responsibility applies to international organizations for activities in the Area carried out by such organizations.

* * *

Article 140

Benefit of mankind

1. Activities in the Area shall, as specifically provided for in this Part, be carried out for the benefit of mankind as a whole, irrespective of the geographical location of States, whether coastal or land-locked, and taking into particular consideration the interests and needs of developing States and of peoples who have not attained full independence or other self-governing status recognized by the United Nations in accordance with General Assembly resolution 1514 (XV) and other relevant General Assembly resolutions.

2. The Authority shall provide for the equitable sharing of financial and other economic benefits derived from activities in the Area through any appropriate mechanism, on a non-discriminatory basis, in accordance with article 160, paragraph 2(f)(i).

Article 141

Use of the Area exclusively for peaceful purposes

The Area shall be open to use exclusively for peaceful purposes by all States, whether coastal or land-locked, without discrimination and without prejudice to the other provisions of this Part.

Article 142

Rights and legitimate interests of coastal States

1. Activities in the Area, with respect to resource deposits in the Area which lie across limits of national jurisdiction, shall be conducted with due regard to the rights and legitimate interests of any coastal State across whose jurisdiction such deposits lie.

* * *

Article 143

Marine scientific research

1. Marine scientific research in the Area shall be carried out exclusively for peaceful purposes and for the benefit of mankind as a whole, in accordance with Part XIII.

2. The Authority may carry out marine scientific research concerning the Area and its resources, and may enter into contracts for that purpose. The Authority shall promote and encourage the conduct of marine scientific research in the Area, and shall co-ordinate and disseminate the results of such research and analysis when available.

3. States Parties may carry out marine scientific research in the Area. States Parties shall promote international co-operation in marine scientific research in the Area by:

(a) participating in international programmes and encouraging co-operation in marine scientific research by personnel of different countries and of the Authority;

(b) ensuring that programmes are developed through the Authority or other international organizations as appropriate for the benefit of developing States and technologically less developed States with a view to:

(i) strengthening their research capabilities;

(ii) training their personnel and the personnel of the Authority in the techniques and applications of research;

(iii) fostering the employment of their qualified personnel in research in the Area;

(c) effectively disseminating the results of research and analysis when available, through the Authority or other international channels when appropriate.

Article 144

Transfer of technology

1. The Authority shall take measures in accordance with this Convention:

(a) to acquire technology and scientific knowledge relating to activities in the Area; and

(b) to promote and encourage the transfer to developing States of such technology and scientific knowledge so that all States Parties benefit therefrom.

2. To this end the Authority and States Parties shall co-operate in promoting the transfer of technology and scientific knowledge relating to activities in the Area so that the Enterprise and all States Parties may benefit therefrom. In particular they shall initiate and promote:

(a) programmes for the transfer of technology to the Enterprise and to developing States with regard to activities in the Area, including, *inter alia,* facilitating the access of the Enterprise and of developing States to the relevant technology, under fair and reasonable terms and conditions;

(b) measures directed towards the advancement of the technology of the Enterprise and the domestic technology of developing States, particularly by providing opportunities to personnel from the Enterprise and from developing States for training in marine science and technology and for their full participation in activities in the Area.

Article 145

Protection of the marine environment

Necessary measures shall be taken in accordance with this Convention with respect to activities in the Area to ensure effective protection for the marine environment from harmful effects which may arise from such activities. To this end the Authority shall adopt appropriate rules, regulations and procedures for *inter alia:*

(a) the prevention, reduction and control of pollution and other hazards to the marine environment, including the coastline, and of interference with the ecological balance of the marine environment, particular attention being paid to the need for protection from harmful effects of such activities as drilling, dredging, excavation, disposal of waste, construction and operation or maintenance of installations, pipelines and other devices related to such activities;

(b) the protection and conservation of the natural resources of the Area and the prevention of damage to the flora and fauna of the marine environment.

Article 146

Protection of human life

With respect to activities in the Area, necessary measures shall be taken to ensure effective protection of human life. * * *

Article 147

Accommodation of activities in the Area and in the marine environment

1. Activities in the Area shall be carried out with reasonable regard for other activities in the marine environment.

2. Installations used for carrying out activities in the Area shall be subject to the following conditions:

(a) such installations shall be erected, emplaced and removed solely in accordance with this Part and subject to the rules, regulations and procedures of the Authority. Due notice must be given of the erection, emplacement and removal of such installations, and permanent means for giving warning of their presence must be maintained;

(b) such installations may not be established where interference may be caused to the use of recognized sea lanes essential to international navigation or in areas of intense fishing activity;

(c) safety zones shall be established around such installations with appropriate markings to ensure the safety of both navigation and the installations. The configuration and location of such safety zones shall not be such as to form a belt impeding the lawful access of shipping to particular maritime zones or navigation along international sea lanes;

(d) such installations shall be used exclusively for peaceful purposes;

(e) such installations do not possess the status of islands. They have no territorial sea of their own, and their presence does not affect the delimitation of the territorial sea, the exclusive economic zone or the continental shelf.

3. Other activities in the marine environment shall be conducted with reasonable regard for activities in the Area.

Article 148

Participation of developing States in activities in the Area

The effective participation of developing States in activities in the Area shall be promoted as specifically provided for in this Part, having due regard to their special interests and needs, and in particular to the special need of the land-locked and geographically disadvantaged among them to overcome obstacles arising from their disadvantaged location, including remoteness from the Area and difficulty of access to and from it.

Article 149

Archaeological and historical objects

All objects of an archaeological and historical nature found in the Area shall be preserved or disposed of for the benefit of mankind as a whole, particular regard being paid to the preferential rights of the State or country of origin, or the State of cultural origin, or the State of historical and archaeological origin.

SECTION 3. DEVELOPMENT OF RESOURCES OF THE AREA

Article 150

Policies relating to activities in the Area

Activities in the Area shall, as specifically provided for in this Part, be carried out in such a manner as to foster healthy development of the world economy and balanced growth of international trade, and to promote international co-operation for the over-all development of all countries, especially developing States, and with a view to ensuring:

(a) the development of the resources of the Area;

(b) orderly, safe and rational management of the resources of the Area, including the efficient conduct of activities in the Area and, in accordance with sound principles of conservation, the avoidance of unnecessary waste;

(c) the expansion of opportunities for participation in such activities consistent in particular with articles 144 and 148;

(d) participation in revenues by the Authority and the transfer of technology to the Enterprise and developing States as provided for in this Convention;

(e) increased availability of the minerals derived from the Area as needed in conjunction with minerals derived from other sources, to ensure supplies to consumers of such minerals;

(f) the promotion of just and stable prices remunerative to producers and fair to consumers for minerals derived both from the Area and from other sources, and the promotion of long-term equilibrium between supply and demand;

(g) the enhancement of opportunities for all States Parties, irrespective of their social and economic systems or geographical location, to participate in the development of the resources of the Area and the prevention of monopolization of activities in the Area;

(h) the protection of developing countries from adverse effects on their economies or on their export earnings resulting from a reduction in the price of an affected mineral, or in the volume of exports of that mineral, to the extent that such reduction is caused by activities in the Area, as provided in article 151;

(i) the development of the common heritage for the benefit of mankind as a whole; and

(j) conditions of access to markets for the imports of minerals produced from the resources of the Area and for imports of commodities produced from such minerals shall not be more favourable than the most favourable applied to imports from other sources.

Article 151

Production policies

1. (a) Without prejudice to the objectives set forth in article 150 and for the purpose of implementing subparagraph (h) of that article, the Authority, acting through existing forums or such new arrangements or agreements as may be appropriate, in which all interested parties, including both producers and consumers,

participate, shall take measures necessary to promote the growth, efficiency and stability of markets for those commodities produced from the minerals derived from the Area, at prices remunerative to producers and fair to consumers. All States Parties shall co-operate to this end.

* * *

2. (a) During the interim period specified in paragraph 3, commercial production shall not be undertaken pursuant to an approved plan of work until the operator has applied for and has been issued a production authorization by the Authority. Such production authorizations may not be applied for or issued more than five years prior to the planned commencement of commercial production under the plan of work unless, having regard to the nature and timing of project development, the rules, regulations and procedures of the Authority prescribe another period.

* * *

3. The interim period shall begin five years prior to 1 January of the year in which the earliest commercial production is planned to commence under an approved plan of work. If the earliest commercial production is delayed beyond the year originally planned, the beginning of the interim period and the production ceiling originally calculated shall be adjusted accordingly. The interim period shall last 25 years or until the end of the Review Conference referred to in article 155 or until the day when such new arrangements or agreements as are referred to in paragraph 1 enter into force, whichever is earliest. The Authority shall resume the power provided in this article for the remainder of the interim period if the said arrangements or agreements should lapse or become ineffective for any reason whatsoever.

4. [This provision establishes the production ceiling for any one year of the interim period and the manner of its calculation.]

5. The Authority shall reserve to the Enterprise for its initial production a quantity of 38,000 metric tonnes of nickel from the available production ceiling calculated pursuant to paragraph 4.

6. [This provision authorizes supplementing production subject to certain conditions.]

7. The levels of production of other metals such as copper, cobalt and manganese extracted from the polymetallic nodules that are recovered pursuant to a production authorization should not be higher than those which would have been produced had the operator produced the maximum level of nickel from those nodules pursuant to this article. The Authority shall establish rules, regulations and procedures pursuant to Annex III, article 17, to implement this paragraph.

8. Rights and obligations relating to unfair economic practices under relevant multilateral trade agreements shall apply to the exploration for and exploitation of minerals from the Area. In the settlement of disputes arising under this provision, States Parties which are Parties to such multilateral trade agreements shall have recourse to the dispute settlement procedures of such agreements.

9. The Authority shall have the power to limit the level of production of minerals from the Area, other than minerals from polymetallic nodules, under such conditions and applying such methods as may be appropriate by adopting regulations in accordance with article 161, paragraph 8.

10. Upon the recommendation of the Council on the basis of advice from the Economic Planning Commission, the Assembly shall establish a system of compensation or take other measures of economic adjustment assistance including co-operation with specialized agencies and other international organizations to assist developing countries which suffer serious adverse effects on their export earnings or economies resulting from a reduction in the price of an affected mineral or in the volume of exports of that mineral, to the extent that such reduction is caused by activities in the Area. The Authority on request shall initiate studies on the problems of those

States which are likely to be most seriously affected with a view to minimizing their difficulties and assisting them in their economic adjustment.

Article 152

Exercise of powers and functions by the Authority

1. The Authority shall avoid discrimination in the exercise of its powers and functions, including the granting of opportunities for activities in the Area.

2. Nevertheless, special consideration for developing States, including particular consideration for the land-locked and geographically disadvantaged among them, specifically provided for in this Part shall be permitted.

Article 153

System of exploration and exploitation

1. Activities in the Area shall be organized, carried out and controlled by the Authority on behalf of mankind as a whole in accordance with this article as well as other relevant provisions of this Part and the relevant Annexes, and the rules, regulations and procedures of the Authority.

2. Activities in the Area shall be carried out as prescribed in paragraph 3:

(a) by the Enterprise, and

(b) in association with the Authority by States Parties, or state enterprises or natural or juridical persons which possess the nationality of States Parties or are effectively controlled by them or their nationals, when sponsored by such States, or any group of the foregoing which meets the requirements provided in this Part and in Annex III.

3. Activities in the Area shall be carried out in accordance with a formal written plan of work drawn up in accordance with Annex III and approved by the Council after review by the Legal and Technical Commission. In the case of activities in the Area carried out as authorized by the Authority by the entities specified in paragraph 2(b), the plan of work shall, in accordance with Annex III, article 3, be in the form of a contract. Such contracts may provide for joint arrangements in accordance with Annex III, article 11.

* * *

Article 154

Periodic review

Every five years from the entry into force of this Convention, the Assembly shall undertake a general and systematic review of the manner in which the international régime of the Area established in this Convention has operated in practice. In the light of this review the Assembly may take, or recommend that other organs take, measures in accordance with the provisions and procedures of this Part and the Annexes relating thereto which will lead to the improvement of the operation of the régime.

Article 155

The Review Conference

1. Fifteen years from 1 January of the year in which the earliest commercial production commences under an approved plan of work, the Assembly shall convene a conference for the review of those provisions of this Part and the relevant Annexes which govern the system of exploration and exploitation of the resources of the Area.

* * *

* * *

SECTION 4. THE AUTHORITY

SUBSECTION A. GENERAL PROVISIONS

Article 156

Establishment of the Authority

1. There is hereby established the International Sea–Bed Authority, which shall function in accordance with this Part.

2. All States Parties are *ipso facto* members of the Authority.

3. Observers at the Third United Nations Conference on the Law of the Sea who have signed the Final Act and who are not referred to in article 305, paragraph 1(c), (d), (e) or (f), shall have the right to participate in the Authority as observers, in accordance with its rules, regulations and procedures.

4. The seat of the Authority shall be in Jamaica.

5. The Authority may establish such regional centres or offices as it deems necessary for the exercise of its functions.

Article 157

Nature and fundamental principles of the Authority

1. The Authority is the organization through which States Parties shall, in accordance with this Part, organize and control activities in the Area, particularly with a view to administering the resources of the Area.

2. The powers and functions of the Authority shall be those expressly conferred upon it by this Convention. The Authority shall have such incidental powers, consistent with this Convention, as are implicit in and necessary for the exercise of those powers and functions with respect to activities in the Area.

3. The Authority is based on the principle of the sovereign equality of all its members.

4. All members of the Authority shall fulfil in good faith the obligations assumed by them in accordance with this Part in order to ensure to all of them the rights and benefits resulting from membership.

Article 158

Organs of the Authority

1. There are hereby established, as the principal organs of the Authority, an Assembly, a Council and a Secretariat.

2. There is hereby established the Enterprise, the organ through which the Authority shall carry out the functions referred to in article 170, paragraph 1.

3. Such subsidiary organs as may be found necessary may be established in accordance with this Part.

4. Each principal organ of the Authority and the Enterprise shall be responsible for exercising those powers and functions which are conferred upon it. In exercising such powers and functions each organ shall avoid taking any action which may derogate from or impede the exercise of specific powers and functions conferred upon another organ.

SUBSECTION B. THE ASSEMBLY

Article 159

Composition, procedure and voting

1. The Assembly shall consist of all the members of the Authority. Each member shall have one representative in the Assembly, who may be accompanied by alternates and advisers.

2. The Assembly shall meet in regular annual sessions and in such special sessions as may be decided by the Assembly, or convened by the Secretary-General at the request of the Council or of a majority of the members of the Authority.

3. Sessions shall take place at the seat of the Authority unless otherwise decided by the Assembly.

4. The Assembly shall adopt its rules of procedure. At the beginning of each regular session, it shall elect its President and such other officers as may be required. They shall hold office until a new President and other officers are elected at the next regular session.

5. A majority of the members of the Assembly shall constitute a quorum.

6. Each member of the Assembly shall have one vote.

* * *

Article 160

Powers and functions

1. The Assembly, as the sole organ of the Authority consisting of all the members, shall be considered the supreme organ of the Authority to which the other principal organs shall be accountable as specifically provided for in this Convention. The Assembly shall have the power to establish general policies in conformity with the relevant provisions of this Convention on any question or matter within the competence of the Authority.

* * *

SUBSECTION C. THE COUNCIL

Article 161

Composition, procedure and voting

1. The Council shall consist of 36 members of the Authority elected by the Assembly in the following order:

(a) four members from among those States Parties which, during the last five years for which statistics are available, have either consumed more than 2 per cent of total world consumption or have had net imports of more than 2 per cent of total world imports of the commodities produced from the categories of minerals to be derived from the Area, and in any case one State from the Eastern European (Socialist) region, as well as the largest consumer;

(b) four members from among the eight States Parties which have the largest investments in preparation for and in the conduct of activities in the Area, either directly or through their nationals, including at least one State from the Eastern European (Socialist) region;

(c) four members from among States Parties which on the basis of production in areas under their jurisdiction are major net exporters of the categories of minerals to be derived from the Area, including at least two developing States whose exports of such minerals have a substantial bearing upon their economies;

(d) six members from among developing States Parties, representing special interests. The special interests to be represented shall include those of States with large populations, States which are land-locked or geographically disadvantaged, States which are major importers of the categories of minerals to be derived from the Area, States which are potential producers of such minerals, and least developed States;

(e) eighteen members elected according to the principle of ensuring an equitable geographical distribution of seats in the Council as a whole, provided that each geographical region shall have at least one member elected under this subparagraph. For this purpose, the geographical regions shall be Africa, Asia, Eastern European (Socialist), Latin America and Western European and Others.

2. In electing the members of the Council in accordance with paragraph 1, the Assembly shall ensure that:

(a) land-locked and geographically disadvantaged States are represented to a degree which is reasonably proportionate to their representation in the Assembly;

(b) coastal States, especially developing States, which do not qualify under paragraph 1(a), (b), (c) or (d) are represented to a degree which is reasonably proportionate to their representation in the Assembly;

(c) each group of States Parties to be represented on the Council is represented by those members, if any, which are nominated by that group.

3. Elections shall take place at regular sessions of the Assembly. Each member of the Council shall be elected for four years. At the first election, however, the term of one half of the members of each group referred to in paragraph 1 shall be two years.

4. Members of the Council shall be eligible for re-election, but due regard should be paid to the desirability of rotation of membership.

5. The Council shall function at the seat of the Authority, and shall meet as often as the business of the Authority may require, but not less than three times a year.

6. A majority of the members of the Council shall constitute a quorum.

7. Each member of the Council shall have one vote.

* * *

Article 162

Powers and functions

1. The Council is the executive organ of the Authority. The Council shall have the power to establish, in conformity with this Convention and the general policies established by the Assembly, the specific policies to be pursued by the Authority on any question or matter within the competence of the Authority.

Article 163

Organs of the Council

1. There are hereby established the following organs of the Council:

(a) an Economic Planning Commission;

(b) a Legal and Technical Commission.

2. Each Commission shall be composed of 15 members, elected by the Council from among the candidates nominated by the States Parties. However, if necessary, the Council may decide to increase the size of either Commission having due regard to economy and efficiency.

3. Members of a Commission shall have appropriate qualifications in the area of competence of that Commission. States Parties shall nominate candidates of the

highest standards of competence and integrity with qualifications in relevant fields so as to ensure the effective exercise of the functions of the Commissions.

* * *

Article 164

The Economic Planning Commission

1. Members of the Economic Planning Commission shall have appropriate qualifications such as those relevant to mining, management of mineral resource activities, international trade or international economics. The Council shall endeavour to ensure that the membership of the Commission reflects all appropriate qualifications. The Commission shall include at least two members from developing States whose exports of the categories of minerals to be derived from the Area have a substantial bearing upon their economies.

* * *

Article 165

The Legal and Technical Commission

1. Members of the Legal and Technical Commission shall have appropriate qualifications such as those relevant to exploration for and exploitation and processing of mineral resources, oceanology, protection of the marine environment, or economic or legal matters relating to ocean mining and related fields of expertise. The Council shall endeavour to ensure that the membership of the Commission reflects all appropriate qualifications.

* * *

SUBSECTION D. THE SECRETARIAT

Article 166

The Secretariat

1. The Secretariat of the Authority shall comprise a Secretary-General and such staff as the Authority may require.

2. The Secretary-General shall be elected for four years by the Assembly from among the candidates proposed by the Council and may be re-elected.

3. The Secretary-General shall be the chief administrative officer of the Authority, and shall act in that capacity in all meetings of the Assembly, of the Council and of any subsidiary organ, and shall perform such other administrative functions as are entrusted to the Secretary-General by these organs.

4. The Secretary-General shall make an annual report to the Assembly on the work of the Authority.

Article 167

The staff of the Authority

* * *

Article 168

International character of the Secretariat

1. In the performance of their duties the Secretary-General and the staff shall not seek or receive instructions from any government or from any other source external to the Authority. They shall refrain from any action which might reflect on their position as international officials responsible only to the Authority. * * *

* * *

Article 169

Consultation and co-operation with international and non-governmental organizations

* * *

SUBSECTION E. THE ENTERPRISE

Article 170

The Enterprise

1. The Enterprise shall be the organ of the Authority which shall carry out activities in the Area directly, pursuant to article 153, paragraph 2(a), as well as the transporting, processing and marketing of minerals recovered from the Area.

2. The Enterprise shall, within the framework of the international legal personality of the Authority, have such legal capacity as is provided for in the Statute set forth in Annex IV. The Enterprise shall act in accordance with this Convention and the rules, regulations and procedures of the Authority, as well as the general policies established by the Assembly, and shall be subject to the directives and control of the Council.

* * *

SUBSECTION F. FINANCIAL ARRANGEMENTS OF THE AUTHORITY

Article 171

Funds of the Authority

The funds of the Authority shall include:

(a) assessed contributions made by members of the Authority in accordance with article 160, paragraph 2(e);

(b) funds received by the Authority pursuant to Annex III, article 13, in connection with activities in the Area;

(c) funds transferred from the Enterprise in accordance with Annex IV, article 10;

(d) funds borrowed pursuant to article 174;

(e) voluntary contributions made by members or other entities; and

(f) payments to a compensation fund, in accordance with article 151, paragraph 10, whose sources are to be recommended by the Economic Planning Commission.

Article 172

Annual budget of the Authority

* * *

Article 173

Expenses of the Authority

* * *

Article 174

Borrowing power of the Authority

* * *

Article 175

Annual audit

* * *

SUBSECTION G. LEGAL STATUS, PRIVILEGES AND IMMUNITIES

Article 176

Legal status

The Authority shall have international legal personality and such legal capacity as may be necessary for the exercise of its functions and the fulfilment of its purposes.

Article 177

Privileges and immunities

To enable the Authority to exercise its functions, it shall enjoy in the territory of each State Party the privileges and immunities set forth in this subsection. The privileges and immunities relating to the Enterprise shall be those set forth in Annex IV, article 13.

Article 178

Immunity from legal process

The Authority, its property and assets, shall enjoy immunity from legal process except to the extent that the Authority expressly waives this immunity in a particular case.

Article 179

Immunity from search and any form of seizure

* * *

Article 180

Exemption from restrictions, regulations, controls and moratoria

* * *

Article 181

Archives and official communications of the Authority

* * *

Article 182

Privileges and immunities of certain persons connected with the Authority

* * *

Article 183

Exemption from taxes and customs duties

* * *

SUBSECTION H. SUSPENSION OF THE EXERCISE OF RIGHTS AND PRIVILEGES OF MEMBERS

Article 184

Suspension of the exercise of voting rights

A State Party which is in arrears in the payment of its financial contributions to the Authority shall have no vote if the amount of its arrears equals or exceeds the amount of the contribution due from it for the preceding two full years. The Assembly may, nevertheless, permit such a member to vote if it is satisfied that the failure to pay is due to conditions beyond the control of the member.

Article 185

Suspension of exercise of rights and privileges of membership

1. A State Party which has grossly and persistently violated the provisions of this Part may be suspended from the exercise of the rights and privileges of membership by the Assembly upon the recommendation of the Council.

2. No action may be taken under paragraph 1 until the Sea-Bed Disputes Chamber has found that a State Party has grossly and persistently violated the provisions of this Part.

SECTION 5. SETTLEMENT OF DISPUTES AND ADVISORY OPINIONS

Article 186

Sea-Bed Disputes Chamber of the International Tribunal for the Law of the Sea

The establishment of the Sea-Bed Disputes Chamber and the manner in which it shall exercise its jurisdiction shall be governed by the provisions of this section, of Part XV and of Annex VI.

Article 187

Jurisdiction of the Sea-Bed Disputes Chamber

The Sea-Bed Disputes Chamber shall have jurisdiction under this Part and the Annexes relating thereto in disputes with respect to activities in the Area falling within the following categories:

(a) disputes between States Parties concerning the interpretation or application of this Part and the Annexes relating thereto;

(b) disputes between a State Party and the Authority concerning:

(i) acts or omissions of the Authority or of a State Party alleged to be in violation of this Part or the Annexes relating thereto or of rules, regulations and procedures of the Authority adopted in accordance therewith; or

(ii) acts of the Authority alleged to be in excess of jurisdiction or a misuse of power;

(c) disputes between parties to a contract, being States Parties, the Authority or the Enterprise, state enterprises and natural or juridical persons referred to in article 153, paragraph 2(b), concerning:

(i) the interpretation or application of a relevant contract or a plan of work; or

(ii) acts or omissions of a party to the contract relating to activities in the Area and directed to the other party or directly affecting its legitimate interests;

(d) disputes between the Authority and a prospective contractor who has been sponsored by a State as provided in article 153, paragraph 2(b), and has duly fulfilled the conditions referred to in Annex III, article 4, paragraph 6, and article 13, paragraph 2, concerning the refusal of a contract or a legal issue arising in the negotiation of the contract;

(e) disputes between the Authority and a State Party, a state enterprise or a natural or juridical person sponsored by a State Party as provided for in article 153, paragraph 2(b), where it is alleged that the Authority has incurred liability as [illegible]vided in Annex III, article 22;

[illegible] any other disputes for which the jurisdiction of the Chamber is specifically [illegible] in this Convention.

Article 188

Submission of disputes to a special chamber of the International Tribunal for the Law of the Sea or an ad hoc chamber of the Sea-Bed Disputes Chamber or to binding commercial arbitration

* * *

Article 189

Limitation on jurisdiction with regard to decisions of the Authority

* * *

Article 190

Participation and appearance of sponsoring States Parties in proceedings

* * *

Article 191

Advisory opinions

The Sea-Bed Disputes Chamber shall give advisory opinions at the request of the Assembly or the Council on legal questions arising within the scope of their activities. Such opinions shall be given as a matter of urgency.

PART XII

PROTECTION AND PRESERVATION OF THE MARINE ENVIRONMENT

SECTION 1. GENERAL PROVISIONS

Article 192

General obligation

States have the obligation to protect and preserve the marine environment.

Article 193

Sovereign right of States to exploit their natural resources

States have the sovereign right to exploit their natural resources pursuant to their environmental policies and in accordance with their duty to protect and preserve the marine environment.

Article 194

Measures to prevent, reduce and control pollution of the marine environment

1. States shall take, individually or jointly as appropriate, all measures consistent with this Convention that are necessary to prevent, reduce and control pollution of the marine environment from any source, using for this purpose the best practicable means at their disposal and in accordance with their capabilities, and they shall endeavour to harmonize their policies in this connection.

2. States shall take all measures necessary to ensure that activities under their jurisdiction or control are so conducted as not to cause damage by pollution to other States and their environment, and that pollution arising from incidents or activities under their jurisdiction or control does not spread beyond the areas where they exercise sovereign rights in accordance with this Convention.

3. The measures taken pursuant to this Part shall deal with all sources of pollution of the marine environment. These measures shall include, *inter alia,* those designed to minimize to the fullest possible extent:

(a) the release of toxic, harmful or noxious substances, especially those which are persistent, from land-based sources, from or through the atmosphere or by dumping;

(b) pollution from vessels, in particular measures for preventing accidents and dealing with emergencies, ensuring the safety of operations at sea, preventing intentional and unintentional discharges, and regulating the design, construction, equipment, operation and manning of vessels;

(c) pollution from installations and devices used in exploration or exploitation of the natural resources of the sea-bed and subsoil, in particular measures for preventing accidents and dealing with emergencies, ensuring the safety of operations at sea, and regulating the design, construction, equipment, operation and manning of such installations or devices;

(d) pollution from other installations and devices operating in the marine environment, in particular measures for preventing accidents and dealing with emergencies, ensuring the safety of operations at sea, and regulating the design, construction, equipment, operation and manning of such installations or devices.

4. In taking measures to prevent, reduce or control pollution of the marine environment, States shall refrain from unjustifiable interference with activities carried out by other States in the exercise of their rights and in pursuance of their duties in conformity with this Convention.

5. The measures taken in accordance with this Part shall include those necessary to protect and preserve rare or fragile ecosystems as well as the habitat of depleted, threatened or endangered species and other forms of marine life.

Article 195

Duty not to transfer damage or hazards or transform one type of pollution into another

* * *

Article 196

Use of technologies or introduction of alien or new species

1. States shall take all measures necessary to prevent, reduce and control pollution of the marine environment resulting from the use of technologies under their jurisdiction or control, or the intentional or accidental introduction of species, alien or new, to a particular part of the marine environment, which may cause significant and harmful changes thereto.

2. This article does not affect the application of this Convention regarding the prevention, reduction and control of pollution of the marine environment.

SECTION 2. GLOBAL AND REGIONAL CO–OPERATION

Article 197

Co-operation on a global or regional basis

States shall co-operate on a global basis and, as appropriate, on a regional basis, directly or through competent international organizations, in formulating and elaborating international rules, standards and recommended practices and procedures consistent with this Convention, for the protection and preservation of the marine environment, taking into account characteristic regional features.

Article 198

Notification of imminent or actual damage

When a State becomes aware of cases in which the marine environment is in imminent danger of being damaged or has been damaged by pollution, it shall immediately notify other States it deems likely to be affected by such damage, as well as the competent international organizations.

Article 199

Contingency plans against pollution

In the cases referred to in article 198, States in the area affected, in accordance with their capabilities, and the competent international organizations shall co-operate, to the extent possible, in eliminating the effects of pollution and preventing or minimizing the damage. To this end, States shall jointly develop and promote contingency plans for responding to pollution incidents in the marine environment.

Article 200

Studies, research programmes and exchange of information and data

States shall co-operate, directly or through competent international organizations, for the purpose of promoting studies, undertaking programmes of scientific research and encouraging the exchange of information and data acquired about pollution of the marine environment. They shall endeavour to participate actively in regional and global programmes to acquire knowledge for the assessment of the nature and extent of pollution, exposure to it, and its pathways, risks and remedies.

Article 201

Scientific criteria for regulations

In the light of the information and data acquired pursuant to article 200, States shall co-operate, directly or through competent international organizations, in establishing appropriate scientific criteria for the formulation and elaboration of rules, standards and recommended practices and procedures for the prevention, reduction and control of pollution of the marine environment.

SECTION 3. TECHNICAL ASSISTANCE

Article 202

Scientific and technical assistance to developing States

States shall, directly or through competent international organizations:

(a) promote programmes of scientific, educational, technical and other assistance to developing States for the protection and preservation of the marine environment and the prevention, reduction and control of marine pollution. Such assistance shall include, *inter alia:*

(i) training of their scientific and technical personnel;

(ii) facilitating their participation in relevant international programmes;

(iii) supplying them with necessary equipment and facilities;

(iv) enhancing their capacity to manufacture such equipment;

(v) advice on and developing facilities for research, monitoring, educational and other programmes;

(b) provide appropriate assistance, especially to developing States, for the minimization of the effects of major incidents which may cause serious pollution of the marine environment;

(c) provide appropriate assistance, especially to developing States, concerning the preparation of environmental assessments.

Article 203

Preferential treatment for developing States

Developing States shall, for the purposes of prevention, reduction and control of pollution of the marine environment or minimization of its effects, be granted preference by international organizations in:

(a) the allocation of appropriate funds and technical assistance; and

(b) the utilization of their specialized services.

SECTION 4. MONITORING AND ENVIRONMENTAL ASSESSMENT

Article 204

Monitoring of the risks or effects of pollution

1. States shall, consistent with the rights of other States, endeavour, as far as practicable, directly or through the competent international organizations, to observe, measure, evaluate and analyse, by recognized scientific methods, the risks or effects of pollution of the marine environment.

2. In particular, States shall keep under surveillance the effects of any activities which they permit or in which they engage in order to determine whether these activities are likely to pollute the marine environment.

Article 205

Publication of reports

States shall publish reports of the results obtained pursuant to article 204 or provide such reports at appropriate intervals to the competent international organizations, which should make them available to all States.

Article 206

Assessment of potential effects of activities

When States have reasonable grounds for believing that planned activities under their jurisdiction or control may cause substantial pollution of or significant and harmful changes to the marine environment, they shall, as far as practicable, assess the potential effects of such activities on the marine environment and shall communicate reports of the results of such assessments in the manner provided in article 205.

SECTION 5. INTERNATIONAL RULES AND NATIONAL LEGISLATION TO PREVENT, REDUCE AND CONTROL POLLUTION OF THE MARINE ENVIRONMENT

Article 207

Pollution from land-based sources

1. States shall adopt laws and regulations to prevent, reduce and control pollution of the marine environment from land-based sources, including rivers, estuaries, pipelines and outfall structures, taking into account internationally agreed rules, standards and recommended practices and procedures.

2. States shall take other measures as may be necessary to prevent, reduce and control such pollution.

3. States shall endeavour to harmonize their policies in this connection at the appropriate regional level.

4. States, acting especially through competent international organizations or diplomatic conference, shall endeavour to establish global and regional rules, standards and recommended practices and procedures to prevent, reduce and control pollution of the marine environment from land-based sources, taking into account characteristic regional features, the economic capacity of developing States and their need for economic development. Such rules, standards and recommended practices and procedures shall be re-examined from time to time as necessary.

5. Laws, regulations, measures, rules, standards and recommended practices and procedures referred to in paragraphs 1, 2 and 4 shall include those designed to minimize, to the fullest extent possible, the release of toxic, harmful or noxious substances, especially those which are persistent, into the marine environment.

Article 208

Pollution from sea-bed activities subject to national jurisdiction

[This article is in all essential respects identical to article 207, *supra.*]

Article 209

Pollution from activities in the Area

1. International rules, regulations and procedures shall be established in accordance with Part XI to prevent, reduce and control pollution of the marine environment from activities in the Area. Such rules, regulations and procedures shall be re-examined from time to time as necessary.

2. Subject to the relevant provisions of this section, States shall adopt laws and regulations to prevent, reduce and control pollution of the marine environment from activities in the Area undertaken by vessels, installations, structures and other devices flying their flag or of their registry or operating under their authority, as the case may be. The requirements of such laws and regulations shall be no less effective than the international rules, regulations and procedures referred to in paragraph 1.

Article 210

Pollution by dumping

1. States shall adopt laws and regulations to prevent, reduce and control pollution of the marine environment by dumping.

2. States shall take other measures as may be necessary to prevent, reduce and control such pollution.

3. Such laws, regulations and measures shall ensure that dumping is not carried out without the permission of the competent authorities of States.

4. States, acting especially through competent international organizations or diplomatic conference, shall endeavour to establish global and regional rules, standards and recommended practices and procedures to prevent, reduce and control such pollution. Such rules, standards and recommended practices and procedures shall be re-examined from time to time as necessary.

5. Dumping within the territorial sea and the exclusive economic zone or onto the continental shelf shall not be carried out without the express prior approval of the coastal State, which has the right to permit, regulate and control such dumping after due consideration of the matter with other States which by reason of their geographical situation may be adversely affected thereby.

6. National laws, regulations and measures shall be no less effective in preventing, reducing and controlling such pollution than the global rules and standards.

Article 211

Pollution from vessels

1. States, acting through the competent international organization or general diplomatic conference, shall establish international rules and standards to prevent, reduce and control pollution of the marine environment from vessels and promote the adoption, in the same manner, wherever appropriate, of routeing systems designed to minimize the threat of accidents which might cause pollution of the marine environment, including the coastline, and pollution damage to the related interests of coastal States. Such rules and standards shall, in the same manner, be re-examined from time to time as necessary.

2. States shall adopt laws and regulations for the prevention, reduction and control of pollution of the marine environment from vessels flying their flag or of their registry. Such laws and regulations shall at least have the same effect as that of generally accepted international rules and standards established through the competent international organization or general diplomatic conference.

3. States which establish particular requirements for the prevention, reduction and control of pollution of the marine environment as a condition for the entry of foreign vessels into their ports or internal waters or for a call at their off-shore terminals shall give due publicity to such requirements and shall communicate them to the competent international organization. Whenever such requirements are established in identical form by two or more coastal States in an endeavour to harmonize policy, the communication shall indicate which States are participating in such co-operative arrangements. Every State shall require the master of a vessel flying its flag or of its registry, when navigating within the territorial sea of a State participating in such co-operative arrangements, to furnish, upon the request of that State, information as to whether it is proceeding to a State of the same region participating in such co-operative arrangements and, if so, to indicate whether it complies with the port entry requirements of that State. This article is without prejudice to the continued exercise by a vessel of its right of innocent passage or to the application of article 25, paragraph 2.

4. Coastal States may, in the exercise of their sovereignty within their territorial sea, adopt laws and regulations for the prevention, reduction and control of marine pollution from foreign vessels, including vessels exercising the right of innocent passage. Such laws and regulations shall, in accordance with Part II, section 3, not hamper innocent passage of foreign vessels.

5. Coastal States, for the purpose of enforcement as provided for in section 6, may in respect of their exclusive economic zones adopt laws and regulations for the prevention, reduction and control of pollution from vessels conforming to and giving effect to generally accepted international rules and standards established through the competent international organization or general diplomatic conference.

6. (a) Where the international rules and standards referred to in paragraph 1 are inadequate to meet special circumstances and coastal States have reasonable grounds for believing that a particular, clearly defined area of their respective exclusive economic zones is an area where the adoption of special mandatory measures for the prevention of pollution from vessels is required for recognized technical reasons in relation to its oceanographical and ecological conditions, as well as its utilization or the protection of its resources and the particular character of its traffic, the coastal States, after appropriate consultations through the competent international organization with any other States concerned, may, for that area, direct a communication to that organization, submitting scientific and technical evidence in support and information on necessary reception facilities. Within 12 months after receiving such a communication, the organization shall determine whether the

conditions in that area correspond to the requirements set out above. If the organization so determines, the coastal States may, for that area, adopt laws and regulations for the prevention, reduction and control of pollution from vessels implementing such international rules and standards or navigational practices as are made applicable, through the organization, for special areas. These laws and regulations shall not become applicable to foreign vessels until 15 months after the submission of the communication to the organization.

(b) The coastal States shall publish the limits of any such particular, clearly defined area.

(c) If the coastal States intend to adopt additional laws and regulations for the same area for the prevention, reduction and control of pollution from vessels, they shall, when submitting the aforesaid communication, at the same time notify the organization thereof. Such additional laws and regulations may relate to discharges or navigational practices but shall not require foreign vessels to observe design, construction, manning or equipment standards other than generally accepted international rules and standards; they shall become applicable to foreign vessels 15 months after the submission of the communication to the organization, provided that the organization agrees within 12 months after the submission of the communication.

7. The international rules and standards referred to in this article should include *inter alia* those relating to prompt notification to coastal States, whose coastline or related interests may be affected by incidents, including maritime casualties, which involve discharges or probability of discharges.

Article 212

Pollution from or through the atmosphere

1. States shall adopt laws and regulations to prevent, reduce and control pollution of the marine environment from or through the atmosphere, applicable to the air space under their sovereignty and to vessels flying their flag or vessels or aircraft of their registry, taking into account internationally agreed rules, standards and recommended practices and procedures and the safety of air navigation.

2. States shall take other measures as may be necessary to prevent, reduce and control such pollution.

3. States, acting especially through competent international organizations or diplomatic conference, shall endeavour to establish global and regional rules, standards and recommended practices and procedures to prevent, reduce and control such pollution.

SECTION 6. ENFORCEMENT

Article 213

Enforcement with respect to pollution from land-based sources

States shall enforce their laws and regulations adopted in accordance with article 207 and shall adopt laws and regulations and take other measures necessary to implement applicable international rules and standards established through competent international organizations or diplomatic conference to prevent, reduce and control pollution of the marine environment from land-based sources.

Article 214

Enforcement with respect to pollution from sea-bed activities

States shall enforce their laws and regulations adopted in accordance with article 208 and shall adopt laws and regulations and take other measures necessary to implement applicable international rules and standards established through competent international organizations or diplomatic conference to prevent, reduce and control pollution of the marine environment arising from or in connection with sea-bed activities subject to their jurisdiction and from artificial islands, installations and structures under their jurisdiction, pursuant to articles 60 and 80.

Article 215

Enforcement with respect to pollution from activities in the Area

Enforcement of international rules, regulations and procedures established in accordance with Part XI to prevent, reduce and control pollution of the marine environment from activities in the Area shall be governed by that Part.

Article 216

Enforcement with respect to pollution by dumping

1. Laws and regulations adopted in accordance with this Convention and applicable international rules and standards established through competent international organizations or diplomatic conference for the prevention, reduction and control of pollution of the marine environment by dumping shall be enforced:

(a) by the coastal State with regard to dumping within its territorial sea or its exclusive economic zone or onto its continental shelf;

(b) by the flag State with regard to vessels flying its flag or vessels or aircraft of its registry;

(c) by any State with regard to acts of loading of wastes or other matter occurring within its territory or at its off-shore terminals.

2. No State shall be obliged by virtue of this article to institute proceedings when another State has already instituted proceedings in accordance with this article.

Article 217

Enforcement by flag States

1. States shall ensure compliance by vessels flying their flag or of their registry with applicable international rules and standards, established through the competent international organization or general diplomatic conference, and with their laws and regulations adopted in accordance with this Convention for the prevention, reduction and control of pollution of the marine environment from vessels and shall accordingly adopt laws and regulations and take other measures necessary for their implementation. Flag States shall provide for the effective enforcement of such rules, standards, laws and regulations, irrespective of where a violation occurs.

2. States shall, in particular, take appropriate measures in order to ensure that vessels flying their flag or of their registry are prohibited from sailing, until they can proceed to sea in compliance with the requirements of the international rules and standards referred to in paragraph 1, including requirements in respect of design, construction, equipment and manning of vessels.

3. States shall ensure that vessels flying their flag or of their registry carry on board certificates required by and issued pursuant to international rules and standards referred to in paragraph 1. States shall ensure that vessels flying their flag are periodically inspected in order to verify that such certificates are in conformity with the actual condition of the vessels. These certificates shall be accepted by other States as evidence of the condition of the vessels and shall be regarded as having the same force as certificates issued by them, unless there are clear grounds for believing that the condition of the vessel does not correspond substantially with the particulars of the certificates.

4. If a vessel commits a violation of rules and standards established through the competent international organization or general diplomatic conference, the flag

State, without prejudice to articles 218, 220 and 228, shall provide for immediate investigation and where appropriate institute proceedings in respect of the alleged violation irrespective of where the violation occurred or where the pollution caused by such violation has occurred or has been spotted.

5. Flag States conducting an investigation of the violation may request the assistance of any other State whose co-operation could be useful in clarifying the circumstances of the case. States shall endeavour to meet appropriate requests of flag States.

6. States shall, at the written request of any State, investigate any violation alleged to have been committed by vessels flying their flag. If satisfied that sufficient evidence is available to enable proceedings to be brought in respect of the alleged violation, flag States shall without delay institute such proceedings in accordance with their laws.

7. Flag States shall promptly inform the requesting State and the competent international organization of the action taken and its outcome. Such information shall be available to all States.

8. Penalties provided for by the laws and regulations of States for vessels flying their flag shall be adequate in severity to discourage violations wherever they occur.

Article 218

Enforcement by port States

1. When a vessel is voluntarily within a port or at an off-shore terminal of a State, that State may undertake investigations and, where the evidence so warrants, institute proceedings in respect of any discharge from that vessel outside the internal waters, territorial sea or exclusive economic zone of that State in violation of applicable international rules and standards established through the competent international organization or general diplomatic conference.

2. No proceedings pursuant to paragraph 1 shall be instituted in respect of a discharge violation in the internal waters, territorial sea or exclusive economic zone of another State unless requested by that State, the flag State, or a State damaged or threatened by the discharge violation, or unless the violation has caused or is likely to cause pollution in the internal waters, territorial sea or exclusive economic zone of the State instituting the proceedings.

3. When a vessel is voluntarily within a port or at an off-shore terminal of a State, that State shall, as far as practicable, comply with requests from any State for investigation of a discharge violation referred to in paragraph 1, believed to have occurred in, caused, or threatened damage to the internal waters, territorial sea or exclusive economic zone of the requesting State. It shall likewise, as far as practicable, comply with requests from the flag State for investigation of such a violation, irrespective of where the violation occurred.

4. The records of the investigation carried out by a port State pursuant to this article shall be transmitted upon request to the flag State or to the coastal State. Any proceedings instituted by the port State on the basis of such an investigation may, subject to section 7, be suspended at the request of the coastal State when the violation has occurred within its internal waters, territorial sea or exclusive economic zone. The evidence and records of the case, together with any bond or other financial security posted with the authorities of the port State, shall in that event be transmitted to the coastal State. Such transmittal shall preclude the continuation of proceedings in the port State.

Article 219

Measures relating to seaworthiness of vessels to avoid pollution

Subject to section 7, States which, upon request or on their own initiative, have ascertained that a vessel within one of their ports or at one of their off-shore terminals is in violation of applicable international rules and standards relating to seaworthiness of vessels and thereby threatens damage to the marine environment shall, as far as practicable, take administrative measures to prevent the vessel from sailing. Such States may permit the vessel to proceed only to the nearest appropriate repair yard and, upon removal of the causes of the violation, shall permit the vessel to continue immediately.

Article 220

Enforcement by coastal States

1. When a vessel is voluntarily within a port or at an off-shore terminal of a State, that State may, subject to section 7, institute proceedings in respect of any violation of its laws and regulations adopted in accordance with this Convention or applicable international rules and standards for the prevention, reduction and control of pollution from vessels when the violation has occurred within the territorial sea or the exclusive economic zone of that State.

2. Where there are clear grounds for believing that a vessel navigating in the territorial sea of a State has, during its passage therein, violated laws and regulations of that State adopted in accordance with this Convention or applicable international rules and standards for the prevention, reduction and control of pollution from vessels, that State, without prejudice to the application of the relevant provisions of Part II, section 3, may undertake physical inspection of the vessel relating to the violation and may, where the evidence so warrants, institute proceedings, including detention of the vessel, in accordance with its laws, subject to the provisions of section 7.

3. Where there are clear grounds for believing that a vessel navigating in the exclusive economic zone or the territorial sea of a State has, in the exclusive economic zone, committed a violation of applicable international rules and standards for the prevention, reduction and control of pollution from vessels or laws and regulations of that State conforming and giving effect to such rules and standards, that State may require the vessel to give information regarding its identity and port of registry, its last and its next port of call and other relevant information required to establish whether a violation has occurred.

4. States shall adopt laws and regulations and take other measures so that vessels flying their flag comply with requests for information pursuant to paragraph 3.

5. Where there are clear grounds for believing that a vessel navigating in the exclusive economic zone or the territorial sea of a State has, in the exclusive economic zone, committed a violation referred to in paragraph 3 resulting in a substantial discharge causing or threatening significant pollution of the marine environment, that State may undertake physical inspection of the vessel for matters relating to the violation if the vessel has refused to give information or if the information supplied by the vessel is manifestly at variance with the evident factual situation and if the circumstances of the case justify such inspection.

6. Where there is clear objective evidence that a vessel navigating in the exclusive economic zone or the territorial sea of a State has, in the exclusive economic zone, committed a violation referred to in paragraph 3 resulting in a discharge causing major damage or threat of major damage to the coastline or related interests of the coastal State, or to any resources of its territorial sea or exclusive economic zone, that State may, subject to section 7, provided that the evidence so

warrants, institute proceedings, including detention of the vessel, in accordance with its laws.

7. Notwithstanding the provisions of paragraph 6, whenever appropriate procedures have been established, either through the competent international organization or as otherwise agreed, whereby compliance with requirements for bonding or other appropriate financial security has been assured, the coastal State if bound by such procedures shall allow the vessel to proceed.

8. The provisions of paragraphs 3, 4, 5, 6 and 7 also apply in respect of national laws and regulations adopted pursuant to article 211, paragraph 6.

Article 221

Measures to avoid pollution arising from maritime casualties

1. Nothing in this Part shall prejudice the right of States, pursuant to international law, both customary and conventional, to take and enforce measures beyond the territorial sea proportionate to the actual or threatened damage to protect their coastline or related interests, including fishing, from pollution or threat of pollution following upon a maritime casualty or acts relating to such a casualty, which may reasonably be expected to result in major harmful consequences.

2. For the purposes of this article, "maritime casualty" means a collision of vessels, stranding or other incident of navigation, or other occurrence on board a vessel or external to it resulting in material damage or imminent threat of material damage to a vessel or cargo.

Article 222

Enforcement with respect to pollution from or through the atmosphere

States shall enforce, within the air space under their sovereignty or with regard to vessels flying their flag or vessels or aircraft of their registry, their laws and regulations adopted in accordance with article 212, paragraph 1, and with other provisions of this Convention and shall adopt laws and regulations and take other measures necessary to implement applicable international rules and standards established through competent international organizations or diplomatic conference to prevent, reduce and control pollution of the marine environment from or through the atmosphere, in conformity with all relevant international rules and standards concerning the safety of air navigation.

SECTION 7. SAFEGUARDS

Article 223

Measures to facilitate proceedings

In proceedings instituted pursuant to this Part, States shall take measures to facilitate the hearing of witnesses and the admission of evidence submitted by authorities of another State, or by the competent international organization, and shall facilitate the attendance at such proceedings of official representatives of the competent international organization, the flag State and any State affected by pollution arising out of any violation. The official representatives attending such proceedings shall have such rights and duties as may be provided under national laws and regulations or international law.

Article 224

Exercise of powers of enforcement

The powers of enforcement against foreign vessels under this Part may only be exercised by officials or by warships, military aircraft, or other ships or aircraft clearly marked and identifiable as being on government service and authorized to that effect.

Article 225

Duty to avoid adverse consequences in the exercise of the powers of enforcement

In the exercise under this Convention of their powers of enforcement against foreign vessels, States shall not endanger the safety of navigation or otherwise create any hazard to a vessel, or bring it to an unsafe port or anchorage, or expose the marine environment to an unreasonable risk.

Article 226

Investigation of foreign vessels

1. (a) States shall not delay a foreign vessel longer than is essential for purposes of the investigations provided for in articles 216, 218 and 220. Any physical inspection of a foreign vessel shall be limited to an examination of such certificates, records or other documents as the vessel is required to carry by generally accepted international rules and standards or of any similar documents which it is carrying; further physical inspection of the vessel may be undertaken only after such an examination and only when:

(i) there are clear grounds for believing that the condition of the vessel or its equipment does not correspond substantially with the particulars of those documents;

(ii) the contents of such documents are not sufficient to confirm or verify a suspected violation; or

(iii) the vessel is not carrying valid certificates and records.

(b) If the investigation indicates a violation of applicable laws and regulations or international rules and standards for the protection and preservation of the marine environment, release shall be made promptly subject to reasonable procedures such as bonding or other appropriate financial security.

(c) Without prejudice to applicable international rules and standards relating to the seaworthiness of vessels, the release of a vessel may, whenever it would present an unreasonable threat of damage to the marine environment, be refused or made conditional upon proceeding to the nearest appropriate repair yard. Where release has been refused or made conditional, the flag State of the vessel must be promptly notified, and may seek release of the vessel in accordance with Part XV.

2. States shall co-operate to develop procedures for the avoidance of unnecessary physical inspection of vessels at sea.

Article 227

Non-discrimination with respect to foreign vessels

* * *

Article 228

Suspension and restrictions on institution of proceedings

* * *

Article 229

Institution of civil proceedings

* * *

Article 230

Monetary penalties and the observance of recognized rights of the accused

* * *

Article 231

Notification to the flag State and other States concerned

* * *

Article 232

Liability of States arising from enforcement measures

States shall be liable for damage or loss attributable to them arising from measures taken pursuant to section 6 when such measures are unlawful or exceed those reasonably required in the light of available information. States shall provide for recourse in their courts for actions in respect of such damage or loss.

Article 233

Safeguards with respect to straits used for international navigation

* * *

SECTION 8. ICE-COVERED AREAS

Article 234

Ice-covered areas

Coastal States have the right to adopt and enforce non-discriminatory laws and regulations for the prevention, reduction and control of marine pollution from vessels in ice-covered areas within the limits of the exclusive economic zone, where particularly severe climatic conditions and the presence of ice covering such areas for most of the year create obstructions or exceptional hazards to navigation, and pollution of the marine environment could cause major harm to or irreversible disturbance of the ecological balance. Such laws and regulations shall have due regard to navigation and the protection and preservation of the marine environment based on the best available scientific evidence.

SECTION 9. RESPONSIBILITY AND LIABILITY

Article 235

Responsibility and liability

1. States are responsible for the fulfilment of their international obligations concerning the protection and preservation of the marine environment. They shall be liable in accordance with international law.

2. States shall ensure that recourse is available in accordance with their legal systems for prompt and adequate compensation or other relief in respect of damage caused by pollution of the marine environment by natural or juridical persons under their jurisdiction.

3. With the objective of assuring prompt and adequate compensation in respect of all damage caused by pollution of the marine environment, States shall co-operate in the implementation of existing international law and the further development of international law relating to responsibility and liability for the assessment of and compensation for damage and the settlement of related disputes, as well as, where appropriate, development of criteria and procedures for payment of adequate compensation, such as compulsory insurance or compensation funds.

SECTION 10. SOVEREIGN IMMUNITY

Article 236

Sovereign immunity

The provisions of this Convention regarding the protection and preservation of the marine environment do not apply to any warship, naval auxiliary, other vessels or aircraft owned or operated by a State and used, for the time being, only on government non-commercial service. However, each State shall ensure, by the adoption of appropriate measures not impairing operations or operational capabilities of such vessels or aircraft owned or operated by it, that such vessels or aircraft act in a manner consistent, so far as is reasonable and practicable, with this Convention.

SECTION 11. OBLIGATIONS UNDER OTHER CONVENTIONS ON THE PROTECTION AND PRESERVATION OF THE MARINE ENVIRONMENT

Article 237

Obligations under other conventions on the protection and preservation of the marine environment

1. The provisions of this Part are without prejudice to the specific obligations assumed by States under special conventions and agreements concluded previously which relate to the protection and preservation of the marine environment and to agreements which may be concluded in furtherance of the general principles set forth in this Convention.

2. Specific obligations assumed by States under special conventions, with respect to the protection and preservation of the marine environment, should be carried out in a manner consistent with the general principles and objectives of this Convention.

PART XIII

MARINE SCIENTIFIC RESEARCH

SECTION 1. GENERAL PROVISIONS

Article 238

Right to conduct marine scientific research

All States, irrespective of their geographical location, and competent international organizations have the right to conduct marine scientific research subject to the rights and duties of other States as provided for in this Convention.

Article 239

Right to conduct marine scientific research

States and competent international organizations shall promote and facilitate the development and conduct of marine scientific research in accordance with this Convention.

Article 240

General principles for the conduct of marine scientific research

In the conduct of marine scientific research the following principles shall apply:

(a) marine scientific research shall be conducted exclusively for peaceful purposes;

(b) marine scientific research shall be conducted with appropriate scientific methods and means compatible with this Convention;

(c) marine scientific research shall not unjustifiably interfere with other legitimate uses of the sea compatible with this Convention and shall be duly respected in the course of such uses;

(d) marine scientific research shall be conducted in compliance with all relevant regulations adopted in conformity with this Convention including those for the protection and preservation of the marine environment.

Article 241

Non-recognition of marine scientific research activities as the legal basis for claims

Marine scientific research activities shall not constitute the legal basis for any claim to any part of the marine environment or its resources.

SECTION 2. INTERNATIONAL CO–OPERATION

Article 242

Promotion of international co-operation

1. States and competent international organizations shall, in accordance with the principle of respect for sovereignty and jurisdiction and on the basis of mutual benefit, promote international co-operation in marine scientific research for peaceful purposes.

2. In this context, without prejudice to the rights and duties of States under this Convention, a State, in the application of this Part, shall provide, as appropriate, other States with a reasonable opportunity to obtain from it, or with its co-operation, information necessary to prevent and control damage to the health and safety of persons and to the marine environment.

Article 243

Creation of favourable conditions

States and competent international organizations shall co-operate, through the conclusion of bilateral and multilateral agreements, to create favourable conditions for the conduct of marine scientific research in the marine environment and to integrate the efforts of scientists in studying the essence of phenomena and processes occurring in the marine environment and the interrelations between them.

Article 244

Publication and dissemination of information and knowledge

* * *

SECTION 3. CONDUCT AND PROMOTION OF MARINE SCIENTIFIC RESEARCH

Article 245

Marine scientific research in the territorial sea

Coastal States, in the exercise of their sovereignty, have the exclusive right to regulate, authorize and conduct marine scientific research in their territorial sea. Marine scientific research therein shall be conducted only with the express consent of and under the conditions set forth by the coastal State.

Article 246

Marine scientific research in the exclusive economic zone and on the continental shelf

1. Coastal States, in the exercise of their jurisdiction, have the right to regulate, authorize and conduct marine scientific research in their exclusive economic zone and on their continental shelf in accordance with the relevant provisions of this Convention.

2. Marine scientific research in the exclusive economic zone and on the continental shelf shall be conducted with the consent of the coastal State.

3. Coastal States shall, in normal circumstances, grant their consent for marine scientific research projects by other States or competent international organizations in their exclusive economic zone or on their continental shelf to be carried out in accordance with this Convention exclusively for peaceful purposes and in order to increase scientific knowledge of the marine environment for the benefit of all mankind. To this end, coastal States shall establish rules and procedures ensuring that such consent will not be delayed or denied unreasonably.

4. For the purposes of applying paragraph 3, normal circumstances may exist in spite of the absence of diplomatic relations between the coastal State and the researching State.

5. Coastal States may however in their discretion withhold their consent to the conduct of a marine scientific research project of another State or competent international organization in the exclusive economic zone or on the continental shelf of the coastal State if that project:

(a) is of direct significance for the exploration and exploitation of natural resources, whether living or non-living;

(b) involves drilling into the continental shelf, the use of explosives or the introduction of harmful substances into the marine environment;

(c) involves the construction, operation or use of artificial islands, installations and structures referred to in articles 60 and 80;

(d) contains information communicated pursuant to article 248 regarding the nature and objectives of the project which is inaccurate or if the researching State or competent international organization has outstanding obligations to the coastal State from a prior research project.

6. Notwithstanding the provisions of paragraph 5, coastal States may not exercise their discretion to withhold consent under subparagraph (a) of that paragraph in respect of marine scientific research projects to be undertaken in accordance with the provisions of this Part on the continental shelf, beyond 200 nautical miles from the baselines from which the breadth of the territorial sea is measured, outside those specific areas which coastal States may at any time publicly designate as areas in which exploitation or detailed exploratory operations focused on those areas are occurring or will occur within a reasonable period of time. Coastal States shall give reasonable notice of the designation of such areas, as well as any modifications thereto, but shall not be obliged to give details of the operations therein.

7. The provisions of paragraph 6 are without prejudice to the rights of coastal States over the continental shelf as established in article 77.

8. Marine scientific research activities referred to in this article shall not unjustifiably interfere with activities undertaken by coastal States in the exercise of their sovereign rights and jurisdiction provided for in this Convention.

Article 247

Marine scientific research projects undertaken by or under the auspices of international organizations

* * *

Article 248

Duty to provide information to the coastal State

States and competent international organizations which intend to undertake marine scientific research in the exclusive economic zone or on the continental shelf of a coastal State shall, not less than six months in advance of the expected starting date of the marine scientific research project, provide that State with a full description of:

(a) the nature and objectives of the project;

(b) the method and means to be used, including name, tonnage, type and class of vessels and a description of scientific equipment;

(c) the precise geographical areas in which the project is to be conducted;

(d) the expected date of first appearance and final departure of the research vessels, or deployment of the equipment and its removal, as appropriate;

(e) the name of the sponsoring institution, its director, and the person in charge of the project; and

(f) the extent to which it is considered that the coastal State should be able to participate or to be represented in the project.

Article 249

Duty to comply with certain conditions

1. States and competent international organizations when undertaking marine scientific research in the exclusive economic zone or on the continental shelf of a coastal State shall comply with the following conditions:

(a) ensure the right of the coastal State, if it so desires, to participate or be represented in the marine scientific research project, especially on board research vessels and other craft or scientific research installations, when practicable, without payment of any remuneration to the scientists of the coastal State and without obligation to contribute towards the costs of the project;

(b) provide the coastal State, at its request, with preliminary reports, as soon as practicable, and with the final results and conclusions after the completion of the research;

(c) undertake to provide access for the coastal State, at its request, to all data and samples derived from the marine scientific research project and likewise to furnish it with data which may be copied and samples which may be divided without detriment to their scientific value;

(d) if requested, provide the coastal State with an assessment of such data, samples and research results or provide assistance in their assessment or interpretation;

(e) ensure, subject to paragraph 2, that the research results are made internationally available through appropriate national or international channels, as soon as practicable;

(f) inform the coastal State immediately of any major change in the research programme;

(g) unless otherwise agreed, remove the scientific research installations or equipment once the research is completed.

2. This article is without prejudice to the conditions established by the laws and regulations of the coastal State for the exercise of its discretion to grant or withhold consent pursuant to article 246, paragraph 5, including requiring prior agreement for making internationally available the research results of a project of direct significance for the exploration and exploitation of natural resources.

Article 250

Communications concerning marine scientific research projects

Communications concerning the marine scientific research projects shall be made through appropriate official channels, unless otherwise agreed.

Article 251

General criteria and guidelines

States shall seek to promote through competent international organizations the establishment of general criteria and guidelines to assist States in ascertaining the nature and implications of marine scientific research.

Article 252

Implied consent

States or competent international organizations may proceed with a marine scientific research project six months after the date upon which the information required pursuant to article 248 was provided to the coastal State unless within four months of the receipt of the communication containing such information the coastal State has informed the State or organization conducting the research that:

(a) it has withheld its consent under the provisions of article 246; or

(b) the information given by that State or competent international organization regarding the nature or objectives of the project does not conform to the manifestly evident facts; or

(c) it requires supplementary information relevant to conditions and the information provided for under articles 248 and 249; or

(d) outstanding obligations exist with respect to a previous marine scientific research project carried out by that State or organization, with regard to conditions established in article 249.

Article 253

Suspension or cessation of marine scientific research activities

1. A coastal State shall have the right to require the suspension of any marine scientific research activities in progress within its exclusive economic zone or on its continental shelf if:

(a) the research activities are not being conducted in accordance with the information communicated as provided under article 248 upon which the consent of the coastal State was based; or

(b) the State or competent international organization conducting the research activities fails to comply with the provisions of article 249 concerning the rights of the coastal State with respect to the marine scientific research project.

* * *

Article 254

Rights of neighbouring land-locked and geographically disadvantaged States

1. States and competent international organizations which have submitted to a coastal State a project to undertake marine scientific research referred to in article 246, paragraph 3, shall give notice to the neighbouring land-locked and geographically disadvantaged States of the proposed research project, and shall notify the coastal State thereof.

2. After the consent has been given for the proposed marine scientific research project by the coastal State concerned, in accordance with article 246 and other relevant provisions of this Convention, States and competent international organizations undertaking such a project shall provide to the neighbouring land-locked and geographically disadvantaged States, at their request and when appropriate, relevant information as specified in article 248 and article 249, paragraph 1(f).

3. The neighbouring land-locked and geographically disadvantaged States referred to above shall, at their request, be given the opportunity to participate,

whenever feasible, in the proposed marine scientific research project through qualified experts appointed by them and not objected to by the coastal State, in accordance with the conditions agreed for the project, in conformity with the provisions of this Convention, between the coastal State concerned and the State or competent international organizations conducting the marine scientific research.

* * *

Article 255

Measures to facilitate marine scientific research and assist research vessels

States shall endeavour to adopt reasonable rules, regulations and procedures to promote and facilitate marine scientific research conducted in accordance with this Convention beyond their territorial sea and, as appropriate, to facilitate, subject to the provisions of their laws and regulations, access to their harbours and promote assistance for marine scientific research vessels which comply with the relevant provisions of this Part.

Article 256

Marine scientific research in the Area

All States, irrespective of their geographical location, and competent international organizations have the right, in conformity with the provisions of Part XI, to conduct marine scientific research in the Area.

Article 257

Marine scientific research in the water column beyond the exclusive economic zone

All States, irrespective of their geographical location, and competent international organizations have the right, in conformity with this Convention, to conduct marine scientific research in the water column beyond the limits of the exclusive economic zone.

SECTION 4. SCIENTIFIC RESEARCH INSTALLATIONS OR EQUIPMENT IN THE MARINE ENVIRONMENT

Article 258

Deployment and use

The deployment and use of any type of scientific research installations or equipment in any area of the marine environment shall be subject to the same conditions as are prescribed in this Convention for the conduct of marine scientific research in any such area.

Article 259

Legal status

The installations or equipment referred to in this section do not possess the status of islands. They have no territorial sea of their own, and their presence does not affect the delimitation of the territorial sea, the exclusive economic zone or the continental shelf.

Article 260

Safety zones

Safety zones of a reasonable breadth not exceeding a distance of 500 metres may be created around scientific research installations in accordance with the relevant provisions of this Convention. All States shall ensure that such safety zones are respected by their vessels.

Article 261

Non-interference with shipping routes

The deployment and use of any type of scientific research installations or equipment shall not constitute an obstacle to established international shipping routes.

Article 262

Identification markings and warning signals

Installations or equipment referred to in this section shall bear identification markings indicating the State of registry or the international organization to which they belong and shall have adequate internationally agreed warning signals to ensure safety at sea and the safety of air navigation, taking into account rules and standards established by competent international organizations.

SECTION 5. RESPONSIBILITY AND LIABILITY

Article 263

Responsibility and liability

1. States and competent international organizations shall be responsible for ensuring that marine scientific research, whether undertaken by them or on their behalf, is conducted in accordance with this Convention.

2. States and competent international organizations shall be responsible and liable for the measures they take in contravention of this Convention in respect of marine scientific research conducted by other States, their natural or juridical persons or by competent international organizations, and shall provide compensation for damage resulting from such measures.

3. States and competent international organizations shall be responsible and liable pursuant to article 235 for damage caused by pollution of the marine environment arising out of marine scientific research undertaken by them or on their behalf.

SECTION 6. SETTLEMENT OF DISPUTES AND INTERIM MEASURES

Article 264

Settlement of disputes

Disputes concerning the interpretation or application of the provisions of this Convention with regard to marine scientific research shall be settled in accordance with Part XV, sections 2 and 3.

Article 265

Interim measures

Pending settlement of a dispute in accordance with Part XV, sections 2 and 3, the State or competent international organization authorized to conduct a marine scientific research project shall not allow research activities to commence or continue without the express consent of the coastal State concerned.

PART XIV

DEVELOPMENT AND TRANSFER OF MARINE TECHNOLOGY

SECTION 1. GENERAL PROVISIONS

Article 266

Promotion of the development and transfer of marine technology

1. States, directly or through competent international organizations, shall cooperate in accordance with their capabilities to promote actively the development and transfer of marine science and marine technology on fair and reasonable terms and conditions.

2. States shall promote the development of the marine scientific and technological capacity of States which may need and request technical assistance in this field, particularly developing States, including land-locked and geographically disadvantaged States, with regard to the exploration, exploitation, conservation and management of marine resources, the protection and preservation of the marine environment, marine scientific research and other activities in the marine environment compatible with this Convention, with a view to accelerating the social and economic development of the developing States.

3. States shall endeavour to foster favourable economic and legal conditions for the transfer of marine technology for the benefit of all parties concerned on an equitable basis.

Article 267

Protection of legitimate interests

States, in promoting co-operation pursuant to article 266, shall have due regard for all legitimate interests including, *inter alia,* the rights and duties of holders, suppliers and recipients of marine technology.

Article 268

Basic objectives

States, directly or through competent international organizations, shall promote:

(a) the acquisition, evaluation and dissemination of marine technological knowledge and facilitate access to such information and data;

(b) the development of appropriate marine technology;

(c) the development of the necessary technological infrastructure to facilitate the transfer of marine technology;

(d) the development of human resources through training and education of nationals of developing States and countries and especially the nationals of the least developed among them;

(e) international co-operation at all levels, particularly at the regional, subregional and bilateral levels.

Article 269

Measures to achieve the basic objectives

In order to achieve the objectives referred to in article 268, States, directly or through competent international organizations, shall endeavour, *inter alia,* to:

(a) establish programmes of technical co-operation for the effective transfer of all kinds of marine technology to States which may need and request technical assistance in this field, particularly the developing land-locked and geographically disadvantaged States, as well as other developing States which have not been able either to establish or develop their own technological capacity in marine science and in the exploration and exploitation of marine resources or to develop the infrastructure of such technology;

(b) promote favourable conditions for the conclusion of agreements, contracts and other similar arrangements, under equitable and reasonable conditions;

(c) hold conferences, seminars and symposia on scientific and technological subjects, in particular on policies and methods for the transfer of marine technology;

(d) promote the exchange of scientists and of technological and other experts;

(e) undertake projects and promote joint ventures and other forms of bilateral and multilateral co-operation.

SECTION 2. INTERNATIONAL CO–OPERATION

Article 270

Ways and means of international co-operation

International co-operation for the development and transfer of marine technology shall be carried out, where feasible and appropriate, through existing bilateral, regional or multilateral programmes, and also through expanded and new programmes in order to facilitate marine scientific research, the transfer of marine technology, particularly in new fields, and appropriate international funding for ocean research and development.

Article 271

Guidelines, criteria and standards

States, directly or through competent international organizations, shall promote the establishment of generally accepted guidelines, criteria and standards for the transfer of marine technology on a bilateral basis or within the framework of international organizations and other fora, taking into account, in particular, the interests and needs of developing States.

Article 272

Co-ordination of international programmes

In the field of transfer of marine technology, States shall endeavour to ensure that competent international organizations co-ordinate their activities, including any regional or global programmes, taking into account the interests and needs of developing States, particularly land-locked and geographically disadvantaged States.

Article 273

Co-operation with international organizations and the Authority

States shall co-operate actively with competent international organizations and the Authority to encourage and facilitate the transfer to developing States, their nationals and the Enterprise of skills and marine technology with regard to activities in the Area.

Article 274

Objectives of the Authority

Subject to all legitimate interests including, *inter alia,* the rights and duties of holders, suppliers and recipients of technology, the Authority, with regard to activities in the Area, shall ensure that:

(a) on the basis of the principle of equitable geographical distribution, nationals of developing States, whether coastal, land-locked or geographically disadvantaged, shall be taken on for the purposes of training as members of the managerial, research and technical staff constituted for its undertakings;

(b) the technical documentation on the relevant equipment, machinery, devices and processes is made available to all States, in particular developing States which may need and request technical assistance in this field;

(c) adequate provision is made by the Authority to facilitate the acquisition of technical assistance in the field of marine technology by States which may need and request it, in particular developing States, and the acquisition by their nationals of the necessary skills and know-how, including professional training;

(d) States which may need and request technical assistance in this field, in particular developing States, are assisted in the acquisition of necessary equipment, processes, plant and other technical know-how through any financial arrangements provided for in this Convention.

SECTION 3. NATIONAL AND REGIONAL MARINE SCIENTIFIC AND TECHNOLOGICAL CENTRES

Article 275

Establishment of national centres

1. States, directly or through competent international organizations and the Authority, shall promote the establishment, particularly in developing coastal States, of national marine scientific and technological research centres and the strengthening of existing national centres, in order to stimulate and advance the conduct of marine scientific research by developing coastal States and to enhance their national capabilities to utilize and preserve their marine resources for their economic benefit.

* * *

Article 276

Establishment of regional centres

* * *

Article 277

Functions of regional centres

* * *

SECTION 4. CO–OPERATION AMONG INTERNATIONAL ORGANIZATIONS

Article 278

Co-operation among international organizations

The competent international organizations referred to in this Part and in Part XIII shall take all appropriate measures to ensure, either directly or in close cooperation among themselves, the effective discharge of their functions and responsibilities under this Part.

PART XV

SETTLEMENT OF DISPUTES

SECTION 1. GENERAL PROVISIONS

Article 279

Obligation to settle disputes by peaceful means

States Parties shall settle any dispute between them concerning the interpretation or application of this Convention by peaceful means in accordance with Article 2, paragraph 3, of the Charter of the United Nations and, to this end, shall seek a solution by the means indicated in Article 33, paragraph 1, of the Charter.

Article 280

Settlement of disputes by any peaceful means chosen by the parties

Nothing in this Part impairs the right of any States Parties to agree at any time to settle a dispute between them concerning the interpretation or application of this Convention by any peaceful means of their own choice.

Article 281

Procedure where no settlement has been reached by the parties

1. If the States Parties which are parties to a dispute concerning the interpretation or application of this Convention have agreed to seek settlement of the dispute by a peaceful means of their own choice, the procedures provided for in this Part apply only where no settlement has been reached by recourse to such means and the agreement between the parties does not exclude any further procedure.

2. If the parties have also agreed on a time-limit, paragraph 1 applies only upon the expiration of that time-limit.

Article 282

Obligations under general, regional or bilateral agreements

If the States Parties which are parties to a dispute concerning the interpretation or application of this Convention have agreed, through a general, regional or bilateral agreement or otherwise, that such dispute shall, at the request of any party to the dispute, be submitted to a procedure that entails a binding decision, that procedure shall apply in lieu of the procedures provided for in this Part, unless the parties to the dispute otherwise agree.

Article 283

Obligation to exchange views

1. When a dispute arises between States Parties concerning the interpretation or application of this Convention, the parties to the dispute shall proceed expeditiously to an exchange of views regarding its settlement by negotiation or other peaceful means.

2. The parties shall also proceed expeditiously to an exchange of views where a procedure for the settlement of such a dispute has been terminated without a settlement or where a settlement has been reached and the circumstances require consultation regarding the manner of implementing the settlement.

Article 284

Conciliation

1. A State Party which is a party to a dispute concerning the interpretation or application of this Convention may invite the other party or parties to submit the dispute to conciliation in accordance with the procedure under Annex V, section 1, or another conciliation procedure.

2. If the invitation is accepted and if the parties agree upon the conciliation procedure to be applied, any party may submit the dispute to that procedure.

3. If the invitation is not accepted or the parties do not agree upon the procedure, the conciliation proceedings shall be deemed to be terminated.

4. Unless the parties otherwise agree, when a dispute has been submitted to conciliation, the proceedings may be terminated only in accordance with the agreed conciliation procedure.

Article 285

Application of this section to disputes submitted pursuant to Part XI

This section applies to any dispute which pursuant to Part XI, section 5, is to be settled in accordance with procedures provided for in this Part. If an entity other than a State Party is a party to such a dispute, this section applies *mutatis mutandis.*

SECTION 2. COMPULSORY PROCEDURES ENTAILING BINDING DECISIONS

Article 286

Application of procedures under this section

Subject to section 3, any dispute concerning the interpretation or application of this Convention shall, where no settlement has been reached by recourse to section 1, be submitted at the request of any party to the dispute to the court or tribunal having jurisdiction under this section.

Article 287

Choice of procedure

1. When signing, ratifying or acceding to this Convention or at any time thereafter, a State shall be free to choose, by means of a written declaration, one or more of the following means for the settlement of disputes concerning the interpretation or application of this Convention:

(a) the International Tribunal for the Law of the Sea established [in Hamburg, West Germany] in accordance with Annex VI;

(b) the International Court of Justice;

(c) an arbitral tribunal constituted in accordance with Annex VII;

(d) a special arbitral tribunal constituted in accordance with Annex VIII for one or more of the categories of disputes specified therein.

2. A declaration made under paragraph 1 shall not affect or be affected by the obligation of a State Party to accept the jurisdiction of the Sea–Bed Disputes Chamber of the International Tribunal for the Law of the Sea to the extent and in the manner provided for in Part XI, section 5.

3. A State Party, which is a party to a dispute not covered by a declaration in force, shall be deemed to have accepted arbitration in accordance with Annex VII.

4. If the parties to a dispute have accepted the same procedure for the settlement of the dispute, it may be submitted only to that procedure, unless the parties otherwise agree.

5. If the parties to a dispute have not accepted the same procedure for the settlement of the dispute, it may be submitted only to arbitration in accordance with Annex VII, unless the parties otherwise agree.

6. A declaration made under paragraph 1 shall remain in force until three months after notice of revocation has been deposited with the Secretary–General of the United Nations.

7. A new declaration, a notice of revocation or the expiry of a declaration does not in any way affect proceedings pending before a court or tribunal having jurisdiction under this article, unless the parties otherwise agree.

8. Declarations and notices referred to in this article shall be deposited with the Secretary-General of the United Nations, who shall transmit copies thereof to the States Parties.

Article 288

Jurisdiction

1. A court or tribunal referred to in article 287 shall have jurisdiction over any dispute concerning the interpretation or application of this Convention which is submitted to it in accordance with this Part.

2. A court or tribunal referred to in article 287 shall also have jurisdiction over any dispute concerning the interpretation or application of an international agreement related to the purposes of this Convention, which is submitted to it in accordance with the agreement.

3. The Sea-Bed Disputes Chamber of the International Tribunal for the Law of the Sea established in accordance with Annex VI, and any other chamber or arbitral tribunal referred to in Part XI, section 5, shall have jurisdiction in any matter which is submitted to it in accordance therewith.

4. In the event of a dispute as to whether a court or tribunal has jurisdiction, the matter shall be settled by decision of that court or tribunal.

Article 289

Experts

In any dispute involving scientific or technical matters, a court or tribunal exercising jurisdiction under this section may, at the request of a party or *proprio motu,* select in consultation with the parties no fewer than two scientific or technical experts chosen preferably from the relevant list prepared in accordance with Annex VIII, article 2, to sit with the court or tribunal but without the right to vote.

Article 290

Provisional measures

1. If a dispute has been duly submitted to a court or tribunal which considers that *prima facie* it has jurisdiction under this Part or Part XI, section 5, the court or tribunal may prescribe any provisional measures which it considers appropriate under the circumstances to preserve the respective rights of the parties to the dispute or to prevent serious harm to the marine environment, pending the final decision.

* * *

6. The parties to the dispute shall comply promptly with any provisional measures prescribed under this article.

Article 291

Access

1. All the dispute settlement procedures specified in this Part shall be open to States Parties.

2. The dispute settlement procedures specified in this Part shall be open to entities other than States Parties only as specifically provided for in this Convention.

Article 292

Prompt release of vessels and crews

1. Where the authorities of a State Party have detained a vessel flying the flag of another State Party and it is alleged that the detaining State has not complied with the provisions of this Convention for the prompt release of the vessel or its crew upon the posting of a reasonable bond or other financial security, the question of

release from detention may be submitted to any court or tribunal agreed upon by the parties or, failing such agreement within 10 days from the time of detention, to a court or tribunal accepted by the detaining State under article 287 or to the International Tribunal for the Law of the Sea, unless the parties otherwise agree.

2. The application for release may be made only by or on behalf of the flag State of the vessel.

3. The court or tribunal shall deal without delay with the application for release and shall deal only with the question of release, without prejudice to the merits of any case before the appropriate domestic forum against the vessel, its owner or its crew. The authorities of the detaining State remain competent to release the vessel or its crew at any time.

4. Upon the posting of the bond or other financial security determined by the court or tribunal, the authorities of the detaining State shall comply promptly with the decision of the court or tribunal concerning the release of the vessel or its crew.

Article 293

Applicable law

1. A court or tribunal having jurisdiction under this section shall apply this Convention and other rules of international law not incompatible with this Convention.

2. Paragraph 1 does not prejudice the power of the court or tribunal having jurisdiction under this section to decide a case *ex aequo et bono,* if the parties so agree.

Article 294

Preliminary proceedings

1. A court or tribunal provided for in article 287 to which an application is made in respect of a dispute referred to in article 297 shall determine at the request of a party, or may determine *proprio motu,* whether the claim constitutes an abuse of legal process or whether *prima facie* it is well founded. If the court or tribunal determines that the claim constitutes an abuse of legal process or is *prima facie* unfounded, it shall take no further action in the case.

* * *

Article 295

Exhaustion of local remedies

Any dispute between States Parties concerning the interpretation or application of this Convention may be submitted to the procedures provided for in this section only after local remedies have been exhausted where this is required by international law.

Article 296

Finality and binding force of decisions

1. Any decision rendered by a court or tribunal having jurisdiction under this section shall be final and shall be complied with by all the parties to the dispute.

2. Any such decision shall have no binding force except between the parties and in respect of that particular dispute.

SECTION 3. LIMITATIONS AND EXCEPTIONS TO APPLICABILITY OF SECTION 2

Article 297

Limitations on applicability of section 2

1. Disputes concerning the interpretation or application of this Convention with regard to the exercise by a coastal State of its sovereign rights or jurisdiction provided for in this Convention shall be subject to the procedures provided for in section 2 in the following cases:

(a) when it is alleged that a coastal State has acted in contravention of the provisions of this Convention in regard to the freedoms and rights of navigation, overflight or the laying of submarine cables and pipelines, or in regard to other internationally lawful uses of the sea specified in article 58;

(b) when it is alleged that a State in exercising the aforementioned freedoms, rights or uses has acted in contravention of this Convention or of laws or regulations adopted by the coastal State in conformity with this Convention and other rules of international law not incompatible with this Convention; or

(c) when it is alleged that a coastal State has acted in contravention of specified international rules and standards for the protection and preservation of the marine environment which are applicable to the coastal State and which have been established by this Convention or through a competent international organization or diplomatic conference in accordance with this Convention.

2. (a) Disputes concerning the interpretation or application of the provisions of this Convention with regard to marine scientific research shall be settled in accordance with section 2, except that the coastal State shall not be obliged to accept the submission to such settlement of any dispute arising out of:

(i) the exercise by the coastal State of a right or discretion in accordance with article 246; or

(ii) a decision by the coastal State to order suspension or cessation of a research project in accordance with article 253.

(b) A dispute arising from an allegation by the researching State that with respect to a specific project the coastal State is not exercising its rights under articles 246 and 253 in a manner compatible with this Convention shall be submitted, at the request of either party, to conciliation under Annex V, section 2, provided that the conciliation commission shall not call in question the exercise by the coastal State of its discretion to designate specific areas as referred to in article 246, paragraph 6, or of its discretion to withhold consent in accordance with article 246, paragraph 5.

3. (a) Disputes concerning the interpretation or application of the provisions of this Convention with regard to fisheries shall be settled in accordance with section 2, except that the coastal State shall not be obliged to accept the submission to such settlement of any dispute relating to its sovereign rights with respect to the living resources in the exclusive economic zone or their exercise, including its discretionary powers for determining the allowable catch, its harvesting capacity, the allocation of surpluses to other States and the terms and conditions established in its conservation and management laws and regulations.

(b) Where no settlement has been reached by recourse to section 1 of this Part, a dispute shall be submitted to conciliation under Annex V, section 2, at the request of any party to the dispute, when it is alleged that:

(i) a coastal State has manifestly failed to comply with its obligations to ensure through proper conservation and management measures that the maintenance of the living resources in the exclusive economic zone is not seriously endangered;

(ii) a coastal State has arbitrarily refused to determine, at the request of another State, the allowable catch and its capacity to harvest living resources with respect to stocks which that other State is interested in fishing; or

(iii) a coastal State has arbitrarily refused to allocate to any State, under articles 62, 69 and 70 and under the terms and conditions established by the coastal State consistent with this Convention, the whole or part of the surplus it has declared to exist.

(c) In no case shall the conciliation commission substitute its discretion for that of the coastal State.

(d) The report of the conciliation commission shall be communicated to the appropriate international organizations.

(e) In negotiating agreements pursuant to articles 69 and 70, States Parties, unless they otherwise agree, shall include a clause on measures which they shall take in order to minimize the possibility of a disagreement concerning the interpretation or application of the agreement, and on how they should proceed if a disagreement nevertheless arises.

Article 298

Optional exceptions to applicability of section 2

1. When signing, ratifying or acceding to this Convention or at any time thereafter, a State may, without prejudice to the obligations arising under section 1, declare in writing that it does not accept any one or more of the procedures provided for in section 2 with respect to one or more of the following categories of disputes:

(a)(i) disputes concerning the interpretation or application of articles 15, 74 and 83 relating to sea boundary delimitations, or those involving historic bays or titles, provided that a State having made such a declaration shall, when such a dispute arises subsequent to the entry into force of this Convention and where no agreement within a reasonable period of time is reached in negotiations between the parties, at the request of any party to the dispute, accept submission of the matter to conciliation under Annex V, section 2; and provided further that any dispute that necessarily involves the concurrent consideration of any unsettled dispute concerning sovereignty or other rights over continental or insular land territory shall be excluded from such submission;

(ii) after the conciliation commission has presented its report, which shall state the reasons on which it is based, the parties shall negotiate an agreement on the basis of that report; if these negotiations do not result in an agreement, the parties shall, by mutual consent, submit the question to one of the procedures provided for in section 2, unless the parties otherwise agree;

(iii) this subparagraph does not apply to any sea boundary dispute finally settled by an arrangement between the parties, or to any such dispute which is to be settled in accordance with a bilateral or multilateral agreement binding upon those parties;

(b) disputes concerning military activities, including military activities by government vessels and aircraft engaged in non-commercial service, and disputes concerning law enforcement activities in regard to the exercise of sovereign rights or jurisdiction excluded from the jurisdiction of a court or tribunal under article 297, paragraph 2 or 3;

(c) disputes in respect of which the Security Council of the United Nations is exercising the functions assigned to it by the Charter of the United Nations, unless the Security Council decides to remove the matter from its agenda or calls upon the parties to settle it by the means provided for in this Convention.

2. A State Party which has made a declaration under paragraph 1 may at any time withdraw it, or agree to submit a dispute excluded by such declaration to any procedure specified in this Convention.

3. A State Party which has made a declaration under paragraph 1 shall not be entitled to submit any dispute falling within the excepted category of disputes to any procedure in this Convention as against another State Party, without the consent of that party.

4. If one of the States Parties has made a declaration under paragraph 1(a), any other State Party may submit any dispute falling within an excepted category against the declarant party to the procedure specified in such declaration.

5. A new declaration, or the withdrawal of a declaration, does not in any way affect proceedings pending before a court or tribunal in accordance with this article, unless the parties otherwise agree.

6. Declarations and notices of withdrawal of declarations under this article shall be deposited with the Secretary-General of the United Nations, who shall transmit copies thereof to the States Parties.

Article 299

Right of the parties to agree upon a procedure

1. A dispute excluded under article 297 or excepted by a declaration made under article 298 from the dispute settlement procedures provided for in section 2 may be submitted to such procedures only by agreement of the parties to the dispute.

2. Nothing in this section impairs the right of the parties to the dispute to agree to some other procedure for the settlement of such dispute or to reach an amicable settlement.

PART XVI

GENERAL PROVISIONS

Article 300

Good faith and abuse of rights

States Parties shall fulfil in good faith the obligations assumed under this Convention and shall exercise the rights, jurisdiction and freedoms recognized in this Convention in a manner which would not constitute an abuse of right.

Article 301

Peaceful uses of the seas

In exercising their rights and performing their duties under this Convention, States Parties shall refrain from any threat or use of force against the territorial integrity or political independence of any State, or in any other manner inconsistent with the principles of international law embodied in the Charter of the United Nations.

Article 302

Disclosure of information

Without prejudice to the right of a State Party to resort to the procedures for the settlement of disputes provided for in this Convention, nothing in this Convention shall be deemed to require a State Party, in the fulfilment of its obligations under this Convention, to supply information the disclosure of which is contrary to the essential interests of its security.

Article 303

Archaeological and historical objects found at sea

1. States have the duty to protect objects of an archaeological and historical nature found at sea and shall co-operate for this purpose.

2. In order to control traffic in such objects, the coastal State may, in applying article 33, presume that their removal from the sea-bed in the zone referred to in that article without its approval would result in an infringement within its territory or territorial sea of the laws and regulations referred to in that article.

3. Nothing in this article affects the rights of identifiable owners, the law of salvage or other rules of admiralty, or laws and practices with respect to cultural exchanges.

4. This article is without prejudice to other international agreements and rules of international law regarding the protection of objects of an archaeological and historical nature.

Article 304

Responsibility and liability for damage

The provisions of this Convention regarding responsibility and liability for damage are without prejudice to the application of existing rules and the development of further rules regarding responsibility and liability under international law.

PART XVII

FINAL PROVISIONS

* * *

Article 309

Reservations and exceptions

No reservations or exceptions may be made to this Convention unless expressly permitted by other articles of this Convention.

Article 310

Declarations and statements

Article 309 does not preclude a State, when signing, ratifying or acceding to this Convention, from making declarations or statements, however phrased or named, with a view, *inter alia,* to the harmonization of its laws and regulations with the provisions of this Convention, provided that such declarations or statements do not purport to exclude or to modify the legal effect of the provisions of this Convention in their application to that State.

Article 311

Relation to other conventions and international agreements

1. This Convention shall prevail, as between States Parties, over the Geneva Conventions on the Law of the Sea of 29 April 1958.

2. This Convention shall not alter the rights and obligations of States Parties which arise from other agreements compatible with this Convention and which do not affect the enjoyment by other States Parties of their rights or the performance of their obligations under this Convention.

3. Two or more States Parties may conclude agreements modifying or suspending the operation of provisions of this Convention, applicable solely to the

relations between them, provided that such agreements do not relate to a provision derogation from which is incompatible with the effective execution of the object and purpose of this Convention, and provided further that such agreements shall not affect the application of the basic principles embodied herein, and that the provisions of such agreements do not affect the enjoyment by other States Parties of their rights or the performance of their obligations under this Convention.

4. States Parties intending to conclude an agreement referred to in paragraph 3 shall notify the other States Parties through the depositary of this Convention of their intention to conclude the agreement and of the modification or suspension for which it provides.

5. This article does not affect international agreements expressly permitted or preserved by other articles of this Convention.

6. States Parties agree that there shall be no amendments to the basic principle relating to the common heritage of mankind set forth in article 136 and that they shall not be party to any agreement in derogation thereof.

* * *

Article 317

Denunciation

1. A State Party may, by written notification addressed to the Secretary–General of the United Nations, denounce this Convention and may indicate its reasons. Failure to indicate reasons shall not affect the validity of the denunciation. The denunciation shall take effect one year after the date of receipt of the notification, unless the notification specifies a later date.

2. A State shall not be discharged by reason of the denunciation from the financial and contractual obligations which accrued while it was a Party to this Convention, nor shall the denunciation affect any right, obligation or legal situation of that State created through the execution of this Convention prior to its termination for that State.

3. The denunciation shall not in any way affect the duty of any State Party to fulfil any obligation embodied in this Convention to which it would be subject under international law independently of this Convention.

Article 318

Status of Annexes

The Annexes form an integral part of this Convention and, unless expressly provided otherwise, a reference to this Convention or to one of its Parts includes a reference to the Annexes relating thereto.

* * *

ANNEX I. HIGHLY MIGRATORY SPECIES

1. Albacore tuna: *Thunnus alalunga.*
2. Bluefin tuna: *Thunnus thynnus.*
3. Bigeye tuna: *Thunnus obesus.*
4. Skipjack tuna: *Katsuwonus pelamis.*
5. Yellowfin tuna: *Thunnus albacares.*
6. Blackfin tuna: *Thunnus atlanticus.*
7. Little tuna: *Euthynnus alletteratus; Euthynnus affinis.*
8. Southern bluefin tuna: *Thunnus maccoyii.*
9. Frigate mackerel: *Auxis thazard; Auxis rochei.*
10. Pomfrets: Family *Bramidae.*

11. Marlins: *Tetrapturus angustirostris; Tetrapturus belone; Tetrapturus pfluegeri; Tetrapturus albidus; Tetrapturus audax; Tetrapturus georgei; Makaira mazara; Makaira indica; Makaira nigricans.*

12. Sail-fishes: *Istiophorus platypterus; Istiophorus albicans.*

13. Swordfish: *Xiphias gladius.*

14. Sauries: *Scomberesox saurus; Cololabis saira; Cololabis adocetus; Scomberesox saurus scombroides.*

15. Dolphin: *Coryphaena hippurus; Coryphaena equiselis.*

16. Oceanic sharks: *Hexanchus griseus; Cetorhinus maximus; Family Alopiidae; Rhincodon typus; Family Carcharhinidae; Family Sphyrnidae; Family Isurida.*

17. Cetaceans: Family *Physeteridae;* Family *Balaenopteridae;* Family *Balaenidae;* Family *Eschrichtiidae;* Family *Monodontidae;* Family *Ziphiidae;* Family *Delphinidae.*

ANNEX II. COMMISSION ON THE LIMITS OF THE CONTINENTAL SHELF

Article 1

In accordance with the provisions of article 76, a Commission on the Limits of the Continental Shelf beyond 200 nautical miles shall be established in conformity with the following articles.

Article 2

1. The Commission shall consist of 21 members who shall be experts in the field of geology, geophysics or hydrography, elected by States Parties to this Convention from among their nationals, having due regard to the need to ensure equitable geographical representation, who shall serve in their personal capacities.

2. The initial election shall be held as soon as possible but in any case within 18 months after the date of entry into force of this Convention. At least three months before the date of each election, the Secretary–General of the United Nations shall address a letter to the States Parties, inviting the submission of nominations, after appropriate regional consultations, within three months. The Secretary–General shall prepare a list in alphabetical order of all persons thus nominated and shall submit it to all the States Parties.

5.28 VIENNA CONVENTION FOR THE PROTECTION OF THE OZONE LAYER.[a] Done at Vienna, Mar. 22, 1985. Entered into force, Sept. 22, 1988; for the United States, Sept. 22, 1988. S. Treaty Doc. No. 9, 99th Cong., 1st Sess. (1985), *reprinted in* 26 I.L.M. 1529[b]

Article 1

DEFINITIONS

For the purposes of this Convention:

1. "The ozone layer" means the layer of atmospheric ozone above the planetary boundary layer.

2. "Adverse effects" means changes in the physical environment or biota, including changes in climate, which have significant deleterious effects on human health or on the composition, resilience and productivity of natural and managed ecosystems, or on materials useful to mankind.

3. "Alternative technologies or equipment" means technologies or equipment the use of which makes it possible to reduce or effectively eliminate emissions of substances which have or are likely to have adverse effects on the ozone layer.

4. "Alternative substances" means substances which reduce, eliminate or avoid adverse effects on the ozone layer.

5. "Parties" means, unless the text otherwise indicates, Parties to this Convention.

6. "Regional economic integration organization" means an organization constituted by sovereign States of a given region which has competence in respect of matters governed by this Convention or its protocols and has been duly authorized, in accordance with its internal procedures, to sign, ratify, accept, approve or accede to the instruments concerned.

7. "Protocols" means protocols to this Convention.

Article 2

GENERAL OBLIGATIONS

1. The Parties shall take appropriate measures in accordance with the provisions of this Convention and of those protocols in force to which they are party to protect human health and the environment against adverse effects resulting or likely to result from human activities which modify or are likely to modify the ozone layer.

2. To this end the Parties shall, in accordance with the means at their disposal and their capabilities:

(a) Co-operate by means of systematic observations, research and information exchange in order to better understand and assess the effects of human activities on the ozone layer and the effects on human health and the environment from modification of the ozone layer;

(b) Adopt appropriate legislative or administrative measures and co-operate in harmonizing appropriate policies to control, limit, reduce or prevent human activities under their jurisdiction or control should it be found that these

a. *See also* Basic Document 5.30, *infra.*

b. Annexes I ("Research and Systematic Observations") and II ("Information Exchange") are omitted.

activities have or are likely to have adverse effects resulting from modification or likely modification of the ozone layer;

(c) Co-operate in the formulation of agreed measures, procedures and standards for the implementation of this Convention, with a view to the adoption of protocols and annexes;

(d) Co-operate with competent international bodies to implement effectively this Convention and protocols to which they are party.

3. The provisions of this Convention shall in no way affect the right of Parties to adopt, in accordance with international law, domestic measures additional to those referred to in paragraphs 1 and 2 above, nor shall they affect additional domestic measures already taken by a Party, provided that those measures are not incompatible with their obligations under this Convention.

4. The application of this article shall be based on relevant scientific and technical considerations.

Article 3

RESEARCH AND SYSTEMATIC OBSERVATIONS

1. The Parties undertake, as appropriate, to initiate and co-operate in, directly or through competent international bodies, the conduct of research and scientific assessments on:

(a) The physical and chemical processes that may affect the ozone layer;

(b) The human health and other biological effects deriving from any modifications of the ozone layer, particularly those resulting from changes in ultraviolet solar radiation having biological effects (UV–S);

(c) Climatic effects deriving from any modifications of the ozone layer;

(d) Effects deriving from any modifications of the ozone layer and any consequent change in UV–S radiation on natural and synthetic materials useful to mankind;

(e) Substances, practices, processes and activities that may affect the ozone layer, and their cumulative effects;

(f) Alternative substances and technologies;

(g) Related socio-economic matters;

and as further elaborated in annexes I and II.

2. The Parties undertake to promote or establish, as appropriate, directly or through competent international bodies and taking fully into account national legislation and relevant ongoing activities at both the national and international levels, joint or complementary programmes for systematic observation of the state of the ozone layer and other relevant parameters, as elaborated in annex I.

3. The Parties undertake to co-operate, directly or through competent international bodies, in ensuring the collection, validation and transmission of research and observational data through appropriate world data centres in a regular and timely fashion.

Article 4

CO–OPERATION IN THE LEGAL, SCIENTIFIC AND TECHNICAL FIELDS

1. The Parties shall facilitate and encourage the exchange of scientific, technical, socio-economic, commercial and legal information relevant to this Convention as further elaborated in annex II. Such information shall be supplied to bodies agreed upon by the Parties. Any such body receiving information regarded as confidential

by the supplying Party shall ensure that such information is not disclosed and shall aggregate it to protect its confidentiality before it is made available to all Parties.

2. The Parties shall co-operate, consistent with their national laws, regulations and practices and taking into account in particular the needs of the developing countries, in promoting, directly or through competent international bodies, the development and transfer of technology and knowledge. Such co-operation shall be carried out particularly through:

(a) Facilitation of the acquisition of alternative technologies by other Parties;

(b) Provision of information on alternative technologies and equipment, and supply of special manuals or guides to them;

(c) The supply of necessary equipment and facilities for research and systematic observations;

(d) Appropriate training of scientific and technical personnel.

Article 5

TRANSMISSION OF INFORMATION

The Parties shall transmit, through the secretariat, to the Conference of the Parties established under article 6 information on the measures adopted by them in implementation of this Convention and of protocols to which they are party in such form and at such intervals as the meetings of the parties to the relevant instruments may determine.

Article 6

CONFERENCE OF THE PARTIES

1. A Conference of the Parties is hereby established. The first meeting of the Conference of the Parties shall be convened by the secretariat designated on an interim basis under article 7 not later than one year after entry into force of this Convention. Thereafter, ordinary meetings of the Conference of the Parties shall be held at regular intervals to be determined by the Conference at its first meeting.

* * *

Article 7

SECRETARIAT

1. The functions of the secretariat shall be:

(a) To arrange for and service meetings provided for in articles 6, 8, 9 and 10;

(b) To prepare and transmit reports based upon information received in accordance with articles 4 and 5, as well as upon information derived from meetings of subsidiary bodies established under article 6;

(c) To perform the functions assigned to it by any protocol;

(d) To prepare reports on its activities carried out in implementation of its functions under this Convention and present them to the Conference of the Parties;

(e) To ensure the necessary co-ordination with other relevant international bodies, and in particular to enter into such administrative and contractual arrangements as may be required for the effective discharge of its functions;

(f) To perform such other functions as may be determined by the Conference of the Parties.

2. The secretariat functions will be carried out on an interim basis by the United Nations Environment Programme until the completion of the first ordinary meeting of the Conference of the Parties held pursuant to article 6. At its first ordinary meeting, the Conference of the Parties shall designate the secretariat from amongst those existing competent international organizations which have signified their willingness to carry out the secretariat functions under this Convention.

Article 8

ADOPTION OF PROTOCOLS

1. The Conference of the Parties may at a meeting adopt protocols pursuant to article 2.

2. The text of any proposed protocol shall be communicated to the Parties by the secretariat at least six months before such a meeting.

Article 9

AMENDMENT OF THE CONVENTION OR PROTOCOLS

1. Any Party may propose amendments to this Convention or to any protocol. Such amendments shall take due account, *inter alia,* of relevant scientific and technical considerations.

* * *

Article 10

ADOPTION AND AMENDMENT OF ANNEXES

1. The annexes to this Convention or to any protocol shall form an integral part of this Convention or of such protocol, as the case may be, and, unless expressly provided otherwise, a reference to this Convention or its protocols constitutes at the same time a reference to any annexes thereto. Such annexes shall be restricted to scientific, technical and administrative matters.

* * *

Article 11

SETTLEMENT OF DISPUTES

1. In the event of a dispute between Parties concerning the interpretation or application of this Convention, the parties concerned shall seek solution by negotiation.

2. If the parties concerned cannot reach agreement by negotiation, they may jointly seek the good offices of, or request mediation by, a third party.

3. When ratifying, accepting, approving or acceding to this Convention, or at any time thereafter, a State or regional economic integration organization may declare in writing to the Depositary that for a dispute not resolved in accordance with paragraph 1 or paragraph 2 above, it accepts one or both of the following means of dispute settlement as compulsory:

(a) Arbitration in accordance with procedures to be adopted by the Conference of the Parties at its first ordinary meeting;

(b) Submission of the dispute to the International Court of Justice.

4. If the parties have not, in accordance with paragraph 3 above, accepted the same or any procedure, the dispute shall be submitted to conciliation in accordance with paragraph 5 below unless the parties otherwise agree.

5. A conciliation commission shall be created upon the request of one of the parties to the dispute. The commission shall be composed of an equal number of members appointed by each party concerned and a chairman chosen jointly by the

members appointed by each party. The commission shall render a final and recommendatory award, which the parties shall consider in good faith.

6. The provisions of this article shall apply with respect to any protocol except as otherwise provided in the protocol concerned.

* * *

Article 15

RIGHT TO VOTE

1. Each Party to this Convention or to any protocol shall have one vote.

2. Except as provided for in paragraph 1 above, regional economic integration organizations, in matters within their competence, shall exercise their right to vote with a number of votes equal to the number of their member States which are Parties to the Convention or the relevant protocol. Such organizations shall not exercise their right to vote if their member States exercise theirs, and vice versa.

Article 16

RELATIONSHIP BETWEEN THE CONVENTION AND ITS PROTOCOLS

1. A State or a regional economic integration organization may not become a party to a protocol unless it is, or becomes at the same time, a Party to the Convention.

2. Decisions concerning any protocol shall be taken only by the parties to the protocol concerned.

* * *

Article 18

RESERVATIONS

No reservations may be made to this Convention.

Article 19

WITHDRAWAL

1. At any time after four years from the date on which this Convention has entered into force for a Party, that Party may withdraw from the Convention by giving written notification to the Depositary.

2. Except as may be provided in any protocol, at any time after four years from the date on which such protocol has entered into force for a party, that party may withdraw from the protocol by giving written notification to the Depositary.

3. Any such withdrawal shall take effect upon expiry of one year after the date of its receipt by the Depositary, or on such later date as may be specified in the notification of the withdrawal.

4. Any Party which withdraws from this Convention shall be considered as also having withdrawn from any protocol to which it is party.

* * *

5.29 CONVENTION ON EARLY NOTIFICATION OF A NUCLEAR ACCIDENT. Done at Vienna, Sept. 26, 1986. Entered into force, Oct. 27, 1986. *Reproduced in* 25 I.L.M. 1370 (1986)

Article 1

Scope of application

1. This Convention shall apply in the event of any accident involving facilities or activities of a State Party or of persons or legal entities under its jurisdiction or control, referred to in paragraph 2 below, from which a release of radioactive material occurs or is likely to occur and which has resulted or may result in an international transboundary release that could be of radiological safety significance for another State.

2. The facilities and activities referred to in paragraph 1 are the following:

(a) any nuclear reactor wherever located;

(b) any nuclear fuel cycle facility;

(c) any radioactive waste management facility;

(d) the transport and storage of nuclear fuels or radioactive wastes;

(e) the manufacture, use, storage, disposal and transport of radioisotopes for agricultural, industrial, medical and related scientific and research purposes; and

(f) the use of radioisotopes for power generation in space objects.

Article 2

Notification and information

In the event of an accident specified in article 1 (hereinafter referred to as a "nuclear accident"), the State Party referred to in that article shall:

(a) forthwith notify, directly or through the International Atomic Energy Agency (hereinafter referred to as the "Agency"), those States which are or may be physically affected as specified in article 1 and the Agency of the nuclear accident, its nature, the time of its occurrence and its exact location where appropriate; and

(b) promptly provide the States referred to in sub-paragraph (a), directly or through the Agency, and the Agency with such available information relevant to minimizing the radiological consequences in those States, as specified in article 5.

Article 3

Other Nuclear Accidents

With a view to minimizing the radiological consequences, States Parties may notify in the event of nuclear accidents other than those specified in article 1.

Article 4

Functions of the Agency

The Agency shall:

(a) forthwith inform States Parties, Member States, other States which are or may be physically affected as specified in article 1 and relevant international intergovernmental organizations (hereinafter referred to as "international organizations") of a notification received pursuant to sub-paragraph (a) of article 2; and

(b) promptly provide any State Party, Member State or relevant international organization, upon request, with the information received pursuant to sub-paragraph (b) of article 2.

Article 5

Information to be provided

1. The information to be provided pursuant to sub-paragraph (b) of article 2 shall comprise the following data as then available to the notifying State Party:

(a) the time, exact location where appropriate, and the nature of the nuclear accident;

(b) the facility or activity involved;

(c) the assumed or established cause and the foreseeable development of the nuclear accident relevant to the transboundary release of the radioactive materials;

(d) the general characteristics of the radioactive release, including, as far as is practicable and appropriate, the nature, probable physical and chemical form and the quantity, composition and effective height of the radioactive release;

(e) information on current and forecast meteorological and hydrological conditions, necessary for forecasting the transboundary release of the radioactive materials;

(f) the results of environmental monitoring relevant to the transboundary release of the radioactive materials;

(g) the off-site protective measures taken or planned;

(h) the predicted behaviour over time of the radioactive release.

2. Such information shall be supplemented at appropriate intervals by further relevant information on the development of the emergency situation, including its foreseeable or actual termination.

3. Information received pursuant to sub-paragraph (b) of article 2 may be used without restriction, except when such information is provided in confidence by the notifying State Party.

Article 6

Consultations

A State Party providing information pursuant to sub-paragraph (b) of article 2 shall, as far as is reasonably practicable, respond promptly to a request for further information or consultations sought by an affected State Party with a view to minimizing the radiological consequences in that State.

Article 7

Competent authorities and points of contact

1. Each State Party shall make known to the Agency and to other States Parties, directly or through the Agency, its competent authorities and point of contact responsible for issuing and receiving the notification and information referred to in article 2. Such points of contact and a focal point within the Agency shall be available continuously.

2. Each State Party shall promptly inform the Agency of any changes that may occur in the information referred to in paragraph 1.

3. The Agency shall maintain an up-to-date list of such national authorities and points of contact as well as points of contact of relevant international organizations

and shall provide it to States Parties and Member States and to relevant international organizations.

Article 8

Assistance to States Parties

The Agency shall, in accordance with its Statute and upon a request of a State Party which does not have nuclear activities itself and borders on a State having an active nuclear programme but not Party, conduct investigations into the feasibility and establishment of an appropriate radiation monitoring system in order to facilitate the achievement of the objectives of this Convention.

Article 9

Bilateral and multilateral arrangements

In furtherance of their mutual interests, States Parties may consider, where deemed appropriate, the conclusion of bilateral or multilateral arrangements relating to the subject matter of this Convention.

Article 10

Relationship to other international agreements

This Convention shall not affect the reciprocal rights and obligations of States Parties under existing international agreements which relate to the matters covered by this Convention, or under future international agreements concluded in accordance with the object and purpose of this Convention.

Article 11

Settlement of disputes

1. In the event of a dispute between States Parties, or between a State Party and the Agency, concerning the interpretation or application of this Convention, the parties to the dispute shall consult with a view to the settlement of the dispute by negotiation or by any other peaceful means of settling disputes acceptable to them.

2. If a dispute of this character between States Parties cannot be settled within one year from the request for consultation pursuant to paragraph 1, it shall, at the request of any party to such dispute, be submitted to arbitration or referred to the International Court of Justice for decision. Where a dispute is submitted to arbitration, if, within six months from the date of the request, the parties to the dispute are unable to agree on the organization of the arbitration, a party may request the President of the International Court of Justice or the Secretary–General of the United Nations to appoint one or more arbitrators. In cases of conflicting requests by the parties to the dispute, the request to the Secretary–General of the United Nations shall have priority.

3. When signing, ratifying, accepting, approving or acceding to this Convention, a State may declare that it does not consider itself bound by either or both of the dispute settlement procedures provided for in paragraph 2. The other States Parties shall not be bound by a dispute settlement procedure provided for in paragraph 2 with respect to a State Party for which such a declaration is in force.

4. A State Party which has made a declaration in accordance with paragraph 3 may at any time withdraw it by notification to the depositary.

5.30 CONVENTION ON ASSISTANCE IN CASE OF A NUCLEAR ACCIDENT OR RADIOLOGICAL EMERGENCY. Done at Vienna, Sept. 26, 1986. Entered into force, Feb. 26, 1987. *Reproduced in* 25 I.L.M. 1377 (1986)

Article 1

General provisions

1. The States Parties shall cooperate between themselves and with the International Atomic Energy Agency (hereinafter referred to as the "Agency") in accordance with the provisions of this Convention to facilitate prompt assistance in the event of a nuclear accident or radiological emergency to minimize its consequences and to protect life, property and the environment from the effects of radioactive releases.

2. To facilitate such cooperation States Parties may agree on bilateral or multilateral arrangements or, where appropriate, a combination of these, for preventing or minimizing injury and damage which may result in the event of a nuclear accident or radiological emergency.

3. The States Parties request the Agency, acting within the framework of its Statute, to use its best endeavours in accordance with the provisions of this Convention to promote, facilitate and support the cooperation between States Parties provided for in this Convention.

Article 2

Provision of assistance

1. If a State Party needs assistance in the event of a nuclear accident or radiological emergency, whether or not such accident or emergency originates within its territory, jurisdiction or control, it may call for such assistance from any other State Party, directly or through the Agency, and from the Agency, or, where appropriate, from other international intergovernmental organizations (hereinafter referred to as "international organizations").

2. A State Party requesting assistance shall specify the scope and type of assistance required and, where practicable, provide the assisting party with such information as may be necessary for that party to determine the extent to which it is able to meet the request. In the event that it is not practicable for the requesting State Party to specify the scope and type of assistance required, the requesting State Party and the assisting party shall, in consultation, decide upon the scope and type of assistance required.

3. Each State Party to which a request for such assistance is directed shall promptly decide and notify the requesting State Party, directly or through the Agency, whether it is in a position to render the assistance requested, and the scope and terms of the assistance that might be rendered.

4. States Parties shall, within the limits of their capabilities, identify and notify the Agency of experts, equipment and materials which could be made available for the provision of assistance to other States Parties in the event of a nuclear accident or radiological emergency as well as the terms, especially financial, under which such assistance could be provided.

5. Any State Party may request assistance relating to medical treatment or temporary relocation into the territory of another State Party of people involved in a nuclear accident or radiological emergency.

6. The Agency shall respond, in accordance with its Statute and as provided for in this Convention, to a requesting State Party's or a Member State's request for assistance in the event of a nuclear accident or radiological emergency by:

(a) making available appropriate resources allocated for this purpose;

(b) transmitting promptly the request to other States and international organizations which, according to the Agency's information, may possess the necessary resources; and

(c) if so requested by the requesting State, co-ordinating the assistance at the international level which may thus become available.

Article 3

Direction and control of assistance

Unless otherwise agreed:

(a) the overall direction, control, co-ordination and supervision of the assistance shall be the responsibility within its territory of the requesting State. The assisting party should, where the assistance involves personnel, designate in consultation with the requesting State, the person who should be in charge of and retain immediate operational supervision over the personnel and the equipment provided by it. The designated person should exercise such supervision in cooperation with the appropriate authorities of the requesting State;

(b) the requesting State shall provide, to the extent of its capabilities, local facilities and services for the proper and effective administration of the assistance. It shall also ensure the protection of personnel, equipment and materials brought into its territory by or on behalf of the assisting party for such purpose;

(c) ownership of equipment and materials provided by either party during the periods of assistance shall be unaffected, and their return shall be ensured;

(d) a State Party providing assistance in response to a request under paragraph 5 of article 2 shall co-ordinate that assistance within its territory.

Article 4

Competent authorities and points of contact

1. Each State Party shall make known to the Agency and to other States Parties, directly or through the Agency, its competent authorities and point of contact authorized to make and receive requests for and to accept offers of assistance. Such points of contact and a focal point within the Agency shall be available continuously.

2. Each State Party shall promptly inform the Agency of any changes that may occur in the information referred to in paragraph 1.

3. The Agency shall regularly and expeditiously provide to States Parties, Member States and relevant international organizations the information referred to in paragraphs 1 and 2.

Article 5

Functions of the Agency

The States Parties request the Agency, in accordance with paragraph 3 of article 1 and without prejudice to other provisions of this Convention, to:

(a) collect and disseminate to States Parties and Member States information concerning:

(i) experts, equipment and materials which could be made available in the event of nuclear accidents or radiological emergencies;

(ii) methodologies, techniques and available results of research relating to response to nuclear accidents or radiological emergencies;

(b) assist a State Party or a Member State when requested in any of the following or other appropriate matters:

(i) preparing both emergency plans in the case of nuclear accidents and radiological emergencies and the appropriate legislation;

(ii) developing appropriate training programmes for personnel to deal with nuclear accidents and radiological emergencies;

(iii) transmitting requests for assistance and relevant information in the event of a nuclear accident or radiological emergency;

(iv) developing appropriate radiation monitoring programmes, procedures and standards;

(v) conducting investigations into the feasibility of establishing appropriate radiation monitoring systems;

(c) make available to a State Party or a Member State requesting assistance in the event of a nuclear accident or radiological emergency appropriate resources allocated for the purpose of conducting an initial assessment of the accident or emergency;

(d) offer its good offices to the States Parties and Member States in the event of a nuclear accident or radiological emergency;

(e) establish and maintain liaison with relevant international organizations for the purposes of obtaining and exchanging relevant information and data, and make a list of such organizations available to States Parties, Member States and the aforementioned organizations.

Article 6

Confidentiality and public statements

1. The requesting State and the assisting party shall protect the confidentiality of any confidential information that becomes available to either of them in connection with the assistance in the event of a nuclear accident or radiological emergency. Such information shall be used exclusively for the purpose of the assistance agreed upon.

2. The assisting party shall make every effort to coordinate with the requesting State before releasing information to the public on the assistance provided in connection with a nuclear accident or radiological emergency.

Article 7

Reimbursement of costs

1. An assisting party may offer assistance without costs to the requesting State. When considering whether to offer assistance on such a basis, the assisting party shall take into account:

(a) the nature of the nuclear accident or radiological emergency;

(b) the place of origin of the nuclear accident or radiological emergency;

(c) the needs of developing countries;

(d) the particular needs of countries without nuclear facilities; and

(e) any other relevant factors.

2. When assistance is provided wholly or partly on a reimbursement basis, the requesting State shall reimburse the assisting party for the costs incurred for the services rendered by persons or organizations acting on its behalf, and for all expenses in connection with the assistance to the extent that such expenses are not

directly defrayed by the requesting State. Unless otherwise agreed, reimbursement shall be provided promptly after the assisting party has presented its request for reimbursement to the requesting State, and in respect of costs other than local costs, shall be freely transferrable.

3. Notwithstanding paragraph 2, the assisting party may at any time waive, or agree to the postponement of, the reimbursement in whole or in part. In considering such waiver or postponement, assisting parties shall give due consideration to the needs of developing countries.

Article 8

Privileges, immunities and facilities

1. The requesting State shall afford to personnel of the assisting party and personnel acting on its behalf the necessary privileges, immunities and facilities for the performance of their assistance functions.

2. The requesting State shall afford the following privileges and immunities to personnel of the assisting party or personnel acting on its behalf who have been duly notified to and accepted by the requesting State:

(a) immunity from arrest, detention and legal process, including criminal, civil and adminstrative jurisdiction, of the requesting State, in respect of acts or omissions in the performance of their duties; and

(b) exemption from taxation, duties or other charges, except those which are normally incorporated in the price of goods or paid for services rendered, in respect of the performance of their assistance functions.

3. The requesting State shall:

(a) afford the assisting party exemption from taxation, duties or other charges on the equipment and property brought into the territory of the requesting State by the assisting party for the purpose of the assistance; and

(b) provide immunity from seizure, attachment or requisition of such equipment and property.

4. The requesting State shall ensure the return of such equipment and property. If requested by the assisting party, the requesting State shall arrange, to the extent it is able to do so, for the necessary decontamination of recoverable equipment involved in the assistance before its return.

5. The requesting State shall facilitate the entry into, stay in and departure from its national territory of personnel notified pursuant to paragraph 2 and of equipment and property involved in the assistance.

6. Nothing in this article shall require the requesting State to provide its nationals or permanent residents with the privileges and immunities provided for in the foregoing paragraphs.

7. Without prejudice to the privileges and immunities, all beneficiaries enjoying such privileges and immunities under this article have a duty to respect the laws and regulations of the requesting State. They shall also have the duty not to interfere in the domestic affairs of the requesting State.

8. Nothing in this article shall prejudice rights and obligations with respect to privileges and immunities afforded pursuant to other international agreements or the rules of customary international law.

9. When signing, ratifying, accepting, approving or acceding to this Convention, a State may declare that it does not consider itself bound in whole or in part by paragraphs 2 and 3.

10. A State Party which has made a declaration in accordance with paragraph 9 may at any time withdraw it by notification to the depositary.

Article 9

Transit of personnel, equipment and property

Each State Party shall, at the request of the requesting State or the assisting party, seek to facilitate the transit through its territory of duly notified personnel, equipment and property involved in the assistance to and from the requesting State.

Article 10

Claims and compensation

1. The States Parties shall closely cooperate in order to facilitate the settlement of legal proceedings and claims under this article.

2. Unless otherwise agreed, a requesting State shall in respect of death or of injury to persons, damage to or loss of property, or damage to the environment caused within its territory or other area under its jurisdiction or control in the course of providing the assistance requested:

(a) not bring any legal proceedings against the assisting party or persons or other legal entities acting on its behalf;

(b) assume responsibility for dealing with legal proceedings and claims brought by third parties against the assisting party or against persons or other legal entities acting on its behalf;

(c) hold the assisting party or persons or other legal entities acting on its behalf harmless in respect of legal proceedings and claims referred to in sub-paragraph (b); and

(d) compensate the assisting party or persons or other legal entities acting on its behalf for:

(i) death of or injury to personnel of the assisting party or persons acting on its behalf;

(ii) loss of or damage to non-consumable equipment or materials related to the assistance;

except in cases of wilful misconduct by the individuals who caused the death, injury, loss or damage.

3. This article shall not prevent compensation or indemnity available under any applicable international agreement or national law of any State.

4. Nothing in this article shall require the requesting State to apply paragraph 2 in whole or in part to its nationals or permanent residents.

5. When signing, ratifying, accepting, approving or acceding to this Convention, a State may declare:

(a) that it does not consider itself bound in whole or in part by paragraph 2;

(b) that it will not apply paragraph 2 in whole or in part in cases of gross negligence by the individuals who caused the death, injury, loss or damage.

6. A State Party which has made a declaration in accordance with paragraph 5 may at any time withdraw it by notification to the depositary.

Article 11

Termination of assistance

The requesting State or the assisting party may at any time, after appropriate consultations and by notification in writing, request the termination of assistance received or provided under this Convention. Once such a request has been made, the parties involved shall consult with each other to make arrangements for the proper conclusion of the assistance.

Article 12

Relationship to other international agreements

This Convention shall not affect the reciprocal rights and obligations of States Parties under existing international agreements which relate to the matters covered by this Convention, or under future international agreements concluded in accordance with the object and purpose of this Convention.

Article 13

Settlement of disputes

1. In the event of a dispute between States Parties, or between a State Party and the Agency, concerning the interpretation or application of this Convention, the parties to the dispute shall consult with a view to the settlement of the dispute by negotiation or by any other peaceful means of settling disputes acceptable to them.

2. If a dispute of this character between States Parties cannot be settled within one year from the request for consultation pursuant to paragraph 1, it shall, at the request of any party to such dispute, be submitted to arbitration or referred to the International Court of Justice for decision. Where a dispute is submitted to arbitration, if, within six months from the date of the request, the parties to the dispute are unable to agree on the organization of the arbitration, a party may request the President of the International Court of Justice or the Secretary–General of the United Nations to appoint one or more arbitrators. In cases of conflicting requests by the parties to the dispute, the request to the Secretary–General of the United Nations shall have priority.

3. When signing, ratifying, accepting, approving or acceding to this Convention, a State may declare that it does not consider itself bound by either or both of the dispute settlement procedures provided for in paragraph 2. The other States Parties shall not be bound by a dispute settlement procedure provided for in paragraph 2 with respect to a State Party for which such a declaration is in force.

4. A State Party which has made a declaration in accordance with paragraph 3 may at any time withdraw it by notification to the depositary.

5.31 PROTOCOL ON SUBSTANCES THAT DEPLETE THE OZONE LAYER, WITH ANNEX A. Done at Montreal, Sept. 16, 1987.[a] Entered into force, Jan. 1, 1989; for the United States, Jan. 1, 1989. *Reproduced in* 26 I.L.M. 1550 (1987)

ARTICLE 1: DEFINITIONS

For the purposes of this Protocol:

1. "Convention" means the Vienna Convention for the Protection of the Ozone Layer, adopted on 22 March 1985.

2. "Parties" means, unless the text otherwise indicates, Parties to this Protocol.

3. "Secretariat" means the secretariat of the Convention.

4. "Controlled substance" means a substance listed in Annex A to this Protocol, whether existing alone or in a mixture. It excludes, however, any such substance or mixture which is in a manufactured product other than a container used for the transportation or storage of the substance listed.

5. "Production" means the amount of controlled substances produced minus the amount destroyed by technologies to be approved by the Parties.

6. "Consumption" means production plus imports minus exports of controlled substances.

7. "Calculated levels" of production, imports, exports and consumption means levels determined in accordance with Article 3.

8. "Industrial rationalization" means the transfer of all or a portion of the calculated level of production of one Party to another, for the purpose of achieving economic efficiencies or responding to anticipated shortfalls in supply as a result of plant closures.

ARTICLE 2: CONTROL MEASURES

1. Each Party shall ensure that for the twelve-month period commencing on the first day of the seventh month following the date of the entry into force of this Protocol, and in each twelve-month period thereafter, its calculated level of consumption of the controlled substances in Group I of Annex A does not exceed its calculated level of consumption in 1986. By the end of the same period, each Party producing one or more of these substances shall ensure that its calculated level of production of the substances does not exceed its calculated level of production in 1986, except that such level may have increased by no more than ten per cent based on the 1986 level. Such increase shall be permitted only so as to satisfy the basic domestic needs of the Parties operating under Article 5 and for the purposes of industrial rationalization between Parties.

2. Each Party shall ensure that for the twelve-month period commencing on the first day of the thirty-seventh month following the date of the entry into force of this Protocol, and in each twelve month period thereafter, its calculated level of consumption of the controlled substances listed in Group II of Annex A does not exceed its calculated level of consumption in 1986. Each Party producing one or more of these substances shall ensure that its calculated level of production of the substances does not exceed its calculated level of production in 1986, except that such level may have increased by no more than ten per cent based on the 1986 level. Such increase shall be permitted only so as to satisfy the basic domestic needs of the Parties operating under Article 5 and for the purposes of industrial rationalization between Parties.

a. *See also* Basic Document 5.28, *supra*.

The mechanisms for implementing these measures shall be decided by the Parties at their first meeting following the first scientific review.

3. Each Party shall ensure that for the period 1 July 1993 to 30 June 1994 and in each twelve-month period thereafter, its calculated level of consumption of the controlled substances in Group I of Annex A does not exceed, annually, eighty per cent of its calculated level of consumption in 1986. Each Party producing one or more of these substances shall, for the same periods, ensure that its calculated level of production of the substances does not exceed, annually, eighty per cent of its calculated level of production in 1986. However, in order to satisfy the basic domestic needs of the Parties operating under Article 5 and for the purposes of industrial rationalization between Parties, its calculated level of production may exceed that limit by up to ten per cent of its calculated level of production in 1986.

4. Each Party shall ensure that for the period 1 July 1998 to 30 June 1999, and in each twelve-month period thereafter, its calculated level of consumption of the controlled substances in Group I of Annex A does not exceed, annually, fifty per cent of its calculated level of consumption in 1986. Each Party producing one or more of these substances shall, for the same periods, ensure that its calculated level of production of the substances does not exceed, annually, fifty per cent of its calculated level of production in 1986. However, in order to satisfy the basic domestic needs of the Parties operating under Article 5 and for the purposes of industrial rationalization between Parties, its calculated level of production may exceed that limit by up to fifteen per cent of its calculated level of production in 1986. This paragraph will apply unless the Parties decide otherwise at a meeting by a two-thirds majority of Parties present and voting, representing at least two-thirds of the total calculated level of consumption of these substances of the Parties. This decision shall be considered and made in the light of the assessments referred to in Article 6.

5. Any Party whose calculated level of production in 1986 of the controlled substances in Group I of Annex A was less than twenty-five kilotonnes may, for the purposes of industrial rationalization, transfer to or receive from any other Party, production in excess of the limits set out in paragraphs 1, 3 and 4 provided that the total combined calculated levels of production of the Parties concerned does not exceed the production limits set out in this Article. Any transfer of such production shall be notified to the secretariat, no later than the time of the transfer.

6. Any Party not operating under Article 5, that has facilities for the production of controlled substances under construction, or contracted for, prior to 16 September 1987, and provided for in national legislation prior to 1 January 1987, may add the production from such facilities to its 1986 production of such substances for the purposes of determining its calculated level of production for 1986, provided that such facilities are completed by 31 December 1990 and that such production does not raise that Party's annual calculated level of consumption of the controlled substances above 0.5 kilograms per capita.

7. Any transfer of production pursuant to paragraph 5 or any addition of production pursuant to paragraph 6 shall be notified to the secretariat, no later than the time of the transfer or addition.

8. (a) Any Parties which are Member States of a regional economic integration organization as defined in Article 1(6) of the Convention may agree that they shall jointly fulfil their obligations respecting consumption under this Article provided that their total combined calculated level of consumption does not exceed the levels required by this Article.

(b) The Parties to any such agreement shall inform the secretariat of the terms of the agreement before the date of the reduction in consumption with which the agreement is concerned.

(c) Such agreement will become operative only if all Member States of the regional economic integration organization and the organization concerned are Parties to the Protocol and have notified the secretariat of their manner of implementation.

9. (a) Based on the assessments made pursuant to Article 6, the Parties may decide whether:

(i) adjustments to the ozone depleting potentials specified in Annex A should be made and, if so, what the adjustments should be; and

(ii) further adjustments and reductions of production or consumption of the controlled substances from 1986 levels should be undertaken and, if so, what the scope, amount and timing of any such adjustments and reductions should be.

(b) Proposals for such adjustments shall be communicated to the Parties by the secretariat at least six months before the meeting of the Parties at which they are proposed for adoption.

(c) In taking such decisions, the Parties shall make every effort to reach agreement by consensus. If all efforts at consensus have been exhausted, and no agreement reached, such decisions shall, as a last resort, be adopted by a two-thirds majority vote of the Parties present and voting representing at least fifty per cent of the total consumption of the controlled substances of the Parties.

(d) The decisions, which shall be binding on all Parties, shall forthwith be communicated to the Parties by the Depositary. Unless otherwise provided in the decisions, they shall enter into force on the expiry of six months from the date of the circulation of the communication by the Depositary.

10. (a) Based on the assessments made pursuant to Article 6 of this Protocol and in accordance with the procedure set out in Article 9 of the Convention, the Parties may decide:

(i) whether any substances, and if so which, should be added to or removed from any annex to this Protocol; and

(ii) the mechanism, scope and timing of the control measures that should apply to those substances;

(b) Any such decision shall become effective, provided that it has been accepted by a two-thirds majority vote of the Parties present and voting.

11. Notwithstanding the provisions contained in this Article, Parties may take more stringent measures than those required by this Article.

ARTICLE 3: CALCULATION OF CONTROL LEVELS

For the purposes of Articles 2 and 5, each Party shall, for each Group of substances in Annex A, determine its calculated levels of:

(a) production by:

(i) multiplying its annual production of each controlled substance by the ozone depleting potential specified in respect of it in Annex A; and

(ii) adding together, for each such Group, the resulting figures;

(b) imports and exports, respectively, by following, *mutatis mutandis,* the procedure set out in subparagraph (a); and

(c) consumption by adding together its calculated levels of production and imports and subtracting its calculated level of exports as determined in accordance with subparagraphs (a) and (b). However, beginning on 1 January 1993, any export of controlled substances to non-Parties shall not be subtracted in calculating the consumption level of the exporting Party.

ARTICLE 4: CONTROL OF TRADE WITH NON-PARTIES

1. Within one year of the entry into force of this Protocol, each Party shall ban the import of controlled substances from any State not party to this Protocol.

2. Beginning on 1 January 1993, no Party operating under paragraph 1 of Article 5 may export any controlled substance to any State not party to this Protocol.

3. Within three years of the date of the entry into force of this Protocol, the Parties shall, following the procedures in Article 10 of the Convention, elaborate in an annex a list of products containing controlled substances. Parties that have not objected to the annex in accordance with those procedures shall ban, within one year of the annex having become effective, the import of those products from any State not party to this Protocol.

4. Within five years of the entry into force of this Protocol, the Parties shall determine the feasibility of banning or restricting, from States not party to this Protocol, the import of products produced with, but not containing, controlled substances. If determined feasible, the Parties shall, following the procedures in Article 10 of the Convention, elaborate in an annex a list of such products. Parties that have not objected to it in accordance with those procedures shall ban or restrict, within one year of the annex having become effective, the import of those products from any State not party to this Protocol.

5. Each Party shall discourage the export, to any State not party to this Protocol, of technology for producing and for utilizing controlled substances.

6. Each Party shall refrain from providing new subsidies, aid, credits, guarantees or insurance programmes for the export to States not party to this Protocol of products, equipment, plants or technology that would facilitate the production of controlled substances.

7. Paragraphs 5 and 6 shall not apply to products, equipment, plants or technology that improve the containment, recovery, recycling or destruction of controlled substances, promote the development of alternative substances, or otherwise contribute to the reduction of emissions of controlled substances.

8. Notwithstanding the provisions of this Article, imports referred to in paragraphs 1, 3 and 4 may be permitted from any State not party to this Protocol if that State is determined, by a meeting of the Parties, to be in full compliance with Article 2 and this Article, and has submitted data to that effect as specified in Article 7.

ARTICLE 5: SPECIAL SITUATION OF DEVELOPING COUNTRIES

1. Any Party that is a developing country and whose annual calculated level of consumption of the controlled substances is less than 0.3 kilograms per capita on the date of the entry into force of the Protocol for it, or any time thereafter within ten years of the date of entry into force of the Protocol shall, in order to meet its basic domestic needs, be entitled to delay its compliance with the control measures set out in paragraphs 1 to 4 of Article 2 by ten years after that specified in those paragraphs. However, such Party shall not exceed an annual calculated level of consumption of 0.3 kilograms per capita. Any such Party shall be entitled to use either the average of its annual calculated level of consumption for the period 1995 to 1997 inclusive or a calculated level of consumption of 0.3 kilograms per capita, whichever is the lower, as the basis for its compliance with the control measures.

2. The Parties undertake to facilitate access to environmentally safe alternative substances and technology for Parties that are developing countries and assist them to make expeditious use of such alternatives.

3. The Parties undertake to facilitate bilaterally or multilaterally the provision of subsidies, aid, credits, guarantees or insurance programmes to Parties that are developing countries for the use of alternative technology and for substitute products.

ARTICLE 6: ASSESSMENT AND REVIEW OF CONTROL MEASURES

Beginning in 1990, and at least every four years thereafter, the Parties shall assess the control measures provided for in Article 2 on the basis of available scientific, environmental, technical and economic information. At least one year before each assessment, the Parties shall convene appropriate panels of experts qualified in the fields mentioned and determine the composition and terms of reference of any such panels. Within one year of being convened, the panels will report their conclusions, through the secretariat, to the Parties.

ARTICLE 7: REPORTING OF DATA

1. Each Party shall provide to the secretariat, within three months of becoming a Party, statistical data on its production, imports and exports of each of the controlled substances for the year 1986, or the best possible estimates of such data where actual data are not available.

2. Each Party shall provide statistical data to the secretariat on its annual production (with separate data on amounts destroyed by technologies to be approved by the Parties), imports, and exports to Parties and non-Parties, respectively, of such substances for the year during which it becomes a Party and for each year thereafter. It shall forward the data no later than nine months after the end of the year to which the data relate.

ARTICLE 8: NON–COMPLIANCE

The Parties, at their first meeting, shall consider and approve procedures and institutional mechanisms for determining non-compliance with the provisions of this Protocol and for treatment of Parties found to be in non-compliance.

ARTICLE 9: RESEARCH, DEVELOPMENT, PUBLIC AWARENESS AND EXCHANGE OF INFORMATION

1. The Parties shall co-operate, consistent with their national laws, regulations and practices and taking into account in particular the needs of developing countries, in promoting, directly or through competent international bodies, research, development and exchange of information on:

(a) best technologies for improving the containment, recovery, recycling or destruction of controlled substances or otherwise reducing their emissions;

(b) possible alternatives to controlled substances, to products containing such substances, and to products manufactured with them; and

(c) costs and benefits of relevant control strategies.

2. The Parties, individually, jointly or through competent international bodies, shall co-operate in promoting public awareness of the environmental effects of the emissions of controlled substances and other substances that deplete the ozone layer.

3. Within two years of the entry into force of this Protocol and every two years thereafter, each Party shall submit to the secretariat a summary of the activities it has conducted pursuant to this Article.

ARTICLE 10: TECHNICAL ASSISTANCE

1. The Parties shall, in the context of the provisions of Article 4 of the Convention, and taking into account in particular the needs of developing countries, co-operate in promoting technical assistance to facilitate participation in and implementation of this Protocol.

2. Any Party or Signatory to this Protocol may submit a request to the secretariat for technical assistance for the purposes of implementing or participating in the Protocol.

3. The Parties, at their first meeting, shall begin deliberations on the means of fulfilling the obligations set out in Article 9, and paragraphs 1 and 2 of this Article, including the preparation of workplans. Such workplans shall pay special attention to the needs and circumstances of the developing countries. States and regional economic integration organizations not party to the Protocol should be encouraged to participate in activities specified in such workplans.

* * *

ARTICLE 13: FINANCIAL PROVISIONS

1. The funds required for the operation of this Protocol, including those for the functioning of the secretariat related to this Protocol, shall be charged exclusively against contributions from the Parties.

2. The Parties, at their first meeting, shall adopt by consensus financial rules for the operation of this Protocol.

ARTICLE 14: RELATIONSHIP OF THIS PROTOCOL TO THE CONVENTION

Except as otherwise provided in this Protocol, the provisions of the Convention relating to its protocols shall apply to this Protocol.

* * *

ARTICLE 19: WITHDRAWAL

For the purposes of this Protocol, the provisions of Article 19 of the Convention relating to withdrawal shall apply, except with respect to Parties referred to in paragraph 1 of Article 5. Any such Party may withdraw from this Protocol by giving written notification to the Depositary at any time after four years of assuming the obligations specified in paragraphs 1 to 4 of Article 2. Any such withdrawal shall take effect upon expiry of one year after the date of its receipt by the Depositary, or on such later date as may be specified in the notification of the withdrawal.

* * *

ANNEX A

CONTROLLED SUBSTANCES

Group	Substance	Ozone Depleting Potential*
Group I		
	$CFC1_3$ (CFC-11)	1.0
	CF_2C1_2 (CFC-12)	1.0
	$C_2F_3C1_3$ (CFC-113)	0.8
	$C_2F_4C1_2$ (CFC-114)	1.0
	C_2F_5C1 (CFC-115)	0.6
Group II		
	$CF_{-2}BrC1$ (halon-1211)	3.0
	CF_3Br (halon-1301)	10.0
	$C_2F_4Br_2$ (halon-2402)	(to be determined)

* These ozone depleting potentials are estimates based on existing knowledge and will be reviewed and revised periodically.

5.32 CONVENTION ON THE CONTROL OF TRANSBOUNDARY MOVEMENTS OF HAZARDOUS WASTES AND THEIR DISPOSAL, WITH ANNEXES I–III & VI. Done at Basel, Mar. 22, 1989. Opened for signature, Mar. 22, 1989. *Reproduced in* 28 I.L.M. 649 (1989)

* * *

Article 1

Scope of the Convention

1. The following wastes that are subject to transboundary movement shall be "hazardous wastes" for the purposes of this Convention:

(a) Wastes that belong to any category contained in Annex I, unless they do not possess any of the characteristics contained in Annex III; and

(b) Wastes that are not covered under paragraph (a) but are defined as, or are considered to be, hazardous wastes by the domestic legislation of the Party of export, import or transit.

2. Wastes that belong to any category contained in Annex II that are subject to transboundary movement shall be "other wastes" for the purposes of this Convention.

3. Wastes which, as a result of being radioactive, are subject to other international control systems, including international instruments, applying specifically to radioactive materials, are excluded from the scope of this Convention.

4. Wastes which derived from the normal operations of a ship, the discharge of which is covered by another international instrument, are excluded from the scope of this Convention.

Article 2

Definitions

For the purposes of this Convention:

1. "Wastes" are substances or objects which are disposed of or are intended to be disposed of or are required to be disposed of by the provisions of national law;

2. "Management" means the collection, transport and disposal of hazardous wastes or other wastes, including after-care of disposal sites;

3. "Transboundary movement" means any movement of hazardous wastes or other wastes from an area under the national jurisdiction of one State to or through an area under the national jurisdiction of another State or to or through an area not under the national jurisdiction of any State, provided at least two States are involved in the movement;

4. "Disposal" means any operation specified in Annex IV to this Convention;

5. "Approved site or facility" means a site or facility for the disposal of hazardous wastes or other wastes which is authorized or permitted to operate for this purpose by a relevant authority of the State where the site or facility is located;

6. "Competent authority" means one governmental authority designated by a Party to be responsible, within such geographical areas as the Party may think fit, for receiving the notification of a transboundary movement of hazardous wastes or other wastes, and any information related to it, and for responding to such a notification, as provided in Article 6;

7. "Focal point" means the entity of a Party referred to in Article 5 responsible for receiving and submitting information as provided for in Articles 13 and 16;

8. "Environmentally sound management of hazardous wastes or other wastes" means taking all practicable steps to ensure that hazardous wastes or other wastes are managed in a manner which will protect human health and the environment against the adverse effects which may result from such wastes;

9. "Area under the national jurisdiction of a State" means any land, marine area or airspace within which a State exercises administrative and regulatory responsibility in accordance with international law in regard to the protection of human health or the environment;

10. "State of export" means a Party from which a transboundary movement of hazardous wastes or other wastes is planned to be initiated or is initiated;

11. "State of import" means a Party to which a transboundary movement of hazardous wastes or other wastes is planned or takes place for the purpose of disposal therein or for the purpose of loading prior to disposal in an area not under the national jurisdiction of any State;

12. "State of transit" means any State, other than the State of export or import, through which a movement of hazardous wastes or other wastes is planned or takes place;

13. "States concerned" means Parties which are States of export or import, or transit states, whether or not Parties;

14. "Person" means any natural or legal person;

15. "Exporter" means any person under the jurisdiction of the State of export who arranges for hazardous wastes or other wastes to be exported;

16. "Importer" means any person under the jurisdiction of the State of import who arranges for hazardous wastes or other wastes to be imported;

17. "Carrier" means any person who carries out the transport of hazardous wastes or other wastes;

18. "Generator" means any person whose activity produces hazardous wastes or other wastes or, if that person is not known, the person who is in possession and/or control of those wastes;

19. "Disposer" means any person to whom hazardous wastes or other wastes are shipped and who carries out the disposal of such wastes;

20. "Political and/or economic integration organization" means an organization constituted by sovereign States to which its member States have transferred competence in respect of matters governed by this Convention and which has been duly authorized, in accordance with its internal procedures, to sign, ratify, accept, approve, formally confirm or accede to it;

21. "Illegal traffic" means any transboundary movement of hazardous wastes or other wastes as specified in Article 9.

Article 3

National Definitions of Hazardous Wastes

1. Each Party shall, within six months of becoming a Party to this Convention, inform the Secretariat of the convention of the wastes, other than those listed in Annexes I and II, considered or defined as hazardous under its national legislation and of any requirements concerning transboundary movement procedures applicable to such wastes.

2. Each Party shall subsequently inform the Secretariat of any significant changes to the information it has provided pursuant to paragraph 1.

3. The Secretariat shall forthwith inform all Parties of the information it has received pursuant to paragraphs 1 and 2.

4. Parties shall be responsible for making the information transmitted to them by the Secretariat under paragraph 3 available to their exporters.

Article 4

General Obligations

1.(a) Parties exercising their right to prohibit the import of hazardous wastes or other wastes for disposal shall inform the other Parties of their decision pursuant to Article 13.

(b) Parties shall prohibit or shall not permit the export of hazardous wastes and other wastes to the Parties which have prohibited the import of such wastes, when notified pursuant to subparagraph (a) above.

(c) Parties shall prohibit or shall not permit the export of hazardous wastes and other wastes if the State of import does not consent in writing to the specific import, in the case where that State of import has not prohibited the import of such wastes.

2. Each Party shall take the appropriate measures to:

(a) Ensure that the generation of hazardous wastes and other wastes within it is reduced to a minimum, taking into account social, technological and economic aspects;

(b) Ensure the availability of adequate disposal facilities, for the environmentally sound management of hazardous wastes and other wastes, that shall be located, to the extent possible, within it, whatever the place of their disposal;

(c) Ensure that persons involved in the management of hazardous wastes or other wastes within it take such steps as are necessary to prevent pollution due to hazardous wastes and other wastes arising from such management and, if such pollution occurs, to minimize the consequences thereof for human health and the environment;

(d) Ensure that the transboundary movement of hazardous wastes and other wastes is reduced to the minimum consistent with the environmentally sound and efficient management of such wastes, and is conducted in a manner which will protect human health and the environment against the adverse effects which may result from such movement;

(e) Not allow the export of hazardous wastes or other wastes to a State or group of States belonging to an economic and/or political integration organization that are Parties, particularly developing countries, which have prohibited by their legislation all imports, or if it has reason to believe that the wastes in question will not be managed in an environmentally sound manner, according to criteria to be decided on by the Parties at their first meeting;

(f) Require that information about a proposed transboundary movement of hazardous wastes and other wastes be provided to the States concerned, according to Annex V A, to state clearly the effects of the proposed movement on human health and the environment;

(g) Prevent the import of hazardous wastes and other wastes if it has reason to believe that the wastes in question will not be managed in an environmentally sound manner;

(h) Co-operate in activities with other Parties and interested organizations, directly and through the Secretariat, including the dissemination of information on the transboundary movement of hazardous wastes and other wastes, in order to improve the environmentally sound management of such wastes and to achieve the prevention of illegal traffic.

3. The Parties consider that illegal traffic in hazardous wastes or other wastes is criminal.

4. Each Party shall take appropriate legal, administrative and other measures to implement and enforce the provisions of this Convention, including measures to prevent and punish conduct in contravention of the Convention.

5. A Party shall not permit hazardous wastes or other wastes to be exported to a non-Party or to be imported from a non-Party.

6. The Parties agree not to allow the export of hazardous wastes or other wastes for disposal within the area south of 60° South latitude, whether or not such wastes are subject to transboundary movement.

7. Furthermore, each Party shall:

(a) Prohibit all persons under its national jurisdiction from transporting or disposing of hazardous wastes or other wastes unless such persons are authorized or allowed to perform such types of operations;

(b) Require that hazardous wastes and other wastes that are to be the subject of a transboundary movement be packaged, labeled, and transported in conformity with generally accepted and recognized international rules and standards in the field of packaging, labelling, and transport, and that due account is taken of relevant internationally recognized practices;

(c) Require that hazardous wastes and other wastes be accompanied by a movement document from the point at which a transboundary movement commences to the point of disposal.

8. Each Party shall require that hazardous wastes or other wastes, to be exported, are managed in an environmentally sound manner in the State of import or elsewhere. Technical guidelines for the environmentally sound management of wastes subject to this Convention shall be decided by the Parties at their first meeting.

9. Parties shall take the appropriate measures to ensure that the transboundary movement of hazardous wastes and other wastes only be allowed if:

(a) The State of export does not have the technical capacity and the necessary facilities, capacity or suitable disposal sites in order to dispose of the wastes in question in an environmentally sound and efficient manner; or

(b) The wastes in question are required as a raw material for recycling or recovery industries in the State of import; or

(c) The transboundary movement in question is in accordance with other critera to be decided by the Parties, provided those criteria do not differ from the objectives of this Convention.

10. The obligation under this Convention of States in which hazardous wastes and other wastes are generated to require that those wastes are managed in an environmentally sound manner may not under any circumstances be transferred to the State of import or transit.

11. Nothing in this Convention shall prevent a Party from imposing additional requirements that are consistent with the provisions of this Convention, and are in accordance with the rules of international law, in order better to protect human health and the environment.

12. Nothing in this Convention shall affect in any way the sovereignty of States over their territorial sea established in accordance with international law, and the sovereign rights and the jurisdiction which States have in their exclusive economic

zones and their continental shelves in accordance with international law, and the exercise by ships and aircraft of all States of navigational rights and freedoms as provided for in international law and as reflected in relevant international instruments.

13. Parties shall undertake to review periodically the possibilities for the reduction of the amount and/or the pollution potential of hazardous wastes and other wastes which are exported to other States, in particular to developing countries.

Article 5

Designation of Competent Authorities and Focal Point

To facilitate the implementation of this Convention, the Parties shall:

1. Designate or establish one or more competent authorities and one focal point. One competent authority shall be designated to receive the notification in case of a State of transit.

2. Inform the Secretariat, within three months of the date of the entry into force of this Convention for them, which agencies they have designated as their focal point and their competent authorities.

3. Inform the Secretariat, within one month of the date of decision, of any changes regarding the designation made by them under paragraph 2 above.

Article 6

Transboundary Movement between Parties

1. The State of export shall notify, or shall require the generator or exporter to notify, in writing, through the channel of the competent authority of the State of export, the competent authority of the States concerned of any proposed transboundary movement of hazardous wastes or other wastes. Such notification shall contain the declarations and information specified in Annex V A, written in a language acceptable to the State of import. Only one notification needs to be sent to each State concerned.

2. The State of import shall respond to the notifier in writing, consenting to the movement with or without conditions, denying permission for the movement, or requesting additional information. A copy of the final response of the State of import shall be sent to the competent authorities of the States concerned which are Parties.

3. The State of export shall not allow the generator or exporter to commence the transboundary movement until it has received written confirmation that:

(a) The notifier has received the written consent of the State of import; and

(b) The notifier has received from the State of import confirmation of the existence of a contract between the exporter and the disposer specifying environmentally sound management of the wastes in question.

4. Each State of transit which is a Party shall promptly acknowledge to the notifier receipt of the notification. It may subsequently respond to the notifier in writing, within 60 days, consenting to the movement with or without conditions, denying permission for the movement, or requesting additional information. The State of export shall not allow the transboundary movement to commence until it has received the written consent of the State of transit. However, if at any time a Party decides not to require prior written consent, either generally or under specific conditions, for transit transboundary movements of hazardous wastes or other wastes, or modifies its requirements in this respect, it shall forthwith inform the other Parties of its decision pursuant to Article 13. In this latter case, if no response is received by the State of export within 60 days of the receipt of a given notification

by the State of transit, the State of export may allow the export to proceed through the State of transit.

5. In the case of a transboundary movement of wastes where the wastes are legally defined as or considered to be hazardous wastes only:

(a) By the State of export, the requirements of paragraph 9 of this Article that apply to the importer or disposer and the State of import shall apply *mutatis mutandis* to the exporter and State of export, respectively;

(b) By the State of import, or by the States of import and transit which are Parties, the requirements of paragraphs 1, 3, 4 and 6 of this Article that apply to the exporter and State of export shall apply *mutatis mutandis* to the importer or disposer and State of import, respectively; or

(c) By any State of transit which is a Party, the provisions of paragraph 4 shall apply to such State.

6. The State of export may, subject to the written consent of the States concerned, allow the generator or the exporter to use a general notification where hazardous wastes or other wastes having the same physical and chemical characteristics are shipped regularly to the same disposer via the same customs office of exit of the State of export via the same customs office of entry of the State of import, and, in the case of transit, via the same customs office of entry and exit of the State or States of transit.

7. The States concerned may make their written consent to the use of the general notification referred to in paragraph 6 subject to the supply of certain information, such as the exact quantities or periodical lists of hazardous wastes or other wastes to be shipped.

8. The general notification and written consent referred to in paragraphs 6 and 7 may cover multiple shipments of hazardous wastes or other wastes during a maximum period of 12 months.

9. The Parties shall require that each person who takes charge of a transboundary movement of hazardous wastes or other wastes sign the movement document either upon delivery or receipt of the wastes in question. They shall also require that the disposer inform both the exporter and the competent authority of the State of export of receipt by the disposer of the wastes in question and, in due course, of the completion of disposal as specified in the notification. If no such information is received within the State of export, the competent authority of the State of export or the exporter shall so notify the State of import.

10. The notification and response required by this Article shall be transmitted to the competent authority of the Parties concerned or to such governmental authority as may be appropriate in the case of non-Parties.

11. Any transboundary movement of hazardous wastes or other wastes shall be covered by insurance, bond or other guarantee as may be required by the State of import or any State of transit which is a Party.

Article 7

Transboundary Movement from a Party through States which are not Parties

Paragraph 2 of Article 6 of the Convention shall apply *mutatis mutandis* to transboundary movement of hazardous wastes or other wastes from a Party through a State or States which are not Parties.

Article 8

Duty to Re-import

When a transboundary movement of hazardous wastes or other wastes to which the consent of the States concerned has been given, subject to the provisions of this Convention, cannot be completed in accordance with the terms of the contract, the State of export shall ensure that the wastes in question are taken back into the State of export, by the exporter, if alternative arrangements cannot be made for their disposal in an environmentally sound manner, within 90 days from the time that the importing State informed the State of export and the Secretariat, or such other period of time as the States concerned agree. To this end, the State of export and any Party of transit shall not oppose, hinder or prevent the return of those wastes to the State of export.

Article 9

Illegal Traffic

1. For the purpose of this Convention, any transboundary movement of hazardous wastes or other wastes:

(a) without notification pursuant to the provisions of this Convention to all States concerned; or

(b) without the consent pursuant to the provisions of this Convention of a State concerned; or

(c) with consent obtained from States concerned through falsification, misrepresentation or fraud; or

(d) that does not conform in a material way with the documents; or

(e) that results in deliberate disposal (e.g. dumping) of hazardous wastes or other wastes in contravention of this Convention and of general principles of international law, shall be deemed to be illegal traffic.

2. In case of a transboundary movement of hazardous wastes or other wastes deemed to be illegal traffic as the result of conduct on the part of the exporter or generator, the State of export shall ensure that the wastes in question are:

(a) taken back by the exporter or the generator or, if necessary, by itself into the State of export, or, if impracticable,

(b) are otherwise disposed of in accordance with the provisions of this Convention,

within 30 days from the time the State of export has been informed about the illegal traffic or such other period of time as States concerned may agree. To this end the Parties concerned shall not oppose, hinder or prevent the return of those wastes to the State of export.

3. In the case of a transboundary movement of hazardous wastes or other wastes deemed to be illegal traffic as the result of conduct on the part of the importer or disposer, the State of import shall ensure that the wastes in question are disposed of in an environmentally sound manner by the importer or disposer or, if necessary, by itself within 30 days from the time the illegal traffic has come to the attention of the State of import or such other period of time as the States concerned may agree. To this end, the Parties concerned shall co-operate, as necessary, in the disposal of the wastes in an environmentally sound manner.

4. In cases where the responsibility for the illegal traffic cannot be assigned either to the exporter or generator or to the importer or disposer, the Parties concerned or other Parties, as appropriate, shall ensure, through co-operation, that the wastes in question are disposed of as soon as possible in an environmentally

sound manner either in the State of export or the State of import or elsewhere as appropriate.

5. Each Party shall introduce appropriate national/domestic legislation to prevent and punish illegal traffic. The Parties shall co-operate with a view to achieving the objects of this Article.

Article 10

International Co-operation

1. The Parties shall co-operate with each other in order to improve and achieve environmentally sound management of hazardous wastes and other wastes.

2. To this end, the Parties shall:

(a) Upon request, make available information, whether on a bilateral or multilateral basis, with a view to promoting the environmentally sound management of hazardous wastes and other wastes, including harmonization of technical standards and practices for the adequate management of hazardous wastes and other wastes;

(b) Co-operate in monitoring the effects of the management of hazardous wastes on human health and the environment;

(c) Co-operate, subject to their national laws, regulations and policies, in the development and implementation of new environmentally sound low-waste technologies and the improvement of existing technologies with a view to eliminating, as far as practicable, the generation of hazardous wastes and other wastes and achieving more effective and efficient methods of ensuring their management in an environmentally sound manner, including the study of the economic, social and environmental effects of the adoption of such new or improved technologies;

(d) Co-operate actively, subject to their national laws, regulations and policies, in the transfer of technology and management systems related to the environmentally sound management of hazardous wastes and other wastes. They shall also co-operate in developing the technical capacity among Parties, especially those which may need and request technical assistance in this field;

(e) Co-operate in developing appropriate technical guidelines and/or codes of practice.

3. The Parties shall employ appropriate means to co-operate in order to assist developing countries in the implementation of subparagraphs a, b, c and d of paragraph 2 of Article 4.

4. Taking into account the needs of developing countries, co-operation between Parties and the competent international organizations is encouraged to promote, *inter alia,* public awareness, the development of sound management of hazardous wastes and other wastes and the adoption of new low-waste technologies.

Article 11

Bilateral, Multilateral and Regional Agreements

1. Notwithstanding the provisions of Article 4 paragraph 5, Parties may enter into bilateral, multilateral, or regional agreements or arrangements regarding transboundary movement of hazardous wastes or other wastes with Parties or non-Parties provided that such agreements or arrangements do not derogate from the environmentally sound management of hazardous wastes and other wastes as required by this Convention. These agreements or arrangements shall stipulate provisions which are not less environmentally sound than those provided for by this Convention in particular taking into account the interests of developing countries.

2. Parties shall notify the Secretariat of any bilateral, multilateral or regional agreements or arrangements referred to in paragraph 1 and those which they have entered into prior to the entry into force of this Convention for them, for the purpose of controlling transboundary movements of hazardous wastes and other wastes which take place entirely among the Parties to such agreements. The provisions of this Convention shall not affect transboundary movements which take place pursuant to such agreements provided that such agreements are compatible with the environmentally sound management of hazardous wastes and other wastes as required by this Convention.

Article 12

Consultations on Liability

The Parties shall co-operate with a view to adopting, as soon as practicable, a protocol setting out appropriate rules and procedures in the field of liability and compensation for damage resulting from the transboundary movement and disposal of hazardous wastes and other wastes.

Article 13

Transmission of Information

1. The Parties shall, whenever it comes to their knowledge, ensure that, in the case of an accident occurring during the transboundary movement of hazardous wastes or other wastes or their disposal, which are likely to present risks to human health and the environment in other States, those states are immediately informed.

2. The Parties shall inform each other, through the Secretariat, of:

(a) Changes regarding the designation of competent authorities and/or focal points, pursuant to Article 5;

(b) Changes in their national definition of hazardous wastes, pursuant to Article 3; and, as soon as possible,

(c) Decisions made by them not to consent totally or partially to the import of hazardous wastes or other wastes for disposal within the area under their national jurisdiction;

(d) Decisions taken by them to limit or ban the export of hazardous wastes or other wastes;

(e) Any other information required pursuant to paragraph 4 of this Article.

3. The Parties, consistent with national laws and regulations, shall transmit, through the Secretariat, to the Conference of the Parties established under Article 15, before the end of each calendar year, a report on the previous calendar year, containing the following information:

(a) Competent authorities and focal points that have been designated by them pursuant to Article 5;

(b) Information regarding transboundary movements of hazardous wastes or other wastes in which they have been involved, including:

(i) The amount of hazardous wastes and other wastes exported, their category, characteristics, destination, any transit country and disposal method as stated on the response to notification;

(ii) The amount of hazardous wastes and other wastes imported, their category, characteristics, origin, and disposal methods;

(iii) Disposals which did not proceed as intended;

(iv) Efforts to achieve a reduction of the amount of hazardous wastes or other wastes subject to transboundary movement;

(c) Information on the measures adopted by them in implementation of this Convention;

(d) Information on available qualified statistics which have been compiled by them on the effects on human health and the environment of the generation, transportation and disposal of hazardous wastes or other wastes;

(e) Information concerning bilateral, multilateral and regional agreements and arrangements entered into pursuant to Article 11 of this Convention;

(f) Information on accidents occurring during the transboundary movement and disposal of hazardous wastes and other wastes and on the measures undertaken to deal with them;

(g) Information on disposal options operated within the area of their national jurisdiction;

(h) Information on measures undertaken for development of technologies for the reduction and/or elimination of production of hazardous wastes and other wastes; and

(i) Such other matters as the Conference of the Parties shall deem relevant.

4. The Parties, consistent with national laws and regulations, shall ensure that copies of each notification concerning any given transboundary movement of hazardous wastes or other wastes, and the response to it, are sent to the Secretariat when a Party considers that its environment may be affected by that transboundary movement has requested that this should be done.

Article 14

Financial Aspects

1. The Parties agree that, according to the specific needs of different regions and subregions, regional or sub-regional centres for training and technology transfers regarding the management of hazardous wastes and other wastes and the minimization of their generation should be established. The Parties shall decide on the establishment of appropriate funding mechanisms of a voluntary nature.

2. The Parties shall consider the establishment of a revolving fund to assist on an interim basis in case of emergency situations to minimize damage from accidents arising from transboundary movements of hazardous wastes and other wastes or during the disposal of those wastes.

Article 15

Conference of the Parties

1. A Conference of the Parties is hereby established. The first meeting of the Conference of the Parties shall be convened by the Executive Director of UNEP not later than one year after the entry into force of this Convention. Thereafter, ordinary meetings of the Conference of the Parties shall be held at regular intervals to be determined by the Conference at its first meeting.

2. Extraordinary meetings of the Conference of the Parties shall be held at such other times as may be deemed necessary by the Conference, or at the written request of any Party, provided that, within six months of the request being communicated to them by the Secretariat, it is supported by at least one third of the Parties.

3. The Conference of Parties shall by consensus agree upon and adopt rules of procedure for itself and for any subsidiary body it may establish, as well as financial rules to determine in particular the financial participation of the Parties under this Convention.

4. The Parties at their first meeting shall consider any additional measures needed to assist them in fulfilling their responsibilities with respect to the protection and the preservation of the marine environment in the context of this Convention.

5. The Conference of the Parties shall keep under continuous review and evaluation the effective implementation of this Convention, and, in addition, shall:

(a) Promote the harmonization of appropriate policies, strategies and measures for minimizing harm to human health and the environment by hazardous wastes and other wastes;

(b) Consider and adopt, as required, amendments to this Convention and its annexes, taking into consideration, *inter alia,* available scientific, technical, economic and environmental information;

(c) Consider and undertake any additional action that may be required for the achievement of the purposes of this Convention in the light of experience gained in its operation and in the operation of the agreements and arrangements envisaged in Article 11;

(d) Consider and adopt protocols as required; and

(e) Establish such subsidiary bodies as are deemed necessary for the implementation of this Convention.

6. The United Nations, its specialized agencies, as well as any State not party to this Convention, may be represented as observers at meetings of the Conference of the Parties. Any other body or agency, whether national or international, governmental or non-governmental, qualified in fields relating to hazardous wastes or other wastes which has informed the Secretariat of its wish to be represented as an observer at a meeting of the Conference of the Parties, may be admitted unless at least one third of the Parties present object. The admission and participation of observers shall be subject to the rules of procedure adopted by the conference of the Parties.

7. The Conference of the Parties shall undertake three years after the entry into force of this Convention, and at least every six years thereafter, an evaluation of its effectiveness and, if deemed necessary, to consider the adoption of a complete or partial ban of transboundary movements of hazardous wastes and other wastes in light of the latest scientific, environmental, technical and economic information.

Article 16

Secretariat

1. The functions of the Secretariat shall be:

(a) To arrange for and service meetings provided for in Articles 15 and 17;

(b) To prepare and transmit reports based upon information received in accordance with Articles 3, 4, 6, 11 and 13 as well as upon information derived from meetings of subsidiary bodies established under Article 15 as well as upon, as appropriate, information provided by relevant intergovernmental and non-governmental entities;

(c) To prepare reports on its activities carried out in implementation of its functions under this Convention and present them to the Conference of the Parties;

(d) To ensure the necessary coordination with relevant international bodies, and in particular to enter into such administrative and contractual arrangements as may be required for the effective discharge of its functions;

(e) To communicate with focal points and competent authorities established by the Parties in accordance with Article 5 of this Convention;

(f) To compile information concerning authorized national sites and facilities of Parties available for the disposal of their hazardous wastes and other wastes and to circulate this information among Parties;

(g) To receive and convey information from and to Parties on:

— sources of technical assistance and training;

— available technical and scientific know-how;

— sources of advice and expertise; and

— availability of resources

with a view to assisting them, upon request, in such areas as:

— the handling of the notification system of this Convention;

— the management of hazardous wastes and other wastes;

— environmentally sound technologies relating to hazardous wastes and other wastes, such as low- and non-waste technology;

— the assessment of disposal capabilities and sites;

— the monitoring of hazardous wastes and other wastes; and

— emergency responses;

(h) To provide Parties, upon request, with information on consultants or consulting firms having the necessary technical competence in the field, which can assist them to examine a notification for a transboundary movement, the concurrence of a shipment of hazardous wastes or other wastes with the relevant notification, and/or the fact that the proposed disposal facilities for hazardous wastes or other wastes are environmentally sound, when they have reason to believe that the wastes in question will not be managed in an environmentally sound manner. Any such examination would not be at the expense of the Secretariat;

(i) To assist Parties upon request in their identification of cases of illegal traffic and to circulate immediately to the Parties concerned any information it has received regarding illegal traffic;

(j) To co-operate with Parties and with relevant and competent international organizations and agencies in the provision of experts and equipment for the purpose of rapid assistance to States in the event of an emergency situation; and

(k) To perform such other functions relevant to the purposes of this Convention as may be determined by the Conference of the Parties.

2. The Secretariat functions will be carried out on an interim basis by UNEP until the completion of the first meeting of the Conference of the Parties held pursuant to Article 15.

3. At its first meeting, the Conference of the Parties shall designate the Secretariat from among those existing competent intergovernmental organizations which have signified their willingness to carry out the Secretariat functions under this Convention. At this meeting, the Conference of the Parties shall also evaluate the implementation by the interim Secretariat of the functions assigned to it, in particular under paragraph 1 above, and decide upon the structures appropriate for those functions.

Article 17

Amendment of the Convention

1. Any Party may propose amendments to this Convention and any Party to a protocol may propose amendments to that protocol. Such amendments shall take due account, *inter alia,* of relevant scientific and technical considerations.

2. Amendments to this Convention shall be adopted at a meeting of the Conference of the Parties. Amendments to any protocol shall be adopted at a meeting of the Parties to the protocol in question. The text of any proposed amendment to this Convention or to any protocol, except as may otherwise be provided in such protocol, shall be communicated to the Parties by the Secretariat at least six months before the meeting at which it is proposed for adoption. The Secretariat shall also communicate proposed amendments to the Signatories to this Convention for information.

3. The Parties shall make every effort to reach agreement on any proposed amendment to this Convention by consensus. If all efforts at consensus have been exhausted, and no agreement reached, the amendments shall as a last resort be adopted by a three-fourths majority vote of the Parties present and voting at the meeting, and shall be submitted by the Depositary to all Parties for ratification, approval, formal confirmation or acceptance.

4. The procedure mentioned in paragraph 3 above shall apply to amendments to any protocol, except that a two-thirds majority of the Parties to that protocol present and voting at the meeting shall suffice for their adoption.

5. Instruments of ratification, approval, formal confirmation or acceptance of amendments shall be deposited with the Depositary. Amendments adopted in accordance with paragraphs 3 or 4 above shall enter into force between Parties having accepted them on the ninetieth day after the receipt by the Depositary of their instrument of ratification, approval, formal confirmation or acceptance by at least three-fourths of the Parties who accepted the amendments to the protocol concerned, except as may otherwise be provided in such protocol. The amendments shall enter into force for any other Party on the ninetieth day after that Party deposits its instrument of ratification, approval, formal confirmation or acceptance of the amendments.

6. For the purpose of this Article, "Parties present and voting" means Parties present and casting an affirmative or negative vote.

Article 18

Adoption and Amendment of Annexes

1. The annexes to this Convention or to any protocol shall form an integral part of this Convention or of such protocol, as the case may be and, unless expressly provided otherwise, a reference to this Convention or its protocols constitutes at the same time a reference to any annexes thereto. Such annexes shall be restricted to scientific, technical and administrative matters.

2. Except as may be otherwise provided in any protocol with respect to its annexes, the following procedure shall apply to the proposal, adoption and entry into force of additional annexes to this Convention or of annexes to a protocol:

(a) Annexes to this Convention and its protocols shall be proposed and adopted according to the procedure laid down in Article 17, paragraphs 2, 3 and 4;

(b) Any Party that is unable to accept an additional annex to this Convention or an annex to any protocol to which it is party shall so notify the Depositary, in writing, within six months from the date of the communication of the adoption by the Depositary. The Depositary shall without delay notify all Parties of any such notification received. A Party may at any time substitute an acceptance for a previous declaration of objection and the annexes shall thereupon enter into force for that Party;

(c) On the expiry of six months from the date of the circulation of the communication by the Depositary, the annex shall become effective for all

Parties to this Convention or to any protocol concerned, which have not submitted a notification in accordance with the provision of subparagraph (b) above.

3. The proposal, adoption and entry into force of amendments to annexes to this Convention or to any protocol shall be subject to the same procedure as for the proposal, adoption and entry into force of annexes to the Convention or annexes to a protocol. Annexes and amendments thereto shall take due account, *inter alia,* of relevant scientific and technical considerations.

4. If an additional annex or an amendment to an annex involves an amendment to this Convention or to any protocol, the additional annex or amended annex shall not enter into force until such time as the amendment to this Convention or to the protocol enters into force.

Article 19

Verification

Any Party which has reason to believe that another Party is acting or has acted in breach of its obligations under this Convention may inform the Secretariat thereof, and in such an event, shall simultaneously and immediately inform, directly or through the Secretariat, the Party against whom the allegations are made. All relevant information should be submitted by the Secretariat to the Parties.

Article 20

Settlement of Disputes

1. In case of a dispute between Parties as to the interpretation or application of, or compliance with, this Convention or any protocol thereto, they shall seek a settlement of the dispute through negotiation or any other peaceful means of their own choice.

2. If the Parties concerned cannot settle their dispute through the means mentioned in the preceding paragraph, the dispute, if the parties to the dispute agree, shall be submitted to the International Court of Justice or to arbitration under the conditions set out in Annex VI on Arbitration. However, failure to reach common agreement on submission of the dispute to the International Court of Justice or to arbitration shall not absolve the Parties from the responsibility of continuing to seek to resolve it by the means referred to in paragraph 1.

3. When ratifying, accepting, approving, formally confirming or acceding to this Convention, or at any time thereafter, a State or political and/or economic integration organization may declare that it recognizes as compulsory *ipso facto* and without special agreement, in relation to any Party accepting the same obligation:

(a) submission of the dispute to the International Court of Justice; and/or

(b) arbitration in accordance with the procedures set out in Annex VI.

Such declaration shall be notified in writing to the Secretariat which shall communicate it to the Parties.

* * *

Article 24

Right to Vote

1. Except as provided for in paragraph 2 below, each Contracting Party to this Convention shall have one vote.

2. Political and/or economic integration organizations, in matters within their competence, in accordance with Article 22, paragraph 3, and Article 23, paragraph 2, shall exercise their right to vote with a number of votes equal to the number of their member States which are Parties to the Convention or the relevant protocol. Such

organizations shall not exercise their right to vote if their member States exercise theirs, and vice versa.

Article 25

Entry into Force

1. This Convention shall enter into force on the ninetieth day after the date of deposit of the twentieth instrument of ratification, acceptance, formal confirmation, approval or accession.

2. For each State or political and/or economic integration organization which ratifies, accepts, approves or formally confirms this Convention or accedes thereto after the date of the deposit of the twentieth instrument of ratification, acceptance, approval, formal confirmation or accession, it shall enter into force on the ninetieth day after the date of deposit by such State or political and/or economic integration organization of its instrument of ratification, acceptance, approval, formal confirmation or accession.

3. For the purposes of paragraphs 1 and 2 above, any instrument deposited by a political and/or economic integration organization shall not be counted as additional to those deposited by member States of such organization.

Article 26

Reservations and Declarations

1. No reservation or exception may be made to this Convention.

2. Paragraph 1 of this Article does not preclude a State or political and/or economic integration organizations, when signing, ratifying, accepting, approving, formally confirming or acceding to this Convention, from making declarations or statements, however phrased or named, with a view, *inter alia,* to the harmonization of its laws and regulations with the provisions of this Convention, provided that such declarations or statements do not purport to exclude or to modify the legal effects of the provisions of the Convention in their application to that State.

Article 27

Withdrawal

1. At any time after three years from the date on which this Convention has entered into force for a Party, that Party may withdraw from the Convention by giving written notification to the Depositary.

2. Withdrawal shall be effective one year from receipt of notification by the Depositary, or on such later date as may be specified in the notification.

* * *

Annex I

CATEGORIES OF WASTES TO BE CONTROLLED

Waste Streams

Y1 Clinical wastes from medical care in hospitals, medical centers and clinics

Y2 Wastes from the production and preparation of pharmaceutical products

Y3 Waste pharmaceuticals, drugs and medicines

Y4 Wastes from the production, formulation and use of biocides and phytopharmaceuticals

Y5 Wastes from the manufacture, formulation and use of wood preserving chemicals

Y6 Wastes from the production, formulation and use of organic solvents

Y7 Wastes from heat treatment and tempering operations containing cyanides

Y8 Waste mineral oils unfit for their originally intended use

Y9 Waste oils/water, hydrocarbons/water mixtures, emulsions

Y10 Waste substances and articles containing or contaminated with polychlorinated biphenyls (PCBs) and/or polychlorinated terphenyls (PCTs) and/or polybrominated biphenyls (PBBs)

Y11 Waste tarry residues arising from refining, distillation and any pyrolytic treatment

Y12 Wastes from production, formulation and use of inks, dyes, pigments, paints, lacquers, varnish

Y13 Wastes from production, formulation and use of resins, latex, plasticizers, glues/adhesives

Y14 Waste chemical substances arising from research and development or teaching activities which are not identified and/or are new and whose effects on man and/or the environment are not known

Y15 Wastes of an explosive nature not subject to other legislation

Y16 Wastes from production, formulation and use of photographic chemicals and processing materials

Y17 Wastes resulting from surface treatment of metals and plastics

Y18 Residues arising from industrial waste disposal operations

Wastes having as constituents:

Y19 Metal carbonyls

Y20 Veryllium; beryllium compounds

Y21 Hexavalent chromium compounds

Y22 Copper compounds

Y23 Zinc compounds

Y24 Arsenic; arsenic compounds

Y25 Selenium; selenium compounds

Y26 Cadmium; cadmium compounds

Y27 Antimony; antimony compounds

Y28 Telurrium; telurrium compounds

Y29 Mercury; mercury compounds

Y30 Thallium; thallium compounds

Y31 Lead; lead compounds

Y32 Inorganic fluorine compounds excluding calcium fluoride

Y33 Inorganic cyanides

Y34 Acidic solutions or acids in solid form

Y35 Basic solutions or bases in solid form

Y36 Asbestos (dust and fibres)

Y37 Organic phosphorous compounds

Y38 Organic cyanides

Y39 Phenols; phenol compounds including chlorophenols

Y40 Ethers

Y41 Halogenated organic solvents

Y42 Organic solvents excluding halogenated solvents

Y43 Any congenor of polychlorinated dibenzo-furan

Y44 Any congenor of polychlorinated dibenzo-p-dioxin

Y45 Organohalogen compounds other than substances referred to in this Annex (e.g. Y39, Y41, Y42, Y43, Y44).

Annex II

CATEGORIES OF WASTES REQUIRING SPECIAL CONSIDERATION

Y46 Wastes collected from households

Y47 Resides arising from the incineration of household wastes

Annex III

LIST OF HAZARDOUS CHARACTERISTICS

UN Class *	*Code*	*Characteristics*
1	H1	Explosive An explosive substance or waste is a solid or liquid substance or waste (or mixture of substances or wastes) which is in itself capable by chemical reaction of producing gas at such a temperature and pressure and at such a speed as to cause damage to the surroundings.
3	H3	Flammable liquids The word "flammable" has the same meaning as "inflammable". Flammable liquids are liquids, or mixtures of liquids, or liquids containing solids in solution or suspension (for example, paints, varnishes, lacquers, etc., but not including substances or wastes otherwise classified on account of their dangerous characteristics) which give off a flammable vapour at temperatures of not more than 60.5°C, closed-cup test, or not more than 65.6°C, open-cup test. (Since the results of open-cup tests and of closed-cup tests are not strictly comparable and even individual results by the same test are often variable, regulations varying from the above figures to make allowance for such differences would be within the spirit of this definition.)
4.1	H4.1	Flammable solids Solids, or waste solids, other than those classed as explosives, which under conditions encountered in transport are readily combustible, or may cause or contribute to fire through friction.
4.2	H4.2	Substances or wastes liable to spontaneous combustion Substances or wastes which are liable to spontaneous heating under normal conditions encountered in transport, or to heating up on contact with air, and being then liable to catch fire.
4.3	H4.3	Substances or wastes which, in contact with water emit flammable gases Substances or wastes which, by interaction with water, are liable to become spontaneously flammable or to give off flammable gases in dangerous quantities.
5.1	H5.1	Oxidizing Substances or wastes which, while in themselves not necessarily combustible, may, generally by yielding oxygen cause, or contribute to, the combustion of other materials.
5.2	H5.2	Organic Peroxides Organic substances or wastes which contain the bivalent-o-o-structure are thermally unstable substances which may undergo exothermic self-accelerating decomposition.
6.1	H6.1	Poisonous (Acute)

UN Class *	*Code*	*Characteristics*
		Substances or wastes liable either to cause death or serious injury or to harm human health if swallowed or inhaled or by skin contact.
6.2	H6.2	Infectious substances Substances or wastes containing viable microorganisms or their toxins which are known or suspected to cause disease in animals or humans.
8	H8	Corrosives Substances or wastes which, by chemical action, will cause severe damage when in contact with living tissue, or, in the case of leakage, will materially damage, or even destroy, other goods or the means of transport; they may also cause other hazards.
9	H10	Liberation of toxic gases in contact with air or water Substances or wastes which, by interaction with air or water, are liable to give off toxic gases in dangerous quantities.
9	H11	Toxic (Delayed or chronic) Substances or wastes which, if they are inhaled or ingested or if they penetrate the skin, may involve delayed or chronic effects, including carcinogenicity.
9	H12	Ecotoxic Substances or wastes which if released present or may present immediate or delayed adverse impacts to the environment by means of bioaccumulation and/or toxic effects upon biotic systems.
9	H13	Capable, by any means, after disposal, of yielding another material, e.g., leachate, which possesses any of the characteristics listed above.

*Corresponds to the hazard classification system included in the United Nations Recommendations on the Transport of Dangerous Goods (ST/SG/AC.10/1/Rev. 5, United Nations, New York, 1988).

Tests

The potential hazards posed by certain types of wastes are not yet fully documented; tests to define quantitatively these hazards do not exist. Further research is necessary in order to develop means to characterize potential hazards posed to man and/or the environment by these wastes. Standardized tests have been derived with respect to pure substances and materials. Many countries have developed national tests which can be applied to materials listed in Annex I, in order to decide if these materials exhibit any of the characteristics listed in this Annex.

* * *

Annex VI
ARBITRATION

Article 1

Unless the agreement referred to in Article 20 of the Convention provides otherwise, the arbitration procedure shall be conducted in accordance with Articles 2 to 10 below.

Article 2

The claimant party shall notify the Secretariat that the parties have agreed to submit the dispute to arbitration pursuant to paragraph 2 or paragraph 3 of Article 20 and include, in particular, the Articles of the Convention the interpretation or application of which are at issue. The Secretariat shall forward the information thus received to all Parties to the Convention.

Article 3

The arbitral tribunal shall consist of three members. Each of the Parties to the dispute shall appoint an arbitrator, and the two arbitrators so appointed shall designate by common agreement the third arbitrator, who shall be the chairman of the tribunal. The latter shall not be a national of one of the parties to the dispute, nor have his usual place of residence in the territory of one of these parties, nor be employed by any of them, nor have dealt with the case in any other capacity.

Article 4

1. If the chairman of the arbitral tribunal has not been designated within two months of the appointment of the second arbitrator, the Secretary-General of the United Nations shall, at the request of either party, designate him within a further two months' period.

2. If one of the parties to the dispute does not appoint an arbitrator within two months of the receipt of the request, the other party may inform the Secretary-General of the United Nations who shall designate the chairman of the arbitral tribunal within a further two months' period. Upon designation, the chairman of the arbitral tribunal shall request the party which has not appointed an arbitrator to do so within two months. After such period, he shall inform the Secretary-General of the United Nations, who shall make this appointment within a further two months' period.

Article 5

1. The arbitral tribunal shall render its decision in accordance with international law and in accordance with the provisions of this Convention.

2. Any arbitral tribunal constituted under the provisions of this Annex shall draw up its own rules of procedure.

Article 6

1. The decisions of the arbitral tribunal both on procedure and on substance, shall be taken by majority vote of its members.

2. The tribunal may take all appropriate measures in order to establish the facts. It may, at the request of one of the parties, recommend essential interim measures of protection.

3. The parties to the dispute shall provide all facilities necessary for the effective conduct of the proceedings.

4. The absence or default of a party in the dispute shall not constitute an impediment to the proceedings.

Article 7

The tribunal may hear and determine counter-claims arising directly out of the subject-matter of the dispute.

Article 8

Unless the arbitral tribunal determines otherwise because of the particular circumstances of the case, the expenses of the tribunal, including the remuneration of its members, shall be borne by the parties to the dispute in equal shares. The tribunal shall keep a record of all its expenses, and shall furnish a final statement thereof to the parties.

Article 9

Any Party that has an interest of a legal nature in the subject-matter of the dispute which may be affected by the decision in the case, may intervene in the proceedings with the consent of the tribunal.

Article 10

1. The tribunal shall render its award within five months of the date on which it is established unless it finds it necessary to extend the time-limit for a period which should not exceed five months.

2. The award of the arbitral tribunal shall be accompanied by a statement of reasons. It shall be final and binding upon the parties to the dispute.

3. Any dispute which may arise between the parties concerning the interpretation or execution of the award may be submitted by either party to the arbitral tribunal which made the award or, if the latter cannot be seized thereof, to another tribunal constituted for this purpose in the same manner as the first.

6. MISCELLANEOUS

6.1 EUROPEAN CONVENTION ON EXTRADITION. Done at Paris, Dec. 13, 1957. Entered into force, Apr. 18, 1960. Europ. T.S. 24, 359 U.N.T.S. 274

The Governments signatory hereto, being Members of the Council of Europe,

Considering that the aim of the Council of Europe is to achieve a greater unity between its Members;

Considering that this purpose can be attained by the conclusion of agreements and by common action in legal matters;

Considering that the acceptance of uniform rules with regard to extradition is likely to assist this work of unification,

Have agreed as follows:

Article 1

OBLIGATION TO EXTRADITE

The Contracting Parties undertake to surrender to each other, subject to the provisions and conditions laid down in this Convention, all persons against whom the competent authorities of the requesting Party are proceeding for an offence or who are wanted by the said authorities for the carrying out of a sentence or detention order.

Article 2

EXTRADITABLE OFFENCES

1. Extradition shall be granted in respect of offences punishable under the laws of the requesting Party and of the requested Party by deprivation of liberty or under a detention order for a maximum period of at least one year or by a more severe penalty. Where a conviction and prison sentence have occurred or a detention order has been made in the territory of the requesting Party, the punishment awarded must have been for a period of at least four months.

2. If the request for extradition includes several separate offences each of which is punishable under the laws of the requesting Party and the requested Party by deprivation of liberty or under a detention order, but of which some do not fulfil the condition with regard to the amount of punishment which may be awarded, the requested Party shall also have the right to grant extradition for the latter offences.

3. Any Contracting Party whose law does not allow extradition for certain of the offences referred to in paragraph 1 of this Article may, in so far as it is concerned, exclude such offences from the application of this Convention.

4. Any Contracting Party which wishes to avail itself of the right provided for in paragraph 3 of this Article shall, at the time of the deposit of its instrument of ratification or accession, transmit to the Secretary–General of the Council of Europe either a list of the offences for which extradition is allowed or a list of those for which it is excluded and shall at the same time indicate the legal provisions which allow or exclude extradition. The Secretary–General of the Council shall forward these lists to the other signatories.

5. If extradition is subsequently excluded in respect of other offences by the law of a Contracting Party, that Party shall notify the Secretary–General. The Secretary–General shall inform the other signatories. Such notification shall not take effect until three months from the date of its receipt by the Secretary–General.

6. Any Party which avails itself of the right provided for in paragraphs 4 or 5 of this Article may at any time apply this Convention to offences which have been excluded from it. It shall inform the Secretary–General of the Council of such changes, and the Secretary–General shall inform the other signatories.

7. Any Party may apply reciprocity in respect of any offences excluded from the application of the Convention under this Article.

Article 3

POLITICAL OFFENCES

1. Extradition shall not be granted if the offence in respect of which it is requested is regarded by the requested Party as a political offence or as an offence connected with a political offence.

2. The same rule shall apply if the requested Party has substantial grounds for believing that a request for extradition for an ordinary criminal offence has been made for the purpose of prosecuting or punishing a person on account of his race, religion, nationality or political opinion, or that that person's position may be prejudiced for any of these reasons.

3. The taking or attempted taking of the life of a Head of State or a member of his family shall not be deemed to be a political offence for the purposes of this Convention.

4. This Article shall not affect any obligations which the Contracting Parties may have undertaken or may undertake under any other international convention of a multilateral character.

Article 4

MILITARY OFFENCES

Extradition for offences under military law which are not offences under ordinary criminal law is excluded from the application of this Convention.

Article 5

FISCAL OFFENCES

Extradition shall be granted, in accordance with the provisions of this Convention, for offences in connection with taxes, duties, customs and exchange only if the Contracting Parties have so decided in respect of any such offence or category of offences.

Article 6

EXTRADITION OF NATIONALS

1. (*a*) A Contracting Party shall have the right to refuse extradition of its nationals.

(*b*) Each Contracting Party may, by a declaration made at the time of signature or of deposit of its instrument of ratification or accession, define as far as it is concerned the term "nationals" within the meaning of this Convention.

(*c*) Nationality shall be determined as at the time of the decision concerning extradition. If, however, the person claimed is first recognized as a national of the requested Party during the period between the time of the decision and the time contemplated for the surrender, the requested Party may avail itself of the provision contained in sub-paragraph (*a*) of this Article.

2. If the requested Party does not extradite its national, it shall at the request of the requesting Party submit the case to its competent authorities in order that proceedings may be taken if they are considered appropriate. For this purpose, the files, information and exhibits relating to the offence shall be transmitted without charge by the means provided for in Article 12, paragraph 1. The requesting Party shall be informed of the result of its request.

Article 7

PLACE OF COMMISSION

1. The requested Party may refuse to extradite a person claimed for an offence which is regarded by its law as having been committed in whole or in part in its territory or in a place treated as its territory.

2. When the offence for which extradition is requested has been committed outside the territory of the requesting Party, extradition may only be refused if the law of the requested Party does not allow prosecution for the same category of offence when committed outside the latter Party's territory or does not allow extradition for the offence concerned.

Article 8

PENDING PROCEEDINGS FOR THE SAME OFFENCES

The requested Party may refuse to extradite the person claimed if the competent authorities of such Party are proceeding against him in respect of the offence or offences for which extradition is requested.

Article 9

"NON BIS IN IDEM"

Extradition shall not be granted if final judgment has been passed by the competent authorities of the requested Party upon the person claimed in respect of the offence or offences for which extradition is requested. Extradition may be refused if the competent authorities of the requested Party have decided either not to institute or to terminate proceedings in respect of the same offence or offences.

Article 10

LAPSE OF TIME

Extradition shall not be granted when the person claimed has, according to the law of either the requesting or the requested Party, become immune by reason of lapse of time from prosecution or punishment.

Article 11

CAPITAL PUNISHMENT

If the offence for which extradition is requested is punishable by death under the law of the requesting Party, and if in respect of such offence the death-penalty is not provided for by the law of the requested Party or is not normally carried out, extradition may be refused unless the requesting Party gives such assurance as the requested Party considers sufficient that the death-penalty will not be carried out.

Article 12

THE REQUEST AND SUPPORTING DOCUMENTS

1. The request shall be in writing and shall be communicated through the diplomatic channel. Other means of communication may be arranged by direct agreement between two or more Parties.

2. The request shall be supported by:

(*a*) the original or an authenticated copy of the conviction and sentence or detention order immediately enforceable or of the warrant of arrest or other order having the same effect and issued in accordance with the procedure laid down in the law of the requesting Party;

(*b*) a statement of the offences for which extradition is requested. The time and place of their commission, their legal descriptions and a reference to the relevant legal provisions shall be set out as accurately as possible; and

(*c*) a copy of the relevant enactments or, where this is not possible, a statement of the relevant law and as accurate a description as possible of the person claimed, together with any other information which will help to establish his identity and nationality.

Article 13

SUPPLEMENTARY INFORMATION

If the information communicated by the requesting Party is found to be insufficient to allow the requested Party to make a decision in pursuance of this Convention, the latter Party shall request the necessary supplementary information and may fix a time-limit for the receipt thereof.

Article 14

RULE OF SPECIALITY

1. A person who has been extradited shall not be proceeded against, sentenced or detained with a view to the carrying out of a sentence or detention order for any offence committed prior to his surrender other than that for which he was extradited, nor shall he be for any other reason restricted in his personal freedom, except in the following cases:

(*a*) when the Party which surrendered him consents. A request for consent shall be submitted, accompanied by the documents mentioned in Article 12 and a legal record of any statement made by the extradited person in respect of the offence concerned. Consent shall be given when the offence for which it is requested is itself subject to extradition in accordance with the provisions of this Convention;

(*b*) when that person, having had an opportunity to leave the territory of the Party to which he has been surrendered, has not done so within 45 days of his final discharge, or has returned to that territory after leaving it.

2. The requesting Party may, however, take any measures necessary to remove the person from its territory, or any measures necessary under its law, including proceedings by default, to prevent any legal effects of lapse of time.

3. When the description of the offence charged is altered in the course of proceedings, the extradited person shall only be proceeded against or sentenced in so far as the offence under its new description is shown by its constituent elements to be an offence which would allow extradition.

Article 15

RE-EXTRADITION TO A THIRD STATE

Except as provided for in Article 14, paragraph 1(*b*), the requesting Party shall not, without the consent of the requested Party, surrender to another Party or to a third State a person surrendered to the requesting Party and sought by the said other Party or third State in respect of offences committed before his surrender. The requested Party may request the production of the documents mentioned in Article 12, paragraph 2.

Article 16

PROVISIONAL ARREST

1. In case of urgency the competent authorities of the requesting Party may request the provisional arrest of the person sought. The competent authorities of the requested Party shall decide the matter in accordance with its law.

2. The request for provisional arrest shall state that one of the documents mentioned in Article 12, paragraph 2(*a*), exists and that it is intended to send a request for extradition. It shall also state for what offence extradition will be requested and when and where such offence was committed and shall so far as possible give a description of the person sought.

3. A request for provisional arrest shall be sent to the competent authorities of the requested Party either through the diplomatic channel or direct by post or telegraph or through the International Criminal Police Organisation (Interpol) or by any other means affording evidence in writing or accepted by the requested Party. The requesting authority shall be informed without delay of the result of its request.

4. Provisional arrest may be terminated if, within a period of 18 days after arrest, the requested Party has not received the request for extradition and the documents mentioned in Article 12. It shall not, in any event, exceed 40 days from the date of such arrest. The possibility of provisional release at any time is not excluded, but the requested Party shall take any measures which it considers necessary to prevent the escape of the person sought.

5. Release shall not prejudice re-arrest and extradition if a request for extradition is received subsequently.

Article 17

CONFLICTING REQUESTS

If extradition is requested concurrently by more than one State, either for the same offence or for different offences, the requested Party shall make its decision having regard to all the circumstances and especially the relative seriousness and place of commission of the offences, the respective dates of the requests, the nationality of the person claimed and the possibility of subsequent extradition to another State.

Article 18

SURRENDER OF THE PERSON TO BE EXTRADITED

1. The requested Party shall inform the requesting Party by the means mentioned in Article 12, paragraph 1 of its decision with regard to the extradition.

2. Reasons shall be given for any complete or partial rejection.

3. If the request is agreed to, the requesting Party shall be informed of the place and date of surrender and of the length of time for which the person claimed was detained with a view to surrender.

4. Subject to the provisions of paragraph 5 of this Article, if the person claimed has not been taken over on the appointed date, he may be released after the expiry of 15 days and shall in any case be released after the expiry of 30 days. The requested Party may refuse to extradite him for the same offence.

5. If circumstances beyond its control prevent a Party from surrendering or taking over the person to be extradited, it shall notify the other Party. The two Parties shall agree on a new date for surrender and the provisions of paragraph 4 of this Article shall apply.

Article 19

POSTPONED OR CONDITIONAL SURRENDER

1. The requested Party may, after making its decision on the request for extradition, postpone the surrender of the person claimed in order that he may be proceeded against by that Party or, if he has already been convicted, in order that he may serve his sentence in the territory of that Party for an offence other than that for which extradition is requested.

2. The requested Party may, instead of postponing surrender, temporarily surrender the person claimed to the requesting Party in accordance with conditions to be determined by mutual agreement between the Parties.

Article 20

HANDING OVER OF PROPERTY

1. The requested Party shall, in so far as its law permits and at the request of the requesting Party, seize and hand over property:

(*a*) which may be required as evidence or

(*b*) which has been acquired as a result of the offence and which, at the time of the arrest, is found in the possession of the person claimed or is discovered subsequently.

2. The property mentioned in paragraph 1 of this Article shall be handed even if extradition, having been agreed to, cannot be carried out owing to the death or escape of the person claimed.

3. When the said property is liable to seizure or confiscation in the territory of the requested Party, the latter may, in connection with pending criminal proceedings, temporarily retain it or hand it over on condition that it is returned.

4. Any rights which the requested Party or third parties may have acquired in the said property shall be preserved. Where these rights exist, the property shall be returned without charge to the requested Party as soon as possible after the trial.

Article 21

TRANSIT

1. Transit through the territory of one of the Contracting Parties shall be granted on submission of a request by the means mentioned in Article 12, paragraph 1, provided that the offence concerned is not considered by the Party requested to grant transit as an offence of a political or purely military character having regard to Articles 3 and 4 of this Convention.

2. Transit of a national, within the meaning of Article 6, of a country requested to grant transit may be refused.

3. Subject to the provisions of paragraph 4 of this Article, it shall be necessary to produce the documents mentioned in Article 12, paragraph 2.

4. If air transport is used, the following provisions shall apply:

(*a*) when it is not intended to land, the requesting Party shall notify the Party over whose territory the flight is to be made and shall certify that one of the documents mentioned in Article 12, paragraph 2(*a*) exists. In the case of an unscheduled landing, such notification shall have the effect of a request for provisional arrest as provided for in Article 16, and the requesting Party shall submit a formal request for transit;

(*b*) when it is intended to land, the requesting Party shall submit a formal request for transit.

5. A Party may, however, at the time of signature or of the deposit of its instrument of ratification of, or accession to, this Convention, declare that it will only grant transit of a person on some or all of the conditions on which it grants extradition. In that event, reciprocity may be applied.

6. The transit of the extradited person shall not be carried out through any territory where there is reason to believe that his life or his freedom may be threatened by reason of his race, religion, nationality or political opinion.

Article 22

PROCEDURE

Except where this Convention otherwise provides, the procedure with regard to extradition and provisional arrest shall be governed solely by the law of the requested Party.

Article 23

LANGUAGE TO BE USED

The documents to be produced shall be in the language of the requesting or requested Party. The requested Party may require a translation into one of the official languages of the Council of Europe to be chosen by it.

Article 24

EXPENSES

1. Expenses incurred in the territory of the requested Party by reason of extradition shall be borne by that Party.

2. Expenses incurred by reason of transit through the territory of a Party requested to grant transit shall be borne by the requesting Party.

3. In the event of extradition from a non-metropolitan territory of the requested Party, the expenses occasioned by travel between that territory and the metropolitan territory of the requesting Party shall be borne by the latter. The same rule shall apply to expenses occasioned by travel between the non-metropolitan territory of the requested Party and its metropolitan territory.

Article 25

DEFINITION OF "DETENTION ORDER"

For the purposes of this Convention, the expression "detention order" means any order involving deprivation of liberty which has been made by a criminal court in addition to or instead of a prison sentence.

Article 26

Reservations

1. Any Contracting Party may, when signing this Convention or when depositing its instrument of ratification or accession, make a reservation in respect of any provision or provisions of the Convention.

2. Any Contracting Party which has made a reservation shall withdraw it as soon as circumstances permit. Such withdrawal shall be made by notification to the Secretary–General of the Council of Europe.

3. A Contracting Party which has made a reservation in respect of a provision of the Convention may not claim application of the said provision by another Party save in so far as it has itself accepted the provision.

Article 27

Territorial application

1. This Convention shall apply to the metropolitan territories of the Contracting Parties.

2. In respect of France, it shall also apply to Algeria and to the overseas Departments and, in respect of the United Kingdom of Great Britain and Northern Ireland, to the Channel Islands and to the Isle of Man.

3. The Federal Republic of Germany may extend the application of this Convention to the *Land* of Berlin by notice addressed to the Secretary–General of the Council of Europe, who shall notify the other Parties of such declaration.

4. By direct arrangement between two or more Contracting Parties, the application of this Convention may be extended, subject to the conditions laid down in the arrangement, to any territory of such Parties, other than the territories mentioned in paragraphs 1, 2 and 3 of this Article, for whose international relations any such Party is responsible.

Article 28

Relations between this Convention and bilateral agreements

1. This Convention shall, in respect of those countries to which it applies, supersede the provisions of any bilateral treaties, conventions or agreements governing extradition between any two Contracting Parties.

2. The Contracting Parties may conclude between themselves bilateral or multilateral agreements only in order to supplement the provisions of this Convention or to facilitate the application of the principles contained therein.

3. Where, as between two or more Contracting Parties, extradition takes place on the basis of a uniform law, the Parties shall be free to regulate their mutual relations in respect of extradition exclusively in accordance with such a system notwithstanding the provisions of this Convention. The same principle shall apply as between two or more Contracting Parties each of which has in force a law providing for the execution in its territory of warrants of arrest issued in the territory of the other Party or Parties. Contracting Parties which exclude or may in the future exclude the application of this Convention as between themselves in accordance with this paragraph shall notify the Secretary–General of the Council of Europe accordingly. The Secretary–General shall inform the other Contracting Parties of any notification received in accordance with this paragraph.

* * *

Article 31

DENUNCIATION

Any Contracting Party may denounce this Convention in so far as it is concerned by giving notice to the Secretary–General of the Council of Europe. Denunciation shall take effect six months after the date when the Secretary–General of the Council received such notification.

* * *

6.2 TREATY OF FRIENDSHIP, ESTABLISHMENT AND NAVIGATION BETWEEN THE UNITED STATES OF AMERICA AND THE KINGDOM OF BELGIUM, WITH PROTOCOL. Done at Brussels, Feb. 21, 1961. Entered into force, Oct. 3, 1963. 14 U.S.T. 1284, T.I. A.S. No. 5432, 480 U.N.T.S. 149

The President of the United States of America, and

His Majesty the King of the Belgians,

Desirous of strengthening the bonds of peace and friendship traditionally existing between their two countries and of encouraging closer economic and cultural relations between the two peoples,

Being cognizant of the contributions which may be made toward these ends by arrangements specifying mutually accorded rights and privileges and promoting mutually advantageous commercial intercourse and investments,

Have resolved to conclude a Treaty of Friendship, Establishment and Navigation, and for that purpose have appointed as their Plenipotentiaries,

The President of the United States of America:

His Excellency Mr. William A.M. Burden, Ambassador Extraordinary and Plenipotentiary of the United States of America in Brussels;

His Majesty the King of the Belgians;

His Excellency Mr. Pierre Wigny, Minister for Foreign Affairs;

Who, having communicated to each other their full powers found to be in good and due form, have agreed as follows:

Article 1. Each Contracting Party shall at all times accord equitable treatment and effective protection to the persons, property, enterprises, rights and interests of nationals and companies of the other Party.

Article 2. (1) Nationals of either Contracting Party shall, subject to the laws relating to the entry, sojourn and establishment of aliens, be permitted to enter the territories of the other Party, to travel therein freely, to reside and establish themselves at places of their choice. Nationals of either Party shall in particular be permitted to enter the territories of the other Party and reside therein:

(a) for the purposes of carrying on trade between the two countries and engaging in related commercial activities; or

(b) for the purpose of developing and directing the operations of an enterprise in which they have invested, or are actively in the process of investing, a substantial amount of capital.

(2) Nationals of either Party and nationals of third countries en route to or from the territories of such Party shall, subject to the reservation in paragraph 1 of the present Article, be accorded freedom of transit for themselves and their baggage through the territories of the other Party by the routes most convenient for international transit. In particular, they shall be free from requirements that entail unnecessary delays and impediments. They shall be subject, however, to regulations with respect to their baggage that are applicable to aliens generally in order to prevent abuse of the transit privilege.

(3) Nationals of either Party, within the territories of the other Party, shall enjoy freedom of conscience; and they shall be at liberty to hold religious services, both public and private, at suitable places of their choice.

(4) Nationals of either Party shall be permitted, within the territories of the other Party, to gather information material for dissemination to the public abroad, and shall enjoy freedom of transmission of such material to be used for publication by the press, radio, television, motion pictures and other means; and they shall be permitted to communicate freely with other persons inside and outside such territories by mail, telegraph and other means open to general public use.

(5) The provisions of the present Article shall be subject to the right of either Party to apply measures that are necessary to maintain public order and protect the public health, morals and safety.

Article 3. (1) Nationals of either Contracting Party within the territories of the other Party shall be accorded full legal and judicial protection for their persons, rights and interests. Such nationals shall be free from molestation and shall receive constant protection in no case less than that required by international law.

(2) To this end they shall in particular have right of access, on the same basis and on the same conditions as nationals of such other Party, to the courts of justice and administrative tribunals and agencies in all degrees of jurisdiction and shall have right to the services of competent persons of their choice.

(3) The provisions of paragraphs 1 and 2 of the present Article shall extend and apply in the same manner to companies. It is understood, moreover, that the right of such access shall be enjoyed without any requirement of registration or domestication:

(a) in the case of Belgian companies not engaged in activities in the territories of the United States of America; and

(b) in the case of United States companies not established in the territories of the Kingdom of Belgium.

(4) If a national of either Party is taken into custody within the territories of the other Party, the nearest consular representative of his country shall on the demand of such national be immediately notified and shall have the right to visit and communicate with such national without arbitrary delay. Such national shall:

(a) receive reasonable and humane treatment in no case less than that required by international law;

(b) be formally and immediately informed of the charges against him; and

(c) be brought to trial as rapidly as is consistent with the proper preparation of his defense, for which he shall enjoy all reasonable means, including the services of competent counsel.

(5) The dwellings, offices, warehouses, factories and other premises of nationals and companies of either Party located within the territories of the other Party shall not be subject to searches or measures other than those permitted by law and in execution of law. Official searches and examinations of such premises and their contents, when necessary, shall be made according to law and with careful regard for the convenience of the occupants and the conduct of business.

(6) Contracts entered into between nationals and companies of either Party and nationals and companies of the other Party, that provide for the settlement by arbitration of controversies, shall not be deemed unenforceable within the territories of such other Party merely on the grounds that the place designated for the arbitration proceedings is outside such territories or that the nationality of one or more of the arbitrators is not that of such other Party. No award duly rendered pursuant to any such contract, and final and enforceable under the laws of the place where rendered, shall be deemed invalid and denied effective means of enforcement by the authorities of either Party merely on the grounds that the place where such

award was rendered is outside the territories of such Party or that the nationality of one or more of the arbitrators is not that of such Party.

Article 4. (1) Property that nationals and companies of either Contracting Party own within the territories of the other Party shall enjoy constant security therein through full legal and judicial protection.

(2) Neither Party shall take unreasonable or discriminatory measures that would impair the acquired rights and interests within its territories of nationals and companies of the other Party in the enterprises which they have established, in their capital, or in the skills, arts or technology which they have supplied.

(3) Nationals and companies of either Party shall not be expropriated of their property within the territories of the other Party except for public benefit and with the prompt payment of just compensation. Such compensation shall be in an effectively realizable form and shall represent the full equivalent of the property taken. Furthermore, adequate provision shall have been made no later than the time of taking for the determination and payment thereof.

(4) Nationals and companies of either Party shall in no case be accorded, within the territories of the other Party, less than national treatment with respect to the matters set forth in paragraph 3 of the present Article and in paragraph 5 of Article 3. Moreover, enterprises in which nationals and companies of either Party have a substantial interest shall be accorded, within the territories of the other Party, not less than national treatment in all matters relating to the taking of privately owned enterprises into public ownership and to the placing of such enterprises under public control.

Article 5. (1) Nationals and companies of either Contracting party shall be accorded, within the territories of the other Party, national treatment with respect to obtaining and maintaining patents of invention, and with respect to rights in trade marks, trade names, trade labels and industrial property of all kinds.

(2) The Parties deem that it is highly desirable to further, through co-operative and other appropriate means, the interchange and use of scientific and technical knowledge, particularly in the interest of increasing productivity and improving standards of living within their respective territories.

Article 6. (1) Nationals of either Contracting Party shall be permitted, within the territories of the other Party, to organize companies for gain upon the same conditions as nationals of such other Party. Nationals and companies of either Party shall be permitted to maintain subsidiaries, branches, agencies and offices within the territories of the other Party upon conditions no less favorable than those accorded nationals of such other Party.

(2) Nationals and companies of either Party shall be accorded national treatment with respect to engaging in all types of commercial, industrial, financial and other activities for gain within the territories of the other Party. The provisions of the preceding sentence shall apply in the case of nationals to activities in an independent or dependent capacity.

(3) Companies constituted under the applicable laws and regulations within the territories of either Party shall be deemed companies thereof and shall have their juridical status recognized within the territories of the other Party, provided that nothing in their charter or corporate purposes is contrary to the public policy of such other Party.

(4) In the case of enterprises situated within the territories of either Party and controlled by nationals and companies of the other Party, such enterprises, whether in the form of individual proprietorships, companies or otherwise, shall in all that relates to the conduct of the activities thereof be accorded treatment no less favorable

than that accorded like enterprises controlled by nationals or companies of the country.

(5) Each Party reserves the right to determine the extent to which aliens may establish, acquire interests in, or carry on enterprises engaged within its territories in communications, air or water transport, banking involving fiduciary or depository functions, or the exploitation of land or other natural resources. However, new limitations imposed by either Party on the extent to which aliens are accorded national treatment, with respect to carrying on such activities within its territories, shall not be applied as against enterprises which are regularly engaged in such activities therein at the time such new limitations are adopted and which are owned or controlled by nationals and companies of the other Party. Moreover, neither Party shall deny to transportation, communications and banking enterprises of the other Party the right to maintain branches and agencies to perform functions necessary for essentially international operations in which they are permitted to engage.

(6) The provisions of the present Article shall not prevent either Party from prescribing special formalities in connection with the establishment of companies or enterprises within its territories which are managed or controlled by aliens; but such formalities may not impair the substance of the rights set forth in paragraphs 1, 2 and 4 of the present Article.

(7) Nationals and companies of either Party shall be accorded national treatment with respect to engaging in scientific, educational, religious and philanthropic activities within the territories of the other Party. They shall be accorded the right to form associations, including non-profit associations, under the laws of such other Party for the purpose of engaging in the aforesaid activities. Nothing in the present Treaty shall be deemed to grant or to imply any right to engage in political activities.

Article 7. (1) The Contracting Parties recognize that it is desirable for conditions of competitive equality to be maintained in situations in which publicly owned or controlled trading or manufacturing enterprises are in competition within the territories of either Party with privately owned and controlled enterprises of nationals or companies of the other Party.

(2) Accordingly, such state-owned enterprises should not be given special economic privileges which could injure the competitive position of such private enterprises. However, this principle shall not be construed to prevent either Party from making such special concessions in aid of state-owned enterprises as it deems necessary during periods of economic crisis, especially to relieve unemployment. This principle, moreover, is without prejudice to special advantages given in connection with:

(a) manufacturing goods for government use, or supplying goods and services to the Government for government use; or

(b) supplying, at prices substantially below competitive prices, the needs of particular population groups for essential goods and services not otherwise practically obtainable by such groups.

Article 8. (1) Nationals and companies of either Contracting Party shall be permitted to engage, within the territories of the other Party, the services of accountants and technical experts of all kinds, executive personnel, attorneys, agents and other specialists of their choice.

(2) Nationals and companies of either Party shall be permitted to engage the services of accountants and other technical experts regardless of the extent to which they may have qualified for the practice of a profession within the territories of the other Party, for the sole purpose of making examinations, audits and technical investigations and rendering reports in the private interest of such nationals and

companies in connection with the planning and operation of their enterprises, and enterprises in which they have a financial interest, within such territories.

Article 9. (1) Nationals of either Contracting Party residing within the territories of the other Party, and nationals and companies of either Party engaged in trade or other gainful pursuit or in scientific, educational, religious or philanthropic activities within the territories of the other Party, shall not be subject to the payment of taxes, fees or charges imposed upon or applied to income, capital, transactions, activities or any other object, or to requirements with respect to the levy and collection thereof, within the territories of such other Party, more burdensome than those borne by nationals and companies of such other Party in like situation.

(2) With respect to nationals of either Party who are neither resident nor engaged in trade or other gainful pursuit within the territories of the other Party, and with respect to companies of either Party which are not engaged in trade or other gainful pursuit within the territories of the other Party, it shall be the aim of such other Party to apply in general the principle set forth in paragraph 1 of the present Article.

(3) Nationals and companies of either Party covered by par. 2 of the present Article, shall not be subject, within the territories of the other Party, to the payment of taxes, fees or charges imposed upon or applied to income, capital, transactions, activities or any other object, or to requirements with respect to the levy and collection thereof, more burdensome than those borne by nationals and companies of any third country.

(4) In the case of companies of either Party engaged in trade or other gainful pursuit within the territories of the other Party, and in case of nationals of either Party engaged in trade or other gainful pursuit within the territories of the other Party but not resident therein, such other Party shall not impose or apply any tax, fee or charge upon any income, capital or other basis in excess of that reasonably allocable or apportionable to its territories, nor grant deductions and exemptions less than those reasonably allocable or apportionable to its territories. A comparable rule shall apply also in the case of companies organized and operated exclusively for scientific, educational, religious or philanthropic purposes.

(5) The provisions of the present Article shall not obligate either Party to extend to nationals and companies of the other Party tax advantages accorded to nationals and companies of any third country on the basis of reciprocity of by virtue of agreements for the avoidance of double taxation. Furthermore, each Party reserves the right to apply special provisions in extending advantages to its nationals and residents in connection with joint tax returns by husband and wife and in allowing to residents of contiguous countries exemptions of a personal nature in connection with income and inheritance taxes.

Article 10. (1) Nationals and companies of either Contracting Party shall be accorded by the other Party the same treatment as nationals and companies of such other Party with respect to payments, remittances and transfers of funds or financial instruments between the territories of the two Parties as well as between the territories of such other Party and of any third country. This treatment shall be not less favorable than that accorded to nationals and companies of any third country in like situations.

(2) Neither Party shall impose exchange restrictions as defined in paragraph 5 of the present Article except to the extent necessary to maintain or restore adequacy to its monetary reserves, particularly in relation to its external commercial and financial requirements. It is understood that the provisions of the present Article do not alter the obligations either Party may have to the International Monetary Fund or

preclude imposition by either Party of particular restrictions whenever the Fund specifically so authorizes or requests.

(3) If either Party imposes exchange restrictions in accordance with paragraph 2 of the present Article, it shall not fail, after making whatever provisions may be necessary to assure the availability of foreign exchange for essential goods and services, to make provision to the fullest extent practicable in light of the level of the monetary reserves and its balance-of-payments, for the withdrawal in the currency of the other Party, of: (a) the compensation referred to in Article 4, paragraph 3, (b) earnings, whether in the form of salaries, interest, dividends, commissions, royalties, payments for technical services, or otherwise, (c) amounts for amortization of loans, depreciation of direct investments, and, to the extent feasible, capital transfers, giving consideration to special needs for other transactions. If more than one rate of exchange is in force, the rate applicable to such withdrawal shall be a rate which is specifically approved by the International Monetary Fund for such transactions or, in the absence of a rate so approved an effective rate which, inclusive of any taxes or surcharges on exchange transfers, is just and reasonable.

(4) Exchange restrictions shall not be imposed by either Party in a manner unnecessarily detrimental or arbitrarily discriminatory to the claims, investments, transport, trade and other interests of the nationals and companies of the other Party, nor to the competitive position thereof.

(5) The term "exchange restrictions" as used in the present Article includes all restrictions, regulations, charges, taxes, or other requirements imposed by either Party which burden or interfere with payments, remittances, or transfers of funds or financial instruments between the territories of the two Parties.

(6) Questions arising under the present Treaty concerning exchange restrictions affecting aliens are governed by the provisions of the present Article.

Article 11. Commercial travelers representing nationals and companies of either Contracting Party engaged in business within the territories thereof shall be accorded within the territories of the other Party treatment no less favorable than that accorded to commercial travelers representing nationals and companies of such other Party with respect to the exercise of their functions.

Article 12. (1) Between the territories of the two Contracting Parties there shall be, in accordance with the provisions of the present Treaty, freedom of navigation.

(2) Vessels under the flag of either Party, and carrying the papers required by its laws in proof of nationality, shall be deemed to be vessels of that Party, both on the high seas and within the ports, places and waters of the other Party.

(3) The term "vessels" as used in the present Treaty, means all types of vessels, whether privately owned or operated, or publicly owned or operated, but this term does not include vessels of war.

Article 13. (1) Vessels of either Contracting Party shall have liberty, on equal terms with vessels of the other Party and on equal terms with vessels of any third country, to come with their cargoes to all ports, places and waters of such other Party open to foreign commerce and navigation. Such vessels and cargoes shall in the ports, places and waters of such other Party be accorded in all respects national treatment and most-favored-nation treatment.

(2) Vessels of either Party en route to or from the territories of the other Party shall be accorded national treatment and most-favored-nation treatment with respect to the right to carry all cargo that may be carried by vessel.

(3) Goods carried by vessels under the flag of either Party to or from the territories of the other Party shall enjoy the same favors as when transported in vessels sailing under the flag of such other Party. This applies especially with regard to customs duties and all other fees and charges, to bounties, drawbacks and

other privileges of this nature, as well as to the administration of the customs and to transport to and from port by rail and other means of transportation.

(4) The coasting trade and inland navigation are excepted from the provisions of the present Article. However, the vessels of each Party shall be accorded by the other Party most-favored-nation treatment with respect to the coasting trade and inland navigation. Moreover, it is understood that vessels of either Party shall be permitted to discharge portions of cargoes at any ports, places or waters of the other Party open to foreign commerce and navigation, and to proceed with the remaining portions of such cargoes to any other such ports, places or waters and they shall be permitted to load in like manner in the same voyage outward, at the various ports, places and waters open to foreign commerce and navigation; but a right to engage in the coasting trade or inland navigation may not thereby be claimed.

(5) Neither Party shall impose any measure of a discriminatory nature that hinders or prevents the importer or exporter of products of either country from obtaining marine insurance on such products in companies of either Party.

Article 14. If a vessel of either Contracting Party runs aground or is wrecked on the coasts of the other Party, or if it is in distress and must put into a port of the other Party, the latter Party shall extend to the vessel as well as to the crew, the passengers, the personal property of crew and passengers, and to the cargo of the vessel, the same protection and assistance as would have been extended to a vessel under its own flag in like circumstances; and shall permit the vessel after repairs to proceed with its voyage upon conformity with the laws applicable alike to vessels under its own flag. Articles salvaged from the vessel shall be exempt from all customs duties unless they pass into internal consumption; but articles not entered for consumption may be subject to measures for the protection of the revenue pending their exit from the country.

Article 15. (1) In all ports of either Contracting Party the masters of vessels under the flag of the other Party, whose crews have ceased to be fully constituted on account of illness or for any other cause, shall be permitted to engage such seamen as may be necessary for the continuation of the voyage.

(2) Nationals of either Party who are seamen may be sent to ports of the other Party to join national vessels, in care of consular officers, either individually or in groups on the basis of seamen's papers issued in lieu of passports. Likewise, nationals of either Party shall be permitted to travel through the territory of the other Party on their way to join vessels or to be repatriated on the basis of seamen's papers used in lieu of passports.

Article 16. The present Treaty shall not preclude the application by either Contracting Party of measures:

(a) regulating the importation or exportation of gold or silver;

(b) relative to its national fisheries and to the products thereof;

(c) relating to fissionable materials, to radioactive byproducts of the utilization or processing thereof, or to materials that are the source of fissionable materials;

(d) regulating the production of or traffic in arms, ammunition and implements of war, or traffic in other materials carried on directly or indirectly for the purpose of supplying a military establishment;

(e) necessary to fulfill the obligations of a Party for the maintenance or restoration of international peace and security, or necessary to protect its essential security interests;

(f) for the protection of national treasures having an artistic, historical or archeological value; or

(g) denying to any company in the ownership or direction of which nationals of any third country or countries have directly or indirectly the controlling interest, the advantages of the present Treaty, except with respect to recognition of juridical status and with respect to access to courts.

Article 17. (1) The term "national treatment" means treatment accorded within the territories of a Contracting Party upon terms of a Contracting Party upon terms no less favorable than the treatment accorded therein, in like situations, to nationals, companies, products, vessels or other objects, as the case may be, of such Party.

(2) The term "most-favored-nation treatment" means treatment accorded within the territories of a Party upon terms no less favorable than the treatment accorded therein, in like situations, to nationals, companies, products, vessels or other objects, as the case may be, of a third country.

(3) As used in the present Treaty, the term "companies" means corporations, partnerships, companies and other associations, whether or not with juridical status, whether or not with limited liability and whether or not for pecuniary profit.

(4) National treatment accorded under the provisions of the present Treaty to companies of the Kingdom of Belgium shall, in any State or possession of the United States of America, be the treatment accorded therein to companies created or organized in other States and possessions of the United States of America.

Article 18. (1) The territories to which the present Treaty extends shall comprise all areas of land and water under the sovereignty or authority of each Contracting Party, other than the Trust Territory of Ruanda–Urundi in the case of the Kingdom of Belgium, and the Panama Canal Zone and the Trust Territory of the Pacific Islands in the case of the United States of America.

(2) It is understood that the present Treaty does not apply to territories under the authority of either Party solely as a military base or by reason of temporary military occupation.

Article 19. (1) Each Contracting Party shall accord sympathetic consideration to, and shall afford adequate opportunity for consultation regarding, such representations as the other Party may make with respect to any matter affecting the operation of the present Treaty.

(2) Any dispute between the Parties as to the interpretation or application of the present Treaty, not satisfactorily adjusted by diplomacy, shall be submitted to the International Court of Justice, unless the Parties agree to settlement by some other pacific means.

Article 20. The present Treaty shall terminate the Treaty of Commerce and Navigation signed at Washington March 8, 1875, and the Convention concerning Trade Marks signed at Washington April 7, 1884.

Article 21. (1) The present Treaty shall be ratified, and the ratifications thereof shall be exchanged at Washington as soon as possible.

(2) The present Treaty shall enter into force one month after the day of exchange of the instruments of ratification.

(3) The present Treaty shall remain in force for ten years and shall continue in force thereafter until terminated as provided herein.

(4) Either Contracting Party may, by giving one year's written notice to the other Party, terminate the present Treaty at the end of the initial ten-year period or at any time thereafter.

In witness whereof the respective Plenipotentiaries have signed the present Treaty and have affixed hereunto their seals.

Done at Brussels, this 21st day of February one thousand nine hundred sixty one, in duplicate, in the French and English languages, both equally authentic.

PROTOCOL

At the time of signing the Treaty of Friendship, Establishment and Navigation between the United States of America and the Kingdom of Belgium the undersigned Plenipotentiaries, duly authorized, have further agreed on the following provisions, which shall be considered integral parts of the aforesaid Treaty:

(1) The provisions of Article 2, paragraph 1, (b), of the Treaty shall be construed as extending to persons who represent nationals and companies of the same nationality which have invested or are actively in the process of investing a substantial amount of capital in an enterprise in the territories of the other Party, and who are employed by such nationals and companies in a responsible capacity.

(2) With reference to the provisions of Article 3, paragraph 2, each Party agrees that, within its territories, the nationals of the other Party shall be entitled to free legal aid on the same conditions as its own nationals.

(3) With reference to Article 3, paragraphs 2 and 3, nationals of either Party having their permanent residence within the territories of the other Party and companies of either Party having their establishment, main or branch, within the territories of the other Party who appear as plaintiff or intervening party before the courts of such other Party shall be exempt from obligation to post security for costs in such instances as nationals and companies of such other Party would be exempt.

(4) The provisions of Article 4, paragraph 3, providing for the payment of compensation shall extend to interests held directly or indirectly by nationals and companies of either Party in property which is taken within the territories of the other Party.

(5) The provisions of the present Treaty do not confer rights to engage in gainful activities except with the authorization to that effect required by the applicable laws and regulations. The two Parties are agreed, however, to entertain in a most considerate manner applications for authorization to engage in activities pursuant to the Treaty.

(6) The provisions of Article 6, paragraph 2, do not extend to professions which, because they involve the performance of functions in a public capacity or in the interests of public health and safety, are state-licensed and reserved by law to nationals of the country.

(7) The provisions of Article 6, paragraph 2, shall not extend to the activity of peddlers and itinerant artisans in the exercise of their occupations as such.

(8) With reference to Article 6, paragraph 3, neither Party shall apply the term "public policy" so as to deny recognition to a company constituted under the laws of the other Party in any situation in which the former Party permits a company with like purposes to be constituted under its laws.

(9) The benefit of the provisions of Article 6, paragraph 3, and of Article 9, paragraph 4, shall not be acquired within the territories of the Contracting Party whose law takes the main establishment into consideration for the recognition of companies, if such establishment is deemed to be within its territory.

(10) The provisions of Article 6, paragraphs 2 and 7, shall not be construed to confer rights with respect to owning real property.

(11) The treatment provided in Article 10, paragraph 1, is designed only to preclude discriminations on the ground of nationality but does not, for instance, preclude different treatment based upon residence requirements.

(12) It is understood that the word "cargo" (or "cargoes") as used in Article 13 shall be deemed to comprehend passengers as well as goods.

(13) The provisions of Article 13, paragraph 2, shall not apply to postal services.

6.3 FOREIGN SOVEREIGN IMMUNITIES ACT OF 1976.[a] 28 U.S.C.A. §§ 1602–1611 (Supp.1989)

§ 1602. Findings and declaration of purpose

The Congress finds that the determination by United States courts of the claims of foreign states to immunity from the jurisdiction of such courts would serve the interests of justice and would protect the rights of both foreign states and litigants in United States courts. Under international law, states are not immune from the jurisdiction of foreign courts insofar as their commercial activities are concerned, and their commercial property may be levied upon for the satisfaction of judgments rendered against them in connection with their commercial activities. Claims of foreign states to immunity should henceforth be decided by courts of the United States and of the States in conformity with the principles set forth in this chapter.

§ 1603. Definitions

For purposes of this chapter—

(a) A "foreign state", except as used in section 1608 of this title, includes a political subdivision of a foreign state or an agency or instrumentality of a foreign state as defined in subsection (b).

(b) An "agency or instrumentality of a foreign state" means any entity—

(1) which is a separate legal person, corporate or otherwise, and

(2) which is an organ of a foreign state or political subdivision thereof, or a majority of whose shares or other ownership interest is owned by a foreign state or political subdivision thereof, and

(3) which is neither a citizen of a State of the United States as defined in section 1332(c) and (d) of this title, nor created under the laws of any third country.

(c) The "United States" includes all territory and waters, continental or insular, subject to the jurisdiction of the United States.

(d) A "commercial activity" means either a regular course of commercial conduct or a particular commercial transaction or act. The commercial character of an activity shall be determined by reference to the nature of the course of conduct or particular transaction or act, rather than by reference to its purpose.

(e) A "commercial activity carried on in the United States by a foreign state" means commercial activity carried on by such state and having substantial contact with the United States.

§ 1604. Immunity of a foreign state from jurisdiction

Subject to existing international agreements to which the United States is a party at the time of enactment of this Act a foreign state shall be immune from the jurisdiction of the courts of the United States and of the States except as provided in sections 1605 to 1607 of this chapter.

§ 1605. General exceptions to the jurisdictional immunity of a foreign state

(a) A foreign state shall not be immune from the jurisdiction of courts of the United States or of the States in any case—

(1) in which the foreign state has waived its immunity either explicitly or by implication, notwithstanding any withdrawal of the waiver which the foreign state may purport to effect except in accordance with the terms of the waiver;

a. For another notable instrument pertaining to immunities, see: International Organizations Immunities Act, 22 U.S.C. §§ 288–288i (1976).

(2) in which the action is based upon a commercial activity carried on in the United States by the foreign state; or upon an act performed in the United States in connection with a commercial activity of the foreign state elsewhere; or upon an act outside the territory of the United States in connection with a commercial activity of the foreign state elsewhere and that act causes a direct effect in the United States;

(3) in which rights in property taken in violation of international law are in issue and that property or any property exchanged for such property is present in the United States in connection with a commercial activity carried on in the United States by the foreign state; or that property or any property exchanged for such property is owned or operated by an agency or instrumentality of the foreign state and that agency or instrumentality is engaged in a commercial activity in the United States;

(4) in which rights in property in the United States acquired by succession or gift or rights in immovable property situated in the United States are in issue;

(5) not otherwise encompassed in paragraph (2) above, in which money damages are sought against a foreign state for personal injury or death, or damage to or loss of property, occurring in the United States and caused by the tortious act or omission of that foreign state or of any official or employee of that foreign state while acting within the scope of his office or employment; except this paragraph shall not apply to—

(A) any claim based upon the exercise or performance or the failure to exercise or perform a discretionary function regardless of whether the discretion be abused, or

(B) any claim arising out of malicious prosecution, abuse of process, libel, slander, misrepresentation, deceit, or interference with contract rights; or

(6) in which the action is brought, either to enforce an agreement made by the foreign State with or for the benefit of a private party to submit to arbitration all or any differences which have arisen or which may arise between the parties with respect to a defined legal relationship, whether contractual or not, concerning a subject matter capable of settlement by arbitration under the laws of the United States, or to confirm an award made pursuant to such an agreement to arbitrate, if (A) the arbitration takes place or is intended to take place in the United States, (B) the agreement or award is or may be governed by a treaty or other international agreement in force for the United States calling for the recognition and enforcement of arbitral awards, (C) the underlying claim, save for the agreement to arbitrate, could have been brought in a United States court under this section or section 1607, or (D) paragraph (1) of this subsection is otherwise applicable.

(b) A foreign state shall not be immune from the jurisdiction of the courts of the United States in any case in which a suit in admiralty is brought to enforce a maritime lien against a vessel or cargo of the foreign state, which maritime lien is based upon a commercial activity of the foreign state: *Provided,* That—

(1) notice of the suit is given by delivery of a copy of the summons and of the complaint to the person, or his agent, having possession of the vessel or cargo against which the maritime lien is asserted; and if the vessel or cargo is arrested pursuant to process obtained on behalf of the party bringing the suit, the service of process of arrest shall be deemed to constitute valid delivery of such notice, but the party bringing the suit shall be liable for any damages sustained by the foreign state as a result of the arrest if the party bringing the suit had actual or

constructive knowledge that the vessel or cargo of a foreign state was involved; and

(2) notice to the foreign state of the commencement of suit as provided in section 1608 of this title is initiated within ten days either of the delivery of notice as provided in paragraph (1) of this subsection or, in the case of a party who was unaware that the vessel or cargo of a foreign state was involved, of the date such party determined the existence of the foreign state's interest.

(c) Whenever notice is delivered under subsection (b)(1), the suit to enforce a maritime lien shall thereafter proceed and shall be heard and determined according to the principles of law and rules of practice of suits in rem whenever it appears that, had the vessel been privately owned and possessed, a suit in rem might have been maintained. A decree against the foreign state may include costs of the suit and, if the decree is for a money judgment, interest as ordered by the court, except that the court may not award judgment against the foreign state in an amount greater than the value of the vessel or cargo upon which the maritime lien arose. Such value shall be determined as of the time notice is served under subsection (b)(1). Decrees shall be subject to appeal and revision as provided in other cases of admiralty and maritime jurisdiction. Nothing shall preclude the plaintiff in any proper case from seeking relief in personam in the same action brought to enforce a maritime lien as provided in this section.

(d) A foreign state shall not be immune from the jurisdiction of the courts of the United States in any action brought to foreclose a preferred mortgage, as defined in the Ship Mortgage Act, 1920 (46 U.S.C. 911 and following). Such action shall be brought, heard, and determined in accordance with the provisions of that Act and in accordance with the principles of law and rules of practice of suits in rem, whenever it appears that had the vessel been privately owned and possessed a suit in rem might have been maintained.

§ 1606. Extent of liability

As to any claim for relief with respect to which a foreign state is not entitled to immunity under section 1605 or 1607 of this chapter, the foreign state shall be liable in the same manner and to the same extent as a private individual under like circumstances; but a foreign state except for an agency or instrumentality thereof shall not be liable for punitive damages; if, however, in any case wherein death was caused, the law of the place where the action or omission occurred provides, or has been construed to provide, for damages only punitive in nature, the foreign state shall be liable for actual or compensatory damages measured by the pecuniary injuries resulting from such death which were incurred by the persons for whose benefit the action was brought.

§ 1607. Counterclaims

In any action brought by a foreign state, or in which a foreign state intervenes, in a court of the United States or of a State, the foreign state shall not be accorded immunity with respect to any counterclaim—

(a) for which a foreign state would not be entitled to immunity under section 1605 of this chapter had such claim been brought in a separate action against the foreign state; or

(b) arising out of the transaction or occurrence that is the subject matter of the claim of the foreign state; or

(c) to the extent that the counterclaim does not seek relief exceeding in amount or differing in kind from that sought by the foreign state.

§ 1608. Service; time to answer; default

(a) Service in the courts of the United States and of the States shall be made upon a foreign state or political subdivision of a foreign state:

(1) by delivery of a copy of the summons and complaint in accordance with any special arrangement for service between the plaintiff and the foreign state or political subdivision; or

(2) if no special arrangement exists, by delivery of a copy of the summons and complaint in accordance with an applicable international convention on service of judicial documents; or

(3) if service cannot be made under paragraphs (1) or (2), by sending a copy of the summons and complaint and a notice of suit, together with a translation of each into the official language of the foreign state, by any form of mail requiring a signed receipt, to be addressed and dispatched by the clerk of the court to the head of the ministry of foreign affairs of the foreign state concerned, or

(4) if service cannot be made within 30 days under paragraph (3), by sending two copies of the summons and complaint and a notice of suit, together with a translation of each into the official language of the foreign state, by any form of mail requiring a signed receipt, to be addressed and dispatched by the clerk of the court to the Secretary of State in Washington, District of Columbia, to the attention of the Director of Special Consular Services—and the Secretary shall transmit one copy of the papers through diplomatic channels to the foreign state and shall send to the clerk of the court a certified copy of the diplomatic note indicating when the papers were transmitted.

As used in this subsection, a "notice of suit" shall mean a notice addressed to a foreign state and in a form prescribed by the Secretary of State by regulation.

(b) Service in the courts of the United States and of the States shall be made upon an agency or instrumentality of a foreign state:

(1) by delivery of a copy of the summons and complaint in accordance with any special arrangement for service between the plaintiff and the agency or instrumentality; or

(2) if no special arrangement exists, by delivery of a copy of the summons and complaint either to an officer, a managing or general agent, or to any other agent authorized by appointment or by law to receive service of process in the United States; or in accordance with an applicable international convention on service of judicial documents; or

(3) if service cannot be made under paragraphs (1) or (2), and if reasonably calculated to give actual notice, by delivery of a copy of the summons and complaint, together with a translation of each into the official language of the foreign state—

(A) as directed by an authority of the foreign state or political subdivision in response to a letter rogatory or request or

(B) by any form of mail requiring a signed receipt, to be addressed and dispatched by the clerk of the court to the agency or instrumentality to be served, or

(C) as directed by order of the court consistent with the law of the place where service is to be made.

(c) Service shall be deemed to have been made—

(1) in the case of service under subsection (a)(4), as of the date of transmittal indicated in the certified copy of the diplomatic note; and

(2) in any other case under this section, as of the date of receipt indicated in the certification, signed and returned postal receipt, or other proof of service applicable to the method of service employed.

(d) In any action brought in a court of the United States or of a State, a foreign state, a political subdivision thereof, or an agency or instrumentality of a foreign state shall serve an answer or other responsive pleading to the complaint within sixty days after service has been made under this section.

(e) No judgment by default shall be entered by a court of the United States or of a State against a foreign state, a political subdivision thereof, or an agency or instrumentality of a foreign state, unless the claimant establishes his claim or right to relief by evidence satisfactory to the court. A copy of any such default judgment shall be sent to the foreign state or political subdivision in the manner prescribed for service in this section.

§ 1609. Immunity from attachment and execution of property of a foreign state

Subject to existing international agreements to which the United States is a party at the time of enactment of this Act the property in the United States of a foreign state shall be immune from attachment arrest and execution except as provided in sections 1610 and 1611 of this chapter.

§ 1610. Exceptions to the immunity from attachment or execution

(a) The property in the United States of a foreign state, as defined in section 1603(a) of this chapter, used for a commercial activity in the United States, shall not be immune from attachment in aid of execution, or from execution, upon a judgment entered by a court of the United States or of a State after the effective date of this Act, if—

(1) the foreign state has waived its immunity from attachment in aid of execution or from execution either explicitly or by implication, notwithstanding any withdrawal of the waiver the foreign state may purport to effect except in accordance with the terms of the waiver, or

(2) the property is or was used for the commercial activity upon which the claim is based, or

(3) the execution relates to a judgment establishing rights in property which has been taken in violation of international law or which has been exchanged for property taken in violation of international law, or

(4) the execution relates to a judgment establishing rights in property—

(A) which is acquired by succession or gift, or

(B) which is immovable and situated in the United States: *Provided,* That such property is not used for purposes of maintaining a diplomatic or consular mission or the residence of the Chief of such mission, or

(5) the property consists of any contractual obligation or any proceeds from such a contractual obligation to indemnify or hold harmless the foreign state or its employees under a policy of automobile or other liability or casualty insurance covering the claim which merged into the judgment, or

(6) the judgment is based on an order confirming an arbitral award rendered against the foreign State, provided that attachment in aid of execution, or execution, would not be inconsistent with any provision in the arbitral agreement.

(b) In addition to subsection (a), any property in the United States of an agency or instrumentality of a foreign state engaged in commercial activity in the United States shall not be immune from attachment in aid of execution, or from execution, upon a judgment entered by a court of the United States or of a State after the effective date of this Act if—

(1) the agency or instrumentality has waived its immunity from attachment in aid of execution or from execution either explicitly or implicitly, notwithstanding any withdrawal of the waiver the agency or instrumentality may purport to effect except in accordance with the terms of the waiver, or

(2) the judgment relates to a claim for which the agency or instrumentality is not immune by virtue of section 1605(a)(2), (3), or (5), or 1605(b) of this chapter, regardless of whether the property is or was used for the activity upon which the claim is based.

(c) No attachment or execution referred to in subsections (a) and (b) of this section shall be permitted until the court has ordered such attachment and execution after having determined that a reasonable period of time has elapsed following the entry of judgment and the giving of any notice required under section 1608(e) of this chapter.

(d) The property of a foreign state, as defined in section 1603(a) of this chapter, used for a commercial activity in the United States, shall not be immune from attachment prior to the entry of judgment in any action brought in a court of the United States or of a State, or prior to the elapse of the period of time provided in subsection (c) of this section, if—

(1) the foreign state has explicitly waived its immunity from attachment prior to judgment, notwithstanding any withdrawal of the waiver the foreign state may purport to effect except in accordance with the terms of the waiver, and

(2) the purpose of the attachment is to secure satisfaction of a judgment that has been or may ultimately be entered against the foreign state, and not to obtain jurisdiction.

(e) The vessels of a foreign State shall not be immune from arrest in rem, interlocutory sale, and execution in actions brought to foreclose a preferred mortgage as provided in section 1605(d).

§ 1611. Certain types of property immune from execution

(a) Notwithstanding the provisions of section 1610 of this chapter, the property of those organizations designated by the President as being entitled to enjoy the privileges, exemptions, and immunities provided by the International Organizations Immunities Act shall not be subject to attachment or any other judicial process impeding the disbursement of funds to, or on the order of, a foreign state as the result of an action brought in the courts of the United States or of the States.

(b) Notwithstanding the provisions of section 1610 of this chapter, the property of a foreign state shall be immune from attachment and from execution, if—

(1) the property is that of a foreign central bank or monetary authority held for its own account, unless such bank or authority, or its parent foreign government, has explicitly waived its immunity from attachment in aid of execution, or from execution, notwithstanding any withdrawal of the waiver which the bank, authority or government may purport to effect except in accordance with the terms of the waiver; or

(2) the property is, or is intended to be, used in connection with a military activity and

(A) is of a military character, or

(B) is under the control of a military authority or defense agency.

6.4 SUPPLEMENTARY TREATY CONCERNING THE EXTRADITION TREATY BETWEEN THE GOVERNMENT OF THE UNITED STATES OF AMERICA AND THE GOVERNMENT OF THE UNITED KINGDOM OF GREAT BRITAIN AND NORTHERN IRELAND, SIGNED AT LONDON ON 8 JUNE, 1972.[a] Done at Washington, June 25, 1985. Entered into force, Dec. 23, 1986. *Reprinted in* 24 I.L.M. 1105 (1985)

The Government of the United States of America and the Government of the United Kingdom of Great Britain and Northern Ireland;

Desiring to make more effective the Extradition Treaty between the Contracting Parties, signed at London on 8 June 1972 (hereinafter referred to as "the Extradition Treaty");

Have resolved to conclude a Supplementary Treaty and have agreed as follows:

Article 1

For the purposes of the Extradition Treaty, none of the following offenses shall be regarded as an offense of a political character:

(a) an offense within the scope of the Convention for the Suppression of Unlawful Seizure of Aircraft, opened for signature at The Hague on 16 December 1970;

(b) an offense within the scope of the Convention for the Suppression of Unlawful Acts against the Safety of Civil Aviation, opened for signature at Montreal on 23 September 1971;

(c) an offense within the scope of the Convention on the Prevention and Punishment of Crimes against Internationally Protected Persons, including Diplomatic Agents, opened for signature at New York on 14 December 1973;

(d) an offense within the scope of the International Convention against the Taking of Hostages, opened for signature at New York on 18 December 1979;

(e) murder;

(f) manslaughter;

(g) maliciously wounding or inflicting grievous bodily harm;

(h) kidnapping, abduction, false imprisonment or unlawful detention, including the taking of a hostage;

(i) the following offenses relating to explosives:

(1) the causing of an explosion likely to endanger life or cause serious damage to property; or

(2) conspiracy to cause such an explosion; or

(3) the making or possession of an explosive substance by a person who intends either himself or through another person to endanger life or cause serious damage to property;

(j) the following offenses relating to firearms or ammunition:

(1) the possession of a firearm or ammunition by a person who intends either himself or through another person to endanger life; or

a. The extradition treaty is at 28 U.S.T. 227.

(2) the use of a firearm by a person with intent to resist or prevent the arrest or detention of himself or another person;

(k) damaging property with intent to endanger life or with reckless disregard as to whether the life of another would thereby be endangered;

(*l*) an attempt to commit any of the foregoing offenses.

APPENDIX I

STATUS OF BASIC DOCUMENTS IN INTERNATIONAL LAW AND WORLD ORDER (AS OF DECEMBER 31, 1989)

For the texts of reservations, declarations, and statements of understanding qualifying the ratification of, or accession to, the multilateral treaties listed herein, see ***United Nations Multilateral Treaties Deposited with the Secretary General.***

1. CONSTITUTIVE/ORGANIC

1.1 CONSTITUTION OF THE UNITED STATES OF AMERICA

1.2 GENERAL ACT FOR THE PACIFIC SETTLEMENT OF INTERNATIONAL DISPUTES

Entry into force: August 16, 1929

Ratified/accepted/approved without qualification: 10

Denmark (4/14/30), Ethiopia (3/15/35), Finland (9/6/30), Ireland (9/26/31), Latvia (9/17/35), Luxembourg (9/15/30), Norway (6/11/30), Pakistan * (7/12/74), Peru (11/21/31), Switzerland (12/7/34)

* India has stated that Pakistan cannot succeed to the Convention as it never applied to Pakistan prior to independence.

Ratified/accepted/approved with qualification: 9

Australia (5/21/31), Belgium (5/18/29), Canada (7/1/31), Estonia (9/3/31), Greece (9/14/31), Italy (9/7/31), Netherlands (8/8/30), New Zealand (5/21/31), Sweden (5/13/29)

1.3 CONVENTION ON THE RIGHTS AND DUTIES OF STATES

Entry into force: December 26, 1934

Signed but not ratified: 4

Argentina (12/26/33), Paraguay (12/26/33), Peru (12/26/33), Uruguay (12/26/33)

Ratified/accepted/approved without qualification: 14

Chile (3/28/35), Colombia (7/22/36), Costa Rica (9/28/37), Cuba (4/28/36), Dominican Republic (12/26/34), Ecuador (10/3/36), El Salvador (1/9/37), Guatemala (6/12/35), Haiti (8/13/41), Honduras (12/1/37), Mexico (1/27/36), Nicaragua (1/8/37), Panama (11/13/38), Venezuela (2/13/40)

Ratified/accepted/approved with qualification: 2

Brazil (2/23/37), United States (7/13/34)

1.4 PACT OF THE LEAGUE OF ARAB STATES

Entry into force: May 10, 1945

Ratified/accepted/approved without qualification: 22

Algeria * (8/16/62), Bahrain (9/11/71), Djibouti (9/4/77), Egypt * (4/12/45), Iraq (4/25/45), Jordan (4/10/45), Kuwait (7/20/61), Lebanon (5/16/45), Libya (1/19/56), Mauritania (11/26/73), Morocco (10/1/58), Oman (9/29/71), Palestine * (9/9/76), Qatar (9/11/71), Saudi Arabia (4/16/45), Somalia (2/14/74), Sudan

(3/28/53), Syria (5/19/45), Tunisia (10/1/58), United Arab Emirates (12/6/71), Yemen (2/9/45), Yemen (Democratic) (12/12/67)

* In 1979 the League of Arab States severed political relations with Egypt and suspended Egypt's membership. Egypt has had no part in the League since that time. Palestine was confirmed a full member in 1976 and is represented by the Palestine Liberation Organization.

1.5 Charter of the United Nations

Entry into force: October 24, 1945

Parties: 159

Original members: 51

Argentina (9/24/45), Australia (11/1/45), Belgium (12/27/45), Bolivia (11/14/45), Brazil (9/21/45), Byelorussian SSR (10/24/45), Canada (11/9/45), Chile (10/11/45), China * (9/28/45), Colombia (11/5/45), Costa Rica (11/2/45), Cuba (10/15/45), Czechoslovakia (10/19/45), Denmark (10/9/45), Dominican Republic (9/4/45), Ecuador (12/21/45), Egypt (10/22/45), El Salvador (9/26/45), Ethiopia (11/13/45), France (8/31/45), Greece (10/25/45), Guatemala (11/21/45), Haiti (9/27/45), Honduras (12/17/45), India (10/30/45), Iran (10/16/45), Iraq (12/21/45), Lebanon (10/17/45), Liberia (10/15/45), Luxembourg (11/2/45), Mexico (11/7/45), Netherlands (12/10/45), New Zealand (9/10/45), Nicaragua (9/6/45), Norway (11/27/45), Panama (11/13/45), Paraguay (10/12/45), Peru (10/31/45), Philippines (10/11/45), Poland (10/24/45), Saudi Arabia (10/18/45), South Africa (11/7/45), Syria (10/19/45), Turkey (9/28/45), Ukrainian SSR (10/24/45), United Kingdom (10/20/45), United States (8/8/45), Uruguay (12/18/45), USSR (10/24/45), Venezuela (11/15/45), Yugoslavia (10/19/45)

* China was originally represented in the UN by the Government of the Republic of China (R.O.C.) on Taiwan until October 25, 1971. Since then, China has been represented by the Government of the People's Republic of China. The R.O.C. is not a member of the UN and has no representation.

Non-signatories admitted under Article 4: 108

Afghanistan (11/19/46), Albania (12/14/55), Algeria (10/8/62), Angola (12/1/76), Antigua and Barbuda (11/11/81), Austria (12/14/55), Bahamas (9/18/73), Bahrain (9/21/71), Bangladesh (9/17/74), Barbados (12/9/66), Belize (9/25/81), Benin (9/20/60), Bhutan (9/21/71), Botswana (10/17/66), Brunei (9/21/84), Bulgaria (12/14/55), Burma (4/19/48), Burundi (9/18/62), Cameroon (9/20/60), Cape Verde (9/16/75), Central African Republic (9/20/60), Chad (9/20/60), Comoros (11/12/75), Congo (9/20/60), Cyprus (9/20/60), Djibouti (9/20/77), Dominica (12/18/78), Equatorial Guinea (11/12/68), Fiji (10/13/70), Finland (12/14/55), Gabon (9/20/60), Gambia (9/21/65), Germany (East) (9/18/73), Germany (West) (9/18/73), Ghana (3/8/57), Grenada (9/17/74), Guinea (12/12/58), Guinea-Bissau (9/17/74), Guyana (9/20/66), Hungary (12/14/55), Iceland (11/19/46), Indonesia (9/28/50), Ireland (12/14/55), Israel (5/11/49), Italy (12/14/55), Ivory Coast (9/20/60), Jamaica (9/18/62), Japan (12/18/56), Jordan (12/14/55), Kampuchea (12/14/55), Kenya (12/16/63), Kuwait (5/14/63), Laos (12/14/55), Lesotho (10/17/66), Libya (12/14/55), Madagascar (9/20/60), Malawi (12/1/64), Malaysia (9/17/57), Maldives (9/21/65), Mali (9/28/60), Malta (12/1/64), Mauritania (10/27/61), Mauritius (4/24/68), Mongolia (10/27/61), Morocco (11/12/56), Mozambique (9/16/75), Nepal (12/14/55), Niger (9/20/60), Nigeria (10/7/60), Oman (10/7/71), Pakistan (9/30/47), Papua (10/10/75), Portugal (12/14/55), Qatar (9/21/71), Romania (12/14/55), Rwanda (9/18/62), Samoa (12/15/76), São Tomé and Príncipe (9/16/75), Senegal (9/28/60), Seychelles (9/21/76), Sierra Leone (9/27/61), Singapore (9/21/65), Solomon Islands (9/19/78), Somalia (9/20/60), Spain (12/14/55), Sri Lanka (12/14/55), St. Christopher and Nevis (9/23/83), St. Lucia (9/18/79), St. Vincent and the Grenadines (9/18/80), Sudan

(11/12/56), Suriname (12/4/75), Swaziland (9/24/68), Sweden (11/19/46), Tanzania (4/26/64), Thailand (12/16/46), Togo (9/20/60), Trinidad (9/18/62), Tunisia (11/12/56), Uganda (10/25/62), United Arab Emirates (12/9/71), Upper Volta (9/20/60), Vanuatu (9/15/81), Vietnam (9/20/77), Yemen (9/30/47), Yemen (Democratic) (12/14/67), Zaire (9/20/60), Zambia (12/1/64), Zimbabwe (8/25/80)

1.6 Statute of the International Court of Justice

Entry into force: October 24, 1945

Note: The Statute is part of the UN Charter. All members of the UN are parties to the Statute. Non-members may become parties to the Statute on conditions set in each case by the General Assembly on the recommendation of the Security Council.

Non-members who are parties to the Statute: 4

Liechtenstein (3/29/50), Nauru (1/29/88), Switzerland (6/28/48), San Marino (2/18/54)

1.7 Convention on the Privileges and Immunities of the United Nations

Entry into force: September 17, 1946

Ratified/accepted/approved without qualification: 101

Afghanistan (9/5/47), Angola (12/8/64), Antigua and Barbuda (10/25/88), Argentina (10/12/56), Australia (3/2/49), Austria (5/10/57), Bahamas (3/17/77), Bangladesh (1/13/78), Barbados (1/10/72), Belgium (9/25/48), Bolivia (12/23/49), Brazil (12/15/49), Burma (1/25/55), Burundi (3/17/71), Cameroon (10/20/61), Central African Republic (9/4/62), Chile (10/15/48), Colombia (8/6/74), Congo (10/15/62), Costa Rica (10/26/49), Cuba (9/9/59), Cyprus (11/5/63), Denmark (6/10/48), Djibouti (4/6/78), Dominica (11/24/87), Dominican Republic (3/7/47), Ecuador (3/22/56), Egypt (9/17/48), El Salvador (7/9/47), Ethiopia (7/22/47), Fiji (6/21/71), Finland (7/31/58), Gabon (3/13/64), Gambia (8/1/66), Germany (West) (11/5/80), Ghana (8/5/58), Greece (12/29/47), Guatemala (7/7/47), Guinea (1/10/68), Guyana (12/28/72), Haiti (8/6/47), Honduras (5/16/47), Iceland (3/10/48), India (5/13/48), Iran (5/8/47), Iraq (9/15/49), Ireland (5/10/67), Israel (9/21/49), Italy (2/3/58), Ivory Coast (12/8/61), Jamaica (9/9/63), Japan (4/18/63), Jordan (1/3/58), Kampuchea (11/6/63), Kenya (7/1/65), Kuwait (12/13/63), Lesotho (11/26/69), Liberia (3/14/47), Libya (11/28/58), Luxembourg (2/14/49), Madagascar (5/23/62), Malawi (5/17/66), Malaysia (10/28/57), Mali (3/28/68), Malta (6/27/68), Mauritius (7/18/69), Morocco (3/18/57), Netherlands (4/19/48), New Zealand (12/10/47), Nicaragua (11/29/47), Niger (8/25/61), Nigeria (6/26/61), Norway (8/18/47), Pakistan (9/22/48), Panama (5/27/47), Papua New Guinea (12/4/75), Paraguay (10/2/53), Peru (7/24/63), Philippines (10/28/47), Poland (1/8/48), Rwanda (4/15/64), Senegal (5/27/63), Seychelles (8/26/80), Sierra Leone (3/13/62), Singapore (3/18/66), Somalia (7/9/63), Spain (7/31/74), Sri Lanka (3/21/77), St. Lucia (8/27/86), Sweden (8/28/47), Syria (9/29/53), Tanzania (10/29/62), Togo (2/27/62), Trinidad and Tobago (10/19/65), Tunisia (5/7/57), Upper Volta (4/27/62), Uruguay (2/16/84), Yemen (7/23/63), Yugoslavia (6/30/50), Zaire (12/8/64), Zambia (6/16/75)

Ratified/accepted/approved with qualification: 23

Albania * (7/2/57), Algeria (10/31/63), Bulgaria (9/30/60), Byelorussian SSR (10/22/53), Canada (1/22/48), China * (9/11/79), Czechoslovakia (9/7/55), Germany (East) * (10/4/74), France (8/18/47), Hungary * (7/30/56), Indonesia (3/8/72), Laos (11/24/56), Mexico (11/26/62), Mongolia * (5/31/62), Nepal (9/28/65), Romania * (7/5/56), Thailand (3/30/56), Turkey (8/22/50), Ukrainian SSR *

(11/20/53), United Kingdom (9/17/46), United States (4/29/70), USSR ** (9/22/53), Vietnam (4/6/88)

* Reservation not accepted as valid by United Kingdom.

** Reservation not accepted by Lebanon.

1.8 Agreement Between the United Nations and the United States of America Regarding the Headquarters of the United Nations

Entry into force: November 21, 1947

1.9 Charter of the Organization of American States

Entry into force: December 13, 1951

Ratified/accepted/approved without qualification: 25

Antigua and Barbuda (12/3/81), Argentina (4/10/56), Bahamas (3/3/82), Barbados (11/15/67), Brazil (3/13/50), Chile (6/4/53), Colombia (12/13/51), Costa Rica (11/16/48), Dominica (5/22/79), Dominican Republic (4/22/49), El Salvador (9/11/50), Grenada (5/13/75), Haiti (3/28/51), Honduras (2/7/50), Jamaica (8/20/69), Mexico (11/23/48), Nicaragua (7/26/50), Paraguay (5/3/50), St. Christopher and Nevis (3/12/84), St. Lucia (5/22/79), St. Vincent and the Grenadines (12/3/81), Suriname (6/8/77), Trinidad and Tobago (3/17/67), Uruguay (9/1/55), Venezuela (12/29/51)

Ratified/accepted/approved with qualification: 6

Bolivia (10/18/50), Ecuador (12/28/50), Guatemala (4/6/55), Panama (3/22/51), Peru (2/12/54), United States (6/19/51)

1.10 Statute of the Council of Europe

Entry into force: August 3, 1949

Ratified/accepted/approved without qualification: 23

Austria (4/16/56), Belgium (8/8/49), Cyprus (5/24/61), Denmark (7/14/49), Finland (5/5/89), France (8/4/49), Germany (West) (7/13/50), Greece (11/28/74), Iceland (3/7/50), Ireland (8/2/49), Italy (8/3/49), Liechtenstein (11/23/78), Luxembourg (8/3/49), Malta (4/29/65), Netherlands (8/5/49), Norway (7/30/49), Portugal (9/22/76), San Marino (11/16/88), Spain (11/24/77), Sweden (7/20/49), Switzerland (5/6/63), Turkey (4/13/50), United Kingdom (7/26/49)

1.11 The Statute of the Organization of the Petroleum Exporting Countries (OPEC)

Current OPEC members: 13

Algeria, Ecuador, Gabon, Indonesia, Iran, Iraq, Kuwait, Libya, Nigeria, Qatar, Saudi Arabia, United Arab Emirates, Venezuela

1.12 Vienna Convention on Diplomatic Relations

Entry into force: April 24, 1964

Signed but not ratified: 1

South Africa (3/28/62)

Ratified/accepted/approved without qualification: 103

Afghanistan (10/6/65), Albania (2/8/88), Argentina (10/10/63), Austria (4/28/66), Bangladesh (1/13/78), Barbados (5/6/68), Belgium (5/2/68), Benin (3/27/67), Bhutan (12/7/72), Bolivia (12/28/77), Brazil (3/25/65), Burkina Faso (5/4/87), Burma (3/7/80), Burundi (5/1/68), Cameroon (5/4/77), Cape Verde (7/30/79), Central Africa Republic (3/19/73), Chad (11/3/77), Chile (1/9/68), China (11/25/75), Colombia (4/5/73), Congo (3/11/63), Costa Rica (11/9/64),

Cyprus (9/10/68), Djibouti (11/2/78), Dominica (11/24/87), Dominican Republic (1/14/64), Ecuador (9/21/64), Egypt (6/9/64), El Salvador (12/9/65), Equatorial Guinea (8/30/76), Ethiopia (3/22/79), Fiji (6/21/71), Finland (12/9/69), Gabon (4/2/64), Ghana (6/28/62), Guinea (1/10/68), Guyana (12/28/72), Holy See (4/17/64), Honduras (2/13/68), Iceland (5/18/71), India (10/15/65), Indonesia (6/4/82), Iran (2/3/65), Italy (6/25/69), Ivory Coast (10/1/62), Jamaica (6/5/63), Jordan (7/29/71), Kenya (7/1/65), Kiribati (4/2/82), Korea (North) (10/29/80), Laos (12/3/62), Lebanon (3/16/71), Lesotho (11/26/69), Liberia (5/15/62), Liechtenstein (5/8/64), Madagascar (7/31/63), Malawi (5/19/65), Malaysia (11/9/65), Mali (5/28/68), Malta (3/7/67), Mauritania (7/16/62), Mauritius (7/18/69), Mexico (6/16/65), Mozambique (11/18/81), Nauru (5/5/78), New Zealand (9/23/70), Nicaragua (10/31/75), Niger (12/5/65), Nigeria (6/19/67), Norway (10/24/67), Pakistan (3/29/62), Panama (12/4/63), Papua New Guinea (12/4/75), Paraguay (12/23/69), Peru (12/18/68), Philippines (11/15/65), Portugal (9/11/68), Rwanda (4/15/64), Samoa (10/26/87), San Marino (9/8/65), São Tomé and Príncipe (5/3/83), Senegal (10/12/72), Seychelles (5/29/79), Sierra Leone (8/13/62), Somalia (3/29/68), Spain (11/21/67), Sri Lanka (6/2/78), St. Lucia (8/27/86), Sudan (4/13/81), Swaziland (4/25/69), Sweden (3/21/67), Switzerland (10/30/63), Togo (11/27/70), Trinidad and Tobago (10/19/65), Tunisia (1/24/68), Turkey (3/6/85), Tuvalu (9/15/82), Uganda (4/15/65), Uruguay (3/10/70), Vietnam (8/26/80), Yugoslavia (4/1/63), Zaire (7/19/65)

Ratified/accepted/approved with qualification: 48

Australia (1/26/68), Bahamas (3/17/77), Bahrain (11/2/71), Botswana (4/11/69), Bulgaria (1/17/68), Byelorussian SSR (5/14/64), Canada (5/26/66), Cuba (9/26/63), Czechoslovakia (5/24/63), Denmark (10/2/68), France (12/31/70), Germany (East) (2/2/73), Germany (West) (11/11/64), Greece (7/16/70), Guatemala (10/1/63), Haiti (2/2/78), Hungary (9/24/65), Iraq (10/15/63), Ireland (5/10/67), Israel (8/11/70), Japan (6/8/64), Kampuchea (8/31/65), Korea (South) (12/28/70), Kuwait (7/23/69), Libya (6/7/77), Luxembourg (8/17/66), Mongolia (1/5/67), Morocco (6/19/68), Nepal (9/28/65), Netherlands (9/7/84), Oman (5/31/74), Poland (4/19/65), Qatar (6/6/86), Romania (11/15/68), Saudi Arabia (2/10/81), Syria (8/4/78), Tanzania (11/5/62), Thailand (1/23/85), Tonga (1/31/73), Ukrainian SSR (6/12/64), United Arab Emirates (2/24/77), United Kingdom (9/1/64), United States (11/13/72), USSR (3/25/64), Venezuela (3/16/65), Yemen (Democratic) (11/24/76), Yemen (4/10/86), Zambia (6/16/75)

1.13 Charter of the Organization of African Unity

Entry into force: September 13, 1963

Signed: 50

Algeria, Angola, Benin, Botswana, Burundi, Cameroon, Cape Verde, Central African Republic, Chad, Comoros, Congo, Djibouti, Egypt, Equatorial Guinea, Ethiopia, Gabon, Gambia, Ghana, Guinea, Guinea-Bissau, Ivory Coast, Kenya, Lesotho, Liberia, Libya, Madagascar, Malawi, Mali, Mauritania, Mauritius, Mozambique, Niger, Nigeria, Rwanda, Saharan Arab Democratic Republic, São Tomé and Príncipe, Senegal, Seychelles, Sierra Leone, Somalia, Sudan, Swaziland, Tanzania, Togo, Tunisia, Uganda, Upper Volta, Zaire, Zambia, Zimbabwe

1.14 The Palestinian National Charter of 1968

In force

1.15 Vienna Convention on the Law of Treaties

Entry into force: May 23, 1969

Signed but not ratified: 23

Afghanistan (5/23/69), Bolivia (5/23/69), Brazil (5/23/69), Costa Rica (5/23/69), Ecuador (5/23/69), El Salvador (2/16/70), Ethiopia (4/30/70), Ghana (5/23/69), Guatemala (5/23/69), Guyana (5/23/69), Iran (5/23/69), Ivory Coast (7/23/69), Kampuchea (5/23/69), Kenya (5/23/69), Luxembourg (9/4/69), Madagascar (5/23/69), Nepal (5/23/69), Pakistan (4/29/70), Peru (5/23/69), Sudan (5/23/69), Trinidad and Tobago (5/23/69), United States (4/24/70), Zambia (5/23/69)

Ratified/accepted/approved without qualification: 31

Australia (6/13/74), Austria (4/30/79), Barbados (6/24/71), Central African Republic (12/10/71), Congo (4/12/82), Cyprus (12/28/76), Greece (10/30/74), Haiti (8/25/80), Holy See (2/25/77), Honduras (9/20/79), Italy (7/25/74), Jamaica (7/28/70), Korea (South) (4/27/77), Lesotho (3/3/72), Liberia (8/29/85), Malawi (8/23/83), Mauritius (1/18/73), Mexico (9/25/74), Nauru (5/5/78), Niger (10/27/71), Nigeria (7/31/69), Panama (7/28/80), Paraguay (2/3/72), Philippines (11/15/72), Rwanda (1/3/80), Senegal (4/11/86), Spain (5/16/72), Togo (12/28/79), Uruguay (3/5/82), Yugoslavia (8/27/80), Zaire (7/25/77)

Ratified/accepted/approved with qualification: 27

Algeria (11/8/88), Argentina (12/5/72), Bulgaria (4/21/87), Byelorussian SSR (5/1/86), Canada (10/14/70), Chile (4/9/81), Colombia (4/10/85), Czechoslovakia (7/29/87), Denmark (6/1/76), Egypt (2/11/82), Finland (8/19/77), Germany (East) (10/20/86), Germany (West) (7/21/87), Hungary (6/19/87), Japan (7/2/81), Kuwait (11/11/75), Mongolia (5/16/88), Morocco (9/26/72), Netherlands (4/9/85), New Zealand (8/4/71), Sweden (2/4/75), Syria (10/2/70), Tanzania (4/12/76), Tunisia (6/23/71), Ukrainian SSR (5/14/86), United Kingdom (6/25/71), USSR (4/29/86)

1.16 Declaration on Principles of International Law Concerning Friendly Relations and Co-operation Among States in Accordance With the Charter of the United Nations

Adopted without recorded vote

1.17 Final Act of the Conference on Security and Co-operation in Europe

Conferees: 35

Austria, Belgium, Bulgaria, Canada, Cyprus, Czechoslovakia, Denmark, Finland, France, Germany (East), Germany (West), Greece, Holy See, Hungary, Iceland, Ireland, Italy, Liechtenstein, Luxembourg, Malta, Monaco, Netherlands, Norway, Poland, Portugal, Romania, San Marino, Spain, Sweden, Switzerland, Turkey, United Kingdom, United States, USSR, Yugoslavia

Signed: 35

Austria, Belgium, Bulgaria, Canada, Cyprus, Czechoslovakia, Denmark, Finland, France, Germany (East), Germany (West), Greece, Holy See, Hungary, Iceland, Ireland, Italy, Liechtenstein, Luxembourg, Malta, Monaco, Netherlands, Norway, Poland, Portugal, Romania, San Marino, Spain, Sweden, Switzerland, Turkey, United Kingdom, United States, USSR, Yugoslavia

1.18 Concluding Document of the Vienna Meeting 1986 of Representatives of the Participating States of the Conference on Security and Co-operation in Europe

Conferees: 35

Austria, Belgium, Bulgaria, Canada, Cyprus, Czechoslovakia, Denmark, Finland, France, Germany (East), Germany (West), Greece, Holy See, Hungary, Iceland, Ireland, Italy, Liechtenstein, Luxembourg, Malta, Monaco, Netherlands, Norway,

Poland, Portugal, Romania, San Marino, Spain, Sweden, Switzerland, Turkey, United Kingdom, United States, USSR, Yugoslavia

2. WAR/PEACE

2.1 DECLARATION RENOUNCING THE USE, IN TIME OF WAR, OF EXPLOSIVE PROJECTILES UNDER 400 GRAMMES WEIGHT

Conferees: 16

Austria-Hungary, Bavaria, Belgium, Denmark, France, Great Britain, Greece, Italy, Netherlands, Portugal, Prussia and the North German Confederation, Russia, Sweden and Norway, Switzerland, Turkey, Wurtemberg

Signed/accepted: 19

Austria-Hungary, Baden, Bavaria, Belgium, Brazil, Denmark, France, Great Britain, Greece, Italy, Netherlands, Persia, Portugal, Prussia and the North German Confederation, Russia, Sweden and Norway, Switzerland, Turkey, Wurtemberg

2.2 CONVENTION (NO. IV) RESPECTING THE LAWS AND CUSTOMS OF WAR ON LAND, WITH ANNEX OF REGULATIONS

Entry into force: January 10, 1926

Signed but not ratified: 15

Argentina (10/18/07), Bulgaria (10/18/07), Chile (10/18/07), Colombia (10/18/07), Ecuador (10/18/07), Greece (10/18/07), Italy (10/18/07), Montenegro (10/18/07), Paraguay (10/18/07), Peru (10/18/07), Persia (10/18/07), Serbia (10/18/07), Turkey (10/18/07), Uruguay (10/18/07), Venezuela (10/18/07)

Ratified/accepted/approved without qualification: 32

Belgium (10/7/10), Bolivia (1/26/10), Brazil (3/6/14), Byelorussian SSR (6/4/62), China (7/9/17), Cuba (4/22/12), Denmark (1/26/10), Dominican Republic (7/15/58), El Salvador (1/26/10), Ethiopia (10/4/35), Fiji (4/2/73), Finland (6/9/22), France (12/6/10), Germany (East) (2/9/59), Guatemala (5/14/11), Haiti (4/3/10), Liberia (4/5/14), Luxembourg (11/4/12), Mexico (1/26/10), Netherlands (1/26/10), Nicaragua (2/14/10), Norway (11/18/10), Panama (11/10/11), Poland (7/8/25), Portugal (6/12/11), Romania (4/30/12), Sweden (1/26/10), Switzerland (7/11/10), Thailand (5/11/10), United Kingdom (1/26/10), United States (1/26/10), USSR (3/7/55)

Ratified/accepted/approved with qualification: 4

Austria-Hungary (1/26/10), Germany (1/26/10), Japan (2/11/12), Russia (1/26/10)

2.3 PROTOCOL FOR THE PROHIBITION OF THE USE IN WAR OF ASPHYXIATING, POISONOUS OR OTHER GASES, AND OF BACTERIOLOGICAL METHODS OF WARFARE

Entry into force: February 8, 1928

Signed but not ratified: 2

El Salvador (6/17/25), Nicaragua (6/17/25)

Ratified/accepted/approved without qualification: 83

Afghanistan (9/2/86), Antigua and Barbuda (1/4/89), Argentina (5/12/69), Austria (5/9/28), Bahrain (12/9/88), Barbados (7/16/76), Benin (12/4/86), Bhutan (2/19/79), Bolivia (1/14/85), Brazil (8/28/70), Central African Republic (7/31/70), China (8/24/29), Cuba (6/24/66), Cyprus (11/29/66), Denmark (5/5/30), Dominican Republic (12/8/70), Ecuador (9/16/70), Egypt (12/6/28), Finland (6/26/29), Gambia (11/5/66), Germany (East) (3/2/59), Germany (West) (4/25/29), Ghana

(5/3/67), Greece (5/30/31), Guatemala (5/3/83), Holy See (10/18/66), Hungary (10/11/52), Iceland (11/2/67), Indonesia (1/21/71), Iran (11/5/29), Ireland (8/29/30), Italy (4/3/28), Ivory Coast (7/27/70), Jamaica (7/28/70), Japan (5/21/70), Kampuchea * (3/21/83), Kenya (7/6/70), Korea (South) (1/4/89), Latvia (6/3/31), Lebanon (4/17/69), Lesotho (3/10/72), Liberia (2/8/28), Lithuania (6/15/33), Luxembourg (9/1/36), Madagascar (8/1/67), Malawi (9/14/70), Malaysia (12/10/70), Maldives (12/27/66), Malta (10/9/70), Mauritius (12/23/70), Mexico (5/28/32), Monaco (1/6/67), Morocco (10/13/70), Nepal (5/9/69), New Zealand (5/24/30), Norway (7/27/32), Panama (12/4/70), Paraguay (10/22/33), Peru (6/5/85), Philippines (6/8/73), Poland (2/4/29), Qatar (10/18/76), Rwanda (5/11/64), Saudi Arabia (1/27/71), Senegal (7/20/77), Sierra Leone (3/20/67), Sri Lanka (1/20/54), St. Lucia (12/5/88), Sudan (12/17/80), Sweden (4/25/30), Switzerland (7/12/32), Tanzania (4/22/63), Thailand (6/6/31), Togo (4/5/71), Tonga (7/19/71), Trinidad and Tobago (11/24/70), Tunisia (7/12/67), Turkey (10/5/29), Uganda (5/24/65), Upper Volta (3/3/71), Uruguay (4/12/77), Venezuela (2/8/28), Yemen (3/17/71)

* The accession by Kampuchea is considered a nullity by Australia, Bulgaria, Cuba, Czechoslovakia, Ethiopia, France, Germany (East), Hungary, Mauritius, Mongolia, Poland, USSR, and Vietnam.

Ratified/accepted/approved with qualification: 37

Australia (5/24/30), Belgium (12/4/28), Bulgaria (3/7/34), Canada (5/6/30), Chile (7/2/35), China (People's Republic) (7/16/53), Czechoslovakia (8/16/38), Estonia (8/28/31), Ethiopia (10/7/35), Fiji (3/21/73), France (2/8/28), India (4/9/30), Iraq (9/8/31), Israel (2/20/69), Korea (North) (1/4/89), Jordan (1/20/77), Kuwait (12/15/71), Libya (12/29/71), Mongolia (12/6/68), Netherlands (10/31/30), New Zealand (5/24/30), Niger (4/5/67), Nigeria (10/15/68), Pakistan (4/15/60), Papua New Guinea (9/2/80), Portugal (7/1/30), Romania (8/23/29), Solomon Islands (6/1/81), South Africa (5/24/30), Spain (8/22/29), Syria (12/17/68), United Kingdom (4/9/30), United States (4/10/75), USSR (4/5/28), Vietnam (12/15/80), Yemen (Democratic) (10/20/86), Yugoslavia (4/12/29)

2.4 Treaty Providing for the Renunciation of War as an Instrument of National Policy

Entry into force: July 24, 1929

Ratified/accepted/approved without qualification: 66

Afghanistan (11/30/28), Albania (2/12/29), Antigua and Barbuda (11/16/88), Australia (3/2/29), Austria (12/31/28), Barbados (11/8/71), Belgium (3/27/29), Brazil (5/10/34), Bulgaria (7/22/29), Canada (3/2/29), Chile (8/12/29), China (5/8/29), Colombia (5/28/31), Costa Rica (10/1/29), Cuba (3/13/29), Czechoslovakia (3/2/29), Denmark (3/23/29), Dominica (7/18/88), Dominican Republic (12/12/28), Ecuador (2/24/32), Egypt (5/9/29), Estonia (4/26/29), Ethiopia (11/28/28), Fiji (5/21/73), Finland (7/24/29), France (4/22/29), Germany (3/2/29), Greece (8/3/29), Guatemala (7/16/29), Haiti (3/10/30), HEJAZ and NEJD (2/24/32), Honduras (8/5/29), Hungary (7/22/29), Iceland (6/10/29), India (3/2/29), Iran (7/25/29), Iraq (3/23/32), Ireland (3/2/29), Italy (3/2/29), Japan (7/24/29), Latvia (7/23/29), Liberia (2/23/29), Lithuania (4/5/29), Luxembourg (8/24/29), Mexico (11/26/29), Netherlands (7/12/29), New Zealand (3/2/29), Nicaragua (5/13/29), Norway (3/26/29), Panama (2/25/29), Paraguay (12/4/29), Peru (7/23/29), Poland (3/25/29), Portugal (3/1/29), Romania (3/21/29), Serbs Croats and Slovenes-Kingdom (2/20/29), South Africa (3/2/29), Spain (3/7/29), Sweden (4/12/29), Switzerland (12/2/29), Thailand (1/16/29), Turkey (7/8/29), United Kingdom (3/2/29), United States (3/2/29), USSR (9/27/28), Venezuela (10/24/29)

2.5 AGREEMENT FOR THE PROSECUTION AND PUNISHMENT OF THE MAJOR WAR CRIMINALS OF THE EUROPEAN AXIS POWERS AND CHARTER OF THE INTERNATIONAL MILITARY TRIBUNAL

Entry into force: August 8, 1945

Ratified/accepted/approved without qualification: 23

Australia (10/5/45), Belgium (10/5/45), Czechoslovakia (9/26/45), Denmark (9/10/45), Ethiopia (10/9/45), France (9/10/45), Greece (9/10/45), Haiti (11/3/45), Honduras (10/17/45), India (12/22/45), Luxembourg (11/1/45), Netherlands (9/25/45), New Zealand (11/19/45), Norway (10/20/45), Panama (10/17/45), Paraguay (11/14/45), Poland (9/25/45), United Kingdom (9/10/45), United States (9/10/45), Uruguay (12/11/45), USSR (9/10/45), Venezuela (11/17/45), Yugoslavia (9/29/45)

2.6 AFFIRMATION OF THE PRINCIPLES OF INTERNATIONAL LAW RECOGNIZED BY THE CHARTER OF NUREMBERG TRIBUNAL

Adopted unanimously

2.7 INTER-AMERICAN TREATY OF RECIPROCAL ASSISTANCE

Entry into force: December 3, 1948

Ratified/accepted/approved without qualification: 19

Argentina (8/21/50), Bahamas (11/24/82), Bolivia (9/26/50), Brazil (3/25/48), Chile (2/9/49), Colombia (2/3/48), Costa Rica (12/3/48), Cuba (12/9/48), Dominican Republic (11/21/47), El Salvador (3/15/48), Haiti (3/25/48), Mexico (11/23/48), Panama (1/12/48), Paraguay (7/28/48), Peru (10/25/50), Trinidad and Tobago (6/12/67), United States (12/30/47), Uruguay (9/28/48), Venezuela (10/4/48)

Ratified/accepted/approved with qualification: 4

Ecuador (11/7/50), Guatemala (4/6/55), Honduras (2/5/48), Nicaragua (11/12/48)

2.8 AMERICAN TREATY ON PACIFIC SETTLEMENT

Entry into force: May 6, 1949

Signed but not ratified: 7

Argentina (4/30/48), Bolivia (4/30/48), Cuba (4/30/48), Ecuador (4/30/48), Guatemala (4/30/48), United States (4/30/48), Venezuela (4/30/48)

Ratified/accepted/approved without qualification: 9

Brazil (11/16/65), Colombia (11/6/68), Costa Rica (5/6/49), Dominican Republic (9/12/50), Haiti (3/28/51), Honduras (2/7/50), Mexico (11/23/48), Panama (4/25/51), Uruguay (9/1/55)

Ratified/accepted/approved with qualifications: 4

Chile (4/15/74), Nicaragua (7/26/50), Paraguay (7/27/67), Peru (5/26/67)

2.9 NORTH ATLANTIC TREATY

Entry into force: August 24, 1949

Ratified/accepted/approved without qualification: 16

Belgium (6/16/49), Canada (5/3/49), Denmark (8/24/49), France (8/24/49), Germany (West) (5/6/55), Greece (2/18/52), Iceland (8/1/49), Italy (8/24/49), Luxembourg (6/27/49), Netherlands (8/12/49), Norway (7/8/49), Portugal (8/24/49), Spain (5/30/82), Turkey (2/18/52), United Kingdom (7/7/49), United States (7/25/49)

2.10 Convention for the Amelioration of the Condition of the Wounded and Sick in Armed Forces in the Field

Entry into force: October 21, 1950

Ratified/accepted/approved without qualification: 129

Afghanistan (9/26/56), Algeria (6/20/60), Antigua and Barbuda (10/6/86), Austria (8/27/53), Bahamas (7/11/75), Bahrain (11/30/71), Bangladesh (4/4/72), Belgium (9/3/52), Belize (6/29/84), Benin (12/14/61), Bolivia (12/10/76), Botswana (3/29/68), Burundi (12/27/71), Cameroon (9/16/63), Cape Verde (6/15/84), Central African Republic (8/1/66), Chad (8/5/70), Chile (11/12/50), Colombia (11/8/61), Comoros (11/21/85), Congo (1/30/67), Costa Rica (10/15/69), Cuba (4/15/54), Cyprus (5/23/62), Denmark (6/27/51), Djibouti (1/26/78), Dominica (9/28/81), Dominican Republic (1/22/58), Ecuador (8/11/54), Egypt (11/10/52), El Salvador (6/17/53), Equatorial Guinea (6/24/86), Ethiopia (10/2/69), Fiji (8/9/71), Finland (2/22/55), France (6/28/51), Gabon (2/20/65), Gambia (10/11/66), Ghana (8/2/58), Greece (6/5/56), Grenada (4/13/81), Guatemala (5/14/52), Guinea (7/11/84), Guyana (7/22/68), Haiti (4/11/57), Honduras (12/31/65), Iceland (8/10/65), India (11/9/50), Indonesia (9/30/58), Iran (2/20/57), Iraq (2/14/56), Ireland (9/27/62), Ivory Coast (12/28/61), Jamaica (7/17/64), Japan (4/21/53), Jordan (5/29/51), Kampuchea (12/8/58), Kenya (9/20/66), Laos (10/29/56), Lebanon (4/10/51), Lesotho (5/20/68), Liberia (3/29/54), Libya (5/22/56), Liechtenstein (9/21/50), Madagascar (7/13/63), Malawi (1/3/68), Malaysia (8/24/62), Mali (5/24/65), Malta (8/22/68), Mauritania (10/27/62), Mauritius (8/18/70), Mexico (10/29/52), Monaco (7/5/50), Mongolia (12/20/58), Morocco (7/26/56), Mozambique (3/14/83), Namibia * (10/18/83), Nepal (2/7/64), Nicaragua (12/17/53), Niger (4/16/64), Nigeria (6/9/61), Norway (8/3/51), Oman (1/31/74), Panama (2/10/56), Papua New Guinea (5/26/76), Paraguay (10/23/61), Peru (2/15/56), Philippines (3/7/51), Qatar (10/15/75), Rwanda (3/21/64), Samoa (8/23/84), San Marino (8/29/53), São Tomé and Príncipe (5/21/76), Saudi Arabia (5/18/63), Senegal (4/23/63), Seychelles (11/8/84), Sierra Leone (5/31/65), Singapore (4/27/73), Solomon Islands (7/6/81), Somalia (7/12/62), South Africa (3/31/52), Sri Lanka (2/28/59), St. Christopher and Nevis (2/14/86), St. Lucia (9/18/81), St. Vincent and the Grenadines (4/1/81), Sudan (9/23/57), Swaziland (6/28/73), Sweden (12/28/53), Switzerland (3/31/50), Syria (11/2/53), Tanzania (12/12/62), Thailand (12/29/54), Togo (1/6/62), Tonga (4/13/78), Trinidad and Tobago (5/17/63), Tunisia (5/4/57), Turkey (2/10/54), Tuvalu (2/19/81), Uganda (5/18/64), United Arab Emirates (5/10/72), Upper Volta (11/7/61), Vanuatu (10/27/82), Vatican City (2/22/51), Venezuela (2/13/56), Vietnam (7/4/76), Yemen (7/16/70), Zaire (2/20/61), Zambia (10/19/66), Zimbabwe (3/7/83)

* The acceptance by Namibia was by the UN Council for Namibia. South Africa does not recognize Namibia's acceptance as having any legal effect.

Ratified/accepted/approved with qualification: 36

Albania (5/27/57), Angola (9/20/84), Argentina (9/18/56), Australia (10/14/58), Barbados (9/10/68), Brazil (6/29/57), Bulgaria (7/22/54), Byelorussian SSR (8/3/54), Canada (5/14/65), China (12/28/56), Czechoslovakia (12/19/50), Germany (East) (11/30/56), Germany (West) (9/3/54), Guinea-Bissau (7/24/86), Hungary (8/3/54), Israel (7/6/51), Italy (12/17/51), Korea (North) (8/27/57), Korea (South) (8/16/66), Kuwait (9/2/67), Luxembourg (7/1/53), Netherlands (8/3/54), New Zealand (5/2/59), Pakistan (6/12/51), Poland (11/26/54), Portugal (3/14/61), Romania (6/1/54), Spain (8/4/52), Suriname (10/13/76), Ukrainian SSR (8/3/54), United Kingdom (9/23/57), United States (8/2/55), Uruguay (3/5/69), USSR (5/10/54), Yemen (Democratic) (5/25/77), Yugoslavia (4/21/50)

2.11 CONVENTION FOR THE AMELIORATION OF THE CONDITION OF WOUNDED, SICK AND SHIPWRECKED MEMBERS OF ARMED FORCES AT SEA

Entry into force: October 21, 1950

Ratified/accepted/approved without qualification: 129

Afghanistan (9/26/56), Algeria (6/20/60), Antigua and Barbuda (10/6/86), Austria (8/27/53), Bahamas (7/11/75), Bahrain (11/30/71), Bangladesh (4/4/72), Belgium (9/3/52), Belize (6/29/84), Benin (12/14/61), Bolivia (12/10/76), Botswana (3/29/68), Burundi (12/27/71), Cameroon (9/16/63), Cape Verde (6/15/84), Central African Republic (8/1/66), Chad (8/5/70), Chile (11/12/50), Colombia (11/8/61), Comoros (11/21/85), Congo (1/30/67), Costa Rica (10/15/69), Cuba (4/15/54), Cyprus (5/23/62), Denmark (6/27/51), Djibouti (3/6/78), Dominica (9/28/81), Dominican Republic (1/22/58), Ecuador (8/11/54), Egypt (11/10/52), El Salvador (6/17/53), Equatorial Guinea (7/24/86), Ethiopia (10/2/69), Fiji (8/9/71), Finland (2/22/55), France (6/28/51), Gabon (2/20/65), Gambia (10/11/66), Ghana (8/2/58), Greece (6/5/56), Grenada (4/13/81), Guatemala (5/14/52), Guinea (7/11/84), Guyana (7/22/68), Haiti (4/11/57), Honduras (12/31/65), Iceland (8/10/65), India (11/9/50), Indonesia (9/30/58), Iran (2/20/57), Iraq (2/14/56), Ireland (9/27/62), Ivory Coast (12/28/61), Jamaica (7/17/64), Japan (4/21/53), Jordan (5/29/51), Kampuchea (12/8/58), Kenya (9/20/66), Laos (10/29/56), Lebanon (4/10/51), Lesotho (5/20/68), Liberia (3/29/54), Libya (5/22/56), Liechtenstein (9/21/50), Madagascar (7/13/63), Malawi (1/3/68), Malaysia (8/24/62), Mali (5/24/65), Malta (8/22/68), Mauritania (10/27/62), Mauritius (8/18/70), Mexico (10/29/52), Monaco (7/5/50), Mongolia (12/20/58), Morocco (7/26/56), Mozambique (3/14/83), Namibia * (10/18/83), Nepal (2/7/64), Nicaragua (12/17/53), Niger (4/16/64), Nigeria (6/9/61), Norway (8/3/51), Oman (1/31/74), Panama (2/10/56), Papua New Guinea (5/26/76), Paraguay (10/23/61), Peru (2/15/56), Philippines (10/6/52), Qatar (10/15/75), Rwanda (3/21/64), Samoa (8/23/84), San Marino (8/29/53), São Tomé and Príncipe (5/21/76), Saudi Arabia (5/18/63), Senegal (4/23/63), Seychelles (11/8/84), Sierra Leone (5/31/65), Singapore (4/27/73), Solomon Islands (7/6/81), Somalia (7/12/62), South Africa (3/31/52), Sri Lanka (2/28/59), St. Christopher and Nevis (2/14/86), St. Lucia (9/18/81), St. Vincent and the Grenadines (4/1/81), Sudan (9/23/57), Swaziland (6/28/73), Sweden (12/28/53), Switzerland (3/31/50), Syria (11/2/53), Tanzania (12/12/62), Thailand (12/29/54), Togo (1/6/62), Tonga (4/13/78), Trinidad and Tobago (9/24/63), Tunisia (5/4/57), Turkey (2/10/54), Tuvalu (2/19/81), Uganda (5/18/64), United Arab Emirates (5/10/72), Upper Volta (11/7/61), Vanuatu (10/27/82), Vatican City (2/22/51), Venezuela (2/13/56), Vietnam (7/4/76), Yemen (7/16/70), Zaire (2/20/61), Zambia (10/19/66), Zimbabwe (3/7/83)

* The acceptance by Namibia was by the UN Council for Namibia. South Africa does not recognize Namibia's acceptance as having any legal effect.

Ratified/accepted/approved with qualification: 37

Albania (5/27/57), Angola (9/20/84), Argentina (9/18/56), Australia (10/14/58), Barbados (9/10/68), Brazil (6/29/57), Bulgaria (7/22/54), Byelorussian SSR (8/3/54), Canada (5/14/65), China (12/28/56), Czechoslovakia (12/19/50), Germany (East) (11/30/56), Germany (West) (9/3/54), Guinea-Bissau (2/21/74), Hungary (8/3/54), Israel (7/6/51), Italy (12/17/51), Korea (North) (8/27/57), Korea (South) (8/16/66), Kuwait (9/2/67), Luxembourg (7/1/53), Netherlands (8/3/54), New Zealand (5/2/59), Pakistan (6/12/51), Poland (11/26/54), Portugal (3/14/61), Romania (6/1/54), Spain (8/4/52), Suriname (10/13/76), Ukrainian SSR (8/3/54), United Kingdom (9/23/57), United States (8/2/55), Uruguay (3/5/69), USSR (5/10/54), Vietnam (7/4/76), Yemen (Democratic) (5/25/77), Yugoslavia (4/21/50)

2.12 Convention Relative to the Treatment of Prisoners of War

Entry into force: October 21, 1950

Ratified/accepted/approved without qualification: 129

Afghanistan (9/26/56), Algeria (6/20/60), Antigua and Barbuda (10/6/86), Austria (8/27/53), Bahamas (7/11/75), Bahrain (11/30/71), Bangladesh (4/4/72), Belgium (9/3/52), Belize (6/29/84), Benin (12/14/61), Bolivia (12/10/76), Botswana (3/29/68), Burundi (12/27/71), Cameroon (9/16/63), Cape Verde (6/15/84), Central African Republic (8/1/66), Chad (8/5/70), Chile (11/12/50), Colombia (11/8/61), Comoros (11/21/85), Congo (1/30/67), Costa Rica (10/15/69), Cuba (4/15/54), Cyprus (5/23/62), Denmark (6/27/51), Djibouti (3/6/78), Dominica (9/28/81), Dominican Republic (1/22/58), Ecuador (8/11/54), Egypt (11/10/52), El Salvador (6/17/53), Equatorial Guinea (6/24/86), Ethiopia (10/2/69), Fiji (8/9/71), Finland (2/22/55), France (6/28/51), Gabon (2/20/65), Gambia (10/11/66), Ghana (8/2/58), Greece (6/5/56), Grenada (4/13/81), Guatemala (5/14/52), Guinea (7/11/84), Guyana (7/22/68), Haiti (4/11/57), Honduras (12/31/65), Iceland (8/10/65), India (11/9/50), Indonesia (9/30/58), Iran (2/20/57), Iraq (2/14/56), Ireland (9/27/62), Ivory Coast (12/28/61), Jamaica (7/17/64), Japan (4/21/53), Jordan (5/29/51), Kampuchea (12/8/58), Kenya (9/20/66), Laos (10/29/56), Lebanon (4/10/51), Lesotho (5/20/68), Liberia (3/29/54), Libya (5/22/56), Liechtenstein (9/21/50), Madagascar (7/13/63), Malawi (1/3/68), Malaysia (8/24/62), Mali (5/24/65), Malta (8/22/68), Mauritania (10/27/62), Mauritius (8/18/70), Mexico (10/29/52), Monaco (7/5/50), Mongolia (12/20/58), Morocco (7/26/56), Mozambique (3/14/83), Namibia * (10/18/83), Nepal (2/7/64), Nicaragua (12/17/53), Niger (4/16/64), Nigeria (6/9/61), Norway (8/3/51), Oman (1/31/74), Panama (2/10/56), Papua New Guinea (5/26/76), Paraguay (10/23/61), Peru (2/15/56), Philippines (10/6/52), Qatar (10/15/75), Rwanda (3/21/64), Samoa (8/23/84), San Marino (8/29/53), São Tomé and Príncipe (5/21/76), Saudi Arabia (5/18/63), Senegal (4/23/63), Seychelles (11/8/84), Sierra Leone (5/31/65), Singapore (4/27/73), Solomon Islands (7/6/81), Somalia (7/12/62), South Africa (3/31/52), Sri Lanka (2/28/59), St. Christopher and Nevis (2/14/86), St. Lucia (9/18/81), St. Vincent and the Grenadines (4/1/81), Sudan (9/23/57), Swaziland (6/28/73), Sweden (12/28/53), Switzerland (3/31/50), Syria (11/2/53), Tanzania (12/12/62), Thailand (12/29/54), Togo (1/6/62), Tonga (4/13/78), Trinidad and Tobago (9/24/63), Tunisia (5/4/57), Turkey (2/10/54), Tuvalu (2/19/81), Uganda (5/18/64), United Arab Emirates (5/10/72), Upper Volta (11/7/61), Vanuatu (10/27/82), Vatican City (2/22/51), Venezuela (2/13/56), Vietnam (7/4/76), Yemen (7/16/70), Zaire (2/20/61), Zambia (10/19/66), Zimbabwe (3/7/83)

* The acceptance by Namibia was by the UN Council for Namibia. South Africa does not recognize Namibia's acceptance as having any legal effect.

Ratified/accepted/approved with qualification: 37

Albania (5/27/57), Angola (9/20/84), Argentina (9/18/56), Australia (10/14/58), Barbados (9/10/68), Brazil (6/29/57), Bulgaria (7/22/54), Byelorussian SSR (8/3/54), Canada (5/14/65), China (12/28/56), Czechoslovakia (12/19/50), Germany (East) (11/30/56), Germany (West) (9/3/54), Guinea-Bissau (2/21/74), Hungary (8/3/54), Israel (7/6/51), Italy (12/17/51), Korea (North) (8/27/57), Korea (South) (8/16/66), Kuwait (9/2/67), Luxembourg (7/1/53), Netherlands (8/3/54), New Zealand (5/2/59), Pakistan (6/12/51), Poland (11/26/54), Portugal (3/14/61), Romania (6/1/54), Spain (8/4/52), Suriname (10/13/76), Ukrainian SSR (8/3/54), United Kingdom (9/23/57), United States (8/2/55), Uruguay (3/5/69), USSR (5/10/54), Vietnam (7/4/76), Yemen (Democratic) (5/25/77), Yugoslavia (4/21/50)

2.13 Convention Relative to the Protection of Civilian Persons in Time of War

Entry into force: October 21, 1950

Ratified/accepted/approved without qualification: 129

Afghanistan (9/26/56), Algeria (6/20/60), Antigua and Barbuda (10/6/86), Austria (8/27/53), Bahamas (7/11/75), Bahrain (11/30/71), Bangladesh (4/4/72), Belgium (9/3/52), Belize (6/29/84), Benin (12/14/61), Bolivia (12/10/76), Botswana (3/29/68), Burundi (12/27/71), Cameroon (9/16/63), Cape Verde (6/15/84), Central African Republic (8/1/66), Chad (8/5/70), Chile (11/12/50), Colombia (11/8/61), Comoros (11/21/85), Congo (1/30/67), Costa Rica (10/15/69), Cuba (4/15/54), Cyprus (5/23/62), Denmark (6/27/51), Djibouti (3/6/78), Dominica (9/28/81), Dominican Republic (1/22/58), Ecuador (8/11/54), Egypt (11/10/52), El Salvador (6/17/53), Equatorial Guinea (6/24/86), Ethiopia (10/2/69), Fiji (8/9/71), Finland (2/22/55), France (6/28/51), Gabon (2/20/65), Gambia (10/11/66), Ghana (8/2/58), Greece (6/5/56), Grenada (4/13/81), Guatemala (5/14/52), Guinea (7/11/84), Guyana (7/22/68), Haiti (4/11/57), Honduras (12/31/65), Iceland (8/10/65), India (11/9/50), Indonesia (9/30/58), Iran (2/20/57), Iraq (2/14/56), Ireland (9/27/62), Ivory Coast (12/28/61), Jamaica (7/17/64), Japan (4/21/53), Jordan (5/29/51), Kampuchea (12/8/58), Kenya (9/20/66), Laos (10/29/56), Lebanon (4/10/51), Lesotho (5/20/68), Liberia (3/29/54), Libya (5/22/56), Liechtenstein (9/21/50), Madagascar (7/13/63), Malawi (1/3/68), Malaysia (8/24/62), Mali (5/24/65), Malta (8/22/68), Mauritania (10/27/62), Mauritius (8/18/70), Mexico (10/29/52), Monaco (7/5/50), Mongolia (12/20/58), Morocco (7/26/56), Mozambique (3/14/83), Namibia * (10/18/83), Nepal (2/7/64), Nicaragua (12/17/53), Niger (4/16/64), Nigeria (6/9/61), Norway (8/3/51), Oman (1/31/74), Panama (2/10/56), Papua New Guinea (5/26/76), Paraguay (10/23/61), Peru (2/15/56), Philippines (10/6/52), Qatar (10/15/75), Rwanda (3/21/64), Samoa (8/23/84), San Marino (8/29/53), São Tomé and Príncipe (5/21/76), Saudi Arabia (5/18/63), Senegal (4/23/63), Seychelles (11/8/84), Sierra Leone (5/31/65), Singapore (4/27/73), Solomon Islands (7/6/81), Somalia (7/12/62), South Africa (3/31/52), Sri Lanka (2/23/59), St. Christopher and Nevis (2/14/86), St. Lucia (9/18/81), St. Vincent and the Grenadines (4/1/81), Sudan (9/23/57), Swaziland (6/28/73), Sweden (12/28/53), Switzerland (3/31/50), Syria (11/2/53), Tanzania (12/12/62), Thailand (12/29/54), Togo (1/6/62), Tonga (4/13/78), Trinidad and Tobago (9/24/63), Tunisia (5/4/57), Turkey (2/10/54), Tuvalu (2/19/81), Uganda (5/18/64), United Arab Emirates (5/10/72), Upper Volta (11/7/61), Vanuatu (10/27/82), Vatican City (2/22/51), Venezuela (2/13/56), Vietnam (7/4/76), Yemen (7/16/70), Zaire (2/20/61), Zambia (10/19/66), Zimbabwe (3/7/83)

* The acceptance by Namibia was by the UN Council for Namibia. South Africa does not recognize Namibia's acceptance as having any legal effect.

Ratified/accepted/approved with qualification: 36

Albania (5/27/57), Angola (9/20/84), Argentina (9/18/56), Australia (10/14/58), Barbados (9/10/68), Brazil (6/29/57), Bulgaria (7/22/54), Byelorussian SSR (8/3/54), Canada (5/14/65), China (12/28/56), Czechoslovakia (12/19/50), Germany (East) (11/30/56), Germany (West) (9/3/54), Guinea-Bissau (2/21/74), Hungary (8/3/54), Israel (7/6/51), Italy (12/17/51), Korea (North) (8/27/57), Korea (South) (8/16/66), Kuwait (9/2/67), Luxembourg (7/1/53), Netherlands (8/3/54), New Zealand (5/2/59), Pakistan (6/12/51), Poland (11/26/54), Portugal (3/14/61), Romania (6/1/54), Spain (8/4/52), Suriname (10/13/76), Ukrainian SSR (8/3/54), United Kingdom (9/23/57), United States (8/2/55), Uruguay (3/5/69), USSR (5/10/54), Yemen (Democratic) (5/25/77), Yugoslavia (4/21/50)

2.14 Uniting for Peace Resolution

For: 52

Afghanistan, Australia, Belgium, Bolivia, Brazil, Burma, Canada, Chile, China, Colombia, Costa Rica, Cuba, Denmark, Dominican Republic, Ecuador, Egypt, El Salvador, Ethiopia, France, Greece, Guatemala, Haiti, Honduras, Iceland, Indonesia, Iran, Iraq, Israel, Liberia, Luxembourg, Mexico, Netherlands, New Zealand, Nicaragua, Norway, Pakistan, Panama, Paraguay, Peru, Philippines, Saudi Arabia, South Africa, Sweden, Syria, Thailand, Turkey, United Kingdom, United States, Uruguay, Venezuela, Yemen, Yugoslavia

Against: 5

Byelorussian SSR, Czechoslovakia, Poland, Ukrainian SSR, USSR

Abstaining: 2

Argentina, India

2.15 Draft Code of Crimes Against the Peace and Security of Mankind

Not yet in force

2.16 Treaty of Friendship, Cooperation and Mutual Assistance

Entry into force: June 4, 1955

Ratified/accepted/approved without qualification: 7

Bulgaria (5/28/55), Czechoslovakia (5/26/55), Germany (East) (5/21/55), Hungary (5/25/55), Poland (5/19/55), Romania (5/30/55), USSR (5/25/55)

2.17 Declaration on the Prohibition of the Use of Nuclear and Thermo-Nuclear Weapons

For: 55

Afghanistan, Albania, Bulgaria, Burma, Byelorussian SSR, Cambodia, Cameroon, Central African Republic, Ceylon, Chad, Congo (Brazzaville), Congo (Leopoldville), Cuba, Cyprus, Czechoslovakia, Dahomey, Ethiopia, Gabon, Ghana, Guinea, Hungary, India, Indonesia, Iraq, Ivory Coast, Japan, Jordan, Lebanon, Liberia, Libya, Madagascar, Mali, Mauritania, Mexico, Mongolia, Morocco, Nepal, Niger, Nigeria, Poland, Romania, Saudi Arabia, Senegal, Sierra Leone, Somalia, Sudan, Syria, Togo, Tunisia, Ukrainian SSR, United Arab Republic, Upper Volta, USSR, Yemen, Yugoslavia

Against: 20

Australia, Belguim, Canada, China, Costa Rica, France, Greece, Guatemala, Ireland, Italy, Luxembourg, Netherlands, New Zealand, Nicaragua, Portugal, South Africa, Spain, Turkey, United Kingdom, United States

Abstaining: 26

Argentina, Austria, Bolivia, Brazil, Chile, Colombia, Denmark, Ecuador, El Salvador, Finland, Haiti, Honduras, Iceland, Iran, Israel, Malaysia, Norway Pakistan, Panama, Paraguay, Peru, Philippines, Sweden, Thailand, Uruguay, Venezuela

2.18 Treaty Banning Nuclear Weapons Tests in the Atmosphere, in Outer Space and Under Water

Entry into force: October 10, 1963

Ratified/accepted/approved without qualification: 116

Afghanistan (3/12/64), Antigua and Barbuda (11/16/88), Argentina (11/14/86), Australia (11/12/63), Austria (7/17/64), Bahamas (7/16/76), Bangladesh

(3/11/85), Belgium (3/1/6), Benin (12/15/64), Bhutan (6/8/78), Bolivia (8/4/65), Botswana (1/5/68), Brazil (12/15/64), Bulgaria (11/13/63), Burma (11/15/63), Byelorussian SSR (12/16/63), Canada (1/28/64), Cape Verde (10/24/79), Central African Republic (12/22/64), Chad (3/1/65), Chile (10/6/65), Colombia (10/17/85), Costa Rica (7/10/67), Cyprus (4/15/65), Czechoslovakia (10/14/63), Denmark (1/15/64), Dominican Republic (6/3/64), Ecuador (5/6/64), Egypt (1/10/64), El Salvador (12/3/64), Fiji (7/14/72), Finland (1/9/64), Gabon (3/4/64), Gambia (4/27/65), Germany (East) (12/30/63), Germany (West) (12/1/64), Ghana (11/27/63), Greece (12/18/63), Guatemala (1/6/64), Guinea-Bissau (8/20/76), Honduras (10/2/64), Hungary (10/21/63), Iceland (4/29/64), India (10/10/63), Indonesia (1/20/64), Iran (5/5/64), Iraq (11/30/64), Ireland (12/18/63), Israel (1/15/64), Italy (12/10/64), Ivory Coast (2/5/65), Japan (6/15/64), Jordan (5/29/64), Kenya (6/10/65), Korea (South) (7/24/64), Kuwait (5/20/65), Laos (2/10/65), Lebanon (5/14/65), Liberia (5/19/64), Libya (7/15/68), Luxembourg (2/10/65), Madagascar (3/15/65), Malawi (11/26/64), Malaysia (7/15/64), Malta (11/25/64), Mauritania (4/6/64), Mauritius (4/30/69), Mexico (12/27/63), Mongolia (11/1/63), Morocco (2/1/66), Nepal (10/7/64), Netherlands (9/14/64), New Zealand (10/10/63), Nicaragua (1/26/65), Niger (7/3/64), Nigeria (2/17/67), Norway (11/21/63), Panama (2/24/66), Papua New Guinea (10/27/80), Peru (7/20/64), Philippines (11/10/65), Poland (10/14/63), Romania (12/12/63), Rwanda (10/22/63), Samoa (1/15/65), San Marino (7/3/64), Senegal (5/6/64), Seychelles (3/12/85), Sierra Leone (2/21/64), Singapore (7/12/68), South Africa (10/10/63), Spain (12/17/64), Sri Lanka (2/5/64), Sudan (3/4/66), Swaziland (5/29/69), Sweden (12/9/63), Switzerland (1/16/64), Syria (6/1/64), Tanzania (2/6/64), Thailand (11/15/63), Togo (12/7/64), Tonga (6/22/71), Trinidad and Tobago (8/6/64), Tunisia (5/26/65), Turkey (7/8/65), Uganda (3/24/64), Ukrainian SSR (12/30/63), United Kingdom (10/10/63), United States (10/10/63), Uruguay (2/25/69), USSR (10/10/63), Venezuela (2/22/65), Yemen (Democratic) (6/1/79), Yugoslavia (1/15/64), Zaire (10/28/65), Zambia (1/11/65)

2.19 Resolution Regarding Weapons of Mass Destruction in Outer Space

Adopted by acclamation, without recorded vote

2.20 Declaration on the Inadmissibility of Intervention in the Domestic Affairs of the States and the Protection of Their Independence and Sovereignty

For: 109

Afghanistan, Algeria, Argentina, Australia, Austria, Belgium, Bolivia, Brazil, Bulgaria, Burma, Burundi, Byelorussian SSR, Cameroon, Canada, Central African Republic, Ceylon, Chad, Chile, China, Colombia, Congo (Brazzaville), Congo (Democratic Republic of), Costa Rica, Cuba, Cyprus, Czechoslovakia, Dahomey, Denmark, Dominican Republic, Ecuador, El Salvador, Ethiopia, Finland, France, Gabon, Ghana, Greece, Guatemala, Guinea, Haiti, Hungary, Iceland, India, Iran, Iraq, Ireland, Israel, Italy, Ivory Coast, Jamaica, Japan, Jordan, Kenya, Kuwait, Laos, Lebanon, Liberia, Libya, Luxembourg, Madagascar, Malawi, Malaysia, Maldive Islands, Mali, Mauritania, Mexico, Mongolia, Morocco, Nepal, Netherlands, New Zealand, Nicaragua, Niger, Nigeria, Norway, Pakistan, Panama, Paraguay, Peru, Philippines, Poland, Romania, Rwanda, Saudi Arabia, Senegal, Sierra Leone, Singapore, Somalia, Spain, Sudan, Sweden, Syria, Tanzania, Thailand, Togo, Trinidad and Tobago, Tunisia, Turkey, Uganda, Ukrainian SSR, United Arab Republic, United States, Upper Volta, Uruguay, USSR, Venezuela, Yemen, Yugoslavia, Zambia

Abstaining: 1

United Kingdom

2.21 TREATY FOR THE PROHIBITION OF NUCLEAR WEAPONS IN LATIN AMERICA

Entry into force: April 22, 1968

Signed but not ratified: 1

Argentina (9/27/67)

Ratified/accepted/approved without qualification: 25

Antigua and Barbuda (10/11/83), Bahamas (4/26/77), Barbados (4/25/69), Bolivia (2/18/69), Brazil (1/29/68), Chile (10/9/74), Colombia (8/4/72), Costa Rica (8/25/69), Dominican Republic (6/14/68), Ecuador (2/11/69), El Salvador (4/22/68), Grenada (6/20/75), Guatemala (2/6/70), Haiti (5/23/69), Honduras (9/23/68), Jamaica (6/26/69), Mexico (9/20/67), Nicaragua (10/24/68), Panama (6/11/71), Paraguay (3/19/69), Peru (3/4/69), Suriname (6/10/77), Trinidad and Tobago (12/3/70), Uruguay (8/20/68), Venezuela (3/23/70)

2.22 TREATY ON THE NON-PROLIFERATION OF NUCLEAR WEAPONS

Entry into force: March 5, 1970

Signed but not ratified: 1

Kuwait (8/15/68)

Ratified/accepted/approved without qualification: 137

Afghanistan (2/4/70), Antigua and Baruda (6/17/85), Australia (1/23/73), Austria (6/27/69), Bahamas (8/11/76), Bangladesh (8/31/79), Barbados (2/21/80), Belgium (5/2/75), Belize (8/9/85), Benin (10/31/72), Bhutan (5/23/85), Bolivia (5/26/70), Botswana (4/28/69), Brunei (3/26/85), Bulgaria (11/3/69), Burundi (3/19/71), Cameroon (1/8/69), Canada (1/8/69), Cape Verde (10/24/79), Central African Empire (10/25/70), Chad (3/10/71), Colombia (4/8/86), Congo (10/23/78), Costa Rica (3/3/70), Cyprus (2/10/70), Czechoslovakia (7/22/69), Denmark (1/3/69), Dominica (8/10/84), Dominican Republic (7/24/71), Ecuador (3/7/69), Egypt (2/26/81), El Salvador, (7/11/72), Equatorial Guinea (11/1/84), Ethiopia (2/5/70), Fiji (7/14/72), Finland (2/5/69), Gabon (2/19/74), Gambia (5/12/75), Germany (East) (10/31/69), Germany (West) (5/2/75), Ghana (5/4/70), Greece (3/11/70), Grenada (9/2/75), Guatemala (9/22/70), Guinea (4/29/85), Guinea-Bissau (8/20/76), Haiti (6/2/70), Holy See (2/25/71), Honduras (5/16/73), Hungary (5/27/69), Iceland (7/18/69), Indonesia (7/12/69), Iran (2/2/70), Iraq (10/29/69), Ireland (7/1/68), Italy (5/2/75), Ivory Coast (3/6/73), Jamaica (3/5/70), Japan (6/8/76), Jordan (2/11/70), Kampuchea (6/2/72), Kenya (6/11/70), Kiribati (4/18/85), Korea (North) (12/12/85), Korea (South) (4/23/75), Laos (2/20/70), Lebanon (7/15/70), Lesotho (5/20/70), Liberia (3/5/70), Libya (5/26/75), Liechtenstein (4/20/78), Luxembourg (5/2/75), Madagascar (10/8/70), Malawi (2/18/86), Malaysia (3/5/70), Maldive Islands (4/7/70), Mali (2/10/70), Malta (2/6/70), Mauritius (4/8/69), Mexico (1/21/69), Mongolia (5/14/69), Morocco (11/27/70), Nauru (6/7/82), Nepal (1/5/70), Netherlands (5/2/75), New Zealand (9/10/69), Nicaragua (3/6/73), Nigeria (9/27/68), Norway (2/5/69), Panama (1/13/77), Papua New Guinea (1/13/82), Paraguay (2/4/70), Peru (3/3/70), Philippines (10/5/72), Poland (6/12/69), Portugal (12/15/77), Romania (2/4/70), Rwanda (5/20/75), Samoa (3/17/75), San Marino (8/10/70), São Tomé and Príncipe (7/20/83), Saudi Arabia (10/3/88), Senegal (12/17/70), Seychelles (3/12/85), Sierra Leone (2/26/75), Singapore (3/10/76), Solomon Islands (6/17/81), Somalia (3/5/70), Spain (11/5/87), Sri Lanka (3/5/79), St. Lucia (12/28/79), St. Vincent and the Grenadines (11/6/84), Sudan (10/31/73), Suriname (6/30/76), Swaziland (12/11/69), Sweden (1/9/70), Switzerland (3/9/77), Syria

(9/24/69), Thailand (12/7/72), Togo (2/26/70), Tonga (7/14/71), Trinidad and Tobago (10/30/86), Tunisia (2/26/70), Turkey (4/17/80), Tuvalu (1/19/79), Uganda (10/20/82), United Kingdom (11/27/68), United States (3/5/70), Upper Volta (3/3/70), Uruguay (8/31/70), USSR (3/5/70), Venezuela (9/25/75), Vietnam (6/14/72), Yemen (5/14/86), Yemen (Democratic) (5/14/86), Yugoslavia (3/5/70), Zaire (8/4/70)

Ratified/accepted/approved with qualification: 1

Bahrain (11/3/88)

2.23 Treaty on the Prohibition of the Emplacement of Nuclear Weapons and Other Weapons of Mass Destruction on the Seabed and the Ocean Floor and in the Subsoil Thereof

Entry into force: May 18, 1972

Signed but not ratified: 22

Bolivia (2/11/71), Burma (2/11/71), Burundi (2/11/71), Cameroon (11/11/71), Colombia (2/11/71), Costa Rica (2/11/71), Equatorial Guinea (6/4/71), Gambia (5/18/71), Guatemala (2/11/71), Guinea (2/11/71), Honduras (2/11/71), Kampuchea (2/11/71), Lebanon (2/11/71), Liberia (2/11/71), Madagascar (9/14/71), Mali (2/11/71), Paraguay (2/23/71), Senegal (3/17/71), Sudan (2/11/71), Tanzania (2/11/71), Uruguay (2/11/71), Yemen (2/23/71)

Ratified/accepted/approved without qualification: 72

Afghanistan (4/22/71), Antigua and Barbuda (11/16/88), Australia (1/23/73), Austria (8/10/72), Belgium (11/20/72), Benin (7/2/86), Botswana (11/10/72), Bulgaria (4/16/71), Byelorussian SSR (9/14/71), Cape Verde (10/24/79), Central African Republic (7/9/81), Congo (10/23/78), Cuba (6/3/77), Cyprus (11/17/71), Czechoslovakia (1/11/72), Denmark (6/15/71), Dominican Republic (2/11/72), Ethiopia (7/12/77), Finland (6/8/71), Germany (East) (7/27/71), Ghana (8/9/72), Greece (5/28/85), Guinea-Bissau (8/20/76), Hungary (8/13/71), Iceland (5/30/72), Iran (8/26/71), Iraq (9/13/72), Ireland (8/19/71), Ivory Coast (1/14/72), Jamaica (7/30/86), Japan (6/21/71), Jordan (8/17/71), Korea (South) (6/25/87), Laos (10/19/71), Lesotho (4/3/73), Luxembourg (11/11/82), Malaysia (6/21/72), Malta (5/4/71), Mauritius (4/23/71), Mongolia (10/8/71), Morocco (7/26/71), Nepal (7/6/71), Netherlands (1/14/76), New Zealand (2/24/72), Nicaragua (2/7/73), Niger (8/9/71), Norway (6/28/71), Panama (3/20/74), Poland (11/15/71), Portugal (6/24/75), Qatar (11/12/74), Rwanda (5/20/75), São Tomé and Príncipe (8/24/79), Saudi Arabia (6/23/72), Seychelles (3/12/85), Singapore (9/10/76), Solomon Islands (6/17/81), South Africa (11/14/73), Spain (7/15/87), Swaziland (8/9/71), Sweden (4/28/72), Switzerland (5/4/76), Togo (6/28/71), Tunisia (10/22/71), Turkey (10/19/72), Ukrainian SSR (9/3/71), United Kingdom (5/18/72), United States (5/18/72), USSR (5/18/72), Vietnam (6/20/80), Yemen (Democratic) (7/1/79), Zambia (10/9/72)

Ratified/accepted/approved with qualification: 9

Argentina (3/21/83), Brazil (5/10/88), Canada (5/17/72), Germany (West) (11/18/75), India (7/20/73), Italy (9/3/74), Mexico (3/23/84), Romania (7/10/72), Yugoslavia (10/25/73)

2.24 Agreement on Measures to Reduce the Risk of Outbreak of Nuclear War Between the United States of America and the Union of Soviet Socialist Republics

Entry into force: September 30, 1971

2.25 Agreement Between the United States of America and the Union of the Soviet Socialist Republics on Measures to Improve the USA-USSR Direct Communications Link

Entry into force: September 30, 1971

2.26 Convention on the Prohibition of the Development, Production and Stockpiling of Bacteriological (Biological) and Toxin Weapons and on Their Destruction

Entry into force: March 26, 1975

Signed but not ratified: 25

Botswana (4/10/72), Burma (4/10/72), Burundi (4/10/72), Central African Republic (4/10/72), Egypt (4/10/72), El Salvador (4/10/72), Gabon (4/10/72), Gambia (6/2/72), Guyana (1/3/73), Haiti (4/10/72), Indonesia (6/20/72), Iraq (5/11/72), Ivory Coast (5/23/72), Liberia (4/10/72), Madagascar (10/13/72), Malawi (4/10/72), Malaysia (4/10/72), Mali (4/10/72), Morocco (5/2/72), Nepal (4/10/72), Somalia (7/3/72), Syria (4/14/72), Tanzania (8/16/72), United Arab Emirates (9/28/72), Yemen (Democratic) (4/10/72)

Ratified/accepted/approved without qualification: 101

Afghanistan (3/26/75), Argentina (11/27/79), Australia (10/5/77), Bahamas (11/26/86), Bangladesh (3/11/85), Barbados (2/16/73), Belgium (3/15/79), Belize (10/20/86), Benin (4/25/75), Bhutan (6/8/78), Bolivia (10/30/75), Brazil (2/27/73), Bulgaria (8/2/72), Byelorussian SSR (3/26/75), Canada (9/18/72), Cape Verde (10/20/77), Chile (4/22/80), Colombia (12/19/83), Congo (10/23/78), Costa Rica (12/17/73), Cuba (4/21/76), Cyprus (11/6/73), Czechoslovakia (4/30/73), Denmark (3/1/73), Dominican Republic (2/23/73), Ecuador (3/12/75), Ethiopia (5/26/75), Fiji (9/4/73), Finland (2/4/74), France (9/17/84), Germany (East) (11/28/72), Germany (West) (4/7/83), Ghana (6/6/75), Greece (12/10/75), Grenada (10/22/86), Guatemala (9/19/73), Guinea-Bissau (8/20/76), Honduras (5/14/79), Hungary (12/27/79), Iceland (2/15/73), Iran (8/22/73), Italy (5/30/75), Jamaica (8/13/75), Japan (6/18/82), Jordan (5/30/75), Kampuchea (3/9/83), Kenya (1/7/76), Korea (North) (3/13/87), Korea (South) (6/25/87), Laos (3/20/73), Lebanon (3/26/75), Lesotho (9/6/77), Luxembourg (3/23/76), Libya (1/19/82), Malta (4/7/75), Mauritius (8/7/72), Mongolia (9/5/72), Netherlands (6/22/81), New Zealand (12/13/72), Nicaragua (8/7/75), Niger (6/23/72), Nigeria (7/3/73), Norway (8/1/73), Pakistan (9/25/74), Panama (3/20/74), Papua New Guinea (10/27/80), Paraguay (6/9/76), Peru (6/5/85), Philippines (5/21/73), Poland (1/25/73), Portugal (3/15/75), Qatar (4/17/75), Romania (7/25/79), Rwanda (5/20/75), San Marino (3/11/75), São Tomé and Príncipe (8/24/79), Saudi Arabia (5/24/72), Senegal (3/26/75), Seychelles (10/11/79), Sierra Leone (6/29/76), Singapore (12/2/75), Solomon Islands (6/17/81), South Africa (11/3/75), Spain (6/20/79), Sri Lanka (11/18/86), St. Lucia (11/26/86), Sweden (2/5/76), Thailand (5/28/75), Togo (11/10/76), Tonga (9/28/76), Tunisia (5/18/73), Turkey (10/25/74), United Kingdom (3/26/75), United States (3/26/75), Uruguay (4/6/81), USSR (3/26/75), Venezuela (10/18/78), Vietnam (6/20/80), Yemen (Democratic) (6/1/79), Yugoslavia (10/25/73), Zaire (9/16/75)

Ratified/accepted/approved with qualification: 8

Austria (8/10/73), China (11/15/84), India (7/15/74), Ireland (10/27/72), Kuwait (7/18/72), Mexico (4/8/74), Switzerland (5/4/76), Ukrainian SSR (3/26/75)

2.27 TREATY BETWEEN THE UNITED STATES OF AMERICA AND THE UNION OF SOVIET SOCIALIST REPUBLICS ON THE LIMITATION OF ANTI-BALLISTIC MISSILE SYSTEMS

Entry into force: October 3, 1972

2.28 INTERIM AGREEMENT BETWEEN THE UNITED STATES OF AMERICA AND THE UNION OF SOVIET SOCIALIST REPUBLICS OF CERTAIN MEASURES WITH RESPECT TO THE LIMITATION OF STRATEGIC OFFENSIVE ARMS

Entry into force: October 3, 1972

2.29 RESOLUTION ON THE NON-USE OF FORCE IN INTERNATIONAL RELATIONS AND PERMANENT PROHIBITION OF THE USE OF NUCLEAR WEAPONS

For: 72

Afghanistan, Algeria, Bahrain, Barbados, Bhutan, Bulgaria, Burma, Byelorussian SSR, Cameroon, Chad, Chile, Congo, Cuba, Cyprus, Czechoslovakia, Egypt, Ethiopia, Fiji, Finland, Gabon, Ghana, Guinea, Guyana, Hungary, India, Indonesia, Iran, Iraq, Jamaica, Jordan, Kenya, Khmer Republic, Kuwait, Laos, Lebanon, Lesotho, Libya, Madagascar, Malaysia, Maldive Islands, Mali, Malta, Mauritania, Mauritius, Mongolia, Nepal, Niger, Nigeria, Oman, Panama, Philippines, Poland, Qatar, Romania, Rwanda, Saudi Arabia, Senegal, Sierra Leone, Singapore, Sri Lanka, Sudan, Syria, Tanzania, Trinidad and Tobago, Uganda, Ukrainian SSR, United Arab Emirates, Upper Volta, USSR, Yemen, Yemen (Democratic), Yugoslavia, Zambia

Against: 4

Albania, China, Portugal, South Africa

Abstaining: 41

Argentina, Australia, Austria, Belgium, Bolivia, Botswana, Brazil, Burundi, Canada, Central African Republic, Colombia, Costa Rica, Denmark, Dominican Republic, El Salvador, France, Greece, Guatemala, Honduras, Iceland, Ireland, Israel, Italy, Ivory Coast, Japan, Luxembourg, Malawi, Pakistan, Paraguay, Peru, Spain, Sweden, Thailand, Togo, Tunisia, Turkey, United Kingdom, United States, Uruguay, Venezuela, Zaire

2.30 WAR POWERS RESOLUTION

2.31 RESOLUTION ON THE DEFINITION OF AGGRESSION

Adopted without recorded vote

2.32 CONVENTION ON THE PROHIBITION OF MILITARY OR ANY OTHER HOSTILE USE OF ENVIRONMENTAL MODIFICATION TECHNIQUES

Entry into force: October 5, 1978

Signed but not ratified: 17

Bolivia (5/18/77), Ethiopia (5/18/77), Holy See (5/27/77), Iceland (5/18/77), Iran (5/18/77), Iraq (8/15/77), Lebanon (5/18/77), Liberia (5/18/77), Luxembourg (5/18/77), Morocco (5/18/77), Nicaragua (8/11/77), Portugal (5/18/77), Sierra Leone (4/12/78), Syria (8/4/77), Turkey (5/18/77), Uganda (5/18/77), Zaire (2/28/78)

Ratified/accepted/approved without qualification: 45

Afghanistan (10/22/85), Antigua and Barbuda (10/25/88), Australia (9/7/84), Bangladesh (10/3/79), Belgium (7/12/82), Benin (6/30/86), Brazil (10/12/84), Bulgaria (5/31/78), Byelorussian SSR (6/7/78), Canada (6/11/81), Cape Verde

(10/3/79), Cuba (4/10/78), Cyprus (4/12/78), Czechoslovakia (5/12/78), Denmark (4/19/78), Egypt (4/1/82), Finland (5/12/78), Germany (East) (5/25/78), Ghana (6/22/78), Greece (8/23/83), Hungary (4/19/78), India (12/15/78), Ireland (12/16/82), Italy (11/27/81), Japan (6/9/82), Korea (North) (11/8/84), Laos (10/5/78), Malawi (10/5/78), Mongolia (5/19/78), New Zealand (9/7/84), Norway (2/15/79), Pakistan (2/27/86), Papua New Guinea (10/28/80), Poland (6/8/78), Romania (5/6/83), São Tomé and Príncipe (10/5/79), Solomon Islands (6/19/81), Spain (7/19/78), Sri Lanka (4/25/78), Sweden (4/27/84), Tunisia (5/11/78), Ukrainian SSR (6/13/78), Vietnam (8/26/80), Yemen (7/20/77), Yemen (Democratic) (6/12/79)

Ratified/accepted/approved with qualification: 10

Argentina (3/20/87), Germany (West) (5/24/83), Guatemala (3/21/88), Korea (South) (12/2/86), Kuwait (1/2/80), Netherlands (4/15/83), Switzerland (8/5/88), United Kingdom (5/16/78), United States (1/17/80), USSR (5/30/78)

2.33 Protocol Additional to the Geneva Conventions of August 12, 1949, and Relating to the Protection of Victims of International Armed Conflicts

Entry into force: December 7, 1978

Signed but not ratified: 37

Australia (12/7/78), Bulgaria (12/11/78), Byelorussian SSR (12/12/77), Canada (12/12/77), Chile (12/12/77), Czechoslovakia (12/6/78), Egypt (12/12/78), Germany (East) (12/12/78), Germany (West) (12/23/77), Greece (3/22/78), Honduras (12/12/77), Hungary (12/12/77), Iran (12/12/77), Ireland (12/12/77), Ivory Coast (12/12/77), Liechtenstein (12/12/77), Luxembourg (12/12/77), Madagascar (10/13/78), Mongolia (12/12/77), Morocco (12/12/77), Nicaragua (12/12/77), Pakistan (12/12/77), Panama (12/12/77), Peru (12/12/77), Philippines (12/12/77), Poland (12/12/77), Portugal (12/12/77), Romania (3/28/78), San Marino (6/22/78), Spain (11/7/78), Togo (12/12/78), Ukrainian SSR (12/12/77), United Kingdom (12/12/77), United States (12/12/77), Upper Volta (1/11/78), USSR (12/12/77), Yemen (2/14/78)

Ratified/accepted/approved without qualification: 59

Antigua and Barbuda (10/5/86), Bahamas (4/10/80), Bahrain (10/30/86), Bangladesh (9/8/80), Belize (6/29/84), Benin (5/28/86), Bolivia (12/8/83), Botswana (5/23/79), Burkina Faso (10/27/87), Cameroon (3/16/84), Central African Republic (7/17/84), Comoros (11/21/85), Congo (11/10/83), Costa Rica (12/15/83), Cuba (11/25/82), Cyprus (6/1/79), Ecuador (4/10/79), El Salvador (11/23/78), Equatorial Guinea (7/24/86), Gabon (4/8/80), Ghana (2/28/78), Guatemala (10/19/87), Guinea (7/11/84), Guinea-Bissau (10/21/86), Guyana (1/18/88), Iceland (4/10/87), Jamaica (7/29/86), Jordan (5/1/79), Korea (North) (3/9/88), Kuwait (1/17/85), Laos (11/18/80), Liberia (6/30/88), Libya (6/7/78), Mauritania (3/14/80), Mauritius (3/22/82), Mexico (3/10/83), Mozambique (3/14/83), Namibia (10/18/83), Netherlands (6/26/87), Niger (6/8/79), Nigeria (10/10/88), Norway (12/14/81), Rwanda (11/19/84), Samoa (8/23/84), Senegal (5/7/85), Seychelles (11/8/84), Sierra Leone (10/21/86), Solomon Islands (9/19/88), St. Christopher and Nevis (2/14/86), St. Lucia (10/7/82), St. Vincent and the Grenadines (4/8/83), Suriname (12/16/85), Tanzania (2/15/83), Togo (6/21/84), Tunisia (8/9/79), Uruguay (12/13/85), Vanuatu (2/28/85), Vietnam (10/19/81), Zaire (6/3/82)

Ratified/accepted/approved with qualification: 19

Angola (9/20/84), Argentina (11/26/86), Austria (8/13/82), Belgium (5/20/86), China (9/14/83), Denmark (6/17/82), Finland (8/7/80), Holy See (11/21/85), Italy (2/27/86), Korea (South) (1/15/82), New Zealand (2/8/88), Oman (3/29/84), Qatar

(4/5/88), Saudi Arabia (8/21/87), Sweden (8/31/79), Switzerland (2/17/82), Syria (11/14/83), United Arab Emirates (3/9/93), Yugoslavia (6/11/79)

2.34 PROTOCOL ADDITIONAL TO THE GENEVA CONVENTIONS OF AUGUST 12, 1949, AND RELATING TO THE PROTECTION OF VICTIMS OF NON-INTERNATIONAL ARMED CONFLICTS

Entry into force: December 7, 1978

Signed but not ratified: 35

Australia (12/7/78), Bulgaria (12/11/78), Byelorussian SSR (12/12/77), Canada (12/12/77), Chile (12/12/77), Czechoslovakia (12/6/78), Egypt (12/12/78), Germany (East) (12/12/78), Germany (West) (12/23/77), Honduras (12/12/77), Hungary (12/12/77), Iran (12/12/77), Ireland (12/12/77), Ivory Coast (12/12/77), Liechtenstein (12/12/77), Luxembourg (12/12/77), Madagascar (10/13/78), Mongolia (12/12/77), Morocco (12/12/77), Nicaragua (12/12/77), Pakistan (12/12/77), Panama (12/12/77), Peru (12/12/77), Poland (12/12/77), Portugal (12/12/77), Romania (3/28/78), San Marino (6/22/78), Senegal (12/12/77), Spain (11/7/78), Togo (12/12/78), Ukrainian SSR (12/12/77), United Kingdon (12/12/77), United States (12/12/77), Upper Volta (1/11/78), Yemen (2/14/78)

Ratified/accepted/approved without qualification: 54

Antigua and Barbuda (10/5/86), Bahamas (4/10/80), Bahrain (10/30/86), Bangladesh (9/8/80), Belize (6/29/84), Benin (5/28/86), Bolivia (12/8/83), Botswana (5/23/79), Burkina Faso (10/20/87), Cameroon (3/16/84), Central African Republic (7/17/84), Comoros (11/21/85), Congo (11/10/83), Costa Rica (12/15/83), Ecuador (4/10/79), El Salvador (11/23/78), Equatorial Guinea (7/24/86), France (2/24/84), Gabon (4/8/80), Ghana (2/28/78), Guatemala (10/19/87), Guinea (7/11/84), Guinea-Bissau (10/21/86), Guyana (1/18/88), Iceland (4/10/87), Jamaica (7/29/86), Jordan (5/1/79), Kuwait (1/17/85), Laos (11/18/80), Liberia (6/30/88), Libya (6/7/78), Mauritania (3/14/80), Mauritius (3/22/82), Namibia (10/18/83), Netherlands (6/26/87), Niger (6/8/79), Nigeria (10/10/88), Norway (12/14/81), Philippines (12/11/86), Rwanda (11/19/84), Samoa (8/23/84), Senegal (5/7/85), Seychelles (11/8/84), Sierra Leone (10/21/86), Solomon Islands (9/19/88), St. Christopher and Nevis (2/14/86), St. Lucia (10/7/82), St. Vincent and the Grenadines (4/8/83), Suriname (12/16/85), Tanzania (2/15/83), Togo (6/21/84), Tunisia (8/9/79), Uruguay (12/13/85), Vanuatu (2/28/85)

Ratified/accepted/approved with qualification: 15

Argentina (11/26/86), Austria (8/13/82), Belgium (5/20/86), China (9/14/83), Denmark (6/17/82), Finland (8/7/80), Holy See (11/21/85), Italy (2/27/86), Korea (South) (1/15/82), New Zealand (2/8/88), Oman (3/29/84), Sweden (8/31/79), Switzerland (2/17/82), United Arab Emirates (3/9/83), Yugoslavia (6/11/79)

2.35 FINAL ACT OF THE UNITED NATIONS GENERAL ASSEMBLY SPECIAL SESSION ON DISARMAMENT

Adopted without recorded vote

2.36 RESOLUTION ON THE NON-USE OF NUCLEAR WEAPONS AND PREVENTION OF NUCLEAR WAR

For: 112

Afghanistan, Algeria, Angola, Argentina, Bahamas, Bahrain, Bangladesh, Barbados, Benin, Bhutan, Bolivia, Brazil, Burma, Burundi, Cameroon, Cape Verde, Central African Republic, Chad, Chile, China, Colombia, Comoros, Congo, Costa Rica, Cuba, Cyprus, Djibouti, Dominican Republic, Ecuador, Egypt, El Salvador, Ethiopia, Fiji, Finland, Gabon, Gambia, Ghana, Grenada, Guatemala, Guinea,

Guyana, Haiti, Honduras, India, Indonesia, Iran, Iraq, Ivory Coast, Jamaica, Jordan, Kenya, Kampuchea, Kuwait, Laos, Lebanon, Lesotho, Liberia, Libya, Madagascar, Malaysia, Maldives, Mali, Malta, Mauritania, Mauritius, Mexico, Morocco, Mozambique, Nepal, Nicaragua, Niger, Nigeria, Oman, Pakistan, Panama, Papua New Guinea, Paraguay, Peru, Philippines, Qatar, Romania, Rwanda, Samoa, São Tomé and Príncipe, Saudi Arabia, Senegal, Sierra Leone, Singapore, Somalia, Sri Lanka, St. Lucia, Sudan, Suriname, Swaziland, Syria, Thailand, Togo, Trinidad and Tobago, Tunisia, Uganda, United Arab Emirates, Tanzania, Upper Volta, Uruguay, Venezuela, Vietnam, Yemen, Yemen (Democratic), Yugoslavia, Zaire, Zambia, Zimbabwe

Against: 19

Australia, Belgium, Denmark, France, Germany (West), Greece, Iceland, Ireland, Israel, Italy, Japan, Luxembourg, Netherlands, New Zealand, Norway, Portugal, Turkey, United Kingdom, United States

Abstaining: 14

Austria, Bulgaria, Byelorussian SSR, Canada,* Czechoslovakia, Germany (East), Hungary, Malawi, Mongolia, Poland, Spain, Sweden, Ukrainian SSR, USSR

* Canada subsequently requested that its vote be recorded as against the resolution.

2.37 Delhi Declaration

Adopted unanimously

2.38 South Pacific Nuclear Free Zone Treaty

Entry into force: December 11, 1986

Signed but not ratified: 1

Papua New Guinea (9/16/85)

Ratified/accepted/approved without qualification: 10

Australia (12/11/86), Cook Islands (10/28/85), Fiji (10/4/85), Kiribati (10/28/86), Nauru (4/13/87), New Zealand (11/13/86), Niue (5/12/86), Solomon Islands (1/27/89), Tuvalu (1/16/86), Samoa (10/20/86)

2.39 Treaty Between the United States of America and the Union of Soviet Socialist Republics on the Elimination of Their Intermediate-Range and Shorter-Range Missiles

Entry into force: June 1, 1988

2.40 Declaration on the Prohibition of Chemical Weapons

Conferees: 148

Afghanistan, Albania, Algeria, Angola, Argentina, Australia, Austria, Bahrain, Bangladesh, Belgium, Belize, Benin, Bolivia, Brazil, Brunei, Bulgaria, Burkina Faso, Burma, Burundi, Cameroon, Canada, Cape Verde, Central African Republic, Chad, Chile, China, Colombia, Comoros, Congo, Cook Islands, Costa Rica, Cuba, Cyprus, Czechoslovakia, Denmark, Djibouti, Dominica, Dominican Republic, Ecuador, Egypt, El Salvador, Equatorial Guinea, Ethiopia, Finland, France, Gabon, Gambia, Germany (East), Germany (West), Ghana, Greece, Grenada, Guatemala, Guinea, Guinea-Bissau, Haiti, Holy See, Hungary, Iceland, India, Indonesia, Iran, Iraq, Ireland, Israel, Italy, Ivory Coast, Jamaica, Japan, Jordan, Kampuchea, Kenya, Korea (North), Korea (South), Kuwait, Laos, Lebanon, Lesotho, Liberia, Libya, Luxembourg, Madagascar, Malawi, Malaysia, Mali, Malta, Mauritania, Mauritius, Mexico, Monaco, Mongolia, Morocco, Mozambique, Nepal, Netherlands, New Zealand, Nicaragua, Niger, Nigeria, Norway, Oman,

Pakistan, Panama, Papua New Guinea, Paraguay, Peru, Philippines, Poland, Portugal, Qatar, Romania, Rwanda, Samoa, San Marino, São Tomé and Príncipe, Saudi Arabia, Senegal, Seychelles, Sierra Leone, Somalia, South Africa, Spain, Sri Lanka, Sudan, Suriname, Swaziland, Sweden, Switzerland, Syria, Tanzania, Thailand, Togo, Trinidad and Tobago, Tunisia, Turkey, Uganda, United Arab Emirates, United Kingdom, United States, Uruguay, USSR, Venezuela, Vietnam, Yemen, Yemen (Democratic), Yugoslavia, Zaire, Zambia, Zimbabwe

3. HUMAN RIGHTS

3.1 American Declaration of the Rights and Duties of Man

Signed: 21

Argentina, Bolivia, Brazil, Chile, Colombia, Costa Rica, Cuba, Dominican Republic, Ecuador, El Salvador, Guatemala, Haiti, Honduras, Mexico, Nicaragua, Panama, Paraguay, Peru, United States, Uruguay, Venezuela

3.2 Convention on the Prevention and Punishment of the Crime of Genocide

Entry into force: January 12, 1951

Signed but not ratified: 3

Bolivia (12/11/48), Dominican Republic (12/11/48), Paraguay (12/11/48)

Ratified/accepted/approved without qualification: 65

Afghanistan (3/22/56), Antigua and Barbuda (10/25/88), Austria (3/19/58), Bahamas (8/5/75), Barbados (1/14/80), Canada (9/3/52), Chile (6/3/53), Colombia (10/27/59), Costa Rica (10/14/50), Cuba (3/4/53), Cyprus (3/29/82), Denmark (6/15/51), Egypt (2/8/52), El Salvador (9/28/50), Ethiopia (7/1/49), Fiji (1/11/73), France (10/14/50), Gabon (1/21/83), Gambia (12/29/78), Germany (West) (11/24/54), Ghana (12/24/58), Guatemala (1/13/50), Haiti (10/14/50), Honduras (3/5/52), Iceland (8/29/49), Iran (8/14/56), Iraq (1/20/59), Ireland (6/22/76), Israel (3/9/50), Italy (6/4/52), Jamaica (9/23/68), Jordan (4/3/50), Kampuchea (10/14/50), Korea (South) (10/14/50), Laos (12/8/50), Lebanon (12/17/53), Lesotho (11/29/74), Liberia (6/9/50), Luxembourg (10/7/81), Maldives (4/24/84), Mali (7/16/79), Mexico (7/22/52), Monaco (3/30/50), Mozambique (4/18/83), Nepal (1/17/69), New Zealand (12/28/78), Nicaragua (1/29/52), Papua New Guinea (1/27/82), Pakistan (10/12/57), Panama (1/11/50), Peru (2/24/60), Saudi Arabia (7/13/50), Senegal (8/4/83), St. Vincent and the Grenadines (11/9/81), Sweden (5/27/52), Syria (6/25/55), Tanzania (4/5/84), Togo (5/24/84), Tonga (2/16/72), Tunisia (11/29/56), Turkey (7/31/50), Upper Volta (9/14/65), Uruguay (7/11/67), Yugoslavia (8/29/50), Zaire (5/31/62)

Ratified/accepted/approved with qualification: 34

Albania (5/12/55), Algeria (10/31/63), Argentina (6/5/56), Australia (7/8/49), Belgium (9/5/51), Brazil (4/15/52), Bulgaria (7/21/50), Burma (3/14/56), Byelorussian SSR (8/11/54), China (4/18/83), Czechoslovakia (12/21/50), Ecuador (12/21/49), Finland (12/18/59), Germany (East) (3/27/73), Greece (12/8/54), Hungary (1/7/52), India (8/27/49), Mongolia (1/5/67), Morocco (1/24/58), Netherlands (6/20/66), Norway (7/22/49), Philippines (7/7/50), Poland (11/14/50), Romania (11/2/50), Rwanda (4/16/75), Spain (9/13/68), Sri Lanka (10/12/50), Ukrainian SSR (11/15/54), United Kingdom (1/30/70), United States (11/25/88), USSR (5/3/54), Venezuela (7/12/60), Vietnam (6/9/81), Yemen (Democratic) (2/9/87)

3.3 Universal Declaration of Human Rights

For: 48

Afghanistan, Argentina, Australia, Belgium, Bolivia, Brazil, Burma, Canada, Chile, China, Colombia, Costa Rica, Cuba, Denmark, Dominican Republic, Ecuador, Egypt, El Salvador, Ethiopia, France, Greece, Guatemala, Haiti, Iceland, India, Iran, Iraq, Lebanon, Liberia, Luxembourg, Mexico, Netherlands, New Zealand, Nicaragua, Norway, Pakistan, Panama, Paraguay, Peru, Philippines, Siam, Sweden, Syria, Turkey, United Kingdom, United States, Uruguay, Venezuela

Against: 0

Abstaining: 8

Byelorussian SSR, Czechoslovakia, Poland, Saudi Arabia, South Africa, Ukrainian SSR, USSR, Yugoslavia

3.4 European Convention for the Protection of Human Rights and Fundamental Freedoms

Entry into force: September 3, 1953

Signed but not ratified: 1

San Marino (11/16/88)

Ratified/accepted/approved without qualification: 7

Cyprus (10/6/62), Greece (11/28/74), Italy (10/26/55), Netherlands (8/31/54), Norway (1/15/52), Switzerland (11/28/74), Turkey (5/18/54)

Ratified/accepted/approved with qualification: 14

Austria (9/3/58), Belgium (6/14/55), Denmark (4/13/53), France (5/3/74), Germany (West) (12/5/52), Iceland (6/29/53), Ireland (2/25/53), Liechtenstein (9/8/82), Luxembourg (9/3/53), Malta (1/23/67), Portugal (11/9/78), Spain (10/4/79), Sweden (2/4/52), United Kingdom (3/8/51)

3.5 Convention Relating to the Status of Refugees

Entry into force: April 22, 1954

Ratified/accepted/approved without qualification: 53

Algeria (2/21/63), Australia (1/22/54), Benin (4/4/62), Bolivia (2/9/82), Brazil (11/16/60), Burundi (7/19/63), Cameroon (10/21/63), Central African Republic (9/4/62), Chad (8/19/81), Colombia (10/10/61), Congo (10/15/62), Costa Rica (3/28/78), Denmark (12/4/52), Djibouti (8/9/77), Dominican Republic (1/4/78), El Salvador (4/28/83), Equatorial Guinea (2/7/86), Gabon (4/27/64), Germany (West) (12/1/53), Ghana (3/18/63), Guinea (12/28/65), Guinea-Bissau (2/11/76), Haiti (9/25/84), Iceland (11/30/55), Ivory Coast (12/8/61), Japan (10/3/81), Kenya (5/16/66), Lesotho (5/14/81), Liberia (10/15/64), Mali (2/2/73), Mauritania (5/5/87), Morocco (11/7/56), Nicaragua (3/28/80), Niger (8/25/61), Nigeria (10/23/67), Panama (8/2/78), Paraguay (4/1/70), Peru (12/21/64), Philippines (7/22/81), Samoa (9/21/88), São Tomé and Príncipe (2/1/78), Senegal (5/2/63), Seychelles (4/23/80), Suriname (11/29/78), Switzerland (1/21/55), Tanzania (5/12/64), Togo (2/27/62), Tunisia (10/24/57), Upper Volta (6/18/80), Uruguay (9/22/70), Yemen (1/18/70), Yugoslavia (12/15/59), Zaire (7/19/65)

Ratified/accepted/approved with qualification: 48

Angola (6/23/81), Argentina (11/15/61), Austria (11/1/54), Belgium (7/22/53), Botswana (1/6/69), Canada (6/4/69), Chile (1/28/72), China (9/24/82), Cyprus (5/16/63), Ecuador (8/17/55), Egypt (5/22/81), Ethiopia (11/10/69), Fiji (6/12/72), Finland (10/10/68), France (6/23/54), Gambia (9/7/66), Greece (4/5/60), Guatemala (9/22/83), Holy See (3/15/56), Iran (7/28/76), Ireland (11/29/56), Israel (10/1/54), Italy (11/15/54), Jamaica (7/30/64), Liechtenstein (3/8/57), Luxembourg (7/23/53), Madagascar (12/18/67), Malta (6/17/71), Malawi (12/10/87), Monaco (5/18/54), Mozambique (12/16/83), Netherlands (5/3/56), New Zealand (6/30/60), Norway (3/23/53), Papua New Guinea (7/17/86), Portugal (12/22/60), Rwanda (1/3/80), Sierra Leone (5/22/81), Somalia (10/10/78), Spain (8/14/78), Sudan (2/22/74), Sweden (10/26/54), Turkey (3/30/62), Tuvalu (3/7/86), Uganda (9/27/76), United Kingdom (3/11/54), Zambia (9/24/69), Zimbabwe (8/25/81)

3.6 Protocol (No. 1) to the European Convention for the Protection of Human Rights and Fundamental Freedoms

Entry into force: May 18, 1954

Signed but not ratified: 3

Liechtenstein (5/7/87), Spain (2/23/78), Switzerland (5/19/76)

Ratified/accepted/approved without qualification: 9

Belgium (6/14/55), Cyprus (10/6/62), Denmark (4/13/53), France (5/3/74), Greece (11/28/74), Iceland (6/29/53), Italy (10/26/55), Norway (12/18/52), Portugal (11/9/78)

Ratified/accepted/approved with qualification: 9

Austria (9/3/58), Germany (West) (2/13/67), Ireland (2/25/53), Luxembourg (9/3/53), Malta (1/23/67), Netherlands (8/31/54), Sweden (6/22/53), Turkey (5/18/54), United Kingdom (11/3/52)

3.7 Convention on the Political Rights of Women

Entry into force: July 7, 1954

Signed but not ratified: 5

Burma (9/14/54), El Salvador (6/24/53), Liberia (12/9/53), Paraguay (11/16/53), Uruguay (5/26/53)

Ratified/accepted/approved without qualification: 47

Afghanistan (11/16/66), Angola (9/17/86), Bahamas (8/16/77), Barbados (1/12/73), Bolivia (9/22/70), Brazil (8/13/63), Central African Republic (9/4/62), Chile (10/18/67), Colombia (8/5/86), Congo (10/15/62), Costa Rica (7/25/67), Cuba (4/8/54), Cyprus (11/12/68), Egypt (9/8/81), France (4/22/57), Gabon (4/19/67), Ghana (12/28/65), Greece (12/29/53), Guinea (1/24/78), Haiti (2/12/58), Iceland (6/30/54), India (11/1/61), Jamaica (8/14/66), Japan (7/13/55), Laos (1/28/69), Lebanon (6/5/66), Luxembourg (11/1/76), Madagascar (2/12/64), Malawi (6/29/66), Mali (7/16/74), Mauritania (5/4/76), Netherlands (7/30/71), Nicaragua (1/17/57), Niger (12/7/64), Nigeria (11/17/80), Norway (8/24/56), Papua New Guinea (1/27/82), Peru (7/1/75), Senegal (5/2/63), Tanzania (6/19/75), Thailand (11/30/54), Trinidad and Tobago (6/24/66), Turkey (1/26/60), Ukrainian SSR (11/15/54), United States (4/8/76), Zaire (10/12/77), Zambia (2/4/72)

Ratified/accepted/approved with qualification: 48

Albania (5/12/55), Antigua and Barbuda (10/25/88), Argentina (2/27/61), Australia (12/10/74), Austria (4/18/69), Belgium (5/20/64), Bulgaria (3/17/54), Byelorussian SSR (8/11/54), Canada (1/30/57), Czechoslovakia (4/6/55), Denmark (7/7/54), Dominican Republic (12/11/53), Ecuador (4/23/54), Ethiopia (1/21/69), Fiji (6/12/72), Finland (10/6/58), Germany (East) (3/27/73), Germany (West) (11/4/70), Guatemala (10/7/59), Hungary (1/20/55), Indonesia (12/16/58), Ireland (11/14/68), Israel (7/6/54), Italy (3/6/68), Korea (South) (6/23/59), Lesotho (11/4/74), Malta (7/9/68), Mauritius (7/18/69), Mexico (3/23/81), Mongolia

(8/18/65), Morocco (11/22/76), Nepal (4/26/66), New Zealand (5/22/68), Pakistan (12/7/54), Philippines (9/12/57), Poland (8/11/54), Romania (8/6/54), Sierra Leone (7/25/62), Solomon Islands (9/3/81), Spain (1/14/74), Swaziland (7/20/70), Sweden (3/31/54), Tunisia (1/24/68), United Kingdom (2/24/67), USSR (5/3/54), Venezuela (5/31/83), Yemen (Democratic) (2/9/87), Yugoslavia (6/23/54)

3.8 Convention Relating to the Status of Stateless Persons

Entry into force: June 6, 1960

Signed but not ratified: 8

Brazil (9/28/54), Colombia (12/30/54), El Salvador (9/28/54), Guatemala (9/28/54), Holy See (9/28/54), Honduras (9/28/54), Liechtenstein (9/28/54), Philippines (6/22/55)

Ratified/accepted/approved without qualification: 20

Algeria (7/15/64), Antigua and Barbuda (10/25/88), Australia (12/13/73), Belgium (5/27/60), Bolivia (10/6/83), Costa Rica (11/2/77), Ecuador (10/2/70), Greece (11/4/75), Guinea (3/21/62), Ireland (12/17/62), Israel (12/23/58), Korea (South) (8/22/62), Liberia (9/11/64), Luxembourg (6/27/60), Norway (11/19/56), Switzerland (7/3/72), Trinidad and Tobago (4/11/66), Tunisia (7/29/69), Uganda (4/15/65), Yugoslavia (4/9/59)

Ratified/accepted/approved with qualification: 15

Argentina (6/1/72), Barbados (3/6/72), Botswana (2/25/69), Denmark (1/17/56), Fiji (6/12/72), Finland (10/10/68), France (3/8/60), Germany (West) (10/26/76), Italy (12/3/62), Kiribati (11/29/83), Lesotho (11/4/74), Netherlands (4/12/62), Sweden (4/2/65), United Kingdom (4/16/59), Zambia (11/1/74)

3.9 Standard Minimum Rules for the Treatment of Prisoners

Adopted unanimously

3.10 International Labor Organization Convention (No. 107) Concerning the Protection and Integration of Indigenous and Other Tribal and Semi-Tribal Populations in Independent Countries

Entry into force: June 2, 1959

Ratified/accepted/approved without qualification: 27

Angola (6/4/76), Argentina (1/18/60), Bangladesh (6/22/72), Belgium (11/19/58), Bolivia (1/12/65), Brazil (6/18/65), Colombia (3/4/69), Costa Rica (5/4/59), Cuba (6/2/58), Dominican Republic (6/23/58), Ecuador (10/3/69), Egypt (1/14/59), El Salvador (11/18/58), Ghana (12/15/58), Guinea-Bissau (2/21/77), Haiti (3/4/58), India (9/29/58), Iraq (7/16/86), Malawi (3/22/65), Mexico (6/1/59), Pakistan (2/15/60), Panama (6/4/71), Paraguay (2/20/69), Peru (12/6/60), Portugal (11/22/60), Syria (1/14/59), Tunisia (12/17/62)

3.11 Communications Concerning Human Rights

Adopted unanimously

3.12 Declaration on the Granting of Independence to Colonial Countries and Peoples

For: 89

Afghanistan, Albania, Argentina, Austria, Bolivia, Brazil, Bulgaria, Burma, Byelorussian SSR, Cambodia, Cameroon, Canada, Central African Republic, Ceylon, Chad, Chile, China, Colombia, Congo (Brazzaville), Congo (Leopoldville), Costa Rica, Cuba, Cyprus, Czechoslovakia, Denmark, Ecuador, El Salvador,

Ethiopia, Finland, Gabon, Ghana, Greece, Guatemala, Guinea, Haiti, Honduras, Hungary, Iceland, India, Indonesia, Iran, Iraq, Ireland, Israel, Italy, Ivory Coast, Japan, Jordan, Laos, Lebanon, Liberia, Libya, Luxembourg, Madagascar, Malaysia, Mali, Mexico, Morocco, Nepal, Netherlands, New Zealand, Nicaragua, Niger, Nigeria, Norway, Pakistan, Panama, Paraguay, Peru, Philippines, Poland, Romania, Saudi Arabia, Senegal, Somalia, Sudan, Sweden, Thailand, Togo, Tunisia, Turkey, Ukrainian SSR, United Arab Republic, Upper Volta, Uruguay, USSR, Venezuela, Yemen, Yugoslavia

Against: 0

Abstaining: 9

Australia, Belgium, Dominican Republic, France, Portugal, South Africa, Spain, United Kingdom, United States

3.13 EUROPEAN SOCIAL CHARTER

Entry into force: February 26, 1965

Signed but not ratified: 5

Belgium (10/18/61), Luxembourg (10/18/61), Portugal (5/28/82), Switzerland (5/6/76), Turkey (10/18/61)

Ratified/accepted/approved with qualification: 1

Italy (10/22/65)

Ratified/accepted/approved without qualification: 14

Austria (10/29/69), Cyprus (3/7/68), Denmark (3/3/65), France (3/9/73), Germany (West) (1/27/65), Greece (6/16/84), Iceland (1/15/76), Ireland (10/7/64), Malta (10/4/88) Netherlands (4/22/80), Norway (10/26/62), Spain (5/6/80), Sweden (12/17/62), United Kingdom (7/11/62)

3.14 CONVENTION ON OFFENSES AND CERTAIN OTHER ACTS COMMITTED ON BOARD AIRCRAFT

Entry into force: December 4, 1969

Signed but not ratified: 2

Holy See (9/14/63), Liberia (9/14/63)

Ratified/accepted/approved without qualification: 105

Afghanistan (4/15/77), Antigua and Barbuda (7/19/85), Argentina (7/23/71), Australia (6/22/70), Austria (2/7/74), Bahamas (5/15/75), Bangladesh (7/25/78), Barbados (4/4/72), Belgium (8/6/70), Bolivia (7/5/79), Botswana (1/16/70), Brazil (1/14/70), Brunei (5/23/86), Burundi (7/14/71), Cameroon (3/24/88), Canada (11/7/69), Chad (6/30/70), Chile (1/24/74), Colombia (7/6/73), Congo (11/13/78), Costa Rica (10/24/72), Cyprus (5/31/72), Denmark (1/17/67), Dominican Republic (12/3/70), Ecuador (12/3/69), El Salvador (2/13/80), Fiji (1/18/72), Finland (4/2/71), France (9/1/70), Gabon (1/14/70), Gambia (1/4/79), Germany (West) (12/16/69), Ghana (1/2/74), Greece (5/31/71), Grenada (8/28/78), Guyana (12/20/72), Haiti (4/26/84), Honduras (4/8/87), Iceland (3/16/70), Iran (6/28/76), Ireland (11/14/75), Israel (9/19/69), Italy (10/18/68), Ivory Coast (6/3/70), Jamaica (9/16/83), Japan (5/26/70), Jordan (5/3/73), Kenya (6/22/70), Korea (South) (2/19/71), Laos (10/23/72), Lebanon (6/11/74), Lesotho (4/28/72), Libya (6/21/72), Luxembourg (9/21/72), Madagascar (12/2/69), Malawi (12/28/72), Malaysia (3/5/85), Maldives (9/28/87), Mali (5/31/71), Mauritania (6/30/77), Mauritius (4/5/83), Mexico (3/18/69), Monaco (6/2/83), Nauru (5/17/84), Nepal (1/15/79), Netherlands (11/14/69), New Zealand (2/12/74), Nicaragua (8/24/73), Niger (6/27/69), Nigeria (4/7/70), Norway (1/17/67), Pakistan (9/11/73), Panama (11/16/70), Paraguay (8/9/71), Philippines (11/26/65), Portugal (11/25/64), Qatar

(8/6/81), Rwanda (5/17/71), Saudi Arabia (11/21/69), Senegal (3/9/72), Seychelles (1/4/79), Sierra Leone (11/9/70), Singapore (3/1/71), Solomon Islands (3/23/82), Spain (10/1/69), Sri Lanka (5/30/78), St. Lucia (10/31/83), Suriname (9/10/79), Sweden (1/17/67), Switzerland (12/21/70), Tanzania (8/12/83), Thailand (3/6/72), Togo (7/26/71), Trinidad and Tobago (2/9/72), Turkey (12/17/75), Uganda (6/25/82), United Kingdom (11/29/68), United States (9/5/69), Upper Volta (6/6/69), Uruguay (1/26/77), Vietnam (10/10/79), Yemen (9/26/86), Yugoslavia (12/12/71), Zaire (7/20/77), Zambia (9/14/71)

Ratified/accepted/approved with qualification: 26

Bahrain (2/9/84), Byelorussian SSR (2/3/88), China (11/14/78), Czechoslovakia (2/23/84), Egypt (2/12/75), Ethiopia (3/27/79), Guatemala (11/17/70), Hungary (12/3/70), India (7/22/75), Indonesia (9/7/76), Iraq (5/15/74), Korea (North) (5/9/83), Kuwait (11/27/79), Morocco (10/21/75), Oman (2/9/77), Papua New Guinea (11/6/75), Peru (5/12/78), Poland (3/19/71), Romania (2/15/74), South Africa (5/26/72), Syria (7/31/80), Tunisia (2/25/75), Ukrainian SSR (2/29/88), United Arab Emirates (4/16/81), USSR (2/3/88), Venezuela (2/4/83)

3.15 Protocol (No. IV) to the European Convention for the Protection of Human Rights and Freedoms

Entry into force: May 2, 1968

Signed but not ratified: 3

Cyprus (10/6/88), Spain (2/23/78), United Kingdom (9/16/63)

Ratified/accepted/approved with qualification: 13

Austria (9/18/69), Belgium (9/21/70), Denmark (9/30/64), France (5/3/74), Germany (West) (6/1/68), Iceland (11/16/67), Ireland (10/29/68), Italy (5/27/82), Luxembourg (5/2/68), Netherlands (6/23/82), Norway (6/12/64), Portugal (11/9/78), Sweden (6/13/64)

3.16 International Convention on the Elimination of all Forms of Racial Discrimination

Entry into force: January 4, 1969

Signed but not ratified: 6

Benin (2/2/67), Bhutan (3/26/73), Grenada (12/17/81), Ireland (3/21/68), Turkey (10/13/72), United States (9/28/66)

Ratified/accepted/approved without qualification: 80

Algeria (2/14/72), Argentina (10/2/68), Bangladesh (6/11/79), Bolivia (9/22/70), Botswana (2/20/74), Brazil (3/27/68), Burundi (10/27/77), Cameroon (6/24/71), Canada (10/14/70), Cape Verde (10/3/79), Central African Republic (3/16/71), Chad (8/17/77), Chile (10/20/71), Colombia (9/2/81), Congo (7/11/88), Costa Rica (1/16/67), Cyprus (4/21/67), Denmark (12/9/71), Dominican Republic (5/25/83), Ecuador (9/22/66), El Salvador (11/30/79), Finland (7/14/70), Gabon (2/29/80), Gambia (12/29/78), Germany (West) (5/16/69), Ghana (9/8/66), Greece (6/18/70), Guatemala (1/18/83), Guinea (5/14/77), Haiti (12/19/72), Holy See (5/1/69), Iceland (5/13/67), Iran (8/29/68), Ivory Coast (1/4/73), Jordan (5/30/74), Kampuchea (11/28/83), Korea (South) (12/5/78), Laos (2/22/74), Lesotho (11/4/71), Liberia (11/5/76), Luxembourg (5/1/78), Maldives (4/24/84), Mali (7/16/74), Mauritania (12/13/88), Mauritius (5/30/72), Mexico (2/20/75), Namibia (11/11/82), Netherlands (12/10/71), New Zealand (11/22/72), Nicaragua (2/15/78), Niger (4/27/67), Nigeria (10/16/67), Norway (8/6/70), Panama (8/16/67), Peru (9/29/71), Philippines (9/15/67), Portugal (8/24/82), Qatar (7/22/76), Senegal (4/19/72), Seychelles (3/7/78), Sierra Leone (8/2/67), Solomon Islands (3/17/82), Somalia (8/26/75), Sri Lanka (2/18/82), St. Vincent and the

Grenadines (11/9/81), Sudan (3/21/77), Suriname (3/15/84), Swaziland (4/7/69), Sweden (12/6/71), Tanzania (10/27/72), Togo (9/1/72), Trinidad and Tobago (10/4/73), Tunisia (1/13/67), Uganda (11/21/80), Upper Volta (7/18/74), Uruguay (8/30/68), Venezuela (10/10/67), Yugoslavia (10/2/67), Zaire (4/21/76), Zambia (2/4/72)

Ratified/accepted/approved with qualification: 47

Afghanistan (7/6/83), Antigua and Barbuda (10/25/88), Australia (9/30/75), Austria (5/9/72), Bahamas (8/5/75), Barbados (11/8/72), Belgium (8/7/75), Bulgaria (8/8/66), Byelorussian SSR (4/8/69), China (12/29/81), Cuba (2/15/72), Czechoslovakia (12/29/66), Egypt (5/1/67), Ethiopia (6/23/76), Fiji (1/11/73), France (7/28/71), Germany (East) (3/27/73), Guyana (2/15/77), Hungary (5/4/67), India (12/3/68), Iraq (1/14/70), Israel (1/3/79), Italy (1/5/76), Jamaica (6/4/71), Kuwait (10/15/68), Lebanon (11/12/71), Libya (7/3/68), Madagascar (2/7/69), Malta (5/27/71), Mongolia (8/6/69), Morocco (12/18/70), Mozambique (4/18/83), Nepal (1/30/71), Pakistan (9/21/66), Papua New Guinea (1/27/82), Poland (12/5/68), Romania (9/15/70), Rwanda (4/16/75), Spain (9/13/68), Syria (4/21/69), Tonga (2/16/72), Ukrainian SSR (3/7/69), United Arab Emirates (6/20/74), United Kingdom (3/7/69), USSR (2/4/69), Vietnam (6/9/82), Yemen (Democratic) (10/2/72)

3.17 U.N. Security Council Resolution 232

For: 11

Argentina, China, Japan, Jordan, Netherlands, New Zealand, Nigeria, Uganda, United Kingdom, United States, Uruguay

Against: 0

Abstaining: 4

Bulgaria, France, Mali, USSR

3.18 International Covenant on Economic, Social and Cultural Rights

Entry into force: January 3, 1976

Signed but not ratified: 7

Algeria (12/10/68), Ireland (10/1/73), Israel (12/19/66), Kampuchea (10/17/80), Liberia (4/18/67), Malta (10/22/68), United States (10/5/77)

Ratified/accepted/approved without qualification: 56

Australia (12/10/75), Austria (9/10/78), Bolivia (8/12/82), Cameroon (6/27/84), Canada (5/19/76), Central African Republic (5/8/81), Chile (2/10/72), Colombia (10/29/69), Costa Rica (11/29/68), Cyprus (4/2/69), Dominican Republic (1/4/78), Ecuador (3/6/69), Egypt (1/14/72), El Salvador (11/30/79), Equatorial Guinea (9/25/87), Finland (8/19/75), Gabon (1/21/83), Gambia (12/29/78), Greece (5/16/85), Guatemala (5/19/88), Guyana (2/15/77), Honduras (2/17/81), Iceland (8/22/79), Iran (6/24/75), Italy (9/15/78), Jamaica (10/3/75), Jordan (5/28/75), Korea (North) (9/14/81), Lebanon (11/3/72), Luxembourg (8/18/83), Mali (7/16/74), Mauritius (12/12/73), Morocco (5/3/79), Nicaragua (3/12/80), Niger (3/7/86), Panama (3/8/77), Peru (4/28/78), Philippines (6/7/74), Poland (3/18/77), Portugal (7/31/78), San Marino (10/18/85), Senegal (2/13/78), Spain (4/27/77), Sri Lanka (6/11/80), St. Vincent and the Grenadines (11/9/81), Sudan (3/18/86), Suriname (12/28/76), Tanzania (6/11/76), Togo (5/24/84), Tunisia (3/18/69), Uganda (1/21/87), Uruguay (4/1/70), Venezuela (5/10/78), Vietnam (9/24/82), Yugoslavia (6/2/71), Zaire (11/1/76)

Ratified/accepted/approved with qualification: 36

Afghanistan (1/24/83), Argentina (8/8/86), Barbados (1/5/73), Belgium (4/21/83), Bulgaria (9/21/70), Byelorussian SSR (11/12/73), Congo (10/5/83), Czechoslovakia (12/23/75), Denmark (1/6/72), France (11/4/80), Germany (East) (11/8/73), Germany (West) (12/17/73), Guinea (1/24/78), Hungary (1/17/74), India (4/10/79), Iraq (1/25/71), Japan (6/21/79), Kenya (5/1/75), Libya (5/15/70), Madagascar (9/22/71), Mexico (3/23/81), Mongolia (11/18/74), Netherlands (12/11/78), New Zealand (12/28/78), Norway (9/13/72), Romania (12/9/74), Rwanda (4/16/75), Solomon Islands (3/17/82), Sweden (12/6/71), Syria (4/21/69), Trinidad and Tobago (12/8/78), Ukrainian SSR (11/12/73), United Kingdom (5/20/76), USSR (10/16/73), Yemen (Democratic) (2/19/87), Zambia (4/10/84)

3.19 International Covenant on Civil and Political Rights

Entry into force: March 23, 1976

Signed but not ratified: 7

Algeria (12/10/68), Honduras (12/19/66), Ireland (10/1/73), Israel (12/19/66), Kampuchea (10/17/80), Liberia (4/18/67), United States (10/5/77)

Ratified/accepted/approved without qualification: 43

Bolivia (8/12/82), Cameroon (6/27/84), Canada (5/19/76), Central African Republic (5/8/81), Colombia (10/29/69), Costa Rica (11/29/68), Cyprus (4/2/69), Dominican Republic (1/4/78), Ecuador (3/6/69), Egypt (1/14/82), El Salvador (11/30/79), Equatorial Guinea (9/25/87), Gabon (1/21/83), Iran (6/24/75), Jamaica (10/3/75), Jordan (5/28/75), Kenya (5/1/72), Korea (North) (9/14/81), Lebanon (11/3/72), Madagascar (6/21/71), Mali (7/16/74), Mauritius (12/12/73), Niger (3/7/86), Norway (9/13/72), Panama (3/8/77), Peru (4/28/78), Philippines (10/23/86), Poland (3/18/77), Portugal (6/15/78), Rwanda (4/16/75), San Marino (10/18/85), Senegal (2/13/78), Spain (4/27/77), Sri Lanka (6/11/80), St. Vincent and the Grenadines (11/9/81), Sudan (3/18/86), Suriname (12/28/76), Tanzania (6/11/76), Togo (5/24/84), Tunisia (3/18/69), Yugoslavia (6/2/71), Zaire (11/1/76), Zambia (4/10/84)

Ratified/accepted/approved with qualification: 44

Afghanistan (1/24/83), Argentina (8/8/86), Australia (8/13/80), Austria (9/10/78), Barbados (1/5/73), Belgium (4/21/83), Bulgaria (9/21/70), Byelorussian SSR (11/12/73), Chile (2/10/72), Congo (10/5/83), Czechoslovakia (12/23/75), Denmark (1/6/72), Finland (8/19/75), France (11/4/80), Gambia (3/22/79), Germany (East) (11/8/73), Germany (West) (12/17/73), Guinea (1/24/78), Guyana (2/15/77), Hungary (1/17/74), Iceland (8/22/79), India (4/10/79), Iraq (1/25/71), Italy (9/15/78), Japan (6/21/79), Libya (5/15/70), Luxembourg (8/18/83), Mexico (3/23/81), Mongolia (11/18/74), Morocco (5/3/79), Netherlands (12/11/78), New Zealand (12/28/78), Nicaragua (3/12/80), Romania (12/9/74), Sweden (12/6/71), Syria (4/21/69), Trinidad and Tobago (12/21/78), Ukrainian SSR (11/12/73), United Kingdom (5/20/76), USSR (10/16/73), Uruguay (4/1/70), Venezuela (5/10/78), Vietnam (9/24/82), Yemen (Democratic) (2/9/87)

3.20 Optional Protocol to the International Covenant on Civil and Political Rights

Entry into force: March 23, 1976

Signed but not ratified: 6

Austria (12/10/73), Cyprus (12/19/66), El Salvador (9/21/67), Guinea (3/19/75), Honduras (12/19/66), Philippines (12/19/66)

Ratified/accepted/approved without qualification: 33

Argentina (8/8/86), Barbados (1/5/73), Bolivia (8/12/82), Cameroon (6/27/84), Canada (5/19/76), Central African Republic (5/8/81), Colombia (10/29/69), Congo (10/5/83), Costa Rica (11/29/68), Dominican Republic (1/4/78), Ecuador (3/6/69), Equatorial Guinea (9/25/87), Finland (8/19/75), Gambia (6/9/88), Hungary (9/7/88), Jamaica (10/3/75), Madagascar (6/21/71), Mauritius (12/12/73), Netherlands (12/11/78), Nicaragua (3/12/80), Niger (3/7/86), Panama (3/8/77), Peru (10/3/80), Portugal (5/3/83), San Marino (10/18/85), Senegal (2/13/78), St. Vincent and the Grenadines (11/9/81), Suriname (12/28/76), Togo (3/30/88), Trinidad and Tobago (11/14/80), Uruguay (4/1/70), Zaire (11/1/76), Zambia (4/10/84)

Ratified/accepted/approved with qualification: 10

Austria (12/10/87), Denmark (1/6/72), France (2/17/84), Iceland (8/22/79), Italy (9/15/78), Luxembourg (8/18/83), Norway (9/13/72), Spain (1/25/85), Sweden (12/6/71), Venezuela (5/10/78)

3.21 Protocol Relating to the Status of Refugees

Entry into force: October 4, 1967

Ratified/accepted/approved without qualification: 72

Algeria (11/8/67), Argentina (12/6/67), Australia (12/13/73), Austria (9/5/73), Benin (7/6/70), Bolivia (2/9/82), Brazil (4/7/72), Cameroon (9/19/67), Canada (6/4/69), Central African Republic (8/30/67), Chad (8/19/81), Colombia (3/4/80), Costa Rica (3/28/78), Cyprus (7/9/68), Denmark (1/29/68), Djibouti (8/9/77), Dominican Republic (1/4/78), Ecuador (3/6/69), Egypt (5/22/81), Equatorial Guinea (2/7/86), Fiji (6/12/72), Gabon (8/28/73), Gambia (9/29/67), Germany (West) (11/5/69), Greece (8/7/68), Guinea (5/16/68), Guinea-Bissau (2/11/76), Haiti (9/25/84), Holy See (6/8/67), Iceland (4/26/68), Iran (7/28/76), Ireland (11/6/68), Italy (1/26/72), Ivory Coast (2/16/70), Japan (1/1/82), Kenya (11/13/81), Lesotho (5/14/81), Liberia (2/27/80), Liechtenstein (5/20/68), Luxembourg (4/22/71), Malawi (12/10/87), Mali (2/2/73), Mauritania (5/5/87), Morocco (4/20/71), New Zealand (8/6/73), Nicaragua (3/28/80), Niger (2/2/70), Nigeria (5/2/68), Norway (11/28/67), Panama (8/2/78), Papua New Guinea (7/17/86), Paraguay (4/1/70), Philippines (7/22/81), São Tomé and Príncipe (2/1/78), Senegal (10/3/67), Seychelles (4/23/80), Sierra Leone (5/22/81), Spain (8/14/78), Sudan (5/23/74), Suriname (11/29/78), Sweden (10/4/67), Switzerland (5/20/68), Togo (12/1/69), Tunisia (10/16/68), Tuvalu (3/7/86), Upper Volta (6/18/80), Uruguay (9/22/70), Yemen (1/18/80), Yugoslavia (1/15/68), Zaire (1/13/75), Zambia (9/24/69), Zimbabwe (8/25/81)

Ratified/accepted/approved with qualification: 29

Angola (6/23/81), Belgium (4/8/69), Botswana (1/6/69), Burundi (3/15/71), Cape Verde (7/9/87), Chile (4/27/72), China (9/24/82), Congo (7/10/70), El Salvador (4/28/83), Ethiopia (11/10/69), Finland (10/10/68), France (2/3/71), Ghana (10/30/68), Guatemala (9/22/83), Israel (6/14/68), Jamaica (10/30/80), Malta (9/15/71), Netherlands (11/29/68), Peru (9/15/83), Portugal (7/13/76), Rwanda (1/3/80), Somalia (10/10/78), Swaziland (1/28/69), Tanzania (9/4/68), Turkey (7/31/68), Uganda (9/27/76), United Kingdom (9/4/68), United States (11/1/68), Venezuela (9/19/86)

3.22 Economic and Social Council Resolution 1235 (XLII)

For: 20*

Against: 0

Abstaining: 4

* Adopted with no roll call vote recorded.

3.23 Declaration on Territorial Asylum

Adopted unanimously

3.24 United Nations Security Council Resolution 253

Adopted unanimously

Algeria, Brazil, Canada, China, Denmark, Ethiopia, France, Hungary, India, Pakistan, Paraguay, Senegal, USSR, United Kingdom, United States

3.25 American Convention on Human Rights

Entry into force: July 18, 1978

Signed but not ratified: 3

Chile (11/22/69), Paraguay (11/22/69), United States (6/1/77)

Ratified/accepted/approved without qualification: 11

Bolivia (7/19/79), Colombia (7/31/73), Costa Rica (4/8/70), Grenada (7/18/78), Guatemala (5/25/78), Haiti (9/27/77), Honduras (9/8/77), Nicaragua (9/25/79), Panama (6/22/78), Peru (7/28/78), Suriname (11/12/87)

Ratified/accepted/approved with qualification: 9

Argentina (9/5/84), Barbados (11/5/81), Dominican Republic (4/19/78), Ecuador (12/28/77), El Salvador (6/23/78), Jamaica (8/7/78), Mexico (3/24/81), Uruguay (4/19/85), Venezuela (8/9/77)

3.26 Procedure for Dealing With Communications Relating to Violations of Human Rights and Fundamental Freedoms

Adopted without recorded vote

3.27 Convention for the Suppression of Unlawful Seizure of Aircraft

Entry into force: October 14, 1971

Signed but not ratified: 6

Burundi (2/17/71), Equatorial Guinea (6/4/71), Kampuchea (12/16/70), Laos (2/16/71), Liechtenstein (8/24/71), Malaysia (12/16/70)

Ratified/accepted/approved without qualification: 106

Antigua and Barbuda (7/22/85), Afghanistan (8/29/79), Australia (11/9/72), Austria (2/11/74), Bahamas (8/11/76), Bangladesh (6/28/78), Barbados (4/2/73), Belgium (8/24/73), Benin (3/13/72), Bhutan (12/28/88), Bolivia (7/18/79), Botswana (12/28/78), Brunei (4/16/86), Burkina Faso (10/19/87), Cameroon (4/14/88), Canada (6/19/72), Cape Verde (10/20/77), Chad (7/12/72), Chile (2/2/72), Colombia (7/3/73), Congo (3/19/87), Costa Rica (7/9/71), Cyprus (6/6/72), Denmark (10/17/72), Dominican Republic (6/22/78), Ecuador (6/14/71), El Salvador (1/17/73), Fiji (7/27/72), Finland (12/15/71), France (9/18/72), Gabon (7/14/71), Gambia (11/28/78) Germany (East) (6/3/71), Germany (West) (10/11/74), Ghana (12/12/73), Greece (9/20/73), Grenada (8/10/78), Guinea (5/2/84), Guinea-Bissau (8/20/76), Guyana (12/21/72), Haiti (5/9/84), Iceland (6/29/73), Iran (1/25/72), Ireland (11/24/75), Israel (8/16/71), Italy (2/19/74), Ivory Coast (1/9/73), Jamaica (9/16/83), Japan (4/19/71), Jordan (11/16/71), Kenya (1/11/77), Korea (North) (4/28/83), Lebanon (8/10/73), Lesotho (7/27/78), Liberia (2/1/82), Luxembourg (11/22/78), Madagascar (11/18/86), Malaysia (5/4/85), Maldives (9/1/87), Mali (8/17/71), Mauritania (11/1/78), Mauritius (4/25/83), Mexico (7/19/72), Monaco (6/3/83), Nauru (5/17/84), Nepal (1/10/79), New Zealand (2/12/74), Nicaragua (11/6/73), Niger (10/15/71), Nigeria (7/3/73), Norway (8/23/71), Oman (2/2/77), Pakistan (11/29/73), Panama (3/10/72), Paraguay (2/4/72), Philippines (3/26/73), Portugal (11/27/72), Rwanda (11/3/87),

Senegal (2/3/78), Seychelles (12/29/78), Sierra Leone (11/13/74), Singapore (4/12/78), Spain (10/30/72), Sri Lanka (5/30/78), St. Lucia (11/8/83), Sudan (1/18/79), Suriname (10/27/78), Sweden (7/7/71), Switzerland (9/14/71), Tanzania (8/9/83), Thailand (5/16/78), Togo (2/9/79), Tonga (2/21/77), Trinidad and Tobago (1/31/72), Turkey (4/17/73), Uganda (3/27/72), United Kingdom (12/22/71), United States (9/14/71), Uruguay (1/12/77), Venezuela (7/7/83), Vietnam (9/17/79), Yemen (9/29/86), Yugoslavia (10/2/72), Zaire (7/6/77), Zambia (3/3/87), Zimbabwe (2/6/89)

Ratified/accepted/approved with qualification: 34

Argentina (9/11/72), Bahrain (2/20/84), Brazil (1/14/72), Bulgaria (5/19/71), Byelorussian SSR (12/30/71), China (9/10/80), Czechoslovakia (4/6/72), Egypt (2/28/75), Ethiopia (3/26/79), Guatemala (5/16/79), Honduras (4/13/87), Hungary (8/13/71), India (11/25/82), Indonesia (8/27/76), Iraq (12/30/71), Korea (South) (1/18/73), Kuwait (5/25/79), Libya (10/4/78), Malawi (12/21/72), Mongolia (10/8/71), Morocco (10/24/75), Netherlands (8/27/73), Papua New Guinea (12/11/75), Peru (4/28/78), Poland (3/21/72), Qatar (8/26/81), Romania (7/10/72), Saudi Arabia (6/14/74), South Africa (5/30/72), Syria (7/10/80), Tunisia (11/16/81), Ukranian SSR (2/21/72), United Arab Emirates (4/14/81), USSR (9/24/71)

3.28 Convention for the Suppression of Unlawful Acts Against the Safety of Civil Aviation

Entry into force: January 26, 1973

Signed but not ratified: 4

Burundi (3/6/72), Congo (9/23/71), Laos (11/1/72), Rwanda (4/4/72)

Ratified/accepted/approved without qualification: 113

Antigua and Barbuda (7/22/85), Argentina (11/26/73), Australia (7/12/73), Austria (2/11/74), Bahamas (12/27/84), Bangladesh (6/28/78), Barbados (8/6/76), Belgium (8/13/76), Bhutan (12/28/88), Bolivia (7/18/79), Botswana (12/28/78), Brunei (4/16/86), Burkina Faso (10/19/87), Bulgaria (2/22/73), Canada (6/19/72), Cape Verde (10/20/77), Chad (7/12/72), Chile (2/28/74), Columbia (12/4/74), Congo (3/19/87), Costa Rica (9/21/73), Cyprus (7/27/73), Denmark (1/17/73), Dominican Republic (11/28/73), Ecuador (1/12/77), El Salvador (9/25/79), Fiji (3/5/73), Finland (7/13/73), Gabon (6/29/76), Gambia (11/28/78), Germany (East) (6/9/72), Germany (West) (2/3/78), Ghana (12/12/73), Greece (1/15/74), Grenada (8/10/78), Guinea (5/2/84), Guinea-Bissau (8/20/76), Guyana (12/21/72), Haiti (5/9/84), Iceland (6/29/73), Iran (7/10/73), Iraq (9/10/74), Ireland (10/12/76), Israel (6/30/72), Ivory Coast (1/9/73), Jamaica (9/16/83), Japan (6/12/74), Jordan (2/13/73), Kenya (1/11/77), Korea (North) (8/13/80), Lebanon (12/23/77), Lesotho (7/27/78), Liberia (2/1/82), Libya (2/19/74), Luxembourg (5/18/82), Madagascar (11/18/86), Malawi (12/21/72), Malaysia (5/4/85), Maldives (9/1/87), Mali (8/24/72), Mauritania (11/1/78), Mauritius (4/25/83), Mexico (9/12/74), Monaco (6/3/83), Mongolia (9/5/72), Nauru (5/17/84), Nepal (1/10/79), Netherlands (8/27/73), New Zealand (2/12/74), Nicaragua (11/6/73), Niger (9/1/72), Nigeria (7/3/73), Norway (8/1/73), Oman (2/2/77), Pakistan (1/16/74), Panama (4/24/72), Papua New Guinea (12/11/75), Paraguay (3/5/74), Peru (4/28/78), Philippines (3/26/73), Poland (1/28/75), Portugal (1/15/73), Qatar (8/26/81), Rwanda (11/3/87), Senegal (2/3/78), Seychelles (12/29/78), Sierra Leone (9/20/79), Singapore (4/12/78), Solomon Islands (4/13/82), Spain (10/30/72), Sri Lanka (5/30/78), St. Lucia (11/8/83), Sudan (1/18/79), Suriname (10/27/78), Swaziland (5/18/88), Sweden (7/10/73), Switzerland (1/17/78), Tanzania (8/9/83), Thailand (5/16/78), Togo (2/9/79), Tonga (2/21/77), Trinidad and Tobago (2/9/72), Tunisia (11/16/81), Turkey (12/23/75), Uganda (7/19/82), United States

(11/1/72), Uruguay (1/12/77), Vietnam (9/17/79), Yemen (8/11/87), Zambia (3/3/87), Zimbabwe (2/6/89)

Ratified/accepted/approved with qualification: 27

Bahrain (2/20/84), Brazil (7/24/72), Byelorussian SSR (1/31/73), Cameroon (7/11/73), China (9/10/80), Czechoslovakia (8/10/73), Egypt (5/20/75), Ethiopia (3/26/79), France (6/30/76), Guatemala (10/19/78), Honduras (4/13/87), Hungary (12/27/72), India (11/12/82), Indonesia (8/27/76), Italy (2/19/74), Korea (South) (8/2/73), Kuwait (11/27/79), Morocco (10/24/75), Romania (8/15/75), Saudi Arabia (6/14/74), South Africa (5/30/72), Syria (7/10/80), Switzerland (5/4/76), Ukrainian SSR (2/26/73), United Arab Emirates (4/14/81), United Kingdom (10/25/73), USSR (2/19/73), Venezuela (11/21/83)

3.29 International Convention on the Suppression and Punishment of the Crime of "Apartheid"

Entry into force: July 18, 1976

Signed but not ratified: 5

Argentina (6/6/75), Jordan (6/5/74), Kenya (10/2/75), Oman (4/3/74), Yemen (Democratic) (7/31/74)

Ratified/accepted/approved without qualification: 76

Afghanistan (7/6/83), Algeria (5/26/82), Antigua and Barbuda (10/7/82), Bahamas (3/31/81), Bangladesh (2/5/85), Barbados (2/7/79), Benin (12/30/74), Bolivia (10/6/83), Burundi (7/12/78), Byelorussian SSR (12/2/75), Cameroon (11/1/76), Cape Verde (6/12/79), Central African Republic (5/8/81), Chad (10/23/74), China (4/18/83), Columbia (5/23/88), Congo (10/5/83), Costa Rica (10/15/86), Cuba (2/1/77), Ecuador (5/12/75), Egypt (6/13/77), El Salvador (11/30/79), Ethiopia (9/19/78), Gabon (2/29/80), Gambia (12/29/78), Germany (East) (8/12/74), Ghana (8/1/78), Guinea (3/3/75), Guyana (9/30/77), Haiti (12/19/77), Hungary (6/20/74), Iran (4/17/85), Jamaica (2/18/77), Kampuchea (7/28/81), Laos (10/5/81), Lesotho (11/4/83), Liberia (11/5/76), Libya (7/8/76), Madagascar (5/26/77), Maldives (4/24/84), Mali (8/19/77), Mauritania (12/13/88), Mexico (3/4/80), Namibia (11/11/82), Nicaragua (3/28/80), Niger (6/28/78), Nigeria (3/31/77), Pakistan (2/27/86), Panama (3/16/77), Peru (11/1/78), Philippines (1/26/78), Poland (3/15/76), Qatar (3/19/75), Romania (8/15/78), Rwanda (1/23/81), São Tomé and Príncipe (10/5/79), Senegal (2/18/77), Seychelles (2/13/78), Somalia (1/28/75), Sri Lanka (2/18/82), St. Vincent and the Grenadines (11/9/81), Sudan (3/21/77), Suriname (6/3/80), Syria (6/18/76), Tanzania (6/11/76), Togo (5/24/84), Trinidad and Tobago (10/26/79), Tunisia (1/21/77), Uganda (6/10/86), Ukrainian SSR (11/10/75), Upper Volta (10/24/78), USSR (11/26/75), Vietnam (6/9/81), Yugoslavia (7/1/75), Zaire (7/11/78), Zambia (2/14/83)

Ratified/accepted/approved with qualification: 12

Argentina (11/7/85), Bulgaria (7/18/74), Czechoslovakia (3/25/76), India (9/22/77), Iraq (7/9/75), Kuwait (2/23/77), Mongolia (8/8/75), Mozambique (4/18/83), Nepal (7/12/77), United Arab Emirates (10/15/75), Venezuela (1/28/83), Yemen (8/17/87)

3.30 Convention on the Prevention and Punishment of Crimes Against Internationally Protected Persons, Including Diplomatic Agents

Entry into force: February 20, 1977

Ratified/accepted/approved without qualification: 36

Australia (6/20/77), Austria (8/3/77), Bahamas (7/22/86), Barbados (10/26/79), Bhutan (1/16/89), Canada (8/4/76), Chile (1/21/77), Costa Rica (11/2/77), Cyprus

(12/24/75), Denmark (7/1/75), Dominican Republic (7/8/77), Egypt (6/25/86), Gabon (10/14/81), Greece (7/3/84), Guatemala (1/18/83), Haiti (8/25/80), Iceland (8/2/77), Iran (7/12/78), Japan (6/8/87), Korea (South) (5/25/83), Liberia (9/30/75), Mexico (4/22/80), Nicaragua (3/10/75), Niger (6/17/85), Norway (4/28/80), Oman (3/22/88), Panama (6/17/80), Paraguay (11/24/75), Philippines (11/26/76), Rwanda (11/29/77), Seychelles (5/29/80), Spain (4/25/88), Sweden (7/1/75), Togo (12/30/80), Uruguay (6/13/78), Yugoslavia (12/29/76)

Ratified/accepted/approved with qualification: 40

Argentina (3/18/82), Bulgaria (7/18/74), Burundi (12/17/80), Byelorussian SSR (2/5/76), China (8/5/87), Czechoslovakia (6/30/75), Ecuador (3/12/75), El Salvador (8/8/80), Finland (10/31/78), Germany (East) (11/30/76), Germany (West) (1/25/77), Ghana (4/25/75), Hungary (3/26/75), India (4/11/78), Italy (8/30/85), Iraq (2/28/78), Israel (7/31/80), Jamaica (9/21/78), Jordan (12/18/84), Korea (North) (12/1/82), Kuwait (3/1/89), Malawi (3/14/77), Mongolia (8/8/75), Netherlands (12/6/88), New Zealand (11/12/85), Pakistan (3/29/76), Peru (4/25/78), Poland (12/14/82), Romania (8/15/78), Switzerland (3/5/85), Syria (4/25/88), Trinidad and Tobago (6/15/79), Tunisia (1/21/77), Turkey (6/11/81), Ukrainian SSR (1/20/76), United Kingdom (5/2/79), United States (10/26/76), USSR (1/15/76), Yemen (Democratic) (2/9/87), Zaire (7/25/77)

3.31 Universal Declaration on the Eradication of Hunger and Malnutrition *

* Adopted apparently by acclamation or consensus.

3.32 Antihijacking Act of 1974

3.33 European Convention on the Suppression of Terrorism

Entry into force: August 4, 1978

Signed but not ratified: 2

Ireland (2/24/86), Malta (11/5/86)

Ratified/accepted/approved without qualification: 6

Austria (8/11/77), Liechtenstein (6/13/79), Luxembourg (9/11/81), Spain (5/20/80), Turkey (5/19/81), United Kingdom (7/24/78)

Ratified/accepted/approved with qualification: 13

Belgium (10/31/85), Cyprus (2/26/79), Denmark (6/27/78), France (9/21/87), Germany (West) (5/3/78), Greece (8/4/88), Iceland (7/11/80), Italy (2/28/86), Netherlands (4/18/85), Norway (1/10/80), Portugal (12/14/81), Sweden (9/15/77), Switzerland (5/19/83)

3.34 Resolution on Disappeared Persons

Adopted without recorded vote

3.35 International Convention Against the Taking of Hostages

Entry into force: June 4, 1983

Signed but not ratified: 14

Belgium (1/3/80), Bolivia (3/25/80), Canada (2/18/80), Dominican Republic (8/12/80), Gabon (2/29/80), Haiti (4/21/80), Iraq (10/14/80), Israel (11/19/80), Jamaica (2/27/80), Liberia (1/30/80), Luxembourg (12/18/79), New Zealand (12/24/80), Uganda (11/10/80), Zaire (7/2/80)

Ratified/accepted/approved without qualification: 35

Antigua and Barbuda (8/6/86), Austria (8/22/86), Bahamas (6/4/81), Barbados (3/9/81), Bhutan (8/31/81), Brunei (10/18/88), Cameroon (3/9/88), Canada (12/4/85), Denmark (8/11/87), Ecuador (5/2/88), Egypt (10/2/81), Finland (4/14/83), Ghana (11/10/87), Greece (6/18/87), Guatemala (3/11/83), Honduras (6/1/81), Iceland (7/6/81), Italy (3/20/86), Japan (6/8/87), Korea (South) (5/4/83), Lesotho (11/5/80), Mauritius (10/17/80), New Zealand (11/12/85), Norway (7/2/81), Oman (7/22/88), Panama (8/19/82), Philippines (10/14/80), Portugal (7/6/84), Senegal (3/10/87), Spain (3/26/84), Suriname (11/5/81), Sweden (1/15/81), Togo (7/25/86), Trinidad and Tobago (4/1/81), United States (12/7/84)

Ratified/accepted/approved with qualification: 21

Bulgaria (3/10/88), Byelorussian SSR (7/1/87), Chile (11/12/81), Czechoslovakia (1/27/88), Dominica (9/9/86), El Salvador (2/12/81), Germany (East) (5/2/88), Germany (West) (12/15/80), Hungary (9/2/87), Jordan (2/19/86), Kenya (12/8/81), Kuwait (2/6/89), Malawi (3/17/86), Mexico (4/28/87), Netherlands (12/6/88), Switzerland (3/5/85), Ukrainian SSR (6/19/87), United Kingdom (12/22/82), USSR (6/11/87), Venezuela (12/13/88), Yugoslavia (4/19/85)

3.36 Convention on the Elimination of All Forms of Discrimination Against Women

Entry into force: September 3, 1981

Signed but not ratified: 21

Afghanistan (8/14/80), Benin (11/11/81), Bolivia (5/30/80), Burundi (7/17/80), Cameroon (6/6/83), Chile (7/17/80), Gambia (7/29/80), Greece (3/2/82), Grenada (7/17/80), India (7/30/80), Israel (7/17/80), Ivory Coast (7/17/80), Jordan (12/3/80), Kampuchea (7/17/80), Lesotho (7/17/80), Madagascar (7/17/80), Netherlands (7/17/80), Switzerland (1/23/87), Trinidad and Tobago (6/27/85), United States (7/17/80), Venezuela (7/17/80)

Ratified/accepted/approved without qualification: 51

Angola (9/17/86), Barbados (10/16/80), Bhutan (8/31/81), Burkina Faso (10/14/87), Cape Verde (12/5/80), Columbia (1/19/82), Congo (7/26/82), Costa Rica (4/4/86), Denmark (4/21/83), Dominica (9/15/80), Dominican Republic (9/2/82), Ecuador (11/9/81), Equatorial Guinea (10/23/84), Finland (9/4/86), Gabon (1/21/83), Ghana (1/2/86), Greece (6/7/83), Guatemala (8/12/82), Guinea (8/9/82), Guinea–Bissau (8/23/85), Guyana (7/17/80), Haiti (7/20/81), Honduras (3/3/83), Iceland (6/18/85), Japan (6/25/85), Kenya (3/9/84), Liberia (7/17/84), Mali (9/10/85), Nigeria (6/13/85), Nicaragua (10/27/81), Norway (5/21/81), Panama (10/29/81), Paraguay (4/6/87), Peru (9/13/82), Philippines (8/5/81), Portugal (7/30/80), Rwanda (3/2/81), Senegal (2/5/85), Sierra Leone (11/11/88), Sri Lanka (10/5/81), St Christopher and Nevis (4/25/85), St. Lucia (10/8/82), St. Vincent and the Grenadines (8/4/81), Tanzania (8/20/85), Togo (9/26/83), Uganda (7/22/85), Uruguay (10/9/81), USSR (1/23/81) Yugoslavia (2/26/82), Zaire (10/17/86), Zambia (6/21/85)

Ratified/accepted/approved with qualification: 45

Argentina (7/15/85), Australia (7/28/83), Austria (3/31/82), Bangladesh (11/6/84), Belgium (7/10/85), Brazil (2/1/84), Bulgaria (2/8/82), Byelorussian SSR (2/4/81), Canada (12/10/81), China (11/4/80), Cuba (7/17/80), Cyprus (7/23/85), Czechoslovakia (2/16/82), Egypt (9/18/81), El Salvador (8/19/81), Ethiopia (9/10/81), France (12/14/83), Germany (East) (7/9/80), Germany (West) (7/10/85), Hungary (12/22/80), Indonesia (9/13/84), Iraq (8/13/86), Ireland (12/23/85), Italy (6/10/85), Jamaica (10/19/84), Korea (South) (12/27/84), Laos (8/14/81), Luxembourg (2/2/89), Malawi (3/12/87), Mauritius (7/9/84), Mexico

(3/23/81), Mongolia (7/20/81), New Zealand (1/10/85), Poland (7/30/80), Romania (1/7/82), Spain (1/5/84), Sweden (7/2/80), Thailand (8/9/85), Tunisia (9/20/85), Turkey (12/20/85), Ukrainian SSR (3/12/81), United Kingdom (4/7/86), Venezuela (5/2/83), Vietnam (2/17/82), Yemen (Democratic) (5/30/84)

3.37 AFRICAN CHARTER ON HUMAN AND PEOPLES' RIGHTS

Entry into force: October 21, 1986

Signed but not ratified: 5

Lesotho (3/7/84), Libya (5/30/85), Somalia (2/26/82), Sudan (9/3/82), Tanzania (5/31/82)

Ratified/accepted/approved without qualification: 36

Algeria (3/20/87), Benin (2/25/86), Botswana (7/22/86), Burkina Faso (9/21/84), Cape Verde (8/6/87), Central African Republic (7/27/86), Chad (11/11/86), Comoros (7/18/86), Congo (1/17/83), Egypt (4/3/84), Equatorial Guinea (8/18/86), Gabon (6/26/86), Gambia (6/13/83), Ghana (2/24/89), Guinea (5/13/82), Guinea-Bissau (3/6/86), Liberia (12/29/82), Libya (3/26/87), Mali (1/22/82), Mauritania (6/26/86), Niger (6/21/86), Nigeria (7/22/83), Rwanda (7/22/83), Saharan Arab Democratic Republic (7/23/86), São Tomé and Príncipe (7/28/86), Senegal (10/25/82), Sierra Leone (1/27/84), Somalia (3/20/86), Sudan (3/11/86), Tanzania (3/9/84), Togo (11/22/82), Tunisia (4/22/83), Uganda (5/27/86), Zaire (7/28/87), Zambia (2/2/84), Zimbabwe (6/12/86)

3.38 DECLARATION ON THE ELIMINATION OF ALL FORMS OF INTOLERANCE AND OF DISCRIMINATION BASED ON RELIGION OR BELIEF

Adopted without recorded vote

3.39 DECLARATION ON THE RIGHT OF PEOPLES TO PEACE

For: 96

Afghanistan, Algeria, Angola, Argentina, Bahamas, Bahrain, Bangladesh, Belize, Benin, Bolivia, Botswana, Brazil, Bulgaria, Burkina Faso, Burma, Burundi, Byelorussian SSR, Central African Republic, Chile, China, Colombia, Congo, Cuba, Cyprus, Czechoslovakia, Djibouti, Dominican Republic, Ecuador, Egypt, El Salvador, Equatorial Guinea, Ethiopia, Germany (East), Ghana, Guatemala, Guinea, Guyana, Haiti, Honduras, Hungary, India, Indonesia, Iran, Iraq, Ivory Coast, Jordan, Kenya, Kuwait, Laos, Lebanon, Lesotho, Liberia, Libya, Madagascar, Maldives, Mali, Mauritania, Mauritius, Mexico, Mongolia, Mozambique, Nepal, Nicaragua, Nigeria, Oman, Pakistan, Panama, Peru, Poland, Qatar, Romania, Rwanda, São Tomé and Príncipe, Saudi Arabia, Seychelles, Sierra Leone, Sri Lanka, Sudan, Suriname, Syria, Tanzania, Thailand, Togo, Tunisia, Uganda, Ukrainian SSR, United Arab Emirates, Uruguay, USSR, Venezuela, Vietnam, Yemen, Yemen (Democratic), Yugoslavia, Zaire, Zambia

Against: 0

Abstaining: 34

Australia, Austria, Belgium, Brunei, Cameroon, Canada, Cape Verde, Denmark, Finland, France, Gabon, Germany (West), Greece, Grenada, Guinea-Bissau, Iceland, Ireland, Italy, Japan, Luxembourg, Malawi, Netherlands, New Zealand, Niger, Norway, Philippines, Portugal, St. Christopher and Nevis, Senegal, Spain, Sweden, Turkey, United Kingdom, United States

3.40 CONVENTION AGAINST TORTURE AND OTHER CRUEL, INHUMAN OR DEGRADING TREATMENT OR PUNISHMENT

Entry into force: June 26, 1987

Signed but not ratified: 28

Algeria (11/26/85), Australia (12/10/85), Belgium (2/4/85), Bolivia (2/4/85), Brazil (9/23/85), Costa Rica (2/4/85), Cuba (1/27/86), Cyprus (10/9/85), Dominican Republic (2/4/85), Finland (2/4/85), Gabon (1/21/86), Gambia (10/23/85), Germany (West) (10/13/86), Guinea (5/30/86), Iceland (2/4/85), Indonesia (10/23/85), Israel (10/22/86), Liechtenstein (6/27/85), Morocco (1/8/86), New Zealand (1/14/86), Nicaragua (4/15/85), Nigeria (7/28/88), Poland (1/13/86), Portugal (2/4/85), Sierra Leone (3/18/85), Sudan (6/4/86), United States (4/18/88), Venezuela (2/15/85)

Ratified/accepted/approved without qualification: 16

Argentina (9/24/86), Belize (3/17/86), Cameroon (12/19/86), Colombia (12/8/87), Egypt (6/25/86), Mexico (1/23/86), Peru (7/7/88), Philippines (6/18/86), Senegal (8/21/86), Spain (10/21/87), Togo (11/18/87), Tunisia (9/23/88), Uganda (11/3/86), United Kingdom (12/8/88), Uruguay (10/24/86)

Ratified/accepted/approved with qualification: 24

Afghanistan (4/1/87), Austria (7/29/87), Bulgaria (12/16/86), Byelorussian SSR (3/13/87), Canada (6/24/87), Chile (9/30/88), China (10/4/88), Czechoslovakia (7/7/88), Denmark (5/27/87), Ecuador (3/30/88), France (2/18/86), Germany (East) (9/9/87), Greece (10/6/88), Hungary (4/15/87), Italy (1/12/89), Luxembourg (9/29/87), Netherlands (12/21/88), Norway (7/9/86), Panama (8/24/87), Sweden (1/8/86), Switzerland (12/2/86), Turkey (8/2/88), Ukrainian SSR (2/24/87), USSR (3/3/87)

3.41 Inter-American Convention to Prevent and Punish Torture

Entry into force: February 28, 1987

Signed but not ratified: 14

Argentina (2/10/86), Bolivia (12/9/85), Brazil (1/24/86), Colombia (12/9/85), Costa Rica (7/31/86), Ecuador (5/30/86), El Salvador (10/16/87), Haiti (6/13/86), Honduras (3/11/86), Nicaragua (9/29/87), Panama (2/10/86), Peru (1/10/86), Uruguay (12/9/85), Venezuela (12/9/85)

Ratified/accepted/approved without qualification: 3

Dominican Republic (1/29/87), Mexico (6/22/87), Suriname (11/12/87)

Ratified/accepted/approved with qualification: 2

Chile (9/30/88), Guatemala (1/29/87)

3.42 Resolution on Measures to Prevent International Terrorism

Adopted unanimously

3.43 Security Council Resolution Condemning Hostage Taking

Adopted unanimously

3.44 Food Aid Convention

Entry into force: July 1, 1986

Ratified/accepted/approved without qualification: 21

Argentina (6/25/86), Australia (6/29/88), Austria (8/26/87), Belgium (6/26/86), Canada (6/23/86), Denmark (6/26/86), EEC (6/26/86), Finland (3/2/87), France (9/21/87), Germany (West) (3/14/88), Greece (6/26/86), Ireland (6/26/86), Japan (12/15/86), Luxembourg (6/30/86), Netherlands (6/26/86), Norway (6/30/86), Portugal (6/30/86), Spain (9/14/87), Sweden (6/25/86), Switzerland (6/26/86), United Kingdom (6/26/86)

Ratified/accepted/approved with qualification: 2

Italy (6/26/86), United States (1/27/88)

3.45 Declaration on the Right to Development

For: 146

Afghanistan, Algeria, Angola, Antigua and Barbuda, Argentina, Australia, Austria, Bahamas, Bahrain, Bangladesh, Barbados, Belgium, Belize, Benin, Bhutan, Bolivia, Botswana, Brazil, Brunei, Bulgaria, Burkina Faso, Burma, Burundi, Byelorussian SSR, Cameroon, Canada, Cape Verde, Central African Republic, Chad, Chile, China, Colombia, Comoros, Congo, Costa Rica, Cuba, Cyprus, Czechoslovakia, Djibouti, Dominican Republic, Ecuador, Egypt, El Salvador, Equatorial Guinea, Ethiopia, Fiji, France, Gabon, Gambia, Germany (East), Ghana, Greece, Grenada, Guatemala, Guinea, Guinea–Bissau, Guyana, Haiti, Honduras, Hungary, India, Indonesia, Iran, Iraq, Ireland, Italy, Ivory Coast, Jamaica, Jordan, Kampuchea, Kenya, Kuwait, Laos, Lebanon, Lesotho, Liberia, Libya, Luxembourg, Madagascar, Malawi, Malaysia, Maldives, Mali, Mauritania, Mauritius, Mexico, Mongolia, Morocco, Mozambique, Nepal, Netherlands, New Zealand, Nicaragua, Niger, Nigeria, Norway, Oman, Pakistan, Panama, Papua New Guinea, Paraguay, Peru, Philippines, Poland, Portugal, Qatar, Romania, Rwanda, Samoa, São Tomé and Príncipe, Saudi Arabia, Senegal, Seychelles, Sierra Leone, Singapore, Solomon Islands, Somalia, Spain, Sri Lanka, St. Christopher and Nevis, St. Lucia, St. Vincent and the Grenadines, Sudan, Suriname, Swaziland, Syria, Tanzania, Thailand, Togo, Trinidad and Tobago, Tunisia, Turkey, Uganda, Ukrainian SSR, United Arab Emirates, Uruguay, USSR, Vanuatu, Venezuela, Vietnam, Yemen, Yemen (Democratic), Yugoslavia, Zaire, Zambia, Zimbabwe

Against: 1

United States

Abstaining: 8

Denmark, Finland, Germany (West), Iceland, Israel, Japan, Sweden, United Kingdom

3.46 International Labor Organization Convention (No. 169) Concerning Indigenous and Tribal Peoples in Independent Countries

Not yet entered into force

3.47 Convention on the Rights of the Child

Entry into force: 30 days after the 20th acceptance

Signed but not ratified: 61 (all on 1/26/90)

Albania, Algeria, Austria, Bangladesh, Belgium, Brazil, Burkina Faso, Byelorussian SSR, Chile, Colombia, Costa Rica, Cuba, Denmark, Dominica, Ecuador, El Salvador, Finland, France, Gabon, Germany (West), Greece, Guatemala, Guinea–Bissau, Haiti, Iceland, Indonesia, Italy, Ivory Coast, Jamaica, Kenya, Lebanon, Mali, Malta, Mauritania, Mexico, Mongolia, Maroc, Nepal, Netherlands, Niger, Nigeria, Norway, Panama, Peru, Philippines, Poland, Portugal, Romania, Rwanda, St. Kitts and Nevis, Senegal, Spain, Sri Lanka, Suriname, Sweden, Togo, Uruguay, USSR, Venezuela, Vietnam, Yugoslavia

4. ECONOMIC DEVELOPMENT

4.1 Articles of Agreement of the International Monetary Fund; Amendment to the Articles of Agreement (July 28, 1969); Amendment to the Articles of Agreement (Apr. 1, 1978)

Entry into force: December 27, 1945

Ratified/accepted/approved without qualification: 151

Afghanistan (7/14/55), Algeria (9/26/63), Antigua and Barbuda (2/25/82), Argentina (9/20/56), Australia (8/5/47), Austria (8/27/48), Bahamas (8/21/73), Bahrain (9/7/72), Bangladesh (8/17/72), Barbados (12/29/70), Belgium (12/27/45), Belize (3/16/82), Benin (7/10/63), Bhutan (9/28/81), Bolivia (12/27/45), Botswana (7/24/68), Brazil (1/14/46), Burma (1/3/52), Burundi (9/28/63), Cameroon (7/10/63), Canada (12/27/45), Cape Verde (11/20/78), Central African Republic (7/10/63), Chad (7/10/63), Chile (12/31/45), China (12/27/45), Colombia (12/27/45), Comoros (9/21/76), Congo (7/10/63), Costa Rica (1/8/46), Cyprus (12/21/61), Denmark (3/30/46), Djibouti (12/29/78), Dominica (12/12/78), Dominican Republic (12/28/45), Ecuador (12/28/45), Egypt (12/27/45), El Salvador (3/14/46), Equatorial Guinea (12/22/69), Ethiopia (12/27/45), Fiji (5/28/71), Finland (1/14/48), France (12/27/45), Gabon (9/10/63), Gambia (9/21/67), Germany (West) (8/14/52), Ghana (9/20/57), Greece (12/27/45), Grenada (8/27/75), Guatemala (12/28/45), Guinea (9/28/63), Guinea–Bissau (3/24/77), Guyana (9/26/66), Haiti (9/8/53), Honduras (12/27/45), Hungary (5/6/82), Iceland (12/27/45), India (12/27/45), Indonesia (2/21/67), Iran (12/29/45), Iraq (12/27/45), Ireland (8/8/57), Israel (7/12/54), Italy (3/27/47), Ivory Coast (3/11/63), Jamaica (2/21/63), Japan (8/13/52), Jordan (8/29/52), Kampuchea (12/31/69), Kenya (2/3/64), Kiribati (6/3/86), Korea (South) (8/26/55), Kuwait (9/13/62), Laos (7/5/61), Lebanon (4/14/47), Lesotho (7/25/68), Liberia (3/28/62), Libya (9/17/58), Luxembourg (12/27/45), Madagascar (9/25/63), Malawi (7/19/65), Malaysia (3/7/58), Maldives (1/13/78), Mali (9/27/63), Malta (9/11/68), Mauritania (9/10/63), Mauritius (9/23/68), Mexico (12/31/45), Morocco (4/25/58), Mozambique (9/24/84), Nepal (9/6/61), Netherlands (12/27/45), New Zealand (8/31/61), Nicaragua (3/14/46), Niger (4/24/63), Nigeria (3/30/61), Norway (12/27/45), Oman (12/23/71), Pakistan (7/11/50), Panama (3/14/46), Papua New Guinea (10/9/75), Paraguay (12/28/45), Peru (12/31/45), Philippines (12/27/45), Poland (6/12/86), Portugal (3/29/61), Qatar (9/8/72), Romania (12/15/72), Rwanda (9/30/63), Samoa (12/28/71), São Tomé and Príncipe (9/30/77), Saudi Arabia (8/26/57), Senegal (8/31/62), Seychelles (6/30/77), Sierra Leone (9/10/62), Singapore (8/30/66), Solomon Islands (9/22/78), Somalia (8/31/62), South Africa (12/27/45), Spain (9/15/58), Sri Lanka (8/29/50), St. Christopher and Nevis (8/15/84), St. Lucia (11/15/79), St. Vincent and the Grenadines (12/28/79), Sudan (9/5/57), Suriname (4/27/78), Swaziland (9/22/69), Sweden (8/31/51), Syria (4/10/47), Tanganyika (9/10/62), Thailand (5/3/49), Togo (8/1/62), Tonga (9/13/85), Trinidad and Tobago (9/16/63), Tunisia (4/14/58), Turkey (3/11/47), Uganda (9/27/63), United Arab Emirates (9/22/72), United Kingdom (12/27/45), United States (12/27/45), Upper Volta (5/2/63), Uruguay (3/11/46), Vanuatu (9/28/81), Venezuela (12/30/46), Vietnam (7/2/76), Yemen (5/22/70), Yemen (Democratic) (9/29/69), Yugoslavia (12/27/45), Zaire (9/28/63), Zambia (9/23/65), Zimbabwe (9/29/80)

4.2 Articles of Agreement of the International Bank for Reconstruction and Development; Amendment to the Articles of Agreement

Entry into force: December 27, 1945

Ratified/accepted/approved without qualification: 151

Afghanistan (7/14/55), Algeria (9/26/63), Antigua and Barbuda (9/22/83), Argentina (9/20/56), Australia (8/5/47), Austria (8/27/48), Bahamas (8/21/73), Bahrain (9/15/72), Bangladesh (8/17/72), Barbados (9/12/74), Belgium (12/27/45), Belize (3/19/82), Benin (7/10/63), Bhutan (9/28/81), Bolivia (12/27/45), Botswana (7/24/68), Brazil (1/14/46), Burma (1/3/52), Burundi (9/28/63), Cameroon (7/10/63), Canada (12/27/45), Cape Verde (11/20/78), Central African Republic (7/10/63), Chad (7/10/63), Chile (12/31/45), China (12/27/45), Colombia (12/24/46), Comoros (10/28/76), Congo (7/10/63), Costa Rica (1/8/46), Cyprus (12/21/61), Denmark (3/30/46), Djibouti (10/1/80), Dominica (9/20/80), Dominican Republic (12/28/45), Ecuador (12/28/45), Egypt (12/27/45), El Salvador (3/14/46), Equatorial Guinea (7/1/70), Ethiopia (12/27/45), Fiji (5/28/71), Finland (1/14/48), France (12/27/45), Gabon (9/10/63), Gambia (10/18/67), Germany (West) (8/14/52), Ghana (9/20/57), Greece (12/27/45), Grenada (8/27/75), Guatemala (12/28/45), Guinea (9/28/63), Guinea–Bissau (3/24/77), Guyana (9/26/66), Haiti (9/8/53), Honduras (12/27/45), Hungary (7/7/82), Iceland (12/27/45), India (12/27/45), Indonesia (4/13/67), Iran (12/29/45), Iraq (12/27/45), Ireland (8/8/57), Israel (7/12/54), Italy (3/27/47), Ivory Coast (3/11/63), Jamaica (2/21/63), Japan (8/13/52), Jordan (8/29/52), Kampuchea (12/31/69), Kenya (2/3/64), Kiribati (9/29/86), Korea (South) (8/26/55), Kuwait (9/13/62), Laos (7/5/61), Lebanon (4/14/47), Lesotho (7/25/68), Liberia (3/28/62), Libya (9/17/58), Luxembourg (12/27/45), Madagascar (9/25/63), Malawi (7/19/65), Malaysia (3/7/58), Maldives (1/13/78), Mali (9/27/63), Malta (9/26/83), Mauritania (9/10/63), Mauritius (9/23/68), Mexico (12/31/45), Morocco (4/25/58), Mozambique (9/24/84), Nepal (9/6/61), Netherlands (12/27/45), New Zealand (8/31/61), Nicaragua (3/14/46), Niger (4/24/63), Nigeria (3/30/61), Norway (12/27/45), Oman (12/23/71), Pakistan (7/11/50), Panama (3/14/46), Papua New Guinea (10/9/75), Paraguay (12/28/45), Peru (12/31/45), Philippines (12/27/45), Poland (6/27/86), Portugal (3/29/61), Qatar (9/25/72), Romania (12/15/72), Rwanda (9/30/63), Samoa (6/28/74), São Tomé and Príncipe (9/30/77), Saudi Arabia (8/26/57), Senegal (8/31/62), Seychelles (9/29/80), Sierra Leone (9/10/62), Singapore (8/3/66), Solomon Islands (9/22/78), Somalia (8/31/62), South Africa (12/27/45), Spain (9/15/58), Sri Lanka (8/29/50), St. Christopher and Nevis (8/15/84), St. Lucia (6/27/80), St. Vincent and the Grenadines (8/31/82), Sudan (9/5/57), Suriname (6/27/78), Swaziland (9/22/69), Sweden (8/31/51), Syria (4/10/47), Tanganyika (9/10/62), Thailand (5/3/49), Togo (8/1/62), Tonga (9/13/85), Trinidad and Tobago (9/16/63), Tunisia (4/14/58), Turkey (3/11/47), Uganda (9/27/63), United Arab Emirates (9/22/72), United Kingdom (12/27/45), United States (12/27/45), Upper Volta (5/2/63), Uruguay (3/11/46), Vanuatu (9/28/81), Venezuela (12/30/46), Vietnam (7/2/76), Yemen (5/22/70), Yemen (Democratic) (10/3/69), Yugoslavia (12/27/45), Zaire (9/28/63), Zambia (9/23/65), Zimbabwe (9/29/80)

4.3 Resolution on Permanent Sovereignty Over Natural Resources

For: 87

Afghanistan, Algeria, Argentina, Australia, Austria, Belgium, Bolivia, Brazil, Burundi, Cambodia, Cameroon, Canada, Central African Republic, Ceylon, Chad, Chile, China, Colombia, Congo (Leopoldville), Costa Rica, Cyprus, Dahomey, Denmark, Dominican Republic, El Salvador, Ethiopia, Finland, Greece, Guatemala, Guinea, Haiti, Honduras, Iceland, India, Indonesia, Iran, Iraq, Ireland, Israel, Italy, Ivory Coast, Jamaica, Japan, Jordan, Lebanon, Liberia, Libya, Luxembourg, Madagascar, Malaysia, Mali, Mauritania, Mexico, Morocco, Netherlands, New Zealand, Nicaragua, Niger, Nigeria, Norway, Pakistan, Panama, Paraguay, Peru, Philippines, Rwanda, Saudi Arabia, Senegal, Sierra Leone, Spain, Sweden,

Syria, Tanganyika, Thailand, Togo, Trinidad and Tobago, Tunisia, Turkey, Uganda, United Arab Republic, United Kingdom, United States, Upper Volta, Uruguay, Venezuela, Yemen, Yugoslavia

Against: 2

France, South Africa

Abstaining: 12

Bulgaria, Burma, Byelorussian SSR, Cuba, Czechoslovakia, Ghana, Hungary, Mongolia, Poland, Romania, Ukrainian SSR, USSR

4.4 Convention on the Settlement of Investment Disputes Between States and Nationals of Other States

Entry into force: October 14, 1966

Signed but not ratified: 6

Australia (3/24/75), Belize (12/19/86), Costa Rica (9/29/81), Ethiopia (9/21/65), Haiti (1/30/85), Thailand (12/6/85)

Ratified/accepted/approved without qualification: 91

Afghanistan (6/25/68), Austria (5/25/71), Bangladesh (3/27/80), Barbados (11/1/83), Belgium (8/27/70), Benin (9/6/66), Botswana (1/15/70), Burundi (11/5/69), Cameroon (1/3/67), Central African Republic (2/23/66), Chad (8/29/66), Comoros (11/7/78), Congo (6/23/66), Cyprus (11/25/66), Denmark (4/24/68), Ecuador (1/15/86), Egypt (5/3/72), El Salvador (3/6/84), Fiji (8/11/77), Finland (1/9/69), France (8/21/67), Gabon (4/4/66), Gambia (12/27/74), Germany (West) (4/18/69), Ghana (7/13/66), Greece (4/21/69), Guinea (11/4/68), Guyana (7/11/69), Honduras (2/14/89), Hungary (2/4/87), Iceland (7/25/66), Indonesia (9/28/68), Ireland (4/7/81), Israel (6/22/83), Italy (3/29/71), Ivory Coast (2/16/66), Jamaica (9/9/66), Japan (8/17/67), Jordan (10/30/72), Kenya (1/3/67), Korea (South) (2/21/67), Kuwait (2/2/79), Lesotho (7/8/69), Liberia (6/16/70), Luxembourg (7/30/70), Madagascar (9/6/66), Malawi (8/23/66), Malaysia (8/8/66), Mali (1/3/78), Mauritania (1/11/66), Mauritius (6/2/69), Morocco (5/11/67), Nepal (1/7/69), Netherlands (9/14/66), New Zealand (4/2/80), Niger (11/14/66), Nigeria (8/23/65), Norway (8/16/67), Pakistan (9/15/66), Papua New Guinea (10/20/78), Paraguay (1/7/83), Philippines (11/17/78), Portugal (7/2/84), Romania (9/12/75), Rwanda (10/15/79), Samoa (4/25/78), Saudi Arabia (5/8/80), Senegal (4/21/67), Seychelles (3/20/78), Sierra Leone (8/2/66), Singapore (10/14/68), Solomon Islands (9/8/81), Somalia (2/29/68), Sri Lanka (10/12/67), St. Lucia (6/4/84), Sudan (4/9/73), Swaziland (6/14/71), Sweden (12/29/66), Switzerland (5/15/68), Togo (8/11/67), Trinidad and Tobago (1/3/67), Tunisia (6/22/66), Turkey (3/3/89), Uganda (6/7/66), United Arab Emirates (12/23/81), United Kingdom (12/19/66), United States (6/10/66), Upper Volta (8/29/66), Yugoslavia (3/21/67), Zaire (4/29/70), Zambia (6/17/70)

4.5 Resolution on Permanent Sovereignty Over Natural Resources

For: 108

Afghanistan, Albania, Algeria, Argentina, Australia, Austria, Bahrain, Barbados, Bhutan, Bolivia, Botswana, Brazil, Bulgaria, Burma, Burundi, Byelorussian SSR, Cameroon, Canada, Chad, Chile, China, Congo, Costa Rica, Cuba, Cyprus, Czechoslovakia, Dahomey, Dominican Republic, Ecuador, Egypt, El Salvador, Equatorial Guinea, Ethiopia, Fiji, Finland, Gabon, Germany (East), Ghana, Guatemala, Guinea, Guyana, Haiti, Honduras, Hungary, Iceland, India, Indonesia, Iran, Iraq, Ivory Coast, Jamaica, Jordan, Kenya, Khmer Republic, Kuwait, Lebanon, Lesotho, Liberia, Libya, Madagascar, Malawi, Malaysia, Mali, Malta, Mexico, Mongolia, Morocco, Nepal, New Zealand, Niger, Nigeria, Oman, Pakistan, Panama, Paraguay, Peru, Philippines, Poland, Qatar, Romania, Rwanda, Saudi Arabia, Senegal, Sierra Leone, Singapore, Somalia, Spain, Sri Lanka, Sudan, Sweden, Syria, Tanzania, Thailand, Togo, Trinidad and Tobago, Tunisia, Turkey, Uganda, Ukrainian SSR, United Arab Emirates, Uruguay, USSR, Venezuela, Yemen, Yemen (Democratic), Yugoslavia, Zaire, Zambia

Against: 1

United Kingdom

Abstaining: 16

Belgium, Denmark, France, Germany (West), Greece, Ireland, Israel, Italy, Japan, Luxembourg, Netherlands, Nicaragua, Norway, Portugal, South Africa, United States

4.6 Declaration on the Establishment of a New Economic Order

Adopted without recorded vote

4.7 Programme of Action on the Establishment of a New International Economic Order

Adopted without recorded vote

4.8 Charter of Economic Rights and Duties of States

For: 122

Afghanistan, Albania, Algeria, Argentina, Australia, Bahamas, Bahrain, Bangladesh, Barbados, Benin, Bhutan, Bolivia, Botswana, Brazil, Bulgaria, Burma, Burundi, Byelorussian SSR, Cambodia, Cameroon, Central African Republic, Chad, Chile, China, Colombia, Congo, Costa Rica, Cuba, Cyprus, Czechoslovakia, Dominican Republic, Ecuador, Egypt, El Salvador, Equatorial Guinea, Ethiopia, Fiji, Finland, Gabon, Germany (East), Ghana, Greece, Grenada, Guatemala, Guinea, Guinea-Bissau, Guyana, Haiti, Honduras, Hungary, Iceland, India, Indonesia, Iran, Iraq, Ivory Coast, Jamaica, Jordan, Kenya, Kuwait, Laos, Lebanon, Lesotho, Liberia, Libya, Madagascar, Malawi, Malaysia, Mali, Malta, Mauritania, Mauritius, Mozambique, Mexico, Mongolia, Morocco, Nepal, New Zealand, Nicaragua, Niger, Nigeria, Oman, Pakistan, Panama, Paraguay, Peru, Philippines, Poland, Portugal, Qatar, Romania, Rwanda, São Tomé and Príncipe, Saudi Arabia, Senegal, Sierra Leone, Singapore, Somalia, Sri Lanka, Sudan, Suriname, Swaziland, Sweden, Syria, Tanzania, Thailand, Togo, Trinidad and Tobago, Tunisia, Turkey, Uganda, Ukrainian SSR, United Arab Emirates, Upper Volta, Uruguay, USSR, Venezuela, Yemen, Yemen (Democratic), Yugoslavia, Zaire, Zambia

Against: 6

Belgium, Denmark, Germany (West), Luxembourg, Norway, United Kingdom, United States

Abstaining: 9

Austria, Canada, France, Ireland, Israel, Italy, Japan, Netherlands, Spain,

4.9 Declaration on International Investment and Multinational Enterprises

For: 23

Austria, Australia, Belgium, Canada, Denmark, France, Finland, Germany (West), Greece, Iceland, Ireland, Italy, Japan, Luxembourg, Netherlands, New Zealand, Norway, Portugal, Spain, Sweden, Switzerland, United Kingdom, United States

Against: 0

Abstaining: 1

Turkey

4.10 CONSTITUTION OF THE UNITED NATIONS INDUSTRIAL DEVELOPMENT ORGANIZATION

Signed: 21

Argentina, Brazil, Chile, Colombia, Ecuador, Egypt, El Salvador, Ghana, Lebanon, Libya, Nigeria, Pakistan, Peru, Romania, Senegal, Thailand, Tunisia, Turkey, Uganda, Yemen (Democratic), Yugoslavia

4.11 DRAFT INTERNATIONAL CODE OF CONDUCT ON THE TRANSFER OF TECHNOLOGY

4.12 CONVENTION ESTABLISHING THE MULTILATERAL INVESTMENT GUARANTEE AGENCY

Entry into force: April 12, 1988

Signed but not ratified: 22

Benin (4/17/86), Bolivia (5/5/86), Colombia (5/27/86), Congo (6/7/88), Dominica (4/29/88), Equatorial Guinea (4/7/86), Fiji (10/3/86), France (7/22/86), Greece (7/18/86), Haiti (9/30/87), Ireland (9/18/86), Malta (9/16/86), Mauritius (11/4/88), Morocco (4/11/86), Norway (6/6/88), Philippines (9/15/86), Poland (1/23/89), St. Christopher and Nevis (4/18/86), Sierra Leone (12/4/85), Sudan (3/10/87), Uruguay (4/8/86), Yemen (10/1/86)

Ratified/accepted/approved without qualification: 51

Bahrain (11/12/86), Bangladesh (3/13/87), Barbados (5/23/86), Burkina Faso (11/2/88), Cameroon (10/7/88), Canada (10/29/87), Chile (3/29/88), China (4/30/88), Cyprus (3/11/87), Denmark (8/18/87), Ecuador (1/15/86), Egypt (9/21/87), Finland (12/28/88), Germany (West) (10/6/87), Ghana (4/29/88), Grenada (1/28/88), Guyana (1/18/88), Hungary (4/21/88), Indonesia (9/26/86), Italy (4/29/88), Ivory Coast (6/7/88), Jamaica (12/15/87), Japan (6/5/87), Jordan (12/16/86), Kenya (11/28/88), Korea (South) (11/24/87), Kuwait (7/6/87), Lesotho (1/30/87), Madagascar (6/8/88), Malawi (5/14/87), Netherlands (10/9/87), Nigeria (3/8/88), Oman (1/24/89), Pakistan (12/1/86), Portugal (6/6/88), Samoa (3/17/87), Saudi Arabia (8/6/86), Senegal (3/10/87), Spain (4/27/88), Sri Lanka (5/27/88), St. Lucia (7/25/88), Sweden (12/31/87), Switzerland (2/8/88), Togo (4/15/88), Tunisia (6/7/88), Turkey (6/3/88), United Kingdom (4/12/88), United States (4/12/88), Vanuatu (7/27/88), Zaire (2/7/89), Zambia (6/6/88)

4.13 OECD GUIDELINES FOR MULTINATIONAL ENTERPRISES

4.14 DRAFT CODE OF CONDUCT ON TRANSNATIONAL CORPORATIONS

4.15 RESOLUTION ON CONSUMER PROTECTION, WITH ANNEX

Adopted without recorded vote

5. EARTH-SPACE ENVIRONMENT

5.1 CONVENTION AND STATUTE ON THE REGIME OF NAVIGABLE WATERWAYS OF INTERNATIONAL CONCERN

Entry into force: October 31, 1922

Signed but not ratified: 11

Belgium (4/20/21), Bolivia (4/20/21), China (4/20/21), Estonia (4/20/21), Guatemala (4/20/21), Lithuania (4/20/21), Panama (4/20/21), Poland (4/20/21), Portugal (4/20/21), Spain (4/20/21), Uruguay (4/20/21)

Ratified/accepted/approved without qualification: 24

Albania (10/8/21), Antigua and Barbuda (10/25/88), Austria (11/15/23), Bulgaria (7/11/22), Chile (3/19/28), Czechoslovakia (9/8/24), Denmark (11/13/22), Fiji (3/15/72), Finland (1/29/23), France (12/31/26), Greece (1/3/28), Hungary (5/18/28), Italy (8/5/22), Kampuchea (4/12/71), Luxembourg (3/19/30), Malta (5/13/66), Morocco (10/10/72), New Zealand (8/2/22), Nigeria (11/3/67), Norway (9/4/23), Swaziland (10/16/70), Sweden (9/15/27), Thailand (11/29/22), Turkey (6/27/33)

Ratified/accepted/approved with qualification: 2

Romania (5/9/24), United Kingdom (8/2/22)

5.2 International Convention for the Regulation of Whaling

Entry into force: November 10, 1948

Ratified/accepted/approved without qualification: 27

Antigua and Barbuda (7/21/82), Australia (12/1/47), Brazil (1/4/74), Costa Rica (7/24/81), Denmark (5/23/50), Finland (2/23/83), Iceland (3/10/47), India (3/9/81), Ireland (1/2/85), Japan (4/21/51), Kenya (12/2/81), Dorea (South) (12/29/78), Mexico (6/30/49), Monaco (3/15/82), Netherlands (6/14/77), New Zealand (6/15/76), Oman (7/15/80), Senegal (7/15/82), Seychelles (3/19/79), Solomon Islands (7/18/85), South Africa (5/5/48), Spain (7/6/79), St. Lucia (6/29/81), St. Vincent and the Grenadines (7/22/81), Sweden (6/15/79), Switzerland (5/29/80), Uruguay (7/15/81)

Ratified/accepted/approved with qualification: 10

Argentina (5/18/60), Chile (7/6/79), China (9/24/80), France (12/3/48), Germany (West) (7/2/82), Norway (9/23/60), Peru (6/18/76), United Kingdom (6/17/47), United States (7/18/47), USSR (9/11/48),

5.3 International Convention for the Prevention of Pollution of the Sea by Oil; Amendments Adopted by the Conference of Contracting Governments to the Convention of 1954; Amendments Adopted by the Assembly of the Inter-Governmental Maritime Consultative Organization

Entry into force: July 26, 1958

Ratified/accepted/approved without qualification: 54

Algeria (1/20/64), Austria (5/19/75), Bahrain (10/21/85), Bangladesh (9/28/81), Belgium (4/16/57), Canada (12/19/56), Congo (9/10/85), Cyprus (6/10/80), Denmark (11/26/56), Djibouti (3/1/84), Dominican Republic (5/29/63), Egypt (4/22/63), Finland (12/30/58), Ghana (5/17/62), Greece (3/28/67), Guinea (1/19/81), Iceland (2/23/62), India (3/4/74), Ireland (2/13/57), Israel (11/11/65), Ivory Coast (3/17/67), Japan (8/21/67), Jordan (5/8/63), Kenya (9/12/75), Korea (South) (7/31/78), Kuwait (11/27/61), Lebanon (5/31/67), Libya (2/18/72), Madagascar (2/1/65), Maldives (5/17/82), Malta (1/10/75), Mexico (5/10/56), Monaco (3/25/70), Morocco (2/29/68), New Zealand (6/1/71), Nigeria (1/22/68), Papua New Guinea (3/12/80), Philippines (11/19/63), Poland (2/28/61), Qatar (1/31/80), Senegal (3/27/72), Spain (1/22/64), Sri Lanka (8/30/83), Suriname (12/1/76), Sweden (5/24/56), Switzerland (1/12/66), Syria (12/24/68), United Arab Emirates (12/15/83), Uruguay (12/9/75), Vanuatu (2/2/83), Venezuela (12/12/63), Yemen (3/6/79), Yemen (Democratic) (5/20/69), Yugoslavia (3/11/74)

Ratified/accepted/approved with qualification: 16

Argentina (9/30/76), Bahamas (7/22/76), Chile (8/2/77), Fiji (8/15/72), France (7/26/57), Germany (East) (1/25/79), Italy (5/25/64), Liberia (3/28/62), Norway

(1/26/57), Panama (9/25/63), Portugal (3/28/67), Saudi Arabia (12/30/71), Tunisia (6/11/73), United Kingdom (5/6/55), United States (9/8/61), USSR (9/3/69)

5.4 CONVENTION ON THE HIGH SEAS

Entry into force: September 30, 1962

Signed but not ratified: 19

Argentina (4/29/58), Bolivia (10/17/58), Canada (4/29/58), Colombia (4/29/58), Cuba (4/29/58), France (10/30/58), Ghana (4/29/58), Holy See (4/30/58), Iceland (4/29/58), Iran (5/28/58), Ireland (10/2/58), Lebanon (5/29/58), Liberia (5/27/58), New Zealand (10/29/58), Pakistan (10/31/58), Panama (5/2/58), Sri Lanka (10/30/58), Tunisia (10/30/58), Uruguay (4/29/58)

Ratified/accepted/approved without qualification: 32

Afghanistan (4/28/59), Austria (1/10/74), Belgium (1/6/72), Central African Republic (10/15/62), Costa Rica (2/16/72), Cyprus (5/23/88), Denmark (9/26/68), Dominican Republic (8/11/64), Finland (2/16/65), Guatemala (11/27/61), Haiti (3/29/60), Italy (12/17/64), Jamaica (10/8/65), Kampuchea (3/18/60), Kenya (6/20/69), Lesotho (10/23/73), Malawi (11/3/65), Malaysia (12/21/60), Mauritius (10/5/70), Nepal (12/28/62), Nigeria (6/26/61), Senegal (4/25/61), Sierra Leone (3/13/62), Solomon Islands (9/3/81), South Africa (4/9/63), Swaziland (10/16/70), Switzerland (5/18/66), Trinidad and Tobago (4/11/66), Uganda (9/14/64), Upper Volta (10/4/65), Venezuela (8/15/61), Yugoslavia (1/28/66)

Ratified/accepted/approved with qualification: 26

Albania (12/7/64), Australia (5/14/63), Bulgaria (8/31/62), Byelorussian SSR (2/27/61), Czechoslovakia (8/31/61), Fiji (3/25/71), Germany (East) (12/27/73), Germany (West) (7/26/73), Hungary (12/6/61), Indonesia (8/10/61), Israel (9/6/61), Japan (6/10/68), Madagascar (7/31/62), Mexico (8/2/66), Mongolia (10/15/76), Netherlands (2/18/66), Poland (6/29/62), Portugal (1/8/63), Romania (12/12/61), Spain (2/25/71), Thailand (7/2/68), Tonga (6/29/71), Ukrainian SSR (1/12/61), United Kingdom (3/14/60), United States (4/12/61), USSR (11/22/60)

5.5 CONVENTION ON THE CONTINENTAL SHELF

Entry into force: June 10, 1964

Signed but not ratified: 21

Afghanistan (10/30/58), Argentina (4/29/58), Bolivia (10/17/58), Chile (10/31/58), Cuba (4/29/58), Ecuador (10/31/58), Germany (West) (10/30/58), Ghana (4/29/58), Iceland (4/29/58), Indonesia (5/8/58), Iran (5/28/58), Ireland (10/2/58), Lebanon (5/29/58), Liberia (5/27/58), Nepal (4/29/58), Pakistan (10/31/58), Panama (5/2/58), Peru (10/31/58), Sri Lanka (10/30/58), Tunisia (10/30/58), Uruguay (4/29/58)

Ratified/accepted/approved without qualification: 40

Albania (12/7/64), Australia (5/14/63), Bulgaria (8/31/62), Byelorussian SSR (2/27/61), Colombia (1/8/62), Costa Rica (2/16/72), Cyprus (4/11/74), Czechoslovakia (8/31/61), Denmark (6/12/63), Dominican Republic (8/11/64), Finland (2/16/65), Guatemala (11/27/61), Haiti (3/29/60), Israel (9/6/61), Jamaica (10/8/65), Kampuchea (3/18/60), Kenya (6/20/69), Lesotho (10/23/73), Madagascar (7/31/62), Malawi (11/3/65), Malaysia (12/21/60), Malta (5/19/66), Mauritius (10/5/70), Mexico (8/2/66), New Zealand (1/18/65), Nigeria (4/28/71), Poland (6/29/62), Portugal (1/8/63), Romania (12/12/61), Senegal (4/25/61), Sierra Leone (11/25/66), Solomon Islands (9/3/81), South Africa (4/9/63), Swaziland (10/16/70), Sweden (6/1/66), Switzerland (5/18/66), Trinidad and Tobago (7/11/68), Uganda (9/14/64), Ukrainian SSR (1/12/61), USSR (11/22/60)

Ratified/accepted/approved with qualification: 14

Canada (2/6/70), Fiji (3/25/71), France (6/14/65), Germany (East) (12/27/73), Greece (11/6/72), Netherlands (2/18/66), Norway (9/9/71), Spain (2/25/71), Thailand (7/2/68), Tongo (6/29/71), United Kingdom (5/11/64), United States (4/12/61), Venezuela (8/15/61), Yugoslavia (1/28/66)

5.6 CONVENTION ON THE TERRITORIAL SEA AND CONTIGUOUS ZONE

Entry into force: September 10, 1964

Signed but not ratified: 22

Afghanistan (10/30/58), Argentina (4/29/58), Austria (10/27/58), Bolivia (10/17/58), Canada (4/29/58), Colombia (4/29/58), Costa Rica (4/29/58), Cuba (4/29/58), Ghana (4/29/58), Guatemala (4/29/58), Holy See (4/30/58), Iceland (4/29/58), Iran (5/28/58), Ireland (10/2/58), Liberia (5/27/58), Nepal (4/29/58), New Zealand (10/29/58), Pakistan (10/31/58), Panama (5/2/58), Sri Lanka (10/30/58), Tunisia (10/30/58), Uruguay (4/29/58)

Ratified/accepted/approved without qualification: 21

Belgium (1/6/72), Dominican Republic (8/11/64), Finland (2/16/65), Haiti (3/29/60), Jamaica (10/8/65), Kampuchea (3/18/60), Kenya (6/20/69), Lesotho (10/23/73), Malawi (11/3/65), Malaysia (12/21/60), Malta (5/19/66), Mauritius (10/5/70), Nigeria (6/26/61), Senegal (4/25/61), Sierra Leone (3/13/62), South Africa (4/9/63), Swaziland (10/16/70), Switzerland (5/18/66), Trinidad and Tobago (4/11/66), Uganda (9/14/64), Yugoslavia (1/28/66)

Ratified/accepted/approved with qualification: 25

Australia (5/14/63), Bulgaria (8/31/62), Byelorussian SSR (2/27/61), Czechoslovakia (8/31/61), Denmark (9/26/68), Fiji (3/25/71), Germany (East) (12/27/73), Hungary (12/6/61), Israel (9/6/61), Italy (12/17/64), Japan (6/10/68), Madagascar (7/31/62), Mexico (8/2/66), Netherlands (2/18/66), Portugal (1/8/63), Romania (12/12/61), Solomon Islands (9/3/81), Spain (2/25/71), Thailand (7/2/68), Tonga (6/29/71), Ukrainian SRR (1/12/61), United Kingdom (3/14/60), United States (4/12/61), USSR (11/22/60), Venezuela (8/15/61)

5.7 CONVENTION ON FISHING AND CONSERVATION OF LIVING RESOURCES OF HIGH SEAS

Entry into force: March 20, 1966

Signed but not ratified: 21

Afghanistan (10/30/58), Argentina (4/29/58), Bolivia (10/17/58), Canada (4/29/58), Costa Rica (4/29/58), Cuba (4/29/58), Ghana (4/29/58), Iceland (4/29/58), Indonesia (5/8/58), Iran (5/28/58), Ireland (10/2/58), Israel (4/29/58), Lebanon (5/29/58), Liberia (5/27/58), Nepal (4/29/58), New Zealand (10/29/58), Pakistan (10/31/58), Panama (5/2/58), Sri Lanka (10/30/58), Tunisia (10/30/58), Uruguay (4/29/58)

Ratified/accepted/approved with qualification: 32

Australia (5/14/63), Belgium (1/6/72), Colombia (1/3/63), Dominican Republic (8/11/64), Fiji (3/25/71), Finland (2/16/65), France (9/18/70), Haiti (3/29/60), Jamaica (4/16/64), Kampuchea (3/18/60), Kenya (6/20/69), Lesotho (10/23/73), Madagascar (7/31/62), Malawi (11/3/65), Malaysia (12/21/60), Mauritius (10/5/70), Mexico (8/2/66), Netherlands (2/18/66), Nigeria (6/26/61), Portugal (1/8/63), Senegal (4/25/61), Sierra Leone (3/13/62), Solomon Islands (9/3/81), South Africa (4/9/63), Switzerland (5/18/66), Thailand (7/2/68), Tonga (6/29/71), Trinidad and Tobago (4/11/66), Uganda (9/14/64), Upper Volta (10/4/65), Venezuela (7/10/63), Yugoslavia (1/28/66)

Ratified/accepted/approved with qualification: 4

Denmark (9/26/68), Spain (2/25/71), United Kingdom (3/14/60), United States (4/12/61)

5.8 THE ANTARCTIC TREATY

Entry into force: June 23, 1961

Ratified/accepted/approved without qualification: 34

Argentina (6/23/61), Australia (6/23/61), Austria (8/25/87), Belgium (6/26/60), Brazil (5/16/75), Bulgaria (9/11/78), Canada (5/4/88), Chile (6/23/61), China (6/8/83), Cuba (8/16/84), Czechoslovakia (6/14/62), Denmark (5/20/65), Ecuador (9/15/87), Finland (5/14/84), France (9/16/60), Germany (West) (2/5/79), Greece (1/8/87), Hungary (1/27/84), Italy (3/18/81), Japan (8/8/60), Korea (North) (1/21/87), Korea (South) (11/28/86), Netherlands (3/30/67), New Zealand (11/1/60), Norway (8/24/60), Papua New Guinea (3/16/81), Peru (4/10/81), Poland (6/8/61), South Africa (6/21/60), Spain (3/31/82), Sweden (4/25/84), United Kingdom (5/31/60), United States (8/18/60), USSR (11/2/60)

Ratified/accepted/approved with qualification: 4

Germany (East) (11/19/74), India (8/19/83), Romania (9/15/71), Uruguay (1/11/80)

5.9 CONVENTION ON CIVIL LIABILITY FOR NUCLEAR DAMAGE

Entry into force: November 11, 1977

Signed but not ratified: 5

Chile (8/18/88), Colombia (5/21/63), Morocco (11/30/84), Spain (9/6/63), United Kingdom (11/11/64)

Ratified/accepted/approved without qualification: 10

Argentina (4/25/67), Bolivia (4/10/68), Cameroon (3/6/64), Cuba (10/25/65), Egypt (11/5/65), Niger (7/24/79), Philippines (11/15/65), Peru (8/26/80), Trinidad and Tobago (1/31/66), Yugoslavia (8/12/77)

5.10 RESOLUTION REGARDING WEAPONS OF MASS DESTRUCTION IN OUTER SPACE

Adopted by acclamation

5.11 HELSINKI RULES ON THE USES OF THE WATERS OF INTERNATIONAL RIVERS

5.12 TREATY ON PRINCIPLES GOVERNING THE ACTIVITIES OF STATES IN THE EXPLORATION AND USE OF OUTER SPACE, INCLUDING THE MOON AND OTHER CELESTIAL BODIES

Entry into force: October 10, 1967

Signed but not ratified: 28

Bolivia (1/27/67), Botswana (1/27/67), Burundi (1/27/67), Cameroon (1/27/67), Central African Republic (1/27/67), Colombia (1/27/67), Ethiopia (1/27/67), Gambia (6/2/67), Ghana (1/27/67), Guyana (2/3/67), Haiti (1/27/67), Holy See (4/5/67), Honduras (1/27/67), Indonesia (1/27/67), Iran (1/27/67), Jordan (2/2/67), Lesotho (1/27/67), Luxembourg (1/27/67), Malaysia (2/20/67), Nicaragua (1/27/67), Panama (1/27/67), Philippines (1/27/67), Rwanda (1/27/67), Somalia (2/2/67), Togo (1/27/67), Trinidad and Tobago (7/24/67), Yugoslavia (1/27/67), Zaire (1/27/67)

Ratified/accepted/approved without qualification: 86

Afghanistan (3/17/88), Antigua and Barbuda (1/26/89), Argentina (3/26/69), Australia (10/10/67), Austria (2/26/68), Bahamas (8/11/76), Bangladesh (1/14/86), Barbados (9/12/68), Belgium (3/30/73), Benin (6/19/86), Bulgaria (3/28/67), Burma (3/18/70), Byelorussian SSR (10/31/67), Canada (10/10/67), Chile (10/8/81), Cuba (6/3/77), Cyprus (7/5/72), Czechoslovakia (5/11/67), Denmark (10/10/67), Dominican Republic (11/21/68), Ecuador (3/7/69), Egypt (10/10/67), El Salvador (1/15/69), Fiji (7/18/72), Finland (7/12/67), France (8/5/70), Germany (East) (2/2/67), Germany (West) (2/10/71), Greece (1/19/71), Guinea-Bissau (8/20/76), Hungary (6/26/67), Iceland (2/5/68), India (1/18/82), Iraq (12/4/68), Ireland (7/17/68), Israel (2/18/77), Italy (5/4/72), Jamaica (8/6/70), Japan (10/10/67), Kenya (1/19/84), Korea (South) (10/13/67), Laos (11/27/72), Lebanon (3/31/69), Libya (7/3/68), Mali (6/11/68), Mauritius (4/7/69), Mexico (1/31/68), Mongolia (10/10/67), Morocco (12/21/67), Nepal (10/10/67), Netherlands (10/10/69), New Zealand (5/31/68), Niger (4/17/67), Nigeria (11/14/67), Norway (7/1/69), Pakistan (4/8/68), Papua New Guinea (10/27/80), Peru (2/26/79), Poland (1/30/68), Romania (4/9/68), San Marino (10/29/68), Saudi Arabia (12/17/68), Seychelles (1/5/78), Sierra Leone (7/13/67), Singapore (9/10/76), South Africa (9/30/68), Spain (11/27/68), Sri Lanka (11/18/86), Sweden (10/11/67), Switzerland (12/18/69), Syria (11/14/68), Thailand (9/5/68), Tonga (7/7/71), Tunisia (3/28/68), Turkey (3/27/68), Uganda (4/24/68), Ukrainian SSR (10/31/67), United Kingdom (10/10/67), United States (10/10/67), Upper Volta (6/18/68), Uruguay (8/31/70), USSR (10/10/67), Venezuela (3/3/70), Vietnam (6/20/80), Yemen (Democratic) (7/1/79), Zambia (8/20/73).

Ratified/accepted/approved with qualification: 4

Brazil (3/5/69), China (12/30/83), Kuwait (6/7/72), Madagascar (8/22/68)

5.13 International Convention Relating to Intervention on the High Seas in Cases of Oil Pollution Casualties

Entry into force: May 6, 1975

Signed but not ratified: 6

Brazil (12/30/69), Greece (4/14/70), Guatemala (11/29/69), Korea (South) (11/29/69), Madagascar (11/29/69), Romania (12/30/69)

Ratified/accepted/approved without qualification: 44

Argentina (4/21/87), Bahamas (7/22/76), Bangladesh (11/6/81), Belgium (10/21/71), Benin (11/1/85), Cameroon (5/14/84), Denmark (12/18/70), Dominican Republic (2/5/75), Ecuador (12/23/76), Fiji (8/15/72), Finland (9/6/76), Gabon (1/21/82), Ghana (4/20/78), Iceland (7/17/80), Ireland (8/21/80), Italy (2/27/79), Ivory Coast (1/8/88), Kuwait (4/2/81), Lebanon (6/5/75), Liberia (9/25/72), Mexico (4/8/76), Monaco (2/24/75), Morocco (4/11/74), Netherlands (9/19/75), New Zealand (3/26/75), Norway (7/12/72), Oman (1/24/85), Panama (1/7/76), Papua New Guinea (3/12/80), Poland (6/1/76), Portugal (2/15/80), Qatar (6/2/88), Senegal (3/27/72), South Africa (7/1/86), Spain (11/8/73), Sri Lanka (4/12/83), Suriname (11/25/75), Sweden (2/8/73), Switzerland (12/15/87), Tunisia (5/4/76), United Arab Emirates (12/15/83), United States (2/21/74), Yemen (3/6/79), Yugoslavia (2/3/76)

Ratified/accepted/approved with qualification: 10

Australia (11/7/83), Bulgaria (11/2/83), Cuba (5/5/76), France (5/10/72), Germany (East) (12/21/78), Germany (West) (5/7/75), Japan (4/6/71), Syria (2/6/75), United Kingdom (1/12/71), USSR (12/30/74)

5.14 Resolution on the Question of the Reservation Exclusively for Peaceful Purposes of the Sea-Bed and the Ocean Floor, and the Subsoil Thereof, Underlying the High Seas Beyond the Limits of the Present National Jurisdiction, and the Use of Their Resources in the Interests of Mankind

For: 62

Afghanistan, Algeria, Argentina, Barbados, Bolivia, Brazil, Burundi, Central African Republic, Ceylon, Chad, Chile, Colombia, Congo (Brazzaville), Congo (Democratic Republic), Costa Rica, Cyprus, Dahomey, Dominican Republic, Ecuador, Ethiopia, Finland, Guatemala, Guinea, Guyana, Haiti, Honduras, India, Iraq, Jamaica, Jordan, Kenya, Kuwait, Lesotho, Malaysia, Maldives, Mali, Mauritania, Mauritius, Mexico, Morocco, Nepal, Nicaragua, Niger, Pakistan, Panama, Paraguay, Peru, Rwanda, Singapore, Somalia, Sweden, Tanzania, Thailand, Togo, Trinidad and Tobago, Tunisia, Uganda, Uruguay, Venezuela, Yemen, Yemen (Democratic), Yugoslavia, Zambia

Against: 28

Australia, Austria, Belgium, Bulgaria, Byelorussian SSR, Canada, Czechoslovakia, Denmark, France, Hungary, Iceland, Ireland, Italy, Japan, Luxembourg, Malta, Mongolia, Netherlands, New Zealand, Norway, Poland, Portugal, South Africa, Ukrainian SSR, United Kingdom, United States, USSR

Abstaining: 28

Burma, China, Cuba, El Salvador, Greece, Indonesia, Iran, Israel, Ivory Coast, Laos, Lebanon, Liberia, Libya, Madagascar, Malawi, Nigeria, Philippines, Romania, Saudi Arabia, Sierra Leone, Spain, Sudan, Swaziland, Syria, Togo, Turkey, United Arab Republic, Upper Volta

5.15 Declaration of the Principles Governing the Sea-Bed and Ocean Floor and the Subsoil Thereof, Beyond the Limits of National Jurisdiction

For: 108 *

Against: 0

Abstaining: 14

* Adopted with no roll call vote recorded.

5.16 Convention On the International Liability for Damage Caused by Space Objects

Entry into force: September 1, 1972

Signed but not ratified: 27

Algeria (4/20/72), Burundi (3/29/72), Central African Republic (4/27/72), Colombia (3/29/72), Costa Rica (3/29/72), Egypt (4/19/72), El Salvador (3/29/72), Gambia (6/2/72), Ghana (3/29/72), Guatemala (3/29/72), Haiti (3/29/72), Honduras (3/29/72), Iceland (3/29/72), Jordan (5/25/72), Kampuchea (3/29/72), Lebanon (3/29/72), Nepal (3/29/72), Nicaragua (3/29/72), Norway (3/29/72), Oman (6/23/72), Peru (4/10/72), Philippines (8/22/72), Rwanda (3/29/72), Sierra Leone (7/14/72), South Africa (3/29/72), Tanzania (5/31/72), Zaire (3/29/72)

Ratified/accepted/approved without qualification: 63

Antigua and Barbuda (11/16/88), Argentina (11/14/86), Australia (1/20/75), Belgium (8/13/76), Benin (4/25/75), Botswana (3/14/74), Brazil (3/9/73), Bulgaria (5/14/73), Byelorussian SSR (12/27/73), Chile (12/1/76), Cuba (11/25/82), Cyprus (5/15/73), Czechoslovakia (9/8/76), Dominican Republic (2/23/73), Ecuador (8/17/72), Fiji (4/4/73), Finland (2/1/77), France (12/31/75), Gabon (2/5/82), Germany (East) (8/30/72), Germany (West) (12/18/75), Hungary (12/27/72), India

(7/9/79), Iran (2/13/74), Iraq (10/4/72), Israel (6/21/77), Italy (2/22/83), Japan (6/20/83), Kenya (9/25/75), Laos (3/20/73), Liechtenstein (12/24/79), Luxembourg (10/18/83), Mali (6/9/72), Malta (1/13/78), Mexico (4/8/74), Mongolia (9/5/72), Morocco (3/15/83), Niger (9/1/72), Pakistan (4/4/73), Panama (6/5/74), Papua New Guinea (10/27/80), Poland (1/25/73), Qatar (1/11/74), Romania (3/5/80), Saudi Arabia (12/17/76), Senegal (3/26/75), Seychelles (1/5/78), Singapore (8/19/75), Spain (1/2/80), Sri Lanka (4/9/73), Switzerland (1/22/74), Syria (2/6/80), Togo (4/26/76), Trinidad and Tobago (2/8/80), Tunisia (5/18/73), Ukrainian SSR (10/16/73), United Kingdom (10/9/73), United States (10/9/73), Uruguay (1/7/77), USSR (10/9/73), Venezuela (8/1/78), Yugoslavia (10/20/75), Zambia (8/20/73)

Ratified/accepted/approved with qualification: 12

Austria (1/10/80), Canada (2/20/75), China (12/19/88), Denmark (4/1/77), Eutelsat (11/30/87), Greece (4/27/77), Ireland (6/29/72), Korea (South) (1/14/80), Kuwait (10/30/72), Netherlands (2/17/81), New Zealand (10/30/74), Sweden (6/15/76)

5.17 Stockholm Declaration of the United Nations Conference on the Human Environment

For: 103 *

Against: 0

Abstaining: 12

* Adopted with no roll call vote recorded.

5.18 Convention on the Prevention of Marine Pollutions by Dumping of Wastes and Other Matter, with Annexes I and II

Entry into force: August 30, 1975

Signed but not ratified: 14

Bolivia (12/29/72), Chad (12/29/72), Colombia (12/29/72), Costa Rica (12/29/72), Kuwait (3/1/73), Lebanon (12/29/72), Lesotho (1/8/73), Liberia (12/29/72), Luxembourg (12/29/72), Senegal (12/29/72), Somalia (4/16/73), Togo (11/21/73), Uruguay (12/29/72), Venezuela (5/30/73)

Ratified/accepted/approved without qualification: 56

Afghanistan (4/2/75), Argentina (9/11/79), Australia (8/21/85), Belgium (6/12/85), Brazil (7/26/82), Byelorussian SSR (1/29/76), Canada (11/13/75), Cape Verde (5/26/77), Chile (8/4/77), Cuba (12/1/75), Denmark (10/23/74), Dominican Republic (12/7/74), Finland (5/3/79), Gabon (2/5/82), Germany (East) (8/20/76), Greece (8/10/81), Guatemala (7/14/75), Haiti (8/28/75), Honduras (5/2/80), Hungary (2/5/76), Iceland (5/24/73), Ireland (2/17/82), Ivory Coast (10/9/87), Japan (10/15/75), Jordan (11/11/74), Kenya (1/7/76), Kiribati (6/3/82), Libya (11/22/76), Mexico (4/7/75), Monaco (5/16/77), Morocco (2/18/77), Nauru (7/26/82), Netherlands (12/2/77), Nigeria (3/19/76), Norway (4/4/74), Oman (3/13/84), Panama (7/31/75), Papua New Guinea (3/10/80), Philippines (8/10/73), Poland (1/23/79), Portugal (4/14/78), Seychelles (10/29/84), Solomon Islands (3/6/84), South Africa (8/7/78), Spain (7/31/74), St. Lucia (8/23/85), Suriname (10/21/80), Sweden (2/21/74), Switzerland (7/31/79), Tunisia (4/13/76), Ukrainian SSR (2/5/76), United Arab Emirates (8/9/74), United States (4/29/74), USSR (12/30/75), Yugoslavia (6/25/76), Zaire (9/16/75)

Ratified/accepted/approved with qualification: 6

China (11/5/85), France (2/3/77), Germany (West) (11/8/77), Italy (4/30/84), New Zealand (4/30/75), United Kingdom (11/17/75)

5.19 Convention on International Trade in Endangered Species of Wild Fauna and Flora

Entry into force: July 1, 1975

Signed but not ratified: 5

Kampuchea (12/7/73), Kuwait (4/9/74), Lesotho (7/17/74), Poland (10/8/73), Vietnam (3/3/73)

Ratified/accepted/approved without qualification: 73

Afghanistan (10/30/85), Algeria (11/23/83), Argentina (1/8/81), Austria (1/27/82), Bahamas (6/20/79), Bangladesh (11/20/81), Belgium (10/3/83), Belize (8/19/86), Benin (2/28/84), Bolivia (7/6/79), Brazil (8/6/75), Burundi (8/8/88), Cameroon (6/5/81), Central African Republic (8/27/80), China (1/8/81), Colombia (8/31/81), Congo (1/31/83), Costa Rica (6/30/75), Cyprus (10/18/74), Dominican Republic (12/17/86), Ecuador (2/11/75), Egypt (1/4/78), El Salvador (4/30/87), Finland (5/10/76), Gambia (8/26/77), Ghana (11/14/75), Guatemala (11/7/79), Guinea (9/21/81), Guyana (5/27/77), Honduras (3/15/85), Hungary (5/29/85), India (7/20/76), Indonesia (12/28/78), Iran (8/3/76), Israel (12/18/79), Jordan (12/14/78), Kenya (12/13/78), Liberia (3/11/81), Luxembourg (12/13/83), Madagascar (8/20/75), Malawi (2/5/82), Malaysia (10/20/77), Mauritius (4/28/75), Monaco (4/19/78), Morocco (10/16/75), Mozambique (3/25/81), Nepal (6/18/75), Netherlands (4/19/84), Nicaragua (8/6/77), Niger (9/8/75), Nigeria (5/9/74), Pakistan (4/20/76), Panama (8/17/78), Papua New Guinea (12/12/75), Paraguay (11/15/76), Peru (6/27/75), Philippines (8/18/81), Portugal (12/11/80), Rwanda (10/20/80), Senegal (8/5/77), Seychelles (2/8/77), Somalia (12/2/85), Sri Lanka (5/4/82), St. Lucia (12/15/82), Sweden (8/20/74), Tanzania (11/29/79), Togo (10/23/78), Trinidad and Tobago (1/19/84), Tunisia (7/10/74), United Kingdom (8/2/76), Uruguay (4/2/75), Venezuela (10/24/77), Zaire (7/20/76)

Ratified/accepted/approved with qualification: 23

Australia (7/29/76), Botswana (11/14/77), Canada (4/10/75), Chile (2/14/75), Denmark (7/26/77), Germany (East) (10/9/75), France (5/11/78), Germany (West) (3/22/76), Japan (8/6/80), Liechtenstein (11/30/79), Norway (7/27/76), Singapore (11/30/86), South Africa (7/15/75), Spain (5/30/86), Sudan (10/26/82), Suriname (11/17/80), Switzerland (7/9/74), Thailand (1/21/83), United States (1/14/74), USSR (9/9/76), Zambia (11/24/80), Zimbabwe (5/19/81)

5.20 International Convention for the Prevention of Pollution From Ships, With Annex I

Entry into force: March 30, 1983

Signed but not ratified: 1

New Zealand (12/23/74)

Ratified/accepted/approved without qualification: 20

Bahamas (3/5/81), Belgium (9/9/82), Denmark (5/9/83), Finland (8/4/86), Germany (West) (8/21/85), Italy (10/1/82), Liberia (2/17/81), Mexico (4/11/80), Netherlands (9/10/80), Norway (7/15/80), Oman (1/24/85), Poland (7/10/81), Portugal (7/8/87), Sweden (6/28/76), Switzerland (12/15/87), Tunisia (5/4/76), United States (9/7/78), USSR (12/30/82), Yemen (3/6/79), Yugoslavia (10/31/80)

Ratified/accepted/approved with qualification: 3

Australia (11/7/83), France (12/31/85), United Kingdom (11/5/79)

5.21 Draft Principles of Conduct in the Field of the Environment for the Guidance of States in the Conservation and Harmonious Utilization of Natural Resources Shared by Two or More States

5.22 Protocol of 1978 Relating to the International Convention for the Prevention of Pollution From Ships, 1973, With Annex

Entry into force: October 2, 1983

Signed but not ratified: 2

Australia (5/30/79), Mexico (6/1/78)

Ratified/accepted/approved without qualification: 40

Antigua and Barbuda (1/29/88), Australia (10/14/87), Austria (5/27/88), Bahamas (6/7/83), Brunei (10/23/86), Bulgaria (12/12/84), China (7/1/83), Colombia (7/27/81), Czechoslovakia (7/2/84), Denmark (11/27/80), Egypt (8/7/86), Finland (9/20/83), Gabon (4/26/83), Germany (East) (4/25/84), Greece (9/23/82), Hungary (1/14/85), Iceland (6/25/85), India (9/24/86), Israel (8/31/83), Italy (10/1/82), Ivory Coast (10/5/87), Korea (North) (5/1/85), Korea (South) (7/23/84), Lebanon (7/18/83), Liberia (10/28/80), Marshall Islands (4/26/88), Panama (2/20/85), Peru (4/25/80), Poland (4/1/86), Portugal (10/22/87), St. Vincent and the Grenadines (10/28/83), Suriname (11/4/88), South Africa (11/28/84), Spain (7/6/84), Switzerland (12/15/87), Tunisia (10/10/80), Tuvalu (8/22/85), United Kingdom (5/22/80), Uruguay (4/30/79), Yugoslavia (10/31/80)

Ratified/accepted/approved with qualification: 14

Belgium (3/6/84), Brazil (1/29/88), France (9/25/81), Germany (West) (1/21/82), Indonesia (10/21/86), Japan (6/9/83), Netherlands (6/30/83), Norway (7/15/80), Oman (3/13/84), Sweden (6/9/80), Syria (11/9/88), United States (8/12/80), USSR (11/3/83)

5.23 Treaty for Amazonian Cooperation

Entry into force: Not entered into force as of December 31, 1989

Contracting parties: 8

Bolivia, Brazil, Colombia, Ecuador, Guyana, Peru, Suriname, Venezuela

5.24 Convention on Long-Range Transboundary Air Pollution

Entry into force: March 16, 1983

Signed but not ratified: 3

Holy See (11/14/79), Romania (11/14/79), San Marino (11/14/79)

Ratified/accepted/approved without qualification: 27

Austria (12/16/82), Belgium (7/15/82), Bulgaria (6/9/81), Byelorussian SSR (6/13/80), Canada (12/15/81), Czechoslovakia (12/23/83), Denmark (6/18/82), E.E.C. (7/15/82), Finland (4/15/81), Germany (East) (6/7/82), Germany (West) (7/15/82), Greece (8/30/83), Hungary (9/22/80), Iceland (5/5/83), Ireland (7/15/82), Italy (7/15/82), Liechtenstein (11/22/83), Luxembourg (7/15/82), Netherlands (7/15/82), Norway (2/13/81), Portugal (9/29/80), Spain (6/15/82), Sweden (2/12/81), Switzerland (5/6/83), Turkey (4/18/83), Ukrainian SSR (6/5/80), United Kingdom (7/15/82), United States (11/30/81), Yugoslavia (3/18/87)

Ratified/accepted/approved with qualification: 5

France (11/3/81), Poland (7/19/85), United Kingdom (7/15/82), United States (11/30/81), USSR (5/22/80)

5.25 Agreement Governing the Activities of States on the Moon and Other Celestial Bodies

Entry into force: July 11, 1984

Signed but not ratified: 6

France (1/29/80), Guatemala (11/20/80), India (1/18/82), Morocco (7/25/80), Peru (6/23/81), Romania (4/17/80)

Ratified/accepted/approved without qualification: 7

Australia (7/7/86), Austria (6/11/84), Chile (11/12/81), Netherlands (2/17/83), Pakistan (2/27/86), Philippines (5/26/81), Uruguay (11/9/81)

5.26 World Charter for Nature

For: 111

Afghanistan, Angola, Australia, Austria, Bahrain, Bangladesh, Barbados, Belgium, Benin, Bulgaria, Burundi, Byelorussian SSR, Canada, Cape Verde, Central African Republic, Chad, China, Cameroon, Comoros, Congo, Costa Rica, Cuba, Cyprus, Czechoslovakia, Denmark, Djibouti, Egypt, El Salvador, Equatorial Guinea, Ethiopia, Finland, France, Gabon, Gambia, Germany (East), Germany (West), Greece, Guinea, Guinea-Bissau, Honduras, Hungary, Iceland, India, Indonesia, Iran, Iraq, Ireland, Italy, Ivory Coast, Jamaica, Japan, Kampuchea, Kenya, Kuwait, Laos, Libya, Luxembourg, Madagascar, Malawi, Malaysia, Maldives, Mali, Malta, Mauritania, Mongolia, Morocco, Mozambique, Nepal, Netherlands, New Zealand, Nicaragua, Niger, Nigeria, Norway, Oman, Pakistan, Papua New Guinea, Poland, Portugal, Qatar, Romania, Rwanda, Samoa, São Tomé and Príncipe, Saudi Arabia, Senegal, Seychelles, Singapore, Solomon Islands, Somalia, Spain, Sri Lanka, Sudan, Swaziland, Sweden, Tanzania, Thailand, Togo, Tunisia, Turkey, Uganda, Ukrainian SSR, United Arab Emirates, United Kingdom, Upper Volta, Uruguay, USSR, Yemen, Yugoslavia, Zaire, Zambia

Against: 1

United States

Abstaining: 18

Algeria, Argentina, Bolivia, Brazil, Chile, Colombia, Dominican Republic, Ecuador, Ghana, Guyana, Lebanon, Mexico, Paraguay, Peru, Philippines, Suriname, Trinidad and Tobago, Venezuela

5.27 United Nations Convention on the Law of the Sea

Entry into force: 12 months after 60th acceptance

Signed but not ratified: 125

Afghanistan (3/18/83), Algeria (12/10/82), Angola (12/10/82), Antigua and Barbuda (2/7/83), Argentina (10/5/84), Australia (12/10/82), Austria (12/10/82), Bangladesh (12/10/82), Barbados (12/10/82), Belgium (12/5/84), Benin (8/30/83), Bhutan (12/10/82), Bolivia (11/27/84), Botswana (12/5/84), Brunei (12/5/84), Bulgaria (12/10/82), Burma (12/10/82), Burundi (12/10/82), Byelorussian SSR (12/10/82), Canada (12/10/82), Central African Republic (12/4/84), Chad (12/10/82), Chile (12/10/82), China (12/10/82), Colombia (12/10/82), Comoros (12/6/84), Congo (12/10/82), Cook Islands (12/10/82), Costa Rica (12/10/82), Czechoslovakia (12/10/82), Denmark (12/10/82), Djibouti (12/10/82), Dominica (3/28/83), Dominican Republic (12/10/82), E.E.C. (12/7/84), El Salvador (12/5/84), Equatorial Guinea (1/30/84), Ethiopia (12/10/82), Finland (12/10/82), France (12/10/82), Gabon (12/10/82), Germany (East) (12/10/82), Greece (12/10/82), Grenada (12/10/82), Guatemala (7/8/83), Guinea (10/4/84), Guyana (12/10/82), Haiti (12/10/82), Honduras (12/10/82), Hungary (12/10/82), India

(12/10/82), Iran (12/10/82), Ireland (12/10/82), Italy (12/7/84), Japan (2/7/83), Kampuchea (7/1/83), Kenya (12/10/82), Korea (North) (12/10/82), Korea (South) (3/14/83), Laos (12/10/82), Lebanon (12/7/84), Lesotho (12/10/82), Liberia (12/10/82), Libya (12/3/84), Liechtenstein (11/30/84), Luxembourg (12/5/84), Madagascar (2/25/83), Malawi (12/7/84), Malaysia (12/10/82), Maldives (12/10/82), Malta (12/10/82), Mauritania (12/10/92), Mauritius (12/10/82), Monaco (12/10/82), Mongolia (12/10/82), Morocco (12/10/82), Mozambique (12/10/82), Nauru (12/10/82), Nepal (12/10/82), Netherlands (12/10/82), New Zealand (12/10/82), Nicaragua (12/9/84), Niger (12/10/82), Niue (12/5/84), Norway (12/10/82), Oman (7/1/83), Pakistan (12/10/82), Panama (12/10/82), Papua New Guinea (12/10/82), Poland (12/10/82), Portugal (12/10/82), Qatar (11/27/84), Romania (12/10/82), Rwanda (12/10/82), Samoa (9/28/84), Saudi Arabia (12/7/84), Seychelles (12/10/82), Sierra Leone (12/10/82), Singapore (12/10/82), Solomon Islands (12/10/82), Somalia (12/10/82), South Africa (12/5/84), Spain (12/4/84), Sri Lanka (12/10/82), St. Kitts and Nevis (12/7/84), St. Vincent and the Grenadines (12/10/82), Suriname (12/10/82), Swaziland (1/18/84), Sweden (12/10/84), Switzerland (10/17/84), Thailand (12/10/82), Tuvalu (12/10/82), Uganda (12/10/82), Ukrainian SSR (12/10/82), United Arab Emirates (12/10/82), Upper Volta (12/10/82), Uruguay (12/10/82), USSR (12/10/82), Vanuatu (12/10/82), Vietnam (12/10/82), Yemen (12/10/82), Zaire (8/22/83), Zimbabwe (12/10/82)

Ratified/accepted/approved without qualification: 23

Bahamas (7/29/83), Bahrain (5/30/85), Belize (8/13/83), Cameroon (11/19/85), Cyprus (12/12/88), Fiji (12/10/82), Gambia (5/22/84), Ghana (6/7/83), Guinea (9/6/85), Indonesia (2/3/86), Iraq (7/30/85), Ivory Coast (3/26/84), Jamaica (3/21/83), Mexico (3/18/83), Namibia (4/18/83), Nigeria (8/14/86), Paraguay (9/26/86), Senegal (10/25/84), St. Lucia (3/27/85), Sudan (1/23/85), Togo (4/16/85), Trinidad and Tobago (4/25/86), Zambia (3/7/83)

Ratified/accepted/approved with qualification: 14

Brazil (12/22/88), Cape Verde (8/10/87), Cuba (8/15/84), Egypt (8/26/83), Guinea-Bissau (8/25/86), Iceland (6/21/85), Kuwait (5/2/86), Mali (7/16/85), Philippines (5/8/84), São Tomé and Príncipe (11/3/87), Tanzania (9/30/85), Tunisia (4/24/85), Yemen (Democratic) (7/21/87), Yugoslavia (5/5/86)

5.28 Vienna Convention for the Protection of the Ozone Layer

Entry into force: September 22, 1988

Signed but not ratified: 6

Argentina (3/22/85), Austria (9/16/85), Burkina Faso (12/12/85), Chile (3/22/85), Morocco (2/7/86), Peru (3/22/85)

Ratified/accepted/approved without qualification: 36

Australia (9/16/87), Austria (8/19/87), Belgium (10/17/88), Byelorussian SSR (6/20/86), Canada (6/4/86), Denmark (9/29/88), E.E.C. (10/17/88), Egypt (5/9/88), Equatorial Guinea (8/17/88), France (12/4/87), Germany (East) (1/25/89), Germany (West) (9/30/88), Greece (12/29/88), Guatemala (9/11/87), Hungary (5/3/88), Ireland (9/15/88), Italy (9/19/88), Japan (9/30/88), Kenya (11/9/88), Liechtenstein (2/8/89), Luxembourg (10/17/88), Maldives (4/26/88), Malta (9/15/88), Mexico (9/14/87), New Zealand (6/2/87), Nigeria (10/31/88), Panama (2/13/89), Portugal (10/17/88), Singapore (1/5/89), Spain (7/25/88), Switzerland (12/17/87), Uganda (6/24/88), Ukrainian SSR (6/18/86), United States (8/27/86), USSR (6/18/86), Venezuela (9/1/88)

Ratified/accepted/approved with qualification: 5

Finland (9/26/86), Netherlands (9/28/88), Norway (9/23/86), Sweden (11/26/86), United Kingdom (5/15/87)

5.29 Convention on Early Notification of a Nuclear Accident

Entry into force: October 27, 1986

Signed but not ratified: 45

Afghanistan (9/26/86), Algeria (9/24/87), Belgium (9/26/86), Brazil (9/26/86), Cameroon (9/25/87), Canada (9/26/86), Chile (9/26/86), Costa Rica (9/26/86), Cuba (9/26/86), France (9/26/86), Germany (West) (9/26/86), Greece (9/26/86), Holy See (9/26/86), Iceland (9/26/86), Indonesia (9/26/86), Iran (9/26/86), Ireland (9/26/86), Israel (9/26/86), Italy (9/26/86), Ivory Coast (9/26/86), Korea (North) (9/26/86), Lebanon (9/26/86), Liechtenstein (9/26/86), Luxembourg (9/29/86), Mali (10/2/86), Monaco (9/26/86), Morocco (9/26/86), Netherlands (9/26/86), Niger (9/26/86), Nigeria (1/21/87), Panama (9/26/86), Paraguay (10/2/86), Portugal (9/26/86), Senegal (6/15/87), Sierra Leone (3/25/87), Spain (9/26/86), Sudan (9/26/86), Syria (7/2/87), Thailand (10/25/87), Tunisia (2/24/87), Turkey (9/26/86), United Kingdom (9/26/86), Yugoslavia (5/27/87), Zaire (9/30/86), Zimbabwe (9/26/86)

Ratified/accepted/approved without qualification: 13

Austria (2/18/88), Bangladesh (1/7/88), Denmark (9/26/86), Finland (12/11/86), Guatemala (8/8/88), Japan (6/9/87), Jordan (12/11/87), Mexico (5/10/88), New Zealand (3/11/87), Norway (9/26/86), Sweden (2/27/87), Switzerland (5/31/88), Vietnam (9/29/87)

Ratified/accepted/approved with qualification: 19

Australia (9/22/87), Bulgaria (2/24/88), Byelorussian SSR (1/26/87), China (9/10/87), Czechoslovakia (9/26/86), Egypt (7/6/88), Germany (East) (4/29/87), Hungary (3/10/87), India (1/28/88), Iraq (7/21/88), Malaysia (9/1/87), Mongolia (6/11/87), Poland (3/24/88), South Africa (8/10/87), Ukrainian SSR (1/26/87), United Arab Emirates (10/2/87), United States (9/19/88), USSR (12/23/86), WHO (8/10/88)

5.30 Convention on Assistance in Case of a Nuclear Accident or Radiological Emergency

Entry into force: February 26, 1987

Signed but not ratified: 49

Afghanistan (9/26/86), Algeria (9/24/87), Austria (9/26/86), Belgium (9/26/86), Brazil (9/26/86), Cameroon (9/25/87), Canada (9/26/86), Chile (9/26/86), Costa Rica (9/26/86), Cuba (9/26/86), Denmark (9/26/86), Finland (9/26/86), France (9/26/86), Germany (East) (9/26/86), Germany (West) (9/26/86), Greece (9/26/86), Holy See (9/26/86), Iceland (9/26/86), Indonesia (9/26/86), Iran (9/26/86), Ireland (9/26/86), Israel (9/26/86), Italy (9/26/86), Ivory Coast (9/26/86), Jordan (10/2/86), Korea (North) (9/26/86), Lebanon (9/26/86), Liechtenstein (9/26/86), Mali (10/2/86), Monaco (9/26/86), Morocco (9/26/86), Netherlands (9/26/86), Niger (9/26/86), Nigeria (1/21/87), Panama (9/26/86), Paraguay (10/2/86), Portugal (9/26/86), Senegal (6/15/87), Sierra Leone (3/25/87), Spain (9/26/86), Sudan (9/26/86), Sweden (9/26/86), Syria (7/2/87), Thailand (9/25/87), Tunisia (2/24/87), Turkey (9/26/86), Ukrainian SSR (9/26/86), United Kingdom (9/26/86), Zaire (9/30/86), Zimbabwe (9/26/86)

Ratified/accepted/approved without qualification: 6

Bangladesh (1/7/88), Guatemala (8/8/88), Jordan (12/11/87), Mexico (5/10/88), Switzerland (5/31/88), Vietnam (9/29/87)

Ratified/accepted/approved with qualification: 22

Australia (9/22/87), Bulgaria (2/24/88), Byelorussian SSR (1/26/87), China (9/10/87), Czechoslovakia (8/4/88), Egypt (10/17/88), Germany (East) (4/29/87), Hungary (3/10/87), India (1/28/88), Iraq (7/21/88), Japan (6/9/87), Malaysia (9/1/87), Mongolia (6/11/87), New Zealand (3/11/87), Norway (9/26/86), Poland (3/24/88), South Africa (8/10/87), Ukrainian SSR (1/26/87), United Arab Emirates (10/2/87), United States (9/19/88), USSR (12/23/86), WHO (8/10/88)

5.31 Protocol on Substances That Deplete the Ozone Layer, With Annex A

Entry into force: January 1, 1989

Signed but not ratified: 16

Argentina (6/29/88), Australia (6/8/88), Austria (8/29/88), Burkina Faso (9/14/88), Chile (6/14/88), Congo (9/15/88), Ghana (9/16/87), Indonesia (7/21/88), Israel (1/14/88), Maldives (7/12/88), Morocco (1/7/88), Panama (9/16/87), Philippines (9/14/88), Senegal (9/16/87), Thailand (9/15/88), Togo (9/16/87)

Ratified/accepted/approved without qualification: 33

Belgium (12/30/88), Byelorussian SSR (10/31/88), Canada (6/30/88), E.C.C. (12/16/88), Egypt (8/2/88), Finland (12/23/88), France (12/28/88), Germany (East) (1/25/89), Germany (West) (12/16/88), Greece (12/16/88), Ireland (12/16/88), Italy (12/16/88), Japan (9/30/88), Kenya (11/9/88), Liechtenstein (2/8/89), Luxembourg (10/17/88), Malta (12/29/88), Mexico (3/31/88), Netherlands (12/16/88), New Zealand (7/21/88), Nigeria (10/31/88), Norway (6/24/88), Portugal (10/17/88), Singapore (1/5/89), Spain (12/16/88), Sweden (6/29/88), Switzerland (12/28/88), Uganda (9/15/88), Ukrainian SSR (9/20/88), United Kingdom (12/16/88), United States (4/21/88), USSR (11/10/88), Venezuela (2/6/89)

Ratified/accepted/approved with qualification: 1

Denmark (12/16/88)

5.32 Convention on the Control of Transboundary Movements of Hazardous Wastes and their Disposal

Participatory information unavailable as of this publication

6. MISCELLANEOUS

6.1 European Convention on Extradition

Entry into force: April 18, 1960

Signed but not ratified: 2

Belgium (12/13/57), Portugal (4/27/77)

Ratified/accepted/approved with qualification: 19

Austria (5/21/69), Cyprus (1/22/71), Denmark (9/13/62), Finland (5/12/71), France (2/10/86), Germany (West) (10/2/76), Greece (5/29/61), Iceland (6/20/84), Ireland (5/2/66), Israel (9/27/67), Italy (8/6/63), Liechtenstein (10/28/69), Luxembourg (11/18/76), Netherlands (2/14/69), Norway (1/19/60), Spain (5/7/82), Sweden (1/22/59), Switzerland (12/20/66), Turkey (1/7/60)

6.2 TREATY OF FRIENDSHIP, ESTABLISHMENT AND NAVIGATION BETWEEN THE UNITED STATES OF AMERICA AND THE KINGDOM OF BELGIUM, WITH PROTOCOL

Entry into force: October 3, 1963

6.3 FOREIGN SOVEREIGN IMMUNITIES ACT OF 1976

6.4 SUPPLEMENTARY TREATY CONCERNING THE EXTRADITION TREATY BETWEEN THE GOVERNMENT OF THE UNITED STATES OF AMERICA AND THE GOVERNMENT OF THE UNITED KINGDOM OF GREAT BRITAIN AND NORTHERN IRELAND, SIGNED AT LONDON ON JUNE 8, 1972

Entry into force: December 23, 1986

APPENDIX II

CITATIONS OF WORLD COURT JUDGMENTS AND ADVISORY OPINIONS

1. Permanent Court of International Justice

1922

Designation of the Workers' Delegate for the Netherlands at the Third Session of the International Labour Conference (Advisory Opinion), 1922 P.C.I.J. (ser. B) No. 1, at 5

Competence of the ILO in Regard to International Regulation of the Conditions of Labour of Persons Employed in Agriculture (Advisory Opinion), 1922 P.C.I.J. (ser. B) No. 2, at 9

Competence of the ILO to Examine Proposals for the Organization and Development of the Methods of Agricultural Production (Advisory Opinion), 1922 P.C.I.J. (ser. B) No. 3, at 49

1923

Nationality Decrees Issued in Tunis and Morocco (Advisory Opinion), 1923 P.C.I.J. (ser. B) No. 4, at 7

Status of Eastern Carelia (Advisory Opinion), 1923 P.C.I.J. (ser. B) No. 5, at 7

S.S. "Wimbledon" (France, Italy, Japan, United Kingdom v. Germany), 1923 P.C.I.J. (ser. A) No. 1, at 7

German Settlers in Poland (Advisory Opinion), 1923 P.C.I.J. (ser. B) No. 6, at 15

Acquisition of Polish Nationality (Advisory Opinion), 1923 P.C.I.J. (ser. B) No. 7, at 6

Jaworzina (Advisory Opinion), 1923 P.C.I.J. (ser. B) No. 8, at 6

1924

Mavrommatis Palestine Concessions (Greece v. United Kingdom), 1924 P.C.I.J. (ser. A) No. 2, at 6

Monastery of Saint-Naoum (Advisory Opinion), 1924 P.C.I.J. (ser. B) No. 9, at 6

Treaty of Neuilly, Article 179, Annex, Paragraph 4 (Bulgaria/Greece) (Interpretation), 1924 P.C.I.J. (ser. A) No. 3, at 4

1925

Exchange of Greek and Turkish Populations (Advisory Opinion), 1925 P.C.I.J. (ser. B) No. 10, at 6

Interpretation of Judgment No. 3 (Bulgaria/Greece), 1925 P.C.I.J. (ser. A) No. 4, at 4

Mavrommatis Jerusalem Concessions (Greece v. United Kingdom), 1925 P.C.I.J. (ser. A) No. 5, at 6

Polish Postal Service in Danzig (Advisory Opinion), 1925 P.C.I.J. (ser. B) No. 11, at 6

Certain German Interests in Polish Upper Silesia (Germany v. Poland) (Jurisdiction), 1925 P.C.I.J. (ser. A) No. 6, at 4

Interpretation of Article 3, Paragraph 2, of the Treaty of Lausanne (Advisory Opinion), 1925 P.C.I.J. (ser. B) No. 12, at 6

1926

Certain German Interests in Upper Silesia (Germany v. Poland) (Merits), 1926 P.C.I.J. (ser. A) No. 7, at 4

Competence of the ILO to Regulate Incidentally the Personal Work of the Employer (Advisory Opinion), 1926 P.C.I.J. (ser. B) No. 13, at 6

1927

Factory at Chorzów (Germany v. Poland) (Jurisdiction), 1927 P.C.I.J. (ser. A) No. 9, at 4

S.S. "Lotus" (France v. Turkey), 1927 P.C.I.J. (ser. A) No. 10, at 4

Readaptation of the Mavrommatis Jerusalem Concessions (Greece v. United Kingdom), 1927 P.C.I.J. (ser. A) No. 11, at 4

Jurisdiction of the European Commission of the Danube (Advisory Opinion), 1927 P.C.I.J. (ser. B) No. 14, at 6

Interpretation of Judgments Nos. 7 and 8 (Factory at Chorzów) (Germany v. Poland), 1927 P.C.I.J. (ser. A) No. 13, at 4

1928

Jurisdiction of the Courts of Danzig (Advisory Opinion), 1928 P.C.I.J. (ser. B) No. 15, at 4

Rights of the Minorites in Upper Silesia (Minority Schools) (Germany v. Poland), 1928 P.C.I.J. (ser. A) No. 15, at 4

Interpretation of the Greco-Turkish Agreement of 1 December 1926 (Final Protocol, Article IV) (Advisory Opinion), 1928 P.C.I.J. (ser. B) No. 16, at 4

Factory at Chorzów (Germany v. Poland) (Merits), 1928 P.C.I.J. (ser. A) No. 17, at 4

1929

Serbian Loans (France v. Yugoslavia), 1929 P.C.I.J. (ser. A) No. 20, at 5

Brazilian Loans (Brazil/France), 1929 P.C.I.J. (ser. A) No. 21, at 93

Territorial Jurisdiction of the International Commission of the River Oder (Czechoslovakia, Denmark, France, Germany, Sweden, United Kingdom/Poland), 1929 P.C.I.J. (ser. A) No. 23, at 5

1930

Greco-Bulgarian "Communities" (Advisory Opinion), 1930 P.C.I.J. (ser. B) No. 17, at 4

Free City of Danzig and ILO (Advisory Opinion), 1930 P.C.I.J. (ser. B) No. 18, at 4

1931

Access to German Minority Schools in Upper Silesia (Advisory Opinion), 1931 P.C.I.J. (ser. A/B) No. 40, at 4

Customs Régime between Germany and Austria (Advisory Opinion), 1931 P.C.I.J. (ser. A/B) No. 41, at 37

Railway Traffic between Lithuania and Poland (Advisory Opinion), 1931 P.C.I.J. (ser. A/B) No. 42, at 108

Access to, or Anchorage in, the Port of Danzig, of Polish War Vessels (Advisory Opinion), 1931 P.C.I.J. (ser. A/B) No. 43, at 128

1932

Treatment of Polish Nationals and Other Persons of Polish Origin or Speech in the Danzig Territory (Advisory Opinion), 1932 P.C.I.J. (ser. A/B) No. 44, at 4

Interpretation of the Greco-Bulgarian Agreement of 9 December 1927 (Advisory Opinion), 1932 P.C.I.J. (ser. A/B) No. 45, at 68

Free Zones of Upper Savoy and the District of Gex (France/Switzerland), 1932 P.C.I.J. (ser. A/B) No. 46, at 96

Interpretation of the Statute of the Memel Territory (France, Italy, Japan, United Kingdom v. Lithuania) (Preliminary Objection), 1932 P.C.I.J. (ser. A/B) No. 47, at 243

Interpretation of the Statute of the Memel Territory (France, Italy, Japan, United Kingdom v. Lithuania) (Merits), 1932 P.C.I.J. (ser. A/B) No. 49, at 294

Interpretation of the Convention of 1919 Concerning Employment of Women during the Night (Advisory Opinion), 1932 P.C.I.J. (ser. A/B) No. 50, at 365

1933

Legal Status of Eastern Greenland (Denmark v. Norway), 1933 P.C.I.J. (ser. A/B) No. 53, at 22

Appeal from a Judgment of the Hungaro/Czechoslovak Mixed Arbitral Tribunal (The Peter Pázmány University) (Czechoslovakia v. Hungary), 1933 P.C.I.J. (ser. A/B) No. 61, at 208

1934

Lighthouse Case between France and Greece, 1934 P.C.I.J. (ser. A/B) No. 62, at 4

Oscar Chinn, 1934 P.C.I.J. (ser. A/B) No. 63, at 65

1935

Minority Schools in Albania (Advisory Opinion), 1935 P.C.I.J. (ser. A/B) No. 64, at 4

Consistency of Certain Danzig Legislative Decrees with the Constitution of the Free City (Advisory Opinion), 1935 P.C.I.J. (ser. A/B) No. 65, at 41

1936

Pajzs, Csáky, Esterházy (Hungary v. Yugoslavia), 1936 P.C.I.J. (ser. A/B) No. 68, at 30

1937

Diversions of Water from the Meuse (Netherlands v. Belgium), 1937 P.C.I.J. (ser. A/B) No. 70, at 4

Lighthouses in Crete and Samos (France/Greece), 1937 P.C.I.J. (ser. A/B) No. 71, at 94

Borchgrave (Belgium v. Spain), 1937 P.C.I.J. (ser. A/B) No. 72, at 158

1938

Phosphates in Morocco (Italy v. France), 1938 P.C.I.J. (ser. A/B) No. 74, at 10

1939

Panevezys-Saldutiskis Railway (Estonia v. Lithuania), 1939 P.C.I.J. (ser. A/B) No. 76, at 4

Electricity Company of Sofia and Bulgaria (Belgium v. Bulgaria), 1939 P.C.I.J. (ser. A/B) No. 77, at 64

Société Commerciale de Belgique (Belgium v. Greece), 1939 P.C.I.J. (ser. A/B) No. 78, at 160

2. *International Court of Justice*

1948

Corfu Channel (United Kingdom v. Albania) (Preliminary Objection), 1948 I.C.J. 15

Conditions of Admission of a State to Membership in the United Nations (Article 4 of Charter) (Advisory Opinion), 1948 I.C.J. 57

1949

Corfu Channel (United Kingdom v. Albania) (Merits), 1949 I.C.J. 4

Reparation for Injuries Suffered in the Service of the United Nations (Advisory Opinion), 1949 I.C.J. 174

Corfu Channel (United Kingdom v. Albania) (Assessment of Amount of Compensation), 1949 I.C.J. 244

1950

Competence of the General Assembly for the Admission of a State to the United Nations (Advisory Opinion), 1950 I.C.J. 4

Interpretation of Peace Treaties with Bulgaria, Hungary and Romania (Advisory Opinion) (First Phase), 1950 I.C.J. 65

International Status of South West Africa (Advisory Opinion), 1950 I.C.J. 128

Interpretation of Peace Treaties with Bulgaria, Hungary and Romania (Advisory Opinion) (Second Phase), 1950 I.C.J. 221

Asylum (Colombia/Peru), 1950 I.C.J. 266

Request for Interpretation of the Judgment of 20 November 1950 in the Asylum Case (Colombia v. Peru), 1950 I.C.J. 395

1951

Reservations to the Convention on the Prevention and Punishment of the Crime of Genocide (Advisory Opinion), 1951 I.C.J. 15

Haya de la Torre (Colombia v. Peru), 1951 I.C.J. 71

Fisheries (United Kingdom v. Norway), 1951 I.C.J. 116

1952

Ambatielos (Greece v. United Kingdom) (Preliminary Objection), 1952 I.C.J. 28

Anglo-Iranian Oil Co. (United Kingdom v. Iran), 1952 I.C.J. 93

Rights of Nationals of the United States of America in Morocco (France v. United States), 1952 I.C.J. 176

1953

Ambatielos (Greece v. United Kingdom) (Merits), 1953 I.C.J. 10

Minquiers and Ecrehos (France/United Kingdom), 1953 I.C.J. 47

Nottebohm (Liechtenstein v. Guatemala) (Preliminary Objection), 1953 I.C.J. 111

1954

Monetary Gold Removed from Rome in 1943 (Italy v. France, United Kingdom, and United States), 1954 I.C.J. 19

Effects of Awards of Compensation Made by the United Nations Administrative Tribunal (Advisory Opinion), 1954 I.C.J. 47

1955

Nottebohm (Liechtenstein v. Guatemala) (Second Phase), 1955 I.C.J. 4

Voting Procedure on Questions Relating to Reports and Petitions Concerning the Territory of South West Africa (Advisory Opinion), 1955 I.C.J. 67

1956

Admissibility of Hearings of Petitioners by the Committee on South West Africa (Advisory Opinion), 1956 I.C.J. 23

Judgments of the Administrative Tribunal of the ILO upon Complaints Made against UNESCO (Advisory Opinion), 1956 I.C.J. 77

1957

Certain Norwegian Loans (France v. Norway), 1957 I.C.J. 9

Right of Passage over Indian Territory (Portugal v. India) (Preliminary Objections), 1957 I.C.J. 125

1958

Application of the Convention of 1902 Governing the Guardianship of Infants (Netherlands v. Sweden), 1958 I.C.J. 55

1959

Interhandel (Switzerland v. United States), 1959 I.C.J. 6

Aerial Incident of 27 July 1955 (Israel v. Bulgaria), 1959 I.C.J. 127

Sovereignty over Certain Frontier Land (Belgium/Netherlands), 1959 I.C.J. 209

1960

Right of Passage over Indian Territory (Portugal v. India) (Merits), 1960 I.C.J. 6

Constitution of the Maritime Safety Committee of the Inter-Governmental Maritime Consultative Organization (Advisory Opinion), 1960 I.C.J. 150

Arbitral Award Made by the King of Spain on 23 December 1906 (Honduras v. Nicaragua), 1960 I.C.J. 192

1961

Temple of Preah Vihear (Cambodia v. Thailand) (Preliminary Objections), 1961 I.C.J. 17

1962

Temple of Preah Vihear (Cambodia v. Thailand) (Merits), 1962 I.C.J. 6

Certain Expenses of the United Nations (Article 17, paragraph 2, of the Charter) (Advisory Opinion), 1962 I.C.J. 151

South West Africa (Ethiopia v. South Africa) (Liberia v. South Africa) (Preliminary Objections), 1962 I.C.J. 319

1963

Northern Cameroons (Cameroon v. United Kingdom), 1963 I.C.J. 15

1964

Barcelona Traction, Light and Power Company, Limited (Belgium v. Spain) (Preliminary Objections), 1964 I.C.J. 6

1965

No judgments or advisory opinions rendered.

1966

South West Africa (Ethiopia v. South Africa) (Liberia v. South Africa) (Second Phase), 1966 I.C.J. 6

1968

No judgments or advisory opinions rendered.

1969

North Sea Continental Shelf (Federal Republic of Germany/Denmark) (Federal Republic of Germany/Netherlands), 1969 I.C.J. 3

1970

Barcelona Traction, Light and Power Company, Limited (Belgium v. Spain) (Second Phase), 1970 I.C.J. 3

1971

Legal Consequences for States of the Continued Presence of South Africa in Namibia (South West Africa) notwithstanding Security Council Resolution 276 (1970) (Advisory Opinion), 1971 I.C.J. 16

1972

Appeal Relating to the Jurisdiction of the ICAO Council (India v. Pakistan), 1972 I.C.J. 46

1973

Fisheries Jurisdiction (United Kingdom v. Iceland) (Jurisdiction of the Court), 1973 I.C.J. 3

Fisheries Jurisdiction (Federal Republic of Germany v. Iceland) (Jurisdiction of the Court), 1973 I.C.J. 49

Application for Review of Judgment No. 158 of the United Nations Administrative Tribunal (Advisory Opinion), 1973 I.C.J. 166

1974

Fisheries Jurisdiction (United Kingdom v. Iceland) (Merits), 1974 I.C.J. 3

Fisheries Jurisdiction (Federal Republic of Germany v. Iceland) (Merits), 1974 I.C.J. 175

Nuclear Tests (Australia v. France), 1974 I.C.J. 253

Nuclear Tests (New Zealand v. France), 1974 I.C.J. 457

1975

Western Sahara (Advisory Opinion), 1975 I.C.J. 12

1976

No judgments or advisory opinions rendered.

1977

No judgments or advisory opinions rendered.

1978

Aegean Sea Continental Shelf (Greece v. Turkey), 1978 I.C.J. 3

1979

No judgments or advisory opinions rendered.

1980

United States Diplomatic and Consular Staff in Tehran (United States v. Iran), 1980 I.C.J. 3

Interpretation of the Agreement of 25 March 1951 between the WHO and Egypt (Advisory Opinion), 1980 I.C.J. 73

1981

Continental Shelf (Tunisia/Libyan Arab Jamahiriya) (Application for Permission to Intervene), 1981 I.C.J. 3

1982

Continental Shelf (Tunisia/Libyan Arab Jamahiriya), 1982 I.C.J. 18

Application for Review of Judgment No. 273 of the United Nations Administrative Tribunal (Advisory Opinion), 1982 I.C.J. 325

1984

Continental Shelf (Libyan Arab Jamahiriya/Malta) (Application for Permission to Intervene), 1984 I.C.J. 3

Delimitation of the Maritime Boundary in the Gulf of Maine Area, 1984 I.C.J. 246

Military and Paramilitary Activities in and against Nicaragua (Nicaragua v. United States of America) (Jurisdiction and Admissibility), 1984 I.C.J. 392

1985

Continental Shelf (Libyan Arab Jamahiriya/Malta), 1985 I.C.J. 13

Application for Revision and Interpretation of the Judgment of 24 February 1982 in the Case concerning the Continental Shelf (Tunisia/Libyan Arab Jamahiriya) (Tunisia v. Libyan Arab Jamahiriya), 1985 I.C.J. 192

1986

Military and Paramilitary Activities in and against Nicaragua (Nicaragua v. United States of America) (Merits), 1986 I.C.J. 14

Frontier Dispute (Burkina Faso/Republic of Mali), 1986 I.C.J. 554

1987

Application for Review of Judgment No. 333 of the United Nations Administrative Tribunal (Advisory Opinion), 1987 I.C.J. 18

1988

Applicability of the Obligation to Arbitrate under Section 21 of the United Nations Headquarters Agreement of 26 June 1947 (Advisory Opinion), 1988 I.C.J. 12

Border and Transborder Armed Actions (Nicaragua v. Honduras) (Jurisdiction and Admissibility), 1988 I.C.J. 69

1989

Elettronica Sicula S.p.A. (ELSI) (United States v. Italy), 1989 I.C.J. 15

APPENDIX III

DOCUMENTARY BIBLIOGRAPHY

Below is a selected list of basic documents collections, both general and covering specific topic areas.

General

Agreements of International Organizations and the Vienna Convention on the Law of Treaties (K. Zamenek ed. 1971)

Basic Documents in International Law (I. Brownlie ed., 3rd ed. 1983)

Basic Documents of International Organizations (S. Chen ed. 1979)

Basic Documents of International Relations (F. Hartmann ed. 1969)

The Consolidated Treaty Series, 231 vols. (C. Parry ed. 1969–81)

Council of Europe, Directorate of Legal Affairs, European Conventions and Agreements, 4 vols. (1971)

Cumulative List and Index of Treaties and International Agreements Registered with the United Nations December 1969 through December 1974, 2 vols. (J. Vambery & R. Vambery eds. 1977)

European Community Treaties (K. Simmonds ed., 4th ed. 1980)

Foreign Relations Law: Documents and Sources, 3 vols. (M. Glennon & T. Franck eds. 1980–)

J. Grenville, The Major International Treaties 1914–1973—A History and Guide with Texts (1974)

J. Grenville, The Major International Treaties 1914–1945—A History and Guide with Texts (1987)

J. Grenville & B. Wasserstein, The Major International Treaties Since 1945—A History and Guide with Texts (1987)

International Human Rights Instruments of the United Nations, 1948–1982 (UNIFO ed. 1983)

International Organization and Integration: Annotated Basic Documents and Descriptive Directory of International Organizations and Arrangements, 2 vols. (P. Kapteyn *et al.* eds. 1981–)

International Organisation and Integration—A Collection of the Texts of Documents Relating to the United Nations, its Related Agencies and Regional International Organisations (H. Van Panhuys *et al.* eds. 1968)

Keesing's Publications Ltd., Treaties & Alliances of the World (A. Day 4th ed. 1986)

The End of the Post-War Era: Documents on Great-Power Relations, 1968–1975 (J. Mayall & C. Navari eds. 1980)

War/Peace

Documents on the Laws of War (A. Roberts and R. Guelff eds., 2d ed. 1989)

Documents on Prisoners of War (H. Levie ed. 1979)

The Laws of Armed Conflicts: A Collection of Conventions, Resolutions and Other Documents (D. Schindler & J. Toman eds., 3rd ed. 1988)

The Law of Naval Warfare: A Collection of Agreements and Documents with Commentaries (N. Ronzitti ed. 1988)

The Law of War—A Documentary History, 2 vols. (L. Friedman ed. 1972)

Major Peace Treaties of Modern History 1648–1969, 5 vols. (F. Israel 1967–80)

Human Rights

Basic Documents on Human Rights (I. Brownlie 2d ed. 1981)

Basic Documents on International Protection of Human Rights (L. Sohn & T. Burgenthal eds. 1973)

R. Friedlander, Terrorism—Documents of International and Local Concern, 3 vols. (1979–81)

Human Rights: International Documents, 3 vols. (J. Joyce ed. 1978)

International Human Rights Instruments: A Compilation of Treaties, Agreements, and Declarations of Special Interest to the United States (R. Lillich ed. 1983)

The International Law of Human Rights in Africa: Basic Documents and Annotated Bibliography (M. Hamalengwa, C. Flinterman & E. Dankwa eds. 1988)

Economic Development

Basic Documents on Human Settlements for Developing Countries (Byggdok Institute ed. 1985)

The International Law of Development—Basic Documents, 4 vols. (A. Mutharika ed. 1978–79)

Earth-Space Environment

International Environment Reporter (1978–)

International Protection of the Environment: Treaties and Related Documents, 30 vols. (B. Ruster & B. Simma eds. 1975–1983)

Manual on Space Law, 4 vols. (N. Jasentuliyan & R. Lee eds. 1979–)

National Legislation and Treaties Relating to the Law of the Sea (United Nations, Legislative Series, 1980)

New Directions in the Law of the Sea, 11 vols. (R. Churchill *et al.* eds. 1973–81)

Register of International Treaties and Other Agreements in the Field of the Environment (United Nations Environment Programme ed. 1985)

Selected Multilateral Treaties in the Field of the Environment (A. Kiss ed. 1982)

The International Law of the Ocean, 2 vols. (S. Oda ed. 1977)

Treaties and Other International Agreements on Oceanographic Resources, Fisheries, and Wildlife to which the United States is Party (Library of Congress, Legislative Reference Service, 1971)

†